Robert Young Pelton's
THE WORLD'S
MOST DANGEROUS
PLACES®

Robert Young Pelton's
THE WORLD'S
MOST DANGEROUS
PLACES®

Fourth Edition

Robert Young Pelton

HarperResource
An Imprint of HarperCollins*Publishers*

THE WORLD'S MOST DANGEROUS PLACES, FOURTH EDITION. Copyright © 2000 by P&A, Inc. All rights reserved. Printed in the United States of America. No part of this book may be used or reproduced in any manner whatsoever without written permission except in the case of brief quotations embodied in critical articles and reviews. For information, address HarperCollins Publishers Inc., 10 East 53rd Street, New York, NY 10022.

HarperCollins books may be purchased for educational, business, or sales promotional use. For information please write: Special Markets Department, HarperCollins Publishers Inc., 10 East 53rd Street, New York, NY 10022.

Inquiries to the author may be addressed to: The World's Most Dangerous Places, P.O. Box 827, 4455 Torrance Blvd., Torrance, CA 90503; URL: www.comebackalive.com; e-mail: ryp@comebackalive.com

FOURTH EDITION

Robert Young Pelton's *The World's Most Dangerous Places* and Mr. DP are registered trademarks of Digital Artists.
Icons & Illustrations copyright © 2000 P&A, Inc.
Photos copyright © 2000 to Individual Photographers as listed on Page 1023

Library of Congress Cataloguing-in-Publication Data
Pelton, Robert Young.
  [World's most dangerous places]
  Robert Young Pelton's the world's most dangerous places / Robert Young Pelton.—4th ed.
    p. cm.
  Rev. ed. of: Fielding's the world's most dangerous places. 3rd ed. c1998.
  ISBN 0-06-273738-4
  1. Travel—Safety measures. 2. Travel—Anecdotes. I. Title: World's most dangerous places.
II. Pelton, Robert Young. Fielding's world's most dangerous places. III. Title.
G151.P44 2000
910'.2'02—dc21   99-056716

---

00 01 02 03 04 RRD 10 9 8 7 6 5 4 3 2 1

To Die-hard Readers

As I sit down for the fourth time to rewrite *The World's Most Dangerous Places,* or *DP,* I can't help think of the black monolith in Stanley Kubrick's film of Arthur C. Clarke's *2001.* Except that I am the curious ape and the black monolith is the enigmatic content of what is about to become the bible of bad news. Yes, I have spent the year traveling to the world's war zones, chatted with rebel leaders, frontline fighters, fishermen, pirates, aid workers, bus drivers, mujahadin, Navy Seals, spooks and thousands more. But I don't begin to understand the total picture until I sit down and begin researching every single area of conflict. It is a sobering experience. Traveling on the ground with the people, where things stink and life is brutal and then sitting down to put it all together. Then we, like those puzzled apes, can wonder whatever happened to this gift called intelligence.

This is simply one book by one man. A best effort at doing what should be done by other, better-funded, much smarter people than I. *DP* has become an annual event like the Doo Dah parade in Pasadena or the fall preview lineup on the networks. *DP* is a much debated view of our world, unrestrained by media giants, boardroom handwringing, and PC angst.

When *DP* first appeared in 1995 as a book, reviewers would ignore it as either a sick joke or an odd marketing gimmick. The mainstream travel and glossy magazines still cock their noses at a book that refuses to recognize the borders and niceties associated with mainstream travel. To those that don't get it, I salute you and wish you Godspeed. Somebody needs to be on those buses in Egypt.

Readers reacted quite differently. The major benefit of the book was to provide, for the first time, a clear—albeit warped—view of the world's least-visited regions. Areas that journalists, spooks and even mercenaries feared to tread. *DP* was a book that took some "dipping into," as one reviewer mentioned, to get the point. Others describe it as a good toilet read, still others carry their coffee-stained and dog-eared copies of *DP* around, always finding something of entertainment and education within.

Journalists and aid workers embraced a book that replaced smoky conversations in country bars. Here at last was a crude but helpful way to get plugged in, to reach out and maybe avoid those first culture shocks that awaited them.

The intelligence "community" was shocked that a nonmilitary dufus and his friends could wander the world and know things that were supposed to be "rumored." They also found much needed meaning and humor in what is usually a grim world of statistics and projections.

To all the world leaders that never bothered to send me a thank you letter and to all the rebel leaders who invited me warmly into their camps, I say you get what you give. So I apologize if you don't see a lot of stories entitled "In a Dangerous Place—The Oval Office."

I thank those who have stuck with *DP* from its rambling, typoed beginnings to its current level of popularity. If you still have a copy of *DP1* with the sneering Chadian gunman, hold on to it—it will be just as funny and cynical ten years from now.

To New Recruits

For those who have never read *DP*, I should provide the standard briefing.

DP is not a travel guide; it is a guide to staying alive, a guide to less-traveled parts of the world and a guide to how to stay safe should you go there.

More importantly, *DP* is a book about learning things firsthand, about ignoring carefully coiffed newscasters and flipping the channel when talking heads regurgitate government policy or debate ethics du jour. *DP* is about stuffing a week's worth of old clothes into a tattered backpack and taking matters into your own hands. I don't care if you work in a hospital or man the front lines. There is no one right answer, no clean take, no big picture, just a lot of people who need to be heard and talked to about what makes this world the way it is. *DP* gives you enough addresses, phone numbers, web sites and backgrounders to intelligently formulate not an opinion but an approach.

I write *DP* for myself. So it's not surprising that I like to think that the readers of *DP* are a lot like me. A traveler who is adventurous, curious, intelligent and skeptical of the sound-bite view of the world our governments would like us to believe. From the thousands of conversations, letters, calls and e-mails I now can tell you that I was right. A lot of people want to know more. And they are okay with handling more than one point of view. The most rewarding thing is that despite rumors of slackers, media numbness and self-centered affluents, there are a lot of smart, inquisitive people out there who not only look under the rug but want to clean up the dirt as well.

Readers and fans of *DP* are not shy about grinding gears or swapping rocks with me. I listen to every comment and even look interested when people are on their second hour of haranguing me on the right of some jackboot state to exist. I have my opinions, you have yours. All are welcome. That's how I learn.

You may wonder why there is so much information on rebels and "the other side" in this book. I am neither left nor right. It's just that these folks have a vested interest in communicating their concerns and you just don't see them on the *Today* show a lot. National governments also want their say in what is reported in *DP*. The government of Colombia was mortified when it discovered it was featured in *DP* (Mr. Pelton, why don't you talk about our beaches?). When I reminded this government that it was running ads asking tourists to stay way from Colombia because it didn't control large tracts of the country and offered to change anything believed untrue, the consternation faded away. Some governments like Cambodia have threatened us, some like Algeria have begged us not to come, some like South Africa have asked us to be kind, and some like Sudan simply won't issue us visas.

As for people who want to focus on the semantic and the hypothetical, my message to them still is go there, keep an open mind, visit both sides, figure it out and get to work. My opinion is just one of many. The world does not need more hot air, just hard work.

What's New in *DP4*

Just about everything—a new publisher, a new sense of expectation, over 30 new stories, new chapters, new takes on dangerous places and hundreds of thousands of miles of travel and adventures crammed into every paragraph. So welcome to *DP4*: No walls, no barriers, no bull.

TABLE OF CONTENTS

List of Maps

Robert Young Pelton's
THE WORLD'S
MOST DANGEROUS
PLACES®

The Author

Robert Young Pelton

Pelton, 45, has chosen an odd career. In high school an aptitude-and-interest test told him he was only suited for three jobs: astronaut, advertising man and adventurer. So much for career counseling. Pelton went on to become a lumberjack, boundary cutter, tunneler, driller and blaster's assistant in addition to his more lucrative occupations as a business strategist and marketing expert. He was not considered for the astronaut program although he has been ejected from many countries at great speed. What Pelton did on his time off turned into a career with the first publication of *Danger Places,* then *Come Back Alive* (Doubleday) (*www.comebackalive.com*) and his autobiography, *The Adventurist* (Doubleday) (*www.theadventurist.com*). He is currently shooting a series of specials for the Discovery Channel, entitled (what else) *Robert Young Pelton's The World's Most Dangerous Places.*

Pelton's articles ride the intellectual and demographic frontier in publications as diverse as the *Harvard International Review* to *Soldier of Fortune* to *Road & Track* to *ABC News.com*. He has been a featured speaker at the *TED* conference (Technology, Entertainment, Design), the Explorer's Club and an Afghan high school. Despite this recent success, Pelton doesn't consider himself a writer or a pundit. "Just a guy trying to figure things out and who has to write things down so he doesn't forget."

Stories about Pelton, his adventures or his books have been featured in publications as diverse as *Outside, Shift, Star, Blue, New York Times, Los Angeles Times, Time, Class, El Pais, Playboy, Sunday London Times, Der Stern, Die Welt, Washington Post, Outpost,* and hundreds of other magazines and newspapers around the world. He has also been featured and interviewed on a variety of networks, including the BBC, NBC, CBS, ABC, ATV, Fox, RTL, CTV, CBC, and seems to appear on entertainment shows like *Oprah, The Late, Late Show, Today,* and *Late Night with Conan O'Brien* only when tourists get blown up or kidnapped.

Not much slows Pelton down; he has survived car accidents, bombings, gunfire, front lines, muggings, illness, aging Russian gunships, attacks by the PKK, SCUDs in Chechnya, two encounters with African killer bees, a plane crash in the central highlands of Kalimantan and a terrorist bomb in Uganda. He attributes his numerous arrests and detainments to his hosts' need to get to know him better and to further his on-the-job survival training. Despite these minor setbacks, Pelton still faces each dangerous encounter with a sense of humor and an irreverent wit.

Pelton is a Fellow of the Royal Geographical Society in London and lives in Los Angeles, California. Contact: *ryp@comebackalive.com*

The Contributors

Wink Dulles

Dulles has spent hard time in Cambodia, Thailand and Vietnam, traveling by motorcycle. He covered the elections in Cambodia and the subsequent breakdown of order in that besieged country, being in-country at a time when few foreigners dared. After the first edition of *DP* was published, he was "invited" back to Cambodia by the government to attend a personal tongue-lashing for his contribution to *DP*. Wink's other notable talents are being mistaken for Mel Gibson and playing a mean guitar. Wink lives on a ranch in Thailand. Contact: *wink@comebackalive.com*

Sedat Aral

Aral has been a "hot spot" photojournalist for more than 12 years. He has covered Afghanistan, Azerbaijan, Bosnia, Chechnya, Georgia, Iran, Iraq, Lebanon, Malaysia, the Philippines and Syria, as well as news stories in his native Turkey. He has worked internationally for news agencies including Reuters and Sipa Press and works on assignment for *Time*. Currently he is a special assignment reporter for the Sabah Media Group in Turkey. He can no longer enter Iran by official routes, having been deported twice for taking photographs. He has had his life threatened in Tunceli for photographing burned Kurdish villages in the region closed to the press, and has been seriously beaten by police after photographing armed attacks on unarmed protesters. Aral lives in London, England. Contact: *sedat@comebackalive.com* or see Sedat's images at Images Sans Frontiers at http://www.imagenet.co.uk/

Jim Hooper

Hooper is a freelance journalist based in the United Kingdom. Wounded twice in Africa (obviously before he had a chance to read *DP*), Hooper is known for showing up where few other people dare. He is the coauthor of *Flashpoint! At the*

Frontline of Today's Wars (with Ken Guest) and *Beneath the Visiting Moon,* a documentary account of his six months with a counterinsurgency unit in Namibia. During the war in Angola, Hooper accompanied UNITA forces on guerrilla operations against Soviet- and Cuban-backed government forces. He also spent considerable time with the contract soldiers of Executive Outcomes in Sierra Leone. He has covered conflicts in Bosnia, Chad, Sudan, South Africa and Uganda. His meticulously detailed articles and way-too-close-for-comfort photos have appeared in a wide range of publications, including *Jane's Intelligence Review,* the *Economist* and the *Sunday Telegraph* of London. Hooper lives in Hampshire, England. *hoop@comebackalive.com*

Rob Krott

Krott, 36, is a former officer and paratrooper who attended Harvard (anthropology). His military career has earned him various awards and decorations from ten foreign governments. Besides his anthropology pursuits (with Richard Leakey's Koobi Fora Project), he finds time to organize parachute jumps for ex-special forces and paratroopers around the world and cover conflicts as a correspondent. He has been on the ground in El Salvador, Guatemala, Sudan, Uganda, Somalia, Bosnia, Myanmar, Cambodia and Angola and continues to work in, or travel on assignment to, the world's most dangerous places. He has served with three foreign armies and lived with a number of rebel groups, including the SPLA in Sudan and the KNLA in Myanmar. He continues to spend a considerable amount of time in Asia, Africa, the Balkans and Latin America. He is a columnist for *Behind the Lines: The Journal of Military Special Operations* and is a senior foreign correspondent for *Soldier of Fortune.* He has been published in *Harpers, Explorers Journal* and *New African.* Krott has an affliction similar to Wink's. Rob is often mistaken for Chuck Norris in his travels. He is hoping some day to be confused with Robert Redford. He keeps *DP* honest with his multipage submissions of corrections, illuminations and anecdotes. He lives in Olean, New York. Contact: *krott@comebackalive.com*

Sarah Richards

Sarah, 26, our first female contributor, lists among her accomplishments riding through Cambodia on a bike and having the crushed foot to prove it. She has written for the *New York Times, The Independent, The Globe & Mail* and *The National Post,* as well as the CBC and other newspapers. Contact: *sarah@comebackalive.com*

Dom Rotheroe

Dom, 35, is a London-based filmmaker who covers hotspots, writes books and collects odd pictures of things. When the republics of Yugoslavia decided on unamicable divorce he went off to the war in Bosnia with £1000 and a Hi-8 camcorder. The resultant documentary, *A Sarajevo Diary,* was nominated for a British Academy Award.

Since Bosnia, Rotheroe has been with the POLISARIO in Western Sahara, investigated cop-killing street kids in Rio, been under fire in East Timor, crossed the blockade around Bougainville and covered the earthquake in Turkey. The focus of all Dom's films has been understanding the situation from the point of view of the people on the ground and telling their story with feeling. And maybe even trying to change at least a couple of people's minds. Rotheroe's articles have been published in *Esquire,* the *Independent,* the *Geographical* and *Adrenalin* in the United Kingdom and in Australia, Portugal and the Netherlands. He is currently working on his first feature film, a savage love story between sexually-abused teenagers. Contact: *dom@comebackalive.com*

Roddy Scott

Scott, 28, graduated from Edinburgh University in 1994. He started his career in journalism working for the London-based *Middle East* magazine. Since then he has covered wars in Afghanistan, Lebanon, Kurdistan, Albania, Kosovo and Sierra Leone. At 25, Scott was the first (and only) outsider to travel with guerrillas of the Revolutionary United Front in Sierra Leone. Despite his enthusiam for adventurous travel and fast living, Roddy still thinks he wants to be a journalist when he grows up. To correct this compulsion, he has contributed a fair volume of darkly humorous insights to *DP4*.

When not bugging RYP to tag along and get shot at or join him in his jail cell, Roddy is a specialist correspondent for *Jane's Intelligence Review* and *Jane's Defence Weekly* as well as a stringer cameraman for London-based *Frontline Television*. His travels have also made him a familiar face to police and militia forces in various countries, who have invariably asked him to stay a little longer while they take a look at his film. At the other end of the spectrum, Scott has become cozy with many of the local bandits, who have rarely stopped him long enough to do anything more than take whatever he had on him. When at home, Scott lives in North Yorkshire, England. Contact: *roddy@comebackalive.com*

WHAT IS
DANGEROUS?

What Is Dangerous?

Yuh Gunna Die

Good—that's out of the way. Now we can talk about when. Funny how we know that the end comes swiftly to sitcoms, lab rats and boy singing groups but it just doesn't seem to apply to us. It can't be possible in this era of Viagra, Barbara Walters, plastic surgery and redesigned Cadillacs that we have any reason to slow down, let alone die. Can't we just keep on "maturing"?

But how will you, after a youth of indiscretions, 20ish flings and 30s stolid seriousness, survive this brave new world of crew-cutted mountain folk, beady-eyed gang-bangers, wobbling asteroids, wild-eyed terrorists and twitchy postal workers? How can you escape the death camp drain of commuting, working, stress, meetings and family? Maybe take a vacation, only to discover brave drunk pilots, myopic bus drivers, defective tail rudders, clapped-out hookers and dope-smoking train engineers? Even if you keep your nose to the grindstone, how will you survive the residual damage of those Twinkies, overcooked bacon, polyester suits, humming cell phones, offgassing carpets and computer screens?

Just how will you work the odds so that you die comfortable in bed, at an impressively advanced age, your far-too-attractive, oversexed spouse looking on tearfully, surrounded by your well-provided-for great-great-great granchildren, looking at your many carefully preserved possessions with eager scientists standing by to preserve your flawless, youthful-looking corpse. Its all about knowing and then beating the odds.

At least that is what we would like to think. But we all know that death comes to one and all; it hovers from that magical point of conception and it stalks us relentlessy through our arrogant youth up into our doddering senility. And one day, when you least expect it, like a prostate exam in an igloo, it gets you.

If you read statistics you would think that most of us will cruise into our 70s with a headful of air and drawer full of Valium. But that's not true. According to the National Center for Health Statistics, Americans should get 76.7 years of good times on this planet. That's two mortgages, 15 car loans paid off and a good deal on that lifetime set of cheap ginzu knives you bought.

You could move to Singapore or Japan and squeeze out a few more years, but I wouldn't call that living. Over all, things are pretty safe and benign for denizens of the Western world.

Yeah, But Can I Get Insurance?

You will be happy to learn that MIT has developed the Tornio scale, a new way to determine the odds of an asteroid hitting the earth and ending life as you know it (maybe that's not so bad after all). Asteroids are measured on a scale of 1 to 10 with 10 being an asteroid capable of causing global catastrophe and 0 being an asteroid with no chance of a collision or too small to matter. There are about 2,000 large asteroids that could come near Earth, although none have actually hit us in a long time. Astronomers predict that a large asteroid hits earth every million years or so. So who's gonna be left to pay off that policy?

So does life suck for everyone else? Not really. Worldwide things are pretty good. Is life outside the West too short to get a 30-year mortgage and too miserable to want one? Depending on who you want to believe, most of the world lives in a mud hut, goes to bed hungry and can't read or write. Worse, the "normal person" lives in a state of perpetual fear from government, hunger, disease, his neighbor, religion and even the weather. Like most things you read, it's half true. Most of the world does not play Doom, log on to CNN for weather reports or even aspire to own a SUV. Most of the world is poor, slightly nervous and a little fatalistic about what's around the corner. But the secret is—they make do. Are they living every moment in fear and apprehension? Not really. It's the West that does that. It is only in developed countries and in the last ten years of baby boomerdom that we have developed this obsession with fear and safety. Because there isn't really anything to fear. Crime is dropping, wages are increasing, life spans are longer, health is better and every segment of society has some benefit provided by the political efforts of bleeding-heart liberals and by the business efforts of cold-hearted capitalists. So let's all take a deep breath, have a group hug and be thankful that we are the longest-lived, healthiest, most protected generation that has ever lived on this planet.

http://www.cdc.gov/nchs/fastats/fastats.htm

So What's the Bad News?

The bad news is that all this safety, caring and sharing, seat belt, Master Card, two weeks to kill society can get itself into a lot of trouble. It's important to understand the relative dangers of normal living to appreciate the numbers that you will read about in later chapters. Danger is relative. Strangely, the dangers that face you when you travel are infinitesimal when compared to just surviving the dangers you face in the nine to five grind, running to the fridge to get your eighth beer, or in the frenetic weekend activities that pass for relaxation. Why? Because we don't think about dying at the 7-11 or watching our kid's soccer game or even watching Leno propped up in bed. But ask any cop–that's where they find dead people all the time.

All right, so let's get to it. What is dangerous and what isn't? Since this is a book about dangerous travel, let's look at the odds. There's a one in 10 million chance of dying in a plane crash. Not bad. The odds of getting killed on a train are 10 times higher, about one in a million. Still good, but not great.

If you think that pilot error or cannibis-smoking railroad engineers are the cause of most accidents, try driving across the country. The chances of getting killed are one in 14,000—worse odds yet. That's dangerous, yet a full third of American drivers don't even bother to buckle up. The recent increase in American speed limits from 55 to 65 has jacked the accident fatality rate to a whopping 44 percent. But we are speeding ahead of ourselves. So what are the odds that we will be one of the 2 million or so people that die every year in the United States?

http://www.disastercenter.com/cdc/

Time

The number one killer of men is that kindly looking fellow, Father Time. Although there is a statistical lengthening of human lives as higher standards of living, safety, nutrition and health care spread to the lower incomes, we are all subject to deterioration of tissues. Most of us can expect to live to our mid-'70s before getting nervous about getting our money's worth on a 5-year carpet. In 1890, the average life expectancy was 31.1 years. Today, it is up to 76.7 years. A whole year more than when the first *DP* came out 5 years ago. Joining the century club is completely possible for the next generation.

Lovers of trivia and calculators should marvel at what the average human body does in one year. We have the ability to walk 1,569 miles, blink 7,884,000 times, breathe 1,040,250 gallons of air, sleep 2,555 hours, yawn 3,650 times, consume about a million calories and do many other less impressive things.

How does one cheat the grim reaper in the long run? First, don't let accidental causes get in the way. Second, exercise and eat right and maintain a positive mental attitude. How is that done? Travel, of course. People who live the longest seem to have an insatiable curiosity as well as a natural love for exploring the world. There are a lot of wiry octogenarians who seem perfectly healthy, have inquiring minds, travel a lot and are always looking for a good time. They stay out of the house as much as possible, fully understanding that the home is the world's most dangerous place for people over the age of 75. And they don't let a lot of doomsday books and warnings slow them down.

http://www.nih.gov/health/chip/nia/aging/geneconnect.html

Accidents

OK, you bought a stack of backpacker guides and stretched your finances to buy that 'round the world air ticket. But how do you live long enough to enjoy all your acquired common sense? First, you have to get through four stages.

Young and Tender

This year, 35,000 children will not make it past the first year of life in the United States. If you make it out of the womb (half didn't) without a major congenital abnormality, there's sudden infant death syndrome to deal with. The next most dangerous incidents are choking, car crashes, ingesting a foreign object, burns or fires and drowning.

Young and Reckless

Young male teenagers in cars seem to have a death wish. Eighteen may be a magic age for most people, but it is a very profitable target demographic for undertakers. Of every 100,000 18-year-olds, 55.5 will die in car crashes.

Middle-aged and Reckless

What is the number two accidental killer of people between the ages of 18 and 49 (after car accidents)? Dying to know the answer? It's accidental poisoning; a curious manner of death, with a rate highest for men aged 37. Most of this poisoning is the result of the deadly side effects of ingesting normal medicines. And, of course, sex kills. HIV claimed over 25,000 people between the ages of 25 and 44 and has become the number one killer for those 25–34. Time to swap that *Playboy* subscription for *Duck's Unlimited*.

Old and Clumsy

The next time you send Gramps downstairs to find his glasses, don't be surprised if he doesn't come back. Falls collect a number of victims in the age group above 75. Although the number pales in comparison to heart disease, it is worth remembering: over 8,000 people died from falls last year and just under half a million from heart disease.

National Safety Council
http://nsc.org/
All the Accidents That Fit
http://www.cdc.gov/nchs/fastats/acc-inj.htm

Disease

Okay, the yoga and meditation lessons are paying off. You are a now a zenlike, cautious, level-headed person. You drive your 6,000-pound sport ute with side, front and back impact bags real slow and tip your hat and smile at anyone who is carrying an automatic weapon.

But there is an insidious killer that few of us have any control over. AIDS is spreading at an alarming rate among young people, so if you are under 45, make sure you pack your leak-tested hazmat suit with extra gaffers tape when you go to Club Med.

When the numbers are totaled up, the leading cause of death caused by medical problems in America is heart disease. Cancer claimed half a million lives, strokes accounted for just under 150,000 fatalities and chronic obstructive pulmonary disease claimed two-thirds of that. It's a long way down to the next killer disease. Are there any trends to give us hope? It seems good living is the nation's number one killer. Just why aren't there sexy commercials telling us to exercise, eat a low fat diet and see a doctor every year?

http://www.cdc.gov/nchs/fastats/deaths.htm

When Ya Gotta Go, Ya Gotta Go	
1. Heart Disease	37.8%
2. Cancer	19.3%
3. Stroke	10.3%
4. Accidents (Non-Auto)	3.0%
5. Influenza (Pneumonia)	2.9%
6. Motor Vehicle Accidents	2.4%
7. Diabetes	1.9%
8. Liver Disease	1.7%
9. Arteriosclerosis	1.5%
10. Suicide	1.4%

Travel

You probably assume that the above stats are just for the sedentary hordes that are content to watch *Wild Kingdom* reruns. So what about those wild-eyed travelers slashing their way through the tropical jungle or rafting down thundering canyons? Is travel dangerous? Not really. The only guaranteed discomfort adventurers will experience is that mad dash to sit and ponder the world's great and varied selection of evacuation devices and the occasional sunburn. (How come Rambo and Indiana Jones never have the runs?) Dr. Richard Dawood put together an interesting chart in *Condé Nast Traveler* using info from the World Health Organization gleaned from a study by Professor Robert Steffen of the University of Zurich. The following table is the incidence of health problems experienced by travelers to tropical destinations (based on a sample of 100,000 people).

Health Problems Experienced (Per 100,000 Travelers)		
Experienced a health problem	55%	55,000
Felt Ill	25%	25,000
Consulted doctor	.08%	8,000
Stayed in bed	.06%	6,000
Unable to work upon return	.02%	2,000
Hospitalized while abroad	.004%	400
Evacuated by air	.0006%	60
Died abroad	.00001%	1
Source: Condé Nast Traveler		

Dawood mentions the results of a study done by the British Consumers Association among 15,972 members which revealed that 15 percent of their members had been sick on vacation. The results are not that surprising when you look at countries where travelers became sick.

When it comes to where you can get Montezuma's revenge, Tut's Trot or Delhi Belly, there are no surprises here. India (60 percent), Egypt (53 percent) and Mexico (40 percent) are the best places to get the runs. The most likely problem affecting travelers to tropical places are diarrhea or intestinal problems, with about 25–40 percent of them being afflicted. Sunburn affects about 10 percent with the Caribbean and Mexico being the most likely place to get fried.

Malaria affected a minuscule number of travelers. Only about 1,036 or about .0000345 percent of the 30 million U.S. residents who traveled abroad contracted the mosquito-borne parasite. About 3 percent of those cases were fatal.

http://www.cdc.gov/ncidod/EID/vol1no2/wilson.htm
http://www.cdc.gov/travel/
http://www.who.int/whr/1999/en/disease.htm
http://www.nsc.org/lrs/statinfo/af80.htm
http://www.healthcarecomputing.com/msrover.html

Accident Facts

We weren't joking in saying that if you want to live longer, stay out of the house. But just don't leave too fast and don't take your car. And don't go charging down those stairs. People between the age of 70 and 90 are attracted to stairs like lemmings to cliffs. But even at younger ages, if you really want to live dangerously, stay at home. Most accidents happen at home. Any student of statistics will tell you that home is where people spend the majority of their time. Each year slippery tile floors, cheap ginzu knives and trendy glass coffee tables do more damage than all the world's terrorists. You even have a 1 in 3 chance of dying in bed. From what? We'll let you get creative on that one.

When should you plan to spend a month in that seminary in solitary? Well, the most dangerous month for accidents is August, with 9,000 unintentional injuries versus a monthly incidence average of 7,500. The safest month is February with only 5,700. Curious to know the other most dangerous months?

Cause of Death	Most Dangerous Month	#	Least Dangerous Month	#	Avg
Car Accidents	August	4,243	January	2,869	3,628
Falls	December	1,145	February	959	1,055
Drownings	July	886	November	147	385
Firearms	November	164	September	83	120
Fire	January	539	June	194	343
Poisoning	August	572	January	412	475

Source: National Center for Health Statistics, National Safety Council also links
http://www.cdc.gov/nchswww/sites/sites.htm

Fly the Friendly Skies

From the moment you grasp your airline seat with sweaty palms to the minute your cab rolls to a stop at your front door, most travelers have a nervous feeling that their life has become more dangerous. The reality is quite the opposite. Remember we told you that fewer accidents happen to people when they travel than when they are at home. Why?

Well, think of who you trust your life to when you travel. For example, your takeoff. If you survive the cab ride you'll arrive in a well-designed, safe terminal complete with sprinklers, emergency exits and in many cases on-site medical staff. (Does your house have this?) When you board the plane, you enter a multimillion-dollar aircraft, the culmination of more than 100 years of aviation safety engineering. Every element and every part of the craft is regulated, inspected, maintained and replaced. Up front, you have two pilots who are the best of their kind. Many American pilots are Vietnam-era pilots who have flown in combat. All have racked up tens of thousands of hours in the air. Every pilot goes through intensive training and regular retraining to stay in top form. You are given flight safety procedures by individuals trained in emergency situations, first aid and other lifesaving procedures. Law mandates that there be a flight attendant for every 50 passengers. After you are aloft you are now under the control of a global traffic network that tracks all major aircraft and weather patterns using a network of computers and fail-safe devices. When you finally arrive at your destination, tired but safe, you meet your driver/guide. Here, things may change. The fact that he is drunk, blind in one eye and drives what used to be a 1957 Chevy still can't take your mind off his gold tooth and missing fingers. So it's off to the rebel camp to meet the guerrillas. "Oh, by the way," he says in his *aquadiente*-laced breath, "the *gobermente* overran the camp yesterday, but I think *el jefe* is still alive."

Regardless of your final destination, travel in the First World is pretty sedentary and predictable. Buses, trains and cars are subject to stringent safety laws in both construction and operation. Hotels have sophisticated sprinkler systems and emergency evacuation plans. Restaurants are inspected by health inspectors, and so on. You can even get your fare back if you are hijacked or killed. Remember that risk and travel are a sophisticated gamble. Nobody plays Russian roulette with six bullets or even two. The trick is to know when the odds are in your favor.

Resources

Minding Your Health Abroad
http://www.masta.org/

World Health Organization
http://www.who.ch

British Airways Travel Clinic
http://www.british-airways.com/travelqa/fyi/health/health.shtml

List of International Health-Related Web Sites
http://www.unmc.edu/Community/ihmec/StdResc/IHWebsite.htm

What Danger Awaits the Weary Traveler?

Be Afraid, Be Very Afraid . . . Not

So is travel dangerous? Not really. One survey says that you are less likely to have an accident on vacation than when you are at home. So what does that mean? That unemployed homeless people live longer than suburbanite workaholics? Other surveys say that most people are injured within a five-mile radius of their homes. So shop more than five miles out? It's hard to sell people on the idea of selling expeditions to the local 7-11 as the most dangerous form of travel, but it's true. If you believe the doom and gloom of the statistics, death is not a Chechen terrorist but comes softly on bunny-slippered feet.

But common sense usually prevails (I said usually). People still buy bus tours to Yemen, there are sex tourists in Cambodia and Uganda's gorillas are still amused by hordes of Tilley-hatted ecotourists. The message is that travel can be dangerous if you want it to be and it can be very safe if you want it to be. Even in a war zone.

The statistics and stories you are bombarded with on tourist misfortune has to be viewed against the staggering numbers of tourists out there at any one time.

In a typical year there are about half a billion tourists or travelers wandering around the world. That's a lot money belts, white shoes, Kodak boxes and cream of mushroom legs. In the mid-1800s Thomas Cook started the package tour and the race was on. Railroads, steamships, buses, hotels, restaurants and prices sprang up to accommodate strangers, and other than a couple of world wars, tourism was on its way to become the world's largest industry.

In 1955 there were only 46 million people traveling from one country to another. Most of them were well-heeled folks "doing the continent" or "taking the sun." Ten years later there were 144 million and today there are 500 million. That's a lot of Samsonite. It also means you read a lot more about misfortune, illnesses and death. These travelers cleaned out their wallets to the tune of $315 billion. Over the next few years tourism is expected to grow around 4.3 percent to 7.1 percent according to the World Tourism Organization. So move back to the rear of the bus.

Besides overcrowding, what do those half a billion people worry about when they travel? Most worry about high prices, safety and dirty accommodations in that order. Price is not this book's bailiwick, but you can figure out what things cost pretty easily these days. For informatin on dirt, you'll have to wait until you check into Pedro's Casa D'Amore before you race the cockroaches for your bath soap.

But safety, now that's an important thing to know about, wouldn't you think? Well, the sad fact is there are no comparative statistics on country or travel safety. I'll say it again in case you don't believe me. There is no way for a traveler to learn the relative safety of his or her destination. Sure you can call up Pinkerton's, Kroll O'Gara or even the State Department and they will give your their best statistical shot massaged with a healthy dose of WAG (wild-ass guess) to let you know if you should pack your Kevlar boxers. But the question I am asked over and over (Is it dangerous?) just can't be answered with statistics. Suffice it to say, the long form answer is the purpose of this book

Now, I am not going to stop you from visiting the local tourist police office in Ouagadougou and you can even twist the arm of the tourism board in Mogadishu for recent robberies, but you will come up dry. Why?

Crime hurts tourism. Tourism means money. Money means overdevelopment. Massive overdevelopment breeds crime. Cheap hotels, cheap bars and even cheaper tourists now crowd the south of Europe, Mexican beaches, budget Caribbean islands and even meccas like Torremolinos, Daytona Beach, Cancun, Las Vegas and Branson. The migratory arrival of pendulous grannies, knob-kneed welders, screaming kids and haggard housewives creates an instant feeding frenzy of snotty-nosed beggars, clapped-out hookers, gold-toothed cops, nimble-fingered teenagers and math-challenged bartenders. Soon all of these subdenizens are tugging at your Fila knockoff shorts, creating the perfect scenario for scams and theft. So understand a basic premise of tourist crime. Tourists breed crime like plastic sneakers breed fungus.

Those Tourists Do the Darndest Things!

Mexican police arrested a 33-year-old American man, Dennis Albert Macchion, for sitting on a hill and firing a high-powered sniper rifle at cars with California license plates. An American tourist died after a bullet smashed through her windshield, struck her in the head and exited through her rear windshield. The 46-year-old woman was sitting between two friends in a pickup truck while driving in Baja California. Over the July Fourth weekend two other drivers reported being fired on between Rosarito and Ensenada. He told police he "did it for fun."

Forget about warfare, hotel bombs and public assassinations. Your biggest danger is having that rental car window smashed in and the Elvis decanter you left in the backseat ripped off. Hey, it was your fault, all the locals know to hide that stuff, so most destinations have no reason to publicize your stupidity to other equally stupid but unexpecting visitors. Remember the $315 billion these turistas spend every year. Some countries live or die based on tourism. If you come across statistics kept by tourist police you will quickly learn that it doesn't seem that bad because (duh) there are tourist police. If you call a government they will tell you that they don't keep statistics because there is no hard line between a tourist crime and a regular crime. When I point out that usually a tourist has a plane ticket and a foreign passport, they say something like "I guess so." The bottom line is that after eight years of doing this book I have found no absolute indicator of crime rates against tourists. I can tell you that tourism breeds crime, and when Arthur Frommer starts complaining about tourist crime on his septuagenarian and low-budget wanderings, look out.

http://www.Nashville.Net/~police/risk/
http://www.fbi.gov/ucr.htm

Stylin' by the Deadly Mile

Now despite the lack of stats on tourist crime, there are plenty of studies on the relative safety of transportation methods that get you to these crime-infested places. Usually these studies focus on countries where they don't have to clear the livestock off the runways before you land. Once again this is akin to conducting STD surveys in convents. But at least it gives you an idea of the relative safety of various modes of transportation, although taking the bus in St. Paul cannot quite be matched up with taking the bus in Calcutta.

By the very definition of travel, you will be forced to choose some form of transportation. Planes are the safest means; cars are the most dangerous. In the United States, the death rate per miles traveled is comforting for those who fly but unsettling for the majority of people who like to drive.

Expect danger every time you decide to get into a taxi; but expect death in a small minivan. You may prefer to travel by bus, cab, rickshaw, trishaw, *becek* or even rollerblades. These are official U.S. statistics—numbers that reflect one of the safest transportation systems in the world. But what about the more typical forms of transportation adventurers will be forced to use?

Type of Passenger Transport	Death Rate (per billion passenger miles)	Passenger Miles (in billions)
Passenger Cars	.89	2393.2
Intercity Buses	.03	23.7
Transit Buses	.01	20.6
Trains	.02	13.5
Airplanes	.01	354.3

To Fly or Drive?
http://www.rvs.uni-bielefeld.de/~ladkin/Incidents/probability.html
UN Traffic Safety Report
http://www.unece.org/trans/main/stapubl/webras.htm
FEVR Links to Traffic Safety Sites
http://www.fevr.org/English_associations.htm#others
NTSB
http://www.ntsb.gov

Minibuses

Imagine what happens when your body decelerates from 60–0 m.p.h. in two milliseconds. Now imagine a forest of rusty seat backs and a plateglass window in your way. Not pretty. Having been at the site of many bus crashes in my travels, I can best compare the scenes to putting a dozen mice in a coffee can along with glass and nails, slamming it against a wall and then shaking it for a few minutes more. Then spray the bloody contents across the path of oncoming traffic. That pretty much sums up the ghastly and confused scene of a *matatu* accident.

I am sure you will never imagine yourself on one of these rickety, belching conveyances, but the first time you need to get from point A to B in countries where gum and deodorant are considered luxury items you will find yourself on a bus.

I would have to say after a lifetime of having my knees wrapped around my neck and old men drooling sound asleep on my shoulder that the most dangerous form of travel in the Third World is the fabled minibus. These are usually small Japanese-made transports with a drivetrain that was originally designed to haul a family of four, but ingenuity and greed prevails, and some will pack up to 16 passengers in one minibus. In 1994, a survey by an English paper found 60 "bus plunges" that caused nearly 1,300 deaths—a number equal to all the air passenger deaths worldwide. A quarter of these accidents were in India.

The minibuses are used primarily for rush hour transportation of poor people to work. Unlike the large, regulated buses, minibuses are run by entrepreneurs who make their money by carrying as many people as many times as they can. For example, in South Africa 60,000 accidents involving minibuses kill more than 900 people every year. In Peru, where they are called "killer combis," the death toll also includes nonpassengers trying to get out of the way of the weaving, speeding vans. The deadly driving style is a result of drivers who must make their money within the two hours of rush hour in order to make a profit on their rental owner's charge. Last year, 375 pedestrians were killed by the 30,000 or so minivans in Lima, Peru. The numbers are not available for most Third World countries. In Europe, 50,000 people are killed in road accidents, and more than 150,000 remain disabled for life according to FEVR. In the United States about 45,000 people lose their lives each year.

A rough estimate puts the chances of a fatality in a minibus, *matatu* or combi at about 30 times the normal U.S. accident rate. So the next time you plunk down between a quarter and fifty cents for one of these rides, consider how much you just sold your life for.

Busplunge.com
http://users.lmi.net/tcs55/index.html
South African National Department of Transportation
http://www.transport.gov.za/
School Bus Accidents
http://www.stnonline.com/core2_files/bbs/accidents.htm

HOW TO SURVIVE MINIBUSES

There is a reason for the multitude of religious symbols, slogans and prayers painted on Third World buses. Once they cram their doors shut and the wobbly wheels start forward, your life is in the hands of a supreme being. If you travel via small buses, remember the following:

- **Don't travel at night. Many bus lines travel at night because it is cooler and the road is less crowded. Drunks, rebels, livestock and hidden washouts all seem to be more prevalant at night. Local drivers also like to sleep at night, usually while they are driving.**

- **Avoid mountainous areas and/or winter conditions. Fly if necessary.**

- **Bring water and food with you; plan for the unexpected, delays and diversions.**

- **Ask whether the route goes through areas frequented by bandits or terrorist groups. You may be surprised to find out who controls the countryside in between major cities.**

- **Sit near an exit or on top. At least make sure you are near an open window. Follow the *DP* rule: Be friends with everyone, your seat mate might be a rebel commander.**

- **There is a reason why you paid 83¢ to travel. You don't buy a lot of brake pads and clutches with that pocket change.**

- **Remember your rooftop luggage is prey for rummagers, slashers and thieves. Put your luggage in a standard trash bag, a canvas duffle or under everyone else's.**

- **Shirt slashers wait for you to doze off and slip out your money pouches. Put your money in your shoes if necessary.**

Taxis

Taxis are not dangerous from an accident point of view but they can be dangerous from a criminal point of view. We are at our most vulnerable when we take cabs. Criminals know this and act accordingly.

There is also one area in the Third World where everyone gets ripped off: Your first ride from the airport into town. After years of negotiation that would make Kissinger or Holbrooke seem like wimps I have managed to pay the local fare. But there is a price to pay. Once the driver knows he will not get $300 in U.S. currency but 300 in the local toilet paper that passes for money (about 8 cents) he then drives into town like a suicidal rally driver. I have learned two lessons. The first is to never piss off a cabdriver and the second is find the oldest driver in the crowd. I figure he didn't get to that advanced age driving like a maniac. (Usually he is just filling in for his son, who is recovering from the time when the brakes failed.)

When you get into a taxi driven by a stranger in a strange land, watch out. The odds for damage to your body, your sense of well-being and your wallet skyrockets. Cabs in most countries have no seat belts, no brakes, no license and no fare limits. In many countries such as Mexico, you may even get robbed in the bargain. In the southern Philippines you could be kidnapped. Taxis can be controlled by telling the driver to drive slowly in his native language. But that does not mean they are bad. Just the opposite. Cabdrivers can be your best friend or your worst enemy, so think carefully about how you treat them. I always ask the cabdriver about his family, the weather, places to see and compliment his rusting place of business. I also leave things in cabs a lot. I always had the driver show up at my room with my wallet or camera and refuse a reward.

Based on courtesy, cleanliness, knowledge and respect for human life, the world's best cabdrivers are in London and the world's worst cabbies are in New York City.

London Taxis
http://www.local-transport.detr.gov.uk/consult/ol/a1.htm
New York Taxi Commission
http://www.ci.nyc.ny.us/html/tlc/home.html
New York City Transportation
http://www.newyorktransportation.com/
Safety Tactics
http://www.tacticsone.com/

HOW TO SURVIVE TAXIS

- **Choose your cab rather than let it choose you. Inspect the car first. Many are just shills for drivers outside. Hire the oldest or the one with the least damage to his car.**

- **Ask staff at the airport how much the ride should cost to go to your city. Inquire about other methods of transportation.**

HOW TO SURVIVE TAXIS

- Always agree on a total fare first and write the price down and show it to the driver. Ask about luggage, airport or time-of-day surcharges

- Keep your luggage in the backseat, not in the trunk.

- Memorize the local words for "no," "yes," "stop here" and "how much?"

- Have the hotel doorman or guide negotiate cab fares in advance when seeing the city. Many private cars also function as taxis, so don't be surprised if a kind person who picks you up wants money.

- It is a global law that cabbies never carry change. Change money at the airport or hotel first.

- Many cabbies will rent themselves out for flat fees. Do not be afraid to negotiate the services of a trusted cabby as guide, chauffeur and protector of baggage.

- Try to establish a rapport with your driver and he may end up being your best tour guide.

Automobiles

If you belive accident statistics, then you would subscribe to the idea that the place you are most likely to meet misfortune is on the road. You need to know that 70 percent of road accidents happen in developing countries. Worldwide half a million people are killed and 15 million are injured in traffic and road mishaps. Traveling from a country where cars have seat belts, air bags and padded dashes to regions where the safety equipment is reduced to a cracked statue of an indeterminate saint probably increases the risks.

International accident rates for travel are clouded by lack of reporting by the large numbers of people who die in vehicle-related accidents and don't have the courtesy to fill out the paperwork after they are dead. Countries like Turkey, Mexico, Pakistan, Australia, India, Egypt and China have horrendous accident rates but do not figure prominently in studies.

Countries like Afghanistan, Somalia, Cambodia and French Guiana wish they had enough cars or roads to have accidents. There is also an odd sleight of hand that pits death per mile of road against death per population total. Both methods have their pitfalls when determining the dangers on the road. Here are a few heads ups for those who wonder if driving is dangerous.

- If stoplights draw crowds just to watch the colors change
- If the little white crosses and flowers are to thank God for making it home alive
- When traffic cops stop you to bum rides and then ticket you for speeding
- When local training for first aid starts by saying "First remove wallet…"
- When cars routinely have bits of clothing flapping from the front bumper

- When an ambulance tells you they need money for gas before they can come and pick up the survivors.

Now, seasoned readers of *DP* will know which one (and only one) of the above is actually not true. The point is that you need to stop and think about the risks you face when you drive in other countries.

Here's what your chances are like outside the country.

International Vehicular Deaths (per 100,000 population)	
India	34.6
South Korea	30.4
Portugal	28.1
Brazil	22.7
Hungary	22.7
Greece	22.0
Venezuela	20.7
Spain	20.5
Ecuador	20.0
New Zealand	19.5
Luxembourg	19.4
Poland	19.2
Belgium	18.4
United States	18.4

Sources: Various; not all countries are included

This time let's look at road deaths based on distance driven instead of population.

Deaths (per 100 million kilometers driven)			
Egypt	43.2	Bahrain	3.2
Kenya	36.0	New Zealand	2.2
South Korea	29.0	Israel	2.2
Turkey	22.0	Taiwan	2.0
Morocco	21.0	France	2.0
Yemen	12.4	Germany	1.9
Austria	10.7	Japan	1.7
South Africa	10.4	Switzerland	1.6
Bulgaria	9.9	Ireland	1.5
Portugal	9.0	Denmark	1.5
Hungary	8.0	Finland	1.4
Macedonia	7.8	Thailand	1.3
Poland	6.3	Netherlands	1.3

Deaths (per 100 million kilometers driven)			
Czech Republic	5.9	Norway	1.2
Spain	5.9	United States	1.1
Hong Kong	4.8	Sweden	1.1
Belgium	3.3	United Kingdom	1.0

Source: IRF, NSC, ASIRT, others (various years)

So it is important to not only view statistics as sketchy but at least feel confident that bad driving is bad driving. The conditions under which you are driving has more of an influence than the country you are in. Alcohol, nighttime, high speeds and bad weather are far more dangerous than cabbing it in Egypt or India.

HOW TO SURVIVE AUTOMOBILES

There is little to be said that hasn't been said in every driver's education class. Speed, booze, bad roads and other drivers kill. Driving in the Third World is not safe, so if possible check out the local Hertz Rent-a-Yak.

- Be familiar with local road warning signs and laws. You can be a good driver and be completely baffled by the sign in Urdu that says "washed out bridge ahead."

- Avoid driving yourself if possible. Usually a local driver may add a few gray hairs but is conversant with local laws, shortcuts and safety matters. Then again, maybe he isn't.

- Avoid driving in inclement weather conditions, at nighttime or especially on weekends. Fog kills, rain kills, drunks kill, other tourists kill. It is estimated that after midnight on Friday and Saturday nights in rural America, three out of five drivers on the road have been drinking. That means if you are one of the sober ones, pray that the other sober driver is coming the other way.

- Stay off the road in high-risk countries. You may think the Italians, Portuguese and Spaniards display amazing bravado as they skid around winding mountain roads. The accident rate says they are just lousy drivers that haven't been killed yet.

- Reduce your speed. This is your biggest edge in staying alive.

- Wear a seat belt, rent bigger cars, drive during daylight, use freeways, carry a map and a good road guide, etc. You're not listening, are you?

- Don't drive at night. You would be surprised what sleeps on the road in the tropics. Most locals never venture outside after dark, let alone drive. In many Central Asian and former Soviet republics drinking and driving is common. I could go on, but you've probably skipped this part, haven't you?

- Don't drive tired or while suffering from jet lag. Don't pull off to the side of the road to nap, don't leave possessions in plain sight and try to park in lighted areas. I can see you're not listening, so just do whatever the hell you are going to do, but don't say I didn't warn you.

National Transportation Safety Board
http://www.ntsb.gov/Surface/Highway/highway.htm
ASIRT
http://www.asirt.org
World Road Rage Survey
http://www.aloha.net/~dyc/surveys/survey2/interpretations.html

Boats

Some parts of the world offer more waterborne transportation than land based. Whether it's tropical archipelagoes like Indonesia or the Philippines or ferries in Hong Kong, the United Kingdom or Bangladesh, people get around on boats. Unlike for planes and cars, there are few helpful statistical heads ups on boat safety. When you consider that most big ships seem to be registered in a bastion of safety and social responsibility—Liberia—then I guess it's okay to be nervous. There are some countries that don't even require enough lifeboats for the number of passengers. Countries like the United States. Even with the popularity of the film *Titanic* you should know that the majority of U.S. passenger vessels that operate within 20 miles of shore and inland waterways are allowed to carry passengers without enough lifeboats and rafts for everyone should they sink. Some have as little as 20 percent of the maximum number of passengers allowed. Quick, there's a sequel in there somewhere. In Seattle, where Starbucks-sloshed, fleece-decked ferry commuters confidently sail to and from work every day, there is a Third World attitude toward marine safety. Most of the ferries have equipment to keep only 25 percent of the passengers out of the frigid Puget Sound waters should one sink. Luckily one never has. The Coast Guard says that in the United States there were 88 fatalities on boats carrying 7 or more passengers in a 30-year period. When *USA Today* looked into domestic ship safety this is what they came up with.

U.S. Ship Accidents	
Passenger vessel accidents in U.S. waters from 1985 through 1995 included:	
Groundings	769
Strikings against solid objects	438
Fires	211
Boat collisions	204
Flooded vessels	194
Sinkings	131
Capsized vessels	38
Explosions	18

Source: Transport Canada/U.S. Coast Guard records

The conclusion is that Stateside and in Canada there is little to fear other than a rough crossing. Going overseas, things change.

Ferries in places like Bangladesh, Haiti, the Philippines and Hong Kong have had major disasters from capsizing due to overloading and collision. In roughly an eight-year period around the world, there were more than 360 ferryboat accidents killing 11,350 people.

The truth is that ocean travel in large ships is so safe they don't even keep death statistics. In 1998, 5.4 million people took vacations on 467 major cruise ships (with 55 more on their way next year), and the only major accident was when 54 people were injured on a shipboard fire aboard the *Carnival Ecstasy*. The only accidental deaths were when 31 crew members were lost at sea during Hurricane Mitch on the *Windjammers Fantome*. A pretty impressive statistic.

Ahoy There Matey!

Hey, who ya gonna call next time you take that dive boat out to Dead Man's Key and spot a speedboat of do-ragged, AK-toting squinty-eyes heading your way? MRM will send in aircraft to drop Specialist Rapid Response Teams to the site of your next hijacking. They are only interested in big money or big cargo gigs, but they just might be bored when you call about your dugout being attacked. Their PR says that each member of the team possess all the specialized skills neccessary to "neutralize" maritime piracy, terrorists and hijack attempts. Hoo yah.

Marine Risk Management, Anti Hijack Service
http://www.marinerisk.com/services/piracy.htm

Those that fancy the life of Joseph Conrad should also know that piracy is still a fact of life in Southeast Asia and other parts of the world. Their targets range from large oil tankers to poor fishermen. The vast majority are attacks against unarmed merchant vessels with ferries and private craft being the small minority. Many are inside jobs and never impact the traveler. Most pirates are armed with submachine guns and use small speedboats to jump the slow-moving vessels. They then commandeer the craft to a safe harbor where they unload the tons of cargo. The major activity centers are in the waters around the Philippines, Thailand, Indonesia, Sri Lanka, Nicarauga, Somalia, Brazil, Sierra Leone and the Mediterranean. Tourists are not immune from pirates either. The Caribbean is the worst spot if you want to end up in the Bermuda Triangle. In the Mediterranean, four Albanian pirates knocked off a boatload of tourists near Corfu a few years back. Two French yachtsmen were kidnapped in Somalia in June of 1998. In the Philippines entire ferryboats are now commandeered by pirates. On my last trip through the Sulu Sea the ferry captain pointed out the bullet hole by the door to the bridge where the last pirates attacked.

The International Maritime Bureau has a piracy bureau in Kuala Lumpur that tracks these things. It said that in 1997 pirates killed 50 sailors in 229 attacks and 400 had been taken hostage. Attacks take place at sea or at anchor and about a quarter of the attacks involved guns. In 1999 attacks had increased overall by 19 percent. According to the Nippon Foundation, a Japanese piracy tracking group, there were 192 reported acts of piracy worldwide and a just under a third were reported along the coasts of Indonesia.

Cruise ships are much safer, with the occasional engine room fire and food poisoning. However, it doesn't provide much comfort to know that the *Achille Lauro* (site of the terrorist takeover that ended in the execution of a wheelchair-bound American, Leon Klinghoffer) sank off the coast of Africa and was dredged up and refurbished for use as a luxury cruise liner.

International Maritime Bureau
http://www.iccwbo.org/IMB/IMB_Piracy_Centre.html
Project on Insurgency, Terrorism and Security/Piracy
http://paladin-san-francisco.com/libpirac.htm
United States Coast Guard
http://www.dot.gov/dotinfo/uscg/welcome.html
National Transportation Safety Board
http://www.ntsb.gov/Surface/marine/marine.htm

HOW TO SURVIVE BOATS

It is hard to provide general safety tips considering the wide range of waterborne craft travelers can take. Large cruise ships have very different safety problems when compared to pirogues. Here is a starting list.

- Know how to swim, or at least how to float. Panic kills.

- Wear or have quick access to a life preserver. Don't assume that the large chest labeled "Life Preservers" actually has usable life preservers in it. Look. You are always better off in a lifeboat because of cold water or sharks.

- Do not take overcrowded boats. Charter your own or ask when the boat will be less crowded. Overcrowding and rough seas are the major reasons for sinking of small- and medium-sized ships.

- Avoid travel in rough weather, or during monsoon or hurricane season.

- Stay off the water in areas frequented by pirates. This applies even to pleasure excursions in places like the southern Philippines, Borneo and Thailand.

- In cold weather remember where the covered life rafts are and if there are exposure suits available. Understand the effects and prevention of hypothermia.

- On large ships pay attention to safety and lifeboat briefings and practice going from your cabin to the lifeboat station with your eyes closed.

- Keep a small carry-on or backpack with your money, papers and minor survival gear (water, energy bars, hat, compass and map). Make it waterproof and a potential life preserver by using one or two garbage bags as a liner.

- Prepare and bring items to prevent seasickness, sunburn, glare and chapped skin.

Flying

Twenty-five million Americans say they are afraid to fly. The rest just lie about it. But the truth is that flying isn't dangerous. It's the crashing part that is. And not many planes crash. Every year you will learn that about the same number of people are killed by lightning as in plane crashes. (Something that should make those nervous flyers think about getting off the ground.) It is even more telling that among the top ten aircraft disasters, most of them occurred when the planes were shot or blown out of the skies or while taxiing on the ground. So view any statistical journey into aircraft danger as proof of the relative safety of this modern marvel. A British study shows that flying is 176 times safer than walking, 15 times safer than car travel and 300 times safer than riding a motorcycle. Statistically, if you were to take a flight every morning you would have to fly for 21,000 years before you would have a deadly crash. Australia can stick all its crashes for the last ten years on one web page (http://www.basi.gov.au/). There are 12,000 (some say 9,000) airliners in the sky making over 15 million flights carrying 1.3 billion passengers. With all that activity, there are only about 40 accidents involving major airlines (including cargo planes) every year. Still, the volume of air traffic and the emerging travel boom in Asia has prompted Boeing to say that there will be a major air crash every week by the year 2010. A dramatic statement, but that still only means 12 more accidents a year at a time when there will be twice as many airliners in operation.

First World Roulette

If you fly any First World airline, your chances of being killed in a crash are one in 4.4 million, according to MIT. If you are on a U.S. carrier, flying coast to coast, the odds are even better, one in 11 million. About two-thirds of major airline crashes have been blamed on flight crew error. When you change from a big bird to a puddle-jumper you have just increased your chances of crashing by a factor of four. Commuter flights (flights with 30 or fewer seats) carry about 12 percent of all passengers. These small planes not only fly lower and take off and land more often, they are piloted by less-experienced, more overworked pilots and are not subject to the same safety standards as large airliners.

Get on a smaller private plane or a charter and the odds multiply again. About 700 people die in small plane crashes each year in the United States. There are so many crashes that the small airplane industry has evaporated because of the resultant litigation. There are 650,000 private pilots in the United States and only 700 out of the 13,000 airfields have control towers. The accident rate for a small plane is about 11 for every 100,000 aircraft hours compared to 0.8 for commercial jets. There are 2 fatalities for every 100,000 hours of operation for small planes. Once again these statistics reviewed against other methods of transportation still look damn good.

Dangerous Trips	

Things look a little different when you eliminate the miles covered and focus on the accident rate based on the number of man-hours exposed to a form of transportation.

Motorcycle	**300.0**
Bicycle	**60.0**
Walking	**20.0**
Automobile	**15.0**
Airplane	**15.0**
Intercity Bus	**6.6**
Train	**4.8**
Transit Bus	**0.1**

Source: Royal Society for the Prevention of Accidents
http://www.rospa.co.uk/

Third World Roulette

Something's bugging you. All this good news about flying but yet it is still covered in *DP*. What is the bad news? Well, the U.S.-based Flight Safety Foundation says that in the last 10 years 70 percent of all accidents involved carriers that between them accounted for 16 percent of all air traffic. A similar statistic exists when safety is examined by region. Over 75 percent of air accidents happen in countries that account for only 12 percent of world air traffic.

Most deaths (over 50 percent) occur when the planes simply fly into the ground. Ouch. Somebody pass the Windex up front.

Even U.S. puddle-jumpers are as safe as houses compared to Third World airlines. If you are flying anywhere in Africa, the chances of crashing are multiplied by 20—about the same odds as getting killed in an automobile accident in the States. Some experts calculate the odds of being killed in a plane crash are less than one in a million for North America, Canada and Western Europe versus one in 50,000 for the dark continent.

Latin America, the Middle East, Asia and Eastern Europe follow Africa as the most dangerous areas of the world. Some number crunchers say that Eastern Europe has the highest accident rate in the world. Not surprising considering that poorer countries fly old aircraft usually purchased from major carriers who have already wrung every useful mile from their abused frames. In the United States the fatality rate can be expressed as 0.5 for every million miles flown; in Russia it is 10 times higher (5.2) and in China it is 20 times higher (10).

New information about the number of air-related deaths has shown that China may be getting better. Airline deaths decreased from at least 642 people in the five-year period between 1989 and 1994 to 37 between 1995 to 1998. China still leads Latin America and Africa in the safety ratings.

Fatal Accidents (per Hundred Thousand Flights)	
Africa	21
Asia	13
South America	8
Central America	8
Europe	5
North America	2
Caribbean	2

Source: *Flight Safety Foundation*

How do you make foreign airlines safer? Well, the Chinese government ordered all airline execs to be flying on their planes when the clocked rolled into the year 2000. Magically, Y2K problems were fixed well in advance. You might be surprised to learn that in 1999, 65 percent of the Chinese fleet are Boeings and 20 percent are Airbus jets with eight A-340s and 20 A-320s on order

Elsewhere in Asia things are improving as well. KAL, whose sterling record of a major crash every year for five years did little to improve bookings, spent $30 million with Boeing to teach their pilots new tricks, like speaking English, the language of air-traffic controllers worldwide, and speaking up when the plane was crashing. Apparently their cultural training says it's rude to point out that your superior is making a mistake. Where is Don Rickles when you need him?

So is flying getting safer? You bet. As many people die in airline accidents as die in animal-drawn vehicles, according to the FAA. In 1946 there were 78 general aviation accidents with 7 fatalities per 100,000 hours of flight time. In 1998 there were 7 accidents and 1 fatality per 100,000 hours. In 1998 there was only one death in 41 accidents, or 0.3 crashes and 0.006 fatalities per 100,000 flight hours, according to the National Transportation Safety Board.

Things are getting better on the private side, despite the JFK Jr. nosedive. There were 37 million private pilots in 1998 who put in the 40 hours to get a license. The FAA issued more than 616,000 flight certificates. In 1998 manufacturers shipped 2,220 planes. Although there are commercial flights permitted out of 300 airports in the States, private pilots fly out of 13,000, which means there is a lot more activity (not as many miles) in the private sector. Small planes have become safer; crashes have dropped in half over the last 20 years, down to 350 a year. One tip: Planes with tail wheels have fewer accidents than those with nose wheels.

What should you really worry about? Around 4,500 passengers are injured by objects falling out of overhead bins.

AirSafe.com
http://www.airsafe.com/
Searchable air-safety information for the airline passenger. Among the crashes covered are celebrity deaths like JFK Jr., Dino Martin's full throttle mind meld, Vic Morrow's last scene, and a whole flapping rudder 737-full of dead rock bands, sports teams, politicians, race car drivers and country singers.

Aviation Safety Network—All the crashes that fit
http://aviation-safety.net/

Royal Society for the Prevention of Accidents
http://www.rospa.co.uk/

Airclaims
http://www.airclaims.co.uk/
An independent source of information on the aviation industry.

Air Data Research
http://www.airsafety.com/
Aviation accident reports and safety equipment.

National Transportation Safety Board
http://www.ntsb.gov/aviation/aviation.htm
Why not curl up with a good diasaster book? On-line descriptions of over 43,000 aviation accidents are on the database. Also in the works, information on road, marine and train safety.

FAA Office of Accident Investigation
http://www.faa.gov/avr/aai/iirform.htm
For those who want the latest crash info, this site covers accidents that have occurred within the last ten days. Please, no liability lawyers.

HOW TO SURVIVE FLYING

Despite all the unnerving statistics, if you have a choice of transportation when traveling long distances, jump on a plane. This applies even in Russia, China or South America. Yes, it is dangerous—but not as dangerous as enduring the kaleidoscope of misery and misfortune that awaits you on the ground.

- Stick to U.S.-based carriers with good safety records.

- Fly between major airports on nonstop flights.

- Avoid bad weather or flying at night.

- You can sit in the back if you want (the rear ten rows are usually intact in case of ground impact but the passengers are usually dead) or above the wing (you may get thrown clear, seat and all) or near an exit (easier egress in case of fire or emergency landing) might be just as advisable.

- Avoid small charter aircraft, dirt strips and non-instrument fields.

- The smaller the plane the higher the risk. The poorer the country, same deal except when foreign carriers operate airplanes in Third World countries.

- Avoid national carriers that are not allowed to fly into the United States.

- Avoid military cargo flights, tagging along on combat missions, or flying over active combat or insurgence areas like Afghanistan.

- Avoid older Soviet or Chinese-made aircraft or helicopters.

- Keep up on what type of aircraft you will be flying on (United States and European is better) and keep in mind you usually get what you pay for.

- After all this, remember that travel by airliner is the safest method of transportation and that your odds of surviving a plane crash are about 50 percent.

- If you are still terrified, remember you can buy flight insurance at 150 airports around the United States. You can get half a million dollars of insurance for $16.65 or you can spend the same amount on four stiff drinks. We recommend the former, but usually end up doing the latter.

Trains

Trains are supposed to be safe. After all, they run on rails, are usually pointed in one direction and rumored to be immune to the inclement weather that dogs airplanes, buses and cars. There's a joke that conductors like to tell: "What is the last thing a bug sees when it hits the windshield of a train?" The answer: Its asshole. What that means is when trains do hit, they hit hard.

What most people don't know is that train safety is the other way around. Most deaths attributed to trains are suicides—people who deliberately kill themselves using a train. In the United Kingdom, where there are historically 25 to 89 deaths caused by trains in a year, there were 250 to 265 deaths of suicides and trespassers. In the United States in 1998, 536 pedestrians were killed on or beside tracks, compared with 431 at crossings. In 1993, there were 626 deaths from crossing accidents and 523 trespassing deaths along the tracks. This is still statistically irrelevant to the 40,000 or so motor vehicle deaths (one killed every 12 minutes for stat nuts).

Trains tend to run into substantial objects like trucks stalled on crossings or other trains coming the other way. But there are very few accidents compared to cars.

Using the death rate per million miles as a guide, American trains are about twice as dangerous as flying, four times safer than driving and a lot safer than local buses. If they have a bar car you can quickly douse your fears as you watch the war-ravaged countryside zip by.

U.S. Trains
http://www.bts.gov/
NTSB
http://www.ntsb.gov/Railroad/railroad.htm
British Trains
http://www.open.gov.uk/hse/railway/rsb9798.htm
Safety Links
http://www.open.gov.uk/hse/org/usa99.htm

HOW TO SURVIVE TRAINS

- Ask locals whether the train is a target for bandits (this is appropriate in Eastern Europe, Russia, Asia or Africa where terrorists, bandits and insurgents regularly target trains).

- Beware of Eastern European train routes where thieves are known to ride as passengers. Sleep with the window cracked open to avoid being gassed.

- Stash your valuables in secret spots, making it more difficult for robbers to locate your belongings.

- The back of the train is traditionally the safest area in the event of a collision. Unless, of course, your train is rear-ended.

HOW TO SURVIVE TRAINS

- Keep your luggage with you at all times if possible. Be nice to the conductor and he will keep an eye out for you.

- Trains are preferable to buses or cars when traveling through mountainous areas, deserts and jungles.

Tourism

A jet ski in Cyprus, a flash flood in Switzerland, a robber in San Francisco, rebels in Uganda, a helicopter in Alaska, a swollen river in Australia, a bus crash in Taiwan, an American sniper in Baja, a creaky boat in Greece, a wall of water in Austria, a mass murderer in Yellowstone, an avalanche in Pakistan. All killers of tourists. None a trend, a statistical blip or even a predictable event. It's pretty much business as usual for tourists or residents around the world when it comes to crime. Tourists are better victims than locals but they are protected more, often travel in groups and take great pains not to get robbed or killed while on vacation.

For the truly paranoid there is APB News (*http://www.apbnews.com/*) where you can find out the crime index for a zip code, listen to police scanners and check out the latest misery before booking your trip.

Tourism Links

Mayhem Morgue
http://www.mayhem.net/Crime/morgue1.html
World Tourism Organization
www.world-tourism.org/
Tourism Offices
www.mbnet.mb.ca/lucas/travel/
Tourist Scams in Europe
www.ricksteves.com/298scam.htm
Tourist Scams in Peru
www.seanet.com/~dg/PeruTravel/SCAMS.htm
Tourist Scams in Russia
www.trans-siberian.co.uk/page64.html
ECPAT (anti–sex tourism)
www.ecpat.net/
Fear of Flying Site
http://www.celebratetoday.com/airdis.html
Books for NGO's
http://www.ngobooks.org

Natural Disasters

Have a nice day. Spoken like a true Californian. Out here we have earthquakes, mudslides, fires, drought and flood. And that's just the attractions at Universal Studio's theme park. The reality is that about 11,000 people die worldwide from natural disasters. Not many of those folks are on vacation. We know that low rates and the hurricane season go hand in hand in the fall and we have a sneaking hunch that blizzards, avalanches and skiing go together. But the nice thing about natural disasters and tourists is that we have a return ticket—the locals don't.

In a typical year there are 600 major natural disasters. In one year there were 200 storms, 170 floods, 50 earthquakes, 30 volcanic eruptions and 150 landslides and forest fires. The bad news is that natural disasters are up 400 percent from three decades ago. That's simply because there are more people and things to get flooded, burned, slid, crushed or blown up.

An average of 400 people are hit by lightning (about 90 die) every year in the United States. The solution? Minimize contact with the ground and get down real low. Don't lie down. The most dangerous places to get hit by lightning, according to the National Climatic Data Center, are open fields and ball fields. What readers may find surprising is the confluence of dangerous places and earthquakes. Unlike hurricanes, fires, volcanoes, typhoons or snowstorms (which have plenty of warnings), earthquakes strike without warning and give you little chance to make an escape. But more importantly, just look at this list of major earthquakes from Reuters and count how many countries are covered in *DP*.

Major Earthquakes		
Earthquakes leading to death tolls over 1, 000 people		
8/17/99	TURKEY	Over 17,000 killed in a 7.4 magnitude quake south of Istanbul in one of the most deadly earthquakes in history.
1/25/99	COLOMBIA	6.2 quake killed at least 1,200 and left 4,500 injured in the central region.
5/30/98	AFGHANISTAN	3,000 dead and 50 villages destroyed in Takhar province.
2/4/98	AFGHANISTAN	4,500 dead in the Rustaq district of Takhar province. The quake measured 6.1.
5/10/97	IRAN	2,000 killed in 7.1 temblor in rural areas of eastern Iran.
5/28/95	RUSSIA	1,989 dead in Russia's worst (est. 7.5 magnitude) earthquake in Neftegorsk and Sakhalin Island.
1/17/95	JAPAN	6,500 killed in central Japan (7.2 magnitude in Kobe).
6/6/94	COLOMBIA	1,000 killed in an earthquake and mudslide in the Paez River valley.
9/30/93	INDIA	22,000 killed, 36 villages destroyed in western and southern India. The first of the five tremors measured 6.4.
12/12/92	INDONESIA	2,200 killed in East Nusa Tenggara by 6.8 magnitude earthquake.
10/20/91	INDIA	1,600 dead, at least 2,000 injured. The quake measured 6.1 on the Richter scale, and was centered close to Uttarkashi, 190 miles northeast of Delhi.
2/1/91	PAKISTAN/ AFGHANISTAN	1,200 dead (Pakistan 200, Afghanistan 1,000), 6.8 magnitude.
7/16/90	PHILIPPINES	2,000 killed, 3,500 injured in 7.7 magnitude quake centered in Cabanatuan.
6/21/90	IRAN	35,000 dead, 100,000 injured. Quake registered 7.7 on Richter scale.
12/7/88	SOVIET UNION	25,000 killed, 18,000 injured. Quake measured 6.9 on Richter scale. Affected area in northwest Armenia.

Major Earthquakes		
3/5/87	ECUADOR	1,000 people killed and several thousand missing in El Reventador, 50 miles east of Quito.
10/10/86	EL SALVADOR	1,500 people killed, 20,000 people injured. Quake measured 7.5 on the Richter scale. Left over 300,000 homeless.
9/19/85	MEXICO	Between 6,000 and 12,000 killed, with 40,000 people injured. Registered 8.1 on Richter scale in Mexico City and adjoining region.
10/30/83	TURKEY	1,300 killed, 500 injured. Over 6 magnitude in the city of Erzurum.
12/13/82	YEMEN	3,000 killed, 2,000 people injured in quake that measured 6 on the Richter scale in Dhamar province, southeast of Sanaa.
6/11/81	IRAN	1,027 people killed and over 800 injured. Measured 6.8 on the Richter scale. The town of Golbaf in Kerman province was destroyed.
11/23/80	ITALY	2,735 people killed and over 7,500 injured in 7.2 quake. The epicenter was at Eboli, but damage was reported over a huge area as far as Naples. Over 1,500 people were reported missing.
10/10/80	ALGERIA	2,590 killed in a 7.3 magnitude earthquake in El Asnam.

Source: Reuters

Making the Best of Nasty Situations

Roll Up to the Magical Misery Tour

We've explored *what* is dangerous; now we should talk about *where* it's dangerous. Remembering to wear a condom in Somalia when chasing a warlord's wife or getting googly-eyed with that cute talib without wearing a burqa in Kabul is kind of where culture collides with travel advice. Fine, so savvy travelers just don't end up in dangerous places, right? Wrong. Travelers live in, work in, travel through and reside in war zones without even knowing it half the time. Let's look at the collision of two trends.

There is a new trend in travel: Intelligent people wanting to explore their world. A land devoid of fast food, hotels, touts, bus tours, concrete dinosaurs or even pay toilets. Before Thomas Cook invented the tour, people were hesitant to just head out and wander around. After all, it was dangerous out there. There were criminals, wars, disease, kidnappers . . . well, you get the point. Things haven't changed much once you explore a little further off the beaten path. When I meet with victims of tragedy overseas, all of them tell me how safe it was, how much research they did and how unexpected the whole event turned out to be. In other words, they assumed that intelligence, planning and dropping a few thou for an adventure tour made them immune from political and cultural realities.

It is my belief that the truly interesting and educational things on this planet occur in areas of high-intensity living. Places where people warn you not to go. But let's go there expecting danger, not thinking we can get vaccinated against it.

Dying to Meet You

I spend most of my time in places where people are fighting wars. It's not something I recommend—it's just what I do. I don't pretend that I can make a major difference, but maybe I can keep a few people safe and help people make heads or tails out of the mess. Warfare is not a bad thing for tourists. It keeps them safe. Our government posts long lists of reasons not to go to places that we consider areas of conflict. Surprisingly, you won't find any information on the United States, a country that is, has been (and continues to be) at war with a number of nations and movements, so then conversely we must assume that we live in a war zone.

You won't find travel advisories for the World Trade Center, Oklahoma or other areas that have seen violent episodes and civilian casualties.

According to the United Nations, of the 85 or so armed conflicts that were fought in the past 3 years, only 3 were between nations. The rest were civil wars or insurgencies. Four million civilians have been killed in wars since 1990 and the death toll rises every minute. The *Journal of Peace* says there are 36 conflicts in 31 places; the National Defense Council says there are 60 nations currently experiencing warfare, insurgencies and violence. So with so much confusion about where and what is dangerous, there is absolutely no guarantee that you might not be the next casualty. If it helps any, the UN also likes to point out that 90 percent of casualties in today's wars are civilians. If you followed events in Bosnia, Kosovo, Sudan, Iraq or Chechnya, it's hard to get enough names for a decent memorial for the soldiers killed.

So the first lesson is to not think of war zones as places with yellow police tape wrapped around them. Many of the countries you can get killed in don't exist yet. There are somewhere around 195 countries these days—but there were only 74 after World War II and only 62 in 1914. It makes sense that little tinpot countries will continue to calve off, creating mayhem and confusion in the process.

The second important lesson is to rethink how wars are fought these days. You won't see long red lines of nicely uniformed soldiers marching slowly into battle so you can step out of the line of fire in time. There aren't even any decent country-on-country wars anymore. The recent rise in non-national warfare, where groups without a country or a geographic link attack nationals from another country, around the world means that you are on the front lines whether you signed up or not.

When they pick up bodies these days, they tend to be young girls in Algeria, old women in Afghanistan or teenage kids in Karachi. Various liberation groups around the world are looking for a few good victims and that could be you.

Where are the hot spots? Usually in destitute countries where things fell apart a long time ago, countries making the rocky transition from dictatorships to democracy and countries that tried to stuff too many ethnic or religious groups into a happy Second World state. According to the UN, Algeria, Afghanistan,

Angola, Myanmar, Burundi, Egypt, Georgia, Haiti, Iraq, Liberia, Mexico, Mozambique, Nigeria, Sudan, Tajikistan, Rwanda and Congo are nations in crisis and in danger of social disintegration. But some of these countries never had enough to disintegrate from.

There are many other civilized countries such as South Africa, Russia, Brazil, Pakistan and the United States where there is just old-fashioned criminal mayhem taking place on a daily basis. There are about 30 wars where more than 1,000 people are killed each year. Seven of those wars kill over 100,000 people a year.

Ever wonder why you don't see much on these places on your local newscast or even on CNN? First of all, the ratings and the PR strategies of low-level conflicts suck. News crews need compliant officials and basic communications to cover stories. Many countries like Papua New Guinea, Sri Lanka, Chechnya and Turkey won't allow journos in for fear they will contest the "official" daily body count. A few folks like *DP* have to sneak in, but we will never go prime time. And in the case of Sri Lanka, even the rebels won't let us in. So these places are assigned to eager but poorly paid stringers who routinely send in casualty reports but never get the big picture. Also, journalists aren't bulletproof anymore. According to the Reporters san Frontiere, an average of 60 journalists are killed each year and more than 125 are detained by local governments who objected to their reports.

Until more official wars start up (with official battlefield tours and air-conditioned press offices), war correspondents will not make as much money as bleached-blonde anchors and gossip columnists. Maybe that's why some of the better war correspondents have opted to embrace hair spray and reduce their fears to being punched out by Sean Penn. For now, the frontline witnesses of history will consist of a lot of scared civilians, ragged soldiers, gonzo stringers and *DP*'ers.

Come Back Alive
http://www.comebackalive.com/
OSAC Database
http://ds.state.gov/osac/
Travel Warnings
http://travel.state.gov/travel_warnings.html

War

What has changed since the last *DP* was being hastily edited from a hotel lobby in Algeria? Well, sadly, not much. Flareups include Angola, Dagestan, Kosovo, East Timor, Chechnya, Eritrea/Ethiopia, East Timor, India/Pakistan, the Caprivi Strip, Guinea Bissau, Casamance in Senegal, the Congo. But none of these are new wars. Just old wounds that flare up and then calm down.

The leader of the PKK was nabbed, Bin Laden and Milosevic are worth $5 mil each, Basayev is worth a mil and, of course, all the dictators Uncle Sam loves to hate are all still firmly in power.

So did any wars go away? Not really. Supposedly the Basques in Spain were happy for awhile, the Peruvians and Ecuadorians kissed and made up over their disputed border, Lesotho got a wake-up call, the IRA stopped bombing (although the bombings continue under splinter groups), things have cooled down in Egypt, Israel is actually trying to make peace, Algeria may be running out of rebels to kill, Saddam hasn't invaded Kuwait recently, West Africa became suspiciously quiet with a brief tussle in Niger, the CIS is its usually cranky, sparky self and the Germans are not poised on the border with France and the Japanese have not promised to invade Hawaii. Things seem to be going swimmingly. Or are they?

I would have to say yes, but on a glacial scale. In 1900 there were 6 democracies and warfare was an accepted part of colonial occupation and old world politics. In 1980 there were 37 democracies and the USSR was backing anyone with a *kefiya* or flip-flops. In 1998 there were 117 democratic nations, with over half of the world's population living in democratic countries. So how come the National Defense Council (who counts 192 nations) says that we have 60 conflicts going on in 1998? This is a drop of 7 since 1997, but a lot more than the 35 conflicts in 1989. The Center for Defense Information says the number of conflicts are in the low 20s. In 1998 they counted 26. The CIA, which should know these things, says there are about 25, give or take a few cruise missile tests here and there. *DP* lists about 80 conflicts, and we are too lazy to list all those tongue-twisting, unpronounceable Transcaucasus cockfights, Somali clan bangs or Myanmarese muddles. The real truth is there are no wars these days. The world is too interconnected by commerce to allow a real slam-bang, roll the tanks, toe-to-toe, do-or-die war. Sure we'll run some tanks around Kuwait, beach our Zodiacs in Panama or even fly over Kosovo, but we are not going to be bayoneted by some blue-eyed mother's sons anytime soon. So read the following list with that in mind.

When you hear the word war be a little suspicious. Yes, India is "at war" with Pakistan, North and South Korea are pissed, Israel doesn't like Syria, but what the hell would either side do with the other if it won?

The sad truth as you review the *DP* list for edition four is that you'll see that most wars are being fought inside countries. In many cases, nary a shot needs to be fired to kill. Starvation, impoverishment, burning villages, no medical care and plain old scare tactics can force people out of their homes and into the grim death camps that await them. Often we assist that evil by rattling our Swiss Army knife, wringing our hands and prevaricating until the dirty work is done. Then we bomb and embargo the victim's country into 2000 B.C. It is the West's reluctance to get into wars that create wars. Our need to lecture the combatants, but not actually show them who's meaner or nastier, lets them get away with murder.

Civilians Killed by Their Own Government		
Soviet Union	62,000,000	1917–1991
China	35,000,000	1949–today
Germany	21,000,000	1933–1945
China (Kuomintang)	10,000,000	1928–1949
Japan	6,000,000	1935–1945
Cambodia	1,000,000	1975–1979
Sudan	500,000	1955–

So for now, expect all these tired, dirty wars to continue for the foreseeable future. Unless we pour mountains of cash on the combatants, expect them to take pot-shots at each other, starve and torture, recruit and harangue and generally become part of the dirty laundry that our shiny white morals will not wash.

http://www.polisci.com/

Watching War Waste

Normally *DP* can get its hands on just about any statistic we want. Want to know how many people slip in bathtubs? No problem. How much shampoo is used? A snap. What the world's biggest taco weighed? Easy. But try to find out how many tourists were snuffed overseas and you will hit a dead end. They are called civilians, visitors, expats, collateral damage, whatever. But no one really wants to tell you how many people were shot, raped, robbed, infected, thumped, chopped up, bombed, barbecued or bitch slapped when overseas. Then there is the problem of matching deaths and mishaps to lack of willing victims. Rather than sail into the dark waters of speculation we have confined ourselves to tracking warfare based on a number of dissonant sources and then exploring the tone and timbre in each region.

At least 110,000 people were killed last year in armed conflicts, according to the International Institute for Strategic Studies (IISS). They also estimate annual worldwide arms sales at $56.9 billion in 1998, up from $56 billion a year before.

As we go to press, 10 international wars and 25 civil wars were being fought in the 191 to 225 countries on this planet. Africa has more hot spots than any other continent, with 11 major conflicts, producing more than eight million refugees.

Eleven of the civil wars were in sub-Saharan Africa with about 55,000 deaths, or 60 percent of the world total deaths from armed conflict, also occurring there.

The IISS estimated 15,000 dead in Ethiopia and Eritrea, 9,000 in the Congo war, and 9,000 in Sierra Leone. Three-quarters of the countries in sub-Saharan Africa are engaged in armed conflict or confronted by a significant threat from armed groups.

Military expenditure in the region totaled nearly $11 billion last year, if military assistance and funding of opposition groups and mercenaries are taken into account.

The United States remains the world's largest arms exporter, accounting for almost half of all arms sold. The military survey estimates that the international arms trade was worth $55.8 billion in 1988. Saudi Arabia was by far the single largest purchaser, importing more than $10 billion, followed by Taiwan. Britain, once the world's second biggest arms exporter, last year sold $9 billion worth of arms—putting it third behind France. So you can see that, until *DP* took out the calculator and death's-head pencil, there was no single "Chart of Wars That Can Kill Tourists Now." We are not going to provide any stirring editorials on the horrors or futilities of war, we just want you to know what's going on. There are lots of unofficial estimates, security service updates and state department warnings, but in our opinion there is no definitive list that reflects rebel, government and civilian casualties. The other thing you would expect is that these "kill" numbers would be changing at the rate of those national deficit billboards. I compared as many statistics as we could find, gave them a fudge factor (fibbing rebels and eager governments) and extrapolated them about two months down the road. Keep in mind that many of the high death tolls are the result of starvation being used directly as a tactic of war. Also, many regions have no official reporting, so we rely on local folks to give us a feel for how busy the morgue is. If you like think tanks check out:

National Institute for Research Advancement
http://www.nira.go.jp/ice/index.html

The International Institute for Strategic Studies
23 Tavistock Street, London WC2E 7NQ, UK
Tel +44(0)171 379 7676 or +44(0)171 872 0770
Fax +44(0)171 836 3108 e-mail iiss@iiss.org.uk
www.isn.ethz.ch/iiss/iisshome.htm

The Center for Strategic and International Studies
http://www.csis.org/

Institute of Strategic and International Studies (ISIS)
http://www.jaring.my/isis/

The Center for Security Studies and Conflict Research
http://www.fsk.ethz.ch/

The National Institute for Strategic Studies
http://www.niss.gov.ua/

War Child
http://www.warchild.

EmergencyNet
http://www.emergency.com

Reliefweb
http://www.reliefweb.int

COPRED
http://www.gmu.edu/departments/ICAR/copred/99conference.html

The DP List

To show you just how much history you may be missing, *DP* has compiled the mother of all lists. In our futile attempt to makes sense of this list, we have used the term *war* to describe instances when police or military are actively campaigning. The gray bars denote areas recovering from warfare with little active fighting.

Country	Type	Cause	Since	With	Killed
AFGHANISTAN	Civil War	Political	1989	Taliban (Pushtun) vs. United Front (Tajiks)	40,000
ALBANIA	Chaos	Political	1998	Local Militias	2,000
ALGERIA	Insurgency	Religious, Political	1992	Islamic Groups vs. Military	100,000
ANGOLA	Civil War	Political, Diamonds	1975	UNITA, FLEC	420,000
ARMENIA	Civil	Religious, Ethnic	1988	Occupation of Azerbaijan	50,000
AZERBAIJAN	Ethnic	Occupation	1988	Nagorno Karabakh	40,000
BOSNIA-HERZEGOVINA	Civil War	Occupation	1991	Serbs vs. Bosnian-Croats & Muslims	250,000
BOUGAINVILLE	See Papua New Guinea				

Country	Type	Cause	Since	With	Killed
BRAZIL	Crime	Economic, Drugs	1992	Drugs, Crime	5,000
BURUNDI	Civil War	Ethnic	1969 1972 1988 1993 1996	Hutu vs. Tutsi	180,000 Since 1993
CAMBODIA	Civil War	Political	1970	Royalists/Khmer Rouge vs. Gov.	2,000,000+
CHECHNYA	(SEE RUSSIA)				
CHINA	Occupation	Political	1950	Tibet	1,200,000
	Insurgency	Ethnic	1920's	East Turkmenistan: Muslim Turkics vs Chinese Ethnics	3,000?
	Territorial Threat	Political	1949	Taiwan	0
	Territorial Threat	Economic	Historic	Spratlys: Contested by Philippines, China Vietnam, Taiwan, Brunei and Malaysia	2
COMOROS	Independence	Economic	1997	Anjouan and Mobeli secede . . . back to France	200
CONGO (BRAZZAVILLE)	Civil War	Political	1995	Old Marxists vs. Gov.	10,000
CONGO (KINSHASA)	Ethnic Political	Ethnic, Political	1998	Kabila vs. Mobutu Supporters	200,000+
COLOMBIA	Drug War, Crime	Ethnic, Political, Ideological, Drugs	1986	FARC, ELN, EZLN, EPL vs. government and Right-wing Squads	30,000
CYPRUS	Ethnic	Territorial	1974	Turks vs. Greeks	N/A
DJIBOUTI	Ethnic	Ethnic, Tribal	1991	Afar vs. Issa Tribes	350
EAST TIMOR	Independence	Occupation	1975	Militias vs. Timorese	212,000
EGYPT	Fundamentalism	Religious	1992	The Islamic Group	700
ETHIOPIA	War	Territorial	1962/ 1999		40,000

Country	Type	Cause	Since	With	Killed
ERITREA	War	Territorial	1973/ 1999		40,000
GEORGIA	Civil War	Ethnic	1991	Abkhazia	30,000
	Civil War	Ethnic	1989	South Ossetia	2,000
GUATEMALA	Banditry	Economic	1968	Disbanded Rebels	100,000
GUINEA-BISSAU	Civil War		1964 1998	Senegalese Incursion	3,000?
HAITI	Poverty	Economic	1994	Overthrow of Military	450–2,000
INDIA	War	Occupation	1989	Kashmir: Muslim vs. Hindu	25,000
	Religious	Religious	1981	Punjab: Sikh vs. Hindu	14,000
	Insurgency	Tribal Rights, Economic	1969	Andhra Pradesh: Maoist Naxalites: Peoples War Group vs. Gov.	80
	Insurgency	Tribal Rights, Economic	1985	Assam: Bodos vs. Bengai Hindus; NDFB vs. BLTF	5,500
	Insurgency	Tribal Rights, Economic	1954	Nagaland, Manipur: Various Tribal Groups	N/A
INDONESIA	Militias	Business Interests	1975	East Timor	SEE EAST TIMOR
	Independence	Occupation	1989	North Sumatra: Aceh Merdaka (Freedom Aceh) vs. Gov.	2,500–20,000
	Independence	Occupation	1950	Mollucas:	10,000
	Independence	Occupation	1963	Irian Jaya: Papua Independent Organization (OPM) vs. Gov.	150,000
IRAQ	Civil War	Religious	1991	Southern Iraq Marsh Gov. Sunni vs. Marsh Arab Shi'a Muslim	250,000
	War	Oil	1991	Gulf War (ongoing bombing)	4,500–45,000?

Country	Type	Cause	Since	With	Killed
	Civil War	Ethnic	1981	Northern Iraq: Kurds vs. Gov.	180,000
ISRAEL	War	Occupation	1948	Jews vs. Muslims	3,800
KOSOVO	Independence	Ethnic	1998	Ethnic Albanian vs. Serb	250–4,500
KURDISTAN	See Turkey & Iraq			Kurds. vs. Turks	37,000
LEBANON	War	Occupation	1982	South: Hezbollah vs. Israeli Defense Force	25,000
LIBERIA	Ethnic	Tribal	1989	Tribal Warfare	200,000
MALI	Ethnic	Racial	1990	North: Arab Turag vs. Black	220
MEXICO	Ethnic, Drugs	Political, Drugs	1994	Chiapas: Zapatistas (14 groups)	200
	Civil War			Guerrerro: EPR	40
MOROCCO	Insurgency	Occupation	1973	Western Sahara: Polisario	2,000?
MYANMAR	Insurgency	Ethnic	1992	Royhinga Muslims	N/A
	Insurgency	Ethnic	1948	Kachin Independence Army	N/A
	Insurgency	Ethnic	1942	Karen National Union	N/A
	Insurgency	Ethnic	1948	Karenni	N/A
	Insurgency	Drugs	1948	Mong Tai	N/A
NAMIBIA	War	Ethnic		Caprivi Strip	2,000
NEPAL	Insurgency	Land, Economics	1996	United People's Front-Nepal (Maoist)	900
NIGER	Insurgency	Ethnic	1991	North: Arab Tuareg vs. Black Gov.	N/A
NIGERIA	Ethnic	Economic	1995	Ethnic Tension	600
PAPUA NEW GUINEA	Insurgency	Ethnic	1988	Bougainville: Mekamui Defence Force; also BRA	20,000
	Crime	Economic		"Rascals" vs. Police/Army	N/A
PERU	Insurgency	Ideological, Drugs	1980	Maoist Guerrillas	30,000
PHILIPPINES	Insurgency	Economic	1969	New Peoples Army	3,500

Country	Type	Cause	Since	With	Killed
	War	Religious	1991	Abu Sayeff	500
	War	Religious Economic	1974	MILF,	5,000
RWANDA	Insurgency	Ethnic	1990	Hutus vs. Tutsi	500,000
RUSSIA	War	Ethnic, Religious	1994–96 1999	Chechnya/Dagestan	80,000 5,000
	War	Ethnic, Religious	1991	Tajikistan	50,000
SENEGAL	Insurgency	Tribal	1983	Casamance (Dioula) vs. Senegalese (Wolof)	1,200
SIERRA LEONE	War, Crime	Rural vs. City, Economic	1991–1999	RUF/Government, UN Accord	50,000
SOMALIA	War	Clan	1978	Ogaden vs. Rahawaine Clan	500,000
	War	Political	1991	Breakaway Somaliland	350,000
SOUTH AFRICA	Crime	Economic	1995	Criminal Gangs	6,000
SRI LANKA	War	Ethnic	1983	Tamil LTTE vs. Gov.	60,000
SUDAN	War	Ethnic, Oil, Religious	1963	Arab North vs. SPLA in South	500,000+
TAJIKISTAN	(SEE RUSSIA)				
TURKEY	War	Ethnic	1984	Kurds vs. Gov.	37,000
UGANDA	Insurgency	Religion	1979	North: Lord's Resistance Army	2,000
	Insurgency	Religion	1995	West: Muslim ADF vs. Gov.	800
	Insurgency	Political	1995	South: Hutus	200
UNITED KINGDOM	Insurgency	Colonial, Religious	1968	Northern Ireland: IRA vs. Gov.	4,000
YUGOSLAVIA	Ethnic		1998	Kosovo	250–4,500
	Ethnic		1998	Macedonia	N/A

SOURCE: DP, VARIOUS

Into the Killing Zones

You bought your flak jacket, got a great deal on a white hardskin Suzuki and swapped your expensive Leica M6s for disposable Nikons. You are on assignment thanks to an ambiguous commitment from a free counterculture city weekly. Your pack is stuffed with film, Power Bars, syringes and phrase books. Now all you have to do is figure out what the hell is going on and, of course, try to remember what a journalist is supposed to do and say in a war zone. If it's your first time, you're in for a treat. You probably read about "the emerging conflict" and arrived about two months too late. If you get a hot tip or stumble onto a flareup, you're in luck. The rule on war coverage is the big money flows for photos and stories when it hits; human interest and "the savage aftermath of war" submission won't even pay for your plane ticket home. So rule one, get in quick.

War zones are pretty easy places to understand, as are their players. One side doesn't like the other side so it bums money from a rich uncle (which they will pay off in favorable trade deals and political favors). There are front lines, kill zones and safe zones, but before you get to stumble around in these you need to get in. You soon find out that no one is impressed by your laminated press card, your reversed New York Yankees hat or even that snazzy, dirtied-up photo vest. You want to play, you pay. War zones are the epitome of entrepreneurial start-ups. Everything from taxis to bottled water costs. The more journos, the more it costs—guides, generators, security, tips, food, you name it. You can blame the big nets for this evil. But you too must pay for your sins. Rule two, bring lots of cash.

If you have a real assignment you'll you have to bring in too much equipment, rent satellite links, order breakfasts, make appointments and do all that stuff you do back home, except at work there is no electricity, phone service, running water or civilization. You need to get permission. But not always from the guy whose picture is on their money. So you need a local fixer. As usual, they are not hard to miss. They will be hovering over you at breakfast the day after your plane arrives. They will rattle off famous journo's names in bad English, roll through a two-inch stack of business cards and give you that smile that says, I ain't going away pal. Okay, Rambo (as all drivers are called), let's get going to the front lines. Rule three: choose your fixer wisely.

But how do you get "in"? How do you actually meet up with the "rebels"? How can you avoid them is a better question. Believe it or not, smart rebels usually have a press office in London, Paris or Washington with unlisted offices in Damascus, Tripoli or Khartoum. To get in, you need permission either from the rebels (who usually are as extraordinarily inefficient and underfunded as they are helpful and incompetent) or the government (which is usually as slick and efficient as it is unhelpful). The rebels will give you a contact name, a place and time to show up, and a letter that just as likely will put you in jail. Naturally, when you show up there will be no one there to meet you and you will discover that you can just take a bus like everyone else does. It's all about rebels pretending to have infrastructure. Rule four: Don't believe a single word anyone tells you.

If you are lucky you will have descended into complete chaos. That means you'll get good stuff: Summary executions, frontal assaults, atrocities, severed heads, all the good stuff. If you arrive too late, you'll have to do it the official way, complete with guide, bodyguard and driver. Then you'll need to be a bona fide journalist.

That means you'll spend most of your time interviewing dull-witted officials and visiting hospitals. Your hosts will load you up with official studies, contact names, military transportation in-country and a tour of what may or may not be the front lines. Naturally, you see more bloodletting and violence at the front row of a Mike Tyson fight than on these tours, which usually consist of more briefings, deserted rebel camps and captured prisoners. But hey, it's a living. Rule five: Just because people are firing guns, it doesn't mean there's a war on.

If you think you'll be the only journo in the thick of things, good luck. The CIA will not invite you to northern Iraq or southern Sudan to discuss long-range planning any more than Kabila will invite you to Kinshasa to discuss his plans for Paris shopping trips. The world of war is a shadowy world of lies, propaganda and circumstantial evidence. As for the bang-bang stuff, remember that traditional wars are fought like Red Rover—you run as fast as you can into the other side, lose a few people and then run back. Then it's the other side's turn. Whoever loses the most people or gains the most ground wins. Usually these wars are designed to create more instability (i.e., loss of investment) than casualties. But you are going to stick it out, wrap it all up, add pathos, plot, insight and story line to your coverage. When you emerge six months later from inside the rebel camps your editor turns to you and says, "Man, where've you been. That's history, not news." Rule six: You make a lot more money stalking celebs than you ever will in a war zone.

Centurion Risk Services
http://www.centurion-riskservices.co.uk
RealWorldRescue
http://www.realworldrescue.com
The Free Lens
http://www.oneworld.org/rorypeck/

HOW TO SURVIVE WAR ZONES

Remember that small wars are not carefully planned or predictable activities. More importantly, land mines, shells, stray bullets and booby traps have no political affiliation or mercy. Keep the following in mind.

- Contact people who have returned or are currently in the hot zone. Reliefweb is a good starting point. Do not trust the representations of rebels or government contacts. Check it out yourself.

- Avoid politics, do not challenge the beliefs of your host, be firm but not belligerent about getting what you need. Talking politics with soldiers is like reading *Playboy* with the pope. Be aware of internal intelligence agents using you.

- Do not engage in intrigue or meetings that are not in public view. They still shoot spies. Listen more than you talk. Getting to know your hosts is important.

- Travel only under the permission of the controlling party. In many cases you will need multiple permission from officers, politicians and the regional commander.

- Remember that a letter of safe passage from a freedom group presented to an army checkpoint could be your death warrant. Understand and learn the zones of control and protocol for changing sides during active hostilities.

- Carry plenty of identification, articles, letters of recommendation and character references. They may not keep you out of jail, but they may delay your captors long enough for you to effect an escape.

HOW TO SURVIVE WAR ZONES

- Bring photographs of your family, friends, house, dog or car. Carry articles you have written or ones that mention you. A photo ID is important, letters with impressive seals are good, but even a high school yearbook can provide more proof of your existence.

- Check in with the embassy, military intelligence, local businessmen and bartenders. Do not misrepresent yourself, exaggerate or tell white lies. Keep your story simple and consistent.

- Dress and act conservatively. Be quietly engaging and affable, and listen a lot. Your actions will indicate your intentions as the locals weigh their interest in helping you. It may take a few days for the locals to check you out before they offer any assistance. Be aware that the people you are seen casually associating with could be the enemy of your host.

- Remember that it is very unusual for noncombatants and nonjournalists to be wandering around areas of conflict without specific permission. If you are traveling, make sure you have the name of a person that you wish to see, an end destination and a reason for passing through.

- Understand where the front lines are and the general rules of engagement, and meet with journalists and photographers (usually found at the hotel bar) to understand the local threats. Don't be suprised if NGOs are not thrilled to see you.

- Carry a lot of money hidden in various places, and be ready to leave or evacuate at any time. This means traveling very light. Choose a place to sleep that would be survivable in case of a rocket or shell attack.

- Visit with the local Red Cross, UN, embassy and other relief workers to understand the situation. They are excellent sources of health information and may be your only ticket out. They also are busy, so don't expect too much.

- If warranted, buy and wear an armored vest or flak jacket. Carry your blood type and critical info (name, country, phone, local contact, allergies) on a laminated card or written on your vest. Wear a Medic-Alert bracelet. Have evac insurance.

- Carry a first aid kit with syringes, antibiotics, IV needles, anesthetics and painkillers as well as the usual medication. It might be wise to use autoinject syringes. Discuss any emergency needs with your doctor in advance.

- Understand and learn the effect, range and consequences of guns, land mines, mortars, snipers and other machines of war.

- Get life and health (and KRE if relevant) insurance and don't lie. Tell them the specific country you will be traveling to. Also check with the emergency evacuation services to see if they can go into a war zone to pull you out.

- Carry a military-style medical manual to aid in treating field wounds. Take a first aid class and understand the effects and treatment of bullet wounds and other major trauma.

MAKING THE BEST OF NASTY SITUATIONS

TIPS FOR NOVICE JOURNALISTS

- Remember that people in wartime are highly unstable emotionally. Many young fighters often can have a blood lust or irrational behavior. Be careful of revenge killings.

- Journalists can be specifically targeted for execution. In many areas journos are considered spies (which they technically are). Areas of ethnic cleansing are very dangerous. Also be aware of kidnapping in the region. If a journalist is kidnapped contact the Red Cross Journalist Hotline, 19 Ave. De la Paix, CH-1202 Geneva, Switzerland, Tel.: 41 22 734-6001, Fax: 41 22 734-8280.

- Carry and show your photos and articles. Do not show gory pictures or articles sympathetic to any side. Point to your name, show them your passport and help them understand your background.

- Travel with an open mind and do not criticize or judge. Do not lie or suggest any affiliation you don't have. In wartime people form alliances based on their gut feelings and the look in your eyes. You will be checked out via computer or phone.

- Try to use a simple notebook and write in your own handwriting as illegibly as possible. Use medium-priced autofocus cameras that are not too painful to replace. Do not make drawings or maps. Ask permission before taking pictures or point to your camera and give an inquiring thumbs up.

- Keep a blank roll of film or videotape handy. When soldiers demand your film or tape, you make the switch and then reload the original.

- Snipers like to home in on lights, bright colors and even decals. Things like cigarettes, head flashlights, video eyepieces, strobe ready lights and press decals can become targets.

In the Land of the Yankee Pig

You don't have to go to a war zone to get killed. Sometimes belligerents will track you down and kill you without your leaving your hotel.

Despite your own political or religious beliefs, you are a symbol to much of the world. Yes, you're a nice person, but your government is not.

Much of the blind anger toward Americans is a direct result of others' perception of our need to control foreign governments. We also support a wide variety of dictators, despots, evil regimes and other nondemocratically elected rulers because we make money from them. The United States also wages financial, moral, covert (and not so covert) operations against enemies of the state, such as the Islamic fundamentalists, drug dealers, unfriendly dictators and gangsters. We do this by supporting (or sometimes creating) opposition forces or countries with money, weapons and military training. This creates a lot of ill will towards "Americans" regardless of their beliefs or background. So when you travel abroad, remember you are paying for the sins of your Uncle. Sam, that is.

You may find it surprising to see how obvious the U.S. "covert" presence is in Third World countries. Terrorist groups keep very good tabs on CIA and other government agents in their countries. And hey, guess what? Spies look just like you. That nice embassy "political section" guy who invited you to the American Club to ask all about your rugged trip through rebel-held area is just doing his job debriefing you for the CIA. Guess what you are now—a spy.

In many turbulent areas such as the Middle East, Southeast Asia, Central Africa and regions where Americans are rarely seen, you will be assumed to be working for or allied with American intelligence agencies. Although I'm Canadian, I have been accused on numerous occasions of being "CIA" in war zones simply because I had no plausible explanation as to why I was there. I made the innocent mistake of showing up in Kabul a few weeks before the United States bombed the hell out of the training camps in Khost. Why was I there? "Oh, just to look around." I was told bluntly by the NGOs and the UN that I should have a better cover story. Sorry for telling the truth guys.

The final problem is that you might be just what the mullah ordered to be held hostage, blown up, sacrificed or made an example of. Bin Laden has a bad habit of giving people permission to kill Americans and Britons "wherever they are found" as payback for the Gulf War.

So accept the fact that any beefy, freckled tourist—Kiwi, Pommy, Canuck, Yank or not—can run the risk of confrontation, kidnapping, detainment or harassment. The good news is that simple execution and murder are rare, since Americans are worth more alive (financially and politically) than dead.

HOW TO SURVIVE BEING A YANKEE PIG

Whether you accept it or not, if you are of European extraction, or were raised on T-bones and Pepsis or wear Gap gear, you will be taken for a Yankee Pig in most of Russia, Asia, Australasia or Central and South America. The Canadian patch on the backpack just doesn't cut it anymore.

So understand that along with your Eagle Creek backpack and ACG Nikes, you carry a different kind of baggage—about 200 years of imperialism, covert action, warfare, occupation and political interference. Even if you don't, a large part of the world just resents the fact that you are so damned affluent and healthy, and they're not. You may not have bombed Laos, smart-bombed innocent Iraqi children, overthrown every Latin America dictator, shot Moros in the Philippines or cut down the rain forests to grow cows for your Big Macs, but the chances are good you will be blamed for it.

- Accept the fact that you can't blend in, but get up to speed on what the locals think of foreign tourists. It could save your life, if not your wallet.

- Dress conservatively, stay away from obvious American brands and logos and do not wear signs of wealth (gold watches, jewelry, expensive cameras, etc.).

- Don't go too native until you actually have met the natives. Some cultures can be affronted by you dressing like Gunga Din with Reeboks.

- Learn or try to use the local language, even if only to say "Thank you" and "Excuse me." Even learning the phrase "I love your wonderful country" can get you a lot farther than "Why the hell don't you wogs learn to speak English?"

- Call the local embassy to find out the do's and don'ts. Often they can recommend a driver or security service in high risk areas.

- Don't wear American flag pins, hand out Uncle Sam decals or argue foreign policy. Focus on learning rather than expostulating. Be proud but keep it to yourself.

- Be compassionate, understanding and noncommittal about the current situation of the country. If you are a target of an anti-American diatribe, ask the person to tell you what he would do if he was president of the United States. He will probably be too shocked at your passive intellectual response to stay angry.

- Simple items like sunglasses, air-conditioned cars and lack of language skills can create barriers and misunderstanding.

- Say hello to everyone you meet on the street and in the course of your travels. Look people straight in the eye and smile. Be polite, patient and helpful.

Viva la Revolution!

Let's play out this scenario: A backward country emerges from decades under a totalitarian regime. Freedom is in the air. Tourist visas are as easy to get as Publisher's Clearinghouse entry forms. Hotels are hosed out and airlines change their names. You, being the adventurous type, are off in a heartbeat, eager to be the first to visit empty temples, scenic wonders, etc. One week later, tanks fill the streets, surly men in cheap uniforms are thumping innocent bystanders, you hear shots every night. One morning, someone kicks in your door, and it's not room service. You are officially an enemy of the people, and you will not be able to try out those bitchin' new Nike ACGs in the mountains after all. You are eating cockroach soup and watching your bruises turn ten shades of purple. What happened?

Students of history and readers of *DP* could tell you that you screwed up. You forgot that the countries most likely to be plunged into civil warfare are newly emerging democracies. Yes, you raving liberal, the most dangerous countries are the ones that still can't figure out how to operate a ballot box. One only has to look. Eastern Europe, the CIS, Latin America, even East Timor are examples of what happens when you pop freedom out of its push-up bra. Things get heavy real fast.

Once the iron hand is lifted, every crackpot faction has a voice and begins organizing. Since there is no effective way to compromise with these well-meaning folks, they simply make their points more clearly by using rifles and shovels. Every colonial entry in Africa has gone through this turmoil. Some, like Liberia and Angola, just don't know when to stop. Other countries, like Yugoslavia, Pakistan, Somalia, South Africa and India, have no clue how to deal with their poverty-stricken masses. The most dangerous transition is from long-term dictatorship to democracy, as was experienced in the Soviet Union. Technically, these are caused by special interest groups putting restraints on leaders and not allowing them to deal with minor uprisings. Division is the natural outcome, splitting the military, religious, regional and business elements into their tiniest elements. Ideally, they form their own spheres of influence, creating the normal political structures found in First World countries. Unfortunately as elsewhere, they adopt the brutal tactics of their former leaders and usually have the tanks and population fired up within weeks. Other groups, like the Mafia, drug runners, terrorists and criminals, make good use of the division and confusion to quickly establish wide-ranging organizations and transportation corridors.

How should you react? Get the hell out of there. Your embassy (if there is one) is your best bet; failing that, your country's best friends' embassy (don't be too picky). If you had done your homework you would have already made friends with the local consul and expats at the bar. If there are no embassies (not uncommon), then you have two choices: NGOs and foreign expats. NGOs will have contingency plans for disasters and you won't be part of it. But they can offer advice or make radio connections for you. Foreign businesses will have long ago shuttered their doors, but if you hang around the golf course you can pick up the local scuttlebutt. It's usually all about getting on a plane ASAP. Failing that, you can try to make local airline connections to at least get you to a less violent area.

Best advice? Get a room at the nicest hotel, stock up on batteries for your shortwave, get a room with a view and a case of your favorite beverage and write that Somerset Maugham novel.

African Conflict and the Media
http://www.c-r.org/occ_papers/occ_af_conf.htm
UN Peace Keeper Training
http://www.un.org/Depts/dpko/training/

HOW TO SURVIVE REVOLUTIONARY PLACES

Although no one can predict a sudden change in government, there are some things that could keep you from appearing on CNN wearing a blindfold.

- Check in with the embassy or NGOs when you arrive to understand the current situation and to facilitate your evacuation if needed. Remember that the local government will typically downplay the danger posed by revolutionary groups.

- Stay away from main squares, the main boulevards, government buildings, embassies, radio stations, military installations, airports, harbor, banks and shopping centers. All are key targets during takeovers or coups.

- If trouble starts, call or have a local contact the embassy immediately with your location. Stay off the streets, and if necessary move only in daylight in groups. Stay in a large hotel with an inside room on the second or third floor.

- Understand the various methods of rapid departure. Collect flight schedules and train information, and ask about private hires of cars and planes. Do not travel by land if possible.

- Do not discuss opinions about the former regime or the current one.

- Do not rely on ATMs, credit cards or traveler's checks.

- Do not trust the police or the army. Remember that there will be many summary executions, beatings and arrests during the first few days of a coup or revolution.

- Hire a local driver/guide/interpreter to travel around town and/or to go out at night. Don't be shy about hiring bodyguards for your residence or family.

- Listen (or have your guide listen) to the local radio station or TV station. Have him update you on any developments or street buzz. When the embassy has set up transport, make your move with your bodyguards or guides.

Fun-da-Mental Oases

There are many countries like Afghanistan, Iran, Iraq, North Korea, Pakistan, Yemen and Syria that would have Rush Limbaugh's head on a stick in less than 15 minutes. These countries might have a Bill of Far Rights, but nothing that would protect your outspoken butt from a lifetime of incarceration or slow execution for sneezing in front of the Big Guy's photo.

They fall into two general categories: Fundamental and mental places. The first is usually a region where Bic shavers, baseball hats and women's legs will never see the light of day. The second are places run by men with Ray-Bans and a distinct lack of humor surrounded by a lot of pictures of them looking stern and wearing Ray-Bans. So let's start with surviving fundamentalist places—places where praying is the national pastime, interrupted by the Friday executions.

I should point out that not all fundamentalists are Islamic. We have our own religious hotheads Stateside, Uganda has the Lord's Resistance Army, and Israel has those guys with the Shirley Temple haircuts. Just look for a lot of basic black, bad haircuts and beards.

But most fundamentalist countries are Islamic. That doesn't mean that Islam demands that its religion come in one flavor. One billion of the world's inhabitants are Muslims and only 18 percent are found in the Arab world. Most live east of Karachi; 30 percent of Muslims are found on the Indian subcontinent, 20 percent in sub-Saharan Africa, 17 percent in Southeast Asia and 10 percent in the CIS and China. There are an estimated 5 million Muslims in the United States. Most Muslims are just like Christians and to a certain extent like Jews, Hindus, Buddhists and whatever. There is a certain purity, elegance and hospitality to Islamic countries—just as there is in Christian and other regions. Most Muslims will tell you that Jews, Christians and followers of their own faith are all "people of the Book" and that there is more to bind us than divide us. So how come everytime I see the word *terrorist* it's usually used to describe some bearded guy in a dress knocking his head on the ground? Well, let's get it out in the open. There has always been a historic antagonism between Christianity and Islam, with the line drawn messily through the Balkans and Transcaucasia and epicentering in Jerusalem. There is the same funny line in the Philippines, a place where the Spaniards just about had a heart attack when they discovered Muslims a few years after they kicked the last of the Moors out of Spain.

This primal distrust between infidel/crusader, Jew/Arab and West/East is still very much a part of world politics. This creates problems for Westerners when they travel to regions where the government has inflamed people against the West. It creates prejudice when the government has inflamed people against the East.

In the land of enlightenment we do a pretty good job of demonizing Muslims. Just watch who Stallone, Willis and Schwarzenegger do battle with in the theaters. There continues to be confusion and distrust generated by the media who are unable to understand the basic similarities between Islam and Christianity. The media focuses on the disparities, and usually the most extreme examples like the Taliban, Mu'ammar Gadaffi and Saddam Hussein. Yet we seem to accept the Saudis, the ethnic Albanians and even the Kuwaitis as somehow "good" muslims.

A government that promotes family values and law and order literally goes ballistic against rulers who have conservative interpretations of—you guessed it—law and order and family values. The presentation of Islamic fundamentalism as a religion rather than a political agenda is one example. The linking of the Koran with politics is another. When was the last time you saw footage of our leader praying at church intercut with his political speeches? Yet we are shown shots of Mecca intercut with AK-47-waving loonies on tanks. Christian fundamentalism is just as dangerous and skewed as any other hard-core belief, but most Americans head into the Muslim world with a negative and dangerous image of Islam and its followers.

So how do you survive fundamentalist places? Open your mind and learn.

Understanding Islam
http://darkwing.uoregon.edu/~kbatarfi/islam.html
Islamic Fundamentalism
http://www.medea.be/en/index089.htm
Al Hayat
http://www.alhayat.com/
Learning Arabic
http://www.arabic2000.com/

HOW TO SURVIVE FUNDAMENTALIST PLACES

When traveling to a fundamentalist-oriented, religiously zealous country, remember to smile, mind your own business, respect their customs and leave your personal opinions at home. Some religions tend to be a little more tolerant of loudmouthed, boorish outsiders, but areas like the Middle East and the Far East are very intolerant. It's touch and go if you are a heathen, risky to be a Jew and better to just be a Christian if you are asked.

- Muslims are more conservative in rural areas and underdeveloped countries. Despite other guidebooks' warnings, Muslims understand that Christians have different customs and won't lop your head off the first time you make a *faux pas* by passing the falafel with your left hand.

- Be very careful in the area of sexual conduct, behavior at religious sites and deportment with women and religious objects. Sexually provocative clothes, obscene gestures, defiling the Koran, theft or insulting the Prophet and women will get you in trouble.

- Do not proselytize, preach or conduct religious functions without permission of the local government. Do not wear religious symbols or use expressions that employ the name of Christ, Allah, God or other religious entities.

- Read and understand the Koran and tenets of Islam. Most Muslims will be impressed that you have read the Koran and if you ask them questions about their religion.

- Feel free to admit that you are a Christian, but express your interest in knowing more about the Koran and the Islamic way of life. Being a "student of all religions" is a good cop-out for the philosophically challenged. But beware that students and older men are very pleased to proselytize the word of Allah to a potential convert.

- If you are Jewish and traveling in a fundamental Islamic country, your life may be at risk by identifying yourself as Jewish or discussing an opposing point of view. Also understand there are strong feelings between Shi'a and Sunni Muslim sects.

- Do not squeeze hands when shaking. You may touch your chest after shaking hands in the traditional Muslim greeting. The left hand is considered unclean because, yes, rural Muslims wash their nether regions with that hand. Muslims also squat to urinate (to keep the pipe straight) and find the Western habit of urinating with legs akimbo and penis pointing far too theatrical for their tastes.

- Dress cleanly and conservatively, and remove your shoes in mosques and temples. Do not point the soles of your feet to your host, and use your right hand to eat, greet and pass objects around. Expect to be kissed on both cheeks by men. Friday is the holy day and anything else you need to know will be communicated to you by your hosts or friends.

- Ask permission before taking pictures; do not insist or sneak photos. Do not take photographs of women, the infirm or the elderly. Don't blow your nose in public. Don't eat while walking around. Don't admire objects in a host's home (he will feel obligated to give them to you). Small gifts are expected when visiting homes. Do not show open affection. Do not show undue attention to women. The list goes on, but don't be paranoid, just respectful.

- Read up on the cultures of each region and ask permission when in doubt.

Mental Places

Okay you've survived war zones, the breakdown of civilization and watching thieves having their hands amputated for stealing bread. Now you are ready for anything. Right? Well, no one is really prepared for the mental places, the places run by mustached loonies, the squalid, retro Marxist hellholes our government warns us against. So, what's it like?

It's Good To Be . . .

Just some of the "Hell No, We Won't Go," Royal Energizer Bunny crowd who save their loyal subjects the cost of wasteful elections and multiparty debates. Select your own from the list of doddering do-nothings, diddling figureheads, brutal dictators, hereditary throne sitters, Rose Bowl parade figurines and "Its my party and I'll rule if I wanna" category.

RULER	POSITION	SINCE
Bhumibol Adulyadej	King of Thailand	1946
Rainier III	Prince of Monaco	1949
Elizabeth II	Queen of the United Kingdom	1952
Fidel Castro	President/PM of Cuba	1959
Hassan II	King of Morocco	1961
Malietoa Tanumafili II	King of Western Samoa	1962
Jean	Prince of Luxembourg	1964
Jaber al-Ahmad al-Jaber al-Sabah	Emir/PM of Kuwait	1965
Muda Hassanal Bolkiah	Sultan of Brunei	1967
Omar Bongo	President of Gabon	1967
Etienne Gnassingbe Eyadema	President of Togo	1967

It's Good To Be . . .		
Mu'ammar Gadaffi	Leader of Libya	1969
Qaboos ibn Said	Sultan/PM of Oman	1970
Taufa'ahau Tupou IV	King of Tonga	1970
Isa ibn Sulman al-Khalifah	Emir of Bahrain	1971
Khalifah ibn Sulman al-Khalifah	Prime Minister of Bahrain	1971
Hafiz al-Assad	President of Syria	1971
Zayid ibn Sultan al-Nuhayyan	President of the U.A.E.	1971
Birendra Bir Bikram Shah Deva	King of Nepal	1972
Jigme Singye Wangchuk	King of Bhutan	1972
Margrethe II	Queen of Denmark	1972
Carl XVI Gustaf	King of Sweden	1973
Juan Carlos IX	King of Spain	1975
Gouled Hassan Aptidon	President of Djibouti	1977
France Albert Rene	President/PM of Seychelles	1977
Ali Abdullah Saleh	President of Yemen	1978
Maumoon Abdul Gayoon	President of Maldives	1978
Hamadou Barkat Gourad	Prime Minister of Djibouti	1978
John Paul II	Pope/Holy See	1978
Daniel Arap Moi	President/PM of Kenya	1978
Jose Eduardo dos Santos	President of Angola	1979
Saddam Hussein	President of Iraq	1979
Teodoro Obiang	President of Equatorial Guinea	1979
Joao Bernardo Vieira	President of Guinea-Bissau	1980
Beatrix	Queen of the Netherlands	1980
Quett Ketumile Masire	President of Botswana	1980
Robert Mugabe	President of Zimbabwe	1980
Mahathir bin Mohammad	Prime Minister of Malaysia	1981
Jerry Rawlings	President/PM of Ghana	1981
Hosni Mubarak	President of Egypt	1981
Abdou Diouf	President of Senegal	1981
Paul Biya	President of Cameroon	1982
Fahd ibn Abdul Aziz al Sauda	King/PM of Saudi Arabia	1982
Lansana Conte	President/PM of Guinea	1984
Maaouiya Ould Taya	President of Mauritania	1984
Hun Sen	Prime Minister of Cambodia	1985
Joaquin Chissano	President of Mozambique	1986
Yoweri Museveni	President of Uganda	1986

Well, quite nice, actually, in places like Syria, Libya, Cuba, Iraq, Iran or even North Korea. It's pretty clean and quiet . . . and cheap. About 200,000 Canadians descend on Cuba each year (there are no figures for Americans visiting

Cuba, because technically you can't go there). They complain about the Americans jacking up the prices. Libya and Syria have some of the nicest uncrowded ruins you'll ever see and North Korea looks like an underbudgeted episode from the *Twilight Zone*. Iran and Iraq are a little nervous about outsiders but the local folks are more desparate to meet you than their government would like. So how do you survive those forbidden places?

Bomb This America
http://www.wildscooter.com/saddam/
National Anthem of Syria
http://www.wildscooter.com/saddam/

HOW TO SURVIVE MENTAL PLACES

Don't be scared off by all those stern-looking posters of Big Brother staring down at you. These countries are poor, a little wacky, very retro and usually safer than an Amish bedroom. Just remember there will be a few things missing—like toilet paper and your rights if you get arrested.

Book a tour with a well-known tour company. They can intervene when you do something stupid. Like talk to a local.

Understand that the local people don't see many tourists and are shy. At the same time, be careful what you say.

Be a little diffident but pleasant with the folks that do walk up to you boldly and want to be your friend. You can start each answer by leaning towards their lapel pin and saying "Check, one, two, check."

All these countries want tourism but they don't necessarily want you to do much other than take pictures and spend money.

Don't talk politics, don't talk about sex, don't talk about government and don't talk about religion too much. Talk about history, weather, geography or your home country and you will make plenty of friends.

Be careful where you point your camera. Always have someone show you around if you are not part of a tour. People can get aggressive very quickly.

Avoid the police. Keep in mind that you will be followed by plainclothes, but that's no reason to get chummy.

Remember to find out which embassy handles your country's interests, so if things do go wrong (usually espionage is the charge) somebody can visit you in jail.

Jackboot Junkets

Now that you have a basic idea concerning religious countries, it's time to move on to those regions run by godless despots. The evil empires, the gold-braided braggarts who run vast chunks of Third World dung heaps—all those countries that have the oxymoronic title of Democratic Republic of Shutthehellupistan. You won't even find much religion (let alone the Trinity Broadcasting channel) in these paranoid backwaters. Not to be confused with the stern military, extra-gold-braid-on-the-hat-please places like Iraq, Libya, Cuba, Syria and North Korea.

These folks allow tourists into their countries so their populace can see and recoil at the evils of a democratic government: the horrors of high-caloric meals, freely elected governments and advanced education. Countries like Tajikistan, Myanmar, Congo, C.A.R. and other little cranky, tin-pot countries are furiously pushing their domains back into the Stone Age and dragging their neighbors along with them.

Why visit these countries? Where else can you take a time machine back to the '50s, the '20s or even the turn of the century (we mean the 12th century)? Imagine meeting people who still herd sheep, break rocks, kill other people and even carve temples, all with no regard for profit, without an education and while they're on the brink of starvation. These places view tourism as the best way to import kidnap victims. So why go?

The answer is simple. You have to go. Somebody has to show these people that there is a world out there full of Pop Tarts, Chevy Suburbans (without bulletproofing), MTV, rotisserie barbecues and fat happy people who actually die of natural causes. Somebody's got to wander around the streets, smiling and waving and showing them we don't order babies for lunch.

If we don't go there, we will maintain our image of drooling sodomites who bayonet and barbecue old ladies for fun. It takes a lot of patience, a lot of money and a lot of *cojones* to travel through the last of the dark kingdoms. Strangely enough, once you connect with the locals most of these places are quite safe, and once the police turn the corner, a lot of fun.

List of Dictators
http://www.thirdworldtraveler.com/US_ThirdWorld/dictators.html
The Dictators
http://www.radicalmedia.com/~liam/norton/dictators.html

HOW TO SURVIVE BRUTAL DICTATORSHIPS

Ever want to see George Orwell's *1984* in real life? Want to see *Killing Fields* Part 2? You haven't traveled until you've been to the world's last "vote for me or die" countries. Here are a few tips to keep you safe:

- Although there is some guy's picture on the money and at the airport, it doesn't mean he actually runs the country.

- Do not discuss politics with anyone. Usually they are no politics to discuss anyway. Yes, you can be paranoid in these places.

- Try not to talk too casually to the locals; they will be questioned later or come under suspicion. Use your guide to select charming visitors to associate with. There really isn't much to talk about in these places anyway. If people stuff letters or postcards in to your hands, do not tell your guide or mail them in-country. They will expect you to mail them once outside the country.

- Most autocratic countries employ surveillance or encourage spying on foreigners. Do not be surprised if you are not only followed but your tails may even argue over who gets to follow you. At least you won't be mugged or pickpocketed.

- On the down side, expect to have your room and your luggage searched while you are out. Remember those letters people stuffed in your hand?

- Telephone and mail are subject to interception and/or monitoring. Be careful what you say. Make sure your room is very secure when you are in it.

- Any violation of the law (imagined or real) will result in severe penalties. There is very little your consulate, lawyer or senator can do for you since you are subject to the laws (or lack of laws) of the country you are in. Stay away from drugs.

- If you are a journalist, activist, eco-activist or infomercial host you will be considered a threat. Contact the freedom groups listed in the back of the book to understand what the risks are. The concept of rights, fair trial or fair treatment are only found on badly dubbed sitcoms imported from the States.

- If you are truly concerned about conditions in these countries, contact the Red Cross, Amnesty International or Reporters Without Frontiers to see what you can do to help. (See our reference section in the back.)

Gimmeyawalletland

Imagine a naked man walking down the street with $100 bills taped to his body. That's what the typical tourist looks like to the residents of nasty places. If it wasn't for tourists the locals would have to rob each other, swapping the same few worthless freshly printed *guidos* back and forth like scores of the local soccer games. You are what they call foreign investment, baby.

The fact that you consider yourself the owner of your camera, wallet, luggage, watch and jewelry is not really a debating point with many of these folks. The concept that you might need to be killed to expedite the transfer of those goods is a really minor detail to some. You don't need to be robbed in these places to lose your money; the police and officials will simply ask for it with a smile.

In many war-ravaged, impoverished places such as Honduras, Cambodia, Liberia, Mozambique or Sierra Leone, the only law is survival of the fittest or the fastest. In countries like Nigeria, Bolivia, Russia and Colombia you might need to hire criminals to protect you from the government. In some places like Mexico, Somalia or Uzbekistan the police will rob you, creating a minor problem in filling out a police report for your insurance company back home.

You demand justice, you say? Well, how much can you afford? That presupposes that there is both a set of laws and a judicial system in place. In most of these places it's cheaper just to hire a hit man than a lawyer.

You had a sense of this when you arrived at customs. The government gets first dibs on what will be your rapidly diminishing resources—the border posts, checkpoints and police stations all will coax your gifts, clothing, cameras, jewelry and folding green from your ownership to theirs. After all it is only a small token of your appreciation for expeditious service, is it not? Consider this part of the local color. Most of the residents of these unfortunate lands must endure the same treatment along with disease, starvation and brutality and, of course, no ticket out. Our best advice is to go with the flow (see "Bribes"), learn the appropriate amounts that will satisfy your wolflike friends and keep your money and assets well hidden, but keep enough of the local currency in the correct denominations for these pleasant encounters.

Here are a few tips to at least stanch the flow and escape with your body parts intact.

International Corruption
http://www.acsp.uic.edu/oicj/pubs/CJI/120413.htm

Transparency International
http://www.transparency.de
Bribe Report from the Ukraine
http://www.usemb.kiev.ua/rso/CrimeDigest9812.html

HOW TO SURVIVE CORRUPT PLACES

Be aware that banditry is a very real danger in areas like Kenya, Somalia, India, Cambodia, Pakistan and southern regions of Russia. Corruption (this assumes that there was a noncorrupt infrastructure to corrupt) is simply the kinder, gentler, slower version of banditry, and can range from ticket clerks mooching spare change to soldiers threatening to lift all of your possessions at military checkpoints.

So lighten up, get change, and please, give generously.

- Understand that "bribery" is normal in many countries, but do not confuse this with theft. Bluster, Negotiate, Smile, Give or Ignore are the watchwords here. Be pleasant. Carry small bills, have cheap gifts (like Mr. DP stickers) and realize that being indignant will just end up costing you more.

- Understand that soldiers at checkpoints are often hungry, sick and impoverished. They will shoot if you don't stop. They can also work themselves into a frenzy if you piss them off. Be cool, smile, pass out the trinkets and just keep talking.

- Meet with and discuss the situation with local embassy staff. Ask them specifically what to do if you are arrested, followed or hassled. Carry their card or at least number and address on you while in country. Ask them for names of military commanders, politicians or anybody important. Write it down. Who you know will help. A name on a piece of paper has more weight than just saying the name.

- Stay within well-defined tourist routes. Lock all luggage and belongings in a secure place. Use a locking canvas duffel or metal box for luggage. Expect and prepare for everything you own to be stolen.

- Never travel in the country alone. Use a local guide to navigate checkpoints and police roadblocks. Always hire a driver recommended by someone you trust.

- Stay inside major cities at major hotels. Eat at well-known, large restaurants. Never travel or go out late at night. Phone ahead to tell people you are coming over and call them again when you arrive home safely.

- Fly between cities and prearrange transportation from the airport to the hotel.

- Prepare for constant intimidation from police and military. Be firm about your innocence and try to lead them to your embassy or safe place. Find and remember to drop the name of a local bigwig if you are frog-marched at gunpoint.

- Remember that police will try to keep items removed during a search. So show them your wallet, watch, and important papers but do not hand anything to them. If the soldier takes your passport into a bunker or building, walk with him (he will wave you back), but insist that you have important information for his superior.

- Don't overtly demand how much money they want. Always offer your bribe as a gift to show your appreciation, to help out with the family, etc. And smile.

Impoverished Paradises

Not all countries are nasty, brutal or full of jabbering zealots. There are lots of places that are really nice—they just seem to have a lot of dead people on the side of the road in the morning. These places have a terminal funk to them. Hazy gray skies, the stench of things rotting, snotty-nosed kids with hands outstretched. These are the tough places, the hard countries that barely survive. Places too pitiful to make fun off. Many of these places, like India, Egypt, Bangladesh, Kenya, Pakistan, Haiti, China and Indonesia, are like this because there are just too many people for the resources available. There are a lot of petty thefts, minor muggings, infectious diseases, scams and a few murders. Most can be traced to the victim tempting the perpetrator and getting what he/she deserved.

In 1950, 33 percent of the world's population lived in the developed, industrialized nations. Today, that share is approximately 23 percent. By the year 2025, it will fall to 16 percent; Africa then will have 19 percent of the world's inhabitants. Today, Western and Southeast Asia are home to more people than any other part of the world. The population of India will overtake that of China early in the next century. This area is also home to the most diverse mix of languages, religions and people in the world, many of whom have been feuding for centuries and who will continue to fight over land, religion and tribal disputes.

As populations grow and standards of living drop, people will live at ever-greater densities, creating more tension. *The World Bank's World Development Report* noted that only Bangladesh, South Korea, the Netherlands and the island of Java have population densities of more than 400 people per square kilometer. By the middle of the next century, one-third of the world's people will probably live at these density levels. Given the current trends, the population density of Bangladesh will rise to a hardly conceivable 1,700 people per square kilometer. Population growth on such a large scale is intrinsically destabilizing. The wars in India show that even minor terrorist incidents can kill hundreds of people. Many of the world's most dangerous places will also be the most crowded and impoverished places.

Poorest People	% of Population in Poverty
Bangladesh	80
Ethiopia	60
Vietnam	55
Philippines	55
Brazil	50
India	40
Nigeria	40
Indonesia	25
China	10

On the African continent, 45 percent of the population is under the age of 15; in South America, it's 35 percent; in Asia, 32 percent. Only 21 percent of the population of the United States and 19 percent of Europe is under 15. Things are not going to get better in our lifetime.

The World Resources Institute reports that only 3 percent of the world's inhabitants lived in urban areas in the mid-18th century. By the 1950s, that proportion had risen to 29 percent. Today, it is more than 40 percent; by 2025, 60 percent of the world's people are expected to be living in or around cities. Almost all of that increase will be in what is now the Third World. The young people tend to migrate to major urban centers seeking Western-style jobs instead of backbreaking menial labor. Once in the city, they find that the competition for jobs is fierce and that petty crime against the more wealthy is the only source of income. But despite this, the cities continue to grow. Mexico City, which had 17 million inhabitants in 1985, will have 24 million by the end of the century; Sao Paulo will jump from 15 million to 24 million Hey, move over, you're using up my oxygen. Tips to survive?

World Bank
http://www.worldbank.org/poverty/library/webguide/regional.htm
International Census Information
http://www.census.gov/ftp/pub/ipc/www/idbnew.html

HOW TO SURVIVE POOR PLACES

Poverty is pretty photogenic until, of course, you smell it. More and more affluent travelers are heading to the Third World on vacation. Should you be afraid, embarrassed, enobled, here's what to consider.

- **Get the guilt thing out of the way early.** You're rich, they're not. They make Nikes and Kmart designer clothes, you wear them. Deal with it or go home and watch informercials for ab machines.

- **You can help.** People who live in poor regions are just as nice, intelligent, witty and interesting as you. Find out what would make a difference and go for it.

- **Be aware of "Poverty Tourism."** Locals who bring in Westerners to do things the locals are completely capable of doing themselves. After all, how many faded Ninja Turtle T-shirts and saggy Care Bear shorts does the Third World need?

- **If you care,** meet with the local aid organizations, schools or government, you will be surprised at how simple and unmet their needs can be—from pencils, to batteries, to 20-cent textbooks.

- **Be aware that money and charity does not fix, only soothe.** Try to understand the overarching reasons for your hosts' conditions. The answer may suprise you.

- **Think about simple, elegant gifts that will be treasured forever:** take photos of their family, or leave your phrase books, guidebook or something from your country. Even teaching someone a song can be a lasting gift.

Terrorist Places

Enough feel-good, we-are-the-world, drum-circle stuff. What about those evil bastards that just want to kill you? The irredeemable, hard-core punks that want to stick a grenade down your shorts to see how long you take to die? The slit-eyed bastard that dreams of cutting you like a goat and bathing his face in your spraying blood. Oh yeah, you Berkeley disbeliever, they're out there. How do we know? Well, our government trained many of them.

There is no simple advice to give on how to avoid being the victim of a terrorist attack. A random bomb attack or murder attempt is simply the most devastating, sickening thing a human can survive. It doesn't make sense; it's evil and inspires terror in anyone that reads about it. When the *Journal of the American Medical Association* (JAMA) interviewed the 182 adults who were inside or around the federal building when the bomb went off in Oklahoma City, they found that half suffered from post-traumatic stress or other psychiatric disorders. *DP* made the State Department report on terrorism in March of 1998 for surviving a bomb attack in Uganda. It's not pretty. And you don't forget.

Although terrorism is specifically designed to capture the world's attention, it poses a lesser threat than disease, car accidents, plane crashes and other afflictions that haunt the traveler.

Statistics are meaningless in understanding terrorism. Our State Department figures show terrorist incidents dropping like an out-of-favor internet IPO stock. They show 273 international terrorist attacks during 1998, a drop from the 304 attacks we recorded the previous year and the lowest annual total since 1971. I guess having our embassies blown up is a positive indicator. They do mention that 741 persons died, and 5,952 persons suffered injuries—the highest death toll ever.

They rack up pipeline attacks, toss out Palestinian actions and exclude most of what passes for political killings. The body count from one act can overshadow hundreds of unreported individual attacks. Don't expect to learn anything other than they are out there. Waiting. Like a protoplasmic liquid, terrorism flows around the world and reshapes itself according to pressures mounted against it. Like water, the harder you hit it, the more it hurts. Just when the experts figure they have it pegged, it assumes new, more frightening images. Beirut, The World Trade Center, Oklahoma City, Tokyo, Kenya and Riyadh sagas have overshadowed hijacking, embassy kidnapping, and airport bombing. In other words, you might just want to travel to Syria, Sudan, Libya, Iran or Afghanistan to escape terrorism now.

MAKING THE BEST OF NASTY SITUATIONS

HOW TO SURVIVE TERRORIST PLACES

There is no real epicenter to terrorism against travelers. Terrorists will seek you out wherever they can. Here are at least a few pointers.

- **Understand what is going on in the world. The OSAC database, Real World Rescue and other free security news sources are ideal.**

- **Don't assume our goverment has any idea of when and where attacks will happen. They have very poor intelligence inside fundamentalist groups. State Department information is not specific and should be regarded as simply warnings.**

- **Highly touristed areas in countries with poor security are ideal for attacks. There are over two dozen groups actively seeking to harm Americans or our interests.**

- **Don't confuse crime with terrorism, military actions with murder, or rebel groups with terrorist groups. Terrorism is directed against innocent people without warning. That usually includes you.**

HOW TO SURVIVE TERRORIST PLACES

- **Be aware of anniversaries (see "Dangerous Days" at the end of each *DP* chapter) and current political events.**

- **Stay away from group tours, expat hangouts, preplanned political events and U.S.-related businesses, hotels and installations.**

Emergency Net (terrorist events updated daily)
http://www.emergency.com/ennday.htm
Patterns of Global Terrorism (updated annually)
http://www.state.gov/www/global/terrorism/
Real World Rescue
http://www.realworldrescue.com

In a Dangerous Place: Northern Albania

Something for Nothing

For Albania's bandits, payday had come at last. As a thousand journalists, aid workers and international observers rushed to the north of the country, the poorest bandits in the poorest country in Europe declared open season the multitude of rich and—more importantly—unarmed foreigners venturing into the country. And a most profitable time they had of it, too. The international media lost cars, satphones, cameras, cash and anything else they happened to be carrying with them when Kalasnikov-wielding figures stopped their cars in the northern Tropoje region of Albania. In one instance, a London staffer of a news agency that had been relieved of its satphone reputably dialed up the stolen phone number. It was duly answered by a man speaking Albanian. With no one on hand who spoke Albanian, the frustrated hack was reported as shouting in English, "Give us our kit back you bastards." Needless to say, the kit, worth several US$100,000s, has yet to be seen.

The expulsion of hundreds of thousands of Kosovar Albanians from their homeland into northern Albania was covered by scores of hacks wielding Betacams and otherwise dripping with cameras. Images of tearful and exhausted refugees duly filled Western television screens and people were duly shocked. I, like the other 1,000 or so hacks, had also made the lengthy journey up to Kukes in northern Albania. Beautiful mountain peaks were complemented by potholed roads and impoverished villages. Kukes, with its one main street and two hotels, was suddenly home to an army of journalists and aid workers, not to mention a few hundred thousand Kosovar refugees. Unsurprisingly, prices had gone through the roof with local flats being let at anywhere between US$100–200 a night, the equivalent of a couple of months' wages for the average Albanian.

North of Kukes is Albania's banditland, a vast expanse of rolling wooded hills and dirt tracks which even the locals think twice about venturing into. They certainly won't talk about the gangs that control the dirt tracks that pass for Albania's roads. "Please don't ask me about these people," an old man begged us, "these are bad times for Albania." Just how bad we were about to find out.

We set out early one morning for a Kosovo Liberation Army (KLA) training camp in the Helshan region, a couple of hours drive north of Kukes. With me are Roger and Bungy, two freelancers for Sky News as well as our interpreter, Donjeta. We hire a local minibus, which is not only cheaper but we hope, a little less conspicuous than a Mercedes taxi for a drive into Albania's Wild West.

The drive, along narrow roads and winding mountain passes, is uneventful. There are hardly any cars on the road. Partly, of course, because relatively few people have cars, and those that have them are not about to risk them driving through banditland. It's a clear and bright day as we clamber from our minibus and trudge the few meters to the gates of the camp. Millings around outside the camp are dozens of local Albanians. Entrepreneurial as ever, they have set up small stalls to sell food and cigarettes to the numerous KLA recruits that pass through the camp. I briefly notice a tall, thin man hidden behind a large pair of mirror reflector sunglasses, clutching an assault rifle, take Donjeta aside and ask some questions. "It's nothing," she says in reply to my slightly disinterested query as to what he had wanted. A short while later we are taken to the camp commander. About 40 years old, slim, with slightly sunken cheeks and graying hair, he introduces himself as Billy and asks what we want. After the usual ritual of us identifying ourselves, we first ask if we can journey into Kosovo with the soldiers to the front lines. If we get permission from Piarko, the regional KLA commander, comes the reply. So, instead, we ask if we can film the training. He agrees and a few minutes later we are trekking across the hillside, pushing leafy branches out of our faces as we make our way through the woods around us. I ask if the area is mined: no, comes the reply. Arriving at a clearing we find about 200 camouflage-clad new recruits, on a rifle range, learning the basics about shooting and using the weapons they will soon be using on the frontlines.

While the group watches, three are lying on ground mats firing AK-47s at targets about 150 meters away. For the next few hours we follow the recruits through their daily training as they repeatedly fire at the white boards at the far end of the range, before trooping back to the camp to strip and clean the weapons. A few interviews later we take our leave for the ride back to Kukes. Our minibus tentatively renegotiates the potholed track as we make our way down the hillside. Reaching flatter terrain the driver speeds up. Ahead of us, a few hundred meters away, there is a white van parked on the grass. Go round it, Roger tells the driver. Our driver cuts across another track towards the Kukes road. A man comes running from the white van, shouting at our driver in Albanian. Ignore him and drive, we chorus to the driver, who duly does so, speeding up. I think those were the guys from the camp gates, Roger says.'

We drive on in an uneasy silence, along the deserted approach to the first bend that will take us back along the mountainous route to Kukes. The silence, though, is shattered a few minutes later by the sound of shots behind us. Glancing back I see the white van we had left behind accelerating to catch up with us. It is only 30 or so meters behind: leaning out the window is the same man who had briefly questioned Donjeta at the camp. His Kalashnikov is still in his hands, and he is now firing it in the air, just above our vehicle. With a blinding ability to state the obvious I say, "I think we've got some bandits behind us." We tell the driver to stop and the white van pulls to a halt in front of us. Two bandits get out of the van and run towards our minibus. The lanky, sunglass-clad bandit opens the front door opposite the driver, jabbing the driver hard in the ribs with his assault rifle. Another pistol-wielding bandit with long dark hair pulls open the driver's door and drags him out, slapping him across the head. Protesting feebly, the driver is dragged to a ditch by the side of the road and a pistol is put to his head. For a split second I think we are soon to be driverless, on a permanent basis. A third bandit with blond hair and blue eyes climbs into the driver's seat. Flourishing his pistol at us he says, "don't move or we'll kill you." Nice to meet you, too. He tries to turn the ignition key but it doesn't work. Our driver is eventually brought back to start the bus using the more traditional method of hot-wiring the engine.

Another van comes up the road. It is just a van full of local people; but they have managed to arrive at the wrong time. Pistols are flourished at the driver and the van is kicked in an effort to encourage the locals to leave the scene of the crime print. Its a matter of seconds before the van full of local people, faces glued to the windows as they briefly catch a glimpse of three Brits being robbed, speeds on its way. The three bandits all climb into our bus and we start driving northwards along the road to Bajram Curri, with the white banditmobile following along behind. In all, it's a 40-minute drive through twisting mountain passes.

I sit quietly and ponder the inevitable loss of all my camera equipment and, in more paranoid moments, my life. Immediately to my right are two of the bandits casually holding their pistols. The third is sitting in the front. Roger is directly behind me and Bungy is at the back of the van. The bandits are relaxed and confident in the knowledge that three feeble journalists are not going to resist. The sad truth is that they are right. Where are we from, they want to know. England, we say, which brings our friendly patter to an end. We pull over on a deserted bend on top of a gorge. "Get out one by one," says the blond-haired bandit. "Leave everything in the van and don't try and hide anything." With a degree of weariness we clamber out one by one. "If you don't give us US$2,000 now we'll kill you all," says the one bandit. We point out that, much though we would like to give him $2,000, we just don't have the cash on us. Traveling in Albania has taught us not to carry too much cash. Another time, maybe?

We are lined up on the grass and told to empty our pockets.'I only have about two hundred lek—two dollars or so—in my pocket. "Keep it and have a beer on me," says the blond-haired bandit with a magnanimous smile. Very generous of you, I mutter as I notice another bandit transfer all our kit from our van to theirs. "If you want your stuff back you will have to pay $2,000," says the Kalashnikov-wielding bandit. "If you come back with the police we'll kill you with heavy machine guns," he says with a wonderful penchant for detail. I wonder if there is any particular difference between being killed by an AK-47 or a heavy machine gun. "We're only doing this for the money," continues the bandit, in what is obviously the standard bandit lecture to idiot foreigners.

While we are herded back into our van, the warnings about the police are reiterated at close-range pistol point. "Don't even think about it," says the blond-haired bandit, cocking his pistol and putting it to my head through the window, sending a brief surge of adrenaline through my body. I wonder why given the comprehensive uselessness of the Albanian police. With that we are sent on our way back to Kukes. I try to ask the driver if he knows who the bandits are and where they live. Glancing back he says, "Please don't ask me this, I have a wife and children, I can't talk about these people. As you can see, here in Albania we have no state, no law, no police and no country . . . we have nothing."

—Roddy Scott

Business Travelers

Professional Victims

Now, you would picture anybody that goes voluntarily into a war zone as a pretty game-faced macho kinda guy. Knife strapped to thigh, grenades taped to chest, spare magazines, first aid kit, last bullet ready for the brain and a sense of *sang froid*. So how come when I get to the blasted airport it's all guys with pocket protectors, cheap briefcases and that just-off-the-bus look? With a look that would sunburn tonsils they head straight to the hotel bar, the local nightclub and even tip the mujahedin at the door. Hey, this is business. War is for pussies.

Believe it or not, the number one travelers to war zones are businessmen (sorry, girls)—people set on selling air conditioners, buying bulldozers, hawking medicine, concrete or even body bags. Hey, this is business. I don't have time to bleed, it ruins the suit.

Doesn't it just seem that everytime you read about someone getting kidnapped, waylaid or massacred, he's a vice president of something or other working in Buttwipeastan? It doesn't have to be this way. There is a booming industry selling safety to business travelers. Companies like Pinkerton's, Jane's and Kroll will give you a blow-by-blow (every day if you like) of every maiming, kidnapping, bombing and attack. Almost all security services are targeted at businesses and businessmen (we're not being chauvinistic here, most victims are men). Yet when I give my talks on travel in dangerous places, I never meet any businessmen. Instead, I run into mostly gung-ho college students and graying, careful spinsters. I figure selling safety to business travelers is like offering sex education classes for monks. They don't see the need. After all, they are not really traveling. They get on a plane, have a couple of drinks, review the file and then meet the driver at the airport. They stay in a swank hotel, have dinner with the customer and then the driver takes them to the meeting the next day. Maybe they'll take in the risque show or just cruise the bars until closing time. Shower, buy a souvenir for the kid, a trinket for the wife and then back home in ten hours. Hey no big deal, just another business trip.

The reality of business travel from the other side is a little different. By flashing that suit, Rolex, President and Megaoil business card, you have become the enemy and the victim. You won't even have to pay the ransom out of your own pocket because they know you have a cash insurance policy for kidnapping.

Business travel is perhaps the most dangerous form of travel. The fact that you represent an American company can make you a target. You also lose the ability to discern about when and where to travel. Most tourists wouldn't consider flying into a Colombian war zone for a week. Yet folks from oil, computer, agricultural and food companies do it regularly. Most victims of terrorism tend to be working on a daily basis in a foreign country in areas where no sane traveler would go.

Finally, by doing business, you tend to frequent establishments and locations where thieves, terrorists and opportunists seek affluent victims—luxury hotels, expensive restaurants, expat compounds, airports, embassies, etc. As a businessperson, you cannot adopt the cloak of anonymity, since you will more than likely be wearing an expensive suit, staying in expensive hotels and have scads of luggage, cash and gifts. If you do business in places like Africa you may be surprised when you call the police for help and discover some don't have gas for their vehicles or bullets for their guns. In some countries like Sierra Leone, a diamond mining center, the police may even show up only to rob you (once they find gas and bullets).

Business travel exposes you to frequent car and air travel and other means of transportation. Many trips are also undertaken in bad weather conditions and at congested travel periods (i.e., Monday out, Friday back). You are fed very carefully through a chain of businesses that cater to businesspeople and become a high-profile target for criminals who prey on business travelers. You make appointments well in advance with complete strangers and you have no idea of where you are going or where you are, and you even tell strangers you are lost. I often shudder when I see oil field technicians, complete with cowboy hats, pointed boots and silver Halliburton briefcases, tossing beer-soaked profanities and Ben Franklins around the world's transit lounges. Can you think of a more inviting target?

News
http://usatoday.com/life/travel/business/ltb000.htm
Weather
http://www.weather.com/travelwise/maps/travelrain.html
Sports
http://espn.go.com/

How to Make a Stiff Drink
http://www.bacardi.com/
Entertainment
http://www.escortservices.com/
Read all about Safety
http://www.groupweb.com/travel/biztravel/advisory_travel.htm

Dangerous Places for Business Travel

Business travelers are by far the juiciest targets for terrorists and thugs alike. They make great kidnap victims as well as willing dispensers of cash for bribes. Any Third World country with oil should be considered dangerous.

Algeria

Algeria is dependent on foreign expertise and open season on visitors. Foreign companies are paying top dollar for oil workers in the south, where it's relatively benign, but Algiers will still make your hair stand up on end.
http://travel.state.gov/algeria.html

Angola

Oil and diamonds shore up this shattered country. The country is looking for investors to help dig them out. However, impotent cease-fires are signed as frequently as bad checks and although the heavy fighting has wound down, the countryside is lawless.
http://travel.state.gov/angola.html

Colombia

Colombia gets five stars for brutality, pervasiveness and ingenuity. The number one spot for expats to go missing for a very long or expensive time. The government wants businesses to absorb the cost of doing business in a war zone. According to the National Police, 2,600 people were kidnapped in 1998, and the new method of miraculous fishing allows rebels to simply grab people at roadblocks.
http://travel.state.gov/colombia.html

Nigeria

Nigeria is floating on oil but its people are dirt poor. I wonder where all that Shell money goes? For now, Nigerians could never be called lazy. They provide some of the best drug mules, scam artists, con men and extortion-based crime. If you get a fax from Nigeria asking for a meeting, run, do not walk, to the nearest bunco squad.
http://travel.state.gov/nigeria.html

Pakistan

Cheap, cheap, cheap is what draws Samsonite-packing deal-makers to this promised land of profits. The government is considered corrupt. Political stability is tenuous and·there is constant warfare and insurgencies.
http://travel.state.gov/pakistan.html

The Philippines

The southern Philippines is where a host of motley terrorists-turned-brigands compete for hostages. They prefer to kidnap the children of rich Chinese but dabble with Westerners when they can.
http://travel.state.gov/philippines.html

Russia

Russia is number two with a bullet for business grief. It is a land of eager protectors and partners who can quickly show you how necessary their services are. A growing quagmire for American businesspeople, many of whom simply walk away. It is faced with extortion, lawlessness and politically instability. It's estimated that there will be more than 120 foreigners killed in Russia this year.
http://travel.state.gov/russia.html

BUSINESS TRAVELERS

Gangsters: The Businessman's Friend

Wherever there is money, there are gangsters. They have an amazing ability to ignore governments and streamline collection procedures. Do not be surprised if your business partner in Eastern Europe or Russia turns out to be a person of ill repute. Italian and Russian gangs are busy establishing links and are now working together in Germany to control a number of businesses: 17 percent of the 776 investigations into organized crime in Germany last year involved attempts to influence politics, big business or government administration. The main activities of organized crime were drug trafficking, weapons smuggling, money laundering and gambling. A while back, police uncovered profits from organized crime in those areas alone totaling US$438 million or 700 million Deutschemarks.

TIPS ON SURVIVING BUSINESS TRAVEL

- Have your host set up transportation, hotel and a driver/bodyguard. These are cheap insurance and insulation from the realities of the Third World

- Don't get too chatty with the locals. All that info about your travel, room, samples and employer is worth money to evil men.

- Avoid restaurants frequented by expats and tourists. Don't make reservations in your own name. Do not sit outside. If possible, enjoy your host's hospitality.

- Dress in business attire, carry a briefcase and dress up only when necessary.

- Make copies of important papers. Separate your credit cards in case you lose your wallet. Keep the numbers, expiration dates and the phone numbers to order replacements. Be careful of credit card fraud, business scams and identity theft.

- Don't reveal home addresses or phone numbers or show your wallet when meeting people. Use your business address or P.O. box.

- Do not discuss plans, accommodations, finances or politics with strangers.

- Wear a cheap watch (or just show the band outward). If driving, wear your watch on the arm inside the car. Leave jewelry at home or in the hotel safe.

- Get used to sitting near emergency exits, memorize fire escape routes in the dark, lock your doors and be aware at all times.

- Kidnappers need prior warning, routine schedules or tip-offs to do their dirty work. Vary your schedule, change walking routes and don't be shy about changing hotel rooms or assigned cabs.

- Stay away from the front or back of the plane (terrorists use these areas to control the aircraft). Avoid aisle seats unless you want to volunteer for execution.

- Do not carry unmarked prescription drugs. Expect for gifts like cigars or alcohol to be appropriated by customs officials.

- Leave questionable reading material at home (i.e., *Playboy*, political materials, *DP* or magazines).

- Carry small gifts for customs, drivers and other people you meet. DP stickers were created for this, but personalized pens are ideal.

- When you call with your plans, assume someone is listening.

- Watch your drink being poured.

- **Do not hang the "Make Up Room" sign on your hotel room door. Rather, use the "Do Not Disturb" sign. Keep the TV or radio on even when you leave. Contact housekeeping and tell them you don't want your room cleaned up.**

Business travel is not more or less dangerous, but people who travel on business tend to be preoccupied with appointments, directions and preparing for meetings. It also exposes travelers to areas where crimes are committed more often, such as nightclubs, downtown areas, banks, ex-pat restaurants and other high-profile spots.

But cheer up, the chances of being kidnapped and returned home safe are the least of your worries. You could end up dead without even being kidnapped, extorted or waylaid. According to International SOS Assistance in Geneva, Switzerland—a company that specializes in health, security and insurance for travelers—a deadly traffic accident is the most likely reason you'll be flown home dead. Cardiac arrest is the second most likely reason. Tropical diseases are the third. Have fun.

Web Resources

Foreign Embassies Worldwide
http://www.embpage.org/
Foreign Embassies in Washington, D.C.
http://www.embassy.org/embassies/index.html
Foreign Consular Offices in the States
http://www.state.gov/www/travel/consular_offices/fco_index.html
Important Phone Numbers when Abroad
http://travel.state.gov/phone_faq.html

Tourists

Fodder for Fiends

The fifth of July 1841 was an auspicious day. It was the day that 570 passengers traveled by Midland rail to Leicester and back for one shilling. Thomas Cook had put together the first organized tour. The passengers were the local temperance association in Market Harborough on their way to attend a gathering in Loughborough. Flash cut to Luxor Egypt, 58 tourists shot and stabbed to death. Click. A busload of kids robbed and raped in Guatemala. Click. Three young female tourists are brutally killed in Yosemite. Click. Eight Greeks killed because they looked like Israelis. Click. Nine Germans killed outside Egyptian museum in Cairo. Click. Uganda 1998—eight gorilla trekkers slaughtered with machetes, Somalis are hijacking passing yachtsmen. Click. Yemen, kidnapping turns ugly as 16 are grabbed and then 4 nice middle-aged people are gunned down in a rescue attempt. Pause for effect. . . . When four tourists were snatched in southern Iran on August 15, 1999, the kidnappers demanded from the front desk, "We need foreigners! How many do you have?"

Lots. So what the hell happened?

Would *DP* be exaggerating if we said that tourists are fodder for fiends? Probably. If your idea of a vacation is two weeks in Orlando and a Howard

Johnson then you probably don't spend too much time worrying about *Interahamwe* unbuckling their pants and slobbering over your wife. The half a billion tourists that wander the globe should worry more about getting a triple-A discount than learning about double-A gunfire. If you spend your time in places where electricity and food is a luxury, you better listen up.

Examine the modern *touristicus domesticus*. They travel in predictably jabbering gaggles, following well-worn trails. Monolingual, they pay little attention to their environment since they are terrified of being left behind or having the bus leave without them. They are usually wearing outlandish colorful plumage. Gray walking shoes sprout cream of mushroom legs marbled with blue veins topped off by what could be a spare tire or a bulging overstuffed money belt. The neck is usually tilted up with a rhythmic swivel bent slightly forward by the weight of their Sears Camcorder and SLR with zoom telephoto, binoculars and silk-screened vinyl camera bag. The right index finger is either pointed at the local attraction or pressing a shutter. The mouth is in a state of continual movement as they talk, not necessarily to each other, but to ensure that they are having a good time and seeing wonderful things. They usually arrive in shiny buses, descending like locusts as they strip souvenir stands clean and cluster in tight groups under the watchful eye of an overly pleasant multilingual guide holding an umbrella.

Nine Day, Six Country African Safari Now Only $42 Million (Airfare Extra)

You thought you'd seen it all on Lifestyles of the Rich and Famous, *you knew rock stars needed a posse, it's understood that bitchy movie stars have demands, but the grand prize goes to Bill Clinton. And yes you paid the bill . . . for Bill. When Clinton and the family decided to see Africa in the spring of 1998, it cost a total of $42.3 million according to the General Accounting Office. The peripatetic Clinton (who has visited 60 countries on 44 trips in office) spent $28 mil on 98 air cargo flights to transport his luggage (which included a bulletproof limo) $2.5 million to bring homeys, posse and press on Air Force One and a million just to refuel helicopters in flight. Two hundred White House aides and 900 military personnel were included . . . just to plan the trip.*

Clinton spent $18.8 million to visit China and 10.5 million to visit Chile earlier. To put this in perspective, Reagan took 24 trips in 8 years and Bush took 21. As of DP4 Clinton has spent 180 days abroad since taking office. (Did someone say a broad?)

Clinton's spokesperson sums up the $4.7 million a day tab as "the price of doing business in a dangerous world."

Tourists are not dumb or bad people, but they are the main source of sustenance for touts, louts and thugs. Some of these tourists do funny things. They sneak away from those bus tour hotels and migrate to seedy places to watch local women take their clothes off. They drink too much. They make friends too easily. They stay out too late. They stagger home at four in the morning singing German drinking songs and get lost. Not bad people, just trusting, naïve people in the wrong place at the wrong time.

There is a subspecies of the *touristicus domesticus*. It is the fabled *touristicus backpackensius*. Unlike the much derided domestic version, this species is more likely to be solitary, but most likely will be seen with a same-sex partner. The key indicators are hiking boots or Nike ACGs, hairy legs with knobby knees (often with scabs from mountain bike spills), T-shirts with politically correct slogans, hiking outerwear (with ski tags still attached) and UV block sunglasses. The older members will have a gray ponytail. They like to think they are independent, even though they bunch up at the same youth hostels and flophouses each night. The key determinant is the right index finger jammed into the same page on their shoestring guides.

These folks are college educated, worldwise and in their minds unlikely to be a victim of any criminal (after all they're not rich and obnoxious, like those other tourists). They are one with the earth and its cultures (they were into world music, waaaay before Sting or Gabriel), giving them a sense of love and harmony.

So what's to worry? Could it be that entire year's supply of money in their "secret" neck pouch? How about that new altimeter, stopwatch, chronometer watch? Those $120 boots are worth a quick $20. And the $400 backpack can fetch another quick ten bucks. These travelers often enjoy entertainment and souvenirs of the narcotic kind, carry everything on their backs and wouldn't be noticed missing for at least a month. Good pickings for the charming bandito or even drug planting *polizia*.

The point of the two cheap shots above is to tell you that it doesn't matter who you think you are. You are a wealthy unarmed foreigner in a land that is not your own. If you are the victim of crime you will hotfoot to your nearest embassy or the next town. You will not be back to file charges or even see what happened to your favorite watch. So consider yourself the ideal victim. And unlike most books who tell you the same dumb stuff, *DP* is going to give you some tricks we don't want you to pass on to your friends.

The good news: The major purpose of crime against tourists is to quickly remove money and other valuables. The perpetrator does not want to hurt you or escalate your brief meeting into assault or murder since the *federales* will be more interested in finding him.

The bad news. Same as the above.

Does it get worse? Well, there is rape. A function of social cultures clashing—usually a result of unaccompanied western women who travel in rural or sexually frustrated cultures. In a world where *Baywatch* and *The Young and the Restless* are the most syndicated shows, one can do little but hope that they remake and syndicate *The Flying Nun* soon to balance things out.

In the case of homicide or brutal attacks, you have to look at the track record of the country you are going to visit. It is not uncommon for bandits to execute robbery victims simply because they won't get caught. Look for countries where they make tourist attractions out of skulls (Cambodia) or eat smoked monkeys (Congo) to give you a heads up.

DP Survival Course: Seven Things That Will Save Your Life

Be alert

Crooks need you to be distracted, lost, in need of assistance or simply in the wrong place. Just adopting the habit of stopping and watching people around (and behind you) will arm you against crime.

Be sober

Alcohol, drugs, jet lag and having too good a time can fuzz your common sense, making you think for one unfortunate moment that you are with cool cats when you're really among wolves. Even pleasant encounters with the locals in bars can lead to ugly bruises and lost pesos if you don't stay in control. Scams begin when the perpetrator thinks he can overcome your better judgment. Bars and nightclubs are also where bad people hang out.

Use it or lose it

Preventing theft begins when you pack. If you are taking too many things or are forced to leave items in your car or hotel, you dramatically increase the chances of losing those things. Travel light, plan on giving away most of the items you bring and perhaps buying local clothes at your destination.

Insure and ensure

I know this is something Marlin Perkins would tell you, but it really does make a difference if your camera, clothes, health and even life are insured against loss when traveling. Traveler's checks are a pain, but worth it for large blocks of cash. Also, credit cards let you do everything from chartering aircraft to buying blowguns, and even medivac insurance ensures that you can be flown to your local hospital if you get hit by a poison dart.

Trust no one, suspect everyone

When you travel, you will meet hundreds of strangers with either pure or unpure thoughts. It all depends on the image you present. If you are interested in their kids, their health and their family, the chances of something evil happening to you decrease. At the same time understand that financial pressures in some countries might force these same people to finger you to a gang of thugs, or pick your pocket.

Stay away from tourists

Tourists attract petty criminals and con artists like dogs attract fleas. It goes without saying that crime occurs at youth hostels, tourist attractions, main plazas, red light districts and other popular spots.

Prevent opportunists

Crime generally occurs after you change $2,000 at the Amex office or your wife hitches up her girdle to get $10 to pay the museum tickets. Zippers on back packs, luggage circling carousels, papers sticking out of breast pockets, fat purses and bulging pockets are "Rob Me" signs. Places like trunks of rental cars, towels at beaches, and daytime hotel rooms are areas where cameras, money, and just about everything of any value should be expected to disappear.

Lock 'em, Fake 'em or Take 'em

Lock 'em Out

The best defense is preparation. By being careful you will avoid unfortunate incidents and wonder what all this fuss is about. Most hotel rooms can be flipped open by a 90-lb. maid, so it doesn't take much for a 200-pound thug to enter your room at night. (That is where you keep all your worldly possessions, isn't it?) Although this is not as pervasive as street robbery, hotel robbery is more serious. Use a wedge, motion detector or chair against the door when you go to sleep. During the day, leave a TV or radio on. Take the room key with you and keep your valuables in the hotel safe. In less-developed countries, leave your valuables with the innkeeper or his family.

Use a retractable cable to tie your bags together even when in your hotel. Put locks on all openings, use twist ties on zippers to keep them together, etc. The harder you make it to steal your things the less chance they will be.

TOURISTS

Fake 'em Out

If you find yourself being trailed by an unshaven man through the back streets of Malta, then it's time for Plan B. Strange as it seems, the act of throwing down your decoy pouch will defuse most situations. (Unless of course the swarthy man is just trying to catch up to you to return the camera you left at the restaurant.)

Assume that your attacker is just after your money. So give it to him, but not much of it. Carry a moneybelt, pouch, wallet and neck pouch with a little bit of money in each place. Protest a lot, and then run like hell in the opposite direction.

When you are being robbed, your attacker may have a weapon. The trick is to keep slowly shuffling backward as you fumble with your decoy pouch or wallet. If you think you can sprint into a safe place, do it. Most thugs will not chase you when other people are around. The attacker is as much of a coward as you. The difference is, he knows what he is doing and you don't.

If you feel mad as hell and decide you aren't going to take it anymore, try this trick I have used with complete success. Simply stick your hand in your shirt or waistband, turn around and start walking forcefully and directly toward your potential assailant. Never take your eyes off him. When he zigs, you zig and when he zags, you zag. In most cases (I repeat "most") he will think you are going to pull something on him and will quickly walk in another direction. Anyway it's more fun than waiting around, knees trembling, to find out what his real intentions are. By the way, I am 6' 6" and 220 lbs.

If you are forcibly restrained or bushwhacked, see the "Take 'em Out" section.

- Sew an inside pocket in your shirt under the arm, extend a pocket to the inside or add a panel to your boxers. Use Velcro fasteners.

- The best place to hide money is within your various possessions: inside backpack tubes, shoe linings, on the back of telephoto lenses, sewn into pant cuffs, the lining of your luggage, in books, etc. You may lose some but you'll end up with something.

- Save your expired credit cards and unused *afghanis* to plump up a decoy wallet. Carry it in your inside front pocket. For you Bernhard Goetz types, try one of my favorite surprises adapted from Iban headhunters—a one-sided razor blade tucked inside backpack pockets.

- Do not carry a purse. But if you must, don't carry any money in it since most thieves stay around only long enough to grab the purse and then run away.

- Gun magazines sell a number of concealable holsters, vests and attachments. They can also be used to carry money.

- Wear your watch on the arm that is inside a car and away from your window. It is better not to wear a watch at all since it is the first thing a thief (or customs inspector) looks at to judge your eligibility as a victim.

Take 'em Out

If you are attacked, your attacker will have the advantage. He will either sneak up behind you, walk up to you and then quickly turn, or he will hit you with a pipe or stick. Violent attacks often are performed by gangs. They will typically continue to kick and hit you while they tear off your possessions and empty your pockets. Quite honestly, you are better off shielding your head and stomach and helping them find what they are looking for. Keep in mind that if you choose to fight you are endangering your life. If you choose to fight back (you big bully) you must also be prepared to see this through until your attacker may become the victim. Not a comfortable thought for tourists out on the town for a night.

Any book that tells you how to be like Jackie Chan is, for lack of a better term, bullshit. People are all animals when attacked. When someone comes at you with an intent to hurt you, the last thing on your mind will be which smooth Kung Fu moves you will use to pulverize your opponent.

Typically, the aggressor will have staked you out and followed you until you were in a place he wanted you to be. At this point everything you do must be reactive. By all means learn the basics of self-defense. Boxing, karate, knife fighting and SEAL training are all fine. They will tell you which parts of the body really hurt when you jab them and a few nasty tricks that will leave your attacker sucking wind through broken teeth. You will only have this opportunity three or four times in a lifetime, and the downside is that if you do get a chance to be Bruce Lee, the locals will gather around and call you the bad guy.

- Do not carry a weapon. In many countries this will make you a criminal and subject to criminal charges, imprisonment and damages to your "victim." Instead, learn to use "soft weapons" like a pen, walking stick, Swiss army knife, flashlight, single-edge razors, etc. You can walk down the street at 4 A.M. with a sharp pen or a walking stick and feel fully armed.

- Be careful of items like pepper spray, mace, short non-folding knives and other offensive weapons. They can be used against you (many people who use pepper spray or mace often spray themselves or inhale the fumes) and will be considered offensive weapons.

- One of the best items is the kubotan (developed by Takayuki Kubota), who created a system of (believe it or not) pen fighting. The kubotan is a five-and-a-half inch long rod often attached to a set of keys. The basic principle behind the kubotan is to apply pressure and intense pain to your opponent.

- Learn to use a sharp object against the groin, upper neck, throat, eyes and nose. All are useless unless your weapon is free and your arm is unrestrained. If you have never practiced these strikes, you will not make a significant impact. The proper thrust is a hard jab "through" the victim followed by as many blows as it takes to incapacitate the victim.

- If you are interested, there are a number of books and courses on self defense. *DP* recommends Tai Kwon Do, karate, boxing and even Thai kickboxing. Even judo, aikido and jujitsu will make you comfortable with violence, reactive instincts and diversion of force. All are part of street survival and more importantly building self-confidence. Once again, consider the consequences of severely beating a stranger in a strange land. You may end up in jail.

- Responses that are always successful in dealing out pain, regardless of relative size or strength, are the heel of the hand under the nose, the bowling ball eyeball grip and the knee in the groin. Keep in mind that if your attacker wasn't pissed or violent before, he will be after you try any one of these attacks.

The Penalties of Self-Defense

Any violent encounter has an emotional after-effect that may turn your trip into a nightmare. On one of my recent expeditions through Borneo, a female member was sleeping in a building on the end of a dock over 100 yards from shore. That night a person slit her sleeping bag, her underwear and began to feel her up. She was in the company of two other males who were sleeping. The next day she reported the incident and the police chief of the small fishing village trotted out the entire male population for her to make an ID. Terrified that she would identify the wrong person, she hesitated. The police said if she did not identify the person, the entire village would be suspect. She identified one man and he was taken away. She was wrong. Fortunately, the villagers knew who it was and brought the guilty man forward. Sorry, that's how the real world works.

It would be unfair to assume that there are specific forms of tourist crime and specific tips to prevent it. Just a quick glance at the clippings that pile up at *DP* and our firsthand experiences would scare anyone from wandering out their front door. But luckily crime is "relative." You stand a much better chance of being murdered or waylaid by a close acquaintance at home than a total stranger when you travel.

But nothing we can tell you can prepare you for the dangers out there. Safari tourists are robbed while on safari in the north of Kenya, while backpackers have sleeping gas injected in their sleeping compartments in Bulgaria. Most thefts on trains happen in stations, usually just before border crossings where thieves hop off before customs (but not before giving the conductor his cut).

Isn't Technology Great?

The new counterfeit-proof $100 bill is now busily being counterfeited in Russia, Lebanon and Syria.

In Colombia and Thailand, young lasses drop scopolamine into overpriced drinks and whores with hearts of gold instruct cabdrivers to take you to their rendezvous, which is a back alley where only your wallet is emptied.

Shirt slashers in Venezuela snick through your shirt and grab your neck pouch; Mexicans spill beer on you while their compadre empties your pocket. Even cops will arrest you for phantom transgressions, and customs officials will tax you for imaginary activities.

Swarthy men will wave pistols at you, urging you to pull over in Italy, Spain and Turkey. Colombian guerrillas, Chechen mafyia, Yemeni tribesmen, Afghan drug runners and Kashmiri mujahedin will kidnap you and maybe release you.

Out-of-work Khmer Rouge will kidnap and then clobber you with a hoe in front of your self-dug grave in Cambodia, while crack heads in Miami will blast you right through your rental car window if you are too slow to find the electric window button.

Believe it or not, it gets worse. A busload of Greek tourists is machine-gunned to death because Egyptian terrorists think they are Israelis. A Palestinian man starts shooting at people at the top of the Empire State Building because he is "despondent." Afghan mujahedin behead a Norwegian tourist after they carve their group's name in his chest. It seems they were supposed to find expats or engineers, but found it was easier to kidnap a hiker. Next year who knows?

So before you weld your door locks shut and burn your passport, remember that despite all the efforts of the world's criminals to ruin your vacation, most tourists will complain about cold French fries and lumpy mattresses. Oh, I almost forgot, the most common problems for travelers are diarrhea and sunburn. So, hey, let's be careful out there.

Dangerous Places for Tourists

Criminals know where, when and how to find tourists. And they know exactly what to say to them. They're nice. They'll ask you where you're from—and then jack you up for your wallet, camera and jewelry. You'll then have to leave town or spend all day in the police station filing a report. You'll have to rebook airline tickets and then hit the VISA or AMEX office to get new credit cards. Chances are you'll never be back to file a charge or testify.

Every year about half a billion people become official tourists. They leave behind about $423 billion in money on the official level. No one knows how much they contribute to the local thugs and con men. Tourists are robbed and beaten in most countries, but many never bother to report the incidents, knowing full well the futility.

Tourists congregate in the same places. They drive in a state of rubbernecking ecstasy. And they are terrified of local law enforcement.

One of the things that bad people want besides your money is your passport. The U.S. Embassy issued 1,100 replacement passports to travelers last year, 1,060 in Italy and 250 in Prague. The most common problem is pickpocketing (about 30 percent of crimes), followed by break-ins into cars. Nobody likes to be considered a tourist; we are travelers, cultural ambassadors yearning to soak up new experiences and sights. In the United States, few local people stray downtown after dark. Unfortunately, many tourists stay in business hotels built downtown and go for early morning jogs or late night strolls. Are they crazy? No, they're just tourists.

Aussie Wuzz He?	
Aussies are arguably about the most adventurous of tourists. Here are their government breakdowns for vacationers based on yearly averages:	
Passports Lost or Stolen	4,460
Detained or Arrested	579
Die Overseas	400
Evacuated for Medical Purposes	184
Hospitalized Overseas	75
Murdered	10
Assaulted	10
Raped	10

Source: Australian government

It seems odd, but the most dangerous places for tourists are where tourists hang out. In Europe, pickpockets and thieves like to hang out exactly where you will:

TOURISTS

the American Express offices (how did they know I just picked up a ton of cash?), popular tourist attractions, main squares and train stations.

Crowds—especially while getting on buses or trains, waiting in line for museums or even going to the bathroom—are ideal areas for minor theft. But the top spot to get ripped off is where the tourists are. It's the ideal place to meet con men, gypsy beggars, pickpockets and other minor ne'er-do-wells.

If you want to meet violent thugs and muggers you will have to wait until the sun goes down and hang around tourist bars. You know, those places where bus tourists sneak you away to down a few drinks and see the local lovelies without the benefit of clothing. Sometimes your new friend will drug your drink or will cause a scene with the bouncer, resulting in your expulsion (minus your wallet). Your new drinking buddies may invite you to a swinging club which just happens to be in a deserted alley.

Trains

In Russia, China, Central and Southeast Asia, Georgia and Eastern Europe, trains are targets of organized thefts and abductions. In Central Asia and Eastern Europe, thieves inject gas into sleeping cars. Pickpockets and petty thieves jump on at one stop, clean out cabins and then jump off at the next stop, usually before a border.

Buses

Buses are prime targets of criminals and terrorists because they hold a lot of people in a confined area, have few exits and generally travel rural routes—also, the unarmed passengers are usually carrying most of their earthly belongings with them. Buses also follow regular routes along remote roads, which allows the civilized bandit to pull off an 11:30 A.M. ambush and make it home for lunch. Checkpoints will shake you down for nonexistent drugs, unexpired visas and lack of special permission for their area. Local thieves will jump aboard, rummage through the roof luggage and then jump off long before you notice your nice frameless pack missing.

Automobiles

Young kids will watch you park in the tourist attraction's parking lot and then swoop down to clean out your trunk. Junkies will smash every single car window along the beach in the Caribbean to find the wallets kept safe and dry inside. Skinny teenagers in cheap leather jackets will wait until you park your new rental car in Moscow before stealing it and hustling it off to Baku.

The Most Dangerous Places for Tourists

Colombia is one of the few countries that not only runs ads telling tourists to stay away but has advised foreign embassies to issue an urgent warning to tourists and businesses about the dangers that await them. Foreign Minister Maria Emma Mejia's public request came a few days after an Austrian and a German tourist were killed by leftist guerrillas in the Darian area. A Russian cyclist was found in a shallow grave in the same area at the same time. He disappeared a year ago and was killed by FARC. Even if you didn't meet Marxist rebels you should know that the murder rate in Colombia is 89.5 killings per 100,000 population—the highest in Latin America. Colombia also is the numero uno place in the world for kidnapping, with more than 1,400 official cases last year. Oddly, some professional security groups, like the Hiscox group, say there were only 1,492 abductions worldwide. Maybe they meant in a week.

In 1997 in Guatemala, band of gunmen forced a tourist bus into the cane fields near the town of Santa Lucia Cotzumalguapa and robbed 16 students and teachers from St. Mary's College in Maryland. Five women were raped. That year there had been attacks on 46 Italians, 13 French tourists, and 35 Swiss travelers. The U.S. Embassy said it doesn't keep such figures. Twelve hundred tour groups visit Guatemala along with 250,000 Americans.

Since 1994, 289 British citizens have died in Thailand, 192 in India, 48 in Indonesia and 24 in Nepal. There have been 415 British deaths in Greece, 233 in Turkey, 378 in France and 1,607 in Spain. Most of these deaths are simple heart attacks, drownings and car accidents.

In a Dangerous Place: Central Asia

Hotel Tajikistan

Dushanbe is about the prettiest city in Central Asia with the ugliest buildings. Wide tree-lined streets with a snowcapped backdrop. The odd German-built apartment or structures are in stark contrast to the land-based version of Russian space junk. Massive slabs of blighted aluminum, rusty steel supports, scabby concrete and stained glass are testament to the Russian talent for blending bad architecture with shoddy construction. Back in the fifties and sixties the Soviets replaced most of the elegant and tumbledown Tajik architecture with their Orwellian/Bauhaus view of the future. Every building must have large slogans and dramatic tableaus of deadly serious workers. But the office and government buildings are Taj Majals when compared to the epitome of Russian nontechnology: the Intourist hotel.

Here in the visitor's first impression of a country is living proof that Russian architecture conspires mightily against Russian construction skills. The abundance of right angles, tile floors and large plazas are all designed to show up the crooked lines, uneven floors, sloppy construction and lack of siting. In this cold and grey city, fountains are big. Or, I should say, what should have been fountains are big. Most are broken, with green slime ponds. Walls of glass doors are bolted or forced shut with chains, hundreds of multiple light fixtures sit empty, with the few that are working containing evil-looking green flickering tubes.

Russian hotels are square, ugly, large and dull because they are supposed to be. It makes putting in extra hours at the Gulag much more attractive. Here hotels are designed with heating but no cooling, have no opening windows but balconies, and assume that all guests will either drink themselves unconscious each night or that the Russian businessmen will spend the night with a local hooker and have to turn the lights off because they are so ugly. This philosophy carries over to Russian bars—dark bars, wicked-witch-of-the-east floor ladies with massive chin warts and deflated tractor-tire–inner-tube sized breasts. Floor ladies that were bred in cages to make sure that nothing of value can be stolen or broken because there is nothing of value in a Russian hotel. Even the crushed and scratched water bottles that appear in my room are reused.

Besides being filthy, dark and ridiculously expensive, these former Intourist hell holes are models of inefficiency. If a job can't be done slow enough by one glacially moving person, there are usually three immobile people to explain why it can't be done at all . . . ever. If you have a complaint, like the four hookers and the policeman that were sitting on my bed when I came in late, the staff has been trained to slowly lift one eyebrow and turn their head to the side as if one of my relatives just died. "Sorry. No Heeengleesh." The same people that bang on my door at 6 A.M. to remind me how much I owe them in perfect Queen's diction.

The staff at this hotel are obviously veterans of the hotel business. They have succeeded in ensuring that the hotel is unpopulated except for the drunk Russian soldiers that are forced to live here. If an unwitting adventurer shows up to claim a room, they have an insidious process of paperwork and withheld features (like water or electricity). Naturally they put me on the top floor because the elevators don't work.

To claim your room, it takes an inordinate amount of thin brown paper, carbon copies, broken pencils and stamps to check me in. I fill out two close-spaced identical forms in triplicate and am handed back four pieces of paper, two receipts, a breakfast chit and a tiny card with my room number. Most of my paperwork has been stamped twice. It takes three people to tear, file and stamp the paperwork that I never actually get a copy of. I ask if there are other tourists here and the young lady says, "Yes, many." According to the book there are two other Westerners and a group of Chinese businessmen. They're slipping.

The guard show me how to override the safety lock on the elevator. It works. The elevator groans upward, the floor numbers in the elevator all akimbo as if someone from Pee-Wee's Playhouse wanted that jumbled effect. The smell is unique. B.O., stale vodka and cigarettes.

I don't actually get a key. I get two pieces of crinkled paper that I am to hand to the grumpy guardian when I get there. I know she is grumpy before the elevator doors grind open painfully. She looks like she was doing just fine sitting with the lights out framed by dead potted plants. I hand her my grubby slips of brown paper and she arthritically files them in a drawer in slow motion.

I still don't get a key. As if I really can't be trusted, she just opens the door for me when I need to get in.

My floor lady is a real beauty: a heavy-jowled, gold-toothed scowling matron who jealously guards a box of battered keys (which itself is locked and requires a key to magically appear from beneath her dirty skirts to unlock). She has dayglo pink socks and a fuzzy white sweater, and I can't stop staring at the large fleshy warts on her face. They're the kind that have three or four black hairs on them. The kind you want to snip off while she is not looking. She shuffles in her soiled slippers in her peculiar hunched-over style mumbling all the way. Needless to say, my room is filthy in a grubby patina sort of way—the look that film producers yearn for when they do stories about junkies or suicides. Every cheap furnishing or object is worn and broken, every surface is diseased with cracks and brown scab. As if to add a touch of literary romance, my toilet paper is actually a yellowing Russian novel shoved behind the rusty water pipe. I think it's a novel, but then again it could be the launch instructions to their nuclear missiles. Now I know why the Russians promoted the publication of literature so much.

If you are used to American hotels, where an eager bellhop hustles up your luggage and jumps around showing you how things work, well you're in for a treat. Here the floor lady glumly shows me everything that doesn't work. The now-familiar crossed-arms sign language for "forbidden" or "broken" seems to be the only and most useful word the Russians don't bother using. If she has no memory of it ever working, she waves her hand as if it is beyond her jurisdiction.

The only thing that American and Russian hotel staffs have in common is the outstretched palm at the end of the tour. I give her some coins and she gives that backup harumph and leaves with my key.

So now I can admire my room in solitude. It is 20" x 20", decorated with a stained overstuffed chair that takes up too much room, a table with a large dirty glass, a chipped ashtray and a tiny TV. The bed looks like a stretcher (though not as wide or soft) and even has a dirty grey blanket to give it that military hospital look. There is also an ancient refrigerator, a heater, a phone, an air conditioner and a lamp. All are broken except the lamp. I really don't know if the lamp is broken because it doesn't have a bulb. The colors are those '50s "made in China" style pastels you see in retro stores these days. Out on my balcony I have a stunning view of a public toilet, a trash fire and a hazy panorama of nondescript box buildings that disappear into the haze.

I was told through sign language and raised fingers that there is hot water between 6:30–7:30 in the morning and between 7–8 at night. Exactly when people don't need it, I guess. She explained very carefully that the reason I don't have any towels is because there is no hot water. When there is hot water she will bring the towels. Uh huh.

Right now there is no water at all, so the brown-throated toilet doesn't flush either. I guess following this logic, she should have taken my russian novel away and returned it when the water came back on.

I find out that although I paid for a deluxe suite I was given a cheaper room, a common scam in most Russian hotels. The price for this hotel is $80–$120 if you prepay in America. I pay $35, but I am sure the folks behind the desk pocketed most if not all of that money.

Dushanbe's wide and empty streets beckon me, but I find out that it is not wise to be out because of the curfew, the shootings and the potential for kidnapping. That's okay. I was looking for a reason to visit the disco anyways. Downstairs, things are jumping. It is pitch black and empty except for a sullen bartender. He obviously knows his stuff. The music is that whiny drank-too-much Russian stuff that they sing before they blow their brains out. Perfect for dancing to. The only good thing is that beer costs 90 cents but tastes like it should cost less.

The light show is really just two alternating flood lights; one red and one green, both spastically unrelated to the lack of beat to the music. Soon after I enter, the music is drowned out by the blaring TV behind the bar—another stern-faced Russian impassively watching deadly dull news about some disaster destroying the country. The bartender politely stares at me, and after one insipid beer I figure I've had enough partying for one night. I sleep for the first time in two days. There is not much noise after 8 P.M. in Dushanbe other than sporadic gunfire.

I am awakened by the hoarse phlegmatic sound of someone trying to hawk up a giant wet lugee. Or is it an oil strike bubbling up under our hotel? Something is coming up from the bowels of the building. I discover the floor lady lied. I have left the tap open by mistake and it would appear that my fantasies are about to be realized—a hot shower after shivering most of the night under my thin smelly blanket.

There is hot water, although technically the hot water is cold now. There is brown water and foul-smelling gas coming from the hot water spigot. In bright anticipation of a hot shower, I let the water run and prepare for a hot shower in the rusty, blackened shower. It takes precisely 30 of the allotted 60 minutes for the water to turn warm. I crack open my one luxury, the hotel-provided shampoo, a bright red fluid that smells like mold. I don't care. Maybe this is a luxury suite after all. Naturally, my towels never show up, so in an act of defiance, I dry myself on the scratchy foul smelling army blanket. Life is good in Tajikistan. At the best hotel in town.

—RYP

Bribes

Stand and Deliver

You can't avoid it. The officious smile, the bad breath, the gold tooth. The expression of true remorse for your condition. Yes, my well-traveled friend, it's time to contribute to the health and welfare of law enforcement around the world. Call it payola, mordida, dash, spiffs, baksheesh, cadeau, processing fees, tea money, fines, gifts or whatever the term, but paying the "bribe" is a regular part of travel in the Third World. It's not their fault, it's not your fault. The country in question just decided to let you pay the smiling official's salary. It's cheaper and more fun that way. And so it goes. So don't get upset when the military, police and government officials expect a gratuity or donation to allow passage or as payment for minor infractions or to issue visas. In some cases, when small, evil, child soldiers forget the social niceties part, it may be your money or your life.

But you, you fearless *DP* reader, are no patsy. You don't need no stinking badges, so you say "stuff it where the sun don't shine" in the appropriate language and drive on. Oops. Your little $10 tip and a tip of the hat has turned into a $50 extortion and maybe even a critical inspection of your personal possessions. You see, you forgot you are playing a game where the other side has already won. Get indignant, yell for your nonexistent consulate, wave your business card around and you may find yourself the proud owner of a mysterious bag of narcotic substance. You still don't get it, do you?

Most travelers who are put in jail actually do break the law. Typically they are involved in traffic- or drug-related offenses. Most of them actually broke many more laws, but the clarity and severity of their infraction demands retribution. Most Third World jails are not meant to hold minor criminals. There just isn't a justice system or infrastructure to feed and clothe, let alone rehabilitate. So most countries have an unofficial method of dealing with these problems and maintaining a police force at the same time. In Tijuana a cop can pull down $6,000 a month on a salary of about a tenth of that. Are they corrupt? No, you are supposed to tip a cop. You never know when you might need one for a serious crime. In Uzbekistan where wide-hatted goons man the streets every 50 meters, figure on a $10 tea money tip to get you through the gauntlet. Don't pay up and it's a trip to the local version of the KGB to invent passport irregularities costing up to a $100.

Keep in mind it serves no purpose for small or poor countries to incarcerate you for lengthy periods of time. It also does not serve the purpose of policemen to spend their time filling out paperwork when they can resolve the problem and teach you a lesson on the spot. From Minnesota to Malaysia to Mexico, I have been amazed at the solid financial education police officers have been given. (Which is better: $100 in your pocket or the policeman's pocket?)

But be forewarned, there are actually officers who do not accept or want bribes. They will have the nerve to get indignant and throw you in jail. The way to tell whether to keep your folding green out of sight or in plain sight is simple. If you are stopped by an officer and he tries to resolve a problem rather than just write you up, handcuff you or arrest you, you are expected to begin the bribe process. This does not mean stuffing cash into his pockets until he says stop. It's important to add a level of social interaction so that all involved have a good time. Get too indignant and you may hurt the feelings of your scrub-faced, beer-bellied friend.

If you feel an opening gambit has been made, then you are expected to explain to the officer your desire for a speedy amicable resolution of your problem. In most cases, the officer will shore your feelings of injustice about his having to take you all the way back to the station (always in the opposite direction you are traveling) to wait for the judge who is typically fishing or out until next week.

If he offers to take the fine back for you or to let you pay it on the spot, then bingo, the chiseling begins. Remember that bribes are a "cash-only" business and the amount you can pay will be limited to the amount of cash you have on you at that moment. Now that you have the rules of the game, please remember that offering any financial inducement to an officer, however innocently, is illegal and can put you in jail.

Delivering a Bribe

One must never discuss money or the amount or the reason for the gift. Typically, you will be presented with a "problem" that can be solved but will take time, money, or approval by a higher authority. You will naturally need to have this problem solved. You may ask if there is a fee that will expedite the solution of this problem, or if the local language fails you, you can point out your urgency and present a passport, ticket or papers with a single denomination of currency tucked inside.

DP's Guide to Bribes	
Minor traffic violation (speeding, imaginary stop signs, burned-out taillights that magically work; usually levied on Fridays or Saturday afternoons).	**$5–$10**
Traffic violations (real stop signs, real speeding tickets).	**$10–$50**
Serious traffic violations (DUI, very serious speeding or racing).	**$50–$500**
Very serious traffic problem (accident with no fatalities).	**$500–$1,000**
Accidents that involve fatalities require the application of funds to a judge, your lawyer, prosecutor and probably the police chief. Costs are usually in the $2,000–$6,000 range, and, yes, they will wait while your credit card clears. You will also be waiting in a jail.	**$2,000– $6,000**
If you are involved in something shady and need to correct the problem, it is wise to hire a lawyer. To make sure you get a lawyer who is sympathetic to the needs of the police, simply ask the police to recommend a good lawyer. The lawyer will negotiate fees for himself, the judge and the police.	**$10,000– $45,000**
Night out and breakfast at the White House	**$500,000**

The Price for Doing Bad Things

Bribes might not work if you are caught by the military, make the local papers or happen to be doing something the government is busy eradicating (usually with U.S. funds) at the time. Smuggling drugs, weapons or people requires the support of a large, covertly sanctioned organization. Freelancers are usually treated roughly with little opportunity to buy their way out. Depending on how big a fish they think you are, you can expect to pay about $12,000 to get out of a South or Central American jail. It is not uncommon to have to pay $30,000–$120,000 to beat a major drug rap.

More importantly you will need the protection of someone who has ensured the affluent lifestyle of the local politician and his family. If you think big you might want to make sure that you contribute to his campaign and keep photos that his political party might be embarrassed by. It always comes in handy if you want to sell or buy a few billion worth of military gear or technology. In most developing nations like Pakistan and Indonesia, the ruling parties and their supporters control exports and purchases. A skim of 15 percent is split between the middleman, who then usually splits his 7.5 percent with his counterpart from the selling country. In nondeveloping nations the ruler simply hires extended family members to pocket everything from oil revenues to bank loans to foreign aid. Now there is another kind of payoff. What if a criminal actually has the nerve to demand money from you or your family? In places like Mexico you'd better be in tight with the police, since many of the kidnappings are both orchestrated and solved by the local gendarmerie.

Other reasons for bribes are to bring in cars, contraband, machine parts, business samples, cash or even a wife. In many countries the police derive their sustenance from local businesses. A recent article in *Newsweek* estimated that in Hong Kong, brothels provide $120–$600 a month. In Bangkok, the city's 1,000 "entertainment houses" pay $600,000 a month to the local police. Strangely, these types of businesses can provide favors to travelers if you find yourself in a squeeze or need help approaching the police on a sensitive issue.

The best way to check out bribes is to contact the local embassy, expats who live in the area, local journalists (not foreign journalists) and local lawyers. It should be stated that in many cases a demand for a bribe can be talked down if you are doing nothing wrong. Many junior customs officials will spot first-timers and shake them down for everything from their *Playboys* to their underwear. Feel free to protest, but when the man with the big hat and gold stars agrees with the peon, it's time to start rolling off the twenties.

Is That a Roll of Twenties in Your Pocket or Are You Just Happy to See Me? Corruption Perception Index

Country	
Cameroon	1
Nigeria	2
Indonesia	3
Azerbaijan	4
Uzbekistan	5
Honduras	6
Tanzania	7
Yugoslavia	8
Paraguay	9
Kenya	10

Source: Transparency International
http://www.transparency.de/

When It Is Better to Give Than to Receive

Many people view bribery as reprehensible and evil. These are usually the ones who have to pay the bribes. Others view the practice as a normal way to supplement meager government wages (you can guess who they are). All countries including the United States have this affliction. Africa is the worst place for bribery, followed by South America and Central America, with northern Europe being the most incorruptible place. Corrupt economies start at the top, not the bottom. The arms trade spins off around $2.5 billion in finder's fees. How do you think Russian leaders make their retirement pay? In Albania 8 percent of all commerce goes in government officials' pockets, Indonesian businesses slip off 20 percent of income to prevent unnecessary hassles, and in Pakistan shopkeepers kill themselves to protest excessive baksheesh demands. Nigeria has one of the worst reputations for *dash*. What would you expect from an oil-rich country that has to import oil and at the same time make its leaders wealthy? So it's not surprising to expect any minor official in most poor African nations to ask for a *cadeau* in exchange for providing a higher level of service. Expats detest this practice because they have to go through customs, and refuse to pay it. Tourists are more easily intimidated and usually have much more to lose if they miss a flight, connection or cruise because of unnecessary delays.

Remember that small bribes are used to facilitate services that can be withheld or denied. Usually tightwads will be processed, but at the back of the line. Obnoxious tightwads who like to make loud speeches about corruption may find themselves with insurmountable visa irregularities ("The stamp in your passport must be green ink for a 15-day visa").

An Exciting New Franchise Opportunity

The Economist *stayed up late to figure out where all the money goes. With a little help from Friedrich Scheider, an economics professor at the Kepler University in Linz, they figure that the global GDP was 39 trillion in 1998. Another 9 trillion goes unaccounted for, based on how much currency is out there. Based on his study of 76 economies and assuming that most dirty dealing is in cash, it is estimated that 15 percent of a country's economy is unreported income. In "emerging" economies, the percentage of black-market activity is about a third. When all is said and done, the study figures that almost 80 percent of Nigeria's GDP is black market, followed by Thailand (70), Egypt (65), the Philippines (50), Mexico and Russia (40). The most honest country? Switzerland, followed by Japan, the United States and Austria.*

A carton of cigarettes will ensure that you are speedily processed in most African countries. A bottle of Johnny Walker will not get you far in a Muslim country but will definitely expedite your exit visa in Colombia. Border crossings into most Central American countries can be made for $100, and you can drive as fast as you want in Mexico if you have a good supply of 20 dollar bills. With such gifts, you may not need a visa entering a country and the customs official may forgo even a cursory inspection of your vehicle.

If you need to be smuggled out of a country, it is a little more complicated. First, the "coyote" will demand about twice the normal fee for your departure and there is no guarantee that he will not turn you in for a reward. Secondly, the matter of securing an exit visa without the benefit of an entry visa will cost you between $100 and $200 in most Asian and Latin American countries. Eastern European and CIS countries can be crossed for as little as $5, with no guarantee that you will not be finked on ten miles down the road.

You don't have to be a criminal to pay bribes. Criminals take great pride in their ability to extract bribes or "protection money" from honest folks. Moscow has 12 major organized crime groups who've been known to extract up to 30 percent of monthly profits from businesses. So the best way to view bribes is as you would tipping. When a country lowers its wages to its police and officials below the poverty line, they look to you to make ends meet.

In summary, using bribery is like kissing in junior high school. Both parties must be willing, but you have to be given an opening before you make your move. If you are brash or unwise, you will be severely rebuked.

Dangerous Jobs

Danger Live: Nine to Five

Don't have time or money for a dangerous vacation? Why not get a dangerous job and make money too? The most dangerous part of some jobs? Getting there. The odds are that you could get your kicks by being splattered on Route 66. Highway deaths accounted for 20 percent of the 6,588 fatal work injuries. According to the U.S. Department of Labor, truck drivers had more fatal injuries than any other occupation, with 762 deaths last year.

Homicide was the second leading cause of job-related deaths, accounting for 16 percent of the total. Robbery was the primary motive for workplace homicide. About half of the victims worked in retail establishments, such as grocery stores, restaurants and bars, where cash is readily available (31,000 convenience store clerks are shot every year). Taxicab drivers, police and security guards also had high numbers of worker homicides. Four-fifths of the victims were shot; others were stabbed, beaten or strangled.

Although highway accidents were the leading manner of death for male workers, homicide was the leading cause for female workers, accounting for 35 percent of their fatal work injuries.

Falls accounted for 10 percent of fatal work injuries. The construction industry, particularly special trade contractors such as roofing, painting and structural steel erection, accounted for almost half the falls. One-fifth of the falls were from or through roofs; falls from scaffolding and from ladders each accounted for about one-eighth. Nine percent of fatally injured workers were struck by various objects, a fourth of which were falling trees, tree limbs and logs. Other objects that struck workers included machines and vehicles slipping into gear or falling onto workers, and various building materials such as pipes, beams, metal plates and lumber. Electrocutions accounted for 5 percent of the worker deaths in a one-year span.

Occupations with large numbers of worker fatalities included truck drivers, farm workers, sales supervisors and proprietors, and construction laborers. Industry divisions with large numbers of fatalities included agriculture, forestry, fishing, construction, transportation and public utilities, and mining. Other high-risk occupations included airplane pilots, cashiers and firefighters.

The Most Dangerous Jobs in America, or Why Don't We See More Action/Adventure Shows Starring These Folks?

1. Truck driver	8. Taxicab driver
2. Farmworker	9. Timber cutter
3. Sales supervisor/proprietor	10. Cashier
4. Construction worker	11. Fisherman
5. Police detective	12. Metalworker
6. Airplane pilot	13. Roofer
7. Security guard	14. Firefighter

Source: U.S. Labor Department

California had the highest total fatalities on the job (601), with Texas finishing second with 497. Florida was a close third with 388. New York City led with the highest number of assaults and violent acts in the workplace (66). Apparently, something about the Northeast provokes violence at work. The District of Columbia reported 76 violent acts and assaults on the job, and Rhode Island had 55. Hawaii had the highest number of work-related highway deaths with 60.

Victims of Violent Crime According to the U.S. Justice Department

Private company	61%
Government	30%
Self-employed	8%
Working without pay	1%

Source: U.S. Justice Department

Who's Out There?

The typical whacko who freaks out at work and starts banging away is typically a middle-aged male over 35, withdrawn, owner of a gun, has served in the military and probably drinks or snorts too much chemical substance.

The Locations Where These Crimes Took Place	
Other commercial sites	23%
On public property	22%
Office, factory or warehouse	14%
Restaurant, bar or nightclub	13%
Parking lot/garage	11%
On school property	9%
Other	8%

What's Danger Worth?

The U.S. Department of State thinks employees who work in dangerous places should receive an additional payment of 25 percent of their normal salary. French companies will pay up to double the standard rate to do business in remote or dangerous places. Americans are the preferred targets. Americans visiting or working in other countries are increasingly becoming targets of anti-U.S. attacks. Latin America is the most likely place for anti-American attacks, with the Middle East just behind.

Don't think that it matters to the private sector paymaster whether you are an American or a former Colombian sent to work in Colombia. You will get preferential treatment: 92 percent of U.S. companies pay the same incremental amount regardless of race or country of origin.

Dangerous Occupations

If you're seeking an adventurous career change and don't particularly like the idea of dodging bullets while you're selling Slurpies and cigarettes, here are a few other jobs you might consider:

Army Ranger

The Ranger course is 68 days and emphasizes patrolling and raiding. The course is being restricted, and very few noninfantry soldiers will be able to attend in the future. Troops from other branches can attend if they are being sent to jobs with a specific need for Ranger skills. The Ranger school is considered the toughest course in the army.

U.S. Army
2425 Wilson Boulevard
Arlington, VA 22210-3385
Tel.: (703) 841-4300

Official Page
http://www-benning.army.mil/rtb/rtbmain.htm

Unofficial site
http://www.airborne-ranger.com/

Bicycle Messenger

There are about 1,500 bicycle messengers in New York City. Messengers are paid between $3 and $30 per trip. The average is about $7, with the messenger keeping half. There are higher rates for rush and oversized packages. Messengers also earn bonuses for working in bad weather. A good bike messenger should make about $125 a day and between $500 and $700 a week. The faster you are, the more you can make, especially during rush hour. You have to supply your own bike (usually a $500 to $1,200 mountain bike), safety gear and health insurance. The messenger company gives you a walkie-talkie and a big bag. Messengers work around the clock and break every rule in the book. Many practice "snatching" or grabbing onto a car or truck to speed up their trip. Contact individual messenger services in large cities for more information.

International Federation of Bike Messenger Associations
P.O. Box 191443
San Francisco, CA 94119
E-mail: magpie@echo.com
Fax: (603) 954 0473
http://www.messengers.org/

Mobil **(Bike Messenger Magazine)**
http://www.mobilecity.com/
Bicycle Messengers Europe
http://www.bme.org/index_m.asp
Background on Bicycle Messengers
http://www.transalt.org/blueprint/chapter14/

Blowout Control

If you like your work hot and dangerous, try containing oil blowouts. The most famous of these workers is, of course, Red Adair's group, which inspired a movie starring John Wayne. Despite the dramatic footage of men covered in oil and being roasted, safety comes first. Red is retired, but the company lives on.

The general idea is that when oil wells catch on fire, or blow out, there is a lot of money being sprayed into the air. So these people have to work fast. Saddam Hussein overtaxed companies from eight countries when he set the Kuwaiti fields alight. There were 732 oil wells in need of capping, but not before US$60 billion worth of oil had disappeared.

Even though the companies can be paid up to a million dollars a job (mostly for equipment and expenses), a more realistic fee is between US$20,000 and US$200,000 to control a blowout. The members of the crew make about US$300 to US$1,000 a day each plus room and board. The work requires a drilling background. It is tough, hard and dirty work. You also can't pick your customers, since blowouts happen anywhere, anytime.

Petroleum Industry Training Service
13, 2115 - 27 Avenue N.E.
Calgary, Alberta, Canada
T2E 7E4
Tel.: 1 (403) 250-9606
Fax: 1 (403) 291-9408
E-mail: webmaster@pits.ca
http://www.pits.ca/internat.html
Boots & Coots
777 Post Oak
Houston, TX 77056
(713) 621-7911
(800) BLOWOUT
http://www.boots-coots-iwc.com/

Red Adair (Global Industries, Inc.)
Corporate Headquarters
107 Global Circle (70503)
P.O. Box 61936
Lafayette, LA 70596-1936
Tel: (800) 900 - 4RED [4733]; (318) 989-0000
E-mail: busdev@globalind.com
Fax: (713) 462-6537
http://www.globalind.com/adair.htm

Bodyguard

Not much danger here, but it sounds dangerous. Big and beefy works for the low-level celebrity stuff, spry and deadly for the high-level political jobs. You can make about $200–$300 a day (when you work), and if you think you'll be working on a yacht in Monte Carlo protecting bikini-clad rich gals, wake up and smell the B.O.

Most bodyguards work for businessmen. You can carry a gun but it'll just wear a hole in your nice dry-cleaned shirts. If you're lucky you can get a fulltime gig where you also get to drive a car, open doors and other step'n'fetchit stuff. Should something go down, you get to throw yourself in front of your employer and spend a few months in the hospital if you get shot. Ex's are the preferred folks here, ex-Secret Service, ex-cops, ex-military, etc. *DP*'s best bet for adventure (but not bucks) is to go south (Latin America) young man, where bodyguarding is serious business. One of our buddies ended up being one of Vesco's bodyguards when he and a pal (ex-navy) were bumming around Costa Rica in the old days. They were hanging out in a bar and were enlisted to make a few sucres standing around looking tough.

International Bodyguard Directory
http://bodyguards.com/
Professional Bodyguard Association
The White House
24 Cumberland TCE
Willington, County Durham
DL15 OPB UK
http://www.qpage.com/host/pba.shtml
International Bodyguard Association
458 West Kenwood
Brighton, Tennessee 38011
Tel.: (901) 837-1915
FAX: (901) 837-4949
http://www.iapps.org/

Executive Protection Institute
http://www.personalprotection.com/
Anvil Crisis Avoidance Group
http://www.anvilgroup.com/
Falcon Global Corporation
55 Pierce Lane
Suite 204
Montoursville, PA 17754
Tel.: (570) 368-8734
Fax: (570) 368-8736
E-mail: falcon@falconglobal.com
http://www.falconglobal.com/

Bounty Hunter

For those of you who can't hold a day job, you might consider bounty hunting. Since the romantic notion of men being brought in dead or alive for a price on their head is almost gone, you end up working for bail bondsmen, not the most romantic of employers. They will pay you a finder's fee so they don't have to cough up the entire amount of the court-imposed bail when their client doesn't show.

The job does not require much training or even much of anything except a pair of handcuffs and a little skip-tracing education. What you get for bringing in bad people is between 10 and 30 percent of the fugitives' bail from the grateful bondsmen. Their clients will not be happy to see you and, in most cases, will try to elude you, since you have neither an attractive uniform nor a big gun. If you have a permit to carry a gun, you are not always allowed to use it. You need a license to operate in Indiana and Nevada, but in other states you are essentially making a citizen's arrest, and if you end up with broken bones or holes in you, it's your problem. Some states don't like bounty hunters; you can't practice your business in Illinois, Kentucky or Oregon, for example. There are less restrictions on bounty hunters than police. You can enter a fugitive's home, cross state lines and secure and transport a fugitive without all that Miranda, constitutional stuff. How? Well next time you post bail, read the fine print. If you are a bad guy you also have some leeway in the legal arena if you feel you were unfairly treated.

There are about 7,000 bounty hunters (2,000 make a living, about 50–100 make a good living at it) in the United States who return about 20,000 fugitives each year. It is estimated that about 35,000 folks jump bail (don't appear in court after paying a security bond) and about 87 percent are brought back by bounty hunters. Most of these hunters don't make much money. The lower the bail, the less serious the crime, the less money they make, the easier the errant crooks or fugitives (don't forget they are innocent until proven guilty) are to find. Bounty hunters have a better return rate than traditional law enforcement: 87 percent vs. 64 percent.

National Institute of Bail Enforcement
P.O. Box 1170
Tombstone, AZ 85638
Tel.: (520) 457-9360
http://bounty-hunter.net/

Western States Bail Enforcement Association
P.O. Box 352
Los Altos, CA 94023
E-mail: webmaster@bounty-hunter.org
http://www.bounty-hunter.org/

Cabdriver

Taxis were introduced in 1907 in New York City. Today, it is a job usually taken by recent immigrants. In New York City, there are 11,787 Yellow Cabs, 30,000 livery cars and between 5,000 and 9,000 illegal gypsy cabs. Cabdrivers are usually independent contractors who lease their cabs from a cab company. In New York, a cabbie pays about $40 a day for the cab and maybe about $20 for gas. He gets to keep everything after that. The term for breaking even is "making the knot." There are no benefits, worker's comp or holidays. The hours are flexible, and you meet a lot of interesting people, albeit briefly. The Lexan dividers in some cabs have been credited with saving lives, but driving a cab is still a dangerous business.

In a recent one-year span in New York City, there were 40 murders of cabbies; most were drivers of livery or gypsy cabs. In a five-year period, 192 drivers were killed. There were 3,892 robberies in that one-year period. The average amount of the theft was $100 in cash.

N.Y. Taxi Commission
Tel.: (212) 302-8294
Fax: (212) 840-1607
http://www.ci.nyc.ny.us/html/tlc/home.html

CIA

It's boom time at the CIA. The agency has been given money to hire new case officers and reopen new overseas offices. You almost think that they nuked the Chinese Embassy in Belgrade just to get some attention and a few budget bumps. Despite all that high-tech crap they keep launching into the air, the CIA's job is still to steal secrets. That's why they finally figured they need more folks on the ground. You know things are bad when the CIA calls *DP* to demand why the new edition is not out yet. We can only imagine legions of spooks pacing the halls waiting for the latest wisecrack from the rebel camps. One KLA recruit was handed a copy of *DP* by his CIA handler before being sent to Albania. Man, times are tough. *DP* supports our L.L. Bean boys overseas, but we always wonder why we never bump into them on the front lines instead of at the American Club.

Well that could be changing. The CIA has their very own venture capital firm to get in on the ground floor, aide groups working diligently to do nothing (just have the local UN point them out for you), freelance journalists carefully taking notes for nonexistent newspapers and even missionaries spreading the word of God and collecting more.

The U.S. intelligence community is comprised of about 100,000 people who work for 28 different organizations. It takes eight agencies just to process and analyze the satellite images sent in by five different intelligence groups. It costs about $28 billion to find out what our friends and enemies are up to. The adventurous, spooky stuff is the Clandestine Service. If you want to be a Clandestine Service case officer, only mention your interest in your first interview. They need folks who have language skills and background in Africa, Central Asia (especially Former Soviet Republics). Entrance salary is between $31,459 to $48,222. Maximum age is 35 and you need to have a college degree. How do we know all this super spooky stuff. Well the CIA has taken to advertising in the *Economist*. For super secret jobs contact:

Chief Career Training Program
P.O. Box 1925
Washington, DC 20013
Tel.: (703) 790-0345
http://www.CIA.gov/

The job category that might attract MBAs/adventurers is what is known as *nonofficial cover*. Opportunity is knocking (or NOCing) for a few lucky business grads. Dissatisfied with the traditional foreign embassy bureaucrat or aid worker as a cover for its operatives, the CIA has decided to get creative. The CIA now recruits young executives through bogus companies, usually based in northern Virginia. The ads appear in major periodicals and newspapers and seek recent business school grads who want to work overseas. The job pays well but requires training. The NOCs are not trained in Camp Peary nor do they ever appear on any CIA database, to keep them safe from moles. Sounds like a great movie plot, so far.

The successful graduates are then posted with real companies overseas. Many large American corporations gladly accept these folks, since they get a real business grad who works long hours for free. Each NOC has a liaison person who must handle the intel that is provided by his charge. Many of these positions are with banks, import-export firms and other companies in such nasty places as North Korea, Iraq, Iran and Colombia. Although the CIA has to cut corners on its $28 billion dollar annual budget and NOCs cost more to train and support, it's hoped they can provide hard information in countries where the embassy is a little light on cocktail party chatter.

If you are exposed or captured, you are officially a spy and not protected by a diplomatic passport.

Typical ad:

Position: Operations Officer (Overseas)
Degree Required: MBA, Master's degree
Majors Sought: Business, Hard Sciences (physics, chemistry, etc.), Liberal Arts
Citizenship Status: U.S. Citizenship is required for federal government employment.
Location: Overseas
Salary: Based on qualifications
Description: The Directorate of Operations is the intelligence collection component of the Central Intelligence Agency. Operations officers are charged with gathering and reporting information vital to the security of our nation. Operations officers carry out their responsibilities by recruiting, training and maintaining networks of agents who provide information about events and issues that threaten or might be potentially harmful to the United States. These officers receive extensive training in specialized tradecraft, interpersonal relations, language skills and reports writing before moving overseas. Supported by administrative and communications specialists, they serve worldwide in diverse and exciting working environments. Although the primary focus of Operations Officers is the collection of foreign intelligence, they are also involved in counterintelligence abroad. They must be concerned with the activities and intentions of hostile intelligence services throughout the world.
Proficiency in a foreign language; full-time private sector work experience.
Type of Schedule: Resumes will be referred to the company. Submit cover letter with resume.
Contact Person: Thomas J. Benning, Recruiter
Address: P.O. Box 12708, Rosslyn Station, Arlington, VA 22209
Phone: 703/905-6349
Fax: 703/482-4188

CIA Employment Office

Career Trainee Division
P.O. Box A2002
Arlington, VA 22209-8727
Tel.: (703) 613-8888
Fax: (703) 613-7871
http://www.odci.gov/cia

To join the Clandestine Service branch of the CIA you need a bachelor's degree along with strong communication and interpersonal skills. Military experience helps. The CIA is keen on folks with backgrounds in Central Eurasian, East Asian and Middle Eastern languages (kind of tells you where the action is, doesn't it?). You need to pass a medical, psychiatric and polygraph test. You must be a U.S. citizen and can't be over 35. The starting pay is $31,459 to $48,222. A lot of the training takes place at the 9,000-acre Camp Peary, outside Williamsburg, Virginia. Here students spend a year at "the Farm" learning how to be spies.

Former CIA operatives can also sign up with any number of security consultants or groups who provide the private sector with intelligence gathering and security.

The CIA's Greatest Hits

The CIA needs a good press agent. We won't even list the botched coups, uprisings, billion-dollar snapshots of the tops of people's heads, the KLA, Kurds, Castro's beard or even their kid's page. But somebody has to base a hit comedy series on the agency. Okay, okay, we will mention the kids page.

6/7/99	U.S. missile delivered by B2 bomber hits Chinese embassy in Belgrade.
7/20/99	U.S. missile hits Sudanese medical factory.
7/7/99	U.S. embassies in Kenya and Dar es Salaam hit by bomb.
5/11/99	India hits nuclear bomb. U.S. military is surprised.
6/25/99	U.S. military gets hit in Dhahran blowing up and killing 19 U.S. troops.
02/13/91	U.S. smart missile hits Iraqi bunker full of civilians.
7/3/88	*USS Vincennes* hits an Iranian Airbus over the Gulf, killing 290 innocent people.

OK, enough spook bashing. The real trend might be the hearts and diapers program underway to sway America's youth to the nefarious dirty work of the CIA.

CIA Kids Page
http://www.CIA.gov/cia/ciakids/index.html
Get a top-level briefing from Spy Guy. Try on a disguise.

CIA Canine Page
http://www.CIA.gov/cia/ciakids/dogs/index.html
Make Bo bark! (Ever wonder what all those billions in covert technology are spent on?)

War Correspondent
Forget Nick Nolte in *Under Fire*, forget Mel Gibson in *The Year of Living Dangerously* forget Dennis Hopper in *Apocalypse Now*, forget David Janssen in *The Green Berets*. Real war photographers and writers are crazier, duller, funnier, sadder, richer, poorer and just about anything more than any cinematic cartoon could create. For every wild-eyed rich boy there is a careful quiet social scientist. For every gray, wrinkled notetaker there is a naïve, heroin-addicted neophyte. The common denominator seems to be the desire to be at the cutting edge of history. To make sense out of chaos and ultimately to drift back into the real world with a collection of old press tags, empty cartridges, unit patches and memories. Fame and self-satisfaction do not pay the rent.

There is not a lot of money to be made—stringers might make $75 a story, $100 a photo. Yeah, maybe you'll be the next Amanpour, Morris, Turnley, Nachtwey or Capa, but don't count on it. War coverage is becoming less and less relevant (and more important) as we head into the "video briefings, police action, kidnapped journos" world of coverage.

How do you get started? Just do it. Save your money, go there, bring your copy of *DP* and ask a lot of questions. When you get back, bang on the door of every newspaper, magazine, TV news group and maybe, just maybe, somebody will send you off somewhere . . . for no money, no guarantees and on your dime. Nice business; too bad it doesn't qualify as a charity.

Writers need to be able to file often and quickly, photographers need reliable ways to modem or courier photos. Most people start in the business by just doing it. Showing up with a cheap camera, new clothes and a hope that no one will discover them for what they are. Keep your ears open and listen. Trade info, dig hard, bring a bottle of booze and spare whatevers, keep it light back at the hotel and you'll do fine.

Reporters Killed 1987–1996	
Europe/Former USSR	128
Middle East/North Africa	94
Asia	85
Africa	51
Americas	41

Source: http://www.rsf.fr

According to Reporters Sans Frontieres, there were 36 journalists reported murdered, 446 arrested and 653 assaulted or threatened because of their work worldwide in 1999. Twice as many journalists killed this year as last year. Most victims are local working stiffs who piss off the government or local bad guys, not the traveling circus of network and feed girls and boys who descend on every breaking story.

"Yeah, That's Nice, but Do They Pay?"

The weekly Mail & Guardian *says that the South African Pan African News Agency (PANA) is looking to be pardoned for their sins, according to an amnesty application handed to the Truth and Reconciliation Commission in 1996. The bogus news agency was created in October 1985 by former Strategic Communications (Stratcom) operative Michael Bellingan. The application was handed to the commission by Bellinga's former associate and former security branch warrant officer Paul Erasmus.*

Bellingan told the commission the security branch set up an "alternative, left-wing media agency" that paid unsuspecting journalists and photographers to write stories and take photographs that were never published but instead ended up in security police intelligence files. Some of the materials were used for intelligence gathering and/or disinformation. "The journalists imagined they were sending news and photographs overseas, but in fact their reports went no further than our files," said Bellingan. In related news, the CIA says it will no longer use accredited journalists to collect intel. What about freelance? Um er, well, ahh, next question please.

The best way for an aspiring war hog to start is to contact one of the many photo or print news agencies to find out who they have in the region and how to file. None will pay your way there or provide equipment or expenses at first, but if you set up a rapport and a stream of saleable submissions you might be on your way. The only advice I can give is *inveniam viam aut facium.*

The Associated Press
International Headquarters
50 Rockefeller Plaza
New York, NY 10020
Tel.: (212) 621-1500
http://www.associatedpress.org

Sygma
322 - 8th Avenue
New York City, NY 10001
Tel.: (212) 675-7900
www.ny.sygma.com
www.sygma-london.co.uk

Reuters
http://www.reuters.com/

Agency France Press
http://www.afp.com

SIPA Press
http://www.sipa.com/

Blackstar
http://www.blackstar.com/

Corbis
http://www.corbis.com

Other Helpful Resources

American Journalism Review (Joblink)
http://ajr.newslink.org/new-
joblinkad.html?9AMB9O

Behind the Lens
http://www.digitalstoryteller.com/
BTV99/contents.html

Committee to Protect Journalists
330 7th Avenue, 12th Floor
New York, NY 10001
Tel.: (212) 465-1004
Fax: (212) 465-9568
E-mail: media@cpj.org
http://www.cpj.org

Reporters Sans Frontieres
Secrétariat International
5, rue Geoffroy Marie - 75009 Paris -
FRANCE
Tel: (33) 1 44 83 84 84
Fax: (33) 1 45 23 11 51
E-mail: rsf@calva.net
http://www.rsf.fr

Society of Professional Journalists
16 South Jackson St.
Greencastle, IN 46135-1514
Tel: (765) 653-3333
Fax: (765) 653-4631
E-mail: spj@link2000.net
http://www.spj.org/

The Free Lens
Rory Peck Trust
7 Southwick Mews, London W2 7JG
Tel.: 44 (0) 171 262 5272
Fax: 44 (0) 171 262 2361
E-mail: rptrpa@dial.pipex.com
http://www.oneworld.org/rorypeck

World War Correspondents Encounter
Encounter Coordinator
The Jose Marti International Institute
of Journalism
General Director
Ave. G No. 503, e/ 21 y 23
Vedado, La Habana, Cuba
Tel.: [537] 32 05 66, [537] 32 05 67
Fax: [537] 33 30 79
E-mail: upec@mail.infocom.etecsa.cu
A one-time event held in Cuba that may
be expanded. Events include tours to
the Border Brigade at the U.S. Navy
base in Guantanamo, Cuba; Playa
Giron, site of the Bay of Pigs Invasion;
and a visit to the Ché Guevara
Mausoleum.

Professional Adventurer

Ha ha, you say. Indiana Jones U, here I come. Is it possible to get a job as a professional adventurer? You know what's coming—adventure isn't a job, it's, well, an adventure you moron.

I make a living being a professional adventurer. Jack Wheeler used to do it in the '80s, Cousteau did it for Nat Geo and then Turner. That goofy alligator guy with the bug eyes, short pants and beerbelly does it for *Animal Planet.* Ranulph Fiennes, Wilfred Thesiger, Sir Richard Burton, Bob Denard, Lawrence of Arabia, Robin Hanbury-Tenison, Mike Williams and Michael Palin have all had a shot at it; most of them never really make the big time either, financially. The more hardcore you are the less time you have to do the cocktail circuit, which ultimately gives you the money to do the adventure thing. Someday somebody will write a decent book about this much-maligned and misunderstood affliction. Hey I did: *www.adventurist.com*

Career advice? Hang out with like-minded people. Don't spend the rest of your life dreaming about it. Do it . . . in your own style.

http://www.comebackalive.com
http://www.rgs.org
http://expeditionnews.com/
http://www.speakers.co.uk/6071.htm
http://www.oceanrowing.com/activearchive/john_fairfax.htm
http://www.theadventurist.com

Delta Force

The 1st SFOD-Delta (Delta Force) began in 1977 as Uncle Sam's sharp edge against terrorism. Today it is estimated to employ between 2,500–8,000 men (and females). Charlie Beckworth was given two years to create an antiterrorism unit similar to European units like the SAS. There are three assault squadrons (A, B and C) made up of 75 people who are split into four- to six-man teams. When they need a lift, they use the Air Force Special Operations Command and the Army 160th Aviation Regiment. It also has its own small air force made of civilian-dressed aircraft that can be converted once in-country. There is also the Funny Platoon, an intel group that uses female operatives.

A $75 million facility on old Range 19 (on McKellars Road) at Fort Bragg is their home. Their specialty is storming buildings or planes, and like the Navy SEALs, they may or may not have been used for a variety of rescue and black ops. The world knows about their botched attempts to rescue the hostages in Tehran and the casualties they suffered trying to take out Aidid in Mogadishu. Delta operatives have spent quite a bit of time cooling their heels in Cyprus trying to rescue hostages or on Howard Air Force base in Panama.

Delta Force prides itself on being the world's best marksmen under all conditions. The latest thrill ride is being invited to sit in the middle of a Delta Force shooting house during CQB (Close Quarter Battle) and watch the team storm the buildings, killing all the paper terrorists without messing a single hair on the guests' heads. Like the Navy SEALs (who often work in conjunction with the Delta Force), the Delta Force can go anywhere, anytime; they just leave the wet jobs to SEAL Team 6, the Navy's version of Delta Force. The FBI has a hostage team that handles domestic terrorist incidents. Delta Force operatives are recruited from the army. The average candidate is around 31 years old, has 10 years of service and has an above-average IQ. Candidates are by invitation only (usually recruited from Green Berets and Rangers) and must go through physical and psychological tests. There is an 18-day formal selection course that mimics the SAS course with the addition of rigorous mental tests after periods of physical hardship and sleep deprivation. If accepted, the candidate then goes through a six-month Operators Training Course. The course includes shooting, air assaults, bodyguarding, high-speed driving, mental sharpening and covert operations. Oh, and those black helicopters everyone talks about. Talk to the Delta Force who conduct urban antiterrorism training.

Sorry you have to start at the bottom.

Army Recruiting
http://www.goarmy.com/
E-mail: ecruiter@usarec.army.mil

Explosives Expert

If Uncle Sam taught you how to blow things up, you might want to try demolishing buildings (no, we don't mean federal buildings). The skill of imploding existing skyscrapers, apartment buildings and large factories has spawned companies that do nothing but take down buildings in a few seconds flat. Controlled Demolition Group holds the world record for blowing up buildings. Although not a dangerous job with the correct training (hell, even I used to work with explosives), it does demand a certain level of attention.

Controlled Demolition Group

Charlesworth House
Richardshaw Road
Leeds, England LS28 6QW
Tel.: [44] (0113) 255-8455
Tel.: [44] (0113) 239-3191
E-mail: marketing@cdg5.discovery-net.co.uk

Green Beret

The Green Berets are the outgrowth of the World War II "Jedburgh teams," special teams that were dropped behind enemy lines to link up with French partisans. They evolved into eight-man Detachment Alpha or "A" teams. Each team member had multiple and overlapping skills. Later the teams would be expanded to 12 men. They were used to train other military or insurgent groups. Despite the shoot 'em John Wayne image, Green Berets are officially known as U.S. Army Special Forces, and they have always been linked with spook work and covert operations. They were created in 1953 by a veteran of the OSS (the precursor of the CIA), and the green beret wasn't officially endorsed until President Kennedy visited Fort Bragg in 1961. To get in, you have to already be a member of the Army and pass the three-week selection course at Fort Bragg. Once accepted there is the Q course, a 3- to 12-month course that teaches the basic skills of counterinsurgency

Criteria for Green Berets

http://www.goarmy.com/sorc/crite-
ria.htm
http://www.goarmy.com/sorc/sorc.htm

John F. Kennedy Special Warfare Center and School

ATTN: AMU-SP-R
Fort Bragg, NC 28307
Tel.: (919) 432-1818

101st Airborne Division

ATTN: RCRO-SM-SF-FC
Fort Campbell, KY 42223
Tel.: (502) 439-4390

Mercenary

You gotta wonder how the job of mercenary became such an icon for the hell-bent-for-leather crowd. These days, working as a soldier in another army is about the same as switching software programming jobs. You've got skills, they've got work, so what's the big deal? Well, its because most people think being a mercenary is about killing people. Ultimately it is, but if you have real skills you are not going to be sitting in a filthy trench with a bunch of bug-eyed local recruits. You are probably going to be back at the base, training, coordinating, planning and not too far out of range from the local nightlife.

You need to have some pretty impressive skills to get work these days. The files of Sandline, MPRI, Vinnel and even the local security guard company are flooded with resumés from thousands of eager, underemployed ex-military types. If you were special forces, worked in an interesting theater and know a few languages, you might stand a chance. If you scraped the rust bits off a refueling barge, you probably won't be getting a call back. There is a lot of security guard stuff for oil companies, training of armed forces, flying, and large-scale planning but not a lot of running around in the jungle in sweaty torn cammo saying "Cover me, I'm going in." Most of these contracts are through Stateside or U.K. corporations. You can try hanging around at the SOF convention, but you better be connected. Worse case, you can read the chapters on mercenaries and decide to keep that 9 to 5 job and live out your fantasies on your vacation instead.

Every once in a while there is a little low-level stuff like recruits for the KLA, Central America or the Caribbean, but it always ends up bad.

Sandline International
http://www.sandline.com/

Military Professional Resources, Inc.
http://www.mpri.com/.

Vinnell Corporation
http://www.vinnell.com

Betac Corporation
http://www.betac.com/

AirScan
http://www.airscan.com/

Armor Holdings, Inc.
http://armorholdings.com/

DynCorp
http://www.dyncorp.com/

Waterborne/Marine Security

Marine Risk Management S.A.
http://www.marinerisk.com/

Pistris
http://www.pistris.com/

Other Sites of Interest

Bob Denard
http://www.bobdenard.com/

French Foreign Legion
http://www.info-france-usa.org/america/embassy/legion/legion.htm

Military Links
http://members.aol.com/rhrongstad/private/mlinknew.htm

International Security Policy and Military Affairs Links
http://www.columbia.edu/cu/libraries/indiv/lehman/guides/isc.html

Mine Clearance

Land mines kill or maim someone on this planet every hour. There is a big demand for former explosives and munitions experts to clean up these killers. Mine clearance personnel are paid about US$90,000 a year. There are about 20 companies that specialize in the detection and removal of land mines. Kuwait spent about US$1 billion to clean up the 7 million land mines sewn during the five-month occupation of Kuwait by Iraq; 83 mine clearance experts have been killed just in Kuwait. If you are looking for big money, be aware that local minesweepers in Angola make only US$70 a day.

NGO Humanitarian Demining Activity Worldwide
http://www.hdic.jmu.edu/hdic/exchange/ngo/

Explosive Ordnance Disposal
http://www.eodmu7.navy.mil/

Ronco
http://roncoconsulting.com/

HALO Trust
P.O. Box 7712
London, SW1V 3ZA, UK
http://www.britannia.com/newsbits/knights.html

Mines Advisory Group
45-47 Newton Street
Manchester M1 1FT, UK
Tel.: 44 161 236 4311
Fax: 44 161 236 6244
E-mail: maguk@cybase.co.uk
http://www.mag.org.uk/

CAMEO Security,
150 Edward Street,
Cornwall, Ontario
Canada, K6H 4G9
Tel.: (613) 936-6815
Fax: (613) 936-6635
http://www.cameo.org/

Mine Clearance Game
http://stud1.tuwien.ac.at/~e9125168/javas/jmine.html

Mine Clearance Dogs
http://www.globalcorp.com/trainingacademy/index.html

Navy SEAL

Specialists in Naval Special Warfare, the SEALs (SEa Air, Land) evolved from the frogman of World War II. The SEALs have been glorified in films and books. Their most recent brush with fame was their less-than-secret invasion of Kuwait City, with the world's press watching and filming with high-powered camera lights. The SEALs were born on January 1, 1962, when they were created by President Kennedy along with the revitalized Green Berets.

In 1989 the SEALs were the first into Panama, using rebreathers and midget subs. In the Gulf War they even used custom-made dune buggies to operate behind enemy lines.

The SEALs go through 27 weeks of intense basic training, either in Coronado, which is near San Diego, or on the East Coast. The training starts with a seven-week exercise and swimming course just to get ready for basic training. Then there are nine weeks of extreme physical and mental abuse. The focus is on teamwork and surviving the constant harassment. The sixth week is "Hell Week," six days of misery and physical torture with little or no sleep. Then there is extensive classroom and underwater training in SCUBA (Self-Contained Underwater Breathing Apparatus) diving. This phase ends with another serious physical challenge. The third and final phase is the UDT and above-water training on San Clemente Island. There is also a six-month probation period.

SEAL teams must practice close-quarter battle drills by firing 300 or more rounds of 9-mm ammunition weekly. Each of the six-line SEAL teams is given 1.5 million rounds of ammunition annually to train its five 16-man platoons. According to the specs on their Beretta 92F pistols, this means they burn out one handgun a year. Their MP5 machine guns last a little longer. The symbol of a SEAL is the gold-plated "Budweiser" pin, the eagle and a trident symbol. SEAL Team 6 specializes in antiterrorist operations. They are controlled by NAVSPECWARCOMDEVGROUP out of Coronado, California.

If you just want to look like a SEAL you can shop at the same place SEALs shop. Be the first on your block to wear a shirt that says "Pain is just weakness leaving your body." Contact: **Bullshirts**, *1007 Orange Avenue, Coronado, CA 92118.*

U.S. Navy Human Resources

2531 Jefferson Davis Highway
Arlington, VA 22242-5161
Tel.: (703) 607-3023
http://webix.nosc.mil/seals/

Official SEALS Site

http://www.chinfo.navy.mil/navpalib/
factfile/personnel/seals/seals.html

West Coast Recruiting/PR

LTJG Tom Greer
Public Affairs Officer
Naval Special Warfare Center
2446 Trident Way
San Diego, CA 92155
E-mail: pao@navspecwarcen.navy.mil
http://www.navy.mil/

Smoke Jumper

If the thought of being parachuted into a raging inferno and having to fight your way back until you can be airlifted out many sleepless nights later appeals to you, then you should try smoke jumping. Smoke jumpers are firefighters who must be in the air within ten minutes and parachute into remote areas to fight fires. Dropped from small planes as low as 1,500 feet in altitude, they quickly must hike to the scene of the fire, and instantly begin to chop and backburn areas to head off forest fires before they get too big. The work is all manual and requires strength, endurance and an ability to work around the clock if need be.

Most smoke jumpers are attracted by the danger and the camaraderie these jobs afford. They are known to be party animals, close friends and hard workers

Although the death of 14 firefighters in Glenwood Springs, Colorado, on July 6, 1994, reminded people that smoke jumping is dangerous, that there are only 387 smoke jumpers in the United States makes those deaths even more significant. The last time any smoke jumpers were killed actually fighting a fire was in 1949 during the Mann Gulch blaze in Montana. During this 45-year period of calm, one jumper pancaked into the ground due to chute failure and another hanged himself when he tried to get out of a tree in which he had landed.

Like most dangerous jobs, the goal is to stay alive and healthy, and you definitely don't do it for the money. Pay for smoke jumpers starts at about $9 an hour, and there is additional pay during fires and with overtime. Most are part-time jumpers who earn the money during the hot summer fire season.

There are nine U.S. Forest Service and Bureau of Land Management regional jumper bases in the West. The supervisors react quickly to fires and send in anywhere from two or more jumpers, depending on the size of the fire. If a lightning strike starts a small blaze, fire jumpers can deal with it quickly and effectively before calling in the water bombers. Supplies can be parachuted in as soon as the jumpers are on the ground. Once done, the jumpers then get to hike out with their equipment or be picked up by helicopter.

Training requires federal certification to fell large trees and to be able to climb in and, more likely, out of trees. They maintain their own chainsaws and other equipment. Their protective Kevlar suits hold their equipment and protect them when landing in trees. Forest Service jumpers use round chutes and jump at 1,500 feet BLM; smoke jumpers use the more modern rectangular chutes and exit at 3,000 feet.

National Smokejumpers Association

Kensington Street
P.O. Box 4081
Missoula, MT 49806
Tel.: (406) 549-9938.
http://www.smokejumpers.com/

UN Peacekeeper

Not many soldiers ask to be UN peacekeepers, and they usually find the idea of talking to a highly trained killer and making him Gandhi for a day even stranger. It's tough enough trying to figure out why someone is trying to kill his closest neighbor, or in our case, why we send pimply kids thousands of miles to whomp Third World revolutionaries. Being a UN peacekeeper means wearing silly blue berets and driving around in white trucks. You can be shot at, but you can't shoot back. You can be insulted, but you can't insult back. In fact, you may find yourself actually helping people kill their enemy as you protect war criminals, maintain archaic political boundaries and provide security for execution squads. You will come under shell fire and gun fire and have to keep up with deadly bureaucratic paperwork. In Bosnia, Canadians were told to return mines they dug up to the armies that planted them. Some scratched their initials on the casings and dug up the same mines weeks later. They must use photodegradable sandbags, and the rules of engagement are so Byzantine that it requires hours to get official clearances to shoot back when they come under fire.

United Nations

Field Operations Staffing
42nd Street and First Avenue, Room 52280-D
New York, NY
Tel.: (212) 963-1147
http://www.un.org/

United Nations Staff College

http://www.itcilo.it/unscp/logo/JS-gbmain.htm

In a Dangerous Place: Central Asia

Southern Tajikistan

Down at breakfast I hand in my food chit and get a greasy sausage, perogis, grapes and Tajik bread. I see the other tourists. One is a large 50ish woman and the other is a young man with the looks of an East German Stasi, complete with long leather coat and small pinched glasses.

After breakfast I sit in the lobby and make some notes. The woman who I had seen at breakfast comes up and asks if I am a journalist. I say no, I am just traveling and looking to hook up with the UN. She is a Swedish journalist and is traveling to the south with the UN this morning. Synchronicity is a big part of travel.

She needs a photographer to cover the refugees returning from the fighting in Afghanistan. It seems I am to become a photojournalist for the next few days. She offers to talk to the UN and see if I can come along.

The man who I mistook as a Stasi agent is in fact a New Yorker and a Field Officer for the UN. Shows how well my judge of character is working. Not only is he going to the south but he has read my book cover to cover and is thrilled that I have shown up.

We have lunch with the UNHCR folks behind their steel-gated compound. John McCallin, the head of the UN mission in the CIS, tells me I am in luck. According to the word on the street there is to be a kidnapping today. So I may be in for some fun. These are the same group of people who were kidnapped by a warlord to ensure the safe passage of his brother out of Afghanistan. The people were stripped and marched through the snow and went through mock executions. Not much fun, but part of the job hazards in Tajikistan. McCallin brushes off the kidnapping as similar to Walter Brennan, croaking out, "Ahve cum to git ma boy." Here there are many private armies, with men getting paid about $5 a day. Many military commanders control government and private armies. There are also plain old-fashioned gangsters and mafyia who do their best to control resources like aluminum and cotton.

My UN host, Jonathan, has spent his time in Herat, Afghanistan, and has come up to help with repatriating thousands of refugees into the war zone while things are calm in Mazar-I-Sharif. He has an apartment for about $300 a month and spends most of his time down south in Shartuz. He makes around 80 grand a year and can salt most of it away. There is also subsistence pay, hazardous duty pay and tax incentives. He figures by the time he is 50 he will have put half a million away. The concept of making your "bundle" is strong motivation in the UN. I sense that there must be something more than money to encourage someone to work in Afghanistan and Tajikistan. It is a good job but it is a hard job, as I am about to see.

These people are Tajiks who fled the fighting in the south of Tajikistan only to end up in the middle of the fighting when the Taliban entered Mazar. The Taliban have been repulsed, but no one knows how long things will be quiet. He has computers, desks, fax machines and all the modern conveniences of home. His work is paperwork heavy and reports must be filed every day to be gathered and collated at headquarters. How many refugees, from where, to which village, how many tons of flour, liters of cooking oil, pounds of sugar, hundreds of blankets and so on all must be requisitioned, shipped, distributed and accounted for under very loose and stressful conditions.

Also, the UN is truly a United Nations of peoples. Thai, British, American, Swedish, Ethiopian and Tajik all work side by side. Jonathan has a degree in geology and a masters in intercultural management

We load up our white, large lettered UNHCR truck and drive at breakneck speed through the warzone.

The south is the site of the heaviest fighting during the civil war. Now it is quiet, except for the occasional battle or killing. The Kurgan Turbe region is the nexus of the conflict for control by the opposition for control of the government. Now Nuri, the leader of Islamic fundamentalist fighters, is in Dushanbe and things have quieted down to the occasional bombing, shooting, and executions of dozens of soldiers. There is still the threat of a kidnapping, so our driver drives a little faster than would be normal. I feel like I am part of the director's cut of *Bullitt*.

We are in a hurry to meet a train with about 310 refugees on board. The Tajik refugees have come from Mazar by truck, barge and train and will be offloaded, fed and then sent off with their goods to their bombed and shattered villages in the region. There have been casualties from the fighting and no one quite knows what kind of condition the refugees will be in.

Finally, down near the southern border, I arrive in a Sergio Leone movie tableau. In a land that is brown and sparse, there is a single building, a water tower and an ancient dilapidated Russian train. The pale blue sky and the dry hills far beyond frame the scene perfectly. The train is comprised of passenger cars, followed by open cars piled high with the refugees' personal possessions.

These refugees have been waiting five years to come home. Back in Afghanistan, 2 people were killed and 20 were wounded in the recent fighting. Their camp was looted and most lost whatever they had brought on their backs from their homes. The children are covered with sores and the people are tired and dirty. Men break down and cry in their relatives' arms as they welcome them back. It is a touching scene and one that reinforces the UN's purpose. Without the intervention of the UN these people would never be able to leave Afghanistan cross through Uzbekistan to rebuild their lives again.

The train passengers have brought with them bicycles, food, blankets, livestock, building materials and whatever food the UN gave them in Afghanistan. It is piled deep in the last nine open box cars.

It seems the Uzbek police, who were charged with the security of the refugees, were actually stealing and looting the refugees' possessions as the Tajiks watched helplessly from the passenger cars in front. The Uzbek police slashed and threw possessions over the side to their friends waiting at the side of the tracks at a predetermined bend.

The Tajiks demand that I photograph the proof of this crime. They hold up slashed bags, empty cases and smashed goods. I suddenly feel like I have a purpose and I lose track of Jonathan. I later find him sitting in his truck with the doors locked, screaming on the radio at the top of his voice. He thinks we can't hear him. He is frustrated by the bureaucracy, the head office is busy reassigning his people to other areas and he is expected to squire around a German delegation. Meanwhile, he is expected, along with 3 people, to get 310 other people fed, housed and organized in a few days.

I offer to shift from my photojournalist duties to chip in with the mammoth job of coordinating people, unloading trucks of flour, blankets, cooking oil, tarps, sugar and other material and to provide security. In the confusion, people are running around stealing food and materials. In the converted schoolhouse, it seems somebody has been stealing blankets through a window sealed with welded rebar. They managed to climb up 10 feet to a window, pull out a 200-pound bale of blankets, smash the metal strapping and then pull each blanket through a 3" x 3" hole in the welded rods. Officially, everyone gets a ration. Each person will get one 50-kilogram sack of flour, 2.4 kilograms of sugar, 3.6 kilograms of cooking oil, one plastic sheet and one blanket. Naturally, only the flour comes in the right size container. So Jonathan must calculate how much will be needed on each night and in each place, organize the arrival and transportation of nine carloads of personal goods and then organize a fleet of trucks to take each family with their goods to the right village. At night he must then fill out the appropriate forms, monitor budgets and assign personnel to make sure he has enough resources. Jonathan is assailed on all sides in his lonely quest to get 310 people transported, fed and tucked in for the night. It is a grind, but urgency and exhausted faces drive us on. The refugees are crowded into the classrooms, women and children are separated from the men. They have that humid funk that refugees have. The women and children sit quietly in one room. It is always reassuring to see the children play as if they were on holiday, contrasting with the dull, tired look on the women's faces. The men have a harder look, as they help with the unloading of the trucks. After hours of carrying the large flour sacks, everyone is dusted white and weary.

Jonathan is the central focus of this ad hoc army of worker bees. Coordinating workers, chasing down thieves, stacking up the next shipments, talking on the radio to headquarters, planning tomorrow's massive unloading, setting up security, even figuring how to divide all the wrong size cooking oil containers into the UN-mandated ration sizes. He is in his element. Late into the night, he says, "It is hard, lonely work but I think it's worth it." The accent was on "think."

That night, we don't go to bed until early in the morning. I sleep on a wooden floor at the UN headquarters and Disa, the Swedish journalist, decides to stay at the UN guesthouse for $24. We decide to eat dinner first. Our host at the UN guesthouse is a tall, deep-voiced, poetic-sounding Somali who is perturbed but gracious that two uninvited supper guests have shown up this late. He explains the proper procedure, the paperwork and the protocol and then sends a houseboy over to wake up the cook.

He is in charge of infrastructure work. In fact, he created this 16-person guesthouse from an old pharmacy for $11,000. It now has plumbing, hot water, carpets and the exotic wall decorations and murals that are popular here.

At the guesthouse we talk about the plight of Tajikistan with our Somali host. The Soviet system created a number of monolithic subsidized systems that still exist. Here only cotton was allowed to be grown and everyone received an education. The central government made sure that bread, fuel, timber and other goods came from factories and regions throughout the Soviet empire. Now, after

Soviet control, the Tajik government still demands that people grow cotton because it is the only major resource they know how to sell. There is no more subsidization, but cotton sells there as if did.

Students, doctors and their families must pick cotton for free. The schools are closed and there are serious fines for not picking your daily quota of cotton. Naturally, this generates no money for the local people, and in a rich agricultural region, there are no staples. It is against the law to grow wheat or corn. The Tajiks speak Tajik and Russian, so they cannot leave to find work elsewhere. So Tajiks are seeing a rapid loss in quality of life after the Soviet system. It is so bad that children cannot walk to school because their parents cannot afford to buy shoes. I ask if our host Tajiks have it worse off than Somalis. He says in Somalia at least they have a government and American oil companies. In his opinion, Tajikistan is very sad and has a long way to go even to get to where Somalia is today. When a Somali feels sorry for a country, it's a good bet that they are in big trouble.

Jonathan compares Tajikistan to the '20s, the era of the Great Depression in America, robber barons, gangsters, and mass poverty. He says they are just going through the same phase. I don't bother reminding him that it took a world war to get things back on track again. Tajikistan could be rich, since it provides a lot of raw resources and cotton, but no one wants to invest in a fractured country at war. So they limp along using the dead Soviet system and hope for some light at the end of the tunnel. But this is an incorrect simile. There is no light and there is no tunnel.

The Somali is more poetic but less optimistic. "It is like a house. If you start from a crooked foundation, the house will never be strong. You have to take it all apart and start again."

The next day, we stop off to send a fax through TACIS, a European aid group, and then return to the lonely rail station. It is chaos. Tons of personal effects are scattered around the rail line as each person tries to coordinate with a open-bed truck that will take them to their village. I take pictures for Disa, who is doing an article on the refugees. Men pose proudly with their chickens. Not quite knowing why they deserve celebrity, they stop and stand straight as boards for their pictures. People still come to search out long-lost relatives, and in between the industry there are tearful reunions and prayers for deliverance.

We accompany some of the families returning to their deserted villages. These villages were bombed and bulldozed by the government troops. The buildings are mud brick with a white plaster veneer. Children have drawn aircraft spitting fire and dropping bombs on screaming people. In the ruins are people making new mud bricks, making tea and rebuilding their homes. On their homes, children have drawn obscene pictures of people with large genitals having sex, a rebirth in an odd way. As I walk around taking pictures, Jonathan says in an offhand way, "Thank goodness they didn't use landmines."

The people are happy as they sit on their blue plastic sheets and rebuild their lives. "This is the part that makes it all worthwhile," says Jonathan.

—RYP

Dangerous Diseases

Souvenirs from Hell

Each time I stop in at my doctor's office (a tropical disease specialist with time in Vietnam), he asks me why the hell I do what I do. Yet, he takes great pains to describe the symptoms of the many tropical diseases that await me in the Third World. His lectures usually center around the lifelong pain and debilitation that can be inflicted on travelers who inadvertently ingest an amoeba, get bitten by a mosquito or become the host for a degenerative bug. I take his advice seriously, and I am as fastidious as I can be in adverse conditions. I am very careful about what I eat and how I sleep, and I follow the rules of common sense when it comes to avoiding infection. Despite this, I have spent nights shivering and delirious, lying in puddles of my own sweat on cement floors in the Sahara desert. I pay his bill gladly and trust to the cosmos and good common sense.

With this in mind, do not assume that this chapter is the be-all end-all reference source for tropical diseases. *Always confer with a specialist before taking any trip.* This way, you understand the odds and the penalties and can make an educated decision on the risks involved. Secondly, *always have full medical tests upon your return.* This means giving a little bit of yourself to the lab to run blood, stool and urine tests. Your doctor may ask you to come back again due to the long incubation time of some of these nasties. This is not hypochondria, but common sense. Early detection will increase your odds of successful treatment.

The odds of coming down with a bug are pretty good once you leave the antiseptic Western world. If you go off on an extended trip (one month or more) you have a 60–75 percent chance that you will develop some illness or problem, most likely diarrhea. Only about one percent of travelers will pick up an infectious disease. I once thought that the locals had built up resistance to the various bugs that strike down Westerners. But once in-country, you realize what a toll disease takes on the Third World. Not only are many people riddled with malaria, river blindness, intestinal infections, hepatitis, sexual diseases and more, but they are also faced with malnutrition, poor dental care, toxic chemicals and hard environmental conditions. The World Health Organization (WHO), in a recent global survey, reported that much of the world's population dies needlessly from preventable diseases due to a lack of access to health care. Of the 52 million people who die each year, infectious diseases kill about 17 million. Infectious diseases are the leading cause of premature death in Africa and Southeast Asia, according to WHO. Of the 11 million victims who are children under the age of five, 9 million die from infectious diseases. About 70 percent of the deaths attributed to cholera, typhoid or dysentery can be blamed on contaminated food. To make matters worse, 30 new diseases have sprung up since 1976, among them AIDS and the deadly Ebola virus. Antibiotics are becoming less and less effective in treating many of these diseases because of resistance due to their overuse.

Ten Least Wanted	
The top ten killer diseases are primarily Third World, celebrity-free, low-visibility killers of children.	
Acute respiratory tract infections	4.4 million
Diarrheal diseases (cholera, typhoid, dysentery)	3.1
Tuberculosis	3.1
Hepatitis B	1.1
HIV/AIDS	1 million +
Measles	1 million +
Neonatal tetanus	460,000
Whooping cough	350,000
Intestinal worms	135,000

Source: *World Health Organization*

DANGEROUS DISEASES

Malaria

Malaria is a very dangerous disease, affecting 500 million people worldwide and killing at least 2 million people every year. The mosquito-borne disease is found in 102 countries and threatens 40 percent of the world's population.

Over a million people (mostly children) in Africa are killed by malaria every year. Two million people worldwide die from it in a one-year period, according to WHO. More than 30,000 European and American travelers will come down with malaria this year.

The female *Anopheles* mosquito is small, pervasive, hungry for your blood, and likes to bite in the cool hours before and after sunset. As they seek out blood to nurture their own procreation, they leave the Plasmodium parasites in your blood system.

Anopheles mosquitoes can be identified by the way they stand head downward when biting, compared to the parallel stance of the benign *Culex* mosquito, Mosquitoes don't venture more than two miles from where they are bred. Only pregnant females feed on blood, biting every two to days to feed eggs. Male mosquitoes eat only nectar and fluids from plants.

Malarial Cycle
Mosquito bites infected human, ingesting a gametocyte
Gametocyte breeds internally, creating oocytes
Sporozoites burst and travel to mosquito's salivary glands
Humans are infected when Sporozoites enter bloodstream
Within 45 minutes Sporozoites penetrate the liver
Within 9 to 16 days merozoites develop and invade red blood and liver cells
Blood cells rupture, releasing gametoctyes and merozoites into the bloodstream, causing the cycle of chills and fevers

Malaria continues to become resistant to the drugs used to prevent and treat it. Malaria is carried by 60 of the 380 types of *anopheles* mosquitoes, which are found primarily in tropical and subtropical areas. There are resistant strains to melfloquine or Larium.

Malarone, supposed to be the new wonder drug from Glaxo-Wellcome, is a brand name for pills containing atovaquone and proguanil. It is legal in Denmark and used for treatment only in the U.K. Some doctors in the U.K. will prescribe it to their patients. The possible side effects of Malarone are headache, abdominal pain, upper respiratory infection, pain nausea or vomiting. Malorone should be started one to two days before entering malarial areas and continued for seven days after. Keep in mind that many people don't develop the symptoms of malaria until after they return from their trip. The symptoms can start with a flu-like attack, followed by fever and chills, then lead to failure of multiple organs and then death.

Name	Usage	Side Effects
Chloroquine (Aralen)	*Not effective in areas where Chloroquine-resistant malaria is found.*	*Has bitter taste; can cause stomach upset and blurred vision*
Mefloquine (Larium)	*Commonly prescribed in North America; 2 percent to 5 percent of users have side effects*	*Usage can cause anxiety, nausea, hair loss, mood changes, and in some cases psychosis*
Doxycycline	*A common and inexpensive antibiotic*	*Causes sensitivity to sun but provides protection against infections; can cause stomach upset, thrush or yeast infections*
Chloroquine w/Progunil (Paludrine)	*Not as effective as mefloquine or doxycycline*	*Can cause nausea, loss of appetite and mouth ulcers*
Primaquine	*New drug*	*Effective against P. vivax and P. falciparum. Can cause nausea and abdominal discomfort*
Atovaquone/Progunil (Malarone)	*New drug*	*Effective against Chloroquine-resistant malaria; can cause nausea, diarrhea*
Fansidar/Fansimef	*For self treatment when malaria is contacted*	*Serious side effects including skin reactions*

Some quik facts:

Roughly 90 percent of malaria cases occur in Africa; 90 percent of travelers who contract malaria do not become ill until they return. Transmission decreases above 200 meters and is rarely found above 3,000 meters.

Malaria is a very real and common danger in most tropical countries. Most malaria in Asian and African areas is quinine-resistant and requires multiple or more creative dosages to avoid the horrors often associated with the disease. The most vicious strain of malaria (*Plasmodium falciparum*) attacks your liver and red blood cells, creating massive fevers, coma, acute kidney failure, and eventually death. There are three other types of malaria in the world: *Plasmodium malaria, Plasmodium vivax* and *Plasmodium ovale* (found only in West Africa).

The *Anopheles* mosquito is the most dangerous insect in the world, and there are few contenders for its crown. Other biting insects that can cause you grief include the *Aedes aegypti* mosquito, which carries yellow fever. His kissing cousins, the *Culex, Haemogogus, Sabethes* and *Mansonia*, can give you filariasis, viral encephalitis, dengue and other great hemorrhagic fevers. Next on the list are tsetse flies, fleas, ticks, sandflies, mites and lice. We won't even bother to discuss wasps, horseflies, African killer bees, deerflies, or other clean biters.

These insects are an everyday part of life in tropical Third World countries. They infect major percentages of the local population, and it is only a matter of time and luck before you become a victim.

Prevention is rather simple but often ineffective. Protect yourself from insects by wearing long-sleeved shirts and long pants. Use insect repellent, sleep under a mosquito net, avoid swampy areas, use mosquito coils, don't sleep directly on the ground, check yourself for tick and insect bites daily and, last but not least, understand the symptoms and treatment of these diseases so that you can seek immediate treatment, no matter what part of the world you are in.

http://www.healthscout.com

The Gift That Keeps On Giving	
Disease	**Annual Deaths**
Infected by malaria	500 million
Infected by HIV	20 million
Infected by AIDS	4.5 million
Acute respiratory infections	4.4 million
Diarrheal diseases	3.1 million
Tuberculosis	3 million
Malaria	2 million
AIDS	1 million

Worms

My least favorite are the helminthic infections, or diseases caused by intestinal worms. Unlike the more dramatic and deadly diseases, these parasites are easily caught through ingestion of bad water and food and cause long-term damage. Just to let you know what's out there, you can choose from angiostrongyliasis, herring worm, roundworm, schistosomiasis, capillariasis, pin worm, oriental liver fluke, fish tapeworm, guinea worm, cat liver fluke, tapeworm, trechinellosis and the ominous-sounding giant intestinal fluke (who's eating who here?). All these little buggers create havoc with your internal organs, and some will make the rest of your life miserable as well. Your digestive system will be shot and your organs under constant attack, and the treatment or removal of these nasties is downright depressing. All this can be prevented by maintaining absolutely rigid standards in what you throw or breathe into your body. Not easy, since most male travelers find wearing a biohazard suit a major impediment to picking up chicks or doing the limbo.

Think of yourself as a sponge, your lungs as an air filter, and all the moist cavities of your body as ideal breeding grounds for tropical diseases. It is better to think like Howard Hughes than Pig Pen when it comes to personal hygiene.

The Fevers

The classic tropical diseases that incapacitated Stanley, Livingstone, Burton and Speke are the hemorrhagic fevers. Many of these diseases kill, but most make your life a living hell and then disappear. Some come back on a regular basis. It is surprising that most of the African explorers lived to a ripe old age. The hemorrhagic fevers are carried by mosquitoes, ticks, rats, feces or even airborne dust that gets into your bloodstream and they let you die a slow, demented death, as your blood turns so thin it trickles out your nose, gums, skin and eyes. Coma and death can occur in the second week. There are so many versions that they just name them after the places where you will stumble across them. Needless to say, these are not featured in any glossy brochures for the various regions. Assorted blood-thinning killers are called Chikungunya, Crimean, Congo, Omsk, Kyasanur Forest, Korean, Manchurian, Songo, Ebola, Argentinian, Hanta, Lassa and yellow fever.

The recent outbreaks of the Hanta and Ebola viruses in the U.S. have proved that North America is not immune from these insect-, rodent- and airborne afflictions. So far, the Ebola Reston virus has only been found in monkeys sent by a Philippine supplier. All monkeys exposed to the virus were destroyed, and officials from the Centers for Disease Control reassured the public that Ebola Reston is a different virus from Ebola Zaire (now called the Democratic Republic of the Congo), the strain that killed 244 people in one outbreak. Still, experts warn that the Ebola Reston strain could mutate into a strain that is fatal to humans. The outbreak of plague in India also has travelers a little edgy about the whole concept of adventurous travel. There are real dangers in every part of the world, and the more knowledgeable you are about them, the better your chances for surviving.

Sex (STDs)

The quest for sexual adventure was once a major part of the joy of travel. Today, the full range of sexual diseases available to the common traveler would fill an encyclopedia. Despite the continual global publicity on the dangers of AIDS, it continues to claim victims at an alarming rate. Of the 34 most affected AIDS countries, 29 are in Africa, where life expectancy has been reduced by an average of 7 years. Whorehouses around the world are thriving, junkies still share needles, and dentists in many Third World countries still grind and yank away with improperly sterilized instruments. Diseases like HIV, hepatitis A and B, the clap, syphilis, genital warts, herpes, crabs, lice, and others that Westerners blame on the Third World, and the Third World blames on the West, are very preventable and require parking your libido. Sexually transmitted diseases are a growing health hazard. According to WHO, 236 million people have trichomoniasis and 94 million new cases occur each year. Chlamydial infections affect 162 million people, with 97 million new cases annually. And these figures don't include the increasing millions with genital warts, gonorrhea, genital herpes and syphilis. The highest rates for sexually transmitted diseases are in the 20–24 age group, followed by 15–19 and 25–29. In many countries, more than 60 percent of all new HIV infections are among the 15–24 age group.

How do you avoid sexually transmitted diseases, some people ask? Well, keeping your romantic agenda on the platonic side is a good start. The use of condoms is the next best thing. Realistically, the chances of catching AIDS through unprotected sex depends on frequency and type of contact. People infected by blood transfusions, prostitutes, frequent drug users, hemophiliacs, homosexuals, and the millions of people who will get HIV this year from heterosexual sex will continue to make HIV a growing danger.

What's in the Bag?

DP reader Dr. Kurt Schultz gives us his pick for his travel meds. The list is provided to give you a starting point to discuss your ideal travel kit with your doctor. Many of these items are available over the counter in Third World countries but may be expired, defective or placebos. Warning. Consult with yout doctor about your own personal needs. Many people require instruction on usage of drugs (its called a medical degree) and most drugs can have side effects, interactions caused by other medications and outside conditions. Many countries prohibit the importation and/or carrying of certain drugs, even for personal use.

1. Bring prescription antibiotics for internal problems. Get a 20-day supply of Cipro or floxin. These drugs are of the fluoroquinolone class, the "patriot missiles" for traveler's diarrhea/dysentery and infectious diarrhea. They are also the drugs of choice for venereal diseases and will kill gonorrhea, chlamydia and most causes of weiner drip.

2. Bring antibiotics for external problems (skin infection/cuts). The dirt in the Third World is impregnated with 2,000 years of feces. Any trivial break in the skin (nick yourself shaving) can lead to a life-threatening cellulitis (a bacterial skin infection). Examples of drugs to bring: Keflex or Augmentin, a 20-day supply. Also good for animal bites.

3. Take malaria prophylaxis as directed by the CDC and WHO. The argument rages as to what is best, but taking nothing is dumb. Sometimes this includes doxycycline, a prescription antibiotic.

4. Get all your vaccinations: get the routine tetanus and measles/mumps/rubella. Make sure you are up to date on your routine vaccinations. You should get both hepatitis A and B, which are very effective (90 percent effective in prevention), and also yellow fever, which is often required to even enter most developing countries.

5. Carry lots of over-the-counter, broad-spectrum antibiotic cream like Neosporin.

6. Anti-diarrheals (but go easy) like Immodium, an over-the-counter diarrhea medicine. The runs is a normal part of acclimatization. Let it flow, drink lots of water, eat less food. If it persists, go to internal antibiotics (#1). It helps to have rehydration powders to recover as well.

7. Buy or make first-aid kids for wound management, abrasion, etc. These kits can be purchased in outdoor stores or over the internet.

8. Carry lots of Tylenol or Motrin for pain control.

9. Tissue adhesive glue. Cool stuff! Glorified Krazy Glue, modified slightly so the drug companies can charge obscene fees. Literally "glue" wounds together. Easy to pack.

10. Ketamine. It would be hard to score, but it's given as an intramuscular shot. You'll need a syringe and to know how to inject it. Disconnects the mind from the body without causing excessive sedation. The military uses this as a "battlefield anesthetic." You can set bones and do major surgery after a single shot. Related to PCP, but without all the freaky side effects and violence.

NOTE FROM *DP*: Although it seems highly altruistic, don't hand out medicines to the locals. Within minutes, the entire village will have a headache and be lined up outside your tent. If you want to leave medicine behind, give it to a doctor or health worker who understands the use and dangers of your gift.

http://www.drugs.com/
http://www.gps4fun.com/main_amd.html
http://www.baproducts.com/fak.htm
http://www.equipped.com/medical.htm
http://www.british-airways.com/travelqa/fyi/health/docs/hitems.shtml

Hepatitis A, B, C

Your chance of getting Hep B if you leave the United States is only 5 percent, unless of course you go for a tattoo at the smack jabbers' rusty-needle convention in the Golden Triangle (and have unprotected sex afterwards with a Thai junkie hooker). All macho bullshit aside, men and women are at equal risk and health workers are at a very high risk when working in Third World countries. Carrier rates among the population in some undeveloped countries are as high as 20 percent of the total population. Many travelers get Hep B without engaging in any high-risk activities because the virus can survive outside the body for prolonged periods. Infection can occur when any infected material comes in contact with mucous membranes or broken skin. Hepatitis A is a viral infection of the liver transmitted by the fecal, oral route through direct contact with infected people, from water, ice, shellfish or uncooked food. Symptoms for Hep A include fever, loss of appetite, dark urine, jaundice, vomiting, aches and pains and light stools. You usually get Hep A in Third World countries with poor sanitation. It is easy to prevent with simple vaccination using one of the two vaccines available. For proper protection the vaccine requires an initial shot (good for three months) and then repeated doses to protect longer term.

DP fan and reader Dr. Susan Hou sent us a polite but firm letter demanding that we expand information on this very easy to catch and very easy to prevent disease. We quote the good doctor (who has knocked around enough to earn a *DP* shirt):

"The majority of people with symptomatic Hepatitis B infection don't die, but spend a month wishing they would. One percent develop fulminate (Webster's: developing or progressing suddenly) disease and die of liver failure. (On the bright side, if you get back to the United States before getting sick, fulminate liver failure moves you to the top of the liver transplant list). Five to ten percent of people become chronic carriers, which means they can infect other people. For women this includes 85 percent of the children they carry who don't get treated. Thirty percent of chronic carriers have ongoing liver disease (chronic active hepatitis). Many progress to cirrhosis and require liver transplants (but start out lower on the transplant list). People with chronic active hepatitis develop liver cancer at a rate of 3 percent per year. The bad news if you get a liver transplant: Hepatitis B is usually still in your body and infects the new liver."

The vaccine for Hepatitis B is 90 percent effective after three doses. See your doctor or a local health clinic for more information before you travel.

AIDS

Perhaps the most dangerous and publicized disease is AIDS. It strikes right at the heart of American phobia—pain for pleasure. AIDS is the terminal phase of HIV (human immunodeficiency virus). HIV is usually the precursor to AIDS, and then the victim succumbs to death by cancer, pneumonia and other afflictions that attack the weakened human immune system. AIDS has roughly a nine-year incubation period.

AIDs was supposed to have jumped from animal to man when humans ate simians in Africa. HIV-1 is a simian immunodeficiency virus (SIV) which causes AIDS. HIV-2 comes from the sooty magabey. The first case of AIDS came from

Africa in 1959. The SIV that spawned AIDS comes from animals that live in Gabon, Cameroon and Equatorial Guinea. Other strains have made the crossover from chimpanzee to man.

Initially brushed aside as "the gay plague" or an "African disease," AIDS has in the last few years become the biggest killer of young American men and women. Washington, D.C., has the nation's highest AIDS rate, far higher than even New York or San Francisco, according to statistics released by the Centers for Disease Control and Prevention. By 1995, the D.C. rate was 185.7 AIDS cases per 100,000 residents. Puerto Rico was second with a rate of 70.3 cases per 100,000, followed by New York, Florida and New Jersey. Nationwide, the rate of AIDS cases is 27.8 cases per 100,000. The CDC says that AIDS is spreading more among women and minorities now, while the epidemic among homosexual white men has slowed. Women accounted for 19 percent of all AIDS cases among adults and adolescents nationwide. A growing number of children are being orphaned by AIDS, which has become the leading cause of death among women of childbearing age in the United States, according to a study in the *Journal of the American Medical Association.* Experts project that about 144,000 children and young adults will have lost their mothers to AIDS by the year 2000. Blacks are six times more likely to have AIDS than whites and twice as likely to have AIDS as Hispanics.

As sobering as the U.S. statistics are, the rate of deaths caused by AIDS in other countries is alarming. WHO said that chronic underreporting and underdiagnosis in developing countries means the actual figure is probably more than 4.5 million. More than 70 percent of the estimated cases were in Africa, 9 percent in the United States, 9 percent in the rest of the American hemisphere, 6 percent in Asia, and 4 percent in Europe. The statistics include only people with active cases of AIDS or those who have died from the disease.

An estimated one million Latin Americans could have AIDS by the turn of the century, according to the Pan American Health Organization. The group says HIV is increasing among women in the Caribbean and Central America and it is expected to increase rapidly, particularly in areas where injection drug use is prevalent. There are currently 2 million HIV-infected people in Latin America and the Caribbean. According to Italy's statistics institute, ISTAT, AIDS has become as big a killer in Italy as road accidents. An estimated 4,370 Italians died from AIDS last year, compared to 6,000 deaths on the roads. For young males between 18 and 29 in Italy, AIDS has overtaken drugs as the second leading cause of death. ISTAT estimates that the number of HIV-infected Italians is at least 100,000. AIDS is also on the increase in smaller countries. WHO estimates that at least 400,000, or one percent, of Myanmar's citizens are infected with HIV. A high number of injection drug users, social tolerance of prostitution and large amounts of cross-border trade with nearby nations make Myanmar's populace more vulnerable. Condoms are also costly and rarely used in Myanmar, exacerbating the problem.

Ministry of Health statistics show that more than 100,000 residents of Zimbabwe have died of AIDS-related causes in the past decade. Another 100,000, or one percent, of the country's population is expected to succumb to AIDS in the next year and a half. AIDS is expected to slow population growth, lower life expectancies and raise child mortality rates in many of the world's poorer countries over the next 25 years, according to a report by the U.S. Census Bureau.

By the year 2010, a Ugandan's life expectancy will decline by 45 percent to 32 years—down from 59 years projected before AIDS. A Haitian's life expectancy will fall to 44 years, also down from 59 years. Life expectancy in Thailand will drop from a projected 75 years to 45. By the year 2010, Thailand's child mortality rates are expected to increase from the current 20 deaths per 1,000 children born to 110 deaths. In Uganda, the jump will be from 90 deaths to 175 deaths out of every 1,000 children born. In Malawi, it will soar from 130 to 210 deaths per 1,000. Overall, premature death rates in those countries will double by 2010 compared with 1985 levels.

In 16 countries—the African nations of Burkina Faso, Burundi, Central African Republic, Congo, Cote d'Ivoire, Kenya, Malawi, Rwanda, Tanzania, Uganda, Congo, Zambia and Zimbabwe, plus Brazil, Haiti and Thailand—AIDS will slow population growth rates so dramatically that by 2010, there will be 121 million fewer people than previously forecast. Thailand's population will actually fall by nearly one percent because of AIDS deaths.

"Zoonosis"

According to journalists, AIDS first began near the Congo-Burundi border, but did it? A 1992 Rolling Stone *article by AIDS activist Blaine Elswood places the blame on polio vaccines grown in primate kidney cells and then injected into humans in 1957 and 1958. Other researchers had injected malaria-tainted blood from chimpanzees and mangabeys into human volunteers. The first AIDS case was reportedly a British sailor (who had never been to Africa) who died in 1959. The case wasn't officially recognized by the Centers for Disease Control until 1981.*

There are two types of human AIDS virus: HIV-1, the most common type, and HIV-2, originally found only in people from Guinea-Bissau in West Africa. HIV-2 is very close to SIV (simian immunodeficiency virus) found in sooty mangabeys. Curiously, SIV is not found in the Asian macaques normally used for research. Sooty mangabeys are commonly eaten by villagers in Africa. There is no hard proof that AIDS came from monkeys or even from Africa, but the preponderance of evidence shows that AIDS may have originated in Central Africa within the past 50 years. AIDS continues to mutate as new strains continue to appear in West Africa and Asia.

Old-Fashioned Diseases

Many travelers are quite surprised to find themselves coming down with measles or mumps while traveling. Unlike the United States, which has eradicated much of the childhood and preventable viruses through inoculation, the rest of the world is more concerned about feeding than vaccinating their children. The recent outbreak of plague in India is a good example of what you should watch out for. Whooping cough, mumps, measles, polio and tuberculosis are common in Third World countries. Although some of the symptoms are minor, complications can lead to lifelong afflictions. Make sure you are vaccinated against these easily preventable diseases.

But don't just run off to be the next bubble boy and spend the rest of your life in a hermetically sealed dome. For travelers, these diseases are relatively rare and avoidable. To put the whole thing in perspective, the most common complaint tends to be diarrhea, followed by a cold (usually the result of lowered resistance caused by fatigue, dehydration, foreign microbes and stress). The important thing is to recognize when you are sick versus very sick. Tales of turn-of-the-century explorers struck down by a tiny mosquito bite are now legend. Malaria is still a very real and common threat. Just for fun, bring back a sample of local river water from your next trip and have the medical lab analyze it. You may never drink water of any kind again.

This is not to say that as soon as you get off the plane you will automatically be struck down with Ebola River fever and have blood oozing out from your eyes. You can travel bug-free and suffer no more than a cold caused by the air-conditioning in your hotel room. But it is important to at least understand the relative risks and gravity of some diseases.

The diseases listed on the following pages are important, and you should be conversant with both symptoms and cures. Please do not assume that this is medical advice. It is designed to give you an overview of the various nasties that possibly await you.

Tropical countries are the most likely to cause you bacterial grief. Keep in mind that most of these diseases are a direct result of poor hygiene, travel in infected areas and contact with infected people. In other words, stay away from people if you want to stay healthy. Second, follow the commonsense practice of having all food cooked freshly and properly. Many books tell you to wash fruit and then forget to mention that the water is probably more filled with bugs than the fruit. Peel all fruits and vegetables, and approach anything you stick in your body with a healthy level of skepticism and distrust. If you are completely paranoid, you can exist on freeze-dried foods, Maggi Mee (noodles), fresh fruit (peeled, remember) and tinned food.

It is considered wise to ask local experts about dangers that await. If you do not feel right for any reason, contact a local doctor. It is not advisable to enter a medical treatment program while in a developing country. There are greater chances of you catching worse afflictions once you are in the hospital. Ask for temporary medication and then get your butt back to North America or Europe.

Remember that the symptoms of many tropical diseases may not take effect until you are home and back into your regular schedule. It is highly advisable that you contact a tropical disease specialist and have full testing done (stool, urine, blood, physical) just to be sure. Very few American doctors are conversant with the many tropical diseases by virtue of their rarity. This is not their fault, since many tourists do not even realize that they have taken trips or cruises into endemic zones. People can catch malaria on a plane between London and New York from a stowaway mosquito that just came in from Bombay. Many people come in close contact with foreigners in buses and subways and on the street from Los Angeles to New York. Don't assume you have to be up to your neck in Laotian pig wallows to be at risk. Many labs do not do tests for some of the more exotic bugs. Symptoms can also be misleading. It is possible that you may be misdiagnosed or mistreated if you do not fully discuss the possible reasons for your medical condition. Now that we have scared the hell out of you, your first contact should be with the Centers for Disease Control in Atlanta.

Dr. Susan Hou recommends that readers leave behind (or take extra) medical supplies for clinics or doctors when they travel. It is a good rule never to give medication, pills or even first aid materials directly to sick people, since most do not know the correct usage or are unaware of side effects. She also suggested giving blood (you can bring your own 18 gauge needle), but don't give blood at high altitudes.

Disease Outbreak News
http://www.who.int/emc/outbreak_news/

First Aid Kits

Adventure Medical
5555 San Leandro St.
Oakland, CA 94621
Tel.: 800-324-3517; 510-261-7414
Fax: 510-261-7419
E-mail: amkusa@aol.com
http://www.adventuremedicalkits.com

Atwater Carey Ltd.
339 E. Rainbow Blvd.
Salida, CO 81201
Tel.: 800-359-1646; 719-530-0923
Fax: 719-530-0928
http://www.destinationoutdoors.com/

Outdoor Research (OR)
2203 1st Ave. South
Seattle, WA 98134-1424
Tel.: 800-467-8197; 206-421-2421
http://www.orgear.com

Wilderness Medical Systems
3336 Harrison Ave.
Suite 331
Butte, MT 59701
Tel.: 800-858-7430; 406-494-8358
Fax: 406-494-7918

Wilderness EMS Training

Wilderness Professional Training (WPT)
P.O. Box 759
Crested Burre, CO 81224
Tel.: 800-258-0838; 303-349-5939;
970-349-5939
Fax: 907-349-1049

Wildernesses Medical Outfitters
2477 County Road 132
Elizabeth, CO 80107
Tel.: 800-569-1854; 303-688-5176

Wilderness Medical Associates (WMA)
RFD 2 BOX 890
Bryant Pond, ME 04219
Tel.: 207-665-2707
Fax: 207-665-2747
http://www.wildmed.com/
course_fact_sheets/wfa_facts.html
http://www.wemsi.on.ca/pamph1.html

Northeastern University, Institute for EMS
145 South Bedford St.
Burlington, MA. 01803
Tel.: 781-238-8400
http://www.ems.neu.edu/

A Rogue's Gallery of Diseases

This list is a simple and incomplete checklist of what to ask your doctor about when planning your trip. The best single source in the world for information on the various bugs and germs is the Centers for Disease Control, available on the web (*http://www.cdc.gov*), by phone (☎ *404-639-3311*) or reprinted in book form. Always consult with a doctor before traveling, before taking medication and to ensure proper precautions are taken. If you are sick within a country, it is wise to have supplementary medical treatment and or evacuation insurance.

African Sleeping Sickness (African Trypanosomiasis)

Found: Tropical Africa.

Cause: A tiny protozoan parasite that emits a harmful toxin.

Carrier: Tsetse fly. Tsetse flies are large biting insects about the size of a horsefly found in East and West Africa.

Symptoms: Eastern trypanosomiasis: two–31 days after the bite recurrent episodes of fever, headaches and malaise.

Can lead to death in two to six weeks. Western trypanosomiasis: produces a skin ulcer within 5 to 10 days after being bitten. The symptoms then disappear in two to three weeks. Symptoms reappear six months to five years after the initial infection, resulting in fevers, headaches, rapid heartbeat, swelling of the lymph glands located in the back of the neck, personality changes, tremors, a lackadaisical attitude, and then stupor leading eventually to death.

Treatment: Suramin (Bayer 205) pentamidine (Lomodine), melarasoprol (Mel B)

How to avoid: Do not travel to infested areas, use insect repellent, wear light-colored clothing and cover skin areas.

AIDS (Acquired Immune Deficiency Syndrome)
Found: Worldwide.

Cause: Advanced stage of HIV (human immunodeficiency syndrome), which causes destruction of the natural resistance of humans to infection and other diseases. Death by AIDS is usually a result of unrelated diseases that rapidly attack the victim. These ranges of diseases are called ARCs (AIDS-related complex).

Carrier: Sexual intercourse with infected person, transfusion of infected blood, or even from infected mother through breast milk. There is no way to determine if someone has HIV, except by blood test. Male homosexuals, drug users and prostitutes are high-risk groups in major urban centers in the West. AIDS is less selective in developing countries, with Central and Eastern Africa being the areas of highest incidence.

Symptoms: Fever, weight loss, fatigue, night sweats, lymph node problems. Infection by other opportunistic elements such as Karposi's sarcoma and pneumonia are highly probable and will lead to death.

Treatment: There is no known cure.

How to avoid: Use condoms, refrain from sexual contact, and do not receive injections or transfusions in questionable areas. Avoid live vaccines such as gamma globulin and Hepatitis B in developing countries.

Amebiasis
Found: Worldwide.

Cause: A protozoan parasite carried in human fecal matter. Usually found in areas with poor sanitation.

Carrier: *Entamoeba histolyica* is passed by poor hygiene. Ingested orally in water, air or food that has come in contact with the parasite.

Symptoms: The infection will spread from the intestines and causes abscesses in other organs such as liver, lungs and brain.

Treatment: Metronidazole, iodoquinol, diloxanide furoate, paromomycin, tetracycline plus chloroquinine base.

How to avoid: Avoid uncooked foods, boil water, drink bottled liquids, be sure that food is cooked properly and peel fruits and vegetables.

Bartonellosis (Oroya Fever, Carrion's Disease)
Found: In valleys of Peru, Ecuador and Colombia.

Cause: *Bartonella bacilliformis*, a bacterium.

Carrier: Sandflies that bite at night.

Symptoms: Pain in muscles, joints and bones along with fever occurring within three weeks of being bitten. Oroya fever causes a febrile fever leading to possible death. *Verruga peruana* creates skin eruptions.

Treatment: Antibiotics with transfusion for symptoms of anemia.

How to avoid: High boots, groundsheets, hammocks and insect repellent.

Brucellosis (Undulant Fever)
Found: Worldwide.

Cause: Ingestion of infected dairy products.

Carrier: Untreated dairy products infected with the brucellosis bacteria.

Symptoms: Intermittent fever, sweating, jaundice, rash, depression, enlarged spleen and lymph nodes. The symptoms may disappear and go into permanent remission after three to six months.

Treatment: Tetracyclines, sulfonamides and streptomycin.

How to avoid: Drink pasteurized milk. Avoid infected livestock.

Chagas' Disease (American Trypanosomiasis)
Found: Central and South America.

Cause: Protozoan parasite carried in the feces of insects.

Carrier: Kissing or Assassin bugs (Triatoma insects or reduviid bugs). Commonly found in homes with thatched roofs. It can also be transmitted through blood transfusions, breast milk and in utero.

Symptoms: A papule and swelling at the location of the bite, fever, malaise, anorexia, rash, swelling of the limbs, gastrointestinal problems, heart irregularities and heart failure.

Treatment: Nifurtimox (Bayer 2502).

How to avoid: Do not stay in native villages; use bed netting and insect repellent.

Cholera

Found: Worldwide; primarily developing countries.

Cause: Intestinal infection caused by the toxin Vibrio Cholerae O group bacteria.

Carrier: Infected food and water contaminated by human and animal waste.

Symptoms: Watery diarrhea, abdominal cramps, nausea, vomiting and severe dehydration as a result of diarrhea. Can lead to death if fluids are not replaced.

Treatment: Tetracycline can hasten recovery. Replace fluids using an electrolyte solution.

How to avoid: Vaccinations before trip can diminish symptoms up to 50 percent for a period of three to six months. A threat in refugee camps or areas of poor sanitation. Use standard precautions with food and drink in developing countries.

Chikungunya Disease

Found: Sub-Saharan Africa, Southeast Asia, India, Philippines in sporadic outbreaks.

Cause: Alphavirus transmitted by mosquito bites.

Carrier: Mosquitoes that transmit the disease from the host (monkeys).

Symptoms: Joint pain with potential for hemorrhagic symptoms.

Treatment: None, but symptoms will disappear. If hemorrhagic, avoid aspirin.

How to avoid: Standard precautions to avoid mosquito bites: Use insect repellent and mosquito nets, and cover exposed skin areas.

Ciguatera Poisoning

Found: Tropical areas.

Cause: Ingestion of fish containing the toxin produced by the *dinoflagellate Gambierdiscus toxicus*.

Carrier: 425 species of tropical reef fish.

Symptoms: Up to six hours after eating, victims may experience nausea, watery diarrhea, abdominal cramps, vomiting, abnormal sensation in limbs and teeth, hot-cold flashes, joint pain, weakness, skin rashes and itching. In very severe cases victims may experience blind spells, low blood pressure and heart rate, paralysis and loss of coordination. Symptoms may appear years later.

Treatment: There is no specific medical treatment other than first aid. Induce vomiting.

How to avoid: Do not eat reef fish (including sea bass, barracuda, red snapper or grouper).

Colorado Tick Fever

Found: North America.

Cause: Arbovirus transmitted by insect or infected blood.

Carrier: The wood tick *(Dermacentor andersoni)*, also through transfusion of infected blood.

Symptoms: Aching of muscles in back and legs, chills, recurring fever, headaches, eye pain, fear of brightly lit area.

Treatment: Since symptoms only last about three weeks, medication or treatment is intended to relieve symptoms.

How to avoid: Ticks are picked up when walking through woods. Wear leggings, tall boots and insect repellent.

Dengue Fever (Breakbone Fever)

Found: South America, Africa, South Pacific, Asia, Mexico, Central America, Caribbean.

Cause: An arbovirus transmitted by mosquitoes.

Carrier: Mosquitoes in tropical areas, which usually bite during the daytime.

Symptoms: Two distinct periods. First period consists of severe muscle and joint aches and headaches combined with high fever (the origin of the term "break bone fever"). The second phase is sensitivity to light, diarrhea, vomiting, nausea, mental depression and enlarged lymph nodes.

Treatment: Designed to relieve symptoms. Aspirin should be avoided due to hemorrhagic complications.

How to avoid: Typical protection against daytime mosquito bites: using insect repellent with high DEET levels, wearing light-colored long-sleeve pants and shirts.

Diarrhea

Found: Worldwide.

Cause: There are many reasons for travelers to have the symptoms of diarrhea. It is important to remember that alien bacteria in the digestive tract are the main culprits. Most travelers to Africa, Mexico, South America and the Middle East will find themselves doubled up in pain, running for the nearest stinking toilet and wondering why the hell they ever left their comfortable home.

Carrier: Bacteria from food, the air, water or other people can be the cause. Dehydration from long airplane flights, strange diets, stress and high altitude can also cause diarrhea. It is doubtful you will ever get to know your intestinal bacteria on a first name basis, but *Aeromonas hydrophila*, Campylobacter, *jejuni Pleisiomonas*, salmonellae, shigellae, shielloides, *Vibrio cholerae* (non-01), *Vibrio parahaemolyticus*, *Yersinia enterocoliticia* and *Escherichia coli* are the most likely culprits. All these bugs would love to spend a week or two in your gut.

Symptoms: Loose stools, stomach pains, bloating, fever and malaise.

Treatment: First step is to stop eating and ingest plenty of fluids and salty foods; secondly, try Kaopectate or Pepto Bismol. If diarrhea persists after three to four days, seek medical advice.

How to avoid: Keep your fluid intake high when traveling. Follow common sense procedures when eating, drinking and ingesting any food or fluids. Remember to wash your hands carefully and frequently, since you can transmit a shocking number of germs from your hands to your mouth, eyes and nose.

Diphtheria

Found: Worldwide.

Cause: The bacterium *Corynebacterium diptheriae*, a producer of harmful toxins that is usually a problem in populations that have not been immunized against diphtheria.

Carrier: Infected humans can spread the germs by sneezing, or contact.

Symptoms: Swollen diphtheritic membrane that may lead to serious congestion. Other symptoms are pallor, listlessness, weakness and increased heart rate. May cause death due to weakened heart or shock.

Treatment: Immunization with the DPT vaccine at an early age (three years) is the ideal prevention; treatment with antitoxin, if not.

How to avoid: Avoid close contact with populations or areas where there is little to no vaccination program for diphtheria.

Ebola River Fever

Found: Among local populations in Congo.

Cause: A very rare but much publicized affliction.

Carrier: Unknown, but highly contagious. In 1989 the virus was found in lab monkeys in Reston, Virginia. The monkeys were quickly destroyed.

Outbreaks in the Congo and Central Africa are a risk.

Symptoms: The virus is described as melting people down, causing blood clotting, loss of consciousness and death.

Treatment: None.

How to avoid: Unknown.

Encephalitis

Found: Southeast Asia, Korea, Taiwan, Nepal, Eastern CIS countries and Eastern Europe.

Cause: A common viral infection carried by insects.

Carrier: The disease can be carried by the tick or mosquito. The risk is high during late summer and fall. The most dangerous strain is tickborne encephalitis transmitted by ticks in the summer in the colder climates of Russia, Scandinavia, Switzerland and France.

Symptoms: Fever, headache, muscle pain, malaise, runny nose and sore throat followed by lethargy, confusion, hallucination and seizures. About one-fifth of encephalitis infections have led to death.

Treatment: A vaccine is available.

How to avoid: Avoid areas known to be endemic. Avoid tick-infested areas such as forests, rice growing areas in Asia (mosquitoes) or areas that have a large number of domestic pigs (tick carriers). Use insect repellent. Do not drink unpasteurized milk.

Filariasis (Lymphatic, River Blindness)

Found: Africa, Central America, Caribbean, South America, Asia.

Cause: A group of diseases caused by long, thin roundworms carried by mosquitoes.

Carrier: Mosquitoes and biting flies in tropical areas.

Symptoms: Lymphatic filariasis, onchocerciasis (river blindness), loiasis and mansonellasis all have similar and very unpleasant symptoms. Fevers, headaches, nausea, vomiting, sensitivity to light, inflammation in the legs including the abdomen and testicles, swelling of the abdomen, joints and scrotum, enlarged lymph nodes, abscesses, eye lesions that lead to blindness, rashes, itches and arthritis.

Treatment: Diethylcarbamazine (DEC, Hetrazan, Notezine) is the usual treatment.

How to avoid: Avoid bites by insects with usual protective measures and insect repellent.

Flukes

Found: Caribbean, South America, Africa, Asia.

Cause: The liver fluke *(Clonorchis sinensis)* and the lung fluke *(Paragonimus westermani)*, which lead to paragonimasis.

Carrier: Carried in fish that has not been properly cooked.

Symptoms: Obstruction of the bile system, along with fever, pain, jaundice, gallstones, inflammation of the pancreas. There is further risk of cancer of the bile tract after infection. Paragonimasis affects the lungs and causes chest pains.

Treatment: Paragonimasis is treated with Prazanquantel. Obstruction of the bile system can require surgery.

How to avoid: To avoid liver flukes do not eat uncooked or improperly cooked fish—something most sushi fans will decry. Paragonimasis is found in uncooked shellfish, like freshwater crabs, crayfish and shrimp.

Giardiasis

Found: Worldwide.

Cause: A protozoa *Giardi lamblia* that causes diarrhea.

Carrier: Ingestion of food or water that is contaminated with fecal matter.

Symptoms: Very sudden diarrhea, severe flatulence, cramps, nausea, anorexia, weight loss and fever.

Treatment: Giardiasis can disappear without treatment, but Furazolidone, metronidizole, or quinacrine HCl are the usual treatments.

How to avoid: Cleanliness, drinking bottled water, and strict personal hygiene in eating and personal contact.

Guinea Worm Infection (Dracontiasis, Dracunculiasis)

Found: Tropical areas like the Caribbean, the Guianas, Africa, the Middle East and Asia.

Cause: Ingestion of waterborne nematode *Dracunculus medinensis.*

Carrier: Water systems that harbor *Dracunculus medinensis.*

Symptoms: Fever, itching, swelling around the eyes, wheezing, skin blisters and arthritis.

Treatment: Doses of niridazole, metronidazole or thiabendazole are the usual method. Surgery may be required to remove worms.

How to avoid: Drink only boiled or chemically treated water.

Hemorrhagic Fevers

Some of the more well-known hemorrhagic fevers are yellow fever, dengue, lassa fever and the horror movie–caliber Ebola fever. Outbreaks tend to be localized and subject to large populations of insects or rats. Don't let the exotic-sounding names lull you into a false sense of security; there was a major outbreak in the American Southwest caused by rodents spreading the disease.

Found: Worldwide.

Cause: Intestinal worms carried by insects and rodents.

Carrier: Depending on the disease, it can be transmitted by mosquitoes, ticks and rodents (in urine and feces).

Symptoms: Headache, backache, muscle pain and conjunctivitis. Later on, the thinning of the blood will cause low blood pressure, bleeding from the gums and nose, vomiting and coughing up blood, blood in the stool, bleeding from the skin and hemorrhaging in the internal organs. Coma and death may occur in the second week.

Treatment: Consult a doctor or medical facility familiar with the local disease.

How to avoid: Avoid mosquitoes, ticks, and areas with high concentrations of mice and rats.

Hepatitis, A, B, Non-A, Non-B

Found: Worldwide.

Cause: A virus that attacks the liver. Hepatitis A, Non-B and Non-A can be brought on by poor hygiene; hepatitis B is transmitted sexually or through infected blood.

Carrier: Hepatitis A is transmitted by oral-fecal route, person-to-person contact, or through contaminated food or water. Hepatitis B is transmitted by sexual activity or the transfer of bodily fluids. Hepatitis Non-A and Non-B are spread by contaminated water or from other people.

Symptoms: Muscle and joint pain, nausea, fatigue, sensitivity to light, sore throat, runny nose. Look for dark urine and clay-colored stools and jaundice along with liver pain and enlargement.

Treatment: Rest and a high-calorie diet. Immune globulin is advised as a minor protection against Hepatitis A. You can be vaccinated against Hepatitis B.

How to avoid: Non-A and Non-B require avoiding infected foods. Hepatitis B requires avoiding unprotected sexual contact, unsterile needles, dental work and infusions. Hepatitis A requires proper hygiene and avoiding infected water and foods.

Hydatid Disease (Echinococcosis)

Found: Worldwide.

Cause: A tapeworm found in areas with high populations of pigs, cattle and sheep.

Carrier: Eggs of the echinococcosis.

Symptoms: Cysts form in organs in the liver, lungs, bone or brain.

Treatment: Surgery for removal of the infected cysts. Mebendazole and albendazole are used as well.

How to avoid: Boil water, cook foods properly and avoid infected areas.

Leishmaniasis

Found: Tropical and subtropical regions.

Cause: Protozoans of the genus Leishmania.

Carrier: Phlebotomine sandflies in tropical and subtropical regions.

Symptoms: Skin lesions, cutaneous ulcers, mucocutaneous ulcers in the mouth, nose and anus, as well as intermittent fever, anemia and enlarged spleen.

Treatment: Sodium stibogluconate, rifampin, and sodium antimony gluconate. Surgery is also used to remove cutaneous and mucocutaneous ulcers.

How to avoid: Use insect repellent, a ground cover when sleeping and bed nets, and cover arms and legs.

Leprosy (Hansen's Disease)

Found: Africa, India and elsewhere

Cause: The bacterium *Mycobacterium leprae* that infects the skin, eyes, nervous system and testicles.

Carrier: It is not known how leprosy is transmitted, but direct human contact is suspected.

Symptoms: Skin lesions, nerve damage that progresses to loss of fingers and toes, blindness, and difficulty breathing.

Treatment: Dapsone, rifampin and clofazimine.

How to avoid: Leprosy is a tropical disease, with over half the cases worldwide occurring in India and Africa. There is no known preventive method.

Loaisis

Found: West and Central Africa.

Cause: The loa loa parasite.

Carrier: Chrysops deer flies or tabanid flies in West and Central Africa.

Symptoms: Subcutaneous swellings that come and go, brain and heart inflammation.

Treatment: Diethylcarbamazine.

How to avoid: Deerflies are large, and their bites can be avoided by wearing full-sleeved shirts and thick pants. Hats and bandannas can protect head and neck areas.

Lyme Diseases

Found: Worldwide.

Cause: A spirochete carried by ticks.

Carrier: The *Ixodes* tick, found worldwide and in great numbers during the summer. Ticks are found in rural areas and burrow into skin to suck blood.

Symptoms: A pronounced bite mark, flulike symptoms, severe headache, stiff neck, fever, chills, joint pain, malaise and fatigue.

Treatment: Tetracyclines, phenoxymethylpenicillin or erythromycin if caught early. Advanced cases may require intravenous penicillin.

How to avoid: Do not walk through wooded areas in the summer. Check for ticks frequently. Use leggings with insect repellent.

Malaria

Malaria is by far the most dangerous disease and the one most likely for travelers to pick up in Third World countries. Protection against this disease should be your first priority. As a rule, be leery of all riverine, swampy or tropical places. Areas such as logging camps, shantytowns, oases, campsites near slow-moving water, and resorts near mangrove swamps are all very likely to be major areas of malarial infection. Consult with a local doctor to understand the various resistances and the prescribed treatment. Many foreign doctors are more knowledgeable about the cure and treatment of malaria than domestic doctors.

Found: Africa, Asia, Caribbean, Southeast Asia, the Middle East.

Cause: The Plasmodium parasite is injected into the victim while the mosquito draws blood.

Carrier: The female *Anopheles* mosquito.

Symptoms: Fever, chills, enlarged spleen in low-level versions; plasmodium falciparum, or cerebral malaria, can also cause convulsions, kidney failure and hypoglycemia.

Treatment: Chloroquinine, quinine, pyrimethamine, sulfadoxine and mefloquine. Note: Some people may have adverse reactions to all and any of these drugs.

How to avoid: Begin taking a malarial prophylaxis before your trip, as well as during and after (consult your doctor for a prescription). Avoid infected areas and protect yourself from mosquito bites (netting, insect repellent, mosquito coils, long-sleeve shirts and pants) especially during dusk and evening times.

Measles (Rubeola)

Found: Worldwide.

Cause: A common virus in unvaccinated areas.

Carrier: Sneezing, saliva and close contact with infected or unvaccinated humans.

Symptoms: Malaise, irritability, fever, conjunctivitis, swollen eyelids and hacking cough appear 9 to 11 days after exposure. Fourteen days after exposure, the typical facial rash and spots appear.

Treatment: Measles will disappear, but complications can occur.

How to avoid: Vaccination or gamma globulin shots within five days of exposure.

Meliodosis

Found: Worldwide.

Cause: An animal disease (the bacillus *Pseudomonas pseudomallei*) that can be transferred to humans.

Carrier: Found in infected soil and water, and transmitted through skin wounds.

Symptoms: Various types, including fever, malaise, pneumonia, shortness of breath, headache, diarrhea, skin lesions, muscle pain and abscesses in organs.

Treatment: Antibiotics such as tetracyclines and sulfur drugs.

How to avoid: Clean and cover all wounds carefully.

Meningitis

Found: Africa, Saudi Arabia.

Cause: Bacteria: *Neisseria meningitis*, *Streptococcus pneumoniae* and *Haemophilus influenzae*. Children are at most risk. There are frequent outbreaks in Africa and Nepal.

Carrier: Inhaling infected droplets of nasal and throat secretions.

Symptoms: Fever, vomiting, headaches, confusion, lethargy and rash.

Treatment: Penicillin G.

How to avoid: Meningococcus polysaccharide vaccine. Do not travel to areas where outbreaks occur (the Sahel from Mali to Ethiopia) in the dry season.

Mumps

Found: Worldwide.

Cause: A virus found worldwide. Common in early spring and late winter and in unvaccinated areas.

Carrier: Infected saliva and urine.

Symptoms: Headache, anorexia, malaise, and pain when chewing or swallowing.

Treatment: Mumps is a self-inoculating disease. There can be complications which can lead to more serious lifetime afflictions.

How to avoid: Vaccination (MMR).

Plague

Found: India, Vietnam, Africa, South America, the Middle East, Russia.

Cause: A bacteria *(Yersinia pestis)* that infects rodents and the fleas they carry.

Carrier: Flea bites that transmit the bacteria to humans. Ticks, lice, corpses and human contact can also spread the disease.

Symptoms: Swollen lymph nodes, fever, abdominal pain, loss of appetite, nausea, vomiting diarrhea, and gangrene of the extremities.

Treatment: Antibiotics like streptomycin, tetracyclines and chloramphenicol can reduce the mortality rate.

How to avoid: Stay out of infected areas, and avoid contact.

Poliomyelitis (Polio)

Found: Worldwide.

Cause: A virus that destroys the central nervous system.

Carrier: Occurs through direct contact.

Symptoms: A mild febrile illness that may lead to paralysis. Polio can cause death in 5 to 10 percent of cases in children and 15 to 30 percent in adult cases.

Treatment: There is no treatment.

How to avoid: Vaccination during childhood with a booster before travel is recommended.

Rabies

Found: Worldwide.

Cause: A virus that affects the central nervous system.

Carrier: Rabies is transmitted through the saliva of an infected animal. Found in wild animals, although usually animals found in urban areas are most suspect: dogs, raccoons, cats, skunks, and bats. Although most people will automatically assume they are at risk for rabies, there are only about 16,000 cases reported worldwide. The risk is the deadly seriousness of rabies and the short time in which death occurs.

Symptoms: Abnormal sensations or muscle movement near the bite, followed by fever, headaches, malaise, muscle aches, tiredness, loss of appetite, nausea, vomiting, sore throat and cough. The advanced stages include excessive excitation, seizures and mental disturbances, leading to profound nervous system dysfunction and paralysis. Death occurs in most cases 4 to 20 days after being bitten.

Treatment: Clean wound vigorously; injections of antirabies antiserum and antirabies vaccine. People who intend to come into regular contact with animals in high-risk areas can receive HDCV (human diploid cell rabies vaccine) shots.

How to avoid: Avoid confrontations with animals.

Relapsing Fever

Found: The louse borne version is found in poor rural areas where infestation by lice is common.

Cause: *Borrelia spirochetes.*

Carrier: Lice and ticks. Ticks are found in wooded areas and bite mainly at night.

Symptoms: The fever gets its name from the six days on and six days off of high fever. Other symptoms include headaches, muscle pains, weakness and loss of appetite.

Treatment: Antibiotics.

How to avoid: Avoid infected areas, and check for ticks.

Rift Valley Fever

Found: Egypt and East Africa.

Cause: A virus that affects humans and livestock.

Carrier: Mosquitoes, inhaling infected dust, contact with broken skin and ingesting infected animal blood or fluids.

Symptoms: Sudden, onetime fever, severe headaches, muscle pain, weakness, sensitivity to light, eye pain, nausea, vomiting, diarrhea, eye redness and facial flushing. Blindness, meningitis, meningoencephalitis and retinitis may also occur.

Treatment: Seek medical treatment for supportive care.

How to avoid: Avoid contact with livestock in infected areas; protect yourself against mosquito bites.

River Blindness (Onchocerciais)

Found: Equatorial Africa, Yemen, the Sahara and parts of Central and South America.

Cause: The roundworm *Onchocerca volvulus.*

Carrier: Transmitted by blackflies found along rapidly flowing rivers.

Symptoms: Itching, skin atrophy, mottling, nodules, enlargement of the lymph nodes, particularly in the groin, and blindness.

Treatment: Invermectin or Diethylcarbamazine(DEC), followed by suramin, followed by DEC again.

How to avoid: Insect repellent, long-sleeve shirts and long pants. Avoid blackfly bites.

Rocky Mountain Spotted Fever

Found: Found only in the Western Hemisphere.

Cause: A bacterial disease transmitted by tick bites.

Carrier: Rickettsial bacteria are found in rodents and dogs. The ticks pass the bacteria by then biting humans.

Symptoms: Fever, headaches, chills, and rash (after fourth day) on the arms and legs. Final symptoms may include delirium, shock and kidney failure.

Treatment: Tetracyclines or chloramphenicol.

How to avoid: Ticks are found in wooded areas. Inspect your body after walks. Use insect repellent. Wear leggings or long socks or long pants.

Salmonellosis

Found: Worldwide.

Cause: A common bacterial infection; *Salmonella gastroenteritis* is commonly described as food poisoning.

Carrier: Found in fecally contaminated food, unpasteurized milk, raw foods and water.

Symptoms: Abdominal pain, diarrhea, vomiting, chills and fever usually within 8 to 48 hours of ingesting infected food. *Salmonella* only kills about one percent of its victims, usually small children or the aged.

Treatment: Purge infected food, replace fluids. Complete recovery is within two to five days.

How to avoid: Consume only properly prepared foods.

Sandfly Fever (Three-Day Fever)

Found: Africa, Mediterranean.

Cause: Phleboviruses injected by sandfly bites.

Carrier: Transmitted by sandflies, usually during the dry season.

Symptoms: Fever, headache, eye pain, chest muscle pains, vomiting, sensitivity to light, stiff neck, taste abnormality, rash and joint pain.

Treatment: There is no specific treatment. The symptoms can reoccur in about 15 percent of cases, but typically disappear.

How to avoid: Do not sleep directly on the ground. Sandflies usually bite at night.

Schistosomiasis (Bilharzia)

Bilharzia is one of the meanest bugs to pick up in your foreign travels. The idea of nasty little creatures actually burrowing through your skin and lodging themselves in your gut is menacing. If not treated, it can make your life a living hell with afternoon sweats, painful urination, weakness and other good stuff. There is little you can do to prevent infection, since the *Schistosoma* larva and flukes are found where people have fouled freshwater rivers and lakes. Get treatment immediately, since the affliction worsens as the eggs multiply and continue to infect more tissues. About 250 million people around the world are believed to be infected.

Found: Worldwide.

Cause: A group of parasitic *Schistosoma* flatworms (*Schistosoma mansoni, Schistosomajaponicum* and *Schistosoma haematobium*) found in slow-moving, tropical freshwater.

Carrier: The larvae of *Schistosoma* are found in slow-moving waterways in tropical areas around the world. They actually enter the body through the skin and then enter the lymph vessels and then migrate to the liver.

Symptoms: Look for a rash and itching at the entry site, followed by weakness, loss of appetite, night sweats, hivelike rashes, and afternoon fevers in about four to six weeks. There will be bloody, painful and frequent urination and diarrhea. Later, victims become weaker and may be susceptible to further infections and diseases.

Treatment: Elimination of *S. mansoni* requires oxamniquine and praziquantel. *S. japonicum* responds to praziquantel alone, and *Schistosoma haematobium* is treated with praziquantel and metrifonate.

How to avoid: Stay out of slow-moving freshwater in all tropical and semitropical areas. This also means wading or standing in water.

Syphilis

Found: Worldwide.

Cause: A spirochete *(Treponema pallidum)* causes this chronic venereal disease, which if left untreated progresses into three clinical stages.

Carrier: Syphilis is spread through sexual contact and can be passed on to infants congenitally.

Symptoms: After an incubation period of two to six weeks, a sore usually appears near the genitals, although some men and women may not experience any symptoms. Some men also experience a scanty discharge. A skin rash appears in the second stage, often on the soles of the feet and palms of the hands. It may be accompanied by a mild fever, sore throat and patchy hair loss. This rash generally appears about six weeks after the initial sore. The third phase of the disease may develop over several years if the disease is left untreated and may damage the brain and the heart or even cause death.

Treatment: Antibiotics are used to treat syphilis, and infected people should abstain from sex until treatment ends. Blood tests should be performed again in three months after the round of treatment. Sexual partners need to be tested and treated. Victims of syphilis should also be tested for other sexually transmitted diseases.

How to avoid: Abstain from sexual activities or use a latex condom.

Tainiasis (Tapeworms)

Found: Worldwide.

Cause: A tapeworm is usually discovered after being passed by the victim.

Carrier: Ingestion of poorly cooked meat infected with tapeworms.

Symptoms: In advanced cases, there will be diarrhea and stomach cramps. Sections of tapeworms can be seen in stools.

Treatment: Mebendazole, niclocsamide, paromomysi and praziqunatel are effective in killing the parasite.

How to avoid: Tapeworms come from eating meats infected with tapeworm or coming into contact with infected fecal matter.

Tetanus (Lockjaw)

Found: Worldwide.

Cause: The bacteria *Clostridiium tetani*.

Carrier: Found in soil and enters body through cuts or punctures.

Symptoms: Restlessness, irritability, headaches, jaw pain, back pain and stiffness, and difficulty in swallowing. Then, within 2 to 56 days, stiffness increases with lockjaw and spasms. Death occurs in about half the cases, usually affecting children.

Treatment: If infected, human tetanus immune globulin is administered with nerve blockers for muscle relaxation.

How to avoid: Immunization is the best prevention, with a booster recommended before travel.

Trachoma

Found: Common in Africa, the Middle East and Asia.

Cause: A chlamydial infection of the eye, which is responsible for about 200 million cases of blindness.

Carrier: Flies, contact, wiping face or eye area with infected towels.

Symptoms: Constant inflammation under the eyelid that causes scarring of the eyelid, turned-in eyelashes and eventual scarring of the cornea and then blindness.

Treatment: Tetracyclines, erythromycin, sulfonamide, surgery to correct turned-in lashes.

How to avoid: It is spread primarily by flies. Proper hygiene and avoidance of fly-infested areas are recommended.

Trichinosis

Found: Worldwide.

Cause: Infection of the *Trichinella spiralis* worm.

Carrier: Pig meat (also bear and walrus) that contain cysts. The worm then infects the new hosts' tissues and intestines.

Symptoms: Diarrhea, abdominal pain, nausea, prostration and fever. As the worm infects tissues, fever, swelling around the eyes, conjunctivitis, eye hemorrhages, muscle pain, weakness, rash and splinter hemorrhages under the nails occur. Less than 10 percent of the cases result in death.

Treatment: Thiabendazole is effective in killing the parasite.

How to avoid: Proper preparation, storage and cooking of meat.

Tuberculosis

Found: Worldwide.

Cause: A disease of the lungs caused by the *Mycobacterium tuberculosis* bacteria or *Mycobacterium bovis*.

Carrier: By close contact with infected persons (sneezing, coughing) or, in the case of *Mycobacterium bovis*, contaminated or unpasteurized milk.

Symptoms: Weight loss, night sweats and a chronic cough, usually with traces of blood. If left untreated, death results in about 60 percent of the cases after a period of two and a half years.

Treatment: Isoniazide and rifampin can control the disease.

How to avoid: Vaccination and isoniazid prophylaxis.

Tularaemia (Rabbit Fever)

Found: Worldwide.

Cause: A fairly rare disease (about 300 cases per year) caused by the bacteria *Francisella tularnesis* passed from animals to humans via insects.

Carrier: The bite of deerflies, ticks, mosquitoes and even cats can infect humans.

Symptoms: Fever, chills, headaches, muscle pain, malaise, enlarged liver and spleen, rash, skin ulcers and enlargement of the lymph nodes.

Treatment: Vaccination is used. Streptomycin primarily. Tetracycline and chloramphenicol are also effective.

How to avoid: Care when handling animal carcasses, removal of ticks and avoidance of insect bites.

Typhoid Fever

Found: Africa, Asia, Central America.

Cause: The bacterium *Salmonella typhi*.

Carrier: Transmitted by contaminated food and water in areas of poor hygiene.

Symptoms: Fever, headaches, abdominal tenderness, malaise, rash, enlarged spleen. Later symptoms include delirium, intestinal hemorrhage and perforation of the intestine.

Treatment: Chloramphenicol.

How to avoid: Vaccination is the primary protection, although the effectiveness is not high.

Typhus Fever

Found: Africa, South America, Southeast Asia, India.

Cause: *Rickettsia*.

Carrier: Transmitted by fleas, lice, mites and ticks found in mountainous areas around the world.

Symptoms: Fever, headache, rash and muscle pain. If untreated, death may occur in the second week due to kidney failure, coma and blockage of the arteries.

Treatment: Tetracyclines or chloramphenicol.

How to avoid: Check for ticks, avoid insect bites, attend to hygiene to prevent lice and avoid mountainous regions.

Yellow Fever

Found: Africa, South America.

Cause: A virus transmitted by mosquito bites.

Carrier: The tiny banded-legged *Aedes aegpyti* is the source for urban yellow fever, and the haemogogus and sabethes mosquito carries the jungle version.

Symptoms: In the beginning, fever, headaches, backaches, muscle pain, nausea, conjunctivitis, albumin in the urine and slow heart rate. Followed by black vomit, no urination and delirium. Death affects only 5 to 10 percent of cases and occurs in the fourth to sixth day.

Treatment: Replace fluids and electrolytes.

How to avoid: Vaccination is mandatory when entering or leaving infected areas.

In a Dangerous Place: The Sahara

The Singing of the Sands

This is a deadly hot place where rain squalls can drop the temperature so quickly they make grown men throw up. Where massive walls of red-brown sand choke and blast everything to a light brown softness. Where camels walk ghostlike through the desert, carrying the dirty white slabs of salt. Where massive mud buildings create a look that is alien as one can get on this planet. A place where paddle wheelers chug down dirty brown rivers, faded yellow earthmovers sit dead and picked like dinosaur carcasses. It was in this Western French place that I first became sick. I remember because I wrote it down as it happened.

I know I am getting weaker. At night I am reduced to lying on the grubby thin mattress. When it gets soaked with my sweat I roll onto the dusty concrete floor in search of coolness. Puddles of sweat crawl slowly out of me like blood from a sniper victim. I spend days sweating on the cement floor of my windowless room. I am too weak to get up. Too tired to eat. Too stupefied by the fever to think straight. I pull myself to the corner with the stinking drain as fluids pour out of my shivering body. I don't know how many star-filled nights I lay on that hard dirty concrete floor. I could see the stars through the open metal door. I could actually see them move. Like a video being played in slow motion. Time has been disconnected. I can hear the sand whispering as the wind moves it over the ground.

When my head rolls to the side the puddles formed by my sweat feels cool. I slip in and out of hallucinations interrupted by spasms of pain emanating from inside me. When will it end? What shall I do? There is no one here to answer. They will be back in a week.

Deep into the night in the deadly godless silence of the Sahara I think I hear two men approaching slowly. They shuffle slowly, banging the metal doors as I hear them search the rooms of the empty encampment. I can hear them coming closer, but I can't move. In the blackness of my cell I can't tell if I am awake or dreaming. A few days earlier, a man jumped through my window and was surprised to find me in the room lying in a dark corner. He fled in terror. Is he back for my life and my money? I wait and listen. My mind and body are wasting away here on the edge of the great Sahara desert. Delirious, sleepless, ill and sickened, I must get to a doctor or I will die. But how?

The steps are getting closer. I cannot move I cannot hide. There is no one to call out to. Just the cold stars that move so slowly through the crack in the rusted steel door. The stars watch me with that cruel curiosity you find in Africa.

Too weak to move, I lie in the dark of the moonless night and await my fate. Finally the steps are at my door. I try to make out a shape or form in the darkness. The door clangs open and reveals a silhouette. Looking up, I see what my nemesis is; just an inquisitive donkey.

Africa can do things like that to your mind.

—**RYP**

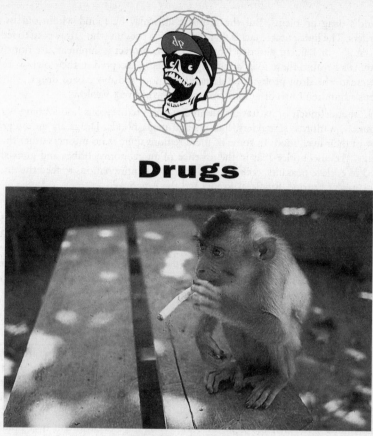

Drugs

War's Bastard Son

Many Western travelers tend to view drugs as a furtive part of their youth or something that affects only inner cities, but the adventurous traveler quickly learns just how vital a role drugs play in the world's most dangerous places. In fact, in many places, danger is a prerequisite to ensure the smooth flow of illegal goods and profits the drug industry needs to escape interdiction. Whenever there is drug activity there is corruption, AIDS and organized crime. Here you'll enter a shadowy world where guests are unwelcome. Typically narco-regions are run by warlords, corrupt politicians, dirty cops or criminals, all of whom can be considered tourism-unfriendly. Mexico City's former police chief built a mansion styled after the Parthenon and stashed away between $1 to $3 billion of corrupt profits during his six-year term. But this is only a small piece of the pie, especially when you consider the Cali cartel made $30 billion last year and the Gulf cartel profited $20 billion by government estimates.

With the increased presence of U.S. government agents and operatives, the drug lords have become more careful and wary of unfamiliar faces—your life could be at risk if you are tagged as someone who should be removed. U.S. government sources spend millions unsuccessfully to try to solve the entire world's drug problems. But the problem also may be found within our own borders. The indisputable fact is that the Bolivian peasant who grows coca to feed his family, or Baluchi gunmen who are paid to protect a shipment, are not the criminals because these folks are doing something accepted in their own world. We create the drug problem by demanding more and more hard drugs, which keeps a hundred or so drug lords around the world very wealthy.

DP spends much of its travel time in drug-infested regions hobnobbing with gunmen, warlords, smugglers, fighters and mafia hoods. Drugs are an integral part of their livelihood. In some of these regions there is no business other than drugs. We also notice that in the absence of an economy, bribes and guns are used to enslave peasants, couriers, politicians and entire nations to feed the drug demands of Europe, Russia, Australia and the Americas.

The drug business would not exist without three major markets, the largest being the United States. Approximately 13 million Americans were users of illegal drugs in 1996, spending $57 billion on illegal drugs—including $38 billion to buy cocaine and $10 billion on heroin.

Approximately 60 percent of federal prisoners are sentenced for drug violations. A quarter to one-half of men who commit acts of domestic violence also have substance abuse problems, many involving illegal drugs.

http://www.nida.nih.gov/in

Heroin

The *Papaver somniferum*, or Eurasian poppy, was introduced to Asia from the Mediterranean by Arab traders in the 12th century and was cultivated for its medicinal properties. This innocent little flower has now grown up to become the half-brother of war. India, Myanmar, China, Pakistan, Laos, Thailand, Mexico, Uzbekistan and Afghanistan are the troubled homes of this gentle, unassuming weed that blows in the wind. Wars have been fought over opium since the 1839–1842 Opium War between Britain and China. Today, the battles are taking place on the streets of St. Louis, Miami, Los Angeles and small-town America. Crime experts say that as turf battles among drug lords decline in the cities, America's small towns are becoming the fastest growing markets. A recent survey found that 47 percent of small-town police chiefs consider drugs a serious problem and two-thirds say drug problems in their area have increased over the last five years. Millions of people are currently enslaved by the byproducts of the opium poppy. And heroin's slaves today aren't just junkies in back alleys. The media recently has had a field day exposing heroin-addicted movie stars and fashion models. Since the drug can now be snorted like cocaine or smoked rather than injected into veins, it has begun increasing in popularity.

Seventy percent of all illicit drugs in the United States are derived from heroin once originating in the land of Chinese drug lords—the Golden Triangle of Southeast Asia but now coming from new competitors in Afghanistan and Colombia. The current purity of heroin found on the street in the United States has jumped from an average of 7 percent in 1984 to 36 percent today, a testament not only to its grip on a nation, but to the seemingly endless world supply of the narcotic. Heroin shipped into the United States comes from at least 11 different countries. The DEA estimates it stops 30 to 40 percent of drugs illegally entering the country.

Heroin starts as fields of beautiful colored poppies. Poppies can be grown in cool plateaus above 500 feet. The plants grow rapidly and propagate easily. Planted at the end of the wet season (in Asia in September and October), the poppy heads are later scraped after the petals fall off. The scraping creates an oozing sap that is removed from the plant and packed tightly into banana leaves. Naturally it doesn't make sense to do all this intensive labor on Fisher Island, so heroin, like coffee and cotton, is an "almost slavery" crop. The crude opium is then transported out of the hills via pony or armed convoys to middlemen. For those who grow opium, few escape its enticing lure. Hill tribe growers swiftly become addicts themselves. Up to 30 percent of Southeast Asia's Hmong tribe is addicted to opium. Most of the income of northern Laos is dope money. In fact, small nickel bags, or *parakeets* as they are called locally, can be used as a form of currency.

The poppy is back big time and is often used in conjunction with cocaine to ease the crash. Purer forms can be smoked instead of injected. There are more than half a million heroin addicts in the United States.

The Golden Crescent

Afghanistan had a massive increase in poppy cultivation under the Talibs, putting it at the top of the list of heroin suppliers. According to the United Nations, Afghanistan cranked out 4,600 tons of opium in 1998. Good weather, encouragement from the Taliban to grow poppy (some say to force concessions from outside groups who will trade reduction of poppy growing for aid dollars) and a need to provide financing either via taxation (the Talibs get 10 percent of all sales to opium dealers which goes for $60 a kilo or 2.2 pounds) or straight sales.

The Taliban is against the consumption of drugs, but not the growing of poppies or exporting of drugs. In Afghanistan poppies bring in about twice what farmers can get for wheat. There are also the usual rumors that eternal bugaboo bin Laden is buying all the raw gum up to finance a jihad. Afghanistan grows most of the poppies and supplies much of the raw paste that becomes Europe's heroin. Poppy cultivation in Pakistan is down to only 50 tons, creating more demand for Afghan goo. Most transport is via Baluchi trafficking organizations operating out of Quetta, Pakistan. These groups place orders with the Afghani processors and arrange for shipment of the drugs from Afghanistan through Pakistan and to Iranian or Turkish buyers who move it through Iran and into international drug channels. Most Afghan opium is destined for processing into heroin in Turkey to be sold in the main cities of Western Europe.

Russia has become junkie central with high demand and short supply lines for not only heroin but also amphetamines. Russian authorities predict that drug use is now accelerating at a 50 percent increase per year and there are now over 2 million drug users in Russia. The Lezgi, Chechen and other trans-Caucasian *mafyia* groups control the drug trafficking and distribution in trans-Caucasia, Central Asia and the Ukraine.

Tajikistan has become one of more lucrative areas for opium and hashish smuggling. A general lack of enforcement and a number of local warlords have made drug smuggling the only industry in Gorno Badakhstan. A kilo of opium can be bought locally between $100 and $120 and can be resold in Moscow 1,800 miles away for between $5,500–$6,000. The presence of 25,000 underpaid Russian military with easy access to air transport to Moscow has made this the main drug highway between Afghanistan and Moscow. The 40,000 or so junkies in Tajikistan can barely get their hands on enough smack before it is whisked out of the country. Curiously, with all this temptation, most drug seizures in Tajikistan are still made by Russian border guards who make about $36 a month. There is minor poppy cultivation near Dushanbe, the southeast region of Khatlon, in the northern Leninabad region and increasingly in Gorno Badakhstan.

Ukraine has become a major conduit for drug smuggling from Central Asia and Turkey to Europe. It is also home to half a million addicts. The poppy growing regions of Central Asia (Kazakhstan, Krygyzstan, Tajikistan, and Uzbekistan) now are involved heavily in heroin trafficking between Southwest Asia and China into Russia and Europe. Tajikistan is a major opium and hashish thoroughfare between Afghanistan to Russia, the CIS, and Europe.

Kazakhstan is vast area is not only a major transshipment region from Tajikistan and China but is home to a woefully understated 17,000 drug users, 6,000 of whom are addicts. It is also a major cannabis growing center (see "Cannabis").

Krygyzstan has over 50,000 addicts and is a transit route from Afghanistan via Tajikistan.

Turkmenistan has a well-established use of opium in its traditional foods and festivals. It also has a well-worn smuggling trail through the Kushka and to Mary. The Karakum Desert provides a direct route from the north of Afghanistan to the Caspian Sea and Russia. Most poppy cultivation is along the Iranian border in the Akhal Velayat.

Uzbekistan is used by the Azeria and Georgian mafia as a Central Asian hub to Russia through its main city of Tashkent. There are about 200,000 addicts and minor poppy cultivation in Samarkand and Syrhandarya. It is also a minor transshipment point from Afghanistan to Kazakhstan.

Turkey is the terminus and major refining center of the Golden Crescent. Three-quarters of Europe's heroin supply comes through or from Turkey. That's about 6 metric tons a month. Turkey's raw product comes from Afghanistan and Pakistan through the northern part of Iran. Drug labs are found primarily in the southeast and in the Mamara region south of Istanbul. Istanbul is one of the world's centers for drug buying and selling. The major player is the PKK, who use a network of Kurds as retail outlets to sell heroin in Europe. Turkish heroin goes for $6,500 per kilo wholesale, and when it gets to Germany or the Netherlands it jumps $35,000. If it gets to North America it can sell for up to $75,000. That's what the dealer pays.

The Abkhaz Route

"Abkhaz route" was allegedly started in late 1993 by Chechen brothers Shamil and Shirvan Basayev. Shamil Basayev led the Abkhaz Brigade during the war and like most enterprising leaders quickly found a use for deadheading empty military transport used to bring in guns with drug transportation shipments going out. It becomes a zero sum game as drugs are used to pay for munitions directly.

The Chechen Commander took a page from the Russians (or did the Russians blame it on the Basayevs) and started using Mi-6 transport helicopters to ship Pakistan-transported drugs from Afghanistan and the Vedenskiy Rayon of

Chechnya to the heliport in New Athens with refueling stops in Dzheyrakh Gorge in Kabardino-Balkariya. From New Athens, Abkhaz trucks deliver the goods to Sukhumi, where they are loaded on Turkish ships and shipped to the port of Famagusta in northern Cyprus. From there the heroin is broken down into small packets and shipped into Europe.

Most of Europe's heroin comes straight from Afghanistan via the Balkan routes. Opium and heroin production are up under the Taliban, and the transit lines are prospering from affluence in Europe and warfare in Central Asia. The northern branch of the Balkan Route is a heroin highway, servicing markets in the Czech Republic, Hungary, and other Eastern European countries.

The traditional route for Central Asian heroin has been the Balkans from Turkey to Austria. Increased demand in Europe, and open borders have expanded the route northward into Romania, Hungary, and the Czech and Slovak republics, and southward through Croatia, Slovenia, the former Yugoslav republic of Macedonia, Greece and Albania. Slovakia is becoming a key conduit for smuggling Southwest Asian heroin to Western Europe.

The Golden Triangle

The Golden Triangle has shrunk to the second largest producer of opium. Myanmar is the world's second largest opium producer, with an estimated 1,300 metric tons, which can produce an estimated one-tenth that amount in pure heroin. In 1995, Laos produced an estimated 180 metric tons of potential opium; its production has slipped to 150 tons in 1998, and it is now the world's third largest potential producer of illegal opium after Myanmar and Afghanistan.

Laos produces a lot of its opium for local consumption. Much of it goes to its 42,000 opium addicts, who consume 60 metric tons each year. Most poppy cultivation is in the Houaphan and Palavek regions. The smack that doesn't enter the arms of the Lao is smuggled out north to China via Luang Namtha and Phong Saly or to Thailand via Oudomsay province.

China is the other major Asia transportation route for heroin. Heading north from the Golden Triangle, most drugs are shipped from Yunnan through Guangxi and Guangdong provinces into Hong Kong for overseas shipments. A smaller amount is smuggled directly into Russia, and some heroin enters Guangxi province from Vietnam.

China has a minor opium crop primarily in the northwest province of Ningxia. There is a conservative government estimate of 380,000 drug addicts in China, but the real total is much higher. A six month crackdown just in Guangdong province netted 7,500 drug dealers and 250 kgs of heroin. Most addicts are in Yunnan province, which also has a skyrocketing AIDS problem due to syringe-needled junkies. Drugs are bad for your health in China. Most drug traffickers are executed by a single pistol shot to the back of the head immediately after trial.

Opium production in China's Yunnan Province is on the decline with a 36 percent drop in production.

Taiwan has more than 60,000 heroin addicts and is a transshipment point for Chinese heroin.

Vietnam has 9,000 villages that produce 2,300 hectares of opium under cultivation. The country also has more than 200,000 addicts (30,000 in Ho Chi Minh City), three-quarters of whom smoke opium while the others inject it.

There are also about 3,000 HIV-positive persons, 80 percent of whom are drug addicts.

Hong Kong (now part of China) continues to be a major money-laundering center, and to a lesser amount, a shipment center.

Indonesia is a minor heroin transit point, primarily for Australia, Europe and the United States.

Cambodia is a major smuggling center from Myanmar, usually via speedboat to Thailand. This new export crop has attracted the attention of the local police and military.

The poppy is regionally cultivated in Third World countries with little or no political, military or police interference. Mexico, Lebanon and Turkey have faded from the scene, replaced by Afghanistan and Myanmar, both of which had bumper crops and governments that see no problem including drug sales in their GNP. Vietnam is the up-and-comer with 3,150 hectares of opium poppy under cultivation (which would yield 25 metric tons of opium gum).

The Americas: Heroin's Brave New World

Poppies can be grown anywhere in the world, so it's surprising that it has taken this long for traditional coca producers to try opium poppies.

Colombia's attempt at diversifying into opium poppy cultivation is going well. Colombia's 6,540 hectares, assuming three crops per year, make it the largest potential opium producer in the hemisphere, putting it slightly behind Laos at 150 tonnes per year. In 1998 Colombia provided 60 percent of all heroin that came into the United States. They are trying to use their cocaine distribution and sales networks to sell an ultrapure form of heroin. Many drug lords, like the Orejula brothers, run their empires from jail, where it's probably safer. A kilo of South American heroin goes for between $85,000 and $195,000—about four times what coke sells for wholesale.

Venezuela, not to be outdone, is busy putting in poppies in the Serrania de Perija frontier region. Mexican drug mafias are strong-arming Huallaga Valley campesinos to plant poppies. The DEA claimed that South American heroin had the highest purity (average 59.3 percent) of any of the samples analyzed under its Domestic Monitor Program.

Mexico remains the second largest Latin American grower of opium poppy with approximately 5,800 hectares under cultivation. Mexico now provides 45 tons of opium, contributing to 42 percent of the heroin smuggled into the United States. The Mexican mafia also controls all drug sales west of the Mississippi.

UN International Drug Control Program
http://www.undcp.org/

Cocaine

Crack is number one with a bullet in the United States. Smoke it and you may get a groovy high or you may turn into a ruthless brute. Crack is big dollars, big profits and big trouble. Law enforcement credits much of the body count in the inner cities to gangs fighting over turf to sell the evil stuff. You only have about five years to wring every nickel out of the 2.1 million coke and crackheads until they die. Crack is cocaine you can smoke, but it is typically cut with anything that grandma left in the cupboard. Crack and cocaine enter the United States by the ton. A kilo of cocaine will sell wholesale for between $10,500 and $40,000.

The coca bush takes two years to mature, at which point the leaves are picked and ground up. A hectare of mature coca bushes can yield around 2.7 metric tons of dry leaf, which in turn yields about 7.44 kilos of cocaine. It takes about 363 kilos of dry leaves to yield one kilo of cocaine. The amount of pure cocaine in the goods depends on the alkaloid level of the leaf. In the Chapare region of Bolivia they have a 0.72 percent alkaloid content. Cocaine goes for about $100 a gram on the street in the United States. Do the math and figure out how much coca eradication equals how much cocaine not smuggled into the States. Unfortunately, despite the valiant efforts of every law enforcement agency in the world, cocaine availability increases every year and prices are dropping.

Most addicts kick the habit by dropping dead. Unlike heroin which will give you ten years of hell, cocaine and crack are more addictive and more destructive. It makes perfect sense that cocaine would be in such heavy demand in civilized countries. There are about 2 million crack or cokeheads in the United States, enough to keep the cocaine trade booming.

Peru is the world's largest producer of coca with 115,000 hectares under cultivation. Although the government likes to blame their problem on the insurgent groups, several senior Peruvian army officers are under investigation and one general was convicted. Drugs have also been found on Peruvian navy ships and air force planes. Even the top security man and President Fujimori's strongman, Vladimir Montesinos, has been fingered in this business. Peru ships its cocaine base to Mexico for processing. Smaller amounts are shipped by land into Chile and Ecuador.

The major markets for South American cocaine producers are the United States and Western Europe. The United States seizes an average of 100 metric tons every year, but admits that it has little impact on drug prices or reduced drug sales.

Colombia's coca production is up to 520 metric tons in 1999, forcing local syndicates to expand distribution into Poland and the Czech Republic. To keep up their number two position, they also import coca base from neighboring Peru and Bolivia. Most Colombian cocaine is shipped in huge multi-ton sea cargo or eight-ton shipments on old 727s to deliver to Mexico, Central America and the Caribbean, where it is broken down into smaller shipments bound for the States or Europe. San Andrés Island, an old stomping ground of *DP,* is one of the major air transshipment points into Nicaragua and then to Mexico. About 80 percent of the cocaine and almost all the heroin nabbed in the United States comes from Colombia. The DEA estimates that Colombian cocaine fetches about $17,500 per kilo (2.2 pounds) wholesale in the United States.

Bolivia is the number three producer of coca and cocaine and slipping in the ranking as Colombia takes over the Bolivian industry. Hectares of coca are grown in the Yungas, Apolo and Chapare regions. Processing centers are in Santa Cruz and Beni. Since coca is used as part of tea, for chewing and for traditional ceremonies, 12,000 hectares of cultivation is allowed legally. The best coca leaves come from Yungas, while almost all coca grown in the Chapare region is for illegal purposes.

Panama, even post-Manny, is still a major transportation center. And no, the Colon Free Zone is not a joke, but a major money laundering center.

Mexico has increased drug production so much that smugglers have switched from cargo planes to cargo ships to meet the demand. The cargo is picked up by high-speed boats that meet them off the coast. Small planes are also used to drop drugs in country. The *contrabandistas* along the border are also eager to smuggle guns, dope or people if the price is right.

Nigeria is a major hub for smuggling by virtue of its corrupt customs and the eagerness of its mules, who will carry cocaine either ingested internally in condoms or on their person. The Nigerians leave South America, often via Rio, then bring the cocaine to Nigeria for sales in South Africa.

The Caribbean island of Aruba, off the coast of Venezuela, is a major drug transshipment point. Shipments funnel in from Colombia, Venezuela and Suriname for transport to the United States and Europe. Also, Vieques Island (Puerto Rico) and the U.S. Virgin Islands are popular delivery points from the islands of the Lesser Antilles. About 30 percent of the drugs that enter Britain come from the Caribbean. Drugs also flow from these islands into their home protectorate of France, and the Netherlands. Cocaine is shipped by sea from South America and then loaded onto aircraft and ships on the ABC Islands. Couriers are also used to transport drugs in 1–2 kilo amounts back to their home countries. They also launder drug proceeds in Aruba, Curaçao, St. Maarten and Bonaire. Antigua and Barbuda are major storage and transshipment points for Colombia, Venezuela, Trinidad and Jamaica. In general, many of the island chains offer ideal smuggling and transfer points due to the large amount of shoreline, number of watercraft and lack of police in the area.

Suriname is the main gateway for cocaine into the Netherlands.

The Dominican Republic is also a convenient stopping-off point for Colombian drugs en route to the United States.

Brazil is a major air transit route for cocaine base from Peru to Colombia.

International Narcotics Control Board
http://www.incb.org/

Cannabis

The weed is not really top priority with the DEA nor is it a major contributor to criminal activity. It is bulky, low margin and can be homegrown easily by cheapskate customers. In many countries, you will find marijuana plants growing wild in backyards, along roads and in fields. The benefits of the cannabis trade are the lack of expensive chemicals to create an end product and a laissez-faire attitude toward personal consumption in many European and Asian countries.

Mexican weed production is down 35 percent to about 6,900 hectares, which can yield 3,560 metric tons of end product. In Mexico coke is it. In 1995, there were 18,650 hectares of cannabis, which produced over 5,000 metric tons of weed.

Colombia is a bit player, but up-and-coming with about 5,000 hectares under cultivation. Most weed is sent by sea to Mexico for land shipment into the United States. Although gringos toke most of Colombia's sensimilla, Colombia is increasing exports to Europe.

Jamaica may be the most visible consumer of ganja, which may contribute to its anemic 305 hectares or 206 metric tons of end product. Maybe there was too much sampling. The drug gangs have also started shipping cocaine.

The Bahamas is a major transshipment point for Jamaican weed and U.S.-bound coke from Colombia.

Guyana is a minor source for cannabis and is a transshipment point for cocaine from Colombia.

Cuba is a minor player with its north shore being a swapping point for Colombian drugs on their way to the States or Europe.

Trinidad and Tobago are major marijuana producing areas with an estimated 24 million marijuana plants found in the forested areas of north, east and south of Trinidad.

The Philippines is a big-time producer and exporter of weed. Grown in northern Luzon and Mindanao, the primary destination of Philippine weed is Japan and Australia.

Central Asia is a major cannabis growing area, with much of the product being turned into hashish.

Kazakhstan studies show that one out of every 14 people in the cities is a cannabis user. Every hippy's dream is the Chu valley, where 138,000 acres of cannabis grow wild. There is an annual crop of 5,000 metric tons. The primary regions for cannabis are the Taldy-Korgan, around the city of Almaty, Kzyl-orda and the south Zakakstan oblasts. There is also the ephreda plant, which grows wild in the mountain ranges of the Zailyiski and Junggar and in the Talky-Korgan and Dzhambyl.

Crack

Crack has replaced heroin as the new "jones" that is dragging down the inner city. Not as addictive as heroin, it has an intense high that is psychologically addictive. In some American cities, three out of 100 first-graders are addicted to crack, thanks to their mothers. In 1995, 18 per 1,000 live births were crack babies. Crack pushes users to violent criminal acts, sexual trading and other desperate measures to feed their habit. According to the Bureau of Justice Statistics, the typical crack user is low-income, white (49.9 percent) and desperate; 35.9 percent are black and 14.2 percent Latino.

Drugs 'n the Hood

Europe

Europe is a major consumer of illicit drugs. Amsterdam, Marseilles and Baltic ports provide easy access for Asian and Central Asian purveyors.

Poland produces 20 percent of the amphetamines sold in Europe and is a major base for Chinese, Colombian and other drug groups looking for a safe, central place to process drugs. There are about 200,000 drug users, and half of them are addicts.

England has an estimated 100,000 heroin addicts and is a major consumer of soft and hard drugs. Most of the heroin comes from Afghanistan via Pakistani organizations. Marijuana comes from Morocco. Cocaine comes directly from South America via Amsterdam.

Italy is home to three major criminal organizations: The Calabrian Ndrangheta, the Neapolitan Camorra and the Sicilian Mafia. All work directly with South American cartels to transport and sell cocaine in Europe. Most cocaine arrives by sea into mafia-controlled ports. There are around 150,000 addicts in Italy and 200,000 cocaine users.

Germany is the one place where cocaine costs more than in the United States and use is up. Its ports of Hamburg, Bremen and Rostock are entry points for drugs, and Frankfurt is the main air terminal used by Europe-bound "mules" from Africa and Central Asia.

Greece has 80,000 heroin users and is a major transshipment point into Europe from Turkey, by road, sea and air.

Bulgaria's lax airport security allows cocaine smugglers access to Europe. It also a main route into Europe from Turkey for West Asian drugs.

Cyprus is an important meeting ground and money laundering center for the Russian mafyia. There are over 20,000 offshore companies, one-tenth of which are Russian. Its central, neutral location and business infrastructure make it the ideal meeting place for drug deals, payoffs and discussions.

The Balkans

The well-maintained roads and compliant customs officials of the former Yugoslavia were the home leg of the long road from the poppy fields of Asia. The war messed up this convenient leg and now most heroin is smuggled through Albania, Macedonia and Bulgaria. About 70 percent of the heroin is smuggled under the direction of the Albanian mafia to customers in Germany and Switzerland. They are bosom buddies with the Italian mafia. The Albanian mafia is comprised primarily of the Kosovar clan. Heroin is also processed in Albania by the mafia to increase profits.

Albania is a mess with the mafia being a stronger force than the government itself. Criminals control most major ports and entry areas, making it a free trade zone for drugs. Cannabis and poppies are also grown domestically. Albanians from the Kosova region are the main smugglers, delivering their wares to retailers in Italy, Turkey and along the Mediterranean.

Trans-Caucasus

The rough-and-ready base of Europe is a natural conduit for anything coming from the foggy mountains of Chechnya, Georgia and other small states.

Chechnya allegedly paid for its revolution primarily with drug funds. The Chechen *mafyia* backed the original war and provided inside military information from corrupt Russian intelligence officers and a flow of weapons or cash. The *mafyia* was able to move heroin from Afghanistan through Iran and Turkmenistan and on up into Moscow and then Europe through Georgia. The Russian military shipped heroin and hash using the Baku-Grozny-Rostov line. The Chechens raided over 559 trains in 1993, looting 4,000 cars and stealing 11.5 billion rubles worth of legal cargo. It is not known how much drugs were taken. There is a nasty rumor that when Dudayev unsuccessfully demanded a higher cut of drug monies from Defense Minister Pavel Grachev, he began to execute train conductors and confiscate all the drugs, prompting Grachev to invade Chechnya.

Armenia is one stop for hashish and opium from Afghanistan on its way to Europe. There are also around 10,000 drug addicts.

Azerbaijan is another rest stop for smugglers from Central Asia, Iran and Afghanistan on their way to Russia or Europe. The drug trade is well entrenched, with the main one being the route from Iran up to Russia and the Baltic states. There is a little side action smuggling drugs into Georgia.

Colombia

Colombia is the world's leading producer and distributor of cocaine, according to the DEA. It is the world's second largest producer of coca after Peru. In 1999 cocaine production was up 28 percent. Business is booming, despite the $300 million Colombia will get from the United States to fight drugs.

Colombia is also a major supplier of heroin and marijuana to the Mexican mafia. In the early '70s, Colombia started out primarily as a grower of pot, with cocaine being a small part of the then $500 million a year export. Pot was mostly cultivated along the Atlantic coast. Today, it is estimated that Colombia's drug industry pockets about $3 billion a year in profits from the drug trade. All this occurs under the protection of the three rebel groups. The ELN generate an estimated $348 million in income linked to drugs through protection of growers, shippers and labs. FARC makes $900 million in protection money for drug growers. The Colombian cartels in conjunction with their Mexican and Cuban distributors have a lock on 75 percent of the world's cocaine, and about 80 percent of the toot goes to Uncle Sam. The DEA figures drug sales pump between $3–5 billion into the Colombian economy, making it the country's biggest export earner. To get an idea of what a narco government is, you have to understand that the entire gross domestic product of Colombia is only $5 billion.

Most coca is grown on 8–20 acre farms. The Colombian farmers get in 3–4 harvests a year. Some farmers are taking the next step and creating coca paste, which sells for about $1,100 per kilo. Most of the 135,000 acres of coca farms in Colombia are in the far south. It is estimated that there are 35,000 farmers in the business of growing coca and poppies. Only about 7,000 families have switched to legal crops in the last two years.

Colombia has 196,000 under cultivation for coca, 2,180 of opium poppy and 5,000 hectares of marijuana under cultivation. Cocaine base is also flown into Colombia for processing via aircraft from Bolivia and Peru. Colombia's 80 metric tons of cocaine and 6.5 tons of heroin is then flown or shipped out to Mexico, Central America and the Caribbean. Ecuador, Venezuela, Paraguay and Haiti are also transshipment points and money laundering centers.

Thailand

Thailand's position in the Golden Triangle is more geographic than economic. It is a net importer of hard drugs and is a major transit route to Western countries. About 50 percent of the opium that enters Thailand from Myanmar heads for the United States. The Thai opium crop is 25 metric tons and is under constant threat by government eradication programs and tough border controls with its northern bad boy neighbor Myanmar. Still, the mule trains get through the rough terrain and insurgents keep the Thai soldiers from truly policing or sealing off the area.

Myanmar

Just under 70 percent of the world's heroin and 60 percent of heroin seized by U.S. law enforcement came from the Golden Triangle. The Golden Triangle is not really a geographic triangle but a loosely U.S.-defined area that covers eastern Myanmar, northern Laos and scattered parts of northern Thailand. The common elements are remoteness and inaccessibility, lack of law enforcement and the right altitude and climate to permit the cultivation of poppies. It may be more accurate to describe the Golden Triangle as just Myanmar.

Visitors to this area will find the locals decidedly reserved and openly belligerent if pressed for details on their trade. The U.S. State Department estimates that Myanmar exports about 2,300 tons of raw opium a year, primarily from the Kachin and north Shan states. Laos moves about 300 tons and Thailand about 30 tons. Currently there is no anti-drug program and even the most visible drug smuggler in the world, Khun Sa, has retired in luxury to Yangon. In fact, the term warlord or drug czar has been replaced by the SLORC with a new title— Leader of National Races—and includes: U Sai Lin aka; Lin Ming-shing of the Eastern Shan State Army (ESSA); Yang Mao-liang, Peng Chia-sheng, and Liu Go-shi of the Myanmar National Democratic Alliance Army (MNDAA-Kokang Chinese); Pao Yu-chiang, Li Tzu-ju, and Wei Hsueh-kang of the United Wa State Army (UWSA); and U Mahtu Naw of the Kachin Defense Army (KDA). All have been fingered by the U.S. government as the men who put the monkeys on the junkies.

For now, the SLORCies are proud of the capture of a ridiculous 100 kilograms of heroin as proof that they are "just saying no" to drugs in Myanmar.

The United Wa Army

Back in 1989, the SLORC generals cracked down on Khun Sa. They overran his base in Ho Mong and subjected him to a list of horrors they felt Myanmar's smack daddy deserved: A mock trial, house arrest, no extradition, a job running the bus system, a nice house to stay arrested in, great medical care, around-the-clock bodyguards and only one round of golf on the Yangon links each week. Despite this cruel and unusual punishment and SLORC's clear message to all aspiring drug lords, the heroin trade still continues in the north.

Today, Khun Sa's Doi Land and Huay Makekahm heroin factories are humming along (they "crank" out 140 kilograms of smack every month) under new ownership, the opium crop is up 10 percent and life is good for the United Wa Army.

The Wa Army is led by two men, former Commie Chao Nyi-Lai and Wei Hsueh-Kang, who operate out of the town of Pan Hsang in the easternmost corner of Myanmar. The Wei Siao brothers, Gang and Long, are supposed to be the majordomos of drug dealing (Gang is wanted in the United States for drug trafficking) after Tei Kung Ming was offed in China. In any case, the Wa boys and the United Wa State Army (an army of between 15,000 to 35,000 men) are in charge. They were trained well since they once provided raw opium to Khun Sa. The two leaders have political ambitions and claim that they want to shift the Wa people into legitimate crops once they have representation within the country of Myanmar. (Probably as soon as Joe Namath plays for the Jets again.) Opium production was up 10 percent in 1996 and instead of one big centralized, high-visibility operation (The big K's downfall) the opium business under the Wa is broken into smaller, more numerous processors.

A third group led by Ai Hsiao-shih and Wei Hseuh-kang specializes in the transportation of raw and processed heroin into China and Thailand.

The Wa and the Shan—or more accurately, the former Khun-Sa factions and Nyi-Lai/ Hsueh-kang—account for 75 percent of the opium leaving thc Golden Triangle. Most of Myanmar's opium is transported in pony caravans along simple trails into China's Yunnan province and eventually to the drug syndicates in Hong Kong, or it moves south through Chiang Mai in northern Thailand down to Bangkok. Once the pony caravans reach minor towns, the heroin is then trucked to major cities, from where it is shipped or flown to the United States or Mexico.

A third route is from Moulmein in southern Burma into Bangkok and, surprisingly, into Malaysia and Singapore. Malaysia and Singapore widely publicize their imposition of a mandatory death penalty for drug smuggling, while also serving as major centers for the export of drugs.

Singapore Swing

Pop quiz: What country has the most executions per million residents? Time's up. Singapore. A happy clean place where one person is executed every nine days on average...and those are the executions they tell us about. Amnesty International figures about 40 people a year have done the rope dance since 1994. Almost all were being punished for drug offenses. They have a long way to go to catch up to China's average of 5 executions a day, but they're trying.

For now the Wa are big wheels in the opium trade. There are plans afoot to turn Khun Sa's big white house into a museum.

Bangladesh, with its harbors and airports, is a growing transshipment point. For now, the country is trying to crack down on the use of phensidyl, a codeine-based cough syrup in vogue with Bangladeshis.

India is a legal producer of opium (in the states of Madhya, Pradesh, Rajasthan and Uttar Pradesh) for medical purposes and is strategically situated between the Golden Crescent to the west and the Golden Triangle to the east. It also supplies processing chemicals to all major drug processing groups. The also produce methaqualone for sale in southern and eastern Africa.

The Hill Tribes

The real dirty work is taken care of by the region's poor but industrious hill tribes. Poppies in the Golden Triangle are grown and harvested by the Lahu, Lisu, Nfien and Hmong tribes, and cultivated among less odious but less profitable crops like maize. Since smart farmers maximize the use of their land and labor, it's not surprising that the annual opium production has tripled in Myanmar in the last ten years. Depending on which drug lord's auspices the farmer falls under, the raw product is sent to processing labs either along the Chinese border (Wa) or along the Thai border (Shan).

The Mong Tai Army

As broken as the surrounding topography, the Mong Tai (Shan State) Army, once led by the now retired Chang Chi Fu aka Khun Sa (Prince of Prosperity) disintegrated into factions in mid-1995 as the drug warlord cut a deal with Myanmar's ruling SLORC. Khun Sa, 63, now lives in Yangon in comfortable retirement. The USDEA was doing backflips when the Kmart of heroin shut down. In August of 1996, street prices for heroin shot up ten times their normal level as supplies disappeared down junkies' veins. For one brief shining moment it looked like the generals had been visited by the do-good fairy. The former headquarters at Ho Mong, nine miles from the Thai border, became a shell of its former glory with the population dwindling to less than 4,000. compared to 18,000 in its heyday. But within the Wa, the new "Wa"-Mart of heroin filled Khun Sa's shoes.

DRUGS

Mexico

Mexico continues to be the financial and transshipment choice of South American drug cartels due to its lax banking laws, corrupt officials and its "don't ask, don't tell" policy of the military and government. The drug business in Mexico is sliced into three cartels; the Tijuana, Juarez and the Gulf. The Tijuana cartel under the Feliz brothers smuggles primarily heroin and majijuana, The Gulf cartel is the coca express and Amada Carrillo Fuentes' group (before he liposuctioned himself to death) used to cover transborder shipments from El Paso to Brownsville. In many cases, the cartels have cut out the beleaguered Colombian middlemen and go right to the source for the coca paste.

Cocaine is smuggled in from South America in large, multiengine cargo jets and large cargo ships. Corrupt customs officials drive new Chevy Suburbans and the ruling class in Acapulco and Tijuana could outbid Bill Gates at any poker game. The downside is that Mexico's border population is coming down with a jones for their product and the U.S. government is losing patience with our biggest narco neighbor.

Belize, Costa Rica, El Salvador, Nicaragua, Guatemala and Honduras are major land, air and sea transshipment routes for Colombian drugs entering Mexico. Mexico snaps up about 50–70 percent of all cocaine from South America. Mexico's corrupt government and long border with the United States make it an ideal entry point for drugs and a major money laundering center.

Mexico produces about 80 percent of the marijuana, 20–30 percent of the heroin and a growing amount of methamphetamines.

Panama

The Darien region of Panama is a hot spot for coca cultivation for the Colombian drug czars. Local Indians are goaded into cultivating crops under the watchful protection of Colombian guerrillas. Recently, officials destroyed more than five tons of cocaine, broke up six coca paste labs and burned down 200 acres of a coca plantation. Still, Panama retains its reputation as an ideal shipment point for drugs and is a major center for laundering drug money.

Peru

Coca is Peru's second largest crop (after maize), with 930 square miles under cultivation. The major areas are the Huallaya Valley and the Apurimac-Enc Valley east of Lima. The 115,300 hectares of coca leaf (60 percent of the world's total coca crop) under cultivation is worth 40–50¢ a kilo (down from $3 in 1994). The drugs are grown by peasants who sell to shippers and processors under the control of the Shining Path, and oddly, enough the Peruvian military.

Russia

Russia's geographical position makes it a major drug producing, shipping and consumption center. Its neighbors make good use of the corrupt and inefficient police and border guards. The Russians quickly motorized the business and Russian Generals made millions sending drugs back to Russia in lead-lined coffins. The trade in Tajikistan sends Tajik agents bearing Russian military supplies—blankets, food, guns, shoes, etc., into Afghanistan. An Afghan dealer swaps the material for drugs and then the Russian soldiers make a one million ruble payment to the border guards. The soldiers then ship the drugs directly into Russia's major cities by military transport (air, rail or road) which is not subject to inspection. The favored route is from Tajikistan Krasnovodsk, Baku, Grozny to Rostov and then on to Europe through Estonia. Defense Minister Pachel Grachev is nicknamed Pasha Mercedes for his high lifestyle and his reputed income from drugs.

Drugs from the Golden Crescent (Pakistan, Afghanistan and Iran) are transported to major centers like Tashkent in Uzbekistan, or through the states of Chechnya, Tajikistan, Georgia and Azerbaijan. There are also major growing areas in southern Russia and the western Ukraine, as well as the states of Uzbekistan, Kazakhstan and Krygyzstan. The presence of foreign troops during the Balkan War has disrupted the once traditional smuggling routes into Europe, which are being replaced by Afghanistan to Tajikistan to St. Petersburg to Cyprus, and then out through ports on the Baltic Sea and Mediterranean.

Russian officials estimate there are about 5.7 million drug users in Russia, with hashish being the drug of choice. A UN report says there may be 100,000 opium poppy fields and more than 2.5 million acres of marijuana under cultivation within the country. Drug-related crime is up 15 percent and 23 tons of drugs were seized in raids last year. About 80 percent of drug dealers arrested in Moscow are Azerbaijanis; the rest are Chechens. Moscow banks are becoming popular with out-of-town drug dealers like the Sicilian mafia and the Colombian cartels to launder money. The total drug business adds up to an unimpressive US$25 million (compared to our US$500 billion narcotics industry). A kilo of hash in Russia goes for as little as US$15, compared to US$200 in Europe. Accordingly, the profit-savvy and brutal Russian gangs are also expanding into Europe and the United States.

Those drugs that don't end up in Moscow or St. Petersburg go through to the Baltics, where eager Scandinavian and Lowlands customers await.

Africa

Africa is not a major consumer of drugs, but it is an important transshipment point. South Africa is a growing consumer of drugs.

Egypt has large opium and marijuana plantations in the remote valleys of the Sinai Peninsula. The flow of cash from the drug trade is supposed to have made the drug cartels' assets an estimated $15 to $60 billion. It is also a transshipment point for Asian heroin on its way to Europe and the United States. Its control of the Suez Canal allow large cargo shipments from the Indian Ocean into the Mediterranean.

Morocco is a supplier to Europe, with 74,000 hectares of marijuana under cultivation.

Nigeria grows cannabis but is known primarily for its courier business. Nigerians supplies South American cocaine and Asian heroin to the United States and Europe. Interpol considers Nigeria the third largest heroin smuggling area in the world. Nigerians also recruit non-Nigerians for the risky business as well. It costs about $5,000 to get five keys of heroin past Nigerian customers inspectors.

South Africa is also a transshipment point for cocaine and heroin and is one of the largest producers of weed, primarily for its own consumption.

East African ports and airports are a transit point for Pakistani couriers as well as sea and air shipments. Often Nigerian couriers will fly into Nairobi to pick up shipments then fly into Europe or the United States. Kenya deals primarily in hashish from Pakistan and heroin from Asia. It is also the major producer of khat, a mild narcotic favored by Yemenis and Somalis.

Yemen is a transit country for hard drugs and consumers of them.

Zambia is a major transit point for methaqualone destined for South Africa.

Zimbabwe grows and exports marijuana to Europe and transships cocaine from South America and methaqualone from India to South Africa.

The Drugstore

It helps to know what you are dealing with if you are going to be in nasty places. *DP* does not endorse the use of drugs since we have a hard enough time staying alive stone-cold straight. A web address is included to provide a variety of sources, but many provide descriptions of all the drugs. It does not imply an endorsement or correctness of the information, just a potpourri of opinions and facts.

Opium

Opium has been used to kill pain, cure diarrhea and even as a social drug since 300 B.C. Today, the legal use of opium is mainly to create morphine and codeine for medicinal purposes. Worldwide, there were an estimated 4,000 metric tons of the stuff in 1995, double the amount produced in 1986.

http://www.pbs.org/wgbh/pages/frontline/shows/heroin/etc/history.html

Heroin

Heroin (from the Greek root, meaning "hero") is the most refined by-product of the opium poppy and causes a sense of power, creates a feeling of euphoria, relieves pain and induces sleep. Heroin has only been around since 1874 and was originally used for medicinal purposes without knowledge of its addictive properties. Today, 65 percent of the world's heroin supply comes from Myanmar, with Laos second. Northern Thailand barely hits the radar screen as a poppy grower. The U.S. government has vacillated between encouraging the production of heroin (as it did in its support of Laotian rebels during the Vietnam War) and condemning it (through its covert military ops in Thailand aimed at stemming the heroin tide washing up on the shores of New York City).

Even in its heavily cut street form (nickel bags diluted with sugar, starch, powdered milk or quinine to less than 10 percent purity), it is highly addictive, and its victims require larger and larger doses and more direct methods of ingestion to deliver a high. In New York City, the street price for a gram of 90 percent pure heroin is about $100, and a nickel bag goes for about $10; its dearth of purity means junkies can snort it instead of having to inject it. Some estimates tag the heroin trade as a US$4 to 10 billion a year business. There are about 600,000 users; half of them are concentrated in New York City. Heroin is becoming more popular; there was a 50 percent increase in heroin-induced overdoses as tracked by ER rooms in a half-year period in the United States.

http://www.health.org/pubs/qdocs/heroin/doaher.htm

Methamphetamine

Meth, crank, or crystal was invented by the Japanese in 1893. The drug also contains ephedrine, found in over-the-counter cold prescriptions. Today it is a homemade drug popular with bikers, truckers and kids. Japan has 600,000 meth heads or tweakers on what they call "shabu." The Philippines is a transit point for crystal meth from China, Hong Kong and Taiwan on its way to local tweakers and into the United States via Guam and Hawaii. Ice, as it is commonly called, is cyrstallized, orderless and smokable. It first appeared in Hawaii in 1989 and came from South Korea, Taiwan and the Philippines. The symptoms are fast and intense euphoria with alertnesss for 8–24 hours. Coming down also includes paranoia, depression, convulsions, hallucinations, aggressive behavior and fatal kidney failure. It is not uncommon to meet serious tweakers in a zombie, sleepless state.

Primarily a cheap, working-class drug, meth can be cooked up at home and can turn a twentyfold profit . . . if you don't blow yourself up in the process of cooking it. Crank got its name when bikers smuggled the powder in the crankcases of their Harley Davidsons.

http://www.nida.nih.gov/Infofax/methamphetamine.html

Morphine

Morphine is bitter to the taste, darkens with age and is derived from opium (at a strength of between 4 and 21 percent). Most of its addicts are former soldiers who were treated with morphine as a painkiller after being wounded in combat.

http://www.bu.edu/cohis/subsabse/morphine/morphine.htm

Codeine

Codeine (0.7 to 2.5 percent concentration of opium) is an alkaloid by-product of the poppy and is found in a variety of patent medicines around the world. In the United States, codeine is only available in prescribed medications. However, these same medicines (i.e., Tylenol with codeine) can be had over the counter in many countries, particularly in Central and South America and Southeast Asia.

http://www.rxlist.com/cgi/generic/acetcod.htm

Cocaine

Cocaine is a bitter crystalline alkaloid obtained from coca leaves. It creates a euphoric effect in users as well as a compulsive psychological need. It has limited medical applications as a local anesthetic agent. It is readily absorbed by the mucous membranes lining the nose and throat. Crack is a derivative of cocaine.

http://nepenthes.lycaeum.org/Drugs/Cocaine/

Marijuana

Mary Jane, grass, weed, or pot is a drug derived from *cannabis sativa,* a tall, leafy plant that is easily cultivated. The chemical that causes the high in pot is THC, or delta 9-tetrahydrocannabinol. More than 400 other chemicals are found in the cannabis plant. Marijuana is usually smoked in loosely rolled cigarettes and is considered a social drug consumed at parties or at home. There are many varieties, with the effects dependent on the amount of THC in the plant. Due to better strains of the plant being cultivated, the marijuana sold today is estimated to be 10 times stronger than the weed sold in the 1970s.

The effect of marijuana varies with the user, but typically results in a faster heart rate, bloodshot eyes and dry throat and mouth. Marijuana can cause acute panic, memory loss and a lack of motivation. Proponents of its use praise its medicinal effects, enhancement of mental powers and increased sensitivity, especially during sex. Others experience drowsiness, giddiness and stupor.

http://www2.druginfo.org/orgs/dsi/Marijuana/MarijuanaMenu.html

Hashish

Hash is derived from the resin of hemp plants. It is stronger than marijuana and can contain up to 50 percent pure THC. It is usually smoked in a pipe or smoked inserted into regular cigarettes. THC is a chemical that usually contains PCP.

http://www.hashish.net/

PCP

PCP, or phencyclidine (also called angel dust), was originally developed as an anesthetic in the 1950s. Today it is illegal, but it is easily manufactured. PCP acts as a stimulant and can stretch time, numb pain centers, and slow body movements. Some users have a sense of power and strength. Overdoses can create violent behavior, which may lead to rash acts when the victim feels invincible (jumping from high places, drownings, car accidents). Heavy users can develop symptoms of paranoia, fearfulness and anxiety.

http://www.arf.org/isd/pim/pcp.html

LSD

LSD is manufactured from lysergic acid, which is a common fungus typically found in grains or bread. LSD was discovered in 1938 and is odorless, tasteless and colorless. It is often in liquid or tab form. Hallucinogenics create a rush of unusual emotions, visions, experiences and sensations. They also increase heart rate, dilate pupils, and increase body temperature and blood pressure. Use of hallucinogens may unmask or exacerbate emotional problems. In some cases, LSD is cut with other drugs to change the high.

http://www.freespeech.org/drugs/

Mescaline

Mescaline comes from the peyote cactus, and its effects are similar to those of LSD, though less extreme. It is usually smoked or swallowed in pill form.

http://nepenthes.lycaeum.org/Drugs/Mescaline/

Psilocybin/Mushrooms

Psilocybin is a hallucinogen found in mushrooms. It is taken in its raw form (mushrooms) or in a powdered tablet.

http://www.erowid.org/plants/mushrooms/mushrooms.shtml

"Khat's Fancy"

Although most countries outlaw the chewing of khat, a mildly stimulating drug, it is still legal in hot, dusty Yemen. It is estimated that half of Yemen's population is moderately drugged for at least part of the day. Khat, or qat, costs about US$3 for a day's hit and is chewed mostly by men. It is issued to soldiers to reduce tension and anxiety. It can also diminish sexual potency, as well as create loss of appetite or gastritis, inflammation of the gums, and quirky side effects. One of the side effects is the perception that the user can regale people with long speeches and stories. They seem inspirational and fascinating to the user, but sound ridiculous to the listener. Khat is a social drug, usually chewed in the afternoon or evening. It is not known to be addictive, but it may prevent users from falling asleep. The leaves of the plant are bitter and are left in the mouth like chewing tobacco and formed into a plug or ball.

Background on Illegal Drugs

U.S. State Department Bureau for International Narcotics and Law Enforcement Affairs (reports on individual countries)
http://www.state.gov/www/global/narcotics_law/1998_narc_report/major/major_countries.html

Ideas on Drug Control
http://csdp.org/edcs/

The DEA
http://www.usdoj.gov/dea/

Photos of Various Drugs
http://www.drugs.indiana.edu/prevention/deapics.html

World of Drugs (maps and statistics)
http://www.lec.org/WOD/

Legal Drugs

http://www.winsite.com/info/pc/win95/demo/powerl98.exe/health_m/drugs.htm
http://www.drugs.com/

DRUGS

Getting Arrested

Oh Won't You Stay...Just a Little Bit Longer

There's a scent of what the hell in the air. Smiling, slovenly cops are chatting up girls, street vendors urge the local weed on you, you only have a few days left and you've been told great and bold stories about the local intoxicants. Anyway, what are you going to do with that bundle of grubby guidos when you get home. You roll off half your wad to the smiling beach boy and you are the proud owner of the island's finest herb. Throwing caution to the wind, you invite the local lasses to your $5-a-night fleabag. As if on cue fully dressed and not even halfway into the carnal depths you intend to plunge into, there is an urgent knock on the door. *"Policia, manos arriba. Tiene armas?"* They go straight to your stash on the dresser and you wonder how it happened so quickly, so cleanly. As you bump your head on the way out you see your beachboy friend with one of those shit-eating grins. Damn.

There are an average of 6,000 Americans arrested in 90 different countries each year according to the State Department. About 1,500 are doing time in foreign jails. The majority (about 70 percent) of the cases are drug related. Mexico and Jamaica are responsible for the bulk of the drug-related incarcerations, filing 72 percent of all drug charges against Americans traveling abroad.

The top five destinations for Americans seeking free room and board are Mexico, Germany, Canada, Jamaica and Great Britain. Last year, Mexico had 525 gringos on ice and had arrested 768 that year. Fifty-five of those weren't happy campers and filed complaints of mistreatment. The Mexican judicial system is based on Roman and Napoleonic law and presumes a person accused of a crime is guilty until proven innocent. There is no trial by jury. Trial under the Mexican system is a prolonged process based largely on documents examined on a fixed date in court by prosecution and defense counsel. Sentencing usually takes 6 to 10 months. Bail can be granted after sentencing if the sentence is less than five years. Pretrial bail exists but is never granted when the possible sentence is greater than five years.

Even those folks have it good. In places like Malaysia and Singapore, move dope and die. Zero tolerance. Deal dope and you'll get the rope. Getting beaten up in a Mexican jail may be inconvenient, but at least the *federales* are trying to teach you a lesson, one you might learn from in later life. In Southeast Asia, there is no later life.

Here are a few survival tips (at the risk of sounding like your mother) for those who don't want to die as a skinny, frazzled, psychotic wimp in a Pakistani jail:

Have nothing to do with drugs or the drug culture.

Those pleasant men in pressed uniforms are employed for a single purpose—to find your drugs. Once they've found them, make no mistake, you will be busted. Once you're tried (if you ever are), you will be going away for a long time. And then it will take a lot of money to get you out. A lot of it. And you'll look different, too. Not good.

Do not take anything illegal through customs, or anything that doesn't belong to you.

Do not be an unwitting mule and carry a package for a friend. Do not think you can sneak a few joints through. Customs officers live by two words: How much? How much is it going to cost you to get out of this mess? How much time are you going to do? How much will it cost to repatriate your remains?

Be careful with unmarked drugs.

Combining drugs or putting prescription drugs into reminder boxes may create questions of legality. Your personal appearance, the quantity of the drugs and the general demeanor of your inquisitor will determine if you are let off.

Avoid driving.

Car accidents are a great way to go to jail. In many countries, the Napoleonic code of justice is utilized. In other words, by law, you are guilty until proven innocent. For instance, if someone smacks into your car in Mexico, you'll go to jail. No witnesses and it may be a long time. Hire a driver and you're off the hook.

Be judicious in your enthusiasm to photograph military or government facilities.

Soldiers in Africa love camera equipment. If you want it back, you'll have to pay a fine. In most of the former Soviet republics, you will be arrested for taking pictures of army bases or airports. We have spent plenty of time fast-talking our way out of jail simply for carrying cameras in countries that demand you have national and regional permits to carry them.

Get the right kind of help.

The U.S. embassy will not lift a finger to get you out of jail. They may assist you, but if you have broken the law in that country, you are expected to do the time. Many countries will assume you are guilty and hold you until trial. It may take an extraordinary amount of time for your case to go to trial, and you may even be required to pay your room and board while in jail. Hire a local lawyer and explore all options for your release, including bribes and being smuggled out. Communicate your case to friends, and tell them to contact journalists in the local and national media. If you really did something stupid and you don't have any money, be prepared for the worst.

Resources

Getting Arrested
http://travel.state.gov/arrest.html

In a Dangerous Place: Mali

C'est l'Afrique

Paris, France—The next morning at the airport was pandemonium. Africans everywhere waving crumpled tickets, brightly dressed women chattering too loudly surrounded by acres of crisp shopping bags. All with Parisian designer logos that contrast with their African block print dresses. Men in expensive suits with huge tribal scars, mountains of luggage in bursting cardboard boxes and metal "caisses" or coffin-sized steel boxes sealed with large brass Chinese-made locks.

Like East Indians with monstrous pastel vinyl suitcases or Asians with their twine-wrapped cardboard boxes, Africans have their metal cases. Not one metal case but stacks of huge military-looking caskets with giant padlocks covered with first class stickers. They contain the fruits of kleptocracy, a unique right of the robber rulers of Africa who brutally divert foreign income like damming off a stream.

I have never been to Africa but I am already learning the class distinctions—the quiet Africans who talk with me while they wait and the noisy garrulous thieves who treat the stewardesses as overpaid waitresses.

The UTA DC-10 traverses the Strait of Gibraltar in seconds. From the French Riviera, over the land of the Moors and descending into the Dark Continent.

The plane descends through the milky haze that shrouds the Sahel. Slowly, faintly as in a dream, the brown landscape begins to rise toward me. Widely spaced, painfully torn trees tied together with thousands of meandering tracks are the only sign of habitation. Then small clusters of brown dots begin to appear. These are the round mud and grass huts of the Bambara. I have never seen a landscape so primitive and exciting.

It begins to hit me as I look past the shiny aluminum wing to the crude huts that this is why I came to Africa. In a microcosm I understand the problem of Africa. This 450 mph, $10 million aircraft has to land on a flyspeck of broken asphalt in the middle of goats and arid nothingness. I have not come from another country but from another planet.

This, truly, is how the first aliens will appear to Westerners: gleaming, streamlined perfection landing just long enough to disgorge its sweaty, disorientated passengers into the heat, red dirt and filth. Above, the silver bird is a massive white triangular thundercloud above the ochre runway. I stop, turn and take a picture.

I am arrested before I can even walk across the hot tarmac to the terminal. Two angry uniformed soldiers run from the terminal and hold me fast.

One of the soldiers roughly grabs for my camera and I hold it away from them. One wags his finger in my face. They smell bad and are not using enough force to convince me to fight back. I am in trouble.

The French UTA ground crew see the commotion and came to my aid. They intervene and use hand motions behind their back to tell me to cool it while they carry on an animated conversation in French with the soldiers. "It is forbidden to take pictures of the airport." This crime is apparently clearly marked inside the terminal that I have yet to enter. The white jump-suited crew asked me if I was taking pictures of the airport, as if to give me an opportunity to say no. I quickly say that I was taking pictures of the giant thunderhead above the plane. A crew member's eyebrow arches. The game is on. They discuss this point in the ongoing shouting match.

Thankfully, Africans are social people even in their suspicion and brutality, and this new interpretation of my crime provokes more heated discussion. This is the first of many times I will be arrested in Africa, but there is no clear resolution to my crime yet. To anger the ground crew is not the goal of my arrest. They expect a direct form of economic penitence from me before I even enter the country. Later, I notice that there are booths to strip-search visitors entering the country.

The pilot of the UTA plane has opened the cockpit window and yells down to see what the commotion is about. I wave at the pilot as if we are old friends. A thought occurs. I explain that I misspoke my bad French. I now correct my confession to say what I meant to say was that I was taking a picture of the pilot, not the plane or the airport. This slows down my captors. We all agree that the pilot is technically not the airport. This new wrinkle and the support of the pilot and crew is gaining me the upper hand. Arresting me would now result in more than a backroom interrogation and search. A deal is finally struck. They frogmarch me up the boarding ladder and into the cockpit. The ground crew scoots ahead to prep the pilot. The pilot greets me with a broad smile and asks why they are arresting this poor fellow for taking his picture. Handshakes and apologies all around. As the soldiers leave, the pilot laughs, shrugs and says "C'est l'Afrique."

—**RYP**

Guns

Itty-Bitty Bang Bang

If you travel to dangerous places you will meet a lot of people with guns. A lot of them tend to be short, under 15 and with that weird, too much real life Doom-or-Quake look that makes you sweat. You didn't like guns to start with, but what do you do when the guy holding it uses it as a pointer at about testicle height? Just relax.

You should know what guns can and cannot do. You should never carry or use a gun in a war zone. You should also know that tension and intimidation are what guns are all about. You are better off respecting guns and acquiescing to their intended role than trying to do a not-quite-as-smooth, Mel Gibson, slap-it-out-of-hand trick to impress your driver.

Television is not a good role model for those who want to learn about guns. On TV, puny handguns fire off hundreds of rounds without reloading, and bullets seem lethally attracted to bad guys. In reality, guns are rather simple and deadly. Imagine throwing a pea-size pebble at someone. Now imagine using a slingshot, projecting that pea-size objective at 1,200 feet per second. Ouch. Bullets are just heavy projectiles that puncture flesh, bounce off and shatter bone and turn people into trauma cases more efficiently than a club.

GUNS

There are more than 200 million guns in the United States. It is estimated that firearm injuries in the States cost about $20 billion in medical costs and lost wages. Firearms send almost 40,000 Americans to their graves each year (19,000 Americans use guns to commit suicide each year, another 18,500 are murdered with a gun, and at least 1,500 more are accidentally shot to death). Gun-related homicides rose 18 percent in the last decade—30 percent among people ages 15 to 24.

The most dangerous handheld weapons are rifles. Handguns require short ranges and careful aim to be lethal. Handguns tend to be the weapons of choice for domestic violence and robberies. Most handguns lose any effectiveness after 25 yards. In fact, the Western movies where men bang away from across the street without hitting anyone are not too far from reality.

Happy Fire

In Los Angeles, 39 people have been killed from bullets fired into the air during Independence Day and New Years Eve shooting. Bullets come down with a velocity of 300 to 500 feet per second. A gun can fire a bullet at 2,700 fps, travel two miles up, and then after a minute land miles or feet away depending on the angle. 77 percent of the victims are hit in the head resulting in a 32 percent mortality rate, according to a study done King Drew Medical Center. Bullets usually fall base first. A velocity of 100 fps will penetrate skin, but 200 fps will break bone and penetrate the skull. There are about 600 to 700 reported incidents of happy fire on New Year's Eve in L.A.

On the other hand, if someone is shooting a rifle at you, you will probably end up dead.

Up until the 1850s, soldiers used muskets. They were smoothbore, and long barreled (about 4–5 feet in length) and could kill a man at 100 meters. Maybe. Loading slowed down the killing process to about eight shots a minute.

In 1855, the Crimean War introduced the Minie Ball, a major advance that pushed the killing range out to 600 yards. By spinning a hollow cavity lead bullet down a rifled barrel, the rifle was born. The French invention meant that armies could now battle without the standard volley, advance and hand-to-hand combat. Armies were slow to adapt the deadly new minié ball, and the Civil War saw armies facing each other 50 to 100 yards apart, firing at point-blank range and then charging with bayonets. In the Civil War 15% or 234,000 men died from Minie Ball bullets.

The next big advances were in the late 1800s, when breech-loading weapons like the Mauser rifle and metal-cased bullets were introduced. The next step was the 1903 Springfield rifle and the later 1917 Enfield. These rifles were deadly out to 1,200 yards and could be loaded and fired quickly.

World War I trenches were typically spaced 300 to 1,200 feet apart and dictated rifle design. The ideal weapon was one that fired accurately, from rest, with a minimum of maintenance and training. The focus was on careful killing of fleeting targets. When fighting got close, bayonets and pistols were the choice. Machine guns were heavy and water-cooled and used for withering fire during assaults or attacks. In 1917 came the introduction of the first semiautomatic weapon that could fire 20 rounds as fast as the trigger could be pulled. The simple Pedersen-device modification to the 1903 Springfield rifle was ordered too late to make a difference in the Great War, but later changed the use of rifles in warfare.

World War II introduced the idea of rapid-fire, portable weapons that could intimidate rather than kill. The M1 Garand (designed by John C. Garand) was a semiautomatic, gas-operated rifle that could fire 30.06 cartridges in eight-round clips. Later, it would be found that the number of rounds fired for every person actually killed was 15,000 rounds, even though the range of engagement closed to half of the World War I distances. Heavy bolt-action rifles were still the infantry weapon of choice, but the Germans and Russians used machine guns and infantry attacks to good effect. The Germans were the first to create the Sturmgewehr (assault rifle), but the first successful version was the postwar Russian AK-47.

Assault weapons provide killing power out to about 600 meters, although battlefield results showed that 350 meters was the maximum practical range in combat. Most firefights occurred with opponents 200 to 300 yards apart. In nasty bush wars most fighting takes place at about 100 meters.

Do You Feel Lucky, Punk?

Twenty-three out of fifty states will issue a carry permit to law-abiding citizens. Twenty-three states do not regulate the open carrying of loaded guns in public. John Lott, author of More Guns, Less Crime, *says that for each year a concealed handgun law is in effect, murders drop an average of 3 percent, robberies by more than 2 percent, and rape by 2 percent.*

Between 1876 and 1885 in Dodge City, only 15 people died violent deaths. There was an average of only 1.5 killings per year. according the book Cattle Towns. *Guns were collected by the sheriff as cowpokes rode into town to get drunk.*

Vietnam and a host of other dirty bush wars introduced the ambush concept of very high rates of fire, light ammunition and firepower. Ammunition had to be light, weapons cheap and easy to fix, and general tactics dictated spraying thousands of rounds during short firefights. The number of rounds per kill tripled from World War II levels to a staggering 50,000 rounds for each kill. In Vietnam, the light and deadly M-16 became the overwhelming choice of ground troops.

The future of rifle design is anyone's guess. Everything from all-plastic intelligent aiming bullets to nonlethal ammunition is being developed. In the meantime, it seems to take a major war to change the face of battle and eventually the use of weapons.

Here's a quick primer on things that go bang:

Handguns

Small weapons with 2"–8" barrels designed for personal protection and intimidating people at close range. Typically, the number of bullets is between 5 to 20. Average is about 8 to 13. Lethal range is from up close to about 50 meters when fired at rest. In combat or tense, moving situations, they are deadly out to about 25 meters. Most people miss when they use handguns as a defensive weapon and hit people when they use them as offensive weapons. Consistent training, long barrel length and small caliber play a big part in attaining accuracy. Dale Towert gathers real-life information that shows caliber and bullet selection make a big difference. His tables show that .22s have a 21 to 34 percent chance of stopping people and .357 Magnums do a much better job at 68 to 98 percent. It all depends on your ammo, the range and most importantly where you shoot the perpetrator. Rifle calibers like .223 Remington and .308 Winchester deliver 93 to 100 percent. Twelve gauges hover at around 98 percent stopping-power effectiveness. Remember the classic words of Robert Ruark. "Use enough gun."

Rifles/Submachine Guns

Modern military rifles are usually fully automatic. They can be fired in single shots or on full automatic. Full automatic is the least accurate but most intimidating. If a soldier is careful when squeezing off single shots, he is probably trying to kill you. If soldiers are using full automatic (common at night and in attacks), it means you have scared the shit out of them or they are attacking. Sniper rifles are the world's most dangerous weapons, simply because they are only used to kill. Rifles are issued to most troops; however, bullets are sometimes not issued to some African troops (or Iraqis). Submachine guns like the MAC-10 and Uzi were designed for spraying fast bursts of pistol-sized (9 mm and smaller) bullets in close quarters. Assault rifles like the AK-47 and AK-74 have high burst rates but longer barrels and better accuracy. Most terrorist or liberation movements carry AK-47 assault rifles because they are cheap, easy to fix and accurate.

Most Asian and African soldiers tend to fire fast and aim high under stress. Middle Eastern and Central Asian countries like Afghanistan and Pakistan breed deadly shots, since they grow up using guns for hunting and engage in warfare at long distances. Jungle fighters like to spray bullets.

Machine guns hold about 20 to 70 bullets and go through them pretty quickly at full auto. An Uzi kicks out 600 rounds per minute but has a maximum clip of 40 rounds. About 10 bullets a second gives you exactly four seconds of looking good until you have to reload. Killing range can extend to 1,400 meters (over a mile with tripod-mounted sniper rifles with scopes) and are effective between 400 and 600 meters. Assault rifles (the ones with large clips and short barrels) are designed to kill between 20 and 200 meters.

http://www.dmoz.org/Recreation/Guns/Manufacturers/

AK-47 (Avtomat Kalishnikova Obrazets 1947g)

If there is one visual symbol or prop that symbolizes the Soviet/revolutionary influence, it is the unmistakable profile of the AK-47. Once it was the hammer and sickle; now it is the banana-shaped clip and pointed barrel of the world's most dangerous rifle.

These weapons are cheap (between $50 and $350), available around the world, rock-hard reliable, and in use from Afghanistan to Zimbabwe. It is estimated that there are about 30 to 50 million copies of the rugged rifle in existence. They can pour out 600 rounds a minute and are designed to be manufactured and repaired in primitive conditions. They use a chromed barrel and the only major defect is the loud click when you change firing rate.

In 1941, the 23-year-old tank commander Mikhail T. Kalishnikov was wounded in the battle of Bryansk by the German invaders. While recuperating, he listened to the complaints of Russian soldiers about their archaic bolt-action rifles. Kalishnikov made use of his downtime to copy the current German machine pistol. His pistol never made it into the arsenal of the Russian army, but in 1943 it got him an entry to compete with other Russian gun designers to create the first Soviet assault rifle. An assault rifle is designed to be light, possess high rates of fire, and do double-duty as an accurate defensive rifle.

His design was chosen based on its durability and simplicity. The AK-47 and variants thereof have been manufactured in 12 countries from Bulgaria to Yugoslavia. The AK-47 and the AKM (a simpler-to-make variant) are sighted in to about 1,000 meters, field-strip down to six parts, fire 30 rounds of the 7.62 x 39 mm cartridge and will deliver three-inch patterns at 25 meters. The rifle is accurate to about 200 meters when fired from the shoulder at rest, and accurate to about 50 yards fired from the hip. The newest version of the classic assault rifle is the AK-74 (adopted in 1974 by the Soviets), which uses a lighter but more accurate 5.45 x 39 mm cartridge.

Kalishnikov was born in the Siberian town of Izhevsk, west of the Ural mountains. Today, Izhevsk is home to Izhmash, a former major arms manufacturing company that exports hunting rifles under the name Kalishnikov Joint Stock Co.

Kalishnikov still designs hunting rifles and has never received a royalty for his innovative design, though he has received many medals for it.

http://www.ak-47.net

M-16

The M-16, or the civilian version called the AR-15, was introduced in 1965. By this time, the light and powerful AK-47 was the best weapon available. In Vietnam, the light and deadly M-16 suffered initially because of ammunition that caused fouling. And the lighter bullet was deflected by brush. After the problem was sorted out, it became the standard issue for all ground troops (replacing the M-14). The M-16 used a lighter (5.56) bullet compared to the Viet Cong 7.62 used in the AK-47. The M-16 round had just as much impact at 200 yards as the AK-47 round.

The M-16 lays down 700 rounds per minute with a muzzle velocity of 3250 feet per second. It comes with 20- or 30-round clips. With a weight of 6.6 pounds, it has been adopted by Asian armies as the weapon of choice.

http://www.colt.com/colt/

The G3

Heckler & Koch are known for high-precision German weapons. A relative newcomer to the arms trade, they were formed in 1949 by three partners; Seidel is the modest one. Originally, the postwar German army used old M-1 Garands and the FAL rifle. The G3 was adopted in 1959 and was the first entirely German designed and made rifle (based on the Spanish CETME). The G3 used the standard 7.62 x 51 NATO cartridge, and its accuracy and durability led it to being adopted by more than 50 other countries. The basic rifle design was made in everything from sniper to .22 caliber versions.

The ultimate H&K version is the PSG1, a $5,000 sniper version for military and police use.

http://www.hecklerkoch-usa.com/

The Uzi

The Uzi is the brainchild of Israeli designer Major Uziel Gal, borrowing heavily from Czech models 23 and 25. The Uzi is designed to spray a room with bullets or be used as an infantry weapon. The 9 mm version has a rate of fire of 10 bullets per second. The magazine inserts through the pistol grip, and the Uzi comes in 16"-long barrel or ultra-compact machine pistol size. The Uzi is also a favorite of the U.S. Secret Service because of its small size and high rate of fire. Originally designed for 9 mm NATO standard ammunition, the Uzi was manufactured in a more powerful .45-caliber format for the U.S. market. Magazines come in 20-, 25- and 32-round capacity (the .45-caliber version comes in a meager 16-round capacity).

http://www.vectorarms.com/indexframe.html

Medium-Range Weapons

When bullets just won't communicate how much you hate people, the military can whip out some other gizmos. Mortars look like tubes with legs on three plates. They are designed to throw shells short distances in a high trajectory. The soldier drops the hand-sized missile down the tube and it fires. When it lands, it spreads shrapnel in a 20- to 60-yard perimeter, depending on the shell. The only good thing about mortars is that you can tell where they come from and they tend to target specific areas.

Artillery is another matter. Artillery sends medium to large shells screaming in waves. The shells are used either to demoralize troops or create havoc before an attack. Artillery kills more people than bullets. If you come under artillery attack, it is not a good sign. You should try to change your travel plans in a direction other than toward the guns.

http://www.janes.com/defence/editors/jmvl99/jmvl99.html

Rockets (RPGs)

Those funny-looking green things on the end of long sticks are RPGs, or rocket propelled grenades. There are also LAWs, or light anti-tank weapons. Even the latest Russian T-90 tank can be taken out with a cheap RPG. LAWs and RPGs give significant range (for the classic guerrilla hit-and-run attack) and cause widespread damage in crowded troop convoys or Sunday Schools. RPGs are very much in vogue in Chechnya and West Africa because they were shipped in by the container and create mayhem for pennies. RPGs are used to attack small- to medium-sized groups of men, trucks and sometimes armored vehicles.

http://www.web.qx.net/warcat/milsf/grenadelauncher.com

Machine Guns

Machine guns were put to good use in the trenches of World War I, where a team of two men with a Maxim could mow down hundreds of attacking troops. The only limitation was how much ammunition they had and if the gun would jam due to the barrel overheating. Travelers will only see the big machine guns at checkpoints and on top of tanks and bunkers. They are used to pin down or decimate large groups of attacking soldiers. They are also mounted on the back of trucks in places like Somalia. Machine guns fire belt-fed ammunition (great for wearing in bandoliers and posing for bad guy pictures) and require a tripod (unless you are Arnold Schwarzenegger) for accuracy. They are loud and require someone to make sure the bullets are feeding properly. They are deadly out to 2,500 meters and can also fire armor-piercing bullets. If you are in an area that has a preponderance of these weapons, you can safely assume you are in an active war zone.

http://www.ffvollmer.com/machineguns.htm
http://www.army-technology.com/contractors/machine_guns/
http://www.guncite.com/gcfullau.html

Long-Range Weapons

Those of you who were lucky enough to see our $5 million cruise missiles go streaking overhead understand why war sucks. Today, there are so many exotic weapons delivery systems that they fill their own Jane's book. Travelers won't come across too many of these weapons, unless they are on the wrong side of Uncle Sam. Some groups, like the Chechens, the Afghans, and the Hutus, like to use Stinger surface-to-air missiles, but they are lethal and unexpected and there is no advice one can give on avoidance except take the train.

http://www.aero.com/catalogues/software/3081.htm
http://www.milnet.com/milnet/weapons.htm

Overnight Delivery, No Signature Required

The toy that gives the medal boys woodies these days is the Tomahawk AGM-86B, a 550 mph, flying "smart" bomb that can be launched from air, land or sea, be programmed onto a target and then deliver a variety of nasty surprises, including a 250 kiloton thermonuclear device. The Tomahawk is 219 inches long, has a 100-inch wingspan, weighs 2 tons, has a range of 1,553 miles, using a solid booster and then a turbojet engine. It was developed in 1972 and has climbed in price from $50,000 to around $2 million a copy. We used Tomahawks in Yugoslavia, Iraq, Afghanistan and Sudan because they perform our "don't ask, don't tell, shut up and roll the video" dirty work of Clintonesque warfare. We used cluster bombs in the camps in Afghanistan, graphite fibers to short out power lines in Serbia and 1,000-pound high explosives against hard targets in Iraq. Tomahawks are supposed to be accurate to within 30 feet using GPS (global positioning satellite), TERCOM or a special terrain way-point radar map and two types of terminal guidance systems: a high-resolution satellite radar image called DSMAC and an Infra-red mapper. The government says it has an 85 percent direct-hit rate. Uh huh, next question.

The Boeing cruise missile uses the same propulsion system but flies faster and smarter. Originally designed to deliver nuclear warheads, the agile cruise missile is now used to accurately deliver high explosives down bunker chimneys or through 3' x 3' windows . . . sometimes.

http://www.fas.org

Resources

DP is a firm believer of being trained and educated no matter what your opinions of guns are. Remember, it's the gun the other guy is holding that is the most dangerous. We do not carry weapons or engage in any hostilities but it's real nice to know what the range of an AK vs. a sniper rifle is. WARNING: Many of the companies do not deal with the public. Sales of weapons are regulated by state and federal law. These are listings for informational purposes.

Assault Rifles, Combat Shotguns (including Sniping Rifles) by John A. Norris $29.95 (ISBN 1-85753-214-7) Brassey's

Eagle Industries

400 Biltmore Drive, Suite 530S
Fenton, MO 63026
Tel.: (314) 343-7547
http://www.eagleindustries.com/
Makers of Mr. *DP*'s favorite pack, loadbearing vests and also other military, SWAT gear.

Knight's Armament Co.

7750 9th Street S.W.
Vero Beach, FL 32968
http://www.knightsarmament.com/
Manufacturer and designer of weapons systems including suppressed 50cal. sniper rifles.

Jonathan Arthur Ciener, Inc.

8700 Commerce Street
Cape Canaveral, FL 32920
Tel.: (407) 868-2200
Manufacturer of sound suppressed firearms and conversion kits.

AWC Systems Technology

P.O. Box 41938
Phoenix, AZ 85080
http://www.awcsystech.com
Manufacturer of sniper rifles and silenced weapons.

Sight Unseen

5444 Corteen Place
North Hollywood, CA 91607
Tel.: (818) 759-8059
Fax: (818) 763-4663
Manufacturers of the remote video sighting system that lets you shoot around corners.

Cheaper Than Dirt

2536 NE Loop 820
Fort Worth, TX 76106
Tel.: (817) 625-7557
Catalog of discounted sporting goods, ammo, holsters, night vision and even a cool night writing pen for $11.97.

GUNS

Brigade Quartermaster

1025 Cobb International Boulevard
Kennesaw, GA 30152
Tel.: (770)428-1248
http://www.actiongear.com
Safari, hunting shooting, and military wear.

TAPCO

P.O Box 2408
Kennesaw, GA 30144
Tel.: (800) 554-1445
http://www.tapco.com/
Hunting, military surplus, books and even bulletproof vests.

Training Courses

Tactical Firearms Training Team

16835 Algonquin Street, Suite 120
Huntington Beach, California 92649
Tel.: (714) 846-8065
http://www.nrawinningteam.com/tftt/

Glock, Inc. (law enforcement and military personnel training)

P.O. Box 369
Smyrna, GA 30081
Tel.: (404) 432-1202

Mas Ayoob's Lethal Force

P.O. Box 122
Concord, NH 03301
Tel.: (603) 224-6814
http://www.ayoob.com

Thunder Ranch

P.O. Box 53
Mountain Home, TX 78058
Tel.: (210) 640-3138
Fax: (210) 640-3183
http://www.thunderranchinc.com/

H&K International Training Division

21480 Pacific Boulevard
Sterling, VA 20166
Tel.: (703) 450-1900 #293

Yavapai Firearms Academy, Ltd.

P.O. Box 27290
Prescott Valley, AZ
Tel.: (520) 772-8262

Front Sight Firearms Training Institute

P.O. Box 2619,
Aptos, CA 95001
Tel.: (800) 987-7719
Fax: (408) 684-2137
http://www.frontsight.com/

The Firearms Training Site

E-mail: aglock45@erols.com
http://www.erols.com/aglock45/
http://www.worldmedia.com:80/caq/
http://www.sirius.com/~gilliams/training.html

NRA Homepage

http://www.nra.org

The Second Amendment Foundation

http://www.saf.org/saf.org

The Citizens Committee for the Right to Keep and Bear Arms

http://www.ccrkba.org/ccrkba.org

The National Shooting Sports Foundation

http://www.wsa.com/ool/misc.files/shootmain.html

Hunting and Firearms

http://www.wolfe.net/~hunter/

Right to Keep and Bear Arms Page

http://www.teleport.com/~dputzolu/rkba.html

National Survey of State Handgun Carry Laws

http://www.primenet.com/~kielsky/states.txt

Electronic GunShop

http://www.xmission.com/~chad/egs/egs.html

American Jousting Alliance

P.O. Box 5360
Pine Mountain, CA 93222
Tel.: (805)242-6904 (805) 242-0927
http://renstore.com/articles/zoppe.shtml
For those who have an aversion to guns, James Zoppe teaches 12th-century-style jousting, sword fighting and other totally archaic and non-mechanized forms of recreation.

In a Dangerous Place: Afghanistan

With the Mujahadin

The fighters at the front lines tell us they are going to fire off some rockets. Rather than use the truck-mounted rocket launcher, or Stalin's Organ, they want to show me how it's done the mujahadin way. The Talibs are like that. "How many would you like us to fire?" I am asked. The morality meter goes off. I just want to observe, not start a spring offensive. He laughs, but I can tell that I may be the first visitor that does order up a custom-made battle. There are rockets in crude stacks and littered all over the side of the road.

What they do is far more frightening than just fire a rocket. The two men pick up a large rock and start bashing the cap of the bottom of a three-foot rocket. They use a stack of other rockets as a workbench. For me, they will fire a rocket "Afghan style" using a handlit fuse instead of the electrical detonator that sends up rockets in groups of 12. They set up a launching platform made of boulders to crudely aim the deadly projectile. The rocket is covered with stones; the fuse is lit. They motion me to come forward and get a better look. I'm no munitions expert, but I know that something that will explode into thousands of pieces of shrapnel being detonated is not a great incentive, so I move forward slowly. Rob, who should know better, goes for a closer look, and when the fighter sees how close we are, says, "No, no. Go back. Go back." The rocket makes a whirring sound and then howls towards the enemy lines. As the fuse ignites the rocket motor, we realize just how powerful this rocket is and retreat in a shower of rocks and pieces of exploded dirt.

Somewhere at the other end of the deadly arc there is an explosion. The mujahedin send up one more rocket and then we hear explosions off in the near distance as the other side rockets back. It is a tit-for-tat war.

This type of warfare reminds me of kids playing war, except they are using Soviet-era weapons of great destruction. There doesn't seem to be any shortage of ammunition, and one fighter estimates that in one day they go through half a container-load of rockets.

The casualty rate seems to be low and the indifference the fighters have toward land mines, rockets and artillery fire makes me think that they might have more accidents from mishandling the ammunition that lies around unprotected.

After a while, there is not a whole lot more to see unless we want to go out on the night operations, but our guide is hungry and our driver is impatient to leave.

—**RYP**

Intelligence

Ignorance Is Bliss

I say it on TV over and over: The most dangerous thing in the world is ignorance. So it's not surprising that the number one question I get is, "How do I get up to speed before entering a dangerous place?"

The ugly truth about traveling to dangerous places is that you are solely responsible for your own safety. Despite what the charming greasy haired embassy staffer says about the beaches in Dagestan or the healthy mountain weather in Colombia or even the uncrowded Roman ruins in Algeria, you need to form your own opinion.

I gave up phoning embassies and recounting the glowing descriptions of their countries. It was like shooting fish in a barrel. These people are based Stateside and have little or no interest in ever returning to the hell they escaped from. But they do make money off of visa applications. In fact, some embassies support themselves solely off expats passport renewals and visa applications.

Most foreign embassies or UN missions will be very helpful, some even refer you to a travel agency that just happens to be owned by their brother-in-law and will send you faded brochures from when cars had fins. But like a hawker outside a clip joint, steel yourself for what you discover once inside.

You may be surprised to learn this, but when you need a straight answer from your government about a dangerous place, you just can't get a straight answer.

Like most bureaucrats, their job is to make it difficult to get in and even more difficult to learn what really is dangerous. Back in the early editions, I was a vocal critic of our State Department's pathetic attempts to keep people informed on dangerous places. Since then, the travel advisories have dramatically improved. I am not saying this is a direct result of *DP* but I am sure that someone was wagging a $20 copy of *DP* done on a shoestring when comparing the budget and information provided by our multimillion-dollar State Department (International Affairs get 1% of the total Federal Budget or 20 billion dollars a year). My opinion is simple: Our tax dollars should provide some meaningful source of information to help people make informed decisions. Their new policy is to simply truncate information on places where they do not have representation, even though the CIA is working overtime gathering information.

Now I would have to say the quality, currency and comprehensiveness of the U.S. travel warnings are the best out there. More importantly, they have responded to pressure groups and added information on aviation, road conditions, children, customs and other matters. But massive government stupidity can still reign supreme, as Y2K warnings were supplied for places like Angola and Eritrea. They still plug in generic information when specific information is lacking. Getting better, but still no competition to *DP* and other private open sources of information.

So what do you do to find out about dangerous places?

Use the Internet.

This sounds like mundane advice, but the Internet provides the most up-to-date information on health, problems, internal contacts and plain old commonsense advice. Don't assume that because it's on the net it's fresh, or even right. Yes, there is even a glowing tourism page for Somalia. Use the sites below as a starting point and then search engines like Yahoo, Excite, Hotbot, Google and others to find more. Keep in mind that search engines are pretty useless these days and you are better off searching within country, region or subject-specific databases on dangerous places.

Then use the magic of e-mail and forums to gather more information and even friends. Post specific questions at places like Black Flag Cafe and you will be surprised at how many intelligent answers you get. Remember, I said specific. So asking someone to plan your trip for you is a little much.

Check things out.

Nag, nag, nag, but accurate knowledge is what separates the quick from the dead. Boning up on news reports and incident reports can at least give a general idea of what is going on, but it won't give you up-to-the-minute information. Remember, things change in war zones about as fast as the fall TV schedule. Contact your local embassy (if there is one) in-country and talk to whoever is in charge of security. You will get a gruff response, but just tell him you are going and ask him to provide some security tips. Tell him you'll buy him a beer when you arrive. Don't be surprised if they recommend that you hire a bodyguard. Embassies don't exist to provide travel tips.

Expect the unexpected.

Don't just focus on getting from point A to B. Don't even assume that the government or even rebel group A will be in charge of the place you are visiting. Learn about first aid and carry a medical kit, learn about short-term survival and carry a small pocket-sized survival book. Buy a language guide, a good map and a guidebook if available. Your local travel specialty store is an excellent place to start. Read my book *Come Back Alive* from Doubleday for more information. Most importantly, understand that the place you are going will be very different from the place you are coming from and you must develop a sense of independence, humor and resourcefulness to return safely. Anything you need or want to make that job easier should be thought of, be conversant with and purchased here.

Train and learn.

How the hell do you train for a trip? The upsurge in tourists and journalists being killed, kidnapped and victimized has spawned a fledgling industry. Crusty old vets of nasty places now can show journalists what to do when guns begin firing and bombs start exploding, They can teach you how to avoid, what to expect and how to survive a kidnapping. They can teach you to learn if you are being followed, how to signal for help, search for carbombs, avoid land mines and how to get yourself out of a nasty situation.

Keep learning.

I can safely tell you that 50–80 percent of what you learned before you went to that fecal muck-streaked place is wrong or out of date. Why? Because it takes about two years for info to be gathered and published in a traditional guide book, about 4–8 months for a magazine story to be published and up to 2–3 months for a newspaper story to run on a remote region. Yes there are live feeds from CNN, but they are not providing survival or travel tips.

When you arrive, find the local watering hole for expats and drop in for a chat. Most expats are surprisingly indifferent or hostile to tourists. They almost resent the fact that you can go back. But many are eager to swap basketball scores or war stories. Ask them pointedly what is going on and what you need to do in case you need Plan B. You will learn that certain aid, NGO and foreign embassies are very helpful in case of emergency. Others won't even answer the polished buzzer. Don't ever assume the U.S. embassies are the friendliest, they aren't. My reception has ranged from being held off at gunpoint to being told to get the hell out of Dodge. On the other hand, once inside, the staff have reason to be paranoid, and with a few warmup jokes, turn out to be pretty helpful in a pinch. The main reason you want to at least register and say hi is to ensure a spot on the chopper if there is a civilian/non-combatant evac. If you don't sign on, you go to the back of the line.

For some reason, embassies and consulates in every war zone have their own vibe, their own sense of welcome and to a certain degree their own reason for existing—none of which usually concerns and assists you, the person they were set up to service.

How do you recover from the cold diplomatic shoulder you are likely to get? Well, ignore them for one. Sometimes the locals outside throwing rocks and chanting slogans are happier to see you than the beleaguered people inside. Once in-country, enlist the help of a local guide, either a friend you meet online, a recommended translator or even a person recommended by a local aid group. Keep an open mind, learn the language, tour the back streets, stay away from tourists and try to absorb as much as you can. Travel in difficult places has become surprisingly easy.

Government Travel Sources

Overseas Security Advisory Council

http://ds.state.gov/travel.html

The Overseas Security Advisory Council (OSAC) began in 1985 when a number of businesses demanded information on overseas security. In 1987 a database of incidents and reports was created, including State Department Travel Warnings, terrorist profiles, anniversary dates, special reports on crime and general information for travelers. The database is free of charge and should be any traveler's starting point for information. They have updated the site to include global news and the latest information on security and links. Keep in mind the information varies widely in quality, currency, and most importantly political perspective.

Bureau of Diplomatic Security
U.S. Department of State
Washington, DC 20522-1003
Tel.: 202-663-0533
Fax: 202-663-0868
E-mail: osac@dsmail.state.gov

To search entire OSAC Electronic Database

http://ds.state.gov/osac/

United States Travel Advisories (Overseas Security Advisory Council)

http://travel.state.gov/travel_warnings.html

Also you can find e-mail and telephone links to U.S. embassies overseas.

Visas

Always contact the embassy in question before you leave. You may also get competing and blatantly wrong information about safety, entry and political conditions inside your chosen destination. Why? Most embassy folks haven't been back to their home countries in years.

Foreign Entry/Visa Requirements

http://travel.state.gov/foreignentryreqs.html

United Kingdom Travel Advisories

http://www.fco.gov.uk/travel/

Based on the dozens of countries included, the foreign office might just as well tell U.K. residents to stay home. A different perspective than the U.S. warnings, with pathetically weak and obscure information for those who must be in-country. It contains helpful statements like, "We believe that there is an increased threat to British interests in Afghanistan from global terrorism. Duh. The information is generic enough that it really doesn't matter if the vague warnings are up to date or not. Well, at least the Web site looks pretty and has a flag from each country. As expected, there is voluminous information about what British consuls can't do for their citizens overseas.

List of missions overseas

http://www.fco.gov.uk/

Canadian Government Travel Advisories

http://www.dfait-maeci.gc.ca/travelreport/menu_e.htm

My native country takes a "Have a good time, eh?" approach to warnings. They also lock step with the U.S. travel warnings and substitute generic information when real information is lacking. They also provide tips for Canadians imprisoned overseas (assuming you have an Internet connection in those Central African prisons).

List of Canadian missions overseas
http://www.dfait-maeci.gc.ca/menu-e.asp

Australian Government Travel Advisories
http://www.dfat.gov.au/consular/advice/advices_mnu.html

I hate to say it, but the most adventurous people on earth (they do have to go a long way to get anywhere) are the least served by their government. It is probably the poorest of the English-language advisories. When East Timor exploded, their advice was, "The security situation in East Timor has become extremely dangerous. The Australian government therefore advises that all remaining Australian citizens should leave now. Australian Consulate Staff will be withdrawn from East Timor today, 8 September. Australian Defence Force aircraft will be despatched to Dili on 8 September to evacuate Australians, including our Consulate staff and approved third country nationals. Australian citizens are very strongly advised to depart on these flights.

"Those who wish to depart should ensure that they arrive at the airport from mid-morning Dili time today 8 September with their Passport, Indonesia Immigration Card and no more than 20 kg of luggage. Those who decide to remain should be aware that after the evacuation of the Australian Consulate, there will no longer be Australian Consulate staff in East Timor to provide consular assistance on the ground to any Australian citizens who decide to remain."

List of Australian Missions Overseas
http://www.dfat.gov.au/missiona/index.html.

Foreign Embassies in the United States
http://www.embassyworld.com/embassy/inside_usa_b.htm

Foreign Embassies in Washington, D.C.
http://www.embassy.org/.

Foreign Embassies in Canada, Abroad and Tourism Offices
http://www.rdm.qc.ca/consulE.html

U.S. Diplomatic Missions Online
http://www.state.gov/www/regions_missions.html

Travel Information

There is no one source of information for dangerous places. You need to search the web and sift through the blizzard of useless flames and opinions to find useful bits.

Tourism Offices Worldwide
http://www.towd.co

Scholars Guide to the Web
http://members.aol.com/Dann01/web-guide.html

Lonely Planet
http://www. lonelyplanet.com
Condensed information on most of the world's countries with input from readers.

Kim Spy Intelligence and Counterintelligence
http://www.kimsoft.com/kim-spy.htm
Good page for links, news and information.

Central Intelligence Agency
http://www.cia.gov/cia/publications/factbook/country.html
Hey, get your money's worth with their comprehensive Country Factbooks (check the date of the information). Sadly, much of the infor on *DP*'s is frighteningly wrong or out of date. While your are searching the database (*http://www.odci.gov/search*) visit the CIA kid's page.

Mario's Cyberspace Station
http://mprofaca.cro.net/
Good gathering point and links for danger/crisis/spy stuff

Crisis Control

314 South Route 94, Suite 19
Warwick, NY 10990
Tel.: 1-800-515-978 or 1-914-858-32
Fax: 1-212-656-1648
http://crisis-control.com/
In order to sell security services, CC tracks current events and advice on security.

Political Resources on the Net

http://www.agora.stm.it/politic/

Security Intelligence News Service

http://www.dso.com/

Real World Rescue

1280 Robinson Avenue, Suite C
San Diego, CA 92103
Tel.: (619) 297 7114
http://realworldrescue.com
Excellent source of information on current conflicts and the training to survive them.

ClandestineRadio Intelligence Web

http://www.qsl.net/yb0rmi/cland.htm
Information and links to radio stations funded and operated by guerrilla groups, opposition parties, and intelligence agencies around the world.

For Journalists/Writers

Project for Excellence in Journalism

http://www.journalism.org/

Pew Research Center for the People and the Press

http://www.people-press.org/link.htm

Online Resources for Journalists

http://www.powerreporting.com/

Finding Data on the Internet

http://nilesonline.com/data/

Federation of American Scientists

http://www.fas.org/

Newsplace

http://www.niu.edu/newsplace/

CPJ Report by Country

http://www.cpj.org/countrystatus/reportsindex.html

Columbia Journalism Review

http://www.cjr.org/

Conciliation Resources

PO Box 21067,
London N1 9WT, United Kingdom
Tel: (44) 171 359 7728
Fax: (44) 171 359 4081
http://www.c-r.org/

The Associated Press

International Headquarters
50 Rockefeller Plaza
New York, NY 10020
Tel.: 212-621-1500
http://www.associatedpress.org

Sygma

322 8th Avenue
New York, NY 10001
Tel.: (212) 675-7900
www.ny.sygma.com
www.sygma-london.co.uk

Reuters

http://www.reuters.com/

Agency France Press

www.afp.com

SIPA Press

http://www.sipa.com/

Blackstar

http://www.blackstar.com/

Corbis

http://www.corbis.com

Other Helpful Resources

American Journalism Review (Joblink)

http://ajr.newslink.org/new-joblinkad.html?9AMB9O

Behind the Lens

http://www.digitalstoryteller.com/BTV99/contents.html

Committee to Protect Journalists

http://www.cpj.org

Reporters Sans Frontieres

http://www.calvacom.fr/rsf/RSF_VA/Acc_VA.html

Society of Professional Journalists

http://www.spj.org/

The Free Lens 1

http://www.oneworld.org/rorypeck

Guerrilla Guide

http://www.GuerrillaGuide.com

Cool Tools

These might help you do a little planning:

Maps
> http://www.parc.xerox.com

Currency Converter
> http://www.xe.net/currency/full/

Flight Tracking
> http://www.thetrip.com/usertools/
> flighttracking

Visa ATM Tracker
> http://www.visa.com/cgi-bin/vee/pd/
> atm/main.html

WorldTime
> http://www.timeanddate.com/world-
> clock/
> also a calendar for any year you choose
> at:
>
> http://www.timeanddate.com/calen-
> dar/

Country Capsules
> http://www3.travelocity.com/destg/
> 0,TRAVELOCITY,00.html

Concierge.com
(Best way into town from 100 airports)
> http://www.concierge.com/travel/
> c_planning/06_airports/intro.html

Altapedia
> http://www.atlapedia.com/
> Online maps of the world and country
> profiles.

Weather Worldwide
> http://www.library.vanderbilt.edu/
> central/staff/fdtf.html

TIme and Date
> http://www.timeanddate.com/

Measurements Converter
> http://www.mplik.ru/~sg/transl/

On-Line Foreign Language Dictionaries
> http://www.facstaff.bucknell.edu/
> rbeard/diction.html

Encarta
> http://encarta.msn.com/

Encyclopedia Britannica
> www.britannica.com

News

Accurate news is only as good as the people on the ground. Coverage on esoteric regions and subjects is best sourced from local Web sites, shortwave radio and newspapers. On a general basis these are good starting points:

BBC
> http://news.bbc.co.uk/hi/english/
> world/
> Your best source for world news and
> background online. Don't forget that
> the BBC also provides much more
> detailed coverage on their shortwave
> services.

YahooNews
> http://www.yahoo.co.uk/headlines/
> world/
> An excellent gathering of newslinks and
> stories with a searchable database.

Matt Drudge
> http://www.drudgereport.com/
> Forget Drudge's self-serving
> muckraking, bookmark his home page
> for the best for news links.

The New York Times
> http://www.nytimes.com/

Nando Nett
> http://www.nandonet.com

AfricaNet
> http://www.africanet.com

ArabNet
> http://www.arabnet.com

Center for Middle Eastern Studies
> http://menic.utexas.edu/menic/
> menic.html

Safety Training

Many of these courses and all this information is available to nonjournalists. There is a blurred line between tourists, stringers and journalists these days with small DV cameras and a trend in khaki adventure wear. The courses are expensive but obviously worth whatever your hide is.

Groups such as Frontline, CPJ and Reporters Respond have no interest in providing travel planning tips to civvies, but if you are trying to break into the impecunious business of war reportage, they can offer some advice.

Centurion Risk Assessment Services Ltd.

Reed Cottage, Fleet Road, Elvetham,
Hartley Wintney, Hants RG27 8AT
(44) 7000 221221
http:www.centurion-riskservices.co.uk
Survival training for journalists, body armor and helmet rental

AKE Ltd.

Mortimer House,
Holmer Road, Hereford. JR4 9TA UK
Tel.: 44 0 1432 267111
Fax: 44 0 1432 350227
E-mail: andy@ake.co.uk.
http://www.ake.co.uk/
Monthly courses on surviving hostile regions in the U.K.

Real World Rescue

1280 Robinson Avenue, Suite C
San Diego, CA 92103
Tel.: (619) 297 7114
http://realworldrescue.com
Provides safety/survival training for journalists and travelers.

Journalist Safety Service and Reporters Respond

Tel.: 31 20 6766771
Fax: 31 20 6624901
E-mail vereniging@nvj.nl
A group that supports journalists in distress and maintains a database on incidents that concern journalists and newsgatherers.

Frontline Television

7, Southwick Mews
London W2 1JG United Kingdom
Tel.: 44 0 171 616 2600
http://www.frontlinetv.com
Freelance agency for reporters in warzone, also provides armored car rental.

Information for Journalists

http://www.ifex.org/

Safety Information and Data on Aircrashes

http://www.airsafe.com/

Committee to Protect Journalists

330 Seventh Avenue
New York, NY 10001
Tel: (212) 465-1004
Fax: (212) 465-9568
E-mail: info@cpj.org
http://www.cpj.org/
A nonpartisan, nonprofit organization founded in 1981 to monitor and protest abuses against working journalists and their news organizations, regardless of their ideology or nationality. Excellent site of interest to travelers. If they are beating up the journalists you can bet you're next.

FreedomForum

www.freedomforum.org
The Freedom Forum is a nonpartisan, international foundation dedicated to free press, free speech and free spirit for all people. The foundation pursues its priorities through conferences, educational activities, publishing, broadcasting, online services, fellowships, partnerships, training, research and other programs, news of interest to journalists and a good links page.

Rory Peck Trust

7, Southwick Mews
London W2 1JG United Kingdom
Tel.: 00 44 171 262 5272
Fax: 00 44 171 262 2162
E-mail: rptrpa@dial.pipex.comhttp://
oneworld.org/rorypeck
A group dedicated to seeking insurance for war correspondents as well as providing grants for assistance. Their publication, "the free lens," is an excellent source of information for front-line shooters.

Health

Center for Disease Control and Prevention
http://www.cdc.gov/
Easily the most comprehensive source for travel information as it relates to health. There is a search panel on the home page and you can also be notified by e-mail.

CDC Travel Health Information
http://www.cdc.gov/travel/

Medical College of Wisconsin Health Link
http://healthlink.mcw.edu/travel-medicine/
Good background information on travel-related illnesses.

Mayo Clinic
http://www.mayo.edu
Large database on travel health

Travel Health Links from Mayo Clinic
http://www.mayo.edu/travel-clinic/links.htm

Natural Medicine and Alternative Therapies
http://www.amrta.org/~amrta

Virtual Hospital
http://vh.radiology.uiowa.edu

Air France Travel Health Information
http://www.airfrance.fr/prod/medaf/Medpax.html

Executive Registry
http://www.med.cornell.edu/nyhexr/exr5.html
An international network of academic medical centers providing physician-to-physician consultation and physician-to-patient consulting service, as well as emergency evacuation services to the executive traveler.

High Altitude Acclimatization Illnesses
http://www.princeton.edu/~rcurtis/altitude.html

International Society of Travel Medicine
http://www.istm.org/
Organization of professionals dedicated to the advancement of the specialty of travel medicine.

International Society of Travel Medicine
P.O. Box 871089
Stone Mountain, GA 30087-0028
Tel.: (770) 736-7060
Fax: (770) 736-6732
E-mail: bcbistm@aol.com

International Travel Medicine Clinic
http://www.hsc.unt.edu/clinics/itmc/travel.htm
At the University of North Texas Health Science Center at Fort Worth.

International Travel and Health
http://jupiter.who.ch/programmes/emc/yellowbook/yb_home.htm

MCW International Travelers Clinic
http://www.intmed.mcw.edu/travel.html

Travel First Aid Kit
http://regina.ism.ca/trakker/Medical/TravMedK.htm

Travel Health Information
http://www.intmed.mcw.edu/ITC/Health.html

Travel Health Information and Referral Service
http://travelhealth.com/
Information on staying healthy when you travel: general guidelines, by country, by disease. Forum and interesting cases.

Travel Health Online
http://www.tripprep.com/
Country-specific health and safety information on immunizations and disease risk.

Traveler's Diarrhea
http://regina.ism.ca/trakker/Medical/TravDiar.htm
You can figure it out from the name.

Travelers Medical Immunization Services
http://www.tmis.com

Open Source

There are a number of companies that provide information on dangerous places. (Funny it must be catching on) For survival guide stuff and this book online go to *http://www.comebackalive.com*

Stratfor, Inc.

http://www.stratfor.com/

Part of a new trend in open source information. Stratfor is a private company that gathers, analyzes and disseminates information on conflict and security for businesses. Essentially doing to the CIA what UPS did to the postal service, except for free. Stratfor, Inc., began in 1995 in Baton Rouge, Louisiana, by now former faculty and students of Louisiana State University, associated with the Center for Geopolitical Studies. The company moved to Austin, Texas, in the summer of 1997, and its staff of 20 has provided accurate (albeit deskbound) open source information and crystal ball-like prediction since then. You can also have them send you analyses via e-mail. Their Global Intelligence Center is an excellent source of news on regional matters.

E-mail: info@stratfor.com
Tel.: (512) 583-5000

Search Database:

http://www.stratfor.com/search/index.htm?section=9

Indigo Net

http://www.indigo-net.com/intel.html
Open source information with a good emphasis on Africa and Europe. You can buy information as needed.

Africa Intelligence

http://www.indigo-net.com/africa.html
Part of the Indigo network.

International Crisis Group

http://www.intl-crisis-group.org/
In-depth analysis of selected conflict areas

Pinkertons

Links to Conflict Resolution Sites

http://www.colorado.edu/conflict/international_links.htm
Not global information, but a lot of good background is available from these mostly academic and think-tank sites.

http://www.pinkertons.com/
I won't belabor you with the history of Pinkerton's, except to say they have been around for a while. Outside of their thriving business in providing security for businesses they now offer a sort of intel-lite all the way up to heavy duty threat analyses. Most travelers will be interested in their Eye on Travel that provides two to five page backgrounders on more than 210 countries. Passport and visa requirements, medical and vaccination information, import/export restrictions, currency and exchange rates, time zones, banking hours, voltage, and commercial holidays. Included are U.S. State Department advisories, consular information reports and travel notices from the British Foreign Commonwealth Office. It costs money, but you can get information on normal countries not covered in *DP*. Don't expect a lot of original or on-the-ground info, but it is an excellent resource for people who want to get their hands on safety information. You can catch their daily risk assessments free at *http://www.ariga.com/pink.htm*.

Pinkerton Global Intelligence Services
200 N. Glebe, Suite 1011
Arlington, VA 22203-3728
Tel.: (703) 525-6111(EST)
Fax: (703) 525-2454
http://www.pinkertons.com/

15910 Ventura Boulevard, Suite 900
Encino, CA 91436-3095
Tel: (800) 232-7465
Fax: (800) 984-4100
E-mail: pinkerton@msn.com

Jane's Intelweb

http://intelweb.janes.com/
Jane's provides a pricey briefing service (a number of which are written by *DP* contributors) which provides exhaustive background on security, military and political developments.

Kroll O'Gara Inc.

900 Third Avenue
New York, NY 10022
Tel: (212) 593-1000
Fax: (212) 593-2631
http://kins.kroll-ogara.com/
Kroll provides comprehensive and specific Country Risk Reports designed for expats or companies doing business overseas. Travelers can purchase Kroll's Travel Watch which covers security and safety information for about 300 cities (including U.S. destinations).

Dangerous Places

http://www.comebackalive.com
The online, searchable database version of this book.

Kidnapping

You're in Good Hands

Kidnapping is an ancient sport designed to embarrass your enemies, find wives, get roads built, ensure peace, force political action and make some serious dough. Of the 8,000 known kidnappings worldwide, 6,500 were in Latin America with over half occurring in Colombia. There are, on average, 10 people kidnapped in Colombia every day. The numbers increase dramatically when narco/terror groups like FARC kidnap an entire army garrison. It's important to state up front that statistics are pretty much worthless when describing kidnappings. Nobody really knows or wants you to know how many people and how much money changes hands. It just encourages people.

Some are multimillion dollar deals with nobody the wiser, and some are quick street abductions with $5,000 payoffs as the same-day profits. If you happen to find yourself as one of the 200 foreigners who get kidnapped overseas every year, there's little for you to do but hope that you'll be well treated.

The ideal victim of a kidnapping is a mid- to high-executive professional working for a multinational corporation overseas. Foreign executives in Colombia will fetch $500,000–$2 million (depending on your point man's negotiating skills), usually in a quick insurance-funded payoff. In Yemen, over

160 foreigners have been kidnapped by tribesmen since 1993. Most are released safely. I said most; four were killed in a botched rescue attempt. Yemenis usually target Italians tourists (over 1,000 Italians visit Yemen every year) and businesspeople. Recently one tourist was shot and injured when a busload of 18 inconsiderate Italians ran a kidnapper's roadblock and were fired on.

In Chechnya there are between 100 and 160 people being held captive at any one time, about a dozen of them foreigners. Everyone is at risk. Some, like the three U.K. and one Kiwi telephone workers, end up decapitated. Chechens don't like to wait for their money. About $20 million in ransoms were paid to Chechen kidnappers from 1996 to '98. If its any comfort, the Granger Telcom workers had 24 armed guards who were overpowered by their 20 attackers. Reality TV and news shows in Moscow show kidnapper's home videos of Chechen kidnap victims, featuring fingers or heads being sawn off.

Kidnappers can come in all shapes and demeanors. For example, Mexicans demand big ransoms but settle for less, Peruvians and Brazilians like quick-and-easy grabs, Filipinos and Venezuelans prefer grabbing kids for cheap bucks, Colombians and Russians go for convoluted, treacherous negotiations with multimillion dollar payoffs, Yemenis and Tajiks treat you like visiting royalty, demanding political concessions, not your wallet. Obscure groups in obscure places like National Front for the Renewal of Chad kidnapped eight tourists to force France to withdraws its troops and to convince Western oil companies to pull out of the country. Yeah, sure, we'll get right on it. One comforting statistic, in the U.S. more than 95 percent of kidnappers are apprehended.

There is an entire business category run by ex-spooks and ex-military intelligence folks that do nothing but return hostages, and most Americans, still putting their picture on milk cartons, will get them back safely.

Give the Chechens a gold star for creativity during the war, commandeering hospitals, buses, airplanes or even ferryboats. Now, it seems they snag just about anyone who has a logo on his hat. In the Philippines about 200–300 people are kidnapped each year, generating about $6 million a year in ransoms just to the 40 or so kidnap groups in Manila who prey on Chinese business families. Down south in Mindanao and Sulu, they don't even keep track. Around 10 percent of them are found dead even after the ransom has been paid.

A New Alternative to Those Tedious Spa Vacations

Former interior minister for Mexico, Fernando Gutierrez Barrios, called newspaper editors in Mexico City to insist that he hadn't been kidnapped but just been "on vacation." He disappeared on December 9, 1997, and reappeared six days later. Witnesses had a few comments on his method of departure after seeing 12 armed men hustle him off the streets in Coyoacan. Officials later found a large withdrawal for $800,000, presumably for spa and bar charges.

Latin America is the most dangerous place in the world for kidnappings. More than 6,000 people are kidnapped in Latin America every year. Colombia accounts for 4,000 of those. Just under half of those kidnappings were carried out by FARC and ELN. Kidnapping is estimated to be a $200-million-a-year, tax-free business in Colombia. And they'll wait for their money. Three missionaries who were snagged in a remote village of southern Panama were held for over five years.

Brazil accounts for 800 kidnappings a year, with 104 in Rio alone. In Mexico, there are as many as 2,000 kidnappings a year where the average ransom is around $5,000 for regular folks, but in the multimillion dollar range for bankers and businessmen. About 100 people are grabbed in Guatemala—mostly children of wealthy families and foreign workers. Ecuador and Venezuela each report around 200 kidnappings a year, and Peru estimates 100 hostages taken annually. In Honduras, primarily around the city of San Pedro Sula, former Salvadoran guerrillas have formed 10 gangs that kidnap about 120 people a year.

Keep in mind that all these statistics don't represent unreported snatches. Colombian groups are considered to be a major exporter of kidnapping to surrounding countries. Their twist is killing the families if they don't get the ransom. If kidnapping slows down, they could always work for a credit card collection agency. Oh, and the latest twist? Police will kidnap the kidnapper's families. I'll raise you a three-year-old and meet your granny.

Don't assume that Europe is safe. There have been 53 abductions since 1989, in Italy, 19 in the U.K. and the same number in Spain. Although the media reports the big cases, most victims are ranchers and small businessmen. Foreign executives who work in the oil and energy industries are tops on most kidnappers' wish lists but aren't numerically high because of the security provided. The new trend is to snatch regular folks and then force their relatives to use their cash card to pay the ransom.

These days, Chubb, Fireman's Fund, AIG and Lloyds of London will write policies designed to make sure you come back alive if you get abducted. The premiums run from US$2,500 to $100,000 a year, depending on where you plan to go and how long you plan to stay. Premiums for coverage of $500,000 to $1 million in most west European countries vary from $3,000 to $5,000 per annum. A policy affording cover for a Russian family with up to seven people in the household is $18,500 for $500,000 of coverage and $33,500 for $1 million. If you tell them you are going to Chechnya you'll get a polite giggle. Lloyds of London has experienced a 50 percent jump in policies written over the last five years, and more insurance companies are looking into offering the coverage. What do you get for your money? Actually, quite a bit. Insurers will pay for the ransom payment, medical treatment, interpreters and even your salary while you are involuntarily detained. The services of a security company to help spring you (sorry, no Rambo for rent here) is included in the coverage.

Chubb has the best deal in town; annual payments total about US$1,000 for every $10 million of ransom payments released. If you are deemed to be "high profile" or the target of previous kidnapping attempts, the premium skyrockets to US$25,000 a year. Kidnapping and ransom insurance for dangerous countries like Colombia cost around $20,000 a year for a million dollar policy, but expect to pay $60,000–$100,000 for a decent-sized policy. Coverage is about half that for Brazil. In addition to insurance, armored cars and armed bodyguards are big in Latin America. Expect to pay between $60,000 and $150,000 for an armor-plated Suburban or Lincoln. Armed bodyguards should run you about $90–$250 a day, depending on the country you're in. One alarming development is the increase in kidnapping of small children of wealthy victims. The only positive note is that the ransom for kidnapped children is a cheap $2,000–$5,000 with usually same-day turnaround to avoid expensive diaper bills.

What, Me Worry?

Should tourists be worried about being kidnapped. Probably not. Expats who live in foreign countries are at most risk, while the casual tourist or in-and-out business visitor are almost risk free. Travelers who journey to remote regions in drug areas face a higher risk. Yes, the folks in Uganda, Yemen and Colombia were tourists. But chalk it up to wrong place, wrong time. Kidnappers need a little lead time to get their act together.

Kidnapping usually involves a group of men hustling you off the street into a car. They grabbed you because for some dumb reason you were profiled in the local paper as an "important executive and rising young star of Widget Exports." You also have a predictable routine for leaving work at the same time and walking the last few blocks from the train station. This makes it easy for the kidnappers to be ready with their car, engine running, gaffer's tape at the ready.

How to Survive a Kidnapping

- Force yourself to be calm and compliant; there is little you can do by reacting violently.
- Do whatever your captors tell you to do without argument.
- Communicate with your captors to make them understand that you want to stay alive.
- Take control of your mental and physical state. Develop a routine that will include mental and physical exercise.
- If you think you can escape, do so, but stop if you are under threat of death or being shot.
- If you are being rescued by armed troops or police, stay flat on the ground. Make it difficult for your captors to drag you away, but do not resist. The greatest risk of death is during a rescue attempt.

You will most likely be blindfolded, gagged and bound. If you squirm or bite they'll thump you a few times to settle you down. Your first destination is a house or country hideout where you are kept in a room with no windows. To prove their point, they may photograph you with a Polaroid or record your voice on a cheap hand-held recorder. They may interrogate you to find out just how much you're worth. Then you will sit and wait, and wait and wait. If they don't get their initial demands, they may cause you pain or remove body parts (little fingers are popular) to get their point across. What will eventually happen? It depends.

About 40 percent of all hostages are released safely after the ransom is paid. Not very good odds. Having an insurance policy will make your chances of generating the necessary number of bucks a lot easier. But you won't have a choice should someone try to storm the joint in a rescue effort. About 34 percent of hostages are rescued from their captives before the ransom is paid. Being saved is perhaps a hostage's greatest threat. Let's say your right wing, NRA-supporting, big-game hunter boss (who voted for Ross Perot) says "Get my boy outta there now!" He sends in a highly trained team of hand-picked ex-SEALS, kicked into action by a cigar-smoking buzz cut. Oops, he just screwed up.

So what if your wife won't return the kidnapper's calls and your boss figures he has really no need for you because the temp is generating twice the business you did? Nearly 11 percent of kidnapping victims are released without payment, either through negotiation or the abductors' realization that he or she will not be paid. In Colombia a mere 3 percent of kidnappers are convicted compared to 95 percent in the United States.

http://www.g21.net/narco.html

Want to know how to avoid being kidnapped? Stay away form suspect places, vary your routine, keep a low profile, stay out of the local papers, avoid society bashes, live low key, use a driver/bodyguard and stay on top of the local threat assessment.

The most dangerous phases of a hijacking or hostage situation are the beginning and, if there is a rescue attempt, the end. At the outset, the terrorists typically are tense and high-strung and may behave irrationally. It is extremely important that you remain calm and alert and manage your own behavior.

Hostage Etiquette/Survival

- Avoid resistance and sudden or threatening movements. Do not struggle or try to escape, unless you are certain of being successful.

- Make a concerted effort to relax. Breathe deeply and prepare yourself mentally, physically and emotionally for the possibility of a long ordeal.

- Try to remain inconspicuous; avoid direct eye contact and the appearance of observing your captors' actions.

- Avoid alcoholic beverages. Consume little food and drink.

- Consciously put yourself in a mode of passive cooperation. Talk normally. Do not complain, avoid belligerency, and comply with all orders and instructions.

- If questioned, keep your answers short. Don't volunteer information or make unnecessary overtures.

- Don't try to be a hero, endangering yourself and others.

- Maintain your sense of personal dignity, and gradually increase your requests for personal comforts. Make these requests in a reasonable low-key manner.

- If you are involved in a lengthy, drawn-out situation, try to establish a rapport with your captors, avoiding political discussions or other confrontational subjects.

- Eat what they give you, even if it does not look or taste appetizing. A loss of appetite and weight is normal.

- Think positively; avoid a sense of despair. Rely on your inner resources. Remember that you are a valuable commodity to your captors. It is important to them to keep you alive and well. For more info, check out advice from the U.S. government at:
  http://www.state.gov/www/about_state/security/security_hostages.html

Kidnap, Rescue and Extortion Insurance (KRE)

Who do you call when someone is kidnapped? Don't call Chuck Norris, Steven Seagal or Jackie Chan. You'll probably end up dead. Don't even call the police; they will jack up the ransom demand and may be in cahoots with the kidnappers. You should call your insurance company, followed by the embassy, and a professional hostage negotiator. *DP* advises that anyone in a hostage situation contact a professional in their home country before they contact the local police. Better yet, educate yourself about kidnapping before you find out the hard way.

Your best bet as an American is to contact the FBI. It is their job to negotiate the release of American kidnapping victims worldwide. They will make sure the country the abductee is in will allow U.S. law enforcement officers to work there and then the local U.S. embassy must invite the FBI in. This can take time depending how backwater you get. There have been some cases where the State Department doesn't want the FBI involved. Since 1990 the FBI has secured the release of 60 victims. If you have purchased KRE, then you get the non-governmental version with all expenses paid. Keep in mind, the FBI does not pay your ransom.

A typical KRE policy with a $1 million limit covers a family of 11 people. In Latin America, business is intertwined with extended family, from grandparents down to grandchildren. An annual policy would cost between $7,000 in Brazil up to a maximum of $26,000 in Colombia. When you cover a business family, you will always schedule each person. Corporations usually buy blanket policies that cover all employees.

In most countries except Mexico and Colombia, unless you work for a large oil company, a $10 million policy for a Fortune 100 company will cost about $350,000 a year. Insurers like Seitlin also can write one-shot, one-month $1 million KRE policies for travelers and businesspeople for between $2,500–$3,000. Is it necessary? Well Seitlin believes you'd be crazy to do business south of Miami without $5–$10 million in KRE coverage. In Colombia, a ransom less than a million is considered a joke. It is estimated that these days about 65 percent of Fortune 500 companies provide kidnap insurance for their employees working overseas.

http://www.emergency.com/latnkdnp.htm
http://www.hiscox.com
http://www.risknet.com/risknet/

Some tips When You Are Invited to Stay Overnight

- Try to avoid countries notorious for kidnapping: Colombia, Mexico, Chechnya and Yemen are just some. Americans doing business for Fortune 100 oil and mining companies in Colombia are at highest risk; low-key backpackers and travelers are usually at low risk.

- Strange as it sounds, the odds of extracting you are better in areas where kidnapping is done in conjunction with the police. Brazil and Mexico are just two countries where kidnapping is a business conducted in conjunction with the local police. Areas where kidnapping is intertwined with Maoist or Marxist ideology are much harder.

- If someone you know is kidnapped, do not contact the police and do not talk to the press. Contact your embassy, the insurance company and/or a security consultancy to take the next steps. If you have a KRE policy, someone will be dispatched to act as a counselor within hours.

- Tape-record or write down any messages and do not commit to anything until the counselor or security help arrives.

- Most security counselors will be ex-CIA, Mossad or other intelligence service pensioners. The British firms pull from their own pool of ex-SAS, Scotland Yard and MI-5 folks.

- Your security counselor will not make any decisions but he will facilitate the process and act as a coach, a mediator and a go-between. They will usually set up a committee that analyzes input and demands and then makes decisions. Usually the decisions are: Pay the money, stall, or negotiate the ransom downwards. Not the best of jobs for amateurs.

- The fatality rate on security-consultant-handled kidnappings is a reassuring 2 percent compared to 9 percent for homemade efforts. Part of the skew is because some kidnap deaths can occur at the attack—the victims may die of illness, heart attack, or they can be killed during rescue attempts.

http://www.ucalgary.ca/MG/inrm/industry/kidnap/kidnap.htm

Who You Gonna Call?

Dying to know which security groups are called by insurance companies when you get kidnapped? Here is DP's insider list. If you can correctly guess which ex-affiliations these groups hold (army, air force, CIA, Mossad, SAS, etc.) we'll send you a free Mr. DP shirt.

- **Chubb uses the Ackerman Group.**

- **AIG uses Kroll Associates.**

- **Cassidy Davis Hiscox Consortium (Lloyds) uses Control Risks Group.**

- **Genesis (Lloyds) uses the Ackerman Group.**

- **Cigna uses Pinkerton's.**

Number of People Kidnapped, 1991–1998	
Colombia	4,040
Mexico	656
Brazil	523
Philippines	460
Pakistan	435
Guatemala	170
Venezuela	107
India	85
Nicaragua	41
Peru	41
All other countries	608

Source: Hiscox Group

KRE Resources

Seitlin & Company

P.O. Box 025220
Miami, FL 33102-5220
Tel.: (305) 591-0090
Fax: (305) 593-6993
E-mail: kandrguy@aol.com
http://www.icanect.net/seitlin/
page2.htm

Seitlin is the largest insurance broker in Florida that also does a ripping business in kidnap/ransom insurance. Luckily he only has to pay out about once or twice a year. Their clients include mostly wealthy Latin American families, corporations that do business south of the border and employees of multinational corporations. He can provide policies from all the major insurance brokers

Asset Security Management

44 171 301 5011 FAX 44 171 481 0351
email: enquiries@asm-uk.com
http://www.asm-uk.com/

Specialists in kidnap insurance and response. Their site contains statistics, advice and case studies.

Chubb Insurance

http://www.chubb.com/businesses/ep/
kr/

Chubb offers kidnap/ransom/extortion (KRE) coverage for busy executives with a healthy level of fear. Extortion can also cover computer hackers, contamination or even a computer virus.

Lloyds of London

1 Portsoken Street
London England, E1 8DF
Tel.: (071) 480-4000
Fax: (071) 480-4170
http://www.lloydsoflondon.co.uk/
http://www.www.hiscox.com

Lloyds, according to the *Independent,* is paying out over $10 million in kidnap claims a year. The Hiscox Group at Lloyd's writes about 5,000 policies a year, about 60 percent of all KRE business. Lloyds uses Control Risks to handle the dirty work, and they become involved in 30 to 40 kidnappings a year. Ransoms paid can range from about $50,000 to over $30 million. The gentleman that paid the $30 million did not have insurance.

American International Group (AIG)

The second largest KRE insurance provider. They use Kroll O'Gara for the negotiation part.

http://www.aig.com

Black Fox International, Inc.

P. O. Box 1187
205 Garvin Boulevard
Sharon Hill, PA 19079
Tel.: (800) 877-2445, (610) 461-6690
Fax: (610) 586-5467
E-mail: jc@black-fox.com
http://black-fox.com/kidnap.htm

Security Resources

Security is big business these days. Americans spend about $90 billion on security every year. We only spend $40 billion on public police. In California there are four times as many private police as there are government police. In countries like Russia and South Africa people don't even bother calling for the police. Areas affected by kidnapping also have a number of local firms that provide security and protection. Inquire at your local embassy or with other multinational companies.

Pinkerton Risk Assessment Services

1600 Wilson Boulevard, Suite 901
Arlington, VA 22209
Tel.: (703) 525-6111
Fax: (703) 525-2454
www.pinkertons.com
fjohns@pinkertons.com

Once on the trail of bank robbers in the Wild West, Pinkerton has gone global and high-tech. Today, you can get risk assessments of over 200 countries on-line or in person. Pinkerton offers access to a database of more than 55,000 terrorist actions and daily updated reports on security threats. For the nonactive, you can order printed publications that range from daily risk-assessment briefings to a monthly newsletter. Their services are not cheap, but how much is your life worth? Annual subscriptions to the on-line service start at about US$7,000, and you can order various risk and advisory reports that run from US$200–$700 each. Pinkerton gets down and dirty with its counterterrorism programs, hostage negotiators, crisis management and travel security seminars.

The service is designed for companies who send their employees overseas or need to know what is going on in the terrorist world. Some reports are mildly macabre, with their annual businesslike graphs charting maimings, killings, assaults and assassinations. Others are truly enlightening. In any case, Pinkerton does an excellent job of bringing together the world's most unpleasant information and providing it to you in concise, intelligent packages.

Unlimited on-line access to their database on 230 countries will run you US$6,000 a year. You will find the information spotty, with a preponderance of information on South and Central America. Many of the write-ups on everything from Kurds to the Islamic Jihad are written by young college students with little in-country experience. On the other hand, there are many holes that are filled by CIA country profiles (available at any library for free).

If you want to save a few bucks, for US$4,000 a year (US$5,000 overseas), you can get a full subscription of daily, weekly, quarterly and annual risk assessments, as well as analysts' commentaries, a world status map and a fax service that keeps you abreast of fast-breaking events.

Cheapskates can opt for the US$2,250 standard package, which eliminates the daily reports sent via fax, but provides you most of the other elements. If you want to order à la carte, expect services that range from a US$30 personalized trip package, to US$250 printouts of

existing risk and travel advisories, to accessing the company's Country Data bank for US$1,000 per country.

Control Risks Group, London

8200 Greensboro Drive, Suite 1010
McLean, VA 22102
Tel.: (703) 893-0083
Fax: (703) 893-8611

83 Victoria Street
London, England SW1H-OHW
Tel.: [44] (171) 222-1552
This international management consulting company specializes in political, business and security risk analysis and assessments, due diligence and fraud investigations, preventative security and asset protection, crisis management planning and training, crisis response and unique problem solving. With extensive experience in kidnapping, extortion and illegal detention resolution, they have handled more than 700 cases in 79 countries. Control Risks has 14 offices around the world including Washington, D.C., London, New York, Bogotá, Mexico City, Bonn, Amsterdam, Manila, Melbourne, Moscow, Paris, Singapore, Sydney and Tokyo. Their international, political and security risk-analysis research department is the largest of its kind in the private sector and has provided hundreds of companies with customized analyses of the political and security risks they may face doing business around the globe. An on-line Travel Security Guide addresses security issues in more than 100 countries.

Emergency Numbers for CRG:

London: (071) 222 1552 or (071) 481 1851 (Nightline)
United States: (703) 893 0083
Australia: (613) 416 1533

Kroll O'Gara

900 Third Avenue
New York, NY 10022
Tel.: (212) 593-1000
Fax: (212) 593-2631
http://www.veriguard.com/ corp_index.html
A security/investigative firm founded in 1972 by Jules Kroll and owned by Equifax (the credit info folks). In

addition to gumshoeing on an international and corporate level.

Kroll has a travel service that provides warnings about crime, medical concerns and even such hazards as missing manhole covers (stolen by the thousands in Beijing to be sold as scrap metal). The reports are compiled from about 270 cities in 89 countries (including the United States). The Travel Watch is produced and distributed by Kroll Associates, a firm offering security and "risk-assessment" to corporate clients. The reports fill one 8-by-11-inch page and are delivered to the computers of about 29,000 travel-agency clients of SABRE, one of the industry's principal electronic reservation systems. Within the first two weeks of offering the reports in June, Kroll Travel Watch reported about 10,000 requests. The reports are free through travel agency requests. For more information or a Travel Watch for your destination, contact your travel agent or purchase the reports from Kroll directly.

Ackerman Group

166 Kennedy Causeway, Suite 700
Miami Beach, FL 33141
Tel.: (305) 865-0072
http://ackermangroup.com/
Mike Ackerman specializes in crisis resolution or hostage return through providing the financial and security resources required to resolve hostage situations safely.

TroubleShooters

United States

Tel.: (352) 343-2406
Fax: (352) 343-3864

Canada

Tel.: (403) 885-5273
Ex-US military folks who freelance for hostage situations and can provide aviation services for overseas extractions. They can provide assistance for executive protection, hostage retrieval and missing person searches.

Interlink Consultants

Seminars and consulting on kidnap prevention and mediation

Interlink Consulting Services
P.O. Box 211302
West Palm Beach, FL 33421-1302
Tel.: (561) 792-0453
Fax: (561) 792-9375
E-mail: info@interlinkconsulting.com
http://www.interlinkconsulting.com/

RealWorld Rescue

Crisis Consulting and Training

http://www.realworldrescue.com/travel.htm

Professional Bodyguard Association

P.O. Box 11493
London, N3 2TH England
E-mail: xsas@msn.com
The e-mail address pretty much says it all. This group will also provide training for groups of up to four protectors. There is also a 800-page Bodyguard Training Manual available for study at home for 45 pounds (payable in Sterling only via bank draft). They are looking to train more Yanks, so they have offered price reduction to offset the airfare costs. For more info, send five one-dollar bills (for postage), and they will send you a prospectus.

Falcon Global

1126 Washington Boulevard, Suite D
Williamsport, PA 17701
Tel.: (717) 321-6220
Fax: (717) 321-6222
Falcon Global has elevated the goon business to a professionally managed level. They can provide security during labor disputes without provoking reruns of Matawa.

Political Risk Services

6320 Fly Road
P.O. Box 248
East Syracuse, New York 13057
Tel.: (315) 431-0511, FAX: (315) 431-0200
Providing international, political, economic and business risk assessments, this company offers forecasts for 148 countries. They claim to be politically and economically nonplussed and employ a network of 250 experts on various countries who provide input for the reports. The series of reports are designed to provide many levels of information, including political stability, investment and trade restrictions, and economic forecasts, and are also

available on CD-ROM. A 50-page printed report on one country costs US$325. Two or more reports are $250 each. CD-ROMs are available by region for $2,000, or you may purchase a CD with condensed reports on hundreds of countries. A monthly 14-page newsletter summary of the latest forecasts is available for $435 per year. A 450-page bound volume, published twice each year, summarizes the current forecasts for 100 countries from all country reports and executive reports. Extensive tables compare and analyze global and regional rankings. Rates are $350 for one volume or $545 for a one-year, two-issue subscription.

Seitlin & Company Insurance

2001 N.W. 107th Avenue, Suite 200
Miami, FL 33172
Tel.: (305) 591-0090, FAX: (305) 593-6993
Providers of insurance for kidnaping, recovery and prevention

Safehouse Hostage Rescue Training

10221 Slater Avenue Suite 112
Fountain Valley, CA 92708
Tel.: (714) 968-0088
http://safehousesecurity.com/hostage_rescue.html

When all else fails:

http://www.corprisk.com/

Yemeni Hospitality

The Yemen Times *reports that between April 1991 and April 1998 there were 124 cases of kidnapping. Of the 146 victims, 124 were foreigners and 22 Yemenis. Over 200 foreigners have been kidnapped to date.*

2000

1/28/00   *An American oil worker is kidnapped in the eastern Marib Province.*

1/26/00   *American is kidnapped in Shobwe province.*

1/17/00   *Two French tourists are kidnapped, released and kidnapped again.*

1999

10/27/99   *Three Americans kidnapped.*

1998

12/30/98   *German tourists kidnapped on December 6, released unharmed.*

12/28/98   *Sixteen tourists—12 Britons, two Americans and two Australians—taken hostage in Abyan province in the largest kidnapping in Yemen's recent history. Four hostages were killed.*

12/14/98   *Armed members of the al-Faqir tribe kidnapped Umar al-Sufi, the 11-year-old son of Hammud Khalid al-Sufi, a GPC member of parliament, outside the boy's school in Sana'a.*

12/6/98   *Four German tourists kidnapped by Bani Dhabyan tribe near the Yislah pass, 60 km south of Sana'a*

11/22/98   *Yemeni businessman Abdel Hakim Hussein Shamsan kidnapped by armed men outside a mosque in Aden.*

10/28/98   *Two European tourists kidnapped by the Ba-Kazim tribe in the Mahfad area of Abyan province; released the next day.*

9/1/98   *The director of projects and construction at the education office in Dhamar is taken hostage by the Hada tribe.*

8/4/98   *President Salih issues a decree imposing the death penalty for kidnapping.*

Yemeni Hospitality

7/30/98   *Four men attempted to kidnap Dutch agricultural project director Mathew Brugman and his wife in Dhamar.*

6/18/98   *Nine Italian tourists kidnapped by the al-Marazeeq tribe near Bir Ali, close to Aden. Mohammad al-Marzuki was demanding a car from the authorities, as promised during another kidnapping of Italians in 1997.*

4/16/98   *David Mitchell, 48, who works for the British Council in Aden, taken hostage.*

4/23/98   *Ukrainian sailor Alexander Bondarenko taken hostage.*

3/1/98   *Tribesmen fired machine guns at a bus carrying about 30 tourists, mostly Germans. One tourist and three policemen escorting the bus injured. Six attackers captured.*

2/18/98   *Dutch agricultural project director Mathew Brugman kidnapped by the Maghrib Ans tribe.*

10/22/98 *Eleven-year-old grandson of the chief Supreme Court judge kidnapped by al-Hada tribe (Dhamar province).*

2/9/98   *Clemens Verweij, a diabetic Dutch tourist with heart problems, kidnapped by Toaiman tribe near Sana'a and taken to al-Mahjaza.*

1/20/98   *German technician working for the health ministry, kidnapped by four armed men of the Bani Dhabyan tribe.*

1/20/98   *Chinese national kidnapped by Bakazem tribe in Shabwah province.*

1/5/98   *Wife of the South Korean consul, their three-year-old daughter and a Korean businessman kidnapped in central Sana'a by members of the al-Hada tribe.*

1997

10/30/97 *American Steve Carpenter, 47, working for a Yemeni al-Hashedi company, is kidnapped in Sana'a and taken to Barat, 160 kilometers north of Sana'a. Held by members of Bakil tribal group.*

10/29/97 *An attempt to abduct the Qatari ambassador in Sana'a, Muhammad Bin Hamad Al Khalifah. Nine people are arrested.*

10/23/97 *Two Russian doctors and their wives kidnapped near Dhamar and held by al-Hada tribe.*

10/16/97 *Briton Henry Thompson (38), working for a Japanese aid agency, kidnapped with his Yemeni interpreter and driver near Anz, 100km south of Sana'a. Held by Sheikh Mubarak Ali Saada of Bani Dhabyan tribe in Marib province.*

10/15/97 *Four French tourists kidnapped by eight tribesmen of Al Salim (Bakil) tribe at the behest of Sheikh Shaya Bakhtan while heading towards Sa'ada, 270 kilometers north of Sana'a.*

8/21/97   *Eighteen Italian tourists in a convoy traveling through Shabwa were attacked by five armed tribesmen who opened fire when the drivers refused to stop. A 32-year-old Italian suffered a broken shoulder.*

8/14/97   *Four Italians kidnapped near Khamir, 100 kilometers north of Sanaa. (Reuter 14–Aug-97).*

8/13/97   *Six Italian tourists kidnapped while on their way to al-Mukalla on the southern coast.*

3/27/97   *Two elderly German couples kidnapped by Jihm tribe while returning from a visit to ruins at Barakesh, 200 km east of Sana'a.*

Yemeni Hospitality

3/1/97   *Seven German motorcycle tourists kidnapped for ten days near Tarim, 750 km east of Sana'a.*

2/1/97   *American oil company engineer held for 17 days in eastern Yemen.*

1996

12/1/96   *Four Polish tourists and their Yemeni guide kidnapped by Beni Jabr tribe 60 kilometers east of Sana'a*

10/1/96   *French diplomat kidnapped for 12 days.*

5/1/96   *Maaz Taha Ahmad Ghanim, aged 20, son of Taha Ahmad Ghanim, the governor of Aden, kidnapped by Khawlane tribe.*

1/26/96   *Seventeen French tourists kidnapped on a bus in Marib*

1995

12/31/95   *American oil worker and three colleagues kidnapped near Janna*

Sources: Various wire services; Yemeni web site.

Land Mines

Boom Times

If there was ever a reason to pay attention in history class, land mines would be it. Why? Because travelers to dangerous places need to know more than the current situation; they must also know why and where wars were fought in the past. There may be peace in Egypt, Mozambique, China, Jordan, the Ukraine or even Belgium, but there are plenty of souvenirs from past wars hiding in the ground. They like to tell people that someone is killed or injured by a land mine every 15 to 20 minutes. Not true. Most land mine victims die in silent agony unseen, unknown and uncategorized.

The world has between 105 and 110 million land mines buried in 64 countries, according to the United Nations. Nobody actually knows exactly how many there are since the people who placed them never bothered to remember their exact location. Yes, sometimes there are detailed maps, but rarely. Consequently, the people who find them remember it for the rest of their lives—if they survive the blast.

Even though land mines maim and kill between 20,000 and 24,000 men, women and children every year, many governments claim they are not a threat to travelers. Even agencies like Greenpeace and the CDC contend the death toll is more like 9,600. Mine clearance groups estimate that the number is 15,000, with about 80 percent being civilians and a third of those being young children. (Some anti-mine groups estimate 37,000 are killed every year.) The truth is there are few little red signs in the boonies and even fewer keeping count of the deaths and maimings. Death by land mine is nasty and lonely. Most victims bleed to death in remote places or are maimed for life. Being injured by a land mine is one of the most traumatic experiences, both mentally and physically, a human can live through.

Eighty-five percent of current mine-related casualties are in Afghanistan, Angola and Cambodia—all sites of past and present dirty little wars where land mines are the perfect weapon. With so many mines, it only takes one false step to be killed or maimed for life. As more and more adventurer-travelers head into the remote regions of Laos, Vietnam, Cambodia and other remote regions, they will learn firsthand of the effects of land mines and UXO, unexploded ordnance.

There are movements afoot to ban land mines worldwide, but that does not solve and will not stop the mines that kill every day. For now, business is booming.

More Than You Ever Want to Know About Mines

The next time someone tells you that it is those crazy Russians and liberation groups that sprinkle the world's mines, you might want to check the receipts of the countries that are buying the land mines. According to *Jane's Intelligence Review*, Iran, Israel, Cambodia, Thailand, Chile, El Salvador, Malaysia and Saudi Arabia top the list. Tsk, tsk, you say. Well, those folks have good reasons to buy those land mines: Iran had a nasty border war with Iraq, Israel gets grief from all of its neighbors, Cambodia had the Khmer Rouge to contend with, Thailand has drug runners, Chile has Paraguay, El Salvador had jungle insurgents, and Malaysia still has vivid memories of a nasty war with Indonesia back in the early '60s. All this is history to journalists but not to the land mines still sitting patiently in the ground.

So just who are those evil amoral people who make these things and where are those nasty places those mines deserve to be put in? The answer may surprise you.

Who Makes 'em	
Country of Origin	**Places Used**
Belgium	Angola, Iraq (Kurdistan), Kuwait, Mozambique, Namibia, Somalia
Brazil	Nicaragua
Bulgaria	Cambodia
Canada	Iraq
Chile	Iraq (Kurdistan)
China	Afghanistan, Angola, Cambodia, Mozambique, Namibia, Somalia
Czech (ex)	Afghanistan, Angola, Cambodia, Mozambique, Namibia, Nicaragua, Somalia
Egypt	Afghanistan, Nicaragua, Iraq

Who Makes 'em	
Country of Origin	**Places Used**
France	*Iraq (Kurdistan), Iraq (Kuwait), Mozambique, Somalia*
Germany (former East)	*Angola, Cambodia, Mozambique Namibia, Somalia*
Hungary	*Cambodia*
Italy	*Angola, Iraq (Kurdistan), Iraq(Kuwait)*
Pakistan	*Somalia*
Romania	*Iraq (Kurdistan)*
Russia	*Afghanistan, Angola, Cambodia, Iraq (Kurdistan), Iraq (Kuwait), Mozambique, Namibia, Nicaragua, Somalia, Vietnam*
Singapore	*Iraq (Kuwait)*
South Africa	*Angola, Mozambique, Somalia*
Spain	*Iraq (Kuwait)*
United Kingdom	*Afghanistan, Mozambique, Somalia*
United States	*Angola, Cambodia, Iraq (Kurdistan), Mozambique, Nicaragua, Somalia*
Vietnam	*Cambodia*
Yugoslavia (ex)	*Afghanistan, Cambodia, Mozambique, Namibia, Zimbabwe*

Source: *Jane's Intelligence Review*

The most industrious and creative producers of land mines are not the Cold War vassal states but the high-tech Western countries who make such a big stink about all those little kids who get blown to bits. There are 100 different companies in 55 countries that make land mines. Of the 55 countries who design and manufacture antipersonnel mines (about 75 percent of all land mines), 36 of the countries allow them to be exported. Keep in mind that many mines are bought through shell companies who import them into "nice" countries and then export them to "nasty" countries. Even Switzerland makes and sells five models, while Iran, Cuba and Myanmar are able only to make one model of land mine. There are billions of mines stockpiled and ready for export should you need them. So, is anyone *not* using land mines?

Well, *DP* has been up on the lines and we watch the kids place them as if they were planning for an Easter egg hunt. But Uncle Sam doesn't like us to watch them in use in places like Guantanamo Bay in Cuba or the oddly named DMZ in Korea. So don't believe all that hair-shirt stuff about not using land mines. They are an integral part of military training for every armed force around the world (except maybe the Papal Guards). Here's a list of where you can shop for the 362 different models of land mines.

LAND MINES

Stumps 'R' Us: Who Designs 'em	
Country	# of Models Sold
United States	37
Italy	36
Russia	31
Sweden	21
China	21
Germany	18
Vietnam	18
France	14
Bosnia Herzegovina	16
Austria	16

Source: Jane's Intelligence Review

How Are They Used?

Mines are a defensive and psychological weapon. When you don't want Omar and his brigands disturbing your sleep, you string a perimeter with trip wires, and sleep tight. If you need to control a rebel activity you mine the waterholes, paths, food patches and storehouses. That way, rebels can eat but only while hopping on one foot using one hand. If you want to mess up an entire country you just drop mines from planes, shoot them from shells, mine waterways, power stations, highways and whatever. This ensures the entire country is plunged into the Stone Age.

Then, of course, your politicians get bored of whatever political manifesto you were protecting and you go home. During hostilities, your mine fields were carefully marked with skull and crossbones, "Beware of mine" signs and carefully fenced off. You backed up these dangerous places with accurate maps showing placement and layout.

Naturally, your land mines were all laid according to preagreed military patterns in a standard defensive area. One such NATO pattern is an A pattern, with one antitank mine surrounded by three antipersonnel mines: one above and one on each side like a triangle with the antitank in the middle. The polite way to kill advancing troops and vehicles.

After the war your nice troops cleaned up all the land mines and handed over the maps to local leaders. Uh huh. If you come from a super nice super PC country you also cleaned up all the dud shells, mortars, chemicals, armories and cap guns you left lying around. Sure, double uh huh. Hey, don't forget all those popped tanks, downed helicopters, shell craters and VD you left behind, too.

Now the war is over, allowing people to live their lives free from fear, safe in their newly created democracy.

That is wishful thinking, since the most effective way to sow land mines is to drop millions of small plastic mines by shell or from aircraft. Small bomblets, 247 to a pod, are dropped as part of cluster bombs. Most rebel groups will put mines in potholes, in detours, along walking paths and in fields; they'll even booby-trap intriguing items that villagers, soldiers or children will pick up. Guerrillas don't follow patterns. Nobody knows how many mortar rounds, artillery shells and discarded ordnance will be discovered by curious children or diligent farmers. No one bothers to keep notes of where mines are planted as booby traps or nightly security perimeters. After the war, whoever loses gets their butts kicked out of the country, booby-traps or blows up every arms cache in sight and leaves behind mountains of useless weapons and material.

Now the shattered economy creates an instant market for the copper and brass used to make mines. Kids will search all day for bombs, mortars, bullets and mines. Many of them like to play with them and see if they can blow them up. I once found a large, shiny, unexploded Urgan missile that some kid had hammered open with a chisel to reveal 12 cluster bombs just waiting to go off.

In the country, mines are used to disrupt agriculture and commerce. When things stop, the mines are sitting in rice paddies, along rivers, in wells and under houses. The overgrown trails and fields soon give up their deadly harvest to ploughs, shovels and children playing.

The problem of land mines is not so much the human cost but the destruction of vast areas of vital food growing and pasture lands.

How Do They Work?

Most people picture the movie cliché of a careless GI hearing a soft click and then sweating buckets while his buddy slides his knife under his boot to keep the detonator depressed on what should be a plate-sized antitank mine. Close, but not quite real. Yes, mines are essentially dumb explosive devices that are detonated by pressure, but weapons designers have learned a few tricks since those World War II movies.

Most mines are antipersonnel devices, cheap, small and designed to maim rather than kill. A wounded soldier is a bigger drain on the enemy than a dead one. Some mines are put just under the ground to blast up while other mines are used above ground to spray debris or ball bearings. These mines are usually planted to protect camps, set ambushes or slow down chasing soldiers. Typically they use a trip wire and are never marked or documented.

A mine contains extremely explosive material that creates a wall of air and debris that expands outward at almost 7,000 meters per second. Some mines add metal projectiles like ball bearings, sharp flechettes or even nails that puncture soft flesh and shred bone into a fine spray. The shock waves are so strong that many victims find their feet still in their boots and their bones turned into projectiles that kill other people.

If you don't die of blood loss, shock or as a result of being turned into Swiss cheese, infection is your worst enemy. The explosion will imbed bits of clothing, grass, mud, dirt and your trusty guide into the shredded mass of meat that used to be your legs. You will need to apply a tourniquet and get to a hospital (yeah, sure, there's probably one around the next sand dune) ASAP. Once you're under medical care, the mashed bits will be quickly amputated, you'll be punched with an IV and given enough morphine to kill a junkie.

Liquid Lunch in a Crunch

*Many times victims of gunshot wounds, mine blasts and injuries caused by
blood loss don't have to die. In order to create an IV solution to provide minimum nutrition and increase blood pressure, it is important to know how to
administer an IV injection. If you do not have a sterile IV solution, one can be
made by taking one liter of sterile freshwater (filtered, then boiled for five
minutes and cooled while covered). Add 25 grams of glucose and 4.5 grams
of table salt. In emergency cases, the juice from a green coconut can be used
with just the salt added.*

Other mines have cute names like Bouncing Betty, because they spring up and
explode at eye level, releasing a lethal explosion of ball bearings, killing
everything within 25 meters and wounding everyone else within 200 meters.
Road mines are so large and powerful that there is a crater and little else left over.
Enough scary stuff; let's get specific. Here are the basic types of land mines used
today.

Scatter Mines

The Soviet-made PFM-1 butterfly-type mine delivers specialized deadly services. These
small mines are sprinkled all over Afghanistan by Russians to injure, but not kill
mujahedin. The idea is that a wounded person slows down two healthy people. These
mines are dropped from helicopters and burrow into the ground using tiny wings. They
explode when twisted or pressed firmly—but not necessarily the first time. These mines
have not found wide usage, but are a disturbing use of lethal force. They do not always
explode when first handled and can actually be kicked, dropped and twisted before they
explode, leading some people to believe that the Russians designed them to kill curious
children. There also are "smart" scatter mines that can arm themselves, detonate without
direct pressure and self-detonate after a specified period. These smart mines are delivered
by cannon, airplane or rocket.

Antipersonnel, Small

Foot soldiers can't carry big heavy mines, so they make a lot of little plastic mines that can
be tucked under footpaths, houses, latrines and rice paddies. These mines are about the
size of an oversized hockey puck and have a pressure-sensitive plate that the victim steps
on. These mines are usually not buried but placed under brush, streams, wet potholes, rice
paddies and mud. The mine takes very little pressure to set it off, and the victim will
usually lose a foot and/or a leg up to the knee. These mines are not designed to kill but
to create serious, incapacitating injuries that effect the morale of the other side. No one
feels gung ho when they see the results of a mine. Top sellers in this category are the
Chinese Type 72, Italian TS-50 and U.S. M14. These mines are very difficult to find,
since many of them use plastic casings and cannot be readily picked up by normal metal
detectors.

Antipersonnel, Large

These killer-blast mines usually pack about 200 grams of explosive (compared to 40
grams in the small category). The best-selling Soviet PMN likes to deliver leg-shattering
wounds caused by small mines with higher explosive content. They are used to maim
groups of soldiers, with severe wounds to groin and buttocks and loss of both legs
common. These and their smaller cousins are the most popular mines numerically. They
cost about US$3 each and can be found still killing and maiming people in most Third
World war zones. There are also large versions of these pressure mines that can kill entire

platoons. These mines are typically buried just under the surface and can be easily found if they have metal parts.

Fragmentation Mines

Mines like the U.S. M18A1 "Claymore" are designed to spray large areas with thousands of ball bearings. Other frag mines like the Russian POMZ-2 explode into thousands of sharp metal pieces. These mines are set up as booby traps (usually with trip wires) and are used to protect camp perimeters or to ambush columns. The mines are placed above ground, on trees, across narrow paths, inside buildings, along roads, or anywhere a group of soldiers would collect. One soldier trips over the wire, and instantly he and his buddies are killed. If the mines are never tripped, they sit waiting for the next victim.

There are also the Bouncing Betty type of fragmentation mines called "bounding" mines. They are designed to be buried in the ground in open areas, and when one of the whiskerlike sensors is triggered, the mine will project upwards and explode ball bearings or shrapnel in a lethal 360-degree radius. The Italian-made Valmara-69 is the most famous example of this mine. The explosion occurs at a three- to five-foot height, maximizing the "kill ratio" (a popular term in all military sales films). Some mines have over 1,000 individual pieces of shrapnel, so the chances of surviving by ducking or turning sideways are slim to none.

These mines are designed to be lethal and are left behind to slow down advancing armies, decimate charges and create maximum casualties.

Antitank Mines

The mines that do the most damage to wartime soldiers and peacetime mine clearance workers are the big plate-sized and plank-size tank killers. These are mines laid down in active war zones to kill and disable vehicles, kill the occupants and destroy the road. The British L9 and the Italian VS-22 are popular mines used in the Gulf War and in other combat zones. Some, like the VS-22, have less metal than a gum wrapper, so don't be too confident when you see the your guards sweep the road.

Road mines are also used in convoy ambushes and can be detonated by radio-controlled explosives. Since these mines are easy to detect and are placed around major transportation corridors, they are usually the first ones to be cleared up (or to be run over).

Other Mines and Hidden Dangers

If you really are kinky about mines, you can pick up a Jane's directory or send for brochures. There are many booby traps that are not technically mines. There are also extraordinary amounts of unexploded ordnance in the ground that may not jump up and bite you, but can be found displayed in villager's homes and souvenir shops.

What are your chances of finding one of these millions of mines? Pretty good if you contribute to *DP*. Not so easy if you stay on the beaten path. Most if not all mined areas are known to locals and their victims tend to be children and women working their daily chores. Soldiers are maimed and mine clearance people do have accidents.

Where Are the Mines?

No one knows. Despite what you read here or elsewhere, no one knows how many mines there are at any one time. Mines are being laid as you read this in places like Angola, Afghanistan, Yugoslavia, Ethiopia, Tajikistan and any conflict where defensive positions are being created. As I write this, mines are being scattered from the air like deadly snowflakes by Russian Antonovs in Chechnya. Eighteen African countries have between 18 and 30 million mines each; Angola has the most, between 9 and 20 million uncleared mines, and even the "lightly mined" countryside of Mozambique (with about 2 million) has turned many small roads into death traps and caused large game to vanish. Somalia has 1 million mines; Sudan has between 1 and 2 million (and growing); and Zimbabwe and Ethiopia have major uncleared minefields (about half a million each). Bosnia Herzegovina, Cambodia and Croatia are the most mined countries in the world, with an average of between 92 and 142 land mines per square mile. This can be misleading, since the mines in Egypt are sitting in the remote northern deserts and the mines in Angola are in small towns and fields. All of East Asia has 15 to 23 million land mines. The Middle East has 17 to 24 million land mines, mainly in Iraq, Iran, Kuwait and the Israeli border. Saddam Hussein went a little overboard during his brief occupation of Kuwait and turned the entire country into a minefield, most of which has been cleaned up at great expense. Europe is home to 7 million mines, mostly along the former Soviet border. During World War I, seven countries fired nearly 1.5 billion shells. Ninety-five percent of them were conventional explosives; the rest were chemical shells. It is estimated that 30 percent of the chemical shells landed without ever exploding and have been sitting around since 1918. Most of the shells were used in Belgium. The Ukraine is home to over a million mines. Russia has both new minefields and World War II fields that were never cleared. Bosnia-Herzegovina has many uncleared fields, and new mines were being laid at a rate of 60,000 a week. At last count, there were 152 mines per square mile in this torn-up land.

Rank	Country	# of Mines	Avg per Sq Mile	Area Found
	The Land Mine Top 20			
1.	Egypt	23,000,000	59	*North toward border with Israel*
2.	Iran	16,000,000	25	*Along border with Iraq*
3.	Angola	15,000,000	31	*Rural areas*
4.	Afghanistan	10,000,000	40	*Scattered by air, also around Kabul*
5.	Cambodia	10,000,000	142	*Rural areas*
6.	China	10,000,000	3	*Along border with Russia*
7.	Iraq	10,000,000	60	*Along border with Iran*
8.	Bosnia-Herzegovina	3,000,000	152	*Throughout country*
9.	Croatia	2,000,000	92	*Throughout country*
10.	Mozambique	2,000,000	7	*Rural areas*
11.	Eritrea	1,000,000	28	*Along border with Ethiopia, rural*
12.	Somalia	1,000,000	4	*Along border with Ethiopia*
13.	Sudan	1,000,000	4	*Southern areas*
14.	Ukraine	1,000,000	4	*Old battlefields*
15.	Ethiopia	500,000	1	*Along border with Eritrea, Somalia*
16.	Yugoslavia	500,000	13	*Throughout country*
17.	Jordan	207,000	5	*Along border with Israel*
18.	Chad	100,000+	6	*Along northern border with Libya*
19.	Rwanda	100,000+	5	*Primarily in north*
20.	Vietnam	100,000+	8	*Southern areas, DMZ*

Source: U.S. Department of Humanitarian Affairs

LAND MINES

Up to a million uncleared mines are left in South America. There are mines in Colombia, Chile and most areas of Nicaragua, Guatemala and even Cuba. Some areas of the Falklands are permanently off-limits because the British could not spare the men to clear the minefields. There is a lot of splattered mutton every week in the Falklands.

Most countries in Southern Africa have large mined areas, as do the entire Horn of Africa, all areas of Middle East conflict and most border areas from the Cold War. Although there are no mines in North America, we did send a few overseas. If you thought the United States didn't do those types of things, think again. Remember that Uncle Sam used to empty out our bomb loads over Laos, leaving millions of cluster bombs for little Laotians to discover. More than 300,000 tons of bombs were dropped on northern Laos during the Vietnam War. No one has any idea how much unexploded ordnance still lies in the jungles of northern Vietnam. The overly cautious should understand that, along with cigarette butts, ammo containers and mixed-race children, land mines are just the litter of war.

A Thousand and One . . . a Thousand and Two . . . BOOM! Places Where They Haven't Counted All the Land Mines	
North, Central and South America	
Mexico	*Reports of land mine injuries, number unknown*
Guatemala	*Under 100,000*
Cuba	*Reports of land mine injuries, number unknown*
Honduras	*Under 100,000, along border with Nicaragua*
El Salvador	*Under 100,000, throughout country*
Costa Rica	*Under 100,000*
Colombia	*In remote areas, under 100,000*
Ecuador	*Along border with Peru*
Peru	*Along border with Ecuador*
Falkland Islands	*Throughout region*
Africa	
Libya	*Less than 100,000*
Uganda	*Along border areas, less than 100,000*
Burundi	*Newly laid mines, less than 100,000*
Zimbabwe	*Throughout country, more than 100,000*
Congo (DRC)	*Less than 100,000*
Namibia	*Less than 100,000*
Western Sahara	*Less than 100,000*
Mauritania	*Less than 100,000*
Senegal	*Less than 100,000*
Guinea-Bissau	*Less than 100,000*
Liberia	*Throughout country*
Sierra Leone	*Throughout country*
Tunisia	*Less than 100,000*

LAND MINES

A Thousand and One . . . a Thousand and Two . . . BOOM! Places Where They Haven't Counted All the Land Mines	
Middle East	
Oman	Throughout country, along borders
Turkey	Eastern areas, along eastern borders
Lebanon	Southern Lebanon, mined daily
Syria	Along border areas
Cyprus	Along Turkish/Greek division
Yemen	Along border areas
Europe	
Germany	In former East Germany, along border areas
Slovenia	More than 100,000
Greece	Less than 100,000
Czech Republic	Less than 100,000
Denmark	Less than 100,000
Latvia	Less than 100,000
Asia	
Belarus	Throughout country
Armenia	Areas of conflict
Azerbaijan	Throughout country
Tajikistan	Border areas
Myanmar (Burma)	Throughout country
Mongolia	Border areas, less than 100,000
Laos	Throughout country, unexploded ordnance

How Do You Get Rid of Land Mines?

There are movements by the UN, military and civilian groups (about 300 groups in total) to ban the manufacture and use of land mines. The chances are good of convincing First World countries of a ban, but the facts are that the most heavily mined countries are a result of dirty wars, not major conflicts. The majority of land mines have been planted in the last 20 years. Currently, 36 nations build land mines and most countries use them. These countries produce about 10 to 20 million units a year. About 2 million new land mines are laid each year depending on what conflicts are raging. The United States budgeted $89 million for land mine warfare in 1996.

The first task a newly stabilized country faces is cleaning up land mines. Traditional land mines are cleared in a variety of ways. In large open areas, tracked vehicles with flailing chains can clear most mines. In less accessible or poorer areas, the old-fashioned metal detector is used. Some new Scheibel-type models can detect many plastic versions. Some countries use the old-fashioned method of probing at a shallow angle with knives. Sniffing dogs can be used, along with a raft of new high-tech methods employing radar, sonar, thermal neutron, microwave, and even satellites. For now, most mines are detected and dug up the old-fashioned way, by hand or the painful way—by foot. Wildly speculative estimates on the costs to remove the world's land mines come in at about $33 billion.

In Cambodia, an on-again/off-again adventure travel destination, estimates hover around US$12 million annually for ten years to remove the 10 million land mines left from the war. There are a few groups like HALO working in Cambodia, but they still have to put up with being kidnapped and harassed by rogue Khmer Rouge bandits. There are 60,000 victims of land mines in Cambodia today, with every 237th Cambodian an amputee. But it is not the pain and disfigurement that ultimately kills. The reality is that unlike handicap-friendly America, losing a limb in the Third World is a fast ticket to poverty, begging, sickness and death.

Land mines can be found in Angola, Afghanistan, Bosnia-Herzegovina, Cambodia, Ethiopia, Eritrea, the Falklands, Iraq, Iran, Laos, Mozambique, Somalia, Thailand, Kuwait and Vietnam. In addition to carefully planted land mines, there is a significant amount of unexploded ordnance in Europe, Southeast Asia and the South Pacific. Don't get smug because you think you know your mines and your history. One mine clearance expert told us they are digging up British Land mines in Mozambique because Qaddafi had his folks dig them up in Libya and sell them to rebels. For those who need to know, there is an excellent book by Eddie Banks titled *Anti-Personnel Mines, A Recognition Guide* ($120, 512 pages, ISBN: 85753-228-7) sold by Brassey's Tel.: *(800) 775-2518, Fax: (703) 661-1501.*

One Small Step . . .

If you can't dig them up and you can't stop them from planting them, what can you do to help? First, write your local and federal politicians to make them aware that the United States and its allies manufacture these insidious killers. If you have experience in explosives or mine clearance, read the "Dangerous Jobs" section to contact a number of mine clearance companies. If you would like to donate money or time to help the innocent victims of mines, contact EMERGENCY, via Bagutta 12, 20121 Milan Italy (Tel.: 39-2-7600-1104, or Fax: 39-2-7600-3719).

There were 7 million land mines laid in Iraq and Kuwait before and during the Gulf War. Kuwait spent $800 million clearing out land mines after the Gulf War.

It costs between $500 and $2,000 per mine to remove them. A few years ago, 80,000–100,000 mines were removed around the world at a cost of $100 million. To remove all the mines in the world would cost $58 billion. Unfortunately, 2 to 5 million mines are put in the ground every year.

A *DP* reader who spends much of his time in mined areas while working for the UN Rapid Response Unit has sent in these tips.

LAND MINES

Wheel of Misfortune:
How to Avoid Land Mines

1. Never be the first on the road before 9 or 10 A.M. Most mines are laid at night to surprise regular convoys or patrols. Try to follow heavy trucks. Keep at least 200 yards behind but do not lot lose sight of the truck.

2. Never take point. (Let others start walking or driving before you.) Keep a distance of at least 60–100 feet to avoid shrapnel. If someone is wounded by a mine, apply a tourniquet immediately to the damaged limbs to prevent death by blood loss. Carry a wound kit and IV equipment if you can.

3. If a mine goes off, DO NOT RUN. Stay where you are, and walk backwards in your own tracks. Retrieve the victim by following their tracks.

4. In heavily mined areas, NEVER leave the pavement (even to take a leak). If you must turn your vehicle around, do so on the pavement.

5. If you have a flak jacket or bulletproof vest, sit on it when driving.

6. Know the mining strategy of the combatants. Do they place mines in potholes (as in northeastern Somalia) or on the off-road tracks made by vehicles avoiding potholes (as in Rwanda, Burundi and Congo)? Ask the locals: Do they booby trap? Do Are they dropped by air? What about UXO (unexploded ordnance)?

7. Mines are usually planted at a shallow depth, with their detonators requiring downward pressure. When trapped in a minefield and only as a last resort, mines can be probed using a long knife or rod inserted at a very shallow angle and with a very gentle touch. Do not touch or remove the mine, but mark it for later removal or detonation.

8. Never touch unusual or suspicious objects. Bodies, money, a camera or even your equipment may be booby-trapped.

9. Travel with all windows open and preferably with doors off or in the back of a pickup truck. This will relieve some of the blast when you hit a mine.

10. If you have reason to believe that there has been mine activity (new digging, unusual tire tracks and footprints), mark the area with a skull and crossbones and the local or English word "MINES." Notify local and/or foreign authorities.

LAND MINES

In a Dangerous Place: Kabul

The Minefields

They say that Kabul is the most destroyed city on earth. I am sure it is. I am getting used to driving by mile after mile of destroyed office flats, elegant buildings and brick houses. The factions of Dostum, Massoud and Hekmatyar duked it out until the Taliban kicked them out. All you hear now is the odd rocket attack and of course the occasional accidental detonation of a mine.

But that's why I was here, to understand about mines and the people who clear them. I had spent a week with the demining dogs. Big burly German shepherds and Belgium Malanoise handled by big burly Afghans.

The Afghans had to grow beards and they looked odd with their U.S. Army green uniforms. The demining program used to be run by Americans and when the money and supplies ran out they just took their old uniforms to the Pakistani tailors in Peshawar. When I first drove along the trunk road to their headquarters my cabdriver's eyes widened at the sight of the great black beards and fearsome looking dogs.

"Talibs?" he inquired wide-eyed.

I laughed and shook my head but he disappeared quickly. Here in Peshawar at the Mine Detection Center, or MDC, the Afghans were actually breeding and training their own dogs to clear land mines in Afghanistan. What was once a $12,000 U.S.-bred and trained police dog was now a $300 Afghan demining dog.

The dogs are trained by one trainer from when they are puppies. The concept is simple. Put a reward with whatever you want the dog to find and he will think he is having fun. In this case a red rubber ball is buried with various explosives, metallic objects and mines. The dog quickly learns to sniff out the telltale scent and is rewarded by his handler.

Then the dogs are trained to walk straight out, sniff and come back. If the dog sniffs a mine he sits and indicates. If they get excited and jump around they could set off the mine.

It's a simple business, but the dog has to know what it is doing. It was time to head out to the mine fields.

Crossing the border between Pakistan and Afghanistan is an instant education as to why the MDC crew is based in Pakistan. This morning there has been a shootout. Something silly, but the young slack-jawed Talibs picked up their battered green rocket launcher and hit the top of a building on the Pakistani side. There was machine gun fire, and then pleading from the Pakistanis to their "brothers to please stop shooting." Within minutes, life on the border was back to normal, or as normal as Torkham can be.

The flow of bent-over, dirty children carrying burlap bags is a flood of brown between tall Pakistani soldiers who stand like sweatered telephone poles above. We are waved through as our presence was aiding the torrent of gunnysacks carrying kids. The kids are carrying scrap, junk, bits of wire, old bullets, tins, anything metal. They are greasy and black and bent over from the weight. You know you are in a poor country when the children smuggle junk.

I spent time in Jalalabad, a few yards down the road from the entrance to Osama bin Laden's compound. I am warned not to walk around, so I do. I am pulled off the street by another demining crew, one that uses manual methods of finding mines. They invite me for breakfast and say, "Only brave men work in the mine fields." They wish they had dogs, but they use metal probes and share a battered mine detector amongst them.

We spend our time in the minefields of Jalalabad finding and blowing up Russian and Italian antitank mines. The Italian mines are made of plastic and have only a tiny metal pin in them. There are also anti personnel mines around each tank mine. Off in the distance the snow-covered mountains of the Hindu Kush frame the Kuchi nomads wandering through the mined pass. "Why do they not trip the mines?" I ask. I am told, "They do."

Often the mines are covered by years of erosion and dirt. But they are also uncovered by the same process. We pull up a silver canister. A Russian mine that listens and feels and then detonates. The batteries have long since gone dead but it is a truly evil invention. Many of the mines are booby trapped by other mines. That's why they are blown in place. The first land to be cleared are roads, followed by habitations then farmlands and then large areas like this. Things are looking good. They will hand over this area next week. When we blow the anti tank mines the buses and cars don't even stop to admire the 60-meter-high mushroom clouds.

I almost make it to Kabul but the demining crew must turn back. The Taliban are impounding their vehicles and we must drive back as soon as possible.

I make my own way back to Kabul, and I arrive at the headquarters of the UN demining program. There are plenty of statistics and handouts, but the bottom line is that under the Talibs they are making good headway. There is no more fighting, and other than being told to leave mines on the strategic hilltops and around the airports, progress is good. But Kabul is not doing so well. These ruins I drive by every day used to be someone's home. The children playing in the blasted streets and ruins are being injured by mines and unexploded ordnance or UXO. Part of keeping them alive is to educate children about mines.

Some 55 percent of land mine victims are children, but about 85 percent of the UXO (unexploded ordnance) victims are children. The most at risk are young men collecting the metal from bombs to sell as scrap. Most injuries are not caused by accidents but occur when kids deliberately seek out weapons of death to sell as scrap for pennies. Now I understand why the Talib checkpoints had mountains of trash along with the degutted cassette tapes.

At 3:20 P.M., a BM-22 Urgan (Hurricane) missile with high explosives slams into Kabul; there is more to come. You get used to rockets, even when you play volleyball here. People look up, measure the distance to the nearest sandbagged bunker and wait for the telltale whoosh. If it's outgoing, the game goes on.

• • •

Today, it's off to the disposal site to see how they get rid of ordnance. I cruise by the closed U.S. embassy in Najibullah Square. As we drive out of town, a silver Taliban Toyota with mirrored windows and chrome roll bars speeds up beside us. A Taliban rolls down the window and stares inside as he drives by. Satisfied, he speeds up and blasts off, scattering children and old men in front of him.

We go to the Polygon, a former military base and tank firing range to the east of Kabul. Mohammad Zahir is a former colonel in the Afghan army and head of the disposal unit. He knows firsthand the problem with incoming rockets. He had a Russian Luna rocket land 500 yards from his backyard two weeks ago.

On display is a spectrum of ordnance ranging from a 500-kilogram concrete-piercing bomb that would demolish a pillbox or building to a 23-millimeter cannon shell fuse that could take off a hand.

The only items that are here are the ones that are determined to be stable. The more dangerous ordnance is destroyed on-site.

To blow up the bombs, they use a ballistic disk to explode into the side casing of the bomb and burn off the explosives.

There is a hodgepodge of ordnance laid out for our inspection. The most ominous sight is an Uragan rocket missile that has been smashed open with a chisel by some local to see what was inside. What was inside were a cluster of 9 or 12 high-explosive bomblets. The man in charge her is Andrew McAndrew, a Scotsman. He is supervising the local Afghans in destroying this deadly harvest.

Noticing my camera, he points to the hills around the blast range. The hills are spiked with silhouettes like Indians waiting for the settlers. They are the nomads and scrap hunters that are waiting for the big bang. The first batch goes off with a devastating bang. As I watch from the bunker I see the hills streaming with running children

They run into the pit after the explosion to grab the red-hot fragments. They are look for the copper drive bands or even the raw steel scrap on the shell casing. They get 20,000 Afghanis for 7 kilograms. They are risking their lives to get 75 cents for 16 pounds of copper. When I approach them I notice a still-smoking 500-pound bomb in the crater.

There are about 60 people in the hole frantically digging and jostling. Small children grab the red-hot shell fragments and grimace, while others dig for the tiny pieces that make the tinkling sound of deadly shrapnel. A fight breaks out in the pit, and one teenager hauls off and starts hitting another with a shovel. When they see me taking pictures, they stop, look up and smile.

I wander over to the HALO Trust offices (Hazardous Area Life Support Organization) and meet Alex, a 28-year-old former officer in the British Army with experience in Bosnia, and with HALO experience in Nagorno Karabakh and now Afghanistan. He is a young, thin man who is the only expat running HALO's Afghanistan operation.

It is the first week of demining after the long winter and Alex is having trouble getting the teams to their northern projects due to fighting. He has a large, plastic-covered map of Afghanistan, and there are a surprising number of green dots for cleared sites and very few red ones.

HALO specializes in mechanical removal of mines and has a selection of heavy equipment that can clear mines in collapsed buildings. They don't work directly with the UN program, but they coordinate their work by slicing up Kabul and other regions. There is a little bad blood between HALO and the UN deminers, who consider the HALO operation a showboat operation with a higher than needed casualty rate. They don't outwardly have any animosity, but Alex does not allow us to take pictures of the armada of white Land Rovers in their compound. Including a bullet proof Range Rover for crossing enemy lines.

The most famous image of demining is Princess Di in Angola visiting HALO and wearing the trademark (and large logoed) body armor and face shield. I am issued the same safety getup and hope that any mines I detonate will not explode upwards, negating the benefit my Hollywood-style getup.

I talk about how the statistics thrown around by outsiders do not reflect the actual truths on the ground. Like many deminers here, Alex believes that there are fewer mines in Afghanistan than the press or even the UN reports.

He gives credit to the Taliban for providing a stable region in which to conduct their operations. He points on the map to the infamous road from Mazar and says "that is an interesting road," refering to the banditry and haphazard safe passage. Alex tells a number of blood-chilling stories about doing business in the lawless regions of Afghanistan. He manages to get through with military bluster and good luck. He remains cheerful despite the daunting task ahead of him.

At the UNICA guesthouse its "bar night" and it's crowded to capacity. There are about 150 foreigners in Kabul and about half of them seem to come for the narrow two-hour window allowed for drinking on Thursday and Friday. I am told that some of the groups have their own private clubs where they drink a homemade brew called *arak*, made of raisins. Outsiders are not welcome at these clubs because they would alert the attention of the Taliban.

The scene is becoming routine. There is a large contingent of French Red Cross workers who had to flee the fighting in Mazar to the north. They view this work as somewhat romantic and have long hair, earrings and seem the lest affected by stress and conditions. They always sit together, and the rest talk shop or spread rumors. It seems we are CIA spies. There is much talk about the two Americans who are ostensibly here to do something on demining, but are neither are journalists or consultants. We are told quite frankly that there are a number of odd people that come through here, and they usually have a better cover story than we do.

For example, they tell me that the U.S. NGO across the street is a front for the CIA, and there have been an awful lot of British and Americans through the bar, none of whom have very good cover stories. But at least I have progressed from mercenary to spy.

The Talibar is the name they give to the small bar at the UNICA guesthouse. It used to be called the "Hard Rocket Cafe" before things eased up here. There is also the "Talibision" that has CNN and the BBC, and the compound has a satellite phone, or a "Talibphone" for UN calls. But back to the discovery.

I discover something interesting. They are drinking ten-year-old booze. The limited selection at the bar of whisky, liquors and vodka came in here in a container in 1991, and they have been drinking it every since. The Chablis turned sour and the Scotch doesn't age. The most cherished alcohol is Dortmunder beer, the only beer that has remained pure and tasty in storage after eight years.

The bar is probably one of the best (well, actually the only) place in Afghanistan for a drink and a chat. Gregory, with UN Habitat from London, likes to man the bar, and Andrew, from Aberdeen, likes to anchor the other end. Andrew McAndrew is 55, an EOD expert and has been here three years. He went into the British army at 18 and came out as a warrant officer. Now he works here to make a difference. His specialty is removing the deadly litter of war—unexploded missiles, bombs, rockets, bullets, fuses, mines and anything that can go bang. He is a quiet man whose favorite line, delivered in a broad Scottish accent, is, "Ah doo wut ahh doo." He is one of the half dozen expats who are working with the demining program in Afghanistan.

The next day I go to school for land-mine awareness. The children range in age from 6 to 13. They play a game: They pull blue or red questions (blue cards are regular questions, red cards are about land mines). They get an activity book. When I ask the girls what they want to be when they grow up, I hear doctor, pilot, stewardess and teacher. When I ask if they think they will ever have those jobs they say, "I will try my best." The children also play a charade about what happens when they collect mines. They all blow up and fall down. The younger children laugh.

After the others go to bed, Andrew, the bomb disposal expert, is having a final drink with me since he is leaving tomorrow and he doesn't know if he will come back. We talk about making a difference. He feels he has made a difference in this world, as unsung or trivial as it may seem. He has spent three years training Afghans to clear, remove and dispose of deadly explosive devices, allowing them to rebuild. Something that will never make headlines or make him rich despite risking his life daily a long way from his wife and home. With the front lines only 12 miles away and the sporadic rocket attacks, he thinks it all might have been a waste. I disagree and encourage him to tell other people how they can make a difference when he gets back to Scotland. Someone has to push back the darkness.

Realizing that he is leaving tomorrow and he is very drunk, he turns to me and says, "Robert, I am so tired."

—RYP

LAND MINES

Military and Paramilitary Organizations

How to Travel Free, Meet Interesting People and Then Kill Them

Adventure stirs deep in the loins of youth and before they had low-cost airfares, backpacks and student discounts, most people got their first trip overseas in uniform. Things have changed.

What can well-trained adventurers do to make this world a better place and tell stories to their grandkids? In the old days, you could ride off to the Crusades, discover the New World or just raise hell in some wealthy potentate's army. Since then, there have been few noble wars to occupy the heroic and romantic. Between our great and not-so-great wars (when Uncle Sam made you volunteer), poets, thugs and the bloodthirsty have volunteered for a variety of romantic causes, from the Russian Revolution to the Spanish civil war.

More importantly, applying your security, medical, engineering or military learned skills to the Third World is just as valid as any civilian skills. The most extreme application would be to join a foreign army or a group that is actively fighting for independence, freedom or any other cause. The KLA was the last manifestation of this age-old tradition, but you will find North American volunteers in Sri Lanka, Kurdistan, Eritrea, Israel, Afghanistan, Kashmir and other conflicts.

Keep in mind that you can lose your American citizenship if you choose to be a mercenary (although no U.S. contract soldier or mercenary has to date) and your chances of being summarily executed by the side of the road if captured are high. So let's start out with the most PC version of military adventure—the Army.

Happiness Is a Warm Gun: The Army/Navy/Air Force

Today's armed forces look pretty good to the hordes of young men and women who can't find jobs. The problem is, these days most young men and women have jobs. Recruitment is down, morale is down, the pay sucks and the idea of being globo-cop is not the idea most people had when they went in. The world is no longer good vs. evil. The world's businesses are just too tightly interwoven and politics too fractured to allow another Axis versus Allies confrontation. A quick look at where Uncle Sam gets to fire guns would result in firing blanks. Sure, there is the quick dash to a Third World wasteland so our soldiers don't get rusty, but most of the current activity of the U.S. military consists of sitting on their behinds overseas or polishing their guns back home.

Sure, the U.S military has officially seen action in Bosnia, Korea, Vietnam, Lebanon, Iraq, Grenada, Panama, Libya, Somalia and Haiti; however, none of these have been official wars. Rather, they were primarily police actions or gun boat diplomacy. That said, there has been covert military action in Angola, Cuba, Cambodia, Laos, Nicaragua, Iran, El Salvador and numerous other areas, and training missions in Uganda, Sri Lanka, Colombia and dozens of other "which end does the bullet come out?" armies we call allies. If their countries actually have gas and airlines we'll train them here. In 1998, Uncle Sam spent $50 million dollars training 9,000 foreign military personnel from over 100 countries. Nice folks like the ones who caused all the ruckus in East Timor. (Okay, class, can we spell D-e-a-t-h S-q-u-a-d)?

In the past, America had a big enemy to unleash its big army on. No more. Today's military is killing time instead of bad guys. In places like Bosnia, Iraq, Lebanon and Somalia, America's finest are now politically correct, overtrained and underpaid flatfoots. With today's booming job market, lack of clear objectives, or even positive role models, it is no surprise that the U.S. military is having trouble attracting the numbers or caliber of soldier it had with the draft. Our current all-volunteer army has lower scores, lower average IQ levels, and gender-modified achievement levels as equipment and technology become more advanced and complicated. Just what would our well-fed, by-the-book, bed-at-night, politically-correct, Geneva Convention–style military do against barefoot mujahedin or female suicide bombers? Unlike the days of the Rough Rider, when bar fighters, intellectuals, noblemen and cowboys joined up to fight the good fight, today's army attracts a totally different crowd. It could be said that today's military, with its too kind, thoughtful, PC nonkillers, does about all it can do to take the adventure out of military service.

What can you expect if you sign up in today's army? The army's nine-week basic training program at Fort Jackson, South Carolina, transforms civilians into soldiers 60 raw recruits at a time. At bases like Fort Jackson, 70,000 military personnel are trained annually, 3 million since the base's opening in 1917.

Upon arrival, you can expect to fill out horrendous amounts of paperwork. You spend the first six days at the Reception Battalion, where you pick up your uniforms, have your head shaved and are given 16-hour doses of KP, or kitchen patrol. The second week is filled with 12-hour days (with reveille at 4 A.M.), drill and ceremony movements, classroom work, land and navigation courses, bayonet assault training and an obstacle course centered around the Victory Tower.

The second month begins with basic rifle marksmanship. You will learn to understand and care for your M-16 like no other physical object you own. You will learn to fire at targets as far as 300 meters away. Based on your performance, you will be called a marksman, sharpshooter or expert. Toward the end of the second month, the weaponry gets serious, with the M-60 machine gun, AT4 antitank weapon and hand grenades. Instead of firing your weapon, you get a taste of what it will be like on the receiving end, as you learn how to move around under fire complete with barbwire obstacles, exploding dynamite and M-60 rounds being fired over your head as you crawl 300 meters on your belly.

The last week of training intensifies with PT testing and working with explosives. The climax is a three-day field exercise, where trainees get to play war by digging foxholes and taking eight-mile hikes with full packs. The last few days are spent cleaning barracks in preparation for the next cadets. How tough is it? New recruits will say very; the old salts will say not as tough as it used to be. Corporal punishment was banned in the mid-1970s, and sexual harassment has been added to the list of subjects taught. Minor punishment is confined to "smoke sessions," for the less than motivated. These semipunitive periods of intense physical training are designed to remind the errant soldier who is in charge. Soldiers are chewed out using the entire spectrum of profanity.

The front-leaning rest position (a push-up that is never completed) is also used as punishment. There is no form of entertainment, since there technically is no rest time. Television, newspapers and radios are taboo. Mail and occasional phone calls are allowed. Three washing machines and five showerheads are considered enough to keep 60 active men clean.

Once out of basic training, you can expect to be posted to an area in line with your specialty. The military is still using technology about 10–20 years behind what you find on the outside. The main focus in the military is changing from '40s-style ground wars to '70s-style rapid-deployment tactics. The army provides lousy pay, good benefits, excellent training and a chance to pack in two careers in a lifetime. As for furthering a cause or making the world a better place, one only has to look at Lebanon, Kuwait, Somalia and Vietnam to see the results of gunboat diplomacy.

Beau Geste: The French Foreign Legion

The more romantic and politically insensitive might want to consider joining the Legion. The Legion is, more or less, France's colonial houseworker, oppressing minorities, liberating missionaries and generally keeping the natives from getting too restless. The Legion knows it does France's dirty work and recruits accordingly. They will take all comers, preferably foreigners and men who will not draw too big a funeral procession. The Legion is tough and disposable.

The best example of the Legion's mind-set is the single most revered object in their possession—the wooden hand of Captain Jean Danjou on display in the museum in Aubagne. Danjou lost his hand when his musket misfired and blew up. He then died with the 59 worn-out survivors defending a hacienda on April 30, 1864, in a small hamlet called Camerone in Mexico. His men, exhausted after a long forced march to evade the 2,000-strong Mexican army, decided to die rather than surrender. His wooden hand was found by the tardy relief column and enshrined to commemorate his courage. Over 10,000 legionnaires died at Dien Bien Phu in 1954 in a similar debacle. One unit suffered a 90 percent loss at Cao Bang, only to have 576 out of 700 killed four years later at Dien Bien Phu.

A normal army would frown upon the lack of reinforcement, bad strategies and resulting waste of manpower. The Legion (like all of French military history) myopically elevates folly into legend and attracts thousands of eager recruits every year. The basic lesson is that with only 75 percent of the Legion being French, they are considered disposable.

Despite its notoriety, the Legion is still the army of choice when young men dream of adventure. The Legion is the tough guy's army, tailor-made for Hollywood film scripts, home for intellectuals, criminals and outcasts. It's a close-knit band of hardy, brutal men who are either escaping misguided pasts or seeking adventure in exotic places and doing heroic deeds. The lure of the Legion is communicated to us via simplistic movies like *Beau Geste,* or simplistic books that romanticize its violence and bloodshed. What they don't tell you is that the Legion has always been brutal and ill-equipped. But you get to learn to be a professional killer and chances are high that you will use those skills on other people.

The Legion was created in 1831 by King Louis Phillipe to assist in the conquest of Algeria. The king correctly assumed that paid mercenaries would not complain about the conditions or political correctness in carrying out his orders. Since then, the Legion has been used to fight France's dirty little wars in Algeria, Indochina, Africa and the Middle East. Although there have been many heroic battles fought in some of the world's most remote and hostile regions, you are better served by reading the multitudes of books about the Legion. The reality today is that the Legion has been downsized and specialized.

The Legion is one of the few action outfits (like the former Selous Scouts of Rhodesia or Oman's mostly British army) which offers the professional adventurer a steady diet of hardship broken up by short bursts of excitement and danger. This format has attracted many of the world's best-trained soldiers, like the SS after World War II or Special Forces vets from Vietnam. The world of adventure is shrinking, however. Today the French Foreign Legion is made up of 8,500 officers and men from more than 100 countries. They no longer have any ongoing wars that require constant replacements. They now focus on picking and choosing from amongst the world's tough guys to enable them to field soldiers who are fluent in many languages and specialities without the religious, political or ethnic barriers that hamper other peacekeeping or expedition forces.

How to Get In

There are 16 Legion recruiting centers in France, the most popular being Fort de Nogent in Paris. Just ask at the police station for the *Legion Etrangere*. The more focused head straight for Aubagne, just outside of the dirty Mediterranean port of Marseille. You will be competing with over 8,000 other eager Legionnaire wannabe's for the 1,500 slots available. Eastern Europeans make up about 50 percent of the eager candidates these days. Candidates are tested for their intelligence and physical fitness, and special skills are a definite plus. If you just murdered your wife's boyfriend the week before, be forewarned that all candidates are run through Interpol's data banks and the Legion cooperates with them to weed out murderers. If you just want to escape the IRS or alimony payments, the Legion could care less. After all, what better inducement is there to staying after your third year in Djibouti than the thought of spending that same time in jail Stateside?

You won't be required to bring an ID or proof of anything; when you sign up, you will be assigned a nom de guerre and a nationality. Being Canadian is popular, and calling yourself Rambo is definitely an old joke.

You must pass the same general standards as the French army, but then the Legion takes over. They will also run on Interpol computers and your home country will get a call. You will learn to march like a mule in hell—long forced marches with heavy packs; jungle, mountain and desert training. You can bail out during the first four months of training, but from then on, you will speak the thick, crude French of the Legionnaire and learn to be completely self-sufficient in the world's worst regions.

There is basic training in Castelnaudary (between Carcassone and Toulouse, just off the A61), commando training in St. Louis near Andorra, and mountain training in Corsica. Four weeks into your training, you will be given the *Kepi blanc,* the white pillbox hat of the Legionnaire. Unlike the Navy SEALs or Western elite forces, the accommodations are simple and the discipline is swift, and other than special prostitutes who service the legion, there is little to look forward to in the mandatory five years of service. Legionnaires can get married after ten years of service.

Once you pass basic training, you will be trained in a specialized category: mountain warfare, explosives or any number of trades that make you virtually unemployable upon discharge (except in another mercenary army). French citizens cannot serve, except as officers. Those French officers who sign on do so for a taste of adventure. In troubled times, the legionnaires are always the first to be deployed to protect French citizens in uprisings or civil wars.

With this international makeup, it is not surprising that Legionnaires today find themselves as peacekeepers, stationed in the tattered shreds of the French empire or with the UN You may be assigned to protect the European space program in Kourou, in the steamy jungles of French Guiana, or to patrol the desert from Quartier Gaboce, in the hot baked salt pan of Djibouti. When it hits the fan as in Kolwezi or Chad, you can expect some excitement, a quick briefing, an airdrop into a confused and bloody scene, followed by years of tedium, training and patrol.

Since the Legion attracts loners and misfits, and because many of them spend their time in godforsaken outposts, it is not hard to understand that the Legion becomes more than a job. In fact, the motto of the Legion is "*Legio Patria Nostra*," or "The Legion Is Our Homeland," which describes the mind-set and purpose. Many men serve out their full 20 years, since they are unable to find equally stimulating work on the outside.

When you get out, you don't get much other than a small pension and the opportunity to become a Frenchman (legionnaires are automatically granted French citizenship after five years). After a lifetime of adventure, and divorced from their homeland, the men of the Legion can look forward to retirement at Domaine Danjou, a château near Puyloubier (12 miles west of St. Maxim, north of the A7) in southern France, where close to 200 legionnaires spend their last years. This is where the Legion looks after its own, its elderly, wounded and infirm. Here, the men have small jobs, ranging from bookbinding to working in the vineyards. Later, they will join their comrades in the stony ground of the country that never claimed them but for which they gave their lives. Remember, the Legion has always been disposable.

Working Freelance

All right, you do your 2, 5 or 20 years and you're out. You keep it high and tight, work out, but selling life insurance or pushing Ralston Purina to pet stores just doesn't have the same edge. Life outside is dull. Life inside was dull but you got to blow shit up, party, shoot at things, jump out of planes, learn cool stuff, hang out with like-minded. You need to get back in.

So who is hiring ex-military experts? Well, technically, nobody. Although historically many countries like Brunei (which uses Ghurkas), the Vatican (which has about 100 Swiss guards) and Oman have armies staffed by paid foreigners (about 360 British officers were "seconded" to the sultan to fight rebels), you will have to be hired out of an existing army (typically the British army) to be considered. Many foreign armies are happy to enlist your services and the Canadian, British or Australian armed forces will even give you citizenship when you are finished. Times are tough, so there are plenty of people who like the idea of paid housing and training. You can expect stringent entry requirements and a thorough check of your background. The real action is in private military corporations (PMCs), which essentially provide outsourced military skills. But don't hold your breath and pack your bags just yet. Yes, those camel lots, oil rigs, pipelines, expat compounds and bigwigs need security, but get in line. It's an old boy's network where few if any employees get dropped in the middle of firefights. Watching cheap black and white monitors in air-conditioned trailers maybe, but just don't expect a lot of heat and light. If you want to get into the shit, keep in mind that late-night 7-11 clerks and bank tellers see more firefights than most marines.

Happiness Is a Hired Gun: PMCs and Mercs

So you did your time in the army and can fieldstrip everything from a Makarov to a Chinese nuclear missile, you can fly an Apache helo or an F-117 blindfolded, you could parachute directly into Saddam Hussein's Jacuzzi without tripping the disco light alarms and can speak 145 languages (including tribal dialects) and swear in 89 of them. You have been trained to kill a man just by twitching your ears, can make explosives out of Rice Krispies and list every LIC and Tango group by acronym alphabetically in Russian. You're under 40, fit and ready to go private. Congratulations, you can now work at Home Depot in the plumbing department or seek employment as a mercenary. If your girlfriend is not impressed with the term *merc,* then how about a contractor for a private military corporation, the new properly spun word for foreign soldiers who work in other peoples backyards.

Well, we may be getting a little carried away, but the bottom line is it won't take long before you start discovering that international security companies are forking over $10,000–$15,000 a month for high-level contract soldiering these days. You only have one problem. Uncle Sam would rather see you work as a Burger King manager than sell your precious skills to the highest bidder. Yes, there are U.S. groups like MPRI and Vinnell who have dull-as-dishwater brochures and who do equally dull things like train foreign armies or write operational manuals for esoteric milspec gear.

Any U.S. citizen entering a foreign army without prior approval (in writing) from both the secretary of state and the secretary of defense will forfeit U.S. citizenship, although Congress has ruled that enlistment in a foreign army is not a clear enough declaration of intent to voluntarily renounce citizenship.

The Hague 1907 Convention banned operation on the territory of neutral states of offices for recruitment of soldiers (volunteers or mercenaries) to fight in a country at war. In 1977, part of a supplementary protocol to the 1949 Geneva Convention on the Protection of Civilian Population in Time of War made freelancers liable to court trial as criminals if they are taken POW. If found guilty, they can be simply shot on the spot as criminals.

The UN General Assembly reached a consensus in 1989 on the recruiting, training, use and financing of mercenaries. If you are interested in volunteering, make sure you understand the laws and penalties that will suddenly apply to you. If you think fighting for money will make you popular and chicks will dig you, think again. On the other hand, if Uncle Sam has spent five years and about half a million dollars turning you into all that you can be, there are employment choices other than flipping burgers or working at Jiffy Lube.

Americans have not always been the ideal volunteers. In fact, the last two great wars showed that the majority of Americans held back until they were pushed into it. But once they were in it, they finished the job. There are two major developments you have to come to terms with.

¿Gringos? No Me Gustan.

First, most foreign armies don't want American volunteers. Americans have an image of wanting too much money, complaining too much, and creating too many political overtones when captured or killed. Unless, of course, our CIA has a vested interest in keeping an eye on things. American mercenaries have fought in Angola, Rhodesia, Guatemala, El Salvador, Nicaragua, Sierra Leone, Myanmar, the Congo, Lebanon, Bosnia and Russia. Many are motivated by religion (black Muslims in the Middle East), background (Croats in Yugoslavia), money (Central America) or a misguided sense of adventure (Angola). The United States is not adverse to hiring or supplying mercenaries, starting back when Benjamin Franklin hired the Prussian officer Friedrich von Steuben to instill discipline into the Continental Army, or when Claire Chennault was hired to give Japan grief with his Flying Tigers. And Americans are not adverse to being mercenaries (we are capitalists, after all). In modern times U.S.-hired mercenaries have been as diverse as the Ray-Banned pilots that flew for Air America, the advisers who trained Nung or Montagnard tribes in Vietnam or the doomed Contras in Nicaragua. There have been Americans in the Congo, Sierra Leone, Rhodesia, Myanmar, Israel and as far back as fliers in World War I, advisers to Haile Selassie in Ethiopia and dozens that fought and died in the Spanish civil war. We are busy training soldiers in Sri Lanka, Uganda and Colombia, so what's the big deal about mercs?

Mercenaries continue to do *our* dirty, or covert work, but our government does not like the idea of *you* running off to fight in other people's wars.

The new solution is to legalize mercenary work. The creation of the private military corporation like MPRI, Sandlines and others are doing a lot of the clean or dirty work countries can't or won't do themselves. For example, Executive Outcomes' brochure promises:

- To provide a highly professional and confidential military advisory service to legitimate governments.
- To provide sound military and strategic advice.
- To provide the most professional military training packages currently available to armed forces, covering aspects related to sea, air and land warfare.
- To provide advice to armed forces on weapon and weapon platform selection.
- To provide a total, apolitical service based on confidentiality, professionalism and dedication.

Today, those who wish to be wild geese or soldiers of fortune will find few clear career paths. You will need the minimum service and training provided by a Western military power. Special forces members, explosives experts, pilots, and officers with training experience and other specialized skills are in demand.

Although the need for foreign volunteers cannot be predicted, there are certain starting points for employment. Make sure you have a contract and remember, even the best-laid plans go awry, as they did for EO in PNG. You should know that EO ended up going tits-up with $19.5 million still owed them by the government of Sierra Leone.

Employment with a Difference

Getting a job in the merc world is a long way from the "Employment with a difference" classified ad placed by Mike Hoare in South Africa when he set out to recruit mercenaries to fight in the Belgian Congo. Having neither the budget nor the time to train men, he put together what he called his "Wild Geese," the name of an ancient Irish band of soldiers for hire. He managed to defeat the Simbas, rescue white women and embarrass the UN. And he received a book and movie deal later.

Remember, if you find a recruiter in a bar who is looking for "a few good men," they are usually filling grunt and junior-officer levels only for second tier gigs. The players have already cut their deal up at the top, and they need to fill in the holes to get paid. Top-level giggers like Executive Outcomes got $20 million for supplying 2,000 soldiers and another $20 million for arms and supplies. Not bad, but don't forget they still paid their ground pounders about $2,000 a month.

There are also horror stories about hucksters preying on the gullible, as in Angola in the '70s. The U.S. government paid to hire mercenaries out of London in their bid to oust the Cuban-supported MPLA. Four groups of 185 men were sent in to fight with the FNLA. It was a disaster from the start. Psychotic officers (like 25-year-old Costas Georgiou, aka "Colonel Callan") executed their own people, few skirmishes were won, and when it was over, 13 mercenaries were put on trial and four were executed by a firing squad (one had to propped up on his stretcher to be shot properly). The high hopes, empty talk and wasted time continue today. Even if you do find someone who has a gig for you, remember that they get paid by the head count, and once in that country you can be turned down, arrested or sent into action on your first day without training, weapons, gear or ammo. The reality is that most experienced mercenaries either use the old-boy network or simply fly to the capital city of an emerging war zone and offer their services directly to the military advisers for whichever side they feel is the most desperate. Their services usually include rounding up cannon fodder like you.

There is also a lot of home-grown soldiering that usually leads nowhere. Some like the Falangists and Chamounists in Beirut in the '80s brought in eager French Falangist Party students, but most look for trained, hardened professionals with special skills. Your paycheck is an occasional bad meal and a place in heaven for fighting the good fight. Young Kashmiris are given a few weeks training and humped off across the mountains to Indian Kashmir to raise hell and end up dead in shootouts. There seems to be no age limit. In Africa, young Ugandan school boys are rounded up and used as porters for rebel groups, kidnapped young girls become part-time pillows and cooks. Isn't war fun?

UN Missions around the World		
Want to save the world? Look good in robin egg blue? Dig white SUVs? The UN may be just the place to spend a vacation. Here is a list of the latest (and longest UN deployments).		
Angola	**MONUA**	**Replaced UNIVEM III ended 6/97**
Central African Republic	**MINURCA**	**Began 4/98**
Bosnia-Herzegovina	**UNMIBH**	**NATO-led IFOR and IPTF**
Croatia	**UNTAES and UNMOP**	
Cyprus	**UNFICYP**	
Georgia	**UNOMIG**	
Haiti	**MIPONUH**	**UNSMIH ended 07/97**
Israel/Syria	**Golan Heights- UNDOF**	
Iraq/Kuwait	**UNIKOM**	
Lebanon	**UNIFIL**	
Macedonia	**UNPREDEP**	
Middle East	**UNTSO**	**Began 1948**
Pakistan/India/Kashmir	**UNMOGIP**	**Began 1949**
Palestine	**UNTSO**	
Sierra Leone	**UNOMSIL**	**Began July 1998**
Tajikistan	**UNMOT/CIS**	**UN observers/CIS**
Western Sahara	**MINURSO**	

Source: UN

Death from Behind a Desk

Because of the old-boy network and need for inside contacts, many soldiers of fortune do not make their money fighting on the ground, but make themselves available for higher-level training and transportation contracts. They might source leased aircraft, arrange weapons transfers, organize rescue attempts, or train eager recruits to shoot guns and blow things up, all the while living in air-conditioned comfort complete with CNN.

Today's mercenary is not a cigar-chomping, muscle-bound adventurer with a bandolier of 50 mm bullets and grenades hung like Christmas ornaments. He is more likely to be an unemployed soldier 30–35 years of age who can't find work with his specialized skills. The pay is good when you have skills and tepid if you don't (mercenaries make between $2,000 and $15,500 a month, depending on skills, rank and type of job, and the benefits); in its glory years, Executive Outcomes took great pains to provide medivac, health and life insurance as well as long-term treatment for the wounded. And the chances of getting killed depend on which side you pick. If you are fighting a bush war, your enemy will take great pleasure in torturing you and parading you around like a three-headed goat. Americans can also lose their passport or citizenship if they fight in the service of a foreign army. Others will most definitely be jailed and tried for war crimes. Mercs are not accorded prisoner of war status under the Geneva Conventions.

Are there any loopholes? If you are hired to invade another country, destroy property, kill or hurt people, or even to destabilize a democratic or undemocratic government, you are breaking the law. If you do not live in the attacked country, have a foreign citizenship, are on a mission to rescue someone, or you're just hanging around a war zone, you can be shot as a spy or a foreign agent. If you are in a country that has declared a state of war, remember it is much easier and cheaper to shoot questionable characters than to fill out the paperwork.

If you want to truly be a volunteer like the German Steiner (the Sudan) or Argentinian Ché Guevara (Uganda, Cuba, Bolivia), remember that Steiner was tried, imprisoned and tortured, and Guevera was ventilated by CIA operatives and dumped in a hastily dug Bolivian grave. When it's over in this business, it's over.

There are some gray areas that afford some (but little) protection. Make sure you enlist in a recognized foreign army. Join a foreign legion like the French Foreign Legion; have a civilian work contract for a recognized government. You could fight with a recognized army in a foreign territory (like our army in the Gulf or Vietnam) that is not technically at war but helping someone else win a war.

The skinniest loophole is offering your services for a higher pay rate in a foreign army where you are seconded to another army. Technically, you can join as a regular service member if there are no local troops with comparable experience. Will that stop the opposing side from parading you around like a zoo animal, then doing a flamenco dance on your testicles? No.

Soldiers of Misfortune

Be warned that there are plenty of cheap movies and bad books attempting to add the luster of righteousness and adventure to the mercenary life. These books tend to be short on facts and long on gun talk. They provide hard-to-find tips like "never handle explosives carelessly" (from the *Mercenary's Tactical*

Handbook, by Sid Campbell) to "take no unnecessary risks" (from the *African Merc Combat Manual,* from Paladin Press).

There are some good books on this nasty business, most long out of print: *The Brother's War,* by John St. Jorre; *Legionnaire,* by Simon Murray; *Mercenary,* by Mike Hoare; *The Last Adventurer,* by Rolf Steiner; *Mercenary Commander,* by Jerry Puren; and probably the most accurate, well-written and depressing of the bunch, the *Whores of War: Mercenaries Today,* by Wilfred Burchett and Derek Roebuck. *Whores,* published in 1977, chronicles the misfortunes of 13 American and British mercs in Angola who were captured, tried and executed or imprisoned. Sobering stuff for wannabes.

Movies like the *Dogs of War* and *The Wild Geese,* and TV shows like *Soldier of Fortune* have some credible origins in real events, and real mercenaries were used as resources to create the scripts as well as advise the filmmakers on location. But somehow, once the cameras rolled, it all turned into pure gun love, complete with sweat, bulging muscles, babes, handheld machine guns and chomping cigars.

Some would-be mercs and real mercs read *Soldier of Fortune* magazine. To be fair, writers, like yours truly and *DP* contributors Rob Krott, Jim Hooper and Roddy Scott, have been published in *SOF.* But in our opinion, *SOF* adds a little too much macho gun-love salsa to what are typically skanky, sweaty, low-budget guerrilla tours with complicated political backgrounds. So what separates the "pass the cigars and keep feeding me ammo" publications from the real thing? Well, we at *DP* like to think that the real litmus test of a publication's readership is always the quality of the ads. Yes, *SOF* is read religiously by a large military readership, but there are those ads that make you wonder just who is *really* reading this adventure mag. You can read more accurate and less titillating books like Tim Spicer's *An Unorthodox Soldier* or Mary-Louise O'Callaghan's *Enemies Within,* about the PNG/Sandline affair, but most neophytes want the machine gun blasting, teeth-gritted look of Hoare's *Mercenary,* which is subtitled, "He was a hired gun in a savage war. One man's shocking true life account of a bloody rebellion." Not bad for a book about a car salesman.

The bottom line is, the merc business is about 99 percent bullshit and 1 percent reality, and the reality part usually sucks. Despite having to buy your own beret, cigars and big knife, you will end up spending time in the most godawful parts of the world, and if a land mine doesn't get you, then the bugs will. If the bugs don't get you, the long arm of the law will.

Any time you leave the apron strings of Uncle Sam's army, you are on your own, and even if you are not in violation of any laws, you will be accused of being a criminal (actually, a criminal has rights—you won't) without any rights and dealt with accordingly.

To be fair, we should inject a little romance and adventure into this much maligned avocation. The true movers and shakers in the mercenary world are the classic megalomaniacs; vicious self-promoters and verbose ex-soldiers who see their role beyond that of a short-term gun toter—as a potential ruler of faraway kingdoms. So our advice, if you are going to get into this nasty business (the retirement program sucks), is to think big, don't take any checks and make sure you remember your hat size when you order your crown.

http://www.cdi.org/ArmsTradeDatabase/CONTROL/Small_Arms/Mercenaries/

The Men Who Would Be King Club

The kingdom-making business has been around for a long time. Men like Englishman (and eventually Rajah) Brooke of Sarawak bought a fast ship with a few naval guns. He used them to chase off pirates in exchange for giant chunks of Borneo. William Walker and a bunch of ne'er do wells ran Nicaragua with a Gatling gun and a few Colt navy pistols. Hell, even I was offered in on a deal to take over a Caribbean island, so there still must be opportunities for adventurers out there.

The late '60s and early '70s were the glory years for mercenaries like "Mad" Mike Hoare, "Black" Jacques Schramme, and Bob Denard. They weren't bright or avaricious enough to grab the main bedroom in the royal palace instead of the barracks the first time around, but it didn't take them long to figure things out. Why support a tin pot ruler so *they* could continue to loot the national treasury to shop in Paris when *you* could loot the treasury and go shopping in Paris yourself? Here is a short list of the folks who thought big.

Equatorial Guinea (1972)

The Dogs of War, by Frederick Forsyth, was published in 1974. Forsyth is said to have modeled the lead character in the book after Denard. In the book and in the film, a group of white mercenaries are hired to take over a West African country on behalf of an industrialist who finds it cheaper to take over the country rather than pay for its mineral resources. The movie ends with the mercenaries suddenly having a change of heart and installing an idealistic and honest leader. Naturally, the book and the film are fiction. Well, not completely, said an investigative report by London's *Sunday Times.* They claimed that *The Dogs of War* was based on a real incident instigated by the author. The *Times* claimed that in 1972 Forsyth allegedly put up just under a quarter of a million dollars ($240,000) to overthrow President Francisco Macias Nguema of Equatorial Guinea. Forsyth was no stranger to the murky world of mercenaries, since he had spent considerable time in Nigeria covering the Biafran civil war. While he was there, he met a Scottish mercenary named Alexander Ramsay Gay. Gay was only too happy to train and equip a small group of men who would set up a homeland for the defeated Biafrans. It is reputed that Gay was able to purchase automatic weapons, bazookas and mortars from a Hamburg arms dealer, then hire 13 other mercenaries along with 50 black soldiers from Biafra. They then purchased a ship called the *Albatross* out of the Spanish port of Fuengirola. The plot was blown when one of the British mercs shot himself after a gunfight with London police. The mercenaries were denied an export permit for their weapons and ammunition, and the ship and crew were arrested in the Canary Islands en route to their target.

Forsyth denies the story or any participation in the plot and admits to nothing more than writing a solidly researched book.

The Sudan (1975)

Rolf Steiner was a member of Hitler's Youth (Hitler Jugend). He joined the French Foreign Legion at the age of 17 in 1950. He fought at Dien Bien Phu and in Algeria and made the mistake of joining the anti-de Gaulle OAS—finding himself a drummed-out corporal chief and a civilian.

In the fall of 1967, Biafra was busy spending oil money and French secret service funds on hiring mercenaries from Swedish pilot Count von Rosen (pilots were paid between $8,000 and $10,000 per month in cash to fly in supplies) and paying Swiss public relations firms to publicize their plight. Money flowed freely; grisly battle-scarred veterans like Roger Faulques were paid 100,000 British pounds to hire 100 men for six months but only delivered 49. He was asked to leave, but Steiner, one of the mercenaries he had hired, chose to stay.

In July of 1968, Steiner asked for and was given a group of commando-style soldiers and had great successes against the Russian-backed Nigerians. He was later given the rank of colonel and given command of thousands of soldiers. This created an instant Napoleon complex and Steiner experienced a series of military defeats and routs. He was reigned in by removal of his Steiner Commando Division, and after an angry confrontation with the Biafran leader, Sandhurst-educated General Emeka Ojukwa, he was shipped out of the country in handcuffs.

Steiner then showed up in the southern Sudan among the Anya Na fighting the Islamic north. He taught agriculture, defense, education and other essential civic skills to the animist tribes. For a brief shining moment, he was their de facto leader, until he was captured by the Ugandans and put on trial in Sudan in the mid-'70s. He was released after spending three years in a Sudanese prison where he was tortured and beaten. His captors' favorite tortures were hanging Steiner by his feet and stuffing peppers up (down?) his anus. Some say he was a crazed megalomanic; other say he tried to apply his skills to aid a tiny struggling nation. He died in South Africa of a kidney ailment.

The Comoros (1978)

"Here, feel the hole in my head" is the way Denard started his conversation with me. He grabbed my hand and rubbed it against the shallow depression under his silver hair. When *DP* met with the elegant-looking gentleman, it was just before his trial for taking over the Comoros. He had to invade, he says, things were going to hell. He was acquitted.

One of the more successful invasion attempts was made by Bordeaux native Bob Denard, who actually managed to run the Comoros Islands between 1978 and 1989. The Comoros are an Indian Ocean island group just northwest of Madagascar. The major export of the long forgotten islands is *ylang-ylang*, a rare flower used in the production of aromatic oils. On May 13, 1978, 49-year-old Denard landed with 46 men in a converted trawler named the *Massiwa*. He had sailed from Europe with his black uniformed crew to claim ownership of this tiny but idyllic group of islands. Denard insists he had more engineers than fighters.

Denard had been here before to train the soldiers of Marxist ruler Ali Soilih. Soilih was busy kicking out Ahmed Abdallah. Abdallah fled to Paris and later, short on funds but high on ambition, offered to cut Denard in on the deal if he would return him to power. The deal was rumored to be worth $6 million. Denard enjoyed his new role as "man who would be king." Soilih was a young despot who appointed a 15-year-old to run the police department, burned all government records, and after a witch doctor told him he would be killed by a white man with a black dog, killed every black dog on the island. Abdallah took all the political heat as his puppet.

Denard, a former vacuum cleaner salesman and policeman, had seen what a few trained soldiers could do in his various adventures as a mercenary in Katanga, Yemen and Benin. This time he was in charge. He landed quietly at night and proceeded to the palace to find Soilih in bed with three girls watching a pornographic movie. Denard shot him, and the next morning drove through town with Soilih's body draped over the hood. Denard had with him a black Alsatian. The crowds cheered and Denard became an able leader of the Comoros for 11 years with 12 other white mercenaries. He took a Comoran wife, bought a villa, converted to Islam and became Said Mustapha Madjoub.

During his reign, South Africa used the Comoros to ship arms to Iraq and monitor ANC training camps in Tanzania, and the French used his islands to ship arms to the right-wing Renamo guerrillas. Finally, after he (or someone else) shot the puppet ruler Abdallah in a heated argument, the tide turned against Denard. His presence angered the other African states to such a degree that the French arranged for Denard's resignation in 1989. Denard, disappointed and back in South Africa, spent his evenings planning his return to paradise. Sounds like a great premise for a sequel. The hole? A piece of shrapnel that nicked a chunk of skull. Nothing really, just a flesh wound.

http://www.bobdenard.com/

The Seychelles (1981)

When *DP* arrived in the Seychelles, we found it hard to imagine taking over a nicer place. Henry Moore–like granite sculptures frame azure blue seas. Laughing creoles, scrawny Italian tourists and lush inland jungles would make the perfect tax-free haven. Dublin-born "Mad" Mike Hoare wasn't really there for the scenery or the beaches. He was hired by persons unknown (most say former premier Mancham in cahoots with South Africa) to take over the Seychelles, a nation of 92 islands 1,000 miles off East Africa. Hoare served in the Royal Armored Corps in World War II and left with the rank of major. He emigrated to South Africa after the war and made ends meet by being a safari guide, car dealer and accountant, until he was hired by Moise Tshombe in 1964 to help him defeat rebels. Hoare put together about 200 male white mercenaries and led probably the last efficient use of a mercenary army in Africa—to save lives and put down a revolt in the Belgian Congo.

Hoare's last big gig (Major Hoare does not work too often due to his high price tag) was a Keystone cops affair that would seem to be the result of a bad scriptwriter rather than real political intrigue. They were supposed to overthrow the socialist government of President Albert Rene of the Seychelles and to take control of the idyllic Indian Ocean archipelago. In December of 1981 their plan of flying in as a visiting rugby team quickly unraveled when customs inspectors found heavy weapons in the bottom of their gym bags. A brief shootout between the 52 raiders and police ensued on the tarmac, with the mercenaries' transportation being quickly hijacked and flown back to safety in South Africa. It was not known for whom or why this was done, but suspicion falls on the South African government. Some analysts believe that Hoare backers were South African businessmen looking for a tax haven. A Durban newspaper charged that several of the mercenaries were South African policemen.

The leniency with which the mercenaries were treated back in South Africa adds to that suspicion. The 44 mercenaries who made it back were put on trial (wearing beach shirts and khakis), not for hijacking the Air India aircraft, which would have meant a mandatory 5 to 30 years in jail; they were charged with kidnapping which requires no mandatory penalty.

The South African cabinet also approved the freeing on bail of 39 of the 44 mercenaries on the condition they keep a low profile and not discuss the coup attempt. Five mercenaries were arrested in the Seychelles, and it is assumed that three others are dead or hiding in the hills.

Others blame ousted Seychelles President James Mancham, who was exiled after Rene's successful 1977 coup. Although Mancham denied the accusation, one of the captured mercenaries had a tape recording of Mancham's victory speech intended for broadcast after the coup. Oops. The soldiers for hire were paid $1,000 each and were promised $10,000 if the coup was successful.

The Comoros (1995)

You can smell the spices in this languorous paradise. The giant curved dhows look right out of *Sinbad*. Things hadn't changed much since the last time Denard was here. They say sequels are never as interesting as the originals, and in this case, they're right. It seems that staring out the window got to be too much for Denard, so at the creaky old age of 66, he decided to give it one more go. On October 4, 1995, Denard and a group of 33 mercenaries (mostly French) rented a creaking fishing trawler and sailed back to the Comoros to recapture his little Garden of Eden where he had been king (actually, head of the Presidential Guard, watching over a puppet ruler) from 1978–1989.

They landed at night and quickly sprung their old buddies out of the islands' main jail; then they captured the two airports, the radio station and the barracks. After that, they rousted the doddering, 80-something Said Mohamed Djohar out of bed. By morning, Denard was on top and Djohar was a criminal charged with misrule and stealing government funds.

Conveniently (too conveniently, some say), two days later, the French government landed 600 troops and after a brief but halfhearted fight, the mercenaries were rounded up and Denard was politely shipped to France where he was tried and acquitted of doing what comes naturally.

Sierra Leone (1995)

Executive Outcomes came into their own when they leapt into the breach and saved Sierra Leone. It wasn't the first time, but it was the best time. The rebels were eating people, smoking ganja in rolled-up Bible paper to get more Jesus in them. There had been other groups in Sierra Leone, like Gurkha Security Guards, who sent in American Robert MacKenzie, son-in-law of the late CIA deputy director Ray Cline. Things got unpleasant when even MacKenzie was killed and eaten by the RUF. GSG pulled out and Branch Energy (Tony Buckingham's company) convinced young Valentine Strasser, the military ruler of the country, to promise some diamond plots, some cash and free reign. EO descended with Belarus-hired pilots and black South African trainers and whipped the slightly spooky but gung-ho Kamajors into shape. EO turned the Kamajors, a rural Mendi militia, into hunter killers. Things quickly came to order and the rebels fled back into the bush from whence they came.

By March 1996, Sierra Leone went to the polls for the first presidential elections in 28 years. And all was quiet in the British version of Liberia. But EO was fired after the International Monetary Fund said that was cheating. Mercenaries, you know, can't have them hanging around. Dogs of War and so on, not exactly cricket, eh wot? The government was overthrown in a coup and Sierra Leone quickly plunged into chaos. Mutilations, terror, murder, looting and starvation were the end result until a peace deal put the rebels in a powersharing arrangement with Kabbah's government in 1999.

Bougainville (1997)

"Your bag makes me nervous" so one of the men behind Sandline told *DP* in a private meeting. The elegant man in the Knightsbridge mews townhouse was not most people's idea of a mercenary. He was, after all, an accountant. But he still got from behind his desk, moved the leather case to point in a different direction and resumed our conversation. Dodgy business, this.

When you hear it from their side, Sandline International and other "private military companies" make perfect sense. No different than 7-11 hiring flatfoots or the pope needing pantalooned police with pig stickers around his country. It was a simple case of economic expediency, if you listen to Sandline when describing what happened in Papua New Guinea. The government needed help and Sandline came to their rescue.

Who else was going to stop the mayhem? The motivation behind the idea was simple as it is denied. Just how does a destitute country come up with millions to put down an uprising? Simple. A few greased palms, handshake agreements and a contract is drawn up to settle the little insurgency problem in Bougainville once and for all.

You see, there was a copper and gold mine, the second biggest hole in the world, being held hostage by a small group of ragged fuzzy-haired natives. Possibly worth serious bucks to a big mining concern (which specializes in doing business in high-risk countries) if they could get it at bargain basement prices. That same mine used to provide half of Papua New Guinea's folding green, but it has been shut down by locals—some armed with rusty Japanese swords, homemade shotguns and slingshots. The local army can't do squat with their undertrained, undermotivated soldiers. So hire some locals to squeal on *el jefè*, do a little low-level intel, fly in a crack squad of commandos and "ka-ching": no more revolution. This is how the screenplay was written, but $36 million dollars later it didn't quite work out that way.

The man in charge of the PNG military not only wanted the money for his own troops, it seems that many of his top officers were related and sympathetic to the rebels in Bougainville. Counterintel supreme. Second boo-boo, white man shows up, lots of used crusty Eastern European gear and things start looking like a bloodbath. Into the slammer and then onto a plane Tim Spicer goes, and the deal is off. Well, not quite. Sandline (who subcontracted to older and less PC brother EO) sues, gets paid in full, the rebels get a peace deal and everyone is happy. The price of copper is in the toilet, the mine is still closed and Francis Ona is happy in his mountaintop kingdom. For those who can't get enough of this tale, you can read Tim Spicer's bio, *An Unorthodox Soldier* and Mary-Louise O'Callaghan's book, *Enemies Within*.

http://www.globalpolicy.org/security/issues/sheppard.htm

The Players

These days, the old Dogs of War business is drying up like blood on a Kinshassa backstreet. Gone are the skull and crossbones patches of Steiner, gone are the nicknames like Black Jack and Mad Mike. The Che Guevaras, Abu Nidals and Carlos the Jackals are now nothing but memories. The last attempt at putting together an old fashioned merc army was with 300 or so drunken Serbs and Europeans shipped in to fight off Kabila. The French put together a motley crew of 300 South Africans, Brits, French, Serbs, Angolans and other nationalities. The new merc scene (or should we say the international security scene) is taking advantage of thousands of laid-off, well-trained soldiers and the need of oil and mining companies to keep things flowing in Colombia, Angola, the Sudan, Congo, Papua New Guinea and other unstable regions. For those who like their action raw and gritty there is no shortage of unpaid volunteer work in Afghanistan, the southern Philippines and Latin America. For now, it seems the job opportunities for scarred, tattooed mercenaries looking through the classified section for "Make Big Money Killing Insurgents" ads are over. You need to e-mail your qualifications to bland looking megacorporations.

But wait. If you are a trained security consultant, there is hope. Believe it or not, you can see many of the major recruiters listed under "Corporate Security" in phone books in Joburg, London, Washington, Miami and Paris. You'll find these euphemistically or acronymically named companies in any big mining or oil center town. These are really the only places where ex- (and current) soldiers are actively recruited for "security" and "training" work overseas. Some times you actually will end up staring at a video monitor in an air-conditioned trailer at an African oil refinery or teaching 18 year olds how to clean a Makarov. With the right credentials, the right background and the right questions you'll get work. Even if you do plug into this world, there is no shortage of experienced people.

Other groups, such as the Ghurkas, the Swiss Guards, and the French Foreign Legion, are not your classic Dogs of War type of mercenaries but vanishing anachronisms. Small but oil-rich countries like Oman or Brunei need outside help to keep things quiet, but usually with the queen's troops on hire, the Ghurkas and the SAS. Even the pope hires mercenaries to keep the Holy See nice and safe. The good news is that right now, stinking rich but "security asset" poor flyspeck states are eager employers but usually by contract through their biggest mineral resource company (which, of course, is blessed by the appropriate ex-colonial country). Other countries like Myanmar, Angola, Croatia, Namibia, Guatemala, El Salvador, Afghanistan and other war-torn regions use foreign advisers (with spooky assistance) supplied by other countries like Iran, Cuba, Libya, Syria, Pakistan, Britain and, of course, the United States to keep their army trained. But in these days of rapid-reaction forces, the UN, and political correctness, the days of the Wild Geese are long gone. These days a mercenary is more likely to be hired by an oil company than a slobbering dictator.

For now, South Africa is the major supplier of mercenaries for work (the RSA will lay off 60,000 soldiers by year 2000) around Africa, and Russia is the biggest source of kill temps in the Caucasus.

Despite the military might available for work for hire, it may surprise you that the real movers and shakers behind the new global security firms are very colorful and wealthy individuals. Here's just a peek at some of the players past and present.

The Back Room

You won't see these guys on the cover of *Soldier of Fortune*, but someday you may see them on the cover of *Fortune*. These are just some of the people who have been linked, however tenuously or incorrectly, with the brave new world of corporate colonialism and the need for private armies. Not that *DP* has any proof or reason to believe that they have anything to do with new trends. They just seem to show up in articles a lot and do business in interesting places.

Tiny Rowland

Former U.K. prime minister Mr. Edward Heath described Rowland as "the unacceptable face of capitalism." Some would simply say that Tiny Rowland didn't really play the games or keep up the appearances that colonial countries do in the Third World. "Tiny" was born Rowland Walter Fuhrhop in 1917 in an internment camp in India. He died in July 1998 at the age of 80 on his yacht of skin cancer. He was worth $405 million when he died from making friends and enemies.

His father was German and his mother Anglo-Dutch. After the first World War, the family returned to Germany where Rowland went to school and later joined the Hitler youth movement. They moved to Britain in 1934, and at a private school he joined the Officer Training Corps and achieved the rank of corporal.

He worked for his father but was interned with his father and other German-born immigrants on the Isle of Man. He spent three months in the Peel camp for high-risk Nazi sympathizers (his brother was fighting in the German army). It is alleged that he was an informer inside the camp and that it earned him special status in his business dealings later.

He moved to Southern Rhodesia after the war and married into the royal family. His mentor was Angus Ogilvy, who hired him to run London and Rhodesian Mining and Land Company, later renamed Lonrho.

His business style was, to say the least, loose. He would simply bribe leaders of African nations to obtain mining rights. He would provide his Gulfstream to fly rebel leaders to press conferences or meetings. He even bought newspapers in South Africa and the U.K. to provide positive coverage of his exploits. One of his partners was Mohamed Al-Fayed who he later had a falling out with. He spent about $50 million fighting Al-Fayed for control of Harrods. He also was responsible for the financial collapse of Australian Alan Bond.

"Tiny" Rowland didn't invent the idea of getting involved in war and politics to make a buck. He just made it respectable. As then-chief executive of the U.K.-based multi-national Lonrho, Tiny made protection payments to Renamo during the early stages of the war to protect Lonrho's agrarian and business investments. When Renamo reneged, Tiny became involved in the political side of things and pushed for a peace agreement.

http://www.c-r.org/acc_moz/vines.htm

Mohamed Al-Fayed

http://www.alfayed.com/

Anthony Rowland Buckingham

Tony (born November 28, 1951) could give James Bond a run for his money. Yachtsman, rallyist, ex-SBS/SAS, businessman, self-made oil and mining tycoon and alleged behind-the-scenes player and author in a number of intriguing scripts, Tony Buckingham is chief executive of Heritage Oil and Gas. He began as a deep sea diver working on offshore oil platform support in various parts of the world and then moved on to put together his own oil deals, which culminated in the establishment of Heritage Oil and Gas, now a listed company on the Toronto Stock Exchange.

Tony likes to have partners and front men. Some of his business partners include Friedland, Salim Saleh of Uganda (Museveni's half-brother,) and Raymond Moi (son of President Daniel Arap Moi).

Tony first hit the radar when in January 1993 Buckingham suggested to the MPLA that Executive Outcomes help clean up the problems at the Soyo complex.

Buckingham and Mann convinced the MPLA to commission Eeben Barlow to recruit a force of South African *Koevet* veterans to capture Soyo from UNITA. Less than 100 men held, then lost, Soyo. Proving to the government of Angola that mercs for concessions was a viable business, EO was off and running. Other gigs followed—Sierra Leone, the alleged rescue of kidnapped foreigners from the OPM in Irian Jaya and the most famous mercenary gig that never happened: Bougainville.

One would never suppose that the April 7, 1996, meeting between Singirok, then PNG defense minister Mathias Ijape and Tony Buckingham at the Cairns Hilton would set the wheels in motion for the Bougainville fiasco, ending up in a very profitable venture for Sandlines, a major corruption probe of the PNG government and peace talks for the rebels. What Tony didn't know was that forces were as busy unselling Sandline to the PNG armed forces as Sandline was selling. Tony Buckingham can be seen on the yachting scene or you might bump into him at antique car rallies. Trivia for journos hot on the trail: Tony owns an appropriately named yacht, *Bit of a Coup*.

http://www.branchenergy.com/
http://www.sandline.com
http://www.thirdworldtraveler.com/New_World_Order/Mercenaries_Minerals.html
http://www.senate.gov/~foreign/reno.htm

Robert M. Friedland

The much belabored and bemonikered ("Toxic Bob," "The Ugly Canadian") billionaire mining king Bob Friedland desperately needs a new PR agent. He has nothing to do with mercenaries or even the idea of private security firms, but somehow he keeps getting wound up in the plot because he is just so damn colorful. Born in 1951, Friedland is a graduate of Reed College in Portland, Oregon, studies mysticism and became buds with

Steve Jobs. After college he worked at the Oregon Feeling Center, obviously an excellent introduction to strip mining and mineral exploitation. He moved to Canada shortly thereafter and became involved in mining ventures, some successful, some not.

One of his ventures was looking for diamonds in Voisey's Bay, Newfoundland, discovering much less glamorous but ultimately more profitable nickel deposits. Inco paid $3.1 million for his find, making Bob richer than he could have ever imagined. Or did it? From that mother lode, he has created Ivanhoe, an investment group for oil and mineral ventures. Since then, his companies show up in a variety of ragtag regions, ranging from Myanmar to Angola.

He became a Canadian in the '80s. He now spends half his time in Sydney where, in 1996, he bought a $7 million luxury villa at Point Piper, some say to make it easier should he need Australian citizenship.

He got the moniker "Toxic" when he used the heap-leach system, the most efficient way to extract gold from ore in the Summitville, Colorado, mine in 1986. There was a spill and the EPA wanted to talk to him about the cleanup bill, but he resigned that same day. Less kind but even more acidic than his former mine is U.S. Interior Secretary Bruce Babbitt's description of Friedland's departure from the scene of the crime: "stealing away in the middle of the night." Friedland, through his Ivanhoe investments, is busy in Myanmar, Guyana, Sierra Leone, Namibia and other developing countries. We're not saying anything, but *Forbes* did a little mining of its own for a 1997 article on Bob and found the words of Edward T. Gignoux, the U.S. district court judge who sentenced Friedland for his drug dealing: "You gave no thought to the consequences for others that could have resulted from this transaction, but only to the large sum of money that you could have obtained."

http://www.essential.org/monitor/hyper/mm0697.09.html
http://www.essential.org/monitor/hyper/mm1194.html#environ

The Front Room

There have been a number of companies that have emerged from the postcolonial vacuum in Africa, Asia and the Pacific. Companies with direct and indirect ties to captains of industry, covertly blessed by former colonial governments and invited by eager, but desperate rulers in exchange for cash or understandings.

The Traders/Soldiers of Fortune

The idea of forming a corporation and then hiring soldiers to provide a little muscle is not a new one. The charter and trade companies are the historical model. The Dutch East India Company, the Northwest Company or the the British North Borneo Company were given mercantile monopolies to develop and exploit "newly discovered" regions. Even when there wasn't a charter, enterprising men like Brooke of Sarawak or Stanford Raffles just sailed over and set up there own little domains. They are all examples of times when entire regions were carved up, exploited and run by corporations with ties to distant sponsors. Their economic interests were slowly replaced by their colonial masters, carving much of the world into the mess its become. In a world where an oil company or mining concern can provide the majority of a country's cash, one would be a fool to think the government calls the shots, particularly when the populace has no idea how governments become governments.

One idea has resurfaced. Since there are still riches to be had and the local government is irrelevant, why not stake out that which is of value and let the rest of the pieces fall into place?

Executive Outcomes (EO)

Nick van der Bergh and Eeben Barlow used to run Executive Outcomes out of Pretoria, South Africa. Executive Outcomes was founded in 1989 by the 17-year veteran and former long-range recon soldier from South Africa's 32nd Battalion. They began the new trend for corporate mercenaries in March, 1993 when UNITA captured a oil storage area in Soya owned by Heritage Oil, Sonangol and a number of other oil concerns. The Forcas Armadas Angolanas (FAA) didn't quite know how to oust the rebels without blowing up the precious oil and drilling equipment. Buckingham, the boss at Heritage, suggested to the powers that be that the state-owned oil company approach Barlow, who despite the impressive sounding name of Executive Outcomes and paladin logo on his card, was a one man band training the South African army and advising a mining company on security.

EO's men attacked with 600 FAA troops and only ended up with 3 South Africans wounded. The facility was retaken and as soon as EO's men left, UNITA retook the facility. It was an important event because it showed that outside "security" forces could be used because they were politically sterile and provided military skills without jeopardizing the stability of tottering regimes.

When UNITA screamed that white mercenaries were fighting in Angola, the oil company mentioned they were just security guards. UNITA soon found out that they were not up against polyester-suited doughnut munchers but ex-South African Defense Force men who had fought *for* UNITA during the 1976-1988 war in Angola. Money changes everything in the merc business.

EO quickly positioned itself as a security service that stabilizes mining operations, allowing governments to write checks based on the smooth flow of raw resources. EO's strength was "using enough gun and enough local intel," creating detailed plans, acquiring and coordinating air support, relying on local militia who knew the turf and paying close attention to the real sources of money: the mine owners and not the Ray-Banned dictators.

After their success in Angola, Barlow made a sales call with his unusual wares in March of 1995 to the beleaguered Valentine Strasser and got busy shortly thereafter. Coincidently, Buckingham was also doing business in Sierra Leone, making it two for two where a "private military company" showed up to clean up rebels. The Koidu diamond mine was held 60 percent by Buckingham/Branch Energy and now by Vancouver-based Diamondworks and 40 percent was held by the government.

The deal to EO was supposed to be worth $35.2 million The fee started off at $1.5 million per month and reduced to $1 million when things cooled down. EO is still owed $19.5 million, but $35 million is a lot of money for a young military dictator to dig up on short notice. Strasser kept promising he would come up with the scratch but did not pay one cent for the services provided by EO from the time they deployed in April–May 1995 to January 1996 when they made their first payment of $3 million. Despite the dunning war behind the scenes, EO saved the day in Sierra Leone. Troops were in-country by April, and they quickly managed to push back the rebels from 36–26 kilometers from the capital in just nine days. They then pushed the rebels out of the Kono diamonds fields (about 216 kilometers east of Freetown) in just two days using helicopter gunships. Their reward was to be fired by Strasser in an effort to save $3 million in fees. Shortly after EO left Sierra Leone, about 3,000 rebels were invited back in to Freetown by coup leader Johnny Paul Koroma.

Dogs of War, Inc., as some called EO, made sure that the world's press knew about this cleaner, brighter, whiter form of pay-as-you-go warfare. The press reacted accordingly and publicly governments recoiled in horror, while privately asking if they could please see a brochure and a price list.

But the rotating circle of military and business friends became a little too obvious. It seemed that the same people showed up in the same countries in the same companies hiring the same military advice. It looked like big money was ganging up with big guns to do a little postcolonial housekeeping. In the meantime, Sandline was taking the forefront in the PMC business, negotiating a little deal in Papua New Guinea to get rid of a seccessionist movement on an island that used to provide over 40 percent of the country's money.

The job in Papua New Guinea was the death knell of EO both financially and politically. Although Sandline subbed the dirty work to EO, it became apparent that they were kissing cousins, and once again there was a large mine involved on the island of Bougainville. The local military arrested their new protectors and an intensive inquiry followed that begged the question: Can you order out national security? And who picks up the bill?

Then, when post-apartheid South Africa began to make noises about stopping mercenary firms, EO had to die, and Sandline stepped into the spotlight.

Commission of Inquiry into Sandline
http://www.datec.com.au/sandline/default.htm

A Profile of Today's Private Sector Corporate Mercenary Firms
http://www.cdi.org/issues/mercenaries/merc1.html

Gurkha Security Guards (GSG)

Reputedly, GSG was a front for the British Government set up to facilitate sending Ghurkas to Sierra Leone to defend the diamond mines. Nick Bell, a former officer in the Gurkha regiment of the British army, managed to provide a few good men. The salary is as high as $8,000 a month. Not bad for the wages of war.

GSG mainly consists of Brits who have had service with Her Majesty's Forces or other security work. Obviously, they lean toward hiring men from Nick's old outfit. His last client was the government of Sierra Leone, which was fighting an all-out war against RUF, a rebel faction. Nick does his recruiting out of hotel rooms in places like Banbury, Oxfordshire, according to the *New African*. They also do mine clearance and other important work.

Job security is a little dicey since the leader of the GSG contingent in Sierra Leone, American Bob MacKenzie, was killed in the Malal Hills in February of 1995. He was also reportedly eaten by the rebels. After MacKenzie was killed, the Ghurkas returned to Nepal. There are a number of companies that provide security to outside countries based in St. Helior, like Frank E. Basil Inc. and Allmakes (Jersey) Ltd.

http://carlisle-www.army.mil/usawc/Parameters/99summer/adams.htm

GSG
Suite 11, Queensway House
St. Helior, Jersey JE4 81Y
Channel Islands, U.K.
Tel.: [44] (1) 534-74-707

Military Professional Resources, Inc.

There is an option for those with a little silver around the temples and a spare tire around the middle. Billed as the "greatest corporate assemblage of Military Expertise in the World," Military Professional Resources, Inc. (MPRI) is a group of former military professionals who train armies and do what retired generals do. They are based in Alexandria, Virginia, and claim to pull in about $12 million a year in assignments. Not bad for an eight-year-old company with 160 employees and about 2,000 topkicks on call. Although their brochure copy would not get them much ink in *Soldier of Fortune*, their terminology sounds ominously like the doublespeak of Executive Outcomes. What does MPRI offer their well-heeled but disorganized customers? Their brochure offers Doctrine

Development, Military Training, War Game Support, and even Democracy Transition. *DP* could not find Advanced Medal Polishing, Golf 101 or Cocktail Party Banter in the list, so we are somewhat suspect of their credentials. However, they are credited with training the Croat army who smacked the bejeezuz out of the Serbs in Krajina province back in August of '95. There were dark rumors about their involvement in Kosovo, training the KLA through former Croat links. If you are tired of wearing your medals at home, contact:

Military Professional Resources Inc.

1201 East Abingdon Drive, Suite 425
Alexandria, VA 22314
Tel.: (703) 684-0853
Fax: (703) 684-3528
E-mail: info@mpri.com
http://www.mpri.com/

Private Military Corporations/Security Firms/Training

Sandline International

Plaza 107
525 Kings Road
London, UK
http://www.sandline.com/

Military Professional Resources, Inc. (MPRI)

1201 East Abingdon Drive, Suite 425
Alexandria, VA 22314
Tel.: (703) 684-0853
Fax: (703) 684-3528
Web site: http://www.mpri.com/
Jobs: http://www.mpri.com/current/personnel.htm

Vinnell Corporation

12150 East Monument Dr., Suite 800
Fairfax, VA 22033-4053
Tel.: (703) 385-4544 -
Fax: (703) 385-3726
Web site: http://www.vinnell.com
Jobs: http://www.vinnell.com/careers.html

Betac Corporation

Betac Corporation
Suite 1100
2001 N. Beauregard St.
Alexandria, VA 22311
Tel.: (703) 824-3100
Web site: http://www.betac.com/
Jobs: http://www.betac.com/careers/default.cfm

AirScan

7017 Challenger Avenue,
Titusville, FL 32780
Tel.: (407) 264-2911
E-mail: airscan@iu.net
http://www.airscan.com/

Armor Holdings, Inc.

http://www.armorholdings.com/
Through their acquisition of DSL they now offer protection of operations in high-risk environments. Their own PR says, "Our security planning and management services enable your team to achieve its business or organizational objectives wherever complex physical risks exist to people or property. Our experience and competence in protecting clients in the world's most difficult environments is matchless."

DynCorp

DynCorp World Headquarters
2000 Edmund Halley Drive

Reston, VA 20191
Tel.: 703-264-0330
Web site: http://www.dyncorp.com/
Jobs: http://www.dyncorp.com/working/careers.asp
Lifeguard
E-mail: jso@deterrent.org

WARNING

Joining any military or paramilitary organization and/or fighting with a foreign army may sub-ject you to prosecution, imprisonment or execution by other countries. If you are a U.S. citizen, you can lose your citizenship and be liable for international crimes. Association or contact with mercenary recruiters and groups can make you subject to investigation by U.S. and international law enforcement agencies.

Happiness Is a Dead Infidel: The Mujahedin

If the Legion seems a little too Euro or confining, you can try the next level down: a mujahedin. The qualifications are that you must be a Muslim, don't mind being completely disposable and hate infidels more than the IRS.

Jihad started with Muhammed 1,500 years ago and was really cooking during the Crusades. It died down for five centuries, and then an almost retro enthusiasm hit in 1979, when the Soviets decided to install a puppet ruler backed by the Soviet army. As with all foreign countries who decided to roll armies into Afghanistan, they forgot that the tribes of Afghanistan love a good fight. In fact, when there is no occupying power, they love to fight amongst themselves.

The 12,000 to 15,000 foreign-born and Afghan-trained "Afghans" are the direct effect of too much money, training and weapons being funneled into one of the world's poorest regions—Pakistan and Afghanistan. The United States decided this would be a great time to give the Russians a bloody nose, prompting them to send in massive amounts of money to support seven mujahedin groups that hated the Russians. All the Afghan groups had to do was provide a head count, a list of weapons, an area of operations, and they were in business. Naturally, the real mujahedin looked upon the money from the infidels warily. The ones that happily accepted the weapons also stockpiled them for sale or use after the Russians left.

The result is that the United States and the Gulf States (through the CIA, through Pakistan ISI) created a new "franchise" of warrior clans armed to the teeth with the common goal of causing the Russians grief. Simple, gun-happy tribesmen were trained in everything from how to make explosives out of fertilizer to how to use Stinger missiles. The CIA not only provided more than enough money; they created an unholy network where these factions could swap war stories and business cards.

Don't think that all these muj came from flyblown deserts. Recruits and funding were actively sought in 28 states in the United States, but the number of U.S. volunteers was minuscule. Most were black and few put up with the austere conditions of the war in Russia.

How to Get In

Most fighters start out as Koranic students from madrassahs, or religious schools. Part of being a Muslim is the need to protect Islam from infidels. Some are more militant about it than others. The concept of jihad is designed to provide a bulwark against oppression or eradication of Islam. There is both defensive and offensive jihad. To be a holy warrior is the highest calling, a straight shot into paradise if you are killed. Don't confuse suicide bombers with holy warriors. It is understood that Allah will choose the time that you will be brought into paradise.

Mullahs will often stress the need for volunteers. Your local mosque in Pittsburgh is not necessarily shipping off recruits to Algeria, but there are more militant groups found in the mosques in suburban New York, Istanbul or London. Volunteers are usually sent directly to the area of conflict and receive whatever training is required on the spot. More promising candidates are sent to Afghanistan, Sudan, Yemen, Iran or six-month advance courses run by Iranian Pasdaran instructors in the Bekaa Valley in Lebanon for more secretive training in explosives, weapons and tactics. Often recruits are sent to Afghanistan for live combat training before being shipped to other destinations. Many of these volunteers are financed by private citizens in the Gulf, the most notable being Osama bin Laden.

Smite the Purple One!

For those of you who like Jihad-Lite, you can become a holy warrior against the most insidious of evils: Barney (or B'harnii, as his unholy named is translated literally by the site). Enter the dark side with tales of horror about the purple saurian that will boil your blood and make you rise up in indignation.

http://www.jihad.net/

Current jihads	
REGION	**HIRING**
Afghanistan	**Taliban**
Algeria	**GIA**
China	**East Turkistan**
Chechnya	**Khattab/Basayev**
Eritrea	**Yemen**
Ethiopia	**Gulf States**
Iran	**Iraq**
Iraq	**North/Kurds**
Israel/Lebanon	**Iran, Bekaa Valley**
Kashmir	**Northern Pakistan**
Sudan	**Khartoum, Iran, Iraq**
Tajikistan	**Fergana Valley**
Uganda	**Sudan**
Uzbekistan	**Tajikistan**
Western Sahara	**Polisario**

You might be surprised that almost all volunteers for jihad will come through camps in Pakistan, Afghanistan, Sudan, Iran and Lebanon. It is one of the reasons why this group has such good contacts around the world. Volunteers usually ship out from Brooklyn, London, Istanbul, Peshawar, Karachi or Gilgit to train and then fight. Private madrassahs are the largest source of volunteers; in Pakistan alone there are 6,000 private religious schools. They end up in the four camps, Zahwar Kali al-Badr (bin Laden's camp), The Harkat ul-jihad al-Islamia (for Pakistanis going to Kashmir), Al Forooq (for training Arabs), and camps near Khost. Although the United States would have us believe that "the Lion" or Osama runs these camps, it is not true. They were funded by the United States in the '80s using the Pakistani ISI, who still pays for and monitors the camps. In 10 years 14,000 young men have been trained here. Harkat al Mujahadeen (Movement of the Holy Warriors) is the front supported by individuals and the Pakistani government.

Life in the camps is pretty austere—up before dawn for prayers, religious studies, weapons training, assault drills, explosives and tactics. Lunch is simple (usually flat bread, sugared tea, rice, bean soup and the odd goat or cow bits). Basic training is short (about two weeks): Equipment is cheap or non existent (there are no uniforms) and the only R&R is soccer or volleyball. You live in tents, use pit toilets, pray five times a day and then get shipped out to a jihad of the trainer's choice. If you are successful you become a shaheed or martyr. If you don't get killed you are still guaranteed a spot in heaven for being a mujahedin. Money? Sorry.

There is no pay, but your hosts will provide simple food, beat-up equipment, transportation and crude shelter. *DP*'s muj friends recommend that you bring your own gear, especially boots. The life of a muj is usually spent sitting around poorly fortified positions, drinking tea, and waiting for your commander to put together an ambush.

Azzam

http://www.azzam.com
http://www.qoqaz.com

Jamaat-e-Islami

Mansura, Multan Road
Lahore, Pakistan
Tel.: 92-42-7844605-9
Fax: 92-42-5419504
E-mail: info@jamaat.org
http://www.jamaat.org

Muslim Brotherhood

http://www.ummah.org.uk/ikhwan/
http://www.ikhwanmuslimoon-jordan.org/

Sites of interest

http://www.unn.ac.uk/societies/islamic/about/war/war4.htm
http://www.islaam.com/jihad/
http://www.moslem.org/jihad.htm
http://www.theatlantic.com/politics/foreign/barberf.htm

Military/Adventure Resources

Books International

69B Lynchford Road
Farnborough
Hampshire, England GU14 6EJ
Tel.: (01252) 376564
Fax (01252) 370181

Books International specializes in military reference books for the modeler, collector, researcher or the curious. You won't find too many cerebral products here, but plenty of hard-to-find illustrated books on past wars, equipment, history and military reference works. Where else would you find an illustrated reference guide to Polish military helicopters or a real life photo book of the Navy SEALs?

Brassey's, Inc.

8000 Westpark Drive
First Floor
McLean, VA 22102
Tel.: (703) 442-4535
Fax: (703) 790-9063

Brassey's is the publisher of choice when British military men want to fill their mahogany bookcases. They are known for their annual *Defence* yearbook that keeps the Brits up to date on the rest of the world. Each issue has essays and intros on the leading political and military topics. If you want to be the model of a modern major general, you should look into their books on biological, nuclear, naval, historical and military warfare. Their annual update of *The World in Conflict* is a must-read for professional adventurers. There are drier books on ammunition, land-force logistics and radar and other technical reference manuals. It is no surprise that their U.S. rep is based in McLean, Virginia.

Covert Action

1500 Massachusetts Ave., NW, #732
Washington, DC 20005
Tel.: (202) 331-9763
Fax: (202) 331-9751

A magazine written by some ex-company folks who have no qualms about telling it like it is. Plenty of facts, numbers, dates, photos and other material to back their statements up.

For Your Eyes Only

Tiger Publications
P.O. Box 8759
Amarillo, TX 79114
Tel.: (805) 655-2009

Billed as an open intelligence summary of current military affairs. Editor Stephan Cole puts together the biweekly eight-page newsletter to provide an excellent update on military, political and diplomatic events around the world. Somewhat right-wing and hardware-oriented, it still provides a balanced global view of breaking events. An annual subscription costs $65 (26 issues). Sample copies are $3 each. Back issues are available for $1.25–$2, depending on how many you order. FYEO is also available on NewsNet: *(800) 952-0122* or *(215) 527-8030*.

Jane's Information Group

1340 Braddock
Suite 300
Alexandria, VA 22314
Tel.: (703) 683-3700
Fax: (703) 836-1593

Jane's is the undisputed leader in military intelligence for the world's armies. About a quarter of a million people subscribe to their annual guide on aircraft, but only about 11,000 need to know what's new in nuclear, biological and chemical protection clothing. Just as teenagers await the new car catalogs in the fall, the world's generals eagerly await the new Jane's reports on weapon systems, aircraft, ships, avionics, strategic weapons and other hardware. Esoteric fans thumb through their yearbooks on "Electro-optics, Image Intensifier Systems" (not to be confused with their guide to thermal imaging systems) or Air-Launched Weapons. Arms dealers never travel without their *World Markets for Armoured and Military Logistics Vehicles*. Prices for the books or CD-ROMs run between $400 and $9,000. If you are buying an update of an existing book or CD-ROM, the price drops about 25 percent. For your money, you get an annual guide, 11 monthly updates and a summary report. Jane's also publishes a monthly intelligence review, *Jane's Intelligence Review*, that provides background on global conflicts, terrorist groups and arsenals.

Jane's Security and Counterintelligence Equipment Yearbook

A new service is *Jane's Sentinel*, a series of regional security assessments with monthly updates and a broadcast fax service. *Sentinel* breaks down the world into six regions and provides reports on physical features, infrastructure, defense and security, as well as general information like maps and graphs.

In case the world is smitten with a bad case of peacefulness, Jane's also dabbles in the mundane. They have guides to airports, the container business and railways.

If you have ever have been torn between buying a Vigiland Surveillance Robot or a Magnavox Thermal Sniper Scope, Jane's makes it as easy as shopping at Victoria's Secret. The book contains an overview and listing of all major equipment used by security, antiterrorist and civil defence organizations.

The New Press

450 West 41st Street
New York, NY 10036
Tel.: (212) 629-8802
Fax: (212) 268-6349
This publisher of "serious books" can be counted on for interesting new books. Their titles include *Civil Wars: From L.A. to Bosnia*, by Hans Magnus Enzensberger, a book that helps readers understand the new forces that shape conflicts, and two books by Gabriel Kolko—*Century of War*, a new view of wars since 1914 with some excellent insights to war after World War II, and *Anatomy of a War*, the story of the Vietnam conflict from the Vietnamese, U.S. and Communist Party viewpoints.

Paladin Books

P.O. Box 1307
Boulder, CO 80306
Your best source for militaria, gung-ho adventure books and such classics as *Advanced Weapons Tactics for Hostage Rescue Teams*. Send for a listing or catalog. Much of the material is flatulent diction, tough-guy fantasies from military manuals or bizarre "get even" tomes. But there are some gems among the stones.

Soldier of Fortune

5735 Arapahoe Avenue
Boulder, CO 80303
Tel.: (800) 877-5207 (subscriptions)
Tel.: (303) 449-3750 (editorial)
The political left imagines the *SOF* reader as a gun-polishing, beer-drinking closet Rambo who actually cleaned latrines in Nam. Well, they are probably half right. It's the other half of the readership and content that is impressive. For every three articles on self-defense, gun control or new fighting knives, there is a good firsthand description of one of the world's dirty little wars. *SOF* does provide some very interesting on-the-ground reporting from countries undergoing Third World turmoil. Their editorial position is somewhat to the right of Ronald Reagan and Wyatt Earp, but the magazine is still an important source

for information on weapons and little-known conflicts. Subscriptions are $28 a year, with newsstand issues going for $4.75

Soldier of Fortune Expo

P.O. Box 693
Boulder, CO 80306
Tel.: (303) 449-3750; (800) 800-7630
Alone in your room, dreaming of foreign adventure and glory? Why not get those army surplus fatigues cleaned and pressed, get a suitable buzz cut, suck in your gut, and hang out with thousands of other "military/survivalist" enthusiasts? Every fall this Expo is more than just row after row of guns and survival equipment; it's also a chance to see real men fire off real machine guns. You get to see things blow up and watch real men fight with pugil sticks; worship real mercenaries, tough guys and heroes up close as you strut around the convention center, terrified that people might think you are actually a wimp; hear speakers tell you why our government can't be trusted and learn what you can do to maintain your God-given right to own metal tubes that propel projectiles.

Behind the Lines

P.O. Box 456
Festus, MO 63028
Tel.: (314) 937-7204
The journal of U.S. Military Special Operations is a bimonthly, 80-page magazine featuring articles on theory, history, development and firsthand accounts of actual missions. $24 per year.

UN Report on the Use of Mercenaries

http://www.unhcr.ch/refworld/un/chr/chr95/thematic/29.htm

In a Dangerous Place: Las Vegas

The 20th Annual Soldier of Fortune Convention

When I spotted the ad for the 20th annual Soldier of Fortune Convention in Las Vegas, everything came flooding back. The crossed daggers, squashed beret and dark sense of another world I will never know. So I went.

I'll confess right up front. I'm a 26-year-old female, Canadian born, living in New York, journalism degree, never killed anyone, never cleaned a Glock, never even had a desire to strangle commie bastards or join the NRA. The only person who could create more friction at the SOF convention would be Hillary Clinton showing up with her boobs popping out of a too-tight cammo.

It goes back to afternoons spent at Dominion News in Winnipeg, a scrubby store of downtown no-goods—but the only gig in town that sold magazines besides feel-good Canadiana like *Maclean's* or *Châtelaine*. Biker bitches, sun-faded postcards, knuckle-dusters—and *Soldier of Fortune* magazine. I was never an avid *SOF* reader. As kids, my brother and I never read the articles. What we wanted was blood, gore, photos that would make us peel over each page slowly, heads held back in anticipation. But more often than not we found infomercials on street-fighting courses given by Chuck Norris look-alikes and cryptic revenge ads in the classifieds. Yawn. Our Lego guns were more fun. But was it just a ruse to hide the real world of mercenary action and adventure from us? What was this world of mercenaries about? Did they really kill people and then snap photos around crusty dead guerrillas with heads popped like dropped watermelons?

When I saw the ad for the annual SOF convention, I knew the time had come to see if the white elephant, the flying pig—the real life mercenary—really existed. And now here I am in the Las Vegas desert, September, hot and ugly as hell and waiting for the Minute of Madness. I'm at a shooting range just outside the city's limits, with an abandoned white van that has been stripped for the demo that sits some 200 yards off in the distance. Leaning up against it is a pathetic-looking mannequin of a soldier with a UN logo, a leftover from the last nuclear test in Nevada.

This is the day guys dressed in cammo allude to, the "just wait till you see it" day when all my questions are supposed to be answered, my doubts quelled by a symphony of 20-odd machine guns lined up on the desert floor. I would be like Saul struck down and reborn as a believer and maybe even a born-again staunch defender of the Second Amendment.

The cranky patriarch dressed in army fatigues, shaved head and mustache who is pacing back and forth in the sand is Peter Kokalis, machine-gun guru and veritable master of ceremonies. As he crosses the sun-baked earth, his right hand rests on a handgun strapped to his black belt, his left hand clutches the mike. The master wants a short burst from each gun so that the audience, a few hundred people perched on bleachers, can learn to appreciate the different sounds. He offers up a synopsis of each gun, peppered with remarks about the user's nationality and skills, then orders his slaves to fire. The further the bullet casings fly from the gun, the louder the shouts from the crowd.

It's just too much for the German TV journalist who is busy having an orgasm, mouth opening and closing like a hungry goldfish, drawing out words with his thick accent. He is ideal target practice material: German. Journalist. Matching turquoise baseball cap and earplugs. "I vood LIKE us to haff a SHOT of YOU vit your GRANDson," he says to Kokalis. The L.A. cameraman wearing a cut-off leopard T-shirt leaps into place. "OKAY," shouts Kokalis, fiddling with a gun. Kokalis' nine-year-old grandson Kody, also dressed in army fatigues and cap, does his best to stay out of gramps' way while he sets up the MG-74 that Kody will be using during the Minute of Madness.

"Now just pretend there are 25 PLO terrorists that are on their way to bombing the U.S. embassy!"

They've come as far away as Sweden for this, a four-day convention of seminars, demos, an expo, storytelling and boozing. The crowd is a mixture of ex-paratroopers, Vietnam vets, retired or working law-enforcement officers, firefighters, militia hacks and lost souls. It's not unusual to be sitting in a seminar and have the speaker field questions from a guy dressed in fatigues berating police guerrilla tactics and a cop inquiring about a bullet's penetration factor. Aside from the German and some local reporters, I'm the only media attending the event. No surprise; SOF is used to bad coverage—especially when it comes to large, New York–based media outlets. After numerous calls to get a media kit, I chalk the lax response time up to my 212 area code. I eventually get a two-page fax of the schedule that changes by the hour.

The central hub of the convention is a glorified gun show. It is home to a mish-mash of gun dealers, Y2K pot and pan salesmen and beef jerky vendors. There's a scattering of fringe vendors selling Nazi marching songs, lingerie and black helicopter paranoia. But mostly dealers with rocambolesque guts, videos of chicks man-handling machine guns, and table after table of guns.

A couple of aisles over from the Refugee Relief International booth, placed strategically at the entranceway, are computer stations running the new Soldier of Fortune first-person shooter game.

There's a buzz of young pimply adolescent males waiting to play. This is the "secret world of the mercenary," complete with a "fanatical terrorist organization" and "explosive missions." I figure this is about as close to blowing someone away as it's going to get at the show. A ferret-eyed programmer from Britain who looks as if he's logged too much time in front of the box is giving a demo.

"Let's make this guy dance."

He sends out a few rounds and the thug wearing denim begins to vibrate across a New York subway platform despite his critical chest wounds. Just as things are getting interesting—when guys start getting their nuts shot off—the flack notices my press card.

Panic.

Suddenly, the purpose of the game is to disarm, not kill. But it takes a little more human dog food before the programmer manages to ding the glasses off a guy's face. From behind me, someone asks why they don't situate the game in a nondescript Midwestern school instead of a subway. The programmer smirks. This game's gonna do all right.

In a nearby booth, and annoyed that the video game is attracting more buzz, is a clutch of young vixens dressed in tight-fitting cammo. I haven't seen any women in 24 hours, and these—all chest, ass and leg—seem to defy the laws of gravity. The least butch female soldiers I've ever seen. Team Savage is a "living tribute" to the U.S. Armed Forces, "particularly" women soldiers. How, I don't know.

Looking at their calendar, I wasn't aware that crawling ass-first through streams and tit-first through the woods of upper New York with guns was a tribute. They've flown down from Manhattan, where they meet once a week at a studio to practice marching drills and "special skills." The calendar they are selling consists of them wearing carefully ripped clothes, painful looks on their face and guns never to be used. At least not as weapons of pain.

Command Sergeant Major Ice, the 27-year-old blonde in charge of parachute operations, has yet to jump from a plane. Nerves.

"I don't want to do that," she replies with refreshing candor. It feels strange to be in the presence of women again. Master Sergeant Panther, with perfect white teeth, gripes that some of the guys tell her to go out in a real field (whether it's with them remains unclear). She doesn't seem to realize that they are in the presence of real Green Berets, SEALs and Rangers, people who don't take kindly to wannabes no matter how many sexy rips there are in your shirt.

Worse, Team Savage is nowhere to be seen at night, when the real action is going down and the boys are showing their prowess. A series of planks strung together by the hotel pool are the stage for the pounding feet of the knife fights. It's dark in Las Vegas, and the sky glows from neon flashing lights ricocheting off the desert stone. Two men, shirtless, wield 6" black rubber knives. Mouths agape, shirtless, they clutch blades covered in red lipstick that leave "cuts" on their opponent's skin. Three cuts per round, best of three rounds. As they lunge, flaccid stomachs jiggle. "Come on! Cut! Be aggressive!"

Names like Bill, Harold, Larry and Alan, the first Native American to compete in the event. All left with bits of cotton ball on their whiskers when it comes time to remove the fake blood. Like a true Western, Alan wins by slaying the white man, and is awarded a 10" blade that only a mother could love. Beaming from the podium, raven hair swept back in a ponytail, he is met with cheers from the audience.

"This has been a really positive experience; this has been the first time anyone from the Hickory Apache reserve has competed in the convention," he gushes, and soon he is talking too much, too long, for a beer-injected audience. Who the hell invited an Indian to a white boy mercenary knife fight, anyways? That's cheating.

It's quickly apparent that here, the past is more active than the present, inseparable yet distinct. The same people, telling the same stories, Vietnam, El Salvador, Guatemala, South Africa, again and again, recited to the rhythm of Sweet Home Alabama played by the hired band at night, in-between beers and plane crash survival courses in the pool. Because there has not been a good war in some time, reminiscing is the only refuge. There are a few poolites who can be overheard telling stories about conflicts in today's news, but these are just visitors, the tick birds that sit on the Cape buffalo's back. In fact, most don't even know where these new adventurers came from or go to. Here at SOF the wellspring is 'Nam, U.S. military service, and all stories must flow from it. Everyone agrees the convention is in dire need of some young blood and new enemies, instead of the old stalwarts—the c-word and a majority of the media.

Colonel Robert Brown, the editor and publisher of *Soldier of Fortune*, wheels about in a wheelchair, his left leg broken in a mundane fall and the words "fuck you" written on his cast. At night, he reclines on a deck chair by the pool, a Pharaoh demanding and receiving the respect of an entourage. He's very deaf despite hearing aids in each ear. It's hard to tell whether he even cares if he can hear what people are saying. He probably knows all the stories by heart, anyway. He rails against our police state (even though the large part of his readership are police and government), he croaks against Second Amendment erosion even though you can buy perfectly good machine guns at the show, and he barks against government incompetence (even though as a magazine publisher he uses *SOF* as a bully pulpit for gun rights). The odd thing is that his stories seem to be about carrying guns in other people's countries.

Vietnam, El Salvador, Nicaragua, Myanmar etc. Brown has refocused his military career into an annual danger junket. "Bob-ka-Bob", as adventurer and Reagan-doctrine-creator Jack Wheeler calls him. He reminisces about Brown's near immolation by Russian napalm on former trips with mujahedin into Afghanistan. He was in Albania a couple of years ago, Bosnia, South Africa you name it. Not really to kill people but to just show up, do something interesting and be Bob Brown. There are many stories, all of which seem to revolve around guns, men and dangerous places. There is almost a standard pattern. Gun love, adventure, man love, danger. All with missing parts that are filled in by little boys' wild imaginations. So is gun love part of this man love? I spend the remainder of Sunday trying to figure that out by popping holes through a target at The Gun Store. Gun stores in Las Vegas all have the same riveting names. I guess the act of pulling the trigger is supposed to be exciting enough. I've never shot a handgun before, and the guys at the gun store are thrilled that a chick wants to try. They give me a .22 Ruger, but I quickly discard it for the KH.40. I begin to understand why some of the conventioneers like playing war so much, although I don't think hole punching will get me much talk time at the pool. What is this gunlove anyway?

Three days earlier, Kokalis gave a seminar titled "In Search of the Magic Bullet"—over an hour of slides of bullet entry-paths, yawing diagrams, brains on morgue tables and other examples of hi-velocity acupuncture. It would be safe to say that Kokalis likes guns. His military job was analyzing foreign light weapons and ordnance. Then he went into wound ballistics. He justifies being a mercenary in El Salvador by saying that he accepted no pay, which makes him a volunteer. So he helped adjust and fix death squad machine guns. Or did he?

Dabbing his forehead with a white Kleenex, he holds the audience in rapture. For 90 minutes, no one dares tell him that he is deep-throating the mike, making it hard to understand his distorted voice in the packed convention room. Kokalis, who is partly deaf from listening to machine guns, could give a shit if he makes others deaf too. Across the hotel hallway, suits are meeting at the Nevada Independent Insurance Agents convention. I wonder how his speech would go over next door. I am snapped out of my musings by Kokalis barking: "Are you anticipating a charging banana tree?" He is puzzled as to why someone would test a gun on a helpless fruit tree—or worse, a phone book. I'm one of maybe three women in an audience of a hundred. Across from me, Little Red Riding Hood's grandmother, sporting a cashmere sweater with a string of pearls, listens intently, hands on her lap. Despite his crabby exterior, Kokalis likes the attention a teacher gets. He has his groupies, including an attractive young Belgian man dressed in desert cammo who sticks to Kokalis like a bodyguard. During the seminar, he sits in the front row.

"Now, if you really want to blow the guts out of someone," Kokalis starts. He pauses at the pedestal, and looks up at the audience. No one says a word. There is an uneasy silence. Has he shattered the glass wall?

"What?" he shoots back. "I'm just telling you like it is. I mean, that's why you're here, not to go hunting rabbits. I look out at you, you look like a bunch of mean, red-neck peckerheads!" Another pause. Followed by a roar of approval. Shock value goes a long way here. I had hoped to minimize my own shock value of attending the show by introducing myself as a Canadian. I thought the neutrality and peacekeeper rep of home would provide me with a nonthreatening entrance point. Little did I know that scribbling "Canada" in parentheses on the green name tag was the equivalent of stamping "SOCIALIST" in red ink on my forehead.

Of course, I wasn't really Canadian or a socialist. After all, I beat my father at target practice at his ranch in Alberta—an act deemed worthy of expulsion in a country that has banned concealed bus passes. Yet the darker secret was about to emerge—that I had moved to New York six months earlier. I was an East Coast liberal, female . . . journalist.

Back at the range, the last of the explosives missed by the machine guns during the Minute of Madness are being detonated. Despite the wall of lead that has been pitched in the air, they still have to detonate the charges by remote control. The white van looks like shrapnel. The machine guns have been spitting out between 200 and 2,500 rounds per second as the loaders feed in belt after belt of 50 cent to a buck shot ammo. The UN man, evil symbol of the New World Order and in bad need of some reconstructive surgery, has mysteriously vanished.

Then, unexpectedly, another explosion. But this one is from behind the front line. I see a clutch of people gathered; excited voices. Suddenly, the whites of Kokalis' eyes are showing, his facial muscles taut as his old body leans forward. A short, overblown man with an NBC press card slung around his neck is slowly sinking into the sand.

He had come with his cameraman to film the Minute of Madness. Saturdays are only slightly less suicidal than Sundays when it comes to local news. The boys at NBC must have gobbed when the press release came through the fax on this one: Men. Guns.

"If you're going to use any footage that makes gun-owners look like shit, I'll personally come after you," Kokalis says to the journalist, jabbing a bony finger in the air. "I've been personally demonized by you people."

The film crew had (unwisely) chosen Crazy Carl to interview. Carl appears every year dressed as a mustachioed French legionnaire, green beret perched on his bald head, full army fatigues. No one quite seems to know where Carl comes from or what he does for a living. But he comes every year, and if you know your military insignia, it would appear he has graduated from every special forces school with a few Boy Scout badges thrown in for good luck. All anyone knows really is that Carl doesn't speak much French for a legionnaire. Screw My-Lai; Carl is the taboo subject of the conference. Bring him up and eyes roll back in their sockets as if gassed. But he is perfect for every naive television crew—the clothes, the mustache—and Kokalis will have none of it. "They will put a spin on it!" he says to Carl. "Having them come out here and pretend they're reasonable people, you're a fool to believe that. Everything they say and record, they're going to clip." The tables have turned, the journalist has been ambushed.

"*You* tell me what an assault rifle is!" Kokalis fires at the journalist, repeating the question endlessly to each cameraman, radio jock and scribe around him. Nobody knows. A blast echoes in the distance as organizers detonate a final explosive missed by the gunners. No one blinks. The L.A. cameraman, who missed the shot, is on his knees pleading for another. "Come on! What is it!" Kokalis pushes. The desert heat—or is it Kokalis'?—is making the journalist flush.

"It's a . . . a . . . what is it?"

Journalists aren't supposed to know anything, just gather information. Then they are experts once they pick through the quotes, footage. No one ever writes a positive piece on the SOF convention. Colonel Brown is still paying off legal bills and bad press from a court case he lost when someone hired a hitman from the classifieds. But the press wants gun love images because it's a big deal in

Manhattan and Washington. Here in the heart of gun territory, low budget vacations and braggadocio are fertile ground for cartoonery.

By now, the ring of conventioneers formed around the scrum is waiting for an outcome in this standoff. Kokalis is rising up like Beethoven, arms pumping the air, readying for his final symphony. He is relentless. As if his audience has more sway than NBC, he makes his point. One that will never make it to the tube. "Do you know what people were demonized in Nazi Germany? The Jews! Well, we are the Jews of this country! We have done nothing wrong! My grandson and I have done nothing wrong! Am I possibly wrong? Did I tell him like it was?"

The crowd cheers. Kody, orphaned in the chaos, squeaks in, "I believe everything you say," looking up at granddad with puppy-dog eyes. And without another word, Kokalis is off, storming through the sand like Patton, heading for his desert encampment.

Cut!

The journalist is in paradise. He can deliver the footage of a crazy gun-loving geriatric with a Major Dad kid in tow. A couple of stock shots of Columbine, teary-eyed prom queens, some obtuse manly quotes form Carl -and voilà. Hard hitting journalism on "America's Love Affair with Guns" and it's Emmy time.

Energized and deafened, the crowd runs across the sand like a land-rush, heading for Kokalis' objet d'art—the white van. They feel their hands along the pock-marked metal in awe. Gun love. I hitch a ride to the hotel in back of a beat-up pickup truck with a sheriff's officer, a welder and a heavy equipment operator. I'm beginning to get a headache from lack of water.

Ken, who spent roughly a year in the Navy, is prepped in fatigues and sucking on a Big Gulp. He is explaining to me the Bible's support of the right to bear arms. He recites verses near perfectly. We talk throughout the trip back to the hotel; he tucks his cap under his legs while my hair blows uncontrollably in the back of the truck. I feel sad because he seems to need love and sounds like he hasn't been with a woman in a very long time. I guess man love can only sustain you for so long. He suggests marriage when we arrive back at the hotel. I decline politely with a stupid girl laugh, but accept a tattered Citizens Rule Book as a gift.

After dinner, Kokalis' hard-bodied Belgian alerts me that if I want to talk to Kokalis I will have to "do it now" (the interview, alas) in his hotel room. I feel like a commando being given marching orders. I'm whisked up 30 flights by elevator, down a short passage and through a door. Kokalis sits in a chair, hands lying on the armrests, another Pharaoh. Across from him is the Belgian, silent, and Ken from the ride back to the hotel. Men trickle in and out of the room. Most pay respect to Kokalis then head for the beer in the tub. Kokalis sips on a Diet Coke. His story is long, technical. He has obviously told it dozens of times. There are few escape hatches for an intimate discussion.

"I don't enjoy it because I'm a warrior," he explains. "I enjoy the excitement, the tightness in the cut, when you're in a tough spot, the rush of excitement in combat. Nothing else can ever approach that. Something else that only men can understand—the love the soldiers have for their fellow soldiers. Bonding that comes from great danger." The two cammoed men in the room nod in sacred agreement. Whew, man love, chapter and verse.

Soon, he will travel to Russia for a double birthday party for himself and Kalashnikov. I can see them now, two old men, blowing out candles on a birthday cake in the shape of a gun in some dank Russian apartment. Kokalis loves Beethoven. He feels a common bond with him. Beethoven was also once deaf, old and smart. Kokalis enjoys that shadow world of reality versus perception. He is a man amongst men, a patriot who would lay his life on the line to fight communism. But then again he could also be Don Knotts, traveling machine gun repairman, who uses the blank parts of his resume to get free beer at conventions. When asked bluntly, with feigned ignorance, how a nonmilitary U.S. citizen can travel to El Salvador and shoot El Salvadorans, he prickles that "there are certain boundaries over which this conversation cannot go."

To him, I'm a journalist, a derider of man love, hater of gun love and all those that worship these sacraments. Had this been asked by one of the crew in the bathroom drinking Coronas, there would have been a chuckle and a reminder to "use less lead on the women and children." A wink and a clink of Coronas, the cue for the next adventure story to begin.

But not for me.

My interview lasts roughly one hour. Kokalis abruptly announces its conclusion, and that he must now tend to his guests. My mercenary? Not really. Kokalis took great pains to point out that he was an unpaid volunteer, that he was a trainer, not a shooter, a repairman not a killer. He was just doing research in the field. But he likes to dance around the question like Salome with John the Baptist.

In the future, organizers hope to move the Soldier of Fortune convention to Phoenix, where there are fewer restrictions on using the dynamite and gasoline explosives they can only dream of using in Vegas during the Minute of Madness Firepower Demonstration. The dogs of war (as the local newspaper headlined the show) no longer feel welcome here. Stunts like rappelling down three story parking lots and firing Magnums underwater in the hotel pool have earned them a bit of a bad-boy reputation.

This year's mishap won't help, either. A shot was accidentally fired from a Scout rifle after a seminar in the hotel. The bullet passed through two walls and ended up piercing a pipe, in of all the gosh-darn places, the hotel office. Could this be a conspiratorial act of a covert troublemaker seeking to tarnish the *SOF* image? We'll never know, but we can discuss it for years to come by the pool. A place where the quiet men in blazers make their introductions and then leave early.

The rules are clear here. I am an outsider, a woman, a journalist, someone who tries to figure out why these guys get together every year and if there's such a thing as a mercenary. Yes, I met my mercenaries, but they did not call themselves as such. They were not the ones you could hear chortling from across the pool. They were the quiet introverts dressed in blazers or clothes from the Gap. The calm men that you meet on the last night of the conference and punch yourself for not having the guts to walk up to earlier. The guy who can calmly give you rank, times, places and dates about his past life. Without embellishment or wild gesticulations. The guy who doesn't dress like Carl, but is still seeking that small sliver of acceptance for his deeds. That soft man love that makes the hard time alone in foreign places real and worthwhile. A profession rooted not in gun love but love for adventure even when there is no clearly scripted story to tell. Here under the overamped hatred of tyranny and government are truer, deeper stories of courage, conviction and maybe a sadness that there are so few who care. I could see that these men were fueled in part by childhood stories of derring-do, exotic locales and maybe even weekends peeking at the gory exciting pictures in adventure magazines. They were good at what they did, they needed the fix of action—and most chose not to build a story around their life to justify it. A life that can be as barren, hard and uncaring as the deserts of Nevada. Did I find what I was looking for? Yup. But if I told you . . . I'd have to kill you.

—**Sarah Richards**

Terrorism

I Hear You Knocking, But You Can't Come In

DP spends a lot of time with terrorists. We sit around and drink tea, talk politics, show pictures of our kids, discuss foreign policy and both scratch our heads at how my hosts became terrorists.

Terrorism can be easily defined as "premeditated, politically motivated violence perpetrated against noncombatant targets by subnational groups or clandestine agents usually intended to influence an audience" as it is by United States Code Section 2656(d).

This is definition is obviously the work of leaders of established and recognized countries, most with democratic political processes. It seems to skirt around groups that we create that are magically labeled "freedom fighters" in our press. Terrorists or freedom fighters. Depends on what week it is. What about the Kurds, the Moros, the Timorese, the Israelis, the Contras, Tamils, Pakistanis, Afghans, and so on? All have been labeled as both. Sometimes we give them money and ask them to help. Sometimes we pay other people to kill them. I haven't figured it out yet, but someday I will.

It should be remembered that the United States of America, Russia, China, France and Israel, along with numerous other now respectable countries, began their road to independence using terrorist methods and actions against their past leaders. Ghengis, Alexander, Caesar, Marx and Mao have all shown that terrorism is just part of the natural element of conflict.

Even today when we fight our remote control wars with smart bombs and crisp debriefings in Serbia, Afghanistan and Iraq, we are sowing terror into the minds of the people we bomb from on high. "Premeditated, politically motivated violence perpetrated against noncombatant targets by clandestine agents usually intended to influence an audience," if I remember correctly. I left out subnational group. Does anyone remember just how few people voted for our last president?

Forgive me and I will put away my soapbox. The point is that labels can blind us to the purpose of a conflict. More importantly, anyone who chooses to die for something should be listened to very carefully and possibly corrective action should be taken.

Today, few can argue that terrorism is a legitimate and sadly productive method to gain international attention, demand concessions and eventually establish legitimate states and political parties. As in Oklahoma City, the World Trade Center and Waco, a few angry men can change the course of history. Despite what the world's governments espouse, there are few minority or splinter groups that can use the existing political process to gain their independence or freedom without resorting to outrageous tactics.

The less potent the group is as a political force and the thinner the support base, the more likely the group will resort to more dramatic methods to secure world attention. The leaders of these groups tend to be from the upper classes, college educated, creative, egotistical and flamboyant almost to the point of ridiculousness. Osama bin Laden, Che Guevara, Yasir Arafat, Khatlah, Abdullah Ocalan, Carlos the Jackal, Abu Nidal and Rafael Sebastin Guillen Vicente—a.k.a., Subcommandante Marcos, the pipe-smoking, wisecracking son of a furniture salesman—are not the exception but the rule.

Are the real bad men the dark silent politicians, theocrats and businessmen who write checks for these groups or provide safe haven? According to our government, Iran, Libya, Sudan, Syria (and its vassal state Lebanon), Pakistan and Afghanistan are where you will see the roots of evil. Or will we? Would the roots of terrorism also be found in Manhattan boardrooms, European gas stations, Dutch oil companies, the Pentagon or even the bedroom of the president? Doesn't Dutch Shell supply the vast majority of income to Syria? Just where does Libya sell its oil? Who wears the diamonds plucked out of Savimbi's Angola? Who injects the heroin that is smuggled through Chechnya? Who toots the coke that fuels the rebels in Colombia? Everyone is guilty. Everyone is innocent. The answers are not that simple

Terror is an emotion that cannot be moderated by legal purpose, thick sheaves of laws or even firm conviction. Aren't innocent but very dead Serbs, Iraqis, Iranians, Afghans, Sudanese and other impoverished peoples as dead and innocent as Americans, British, Australians and Canadians? The difference is that we are right and they are wrong. Right?

The U.S. State Department estimates that about 21 percent of world terror is directed against the United States. Most of it is result of our support of Israel and Saudi Arabia, oil projects in South America and Africa, attacks on Muslim countries, and just generally being the biggest bully on the block. Of course, the State Department turns a blind eye toward Oklahoma City. The discussion of internal terrorist acts is not one that any government wants to address simply and plainly. It is much easier to demonize swarthy leaders, make vague accusations about support for terrorism and then punish their people for not electing them. Is killing innocent people terrorism when it effects no change in their government or political stance?

But that is where I leave it. Terrorism is the most feared tool of established democracies because it forces them to subvert the clean ideals that they pride themselves on. It creates a police state, a state of fear, harsh punishments and tight controls. As one example, even though there have been few if any hijackings on U.S. soil, all passengers and their baggage must be checked as if they were potential terrorists. Does terrorism work? You bet.

Terrorism 101

There are various proven methods of gaining the world's attention. The first is to blow something big up, preferably with American citizens inside. Embassies do just fine if you can't get close enough to an army barracks. This one act can move you right up to the top of the wanted list. Luckily, most bomb attacks are silly little hole punchers that create a lot of broken glass and a few cuts.

The second most heinous act is to kidnap then execute Americans while they are abroad. This will guarantee at least two to five minutes on CNN every night, with 30-minute repeats every half-hour until the situation is resolved. If you can, grab politicians or military or embassy workers. You can get your mug and demands on every major news network around the world. Kidnapping has been getting tougher now that people are savvy.

The third common method is usually hijacking; the least effective acts are direct attacks on military or police forces. They like that because that's all they train and are armed for. Pulling up with a Ryder weekend special packed with fertilizer and fuel oil is just plain unsporting.

You could try sending a polite, well-written political proposal with workable, fair solutions to the ruling party. But I have a feeling that won't even get you a return phone call. You gotta have a gimmick, and fear among the populace will definitely get you attention.

Terrorism: Bigger Than Internet Stocks!

You may have noticed that terrorism has shifted a bit. Times are tight in the bad boy club, so you aren't seeing much action out there. Somewhere along the line somebody in Washington took a page from *DP* and realized that if you just paid the terrorists to sit down and shut up instead of giving the government all that money to fight them, things worked out just fine. That's why you see casinos crammed with Israelis on the Gaza Strip. But now we have another kind of problem. It seems that there is a new generation of self-funded (usually by kidnapping or extortion), self-sufficient groups, some even with their own country, thank you very much—and some that don't even want a country, thank you very much.

These are the narco and fundamentalist groups that can make money just by creating giant no-go zones. Colombia, Afghanistan, the Caucasus, Central Africa, the Horn and large tracts of Kurdistan are simply entrepreneurial rebel zones where everything from smack to color TVs move in splendid, untaxed (by the government) isolation. Luckily most of these groups are too busy making money to really attack the United States.

There is another level of terrorism activity that doesn't make the headlines but is necessary for the ongoing support of organizations and activities. If terrorist groups are not funded by a government (such as Iran, Iraq, Libya or private sources), they must resort to extortion (demanding money in exchange for lack of violent attacks), robbery (theft of money or possessions by force or threat of force), kidnapping (abducting people who then are released in exchange for negotiated amounts of money) or drug or weapons smuggling (payment for safe transport of illegal goods). Other groups are for hire and will conduct assassinations, kidnappings, warfare, protection, bombings or other criminal attacks for a fee. Many times these acts are carried out under the name of a terrorist group but are simply criminal acts. They would provide spectacular sound bites and video clips for a fee and/or a piece of the action. All that was missing was a director and a producer.

It is important to note that terrorists would like to attack at the heart of the intended enemies' strongholds but are neither strong, wily or powerful enough. Worse yet, there are few terrorist groups who can handle the ideologically numbing bureaucracy it would take to pick up the trash and clean out parking meters, pick up stray dogs and listen to zoning meetings. Just look at the poor Palestinians who are now faced with beating their own people to quell rioting and protect Israelis. So most groups content themselves with chipping away at the public confidence, gaining a hollow importance but taking no real steps toward bettering the plight of the people they represent.

Our government's biggest bugaboo is Osama bin Laden, a man who takes great pleasure in kicking the United States in the shins to remind us we should stick to our home turf and not mess around in the Middle East. Can one man keep the most powerful country in the world flummoxed and chasing its tail? Sadly, yes. Terrarism works best for those who have no ultimate political solution.

Terror Mutates

The pure ideology of '70s terrorism is slowly evolving into a cash-based, self-centered ideology better suited for the '80s than the new millennium (we never said terrorists are up on trends—after all, they do spend a lot time in hiding).

Gray-haired academics spouting Marx in jungle camps now have to resort to the purest of entrepreneurial pursuits to make ends meet.

Despite the lack of big-time sponsors, terrorism will continue to be a threat to all Western travelers. Westerners are high-profile pawns in the publicity game. The savvy traveler needs to understand the difference between the Algerian terrorist (who will cut your throat without even rifling through your pockets), a Mexican terrorist (who has no reason to harm an American tourist), a Filipino terrorist (who will trade you like a used car salesman), a Kurdish terrorist (who will use you as a political pawn and usually release you unharmed and well fed), a rogue Khmer Rouge gunmen (who wants his $10,000 or you get whacked) or a plain ol' thug who may have been fighting for some funky acronymic rabble, but just likes the Rolex you have and can't be bothered asking you politely for it. Terrorism may also be faceless in the case of bombings in Paris, Tel Aviv, Karachi and other urban centers. So keep in mind that carrying around a copy of Mao's little red book or Qaddafi's green book or even Carlos' black book won't get you as far as carrying a Gold card. Money is the primary goal of most terrorism groups in the Third World, publicity is second, and achievement of political objectives is a distant third. From Colombia to Kashmir, bad guys are taking the money and running.

For those who want to understand more about the aims of various political, terrorist or freedom groups, they can be contacted at the addresses at the end of this chapter. Keep in mind that any contact with this group may put you under the direct scrutiny of U.S., European and Israeli intelligence agencies and lead to criminal charges being filed if any collusion or support is proven.

http://www.state.gov/www/global/terrorism/1998Report/appa.html
http://www.state.gov/www/global/terrorism/1999Report/appa.html

The MisFortune 500

Terrorism is big business these days. These are the players left in the game. Yes, there are many more terrorist groups listed by the State Department, but *DP* and our contributors have visited with most of them and here are our picks for the next few years.

Group	Leader/Goals	Cause	Location	Size	Began
Al Quds	Osama bin Laden and a network of Gulf contributors	Removing America from Saudi Arabia	Based in Jalalabad. Travels to Yemen, Sudan and Tajikistan	Loosely grouped	1992
Hezbollah	Nasrallah and Fadlallah lead a religious/political party with military and information wings. Funded and controlled by Iran	Anti-Israel, Shia Islamic fundamentalists	Operates out of Lebanon with cels in Argentina, U.S. and Europe	Thousands	1982
PKK	Pro Kurd alleged to be funded by extortion of Kurdish businesses in Europe and drug transshipment	Kurdish homeland in SE Turkey	Military base is Zap, Northern Iraq	10,000–15,000	1974
NPA	Left-wing workers group in Philippines		Northern Philippines, Negros and Mindanao	3,000	1947
Sendero Luminoso	Maoist meanies who baby-sit coca trade	Maoist drug production	Peru http://www.csrp.org/	300	1967
GIA	Loose groups of cels backed by Iran, Sudan and French based Algerian expats	Islamic fundamentalists	Algeria	1,500	1992
Islamic Group	Iran and Sudan supported and trained fighters. Doddering since leader Sheik Al Rahman was imprisoned in the U.S.	Islamic fundamentalists	Egypt	Al Minya area	1975
Hamas	Palestine political party with military wing backed by Saudis, Sudanese Iran and expats	Islamic/anti-Israel	West Bank, Gaza Strip	Thousands	1987
Harakat Mujahadin	Islamic group supported by Pakistan that seeks independence of Kashmir	Islamic/anti-India	Muzaffarabad, Pakistan Raiwind in Punjab	300	1980?
RIRA	The real IRA.	Anti-U.K.	Military wing of the 32 County Sovereignty Committee	Hundreds	1997

TERRORISM

Group	Leader/Goals	Cause	Location	Size	Began
Tamil Tigers	Ethnic independence group	Tamil homeland in Sri Lanka	Northern tip of Sri Lanka	10,000	1983
FARC	Communist rebel group, controls most drug shipments in Colombia.	Anti-U.S, antigovernment	Colombia and border areas	7,000	1966
National Liberation Army	Maoist-Marxist-Leninist group seeking to overthrow government but gets funding from kidnapping and drugs	Antigovernment	Rural parts of Colombia	3,000	1963
EPR	Mexican bad boys	Antigovernment	Oaxaca, Mexico	300	1996
The Extreme Right	U.S.-based militia, activists acting in singular events	Antigovernment	West and South	?	1776

Resources

State Department Report on Global Terrorism
www.state.gov/www/global/terrorism/ 1998Report/1998index.html

Terrorism Research Center
www.terrorism.com/

ICT Terrorism
www.ict.org.il/

KimSpy
http://www.kimsoft.com/kim-spy.htm

Clandestine Radio Listings
http://www.subnet.virtual-pc.com/ yo379459/clandestine.html

Mario's Cyberspace
http://mprofaca.cronet.com/ index1.html

Stratfor
www.stratfor.com

Good Links Page
http://rvl4.ecn.purdue.edu/~crom-well/lt/terror.html

Who's Minding the Store?

Want to know who is really behind that terrorist group? The Web allows you to find out who gets the bill every month for that rabid, foaming-at-the-mouth hate site. Just type in:
http://www.ibc.wustl.edu/ibc/domain_form.html

Jane's ($325 per year)
http://catalogue.janes.com/ terr_watch.html

Studies in Conflict & Terrorism
Department of International Relations
St. Andrews University
St. Andrews KY16 9AL Scotland, UK
US (215) 625-8900

The World in Conflict ($39.95)
by Dr. John Laffin (ISBN 1-85753-216-3) Brassey's
A roundup of the world's wars, the combatants tactics and background.

Patterns of Global Terrorism
http://www.usis.usemb.se/terror/ index.html
Annual report on global terrorism.

Terrorism
http://www.terrorism.com/

Low Intensity Conflicts
by CSM James J. Gallagher, $14.95 (ISBN 0-8117-2552-9) Stackpoole Tel.: (800) 732-3669
A good manual for soldiers or journalists who want to understand various attack formations, ambushes, peacekeeping operations and even how checkpoints are set up.

U.S. Army Special Forces Handbook
The best, the smallest and translated into more Third World languages than you'll ever know. Also you will need the ST 31-91B Medical Handbook in case you didn't pay close attention to the Handbook. Worst case, there's always the Army Chaplain's Handbook.

http://www.netside.com/~lcoble/books/ booklist.html
http://www.paladinbooks.com/

Terrorism Research Center

> *http://www.infowar.com/*
> *Tel.: (813) 393.6600*
> *Fax: (813) 393.6361*
> *E-mail: infowar@infowar.com*
> Links to info on privacy, espionage, terrorism and much more.

FEMA Fact Sheet

> *http://www.fema.gov/fema/ter-rorf.html*
> Terrorism help and tips from FEMA.

Hate Groups, Terrorists, and Radicals

> *http://www.xensei.com/users/hubcom/hate.htm*

Terrorist Weapons

> *http://www.onestep.com/milnet/tweaps.htm*

Terrorist Use of Chemical Weapons

> *http://groucho.la.asu.edu/~godber/research/cwpaper.html*

Counter Terrorism

> *http://www.counterterrorism.com/*

Terrorist Profile Weekly—The Terrorist Fanzine.

> *http://gopher.well.sf.ca.us:70/1/Publications/online_zines/Terror*

Terrorism and Counterterrorism

> *http://www.spystuff.com/listsites.html*

Bureau Of Diplomatic Security: Reward Info for Criminals

> *http://www.heroes.net/content.html*

Terrorist's Handbook

> *http://pilot.msu.edu/user/snooktyl/*

Pyrotechnics, Fireworks, Explosives

> *http://www.amazing1.com/fire.htm*

Jolly Roger's CookBook

> *http://www.voicenet.com/%7Ewizkid/jr.html*

The Big Book of Mischief

> *http://www.cybercity.hko.net/berlin/solon/bigbook/MAIN.html*

Revenge Page

> *http://www.cs.uit.no/~paalde/Revenge/*

Defense, Aircraft and Counter-terrorism Page

> *http://crisny.org/users/siegelm/defense.html*

Virtual World of Spies and Intelligence

> *http://www.dreamscape.com/frank-vad/counter.html*

Terrorism Research Center

> *http://www.geocities.com/CapitolHill/2468/trc2.html*

Counter-Terrorism Page

> *http://www.emergency.com/cntr-terr.htm*

Terrorist Profiles

> *http://vislab-www.nps.navy.mil/%7Egmgoncal/tgp2.htm*

Domestic Terrorism

> *http://enhtech.com/veterans/vjv1n4/vj2.html*

Most Wanted

> *http://www.MostWanted.com/*

Cyber Muslim

> *http://www.uoknor.edu/cybermuslim/cy_jihad.html*

Center for Terrorism in India

> *http://rbhatnagar.csm.uc.edu:8080/india_terrorism.html*

Perilous Times—Terrorist Page

> *http://www.teleport.com/~jstar/ter-ror.html*

Terrorist Profile Weekly Archives

> *http://www.site.gmu.edu/~cdibona/tpw.html*

Intelligence Web

> *http://www.awpi.com/IntelWeb*

Index of Terrorist Groups

> *http://www.site.gmu.edu/~cdibona/grpindex.html*

Society of Competitive Intelligence Professional Homepage

> *http://www.scip.org*

All Intelligence and Counter-intelligence Agencies

> *http://www.kimsoft.com/kim-spy.htm*

Other People, Other Voices

These are not terrorist sites but rather communication tools used to circumvent the barriers the traditional media puts up.

Television

Two groups have television stations that we know of: The PKK has MED-TV a satellite station that conveniently goes on the blink every once in a while.

MED-TV

The Linen Hall, 162-168 Regent Street
London W1R 5AT
Tel.: [44] (0) 171-4942523
Fax: [44] (0)171-494-2528
E-mail: med@med-tv.be

MED-TV is the world's only satellite channel that broadcasts Kurdish programming to receivers in Europe, North Africa and the Middle East.

Radio

Most rebel groups have radio stations or transmitters. Whether it's Foday Sankoh of the RUF (Sierra Leone), who used to broadcast from a transmitter in his hotel suite in the Abuja Sheraton, or Charles Taylor's hip-hop KISS-FM in Monrovia, radio has been used to send boring pap (VOA), transmit bullshit (Marxist drivel), whip up people to a frenzy (Milles Collines, Burundi) and to play music with revolutionary themes.

Clandestine Radio Stations

http://up4c03.gwdg.de/~kuhl/cla

Adventure Calls

Life Is Not a Job

Everybody has a different idea of adventure. It could be bird-watching or it could be parachuting into jungles to fight with rebels. It sure as hell ain't moving memos from the "in" to the "out" basket. But most of us spend the large part of our waking lives working to not work. Our puritanical background says that in the typical 2,000 hours of labor we provide each year, we might be able to squeeze two weeks or 336 hours of real living. The Travel Industry Association of America says that 98 million people took adventure vacations. But how many took adventure jobs? Adventure is not about papering your gray Herman Miller foxhole with cool pictures ripped out of magazines. Adventure is about pushing yourself, discovering your own worlds, writing your own itinerary. But for those who want to walk before they run, it's a good way to start. Adventure is about living adventurously 24/7, 365 days a year, year after year until you drop dead with a smile on your face. Now get back to work.

Head Banging for Bucks

Bungie jumping started on the island of Vanuatu. The Pentecost Jump, or naghol, started on Pentecost Island as a fertility rite in April and May to guarantee a good yam harvest. Men of the village erect crude scaffolds, measure vines, and then jump. Naturally, the tough guys are the ones that smack their head on the soft dirt piled at the bottom. The intrepid travelers who have made it to the former New Hebrides were usually hit up for a donation of around $50. It seems those days are over. Now local chiefs are charging 5,000 vatu ($38) for spectators, 25,000 vatu ($192) for a still camera, 40,000 ($307) for a video camera and a million vatu or $7,692 for TV crews. Contact: Vanuatu Tourist Office, Box 209, Port Vila, Vanuatu, Tel.: 011 678 22 813 Fax: 011 678 23 889, E-mail: tourism@vanuatu.com.vu.

Expeditions

The first big step for most people is actually creating a cool venture, an expedition. There is no one way to join or organize an expedition. By definition, all you have to do is walk out your door. Most expeditions have goals, structure, deadlines, budgets, and so forth, and require more planning than execution. Most are scientific in nature. Many are adventurous or exploratory, with little of the painstaking information recording required of expeditions in the old days. Expeditions are simply formalized trips. Like any great endeavor, they should have an objective, a unique sense of purpose and maybe a dash of insanity. A lot of people dream about doing great things and being lauded for their superhuman status.

An expedition is a way to say "Here is what we said we would do, and here is what we did." There is little to no reward for climbing Mt. Everest blindfolded or swimming the Atlantic while towing a barge. There is far more reward in being an actor portraying the adventurer. Sigourney Weaver (as Dian Fossey) and Patrick Bergen (as Sir Richard Burton) put more in the bank than their real-life counterparts ever made in a lifetime—a sobering thought. Fame does await the bold. And after that fame comes an endless procession of rubber chicken dinners and outdoor store openings. The more literate of them will write a book that will grace remainder lists for years to come. So consider an expedition as a good use of your skills and talents, with the only reward being the satisfaction of fellowship, a job well done and a better understanding of our world. Along the way, you will enter an elite club of men and women who have tested themselves and found themselves to be comfortably mortal.

Now a warning to the adventurous who view expeditions as an interesting way to see the world. All expeditions have some hardship involved. In fact, more and more of them seem to feature physical discomfort. Rannulph Fiennes' jaunt to the pole on skis is an example of this craziness. He could have flown, but he wanted to do something that had never been done before. Other expeditions, like the recent attempt to climb Mt. Kinabalu in Borneo the hard way, turned into a fiasco because a group of men decided to do whatever they felt like and got lost. They were found later, close to starvation on a mountain that is routinely climbed by schoolchildren. Expeditions are usually led by tough, experienced men who think there is nothing unusual about forcing physical and mental discomfort on others. So it is not surprising that many expeditions tend to be run either by emotionless, sadomasochistic, raving egomaniacs—men who were dressed as girls when they were young or questionable characters with overstated credentials—who are forced by their lack of job skills to make their living in godforsaken places.

If you can combine all these characteristics into one person, then you stand the chance of mounting a successful expedition.Why would someone want to walk to the North Pole, bake in the Sahara or pick ticks out of their private parts, you may well ask? The answer is always unsatisfactory. Most expedition junkies are always testing themselves, proving other people wrong and seeking to top themselves in their next harebrained adventure.

Why do I sound so cynical here? Maybe because I have watched various expedition leaders lose it and seen many of my well-trained friends throw their hands up in disgust. The biggest single enemy of the expedition is bad chemistry, usually caused by the fearless leader's inability to lead men by example rather than brute force.

Shark! Shark!, Tartar Sauce! Tartar Sauce!

About 50 people will be attacked by sharks in a typical year. Shark attacks have been declining since 1995, possibly due to the demand for sharks as food rather than TV stars. Divers are 18 percent of victims. Surfers make up 69 percent. Sharks signal their defensive attack through exaggerated, jerky movements. Look for an arched back, lifting of the head, and figure-8 loops. Tips on avoiding attacks: Sure, stay out of the water.

Source: ISAF www.flmmh.ufl.edu/Fish/research/ISAF/shark.htm

Whenever Discovery Channel wants to goose the ratings they lay on Shark week. Why? Who cares. Well, I guess you do.

My more pleasurable expeditions have always seemed leaderless, where the group reacted in unison, allowing creative interpretation of directions, deadlines and goals. Also, you must truly know your fellow expedition members. Men and women react very strangely under stress. Some revert to childish whining, others become combative, and still others simply lose it both mentally and physically.

The best way to see if you have picked the right partners in an expedition is to have a dry run that includes at least 48 hours without sleep, in adverse conditions. Sleep deprivation, combined with some mental and physical abuse at the 36-hour stage, will show a person's real mettle. Strangely enough, in my experience, white-collar workers, physical fitness nuts, city dwellers, businessmen, triathletes and sportsmen do very poorly in the ill-defined, noncompetitive expedition environment. People with military experience, medical personnel, aboriginals, photographers, blue-collar laborers, and folks with rural backgrounds do very well.

The attributes to look for are experience in hard conditions, physical fitness, a sense of humor, a levelheaded approach to stress, pain and discomfort, and a genuine desire for knowledge and fellowship.

Expedition members should be chosen for specific knowledge, such as medical, language or bush lore; always get references. Members should never be chosen for prestige, ability to provide funding, or university credentials, and absolutely stay away from taking on journalists, relatives of backers and good-looking members of the opposite sex.

How to Launch an Expedition

1. **Pick a region or topic that is newsworthy or beneficial to sponsors.**

2. **Select a specific task that you will accomplish, and one that will make the world a better place or create publicity.**

3. **State specifically how you will generate publicity (book, speeches, press releases, photographs, magazine articles).**

4. **Write a one-page query letter that states your purpose, method of execution and perceived result. Ask for a written show of support (do not ask for money) and other people who should be made aware of your expedition.**

5. **Gather letters of support from high-profile politicians, community members and scientists, and include them in your proposal.**

6. **Write an expedition plan (much like a business plan), and explain the benefits to the backers and sponsors.**

7. **Create a sponsorship program. Tell and show the primary sponsor what they will get, secondary sponsor and so on. As a rule of thumb, ask for twice as much money as you predict you will need, and come up with something to present to a recognized nonprofit charity at the end of your expedition.**

8. **Once you have your expedition goal figured out and a raison d'etre, send a one-page press release and your outline to all news organizations, telling them your intentions and that you need sponsors. It is important to set a date to let sponsors know that you are going with or without their funds.**

9. **Gather lists of potential sponsors, and then phone to get the owner, president or founder's name. Send in your pitch, along with any early PR you generated. If the president or owner likes it, they will delegate it downward. If you send it in blind, most companies will put you in the talk-to-our-PR-company-who-then-promises-to-talk-to-the-client loop.**

10. **Follow up with a request for a meeting (money is never pledged over the phone), and thrill them with your enthusiasm and vision.**

11. **Send a thank-you letter with a specific follow-up and/or commitment date. Promise to follow up with a phone call on a certain date and time.**

Do this thousands of times, and you will have enough money to do any harebrained thing you want.

Just as Columbus had to sweet-talk Isabella after the banks turned him down, you have to be creative and ever hopeful. Remember, everyone interested wishes they could go with you, and their investment is just a way of saying I am part of this adventure.

The best sources for tough expeditions are the Royal Geographical Society in London and the National Geographic Society in Washington, D.C. Local newspapers will carry features on "brave young men and women" who are setting out to do whatever has not been done. In most cases, they will be looking for money (always an automatic entree into an expedition) or someone with multiple skills (doctor, cook, masseuse) to fill out the team. Be careful, since it all comes down to personality fit. Many people have never spent more than a weekend in close proximity to their spouse, let alone a total stranger; shakedown cruises are well advised, and go with your first impression. Things usually only get worse.

Hit and Run

The average speed on junior and intermediate ski slopes is a carlike 25 to 40 miles per hour. So it's no surprise that when skiers hit each other and trees, things go pop. Even so, only 33 people a year die in a typical ski season from skiing-related accidents. But when adventurous yuppies think that they might actually get hurt, stuff happens. The nonprofit group Ski Hit and Run Reward Inc. is offering a $1,000 bounty for the identification of reckless skiers. Men are involved in 90 percent of ski accidents, usually people who are in the "tuck" position traveling at high speeds. Other solutions include mandatory wearing of helmets. In Albertville, France, speeders or reckless skiers can be fined up to 100,000 francs or spend a year in jail.

The up side is that you can be the first person on your block to pogo-stick to the North Pole, balloon across the Sahara or kayak Lake Baikal. Fame and fortune may await. You will need lots of money, time and the enthusiasm of a Baptist preacher. Remember that 99 percent of your time will be spent raising funds and planning. The best single source in the world is the Expedition Advisory Centre of the Royal Geographical Society in London.

Expeditions are usually funded by universities or governments, and there are no real grapevines other than reading scientific journals, staying in touch with universities or talking to expeditioners and outfitters. Most participants will be scientists and will often bring interns (for a fee) to help defray costs. The best way to find out what is happening is to contact a university directly to see if any expeditions are being mounted.

Adventure Magazine

    http://www.adventure-mag.com/home.htm

Expedition Planning

The National Geographic Society

The august and venerable National Geographic Society has become the best and most popular means for the world to understand itself. Back in 1888, it was simply a group of philanthropists who wanted to increase and diffuse geographical knowledge. Since then, they have funded almost 5,000 expeditions and educated and entertained hundreds of millions, and today they are the largest geographic group of any kind on this planet. They manage to maintain a rough edge and an accessible front. Unlike the tiny, musty adventurer's clubs, the National Geographic Society has gone global. You can sit in your own musty den and travel to more countries, experience more expeditions and learn more about our world, thanks to their efforts.

Many adventurers were weaned on their yellow tomes. A generation further back was titillated by sights of unclothed natives and exotic locales. If any magazine could be called adventurous, it would be good old *National Geo.*

National Geographic Society has 9.7 million members in almost 200 countries. Over 44 million people read each issue of the magazine, 40 million watch their documentaries on PBS and 15 million watch "On Assignment" each month. Though not exactly an elite group, being featured in or by a National Geographic publication thrusts you into the mainstream of adventure/entertainment. If you are written up or have an article in the *National Geographic Magazine*, you can work the rubber chicken circuit for the next decade. If you are featured on any of their television specials, like Jacques-Yves Cousteau ("The Voyages of the Calypso") or Bob Ballard ("The Search for the Titanic"), you can contemplate licensing and even starting your own TV series.

Despite being Valhalla for adventurers, the National Geographic does its bit to generate content. In 1992, the Society awarded 240 grants for field research and exploration. The Nat Geo is also on a mission to create higher awareness of geography among students, because they would have little product to sell if people didn't know the difference between Bahrain and the Bahamas. If you are young and a whiz at geography, you can try to join the 6 million people who take part in the National Geographic Bee.

The National Geographic is probably the biggest and best source for just about any information about the world and adventure. They offer a staggering range of books on everything from the Amazon to Zaire. They now offer *World,* a kid's magazine with 3 million readers a month, *Traveler Magazine* with another 3 million and *National Geographic Explorer* (8 million viewers a month), a radio station (a million listeners a day) and home videos with 5.4 million viewers a year. You wouldn't think there was enough adventure, geography and science info out there, but Nat Geo just keeps on churning it out with CD-ROMs, Geoguides, popup action books, news features, on-line services, globes, atlases, a museum and more. How do they do it? For starters, they pull in about half a billion dollars in tax-free income. Just call *(800) 638-4077* for a catalog of what interests you and join today.

National Geographic Research and Exploration Quarterly

1145 17th Street NW
Washington, DC 20036
Tel.: (800) 638-4077
A quarterly journal with a definitely scientific bent. Better laid out and illustrated than other dry journals.

National Geographic Magazine

1145 17th Street NW
Washington, DC 20036
Tel.: (800) 638-4077
The old standard (requires membership) at $21 a year is still a great bargain. The editorial stance is getting tougher, with more articles on pollution, politics and natural threats, in addition to the standard "purdy" pictures. The magazine has launched a small but well-traveled group of photographers who capture the world for a handsome fee.

The Royal Geographical Society

1 Kensington Gore
London, England SW7 2AR
Tel.: [44] (71) 589 5466
The fabled exploration society still requires nomination by an existing member to join. When in London, nonmembers can visit the Map Room in their creaky Victorian headquarters on Hyde Park near Albert Hall. They also have an impressive photo archives and reference book selection.

The Royal Geographical Society Magazine

Stephenson House, 1st Floor
Bletchley, Milton Keynes
MK2 2EW
Tel.: (0908) 371981
A monthly magazine that is a lot drier and a lot less pretty than a *Nat Geo* publication but much tougher and smarter in its editorial focus. Covers expeditions, environment, travel, adventure—all with a scientific bent.

RGS Expedition Advisory Centre

1 Kensington Gore
London, England SW7 2AR
Tel.: [44] (71) 5812057
Contact the Expedition Advisory Centre. Don't be shy about calling or ordering any one of their excellent (but very British) books on expedition planning. They have an incredible selection of how-to books, and you can also get listings of past expeditions, contact other people interested in expeditions and get in touch with experts who have been to your area of interest. They do not sponsor expeditions but have a handbook on how to raise money.

Expedition Organizers

If you would like to do more than wander around a country, try joining an expedition. Americans haven't quite caught on to this method of travel, but Europeans and the Japanese are crazy about it. Accordingly, they offer a lot more variety than some of their Stateside counterparts.

South American Explorers Club

126 Indian Creek Road
Ithaca, New York 14850
Tel.: (607) 277-0488
http://www.solutions.net/rec-travel/south_america/s_am_explorers_club.html
The nonprofit South American Explorers Club is a source of travel information about South and/or Central America. There are Clubhouses in Lima, Peru; Quito, Ecuador; and Ithaca, New York.

Royal Geographical Society of Australasia

c/o State Library of South Australia
North Terrace
Adelaide, South Australia 5000
Postal Address:
GPO Box 419
Adelaide, South Australia 5001
Tel.: (08) 207-7265/207-7266,
Fax: (08) 207-7247
http://www.asap.unimelb.edu.au/asa/directory/data/301.htm

Scientific Expeditions

http://wk122.nas.nasa.gov/NAS/FAST/FASTtreks/index.html
An online, interactive exploration into data. FAST Expeditions allow FAST users to load datasets and scripts into FAST from the World Wide Web. Comes with instructions.

Randall's Adventure & Training

60 Randall Road
Gallant, Alabama 35972
Tel.: (256) 570-0175
Fax: (256) 538-6418
http://www.btb.com/kjslavin/
Jeff runs tours and training into the Amazon basin from mild to wild. Personalized courses for groups, hardcore training for adventure racing teams and, of course, eco-tours.

Running with the Bulls

Have you ever dreamed of being one of the corredores in the annual encierro of Pamplona? Probably not, but many of us have dreamed of running with the bulls ever since we read Hemingway's account of it in The Sun Also Rises. *Little did he know that he would elevate the running of the bulls in the medieval city of Pamplona to the level of the Holy Grail for adventurers. Twelve people have been killed in the run. No one bothers to keep track of the trampled, tripped and torn. The consumption of alcohol is considered to be mandatory, and the cost and scarcity of hotel rooms means that sleeping is completely on a "when available/as needed basis."*

The running of the bulls is part of the Festival of San Fermin, July 6–14, every year in the Spanish province of Navarre. As if it matters anymore, Saint Fermin was martyred in the third century.

The bulls are let loose from a corral about 800 meters away from the bull ring, and they run through the barricaded streets on their way to it.

A rocket is fired off to start the run on Calle Santo Domingo at 7 A.M. on the seventh day of the seventh month. Don't eat breakfast first, since it is customary to celebrate afterward with hot chocolate and deep-fried churros, essentially a long Spanish donut. Get there early. The students from the local university tend to be the most enthusiastic members of the crowd. Foreigners are usually too damn serious. The course is a lot shorter and tighter than most people expect it to be. Novices (or Los Valientes, the Brave Ones) get about a five-minute head start on the bulls but are quickly overtaken. The most dangerous part of the course is the tight turn onto Estafeta Street. Here, bulls and corredores discover that two objects can't occupy the same place at the same time. The lack of space is aggravated by lines of policemen who prevent the more timid from bolting over the barricades. The bulls are prodded on by the less valiant (those running behind or spectating) who smack them with rolled-up newspapers. Once bulls and runners stream into the bull ring, free-form amateur bullfighting breaks out. Once you get bored, head into the old quarter for breakfast or to the cafes to continue your celebrating. If you end up feeling like a Union 76 ball on a car antenna, the Red Cross is nearby to attend to any minor injuries.

If for some strange reason you do not spend the evening drinking and carousing, the best accommodations are to be found in the nearby town of Olite, about 40 kilometers away.

In July of 1995 an American from Chicago was gored in the chest and thrown 23 feet in the air, becoming the first fatality in over 20 years.

Sounds like a great concept for a Reebok commercial.

Adventure Racing

Pity the adventure racer. Once the domain of quirky, superfit international party animals who never even knew what jogging was, the sport is filled with hatchet-faced triathletes wearing the latest in injection-molded gear. It just seems the teamwork and fun has been trained out of it.

First it was the Hash House Harriers who ran up mountains as an excuse to booze it up, then it was the crazy Kiwis and their Southern Traverse, then it was the wild and woolly Camel Trophy and then the competitive Raid Gauloise, followed by the PC sounding Eco-Challenge—now adventure racing has submutated into dozens of weekend events around the world. Events like the Warn Challenge, Trans Borneo, Trans Pen have come and gone. I will be the first to admit that I have been in a few of these, but ultimately they are not the most rewarding way to learn about yourself and your limits. Like a poorly paid actor in a gala adventure show, you feel insulated from the locals and end up stuffing more than a little money in to the resorts', airlines' and organizers' pockets. Stung by eco-critics, most now include an ecological project or benefit to their host country.

On the good side, many of these events allow you trample through the jungle, raft rivers and ride bikes in places you couldn't normally get to or have the time to organize. If you really want to see what you are made of, keep in mind that you are the spandex version of a celebrity lab rat, where each course has been designed to cause just enough grief to make it look good for TV. Probably the most daunting part of these races is wading through the hyperbole.

Jungles are "green infernos" or "impenetrable," deserts and mountains are "forbidding," rivers are "raging" or thundering, tropical paradises become "harsh environments" and even insects become deadly. Also, the competition is not just in the wilderness; the popularity of these races has created a race to grab the top teams and favorite spots.

A word of advice: Make sure you contact a few participants to get the latest before you plunk down your money.

Burn

In-depth coverage of adventure racing with info on upcoming races, equipment tips and classifieds.

http://www.burnmagazine.com

Plateau Adventure Racing Journal

http://www.plateaumagazine.com/

AdventureTime

Good links to everything from Underwater Hockey to Streetluge

http://www.adventuretime.com/links/index.html

Adventure Races

The Southern Traverse

http://www.southerntraverse.com/
The Southern Traverse began in 1989 and was based on the first Raid Gauloises or Grand Traverse, held in the Southern Alps on the South Island.

Marathon des Sables

Begun in 1986 with about 500 competitors from around 30 countries, running across 200 miles of North Africa sand in April. You carry all your gear, get hot, eat sand and then go home. There is also a newsletter online.

Gadams Group, Ltd.
P.O. Box 29903
Richmond, VA 23242
Tel: 202.478.0218
Fax: 202.478.0218
E-mail: info@sandmarathon.com
http://www.sandmarathon.com

The Eco Challenge

Big TV deal, lots of sponsors and well-heeled yuppies meets copy of Raid Gauloise. The Beverly Hills–based organizers have grabbed the market for adventure racing. By now the idea of watching hours of young urban professionals complaining about blisters should be old hat, but people love it. A fee of $12,500 gets 4 into the 8-to-12-day race. (Don't forget airfare, gear and supplies.) You can also take one of their training courses, sponsor a team or take an oxymoronic package/adventure tour. Contact:

9899 Santa Monica Blvd., Suite #208
Beverly Hills, CA 90212
Tel.: 310-399-3080 ext. 4000
Fax: 310-399-3584
E-mail: ecochallenge@earthlink.net
http://www.ecochallenge.com/

Camel Trophy

The Camel Trophy is going through an identity crisis. The original big endurance event that allowed normal people to compete in the "toughest test of man and machine" began in 1980. You won't read about the accidents, mutinies, fights and helicopter crashes, but it sold cigarettes like crazy (except in the United States for some reason, where Joe Camel ruled). First it was a bunch of crazy Germans re-creating a macho cigarette ad in the Amazon. Then it became a cigarette commercial with Land Rovers, then it became a clothing ad named after a cigarette with family station wagons. Now it's a bizarre combination of music, 40 people for three weeks in rubber rafts, bouncing between tropical islands. Is it still a cigarette ad? Well, for some reason the organizers still think the Canary Islands is a country and the only countries that can enter come from big R. J. Reynolds' markets. You won't see Canada or Mexico among the countries, but somehow Luxembourg and Belgium are in. Go figure.

You need to apply at the Worldwide Brands HQ in the country you reside it.

Camel Trophy Applications
Worldwide Brands Inc.
P.O. Box 124
Staines, Middlesex TW18 4LL
http://www.cameltrophy.com/

Raid Gauloise

Gerard Fusil started the Raid in 1988 because he thought the Camel Trophy was too easy. He introduced the idea of multiple sports instead of the sleep deprivation and brutal pushing of the Camel event. What was lost was the international teamwork and what was gained was a greater sense of athletics (and of course income from paying teams).

After the originator of the event left to start a new race, things got a little loose for the last race. A blizzard of negative articles about organizational snafus may have put the venerated Raid in jeopardy.

46 bis, rue de la Republique
92170 Vanves
Tel: 33 (0) 141 081470
Fax: 33 (0) 141 081488
E-mail: info@raid-gauloises.com

United States

470 S. Wetherly Drive

Beverly Hills, CA 90211
Tel.: (1) 310 271 83 35
Fax: (1) 310 270 83 65
E-mail: nfusilraid@earthlink.net
http://www.raid-gauloises.com/

Elf Adventure

There is just something magical about oil and cigarette companies sponsoring adventure racing. What's next, the Strip Mining and Waste Management Adventure? In any case, if you wondered where Gerard Fusil ended up its here. Fourteen, seven-member coed teams do a 350-mile mazed sports race in an exotic country where "machetes are mandatory equipment" (stop me if you've heard this before). Competitors must brave the elements, not be eaten by wild animals, stung by insects, etc., etc. A memorable line from a press release: "More than one racer has described snake sightings, and the caves house bats." Egads.

You can contact race organizers at:

Gerard Fusil Company
1, villa Marie Justine
92100 Boulogne – Paris – France
Tel.: 33.1.41.31.74.74
Fax: 33.1.41.31.05.91

Or for some odd reason contact the oil company at:

ELF AQUITAINE
Tour ELF
2, place de la Coupole
92078 Paris La defense – France
Tel.: 33.1.47.44.38.29
Fax: 33.1.47.44.24.30

Stateside it's

CSM
Bell Canyon, CA
Tel.: (818) 883-7891
E-mail: CSMlh@aol.com
http://www.elf-aventure.com/

Beast of the East

Their Web page is a good link to a number of regional events, including the SEAL adventure Challenge (yes, people pay $125 to go through a recreation of hell week), the beast of Alaska and others.

http://www.beastoftheeast.com

The Salomon X-Adventure

The "Cross" adventure is a series of events in Europe and Japan culminating in a fall event somewhere in the world. It's the usual man against nature gig: Six sports over a 30-hour period. Salomon also owns Taylor Made. So how come no Extreme Golf guys?

http://www.salomonsports.com/

Hi-Tec Adventure Racing Series

The boot manufacturer sponsors a number of mini endurance races around the country. A good way to get into the sport.

http://www.mesp.com/ars.htm

Canuck Adventure Racing World

In a country where just trying to get to work can be an endurance race, there are people who want more. The best single site to bookmark if you are into adventure racing. Excellent links page, with 30 different adventure races along with links for adventure teams and gear.

http://tor-pw1.netcom.ca/~ceaston/index.html

United States Adventure Racing Association

http://www.usara.com/home.htm

DP's ratings.

There is no single reliable source of safety, deaths, casualties, or misfortunes. So don't look for one here. Our ratings are entirely personal and completely changeable depending on when, where and why you are there. In really dangerous lands there aren't a whole lot of bureaucrats with clipboards keeping count. The U.S has a very comprehensive system of travel warnings but conveniently overlooks the dangers within its own borders. India will be generous in counting Pakistan casualties in Kashmir but be stiff lipped about its own dead. Even tourists killed in army rescues are considered casualties by terrorist actions.

So we essentially threw all the official statistics in the dumpster and used our own research. How do we rank these places? First of all we travel without a protective shield, we have the ability to compare disparate places within narrow time periods and we grind through massive piles of documents to determine just what is going on around the world. So with this caveat in mind, here is how you can interpret our ratings:

★★★★★   **Apocalypse Now**

A place where the longer you stay, the shorter your existence on this planet will be. These places combine warfare, banditry, disease, landmines and violence in a terminal adventure ride.

★★★★   **Very Nasty Places**

Danger here may be more regional, slightly more definable and maybe even avoidable. But you won't see insurance salesmen holding any conventions soon.

★★★   **Dodgey Places**

Three stars designates places with very specific problems, usually avoidable. Danger may also be sporadic, seasonal or local. They may even have some freshly looted televisions to watch the local news on.

★★   **Heads-Up Places**

Danger lurks in these places, but usually the violence is very contained or is easily identifiable.

★   **Bad-Rep Lands**

Places that are not really dangerous but have a bad rap for isolated incidences. But if you try hard enough, you could get waylaid or interred.

The Hands ✋

DP gets a perverse thrill from listing ridiculously safe places that get a bad rep. Usually thanks to the U.S. State Department. And we need to have a little comic relief sometimes. So you'll countries run by guys with green polyester uniforms and regions where *Baywatch* is still an artillery position.

So, five hands would mean you would be one of the few outsiders ever to enter this crumbling bastion of Cold War paranoia. A place where the fearless leader has the highest rating TV show (well actually the only TV show), bestselling book (usually in green or red), bestselling record (not actually him singing but people singing about him), coolest poster (love those Ray Bans) and the biggest house on the biggest hill.

One star means that despite the fear and loathing it really is a fun place.

DANGEROUS PLACES

Dangerous Places (Short and Sweet)

The Grim Reaper's Cheat Sheet

We have been noticing that a lot of people never actually read *DP*. We don't blame them. Not many people can take both barrels of all the world's woes. So they dive in and out of it like a box of mental munchies looking for those neat little knowledge nuggets hidden inside. Some read it on the subway, trolling for intellectual members of the opposite sex. Others keep *DP* carefully tossed on their coffee, table artfully dog-eared and stained from their last trip to Cambodia. Some rebels insert it on their office bookshelf to remind their boss that going postal is only an argument away. In candid recognition of this, we have created a very short, highly opinionated, condensed version of the book that will keep you swimming with free lattes and sagacious companionship. If you are in the mortuary or arms business it might also be a good lead generator. So just what the hell is going on in this crazy, mixed up world?

Afghanistan	Northern Tajik fundamentalists stare at backcountry Pahktun fundamentalists from decades-old front lines. The only country where religious students know how to drive tanks. And getting stoned means exactly that.
Algeria	Muslim fundamentalists are mad because they were cheated out of a 1992 election victory. Ginzued bodies and heads on sticks make this the Jihadsicle capital of the world.
Angola	A civil war between pouting egos (Diamonds vs. Oil). Here, warfare and diamonds are forever.
Bosnia-Herzegovina	"Hunted" war criminals who have popular TV shows. Ethnic cleansing with no messy residue.
Bougainville	Fuzzy-haired rebels with rusty shotguns fighting for a flyspeck-size island. Mercenaries spanked and turfed. Where's Gilligan and the Professor to sort this all out?
Burundi	Rwanda, the sequel. Same story, different location. Nobody cares.
Cambodia	Hidden land mines, Khmer Rouge stragglers, plagues of Vietnamese whores, raped temples, a lonely dictator and a sad king in exile. But hey, who cares? Strap on your backpack cause its cheap, cheap, cheap.

Chechnya	Russia says, "How about 2 out of 3?" The chechens oblige. Kidnapping replaces homestays as the biggest tourist concept.
China	Made in China now includes our high-tech war toys. Remember when we used to worry if they all jumped at the same time?
Colombia	The nastiest place in the Western Hemisphere: drugs, kidnapping, murder and terrorism. Truly a hot spot for adventure ecotourism.
Congo, Kinshassa	Nasty, large, central African hellhole run by whomever has the most ammunition (not to be confused with the other Congo).
Congo, Brazzaville	Nasty, small, central African hellhole run by whomever has the most ammunition (not to be confused with the other Congo, above).
Corsica	Swarthy men who want to have their own country of swarthy men. Tourists are guaranteed to have a blast.
Cyprus	Turks versus Greeks separated by a very faded blue line. The UN mission that keeps on going and going and going . . .
Djibouti	The hottest, lowest place in Africa doesn't seem like it would be worth fighting over, but the Afars and the French Foreign Legion do.
Egypt	The wellspring of old time fundamentalism. For now, rebels like to hide in the weeds along the Nile and take potshots at tourists. Could this be a new theme park ride?
Haiti	Decades of brutal dictatorship, crime and corruption in this hemisphere's poorest country briefly interrupted by some good old-fashioned gunboat diplomacy.
India	Seven revolts, hundreds of languages, countless religions and manufacturing more people daily than China in half the space.
Indonesia	A military dictatorship with great surf. Real bad losers when pieces of former country fall off. Some folks in Aceh. Kalimantan and Irian Jaya mean great deals on travel coming up.
Iran	The Ditech funding of terrorism. Gotta a jihad? Need a loan? Call 1-800-AYA-TOLLA
Iraq	A one-man demolition derby that could teach our leaders about longevity.
Israel	Five billion dollars a year is all it takes to have your place in the Middle East sun.
Kenya	Safari heaven has become hell. Embassy bombings, shifts, Islamic riots, plenty of crime, AIDS and great deals on those great leopard print muumuus.
Laos	Chao Fah rebels and more unexploded ordnance than a canceled Fourth of July celebration.
Lebanon	Hey, was that a rocket attack or is it a national holiday? Nice tourist place that is the home of Hezbollah, the UN and a nasty little spat down south.
Liberia	A West African cesspool run by an escaped federal felon with a warrant for his arrest.
Malaysia	Clean, modern place surrounded by vicious seaborne pirates.
Mexico	The only place that has rebel tours. Nice beaches, nasty criminals.

Morocco	The Polisario still conduct sand wars.
Mozambique	More land mines than people. All sold out of "watch your step" signs.
Myanmar	More generals than a GMC truck dealer. Everybody's happy, except of course most of the people who live here.
Namibia	Nice place for a safari except for the nasty Caprivi Strip (hint, it's not a men's club).
Northern Ireland	Keep your fingers crossed, and kiss your four-leaf clover. Let's hope shopping in London doesn't get exciting again.
Pakistan	Military-run country with fierce mountain tribes in the northwest. Fierce desert tribes in the south. Fierce Muslim tribes in the northeast. You get the picture.
Papua New Guinea	Remote jungle paradise terrorized by "Rascals," kidnappers and thugs. Is Bougainville a separate country? Depends on who you ask.
Philippines	In the south, Muslims vs. Christians. In the north Commies vs. land-owners. Rebels that still love Kenny Rogers and Air Supply. Kinda says it all.
Peru	The government has faded, Tupac has faded and Shining Path is not so shiny. So just who does move all those drugs now?
Russia	Discos, limousines, drugs, cigarettes, cheap booze, gangsters, gunfights . . . so where's Coppola and Scorsese?
Rwanda	No one left to kill anybody. They'll need about ten years to build up enough people to start panga-whacking again.
Sardinia	Swarthy gangsters import drugs, kill people, make money. See Chechnya and Corsica and Russia and . . .
Senegal	*Casamance* is still hiding in the swamps.
Sierra Leone	A prez named Johnny hooks up with a rebel leader named Foday. Is this half of a new doo-wop group?
Somalia	The land of Mad Max, or "My Toyota can whip your Toyota." The only country run by an AWOL marine from Orange County, California.
South Africa	Mandela promised them jobs, homes and cars. And now they're using AKs to get them.
South Korea	The world's most militarized "Demilitarized Zone."
Sri Lanka	Suicide frogmen, self-annihilation for chicks and cyanide pendants are popular here.
Sudan	If only the Dinkas and Nuers would decide the decades-old war by challenging the Arab north to a pickup basketball game.
Suriname	Rebels in the jungle, crime, drugs, corruption. Business as usual in the south Caribbean.
South Africa	Fear central. You don't need to go to the game parks to see how animals prey on their own kind.
Tajikistan	A poor, wartorn ex-Soviet republic jammed between Afghanistan and Kyrgyzstan known for smuggling, kidnapping, corruption and crime. And those are the good points.

Turkey	The PKK said everyone will become a human bomb. Some of them said OK, you go first. So if the PKK is all over, why does the army keep invading Syria?
Uganda	Rebels, gorillas, guerrillas, terrorists, whackos and, according to Condé Nast, a great place to visit.
United States	Land of Jerry Springer, Bill Clinton and Fox reality shows. And we tell other people how to run their country? Over 70 people killed a day and over 220 million guns ready to party. Do you feel lucky, punk?
Western Sahara/ Morocco	This sand ain't your sand, this sand is my sand. No, this isn't Coney Island on a long weekend.
Yemen	The ultimate homestay vacation. (See Chechnya)

Kabul

Afghanistan
★★★★

Talibision Comes to Kabul

Somehow the stalwart brave mujahedin of Afghanistan have gone from lusty freedom fighters to Amish with AK's. The same fundamental drive that pushed the Russians out of this impoverished land has created the Taliban.

We didn't really care when we dumped billions worth of cheap Russian and Chinese armament on Hekmatyar in the '80s. Even if he did call us evil and corrupt. We didn't mind when he closed the cinemas and made the burqa mandatory. Even when the Talibs called Hekmatyar a Western puppet and used those same arms to take over 90 percent of the country. We forgot about the rapings, murders and mayhem the out-of-control muj factions brought on their own people. Suddenly peace broke out and a different breed of journos entered. The International Committee of the Red Cross (ICRC) flew 120 journalists into the Kabul to see if the Talibs would begin executing everyone in sight. Nothing happened.

Then, with the unparalleled safety of a oddly peaceful Kabul, more timid journalists entered to do human interest stories. For some reason the Talibs

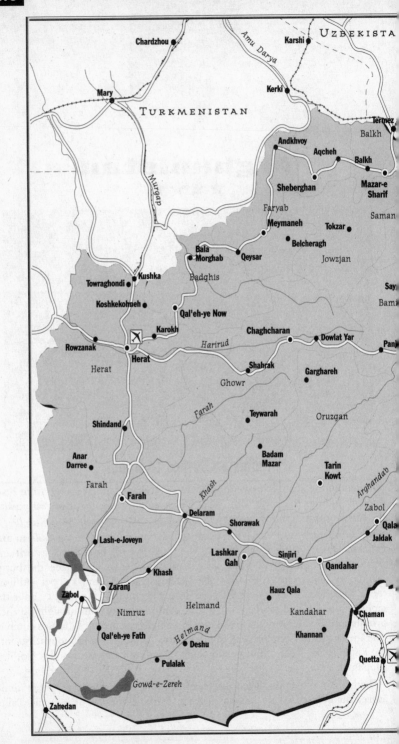

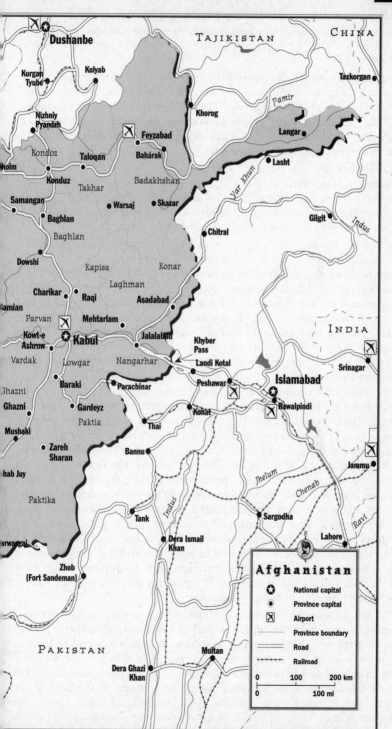

Afghanistan

- ✪ National capital
- ● Province capital
- ☒ Airport
- ⋯⋯ Province boundary
- —— Road
- ┼┼┼ Railroad

| 0 | 100 | 200 km |

| 0 | 100 mi |

would allow NGO-sponsored journos but not let independent journalists in. Every journalist had to have an angle. Prohibitions about talking to women and a crackdown on what the Talibs considered lax morality piqued the interest of scribes.

The highlight of this access to Kabul was the UN's Emma's and CNN's Christiane's little bitch-slap tussle with the Talibs for filming "nekkid wimmin" and entering a sterile operating room. The UN had declared war on a country at war. The "gender junkets" began. Emma and her private UN planes began disgorging notebook-wielding females intent on documenting the lack of women's rights while rockets rained down.

The *Taliban* (literally "religious students" or "seekers of truth") who once appeared as God-fearin', upstandin', rag-headed Gary Coopers suddenly appeared as cross-eyed, brutal, morose and wacky Ike Clanton boys. These are the same Afghans who kicked out the Russians, who were armed by us (via the Pakistan ISI) and still wonder why the United States doesn't like them.

Gone were the network war hogs who hiked in from Peshawar and wrote stirring tales of muj bravery. Now sleek white UN turboprops off-loaded female journalists in waiting chauffeur-driven black Mercedes. Over lunch and dinner at the UN mansion (with exercise room, satellite television and bar) they chronicled the horrors of the lack of health care, the treatment of women and generally how life sucked and apparently just for women. There was even a standard journo junket. The first stop was to see Mullah Qalaamuddin, the deputy head of the Religious Police (the Department for the Promotion of Virtue and the Prevention of Vice), where every writer was assured to get a few giggles from the latest *fatwah:* no paper bags, no white socks, four fingers of beard and no picture-taking. Then off to a barber for a little humor, a clandestine visit to a girl's school, pack a lunch for the Friday executions and then back to Peshawar to file. The object of their journalist lust? The dreaded *burqa,* a garment worn by every women outside of cosmopolitan Kabul for centuries but suddenly held up as being a sign of the devil in Kabul. Not many paid attention when Hekmatyar made it mandatory long before the Talibs showed up. The writers never really mentioned that they were in the most destroyed city on earth, a militarily occupied zone with a war raging 15 kilometers to the north, rockets raining into the city and young men are pressganged. Somehow in their zeal to create women's rights in a country staggering to its knees, they forget to mention the complete lack of jobs, housing, medical care, health services and education for men (who must provide for their women and children) let alone women. The articles inflamed the world and shut down any aid to the wartorn region. How did the Taliban get lynched on women's rights? It's akin to taking the KKK to task for not providing minority scholarships.

The *Taliban* started as collection of 40-something-year-old mullahs and eager religious students from Kandahar. The Taliban is neither a political party, army or puppet-of-the-month splinter group. It is the most orthodox (and some Muslims say, most over-the-edge) Islamic movement ever to learn how to run a country from scratch. Devoid of press agents or even graphic designers, they have raised their white flag across Afghanistan, leaving tiny pockets of resistance in the Hazari and occupied cities and the forbidding mountainous north. The Northern Alliance's "minister of defense," Ahmed Shah Massoud, still holds the forbidding Panjshir Valley (his old stomping ground against the Russkies) and it looks like he will be experiencing déjà vu as he battles a much larger army from his mountain strongholds. Massoud has been fighting wars in Afghanistan since the '70s, so he is a good long shot if his Iranian and French supporters will add a few zeroes to their checks.

Despite the Northern Alliance's lack of alliance, money or territory, they are still the recognized government of Afghanistan—something that will probably change when the Talibs welcome Hooter's franchises, Marilyn Manson concerts and martini bars. The Taliban don't have a lot of friends. Only three countries recognize their control (Saudi Arabia, Pakistan and the UAE) and everyone else just mumbles and keeps walking. Unocal desperately wants to build a pipeline from Turkmenistan to the south but the State Department has been dangling it as bait for women's rights and Osama bin Laden's head. For now the Taliban have brought peace and stability to the areas they have conquered—something that has never happened in the last twenty years. They also bring a draconian form of sharia or islamic law that fills the stadium (rebuilt with UN money) in Kabul every Friday at 3:30 P.M. to cheer as thieves are amputated, killers are shot and bad people are flogged. Hey there's nothing on the television or at the theaters, anyway.

Modern Afghan misery began in 1978, when Noor Taraki attempted to import communism into Afghanistan with the aid of the Soviet Union. His successor, Babrak Karmal, asked Moscow for troops, thus signaling the beginning of the conflict. Marxism was met with mortars, machine guns and the primitive flintlock rifles of the mujahedin, or holy warriors.

Eighty-five-thousand Soviet soldiers invaded Afghanistan. Their pretext was that the puppet ruler, Karmal, needed help. The official demand for this intervention was sent from Kabul and signed by Karmal, who could not have been in the Afghan capital at the time because he was riding into Kabul with a Soviet army convoy. Meanwhile, Gulbuddin Hekmatyar spent the Russian war safely in Peshawar, squirreling away the massive arms shipments, while Massoud was fighting in the mountains of the Panjshir.

The conservative Muslim mujahedin put up an unexpected and bitter resistance to the new government. Soviet troops, armed to the teeth with Moscow's most modern materials of doom, were picked apart on the ground by elusive rebel mujahedin guerrillas, employing antiquated weapons that had been state of the art when Janes first started publishing their guide to all the world's blunderbusses. Later, the rebels, backed by the CIA and supplied through Pakistan, began picking Soviet gunships out of the sky with a couple of thousand U.S.-supplied Stingers and other surface-to-air rockets. The Stingers soon shut down the Russian gunships and supply aircraft. Convoys were easily ambushed. Russia had its very own Vietnam, but without the cool antiwar songs and concerts back home. More importantly, the seed of the Taliban was planted by the United States.

Say what? you exclaim. The Taliban, an American idea? When Afghanistan was invaded by the Soviets in 1979, President Jimmy Carter provided the mujahedin with US$30 million in covert aid. This manifested itself in the form of the Pakistani secret service, or ISI, supplying selected rebel commanders with old Soviet arms procured from Egypt. The Pakistanis carefully chose southern commanders who were Pushtun and had ethnic ties with Pakistanis across the border. Many of these commanders, like Gulbuddin Hekmatyar, were virulently anti-American and hard-line Islamics. They knew that the Russians would be gone and then there was going to be a power grab. He and others kept brand-new weapons in their original containers in large storage yards waiting for the day. The Russians would leave.

As covert military aid to the mujahedin increased under the Reagan administration, so did the carnage and the number of refugees. By 1985, the Afghan rebels were receiving US$250 million a year in covert assistance to battle the by now 115,000 Soviet troops. This figure was double 1984's amount. The annual amount received by the guerrillas reached a whopping US$700 million by 1988. There were even shipping Tennessee mules to Afghanistan to carry all the weapons in the hills. Even today Afghanistan is littered with the abandoned one-way shipping containers used to bring all that weaponry into the country. In all, the Soviets lost with 14,453 dead (the real number is closer to 35,000). Probably the most expensive funerals the United States ever created. Even after the Soviets withdrew from Afghanistan, the spook bucks kept flowing. In 1991, anywhere from US$180 million to US$300 million was funneled into Afghanistan by the CIA via the ISI. In all, the CIA spent about US$3.3 billion in rebel aid over the course of the war. Traditionally each region elected a leader based on his social contacts and ability to defend their region. Now the system was out of kilter. Small-time commanders now controlled massive arsenals and large numbers of paid "volunteers." These commanders began to consolidate trade, smuggling and businesses under their control. Traditional law enforcement or tribal control was in disarray. By 1988 there was no law in afghanistan except the gun.

An initial agreement to end outside aid was signed in April 1988, by Afghanistan, the USSR, the United States and Pakistan. The accords were signed on the condition that the USSR pull out its troops by the end of the year. The Soviets' withdrawal occurred in February 1989. Another agreement, signed between the Soviet Union and the United States in September 1991, also sought to arrange the end of meddling into Afghanistan's affairs by the two superpowers. By the middle of April 1992, mujahedin guerrillas and other Islamic rebels moved in on Kabul and ousted President Najibullah. A 50-member ruling council comprised of guerrilla, religious and intellectual leaders was quickly established to create an Islamic republic. It fell apart in violent warfare and factional squabbling. After all, this was Afghanistan, a place where even minor personal disagreements can lead to gunfire and blood feuds. Politics and unlimited access to weapons just added gasoline to the fire.

The fighting had created large numbers of refugees in Quetta and Peshawar. In mountainous Kabul it was traditional for students to be educated in warmer Peshawar and then return to work in the summer. These Afghans were educated in madrassahs, or religious schools. Now with millions of refugees stuck in Pakistan where they were treated roughly, the religious teachers, or mullahs, urged the young men, or Talibs, to return to Afghanistan to drive out the corrupt Western leaders.

This patchwork of Westernized and armed warlords with no wars to fight had become despots, thieves and drug lords. They became greedy and violent, mocking the initial purpose of jihad.

The Talibs began during a small border incident in Spin Boldak under the leadership of Mullah Omar and Mullah Rabbani. They came from the poor south, all had fought the Russians and most had been severely victimized. They had known no traditional schooling, media or education and many had fought against the Russians to make a new Afghanistan. The Taliban was a small group from the Maiwand district of southern Afghanistan, led by a group of 30 former religious students who had studied together in the provincial madrassahs from Kandahar and Helmand provinces. Their leader was one-eyed, 35-year-old Mullah Muhammad Omar. The uprising began when they attacked the highway checkpoints manned by their followers—extortion, robbery and rape were daily occurrences. These atrocities not only angered the common people but they cut into the business of influential traders based in Quetta, Pakistan, and in Kandahar. These traders financed the initial campaigns of the Taliban to clear Kandahar of the warlords.

Starting small with donations from Pakistani and Saudi businessmen they swept like a dust devil from the south all the way to the foothills of the Panjshirs. They used bribes, tanks, suicide charges and discussion to win over region after region. Businessman and former mujahedin Usama bin Laden donated around 2,000 Toyota Hiluxes and worked with the Taliban to create a new form of blitzkrieg. The flat arid south was perfect for rapid movement of self-contained lashkars of Talibs. He counseled Mullah Omar on tactics, government and even policy. Afghanistan was destined to become an emirate and an Islamic state with shari'ah as its law.

In the summer of 1998 they finally pushed Uzbek warlord Dostum all the back to Ankara (for the second time), scared Hekmatyar back to Tehran and had walled up Massoud in the Panjshir mountains. Many will say that their rapid drive to Kabul was funded and planned by the Pakistani ISI. It is plainly obvious that once they entered Kabul they had overextended their support base and are now fraying at the edges as Massoud plays a seesaw war across the Shomali plains just north of Kabul.

The Taliban's power base still remains in the Durrani and Pushtun provinces of southern Afghanistan and Pakistan. The Taliban has effectively created a Pushtun power base that represents a group of 15 to 17 million people, of which 10 million live in Afghanistan and the rest in Pakistan. The urban and northern Hazaris (who are Shiite) and the northern Tajiks do not see eye to eye with the Taliban. The Uzbeks are frantic and have locked down their borders and invited in the Russians. Tajikistan has began supporting Massoud covertly by allowing him to move supplies and people across their border. Iran has mobilized troops but will not spark a war like the eight-year war they had with Iraq. Turkmenistan is playing it cool. It is still (along with Iran) a porous border for drugs, people and contraband.

Worse, the northern Central Asian states know that they are the only barrier between the Taliban and a quick march to Moscow. "The Russians must pay," as one Taliban said to me. As I made fun of one Talib's "military issue" plastic sandals, I was told, "Inshallah, with these sandals we shall march to Moscow."

The Taliban is in control of the majority of the third-poorest country in the world, which is something like winning third prize at Rotarian bingo. It might cost more to get rid of it. Even though these religious students have the Koran down pat, they need to cram Politics for Beginners and Economics 101 if they want to get a degree in Political Correctness. Their down home Pakhtun brand of Islam is a little rough for the more sophisticated northern Tajiks, big-city dwellers, Uzbeks and the rest of the world. Their frontier justice has brought relief from two decades of warfare and oppression, but things are changing for the black-turbaned Talibs. The battle still rages back and forth in the north as Massoud defends his home turf from what he considers to be yet another foreign backed enemy.

The Taliban

The black-turbaned Taliban are a PR agent's worst nightmare. A visual mix of Darth Vader gansta rappers and rejects from a Bible play, they come to press conferences with Noriega-style Ray Bans, scruffy beards, long black robes, armed bodyguards and an attitude that makes Louis Farrakhan seem like Mr. Rogers. The Taliban are not bad guys, they're just a little rough around the edges and they don't get out much. Maybe a guest shot on Oprah with a sensitivity coach would help them "address their issues." Their leaders are primarily 40-something muj selected from the Durrani tribes from the backwater southern provinces of Helmand and Uruzgan. They are a simple, pure people led by very religious but culturally isolated mullahs who want outsiders out of Afghanistan and to establish a pure Islamic state. They are simply mad as hell at foreign intervention and ain't gonna take it any more. The funny thing is their northern enemy says they are just the latest Pakistani-backed stooges in this too-long-running war movie/soap opera.

Why are they mad as hell and not going to take it anymore? Well, when they started their leader was one-eyed, 35-year-old ex muj commander Mullah Muhammad Omar. Trucks driving towards Kabul from southern Pakistan were forced to pay a toll of 2 million afghanis (about US$250–300) to cross the checkpoint. Charging tolls is generally accepted in Afghanistan, but other, more repulsive things happen that could not be ignored. The gunmen would force young boys who have the misfortune to pass through the checkpoints to undergo a mock public marriage and then sodomize them repeatedly. A sort of *Deliverance* meets *Rambo, Part 2*.

Outraged by the treatment the warlord dealt to his own people, the local Taliban or students of the madrassah, took action. They strung up the miscreants from the barrels of their tanks. These atrocities had not only angered the common people but they cut into the business of influential traders based in Quetta, Pakistan, and in Kandahar. These traders with links to the Pakistani government financed the initial campaigns of the Taliban to clear Kandahar of the warlords. Thus began the direct involvement of Pakistan, which saw that tight business, religious and ethnicity connections could force out or marginalize Tajik, Hazari and Uzbek elements in Afghanistan. That's the story of the Talibs as told to *DP* by the Talibs. Other sources say that the Talib, led by Mullah Omar and 11 students from Kandahar, got rid of some thieves in the town of Sing Hissar and then overthrew the governor for not doing his job. There is also the one about the dream and yadda yadda. Either way, don't wait for the movie version.

The Talibs also drew support from the madrassahs in the refugee camps of Baluchistan and Peshawar, where thousands of young Afghan refugees were studying. The Pakistani madrassahs in the south were supported by businessmen and religious leaders who had connections with the Pakistani religious party Jamiat-i-Ulema Islami, led by a member of Bhutto's government, Fazlur Rahman. The Talib's brand of Islam is the strict, old-fashioned Sunni Deoband school—so strict that the leaders forbade their pictures from being taken. It has been traditional that Afghans be encouraged to seek out knowledge; *Talib* means "seeker" in Arabic. The madrassahs started operating in the northwest frontier regions of British India around the early part of the 20th century. Up until 1947 partition of India and Pakistan, Afghan religious students dreamed of learning in the Islamic centers in Deoband and Delhi. When it became difficult to travel from Afghanistan through Pakistan to India some scholars of the Deobandi school opened madrassahs in Lahore, Karachi and Akora Khattak in NWFP. With the establishment of these madrassahs, there was a steady flow of Afghans studying in Pakistan.

There is also a current movement to restore the ancient learning centers of Bukhara in what is now Uzbekistan. But this religious goal has been overshadowed by the Taliban's new military and political image.

The transition of the term *Taliban* from that of students to military was when the Taliban captured the Afghan–Pakistani border town of Spin Boldak in October 1994. It didn't take long, about two to three hours. In two days the entire city of Kandahar fell to the Taliban after weak resistance. In November and December, the provinces of Uruzgan to the north and Zabol were taken by troops riding in the back of pickup trucks waving the Koran. The Talibs had revolutionized warfare by using pickup trucks bought by Osama bin Laden. They formed a Rat Patrol strategy, loading men, ammunition and supplies on the Toyota Hiluxes. Within hours they could surround towns or military positions, or change their own positions, a radical departure from the sandals and RPG war fought against the Russians in the mountains.

In January, the Taliban took over Afghanistan's major poppy growing center, Helmand, without a single shot fired. In late January and February, Ghazni and Maidanshahr came under Taliban control, erasing Hekmatyar's supply line to his position at his base of Charasyab south of Kabul and in Logar province. On February 14, Hekmatyar fled Charasyab. All this was accomplished with an army of less than 3,000 ill-equipped, ill-trained but eager Talibs.

Estimates put the Taliban army at 20,000–30,000 men (about half volunteers and half conscripts) and their holdings at about 80–90 percent of the country—the largest unified area since the Soviets occupied Afghanistan. The Northern Alliance is evenly matched with 40,000 men and less heavy weapons. Oddly, the north will tell you that Pakistan is behind the Talibs, and the Talibs will tell you that Pakistan is behind the destruction of Afghanistan. Go figure. The Talibs will tell you that Massoud is a Russian, Iranian and Indian stooge, and Massoud will tell you that the Talibs are American, Pakistani and Saudi stooges. Go figure. Neither of them have a pot to piss in.

The first setback for the Taliban came in May of '97 when Dostum assassinated Abdur Rehman Haqqani, a close ally of his number two, General Malik Pahlawan, because he wanted to negotiate a settlement with the Taliban. Malik turned on Dostum and formed an alliance with the Taliban allowing them into Mazar-i-Sharif. When the Taliban began to disarm the Shiites in their most holiest of cities (the prophet Ali is buried in Mazar-i-Sharif and the Taliban are Sunnis who view the Shiites as a cult), a battle ensued forcing the Taliban to retreat and creating the first major setback in their 18-month history.

In 1998 and 1999 the Talibs pushed northward across the Shomali plains into the very headquarters of Massoud's Northern Alliance. It seemed all over until under *DP*'s buddy Commander Daoud they pushed the Talibs all the way back into Kabul. The people were initially terrified of these black-turbaned übermensch but once they got a taste of the Taliban they rose up and defeated them soundly. The Talibs have changed their holier-than-thou agenda, and now it is not uncommon to see them laying land mines, pressganging women to be married off and plain old looting and stealing. Although the Talib high command says they will discipline anyone caught doing these things, it's starting to sound like a press release.

The overall structure of the Talibs is under scrutiny as well. The Talibs are traditionalists, or orthodox, who want to return to the purity of the teachings of the Koran and the Sunnah—the practice of the Prophet. This sense of purity rejects non-Muslim interference and traditional political structures. The Talibs are also confused with Islamic fundamentalists (like the Wahabi) and more moderate Islamists (like Rabbani and Massoud) who follow the teachings of the *iqwan*, or Muslim Brotherhood, at the Al-Azhar University in Egypt. The strength and the weakness of the Taliban is its foundation along regional affiliations rather than pure political parties. This ensures that unless the Taliban changes they cannot conquer or hold anyone past their own ethnic, regional and religious support base.

Many attribute the Taliban's success to Pakistani military management and control. Although *DP* met with captured fighters from Yemen and Pakistan, we didn't see any Pakistani officers as the north promised us. There is an undeniable influence of Pakistan with the Talibs. The highest decision-making body in the Taliban is the Shura, which reportedly numbers 30 but has grown to include leaders from areas that have come under the Taliban's influence. The problem is that Omar is not a emir (someone who has undergone supervised religious studies for eight to nine years) and not even a mullah (about four to five years of religious study) and therefore technically not able to issue *fatwahs*. He has a reputation similar to that of a TV evangelist (although Omar has only apparently been interviewed only once TV, by *DP* of course) who talks the talk but can't quite get his followers to walk the walk.

Many of his decrees and rules are quite baffling to the world Muslim community who view his religious credentials as about as credible as Tammy Faye Baker's. Still, those who have met him have all agreed on his strong charisma and vision for Afghanistan. The inner core of the Shura is limited to eight members, of which a group of four leaders, all from Kandahar, one-eyed Maulvis Umar, Muhammad Rabbani, Muhammad Abbas and Borjan, are considered the brains behind the Taliban. Osama bin Laden is more involved in the decisions of the Taliban than most western intelligence services want to admit.

http://www.taleban.com

The Taliban Can and Can't List

Confused by dress codes? Baffled by protocol? Now the Taliban have made it easy for social klutzes to follow the rules.

No music	Say good-by to old favorites like "I Left My Hand in West Kabul"
No theater	"Achmed, Get Your RPG" closed after ten years
No TV	No 24-hour All Mullah, All the Time, Talibvision
No movies	Debbie can't do Kandahar
No book reading	Can't read DP to find out what you can't do

The Taliban Can and Can't List

No soccer	Watch the Jihad All-stars play buzkashi
No drinking	No Colt 45 unless it really is a Colt 45
No paper bags	No sneaking Colt 45s in a bag
No flying kites	No Afghan space program
No photography	Rides on Xerox machines are definitely out
No videos	Debbie can't do Herat either
No foreigners with Afghan women	No paper bag jokes
No recycling the Koran	See paper bags
No white socks for females	No coed cheerleading, either
No schooling for females	Tiny Talibettes have to figure things out themselves
Men must grow beards at least four fingers long	Bic is out of business

Source: Radio Shariat, Kabul, DP

In Taliban areas, soccer, volleyball and even chess have been banned because they cause youths to miss some of their five daily prayers. Women must wear the *burqa*, a kind of shmoo-sack slash veil that covers the entire body, and men must have long beards, something that shocks naïve journos but is quite normal outside of Kabul. Western pleasures like trashy novels, MTV, movies, beer and Nintendo are all forbidden. The idea is to not divert people's minds from God and family. Come to think of it, these guys might be on to something. To contact the Taliban stateside get ahold of:

Mulawi Abdul Hakeem Mujahid or Noorullah Zadran
55/16 Main Street
Flushing, NY
Tel.: (718) 359-0457
News Hotline: (718) 762-8095
Fax: (718) 661-2721
Web site: www.taleban.com
E-mail: AMujahid@aol.com

Nonofficial site:
http://www.ummah.net/Taliban/

Friday Night Specials

The most publicized change is the practice of public executions. A step up from the extrajudicial killings and rapes that occurred before the Taliban but it's the packed crowds in the UN-rebuilt sports stadium that makes it odd. Victims are judged by a *shura* and in murder cases the victim's relatives get to execute the killer with a machine gun or knife. In some cases the killer's father must do the killing and buy the bullets used to end his son's life. Public amputations of thieves' hands are common and are performed by doctors who administer a painkiller first. Sometimes the hands are put on display in an odd form of saying "Welcome to Kabul." For local listings of the executions in your area stay tuned to Radio Shariat.

http://www.afghanradio.com
http://www.amnesty.org.uk/news/press/eje.shtm

How 'bout two out of three?

Life is never boring for the former BBC correspondent in Kabul, William Reeve. Other than covering the regular rocketings, feuding aid workers and contributing to the slowly diminishing whiskey supply at the UNICA guesthouse he gets to cover the odd walling, the execution of sexual miscreants by pushing a wall over on them. Being a homosexual is punishable by death in Afghanistan. Walling, or rajim, is supposed to be death by stones but with the time restraints of the modern world, the Talibs figure pushing over a whole wall of cinderblocks gets the job done quicker with less mess to clean up afterward.

Reeve covered the walling of an 84-year-old man who had been accused of molesting a 12-year-old young boy at guesthouse in Maidan Shahr. The man protested that he didn't even have sex with his wife, let alone the boy, but the Talibs apparently tortured him into a confession. Witnesses initially said that he was dead, but as luck would have it, they discovered when the rubble was cleared away 30 minutes later that the 15-foot wall did not kill the man as originally planned. He was let go. Someone who survives a walling is considered innocent of the crime.

Mullah Mohammed Omar

One-eyed Mullah Omar is Commander of the Faithful, top dog and head cheese of the Taliban and of Afghanistan. Omar is not so much the political leader of the Taliban as he is the poster boy and religious diviner. He is Afghanistan in a microcosm. Wounded war hero, politician, religious leader and visionary shaper of the new Afghanistan. Omar was born the son of a poor farmer in 1962 in Uruzgan or the Mewand district in SW Afghanistan. He wanted to study the Koran, but the jihad against the Russians interrupted his studies. He was wounded four times in one firefight, losing his left eye. His friends say he was a pretty good shot with an RPG. He then ascended the ranks to be the chief commander in the Harakat-i-Inqilab-i Islami party of Muhammad Nabi Muhammad. On April 3, 1996, over 1,000 Muslim clergymen chose Mullah Omar to be the "Amirul-Mumineen" (Supreme Leader of the Muslims). Depending on who you talk to he is the little man pulling the levers in *The Wizard of Oz* or a charismatic diviner of truths. *DP* set up the world's only taped interview with him and lets just say he's a nice guy but he rambles a bit when it comes to the jihad stuff. He can usually be found in the newly undecorated governor's mansion in Kandahar holding court.

Mullah Omar
Kandahar, Islamic Emirate of Afghanistan

Ahmed Shah Massoud/The United Front

The "Lion of Panshir" was born in 1952 to an army officer. He is credited with being the main reason the Russians hightailed it out of Afghanistan. He lives with his wife, son, and two daughters in Taloqan. His family home is in Rokas in the Panjshir valley. He perfected the Afghan style of guerrilla warfare and has a personal charisma that kept squabbling factions together. Currently he is supposed to be Rabbani's defense minister in an ever shuffling government lineup. The truth is that Commander Ahmed Shah Massoud holds all the cards. He personally controls and leads a well-trained 6,000–10,000-man army and is surrounded by commanders who have been fighting for three decades. He also has surrounded himself with young twenty-something commanders like Doaud, who pushed back the Talibs from his headquarters in Taloqan. Massoud is one of those leaders who is morally and financially pure, motivated only by a burning resolve to give his people a democratic government of their own choosing. He operates as "the minister of defense" in a government that has the same continuity as a pickup basketball game. He is ultimately a Tajik and a man with great personal charisma, energy and tenacity. For now he has surrounded himself with bright young men and hardened commanders, some of whom swap sides depending on who is winning. He is prepared to head into the hills and fight a guerrilla war—as he was almost forced to last year—despite his tiny real estate holdings (Massoud has about 40,000 soldiers). The alliance will tell you that the 80/20 stuff you hear is a little wrong. Population-wise they like to think that they represent about 30 percent or more of the population, considering the Taliban don't really occupy large parts of rugged Afghanistan. He is hurting from recent losses of tanks, helicopters (down to 12 from around 45) and only about 4 operating gunships (not including the 2 on the river outside his house in the Panjshir)

Although he stills wears the jaunty *pakool* (adopted from his early years in Nuristan) he is getting a little gray around the temples and close friends says that he feels a little more embattled after almost three decades of constant fighting. He still has a nice collection of armor, artillery and even has about 20 SCUD-Bs stashed in the Panshir valley. Vague rumors say that he was handed $50 million from a high-ranking American diplomat to squeeze the Taliban militia, that he has Iranian backing and now French help. *DP* didn't see much evidence if he did. The truth is the Northern Alliance often has a hard time scratching up the $420 it takes to refuel their helicopters before they take off from Dushanbe for Taloqan. They do have a new supply base at Sher Qila, situated on the other side of river Oxus inside Tajikistan. and there are plenty of piles of new mines, rockets, AKs and bullets to be seen.

His soldiers make around 15,000 northern afghanis a month(a 56-kg wheat ration). Massoud wants to fight the Taliban on as many fronts as possible but attributes the Taliban's success to support by the Pakistani Secret Police (ISI), something he knows firsthand since he was originally trained by the ISI when he was a student in Peshawar.

Massoud is the third of six sons of a well-off Tajik army officer. He was raised in Kabul and attended the French Lycée Istiqlal secondary school. He studied at the Polytechnic college, where he also met Rabbani. There he also met Hekmatyar, who was the most dominant figure in the Afghan student group. He along with other Afghan refugees were trained in a one-month course by the ISI in the Cherat army camp near Peshawar. Massoud was sent into Afghanistan in July of '75 with 30 other Afghans, resulting in half of his comrades being arrested or killed. Two months later, Massoud formed an alliance with Rabbani, who led the Jamiat-i-Islami (Islamic Society), and Hekmatyar formed the hard-line Hezbi Islami group.

In 1976 Pakistan backed Hekmatyar and turned against Rabbani, resulting in arrests and torture and murder of some of Massoud's friends as spies. He never forgave Hekmatyar and the Pakistanis for their treachery.

Daoud was killed in a military coup that brought the Communists to power in 1978 and Massoud returned to the Panjshir in the spring of '79 to join the growing revolt. He battled against government troops and was wounded in the leg. Within a year Massoud became the leader of the Panjshir. When the Russians invaded to prop up the Communist government, they tried unsuccessfully to wrest the strategic valley from the rebels.

Hekmatyar was the main recipient of the CIA and ISI's largesse and kept his base inside Pakistan while Massoud fought the Russians in the mountains with his army of 8,000 men. After the fall of the Russians, a civil war broke out with Pakistani-backed Hekmatyar and Rabbani. For now Massoud takes the long-term view, hoping that Afghanistan will be run by its own people and that the outside meddling of Russia, the United States or

Pakistan will slowly bleed to death. Today the government has created the more rebellious sounding United Front of Afghanistan, a loose collection of minorities and political interests against the Talibs.

Journalists who want to enter northern Afghanistan or contact Massoud can try to reach him through his younger brother Ahmad Walid Massoud at the Afghan embassy in London; call *(0171) 589 8891*. Wally will provide assistance only to mainstream and credentialed journalists, aid workers, etc.

http://www.afghan-government.com/

Embassy of the Islamic State of Afghanistan (UK)

31 Prince Gate London SW7 1QQ
Tel: 0171) 589 8891
Fax: (0171) 581 3452
http://www.afghan-government.com/

Dr. Abdullah (Official Representative in New York)

00 873 761 8942 75/ 873 614 780 73
UK mobile 0370 890 372

Engineer Ishaq (Representative in Panjshir Valley)

873 762 0175 33
Fax: 873 762 0175 34

Jamiat-i-Islami (Islamic Society)

The Jamiat-i-Islami (Islamic Society) is influenced by the thinking of Pakistani theologian Abul Ala Maududi and Egyptian thinker Sayyid Qutb. It is the party of the current official but diminutive government of Rabbani and Massoud. Afghan Islam began on the campus of Kabul University in the mid-1960s as a reaction to the Marxist trend among the students. The professor trained at Cairo's Al-Azhar University, Burhanuddin Rabbani, attracting students of science, engineering and medicine. Hekmatyar (Kabul University) and Massoud (Kabul Polytechnic) were both engineering students who began their political careers on Kabul campuses. The party of Rabbani and Massoud pushes a revolutionary but modern form of Islam.

http://www.jamiat.com/
Sat phone: 873-761-613-932
Fax: 873-761-613-933
E-mail: administration@jamiat.com

The Unemployed Warlords for Hire Department, Or "It Ain't Over until the Fat Man Swings"

The Talibs told *DP* that if they catch any of the '80s-era warlords, including Massoud, Dostum or Hekmatyar, they will hang them from the nearest tall structure. Even Najibullah and his brother thought they could kiss and make up before they decorated a traffic post with their battered and decorated bodies. So since *DP* is mindful that everyone needs a job to get by, it might be appropriate to see if anyone has a job for these hardworking guys:

Gulbuddin Hekmatyar

Hekmatyar has been assassinated more times than Monica Lewinsky's character. Dumped by the ISI in favor of the Taliban in 1994, he still plays the part of fiery muj leader. Somehow he always pops up alive on the radio a few days later haranguing his detractors. He was rocketed when he was sworn in as PM at the Kabul Intercontinental (after a live radio interview by a *DP* fan and journo Haneef) and even as we go to press he was supposedly gunned down on the streets of Mashad, Iran. Hek is the late-40-something "rebel without a pause" from Baghlan who came to prominence as the most favored of the 12 Afghan rebel factions nurtured by the CIA. He is originally from Baghlan and is the head and founder of the Hezbi Islami group. He first studied at the Afghan military academy, then switched to the engineering department of Kabul University in 1968. Some of his friends call him "Engineer Hekmatyar" but he never graduated from Kabul University. Hekmatyar spent four years in the communist PDPA (People's Democratic Party of Afghanistan), which was made up of both Parchami and Khalqi groups. In 1972, Hekmatyar was jailed for killing a Maoist student, but then fled to Peshawar, Pakistan, where he founded Hezbi Islami. In 1974, until 1976, he was trained by the ISI to overthrow President Davd. He has changed alliances and benefited greatly in his position as leader of the Pashtuns until recently when the Taliban became the major Pashtun group. Hekmatyar was once Rabbani's prime minister, but broke away and began a yearlong siege of Kabul. His army was trashed in March 1995 by the Taliban and he is still looking for a sugar daddy. Detractors point out that Hekmatyar spent the Russian war safely in Peshawar stockpiling CIA-supplied weapons and money while Massoud was fighting in the mountains with weapons stolen from dead Russians. His forces were the major beneficiary of weapons from Pakistan and once bragged that he could fight a war for 25 years without ever needing supplies. His arms caches are now in the hands of the Taliban. Be careful before you trash talk about Hekmatyar because he still has a lot of fans in Pakistan; in fact, one of them tried to off the Taliban mullahs while *DP* was there. Hek, Dostum and Massoud were blamed for the more than 50,000 people who have been killed in Kabul during the factional fighting after the Russians left.

Hezb-e-islami.
http://www.hezb-e-islami.org/

Sayed Jafar Naderii

Jafar is a journo's dream. On the surface he is an Ismaeli who controlled Baghlan province and kept it safe from the turmoil that surrounded it. He's a former pizza delivery boy, Hell's Angel and rock-and-roll warlord who controlled the strategic and profitable region of Puli Khomri. His father brought him back and he became a general in his 20s. He could barely speak the local language. The Talibs kicked him out in August of 1998 and trashed his luxury compound. He was in town from his new base in London when *DP* was in Dushanbe. He's looking for a way to get back into things, no doubt, but we didn't notice any "warlord wanted" ads in the local paper. He used to control a private army of Kayanis who kept things nice and calm.

Sayed was famous for being a fan of Jon Bon Jovi, sex, drugs and rock and roll. In a region where you might think that the wheel is new invention his snappy interviews, interesting choice of '80s disco decor and pure love of the game made him the holy grail for rock-and-roll journos doing the Afghan thing.

His most famous attributed statement was when asked why he left New Jersey to return to Afghanistan and become a warlord: "Because I can fuck or kill anyone I want."

Ooooh kay.

General Rashid Dostum

Roly-poly Rashid got caught up in his own web of intrigue when his second in command defected to the Taliban on May 25, 1997, and had to hightail it to Ankara. Dostum used to control eight provinces in the north and ran his little kingdom out of his hometown and western military headquarters of Shebergan, Jozjan province, 80 miles from Mazar. Detractors will tell you that Rashid is an old-time commie warlord who is propped up by Uzbekistan and drug transportation from the hash- and poppy-rich fields around Mazar-i-Sharif. He was a man with a grade school education surrounded by gangsters. He packed his bags, family and flunkies and flew out to Ankara, Turkey, where he bravely proclaimed, "The war is not over." He promised to return "when the conditions are right." The conditions were right on September 12, when Dostum blasted his way into

Mazar and sent Malik packing. Then of course the Talibs blasted him out of Mazar and he had to check if he could keep his lease on his bulletproof Beemer and swank pad.

Dostum, the former military commander under Najibullah, is now looking after the Uzbeki's interest in northern Afghanistan. The sight of his boss swinging in the breeze has not made him a fan of the Taliban or homesick for Afghanistan.

President Burhanuddin Rabbani

Technically not unemployed (after all he is the official president of Afghanistan) Rabbani is a former theology professor from Kabul and the former official political leader of Afghanistan (although his term has legally expired), but one wonders what he has been leading. A highly educated man, Rabbani made an attempt to build a bridge between opposing forces when he named Hekmatyar prime minister in 1993 and again in 1996. But there is little room for compromise in this fundamentalist country. He is backed mainly by the Tajiks in the north (3.5 million people, or about 25 percent of Afghanistan's population) and maintained his power only with the military might of Massoud. His Jemiate Islami party is the only non-Pathan party in Afghanistan. Apparently Rabbani's biggest skill is the ability to put an entire room of feuding warlords to sleep once his starts in on one of his monotonal marathon speeches. He can be found in Faizabad in northern Afghanistan.

http://frankenstein.worldweb.net/afghan/Politics/wl_profile.html

Mujahedin, "Afghan" and the Camps

Warlords have to start somewhere. There is no formal way to become a commander or leader; you just have to have the chops and then other people will follow. The Pathans encourage a culture of independence and being "strong" fighters.

The Wiley Pathans (called Pakhtuns in their own language) are not a generic group of evil-looking, bearded men waiting perpetually in ambush along Afghanistan's mountain passes. The Pathans are a group of tribes that make up 40 percent of Afghanistan's populace and 13 percent of Pakistan's. They are primarily rural, clan based and aligned in major ethnic or geographic alliances. Their love for freedom, guns and adventure are probably their most publicized traits but they are also loyal, honest and moral.

Years of war and over $3 billion in covert U.S. aid have created three new warrior castes in Afghanistan. The older generation of Afghani mujahedin are Tajiks and Pathans who spent their young lives in nomadic columns killing Russians in the early '80s. The second group are the infamous "Afghans"—the people the CIA (through the Pakistani secret service) hired and trained to fight the Russians. They are called "Afghans" because they are not Afghani. (Stay with me, this stuff is complicated). These "Afghans," estimated to be around 5,000 in total, were primarily Baluchis, Algerians, Egyptians, Saudis, Filipinos and Palestinians. Most of these men have returned to their home countries and are wreaking havoc everywhere from Zamboango, Philippines (Abu Sayeff), to Algiers, Algeria (GIA) and Manhattan, New York (World Trade Center bombing).

Both these groups were well trained, impoverished and savvy in the arts of deception, marksmanship, explosives and terror, and they have been in great demand in other parts of the world by Iran and Sudan for their absolute devotion to jihad.

The third group or new generation of mujahedin are youngsters who grew up in the squalid, mud-walled refugee camps of Peshawar and Quetta. These are the young men who grew up under the brutality of the warlords and are heeding the call of the Taliban.

http://www.subcontinent.com/sapra/terrorism/tr_1998_11_001_s.html

The Artist Formerly Known as Cat

If you are wandering through Kabul and you think a cat is being boiled alive, you probably just heard the Taliboogey. Highly amplified chantings and singings without musical accompaniment blasted from loudspeakers, usually outside Talib military barracks. One of the big hits a few years back was a bootleg version of a song by Cat Stevens, now called Yusuf. Yusuf first wrote the song for mujahedin fighting the Soviets in 1979. The version had been recorded when Yusuf did a live performance in the '80s in Pakistan. He recently recorded an album of freedom songs for Bosnia. Cat, or Yusuf, was born a Roman Catholic and lives in London.

Osama bin Laden

Osama bin-Laden was born in the city of Riyadh in 1957 the youngest son of Muhammed bin Laden. He was raised in Medina, Munawwara and Hijaz. He went to school in Jedda before studying management and economics in King Abdul Aziz University. Although he describes himself as construction engineer and an agriculturist, he is more famous for being America's biggest nightmare.

He fought against the Russians in Afghanistan between '79 and '89 and raised a number of volunteers from Arab countries. He also helped build tunnels, roads and bunkers using heavy construction equipment he donated. You can visit the huge tunnels he blasted into the Zazi Mountains of Bakhtiar Province for guerrilla hospitals and arms dumps. He still likes to hang out in air-conditioned, cruise-missile-proof caves.

In 1994 he was kicked out of Saudi Arabia and hung out with Hassan al-Turabi, leader of the National Islamic Front. He built the Port Sudan roads (paid for in sesame seeds) invested in agricultural projects and built three training camps for mujahedin.

In May 1996 he was expelled from Sudan and hung out in southern Yemen and some say Afghanistan as well. He came to the world's attention in April 1996, February 1997 and February 1998 when he gave a round robin of interviews to the world's press. He has been fingered for the November 13, 1995, Riyadh Bombing, the June 25, 1998, bombing in Dhahran of the Al-Khobar towers and a number of other events that range from trying to kill the pope, blowing up airliners from the Philippines, the assissination attempts in June 1995 of Egyptian President Hosni Mubarak in Sudan and in June 1993 of Jordan's Crown Prince Abdullah.

Bring me the head of Clinton!... But can you make that two-day instead of overnight?

Peshawar-based Afghan scholar Abdul Rahim Muslim has offered a reward to anyone to bring him the head of Clinton according to the Afghan Islamic Press (AIP) "If anyone kills Clinton I will pay a reward of five million afghanis," Rahim rants; "If America sets the price of Osama bin Laden at $5 million, then we can set the price of the American president at five million afghanis" (about $113).

What drives Binny? Well, some say that he always wanted to one up his older brother Salim, who was killed in a hang glider accident in Texas in 1989. He is one of 53 children and the only son of one of his father's 10 wives. Technically he is half Palestinian on his mother's side and half Yemeni on his father's side. Osama was never really taken seriously by the mujahedin in the early days and was even ridiculed as a spoiled brat who expected respect in exchange for his dollars. Osama is no slouch in the toy department—he owns a Gulfstream G-8 business jet. His organization, called "the base" or Al-Qaida, is unique in that there is no government behind it. Essentially, terrorism meets entreprenurialism. In 1997, bin Laden's new Terrorists 'R' Us concept was blown apart when moneyman Sidi al-Madani al-Ghazi Mustafa al-Tayyib was busted and squealed. The CIA has been bragging that they have been tracking his satphone calls as well.

What Osama lacks in popularity in the West he makes up for in directness. In his May 26 ABC interview with John Miller, bin Laden simply said, "Leave Saudi Arabia or die. . . . Allah ordered us in this region to purify the Muslim land of all nonbelievers, and especially in the Arabian Peninsula. . . . We believe that the biggest thieves in the world and the terrorists are the Americans. . . . We do not differentiate between those dressed in military uniforms and civilians; they are all targets in this fatwa." The only thing that bin Laden might have overlooked is that he is not a mullah since his degree was in economics and agriculture not religion. It is a bad habit he shares with his close friend Mullah Omar, who is also technically not a mullah.

So let's just say Binny is the bearded Ross Perot of the Middle East. Technically Binny Bang Bang (he keeps going an going and going and going . . .) can now join Castro and Qaddafi for drinks at the Bad Boy's Club, unless the United States keeps turning off his cash flow. A man with 40 brothers, 13 sisters and wealthy patrons can probably play hide the pickle longer than the State Department can. For now bin Laden is a right-wing billionaire (or millionaire or even destitute, depending who you talk to) who combines industrial activity with political activism. Although Laden's chances of creating a hardline Saudi government are about the same as Perot's presidential bid, he's doing just fine in sunny Afghanistan. Laden found a friend in the former jihad buddy Mullah Omar and the Taliban and intends to stay in Jalalabad with about 50 of his family members, his four wives, five kids and twenty truckloads of bodyguards. A tip to up-and-comers, son Muhammed bin Laden (born 1984) is expected to be the heir apparent. To visit Binny just turn left after you leave the last checkpoint heading east out of town. He originally came here from Sudan and gathered around him a group of 200 or so Arab fighters who were trapped inside Afghanistan. They formed the core of a fighting group and bodyguard that ensures that only the quick or the dead will make a snatch attempt to get the $5 million the U.S. government has offered for his arrest and conviction. He can be contacted through 39-year-old Zainul Abideen, alias Abu Zubaida in Pakistan or Harkatul Mujahideen, in the NWFP. In case you wonder what he thinks of Yanquis, his June and February 1998 *fatwah* cut to the chase: ". . . kill[ing] the Americans and their allies—civilians and military—is an individual duty for every Muslim who can do it in any country in which it is possible to do, in order to liberate the al-Aqsa Mosque and the holy mosque [Mecca] from their grip . . ." Oh, and one other thing: Don't offer him a Pepsi.

Taliban Says Stone Clinton to Death

Another major setback in Hillary's on- again off-again secret election bid in Afghanistan came in a weekly newspaper published by the militant Islamic group Harakat ul-Ansar. Mullah Omar was quoted as saying that Clinton should be stoned to death for becoming involved with a woman who is not his wife. "Clinton is a confessed sinner and a bad person," Omar was quoted as saying "It is absolutely not possible to negotiate with such a person and he should be removed [from power] and stoned to death. He is of bad character." Hillary then decided to run in New York.

Pakistan

If you look on most maps, you will see a distinct border between Afghanistan and Pakistan. T'ain't so. Anyone with a pony or a pair of Reeboks can skip over the border and back. (Just don't try this at the official border crossings. Also, watch out for those land mines.) Even though the Durand line was created as an official demarcation between the two countries, it is not recognized by either of the Afghanistan or the Pathan tribes whose homeland it divides. Pakistan has absorbed most of the refugees created by the fighting in Afghanistan and keeps warm ties to whoever is in power. During the time Uncle Sam was supporting the mujahedin, Pakistan diverted arms to the mullahs rather than the various tribal chiefs, who were less religious but equally warlike. More specifically, the Pakistani government of General Zia—killed in a plane crash on July 18, 1988—supported the Ghilzai tribe from eastern Afghanistan, where most *mujahedin* leaders came from. The southern Durranis still support the Afghani royal family of former king Zahir Shah who lives in splendid luxury in Rome. There is also an intense desire for statehood among the Pathans for "Pahktunistan," with a bent toward Afghanistan that might remove most of the NWFP and the tribal areas from the map of Pakistan.

The Afghans

Any visitor to the Afghan refugee camps can't help notice thousands of men between 15 and 60 years of age just sitting around in the teahouses. They are out of work mujahedin. Veterans of the war against the Soviet Union, various Afghan warlords and the latest fighting between Talib and Massoud. Killers with hard, deeply lined faces. None had jobs. Ask anyone what they did in the war and you'll get enough for 20 action movie scripts.

Virtually every male in Afghanistan old enough to lift a rifle fought against the Russians. But Afghanis weren't the only ones. The other "Afghans" included more than 3,000 Algerians who fought in Afghanistan, as well as 2,000 Egyptians. Hundreds, if not thousands, of others arrived from Yemen, Sudan, Pakistan, Syria and other Muslim states.

In all, according to some estimates, 10,000 Arabs received training and combat experience in Afghanistan—of whom nearly half were Saudis. A big chunk of the financial backing for the Afghan warlords came—and continues to come—from the fundamentalist Wahhabi sect in Saudi Arabia.

The war in Afghanistan graduated a lot of students, and many are continuing their education in places as far away as Bosnia, the Philippines and the United States. In fact, fighters trained in Afghanistan have surfaced in at least a dozen different struggles, including conflicts in China, Kashmir, Chechnya and Algeria. More than 1000 veterans of the war in Afghanistan fought in Bosnia. Abu Sayyaf, a radical new Islamic group comprised of "Afghanis," has emerged as the principal Muslim guerrilla movement in the Philippines. Ramzi Ahmed Yousef, the mastermind behind the 1993 bombing of the World Trade Center in New York City, is an Iraqi who was trained in Afghanistan. In Algeria, the last two leaders of the radical Armed Islamic Group (GIA) were Afghan veterans.

And wherever the "Afghans" go, the conflicts become bloodier, and Islamic "justice" becomes unjust. Whereas 9 journalists were killed in Algeria by Islamic extremists in 1993, more than 50 were assassinated in 1994-1995. In the Philippines, Abu Sayyaf staged one of the most brutal attacks in the country's two decades of Muslim separatism when, in April 1995, 200 heavily armed Islamic guerrillas attacked the southern town of Ipil, killing 50 and razing the city. Yousef himself was involved in a plot to assassinate Pope John Paul II and was linked to the bombing of a Philippines Airlines plane in December 1994.

When Afghanistan's Taliban ave finished their task of uniting the country, one can only wonder what the 20,000 unemployed Talibaan will do. Revolution anyone?

Boy, if you hate crowded hiking trails and booked hotels, have we got a place for you. Although the U.S. State department says don't go, the Talibs say don't go and the north says don't go, Afghanistan is number one with a bullet for people who want to visit dangerous places. There is no U.S. embassy at the moment (hell, there's no anything at the moment), The NGOs keep their bags packed and no one quite knows who's in charge at any one time. The Talibs are here to stay, but that doesn't mean there is an long-term sense or logic regarding their entry policy for foreigners.

Journos and scribes are officially welcomed by the Taliban and then never given visas to enter. The Red Cross needs Talib approval for all journos before you can book a flight. Same goes for the UN. There are a number of restrictions, advance notice and permission requirements so contact:

Flight Operations UNOCHA/UNDP Islamabad
> *Tel: +92 (51) 211451-5*
> *Fax: +92 (51) 211450*
> *E-mail: unocha@undpafg.org.pk*

Once inside journos have to comply with a two page list of do's and don'ts, which oddly enough includes having your picture taken in a place where taking pictures of living things is forbidden. Being beaten every time you whip out a camera does put a damper on bringing in a Betacam crew. If you are sponsored by an NGO you must only cover the activities of that group. If you somehow get it just to look around, you must stay at the Intercontinental, hire a guide and a driver who maintains his lonely vigil in the lobby. Figure on doubling the rate when you go to the front lines. Strangely, if you are not a journalist there are no laws to restrict your movement. And techncially, once outside Kabul you are free to do what you like (other than photograph people or, as a male, interview women). In the north, you must register in Mazar and stay at the UN guesthouse, whereas journos are forbidden from staying with the UN in Kabul. You will find the Taliban both pleasurable, exasperating and sometimes brutal, depending on circumstances.

DP called the embassy to get the latest travel stats. Apparently, Afghanistan is where all the journos were headed to earn their spurs. When asked who is going to Afghanistan, our contact replied, "Lots of journalists." The embassy needs $60, a couple of photos and a letter from your company saying why you want to be Afghanistan bound. If you enter from Peshawar, don't forget you need to arrange a double or multiple entry visa, a Khyber Pass permit and a gunman from the Khyber Tribal Agency office in Peshawar to get to Torkham. For some odd reason going back doesn't require this. You also need an exit visa (which can eat up half a day) if you leave from Kabul.

Pleasure tourists may find their visa request turned down unless they are truly persuasive. or bum a ride with an NGO car. The border crossings are as mercurial as they are dangerous. *DP* narrowly missed being caught up in a shootout at Torkham between slack-jawed Talib boyguards and veddy British and veddy nervous Pakistani border guards. After the Talibs rocketed the top of the Pakistani post and shot through a demining vehicle, calm was restored and the Talibs went back to whipping urchins with their steel cables.

The Taliban-friendly U.S. embassy (locked in their usual time warp) told us that Massoud was getting support from "Russia and the Soviet Union" and when pressed for advice on how to stay safe, they came up with "Don't steal anything." Any other advice? "Well, you might have to grow a beard, or if you are a woman you might have to wear the chador, well no, now that I think of it, I guess Diane Sawyer didn't have to." We assume he meant the chador not the beard.

The London Afghan Embassy is run by Massoud's brother Wali. He can get you a journo visa for the north but can't do much about arranging a flight in. Tajikistan and Pakistan are your only safe bets for getting into the north. But just getting into and out of Tajikistan is its own nightmare (see the "Tajikistan" chapter).

All border crossings except Termez in Uzbekistan are technically open, but the embassy recommends that travelers use the crossings from Pakistan, Iran and Tajikistan only. The best way into the north and the south is from Pakistan. The intrepid can stroll into Afghanistan over the many mountain trails that connect the two countries in the north and along the Khyber Pass. Since these are usually drug smuggling routes, all travelers will be suspect. A few years ago the DEA (via the Pakistani antidrug agency) was actually offering tribesmen a bounty on any gringos caught buying drugs, so shop for souvenirs with caution.

Afghans are quite hospitable and will offer food and whatever lodging they have. You are expected to reciprocate with some type of gift or remembrance. Photos of your family are great icebreakers and gifts like flashlights, medicine or even clothes are received well. Make sure you pick the right guide, one on good terms with the tribes who control the regions you will be passing through. You will probably be the only tourist in Afghanistan. Camels can be rented to carry heavy gear for US$10 dollars a day, and guides go for about US$20 a day, plus *baksheesh* (a tip). Travelers would be ill-advised to go gem hunting or arms collecting in the hills at this time due to the prevalence of land mines—still the number-one killer and maimer of humans and other living things—and the propensity of Afghans to kidnap foreigners for a few quick dollars.

Most of the country is in the hands of the Taliban, who also control the entry and movement of all outsiders. The northwest is in the hands of the Tajiks and the Wahkan corridor is a no-man's-land under any condition due to the mountainous terrain and drug smuggling. Those who want to meet the Taliban can also contact them in Pakistan.

Afghanistan is sort of an Adventureland notch for journos—a place where you can take a cab to the front lines and be home in time to shop for carpets on Chicken street. The Talibs view most journos with a jaundiced eye since the rash of gender junkets trashed their ideas on women's fashion and law and order.

Although they told me that DP was the first North American the Taliban had talked to long ago, I am sure the thrill has long worn off as everyone from *National Geographic* to *Dateline* does their prerequisite Afghan Taliban adventure story. Areas under Talib control are safe but expect major league hassles from Talibs who want to know what your business is. Try taking pictures of them and you may end up walking like a chicken. The north is still wild and wooly and the last time I tried to get around on a fuel convoy I was told that I might be stopped by brigands and "teased" like one of their drivers was a while back. I learned later that this is a polite way of saying sodomized. Soooeii.

The favored modes of travel are by minibus (cheap and available in all small towns), private car (not as available) and pack animals, which are slow and a great way to see what land mines can do. There is no law inside Afghanistan other than the Taliban's industrial-strength version of *sharia*, usually mixed in with a little local tribal law and whatever the local commander feels like doing with you that night. If he wants you to watch a Ned Beatty movie with him decline, politely. (no more *Deliverance* jokes from here on in.)

It is helpful if Westerners understand Afghan culture and have a basic understanding of the Pakhtun (Pathan) language. Most important is knowledge of the customs of Islam. Despite what you read in the press most Afghans (and not just the Taliban) are devout Muslims and adopt traditional dress and customs. Currently, there is little animosity toward Westerners, but you will be lectured continuously on Islam and considered an oddity for not embracing what is essentially the only religion in Afghanistan. Any major affront to Islam could result in severe punishment or a sound beating. Travel only with the permission of each local commander and be prepared to drink a lot of tea.

Abdul Hakeem Mujahid is your man if you want to get into Talib-held areas. The Taliban's ambassador in Pakistan now works out of a small office in a third-floor walkup in Queens, New York.

Embassy Locations

Because there is no U.S. embassy in Afghanistan and no country represents U.S. interests here, the U.S. government is unable to provide normal protective services to U.S. citizens in Afghanistan (as if they would even if they had an embassy). The nearest U.S. embassies and consulates are in Pakistan and Tajikistan. The telephone number for the (very helpful if you want reasons to stay out of Afghanistan) but under siege U.S. embassy in Islamabad, Pakistan, is: *[92] (51) 826-161/179.* There is little they can do for you once you are in Afghanistan.

U.S. Consulate in Peshawar, Pakistan
Tel: [92] (521) 279-801/2/3

U.S. Embassy in Tashkent, Uzbekistan
Tel: [7] (3712) 771-407/771-081

U.S. Embassy in Dushanbe, Tajikistan
Tel: [7] (3772) 21-0356/-0360/-0457

U.S. Embassy in New Delhi, India
Tel: [91] (11) 600-651

The bus system still operates, taxis are cheap (*DP* paid $25 to go the 200 miles from Torkham to Kabul) and depending on how many crashes Ariana has there are airliners flying in and out of the southern cities. Last time we checked the one-way fare from Kabul to Dubai was $175. Ariana, which was once run by Pan Am, now has three Boeing 727s, three Antonov 24s and is buying a wide-bodied Boeing 747 from Kuwait Airlines. The airport at Kabul is blown to bits but open. Ariana flies a lot of unknown cargo to Dubai, so it's hard for foreigners to buy tickets. Most journos drive in or fly on the Peshawar-based Red Cross and Islamabad-based UN flights.

Ariana Airlines

3rd Floor, Dudley House,
169 Piccadilly
London W1V9DD, UK
Tel.:+44-171-4931411
Fax:+44-171-6291611
Web site: http://fly.to/ariana
E-mail: arianaaf@brain.net.pk

Drugs

Despite the don't ask–don't tell antidrug stance of the Taliban, Afghanistan is the major poppy growing nation in the world (after Myanmar) and a major transporter. The latest word on the street is that bin Laden is buying up raw opium and using it to fight a second front in his war against the West. About $350 of opium gum can be refined into herioin worth a street price of $70,000 in New York. Farmers in Helmand and Nangarhar provinces grow poppies, which are cut to ooze gum. The gum is gathered and send to the 60 or so labs in the southeast and east of Afghanistan. Wrapped tightly in plastic or in glass jars it is shipped to Pakistan across Iran or through Turkmenistan to Turkey or north to Tajikistan, where the Russian military expedites its shipment to Moscow.

Afghanistan is the largest grower of poppies (4,600 tonnes in 1999 compared to 1,300 tonnes from Myanmar) and the largest exporter of hashish in the world. Up to 14 metric tons of hashish have been seized by the border states of Uzbekistan, Turkmenistan, Kyrgystan, Tajikistan and Kazakhstan. Badakhshan borders Tajikistan, where Russia has deployed 25,000 troops to help fight antigovernment Islamic guerrillas believed to have bases in Afghanistan. Strangely, Osama's efforts to corner the market has pushed the price down to $37 a kilo (2.2 lbs.) from $60.

http://www.afghan-politics.org/Reference/Drugs/drugs_main.htm

The Khyber Pass/Tribal Areas

The Khyber Pass is still controlled by tribal chiefs who make a living by shipping drugs, shaving a few rupees from truck drivers and kidnapping folks that ply this historic route. Robbery, shootouts, murder, extortion and/or kidnapping are an everyday occurrence for the unwary, and it has only been the lack of foreigners that have kept this region out of the headlines.

http://www.javed.com.pk/Peshawar.html

The Camps

Afghanistan has always had training camps for mujahedin. We know this because the United States paid for them to be built and expanded back in the '80s. So it wasn't that hard to cruise missile them on August 20, 1998, and it wasn't that hard to rebuild them in Khost and outside Jalalabad, Kabul and Kunduz by December, five months later. Osama, the son of a Saudi construction maven from Yemen, just can't stop building. He has about 3,000 people on the payroll in Afghanistan and is building everything from mosques to government buildings. Tomahawk missiles also hit Jamiatul Mujahideen and Harkatul Ansar camps, both run by Pakistanis, almost 21 kilometers away from Osama's exclusively Arab camp in Khost. The Salman Farsi camp and the Badar 1 and Badar 2 are for the training of Arabs, while the Pakistani-run camps of Pakistani-based Harkatul Mujahideen (former Harakatul Ansar or HUA) and Harkatul Jihad Al-Islami. Osama is one of the benefactors of the Harkatul Mujahideen who teach volunteers from as far away as North America, the Phillipines, Bosnia and Algeria to fight low-intensity terrorist wars.

Missiles also hit the ten-year-old Jamiatul Mujahideen camp commanded by the Kashmiri Mufti Bashir. This camp was for training up to 250 volunteers from Kashmir and Pakistan to fight in Kashmir, a war the Pakistani ISI funds and provides training for.

Fashion

Females have become the latest pawns in the war in Afghanistan. Reacting to a report by *DP*'s co-resident at the UNICA guesthouse Zohra Rasekh, the Physicians for Human Rights and other junket journos have declared war on the Afghan people. By focusing on the *burqa* as a symbol of evil (something Zohra, a woman, forgets to mention she didn't have to wear in Kabul), she has demonized Afghan culture and blamed it on the Taliban. Any visitor to the north will tell you that the *burqa* is a part of Afghan life except in once-cosmopolitan Kabul.

The report goes on to clinically document the lack of health care for women as if the author has comparable statistics from Afghan women in Rochester, Minnesota. "PHR explored the reasons for decreased access to health care services. Of the 40 women interviewed, 87% (33 of 38) reported a decrease in their access to health services. The reasons given included: no chaperone available (27%), restrictions on women's mobility (36%), hospital refused to provide care (21%), no female doctor available (48%), do not own a burqa (6%), and economics (61%)." Taken the other way DP finds it amazing that 52% of afghan women had access to any doctor male or female. Women and their rights are being used as a pawn in this war but the endgame is they have lost either way. The lack of aid because of the way their unelected government treats them and another generation lost to poverty and hopelessness.

http://www.rawa.org/
http://www.phrusa.org/campaigns/af_exec1.html

Tribes

Most people are unaware that Afghanistan is still a land of tribal chiefs and feudal kingdoms. This is the land of *badal*, where every Afghan man must avenge a wrong, no matter how slight and how long it takes. Every major tribal home in Afghanistan is a small stone-and-mud fortress, and each person must stand watch in the tower. Tribes have been keeping score over how many of each other they have whacked, with a rivalry that approaches USC-UCLA fervor. They also take their tribal codes and Islam seriously. When *DP* was cruising through one tribal area, we were told a tribe member had seen a young woman and a man from another tribe kissing on a hillside. The father of the girl captured a cousin of the object of her affection, tied them both to a tree and pumped 75 bullets into them.

Guns

When it comes to gun love, the Afghanis have no equal. Afghanistan has more guns per capita than anywhere else on earth. England allowed the Pathans to manufacture their own guns 200 years ago, and the CIA delivered enough weapons to keep the region swimming in weaponry for years to come. But this was all dwarfed by the stockpiles of weapons the Russians abandoned or lost in the ten years of warfare. One Afghan gunman philosophically pointed out to *DP* the unique relationship Afghanis have with their ballistic toys when he said, "You have your cameras, and we have our guns."

If the containers and warehouses full of pristine weapons aren't enough, the Affridi tribe of Afghanistan and Pakistan still pumps out about 900 to 1,200 copies of modern weapons a day in its gun factories in Darra Adam Khel.

Happiness Is a Worn Gun

For those who can't resist a bargain, the best place to buy guns is actually just outside Afghanistan in Pakistan. You can hire a gunman for about $20 a day, but if you want to shop for that special hard-to-please someone, take along an Afghan guide and go visit the Smugglers Bazaar (20 minutes east of Peshawar) in Darra (about 40 minutes south of Peshawar). Although Darra has been officially closed for two years to outsiders you can still buy a worn but serviceable AK-47 for $200. Pros know to buy the short Chinese-made assault versions, since their barrels don't heat up as much and they can be concealed under your shwaler qamiz. These go for about $375–$1,000 Chinese- and Russian-made pistols are between $10–$100, with the Pakistani-made knockoffs at the low end of the price spectrum.

Rambos can pick up Chinese and Russian rocket launchers for just under a grand and rockets by the case for 400 rupees (US$125) each. Grenades are a bargain at US$3 each. Perfect for that kidnap scenario when you threaten to pull the pin. Other items for sales at bargain basement prices include land mines, antiaircraft guns, bazookas, Stalin Organ–style rocket launchers (the self-propelled kind) and even lovely used Russian T-55 tanks.

Wanna-bes who don't want to be arrested in Darra can head north of Peshawar to Sakahot and see guns being made from cheap pig iron. Lookee loos who appreciate the smell of cordite and the sound of tinnitus can arrange to fire automatic weapons in the nearby gorge. One banana clip of 30 bullets will set you back about ten bucks. Cheap, even by Coney Island standards. The hottest selling items are still the pen guns that fire a single bullet and can be used to write ransom notes. They are a measly six dollars. Naturally, you will need a complete Soviet era–uniform, bayonets, combat gear, watches, boxes of uncirculated rubles (wrapped and still in serial number order) and medals to complete your Cold War GI Joe play kit.

Kidnapping: Part One

The Afghans are among the most hospitable people in the world. In fact, some may invite you to stay with them for a long, long time, unless you or your relatives can cough up the ransom. Kidnapping is actually a tribal tradition that goes back before recorded time. It is an easy way to get a wife, get your goats back or make some extra money in lean years. Recently, kidnapping has been a means to bring attention to tribal disputes or grievances. Locals, expats and tourists are routinely kidnapped in Afghanistan and near the border with Pakistan. Ransoms run from US$2,000 up to US$50,000 and more for foreign workers. The positive side to this is that if you're traveling under the protection of one tribe and are kidnapped by another, your host tribe has an obligation to free you. The people in the greatest danger are foreign workers who travel in a predetermined route or stay in a fixed place.

http://travel.state.gov/afghanistan_warning.html

Kidnapping: Part Two

Maybe its ironic that the United States has sent special forces to Peshawar to kidnap bin Laden should he stick his foot outside Afghanistan. The main problem is that any foreigner is going to be considered a suspect kidnapper. Even when *DP* was in Kabul just before the missile attacks we were told flatly by the NGOs to use a better cover for our spying.

Mines

The Russians buried and dropped about 12 million mines in the ground. Some say at the current removal rate it will take 20,000 years to remove all the mines. HALO figures that 640,000 mines have been laid since 1979. In 1998 they cleared 100,000 individual items of unexploded ordnance, or UXO. HALO has 1,300 Afghan deminers working under the supervision of only two expats clearing the towns and countryside. They are working feverishly to demine the 95 percent of the country under peace so that more than 3 million Afghans can return to their formerly mined villages. There are currently 300,000 Afghans waiting to rebuild or move back into their homes in Kabul.

Most deminers will tell you privately that the UN estimate is a little over the top but makes them look good when they do it faster. There are more than 50 different kinds of mines, and not just Russian made. There are RAP-2s from Zimbabwe, and even NR-127s made in Belgium. There are neat battery-powered multicensored mines that blow up when they feel vibration. According to the UN, 162 of Afghanistan's 356 districts are affected by mines. The most dangerous areas for mines are Helmand with 5 major fields, Kandahar with 47, Paktia with 118, Logar with 53 and Herat with 86. The areas affected are grazing land, irrigation systems, agricultural land and cities. Both the Taliban (who promised me they didn't and wouldn't use mines back in the bad old days) and the northern alliance is busy putting new ones in as you read this.

The UN estimates it needs $185 million to carry out all its programs, including demining. Afghanistan currently has the world's largest demining program and in seven years has destroyed over 200,000 devices, but has cleared only 80 square kilometers. The most heavily mined areas are security zones around the major cities along the Iranian and Pakistani borders (Herat, Kandahar, Jalalabad and Khost). Follow the basic rules and you will survive: Do not wander off hard surface (even when taking a leak). Learn to squat at the edge of the road to urinate like the locals do. Do not travel in snow. Land mines were laid in strength along mountain passes and can be more sensitive with ice and snow cover. Do not turn over or pick up any items, do not inspect abandoned military vehicles, do not run up a hill to get a better vantage point . . . and the list goes on.

http://www.un.org/Depts/Landmine/program/Afghan/partners.htm

I Guess I Should Have Stayed at Home Department

What were people in Afghanistan doing when they were killed or injured by a land mine.

Fetching water	20 percent
Traveling	15 percent
Fighting	13 percent
Playing with a mine	8 percent
Demining	4 percent

GETTING SICK

Even though things are settling down, medical care is not Afghanistan's strong point. Health care is available in the major cities through aid groups. Many prescription drugs and antibiotics (not opiates) can be bought over the counter. They will be old and dusty and we do not recommend self-medication. A traveler with a serious condition should seek help in Pakistan or Iran. Better yet, take the next flight home or to London. Expect that the most basic medical care is limited or nonexistent with war wounded and children getting priority treatment. Malaria (primarily the benign vivax form) is present below 2,000 meters (6,562 feet) between May and November in the southern area and falciparcium strain occurs in the warmer south. Chloroquine-resistant falciparcium has been reported. Rabies, tick-borne relapsing fever and cutaneous leishmaniasis are present.

NUTS AND BOLTS

Electricity (when you can find it) is 220v/50Hz. The official languages are Pashtu (mostly in the south and east) and Dari Persian (in the north and west). Many people speak English and some Russian. The money is the Afghani and the black market is the only real place you can exchange notes. Figure on a U.S. dollar getting you 44,360 afghanis. Be forewarned that there are two afghanis. One, called Dostum money, is used in the north and is one-tenth of the value of the Talib afghani used in the south. They look identical except for the spacing between the type on the front. The way to remember is the type of the northern or Dostum money is "allied" or together and the south is apart.

The money changers are fair since this is how all people change money. Try not to use U.S. $100 bills printed before 1993 since many money changers won't take them. When shops are open they start at 8 A.M. and close between noon and 1 P.M. and then reopen until 4:30 P.M. Some shops are closed Wednesday and Friday. Traffic drives on the right and the normally paved roads are full of potholes from shells and disrepair. Jalalabad is the main smuggling area for cars, electronic goods and drugs into Pakistan, so be judicious when asking questions or taking photographs.

Web Sites
http://www.agora.stm.it/politic/afghanistan.htm

DANGEROUS DAYS

11/9/99	Mullah Omar offers Massoud a truce if they can both go and fight the Russians in Chechnya.
12/15/98	New training camps are operational in Khost, Jalalabad and Kabul.
8/20/98	Seventy $1.5 million Tomahawk cruise missiles are dropped on Harakatul Mujahedin camps in Khost (94 miles south of Kabul, near the Pakistani border) in retaliation for the bombings of U.S. embassies in Kenya and Tanzania in August, which killed more than 230. Salvaged cruise missiles are traded to Chinese generals for a small mountain of small arms.
8/20/98	Bill Clinton tells of air strikes against Sudan and Afghanistan while on vacation in Martha's Vineyard .
10/30/97	Emma Bonino and Christiane Amanpour are beaten and detained by the Taliban for photographing women in a hospital.
9/97	Over 120 journalists enter Kabul to cover Taliban's occupation of Kabul.
9/27/97	The Taliban enter Kabul.
9/12/97	Dostum returns to Mazar-i-Sharif after heavy fighting and looting.

5/28/97	Taliban forces retreat from Mazar-i-Sharif after losing 100 men in 18 hours of fighting. This marks the first retreat in the Taliban's history.
5/24/97	General Malik Pahlawan turns against warlord Rashid Dostum opening the city to the Taliban. The Uzbeks and Tajiks revolt when the Taliban tries to disarm them.
9/27/96	The Taliban drive Massoud, Rabbani and Hekmatyar out of Kabul exactly one year after their founding.
6/19/96	Pakhtun leader Hekmatyar signs a peace pact with former enemy Rabbani becoming Prime Minister in Kabul.
9/11/96	Hekmatyar's Hezbi-Islami arms depot is captured in Paktia.
4/3/96	Mullah Omar is proclaimed Amir-ur-Momineen.
9/5/95	The Taliban capture Herat and begin imposition of strict sharia.
9/19/94	The Taliban emerges from the southern province of Kandahar.
1/119/94	Hekmatyar lay siege to Massoud and Rabbani in Kabul, turning the city into rubble.
04/15/1989	Najibullah leaves. Rebels beginning battle of Kabul as factions war for control.
2/15/1989	The last Soviet soldier leaves Afghanistan.
1988	Gorbachev announces Soviet withdrawal from Afghanistan.
1986	Soviets install Najibullah as the 100,000 Soviet soldiers fight against seven U.S.-backed rebel factions.
12/1979	Moscow turfs the socialist government and installs Babrak Karmal. Soviet troops enter Afghanistan to prop up Karmal.
1978	Socialists under Hafizullah Amin stage a coup in Kabul. Moscow begins to send aid.
1973	King Zahir Shah is overthrown.

In a Dangerous Place: Afghanistan

Just Another Day

The shockwaves first wake me from a slumbering sleep. Fractionally later the sound reaches me, a dull sounding *bduuumf*. Scrambling off my mattress I lurch towards the window, just in time to see a gray mushroom cloud reaching towards a clear blue sky.

It is an early morning wakeup call from the Taliban. They have just bombed Taloqan for the umpteenth time that week. I had arrived in northern Afghanistan a week earlier. It is the last part of the country held by Ahmed Shah Massoud, the legendary Tajik commander. He is now the last serious opposition to the Taliban goal of conquering the whole of Afghanistan by force.

The Taliban have not taken too kindly to this. In fact, their displeasure had been fairly obvious for most of the week as they had rained down bombs on the town.

It is a matter of seconds to grab my equipment and head for the direction of the dissipating smoke. A crowd had gathered around bomb site. Rushing down a narrow alleyway I can already hear female shrieks of grief. A young boy runs past me crying. Emerging at the place which would have been the courtyard of the house, I see only rubble, desolation and a very large crater. Turban-clad men are digging into the rubble in an attempt to find survivors; or failing that, the bodies at least. The family had just been making breakfast when the bomb brought their home crashing down on top of them. A two-year-old girl, her mother and her grandmother have all been killed. The father is still under the rubble somewhere. Sudden cries from the excavators amid rubble being flung aside indicate that the father has been found. His unconscious body is quickly loaded onto a stretcher and rushed to what passes for the hospital. There is no electricity, no running water and the normal transport is a horse and cart for the rich, a donkey for the lucky and foot for everyone else.

Civilian casualties, though, are by no means the sole casualties in Afghanistan's most recent war. The following day as I drive back from an afternoon of filming at the front line my car passes a donkey carrying a stretcher. I stop to see what's happening. Loaded on the stretcher is a young majahedin, or to be more precise, a bloody lump of flesh. He has been blown up by a mine. Amazingly, he is still alive, though his body appears to be irredeemably shattered and his bones are protruding from his legs. His father is weeping uncontrollably with grief beside the stretcher.

We put him in our car and drive as fast as possible for the hospital. It will make little difference, though. He will die some hours later. A few days later I am at Bangi, a small village near the front line. I meet Pir Muhammad, the commander for the area. The village is typical in its mud-built walls and houses. People, though, are few and far between. Young children stand at doorways watching the mujahedin. Uniformly they are barefoot and shy. The bolder ones are soon helping the mujahedin unload weapons from the Russian-made jeeps. Soon all the children are stumbling under the weight of ammunition boxes as they carry the boxes down dusty alleyways to various houses in the village. One child is carrying RPG warheads. He cannot be more than five years old and the warhead is not much smaller than he.

Later I am driving towards the front with some of the mujahedin. There isn't much in the way of a road as we bump our way across the potholes. The discussion, over the sound of Indian music, revolves around my camera and whether they can have the pictures I take of them. I promise to bring the pictures back when I return. A Taliban tank spots our vehicle. The first intimation that I have of this, though, is the feeling that some invisible hand has reached out and rocked the entire car. Fractionally later, a messy cloud of smoke billows up about six meters behind the car and there is a dull crashing sound. "Fast," the mujahedin in the passenger seat screams to the driver. Suddenly we are speeding down the track, past deserted houses and fighters crouched in small orchards, as if we were in the last lap of the Camel Trophy race.

We reach the house where the local commander is billeted. he has watched our manic drive with amusement. We are invited in for tea. There are about 30 fighters billeted in the building and we all troop upstairs. There are mattresses on the floor around the edge of the room. An assortment of weapons are heaped casually in a corner. We have a perfect view of the sprawling orchards and fields that make up this part of the front line. It is still beautiful, despite the war. Conversation is interrupted only by the occasional squawk of a field radio. After tea it is time for the drive back.The end of another day in Afghanistan.

—**Roddy Scott**

Albania
★★★

The Return of the Albaniacs

In just a few short years Albania has had the distinction of changing from a country with the most paranoid and overcontrolled communist state ever to a country without a state.

It was tricky, but Albanians have risen to the challenge to become Europe's most lawless people at the turn of the century. Hey, look on the bright side. A holiday in Albania means none of the usual hassle with the cops. The chances of being arrested for dope in Bajram Curri—zilch. The possibility of being stopped for drunk driving—less than zilch. You're a wanna-be aspiring arms dealer? An AK-47 assault rifle was going for about US$50 in Tropoje.

Yes, the country where everything and anything goes can be reached for as little as US$200—if you live in Europe. There is, however, a slight catch in all this, which I guess I better mention. Being a foreigner, unless you happen to know a couple of the local banditos, you stand an excellent chance of being fleeced. The minute you walk in the door or open your mouth the $ signs will start ringing for just about everybody there—except you. In a country where the cops are the bandits (in the north, anyway) you might find yourself buying dope one minute and then explaining to your dealer's superior (cop, that is) just what you're doing with a few grams of hash.

The crisis in neighboring Kosovo brought foreigners flooding into Albania. The capital, Tirana, suddenly had hundreds of smart land-cruisers driving up and down its dilapidated boulevards. The mafia licked its lips and relieved as many of the occupants of their cars as they could. The head of the World Bank was one of many who had his car stolen at gunpoint in central Tirana one fine evening. Western Europe sent a multinational police force to advise and help their Albanian colleagues. No match for the mafia, though, they too joined the list of people whose cars were stolen by gun-toting Albaniacs in central Tirana after dark. Albania's fun all began in January 1997, when the inevitable end of pyramid investment schemes vaporized more than half of the Albanian population's savings. Having no one to blame except their own greed and gullibility, the people quickly blamed the government. Soon the riots and the looting escalated into full-scale anarchy. The "Albaniacs" were born. Thousands of repressed, newly impoverished people attacked, looted and burned banks, jails, museums, government buildings and armories until all were picked clean or destroyed. And the fun has pretty much continued ever since.

The concept of law and order is a quaint and outdated notion in today's Albania. Crooks arrested by the police are quickly released by the courts, leaving Albania with the distinction of being the one European country where policemen keep a low profile, while Kalashnikov-wielding bandits drive around in stolen UN pickups. And it's been a busy and profitable year for the Albanian gangs, especially the guys in the north of the country. There have been refugees to fleece, guerrillas to supply, foreigners to rob, feuds to conduct and homes to loot. Who says crime is easy? But never fear, their mates in the south have been busy, too. There have been refugees to smuggle out, large amounts of drugs to deliver and officials to bribe and intimidate. You know things are on the downhill slope when the Albanian prime minister comes out with comments like "the only modern thing about the port of Durres is the way money is made in dishonest ways." And when the first word that NATO's supreme commander, General Wesley Clark, learns in Albania is "baksheesh," things are pretty rock bottom. With customs and harbor fees yet another outdated notion in the land of the Albaniacs, ships with heavily armed crews cruised into Durres, forcing officials and the rest of the unhappy gang to unload their wares at gunpoint. Fearing that Albania would become the laughing stock of Europe's policing fraternity, the government ordered commandos to take over the port in August 1999. With the police banned from the port, things have become trickier for the mafia, supposedly.

Its been boom time in Albania for much of 1999. Albanians might say that they hate Slobadan Milosevic, but they love the guy really. Slobo's rather silly notion that he could take on NATO in a game of "you hit me, I hit you" gave Albanians the chance to apply their "Albanian school of higher business" from theory into practice, sending the Albanian economy into a boom. Okay, Okay, so it was a boom for guns, drugs, refugee smuggling and banditry. But lets not be too

BOSNIA-
HERZEGOVINA

SERBIA

Valbonë

Han i Hotit

Lake
Scutari

Bajzë
Koplik

Shkodër

Drin

2

Bajram
Curri

Laqi i
Roman

1

Laq i të
Dejës

Pukë

4

Ligeni i
Fierzës

Kukës

Buena

Adriatic
Sea

Shëngjin

Lezhë

Rrëshen

Zall-Reç

6

Drini i zi

3

Milot

Rubik

Laç

Burrel

7

Peshkopi

Klos

8

Krujë

5

Mat

9

Shijak

10

Mat

Durrës

Tiranë

11

MACEDONIA

Kavajë

12

Librazhd

Rrogozhinë

Elbasan

Shkumbin

Lake
Ohrid

Cërrik

Lushnjë

13

Gramsh

Pogradec

17

Lake
Prespa

Seman

Qyteti
Stalin
(Kuçovë)

16

Fier

14

Berat

Osum

Devoll

Maliq

15

Korçë

19

18

Ballësh

Vjosë

Selenicë

Vlorë

Mavrovë

21

Çorovodë

Strait of
Otranto

N

Këlcyrë

2

Ersekë

25

Tepelenë

22

Përmet

24

Gjirokastër

Delvinë

GREECE

Sarandë

23

ALBANIA

Albania

⊛ National Capital

◉ Region Capital

● Secondary City

Primary Road

Railroad

Administrative Border

0   25 km

0   25 mi

finicky, now, shall we? It's all demand led and we're all supposed to support the free market these days.

A war to supply has kept the arms dealers busy, making more than a few millionaires in the country. Of the 1 million weapons and 1.5 billion rounds of ammunition looted in 1997, more than a few found their way to the Kosovo Liberation Army—for the right price—fighting the Serbs in neighboring Kosovo. Tons of weapons went by the tractorload to the KLA camps of Papaj and then Padesh in the far northeast of Albania. Naturally there were more than a few tiffs and arguments about who should be controlling the lucrative gun trade up in Bajram Curri, where scores tend to be settled firmly and permanently. Blood Feuds R Us. What do you do if your brother is shot dead in an ambush and you are the chief of police in Bajram Curri? Why, it's simple. You resign your post and go after the culprits. That, at least is the story of Fatmir Hakraj, who was chief of police and his brother was ambushed and killed. Going back to the police station, he resigned and walked out—wasting a fellow policeman, who was suspected of complicity in the murder, as he left the station. Then, so history relates, he zapped another eight people—one person for every bullet hole in his dead brother's body. Mission accomplished, he rejoined the police. That's the Albanian justice system for you. Er, quite.

There was a bit of a property boom, too. The en masse expulsion of as many as 700,000 Kosovar refugees from their homes, by the Serbs, sent real estate in Albania to its highest value since Albanians were allowed to own property. Thousands of tired, semistarved and beaten Kosovars found themselves on the other side of the border, wondering where they would be staying for the rest of their lives. At least in the short term they had nothing to worry about. In a spirit of true generosity Albanians vacated their homes for the fleeing and demoralised Kosovars. Their Albanian kith and kin were given a roof over their heads. And the price? Why, merely three times the normal rent! For the inhabitants of Kukes, in northern Albania, one of the most forgettable towns in existence, it was boom time with a vengeance. The traditionally richer Albanian Kosovars found themselves forking out DM1,000 a month for accommodations. A discount compared to the US$200 a night the international media were being charged. For those Kosovars that could afford it the price of a ferry ride—with false papers—from Vlora to Italy was a mere US$1,100.

As for Albania's more traditional hardworking bandits, there's a good chance that most of them will be nearing nervous exhaustion. The sudden influx of large numbers of journos, aid workers and the like left them horribly overstretched. Extra family members had to be called up to cope with the work schedule. It was tough, but they knew that they had their reputations to consider. Doubtless they will all now be having a well-earned rest. In an effort to clamp down on crime in the north of the country, the government sent a special forces unit to Bajram Curri. The commander of the unit asked permission to kill about 20 people leading the gangs. The government said "no" and the special forces all went home, leaving business as usual in Bajram Curri.

To be honest, Albania's bandits and gunrunners weren't the only people to benefit from the Kosovo crisis. Albania's economy in general got an unexpected boost from the bombing campaign and the influx of half Kosovos population. Albania's central bank has done a bit of adding up and reckons that the country has been left with a whole US$30 million more in its second quarter of 1999 (about the same Uncle Sam spends on one night of Baghdad pyrotechnics!). Aid agencies flooded to Albania to set up camps and hospitals for refugees. By far the best camp, with its own hospital, E-mailing system and meals three times a day, was the camp established by the United Arab Emirates. Other aid agencies were of a less orthodox type. The Islamic Revival Foundation, for example, had more than just food on the menu when Albanian police dropped round for a chat one day. Guns and bombs were found in one raid. Suspicious types began to hang round the U.S. embassy and memories of Nairobi began to make diplomats a leeetle bit nervous. Yes, you've guessed it: the Osmana bin Laden fan club had arrived in Albania to join in the fun. Having taken advantage of Albania's lax immigration regulations (most people want to leave, not enter), they asked directions to the U.S. embassy, no doubt wanting to inquire about travel to the States. Americans began describing themselves as Canadian and avoided the embassy. Meanwhile, back at the ranch in Tirana, what passes for government has been going about its daily business. In December 1998, former premier Sali Berisha took time out from calling the current premier, Pandeli Majko "mentally deranged" and sat down at a table with him. For his part, Majko temporarily stopped calling Berisha's Democratic party a "maternity ward for crime." How heartwarming.

Not that much has subsequently happened. The shrewder political analysts aren't putting any money on anything as radical as a normal government emerging. Ever. Not to say that the government has not been making the right kind of noises. In a visit to Tropoje the minister for jokes (law and order) declared that the government would "mercilessly . . . attack anyone who will dare cycle crime in this district." History does not relate what the local bandits had to say about this . . . that is, when they had stopped laughing.

On a more serious note, Albania is one of DP's tips for future Balkan wars. We all know that things are not cool in Albania just at the moment, but they could be getting even less cool (or a lot hotter) in the future.

By late October 1999, Pandeli Majko sensibly decided that he'd had enough as premier of the Albaniacs. What was it? The abysmal salary? He couldn't take the name-calling? Whatever it was, he resigned ostensibly to make way for a new coalition government. But the kids in his party (the Socialists) decided that they couldn't be bothered to include the Democrats led by Sali Berisha in anything as exotic as a coalition government. Berisha was not chuffed.

Of course, we at DP should point out that there is no such thing as a government in Albania.

But lets not travel down the path of abuse for its own sake, shall we? There are serious issues here. For Socialists, by the way, you should read "Tosks," being the ethnic boys and girls who live in the south of Albania. For Democrats you should read "Ghegs," being the kids who live in the north. And this is where things start getting complicated and going wrong. The Tosks and the Ghegs like each other about as much as Kosvovar Albanians like Serbs. And their respective leaders, Sali Berisha and former premier Nano, like each other even less on a personal basis. And there's nothing they get more kicks from than merrily feuding away.

So, what's all the hassle then? After all, they've had years to feud away to little avail. The hassle is that things have changed of late. By a small coincidence the

Kosovar Albanians are also Ghegs, and now that there are no Serbs to boss them around people are getting a tad worried that they might start supporting their kith and kin in northern Albania against the southern Tosks. One minor clash might be all that is needed for third series in DP's ongoing saga of "Return of the Albaniacs." Stay tuned.

Albania is the country where most of the population would rather be living somewhere else. Fifteen percent of the 1991 population have left the country . . . mostly as illegal immigrants for the European Union. Blood feuds are now making a popular comeback, replacing a nonexistent judicial system. None of which should be any surprise, as Albania is one of the poorest countries in Europe and has vacillated between communism, democracy and anarchy since it proclaimed independence on November 28, 1912, after a history of Roman, Byzantine and Turkish domination.

Order totally disintegrated in Albania in early March 1997, when rage over collapsing investment schemes—in which half the population lost their entire life savings—plunged Albania into anarchy. Albanians pillaged hundreds of thousands of weapons from government armories during the chaos. Some 500,000 of these weapons remain in the hands of private citizens. Since then Albania has calmed to a more normal state of affairs of daily robbery and smuggling. The mafia has taken the opportunity to get a bit more organized. Almost 70 percent of the drugs reaching Germany and Switzerland come via Albania. Busy bees, as ever, alliances have been forged with the Sicilian mafia in the form of the Sacra Corona Unita (United Holy Crown . . . un-holy surely?), to facilitate the smuggling of . . . well, pretty much anything, actually, to Italy.

To all intents and purposes Albania is now run by the international community. NATO is trying to train what passes for an army, the Italians are trying to teach Albanian customs officers the meaning of the word *honest* and police officers the meaning of the word *law*. And the UN is trying to help the burgeoning number of aid agencies operating in Albania.

Ex- Prime Minister Pandeli Majko

A man given an unenviable task who then quickly bailed. He was in charge of a country that was in a shambles—when he was actually in charge, that is. The head of the Socialist Party, he came to power in the aftermath of 1997's anarchy. At 31 he was the youngest prime minister in Europe. He quickly grew up and quit learning on the job that there really is no government in Albania. To find out who's in charge check out:

http://president.gov.al/
http://www.hri.org/news/balkans/ata/
Email: postmaster@minjash.tirana.al

Sali Berisha

The man who thought that pyramid schemes were a sound basis for an economy. Now heading up the opposition, he spends most of his time sulking in the north of the country and wondering if it's time to make a comeback. Charismatic Berisha played hardball during the unrest but finally gave in to demands that he set up an interim government until new elections could be held. He's a lucky guy. On June 4, 1997, someone chucked a grenade at Berisha during a campaign appearance. The assailant's aim was perfect, but he forgot to pull the pin—or, in the Albaniac tradition of weapons proficiency, perhaps didn't realize there was a pin that needed to be pulled.

E-mail: presec@presec.tirana.al

Criminal Gangs

Albania's gangs are the envy of gangs all around the world. Whereas in places like Turkey and Russia gangs tend to be in cahoots with the politicos, in Albania much of the time they simply don't bother. There is no government. Well, most of the time. The idea of the government cracking down on them is laughable. Government authority barely goes north of Tirana (or south, for that matter). Local mafias and criminal gangs took over the southern half of Albania in March 1997. And they've stayed put ever since. As for the north . . . well, the less said the better, quite frankly. Certain criminal clans run whole sections of the economy in the form of smuggling cigarettes and coffee.

In 1999 it was the boys in the north of the country who got most of the limelight, robbing anyone they could at gunpoint. Not to be outdone, the Vlora mafia were sending ferryloads of Kosovar refugees to Italy on forged documents for US$1,100 per person. The local police, suffering temporary (or is it permanent?) illiteracy, didn't manage to spot any of the fake documents. Only acidic telephone calls from the Italian Foreign Ministry managed to put a slight stop to such blatant racketeering.

NATO

The arrival of thousands of NATO troops almost made Albania an honorary member of the alliance. Well, it might have done if the Albanian army had managed to keep any of its weapons after 1997. I jest, but you take the point. Albania's army is, like everything else, shambolic. Now NATO is training—sorry, trying to train—the army. NATO troops were about the only people who were not robbed in Albania. Yes, even the Albanians thought twice about trying to snaffle an Apache.

http://www.nato.int/pfp/al/albania.htm

The Albanian government no longer requires visas of U.S. citizens for stays up to 30 days. A passport is required. A US$10 airport fee must be paid to Albanian customs officials upon departure. However, depending on where you enter and where you leave from, nobody really bothers looking at the time you have spent in the country. The ferry between Corfu and Sarande is working in the south again. For specific entry/exit requirements, travelers can contact the following:

Embassy of the Republic of Albania

2100 S Street, NW
Washington, DC 20008
Tel.: (202) 223-4942
Fax: (202) 628-7342
http://www.embassyworld.com/embassy/albania1.htm

Albania used to have a low rate of crime . . . a long, long time ago. However, crimes against tourists (robbery, mugging and pickpocketing) are waiting to happen, especially on city streets after dark. Credit cards, personal checks and traveler's checks are rarely accepted in Albania. In addition, hotel accommodations outside Tirana are very limited, and even confirmed reservations are sometimes not honored. Transportation is rudimentary and, in a word, sucks. The roads are rubbish (where they exist), and if you want to be remotely comfortable you should hire a land cruiser. The infrastructure in the south is generally better than the north. Hotels are either upscale or cockroach motels. Most folks stay with the locals.

U.S. Embassy

Rruga E Elbasanit 103
Tirana, Albania
Tel.: (355-42) 32875.

The North

The most lawless place in Europe. A drive into northern Albania will take you back to the Wild West. Once you go north of Krume, on the Bajram Curri road, you're in bandit country. And driving in a land-cruiser, you might as well put up a sign saying "rob me." Unless you're with a local who knows the gang, consider yourself fair game. A police escort, perhaps? you might be thinking to yourself. Unlikely to be of any assistance, DP can inform you. Hacks with a police escort suddenly discovered their escorts didn't know where the safety catch on the AK was. The bandits did, though.

Tirana

Fine during the day. It's after dark that you should be careful. The number of foreigners—including foreign police officers helping to train the Albanian police—who have had vehicles stolen at gunpoint is considerable. Definitely not advisable to carry large quantities of cash. The slight hitch is that credit cards are rarely accepted. The Tirana International hotel does accept credit cards, though. Muggings and theft are common.

Everywhere Else

The south is much calmer these days. The boys in blue might be stretched in a bit of a thin line, but they are still there . . . ready to go off duty at a moment's notice. There are still at least 500,000 unaccounted for weapons floating round he country. Efforts by the police to arrest unauthorized and armed men have met with little success. But generally speaking, there is less risk traveling in the south.

Pyramid Schemes

Imagine hundreds of thousands of drunken, armed Americans terrorizing the streets of Washington after Tupperware and Amway go bankrupt. Well, that's what happened in Albania in 1997. Some of the Albanian investment schemes involved the mafia laundering the proceeds of smuggled oil from Libya and Iraq to Serbia via Montenegro. Pyramid schemes were then used to launder the dirty oil money, which was then unloaded into the Albanian national bank. This got the government involved, as the boys in office borrowed the cash to help pay off its massive national debt. Liking what they saw, the Albanian people started getting into the pyramid game by investing their life savings in the schemes. When the smaller pyramids—such as Gjallica, Sudja, and Populli—started going broke, investors wanted their money back. Oops. Meanwhile, the larger schemes saw what was happening and pooled their resources in an attempt to get a license as a private bank. Mafia cash is the suspected reason why pyramid companies such as Vefa survive.

Camera Crews

The list of networks robbed by Albanian bandits grows ever longer. The BBC, the Associated Press, Sky TV . . . you name them and they'll probably be on the list. In 1997 it was all in the south of the country. In 1999 the northerners had a chance to catch up on what they had missed out on. Satphones, Betacams, cash, computers . . . the paraphernalia of modern journalism in dodgy places was all gratefully received by the Krume and Bajram Curri gangs.

Glow Worms

In April 1997, the director of the Albanian army's chemistry unit, Colonel Asllan Bushati, appealed to some folks who unwittingly stole radioactive materials and lethal chemicals from four military bases to return the hazardous material, including cobalt and strontium, to the authorities. The bandits were also implored not to abandon the material in a field, as the radiation could enter the human food chain.

There is one doctor for every 574 people in this country of 3.3 million inhabitants.

Condé Nast Traveler naively touted Albania as "The Next Place," and it may be if you make your vacation plans 12 years ahead. In the meantime, the country will have some growing pains to ride out. The government estimates that 750,000 weapons and 3,600 tons of explosives were looted from over 1,200 army depots. So far only 25,000 have been returned. Vulnerable to riots, mayhem and anarchy, lowly Albania lies at the southeastern end of the Adriatic Sea. It gained its independence from Turkey in 1913 and became a Stalinist communist state in 1944. Its first multiparty elections were held in 1991. And it's been pretty rough sailing since. The country possesses Europe's least developed transportation system. In fact, private cars were prohibited until 1991. The telephone system is antiquated, so expect connections to take a long time. For international calls your best bet is to go to the Tirana International Hotel. Muslims comprise about 70 percent of the population, while Greek Orthodox account for 20 percent and Roman Catholics 10 percent. Ninety-eight percent of the population is ethnic Albanian, officially, although ethnic Greeks in Albania contend their own group makes up about 10 percent of Albania's population. Marijuana is widely grown in Albania. There is one doctor for every 574 people in this country of 3.3 million inhabitants. The official language here is Albanian, and the currency is the New Lek. And for one buck you will be the proud owner of about 140 Lek.

ALBANIA

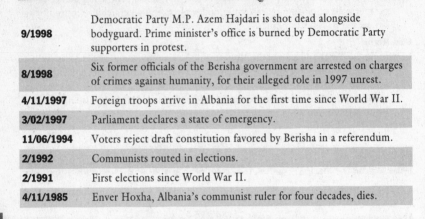

9/1998	Democratic Party M.P. Azem Hajdari is shot dead alongside bodyguard. Prime minister's office is burned by Democratic Party supporters in protest.
8/1998	Six former officials of the Berisha government are arrested on charges of crimes against humanity, for their alleged role in 1997 unrest.
4/11/1997	Foreign troops arrive in Albania for the first time since World War II.
3/02/1997	Parliament declares a state of emergency.
11/06/1994	Voters reject draft constitution favored by Berisha in a referendum.
2/1992	Communists routed in elections.
2/1991	First elections since World War II.
4/11/1985	Enver Hoxha, Albania's communist ruler for four decades, dies.

In a Dangerous Place: Albania-Kosovo Border

UCK: Utter Chaos in Kosovo

Access, they say, is everything. And never more so than in a war zone. So when NATO started its bombardment of a defiant Slobodan Milosevic, the hacks slung out of Kosovo naturally looked for a way back in. For this we all needed the good offices of the Kosovo Liberation Army (KLA), more often known by their cyrillic initials U«K, (Ushtria «lirimtare E Kosoves). It is a bright and sunny morning as we set out from Bajram Curri in northern Albania. We're bumping along in the back of a British- made Land Rover which, given that it is being driven by northern Albanians, is almost certainly stolen. It has "police" written on the side, although the hawk-faced older man and the two jean-clad youths with pistols stuck in their pockets constituted the most unlikely bunch of policemen I had ever seen, well . . . except maybe in Africa.

Beside me in the back two Kalashnikov assault rifles lie on the floor of the Land Rover. We are heading for the border, in an attempt to cross into Kosovo with the KLA guerrillas and cover the ongoing war, as NATO bombardments rose to ever greater levels of severity. Days previously I had watched Nato bombers hit Serb positions near the Kosovar town of Djackova. The bombers were just visible: appearing like small silverfish in a clear blue sky. High-pitched keening sounds had preceeded vast plumbs of earth rising into the sky. If there were any surviving Serb soldiers they must have had some deity watching over them. The bombs had hit in quick succession, the earth sprouting brown fingers as columns of dust and smoke rose into the air one after another. And as our Land Rover bumped along the potholed track that led to the KLA border camps I mused on how much damage the NATO bombardment was doing to the Serb troops. Certainly, the KLA were making little headway in their battle against the Serbs. Neither had they been particularly accommodating to journalists.

We pull up at the KLA camp of Padesh. The opposite hilltop is Kosovo. The area is littered with tents and KLA soldiers are cooking breakfast over fires. For the most part they are young. Many of them have come from abroad, volunteering after the NATO strikes and mass deportations began. We slither down a hilltop and approach a farmhouse, looking for the now notorious KLA press officer whose unhelpfulness to hacks was already legendary. A youth emerges form the old stone house. Dressed in combat fatigues, a straggling beard and a peaked cap. "You are journalists?" We are indeed. "Very well. There are a number of regulations concerning the activity of journalists in our areas." We have just met the press officer. His voice is a toneless monotone, the archetypal bureaucrat, I cannot help thinking while he recites the rules as if he has learned them by rote. "Perhaps you would like to read the rules later; but let me tell you that journalists are only allowed here between 11 A.M. and 3 P.M." I look at him in disbelief. It sounds a bit like hospital visiting hours. And as for reading the rules, which probably verge either on the idiotic or are simply common sense mixed with a dose of security for all concerned, there is nothing I would like to do less. But, my whims are—quite rightly—irrelevant here. My train of thought is broken into by the press officer: "Now, to enter Kosovo you must fill out an application form." This is getting worse.

The press officer disappears briefly into the stone-built farmhouse and re-emerges clutching two forms. "If you would like to sit down at the table," he says pointing to a dilapidated-looking wooden table with benches either side, "you can fill out these forms. Your applications will be duly considered and we will let you know the result tomorrow." We sit down to fill out the forms. From a nearby hilltop, a firefight erupts. The sound of small arms echoes across the valley, interspersed by occasional chatter of a heavy machine gun. The noise reaches a crescendo and suddenly quiets, only to start again minutes later. The situation feels surreal. Filling out application forms in the middle of a war zone. And if the KLA had numerous small arms there was one thing they lacked: heavy artillery. But the Serbs didn't. We can hear the scream of the first shell for seconds before its impact. A dusty plume of smoke gathers some 400 meters away on the hilltop opposite, which is technically Kosovo. The Serbs are shelling the road the KLA use for bringing in supplies.

A group of KLA soldiers, laden with ammunition clips and assault rifles, trudge up the hill toward us. Beads of perspiration have formed on their foreheads, below their helmets. I know one of them. He is a former British Royal Marine commando called Ronnie, who has linked up with the KLA. They are returning from the front line for two days rest in what is technically Albania. "I tell you it's crazy on down there," says Ronnie with a jerk of his head in the direction of the front lines. "I've seen more action in two days here than I saw in the whole of the Falklands war." "Oh yeah," adds Ronnie, "you see where all those shells are landing . . . well that's the road you're going to be taking. Have fun mate." He picks up his assault rifle and troops back up the hill, heading for the another camp called Papaj. For the next ten minutes there is a steady scream of incoming shells, which nobody pays much attention to as they all seem to fall just out of range. It all seems to resemble scene from Monty Python as I list the equipment I want to take to the front lines, write out my passport number and stipulate the number of days I want to spend in Kosovo—whilst just 400 meters away there is the steady howl and then *budumfff* of incoming shells landing. I finish my application form and add my signature with a flourish. "Yes, please come back at 11 A.M. tomorrow morning," says the press officer.

With some resignation we make our way back to the car and head back to Bajram Curri for another night in Banditville. The following morning we return to Padesh and are greeted by a different officer. He has come from Switzerland and speaks to us in French. "Yes, your applications have been approved," he says handing me a piece of paper, which turns out to be a one-day permit to "enter Kosovo." "As you know," says the officer, "entry hours to Kosovo are between 11 A.M. and 3 P.M. If you would like to wait a while, we will prepare an escort for you." I pull my flak jacket and helmet from my backpack, check my equipment and then sit down on the grass. An hour or so later the "escort" is ready. We walk for about 20 minutes. Just as I am about to step over a piece of fencing wire lying on the ground the officer jumps ahead. Holding out his palm in a vertical stop sign says with a smile, "Alors, you are now entering Kosovo. Do you have your passport and the correct visa?" Yes, ha ha, very funny. We trudge further through trees and bushes. I am constantly scanning the ground in front of me for any signs of freshly moved earth, the usual indicator of mines. It's probably a futile exercise, but it helps calm my paranoia.

We reach the KLA barracks that had days earlier been mistakenly precision bombed by NATO, killing seven KLA soldiers. Almost a quarter of the barracks has been reduced to rubble. There are only a few KLA soldiers milling around the place. Most are now at the front lines. I ask if we can go to the front lines. The officer looks at his watch. "Maybe another time. We must return soon." I look at him and wonder if he is terminally stupid, or just mentally retarded. Apart from a bit of film of the barracks I have done nothing, and certainly do not have what we hacks like to call "a story." I wonder what he thinks the point of bringing journalists into Kosovo is, if he can think at all.

We have lunch, which consists of a good soup, at the barracks. "So, if everybody is ready we will now return," says the officer.

—**Roddy Scott**

Algeria
★★★★★

The Triangle of Death

Ever since one of the 20 companions of Hercules founded a trading center here, Algeria has been rocked by rebellion and warfare. The Romans, Vandals, Hafsids, Merenids, pirates (the famous home base of Barbarossa, aka Red Beard and the Barbary pirates), Spanish, Arabs, Turks and French all pillaged, abused and destroyed the former breadbasket of the Roman Empire. The current killing is gaining rapidly on the 250,000 body count racked up by the French in their eight-year "Vietnam" from 1954–1962. Today the war is a sick soap opera where the former terrorists (FLN) and current leaders let the new rebels (GIA) destroy their own people and future political legitimacy. There is also firm suspicion that the body count is helped by right-wing killers who play tit-for-tat.

Most of the killing takes place just outside Algiers and in Algeria's Mitidja Plain. This fertile, and now dirt-cheap and deadly, farmland stretches southward from the outskirts of Algiers, and is called the Triangle of Death. An apt name for what may well be the most deadly real estate since Cambodia's Killing Fields. This is the stomping grounds of the insurgent Armed Islamic Group (GIA), the radical, genocidal rebel group trying to oust the presidency of Abdelaziz Bouteflika and

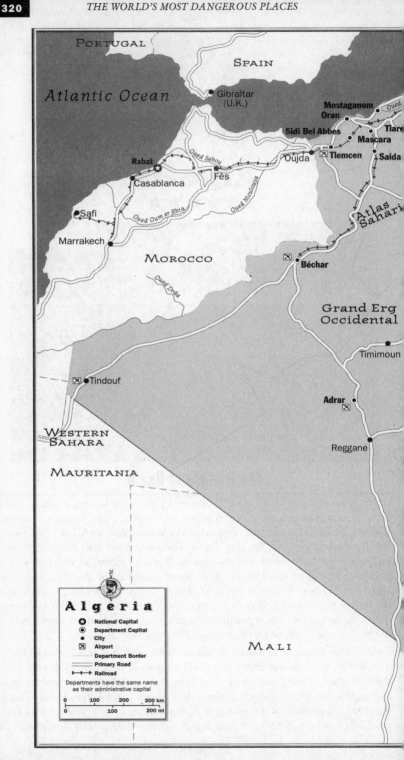

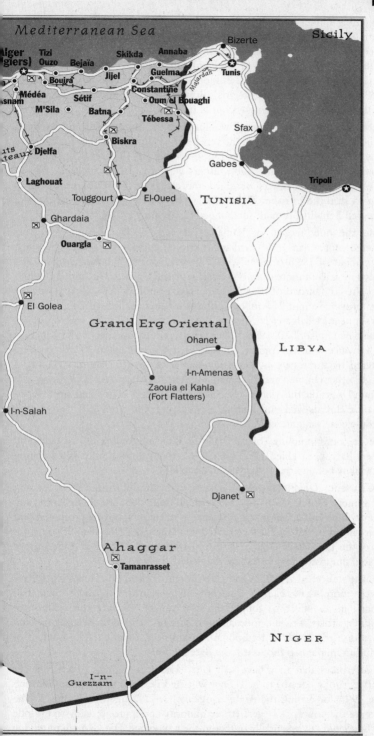

the lingering influence of Liamine Zeroual, Algeria's most recent leader. Between 80,000 and 120,000 people have died (with at least 500,000 displaced), many of them fertilizing this valley with their blood. Here, the most common item can become an executioner's weapon: rusty knives, axes, homemade bombs, hoes, grenades fashioned from Coke cans and rakes. All are used to slaughter old men, schoolgirls, farmboys, teachers and anyone else who gets in the GIA's way, or even stays out of it.

In February 1997, the GIA said it would "slash the throats of all apostates and their allies" and set "explosions in the very heart of Algiers and Blida." They have certainly made good on their threats. On September 22, 1997, in Bentalha, eight miles south of Algiers, some 300 villagers were killed in a six-hour orgy of violence as army helicopters observed the slaughter from overhead, doing nothing to stop the carnage. The guerrillas slipped away at sunrise as easily as they entered Bentalha, though surrounded by the army's tanks.

During the holy month of Ramadan in early 1998, Muslim insurgents slaughtered more than 1,200 civilians (some estimates say 2,000). The worst single incident of 1998 occurred on January 11 during Ramadan, when GIA extremists massacred more than 100 civilians in Sidi Hamed. On April 11, 1999, rebels slashed the throats of 18 civilians at a fake roadblock in the Zelamta area of Mascara province about 250 miles southwest of Algiers. Ten civilians had their throats slit near Mellah area in Mascara Province about 187 miles west of Algiers the same day. On April 27, 1998, GIA guerrillas cut the throats of 43 villagers in Madea Province, south of Algiers. On May 14, 1997, more than 30 villagers were slaughtered by the rebels in the sleepy hamlet of Douar Daoud, including 2 infants, 15 other children and 7 women. On April 16, the bodies of 4 young girls were found outside the village of Chaib Mohammed. They had been raped before their throats were slit. During only one week in April 1997, more than 140 people were slaughtered.

These are only samplings of the daily nightlife in Algeria. More than 100 foreigners have been killed here since 1992, though none were killed during 1998 (namely because there were none left to kill).

The GIA sends *DP* crudely assembled and energetically written faxes claiming that all singers, artists, journalists, soldiers and policemen are nonbelievers, and that they will be killed. There was no mention of lawyers, boxing promoters and used-car salesmen, but take it for granted you are marked for death if you enter Algiers or the Triangle of Death. (Despite the warnings, *DP* visited Algiers to see these rabid dumpster dogs and share the negative vibes.)

Since the cancelled 1991 Algerian elections, radical fundamentalists have murdered more than 22,000 innocent people, including more than 100 foreigners, in an effort to topple the government. Among the victims are playwrights, artists, singers, journalists, politicians, and even schoolgirls who refuse to don the *hejab,* or traditional Muslim head covering. The number of slain Muslim militants is thought to be over 20,000.

The GIA brags that they have sent Cheb Hasni (a popular Algerian singer whom they shot to death) to hell. They whacked Berber singer Lounes Matoub in June 1998 for dissing the Arabic language (see "Dangerous Things"). The Berbers are the country's largest ethnic minority and a group ready to explode after a July 1998 law essentially outlawed their language. The GIA communique to *DP* went on to say, "Now we will start with the journalists, the poets and the soldiers. Belly dancing is a prayer to Satan. When Satan's messengers give a direction to people, they dance." They ask that if you dance, please stay out of Algeria. Not an entirely surprising request in post-disco Algeria.

The fundamentalists' threats are not just the rhetoric of bored bullies. Journalists are under a direct threat of immediate execution if they enter the country; more than 70 have been killed and 700 have fled. Wearing glasses, Western clothes or even looking educated can make you a target. It is estimated that the entire wealth of this country of 28 million is in the hands of only about 5,000 people.

Algeria is no stranger to hatred and death. Eight years of cruel warfare with the French started back in 1954. During this period, a quarter of a million people were killed and more than a million *pied noirs* (black feet), or white colonists, were forced out. Despite the messy divorce, Algeria's 133-year marriage to France has made it more French than Arabic.

France has always had a love-hate relationship with Algeria, due more to its geographical proximity than to its cultural dissimilarities. In Algeria, Russia has found a major customer for its military hardware and expertise, and Italy makes sure Algeria continues to pump out the oil and gas it needs to keep those Fiats and Ferraris topped off.

Algerian militants are training at military bases in Sudan, and financially supported by Iran. Most of the trainees were veterans of the Afghan war and traveled to Sudan via Iran. These militants are trained to add to the core of the underground Islamic fundamentalist movement held responsible for the killing of hundreds of members of Algeria's security forces. For now the world pretends that Algeria doesn't exist.

Algeria has become now the world's second most dangerous place for travelers, after Chechnya. Not much of a tourist bullet point, but that's the only good news we found. It is still a country where whacked-out fundamentalists and ultraright terrorists turned military turned government fight to the bitter end.

The rebel groups, seeming bored with killing and barbequeing helpless villagers, occupy themselves by blowing each other away. The FIS and GIA and splinter groups of the GIA have decided to take out each other. The resulting civil strife is similar to that in Somalia and southern Lebanon.

A Day at the Office

"Expat workers travel from the living quarters compound to the worksite only a couple of kilometers away under heavy military escort," wrote an American expat to DP who works for Sonatrach, the Algerian Oil & Natural Gas Co. "We are not allowed to leave the worksite or the compound without this escort. A ship docks twice a week at the worksite for expats only and crosses to Cagliari, Sardinia, for R&R or for flights out. For the army, guarding expats is better than fighting terrorists in the mountains. The army will not win until they learn and are willing to fight at night."

Abdelaziz Bouteflika and the Government ("The Power")

Ex-president Liamine Zeroual's former foreign minister Abdelaziz Bouteflika is calling the shots these days, by default. The April 1999 elections were billed as democratic; however, on April 14, 1999, two days before the election, Bouteflika's six opponents pulled out of the race en masse to protest Zeroual's refusal to meet with them over charges of election fraud. The fact that Zeroual refused to let foreign monitors have a peek at the process propped up the crybabies' claims. It ain't the first time ole' Zeroual's tilted the scales. His, and the army's, cancellation of 1991 elections the Islamic Salvation Front (FIS) was well on its way to winning set off the current Muslim extremist campaign of throat-slashing and chainsaw manicures in the Algerian countryside. Bouteflika once served as right-hand man to Houari Boumedienne, the army colonel who, in 1965, overthrew Algeria's first civilian president, Ahmed Ben Bella. When a reporter asked Bouteflika if it was time for the army to surrender political power, he replied, "Not yet."

The military is directly in control of the High Security Council, with General Khaled Nezar, the leader of the Algerian military, pulling the strings. Security forces have made huge gains in 1999 against the GIA, forcing the guerrillas to concentrate more on military targets than innocent peasants. But with Bouteflika's dream, come-from-behind victory, no jugulars will be safe in Algeria any time soon

Algeria: Africa's Burma?

Liamine Zeroual's annulment of the 1991 elections, which the FIS appeared to be winning hands-down, has traditionally been met with the same international condemnation that Burma's SLORC rulers faced after dishonoring the results in that country's elections in 1989, which the National League for Democracy had won hands-down. But little known, or equally remembered, was the FIS pronouncement at the time that should they win, the elections would be Algeria's last.

The Also-rans

Ex-premier Mouloud Hamrouche, former foreign minister Ahmed Taleb Ibrahimi, Islamic Movement for National Reform candidate Abdallah Djaballah, former Zeroual consultant Youcef Khatib and representatives of ailing Socialist Forces Front (FFS) leader, Hcine Ait Ahmed and ex-prime minister Mokdad Sifi, were the six dudes who pulled out of the race at the 11th hour alleging the army was pressuring voters and handing out dummy ballots pressed with the government seal. They claim they will not recognize Bouteflika's presidency. Now, let's see who else won't. Seventy-five percent of Algeria's population is under 30 years old, the golden years of angst. Hold onto your seats.

The Final Tally

Although Abdelaziz Bouteflika was the only candidate in the April 1999 elections, he received only 74% of the vote. We have to assume the other 26 percent went to Pat Robertson or Pat Paulsen.

Islamic Salvation Front, Front Islamique du Salut (FIS)

The Islamic fundamentalist FIS, founded in March 1989, was once a strong political party that should have been in power, but was banned by the Algerian government after the

1991 elections were voided. The FIS signed a peace agreement on September 24, 1997, to essentially show that the GIA is conducting the grisly killings.

FIS leader Shaykh Abassi Madani (who did his doctorate at London's Institute of Education) and his hawkish deputy, Ali Belhadj, were released from jail and transferred to a cushy villa under house arrest in an effort to strike a compromise with the fundamentalists, but put back in jail after the government refused to meet the leaders' demands. But in another conciliatory gesture to the rebels, Madani was freed on parole in July 1997, although his influence over the rebels has waned. Most consider Abdelkader Hachani the next FIS leader until he was killed on Nov. 22, 1999. Hachani was sentenced in July 1997 to five years in prison, but was then freed by authorities. Ali Belhadj (b. 1955) was a former teacher and Imam of a mosque. He was imprisoned twice before for antigovernment views.

The government's policy of attacking and jailing FIS leaders has had the same effect Hercules had on the Hydra. Instead of one unified Islamic group, they now had dozens of smaller groups, each with a different agenda and approach.

Armed Islamic Group, Groupe Islamic Armee, el-Djama'a el-islamia el Mosalaha (GIA)

The GIA, numbering between 20,000 and 25,000 fighters are organized into tiny, unrelated and sometimes warring divisions. Some say their headquarters is in the Hatatba Mountains 50 miles south of Algiers. At its core are some of the most heartless and cruel men on earth: Algerian veterans of the Afghan war, or mujahedin. They're hard, brutal religious zealots trained in Sudan, battle-tested in Afghanistan and bankrolled by Iran.

Formed by Djamel Zitouni, alias Abou Aberrahmane Amine, the GIA split away from the FIS, disagreeing violently with its softer position. Zitouni was killed on July 16, 1996, during infighting that led to the split of the GIA into three factions. The "mainstream" GIA is now led by Miloud Hebbi or Slimane Mehrezi, depending on who you talk to. The faction that followed Zitouni is led by Antar Zouabri (aka Abu Talha), and is considered one of the most brutal. It was rumored he was killed in a July '97 shootout with the army, but Zouabri apparently rose from the dead to continue severing jugulars. It probably doesn't matter since the GIA has lost at least 12 leaders and/or commanders in five years. Realistically, no one knows the actual structure or leadership of this phantom organization.

One thing for sure, its most dreaded unit is called the Phalanx of Death, and it consists of many of the guerrillas based in the mountains in the southeast of Algiers. Phalanx commander Bekati Rabah (aka Abdelfattah) was whacked by government security forces in August 1998 while secretly visiting his family about 275 miles west of Algiers.

The government has had some other recent successes in blowing away GIA leaders. On August 12, 1998, security forces shot and killed Eulmi Hamou, 30, GIA commander for the regions of Constantine, Skikda and Guelma in the east of the country, after a month-long manhunt.

There is another GIA group led by Mustafa Kertali, that performs its massacres under the banner of the Islamic Movement for Preaching and Jihad (MIPJ). Kertali is believed responsible for whacking Zitouni. When politicians and academics are in the news for being dead, MIPJ is most likely to have written the headlines. Other leaders included El Mansouri El Miliani, Abdullah Qalek, Abdel-Haq Ayadia and Djafar El Afghani.

Few if any journalists have dared meet with the GIA because of its hatred toward Westerners and its lack of a clear focus or agenda. Some journos believe that the cut throats and cold-blooded massacres of rural peasants has more to do with a major land grab than politics, much the same way the PKK terrorizes small villages that might interfere with its lucrative heroin routes. The GIA has razed some 1,000 schools and executed at least 200 teachers. Of the 100-plus foreigners killed by militants in Algeria since 1992, most were victims of the GIA. The current leaders of Algeria are under a death sentence decreed in a *fatwa* by Sheik Abedel-Haq el Ayadia, one of the founders of the GIA. The *fatwa* is all encompassing and includes the people who support the government, including foreign workers and journalists.

The Italian mafia in Sicily and Naples are rumored to be the main hardware suppliers of the GIA arsenal. The law of the GIA is the Hadith el Quran (Koran) much like the Taliban's countrified version of shari'ah or Koranic law. The fighters can be found in the Algiers region and in the twisting backstreets of Algiers. One minor lifesaving point: The GIA is said to steer clear of Americans or Germans because their countries granted asylum to their leaders. No foreigners were killed by the GIA in 1998 in Algeria.

Partly due to criticism from Islamic extremist groups abroad against the GIA's campaign of attacking civilians—and partly due to recent army successes against the terrorists—defections in the GIA are continuing to add up. Dissident GIA leader Hassan Hattab in May 1998 publicly dissed GIA faction leader Antar Zouabri for his slaughter of civilians and in September 1998 split from his boss and created a new GIA offshoot, the Salafi Group for Call and Combat, charged primarily with attacking security force elements. Despite the defection from Zouabri, Hattab's faction continued to blow away Algerians throughout 1998. It was Hattab who whacked popular Berber singer Lounes Matoub in June 1998, an act that made Hattab the Mark Chapman of Algerian pop.

Now It Makes Sense

If you ever wondered how Muslim fundamentalists can justify killing and maiming in the name of God, this recent GIA fax to al-Hayat in London should clear things up for you: "We are that band, with God's permission, who kill and slaughter and we will remain so until the word of religion has prevailed and the word of God is raised high. Let everyone know that what we do in killing and slaughter and burning and pillaging is close to God." Might al-Hayat consider a rebuttal from the pope?

The Army and the "Eradicators"

Groups of 5 to 10 men in plain clothes work the inner city, while 35,000 troops man an "infernal arc" in the Mitidja between Algeria, Blida, Laarba and Medea. Out in the countryside, small groups of soldiers travel in helicopters and armored personnel vehicles to track down fundamentalists. It's clobbering time in Algeria. The annual U.S. report on human rights said there was "convincing evidence" of systematic torture and executions of suspected GIA and FIS insurgents. The right-wing groups are called "eradicators," the cops that guard the cities in the black ski masks are called "ninjas." According to some recent estimates, there are at least 5,000 local so-called "self-defense" or "patriotic" groups in place across the country. The GIA now almost invariably skips villages where these groups are well organized and well armed.

The Cops

Police and security forces in Algeria consist of three organizations: (1) the national police (DGSN); (2) an agency of the ministry of the interior, Gendarmerie (MOD); and (3) the communal guards, similar to village or small-town police with limited training and equipment. There is an ongoing problem with the terrorists infiltrating the ranks of all three. In addition, the terrorists have obtained hundreds of police uniforms and badges and have masqueraded as police to carry out terrorist and criminal operations. Some of these operations have included assassinations of GOA officials by terrorists operating fake police checkpoints. Throughout the war, terrorists have targeted GOA officials, journalists, foreigners and randomly selected Algerian citizens. But the cops and security forces have borne a large proportion of the targeting and, as such, suffered numerous casualties. The large number of deaths within the police forces, coupled with the uncertainty about fellow officers' loyalties, have resulted in low morale in the police ranks.

Algeria is calming down. The massacres have not stopped and the danger is still there, but fewer people die these days. Algeria does not issue visas to persons whose passports indicate previous travel to Israel or South Africa. Both "tourist" and business visas cost US$30. There isn't a predetermined length of stay. Instead, you must request the length of and reason for stay on the visa application. Visas permit entry into Algeria at authorized checkpoints by air, land or sea. At press time, Americans and other foreigners were permitted entry into Algeria from Libya, Mali, Tunisia, Niger and Mauritania. There is no entry into Algeria from Morocco. *DP* went in as a tourist, denying ourselves the luxury of an armed escort.

Journalists should transit through Paris because the city is a hub of numerous contacts of all political leanings within the Algerian expat/exile community. Among these folks are a number of Algerian journalists who can be contacted through French journalists. Journalists need six photos, your CV, two completed forms, a $32 money order made payable to the Embassy of Algeria, and you must tell them if you have been to Algeria before and wait two to three weeks. They probably just want to run your articles through the spellchecker.

On our way to Algeria for the blood-soaked local elections, someone from the foreign news desk of CBS called to see if we could send some of our footage back. When we told him that *DP* was going on a tourist visa and not as a heavily guarded journo he quickly hung up.

For more information concerning entry requirements, crazy travelers may contact:

Embassy of the Democratic and Popular Republic of Algeria

2137 Wyoming Avenue, NW
Washington, DC 20008
Tel.: (202) 265-2800
Fax: (202) 265-1978
E-mail: embalgus@cais.com

Tourists may be restricted in their movements and either monitored or escorted by the military. Theoretically, tourists are permitted in Algiers, the highway leading to Oran, as well as Oran itself and other towns along the coast, including Tlemcen. The border area northeast of Nefta on the Tunisian border may also be accessible, as well. Restricted areas include a huge swath of real estate in the Grand Erg Occidental with El Golea as the nucleus.

If a journalist wants to visit another area of the country other than Algiers, travel is restricted to air (via the domestic carrier, Inter-Air Services), and the itinerary must be cleared by authorities beforehand. In all likelihood, travel outside Algiers will be with a police or military escort. Even with an armed escort, travel in the Algerian countryside is hazardous. Journalists are not permitted to freely report on the civil war. For journalists, the best advice is to conduct business in your hotel, and have your interview subjects visit you at the hotel. Journalists are monitored and are usually assigned police or military escorts. It is illegal to move outside Algiers without them. Permission for independent travel is rarely granted. Those who slip away from their escorts and travel outside Algiers will be deported.

The government has rigorously enforced a late-night curfew in the central region around Algiers. Roadblocks are located at most of the major intersections and many others. The government isn't the only one setting up the blocks. Fake roadblocks are also set up by the GIA and others for the purposes of robbery and murder. There has been a slew of robbery and assault incidents involving foreigners, especially in the far southern region of Algeria near the border with Niger. Algeria south of Tamanrasset is particularly dangerous.

The two routes south across the Sahara are closed (there is an alternate route through Mauritania to Senegal). Foreign oil workers in the south bypass the north altogether, flying directly into their installations and living in highly secured compounds. Control Risks Group, a business consultant to companies doing business in foreign countries, rates Algeria as the most dangerous place in the world to do business. About 2,000 French citizens, mostly businessmen and diplomatic staff, remain in the country.

You can visit with one of the FIS leader in America. Anwar N. Haddam, president of the FIS Parliamentary Delegation Abroad, is currently in prison in Manassas, Virginia. Call (703) 792-6420

DP's Tips on Surviving Algeria

1. The government of Algeria is not wild about tourists. Even accredited journalists will be allowed entry only after approval from Algiers.

2. All accredited journalists are met on arrival by a protection team supplied without charge by the government.

3. In Algiers, journos can only stay at the Hotel al-Jezzair call: [213] (2) 59-10-00 or the Hotel Aurassi call: [213] (2) 64-82-52. Both are guarded 24 hours a day.

4. During your stay, you will be escorted at all times by the "ninjas," black-uniformed security police. You will be driven to meetings and escorted back to your hotel. The teams only operate in Algiers. For trips outside the city, taxis can be hired for about $60 a day from your hotel.

5. Those who want to wander around town will be given walkie-talkies. Do not wear these conspicuously. Do not stay in one place any longer than ten minutes (the typical time it takes locals to alert GIA gunmen).

6. You will be allowed to walk around town unescorted or to leave Algiers only if you sign a disclaimer.

7. The most dangerous place in Algiers is the Kasbah. One Western journalist went there unprotected and was shot within five minutes.

8. If you are in Algiers, say hello to the U.S embassy staff—major consumers of DP T-shirts and stickers, as well as all-around good sports.

9. The police emergency telephone number is 17, and ambulance is 62-33-33.

With terrorists in the north and bandits in the south, most of Algeria is dangerous. The Zabarbar Forest, Blida Mountains and the Jijel region are frequently napalmed by the government in their quest to rid themselves of fundamentalist pockets. MiG-23s regularly drop napalm on remote regions used by the terrorists for their bases of operations.

Algiers

A global study conducted by an international business group, Corporate Resources Group, rated Algiers the worst city in the world. The group based its findings on criteria such as quality of life, security, public services, mental and physical care and facilities, and political and social stability. They could have saved their money. Every night an average of 50 people are killed in the city of Algiers. There are also frequent bomb attacks in crowded public areas such as markets and mosques.

Schools

In addition to journalists, teachers are a favorite target of Muslim militants. It's not unusual for two a week to be whacked in Algiers, and, as of mid-1996, some 700 schools had been razed by fire or sabotaged. Teachers are often murdered by guerrillas in front of their schoolchildren.

Massacres

Between 75,000 and 100,000 people were killed in extremist violence since 1992. The month of Ramadan is the most deadly time. The MO for Muslim rebels is to attack small villages (*mechtas* or *dovars*) with knives and machetes and go for the jugular. The daily attacks take multiple lives. Children, women and old folks make the most convenient targets, their throats slashed like the livestock hanging on hooks behind those scrumptious displays of designer olive and feta salad at the deli in Von's. In the first two months of 1999, more than 200 civilians had their throats slashed. Besides throat slitting, survivors describe dismemberment by chain saw, villagers being burned alive, the decapitation of babies and the disembowelment of pregnant women. It would be superfluous to get into the incidents (hundreds of villagers are routinely slaughtered during a single massacre), which are clumped together like basketball games during a strike-shortened NBA season. Most massacres are the work of the Armed Islamic Group—though security forces have also participated in their fair share, many dressed as rebels, or working in the GIA deep cover for the government. One of the GIA's bloodiest massacres took place on September 22, 1997, in Bentalha, eight miles south of Algiers. Some 300 villagers were killed in a six-hour orgy of violence as army helicopters observed the slayings from overhead, doing nothing to stop the carnage. The guerrillas slipped away at sunrise as easily as they entered Bentalha. Much of the daily carnage takes places southwest of Algiers, in and around Ain Defla Province, Tlemcen and Relizane. On March 21, 1999, Muslim rebels cut a little deeper with their knives and beheaded four women and then impaled their heads on stakes off a road near Emir Khaled town in Ain Defla.

Bandits

As if the terrorists weren't enough, there are also numerous incidents of banditry and assault involving foreigners that have been reported in the far southern region of Algeria near the border with Niger. Bandits have robbed, assaulted, kidnapped and killed travelers in Algeria south of Tamanrasset.

Being a Journalist

At least 70 journalists have died in Algeria since 1993. Foreign journalists were forbidden to leave their hotels in Algiers without an armed escort for protection against attack. That's the government line. More than likely, it's also to keep them from having a chat with the bad guys. Journos caught sneaking out without their baby-sitters are deported and not let in again.

You must understand that it isn't completely your skin they are trying to save. Since outside hacks have such high PR value when dead, the GIA gets all dreamy eyed and weak in the knees thinking of your recently butchered carcass on the cover of *Newsweek*. If they have to take out an entire post office, office building or nursery school to get you, that's okay, too.

www.cpj.org

Speaking

On July 5, 1998, a new law came into effect making Arabic the only language permitted for use in public life, including all business transactions/meetings, government procedures/sessions and political party rallies. Any breach of the law carries a US$170 fine. The first problem is that most high-ranking bureaucrats and prominent business people can't speak Arabic, only French. The Berbers (who comprise 20 percent of Algeria's population), for one, were outraged. The previous month, the popular Berber singer Lounes Matoub was whacked by Muslim militants. His life expectancy wasn't helped after he described the Arab language as "uninteresting . . . unsuitable for knowledge and science." The law makes it illegal for the secular-minded Berber speakers of Kabylia to hold rallies in their own region in their own language. Protesters in Kabylia tore down Arabic signs and rampaged through government-owned shops. *C'est la vie.*

Berber Party
http://www.rcd.asso.fr/

Bombings

In 1997, 177 bombings in Algeria killed 412 civilians and injured 1,572 others. Twenty-seven of the bombs were booby-trapped cars and trucks. High schools, markets and cafés are popular targets

Being a Kid

The GIA likes bombing youth centers and slicing the throats of pop singers and youth idols. The GIA believes that schooling for kids is an "obstacle to the Holy War in Algeria." The youth of Algeria have only two choices in life: join the GIA or join the Algerian military regime. Most just want to find a decent disco. Seventy-five percent of all Algerians are under 30, between 70 percent and 84 percent of whom are unemployed.

Criminals

As if getting your throat slit wasn't bad enough, the threat of theft is increasing in Algeria. The most frequent crimes involve the theft of auto parts from parked cars. Car windows and trunk locks are frequently broken in the hope that the thief will find something of value within. Home burglary is an increasingly serious problem, and most residences of foreigners are protected by alarm systems, watchdogs and/or guards. Experienced expatriate residents should venture out into the city with only a minimum amount of cash carried in a carefully concealed location. Vehicles are not generally parked in unguarded locations because of theft and vandalism.

GETTING SICK

Hospitals and clinics in Algeria are available, but limited in quality. Your best bet is to ask to be taken to the Ain Naadja Military Hospital in the suburbs of Algiers. If you have the choice or the time, ask to be taken to a military hospital instead of the closest public one. You may find a hand grenade in your bedpan. If you are seriously wounded, you stand a better chance by being flown out to nearby France, Britain or Germany. Medicines can be difficult to get and expensive. Don't expect much outside of the major cities. A 24-hour chemist is located at *19 rue Abane Ramdone: 63-36-31* or *2 rue Didouche Mourad: 63-47-43.* There is a civilian hospital, Hôpital Mustopha near *place de Mer: 66-33-33* (ambulance also available at this number).

Algeria, with a population of just under 29 million people, is the size of Europe with a climate that varies from arid to semiarid. The coast gets wet winters and hot summers. Cold winters characterize the high plateau. Sunni Muslims make up 99 percent of the population; virtually all are of Arab-Berber descent.

The currency is the Algerian dinar. Change your money at the hotel (you don't just walk around and get change here). Electrical current is 137/240V with the European two-pin plug. Phone and fax service is available from major hotels and businesses, but you may have to wait for a free overseas line. Most people speak French and Arabic. English is spoken only in the main cities and in big hotels and businesses.

The workweek in Algeria is Saturday through Wednesday, at least for those who work; 84 percent of Algerians between the ages of 15 and 30 are jobless, and inflation is at 55 percent. Factories are functioning at 50 percent capacity. In addition, Algeria has the lowest farm yield of any Mediterranean country, forcing it to import two-thirds of its food.

Traveler's checks and credit cards are acceptable in only a few establishments in urban areas. Currently, the government of Algeria requires all foreigners entering the country to exchange US$200 into local currency. Documentary proof of legal exchange of currency is needed when (or if) you leave Algeria. It is rarely checked.

Embassy Location

U.S. Embassy

4 Chemin Cheikh Bachir El-Ibrahimi
B.P. 549 (Alger-Gare) 16000, Algiers
Tel.: [213] (2) 69-11-86, 69-18-54,
69-38-75, 69-14-25

Government Agencies

Office of the President

Presidence de la Republique
El Mouradia
Algiers, Algeria
Tel.: [213] (2) 60-03-60

Office of the Prime Minister

Palais du Governement
Algiers, Algeria
Tel.: [213] (2) 63-23-40

Ministry of Defense

Avenue des Tagarins
Algiers, Algeria
Tel.: [213] (2) 61-15-15

Ministry of Foreign Affairs

6 Rue 16n Batran
El Mouradia
Algiers, Algeria
Tel.: [213] (2) 60-47-44

Press Agencies and Newspapers

(note: many are in French)

Agence France Presse (AFP)

6 Rue Khettabi
Algiers, Algeria
Tel.: [213] (2) 63-37-02

Algerian Press Service (APS)

20 Rue Zouieche
Kouba
Algiers, Algeria
Tel.: [213] (2) 68-05-30

Associated Press (AP)

4 Avenue Pasteur, BP 769
Algiers, Algeria
Tel.: [213] (2) 63-59-41

El Djazar

http://www.djazaironline.net/

El Khabar

1 Rue Bechir Attar
Algiers, Algeria
Tel.: [213] (2) 66-19-31/32
http://www.elkhabar.com/

Le Matin

1 Rue Bechir Attar
Hussein-Dey
Algiers, Algeria
Tel.: [213] (2) 66-30-13/14
http://www.lematin-dz.com/

ALGERIA

Reuters

6 Boulevard Mohamed Khemisti
Algiers, Algeria
Tel.: [213] (2) 64-46-77

El Watan

1 Rue Bechir Attar
Algiers, Algeria
Tel.: [213] (2) 66-26-41/42/44
http://www.elwatan.com/

12/30/99	400 people are killed in 4 villages at the start of Ramadan. The worst massacre in the six year civil war.+
4/16/99	Abdelaziz Bouteflika is elected president after his six contenders dropped out of the race two days earlier charging widespread election fraud. Massive protests engulfed Algiers and other cities.
6/5/97	President Liamine Zeroual's government is reelected; the FIS is banned from participating in the polls.
5/5/95	Islamic extremists kill five foreigners working at a pipe mill at an industrial zone in the Ghardaia region of northern Algeria. The victims were identified as two Frenchmen, a Canadian, a Brit and a Tunisian.
12/91	The first parliamentary elections ever held in Algeria are won by Muslim fundamentalists. The elections were nulled by the government, tossing Algeria into civil war.
4/20/80	Berber spring. Berber ethnic protests are held in Tizi Ouzou.
8/20/55	Algerian independence fighters launch their first armed offensive against French forces in eastern Algeria.
11/08/42	U.S. and British forces land in North Africa.

In a Dangerous Place: Algeria

Rock the Casbah

"The butchers' federation, concerned their trade was getting a bad name, urged journalists 'whose vocabulary has failed them' to use other terms like cruel, bloody, barbarous, ferocious or savage to describe the killings.

"The butchers issued the statement, which was faxed to Reuters on Tuesday, in reaction to the massacre of 58 foreign tourists in Luxor last week and continuing violence in Algeria that has killed at least 65,000 since 1992."

I am in Algiers, the most dangerous city in the most dangerous place in the world. At least that's what the security firms, the journalists and insurance people tell me. I'm here on a tourist visa, without a bodyguard, looking to find out who is doing all the killing. The leaders of the FIS have told me that the military has sent recruits to Afghanistan to be recruited back into the GIA and that the government and the fundamentalists are engaging in a holy dance of horror.

I all I know is the Russian hookers in the lobby bar are slowly moving over to me and I need an escape route.

I am saved by Mr. Ray Ban. I don't know his name because he never tells me. He is the head of security for the city of Algiers and he is accompanied by a unsmiling bodyguard. He sits between me and a slowly slinking, badly bleached blonde with bad teeth.

He very politely and very firmly wants to know what I am doing here. I tell him I am a tourist, but he smiles and asks to see my passport. He then says "your passport says you are a tourist, but I think you are a journalist."

"All journalists must have a security detail."

Now it's pretty much impossible to prove that you are not a journalist, since both tourists and journos carry cameras, notepads and video cameras. To prove who I am I go up to my room and get a T-shirt and my book. Upon seeing my photo on the cover he smiles broadly and says "hah you are a journalist." I am wearing what looks like a journalist's jacket in a publicity shot. I explain that a journalist works for a news organization and that writers are unemployed artists who have no agenda other than understanding the world better. I should have known better than to pull up at the American embassy alone in a taxi. Ringed by armed men in golf shirts I was told politely to get the hell out of Dodge. Worse, one of them recognized me when I asked him for tips on traveling in Algeria. He laughed: "Hell, man, we never leave the compound. We read your book to figure out what's going on." The guy in charge was not as impressed. That's why Mr. Ray Ban and Beef were here.

When he sees the T-shirt he sees Algeria right next to Afghanistan and Albania and he says, "No, no, no, this must be changed. Algeria is not Afghanistan or Albania. It is not dangerous here. I think you should leave tonight for your bad deeds, making people think Algeria is dangerous."

I ask him, "If he is head of security and it is not dangerous, why does he have a bodyguard?"

Before he leaves, he writes down three places I am allowed to go and he says that I must use the same cabdriver as I had today.

The next morning I notice four men sitting in one car outside the hotel. Disingenuously he has selected his bodyguard of last night as one them. I give them the slip, wave through the hotel security guards. and flag down a cab outside the hotel. The three places he wrote down are not where I will be going. The cabdriver asks, "Vous et seul?" (You are alone?) I tell him to keep going and don't worry, my friends will catch up with me later. I decide to stop in at the Hotel Aurassi, where the journos are waiting to go on their now daily ritual of visiting massacre sites.

Inside it is a babbling zoo. There are even more Betacams, Canons, and Nikons with fat telephoto lenses are strewn everywhere. Piles of cables, mike booms and luggage are piled in between people chattering on cell phones in French, English, Spanish and Arabic. There is a desk in front where journalists must sign up for tours. A large pad of paper lists the tours for today. It seems there are a number of massacre sights to be visited and if they are lucky there is firefight going on where the army has the rebels holed up in the mountains. They journos get to go there in tourist buses. One novice tells me how they will be taken in bulletproof vans to the fighting. I point out that the blue-and-black bulletproofed Nissan Patrols are for the ninjas and that he will be riding in the large windowed very unbulletproofed tourist bus in front. I take some video shots of the circus and one female producer for WTN says, "Don't take my picture. If my mother knew I was here she would kill me." The crowd is made of seasoned vets, eager freelancers and nervous staffers, some on their first blooding assignment away from the home desk. One eager young photographer who befriends me is a former mercenary and special forces soldier eager to get some gory shots for his French photo agency. He describes his frustration at seeing crusty brown puddles, dull-eyed survivors and no bang bang. They are envious of the fact that I will be cruising around the countryside and the killing zones without a bodyguard. They are resigned to their government organized Cook's tour.

Some journalists own my book and are surprised to see me in the flesh. Other think its the damned funniest story they've heard all week.

As I talk with the journos before they head off on their Magical Massacre Tour I bump into Mr. Ray Ban. He wants to know why I am here and not where he told me to go. I fudge and say that I was looking for a friend of mine and that I was just leaving. For er uh, one of the three places he mentioned. I forgot what they were because I threw the piece of paper away. He watches me get into the wrong cab and wags his finger at me. He says something on the walkie-talkie and watches me disappear.

I head straight into the killing zone. I have a fair sense of security because most massacres happen at night. There is a danger of fake roadblocks but I have a sense that there will be no "phony" policemen while the journos are here. In fact, I am becoming disturbingly confident that not much of anything is going to happen while the journos are in-country. Along the way I stop at a restaurant. The owner is thrilled to have a Western customer; he even turns the fountain on for me. He tells me he has not seen a tourist since 1992. I watch a duck swim in the fountain while a cat comes closer to drink. Every time the cat gets close the duck flaps around and scares it off. There is a scabby dog that chases the cat away and drinks at the fountain. I get a bit of insight. The duck is not afraid of the dog who can easily kill it because it thinks it scares the cat away. Kind of a weird microcosm of what is happening in Algeria. The people are meant to be more afraid of the Islamists than the government so they will run to the people who they think will scare the rebels away. Right into the smiling jaws of the military.

Along the way I stop and talk to many Algerians. I like them a lot. They are proud of their land, their history. It is when you pull out a camera or a notebook they draw back. All refuse to be photographed. I assume it is because of the terrorists. Later one older man fishing off a pier sees me and says, "Take my picture and talk to me. I am not afraid of the government."

Somewhat stunned by admission that the government is who they fear and not the GIA, I talk to him. He worked overseas as an engineer and has worked in many communist countries. He is used to the black cloak of fear and in his retirement he quite frankly doesn't give a damn. Even my cabdriver cautions him to watch what he says. My driver also continues to scan the village looking for people who may be overly interested in our presence.

When asked about *les affreux,* or the terrible ones, the old man tells me that the GIA is just one more of the many problems Algeria has had. "It is like a baby, it is small and weak then it grows into a teenager, ugly and strong and then it gets old and dies. And then another is born." He is glad that I am here and that I can see with my own eyes that the people of Algeria are not afraid. I ask him if the West should help. He says this is an Algerian problem and Algerians must fix it. A phrase I will hear again and again.

My driver interrupts and asks if I have enough pictures and can we please go back. He politely tells me that every time I get out of the car he counts how long it is taking the mujahedin to find their rifles. Acceding to his request we head back into town. He thanks me and guns it. It is so tense the soldiers don't get out of their bulletproof trucks to inspect passports and papers. Buses packed full of tired women and old men are waved into a large walled compound to be searched.

I have returned from the killing zone . . . or have I?

I stop at what looks like a bogus McDonalds. Inside the young boy gives me a free orange juice and I give him a *DP* sticker for his cash register. As I turn to leave I walk straight into Omar and Kamel. I know their names because I ask them what their names are. They are two plainclothes police who are as surprised to see us as I am to see them. It seems this quaint little restaurant is directly across the street from their headquarters. Politely holding us back with their outstretched hands, they radio in for instructions. They have to repeat their request because the person at the other doesn't believe that they have found a tourist in this area. When they realize I am listening, they switch from French to Arabic. While they are trying to convince their boss that they have found a tourist, I scuttle sideways like a crab down the sidewalk with my driver in tow. They scuttle with me with their upraised palms pressed against me like a crossing guard. When they hit a light pole I keep scuttling. Not knowing how to keep smiling, working the walkie-talkie and scuttling. They resort to chasing after us. As we jump in the car we start to pull away, only to see Omar and Kamel jump into the backseat with us as we are moving. I introduce myself. They smile and tell me their names. They politely suggest to my driver that we head to the police station. They keep smiling and say, "Pour votre securité, messeur." (For your security, sir.)

Inside the military HQ you are greeted by a rogue's gallery of glum-bearded mujahedin. A few have a line drawn across their picture with the words *Tuer* or *killed*. I am separated from my driver and plopped in the some high-ranking person's office. The office is neat with few accessories. There is obviously not much crime or much of anything else to occupy the military police here.

After a little polite banter and questions the chief gives me the general gist that I am in big trouble and he wants to know why I am here. I explain that I am not in trouble because I am tourist and as far as I know there are no laws against tourists sightseeing in Algeria.

After we go around in semantic circles about his telling me I am in trouble and I telling him that no I am not, two disheveled men poke their head in the door and demand my passport. They yank my passport out of my hand and start yelling at Kamel and Omar, who are trailing them like dogs. My meek friends remind them that I speak French and the conversation switches to Arabic again. What the cause of this heated discussion is I don't know. One of fat 40-something men sticks his head back in, grabs my Leica camera and starts yelling in French that I have been taking pictures of the "Post." I tell him "I take pictures of everything because I'm a tourist and give me my goddamn camera back." I grab my camera back and he yells for a little longer. Then they move into another office and I can hear them yelling at each other in Arabic.

Finally, after spending 20 minutes with the police chief, I am moved to another office. It is a gray painted cell with one tiny window propped open and a messy desk in the center. Behind the desk is a cot with a disheveled mattress. There are more file cabinets here than the chief's office. The desk is piled high with thick dossiers and paperwork.

There is a map, and I peruse the thick files and documents on the desk. A lot of in depth information on people and their activities. But I don't have time to do a lot of reading. One of the disheveled men comes back. He is wearing gray sweatpants, a Fila T-shirt and sandals. It looks like he might have been sleeping here before we were dragged in. He takes my camera and peers in all the glass orifices as if there is something inside. He then puts it down on the desk and starts typing out a large form.

I keep up a light banter in my bad French and wonder why with all the beautiful scenery and sights outside his office he doesn't take some pictures and put them on the wall.

He turns to me coldly and says flatly in perfect English, "Monsieur, you are not in a hotel."

I ask him where he learned his English. He turns again in the same agitated manner and says, "When I was in the what you call the Marines, I was trained by the Americans."

I realize who I am talking to. I am talking to an "eradicator"—the secret police who take care of the dirty work the government needs done. Although I have no proof, it dawns on me that this is a man who works at night, has no uniform and is the one in charge of the police and the plainclothes security guards.

He asks me the same questions the police chief has asked me. Why am I here? What am I doing here? Where is your security detail? I respond in my usual fashion. He goes out for another shouting match with his friend and then after a few crackles on the walkie-talkies he comes back in a funk.

He grabs a stack of forms, inserts well-worn carbons and jams them angrily in his manual typewriter. He wants to know my mother's maiden name and where my father was born. After having me sign the form, we were free to go back, and quickly. I find out later the interrogation of my driver was very different than mine. He was asked to list every person I had talked too, every picture I had taken, every place I had been and what I had talked about. He assured me that I was just a tourist taking pictures of the scenery.

Like the driver I had yesterday, he told me that I should be with the military and not on my own. "This is very dangerous." I tell him to drop me off at the journo's hotel.

As he drops me off he says, "Messeur Robert, you know I like traveling with you. It's dangerous but I like it. Where do you want to go tomorrow?" I give him a conspiratorial grin and tell him to meet me at seven outside the hotel and we'll find out.

Inside I meet up with an American and French journalist. They suggest we go to dinner. Their real goal is to interview the person who has now become "the only tourist in Algeria," a story every bored journo wants to file for some much needed local color. On the way to get a cab, who do I bump into again but Mr. Ray Ban. He politely asks me where I was today. I fudge and say I don't remember the name of the place. He waves his walkie-talkie at me and says, "My friend, today you were lucky. Don't do it again." Mr. Ray Ban is either my nemesis or my guardian angel.

We get into a cab and wait for Mr. Ray Ban to line up our escort for my journo friends. I have never had a police escort, so this should be fun. The experience is kind of like a low-budget roller coaster ride. You sit politely waiting for takeoff and then the screeching of tires from the police details lets you know the ride has begun. And then you're off. Down the twisting curving streets of Algiers at ridiculously high speed. A nice way to dodge snipers, but an ideal way to end up wrapped around a light pole. Our escorts consist of four men split between two cars. They wear tight pants, gold chains and photo vests to hide their pistols and machine guns. They have obviously been trained in executive protection and evasive driving. We careen through the streets at thrill-ride speeds as our escorts swoop, dodge and swerve. Meanwhile, our cabdriver, untrained in any method of driving, labors to keep up without being rear-ended or sideswiped by our energetic dodge 'em car escorts.

We end up at the restaurant. It is closed because the power is out to a large section of the Casbah, exactly the scene that happens before the massacres in the villages when the phones and power are cut and the wholesale slaughter begins. Our guides park in front and behind us, blocking us in with their lights on. I feel nervous. The dreaded Casbah is just behind us. We are well-lit sitting ducks with groups of shouting policemen arguing and discussing which restaurant we should go to next. I am wondering if the terrorists up in the Casbah behind us are holding up their attack, thinking this is so obvious a target that it must be a setup.

Finally after ten minutes of arguing and yelling and walkie-talkie-ing we are off to another restaurant. Inside is the quaint colonial fin de siècle ambiance of a Moorish palace. My two journalist friends interrogate our waiter about politics. He mumbles in a low voice while a visible line of sweat appears on his upper lip. I realize this is one of the few times the journalists get to talk to "the man on the street." His opinion of politics is that the no one likes the government but that they will win the elections by any means possible. He coughs slightly and excuses himself. Our bodyguards wait patiently outside, but our waiter knows that this does not mean he is unwatched. As we leave, we tell the driver to drop me at the Hotel al D'Jessair and then take the two female reporters back to their hotel.

The security guards have a snit. "Can't do it." Why? They left with three journalists they must come back with three journalists. I explain I am a tourist and that they actually left with two journalists and one tourist and will come back with two journalists. I will walk.

Confusion reigns. Walkie-talkies crackle. They have never just dropped anyone off before and they have never heard of anyone just walking back to the hotel. Mr. Ray Ban comes to the rescue. Oh it's that tourist again. Yeh. Just drop him off.

I now know that I must seek out fear. Where are the most dangerous places? I head straight for the journalists compound. In Algeria the journalists are grouped together in a heavily guarded, walled compound. My driver cruises in past the heavy security and I pick a newspaper office at random. It seems things are serendipitous. I have chosen the offices of *El Watan,* a newspaper run by Omar Belhouchet, a defiant man who has survived an assassination attempt while picking his daughters up from school. I have dropped in without an appointment, so as I wait in a side office, I rummage through their archives. I learn that the journalists are not only not allowed to wander freely, they are forbidden from taking photos unless the military approves. Most photos are taken from the hip without the military knowing. In many cases, the military has sanitized the massacre sights before the journalists are allowed in. A young women photographer going through some files views me suspiciously. Some photos are ludicrous. A soldier points to a severed finger on a mantle. Dead terrorists are unrecognizable shredded cadavers. Most pictures are of dead people lying in pools of blood. Two photos raise questions. One is of new military equipment, badges, guns and rifles taken from a bogus checkpoint supposedly manned by the GIA. Another is off a collection of rusty swords, ornate sheep-killing knifes and homemade daggers found at a massacre sight. I am interrupted by the appearance of an interpreter and she answers some preliminary questions. "Who are the GIA?"

"They are an enigma," she answers. "Nobody knows who they are."

She cautions me against asking the director any political questions.

The director comes down and answers my pointed questions strongly and without pausing. He tells me is a journalist because without journalists the people of Algeria would only have the government's point of view. The people would know nothing.

I ask him if having the Western journalists here is good for the image of Algeria. He says the government will not let the foreign journalists into the areas that are really dangerous, but this is for the benefit of the elections. Normally foreign journalists are not welcomed by the governement. None are allowed to wander freely.

I ask him if the UN or other groups should get involved in Algeria's problems. He says Algeria has a history of repulsing outsiders and that Algeria will and must solve their own problems.

I mention that it seems that he has become a combatant in this war. He replies that if he has it is because he is fighting against apathy and ignorance.

I ask him who tried to kill him. He says he doesn't know. I ask again if it is the government or the fundamentalists who tried to kill him and he says he does not know. He does not want to forward any suspicions to me and I understand why. He was given a message and he got the point.

As I pack up the interpreter says, "I thought you said you weren't going to ask any political questions." I say that what we talked about was about life, death and freedom.

Politics, life and freedom are dangerous in Algeria.

I head to the most dangerous place in the most dangerous city in the most dangerous country in the world. There is no argument that the nexus is the

Casbah. It is dusk and my goal is go to the mosques to see if I can link up with anyone from the GIA.

As I walk into the Casbah, I take pictures of people to give me something to do. The people scatter like frightened pigeons when I raise my camera. One group of young men dives behind a doorway and then seeing that I am walking further into the Casbah, they rush up and prevent me from continuing. They say, "Are you crazy man? Do you know where you are going?"

I say I just want of see what's going on. They forcefully push me back and says, "Go now, go as quickly as you can"

I disappoint them by sitting down with them and sharing a cigarette. Their eyes scan the street as they talk to me. They do not want me here. They shake their heads and say, "Man you are crazy." I ask them why they are here. They say, "We live here, but you don't have to." One man asks me to take him with me to America. I am becoming used to the curious habit Algerians have of scanning the surroundings while answering your questions. After a while I realize that I am endangering them just by sitting with them, so I thank them and move on. Danger is sad here.

The next day is election day and I decide to play journo and sneak on the buses.

Instead of the typical massacre site tour the journos will be visiting a variety of voting stations to watch the elections unfold around Algiers. The polls open and we wait, and wait and wait. An old women shows up and walks stiffly to the ballot booth. The journalists mob her and make her drop her ballot again and again. Bewildered by the attention, she leaves muttering. The young people manning the voting offices sit bored. Ten minutes later, an old man wanders in and is also baffled by being the focus of bright lights and all the media attention. There doesn't seem to be a rush to the polls to vote. In fact, we wonder where everyone is since the streets are deserted on a day the government has decreed that all business must cease.

We move on to four other voting stations. On one visit a man is dragged yelling and kicking by security guards into a side room. When we ask our escorts what the problem was, they say "What problem?" The man reappears a few minutes later, flushed but calmer. He takes great pains to tell us that there was no problem, a simple misunderstanding. At another location, an old man stumbles up to me and tells me he has a letter from Franklin Roosevelt for helping out in World War II. The old man has to pause to collect his words, but our escort hisses to the old man in Arabic, "Keep talking, keep talking." At another station, an old women lectures the journalists and says, "Why are you taking my picture? You are just going to make trouble for everyone here. Go away." It is apparent that only the aged and the fearless have come out to vote. We didn't see any fearless people.

Back at the hotel I step off the journo tour bus and walk smack into Mr. Ray Ban. Busted. He gives me a smug look and wags his finger. I offer to buy him a coffee and he accepts. Satisfied that I am finally leaving in a few hours, he writes his name down for me so I can send him a copy of my book. He says he has been talking to the other reporters and says, "You are not a journalist are you?" I say no. I am just here to visit Algeria. He shakes his head and says he must get back to work. He smiles and shakes my hand.

Later I read the results of the vote. The papers said the government's RND party had won with a majority. They say that over 45 percent of the population had turned out to vote. In a city of 3 million people, I had been to five polling stations and seen less than 30 people vote. When I return, my journo friends are amazed at my deeds. I tell them that it was quite a mild trip and I truly enjoyed the scenery and the people of Algeria. They think I am being brave, but I know what real bravery is.

Soon after the journalists left, the killing began again. Sixteen people were murdered just south of Algiers. Ten of the victims were children, one a seven-month-old baby.

—RYP

Angola
★ ★ ★ ★ ★

Movin' on Up

Angola is moving up. Not on the civilization scale, but on the radar of coming global catastrophes, joining the likes of Congo, Somalia or the Sudan. There are five-star examples of ethnic cleansing, starvation, devolution, greed, etc. It doesn't take long to figure out what's wrong with Angola. It's one of those rich African countries led by swaggering charismatics that somehow remains eternally poor. Angola has some of the richest alluvial and kimberlite diamond deposits in the world and can pump out 2 billion barrels a day of black gold. So it makes perfect sense that this is the site of Africa's longest running civil war, a place where the average Angolan is happy to see his 50th birthday, has one doctor per 13,500 people and can dream of someday moving to the west side to some wealthier, safer nation like . . . let's say . . . Sierra Leone.

But things are looking better. UNITA has been carefully buying weapons, major offensives have begun in the countryside, oil workers are kidnapped more frequently, land mines are being placed nightly and they get their own chapter in

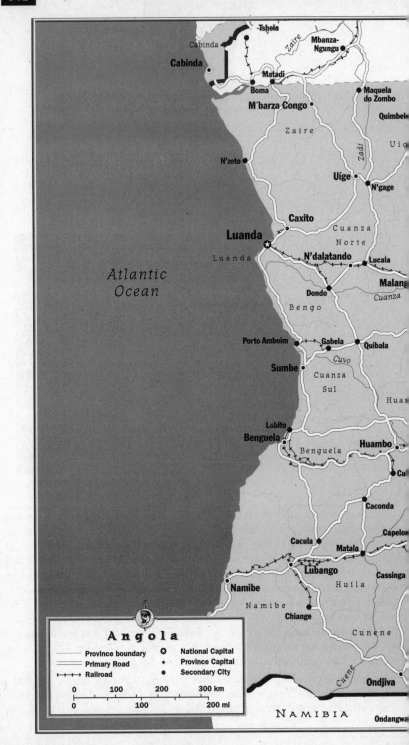

Atlantic Ocean

Tshela
Cabinda
Cabinda
Matadi
Boma
M'barza Congo
Zaire
Mbanza-Ngungu
Maquela do Zombo
Quimbele
Zadi
Uíg
N'zeto
Uíge
N'gage
Caxito
Luanda
Cuanza Norte
Luanda
N'dalatando
Lucala
Malang
Dondo
Cuanza
Bengo
Porto Amboim
Gabela
Quibala
Sumbe
Cuvo
Cuanza Sul
Huai
Lobito
Benguela
Huambo
Benguela
Cu
Caconda
Capelo
Cacula
Matala
Lubango
Cassinga
Namibe
Huíla
Namibe
Chiange
Cunene
Ondjiva
Cuene

Angola

Province boundary	✪	National Capital
Primary Road	•	Province Capital
Railroad	•	Secondary City

0   100   200   300 km

0   100   200 mi

NAMIBIA   Ondangwa

ANGOLA

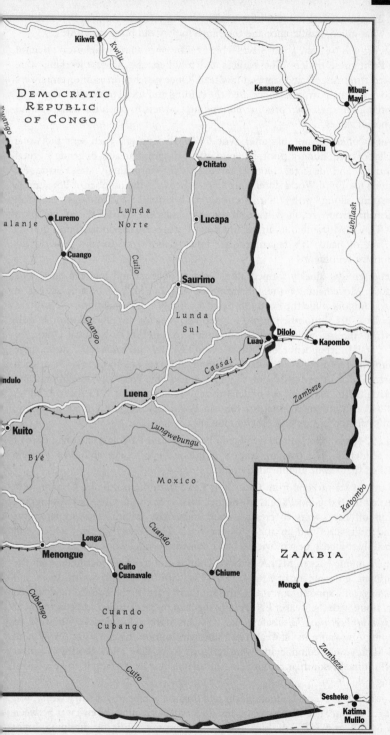

DP. Things are looking good for a full-scale war again in Angola. It just shows you what greed, indifference and too much money can bring on in Africa.

Angola was basically about slaves—big healthy ones who brought top price for the Portuguese traders. The biggest and toughest and hardest working were yanked from Angola and shipped to Brazil. Once other sources of revenue were discovered, the Portuguese increased the cultural and social tone of the region by emptying out their own prisons and sending convicts to teach the natives about European values.

When coffee became big after World War II, Portugal then sent the usual flotillas of tired, hungry, poor, illiterate riffraff to spread an aura of gentle cultural sensitivity and delicate colonial harmony. Not surprisingly the Portuguese formula for Third World dominance led to chaos. As the number of Portuguese increased, along with their hectares of bountiful landholdings, Angolan nationalist groups revolted in an effort to gain independence for the colony. As in East Timor, Mozambique, Brazil and other Portuguese cesspools, things quickly got out of hand. It's amazing what forced labor and brutality can do for nationalist sentiments.

Rebel groups quickly formed along ethnic, political and regional lines. The Popular Movement for the Liberation of Angola (MPLA) became strong in central Angola while the northern-based Union of the Populations of Northern Angola (UPNA) morphed into the National Front for the Liberation of Angola (FNLA). Internal wrangling led southerners to spin off the National Union for the Total Independence of Angola (UNITA). By the early '60s, these three groups started using their outside training and weapons to bang away at each other. The northern tribes of the FNLA had the West and neighbor Zaire backing them. The commies under Russia were backing the MPLA and UNITA was a poorly disguised shell for the old Portuguese regime but soon became South Africa's tool to fend off communism.

In 1974, a kindlier, gentler regime in Portugal gave Angola its first real taste of independence. The pouting leaders didn't see eye to eye and their backers brushed them aside and invaded in 1975

South Africa invaded from the south, Zaire from the north and Cubans were shuttled in to pay Fidel's bills to Mother Russia. Even the CIA started snagging riffraff off the streets to create instant mercenary armies. This scenario was wonderfully captured in the '70s-era book *The Whores of War,* which will hopefully someday be a movie—a black comedy starring white people.

The commie-backed MPLA grabbed Luanda and handily proclaimed itself the legitimate government of Angola. UNITA, with the help of South Africa and Washington's spooks, controlled the southern part of the country and waged war, along with the weaker FNLA (and the help of the classified ad department at *Soldier of Fortune).* Ultimately the Russians were a lot more committed to keeping Angola for its oil wealth and strategic position. By early '76, Angola and the MPLA went commie and were resigned to battling a low-level war against UNITA in the south and southeast. All they had were diamonds to keep them going.

Cut to 1991. Russia is ideologically and financially tapped out and a weary, war ravaged country negotiates a cease-fire, theoretically ending the civil war between the MPLA and UNITA. Elections in '92 surprise rebels by dumping Jonas

Savimbi and his now largely economic rebel group UNITA. Accordingly, Savimbi renews hostilities in October 1992.

The UN Security Council voted on September 26, 1993, to hit Savimbi where it hurts, in his pocketbook. Economic sanctions against UNITA forced them to accept its defeat. Savimbi was offered and accepted the nation's vice presidency in 1994. To make things more friendly, UNITA was even formally legalized by the government on March 11, 1998.

But Savimbi was only stalling for time. He used the lull in the fighting to build up UNITA forces and to siphon income from his oil and diamond fields in the north. With the 1994 Lusaka Protocol, UNITA won four years of breathing space while the government imploded through its corruption and ineptitude. In December 1998, Savimbi and his boys upped the ante and went back on the offensive to ensure that peace doesn't get in the way of killing. Soon political positions were brushed aside as Western countries cut their deals with whoever controlled the oil at the time. Today 95 percent of Angola's paycheck is for oil it sells. It doesn't look like things are going to get better as diamonds and oil drive the self interest of fat cats while the lifestyle of the people descends into levels not ever worth measuring on Western quality-of-life charts. Meanwhile, Angola, a country in name only, is barely supported by privately owned mines and diamond fields, outposts protected by mercenaries, under siege by ragtag rebels. The Cabinda enclave is essentially Gulf and Chevron fighting a private Fort Apache–style war against the rebels.

Today, Angola has the highest percentage of amputees in the world. Enthusiastic aid groups say nearly 40 percent of the population is estimated to be missing limbs. The 20 million explosives left buried in the soil will continue to kill and maim for years to come. There are perhaps only 11 million people left in Angola, and more than enough land mines, famine, drought and pestilence to kill every one of them at least twice.

Oil against diamonds. War against starvation. Misery against hopelessness. When you look for a bad guy, the dirty finger always swings towards Savimbi. Or should it point at the gray men who buy his diamonds? The 1994 Lusaka protocol gave Angola what the world, and the UN, thought was peace. Rather, it was a disguise of stability that played perfectly into the hands of Jonas Savimbi's UNITA rebels (the diamond boys) in their ongoing fight against the MPLA (the oil boys). The 18-month UN demobilization effort was nothing short of paid R&R for the insurgents. Savimbi used the breather to grab more Angolan real estate, of which UNITA controls about two-thirds in Angola. And while "disarming" after the 1994 accords, UNITA was secretly buying tanks and heavy artillery from Ukraine. The full-scale fighting that erupted anew in December 1998 has been less about ideology than about a grab for cash and power. UNITA funds its efforts with some $500 million a year in diamond sales from mines in northern Angola, despite international sanctions against the guerrillas. The government has mortgaged oil sales to reap about $1 billion for arms purchases. It's all about the Benjamins here.

Some half-million people have been killed in the ongoing battle since Angola's independence from Portugal in 1975. Angolans have watched their currency fall in value more than 2 million kwanzas to the dollar. The government is entirely out of foreign exchange reserves. And there are no genuine efforts to end the fighting. Savimbi is demanding negotiations. Dos Santos says no deal, as Savimbi hasn't honored any peace accords in the past. There is no prospect of either side winning an outright military victory. As UN Angola mission leader Alioune Blondin Beye discovered before he was splattered in a plane crash in a last-ditch effort to reach peace in June 1998, neither Savimbi nor dos Santos want peace. Too many folks are getting rich off murder and maiming. Meanwhile, dos Santos, funded with gifts of tens of millions of dollars from oil companies, has spruced up Luanda's streets lining foreign embassies for the new millennium. Just another disguise in the sinkhole of Africa.

Jonas Savimbi/ Uniao Nacional Para Independence de Angola/National Union for the Total Independence of Angola (UNITA)

Headed by Jonas Savimbi (call him "Doctor" or he gets pissed), the mainly Ovimbundu UNITA has been fighting various Angolan governments and groups since its creation in 1966. He was born in 1933 as a stationmaster's son in the town of Andulo, in Bie province. Considering the number of people his brand of socialist politics has killed, it may be surprising to learn that Savimbi was a graduate of the School of International Politics at Lausanne University in Switzerland (though this is questioned by many). He speaks Portuguese, French and English. He's also called charismatic, psychotic, a liar and many other things. In any case, he is large and in charge. Educated in guerrilla tactics in China, he has vowed to topple the formerly Cuban- and Soviet-backed government. The classic revolutionary, a cross between Ché and Austin Powers, Savimbi draws support from the countryside and uses Angola's large size, dislocation and tattered state-run infrastructure to his full advantage. Savimbi's control of the diamond mines in the northern diamond-producing area of Lunda Norte near Cafunfo has funded his Maoist-style resistance movement. Once backed by the CIA and welcomed at Ronald Reagan's White House as an anticommunist freedom fighter, Savimbi has reemerged as an international rogue, but a successful one at that. He controls nearly 70 percent of the country and has an upper hand in the current hostilities, largely due to his "peacetime" arms procurements from Romania, Ukraine and Bulgaria. His troops are more disciplined and skilled than the FAA, although UNITA is having a hard time scratching up new recruits. UNITA troops are estimated to between 30,000 and 70,000, depending on who you talk to. Many were trained by South African special forces, leaving their signature SADF booby traps anywhere the sun don't shine. But UNITA is in want of air power and fuel supplies. UN sanctions against the rebels (including diamond sales and fuel procurement) have had an impact one the group, which has transformed itself from a guerrilla insurgency into a conventional mechanized force. And although diamond revenues in 1997 amounted to some $500 million, the guerrillas' 1998 output was closer to $250 million, as the land has been ravaged by years of extraction and the handiwork of illegal diggers, or *garimpeiros*. Depopulation of the countryside has made conscripts hard to find, but it seems to be part of the plan. To make up for lost riches and as a safeguard should Namibia get sucked into Angola's conflict, the rebels are training an estimated 600 Caprivian seccessionists in southeastern Angola. UNITA's on a roll, their tactics highly effective, if somewhat macabre. It seems that the locals have been lending a hand to UNITA and sometimes arms and feet. In vogue at the moment is driving entire populations from villages into the urban centers of Huambo, Malanje and Cuito, forcing the government to divert precious resources into feeding refugees staggering into these cities with their arms hacked off—a scene right out of *Night of the Living Dead*. Malanje's population has swelled by more than 150,000 in recent months. UNITA's deliberate downing of two UN aircraft just after Christmas should leave no doubt as to the global isolation that UNITA wishes to be left alone in to make its money.

UNITA Web Site
www.kwacha.com

José Eduardo dos Santos/ Movimento Para Libertacao de Angola/the Popular Movement for the Liberation of Angola (MPLA)

Started in 1956, the Marxist-dominated (but really ethnically Kimbundu) MPLA party is now a bootlace regime held together by the soft-spoken and educated José Eduardo dos Santos. He was propelled to power via a slam-dunk election masterminded by a Brazilian public relations company. Cuban troops back in the '70s also helped. Dos Santos promised to drop the unpopular dogma of Lenin and embrace free-market principles. The idea is that Angola can transcend tribal affiliations and become a happy, peaceful, wealthy country. Now you know how hopeless the situation is. The MPLA won the September 1992, elections, supervised by 800 outside observers. Dos Santos' archrival, Jonas Savimbi, went back to his base in Huambo and continued to kill his countrymen in the name of peace. The MPLA controls only about a third of Angola, basically only the major cities.

MPLA Web Site
www.angola.org

Angolan Armed Forces (FAA)

Dos Santos' government is propped up by petroleum and diamond exports extracted and managed by foreign firms and the Angolan Armed Forces (FAA). The FAA is busy packing over US$1 billion to buy arms with, which has been distributed in the old-fashioned Joey Mobutu Trickle-Down School—five for me, one for you. Senior officers are like kids in a candy store, profiting from giant commissions on arms purchases from Belarus. The generals and the politicos are making hundreds of millions off the war, while junior officers sell fuel, weapons and uniforms to UNITA guerrillas so they can eat and catch a video. Some $200 million has been recently paid to senior military officers in weapons-deal kickbacks. The governor of Malanje Province was taking in salaries and military supplies for 11,000 men in 1999 to defend the city, though he had only 1,000 men registered, and actually only a few hundred mustered. The army has also been pressganging youths into the war. In July 1999, the army called up men born in 1978 to fight UNITA, expecting to round up some 30,000 more soldiers. Instead, only 7,000 showed up for a haircut. So they've started knocking on doors. The pickings are ripe. Well more than half of Angola's 11 million people were born after independence in 1975. Soldiers move from school to school, corralling in kids as young as 15 to fight the good fight. A number of the new refugee camps are populated only by women and small children. It's a good time for that trip to Disneyworld.

Frente Nacional Para Libertacao de Angola (FNLA) National Front for the Liberation of Angola

This U.S.-backed group was created in 1962 to combat communist influence. A northern group once allied to Zaire (Congo), they began as Union of the Populations of Northern Angola but split into the southern-aligned UNITA and the northern-aligned FNLA.

FLEC/Front for the Liberation of Cabinda

Still crazy after all these years. There are 13 rebel groups trying to liberate this tiny 4,400 square mile area from Angola. The locals want a piece of that big-money oil action (Cabinda provides 60 percent of Angola's oil output of 600,000 barrels per day) and they will keep attacking until they get it. They battle Congolese and Angolan troops as well as foreign "security guards" hired to protect the land-based oil installations. There are also a number of offshore oil platforms in operation. In July 1999, the leader of the Cabinda

Enclave Liberation Forces, Anonio Bento Bembe, was taken prisoner by being offered $12.5 million for his two Portuguese and two French hostages. The foreigners, all employees of French company Bouygyes S.A., were kidnapped March 10, 1999. When he showed up, he was introduced to an Angolan elite army unit which captured him and then ten days later freed the hostages.

Mercenaries/Diamonds/Oil, Oh My

The now defunct Executive Outcomes (EO) was the hugely successful South African based temp agency for international dogs of war. The Angolan government used about 500 EO "advisers" to fight against UNITA in the early and mid-1990s, and it paid off when the rebs made peace with the MPLA in November 1994. The joke was that most of the EO bunch came from special forces that fought with UNITA against the MPLA in the '70s, but it came with a price tag of about US$23 million. A number of EO personnel remained in Angola after 1994, working in the civilian sector should they need to be mobilized again. Former EO directors have secured contracts with the dos Santos government for training soldiers and pilots. Other former EO mercs have been brought aboard as pilots and aircraft technicians to fly and service Luanda's new MiGs. Diamondworks has brought in professional help so that anything not bolted down stays around. You should know that Diamondworks and Branch Energy have had kidnap attacks against their installations in Angola and guess which company (which has been directly linked through ownership, board membership and association) they call to sort things out?

Sandline International

www.sandline.com

Diamonds

The chairman of De Beers, Nicky Oppenheimer, once said that diamonds were intrinsically worthless "except for the deep psychological need they fill." So why are there diamond wars in Africa? The diamond war is waged on two fronts. One side is De Beers who has been spending spend hundreds of millions in 21 languages since 1948 trying too convince folks that "A Diamond Is Forever" and then carefully controlling the value by purchasing the bulk of the diamonds dug up around the world. On the other front are the thousands of impoverished miners *garimpeiros* Angolan, Sierra Leonean and Brazilian freelance miners that dig up, steal or smuggle diamonds. And of course the rebels and companies that violently control those mines to the detriment of the populations they war against.

Unlike oil, which takes major investment, a mildly stable transportation system and some sense of international propriety, diamonds are a rebel's best friend. Extracting diamonds can be a free-for-all in Angola. Punch a few holes, hire a few mercs with a secured perimeter find an eager Lebanese buyer and you are in business. Not quite. Diamonds, functionally useless outside of adorning grinding wheels can only maintain their value in an odd monopoly created and controlled by DeBeers.

Angola produces 15 percent of the world's diamond output and 70 percent of all rough diamonds are sold through De Beers' Central Selling Organisation (CSO) at 17 Charterhouse Street in London to wholesalers and diamond buyers. Angola's rocks are among the highest quality diamonds in the world, costing three times as much per carat as South African diamonds. That's why De Beers even sucks up the less-than-perfect rocks smuggled out or stolen by locals.

In 1997, Angola produced about $1 billion worth of diamonds—$500 million in 1998. At the center of this lucrative trade is the diamond transnational De Beers, its London-based CSO and Russian mining giant Alrosa. Diamonds are UNITA's main source of revenue and De Beers has been buying UNITA alluvial diamonds on the open market since the rebels took control of the Cuango Valley in 1992. UN sanctions imposed on the insurgents in July 1998 prohibited unofficial Angolan diamond sales. Now De Beers is getting a look-see by rights groups such as Global Witness, who haven't seen any indication the diamond moguls have taken their hands out of Jonas' cookie jar. De Beers insists it is only buying only government diamonds. But there's no hiding the fact that De Beers has bought directly from the rebels in the past, acting as de facto financiers of rebel groups through middlemen. But then again it's no secret that Shell and other oil companies finance the other side through oil royalty checks cut to dictators, rebels and strongmen.

Oil

What keeps the tanks rolling and the soldiers eating and the bombs falling in Angola? Oil, friend. Black gold. Texas tea. Angola's war pits oil against diamonds. The rebs have the diamonds, dos Santos has got the oil. Angola pumps some 775,000 barrels a day, much of it from the billion-barrel Girassol oil field. Other deepwater finds in recent years should up the daily tally to 2 million barrels a day by 2010. Also offshore are thought to be the largest untapped oil reserves on the planet, which would make it 3 million barrels a day—over a third of Saudi Arabia's production. Whoa, we could be talkin' about a lot of limos in Luanda. And it may just happen that way. The diamonds are fading fast and they're in a war zone. The oil's offshore, and there's a lot of it. Oil is also a weapon here; UNITA tanks have run out of oil during major assaults, leading UNITA's top researchers to see if they can be run on hot air.

Rain

The UNITA headquarters in Andulo has yet to be taken despite three offensives in 1999. The government needs the ground to be dry so their lumbering vehicles can support the attacking troops. On the other hand, the hit-and-run tactics of UNITA are helped by the rain. Angola gets between 9 and 12 inches of rain a month in the rainy period between October and March. Naturally, it is not unusual to have years of drought, which causes countrywide famine.

Passport and visa required. Persons arriving without visas are subject to possible arrest or deportation. Tourist/business visas take two days and require an application form, US$30, a letter stating purpose of travel, and one color photo with your name printed on the back. Applications by mail require a prepaid return envelope. Yellow fever and cholera immunizations are required. As of mid-1999, the Angolan embassy in Washington was still issuing tourist visas, but they advise strongly that you fly directly into Luanda and do not dillydally out of Luanda, Lobito, Benguela or Namibe. The Angolan Ministry of Hotels and Tourism is the best source for people looking to book Shriner conventions there.

Land borders may or may not be under government control. Folks caught tiptoeing in will be incarcerated if they don't hit a land mine first.

For additional information, contact the following:

Embassy of Angola

1615 M Street NW, Ste. 900
Washington, D.C. 20036
Tel: (202) 785-1156
Fax: (202) 785-1258

The Permanent Mission of the Republic of Angola to the U.N.

125 East 73rd Street
New York, New York 10021

Tel: (212) 861-5656

There is little infrastructure left in Angola. Most roads are closed or mined or both. Wandering bands of armed thugs will stop and rob any travelers found in the countryside.

Make sure you have extra passport-sized photos for special permits required to travel around the country outside Luanda. Permits are available at the Direcao de Emigracao e Fronteiras in Luanda. Most folks you run into here will be in the oil patch. There are plenty of roadblocks, and chances are one of them might be a group of thugs who want your car. There have been carjackings against foreigners coming from the airport. You can't blame these folks for being a little riled up at whitey. After all, the Portuguese yanked about 3 million mothers' sons from Angola during the slave days and the Western world has done a good job of killing whoever was left.

Travel anywhere in Angola is considered unsafe because of the presence of undisciplined armed troops and land mines, as well as the possibility of sudden outbreaks of localized combat or a direct attack by armed soldiers or civilians. Travel in many parts of the capital city is relatively safe by day, but considered unsafe at night because of the mounting incidence of armed robberies and carjackings. The presence of police checkpoints after dark, often manned by armed, poorly trained personnel, contributes to unsafe nighttime travel. Police at checkpoints actively solicit bribes and have used deadly force against vehicles for not stopping as requested. The most dangerous spots in the country are currently the cities of Huambo, Cuito and Malanje.

The Northeast

Lunda Norte and Lunda Sul Provinces in the northeast are extremely hazardous for foreigners. The diamond areas around Lucapa are major stages for violent crime. About 50 to 100 people used to be murdered in Lucapa each week. Despite the attempt to legalize and control diamond mining, most stones are smuggled out of the country, with perhaps 20 percent of the hauls actually going through official channels.

Cabinda

About 13 independence groups, a.k.a. poorly dressed armed men, dream of the day when they can snag a Westerner and swap him back for a few mil. See FLEC under "The Players."

Not Eating

In Huambo, about 520 kilometers southeast of Luanda, which has been under siege by UNITA rebels since the breakdown of the Lusaka Protocol peace accords, 16.7 percent of children under five are malnourished, compared to 3.7 percent in April 1995. Overall in Angola, as of mid-1999, only 56,000 tons of cereals—out of an estimated 180,000 tons in international emergency food assistance needed through April 2000—have been pledged. There are about 1.7 million people displaced by the fighting in Angola.

Land Mines and Booby Traps

Human Rights Watch says there are 20 million land mines in Angola. The UN figures there are 12 million. Norwegian People's Aid is the largest demining group in Angola and along with HALO Trust and Mines Advisory Group, two British mine-clearing companies, they are the lucky guys who have the thankless job of clearing them out. They find a lot more unexploded ordnance than land mines. A new generation of booby-trap mines designed to blow away the engineers trying to demine the country have been making regular appearances. They're no larger than a cigarette pack and can be motion or light sensitive. Made in South Africa, they can be set off by the magnetic influence of a deminer's detector. Overall, about 120 people a day are killed in Angola by land mines. About 200 mine fields (of a total of 2,229) have been cleared since 1995, but new mines are laid every day. It takes a day to remove a mine that takes 15 minutes to place. There are 60 types of mines, and during 1998 there was an average of 11 mine incidents a month, killing 5 people and maiming the rest.

Diamond Mining

Diamond mining in Angola is one of the world's most dangerous occupations, and it has nothing to do with hard hats and cave-ins. On November 8, 1998, some 50 UNITA rebels attacked the diamond mine at Yetwene, killing two British nationals and a Portuguese. Two Filipinos, a Briton and a South African were kidnapped. Despite the best efforts of Sandline and Tim Spicer on behalf of Diamondworks, nothing has happened. In all, five expats were killed and another five taken hostage. Security is a nightmare for mining companies. Ambushes and kidnappings have become routine.

Diamondworks

www.diamondworks.com

Thugs

Violent crime exists throughout the country. Armed robbery occurs in Luanda both day and night. Travel outside Luanda is not safe. In a country where police make the equivalent of $5 a month, there is little incentive to follow the straight and narrow. In Angola, crime does pay—at least a lot more than the cops make.

Shoplifting

Angola doesn't possess a formal prison or penal system. Most "law" offenders are simply beaten or executed.

GETTING SICK

Don't. Travelers are advised to purchase medical evacuation insurance. Malaria in the severe falciparum (malignant) form occurs throughout the entire country and is chloroquine-resistant. Tungiasis is widespread. Many viral diseases, some causing severe hemorrhagic fevers, are transmitted by ticks, fleas, mosquitoes, sandflies, etc. Relapsing fever and tick-, louse- and fleaborne typhus occur. Sleeping sickness (human trypanosomiasis) is regularly reported. Foodborne and waterborne diseases are highly endemic. Bilharziasis is present and widespread throughout the country, as are alimentary helminthic infections, the dysenteries and diarrheal diseases, including cholera, giardiasis, typhoid fever, and hepatitis A and E. Hepatitis B is hyperendemic; poliomyelitis is endemic and trachoma widespread. Frequently fatal arenavirus hemorrhagic fevers have attained notoriety. Rats pose a special hazard; lassa fever has a virus reservoir in the commonly found multimammate rat. Use all precautions to avoid rat-contaminated food and food containers. Ebola and Marburg hemorrhagic fevers are present but reported infrequently. Epidemics of meningococcal meningitis can occur. Echinococcosis (hydatrid disease) is widespread in animal breeding areas. The health system has collapsed. Three million people are at risk of famine, and, at its peak, more than 10,000 people were wounded a day during the war. There is one doctor for every 13,489 people. Angola has the highest infant mortality rate in the world, as well as the greatest number of amputees—not from sickness, but from mines.

Angola is a developing African country that has been plunged into civil war since its independence from Portugal in 1975. On May 19, 1993, the United States recognized the government of the Republic of Angola, and a U.S. embassy was established in Luanda on June 22, 1993. Facilities for tourism are virtually nonexistent. There are severe shortages of lodging, transportation, food, water and utilities in Luanda and other cities in the country. Shortages result in a lack of sanitary conditions in many areas, including Luanda.

The largest ethnic group, the Ovimbundu, comprises 37 percent of the population (and the essence of the UNITA forces) and lives mainly in the central and southern parts of Angola. The Kimbundu are the second-largest group, comprising about a quarter of Angola's population. They are primarily found along the coast and make up most of the MPLA. Finally, the Bakong account for 13 percent of the population. They live in the north and constitute the core of the FNLA forces. About one percent of the population is of mixed race, many of whom control key positions in government and business, further compounding ethnic problems. Before the war, as many as 330,000 Caucasians lived in Angola; perhaps 30,000 remain.

Per capita income in Angola was only about US$770 back in 1993; 75 percent of the people are engaged in subsistence agriculture. Life expectancy is a low 44 years, and more than half of the population is illiterate. The highest rainfall is in April; the coolest and driest time to go is July through September.

Money Hassles

There are a number of counterfeit Angolan $100 notes in Luanda. The notes are printed on the same paper that the real currency is. The counterfeit notes have 1990 and 1993 dates.

Registration

U.S. citizens who register at the U.S. embassy's consular section, which can now extend full consular services, may obtain updated information on travel and security in Angola.

Embassy Location

U.S. Embassy

*On Rua Houari Boumedienne
in the Miramar area of Luanda.
P.O. Box 6468
Tel: [244] (2) 34-54-81 and 34-64-18
(24-hour number)
Fax: [244] (2) 34-78-84*

Consular Section

*Casa Inglesa, First Floor
Rua Major Kanyangunla No. 132/135
Luanda, Angola
Tel: [244] (2) 39-69-27
Fax: [244] (2) 39-05-15*

1/27/00	UNITA asks for peacetalk saying neither side can win a military victory.
1/99	The UN withdraws its final 1,200 observers and peacekeepers from Angola.
12/98	The Lusaka Protocol peace accords crumble. UNITA resumes full-scale civil war against the dos Santos government.
11/8/98	Five foreign nationals are killed and another five kidnapped after UNITA rebels attack the Yetwene diamond mine in northeast Angola.
7/1/98	The UN places economic sanctions on UNITA in an effort to curtail its diamond mining profits and derail its ability to make war.
3/11/98	The Angolan government legalizes the rebel group UNITA.
11/20/94	The Lusaka Protocol peace accords signed.
1/89	Cuban troops withdraw from Angola under pressure from South Africa.
11/11/75	Angola wins its independence from Portugal.
1966	U.S.-backed Frente Nacional Para Libertacao de Angola (FNLA) founded.
1961	War starts.
1956	The Movimento Para Libertacao de Angola (MPLA) founded to end 300 years of Portuguese occupation.
1482	Portuguese build forts along the coast of Angola.

Bosnia-Herzegovina
★★

War Criminals United

Imagine a country where the various inhabitants have tried very hard to kill each other for nearly four years. Imagine hundreds of thousands of people being killed to the satisfaction, even glee, of the different sides. Imagine death camps being set up, women raped, and massacre after massacre happening year in, year out, all documented by the news crews.

It's a place without any goodies, just various shades of gray and black. I mean, this is the kind of war where one of the protagonists came out with the following comment: "We would never rape Muslim women...they're too ugly." Get the picture?

Okay, then imagine some idiot coming along with a very big stick and an even bigger checkbook who tells everybody that they have to live together in peace and friendship, and just kinda ignore the last few years of slaughter. Welcome to Bosnia. For the inhabitant, read Muslims, Croats and Serbs. For the idiot telling

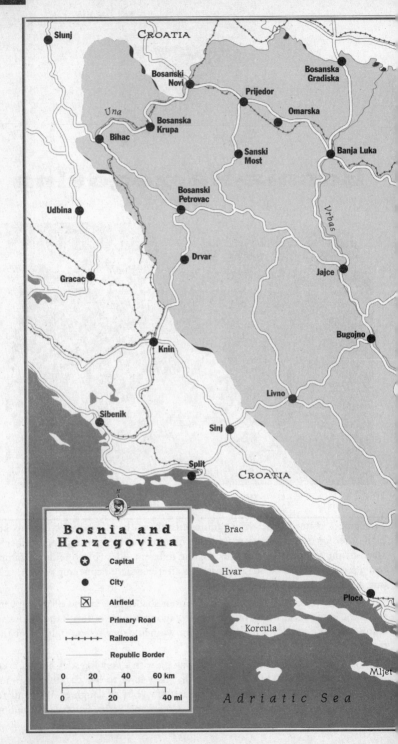

Slunj

CROATIA

Bosanski
Novi

Prijedor

Bosanska
Gradiska

Una

Omarska

Bosanska
Krupa

Bihac

Sanski
Most

Banja Luka

Bosanski
Petrovac

Udbina

Vrbas

Drvar

Jajce

Gracac

Bugojno

Knin

Livno

Sibenik

Sinj

Split   CROATIA

N

Bosnia and Herzegovina

Brac

⭐ Capital

Hvar

● City

🗵 Airfield

Ploce

Primary Road

┼┼┼┼┼ Railroad

Korcula

Republic Border

Mljet

0   20   40   60 km

0   20   40 mi

Adriatic Sea

them to live together, read the "international community," helpfully backed by about 30,000 NATO troops (8,000 of which come from the United States). It's pretty hard to believe, really. I mean, for 44 months the various sides try as hard as they can to prove that they have about as much desire to live together as Bill does in moving in with Monica, and what does the "international community" want? A multi-ethnic, multi-tolerant Bosnia! It does make you wonder. None of which is to say that a flawed peace is worse than all-out war. It just means that no one should be very surprised if it all starts over again once the "international community" loses interest and pulls out.

Of course, the popular view is that the war ended when NATO launched a bombing campaign against the Bosnian Serbs. The United States and Europe, the fiction goes, could no longer ignore the casualties and the atrocities (though they'd done a pretty good job of ignoring just that for the previous three years). Thus, heroic NATO bombed; the Serbs said "We surrender" and came to the table.

What is not mentioned is the fact that the Croats had been rearmed and trained for the previous year or so by the Germans with United States complicity. Even less is said about the fact that NATO's bombing campaign coincided with a masssive Croat offensive (retaking the Krajina region) that had the Serbs back-pedalling so fast they never really knew what hit them. Thus the "Dayton Accords" were born in November 1995, with a bit of additional vicious arm twisting by Richard Holbrooke, just to make sure that everyone agreed in the right spirit of reconciliation and friendship. It's really all very heartwarming.

Where did it all go wrong? Good question. How far back do you want to go? To a Serb nationalist whacking an Archduke in 1914? That's a start, I guess. Of course you could always trek a bit forward to World War II for a few really nasty massacres involving Croatian Ustashe, Muslim Nazis and Serbian partisans. Oh, what the heck! Why don't we all just go back to sometime in the 14th century when the Turks invaded the place. Let's just say it went wrong whenever the locals said it went wrong—hey, they're the guys who were fighting. You gonna call them liars? You mean, they don't know why they were fighting? If you want a more recent starting point, I guess we could always take the breakup of Yugoslavia. But to keep it very very simple, let's just say that various elites played the nationalist card to get their own little fiefdoms.

Top of the list was Franjo Tudjman, who started the ball rolling by declaring Croatia independent. It might not have mattered (it probably would have) if Germany hadn't recognized the bloody place. Suffice to say the Bosnian Muslims didn't like the idea of living in a federal republic dominated by Serbs and ruled by Belgrade. For their part, the Bosnian Serbs didn't hitch with the idea of living as a minority in a Muslim-dominated state. Oh, and the Croats didn't want to live with either of them as another minority. So they all spent the next 44 months duking it out with artillery to get each other's population statistics down. The Dayton Peace Accords seem to be the closest thing to an event worth celebrating.

This peace plan, which went into effect in January 1996, called for the stationing of 60,000 NATO troops in Bosnia, including 20,000 American soldiers. Bosnia's various armies pulled back to 2.5 miles from the 600-mile-long confrontation line, permitting NATO's Implementation Force (IFOR) to move between the warring factions. The Dayton accord requires that the Bosnian Serb army leave the suburbs of Sarajevo, and the Bosnian Croats have to cede their conquests in the country's northwest. The armies were then permitted to enter each other's evacuated territories during March 1996. The accords have bought some time, but Muslims are still forbidden by Serbs from reentering their homes, war criminals go on with their daily business, and bleached skeletons are uncovered by heavy rain. Land mines lurk in the dark woods, and hatred still festers in the hearts of the combatants. Nothing has really changed.

Currently, Bosnia is divided into two areas: the Muslim Croat federation and the Serb Republic. Supposedly, the country is "multi-ethnic," which is a misnomer if there ever was one. Each region is run by its own parliament while, just to keep everyone happy, there is a shared presidency so everyone can sort of take turns at being Prezzy. How nice. Under provisions made by the Dayton Accords, refugees are theoretically allowed to return to the homes they were expelled from. But generally speaking, about the only thing that unites the various groups is a determination to stop this happening. Bosnia is overseen by the Office of the High Representative (OHR), whose job it is to make sure that everybody plays ball with the Dayton Accords. A load of fun that must be.

Just to make sure that everybody stays best pals, there are about 30,000 NATO troops in Bosnia these days. They go under the name of Stabilistion Force, or SFOR for short. So for now, Bosnia is held together, just, by the Dayton Accords, which was signed by Slobodan Milosevic, Franjo Tudjman and Alija Izetbegovic, which rather goes to show who was pulling the strings all along. In September 1996, Bosnia held elections for the collective presidency that was established by the accords. Are they all happy boys? Well, apparently not.

It seems that Franjo forgot what he signed up to; in October 1999 he decided that Bosnia should really be split in three, and made a statement to that effect, which must have left Richard Holbrooke choking over his soup when he heard the news. Stay tuned for *Bosnia: Return of the Croats,* coming to a screen near you anytime soon.

So far, so good, you might be thinking. What will I see on a tour of Bosnia? Well, that rather depends on where you go. Much of Sarajevo has been rebuilt and it's actually quite a hip place to hang around these days. An army of aid workers, overly paid UN officials and about 30,000 NATO peacekeepers in the country means that Sarajevo is the place to hang out, even if most of the locals can't afford a cappuccino in the cafés. A must for any wanna-be tourist is Pale, the wartime HQ of the Bosnian Serbs. Well, actually, it probably isn't that much of a "must." Pale is pretty much "War Crimes City." It's where all those nice guys who spent most of the war indulging in a bit of ethnic cleansing now like to hang out in retirement. Actually, you can't really even say that they're retired. The ethnic cleansing might be over for the moment, but there's loads of racketeering and smuggling to keep all the guys busy. Take everybody's favorite psychiatrist, Radovan Karadzic: well, he's retired from politics, which is to say that he's been banned from holding any political office under the Dayton Accords. But that hasn't crimped his style—well, not much. He might be the most wanted man in Bosnia, but guess what? NATO troops just don't seem able to get hold of him. It's a bit like the Scarlet Pimpernel, just the reverse: "They don't seek him here, they don't seek him there . . ."

So, in the meantime Radovan's been able to carry on with business as usual, in the lucrative business of smuggling and extortion. And just to make sure that NATO doesn't get any silly ideas, he trundles round the place with a massive entourage of bodyguards—about 400 all told. Kinda hard to miss, really. That's not to say that all the war crimes have been having an easy time drinking cognac in safety.

In January 1999 Dragan Gagovic was most unfortunately shot dead by French peacekeepers. Perhaps it had something to do with the fact that he tried to run over the French soldiers as they moved in to arrest him? You never know. But the chances are that they would never have tried to arrest him if it hadn't been for the fact that he'd done the usual spot of rape and ethnic cleansing in the town of Foca in 1992 and 1993.

Another war crime to bite the dust in a less dramatic fashion was Serb army bigwig Momir Talic. You almost (but not quite) feel sorry for the guy. I mean, there he was off on a quick trip to Vienna on another "how-Muslims-Serbs-and-Croats-can-all-live-together course" when a couple of Austrian security goons arrest the guy. Why? Well, it turns out there'd been a nasty little "go-straight-to-prison-card" (a sealed indictment, to you) waiting for him in The Hague. And nobody had thought to tell him—how unsporting! Talic, who is a buddy of Ratko Mladic, did his share of ethnic cleansing when he commanded the 1st Krajina Corps during the war. The Serbos back at base were not chuffed in the slightest when they heard the news. In fact, they got distinctly sulky about the whole affair and huffed and puffed for a while before skipping on some of those tiresome confidence-building conferences that everyone likes to go to in Sarajevo.

So, with poor old Radovan and his Frankenstein sidekick, Ratko, out of the picture who's running the Serb show these days? A number of different people is the answer—with Radovan pulling the strings behind all of them. It kinda alternates between the strappy and the less strappy guys who hang around in Pale and Banja Luka. For a while, Nikola Poplasen had a stint at the helm of dear old Republic Serbska. But, you know, Carlos Westendorp—the West's big cheese in the area—didn't like his attitude. So he fired him, as he can under the Dayton agreement. The current Bosnian Serb President is Momcilo Krajisnik, and guess what? Surprise! He's another of Radovan's pals.

With a mass demobilization of troops and poor economic conditions, there has been an increase in crime. Police response to an emergency is often inadequate because law enforcement and civil authority have not ben established in many places. Anti-American sentiments run high throughout the country, particularly in Serb-controlled areas. Profiteering and extortion seem to be the basis for wealth in Bosnia these days.

Just across the border, the Belgrade Boys have got a leetle bit of inflation, which is running at a steady 70–90% for the Yugoslav dinar. All sides in the civil war have been implicated in human rights abuses, especially ethnic cleansing (a new euphemism for genocide) of towns and villages where entire populations were forced to flee to avoid murder, rape and torture. What seems even more ironic in all this senseless carnage is that the Serbs, Croats and Muslims are all south Slavs of the same ethnic stock. These people look alike, speak the same language and managed to live as neighbors for years. Over a million people have been displaced by the war and a million have left their homeland as war refugees. The dead total: 210,000; the wounded: 200,000. Many historic cities have been destroyed and 20 percent of Bosnia's homes leveled along with half the nation's schools.

Bosnia is a country where none of the inhabitants want to live next door to their neighbor. They spent 44 months in a civil war, trying their best to kill one another. Now they are supposed to live side by side and be nice to each other. The place is kept going by large amounts of aid being poured in by the European Union, United Nations and the United States, which keeps some of the people happy, some of the time. Those who do not do what they're told don't get any aid. It's simple. So they smuggle instead.

The Serbs

Officially "the Baddies" of the war, much to their own outrage. By far the worst massacres were at the hands of Serb forces. As many as 7,000 Muslims were killed when Serb troops overran the UN designated "safe haven" of Srebrenica. The Serbs just feel that no one sees their point of view; but as this involves paranoid rhetoric about a global "Muslim plot," this not is not very surprising.

E-mail: info@mvp.gov.ba
Web sites: http://www.wcw.org/icty/suspects.html; http://www.pdos.lcs.mit.edu/~dean/plavsic_bio.html

Slobodan Milosevic

Born in 1941, Slobodan Milosevic has turned out to be one of the great political survivors of the twentieth century. After all, how many people do you know who have lost four wars, have US$5 million on their heads, have been indicted by an international tribunal, and are still in power? He moved from being a communist apparatchik in the late 1980s to a Serbian nationalist just as Tito's Yugoslavia began to fall apart at the seams. At school he was remembered for being bossy and organized. At university he was in charge of the ideological section of the communist party—a bundle of laughs that must have been. He married Mirjana Markovic and they have had two nice children. By 1984 Slobo had crawled his way up the political ladder to be the head of Belgrade Communist Party. During his eight years in power, there have been four wars in the former Yugoslavia and over 300,000 deaths. Is it just that the guy is misunderstood? Slobo is the archetypal politician, which is to say that he will use anything to get and stay in power. Reading the sign of the times in the 1980s, he used Serb nationalism to get his place at the top. The problem was that there was a fair amount of Croatian nationalism as well. Germany helped with the destruction of Yugoslavia and the rise of Serb nationalism by recognizing Croatia. That got the initial bloodbath going. And on and off it has continued ever since. According to recent reports, he lives in the bunkered command center Crna Rijeka in the region of Jans Pijesak.

http://www.sps.org.yu/engleski/ljudi/smilosevic.html
http://www.wcw.org/icty/suspects/Ratko_Mladic.html
http://www.serbia-info.com
http://www.mvp.gov.ba/
http://www.un.org/icty/indictment/english/24-05-99milo.htm

General Ratko Mladic

The man who said, "we would never rape Muslim women . . . they're too ugly," which I guess speaks volumes about the guy. Quite what Muslim women have to say about him is not known to *DP*. But if words like "murderer," "ethnic cleanser," "killer" and "complete and utter bastard" are among them, then they will not be alone in holding such opinions. Mladic is an indicted war criminal, held to be responsible for the deaths of some 7,000 Muslim men when Serb forces took the supposed "safe haven" of Srebrenica. (That's just the most well-known deaths). The international community tried to tell him what to do; he didn't like it and pretty much said "watch this folks" and proceeded to sit back and watch his troops systematically gun down thousands of unarmed Muslim men and boys. He was also responsible for the shelling of Sarajevo throughout much of the war, in which 10,000 people died. As you can see, he's a really nice guy.

http://www.pdos.lcs.mit.edu/~dean/mladic_bio.html
http://www.un.org/icty/index.html

Radovan Karadzic

A former psychiatrist turned indicted war criminal who spent a bit of time in between as the rebel Serb leader during the civil war. Karadzic was the leader of the rebel Serb Republic until he was barred from office as a wanted war criminal. He might be retired from politics, but he's still a busy guy. There's smuggling to organize, debts to collect and The Hague to avoid. Should he leave Bosnia, there's a comfy little room waiting for him in The Hague. He can even stay there for the rest of his life if he wants, it's all free.

http://www.wcw.org/icty/suspects/Radovan_Karadzic.html

"Arkan"

Arkan (or Zeljko Raznatovic, to give his real name) made his reputation in Croatia in 1991 when he formed his "Tigers" militia. Wanted for the Vukovar massacre (one of the worst episodes in the Croatian war) by the international tribunal based in The Hague, Arkan has of late taken to appearing on CNN and emphasizing that he's really just your average family man (he probably is, in the Balkans). But his relations with CNN have not always been so good. In 1997 he threatened to sue the company when CNN ran a story, "Wanted," in which poor old Arkan was accused of being all sorts of nasty things, like a murderer, for instance. The poor guy must have been heartbroken. You won't be surprised to hear that CNN wasn't really that worried about being taken to court. In 1991 Arkan served six months in a Croatian slammer for possession of arms. So I guess that technically he had a criminal record. Not that it affected his career prospects too much. Actually, in his youth Arkan was known as a bit of a wild kid (no surprise that, I guess). He obviously saw the civil war coming, so to get a bit of practice he spent much of his time robbing banks. It has stood him in good stead ever since. Other things in his busy schedule include sitting in the Belgrade parliament (when he's not busy organizing ethnic cleansing). Poor Arkan was gunned down in the Intercontinental Hotel on January 14, 2000.

http://www.interpol-pr.com/
http://www.fas.org/irp/world/para/sdg.htm

Nikola Poplasen

Another hardline Serbian nationalist. Well, that makes a change! Can't be doing much with all these hand-wringing liberals all over the place. He replaced the more moderate Biljana Plavsic as the President of the Serb Republic who just showed too many signs of moderation. Poplasen established his credentials by inviting the charming and urban Vojislav Seselji (rabid and vicious, some would say, but at *DP* we don't say that kind of thing) from Belgrade to Banja Luka. Seselji wasn't too popular, though, and was escorted from Bosnia by NATO troops after the OHR declared him very PNG. Poplasen wasn't too popular either, for that matter, being viewed as something of an "obstacle towards peace." In 1999 he was sacked as the president of the Bosnian Serbs by the top Western peace envoy, Carlos Westendorp.

http://www.cdsp.neu.edu/info/students/marko/velsrb/velsrb1.html

The Muslims

Officially "The Victims" of the Bosnian war. Probably debatable. Underdogs might be a better description. It was partially the desire of the Muslims to create a separate state as Yugoslavia collapsed—in which the Serbs would have been a minority, rather like the Muslims would have been a minority in a "greater Serbia'—that left the Serbs heading to the high ground around Sarajevo with the artillery.

http://www.islamworld.net/bosnia.html

Alija Izetbegovic

Izetbegovic was elected president of Bosnia in 1992. For much of the civil war he hung around in Sarajevo, getting shelled like everyone else. Aged 70, he's also knocking on a bit, but hanging in there. When the war ended and everyone started picking up the pieces, Izetbegovic was elected as the Muslim rep for the collective presidency for the Bosnia Social Democratic Party, led by Zlatko Lagumdzija, who served as the deputy prime minster in Bosnia's Muslim-led government before he was wounded in 1993. The party is an amalgam of two opposition parties, the Social Democratic Party and the Social Democrats, which draw support from all ethnic groups in Bosnia. That's why they're the opposition. They hold a whole 25 of the 140 seats in the lower house of Bosnia's Muslim-Croat federation.

http://www.vu.nl/~frankti/archive/1992/english/izetbegovic.html

The Croats

The guys who seem to have got away with it all. The boys back in Zagreb have had a pretty good time of it really, especially when it comes to being not indicted for too many war crimes. The largest mass expulsion of any of the three ethnic groups was carried out by the Croats when they took the Krajina region. In a matter of days 600,000 Serbs were expelled from their homes.

Franjo Tudjman

He came to power in the first multi-party elections in 1990 and stayed in power until his death. Sensible chap. In his youth he spent a few years in the slammer for being a Croat nationalist. For the Croats he's the man who retook the Krajina region. For the Serbs, he's the guy who made 600,000 of them homeless. They will probably be taking some consolation in the fact that Tudjman's is six feet under. The 77 year old is dead of stomach cancer. Get the violins out.

The Montenegrans

If you want to place bets on where the next war in the Balkans is going to be, then this is the current favorite: Montenegro. It's the last republic in what was the Federation of Yugoslavia. And in all likelihood its only a matter of time before its hip and trendy Prezzy, Milo Djukanovic, decides he wants complete independence for his people, leaving poor old Slobo as president of a rather bankrupt Serbia. Not that anyone's betting Slobo will take any of this lying down. There is already speculation that Montenegro will dump the dinar and go for its own currency pegged to the German DM. This is no big surprise when you consider that the Yugoslav dinar is streaking all about the place at 70–90 percent inflation. Sections of the Yugoslav (Serb, really) army are based in Montenegro, but the police force is loyal to Djukanovic. All in all it makes the place a hot future favorite for mortars at breakfast. Milo Djukanovic is not a popular guy in Belgrade just at the moment. He didn't get into Slobo's good books when he won the elections beating Slobos boy, Momir Bulatovic. In a fit of sulks, Bulatovic organized a rally of 8,000 fellow goons who quickly started rioting. Djukanovic is even less popular now for giving tacit support to NATO's bombing campaign in Kosovo. Slobo refuses to recognize Djukanovic, and just to turn the screw, he won't give any tax revenue or customs due to the small republic. But given that most of Serbia no longer has a financial system, it's unlikely that Djukanovic minds too much. Montenegro is the last republic that is still part of the Yugoslav federation. If—or as some are saying—when it decides that Slobo ain't their kind of guy it will leave Serbia as a federation of republics without any republics in it.

http://www.montenegro.org/

NATO

There are currently 30,000 NATO troops in Bosnia trying to make the glue stick in the peace process. Another little chore for the NATO troops is to arrest any war criminals they happen to come across in the line of duty. You know, like if they bump into Ratko or any of his mates having a quick beer somewhere. Quite when NATO forces will pull out of Bosnia is not yet known. The current NATO chief is United States Army Lieutenant General Ronald Adams.

http://www.nato.int/ifor/ifor.htm

Louise Arbour

Not the popular kid in town, I'm afraid. Well, in some areas, at least. Louise Arbour has the job of investigating and then assembling all the evidence of war crimes. After that, all she has to do is prosecute the guilty parties. In Bosnia—and now Kosovo—it's a job that's likely to keep her employed for the next hundred years or so. Hey, at least she'll never be unemployed!

You can now fly directly to Sarajevo. Alternatively you can drive.

Your best bet is to hire a car.

The Hague

Not dangerous as in "dangerous," perhaps. But it's the one place where quite a lot of people are trying to avoid going. The Hague tribunal was set up to try war criminals, mainly after the Bosnian war. Officially, The Hague has about 76 people on its books, with prepaid reservations for accommodation. Unofficially, there may well be more. There have been two types of indictment: open indictments and sealed indictments, the latter of which are issued in secret, just so the war criminal in question stays nice and relaxed . . . until someone knocks on his door.

The Serb Republic

This does rather depend on who you are. If you're Russian, you'll find yourself downing cognac with the boys and being given a guided tour. Being a Yank or a Brit, though, is another matter. In fact, these days, being from any NATO country will probably mean you are PNG. Nasty looks will be the least of it. They're not happy bunnies.

Anti-Personnel Mines

In 1998 around 10 people were being hurt or killed a month by anti-personnel mines. Not bad compared to the 100 a month of 1997. There are mines galore in Bosnia, so if you stray off the track you'll quite possibly earn the nickname Stumpy for the rest of your days. Around Sarajevo there are 1,200 mine fields alone. Altogether there are about 30,000 mine fields. But don't get too wound up by all this. After all, a mine field can consist of as little as 5mines . . . or 3,000 mines. If in doubt, ask the locals. Or look for the three-legged cows grazing the field—always a good indicator.

Being a War Criminal

Or is it? Being a war criminal. Dangerous? I mean, actually most of the war criminals seem to be pretty well off. There are at least 40 indicted war criminals swanning around in Bosnia, and a number of sealed indictments, which do not reveal the identity of the accused (until NATO troops theoretically storm into his bedroom one morning). Only about 20-something war criminals have actually been arrested in the last four years or so. The boys at the very top of this list are the two R's: Radovan and Ratko. And it doesn't look like they're in any hurry to be on a free flight to The Hague, either. For that matter, it doesn't look as if NATO is exactly desperate to get them.

http://www.wcw.org/icty/suspects.html
http://www.igc.org/balkans/tribunal.html

The Web/Berserkistan

A defunct but very interesting experiment by DPer Jim Bartlett in war coverage from the front lines and on the ground.

http://www.imisite.org/berserk/

Bosnia covers a total of 19,776 square miles. The country runs a few miles of coast on the Adriatic Sea but is mostly landlocked. Bordered by Croatia, Serbia and Montenegro, it has a population of 4,408,000. The people of Bosnia-Herzegovina declared their independence in March 1992, and it's gone downhill ever since. Yugoslavia was held together by the big bear hug of Tito for 45 years, but now it's a crazed out-of-control multi-headed monster of religious and ethnic groups forced to live together—all harboring long-standing grudges that go back to the Middle Ages. About 44 percent of the people are Bosnian Muslims, 31 percent are Serbs, and Croats account for 17 percent. The remaining 8 percent includes Gypsies, Ukrainians and Albanians. Religiously, Slavic Muslims make up 40 percent of the population, Orthodox 31 percent, Catholics 15 percent and Protestants 4 percent. The official language is Serbo-Croatian, or Bosnian, written in Latin and Cyrillic. The Bosnian dinar is the monetary unit, with 100 paras to the dinar. Credit cards are now accepted in the Sarajevo; but the currency of choice is the German Deutsche Mark.

10/5/95	U.S. brokers Bosnia cease-fire
9/18/95	Muslim-Croat alliance sweeps Serb strongholds he offensive reduces Serb holdings in Bosnia from some 70 percent to 55 percent.
8/30/95	NATO assaults Bosnian Serb targets
8/28/95	Shells rip into Sarajevo marketplace, killing more than 35
8/19/95	3 U.S. diplomats and a French UN soldier die on peacekeeping mission when their armored vehicle slides of a road near Sarajevo
7/11/95	Srebrenica falls to Serbs
5/25/95	NATO launches air strikes against Bosnian Serbs.
12/20/95	The United Nations hands over control to the North Atlantic Treaty Organization. Operation Joint Endeavor, NATO's largest military mission since its founding in 1949.
7/25	Radovan Karadzic and Ratko Mladic indicted for war crimes.
7/11/94	Serbs seize Srebrenica.
2/6/94	A mortar explodes in Sarajevo's central market killing 68 people.
8/12/92	Stories and images emerge of emaciated Muslims being held in Bosnian Serb prison camps
4/92	Bosnian Serbsbegin siege of Sarajevo from the surrounding high ground
2/29/92	Bosnia-Herzegovina declares independence and the Bosnian Serbs declare their own separate state.
12/9/91	Rebel Serbs declare independence in Krajina region of Croatia.
6/27/91	Croats and Serbs begin fighting in Croatia.
6/25/91	Croatia and Slovenia proclaim indepedence from Yugoslavia. The Yugoslav army attacks Slovenia.
2/8/84	The XIV Winter Olympic Games open in Sarajevo There were 1,510 athletes from 49 nations compete

Bougainville
★

Jungle Boogie

The island of Bougainville is really part of the North Solomons, a name that is more indicative of its true geographic and ethnic alignment than its current position as an eastern outpost of Papua New Guinea (PNG). True, PNG is an autonomous country, but Australian business interests call the shots and cash the checks here. There is a lot of potential wealth in PNG, but it needs big cash to punch the big holes it takes to pull out the buried mineral wealth, something the T-shirt, flip-flop wearing natives don't have a lot of.

The Western history in the islands started when Louis Antoine de Bougainville generously gave his name to the big island (and the colorful, thorny, flowering bush that comes from the region). When he approached the smaller island to the north, he was greeted by cheers of "Buka, buka," which loosely translated means. "What? What?" He promptly named the island Buka.

The lush islands were traded like baseball cards between the French, British, Germans, Japanese and Australians without anyone bothering to ask the locals their opinion until, in 1964, copper was discovered in Panguna.

Overnight, Bougainville copper created an instant metropolis and the money flowed—flowing out of Bougainville and into Australian and PNG pockets. Laborers and technicians were flown in to work the mine, but only one in five of the 4,000 laborers was a foreigner. Although a few folks benefited, the quality of life for the people actually decreased as pollution from the mine began to destroy their pristine homeland.

In 1987, the Panguna Landowners Association, led by Pepetua Sereo and Francis Ona, was formed and they wanted their slice: $10 billion dollars and back payment of mine profits. A year later, after they were rebuked, the Bougainville Revolutionary Army was formed and the mine began to experience a number of shutdowns due to demonstrations, attacks and sabotages.

The mine was shut down in 1989 and the army was sent in to clear things up. Large numbers of people were rounded up and moved to 40 "care centers," or concentration camps. The press was kept out to make sure the term *civil war* didn't hit the papers. A recent sprinkling of gonzo journos have snuck into the south to tell the real story.

So far it is estimated that 7,000–10,000 citizens and soldiers have been killed in this conflict, with neither side offering an accurate body count. The blockade caused the expected suffering and deaths among the 12,000 noncombatant population as well. In 1997, the situation came to a head as London-based Sandlines brought in the mining companies' best friend: mercenaries from Executive Outcomes (fresh from their successful handiwork in Sierra Leone) to do a little surgical killing.

The tables turned when the army locked them up and mutinied. They were incensed that the government would spend $34 million on a contract for 40 South African mercenaries complete with infrared-equipped helicopter gunships instead of on equipment for them. For now, things have become more conciliatory between PNG and BRA, and the military blockade has been lift

In 1997 and 1998 unarmed troops began landing on the island to set up a peace monitoring group Australia sends 300 troops and kicks in $50 million a year to "monitor" the peace process. Things are slowly coming back to subnormal as aid groups endlessly interview locals and try to decide what needs to be done first. For now, Bougainville, with its totally destroyed Western veneer and *Heart of Darkness* past would be a perfect movie set for a post-apocalyptic film.

Bougainville can be considered the ultimate tropical getaway: No crowded hotels, no beach vendors and nothing but dark-faced ex-rebels and overly cheerful Aussie peacekeepers. The mine used to provide 45 percent of PNG's folding green, but for now it's just a big hole in the ground as homespun rebels keep the army at bay.

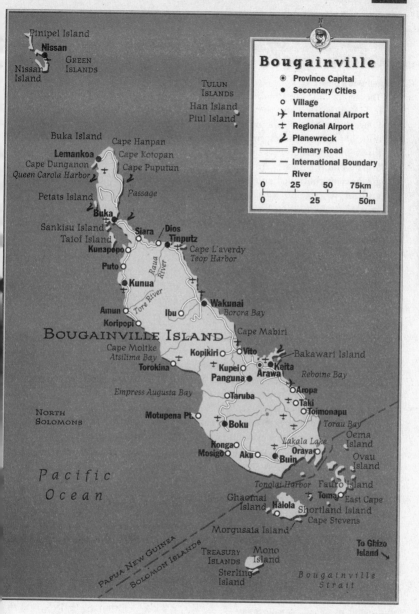

The Land Down Under

The land of Crocodile Dundee and Bazza MacKenzie is spending 100 to 120 million to build Bougainville, rather an odd turnabout considering they were busy helping PNG kill Bougainvilleans before. The locals complain that most of the money is just being spent on Australian firms to build expensive-to-maintain hospitals, schools and other infrastructure that will require outsiders to run and maintain. Francis told *DP* that for the same $6,700,000 the Aussies are spending to build a hospital in the non-affected and government controlled northern town of Buka, they could hire teachers and buy textbooks for every affected village on the island.

The Australians have taken a page out of the American book and pretend that they are spearheading a multinational peacekeeping force, when in fact they only have token representation and investment from the islands of New Zealand, Fiji and others.

AidWatch
http://www.toysatellite.com.au/aidwatch/reports/bougain.htm

Ausaid
http://www.ausaid.gov.au/country/png/bougainville.html
http://www.unpo.org/member/bougain/bougain.html

Francis Ona

The President of Mekamui lives in the village of Guava (a local word for "big hole") near the Panguna mine. The road that leads up to the mine is littered with downed power pylons, ditches and a tight squeeze through a landslide-covered section. Francis and his aligned chiefs have created the Mekamui National Chief's Assembly and its armed forces as the Mekamui Defense Force. Despite what you hear from the peacekeepers, Francis views them as interlopers and invaders. They have graciously made big red lined "No fly" zones for their orange Hueys because Francis and his boys like to shoot at them. There are also a number of shooting incidents each week that never really make the news.

Francis claims that he received his presidential support from the 700 chiefs and other supporters who met in Panguna on July 28–31, 1998.

E-mail: RosieK@bigpond.com

Martin Miriori/Bougainville Interim Government (BIG)

It seems Martin, who has been living in exile in Holland, has a little bad blood on the island of Bougainville. Something about living very well, handling aid money and other stuff that keeps him conveniently away from his homeland. Martin is also the guy that wrote a very creative press release about *DP* being mercenaries and being bounced out of the Solomons. When confronted on the phone by *DP*, he was all love and kisses. Yes Martin will make a fine politician.

E-mail: V.john@uts.edu.au (Vikki John, Bougainville Freedom Movement)

Bougainville Revolutionary Army (BRA)

BIG/BRA is led by Jospeh Kabui and Sam Kauona, former leaders under Francis Ona. The BRA have broken away from the former truck driver turned president. The BRA are part of the peace talks and are credited with giving *DP* a tense and less than peaceful send-off in Arawa. The BRA started as a rag-tag group of determined rebels who forced concessions from the main government in PNG. When Francis Ona put his foot down and refused to negotiate with what were his former enemies, the Kiwi/Aussie delegation provided funds for the military leader Sam Kauona to attend. Francis says he was paid $17,000 to start talking peace. The Bougainville Interim Government (BIG) is the political side of the BRA. They declared independence in May of 1990. The PNG Government reacted by imposing a complete economic and communications blockade. For now the rebels are fighting a bush war without any outside help. The island of Bukato is under government control as are many areas of the island of Bougainville, but the BRA still controls areas in the south and center of the island. At last count 67,300 Bougainvilleans are currently living in 49 governnent-run care centers in Bougainville. The BRA have taken hostages (usually government defense soldiers) and have been accused of executions. For now, the BRA has an office in Buka and Arawa and requires that all visitors get their permission before landing on Bougainville. They are not crazy about journalists.

There is no real animosity between the two factions of Ona and Kabui because most of the rebels are related to each other.

Australian Foreign Affairs and Trade
Web site: http://www.dfat.gov.au/geo/spacific/png/bougainville/

Rebels

It is hard if not impossible to tell the "boys" from the boys. The "boys" is how the locals describe the fighters who fought for the last decade against the PNGDF troops. Just about anyone between the age of 10 and 40 can be considered a former rebel. There is still much bad blood between the government, BRA and Ona factions on the island. This is exacerbated by the lack of jobs, economic incentives and infrastructure, as well as old feuds.

The rebels come down to the village to do their shopping every day. How can you tell who the rebels are? Look for the scrape marks on the side of the vehicles.

Papua New Guinea Defence Force (PNGDF)

They sat for months bored and trapped in grubby buildings and outposts. There were less than 750 soldiers on the island of Bougainville who couldn't leave for "peacekeeping purposes." Now they have all been sent home.

Bougainvilleans

There are only 170,000 Bougainvilleans left on the island. All have some sense of PST from the conflict and all are willing to get past it. They are 19 different languages, hundreds of chiefs and villages but most are related through marriage. Bougainville has also experienced ethnic cleansing by the flight of "rusties," or PNGers, during the conflict.

http://www.hartford-hwp.com/archives/24/157.html

The Panguna Mine

The Bougainville Copper Mine (BCL) in Panguna sits high in the clouds. This huge open-pit mine is jointly owned by the PNG government and the Australian mining company CRA (Conzinc Rio Tinto). In November 1988, the BRA blew up power pylons and other installations, forcing operations to shut down. When the BRA began to attack government offices and non-Bougainvilleans, PNG Riot Squad Police were deployed in December 1988, followed by three companies of regular PNGDF troops which arrived in March 1989.

Fame

GILLESPIE REJECTS BOUGAINVILLE ENTRY CLAIMS

CANBERRA, Australia (March 9, 1998, PACNEWS)—Australian civil rights lawyer Rosemarie Gillespie has angrily rejected claims that she helped four foreign nationals who tried to enter Bougainville illegally through the Solomon Islands.

Gillespie says it was she who alerted the Sydney-based National Coordinator of the Bougainville Freedom Movement, Vikki John, about the entry attempt and this led to

Solomon Islands police preventing the four men from crossing the border into Bougainville.

Gillespie, a vocal supporter of Bougainville independence, was appointed Research Officer for the breakaway Bougainville Interim Government in 1995.

She entered Bougainville four times during the war, carrying medicine and other humanitarian supplies, and did much to publicize the plight of the Bougainville people to the outside world.

In a statement issued Sunday, Gillespie says she was approached in January by an American writer, Robert Pelton, who wanted to interview rebel leader Francis Ona for a new edition of his book, *The World's Most Dangerous Places*. She said she repeatedly told Pelton and his three colleagues that the time was "not right" to visit Ona and that they should not do so unless they were invited.

She said she was concerned when she learned that one of the men, Rob Krott, was a former member of the U.S. Special Forces and had served as a mercenary in several countries.

"I raised the alarm when they would not take notice of me," she said. Gillespie said allegations made against her by the Secretary of the Bougainville Interim Government, Martin Miriori, and others were nonsensical and defamatory and she is threatening legal action.

http://www.amnesty.org/ailib/aipub/1997/ASA/33400197.htm

Jap Crap

If you do make the trip to Bougainville you might want to visit a piece of history. Near the village of Aku (24 kilometers before Buin) about an hour walk from the road, lies the wreckage of Japanese Admiral Yamamoto's Betty Bomber. He was shot down on April 18, 1943, by U.S. P-38s. All around the island are other relics of World War II. Buin is full of Japanese equipment and fortifications. A downed and very dead American pilot was found in his Corsair in 1968 just half a kilometer from Buin-Kangu Hill road. The mangrove swamps on Sohano Island near the Buka passage to the north are also full of old equipment, including a Japanese fighter. Green Island was a dumping ground for U.S. equipment after the war.

There are flights to Buka from Port Moresby. Buy your ticket to Arawa (the main town on the island). If you think you can just pop up the mountain for a chat with "Cranky Franky," as his detractors call him, forget it. *DP* was the first outsider in two years to meet with Francis and we were told there would be everything from snipers to skulls on sticks on the road up. Was there? Depends if you have an invitation.

You can now fly in on a selection of small- to medium-sized planes that fly out of Buka. There is usually a waiting period for seats out. Fuel is scarce. You can try hitching rides. Rains will wash out or flood most of the bridges and roads.

News Links for the Region

http://pidp.ewc.hawaii.edu/pireport/news_links_text.htm

You need a PNG visa and of course permission to enter Bougainville, which will be automatically denied. Aid workers are not restricted. You are also supposed to have permission from the BRA office in Buka to enter Bougainville. If you buy your ticket quick and don't make a fuss, they won't catch you until you've been and gone.

Port Moresby, PNG

As if it matters, there is a major crime problem with "rascals" or thugs in the main cities of PNG. There is also rape, robbery, carjacking, theft, mugging and the usual symptoms of primitive society forced to deal with Batman T-shirts and the Spice Girls. If you want more background call the Embassy Duty Officer at *(675) 321-1455, Fax: (675) 321-1593.* If you get thumped or waylaid call *(675) 693-8799* for help.

Our hardworking embassy in-country tells us not to patronize disreputable bars, proposition women, stay out after midnight or visit cemeteries, dead-end streets or the remote bush. If you would like this in the crystal-clear language of our government: "PNG is experiencing incomplete transition from subsistence agriculture" in a country that has "unifying elements that are counterbalanced by social strains." Thanks, guys.

Have Gun/Will Travel

Sandline International won their court case against the government of PNG. It seems that even if you change your mind about the tune, you must still pay the piper. Sandline was brought in to clean up PNG's nasty rebel infestation. To do that they subbed out the dirty work to Executive Outcomes (EO), a now defunct mercenary firm out of South Africa. EO flashed a card almost identical to TV's Paladin, or a knight's chess piece. The company's form of security for mining operations was part of a new trend in "outsourcing" security services to stabilize entire countries as evidenced in Angola and Sierra Leone. When PNG prime minister Julius Chan brought in the hired guns, he neglected to tell folks that he actually owned a piece of a mining security firm that took care of some nasty business in PNG. Well, enough dirt. What do you get for $36 million (up from the original fixed price of $32 million) these days? Well, first you get an ever so euphemistic proposal with statements like: "This operation is highly sensitive and needs to be carried out with a precision that will completely disable the enemy command structure with minimum collateral damage in order to make it acceptable to the Government and people of PNG and to world opinion."

Nicely put, but how exactly did they intend to snuff out the fuzzy-haired little buggers so the big boys can cash their checks?

"To achieve this, the military imperative is the ability to gather high-grade, specific intelligence about the location, capacity and intentions of the enemy force, particularly their C31 assets and match that intelligence with a strike capability, the key ingredients of which are: firepower, mobility, precision, speed and surprise." What this means is that EO's air wing would bring in one fixed-wing aircraft carrying $4 million worth of electronic eavesdropping and sensing gizmos to take pictures and record sounds and then send in troops and helicopter gunships to wax the leaders. Soldiers would be paid around $13,000 a month and get full medical and insurance benefits and rapid evacuation via EO's jet aircraft to Australian hospitals.

The PNG government had to pony up all logistic support, including fuel, accommodation, food and medical supplies for all personnel. It also included three secret trips by team leader and now jailbird Tim Spicer.

The deposit of $15 million was cashed. The mercs were tossed. The East German gunships are sitting gathering dust in Australia. Sandline sued and won. The mercs are all back here killing time instead of islanders. When *DP* asked Sandline if they had a message for Ona, they asked quite politely that they give them credit for forcing the peace process. Ona wishes they could have tussled in the thick green jungles of his backyard. "We would have liked to whip those boys," he said chuckling.

Sandline International
www.sandline.com

Hey, you're on a tropical island with no sanitation and no doctors. What could go wrong? It might be illuminating to know that of the 80,000 Japanese troops on these islands during World War II, 23,000 were taken prisoner, 20,000 were killed, and a staggering 37,000 died of starvation and disease. Malaria is a major problem. If you need help, there is a tiny clinic in Akampos, but you best get off the island to Gizo for anything more than a Band-Aid.

There are no nuts or bolts. There are very minimal services on the island of Bougainville. Like the great words from *Gilligan's Island*, "No phones, no lights, no motorcars. Not a single luxury." Things are improving daily. Bougainville is 200 kikometers long and an average of 80 kilometers wide, yet there are 19 different languages spoken. Thankfully, a pidgin form of English is one of them. It is only 20 kilometers from the Solomons, but is connected politically to PNG. It is mountainous terrain covered with tropical jungle, complete with misty mountains and steaming vents. The highest point is actually an active volcano, which adds a bit of drama to the whole affair. Most of the 156,000 residents live along the coast, with about 12,000 people living in the embargoed area of south Bougainville.

Embassy/Contacts

Passport, onward/return ticket and proof of sufficient funds required. Visitor's permit issued on arrival for stay up to two months in one-year period. Remember, you will probably be refused entry to Bougainville, so ask first about prevailing conditions and don't expect an intelligent answer.

Contact Papua New Guinea Embassy
Third Floor, 1615 New Hampshire Avenue, NW, Washington, DC 20009
Tel: (202) 745-3680
Fax: (202) 745-3679.

Embassy of the United States of America
P.O. Box 1492
Port Moresby, Papua New Guinea
Tel: 321-1455
Fax: 321-3423.

Papua New Guinea Consulate

Suite 2700, 145 King Street West
Toronto, Ontario M5H 1J8
Tel: (416) 865-0470
Fax: (416) 865-9636.tan

Martin Miriori (International BIG Secretary in Europe, NL)

Tel: +31-55-577-99-60
Fax: +31-55-577-99-39
E-mail: UNPOnl@antenna.nl
(Unrepresented Nations and Peoples Org.)

Bougainville Freedom Movement (BFM)

Sasha Baer or Vikki John
P.O. Box 134, Erskineville NSW 2043,
Australia
Tel:+61-2-9558-2730
E-mail: V.John@uts.edu.au

Bougainville Interim Government (BIG)

Moses Havini (International Political Representative in Asia/Pacific)
PO Box 134, Erskinville, NSW 2043,
Australia
E-mail: tuluan@ar.com.au
Tel./Fax: +61-2-9804-7632,
Mobile: +61-(0)414-226-428

Rosemarie Gillespie, Overseas Research Officer

24 Garling Street
Lyneham ACT 2602 Australia
Tel: [61] (6) 257-1298

Map of Bougainville

http://www.datec.com.au/png/
mapframe.htm

Max Watts—(specialised Journalist)

P.O. Box 98, Annandale NSW 2038,
Australia
Tel: +61-2-9564-1147
Phone/Fax +61-2-9818-2343 (work)
E-mail: RosieK@bigpond.com

Bougainville Interim Government—Solomon Islands

Martin Miriori, Netherlands
Tel: [31] (55) 577-99-60
Fax: [31] (55) 577-99-39
E-mail: unponl@antenna.nl
(c/o Robin Sluyk)

Resources

http://www.hartford-hwp.com/
archives/24/index-w.html

Sandline Inquiry

http://datecbne.datec.com.au/
sandline.nsf

AusAid Bougainville

http://www.ausaid.gov.au/country/
png/bougainville.html

PNG Links

http://coombs.anu.edu.au/
SpecialProj/PNG/Index.htm

The National

http://www.wr.com.au/national/

Post Courier

http://www.wr.com.au/national/

Tok Pisin

http://www.abc.net.au/ra/png/
pnghome.htm

7/1/99	PNG government offers vote on "limited autonomy" for Bougainville.
12/9/98	Bougainville leaders announce that they will ignore the vacuum created by the adjournment of the PNG Parliament and will form their own Bougainville People's Congress.
11/97	Three hundred peacekeepers arrive on island, which costs $50 million a year.
1/23/98	Lincoln Agreement is signed at Lincoln University in Christchurch, New Zealand.
7/18/97	Burnham peace treaty is signed in Burnham, New Zealand.
4/15/97	Day that Executive Outcomes would be ready to swing into action.
1997	PNG government hires Sandline International.
10/14/96	Premier Theodore Miriung assassinated.

1/30/96	Rebel leaders and their delegation are ambushed, returning by boat to Bougainville from the Cairns peace talks.
5/17/90	Francis Ona declares independence for the Republic of Bougainville.
2/14/90	St. Valentine's Day massacre, in which PNGDF drops five bodies from Iroquois helicopters.
6/89	PNG Government announces a state of emergency, and in July four Iroquois helicopters are received from the Australian government.
1/89	Violence erupts.
11/88	Sabotage of mines begins.
1987	Pepetua Serero and her first cousin, Francis Ona, demand compensation (K10 billion in compensation, a 50 percent share in BCL profits and greater environmental protection) from the Panguna mineowners Bougainville Copper Limited (BCL), a subsidiary of Conzinc Riotinto Australia (CRA).
9/75	Unilateral declaration of independence.
1974	The Bougainville Copper Agreement is signed with some resentment on the part of the Bougainvillean landowners.
9/1/75	Independence Day.

In a Dangerous Place: Bougainville

Bugurup

The 10th or 20th time the boat's engine refuses to restart, Russell throws the lump of metal he calls an anchor into the water. Metal and rope separate faster than Yugoslav republics, and I stare, unsurprised, at the loose soggy knot that floats back to the surface. It could't really be any other way. We are now adrift in the South Pacific and no one's singing. The only thing left is for us to sink, and I start wondering exactly when that will happen.

Wondering when things will happen has been our main source of entertainment for five weeks now, and in the next five will change my philosophy of life. I now believe people to be divided into three basic types. The vast majority are Brians, who tend to look on the bright side of life. Then there are the Murphys, who believe that anything that can go wrong—Slavs, (Luton) supporters, filmmakers. And last, there are those who know that Murphy was an optimist—filmmakers trying to make a documentary in Bougainville. Bougainville is an island 600 miles east of the capital of Papua New Guinea and only 6 miles west of the Solomon Islands. Despite the fact that its geographic, ethnic and cultural links are patently with the latter, in the first half of the century it was made part of PNG during the close-your-eyes-and-draw-a-line-on-the-map-somewhere territorial carve-ups by the colonial powers that have kept arms dealers in profit ever since. While there were muted demands for self-determination when Papua New Guinea got independence in 1975, it was the excavation of the world's biggest copper mine on the island that finally catalyzed the locals into rebellion in 1989. A people whose life, soul and tradition is the land they own grew increasingly fed up with the huge hole appearing in the middle of their island, the damage its chemicals were doing to the environment they lived off and the minimal compensation they were getting for it.

When their demands were ignored, the landowners decided to close the mine with force, Papua New Guinea sent in a heavy military response, the Bougainville Revolutionary Army was formed and a war for independence started in earnest. Since then the Papua New Guinea Defence Force has maintained a sea blockade around the island with a shoot-to-kill policy, one of the reasons why only a smattering of journalists have got in since and why most of the world has never heard of Bougainville. Gizo in the Solomons is the gateway to Bougainville and Bishop Zale is the man with the key, a priest of the airwaves who constantly relays messages to and from the island on his shortwave radio. He greets our still fresh and eager faces with a broken-toothed smile and tells us that the seas are too rough for boats to come for us from Bougainville at the moment. Tomorrow maybe. We set off to explore Gizo.

By lunchtime we are finished. Gizo is the second largest town in the Solomons and a pretty one, with reefs and truly emerald isles scattering the vivid shades of blue around it. But with only 4,500 people, two streets and one bar there isn't a whole lot to do. The life here is all underwater at some of the best dive sites in the world, a wholly different planet of which we get a tantalizing glimpse on what we can stretch out of the budget. The rest of the time Carlos, the soundman, Alex, a photographer, and I spend reading, sitting in the bar, patronizing the local cinema (where a large TV plays pirate Z-videos that make Van Damme movies look like *Citizen Kane),* sitting in the bar, listening to the cluck of the geckos, reading, sitting in the bar. . . .

As the days trudge by we begin to realize that the bishop belongs to the Church of Godot. When the weather clears there are boat engines that need to be fixed. We duly fork out and are told, "Tomorrow maybe." But then our captain vanishes without a trace to another island. Other excuses follow until one fine day, four weeks after our arrival, "Tomorrow maybe," actually becomes "Tomorrow." Newly versed experts in Beckett as we are, we don't believe the word, but nevertheless turn up at the waterfront at six the next morning for a covert rendezvous with our new captain who has been described as dreadlocked and fat.

Five hours later someone finally approaches us and, as we should have expected all along, he is close-cropped and thin. We don't care—he has a boat and right now he can take us where he likes. Which turns out to be a nearby island that even at low tide just the three of us make as crowded as Malibu Beach when surf's up. As our only link with the world assures us that another boat will be along soon and chugs into the distance, we wonder how many nights we'll have to spend on our shadeless little Alcatraz. Various atavistic scenarios flash before us, envisioning a quick regression to *Lord of the Flies* territory, maybe still hiding out here in 20, 30 years like diehard Japanese soldiers while our mothers and producers are flown overhead, trying to assure us that the war is over. "No!" we will scream back defiantly. "It's a trick! The war is still there and we still have to film it!" Inexplicably, though, a boat does appear almost immediately. It even has a hefty, dreadlocked skipper at the helm. This is Russell, soon to be known as the Dead Albatross for his curse on all things maritime. He is relentlessly optimistic and assures us the trip to Choiseul Island. The northern part of the Solomons, from which the BRA will take us through the blockade, is only four hours. No worries. Everything will be fine. And indeed it is, for an hour. Then the engine breaks down for the first time. Russell isn't phased when it refuses to restart and decides we just have to wait a little bit.

BOUGAINVILLE

No worries. For the next two hours he manages to get it going intermittently, each time with a blindly faithful grin that it will never break down again, and takes us one step forward while the rest of the time the current confidently washes us two steps back. When the engine finally throws in the towel, the Albatross does the same with his unattached anchor and I realise that anything that can,t go wrong will. Some hours later a local fisherman tows us to the nearest island where we spend the night while repairs are paid through the nose for at a nearby logging camp. Before we go to sleep in the dusty pungency of a copra shed, the Albatross promises, "Tomorrow everything will be 100 percent okay. I am skipper for all weathers. Just two hours to Choiseul now. No worries." Strangely, I almost believe him. I guess it's better than crying. Two hours into the next leg of the voyage of the damned there is still no land to be seen ahead of us. Or to any side of us, for that matter. The Albatross assures us that's because it's too cloudy, though my swiftly crisping skin tells me otherwise. Still, we relax slightly in the knowledge that time here is not the one we know, and a two-hour trip will invariably be at least twice that, just as tomorrow really means next week. Some years later Carlos glances at the afternoon sun to our right. . . . Our right? As we're meant to be heading north, this seems a little odd. He looks at the compass on his all-singing, all-dancing watch. Back at the sun. Back at his watch. "Russell, we're heading southwest." None of us really believe—none of us really want to believe this. But the fact is inescapable—the Albatross has been cheerfully steering us into the middle of nowhere, straight into the great wide ocean. We have no idea for how long or how consistently, but rapidly do a U-turn and head northeast, hoping to hit Choiseul at least somewhere along its coast before it gets dark. The Albatross still won't admit the reasoning of compass, sun and total absence of land, but he clearly isn't sure enough of himself to protest and pretends he's changing course just to make us happy. He shrugs and grins—no worries. I flinch because now I know something bad is going to happen. And sure enough, the engine dies within five minutes. In brief spurts of life thereafter, it struggles to push its heavy cargo through increasingly choppy seas, but with the Albatross in charge it's a Sisyphean task. The only advice I can give about malfunctioning machines is, "Hit it." And again. But it's been clear since we set out that Alex, and especially Carlos, know more about this engine than the Albatross. Any polite deference to our supposed skipper is jettisoned in direct proportion to the amount of water we're taking on board. Carlos moves to the stern and instructs the Albatross on exactly how to treat the motor to keep it alive.

Alex, meanwhile, who has read enough horror stories of people adrift on the ocean for this to be his worst nightmare, has bypassed the agnostic in himself and started silently praying. And it seems to be answered. Ahead of us he spots a cloud that he likens to a flying turtle. As I watch, it fills out into something remarkably like a dove. I remember a story about an ark and an olive branch and there—that's not a mirage is it?—just beneath the cloud—is that?—it must be—yes, yes—I think—land! And then the dolphins come. A school of 30 or more, surrounding us, comforting us, coiling in and out of the blue, and leading us, yes, it must be, leading us to land. Hallelujah! The sight of it is so beautiful that it almost makes everything seem worthwhile. I grin, Alex grins, Carlos grins, the Albatross, as ever, grins. And then he has to, doesn't he? He has to say it, "You see—no worries!" As the dolphins vanish, I wonder if I should make a sacrifice of the Albatross to appease whichever god we've so clearly pissed off—Yahweh, Allah, Neptune, any will do. Just give me the excuse. The dim sanctuary of terra firma dissolves as the sun slips down, dragging with it the dregs of our hopes. In the distance Alex spies a trawler. He ties his T-shirt to an oar, waves an SOS from the bow, and I realize we're on the raft of the Medusa. The trawler speeds off, the night settles down and the engine's heroic bursts get shorter and shorter. Carlos makes it clear that it's going to die eternally under this weight. Something has to go. I have my own ideas on making the boat lighter, but, with only a half pack of custard creams and tin of tuns on board, we might need to cannibalize the Albatross later. He agrees with Carlos, though, and says we'll have to lose either some of the petrol or the beer. Excuse me? Beer? What bloody beer?

And so it turns out that the mysterious boxes under all our luggage are not medicines or schoolbooks or clothes for the people of Bougainville, but enough cans of beer to keep a coachload of Liverpool fans happy, well, at least half the way to Wembley. It isn,t even going to cheer up the soldiers of the BRA, just to a bar in Choiseul, and so, sacrilegious though it seems, presently we are leaving a trail of bobbing Solbrew in our wake. Even this isn't enough, though, and a 200 liter drum of petrol soon joins its tiny alcoholic cousins. At least the engine chugs constantly now, but to make up for it the Pacific spews more of itself into our faces. Captain Carlos (for such he has become) constantly barks compass directions at the Albatross who hasn't even mastered the notion of steering towards a particular star and veers off course every few minutes. The rest of us try to peer through the barrage of waves for any sign of the land we pray we're zigzagging towards. Phosphorescent algae plays tricks with our eyes, suggesting cozy little villages on the horizon before hurling itself into the boat—but finally the consensus comes that faint lightening of the sky over there is some sort of life. It could just be a ship leading us into uncharted waters, but Crusoes can't be choosy.

Just before midnight, we pull into a small village, which suddenly seems the acme of civilization, and a couple of dim figures on the beach assure us that we have in fact reached Choiseul. I decide to remember Carlos in my will, shine my torch on the two figures and find the welcoming insignia of the Royal Solomon Islands Field Force. At least the Albatross has been consistent. Not content with frazzling, half-drowning and completely scaring us, he has now delivered us into the hands of the Solomons border patrol, whose current main occupation is stopping journalists like us from crossing to Bougainville.

Seeing us arrive at dead of night with a Bougainvillean, on an island that sees about ten tourists a year, naturally arouses some suspicion. Names are taken, passports checked, but right now we don't really care. It would be a blessing if they deported us. We are denied even that way out, though. Of course no one really believes we're just tourists who've paid the Albatross to boat us around, but no one really cares either. In general the Solomon Islanders' sympathies are with the Bougainvilleans, and it's quite clear there are ties between the BRA and the Field Force. One of them even offers to take us to our rendezvous with the rebels, and the next morning turns up drunk after an all-night binge, no doubt on some of the beer we didn't find when we were throwing things overboard. In true yeasty tradition, he mumbles about wanting us to trust him. He'll see us all right. Then, in even truer yeasty tradition, he disappears for good. For the next few days we are shunted from village to village, awaiting boats that never turn up to fulfill arrangements that change by the hour.

Finally a horde of heavily armed BRA do turn up at our fourth resting place in as many days, and when we make it clear that we're either on their first boat in or on the next plane out, they hurry us to the beach. As, with relief, I watch the Albatross dwindle to a squat speck on the shore, I realize that it's been such an effort just to struggle through the "Maybe tomorrows" of the Bougainvillean network that I've utterly forgotten the main danger of the whole enterprise—the Papua New Guinea Defence Force and its gunboats on the border. It comes home with a shock as the three BRA boats we're heading in with stop in the middle of the sea and a short prayer for a passage that won't "bugurup" is offered. I look at the five armed men on my boat, at the canisters of petrol stacked around me and realize that it isn't really a case of the PNGDF catching us—just one stray bullet will be enough to fry us. The burnt scar tissue twisting the face of the guerrilla next to me is eloquence itself. Still, the Albatross isn't aboard, so maybe we stand a chance. As we set off at the speed we've been looking for since we left Gizo, getting the back-slamming, bum-battering, bollock-breaking ride of our lives, it becomes obvious that these people do know what they're doing. It doesn't, of course, stop our boat breaking down on the wrong side of the border, but no gunboat appears on the horizon, and by nightfall we have actually staggered onto Bougainville, disproving all our theories that it was really some never-never-never again land at the end of a concocted rainbow.

The plan is to make our way to Guava, the mountain base of Francis Ona, leader of the Bougainville revolution and president of its self-declared republic. He, at least, we have been told, is awaiting us. Plans, however, not being worth the optimistic electrons they're dreamt up with on Bougainville, this gets stamped down on morning one. Instead we are intercepted by a group of officials headed by a member of Military Intelligence who soon reveals himself to be proof incarnate that that term is an oxymoron. Suspicions of white visitors is high since PNG hired a British company, Sandline, at the beginning of the year to supply mercenaries to finish off the BRA. Media exposés, followed by protests in the PNGDF (who'd sort of admitted they were beaten anyway) and domestic and international protests soon scotched this idea, but it's clear that we, as Brits, are being regarded as possible spies in the vanguard of a future attempt. That may be fair enough, but what I find rather staggering is that the Military Stupidity official doesn't even know the basic facts about Sandline and the expert force, which could well have proved to the greatest threat to Bougainvillean independence yet. His line of interrogation includes such gems as, "Do you have anything to hide?" and "Is there anything you're not telling us?"—cunning traps that I just manage to avoid falling for. In the end I decide he's just trying to throw his weight around to impress us (at least I hope so for the Bougainvilleans' sake), while achieving exactly the opposite. What he does make obvious is the success of eight years of PNG blockade in keeping many of the islanders out of touch with the rest of the world. Despite the fact that in those years there have been fewer journalists here than you'd have found on a quiet day in the Sarajevo Holiday Inn, the officials ranked before us seem to have decided that said journalists' ability so far to change the minds of their governments about the war means they're a waste of time. We don't pretend that we'll make any difference either, but do point out that if it wasn't for those journos, even fewer people in the world would know Bougainville existed. And that if some of the journos hadn't broken the Sandline story, a lot of Bougainvilleans might well be dead by now. And that killing the messenger tends to be counterproductive anyway.

—**Dom Rotheroe**

Brasilia

Brazil
★★

Street Kids Named Desire

Imagine a country where the most dangerous criminals are those that are supposed to protect you; a place where you are always the prisoner. Could it be Hell?

Close.

It's Brazil, where the most dangerous people are cops, anyone who ever was a cop, and anyone who ever thought of becoming a cop—not to mention all off-duty cops. In April 1997, 17 cops went on trial for the massacre of 21 residents of a shantytown in Rio. The victims' crime? Living in a neighborhood where some police officers were killed.

In May 1999, a São Paulo court overturned the 59-year prison sentence given a former police officer who was videotaped shooting at slum dwellers. The cop was one of eight caught on tape in 1997 beating the crap out of three men with nightsticks at a São Paulo roadblock. After the gendarmes allowed the victims to return to their car, the convicted officer decided to take some target practice and killed a 27-year-old mechanic in the back seat.

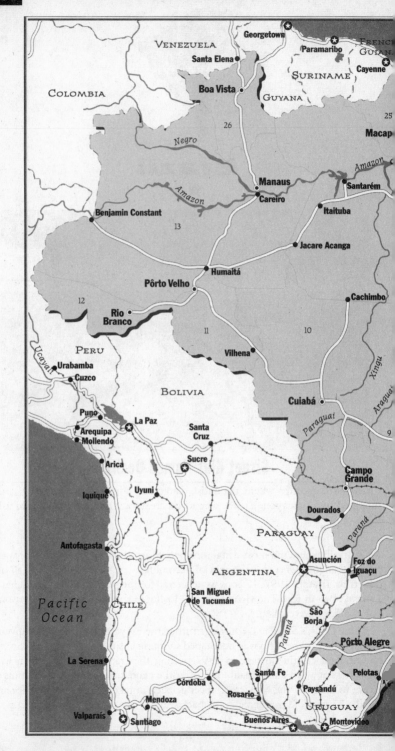

BRAZIL

BRAZIL

Atlantic Ocean

Brazil

- National Capital
- State Capital
- Secondary City
- State Border
- Primary Road
- Secondary Road
- Railroad

| 0 | 250 | 500 | 750 km |
| 0 | | 250 | 500 mi |

Belém

São Luís

Santa Inês

24

Fortaleza

Pôrto Franco

Teresina

22

21

Picos

Natal

20

João Pessoa

Miracema do Norte

23

19

Recife

Juàzeiro

18

17

Maceió

rupi

15

Barreiras

16

Aracaju

Ibotirama

Salvador

Brasilia

Vitória de Conquista

oiânia

Pirapora

Montes Claros

Pôrto Seguro

berlândia

8

7

5

Belo Horizonte

Vitória

Volta Redonda

Niterói

ão Paulo

Rio de Janeiro

iritiba

Santos

Florianópolis

io

Tocantins

Tocantins

São Francisco

States of Brazil

1. Rio Grande do Sul
2. Santa Catarina
3. Paraná
4. Mato Grosso do Sul
5. São Paulo
6. Rio de Janeiro
7. Espírito Santo
8. Minas Gerais
9. Goiás
10. Mato Grosso
11. Rondônia
12. Acre
13. Amazonas
14. Parâ
15. Tocantins
16. Bahia
17. Sergipe
18. Alagoas
19. Pernambuco
20. Paraíba
21. Rio Grande do Norte
22. Ceara
23. Piauí
24. Marnahão
25. Amapa
26. Roraima

Note: Brasilia is surrounded by a federal district

During the same month, hundreds of Rio slum residents rioted after the police shooting and killing of a 15-year-old boy. It was the third child shot by police in as many days.

Just another day in the office with Brazil's finest.

Rio de Janeiro is a continuing source of petty crimes committed by street kids barely out of pajamas. Shopkeepers pay the cops to pick off the toddler thieves like coyotes on a Wyoming sheep farm. About five children are murdered a day, according to the University of São Paulo. Treated like vermin, most street urchins have a short life span. Many work for drug dealers; they sniff glue and gasoline to kill their hunger pangs. There is little sympathy on behalf of Rio's citizenry for these prepubescent dope peddlers, and it's unlikely that the police, who knock them off on a regular basis, will be convicted for what is generally viewed as a socially beneficial act.

Is is estimated that there are 7 million kids living on the streets in Brazil. Hunted by death squads like rats in a sewer, they subsist by begging, stealing and deionizing themselves on petrol-based solvents. Are they a threat? You bet.

Other criminals in Brazil fall under the umbrella of nebulous quasi-terrorists. One street gang, with visions of sugarplums and Abu Nidal, menacingly calls itself the Commando Vermelho (Red Command). This "terrorist" group strikes in a sporadic fashion, but its actions are essentially criminal activities. In fact, the Red Command may be no more than a gang operating under a nom de guerre. And the absence of any identifiable pattern in the crimes suggests most are the work of individuals rather than any organized group.

There's a huge difference in living standards between the developed south of Brazil and the northeast. Consequently, there has been massive migration to Rio's and São Paulo's slums. This has caused a sharp increase in urban violence. A group of neo-Nazi nasties called *Carecas do Brasil* (Skinheads of Brazil) operate with two other extremist clubs out of São Paulo and specialize in brutally beating *Nordestinos* (northeasterners) along with Jews, blacks and gays, not to mention murdering street kids.

The poverty-stricken lower classes have essentially seen zero benefits from the past growth of the economy. About half of all Brazilians are black, and they make, on average, about half of what the whites make. In Brazil, nearly one-fifth of the population is illiterate. The country also has one of the world's most disparate income distributions: 60 percent of the national wealth is possessed by one percent of the population, with maybe 50 percent of the population living in poverty. Since World War II, the purchasing power of Brazil's minimum wage has been cut in half. Because of widespread inefficiency and corruption, only 8 percent of the government's social spending reaches the poorest of the population. In Rio, poor families have become squatters on empty lots and in abandoned and partially completed housing complexes. Brazil's underbelly is also being corroded by the spread of drug abuse and such diseases as AIDS, bubonic plague and cholera—a few good reasons for a lot of crime.

You might expect a little mayhem in a country where 20 percent of the population lives in extreme poverty and another 20 percent is said the be "barely surviving." In one 9-month period, there were 6,012 murders in Rio alone. These days, about 18 people are murdered each day in Rio. In São Paulo, 25 people are killed every day. About 90 percent of all the violent crimes in Rio are committed against or by minors. Most of the violence can be linked to drugs and theft. Teenage drug bosses have set up their narco shops in the favelas, the slums in Rio's surrounding hillsides, and loaf around in sandals toting automatic rifles. In February 1997, police found a gang of street kids in possession of an antitank rocket launcher, antitank rockets and machine guns. Eeks! Such weaponry might help explain the ease Brazilians enjoy stealing cars. Auto thefts average a whopping 3,000 per month in Rio, and a simply staggering 10,000 per month in São Paulo.

Try, Try Again

A mathematics teacher, down on his luck, attempted suicide July 9, 1997, by detonating a bomb he was carrying aboard a TAM airliner. The blast killed another passenger, who was sucked out of the aircraft, but not the bomber himself. Not pegged as the culprit, the man was set free, only to wind up in a São Paulo hospital the next day–still quite alive–after being run down by a bus in another suicide attempt.

Hit Squads

Despite their reputation for tardiness and diffidence in daytime law enforcement, the Military Police are famous for off-hours overzealousness. Human rights groups estimate there are two police-committed killings a day on average in Brazil. About 200 police officers are fired every year for their participation in organized kidnapping, corruption and death squads. The Vigario Geral shantytown massacre on August 30, 1994, is probably the most famous example of their devotion to cleaning up the streets. That night 21 men, women and children were murdered by at least 30 masked gunmen believed to be police officers acting in vengeance for 4 officers killed two days earlier in the shantytown.

But while the Policia Militar (usually retired or off-duty police officers) spend their off-hours in hit squads eliminating street kids, the hit squads are being hunted by other less violent but equally eager hit squads. Brazil has created a force to police the police force, a federal police unit tasked with investigating and eliminating death squads all over the country. Death squads and drug traffickers are considered major contributors to Rio's murder rate of more than 60 per every 100,000 people.

Rather then retaining attorneys to handle legal matters, Brazilians prefer hit men. The tab reads like a restaurant menu. Want to off an impoverished peasant? This week's special is only US$70. But if you want to take out a prominent politician, expect to pay for the caviar: about US$20,000. About half of the 12 killings a day in São Paulo are contract snuffings.

http://www.state.gov/www/global/narcotics_law/1998_narc_report/major/Brazil.html

Youth

The street kids, or "street urchins," are often themselves the target of death squads. In the first five months of 1997, 239 children between the ages of 7 and 16 were murdered in São Paulo, a huge jump over 1996. During all of that year, 337 kids were whacked. About 80 percent of the kids murdered in Brazil live in squalor, and more than 90 percent are connected to the cocaine trade. In Rio, the scene is even uglier. Between 1987 and 1997, some 6000 street kids were murdered by death squads.

http://www.streetkids.org/brazil/brazil.html

Teenage Drug Gangs

Prepubescent drug gangs in Rio are involved in an estimated 90 percent of all the city's violent crimes. Hundreds of drug dealers operate in the hillside slums ringing the city. A popular activity for the teens these days is setting street people on fire. During a two-month period in 1997, street kids set at least four people ablaze, killing all of them.

http://www.uetigers.stier.org/library/gs10brozlatam.htm

A passport and visa are required. Tourist visas are valid for 90 days, must be obtained in advance, and are free of charge (although there is a US$20 processing fee levied on Americans). Minors (under 18) traveling alone, with one parent or with a third party, must present written authorization by the absent parent(s) or legal guardian, specifically granting permission to travel alone, with one parent or a third party. This authorization must be notarized, authenticated by the Brazilian embassy or consulate and translated into Portuguese. If you are caught entering illegally, you must leave the country voluntarily within 3 to 8 days. The Ministry of Justice can hold you for 90 days before deporting you.

For current information concerning entry and customs requirements for Brazil, travelers can contact the following:

Brazilian Embassy

3006 Massachusetts Avenue, NW
Washington, DC 20008
Tel: (202) 745-2700
Fax: (202) 745-2827
Web site: http://www.brasil.emb.nw.dc.us/

Brazil also has consulates in Los Angeles, San Francisco, Houston, Miami, New York, Chicago and San Juan.

Rio

Rio likes to party, so it's no surprise that the areas surrounding beaches, discos, bars, nightclubs and other similar establishments are dangerous, especially at dusk and during the evening hours. Prime targets in Rio are the popular beaches and neighborhoods of Copacabana and Leme. The most dangerous areas of the city are hillside slums (favelas), where drug gang shootouts and cop atrocities are routine. Gang warfare, drug trafficking and robberies claim about a 18 lives each day in Rio.

"I Gave at the Office"

The most dangerous thing to tell a crook in Brazil. Thugs in Brazil aren't particularly thrilled when, after they've gone to all that trouble to jack you up, they discover you've read all those crime safety brochures and left all your valuables and cash back in the hotel safe. It's best to keep about US$30 in local currency on hand for a potential donation to the local black economy. Muggers often respond violently if you're only carrying a Bic lighter and a New York subway token.

São Paulo

There were 4,500 murders in São Paulo in 1996—and that was a year in the city that was, in John Lennon's words, "giving peace a chance." Through the first three-and-a-half months of 1998, 2,130 folks were murdered in São Paulo, about 25 homicides a day. In March 1998 alone, there were 771 murders and a whopping 10,700 cars stolen. Each day in the city there are about 340 violent robberies. Though 140,000 suspects are caught and jailed each month, most don't remain behind bars because their crimes are "never properly investigated," according to São Paulo's state council on crime.

Ciudad del Este, Paraguay

This smugglers' boomtown is technically in Paraguay along the border with Brazil and Argentina, but may as well be in Brazil. This is a major base for drug traffickers smuggling Bolivian cocaine via hidden landing strips cut out of the jungle. More than US$12 billion moves through here a year. As the Brazilian drug lords have been pushed out of the shantytowns of Rio, they've found a convenient base in Ciudad del Este. In fact, this place has it all—murder, mayhem and even Islamic fundamentalist guerrillas, who are suspected of using the city to launch bombing attacks against Israeli and Jewish targets in Argentina. There are about 200 murders a year in this city of 100,000, most of the executions identical in appearance with Brazilian gangland slayings. It costs US$500 to bribe a customs official in Ciudad del Este, and a bogus passport can be had for US$5,000. The city is also a channel for smuggled electronics goods and computers from Miami and stolen cars from Brazil. It's estimated that half the cars on Paraguay's roads were stolen in Brazil.

Ciudad del Este is a tax-free center and popular with Paraguayans for its bargains on consumer goods. The 400-yard bridge is usually packed with trucks and passenger cars stuffed with brand-new goods bought in Brazil. It is also a great place to pick up bogus U.S. dollars, antiaircraft guns, rare and endangered animals, weapons and drugs. The area is also called the "Triangle"—the frontier area between Argentina, Brazil and Paraguay—a South American Barbary Coast rough-and-ready area with a Shiite Muslim community of about 6,000 people. Lebanese, Syrians and Iranians came here in the early 1980s and brought with them a New World cell of Hezbollah. Hezbollah trains local recruits in the jungles around the main city of Foz do Iguacu and gets its support from both the local merchants and Iran. To combat Ciudad del Este's emergence as the globe's hub of nastiness, the FBI is opening an office in Brasilia. But Ciudad del Este makes Waco look like a warehouse for Mormon pamphlets.

Rio's Airport

There are probably more cash transactions each day at Rio de Janeiro's international airport than at a typical Rio bank. So why not jack up the airport? In March 1999, five gunmen tried to rip off bank security guards at the airport in a hail of gunfire in the international terminal, forcing panicked travelers to hit the deck while queued to get aisle

BRAZIL

seats in the nonsmoking section. Four people in the check-in area were wounded, including an Argentine tourist.

Brazil's Roads

Brazil possesses the world's worst highway safety record. More than 50,000 people are killed and another 350,000 injured every year on Brazil's roadways. To put things in perspective, the United States has 10 times as many vehicles as Brazil—198 million to Brazil's 20 million—but only about 41,000 traffic deaths each year. At least a third of Brazil's 50 million motorists don't have a driver's license. And those who don't die in an accident die of old age sitting in traffic. São Paulo is home to some 5.1 million cars, a number that grows by 800 each day. It's not uncommon in the world's second largest city for traffic jams to stretch 140 miles. During a typical rush hour, traffic jams average 53 miles in length. How bad is it in Brazil? At an Indy Car Grand Prix in Rio a few years ago, Brazilian veteran race driver Emerson Fittipaldi took a helicopter to the track.

Kidnapping

Kidnapping in Rio and São Paulo has become a pastime in the last few years. And it's as easy as stealing an apple off a produce cart. Reported kidnappings doubled annually in the mid-90s. Authorities believe the actual number was far greater. Many in Brazil have no faith in the police to handle kidnapping situations competently and successfully. It's part of a vicious cycle, giving kidnappers the confidence for carrying out their activities. But the cops are getting hip and now approach kidnappings with a "take no prisoners" attitude. Besides the increasing extrajudicial whacking of kidnap suspects, cops are now retaliating to kidnappings by busting the members of kidnappers' families. The game's the same: you show me yours and I'll show you mine.

Highway Robbery

Organized gangs of highway banditos prey the route linking São Paulo and Rio and other roads. Police say that highway robbery has "exploded" over the past six years; the gangs have become more sophisticated than drug traffickers. The usual MO is for the thugs to place rocks or other obstacles on the road during the wee hours, forcing drivers to stop. Their biggest caches are loads of cargo and electrical appliances snatched from commercial vehicles.

Designer Death Squads

In Brazil, death squads are like bowling teams anywhere else. Besides murder gangs comprised of former and current police officers (see "The Players"), there are also death squads made up of congressmen and even, believe it or not, taxi drivers. In February 1999, an investigation into allegations that Congressman Hildebrando Pascoal is the chairman of the board of a death gang responsible for murdering at least 30 people since 1985 was initiated by the Supreme Federal Tribunal, the nation's top court. Death squads are active in at least 9 of Brazil's 27 states. In Acre, a death squad composed entirely of taxi drivers is thought to be roaming around whacking people after fender benders. The Acre taxi hit team has killed at least five people, usually folks involved in accidents with a cab. Steer clear of taxis in Acre, and if you've gotta take one, it'd be a good idea to leave a real good tip.

Being Famous

Cover your ass if you get your face on a couple of magazine covers in Brazil. In August 1998, TV soap star Gerson Brenner was shot in the head during a highway robbery. In late March 1999, Mariana Moraes Rangel, South America's 800-meter freestyle swimming champion, was shot and wounded by thugs attempting to steal her car in Rio de Janeiro. That same month, Wellington Di Camargo—the composer brother of a member of the popular country music singing duo of Zeze Di Camargo and Luciano—was snatched by a kidnapping gang. He was freed after a US$300,000 ransom payoff. The cops quickly nabbed 15 of the perps as they tired to drive into Paraguay. At least 2 of the kidnappers were cops. And you wonder...

Police Strikes

...why cops moonlight as body snatchers. In 1997, police strikes spread to 15 of Brazil's 27 states. Police, more than 30,000 of them, have been demanding higher wages, which typically start at below the poverty level. And it seems that everyone is taking advantage of the picketing policemen. Robbers hit eight banks in Recife in one day. Motorists have been parking in restricted zones and barreling the wrong way down one-way streets. Police in Brazil make between $74 and $384 a month. This has not only attracted fewer desirable candidates for the country's forces, but also increased corruption. The flunky flatfoots have been clashing with army troops sent in to replace them.

Judges

And speaking of salaries, Brazil's 750 federal judges staged a one-day walkout on March 17, 1999, over foot-dragging on the implementation of a promised salary increase for the magistrates. The government-pledged raise? One hundred times the minimum official salary. If the judges don't get what they want, expect a lot of hung juries. Literally.

Flak

Between January and May 1999, more than 44 people were killed by stray rounds of gunfire in Rio de Janeiro. Most of the strays come from gang battles in Rio's streets, mostly in the city's favelas (hillside slums). But some of the flak is spat from the weapons of police officers in the heat of battle with dope pushers. Kevlar thongs may become all the rage on Rio's beaches.

Organized Crime

Some 65 mafia leaders from the Cosa Nostra, Camorra, N'Drangheta and La Sacra Corona Unita mobs have bases of operations in Brazil. Most of the mobsters make Rio their headquarters. Sixteen mob bosses have been jailed in the past four years in Brazil; 12 were arrested in Rio. The crooks have been taking advantage of Brazil's chaotic three-year economic program and the lack of legislation against organized crime. The Italians aren't the only boys in town. Gangsters from Russia, Korea, Japan and Nigeria have also set up shop in Brazil.

Land Disputes

During 1995 and 1996, 1.3 million people were involved in 1304 violent incidents over land disputes in Brazil, 750 in 1996 alone. That's the highest number since 1985. More than 112 people have been killed since 1995, and 976 died between 1985 and 1996. More recently, there's been quite a bit of fighting between Indians and settlers in Brazil's northern state of Roraima in 1998 and 1999. The battle is over border demarcations in a 4.12 million acre area reserved for natives. Eco-trekkers beware—these guys aren't chucking spears and throwing beer bottles at one another. They are quite well armed. And the Landless Workers Movement (MST) invaded and seized 244 property sites in the first four months of 1999, a 40 percent jump over the same period in 1998. Fully one-third of the occupations have been working ranches, which are usually razed and the cattle destroyed. When the cops show up, things turn nasty. This isn't difficult to imagine in a country where one-fifth of the population owns 90 percent of the land.

Body Parts

The business of murder for body parts is thriving in Brazil. Even public health hospitals have been allegedly running body parts businesses. Homeless street kids are abducted and slain for kidneys, livers and other viscera that hasn't rotted from glue fumes.

Being a Cop

Between 1992 and 1998, some 940 police officers were whacked in the line of duty in São Paulo alone. Nearly 14,700 were injured. Now that's protecting and serving.

Being a Security Guard

And where do the bad guys get all those guns to kill all those cops? They simply pop guards working for private security firms, a growth industry in Brazil. Bodyguard services cost between US$40 and US$100 per hour. Want to armor that limo? Armoring a vehicle here costs a minimum of US$30,000. A growing number of business execs in São Paulo eschew ground transportation altogether. They shell out US$800 an hour to commute to work by helicopter.

Medical care varies in quality, particularly in remote areas. Cholera has been reported in the Amazon Basin region and northeastern Brazil. Some cholera outbreaks have also been reported in major cities. However, visitors who follow proper precautions about food and drink are not usually at risk.

Brazil has a population of 155 million and possesses the world's largest rain forests. The population is 80 percent Roman Catholic and speaks Portuguese, Spanish, English and French. The climate ranges from tropical to semitropical with a temperate zone in the far south. The literacy rate is about 81 percent.

Air service runs efficiently throughout the country, as does railroad service. The telephone system is adequate, particularly in the major cities, including Rio, Brasilia, São Paulo, Recife and Salvador. Taxis abound in most urban areas. Tipping isn't necessary. Taxis are best hired from your hotel. Radio taxis are more reliable, and trustworthy, than meter taxis. When tipping in restaurants, 5 percent is usually considered appropriate.

Don't wear the colors of green and yellow, the colors of Brazil's flag. You'll be instantly pegged as a tourist. Taking the Metro isn't advised. Credit cards are widely accepted except for the remote boonies. The currency is the real, which is roughly equal to the U.S. dollar. The electrical current is 126V throughout most of the country and 22V in Brasilia. The local time is 3 hours behind GMT.

http://www.aaa.com.au/images/logos/searches/br.shtml
http://www.gazeta.com.br

Emergency Numbers

Local 911-type police numbers include the following:

Rio tourist police
  Tel: 511-5112

Fire
  Tel: 193

Military police (patrol)
  Tel: 190

Civil police (investigations)
  Tel: 147

The U.S. embassy is located in Brasilia:

Avenida das Nacoes, Lote 3
Tel: [55] (61) 321-7272

There are consulates in the following:

Rio de Janeiro

Avenida Presidente Wilson 147
Tel: [55] (21) 292-7117

São Paulo

Rua Padre Joao Manoel 933
Tel: [55] (11) 881-6511

Porto Alegre

Rua Coronel Genuino 421 (9th floor)
Tel: [55] (51) 226-4288

Recife

Rua Goncalves Maia 163
Tel: [55] (81) 221-1412

There are also consular agencies in the following:

Belem

Avenida Oswaldo Cruz 165
Tel: [55] (91) 223-0800/0413

Salvador de Bahia

Avenida Antonio Carlos Magalhaes S/N
Edificio Cidadella Center, Suite 410
Candeal
Tel: [55] (71) 358-9195

Manaus

Rua Recife 1010, Adrianopolis
Tel: [55] (92) 234-4546

Fortaleza

Instituto Brasil-Estados Unidos (IBEU)
Rua Nogueira Acioly, 891
Aldeota
Tel: [55] (85) 252-1539.

Burundi
★★★★★

The Problem

Each day at nightfall in Burundi's capital of Bujumbura, the streets are empty. Grenade blasts (grenades can be had for a mere US$7) and machine-gun fire from both the city and the surrounding hills shatter the night silence. Occasionally, there is screaming and crying. The impression is that you're suddenly being caught in the middle of an invasion. Then, in the morning, it is calm. You're surprised to discover that corpses do not litter the streets. There is little, if any, evidence of fighting. When inquiring among locals about the cause of the evening's disturbance, you will be answered with two words: "Burundi's problem." It would seem "the Switzerland of Africa" has a bit of a problem. A problem that has existed for over 30 years.

It wasn't always like this. The Twa pygmies used to live in peace under the triple canopy rain forest. The pastoral Bantu Hutus migrated into this fertile region and were followed by the tall-nomadic Tutsis. The Tutsi immediately showed the less warlike folks how things should be run and gained the favor of the colonial masters.

Burundi endured one of Africa's worst tribal wars in 1972. War is not the right word. Genocide fits better. It all happened after King Ntaré V returned in April of that year. Usually, when the president of the country promises safe conduct to a returning monarch, the chances are pretty good the red carpet will be rolled out. Well, that wasn't exactly what Burundi president Michel Micombero had in mind for the return of the man he overthrew. Not even a party. No sooner had Ntaré V stepped off the plane than he was judged and executed by Micombero. Hell of a homecoming. What happened afterward defies explanation.

Thousands of invading exiled Hutus attending Ntare V's return to Burundi were slaughtered by the rival Tutsis. But the Tutsis didn't stop there. Over the next eight weeks, nearly a quarter of a million native Burundi Hutus were massacred by the Tutsis. The genocide was followed by coup after coup after coup, until Burundi's first democratically elected leader, Melchior Ndadaye, a Hutu, assumed the presidency in June 1993. All's well that ends well? Hardly.

Tutsi paratroopers assassinated Ndadaye on October 21, 1993, abruptly ending the four-month experiment with democracy in the central African state. The predawn coup was led by army chief of staff Colonel Jean Bikomagu and former president Jean Baptiste Bagaza, who was himself overthrown in 1987. The paratroopers arrested Ndadaye and detained him at the Muha barracks on the outskirts of Bujumbura before executing him. The coup was the fifth since the country's independence in 1962, and led to unprecedented violence and death. More than 200,000 deaths were caused by the unrest, equaling if not exceeding the casualties that occurred in the 1972 genocide that swept the country. Tribal massacres drove nearly a million Burundians into neighboring countries to escape the slaughter.

The coup collapsed, but it hardly made any difference. Burundi itself had already collapsed. Ethnic fighting between the Hutus and the minority Tutsis, who controlled the military and have dominated politics since Burundi's independence from Belgium in 1962, continued to ravage the country. Pictures revealed hundreds of bodies, devastated towns, destroyed farms and a countryside that had been set on fire. Corpses littered the landscape, after the army stood by and watched as Tutsis and Hutus slaughtered each other. Thousands of Burundians marched through the streets of Bujumbura, urging the remnants of Ndadaye's government to emerge from hiding and lead the country from the chaos caused by the military revolt. As many as 500,000 refugees had fled to Rwanda alone.

But even the foiled coup failed to bring stability to Burundi. The presidents of both Burundi and Rwanda were aboard a plane that was blasted out of the sky by rocket and gun fire as it was landing at Kigali airport in Rwanda on April 6, 1994. Intense fighting broke out in neighboring Rwanda. During the ensuing 14-week civil war in Rwanda, Tutsi rebels swept across the country, decimating the mainly Hutu government.

On April 29, 1994, hundreds of people fled shelling in Bujumbura, after the expiration of a government ultimatum to militants to turn in their weapons. Although Burundi escaped much of the 1995 fighting between the two ethnic groups, Hutu militants of the "People's Army" declined to comply and surrender their weapons.

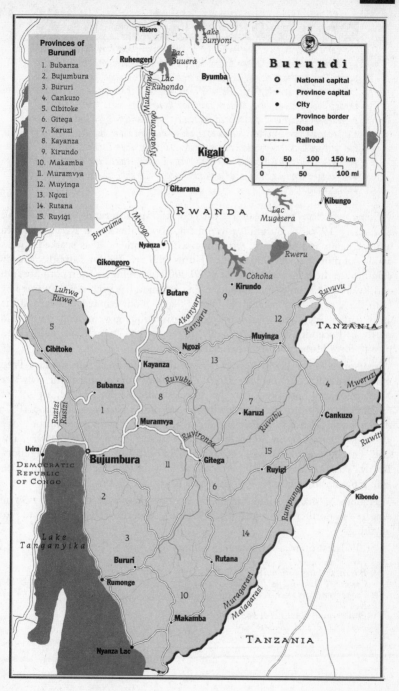

Provinces of Burundi

1. Bubanza
2. Bujumbura
3. Bururi
4. Cankuzo
5. Cibitoke
6. Gitega
7. Karuzi
8. Kayanza
9. Kirundo
10. Makamba
11. Muramvya
12. Muyinga
13. Ngozi
14. Rutana
15. Ruyigi

Burundi

⊙ National capital
• Province capital
• City
Province border
Road
Railroad

| 0 | 50 | 100 | 150 km |
| 0 | 50 | 100 mi |

The Trash War

The morning was foggy, and we had driven up the slippery slopes from Tanzania. When we camped for the night, we saw no one. Now we were surrounded by a circular wall of people. They pressed in slowly, curious to see what these visitors might have. They began to touch at first, and then grab. Fighting back, we chased them off. As they ran and tripped, they grabbed anything they could pry loose—empty water bottles, scraps of paper. As the bolder ones tried to grab and run back into the crowd, they were immediately pounced upon by other Hutus, who ripped and tore whatever meager trophy they had retrieved until they possessed minuscule scraps in their hands. The Hutus were stealing trash, fighting for trash. As we quickly jumped in our vehicles and drove off, we watched them continue to beat and fight each other for trash until, finally, the battle was lost in the fog.

Violence, perhaps a precursor to a total breakdown in Burundi, again broke out in January 1996, as Burundi government troops attacked a Rwandan Hutu refugee camp and killed 20, wounding scores of others. This sparked a mass exodus of more than 14,000 terrified Hutus who beat tail for Tanzania, already crammed to the brim with more than 700,000 Hutu refugees from both Burundi and Rwanda. Although the Burundi ruling coalition has been sternly warned by both the United Nations and the United States about ethnic violence, and the army particularly about overthrowing the precarious government, the raid in northeast Burundi was seen as a highly choreographed attempt in a multiphased plan to force Hutu rebels into permanent exile.

Strongman Major Pierre Buyoya became the president of Burundi in a Tutsi military-backed coup in July 1996. The Hutu former president Sylvestre Ntibantunganya hotfooted it to the American ambassador's home, a place we remember well from our pleasant lunch. He didn't emerge until June 1997. Another coincidence is that we also met the new prez (and former major in the army) at a whoop-up in '91 while he was president (from 1987 to 1993). The only change we found was an embargo imposed by Burundi's neighbors. Buyoya's army of some 20,000 men will be busy fighting the 3,500 Hutu rebels who represent the 85 percent of Burundians who are Hutu.

Gentlemen, sharpen your machetes. Because pencils at the peace talks in Arusha—in northern Tanzania—in 1999 don't seem to be sharp enough to sign anything.

For the latest on peace in Burundi, contact:

Farah Stockman
Internews International
Criminal Tribunal for Rwanda
Phone from Africa: 057-4207/11; ext 5235
Fax: 057-4000
Phone from USA:1 (212) 963-2850; ext 5235
Fax: 1 (212) 963-2848/49

BURUNDI

The 1:30 to Paris

Our arrival was not an important event, but reason enough for lunch at the embassy. After a brief tour, including meeting the grizzled marine security officer, we had lunch high up in the hills overlooking Bujumbura. In between polite conversation, a silence would fall as an airliner took off from the airport. Without looking, our hosts would rattle off the flight and carrier, as if repeating a religious chant.

It was much easier when only Twa pygmies lived in the virgin forests. The invasion of Hutus and then Tutsis would make Hitler take notes and force Darwin to rethink his theory. The human species in Burundi should be separated into the quick and the dead. This majority agrarian Hutu nation has been ruled by the minority Tutsis since independence from Belgium in 1962. More than 180,000 people (many say more than 200,000) have died in Burundi since 1993 in civil wars between Tutsis, who control the 18,000-20,000-man-strong military, and majority Hutus—and a million more made refugees. (According to some estimates, some half a million people are reported to have been killed—mostly Tutsis—in 1994 alone.) Burundi's president, Pierre Buyoya, has been struggling to maintain peace since he was chosen by the military in July 1996 to step back into office after successive Hutu-controlled governments—the last one led by Hutu president Sylvestre Ntibantunganya—failed to restore order in this carnival of massacres. Buyoya first seized power in a 1986 coup and led Burundi to free elections in 1993. Hutu Melchior Ndadaye was elected president but assassinated by Tutsi paratroopers four months later. Then the carnage began.

As part of Buyoya's security plan and in a move reminiscent of South Vietnam's "Strategic Hamlet" program of the 1960s, more than 600,000 people—Hutus and minority Tutsis—have been rounded up by the government and placed in some 200 camps dotting the countryside, to the outrage of the United States and the subdued disapproval of the United Nations. The Hutus, encamped by force, live a more cramped existence than their fellow Tutsis, who mostly come to the camps by free will in fear of Hutu rebel attacks. For their part, the Hutu rebels that formed the army of the Ndadaye government (and the ex-armed forces of Rwanda and Zaire) are returning to Burundi from their camps and bases in Congo and Tanzania for their revenge. Buyoya is in no mood for compromise, though. He hasn't committed himself to new elections nor one day sharing power with the rebels. But Major Buyoya proposed in June 1999 the setting up of a transitional government to run the affairs of state for the next ten years, during which the head of state will be assisted by two vice presidents—one each from the two major ethnic camps, Hutus and Tutsis. Meanwhile, Buyoya's been busy beefing up his 20,000-man army for more bloodshed.

The good news is that at the 1999 peace talks in Arusha, Burundi's 18 warring political parties have decided to consolidate into only 3. The bad news? They consolidated into the government, the Tutsis and the Hutus. Square one. Again.

Death Wish Democracy

Since October 1993–when Burundi's first elected president, Melchior Ndadaye was assassinated–out of the 81 members of the 1993 parliament, 23 have been murdered. While many in Burundi want democracy, it seems only fools should have any dreams of running it.

The Hutus

Hutus, a Bantu race, comprise about 85 percent of Burundi's population and were the victims of a Tutsi-led mass genocide campaign in 1972. After President Ndadaye was overthrown and executed in an abandoned coup effort in October 1993, the Hutus went on a stampede. When it was over, nearly a quarter million corpses were left in the wake. The leader of the Hutu rebels, the National Council for the Defense of Democracy (CNDD)—its armed wing is called Forces for the Defense of Democracy—is Leonard Nyangoma, a former interior minister.

The Tutsis

The Tutsis are originally Nilotic herdsmen from the north. The Tutsi-led military junta purged the military and bureaucracy of Hutus from 1964 to 1972. In 1972, a large-scale revolt by the Hutus killed several thousand Tutsis. The Tutsi machine followed with the mass extermination of selected and unselected Hutus. Any Hutu with an education, a decent job or any degree of wealth was arrested and murdered, most in a horrifying fashion. More than 200,000 Hutus were slaughtered in the ensuing three months. The Tutsi army's makeshift trucks could be seen in the streets packed with the mutilated corpses of Hutu victims.

Pierre Buyoya and the Government

Major Buyoya survived more than two years of sanctions imposed on Burundi by Ethiopia, Tanzania, Kenya, Uganda, Rwanda, Zambia, Eritrea and the Democratic Republic of Congo after seizing power from the civilian government in July 1996. How effective were they? Though no commercial flights were permitted into Burundi, planes from Belgium and the United Arab Emirates landed regularly with the staples Burundians needed to survive: Moët & Chandon champagne, American bourbons and Scotch whiskeys, French cheese, stereos, VCRs and Celine Dione CDs. The sanctions have been blamed for the continuing violence in Burundi. But now that they have been (at least temporarily) lifted, rebel leaders who supported the embargo have intensified their campaign against the government. As one aid worker said: "If things don't improve soon with the lifting of the sanctions, then this government will have a problem." (It must've been his first week in-country.) But the embargo was at least effective enough to prevent luxury items from reaching Burundians, like food and medicine—forcing Buyoya to toke on the peace pipe at Arusha.

http://www.burundi.gov/presi.htm

Laurent Kabila and the Democratic Republic of Congo (DRC)

Burundi is also no stranger to exporting misery. Buyoya's Burundi troops have less than covertly been involved in the DRC's civil war, aiding rebels (including Ugandan and Rwandan forces) seeking to depose Kabila. Kabila's pissed that Buyoya's helicopters are ferrying DRC guerrillas on sightseeing flights around the Congo countryside. Although Rwanda and Uganda publicly admit to aiding the Congolese rebels, Buyoya is a little more hesitant to do so. As DRC defense staff chief Faustin Munene reminded Buyoya in May 1999: "Congo will not hesitate to attack Bujumbura which, by the way, is only a few kilometers" from the DRC. Sorta like a "Subway Series" African war.

Party for the Reconciliation of the People (PRP)

Led by Mathias Hitimana, now under house arrest, the Hutu dissident group opposes the oppression of the Hutu people by the government. The group, a champion of Hutu dissidents, is a frequent instigator of street clashes with government security forces.

BURUNDI

National Liberation Front (NLF)

The armed wing of the Hutu Party of Liberation is based and prevalent in the northwestern province of Cibitoke. They are hostile to foreigners, especially white expats, and killed three Swiss Red Cross workers when they ambushed and machine gunned a clearly marked Red Cross vehicle in June of '96.

National Council for Defense and Democracy/Conseil National Pour la Defense de la Democratie (CNDD)/FORCES POUR LA DEFENSE DE LA DEMOCRATIE (FDD)

The main Hutu rebel group has now split into two factions: the CNDD of Leonard Nyangoma and the CNDD/FDD of Jean-Bosco Ndayikengurukiye. FDD lost most of its rear bases in the eastern DRC when Kabila came to power and pushed the rebels into western Tanzania. They operate from in and around the refugee camps. The FDD have again found rear bases in the eastern Congo and are helping Kabila's troops against the RCD.

This Hutu faction—led by Leonard Nyangoma—which stages most of its attacks on Burundi villages from bases inside Tanzania, is perhaps Pierre Buyoya's biggest threat. The FDD (CNDD's armed wing) has been recently battling government troops in the provinces of Makamba, Ruyigi and Rutana. The CNDD/FDD has accused the international community of ignoring the massacre of more than 100 civilians allegedly by the Tutsi-dominated army, in Ruyigi province on April 10, 1999. Another CNDD/FDD leader, Jerome Ndiho, based in Brussels, says his faction won't participate in the peace process, although he's been invited to do so. But Nyangoma has indicated his willingness to talk. Nyangoma is generally recognized as the CNDD/FDD leader, while the harder-line Ndiho is seen as something of a splintered rogue.

PARTI POUR LA LIBERATION DU PEUPLE HUTU (PALIPEHUTU):

This is the longest established Hutu rebel group independent from CNDD/FDD. There are regional rivalries between the two groups. CNDD members come from the southern Bururi region and PALIPEHUTU are recruited from the central Muramvya area. PALIPEHUTU, led by Cossan Kabura, has had successes in fighting around Bujumbura. Its armed wing is the Forces nationales de liberation (FNL).

Front Pour la Liberation Nationale (FROLINA)

Another Hutu rebel group, closely linked to PALIPEHUTU. Its armed wing is the Forces armees du peuple (FAP).

UNION POUR LA LIBERATION NATIONALE (ULINA)/FORCES DE LIBERATION NATIONALE (FALINA)

ULINA and its armed wing FALINA are an umbrella group bringing together Hutu rebel groups, with the exception of CNDD/FDD. PALIPHUTU has recently issued statements urging all anti-government forces to join the movement.

Though all of Burundi's entry and exit points are sealed off on any given day, theoretically one can get into Burundi by air, road or lake ferry. Keep in mind the airport in Bujumbura opens and closes like an L.A. rave club. By land from Rwanda, you can get in from Butare as well as Bujumbura. Expect to have your belongings searched on both sides of the border. From the DRC, you can get into Burundi from Bakavu via Uvira. You can also get to Bujumbura from Bakavu via Cyangugu in Rwanda. On Lake Tanganyika, you can get in from Tanzania. (Few travelers stay long in Burundi. Most are in transit between Tanzania and Rwanda.) However, at press time, all land crossings were closed to foreigners.

A passport and a visa are required. Only those travelers who reside in countries where there is no Burundian embassy are eligible for entry stamps, without a visa, at the airport upon arrival. These entry stamps are not a substitute for a visa, which must subsequently be obtained from the immigration service within 24 hours of arrival. Visas cost from US$30 to US$60, depending on the anticipated length of stay. Travelers who have failed to obtain a visa will not be permitted to leave the country. Multiple entry visas valid for three months are available in Burundian embassies abroad for US$11. Evidence of yellow fever immunization must be presented. Also, visitors are required to show proof of vaccination against meningococcal meningitis. Additional information may be obtained from the following:

Embassy of the Republic of Burundi

2233 Wisconsin Avenue, NW, Suite 212
Washington, DC 20007
Tel: (202) 342-2574

Permanent Mission of Burundi to the United Nations in New York

Tel: (212) 687-1180

Burundi has a good network of roads between the major towns and border posts—when they're not mined. Travel on other roads is hazardous, particularly in the rainy season. Public transportation to border points is often difficult and frequently unavailable, but it is improving. There has been a proliferation of modern Japanese-made minibuses in recent years. They're usually not terribly crowded and are far less expensive than taxis. These buses leave terminals *(gare routière)* in every town in the early morning through the early afternoon, and depart when they are full. They display their destinations on the windshield. The government-owned OTRACO buses are mainly found in and around the capital of Bujumbura. Total road miles are 3,666; but only 249 of them are paved. There are six airfields in the country, only one with a permanent surface.

The border with the DRC is closed temporarily to prevent Hutu rebels from crossing into Burundi. Route 1, the main highway linking Bujumbura with the rest of the country, is frequently closed because of land mines placed by Hutu rebels, usually northeast of the capital. The road is also the site of frequent ambushes. More than 125 people, mostly civilians, were killed in more than 20 ambushes early in 1996.

There is an eight-mile cordon sanitaire, or clean line, around the city of Bujumbura as well as a midnight curfew. Life may go on as normal during the day, but the killing begins at night. As many as 100 people die every week in Burundi, mostly because of attacks by Hutu insurgents from their bases in the refugee camps in the DRC and Tanzania, and because of army reprisals against local Hutus.

Bujumbura

Sporadic violence remains a problem in the capital, Bujumbura—better known to locals as "Tutsiville," as the Tutsis have slaughtered most of the city's Hutus or sent them fleeing into the hills—as well as in the interior, where large numbers of displaced persons are encamped or in hiding. Warfare in neighboring Rwanda has caused thousands of Rwandans to flee to Burundi and other countries in the region. The U.S. embassy has reiterated the importance of using extreme caution, with no travel to the troubled neighborhoods of the capital and none but essential travel in the city after dark. In May

1999, the British Foreign and Commonwealth Office advised against all travel to Bujumbura. (In March, the State Department urged U.S. citizens to defer all travel to Burundi and recommended that all U.S. citizens in Burundi leave the country, citing the March 1999 Hutu rebel killings of U.S. citizens in southwestern Uganda.) There is a midnight to dawn curfew in the city and regular reports of armed robberies and carjackings. Armed Tutsi thugs and army soldiers comb the streets after dark, preying on the remaining Hutu militiamen. The Hutus, for the most part, have fled into the surrounding hills and each morning stream down into the capital to go to the market or do other chores before heading back to the hills before dark—to keep from being shot. As one journalist notes: "At 8 P.M., a Burundian must already be where he plans to spend the night." Burundi periodically has closed its land borders without notice and suspended air travel and telephone service in response to political disturbances.

The Border with Tanzania

At least 1,500 Hutu rebels surged across the border from their base camps in Tanzania in March and April 1997, and are engaging government forces in the southern provinces of Bururi and Makamba.

Route 7

Strategic Route 7, which snakes southeast from Bujumbura, is closed, due to continued rebel attacks, effectively cutting off the entire south of the country.

Crime

Street crime and muggings in Burundi pose a high risk for visitors, as *DP* knows first-hand. Crime involves muggings, purse snatching, pickpocketing, burglary and auto break-ins. Criminals operate individually or in small groups. There have been reports of muggings of persons jogging or walking alone in all sections of Bujumbura, especially on public roads bordering Lake Tanganyika. You've got to be pretty desperate to jack up a jogger. Most health nuts in the world leave their credit cards at home and carry just enough pocket change for a post-jog latte at Starbucks.

Bujumbura U.S. embassy sources report that dangerous areas for criminal activity in Bujumbura are the downtown section, the vicinity of the Novotel and the Source du Nil hotels, and along the shore of Lake Tanganyika. The majority of the criminal incidents in the Burundian capital consist of muggings, purse snatchings, and auto break-ins (to steal the contents).

Refugees

There's no place like home. And that's why few Burundians want to go back. As of mid-1999, 489,658 Burundians continued to live outside the country—457,000 in Tanzania alone—of which 200,000 constituted "old caseload" refugees who had arrived in the 1970s and have assimilated into local communities. Some 30,000 refugees remain in the DRC while the rest are spread in smaller numbers in Rwanda, Zambia, Kenya, Congo (Brazzaville), Angola, Malawi and Cameroon. By April 1999, 195,640 Burundians had returned home since 1996 (114,558 from the DRC, 75,501 from Tanzania and 5,581 from Rwanda). The provinces with the highest number of refugees still in Tanzania include Muyinga (54,585), Makamba (46,303), Ruyigi (34,030), Kirundo (28,302) and Karuzi (20,446).

http://www.UNHCR.cb/world/afri/burundi.htm

Guns

Burundi has been flooded with weapons over the past two years. Most of the guns are being provided by China, France, North Korea, Russia, Rwanda, Tanzania, Uganda, the United States and the DRC.

Land Mines

Land mines are becoming a very popular way of killing people, and Hutu rebels are becoming accomplished gardeners and landscape architects. The main artery out of Burundi is the road to Kigali, Rwanda—Burundi's highway to hell. It makes Cambodian roads look like D.C.'s Beltway. This road has been subject to daily ambushes and the nightly planting of land mines. Hutu rebels plant land mines like cheap perennials. Sort of the African version of Dutch tulip fields. This and other roads in the country are regularly closed while military operations are carried out, meaning they're closed a lot.

Ears

Yeah, you heard that right, if you can hear at all. An increasing amount of Burndians (Hutus and Tutsis) are getting theirs hacked off. Hutu rebels are slicing off the ears of villagers they feel sympathize with the government, both Hutus and Tutsis. As one-eared villager explained after he and 20 others had their ears chopped off by Hutu rebels just east of Bujumbura on April 16, 1998: "The rebels told me, 'If you had ears, you would have listened to what we have been telling you. But you don't listen, so now we are cutting off your ear.' "

http://www.amnesty.org/ailib/countries/index116.htm

Humanitarian Aid

In May 1999, rebels attacked a therapeutic feeding center run by the Italian NGO GVC. Food and drugs from a nearby health center were stolen along with some 45 cows. Four government soldiers were killed and seven injured during the attack. Three Swiss Red Cross workers were shot dead by NLF rebels while traveling in a clearly marked Red Cross vehicle in June 1996. In April 1998, Bent Nielsen, director of the Adventist Relief and Development Agency, was stabbed and shot to death while his vehicle was carjacked. NGO work is a hazardous occupation in Burundi. But if you want to gamble with your life anyhow, you can contact:

Office for the Coordination of Humanitarian Affairs (OCHA)
Bujumbura, Burundi
Tel: (257) 218034 or 219157/8
Fax: (257) 218035
E-mail: dha@cbinf.com
Web site: http://www.reliefweb.int/IRIN

Street Demonstrations and Clashes

Minority Tutsi youths regularly engage with the military and police in street protests in Bujumbura. Although the protests are not anti-U.S. in nature and Americans and other foreigners are rarely targeted, stay off the streets during any public rally. Relatively peaceful demonstrations can turn violent.

Northern Burundi has been in the throes of one of the biggest typhus outbreaks since World War II, mostly due to overcrowded camps and unhygienic conditions. The reported cases have surged to more than 20,000 since October 1996, when the outbreak was first observed. If that's not bad enough, aid groups say that 40,000 children are suffering from malnutrition and that around 300,000 people now face famine. Shortly after the coup in July 1996, Ethiopia,

Tanzania, Kenya, Uganda, Rwanda, Zambia, Eritrea and the Democratic Republic of Congo slapped an embargo on Burundi, which has caused most of the food shortages.

There are 14 hospital beds and 0.5 doctors for every 10,000 people. Yellow fever and cholera immunizations are required. Inoculations for tetanus, typhoid and polio are also recommended, as are gamma globulin shots and malaria suppressants. Doctors and hospitals often expect immediate cash payment for health care services. U.S. medical insurance is not always valid outside the United States. Supplemental medical insurance with specific overseas coverage, including medical evacuation coverage, has proved to be useful. The Centers for Disease Control recommends that travelers to Burundi receive the meningococcal polysaccharide vaccine before traveling to the area.

A per capita annual income of around US$150 makes the country perhaps the poorest in Africa, even more impoverished than neighboring Rwanda. Despite Burundi's tiny size (six and a half million people in 10,747 square miles), the country is divided into 15 provinces, each administered by a civilian governor. The provinces are subdivided into 114 communes, with elected councils in charge of local affairs.

Burundi's climate varies from hot and humid in the area of Lake Tanganyika, with temperatures around 86° F, to cool in the mountainous north, about 68° F. The long rainy season runs from October through May.

Hutus comprise about 85 percent of the population. About 14 percent are Tutsi. Kirundi and French are the official languages; Swahili is also spoken; English is rare. Indigenous religions are held by 34 percent of the population; Roman Catholics make up 61 percent of the population; Protestants account for 5 percent. The literacy rate is about 50 percent.

The currency in Burundi is the Burundi franc (BFr). The electrical current is 220/240V.
http://www.burundi.gov.bi

Embassy Locations

U.S. Embassy in Burundi

Ave des Etats-Unis
B.P. 34, 1720, Bujumbura
Tel: [257] (2) 22-34-54
Fax: [257] (2) 22-29-26

Burundian Embassy in United States

2233 Wisconsin Avenue, N.W., Suite 212
Washington, D.C. 20007
Tel: (202) 342-2574

Burundian Embassy in Canada

151 Slater Street, Suite 800
Ottawa, Ontario, Canada K1P 5H3
Tel: (613) 741-7458
Telex: (369) 053-3393
Fax: (613) 741-2424

BURUNDI

1/20/00	Burundi promises to close 10 of it's 40 "regroupment" camps after Nelson Mandele acts as a mediator.
7/25/96	Pierre Buyoya succeeds Sylvestre Ntibantunganya in a bloodless coup.
4/25/94	A military coup in Burundi fails when soldiers, fearing the triggering of a tribal bloodbath similar to the one in neighboring Rwanda, refuse to participate in the military mutiny.
4/6/94	A plane carrying the presidents of both Rwanda and Burundi is shot out of the sky as it attempts to land in Rwanda.
10/28/93	Foreigners in Burundi are evacuated to Bujumbura, as concern over tribal violence associated with a failed military coup grows.
10/28/93	Six government ministers are confirmed murdered during a failed coup in Burundi.
10/21/93	Paratroopers overthrow President Melchior Ndadaye and execute him.
6/2/93	Melchior Ndadaye becomes Burundi's first democratically elected president.
11/6/76	Lieutenant Colonel Jean-Baptiste Bagaza leads a coup and assumes the presidency, suspending Burundi's constitution.
4/19/72	Natré V returns to Burundi and is executed by President Micombero, sparking one of the bloodiest wars in African history.

Phnom Penh

Cambodia
★★

Come Here, Rouge!

Pol Pot's dead.

Khieu Sampahan and Nuon Chea have "retired" in Ieng Sary's get-rich-quick limbo for aging mass murderers—the former Khmer Rouge (KR) headquarters of Pailin in western Cambodia. And Kaing Khek Iev—known by his revolutionary name of "Duch" and the former proprietor of Phnom Penh's infamous Tuol Sleng Prison, where at least 14,000 Cambodians and 8 Westerners were tortured for months before being executed—surfaced as a born-again Christian and then snuck back off into the jungle after doing a kiss-and-tell for Western reporters in May 1999 about KR atrocities during Pol Pot's murderous 1975–1979 reign. He was "caught" by the army a few days later and whisked off to Phnom Penh.

Perhaps reluctantly—no, decidedly reluctantly—and assuredly without the zeal that would normally be exhibited by a "democracy" in rounding up the perps of a genocide that wiped out a quarter of Cambodia's population in the mid- and late-1970s, Phnom Penh has been shouldered with yet another burden: what to

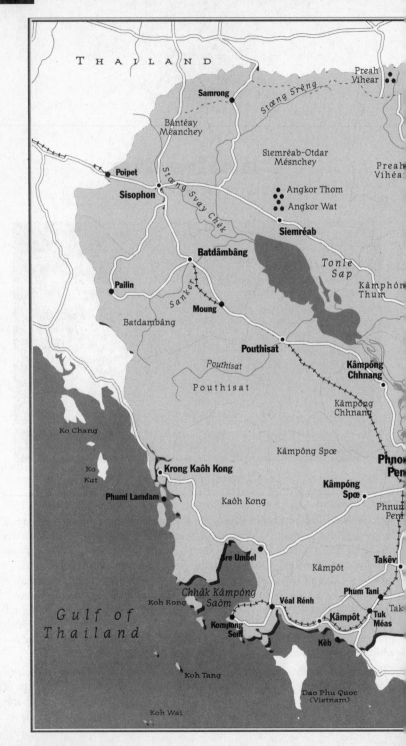

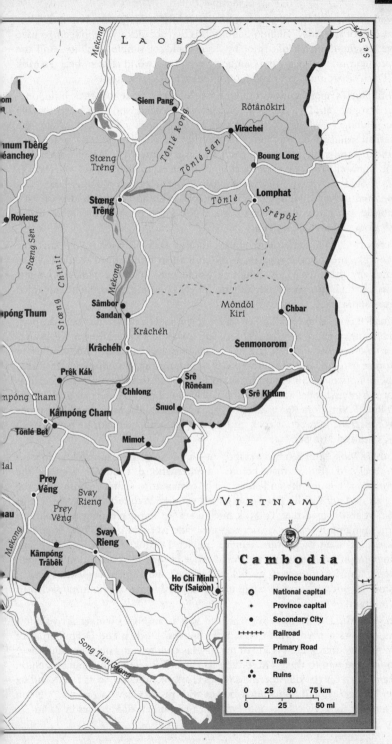

LAOS

Siem Pang

Rôtânôkiri

Virachei

Stœng Trêng

Boung Long

Stœng Trêng

Tônlé Kong

Tônlé San

Tônlé

Srêpôk

Lomphat

Rovieng

Stœng Sên

Stœng Chinit

Mekong

póng Thum

Sâmbor

Sandan

Krâchéh

Môndól Kiri

Chbar

Krâchéh

Senmonorom

Prêk Kák

Chhlong

Srê Rônéam

Srê Khtum

póng Cham

Snuol

Kâmpóng Cham

Tônlé Bet

Mimot

Prey Vêng

Svay Rieng

Prey Vêng

VIETNAM

Svay Rieng

Kâmpóng Trâbêk

Ho Chi Minh City (Saigon)

Song Tien Giang

Cambodia

———	Province boundary
⊕	National capital
•	Province capital
●	Secondary City
++++	Railroad
===	Primary Road
- - -	Trail
••	Ruins

0   25   50   75 km

0   25   50 mi

do with its expanding collection of former Maoist executioners, responsible for the deaths of at least 1.7 million Cambodians two decades ago, who seem to have arrived at the doorstep of justice by default and/or simple stupidity. And the government is in no hurry for Cambodians and the world alike to hear Ta Mok and Duch sit around a courtroom campfire and tell ghost stories.

Until Duch's apprehension, Phnom Penh's biggest prize was their little, one-legged trophy called Ta Mok—a very nasty KR general who goes by the handle "the Butcher"—who's rotting away in a Phnom Penh jail while the "international community" discerns whether Cambodia's judicial system can handle a purse-snatching case, much less a genocide trial. While Cambodian prime minister Hun Sen, Washington and Kofi Anan bicker over whether Ta Mok should be tried in Phnom Penh, The Hague or Disneyland—and prosecuted by part-time cyclo drivers or folks with an actual law degree, or a combination of the above—the former KR killer is withering away like a mushroom under a midday sun.

If convicted, a life sentence would last about a week (Ta Mok is 75). And how do you execute a one-legged man? A Cambodian firing squad would have an excuse why they missed. A guillotine would only lower Ta Mok's IQ a few points. He'd just get another prosthetic. Surely a bowling ball could be smuggled in from some place.

Initially Prime Minister Hun Sen said that it would be best to just bury the past, in the name of national reconciliation, and leave the geriatric former KR leaders alone to drop dead of heart attacks and colon polyps in Pailin while tending to their rose gardens. But pressure from the "international community" (read that as the donors of US$5 billion in aid to Cambodia) to bring these ex-guerrillas before an international war crimes tribunal has put Hun Sen, the marginal winner over Prince Norodom Ranariddh in 1998 elections amidst widespread allegations of voter fraud, between a rock and hard place—in other words, between Ta Mok's head and his peg leg.

With Ta Mok, Hun Sen had a scapegoat—a way to affix accountability, do it his own backyard (rather than before an international tribunal), appease the international community and allow the government to simultaneously bury the KR past and permit the Pol Pot regime's veridical architects to remain free in Pailin. It also helped that Ta Mok hired a lawyer and is pleading not guilty to charges ranging from war crimes and genocide to jaywalking. That, of course, puts the onus on the government to convict Ta Mok. Even a junior college biology major in a barrister's wig could prove beyond reasonable doubt enough to retire Ta Mok forever to his beloved jail cell and Khmer-language Voice of America broadcasts—and he could do it without dusting off too many skeletons in the closet.

Ah, but Mr. Duch—now 56, who laid low as an NGO worker for past few years—throws a wrench into Hun Sen's spokes. Duch is the Deep Throat of Cambodian politics. He's ready to tell all—his own role at Tuol Sleng and those who ordered him to do it. (According to Duch, KR second in command Nuon Chea ordered him to kill Americans James Clark and Michael Scott Deeds and six other Westerners and "burn their bodies with tires to leave no bones.") Nuon Chea might think twice about investing in any shuffleboard arcades in Pailin.

These are the kinds of admissions that strike fear into Hun Sen, because he'll be left with few options but to kindly invite Pailin leader (and former Brother #3), Ieng Sary, former KR ideological mouthpiece Khieu Samphan and Nuon Chea to Phnom Penh (all free men) for a working lunch at the Cambodiana followed by traditional Cambodian dance performance and a nice little cultural show—a genocide trial.

When Ieng Sary "surrendered" to the government in August 1996, his punishment was leadership of the antonomous, personal fiefdom of Pailin—including the command of the 5,000 KR fighters who switched shoulder patches along with him. And there's no reason to believe Sary and his boys won't change uniforms again if he's asked to challenge in court anything more serious than a parking ticket. If international pressure becomes such that Hun Sen is forced to "arrest" Ieng Sary, Khieu Samphan and Nuon Chea, this shrewd prime minister will flip another ace from his sleeve (he's got enough of them to keep warm in Alaska) and tell the world: "You want 'em? Come and get 'em."

Anywhere that a hundred of Interpol's most wanted fugitives can safely call home is somewhere you wouldn't want to live. Perhaps no country on earth has so brutally suffered from as many forms of conflict over the past 35 years as has Cambodia—civil wars, border wars, massive bombardment via a superpower's B-52s, a deforestation rate considered unparalleled anywhere in the world, an autogenicide unprecedented in its savagery.

With the help of the United Nations, Cambodia began crawling back into the world on its knees in 1993, literally, as so many of the country's citizens are missing limbs after accidental encounters with one of the perhaps 6–10 million land mines still buried beneath the countryside's topsoil. (Though the number's been cut in half over the last two years through demining efforts and education, more than 150 Cambodians a month step on land mines. One in every 256 Cambodians is a land mine victim.) And those not missing arms or legs are most assuredly missing relatives, victims of Pol Pot's murderous regime. Many of Pol Pot's victims who survived the genocide today roam Phnom Penh's trash-laden boulevards like zombies out of a George Romero film. Some are hideously disfigured; nearly all are penniless and they follow Western tourists like gulls behind a trawler, begging for handouts.

In many areas across the neon-green Khmer countryside, bones spring from the earth like desert cacti, still shrouded with the tattered garments their owners were clothed in on the day they were slaughtered—a testament to the KR's demonic wrath. Red signs depicting skulls and crossbones are tacked to trees, sharing the bark with bullet holes, warning of land mines.

Since 1993, peace in Cambodia has been fragile at best, nonexistent most of the time. The shit hit the fan over the weekend of July 5, 1997, when Hun Sen bitch-slapped First Prime Minister Norodom Ranariddh and seized sole power of the shredded government in a bloody coup d'etat that killed at least 60 people and caused $76 million in damage to the frail economy. The Phnom Penh airport was once again riddled with bullet holes and mortar blasts. (In the nine months that followed the coup, nearly 100 of Hun Sen's political opponents were tortured, killed, or simply disappeared.)

The move cost Cambodia admission into the powerful Asian trade bloc ASEAN and the world a helluva lot more: the $3 billion UN effort in 1993 to bring peace to Cambodia. The Khmer Rouge became a sideshow, for the first time in Cambodian politics, as thousands of Phnom Penhoise, including soldiers, took to the streets in a covetous frenzy of looting, murdering and pillaging. Tanks could be seen rattling down Norodom Boulevard packed to turret with stolen refrigerators, stereos and motorbikes. Car dealerships were gutted as military officers hot-wired spanking new Mercedes and Land Cruisers and sped off to the rice fields. Corpses were strewn in the streets of Phnom Penh. Terrorized tourists and expats hightailed it for the Hotel Cambodiana and, finally, Bangkok and Singapore. Aboard C-130s, they were forced to land at an airport without radar equipment—it had been swiped by Hun Sen's best. Bullets and rockets ricocheted off the ancient temples at Angkor as soldiers of both sides sought solace behind the fabled bulkheads of 900 years of history.

Greed became the new face of danger in Cambodia—hidden behind the fancy and bombastic acronyms of its political parties and the sound bites of democracy spewed by corruption's elected guardians. When the middle-aged little boys in Windsor knots don't get their way, they pull out their guns, in which Cambodia is awash. Just a few weeks prior to the coup, Cambodia's most prominent businessman, Teng Boonma, got pissed off with the service aboard a Royal Air Cambodge flight from Hong Kong to Phnom Penh. Did he complain at the ticket counter upon arrival? No. Instead, he shot out a tire of the Boeing 737 with his bodyguard's AK while the Pratt & Whitneys were still spinning. He was not detained. So Hun Sen took the cue, flipped the world the bird and blew out the tires of democracy.

But Hun Sen is a survivor, if nothing else. New elections in 1998 solidified his grasp on power, sole power. For now, the Khmer Rouge is dead, and Cambodia is enjoying relative peace for the first time in some 35 years. The country entered ASEAN in April 1999, the final Southeast Asia nation to do so.

DP just got back from circumnavigating the country by motorcycle (at the end of 1998) and can report that…well…that it's possible—an unimaginable journey even a year ago.

Though Cambodia has ridded itself of the KR and been given a kick-start of legitimacy by its neighbors, it remains a culture of violence (two out of every three Phnom Penh households possesses at least one firearm). Though crime is down slightly in the capital since the aftermath of the 1997 coup, Phnom Penh remains one of the most dangerous cities in the world.

Don't be fooled. With the demise of the Khmer Rouge, there is emerging the perception of Cambodia being more peaceful. In reality, with the demise of the Khmer Rouge, the violence simply doesn't make as many headlines.

Rebel Etiquette

In 1992, UNTAC issued a pamphlet to its soldiers and workers listing helpful Khmer phrases for use in the event of being detained or robbed by the KR. Translated, a couple read:

• *That's a very nice gun, sir. I'd be honored to give you the gift of my truck.*

• *My watch is very expensive; that's why it makes me very happy to present it to you as a gift.*

Pol Pot died unceremoniously in a jungle shack on April 15, 1998, and was burned like trash, nearly a year after Hun Sen had quite dramatically taken over Cambodia's government. At first he was an international pariah, but the July 1998 elections "legitimized" Hun Sen's coup and the former KR turncoat has since turned his attention to getting back the foreign aid that accounts for half of the Cambodian budget—and to dealing with loud calls from the international community to bring former high-ranking Khmer Rouge cadres to justice in a court with John Grisham credentials. Of course, this is at the risk of reigniting the revolutionary flame in Pailin, where most of Pol Pot's henchmen are living freely and shooting craps at the Riviera Casino. But rifles could well replace the dice should the prime minister fire off anything more than sound bites. At the moment, Cambodia may be politically safer than a year ago, but don't put this theory to test on the streets. During a two-week period in October 1998, there were more than 15 armed robberies of foreigners in Phnom Penh.

Ta Mok

The man with Star Wars–sounding name and probably the most brutal rebel leader alive is cooling his heels and tuning into Voice of America broadcasts from his tiny, stinking Phnom Penh prison cell. Thinking he'd cut a defection deal with Hun Sen, Ta Mok was busted on March 6, 1999, near the Thai border. The one-legged Ta Mok had been running what was left of the Khmer Rouge out of Anlong Veng and is known for scores of atrocities and cold-blooded murders of his own people and Western tourists. Ta Mok was the one that carried out Pol Pot's execution plans. Now, the former KR's ranking general is a can of worms and the center of an international debate on who should open it up and where. Hun Sen would like to see Ta Mok quietly tried for tax evasion in a Phnom Penh court presided over by barbers and cyclo drivers turned judges, and hopes that he simply dies of old age before they get to the juicier charges: genocide, kidnapping and murder.

The Khmer Rouge, or NADK (National Army of Democratic Kampuchea)

The Khmer Rouge is dead for now with maybe a couple of thousand KR running around the jungles of Anlong Veng still playing revolution. The KR's legacy is still shaping Cambodia's future. Like the Afghans, the KR was another CIA Frankenstein, and responsible for between 1.7 to 2 million deaths during their vicious, extreme and xenophobic experiment in radical collective agrarianism between 1975 and 1979 in a genocide unparalleled in modern times. Perhaps a quarter of the Khmer population perished from executions, torture, disease, starvation and exhaustion in only four years at the hands of the KR. The KR and leader Pol Pot were ousted from power in January 1979 by the Vietnamese and retreated to Cambodia's western jungles, where they fought a war of attrition against the government, slaughtering ethnic Vietnamese and abducting foreign tourists, until early 1999. In the KR's final years, starting with the August 1996 defection of Brother #3 Ieng Sary, some 15,000 guerrillas defected to the government side, reducing the KR to an armed barbershop quartet. The defecting rebels were played like cards by Hun Sen and Ranariddh before the July 1997 coup. After the coup, KR completely disintegrated, as the last remaining holdouts—Khieu Samphan and Nuon Chea—scrambled to cut deals to save their asses. Khieu Samphan, Pol Pot's former spokesman and nominal leader of the Khmer Rouge, had closed a deal with Ranariddh—granting the KR henchman amnesty and a significant role in a Funcinpec political alliance—just hours before the putsch began. That deal died with the coup, but Khieu Samphan is now living comfortably, along with Nuon Chea, in the former KR headquarters—now the semiautonomous zone run by Ieng Sary—of Pailin. Another KR bigshot, Son Sen, was reportedly shot dead by Pol Pot. As for Pol Pot himself, he was put on a show trial by the remaining KR forces in July 1997 and sentenced to life under "house arrest." He died under mysterious circumstances close to the Thai border on April 15, 1998. Unlike some other insurgencies across the globe, the Khmer Rouge never built a Web site, but a Yale research team has put together a biographical database for the Web containing about 6,000 biographies of Khmer Rouge leaders and their victims. More are being added. There is also a geographical database of maps of the killing fields and mass graves, as well as an archive of more than 6,000 photos of KR victims after their arrest. Check out:

Yale Research Database
http://www.yale.edu/cgp

Hun Sen

Cambodia's prime minister, the one-eyed Hun Sen (few Cambodians have two of everything they should have), is a Khmer Rouge soldier who pulled a Benedict Arnold and switched sides in 1997 and was installed as Cambodia's puppet president by the Vietnamese after their defeat of the Khmer Rouge in 1979. He is shrewd, power hungry and paranoid, and disdains the press. He ruled alone until the 1993 elections but was named co-premier despite losing the elections to Prince Norodom Ranariddh. Hun Sen grew up the son of a peasant near the Vietnamese border, though he's better known these days as the son of a bitch who staged the violent July 1997 coup that ousted First Premier Ranariddh. During calmer times, he enjoys an occasional cigarette—48 a day—lobbing grenades at opposition figures and naming schools after himself. Not known for his subtlety, he was busy executing Ranariddh supporters after the coup but doesn't quite know what all the fuss was all about. Hun Sen emerged the winner in the elections called for July 1998, polls that met with widespread charges of tampering and fraud. Just politics as usual in Cambodia.

Prince Norodom Ranariddh

Ranariddh was Cambodia's first prime minister before being deposed by Hun Sen on July 5, 1997. The king's son and born with a silver spoon, Ranariddh—before the coup—ran the country as if he were hosting a dinner party. Although painted as the good guy during the crisis of '97, Ranariddh's hands are dirty with his courting of the Khmer Rouge. To buy votes for the 1998 elections, Ranariddh's olive branch to the KR were offers of wristwatches, money, new legs and senior positions in the Cambodian military. He struck deals with KR monsters such as Ieng Sary and Khieu Samphan. Ieng Sary's punishment for the death of 2 million Cambodians was his own little fiefdom in western Cambodia and all the pretty little gems and hardwood forests that came with it. Ranariddh is still leader of the FUNCINPEC party and holds the position of speaker of the general assembly.

Ieng Sary

Former KR big shot Ieng Sary—Brother Number Three, foreign minister in Pol Pot's '75–'79 regime and a butcher in his own right—initiated the mass KR defections in August 1996 and was rewarded by the government with a royal pardon for his genocide crimes and the leadership of the former KR headquarters of Pailin, which Sary rules with virtual autonomy from Phnom Penh. Sary and his boys have swapped shoulder patches, but that's about all. He occasionally trots on over to Bangkok for medical treatment, as he did when *DP* was in town to interview him. His son, Ing Vouth, took one look at the motley *DP* crew in late 1998 at Pailin police headquarters and spat pebbles and dust from his shiny new smuggled SUV in a dash to get back into town. Perhaps he was expecting Nate Thayer or Ted Koppel.

Kaing Khek Iev, or "Duch"

Duch was the director of Phnom Penh's infamous Tuol Sleng detention center, or S-21, where perhaps 16,000 Cambodians and 8 Westerners were brutally tortured before being carted off to the killing fields at Choeung Ek for execution. Western reporters tracked down Duch in the spring of 1999 in Battamabang, where he'd been working for three years as an NGO worker under an alias. A born-again Christian, Duch confessed his crimes to the media and offered to blow the lid off the chain of command and the secretive flow charts of Pol Pot's genocide machine at an international war crimes trial.

King Norodom Sihanouk

In 1941, the French made Prince Sihanouk king of Cambodia, believing they had installed another loyal puppet on the throne who'd do anything they asked of him for the price of a lavish existence. Instead, King Sihanouk moved in the direction of Cambodian independence. In 1953, he declared martial law and dissolved the parliament. On November 9, he proclaimed Cambodia an independent state. But internal divisions continued to hamper the solidarity among the nation's leaders. In 1955, Sihanouk abdicated the throne in favor of politics. Politically, Sihanouk has vacillated between the right and the left throughout his career (intermittently supporting the Khmer Rouge and its foes alike). Known for bending with the wind, he is nonetheless still worshiped by the core of the Cambodian people. Ill with cancer, he resides primarily in Beijing and Pyongyang, North Korea. His relationship with the late North Korean leader Kim Il Sung was deep and lasted for decades. In the name of national reconciliation, he pardoned Khmer Rouge henchman Ieng Sary in 1996. These days, Sihanouk spends most of his time being sick in Beijing, quashing reports he is considering abdicating. and shaking his head over the sorry state of his realm.

Sam Rainsy

Sam Rainsy, a brilliant, French-educated free market reformer, outspoken government critic and ardent anticorruptionist, is the darling of Western diplomats. Rainsy was stripped of his MP position in parliament and expelled from Funcinpec in May 1995. On November 9, 1995, Rainsy launched a new political party in Cambodia called the Khmer Nation Party (KNP) and later humbly renamed it The Sam Rainsy Party. Rainsy formed an alliance with Ranariddh in the run-up to the '98 elections, but has gotten a lot less press since the elections, in which he ran a distant third. (But Rainsy tallied enough votes that, combined with Ranariddh's support, he still remains Hun Sen's enigma.) Sammy boy's had a number of brushes with assassination. On March 30, 1997, three or four grenades were tossed into a demonstration he was leading in front of the parliament building, killing 19 and wounding 120, including Rainsy himself.

Pol Pot (Saloth Sar)

After becoming the victim of a KR mutiny the previous year and put under "house arrest," Pol went to the great piss Pot in the sky on July 15, 1998. KR Brother #1 was chairman and CEO of the 20th century's most brutal and xenophobic government on the planet. Before an autopsy could be performed, Pol Pot's corpse was tossed into a tire-and-easy-chair bonfire by his former buddies less than a kilometer from the Thai border. There was no eulogy and few mourners (just his ex-ammo porter wife, his two kids, a few low-ranking KR cadres and fewer reporters). As his frail, disease-riddled frame was reduced to cinders, his right arm, its fist clenched, could be seen pointing to the sky. It's widely thought Pol took his own life. He was suffering from cerebral malaria, but still he was cerebral enough to realize that capture by government troops was imminent.

Pol's real name was Saloth Sar. He was born to well-off rice farmers, went to Paris on a scholarship to study electronics and came back a Communist. Back home he taught history and geography. He helped to organize the Khmer Rouge in '63 and his little cadre took off during the Vietnam War when U.S. bombers carpet bombed their homes. In 1975, about 70,000 KR rebels overthrew Lon Nol and Year Zero began. The mayhem began in earnest and only stopped when the Vietnamese army invaded and took Phnom Penh in January 1979.

http://www.cybercambodia.com/dachs/index.html

A passport is required. An airport visa valid for a 30-day stay is available upon arrival at Phnom Penh's Pochentong Airport from the Ministry of National Security for US$20. You can also apply to:

http://www.embassy.org/cambodia/

General Direction of Tourism

Chief of Tour Service Office
3 Monivong Street
Phnom Penh
Tel: 855-23-24607 or 23607
Fax: 855-23-26164 or 23-26140.

You will need to send the following: full name, passport number, photocopy of the front section of your passport, date and place of birth, arrival and departure dates and itinerary. They will confirm receipt of application. Visas will then be issued on arrival at Pochentong Airport. You will need two passport-sized photos. Visas are good for stays up to 30 days.

Visa extensions can be applied for, but not necessarily granted, in Phnom Penh at the following:

http://www.cambodia-web.net/

Foreign Ministry

240 Street and Samdech Sothearos Boulevard
Phnom Penh, Cambodia
Tel: 24641 or 24441

General Direction of Tourism

3 Monivong Street
Phnom Penh, Cambodia
Tel: 855-23-723607
Fax: 855-23-426164 or 426140

Phnom Penh Tourism

313 Samdech Sothearos Boulevard
Phnom Penh, Cambodia
Tel: 723949, 725349, or 724059
Fax: 885-23-426043

You can also arrange for visas in Vietnam. Allow three to five days for issue. Various Saigon tour operators run boats up the Mekong River from Vietnam to Phnom Penh. However, occasionally, these excursions are canceled due to lawlessness and bandit attacks on river-going vessels.

From Thailand

Entry by land from Thailand is legal at the Aranyaphrathet/Poipet checkpoint and at Trat in the corner of Thailand's southeast. The Poipet checkpoint is becoming popular with adventure-type backpackers seeking to go overland to Siem Reap and the temples at Angkor. Pickup trucks packed like sardine cans make the grueling sunrise-to sunset-journey to Siem Reap along dilapidated National Route 6. Visitors in Thailand can also briefly enter Cambodia from Sisaket along Highway 221 to the ancient, mountaintop Khmer temple of Preah Vihear on the Thai–Cambodian border; but visitors cannot proceed any further into Cambodia. Between Preah Vihear and Siem Reap is the most heavily mined swath of Cambodia.

From Vietnam

Crossing into Cambodia from Vietnam is very popular with budget travelers. There are several border checkpoints, but at the time of this writing, only one is usable by foreigners: the Moc Bai-Bavet checkpoint on Route 1. A bus leaves at dawn daily except Sundays from both Phnom Penh and Saigon; it's a hellishly crowded affair, and very slow with frequent stops. Once the bus reaches the border there can be a wait of several hours while the authorities on each side pour over travel papers, visas, and every box and basket on the bus in search of contraband. Total travel time is about 12 to 13 hours, if the bus doesn't break down. Verdict: not recommended.

A better way is to catch a "share taxi" to the border from either side; from Phnom Penh the fare can be as low as US$5 per person if the car is full. Upon arrival at the border, simply walk to the other side and stick your thumb out for the next taxi or private car willing to ferry you the rest of the way. This cuts a good four hours off the bus trip, and is usually much more comfortable. Be sure the price is agreed upon before getting into the car.

From Laos

At press time, there are no border crossings open to foreigners to Cambodia from Laos. This is probably because the northeast of Cambodia is mostly thick jungle with little population, no infrastructure and no roads connecting the region with Phnom Penh. Theoretically it should be possible, but again you would be entering illegally if your visa (assuming you had one in advance) was not stamped. If you must do it legally, the best route would be along the Mekong River, as there is sure to be a checkpoint for the locals, or along a well-traveled logging road.

Intercity buses are officially off limits to foreigners and trains are often restricted to Cambodian citizens (though it is now possible to take the train to Kompot from Phnom Penh—just be persistent!). By road, Siem Reap can be reached from Phnom Penh via share taxis (or rented motorcycle), which take National Route 5 to Battambang and then swing east around the Tonlé Sap Lake. The trip is long and arduous, however, and security on the Sisaphon-Siem Reap leg is chancy, especially after dark. National Route 6, the most direct road from Phnom Penh, is still highly insecure between Kompong Thom and Siem Reap.

By air, Royal Air Cambodge (owned by Malaysian Air Service) flies new Boeing jets and ATR turboprops to Siem Reap from Phnom Penh several times daily and several times weekly to Sihanoukville, Battambang, Ko Kong and Rattanakiri. Siem Reap is also accessible by air from Bangkok via Bangkok Airways.

There are now several companies running a speedboat service to Siem Reap via the Tonlé Sap River. The trip takes about five hours from Phnom Penh; foreigners pay US$25, Khmers 50,000 riel, one way. Two types of boats make the run: long, enclosed boats bought second-hand from Malaysia, and comparatively new, smaller speedboats with twin outboard engines run by a Chinese company. The long boats are the more comfortable, with aircraft-like interiors, air-conditioning, and real (if tiny) toilets. Be sure to bring toilet paper, as none is provided. Earplugs are also a good idea, as the drone of the engine competes with torturous, tinny and continually repeating Khmer karaoke videos played at top volume. The smaller speedboats are supposedly a bit faster, but the double-row bench seats get uncomfortable after an hour, and the "toilet" is a roofless box at the stern. Both boats depart every day at 7 A.M. from the Psar

Toit area north of the Japanese Bridge. A free shuttle to the pier leaves about 6:30 A.M. from the Capitol Hotel.

Travel to Siem Reap is also possible on the slow cargo boats, which depart Phnom Penh regularly and take a full 24 hours. The boat anchors in the middle of the river for the night; travelers must bring their own sleeping gear. Price is about 3,500 riel one way.

Siem Reap

Travel in areas of Siem Reap province outside the Angkor complex can be highly dangerous, as bandits prey upon large parcels of the province. Visitors traveling outside urban areas are urged by Western embassies to exercise caution and restrict travel to daylight hours and only in vehicle convoys to enhance security.

Pailin

Pailin, only 20 kilometers from the Thai border in western Cambodia, is the former Khmer Rouge headquarters and now a semiautonomous zone run by Ieng Sary and other Khmer Rouge defectors. Westerners are both an oddity and a curiosity here, as only a few short years ago they would have been abducted and/or executed well before they got this far into KR territory. To preserve their fragile coexistence with Phnom Penh, the former KR—though they remain suspicious of foreigners—take pain to ensure that the rare visitors here have a safe stay. But the 80-kilometer stretch of roadway between Battambang and Pailin is flanked by huge quantities of land mines—right to the edge of the road. Don't even think about finding a bush to pee behind.

Phnom Penh

Although things have returned to normal after the coup, "normal" in Phnom Penh is daily occurrences of armed robbery, banditry and murder. Armed bandits dressed as soldiers prey on foreigners. During a two-week period in October 1998, 15 foreigners were the victim of an armed robbery. An American tourist was robbed and shot dead just prior to the July 1997 uprisings. A Canadian was also killed photographing looting in the city. Soldiers will have no scruples about shooting you should you end up in the wrong place at the wrong time. Stay off the streets after 10 P.M.

Rattanakiri

Due to its sheer remoteness in the northeast of Cambodia, and because of a lack of infrastructure and a nonexistent security apparatus, travel here should be done very cautiously. In April 1997, three foreign aid workers—two American women and a Frenchman—had their NGO 4-wheel-drive vehicle shot at and halted in the province by heavily armed men in military uniforms. They were robbed and their vehicle was set ablaze and destroyed.

Land Mines

UN officials and demining experts estimate that between 5 and 6 million mines are scattered around the country. The Russian PMN2 antipersonnel mine is most common in Cambodia. Between 150 to 500 people are killed or maimed every month. It is estimated that one person in 256 in Cambodia is an amputee because of an injury from land mines. The government says it needs US$80 million to clear them. The most heavily mined areas are Kampong Thom, Siem Reap, Kampong Chang, Kampong Speu, Koh Kong, Oddar Meanchey, Batneay Meanchey, Battambang and Pursat. As of 1999, the Cambodian Mine Action Center had only cleared perhaps 10 percent of the old minefields in Cambodia. The good news is that it is expected that it will take 10 to 20 years to clear them all out instead of the 100 years originally expected. Only about 100 square miles of the 1,160 square miles of mined areas have been cleared.

Clearing Mines

While *DP* was in Cambodia a few years ago, a group of 29 mine disposal workers was attacked by the Khmer Rouge in Siem Reap province. The Mines Advisory Group was accused by the KR of laying mines. The 10 gunmen made off with an English mine clearer—Christopher Howe—and his interpreter. A man who was arrested later said he was paid US$20 to show the KR where the mine clearers would be working that day. A group of three women who went to negotiate the Brit's release were themselves taken hostage, and all five were taken to Anlong Veng, the former KR camp run by Ta Mok. Howe and his interpreter have not been heard from since.

Big News

Nate Thayer, a journalist who works for *Far Eastern Review,* had spent ten years of his working career waiting for one story: Pol Pot. Then he was given the chance to take cameraman David McKaige. He had made over 40 trips into the jungles of Cambodia to cover the Khmer Rouge and now it seemed the holy grail would be his. The U.S.-based ABC News learned of his scoop and Washington-based *Nightline* offered to pay $350,000 for worldwide exclusive rights to his footage. ABC then chartered a DC-10 to fly Ted Koppel and his crew to present the story. On the way out the airport was shut down and Koppel's assistant called *DP* to get him out. We did and the final words as the small plane left the ground were, "If they think that pilot is going to get $23,000 he's crazy." They said they owed us big, and naturally nothing has ever transpired.

Thayer went public with his nonpayment and ABC finally coughed up the check... after they had won a Peabody using Thayer's dramatic film.

Crime

There are frequent armed thefts of vehicles, armed extortion attempts and numerous incidents of petty crimes, such as those from hotel rooms and purse snatching. Automatic weapons abound in Cambodia, and are possessed and used by numerous citizens, even within Phnom Penh. In one summer month, 75 cases of robbery were reported in Phon Penh, 69 resulting in the death of the victim. In 1997 there were 700 crime-related deaths in Phon Penh, 2,100 for the entire country.

The Khmer Rouge does not have a retirement plan, so many former KR guerrillas are roaming the country with their weapons looking for spare change. An Aussie expat told an *Outside Magazine* journalist, who was in Phnom Penh doing a story with *DP* contributor Wink Dulles in late 1998, the best way to survive an armed robbery: "Immediately lie down on the ground. Put your hands on the back of your head, and don't say anything or look at them. You speak, wham, they hit you in the head with a pistol, mate. And they really don't like you looking at them. Mostly, it's police officers that are robbing you, so they don't want to be seen. Just keep your head down, don't speak, and let them take whatever they want. Mostly, they're not bad blokes—they usually leave you a thousand riel to get home." In other instances, foreigners are the victims of teenaged *bong thom* (big brother) gangs.

Guns

In May 1999, Prime Minister Hun Sen rolled a bulldozer over 4,000 handguns and automatic weapons in a ceremony at the National Stadium to show the world that Cambodia was voluntarily disarming itself. Hardly. Of the half million handguns and automatic rifles in circulation in Cambodia, only about half are in the hands of the army and police. And only about 10 percent of the remaining weapons are registered. Nearly 70 percent of all Phnom Penh households possess at least one firearm. And schoolyard arguments are often settled by an angry parent tossing a hand grenade or firing a pistol into the air.

Hooligan Haven

The Interpol representative's office in Cambodia believes that at least 100 of Interpol's most wanted criminals are hiding in Cambodia. The fugitives are said to be taking advantage of Cambodia's relatively lax legal system and the present inability of Royal Cambodian Government (RCG) law enforcement agencies to meaningfully fight crime. Interpol was further reported to be concerned that the apparent influx of criminals may signal a rise in organized crime activities in Cambodia—a country that has already seen an upsurge in international drug trafficking attributable to deficient law enforcement abilities.

In addition, police have launched a major investigation into the operations of a Phnom Penh-based company linked to Yoshimi Tanaka, a Japanese Red Army member, on charges of using counterfeit U.S. dollars. Police in Phnom Penh believe that Kodama International Trading (KIT), run by Tang Cheang Tong, a Japanese citizen of Khmer-Chinese origin, helped Tanaka launder fake U.S. currency through its export-import operations. Tanaka was arrested on the Cambodia-Vietnam border on March 24, 1996, by Cambodian police, Interpol officials and U.S. federal agents after being accused of disposing of counterfeit dollars in the southeastern Thai resort of Pattaya. Cambodian customs officials and police were at various times offered up to US$40,000 in bribes to let him cross the border. Notorious as one of Japan's best-known fugitives, Tanaka was also wanted for his role in the 1970 hijacking of a Japanese airliner to Pyongyang, North Korea.

Car and Motorbike Jackings

There's been a surge in armed carjackings and forcible rip-offs of motorbikes in Phnom Penh. Even the police are not immune to becoming victims. In many instances, the victims are shot.

Grenades

In March 1999 alone, there were more than eight grenade attacks in Phnom Penh. Most attacks are against ethnic Vietnamese shop owners. On March 25, a grenade exploded in a government compound just as Prime Minister Hun Sen's motorcade was passing. You might just want to wait until you get to Saigon for that bowl of *pho.*

Trains

Though trains have been a no-go since the days Western tourists were being corralled by KR guerrillas and marched off into the forest, it is indeed possible these days to take the Phnom Penh/Kompot-train. Banditry still remains a possibility. Now that the KR is gone, bandits have risen to the opportunity and taken their place. But for the first time since 1994, foreigners can actually buy a train ticket.

Buses

Due to the high incidence of banditry, Western tourists are prohibited from traveling aboard local buses. Only the bus to Saigon is open to foreigners.

Timber

The Khmer Rouge formerly earned about US$10 million a month in timber sales to Thailand before their ranks were decimated by defections, according to Global Witness. And it would be fair to say that someone has taken their place. The government of Cambodia has authorized soldiers to open fire on logging trucks or boats taking lumber out of Cambodia.

Outside of the major cities, you are out of luck here. It would be best to fly to Bangkok or Singapore for treatment of serious wounds or diseases. You can expect malaria and other tropical bugs endemic to Southeast Asia. There is one doctor for every 27,000 people in Cambodia.

Update all your shots and take the usual precautions for malaria and other tropical diseases. There are many virulent strains of malaria that are resistant to all prophylactics. Inoculations are not required unless you're arriving from an endemic area.

Dr. Gavin Scott is Phnom Penh's senior Western doctor and the only native English speaker. He can be contacted at the **Tropical & Travelers Medical Clinic** *(No. 88 Street 108, tel., 366802).*

There is no truly modern hospital facility in the country. You will need to buy your own drugs (usually expired). It's best to stock up in Bangkok, where many useful preparations can be had over the counter. Dangerous snakes include vipers, cobras and king cobras, hanumans and banded kraits.

Hospitals in Phnom Penh

SOS International Medical Center

83 Issarak Boulevard
tel., 015-912-765, 364127.
Emergency medical care, up to limited Western standards.

Access Medical Services

203 63rd Street
tel., 015-913-358.
Australian nurse; vaccinations.

Clinique Borei Keila

172 Tehcoslavaquie
tel., 360207.

Maternite Somphop Panya

282 St. Kampuchea Krom
tel., 366046.

Polyclinic and Maternity Psar Chas

38-40 110 Street
tel., 426948, 360436.

Raffles Medical Center

Sofitel Cambodiana
313 Sisovath Boulevard Office 3,
Ground Floor.
tel., 017-204088, 426299 (ext. 631/7).

Calmette Hospital

Monivong Boulevard
tel., 723173.
This is the best facility in the country, although it's hardly up to Western standards.

European Dental Clinic

195A Norodom Boulevard
tel., 62656, 018-812-055.

Kantha Bopha-II

Pediatrics Hospital
Vithei Oknha Chun.

Polyclinic and Maternity Angkor

75 St. Oknha Pich
tel., 018-811237.

Polyclinique Aurore

58-60 113 Street
tel., 018-810339.

Visalok Polyclinic

80 Monireth Boulevard
tel., 427069, 365160.

Americans can register at the U.S. embassy in Phnom Penh and obtain updated information on travel and security within Cambodia.

Embassy Locations

U.S. Embassy

No. 20, Mongkol Iem Street (Street 228)
Phnom Penh, Cambodia
Tel.: [855] (23) 26436 or (23) 26438
Cellular: 018-810465
Fax: 855-23-27637
The consular entrance to the U.S. embassy is located at *16 Street 228 (between Street 51 and Street 63)*. The embassy is able to offer essential consular services.

Cambodian U.N. Section

866 U.N. Plaza, Suite 420
New York, NY 10017
Tel.: (212) 421-7626

1/18/00	Former Khmer Rouge Commander now serving in Cambodian Army arrested for murder of three western tourists abducted in July, 1994.
5/14/98	Nate Thayer, who has a world exclusive interview, goes public with ABC News nonpayment for $350,000 rights for exclusive rights to his film. ABC *Nightline* wires the money after accepting a Peabody Award.
4/ 15/98	Pol Pot dies at age 73 after 19 years of hiding; cremated four days later.
7/5/97	Hun Sen ousts Norodom Ranariddh in a coup that kills more than 50 people.
3/30/97	A grenade blast rips through a demonstration organized by the Khmer Nation Party, killing 19 and wounding 120 others, including an American political consultant.
6/18/96	Ieng Sary, a top Khmer Rouge leader, defects to the government, bringing with him 1,000 KR guerrillas, their weapons and 20 tanks.
1/15/95	American Susan Hadden is killed by the Khmer Rouge near Banteay Srei temple.
7/26/94	Three Western tourists bound for Sihanoukville by train are taken hostage by the Khmer Rouge and subsequently executed.
4/11/94	Three Westerners are taken hostage along Route 4 in southern Cambodia by the Khmer Rouge and subsequently executed.
1/7/79	Vietnamese take Phnom Penh and install Hun Sen as prime minister of Cambodia.
4/17/75	Pol Pot and Khmer Rouge roll into Phnom Penh and seize control of Cambodia.

10/9/70	Cambodian monarchy abolished. The country subsequently is named the Khmer Republic.
11/9/53	Independence Day.
6/19/51	Army-people solidarity day celebrates the founding of the Cambodian People's Armed Forces.
2/3/30	Founding of the Indochinese Communist Party (ICP).
5/19/28	The birthdate of Pol Pot, late leader of the Khmer Rouge.
5/24/563 B.C.	Birth of Buddha.

In a Dangerous Place: Pailin

Fear and Loathing in Cambodia's Las Vegas

Pailin, Cambodia—It's 6 P.M. and the Riviera Casino in Pailin, the former—and arguably the current—Khmer Rouge headquarters in western Cambodia and the world's most forbidden place from 1980 until . . . well . . . say, yesterday, is getting ready to party.

Half this dusty frontier backwater's inhabitants, employees of the casino, are dressed up like Fred Astaire sneaking out of a brothel. Milling around the parking lot smoking cheap Thai cigarettes and decked out in listing black bow ties, dinner-dance shirts, electric lime cummerbunds and 10W-40 weight prom-rental trousers, Pailin's labor pool of five-card stud dealers, bar-backs and Johnnie Walker comfort queens looks like a concession of cotton candy vendors at a refugee camp, or an audition for some back-alley vaudeville act.

They're surrealistically out of place. Though the sign on the marquee announces the casino is open 24 hours, another more hastily scrawled message taped to the glass door reads "closed." One bored Cambodian hostess laments, "The Thais don't come today. We have no customers."

Except me.

I've just ridden a motorcycle 400 kilometers from Phnom Penh along the world's longest sustained motocross track, over bombed-out bridges and a moonscape more like a low-pressure trough on the South China Sea than an actual road. Detonated Claymore antitank mines littered the side of the rutted track from Battambang like rusting bedpans (huge quantities of live mines are buried everywhere). A few were propped up on sticks, as a testament to Pailin's impenetrability, or as a warning of it. Disemboweled armored personnel carriers were canting permanently in roadside gullies. Peasants stoically worked cassava patches inside roped-off, active mine fields.

It's taken me three days to get here. I'm caked with red Cambodian clay and I smell like the congealing of an unstable fossil fuel and a day-old electrical fire. I'm here to get down with the Khmer Rouge and boogie with the guerrilla bad boyz at baccarat, bingo and debauchery.

But the Riviera possesses none of the glitz of Vegas or Monte Carlo. Nor even the lipstick-smeared, plastic-cocktail-cup ambiance of those raunchy slot-machine roadhouses that pinprick a Nevada map like Third World sidewalk cigarette vendors. Rather, the Riviera looks like a strip mall bowling alley in the part of town where your neighbors sell hubcaps or run a police department impound lot.

Erecting a casino in the hub of a movement that was responsible for some 2 million Cambodian deaths during its genocidal rule of the mid- and late-1970s may appeal to some, but a Mirage it will never be. Rather, a casino in Pailin is like opening a peep show in Hitler's Berlin bunker.

Pailin's gendarme commander, undoubtedly a former high-ranking KR cadre, is drunk—but not as twisted as his uniformed, middle-aged charge, who's fondling the barely ripened buttocks of one of the casino's handful of "service girls" to the tedious electronic drumbeat of a whiny Khmer pop tune, a song so saturated in reverb, it appears to have been encrypted.

With the casino closed, the police chief has figured it's a good time to open the Riviera's disco, which is nothing more than what the Riviera's restaurant becomes after its last dinner patron has slurped up his "moum banjuok." The Bee Gee-esque disco ball hanging from the dining room ceiling like a forgotten Christmas ornament becomes awash in lasers. The former rebels, with their impromptu dates in tow, then form an oozing, Apsara-like queue on the dance floor—a moving bas relief, like the oscillation of a single-celled organism in a Petri dish. It's a cross between Cambodian traditional dance, an invertebrate's mating ritual, and doing a Brazilian samba with wet nail polish on.

My partner on this expedition, *Outside Magazine* writer Patrick Symmes, finds this all amusing enough to snap off a few frames on his Nikon. The portly, bun-squeezing gendarme isn't amused, as the object of his affection—and Symmes' 35 mm—is most certainly not his wife. After Symmes excuses himself for the toilet, Captain Buns snatches Symmes' camera from our table. Instinctively, I snatch it back from him.

The dancing abruptly stops as Captain Buns and I straddle the abyss of an international incident. But the bomb is quickly defused when Pailin's top cop gets between us and grandly gestures through an interpreter: "You foreigner are welcome to Pailin!" He implores us to select among his jumbo fleet of wet-leased concubines.

In a slurred blend of Khmer and Thai, Captain Buns apparently mutters to me: "Two years ago you would have been shot for that."

Instead, we join the former guerrillas and their China-doll hookers on the dance floor and party the night away, Cambodian style, to a continually repeating, 50-cent karaoke video. Have times changed.

Actually, a few years ago, Symmes and I would have been shot 80 klicks out of Phnom Penh.

—**Wink Dulles**

Chechnya (Ichkeria)
★★★★★

The Return of Howling Wolf

It seemed only a matter of time before the fiercely independent Chechen people would rise up against "Mother Moscow."Again. The Chechens have been conquered, neglected, abused and banished by everyone from the Ak Koyonlu and the Horde of the White Sheep to Georgian boy-turned-snuffmeister; Joey Stalin. During WW2 Stalin stuffed the Chechens in boxcars and sent them to Siberia and northern Kazakhstan (along with the Tartars) for being German collaborators. Well they weren't actually, but; hey a dictator can never be too careful you know. So it's not surprising the Chechens have a mean streak as wide as the mountainous border that divides the southern part of their country.

After they were repatriated by Kruschev in the 50's the Chechens, hardened and without any means of earning a living, set about forming the largest criminal gangs in the former Soviet Union. Keep in mind that in Russia, one has to be careful before calling someone a crook. The Chechens were as far from the Marxist, there-is-no-God, one-size-fits-all Soviet model as a people could be.

Why? First, Chechens aren't even Chechen (they are *Nuokhchi*, or sons of Noah); they speak a unique language- *Nakh*; they are Muslim; they are more entrepreneurial than Donald Trump and tougher than a hung over hockey team. More importantly they have kept their national identity intact. Chechen loyalties are to one of the more than 100 *teips,* or clans, that constitute Chechen society, not to the fat-bottomed thieves in the Kremlin. Think of teips as similar to the city states of Athens. Warring in peacetime, peaceful in war. Left to their own devices and sitting on the nexus of the east and west, the Chechens thought and acted just like the lone wolf that has become their national symbol.

The Russians considered them the toughest, baddest people in the former Soviet Union. But bears don't kill wolves, packs of wolves kill bears. Russians are quick to accuse the Chechens of blowing up apartments, running drugs, hijacking airliners and school buses and other abuses, and of then hotfooting it back to Chechnya to hide out in their inaccessible mountain villages.

So *DP* thought it was strange that the news media were quick to recast the ornery Chechens as the heroic-defenders-of-their-homeland underdogs in the West in the '94 -'96 war. You didn't hear much about the rumblings in Chechnya and the *contractistya*'s hired by the Russian army to start a revolution. But when the sham civil war started the empire struck back. Russian defense minister Pavel S. Grachev boasted that a single paratroop regiment would need only a couple of hours to wipe out the rebellion. Darth Vader he ain't.

Outnumbered by five (more likely ten) to one, the Chechen irregulars, along with volunteers, waged a guerrilla war from the mountains. The Russians seemed to have completely forgotten the lessons they learned in Afghanistan, as their forces hid in their newly built forts along the major highways using vulnerable supply and patrol convoys. Then when the Chechens came out of the mountains to kill the Russians in Grozny, it was all over.

It was a story the Western media loved—peasants armed with sticks and shovels defiantly dancing around bonfires in central Grozny, seemingly holding off the entire might of the Russian bear. Wolf-like Chechen fighters, unshaven and dirty, waving their flag while strafing fighters soared overhead turning their parliament into Swiss cheese. Meanwhile, the most feared army in the world turned out to be shivering, underfed, stoned, confused and mostly prepubescent.

Although the vastly superior Russian forces eventually took the Chechen capital in February 1995, they faced a low-budget Afghanistan for the next 20 months. The Chechen insurgents—many of them former Soviet soldiers trained in mountain guerrilla fighting—dug into the hills and waged a long and fierce battle of attrition against an undisciplined, underaged band of Moscow's best. And, in true Afghanistan form, the Russian army set up a puppet government, while the rebels regrouped in the hills.

Between 1,500 and 3,000 Chechen fighters in three groups fought this pocket *gazavat,* or holy war. Dzhokhar Dudayev ran his tiny rebel army from his "secret" base in Roshni-Chu, about 45 minutes south of Grozny, until he was hit by a Russian missile, which homed in on his satellite phone in a clearing 20 miles southeast of Grozny in April 1996. In February 1995, the Russian army needed 38,000 troops just to keep the lid on Chechnya, and the Interior Ministry had deployed an additional 15,500 men. But an aggressive drive by the Chechen fighters on August 6, 1996 (Yeltsin's inauguration day) reversed the war, driving

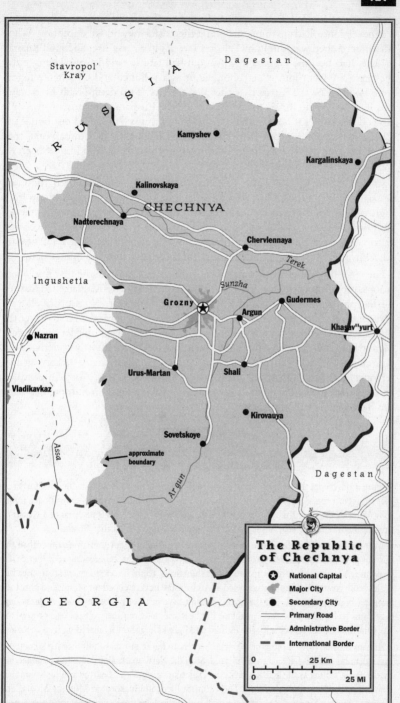

The Republic
of Chechnya

National Capital

Major City

Secondary City

Primary Road

Administrative Border

International Border

0   25 Km

0   25 Mi

thousands of Russian troops and civilians out of Grozny. It seems the Russian had never controlled anything, including their drinking and self deception. When Alexander Lebed was sent in by Yeltsin to work out a cease-fire, he found Russian soldiers had become demoralized, vanquished and lice-ridden weaklings. After the cease-fire went into effect, sporadic firing continued and Chechen refugees were bombed by the Russians as they fled the city. Two daring raids by Basayev and Raduyev inside Russia quickly reminded the Russians that Moscow was only a bus ticket away for holy warriors. A peace treaty was hammered out but as the Chechen commander told DP Lebed warned them they had three years, they better be ready. In the meantime all the money slated for rebuilding Chechnya was siphoned off and stolen.

So in October of 1999 the Chechens were ready. One-hundred thousand Russians rolled in fueled by promises of quick victory and a budget bump from higher oil prices. On paper it looked good Russian tanks swept through miles of flat northern plains encircling cities, pounding them to rubble and then declaring victory. The problem was the Chechens weren't fighting. When DP was in Chechnya the Russians pounded Argun for three days after the fighters left.

The second war was pretty much a bigger budget remake of the first war. More troops, more fireworks, more rhetoric and more dead. The Russians had learned media spin from ex-CIA director Bush and his Gulf War. No journos allowed (except on escorted bus tours) was the rule. Few if any journos dared to cover the war from the rebel side, terrified of stories of kidnapping, murder and deceit. Meanwhile the Russians pounded their own people (mostly elderly, poor Russians who had been given flats in Grozny) while claiming victory against terrorists. DP was in the bunkers with the "terrorists" eating pumpkin pancakes and wondering why the media didn't give a shit about a war in Europe that made the Balkans pale in comparison.

Forget oil, forget the mafiya, forget global strategy, forget islamic fundamentalists, forget all that strategic Trans Caucasian gobbledy gook. The war (s) in Chechnya are about Russia trying to hold on to the frayed tatters of their Soviet pipedream. Chechnya is just one of a cluster of tiny southern republics that don't want to be under the skirts of Mother Russia.

War has always been the way to keep Russians complaining about something other than the corrupt government. A bear looks pretty docile and weak when its hibernating so its better if it looks tough and pissed. It rears up and makes those nasty teeth. It used to growl at America but we kicked its teeth in. Then they growled at Afghanistan but it stepped on a trap. And now they are growling at Chechnya. But that growl doesn't have teeth or brains anymore. At press time it remains to be seen how bad a mauling the bear will get from the wolf packs. For now the Russians military contents itself with a sound and light killing show while hiding its true losses.

It took a while (four months) for Yeltsin backers to figure out that Putin needed something more than his lack of charisma to get elected. So voila. Nasty apartment bombings (engineering by the Putin's buds at the FSB), attacks on Dagestani villages and Basayev and his volunteers come running. So its Wag the Wolf: The Ultimate Election Blockbuster! Mug the Media: The Ultimate Horror Story! Both films are now playing in Chechnya. Ex-spy Putin took a page from ex-spy Bush and ex-caught-in-the-bush Clinton to create a media-blind election event.

Smash the terrorists! (bomb the old people), Win the war! (lock up the journos), Conquer Chechnya! (stay out of the towns), War without Casualties! (burn them in piles) and so on.

For now, Chechnya is a nice place if you sell Grad Rockets and have one of those 50's era basements.

http://www.cdi.org/issues/Europe/ncaucasus.html

Vladimir Putin

Short, dour, evasive and eager to act tough. Putin's ratlike glowering persona is the opposite of Yeltsin's doughboy greed. The problem is they are backed by the same people. Putin was a spy and that guides most of his thinking. He sees great treachery in Chechnya and would rather turn it into a parking lot than negotiate. He talks and acts tough, some say so that the military doesn't dump him. Others say he is mean SOB and likes to have an enemy. Or if you would like the Chechen view of Putin (from an avowed terrorist) "The problem with Putin, is that he is very small. So the distance from his heart to his asshole is too little." Looks like we won't seem much hugs and kisses anytime soon.

Boris Badenov

The first time Boris was mad as hell and he wasn't going to take it anymore, he forgot that the massive army of Stalin and Brezhnev is long gone. When Boris pushed the button, all he got was a bunch of sparks and fizzles. The second time he took a page right out of Clinton's *Wag the Dog* playbook. Except Boris was benched by the money boys and glum Putin fielded. Feeling the heat of embezzlement accusations and personal wrongdoing Boris gets a "Get Out of Jail Free" card and to keep his swindled millions. With Boris's liver looking like the houses in Grozny, it is now up to favorite son Putin ("whore" in a number of languages) to bang the drum and deflect attention from Russian's slide into oblivion.

The Chechens

No matter what happens, who wins or who claims to be in charge, the Chechens will endure as they have since they sprang from Shem the son of Noah. Mountain-bred and mean as polecats, the Chechens are an unaligned assortment of major clans that are constantly fighting for influence and shifting alliances with other clans. Each clan is led by a spiritual mystic. Some adhere to a Sufi mysticism branch of Sunni Islam called Muridism. This branch of Islam divides its followers into sects led by local feudal leaders. They are united only in their opposition to domination by outsiders.

They are not fundamental muslims. About half of Chechens belong to a Sufi brotherhood or tariqas. The two Sufi tariqas that spread in the North Caucasus were the Naqshbandiya and the Qadiriya. The Naqshbandiya in the North Caucasus is particularly strong in Dagestan and Eastern Chechnya, whereas the Qadiriya has most of its adherents in the rest of Chechnya and Ingushetia. Basayev and his foreign volunteers led by Khattab defend and control the eastern part of Chechnya. There are also elements of mysticsm mingled with islam in remote mountain areas.

Above all this is the *teips* or clans are based on land more than blood and they all have an uneasy relationship in peace and are bonded together during war. But its not that simple Commanders can be aligned to *teips*, religions, political allegiance, financial goals or a mixture of all.

During the war, the Chechens' military chain of command is like a pickup basketball game working towards a grand plan. If units of irregulars met up with each other, it was purely by happenstance. They go out and fight, then come back to eat and sleep. The fighters buy their own weapons, train on Russian conscripts and are about as coordinated as a demolition derby, but equally as destructive and resourceful. The man with the plan is Maskhadov but the man with the juice is Basayev who makes up for his lack of diplomatic skills by his ability to turn any firefight into a Russian bloodbath.

Chechen Republic of Ichkeria Homepage
http://www.chechnya.org/

Nashqabandi
http://www.naqshbandi.org/

Shamil Basayev

The million dollar man. Or so the Russians think by, putting that price on his head. Basayev thinks its an insult. Shamil Basayev was born in 1963 in Vedeno, Vedeno District, Chechen Republic. Vedeno is famous for the fortress where the great Chechen leader Iman Shamyl surrendered to Russian forces 100 years earlier. He is married to two wives and moves around quite a bit. He has three brothers. One was killed during the fighting in Vedeno at the beginning of 1995. An older brother, Shirvani Basayev, was a commandant of the city of Bamut.

In 1987, Basayev enrolled at the Moscow Institute of Land-Tenure Regulations Engineers. In August 1991, in one of history's stranger events, he defended Boris Yeltsin with a couple of hand grenades during the takeover of the White House in Moscow. In 1991, he returned to Chechnya from Russia and joined the Confederation of the People of the Caucasus (KHK), working his way up to commander in 1992. He fought in Abkhazia against the Georgians and Russians in August of 1992. He also fought alongside the Azerbaijanis in Nagorno-Karabakh. He went to Afghanistan between April and July 1994 for training at the Khowst camps. In the summer of 1994 he fought at Dzhokhar Dudayev's side. His most famous action was on June 14, 1995, when he took the hospital in the city of Budyonnousk, Russia. He says he was actually on his way to Moscow but ran out of bribe money. His goal was to destroy Yeltsin's credibility at the upcoming June 16 G-7 Summit in Halifax, Canada. During the standoff with 150 heavily armed Chechens, an old woman walked up to the Chechens in the hospital and asked them what the name of the movie they were shooting was. It got weirder. On the 18th, Victor Chernomyrdin, the Russian prime minister, appeared live on Russian television to conduct hostage negotiations with Basayev. His daring raid worked and the process of peace negotiations began.

In April 1996, he was elected commander of the armed forces of the Chechen Republic. In December 1996, he left the post of the commander in order to be a candidate for president of the Chechen Republic in forthcoming elections. On January 27, 1997, he pulled in only 23.5 percent of the voters, finishing in second place behind the winner, Aslan Maskhadov.

Then, in late 1997, Maskhadov issued a decree appointing Shamil Basayev acting premier for the duration of Maskhadov's trip to Turkey. Shamil Basayev had just resumed his post of first deputy premier. (Since Basayev had submitted his resignation from the post back in the summer, Maskhadov refused to sign the decree on Basayev's resignation.) In early December, President Aslan Maskhadov announced that he would transfer some of his authority as premier to First Vice Premier Shamil Basayev.

On January 1, 1998, Maskhadov dismissed his cabinet and tasked Basayev with forming a new government with 22 ministers instead of the then 45. Maskhadov expected to remain both the president and prime minister of Chechnya. However, Basayev was increasing his powers and influence, and let it be known he preferred to become Chechnya's prime minister.

In Augsut of '99 when Russian units attacked Chechen villages in Dagestan he and Khattab put together a crusading group of fighters to push back the Russians. This was one of the triggers of the '99-'00 war along with the apartment bombings that Moscow blamed on the Chechens but never actually proved. He lost his right foot in the Feb. '00 retreat from Grozny.

http://www.-cgsc.army.mil/milveu /english.mayjjun97/finch.htm

Ibn-ul-Khattab

Basayev's diminutive but fierce bosom buddy (born 1970 in the Arabian Gulf) is a curly-locked, dark-skinned Bedouin named Khattab, an Emir (or Commander) of the Foreign Mujahideen Forces in the Caucasus. Kahttab (his nom de guerre) has a Dagestani wife living in the settlement of Kara-Makhi in Dagestan. Although not as well known as Basayev, Khattab is a mujahedin's mujahid. He is also called "one-armed Akhmed" and "the Black Arab,"

In 1987, when he was 18, he left the American High School began his jihad in Jalalabad, Afghanistan, he was originally going to be a surgeon but became a mujahid instead. He liked fast cars and came from a wealthy family. He last two fingers from his right hand when throwing a home made grenade. He often wears a bandage or driving glove on his right hand. He fought in Tajikistan from 1993 to 1995 and then returned to Afghanistan where he met Basayav Khattab put together a group of volunteers and headed to Chechnya.

Khattab says he says he took part in actions in several Persian Gulf countries against French and other Israeli citizens. Despite being wanted by Interpol, Khattab is both shy and media savvy. He has taken to videotaping every action his men take part in.

His most famous actions are the attack and complete annhilation of (and videotaping of) a Russian armored convoy near the villages of Serzhen-Yurt and Yarysh-Mardy in the spring of 1996. You can see some of the carnage on the *www.azzam.com* site. After the Russians retreated, Khattab set up a training camp during the winter of '96-'97. His training school was near the village of Serzhen-Yurt, Vedeno Rayon, where he and several of his senior veteran "Afghan" and "Bosnian" mujahedin taught black skills.

He escaped an assassination attempt in June 1997 while driving a jeep near Benoy, some 70 kilometers south of the capital, Grozny. A remote-control land mine blew up. missing the jeep by seconds. Khattab was not hurt.

His school trains and indoctrinates some of the most promising Chechen youth, all war veterans, to become the core of Chechnya's current intelligence, special and terrorist forces. For some reason, the school also has a special department training Algerians and French maghribis for terrorist operations in France.

It is no surprise that the apartment bombings in Moscow combined with Khattab's sudden lack of visibility with journos in-country to interview him led to direct suspicion of his graduates being involved in the attacks.

The mainstream Chechen leaders have been publicly distancing themselves from Khattab since January 1997, particularly Maskhadov, under whose command Khattab once fought. This has led to Basayev's split from Maskhadov and brotherlike relationship with Khattab.

http://www.qoqaz.net/

Aslan Maskhadov

Although not born in Zebir-Yurt, Maskhadov moved with his parents at the age of six to the Nadterechny district of the Chechen-Ingush Autonomous Republic. He is a graduate from the Tbilisi Higher Artillery College in 1972, and then the Kalinin Military Academy in Leningrad, where he graduated in 1981.

He was a platoon commander in the Far East and served in Hungary as a battery commander and then as a regiment commander. He was a colonel in a missile and artillery force during the attempt to capture the television tower in Vilnius in January 1991, which was part of Soviet leader Mikhail Gorbachev's attempts to put down independence in the Baltics.

After the breakup of the Soviet Union, Maskhadov served in the Chechen Armed Forces from 1992 to 1996. In December 1993, he was promoted to chief of staff and served as prime minister in the Chechen coalition government from October 1996 until January 1997.

He is primarily responsible for hammering out an agreement with the Russians at Nazran in June 1996 and in Novye Atagi from June 28 to July 4, 1996. On August 31, 1996, following talks with former Russian Security Council Secretary Aleksander Lebed, he signed the Khasavyurt agreements, buying time for Chechnya. He was unceremoniously replaced in the government during the fall of 1999 as Russian troops invaded what used to be his country. Maskhadov is married and has a daughter and a son.

Maskhadov became Chechnya's president as a result of the January 1997 elections. Maskhadov is a moderate and perhaps the man best suited to restore some semblance of order to Chechnya. Maskhadov was grudgingly endorsed by Moscow as the lesser of a dozen evils something that has caused the split between more militant groups led by Basayev. He is revered by Chechens as a fighter and the man who won the Chechen war, and equally as a diplomat who ended it. Maskhadov is a good military strategist with the personality of a piece of cardboard. *DP* spent a few hours doing the obligatory interview and didn't get too much that would be considered profound. He had been elected by a large majority of Chechen voters and controls acess into Chechnya but not the main fighting force. That is when you must talk to the man who calls the shots: Basayev.

The General Representative of the President of the Chechen Republic—Ichkeria First

The Coordinator
Zulay Khamidova
Tel: [90] (212) 257-68-15
Fax: [90] (212) 257-68-17
E-mail: dbolat@dominet.com.tr

Ambassador at Large of the Chechen Republic
Prince Charles Tchkotoua
Tel: [44] (171) 352-3597
Fax: [44](171) 352-8968

Caucasian-Chechen Information Committee
Ankara, Inkilap sok. No. 15/8
Tel./Fax: [90] (312) 431-5115

IHH (Insan Hak ve Hürriyetleri)
Tel./Fax: [90] (212) 631-3368
http://www.ihhvakf.org

Salman Raduyev

Raduyev is the poster boy for "Chechen extreme" and the son-in-law of the late Dudayev. In January 1996, he led a Lone Wolf team in taking 3,000 hostages at a hospital in the Dagestan town of Kizlyar. Russian forces surrounded the village and pounded the rebels and hostages for several days before suffering the ultimate humiliation. Raduyev broke through the Russian perimeter with his fighters and 100 of the hostages and made a successful run for the Chechen town of Pervomaiskaya. Although the Russians claimed one of its snipers killed him in March 1996, Raduyev returned to Chechnya in July and claimed responsibility for a series of trolley blasts in Moscow. Reporters noticed that Raduyev had lost his left eye in the March attack and had gotten his mug rearranged by plastic surgeons in Europe after recuperating in the Middle East. He had been shot in the cheek and the bullet came out his eye. Ouch.

He also escaped another assassination attempt in April 1997, when he was badly wounded when his car was blown up. Stallone and Schwarzenegger should take notes. Raduyev and his boys are the most radical of the Chechen separatists and don't recognize the legitimacy of Maskhadov's government. Attempts on his life have been courtesy of Russian intelligence (could there be such a thing?). In July 1997, they did it again when a van filled with explosives blew up as Raduyev's car was supposed to pass by.

Raduyev continues to stir up trouble in the Chechen countryside and just like *DP* believes that Dudayev (and Elvis) is still alive. Raduyev can be found in his headquarters in Grozny. My favorite Raduyev quote: "Russia needs the pipeline, but we'll explode it." He was described to *DP* by his Chechen commanders as not being "quite right in the head" after the bullet went through it.

Iman Shamyl

You would think Russia would have learned. This war is neither the first or second conflict in Chechnya. Russia first conquered Chechnya and Dagestan between 1825 and 1859 and had to deal with a fighter named Iman Shamyl. He finally surrendered to Tsar Alexander II, but the fighting continued as Russian columns continued to be attacked in the 1860s. The North Caucasus resisted by force the imposition of Soviet rule between 1917 and 1921, with sporadic clashes continuing into the 1930s. He was known for daring raids behind Russian lines, fighting against massive odds and oddly enough for surrendering and living out his life in comfort in Russia.

Tartars

Not the stuff the dentist scrapes off your teeth, but a group of about 180,000 people who were shipped off along with the Chechens by Stalin. The Tartars fought alongside Chechen rebels against the Russian government. Of the current community of 6 million Tartars, 250,000 are found in the Crimea, but their sympathies lie with the Chechens.

Dzhokhar Dudayev

Looking and acting surprisingly like Boris Badenov of *Rocky and Bullwinkle* fame, Dzhokhar (pronounced Jokar) Dudayev was a Muslim and a former general in the Soviet air force. He was a member of the Myalkhir Hill Clan, a very unpopular clan amongst other Chechens. The Myalkhir Hill Clan is poor, feisty and treacherous—sort of the Chechen equivalent of our white trash without the mobile homes.

Dudayev delivered on his promise of a *gazavat*, or holy war, when Moscow invaded his tiny gangster kingdom. Dudayev hated Russians (who weren't too fond of him, either— even those opposed to the war and Boris Yeltsin alike).

Dudayev's men were led by Basayev, veterans of the war in Abkhazia, where they are mildly related and supportive of the 20-odd clans that are fighting the Russians there. Dudayev's son was killed during the Russian assault on Grozny. Dzhokar Dudayev was elected president of the self-proclaimed Chechen Republic on a nationalist separatist platform in October 1991, and immediately told Russia to get stuffed. He knew the strategic and economic value of not only the pipelines but the smuggled contraband that crosses Chechnya. It took a year and a half for Moscow to figure out what to do. In April 1993, Dudayev disbanded the Chechen parliament. The next month, a series of skirmishes developed into war leading to heavy street fighting in Grozny during the summer of 1993. Moscow still hadn't figured out what to do, so they did what they do in all emerging fistfights—they bet on both sides. Both Chechen loyalists and Chechen independence groups used Russian equipment, soldiers and mercenaries. The alliance that swung the tide was the Chechen mafyia, which backed Dudayev and provided intel from corrupt intelligence officers and a flow of weapons. DP can confirm that Dudayev is dead but his spirit is very much alive throughout Chechnya.

Monopoly

You know the game where you have to control all the little squares. Well, it's the same basic idea here. Aslan Maskhadov considers access to the Caspian Sea to be "vitally necessary for Ichkeria." They want to create an "imanate." The problem is, there is a place called Dagestan in the way. Basayev's attempts to declare Dagestan independent and toss out the Russians didn't work, and it appears the locals weren't too thrilled about being bombed and shelled. The Chechens also like the idea of the Black Sea being part of Ichkeria. The Chechens are cozy with Abkhazian rebels and it's conceivable that they could kick the Russian peacekeepers out. Now what about Georgia, you say? Well, Georgia hates the Russians more than it hates the Abkhaz rebels or Chechens, so it's conceivable that there could be one fat happy corridor from the Caspian to the Black Sea. The problem is that Russia has designs on getting Georgia back by hook or by crook. More likely by crook. Whoever wins would create a freeway for drugs, oil, smuggled goods and whatever else needs to get from Afghanistan through Turkey and into Europe and Russia.

The Russian Army

The Russian army, since the czarist era and through the Soviet period, has always relied on brute force and sheer numbers to win wars—which they haven't been doing a lot of recently. Tactically deficient , morally corrupt and technologically marginal, the army has always relied on overpowering numbers of undertrained, underfed troops to take home battlefield trophies. Even during the Soviet era, there was little need to train elite commando units, as there weren't any uprisings for them to put down.

By the time the Russian army was booted out of Grozny, its soldiers were lice-ridden and begging for food in the capital. To get through their roadblocks, all it took was a loaf of bread. If you threw in some Camel cigarettes or vodka, they'd roll out a red carpet and give you an armed escort (big deal). Even DP's muj buddies could pay $1400 to cross Russian lines to fight and get a ride in the Commanders car tossed in.

Chechnya is currently republic within Russia..but don't take any bets on how long. Depending on what's going on you need either a Russian visa or a Chechen bodyguard. (About ten is a safe number) Right now its only volunteers, stringers and live fast, die young, types (and DP of course) who enter rebel-held Chechnya. Reporters are allowed to work in the country only on trips organized by the Chechen Interior Ministry. If you hang with the Russians you won't get close to much. If you are in the south with the rebels you'll be too close. Take your pick.

For current information on visa requirements, U.S. citizens can contact the Russian consulates in New York, San Francisco or Seattle, or the Russian embassy in Washington, D.C.:

Russian Embassy

Consular Division
1825 Phelps Place NW
Washington, DC 20008
Tel: (202) 939-8918, 939-8907, or 939-8913

Entry into Chechnya should only be attempted by journalists or aid groups with heavy protection. Journalists must get permission from the Chechen Interior Ministry. Usually through Chechen contacts in Istanbul or Baltic countries. Today, journalists seeking entry into Chechnya or other information should contact one of the following representatives.

SBC International

    http://www.sbcif.com/

IHH

    Macar Kardesler
    Caddesi Hulusi Noyan
    Sokak No.23, Fatih
    Istanbul
    Tel./Fax: [90] (212) 631-3368
    http://www.ihhvakf.org

Chief Advisor on Foreign Affairs

    Tel: 90-212-257-3616 or 90-212-257-6815
    Cell phone: 90-212-532-27147177
    Fax: 90-212-257-3286

Also, what's an emerging republic without a web site? Start with:

    http://www.amina.org
    http://www.kaukaz.org

There is no way to safely get around in Chechnya until things improve dramatically. There is a very high threat of kidnapping (that means journalists). Journalists can only travel in Chechnya on escorted junkets and still run the risk of running into firefights, being bombed by all manner of evil things or just being shot by a drunk Russian soldier.

The Entire Country

Military activity is not predictable and occurs in all regions without notice. Most of the 400 villages are heavily armed and very jumpy. The area is under martial law, if you could call it that.. For those who like political subtlety, the area north of the Terek river is pro-Russian and does not grumble, the lowland middle of Chechnya is under heavy occupation, and all bets are off in the mountainous southwest.

Grozny

Groszny was blown to hell in the first war then reblown further to hell in the latest war. People do survive here but only if you consider not being dead, surviving

Being a Chechen Civilian

More than 80,000 civilians have been killed or are missing in the first war. It remains to be seen how many have died in this one. Another 150,000 or so are refugees. Either Russian pilots are bad shots or they feel the odds are better at snuffing unarmed civilians. Markets (bazaars), medical facilities and civilian cars on the roadways—some sites hit multiple times—were the Russians' favorite targets. The Russians like funeral processions, busloads of children and even empty roads. Nobody told them that the rebels move at night and only civilians are desparate enough to move during the day.

Being a Russian Civilian

Almost half the 20 - 40,000 people trapped and being bombarded inside Grozny were Russians. When Basayev took over a Russian hospital in Budyonnovsk in June 1995 the Russian special forces splatters dozens of screaming Russian hostages in their failed efforts to kill terrorists. Same story when Radayev got busy in Kizliar in January 1996. Russian forces killed hundreds of Russians in their efforts to win them back. Most of the Russian troops in Chechnya are dog assed farm boys conscripted into the Russian army, forced to pay protection money to their officers and even for food. Fun place huh?

Kidnapping

Kidnapping here is not pretty. Well-known aid maestro Fred Cuny is executed, and even his decomposed body is being ransomed for $200,000 to the Soros Foundation; Red Cross workers were shot point-blank in the head with silenced weapons; phone workers were kidnapped and then found decapitated; kidnappers send videos of victims' fingers and ears being sliced off to speed up payments. Things are ugly in Chechnya. The problem is that most of the kidnapping is done by Russians. Russians sell back dead Chechen fighters, split ransoms with their victims, snatch journos from Ingushetia, Georgia and Dagestan and then keep them in safehoues inside Chechnya. There is even a wholesale business as victims are swapped like baseball cards.

So far about 1200 people have been officially kidnapped since 1994. The *Economist* figures Chechen warlords made $8 million from ransoms in a year. Some say $20 million. It seems that the film *Prisoner of the Mountain* has turned into an infomercial.

Not much help to speak of here. Chechnya is a fairly healthy place, but with very limited medical resources and facilities.

Chechnya is a self-proclaimed republic in Russia with a population of 950,000 people lying just to the east of the principal road crossing the central Caucasus, ranging from the plains and foothills into the alpine highlands. Its neighbors are Dagestan to the east, the Turkic-speaking Kumyk people of Russia to the north, the Ingush to the west and the southern Ossetians and Georgians to the south. Grozny is the largest city and capital with an official peacetime population of about 400,000, depending on how severely it's getting pounded at any given moment. It was generally depopulated as a result of the Russian bombing. The DP Investor reccomends going big on retirement time shares in Grozny right now.

Chechen is the principal language, spoken by some 97 percent of the population. Russian is spoken by all. Ingush is a closely related language understood by most Chechens. Chechens and the Ingush are almost entirely Sunni Muslims of the Hanafi school. The currency is the Russian ruble and the US Dollar. The electricity is 220V/50Hz, if you can find it.

1/28/00	Khattab threatens to attack inside Russia . . . again.
12/31/99	Boris Yeltsin resigns putting Putin in charge.
10/1/99	Russians invade Chechnya . . . again.
9/9/99	A series of explosions in Moscow apartments is blamed on Chechens.
8/10/99	Dagestan declares independence after Basayev takes control of selected villages and towns.
7/99	Basayev and Khattab begin operations in Dagestan.
1/97	Maskhadov elected president of the Chechen Republic.
8/31/96	Lebed and Maskhadov sign peace treaty ending the war in Chechnya.
1/97	Two Russian journalists are kidnapped, beginning a long list of kidnap victims in Chechnya. Reconstruction is stopped and aid workers move out.
8/06/1996	Chechen fighters reverse the war, driving Russian troops out of Grozny.
3/31/1996	Yeltsin announces peace plan and says all Russian military operations will be suspended.
1/16–19/96	Pro-Chechen commandos hijack a Black Sea ferry at the Turkish port of Trabzon, taking 150 hostages, most Russian tourists. Hostages are later released after the hijackers claim their aim of drawing worldwide attention to Russian atrocities in Chechnya is achieved.
1/17/96	Russian troops attack Chechen fighters and their hostages die in the village of Pervomaiskaya on the Chechnya–Dagestan border. Eighteen hostages are reported missing by Moscow, which also claims killing 153 Chechens and taking 28 prisoner.
1/9–24/96	Chechen commandos, led by Salman Raduyev, take 2,000 people hostage at a hospital in Kizliar in the republic of Dagestan.
6/14–20/95	Chechen fighters take the southern Russian town of Budyonnovsk and 1,500 hostages in a hospital. Russian forces free 200 people on the 17th, but at least 150 are killed. Talks are held between Chernomyrdin and Shamil Basayev. Negotiations for the withdrawal of Russian troops in Chechnya begin.
2/9/95	Former Soviet leader Mikhail Gorbachev describes the campaign as a huge mistake that would cost the country dearly.
4–8/94	Kidnappers from Chechnya carry out a series of hostage seizures of civilians in southern Russia. Russia blames Dudayev, and calls on Chechens to topple him.
6/92	Chechnya and Ingushetia split, Ingushetia remaining in the Russian Federation.

11/91	Yeltsin declares a state of emergency in Checheno-Ingushetia and sends troops to Grozny. Troops are blocked at the airport, parliament overrules his declaration, and Yeltsin pulls them out after three days.
10/91	Dudayev launches a campaign to topple Moscow's temporary administration, attacking government offices and holding mass rallies. He wins 80 percent backing in presidential polls and unilaterally declares Chechnya independent.
9/5/91	The government of Checheno-Ingushetia, which supports the August hard-line coup against Mikhail Gorbachev, resigns. Soviet air force general Dzhokhar Dudayev leaves Estonia and is installed as national leader.
2/26/44	Hundreds of thousands of Chechens are deported by Soviet dictator Josef Stalin with other Caucasus peoples to Soviet Central Asia. Many die during the journey or in exile. After Stalin's death, they are allowed to return home in 1957.
1934	Chechnya merges with neighboring Ingushetia in Checheno-Ingushetia.
1921	Chechnya becomes part of Russia's Mountain Republic, which is formally incorporated into the Soviet Union in 1924.
1859	Chechnya is incorporated into Russia.
1817–1864	Imperial Russia fights a 40-year war to conquer mountainous lands between itself and newly acquired Georgia, defeating the Chechens and other Muslim peoples.

In a Dangerous Place: Chechnya

Leaving the Terrible

GROZNY, CHECHNYA - I like sleeping in the house on the wood floor with the rest of the Chechen mujahadin. I didn't want to stay in a basement. The basements are hot, damp, and foul, like a tomb. Like defeat. Like death. The house is clean, happy, a human place. A bright, victorious brave place; a place of warm humanity. I would rather die as an honored guest than a frightened rat.

I am staying as the guest of Commander Turpelovali in his newly built house in the southern suburbs of Grozny. His fighters talk and laugh in the main room where the heat is. RPK machine guns, ammo belts, spare magazines and AKM-74 "Automats" (as they call them here) are strewn around the house. The modern, airy house is always full of mujahadin. The bearded fighters wearing bulky cammo jackets, utility vests and waterproof pants come and go throughout the day and night.

When they enter from the cold the routine of the fighters inside is automatic: Stand up, hug, single buss and then stand with one arm on each other's shoulder as they warmly greet each other. They are like old friends. More importantly, they are still alive. There is an obligation to update one another on what is happening; to convince each other that they are winning; to remind each other of

Russians lies and incompetence. Here the nighttime is the daytime; the working time; the time to kill Russians. Again.

It is time for war in Chechnya. Again. I have entered this war against all warnings. There are hundreds of journalists taking bus tours in the north, in Russian controlled Nazran. There, the media machine endlessly interviews refugees, stepping inside the border to dateline their stories "Chechnya." Here on the rebel side there are two Russian stringers inside and a Turkish TV crew and two journalists I am bringing in. To enter Chechnya we have had clandestine meetings in the side streets of London and Istanbul. We have met with the Chechen mafiya in the devastation of Turkish earthquakes and we have been inserted into the pipeline of fighters and supplies that enter Chechnya. We have spent a week in a smoke-filled hotel in Tbilisi listening to the tales of Chechens waiting to go in and the stories from escaping journalists. I say escaping because no one simply leaves Chechnya. They escape.

In the hotel we meet a photographer who was abandoned by his crew once they learned about the true conditions inside Chechnya and they left in a hurry, leaving him to walk out 40 kms. He spent five days hiking and pushing his car through the snow avoiding gunships. Now, he is glad to be alive. He confesses that he was so scared he forgot to take pictures.

The story here is that it is easy to get into Chechnya. It is getting out that is difficult.

Early one morning we are told it is time to go. We are driven over a snow covered mountain pass, walk through steep gorges littered with air-dropped mines and after a long day we are inside the most southerly edge of Chechnya.

We will need protection and transportation. A car is chosen. Two eager young fighters are pressed into service. A pair of furry-faced and, as to find out, completely insane mujahadin are recruited to drive us through the Argun Gorge continually shouting "alluaha akbar!" at each other and giggling uncontrollably. It will be a wild ride. They are foreign volunteers who have come to fight jihad: A holy war. They are here for a good time but not for a long time. A holy warrior is guaranteed a place in heaven so they are happy. They stop to blast away at a white rabbit. One muj shoots rapid fire directly at the other muj who is dashing and slipping through the sparking and ricocheting bullets on the icy road trying to catch the rabbit. The rabbit and the mujahadin survive. I am about to learn it takes a lot to kill people here.

After three hours of driving we stop to relieve ourselves and to stretch. I don't see the war, I feel it. There are no lights. There is no electricity here. I hear the sound that will be with me for the next week. The continual dramatic sound of bombardment. The pounding of subsonic kettle drums, pressure waves smacking on my face. Deep violent rythms shaking the ground. Karumps, Blams, Badoom's. There is no English word to describe the sound. I am entranced by the symphony of death.

"Grozny," says one of the mujahids in a rare, serious mood as he nods toward the city. We are still 40 kms from Grozny but the sound travels easily through the clear cold night. Finally I see it. Tall columns of dirty orange flames rise in slow motion. Scud missiles are landing on Grozny. A city where there are between 10,000 and 40,000 civilians still inside. Our destination.

Grozny is the epicenter of Russian rage. The stubborn center of Chechen hopes. But Chechnya is an evil place if you listen to the Russians. A land of bandits and terrorists. A people that must be erased from the earth.

To the outside world, Chechnya is a place where journalists are killed (18 so far), arrested (nine in a recent week), kidnapped (more than 1200 people have been abducted to date) and innocent aid workers and expatriates are executed without mercy, A place that few outsiders dare to witness the evil that is within.

I would have thought that anyone who would dare to explore this frightening place would have the support of the world's media. None hired me, none supported me, not one even encouraged me to go.

A typical e-mail:

"I'm a world assignments editor for BBC news and the line manager for _____ in Moscow. I understand you've been asking his advice on going to Chechnya. Our view, and that of the British Foreign Office and numerous experienced and expert people in Moscow, is that it's mad to contemplate a trip to Chechnya. Not only are there serious risks of the obvious kind attendant upon any battlefield situation, but the risk of kidnapping for ransom is extremely high, not only in Chechnya, but also in the neighboring republics of Ingushetia and Dagestan (Some British Telecom engineers working on a contract in Chechnya, and with the highest guarantees of official protection, were kidnapped and beheaded a few months ago). At the moment we only approve visits by our people under the most carefully researched and heavily guarded circumstances, and that means either the Russian army or absolutely top-level guarantees from the Chechen authorities. We regard Chechnya as the most dangerous place in the world for western journalists to work.

Our strong advice is - keep away."

But I am here. In Chechnya; the most dangerous place in the world. Where observers have counted 6000 impacts per hour, up to 200 airstrikes a day. Where over 100,000 Russian troops grind toward a tiny breakaway republic, destroying everything in its path. An already shattered land where napalm, phosphorus, cluster, shrapnel and high explosive bombs rain down on half-a-million civilians. Where Grad rockets, Scud missiles, and 9000-pound bombs thunder down on women and children creating massive craters and vaporizing unsuspecting citizens. A place that can be called without little fear of exaggeration, "Hell on earth."

- - -

There is no way to avoid Grozny. This war is focused on it. So it is not surprising that the total effort of my Chechen hosts is to get me inside Grozny before it is surrounded. I make it in but the journey is not easy. It is an act of pure faith on their and my part that I will, no I must, stay alive. Grozny is an eerie place. Other than the trapped people and the fighters, we are alone in this city.

One morning one of the fighters came in with an armful of bread. He has news for me, "They have just bombed the marketplace. There are many casualties. Quick. Come." The market is 500 meters away. When we arrive there is a white car burning and the topsy-turvy debris of an explosion. A tiny gray puppy staggers around the deserted market stalls not quite knowing what is going on. A few fighters stand around and some old men stare with their hands in their leather jackets. Rockets and bombs are not new experiences for them but having outsiders to witness it is. They have moved the three victims to a nearby building. A young man and two children. I watch the young man die as a female Chechen doctor labors in vain to put together his shattered face into a recognizable shape. The injured children have been taken to a nearby apartment building

I don't need directions. Around the corner from the burning car there is a large splatter of blood thickening on the ice. A trail of blood winds its way to a nearby apartment. At first I think they are in the basement but the Chechens are in the apartments and out on the street looking for me. They are not cowering, they are mad. I must come and see what has been done.

Inside the stairway it is dark and cold. Normally people light candles for us but the old people navigate perfectly in the dark. I use the railing to guide myself.

The unheated apartment is dark and the people urge us towards the light. There is a single window illuminating the bed. Inside is a young girl in silent pain with tears running down her face. Her thigh has been gashed by shrapnel. Her mother is angry and distraught, "Why are we being bombed? Are we terrorists? Is she a terrorist? She was just going out to get water. I knew this was going to happen." She breaks down sobbing. The girl just looks up silently. The golden light from the missing window catches a tear as it rolls down the eight-year old's face.

I am crowded in the small apartment by more elderly people. For some reason they do not care that there is no light in the stairwell or the apartment. Looking closely at one older woman I discover she is blind. They do not blink or shade their eyes when they enter the front room where the girl lies. They are all Russians. They are all old. They are all blind.

This is an apartment for the infirm and the blind.

. . .

The daytime is the time to relax, warm stiff bodies in the sun and talk with friends about surviving the night before. The daytime is when the Russians bomb. The fighters only look up when the jets are close. The kids don't even pay attention. I watch the skies with rapt attention.

I soon learn the routine: The Russian jets are guided by the constantly hovering spotter planes. The drone and glint of the four-engine spotter plane draws lazy circles in the pale blue sky. Two minutes later two jets streak in. Four bombs will strike the center of the wide arc. The Chechens tell me to watch ahead of the sound. Where the bright flash of silver reveals the dart-shaped jet bombers. Watch for the flares to divert SAMs to signal the release of the bombs and then watch the black bombs descend in a slow arc onto their targets. If they are oval you are OK, if they look round you are about to be hit. Will people die? Inshallah - "If God wills it." Some things are not in their hands.

During the day we are hunted. The Russians strike at anything that moves. At night the attacks are impersonal. When the rockets and missiles fall. Like now. The heaviest it's been in a long time.

In the unheated space off the main room in Commader Turpelovali's house I listen first to the conversation and then to the explosions outside. They said they would wake me if the city falls. But for now they advise me not to worry, "It's just the Russians calling us," they say. "Russian telephone calls" is how the

Chechens refer to the rocket attacks. I am not worried, I am fascinated by the sounds of war.

After a week in rebel held Chechnya, I can identify the different munitions being dropped on me by their sound. The flat bubble burst of 500-pound bombs, the violent wham of 1000 pounders, the angry double whumps of the Grad rocket barrages, the freight-train screaming of artillery shells, the flat slam of the tanks and even the almost subsonic shudder of Scuds that shake the ground. Tonight they are using Grad or Hail rockets. Normally each barrage of 40 rockets is used to destroy a square kilometer of artillery or marching troops but here they annihilate houses, children, dogs, old people, trees and dirt. Tonight I lie and listen to the explosions move closer and further away as if they are looking for me. Like a confused giant's footsteps, crushing the land with each thunderous step.

They the dramatic soundtrack to the violent hell that is "Grozny." In English, "Grozny" means "The Terrible", "The Frightful", "The Fearsome". The name was taken from Ivan Grozni in 1818 when the Russians built their fort on the river in the spring to protect them from the Chechens. Now it is a prison for trapped civilians and a killing ground for exhausted Russian soldiers. Tonight I count an average of 18 barrages of 40 rockets every sixty seconds. I don't bother counting the artillery or tank shells. I am tired of counting the explosions and drift off to sleep.

- - -

When I awake in the morning my host tells me our neighborhood was hit pretty hard last night. It would have been difficult to miss but here discussing being bombed is like talking about the weather. The violent night was probably due to the sat-phone call we made about the kidnapped French journalist. They say that's how the Russian artillery knows where the commanders are. By the signals coming from their radios and sat phones. I didn't even notice. What woke me up was the dead silence. This morning is quiet. Too quiet. The commander says we are leaving the city this morning. He has been up all night. "You should have left last night but your guide said he was tired." I kick my perpetually slumbering and sometimes guide out of his bed and tell him to get ready. The Russians advanced last night to within two and a half kilometers of the house. Straight through the Chechen lines. The night before I had given a friend, an American volunteer, my video camera to shoot some combat footage and he promised to come back this morning. But now I must leave. The Russians overran his position during the night. He was part of twenty Chechens against 5000 Russians. Is he dead or alive? "Inshallah" is the only answer my host can give me: If Allah wills it.

Waiting for the Lada to be readied, I walk through the deserted streets of Grozny. There are no sounds except for the barking of dogs. My breath steams just like the urgent animals that skulk through the streets. The abandoned dogs are well-liked here because they bark at approaching Russians. I can see the dogs off in the haze as they nervously forage like apocalyptic commuters. They keep their distance as if embarrassed that they did not warn us. Up above the crows sit silently in the trees, waiting. Is this what it will look like at the end of the world? Nervous dogs watched by patient crows? In the summer the dogs eat the dead Russian soldiers, then the Chechens shoot the dogs. They go mad for human flesh they say.

I walk back to our house. Its easy to think when there is no noise of war. Why did I stay in a house instead of a bunker? Journalists who covered the last war bragged about their time in the bunker. To me it was an admission of defeat, of imminent death. Here above ground, in the sun I was immortal. For today at least. Others were not. Its better I don't think and concentrate on surviving.

Around our unscathed headquarters there is the evidence of last nights mayhme. Houses randomly broken and smashed like bad teeth. Am I trying to prove something? That I can not die because this is not my war? That I must survive to bring the truth out? Lost in my silent reverie I am surprised by two well-dressed, middle-aged Russian women walking by me. They are heading out to do their morning shopping like nothing is going on. It's important for the people trapped here to ignore the war. If they didn't they would go mad. The women stop and talk, not surprised in the least to see a foreigner just hanging around the deserted streets. It is the same story, "We live here, where should we go?" They have no money so they stay and wait. For what? They do not know.

The commander comes out and points at them: "Russians." This is not a war against just Chechens. The women feel comfortable around the commander. After all, he is their neighbor, their protector from the Russians. If the Russians come they will beg, steal, rape and loot and some say worse. For some reason I give one of the women a kiss on the cheek, she blushes deeply. Just a small act of warm humanity in this bleak monochrome hell.

The Commander laughs at the woman's embarrassment. He decides he wants to dance. His men start clapping as he flails his arms around and kicks out his feet. Slapping his heels with his hands, thrusting his arms into the air, he is energized. It is a happy, defiant, manly dance. His men accompany his shouting and clapping by firing their AK's. Not too many bullets are fired, they will need them. When he is done, Turpelovali tells me that he recommends his men dance everyday. He is worried that people here have not been dancing as much as they should.

I escape Grozny one hour before the Russians surround it.

- - -

SHALI, CHECHNYA - I have made it to Shali a few kilometers south and east of the Russians surrounding Grozny. In the town center life seems to go on as if the Russians were a thousand miles away. Here in the main square the center of attraction is the arms market. A grandiose term for a loose cluster of about 100 men and fighters huddled around various lethal toys. The star of the show is a white hatchback Lada with a 50-caliber antitank gun sticking out of the back. A tall scarred man under a large white sheepskin fright wig glares at me as I take a picture. He wags his finger at me and disappears into the crowd. Plastic explosives foraged from T-90 explosive armor is sold by the slice like bread. Hand grenades are five dollars. AKM-74s are $500, AK 47s are a meager $250. As the Russians come closer the prices will drop. They tell me to buy the Automats with the pink tourniquet tubing on the stocks, the Aks taken from dead Russians.

The fighters don't want me taking pictures of the arms market. As if this was a dark secret they didn't want the outside world to know. The Russians are selling weapons to the Chechens. The local people don't like the arms market here either. They have asked the fighters to move but they refuse. They won't have to worry for long, the Russians are coming. No the fighters laugh, the Russians are here. I want to go to the front lines to see the Russians. They joke and tell me to wait, maybe the front lines will come to me.

There is much going on now. Everyone comes through the main square. There is Commander Basayev's Land Cruiser, Khattab, the head of the foreign mujahadin came through this morning, the head of parliament is in that bunker. Everyone comes to Shali.

As Russian tanks began their encirclement, we probe the edges of Shali to find the front lines. On one street the houses are smashed down as if by an angry fist. Women and old men dutifully pick through the rubble to rescue their possessions. We are warned to leave: Russians are coming down the road. We try to take another route to the edge of town but we are waved back. There are 40 tanks approaching. We are trapped.

We must now make our escape plans but we have to be off the streets. Even in these conditions our bodyguard is worried about us being kidnapped. It's not about money anymore. We could be traded for safe passage through the Russian lines. Those who have nothing, have nothing to lose. We have just come from a place where sixteen Spetznatz prisoners were executed because their Russian commanders refused to trade them for the safe passage of Chechen civilians. Everything has a value and a purpose here. And timing is everything.

- - -

To get us off the streets we are driven down the street to a quiet house on the edge of town. We are invited for tea and lunch by a Chechen family. The woman of the house wanted to make sure I had enough homemade jam and fresh bread to eat. "Would I like more tea?" she asked. "No, thank you," I said. I have to leave before the Russians arrive. Tank fire was exploding down the street. I asked the family what they would do. "What can we do?" they answered. An old man had learned there were foreigners in the house. He asked permission to come in and asked me to point my video camera at him. He took off his fur hat and asked very politely if America could help them. "We are weak, you are strong. Please protect us."

Before I left, the man of the house gave me a gift of a handkerchief. The Chechen family apologized for not having more to give me. When I tried to give them something they waved me away and said, "We are Chechens, this is our custom."

We retreat to the center of Shali. Somehow it seems normal here. I realize why. Other than the armed men and the Chechen flag this looks like the prototypical town square from a Universal Studios set. The local commander pulls up in a black Volga. He has had his lower lip shot away in the last war and a doctor has done a crude job of patching it together. He is surprised to see a foreigner as I muscle my way through the fighters to his presence. He laughs when he hears my request to go up to the fighting.

"You want to go to the front?"

"Why not?"

"Do you dare?" He asks.

· · ·

We pile into the back of his black Volga, a lush battered car, complete with tinted windows. The fighter in the front seat radios the front line. The only word I recognize in Chechen is "normaal." Pronounced with that flat second syllable. However, his communication is uncomfortably phrased as a question not as a statement. I guess it's reassuring to know they don't want to get killed. The fighter's favorite expression has been, "If we die, we win." He pulls over and stops. There are casual and then more urgent exchanges on the radio.

Not once but many times I hear the question, "Normaal?" He waits, listening carefully to the Motorola radio. There is no answer. He asks again, "Normaal?"

It is now more urgent, as if saying it would make it so. There is a response from the other side and the fighter in the passenger seat signals to the driver. He flicks his head forward with grim resolution.

It appears that things are calm so we can go. Or are they? We leave the center of Shali, drive past the arms market, the food market, turn left, right and then out into an open field less than two kilometers from the center of town.

The sun blasts a deep yellow light through the cracked windows of the Volga. We skirt the tree line of the field. Twelve kilometers to the north is Grozny. It is marked as always by lazy black columns of smoke that rise up and flatten into dark bands when they hit 1000 feet.

We know the Russians aren't far away. We see them in the distance. We see them in the sky. All day long we keep running into Russian tanks and troops towards and around the city. Now I am heading to the front lines but there is something very wrong. I try to hold on to my sense of direction using the giant black pillars of smoke and the setting sun as indicators. I am having a hard time calculating or more accurately, believing my calculations. We are just ahead of the advancing Russians. The Russians are already surrounding us.

We slither through the edge of the stubble field. Our driver spins the wheel back and forth as he slides sideways on the gooey muck.

It had never dawned on me to ask just exactly what was happening on this front line. I was told there was shooting and Russians. The sun is setting highlighting a tall black cloud with a blazing red base less than two kilometers away. The oil refinery we drove by this morning has been hit by a Scud missile. Now it is in Russian hands.

Our driver listens, scans the sky for Hind 24 gunships and moves forward. He drives faster and faster. He is really staring at something and spending more time peering intently out the cracked window than on the road in front of him. Damn that makes me nervous. Gunship? Russians? False alarm? He doesn't answer.

As we turn left along the edge of the stubble field, I see a tiny head popping above the brush on the side of the road. Russians? Chechens? The driver slows down. Chechens. Relief. But wait, they are facing the direction we just came from. Why would fighters be facing towards the direction we just came from? What are they are defending?

The car edges against the trees that separate the fields. I don't know why but I am thankful for the row of trees. I still have no idea which way the enemy is. A nervous Chechen fighter is reason enough to be nervous.

I was told there is shooting here. But it's now deadly silent. The same silence I heard this morning. There are freshly dug positions to defend the city. A few hundred yards away I can see the wooden barns and the newly rebuilt brick houses are glowing red in the setting sun.

At either end of the trench are hills made from the piled up dirt. On these hills sit the machine gunners who have an excellent field of fire. A perfect spot for destroying Russian tanks and armored vehicles. The steep angle will expose the blind tanks and slow down the six-wheeled BMPs. There is also cover of the trees where the fighters can escape when things get too hot. The fighters only have a small black plastic bag with some fresh rolls bought in the market. They have dutifully set up in the slit trenches with their guns and they look fierce. Still, something is odd. They are here to defend Shali but they are staring at Shali. They pose for pictures and someone says, "Gunship." I hear a low deep mechanical noise. It isn't the sound of a Hind gunship. It is different. Above the low thrum is the metallic clanking and grinding sound of tanks.

The man in charge sends his second-in-command up to the top of the left ridge to get a better look. He looks, puts his binoculars down and looks again. He yells down, "Tanks." Lots of them it would appear by his gesticulations. Coming directly towards us on our left and right. When he comes down off the hill there is a hurried conference. I ask how many tanks. I hold my fingers up and ask, "One? Two?" He holds up both of his hands and I say, "Ten?" He shakes his head and smiles then flashes his outspread fingers three times. He means thirty. Now the slow steady rumble resembles the beat in a horror film. I look back at the line of defenders. Eight men, one RPG, two machine guns and the rest are armed with AKs. We have to go before we are cut off. The commander says, "We will not give Shali to the Russians." What else can they say? I know that their spirit may not be lagging but the sheer numbers of approaching Russians is going to make this a long night. I have a decision to make. Stay and be part of the battle first-hand or leave. The Commander makes the decision for me. They don't want dead journalists. It is time to go.

- - -

Back in Shali there is nothing to indicate that the town is being surrounded by Russians. But there is an odd transition from the clear sunshine of day to the darkness and cold of night that makes the possibility more ominous.

Daylight is dwindling and we must find a place to stay. I have learned by now, nighttime is the killing time. We stop to buy some food. Warm sausage-filled buns, bread and even Snickers bars-five for a dollar. We are taken to a house, not a safe house, just a house. But it is less than 500 yards away from the front line position we just left.

Ibrahim, the young man of the house, is happy to see us and opens the green metal gates as if we are entering a luxury resort. It is now 6:30 p.m. It is pitch black and the mud has turned to rock-hard ice. As if to signal the arrival of night, a thunderous volley begins. It is the Russians softening up the front lines a few hundred yards away.

Inside the dimly lit house the windows rattle and the yellow kerosene lantern flickers with each rocket and bomb blast. There is a simple metal stove to heat the room. I teach Ibrahim English and he delights in constructing simple sentences from the handful of words he learns-"wall," "window," "door," and "roof."

Using his new words, he takes my flashlight and shows me the damage done to his house in the last war when a Russian gunship attacked a tank parked behind his front gate. The gate is still perforated with shrapnel marks. I ask him what he will do when the Russians come. "If my family needs me I will stay. If they do not, I will fight."

The tanks are now firing just a few streets behind the house. It sounds like the last stand for the fighters on the line. When I mention the futility of this kind of defense, our guide and driver tells us that it is normal for a handful of Chechens to take on a few thousand Russians. They don't really have a choice. It is hard to know whether the idea of eight lightly armed soldiers holding off a juggernaut of Russians is a fable or true. Here it is true.

In the next house a group of young women are scraping kernels off corn. This is part of the harvest dance to celebrate a good crop. They dance with just handclaps for accompaniment even though the Russians are battling furiously with the Chechens. The sound of light-arms fire resembles popcorn popping next to the massive concussion of the tank shells.

At midnight I am standing on the balcony with Ibrahim. He is 19 years old, studying Arabic. He says he likes to learn. His mother is frail and thin. I can see her through the diagonal metal bars. She is sitting inside by the stove. Lit by the yellow glow, she says nothing, just sadly stares into the flames holding the side of her face with her hand. Two wars in one lifetime are too many.

In the star-filled night a tiny streak of flame whizzes by. A cruise missile. It lands to the south. There is a dull white glow on the horizon and a deep delayed boom. Two more streak by as we stand outside. The time between the glow and the thunder is about 14 seconds. "Grozny," Ibrahim says. He tells me they are also using gas in Grozny and Argun. Our guide told me he overheard terrified requests for gas masks and saw two young victims who the doctors said have lost their sight. It probably doesn't matter. There is war here in Europe and there are no witnesses. An evil combination. I go to sleep and wait for the window of opportunity from 2:00 a.m. to 5:00 a.m. when the Russian soldiers sleep and the rocketing stops. That is when we must make our escape.

As the night goes on the bombardment gets uncomfortably erratic. Explosions are coming from every direction. Grad and Uragan rockets are flying over our house towards the town. Rockets coming from the town are softening up the lines. Tanks are firing in the fields behind us. The small-arms fire from the trenches has stopped. Something is happening. Then that deadly silence. Again. We should leave. Now. We pack quickly, exchange gifts with the family and leave. How can you say goodbye to friends who you share surviving with? They cannot flee with us, this is their home. So they stay and wish us good luck. But we cannot never completely leave them. They always remain with you. As strong as a wedding or first kiss. They are concerned that we have enough food so they give us more food as we leave. The Chechens ask for nothing and give all.

Outside the green gates the streets are empty. We look for cars that might signal an escape route. One jeep rushes towards us and slams on the brakes. The driver says he tried to leave but turned around because the bombardment was too much. The Russians are taking the city.

- - -

We carefully crawl through the streets of Shali looking for a way out. The town square is now empty. The commander's bunker no longer has mud splattered Land Cruisers parked outside. The kerosene lanterns that make the yellow squares in the windows are extinguished. There is not even the barking of dogs. We drive slowly towards the southern road, towards the mountains, towards Georgia and perhaps safety. We have driven well past where the tanks were today. We probe nervously for Russians. None are to be seen.

We begin to drive slowly and we reach the outskirts of town. We stop, turn the lights off and wait and listen at the start of the road out of town. There is no sound. Ahead is a straight section of road that crosses the plains and then winds along the gorge into the comparative safety of the mountains. The section ahead of us is very open and very exposed. The same place where we saw the Russians at dusk. We are at a dead stop in perfect blackness straining every receptor in our body.

Suddenly, off the right front corner of the car we are illuminated by a bright sparkling light that streaks toward the heavens. At the top of the arc the flare suddenly stops and seems fixed in place. We are uncomfortably illuminated. No, we are terrified. The light is bright, too bright, painfully bright, industrial bright, no military bright. Shit. Russians. Then another 50 meters down the road another sparkling brilliant arc of light ends up hanging in the sky. Then the same distance further down the road there is another and then another, until there is a long line of illumination flares 50 meters apart floating slowly to earth. Marking the Russian front lines. A festive line of lights that also marks our path to freedom. Off to the right across the river that separates us there are tanks and soldiers visible under the ghostly light. The Russians know something is out there but there is no moon and we are as still as death. The soldiers and tanks are advancing at a steady pace directly 300 meters from the road. There is a constant grumble of turbines and diesel engines. The Russian advance extends along the road for about three kilometers with illumination flares creating a string of brilliant pure white lights that extend into the distance.

We discuss our next move. Return, go forward or run to the side of the road. We are with Chechens so I know we will go forward. If they begin to rocket we must leave the car immediately. We decide who will get out which door. But there are tanks and APCs with 12.7mm heavy guns. There will be no time to get out of the car. I don't even bother to tell the driver that his seat doesn't go forward. My only hope will be to roll out the back. I hook my finger on the rear hatch release and wonder how quickly death will come.

I have never seen a scared Chechen but I can see the look in our guide's face. The driver says, "At this point only Allah will decide whether we will live or die." He starts the car and gently puts the car in gear and starts to move slowly forward. He covers the yellow choke light and we hold our breath. There is no moon and I cannot see the road. There is a river on our right and as we pick up speed we are getting closer to the front line. We are driving in a parallel path but moving closer to the Russian line. It is tense.

Off to the right are the sparks of a rocket motor being ignited. Shit! Duck! But the rockets are not for us. We are too close. I can't stand it. We are moving closer and closer to the front line. Why don't the Russians open fire? Why can't they see us? We are now only 100 meters from the Russians. More rockets ignite and howl overhead but we are spared again. And then mercifully the road turns eastward away from the front lines. We pick up speed. Are we safe? We are still in Chechnya, how could we be safe?

Then it sinks in. The Russians have now surrounded Shali and are focused on cutting off the only road out of Chechnya. The one we need to escape on. We must get to the border as quickly as possible before the Russians storm up the road or they land paratroopers in the mountains, cutting off our escape.

- - -

We try to escape to the Georgian border that night. Avoiding a blown out bridge, our car breaks down in a riverbed. The suspension strut has been sheared off by a rock. We walk back to the small village of Duba Yurt, where a friend of our driver will try to fix the car.

Walking in the frigid night is invigorating and crisp. Down below us on the plains we have just driven across there is now a battle going on. In older days correspondents would sit on a hill with binoculars and send dispatches of poetic prose about sacrifice, bravery and loss. There is no one to witness the fall of Shali except us. But this is just one of many Russian advances. At great cost. Down below there are the dirty boiling orange flames of eight burning armored vehicles. The sounds of firing and explosions seem very far away. I am watching a one-sided war where an angry drunken giant is using a club to kill a mosquito.

Up above us in the village ahead each house has one window dimly lit by a kerosene lamp. It seems normal here. The streets are icy and narrow as we climb the hill. Our guide calls out at a gate and an old lady answers and opens the gate. We are invited in. They light a fire in the stove and invite us to rest.

That night there are a number of rocket and missile attacks, some close, some far away. I am concerned that the strategic heights of Duba Yurt will be the Russians' next target. Our guide tells us to relax, the Russians will not make it up the hill tonight. He was in the Soviet military, he knows how slow they are. The owner of the house tells us that since the war began there have been 40 direct hits on this village of 35,000. Mostly bombs but also Scud missiles. Only two families have moved away. I am comforted despite the explosions outside and sleep the sleep of the dead.

The morning light reveals that we on a height that overlooks Grozny and the Argun Gorge. With the morning also come the jets. I time the air strikes. We are hit on average about every 15 minutes. Sometimes more, rarely less. Some say they are attacking the road. Others say they are attacking the hills behind us. Others say they are trying to kill the villagers. The truth is they are attacking anything. Cars on the road, groups of villagers gathering water, empty houses, packed houses, whatever the Russian pilots choose. Wherever their explosives land.

I go outside to get a better view from the top of the hill. They have cleaned our muddy boots as a sign of respect, a local Chechen custom. Somehow war does not affect this place. Behind the house, men are loading firewood onto a truck. The thin and pretty young wife feeds the chickens. The children slide on the ice and laugh when they fall. Here the bombing is new to the children. They pause to watch the Su-24 jets streak over. I climb the hill behind our house to take in the panorama of rural Chechnya. It is a peaceful scene. The blue sky, the forested hills, the cluttered rows of houses with smoke coming out of their chimneys, the tall spires of red brick mosques contrasting against the snow-capped mountains to the south. A beautiful place to fight a war. A place worth defending.

There are now artillery shells flying over my head. Angry, deep, howling buzz-saw sounds that streak overhead and explode in distant disconnected gray puffs. These shells come from behind me and are destined for the large cement factory over a mile in front of us. The Russians are making sure there will be nothing left no matter who wins. Nobody will win this war.

Then the ground shakes. A gray and white mushroom cloud rolls up to the heavens. Then another. The jets are bombing the hills around us. It is my turn to be the target. My guide pleads with me to go back inside the house.

Sitting inside, we are never without fresh tea, firewood and people watching us like we are aliens from space. The windows and teacups rattle as the village is bombed. I am worried that they are forming a crowd and we will get a direct hit.

It is Sunday in the village of Duba Yurt. Just like any other day, men are standing around talking, firewood is being cut, livestock fed. Women walk house-to-house to visit, children play with homemade toys: wooden wheels on the ends of sticks. Chickens stroll around the yard and young mothers play with babies dressed in those antique white bonnets.

They look up when they hear the sound of the jets. Teenagers time the space between the jets and the explosions. Some are close and some are distant. Today they have bombed the graveyard, some cars on the road and even the hills around the house.

- - -

Waiting in the only room heated by the stove, I hear what sounds like classical chorale. More of a dirge. It is a deep sad sound that rises slowly in arching harmonies. I am fascinated. The house next door is a new red brick compound with punched tin circles and wheels that decorate the gables of the house. My hosts don't want me to venture out but I am curious.

It cannot be a recording; there is no electricity. An older woman invites me to the house. In a covered area there are about a hundred men with heavy lambswool hats and black leather jackets walking slowly in a circle, singing. Some keep a basso profundo beat, others wail, others chant in a deep rhythmic guttural chant. All of the men shuffle and stamp their feet on the concrete floor until it vibrates. They change directions and move in a tight circle.

It is a funeral for an older woman. The men are asking Allah to forgive her sins. But it is more. It is a celebration of life, of sorrow and of death, uninterrupted by the bombs and rockets that fall outside. It is the inner strength of the people emanating from their voices and movements.

Young and old, in tall hats, high boots and cheap leather jackets they stamp their feet and sing with a deep force ignoring the bombing outside. Ignoring the Russians, ignoring the war. Outside the Russians are destroying their land, killing their people and virtually wiping out their existence. But this age-old ceremony tells me that the Chechens will endure against the godless, stateless Russians.

- - -

The sun is setting, the car is repaired and it is time to go. We pack our bags as the last rays of light disappear. The trip should take us five hours getting us to the southern border of Chechnya between eight and midnight. But the arrival of the Russians in the valley has changed things. The people want us to go and to reach the outside world with our tapes and stories. If the Russians capture us they will take all these things and call us spies. After all we are with the terrorists.

As we leave the village there is no bombing. Just silence. I am now connecting the lack of violence with the prelude to something awful. As we come to the main road there are more vehicles. Military vehicles driving southward towards the mountains in a hurry. They rush by us without even stopping. Back on the same blown out bridge where the car broke, there is a jam of trucks and cars trying to get across. There are men walking, directing traffic through the thick mud. Women with heavy bags make their way through the muck. The trucks slip and slide in the deep mud not yet frozen in the chilly night. Our guide does not know the way but he stops to ask people as we make a number of false starts. He has now adopted the phrase, "Robert, no problem."

We find the right road out of town. Our lights illuminate the destruction from today's bombing. The houses along the road are smashed into small pieces of wood and brick, the trees angrily scarred and knocked down by the blasts. We pass a bombed graveyard and destroyed car. The Russians making sure that even the deceased Chechens are dead.

We climb slowly as we wind along the Argun River. In Shatoi near the blasted bridge there is a row of candles like a religious service. It is the market. The people do not come out during the day for fear of being bombed so they are lined up in a row of tiny stalls lit by tiny votive candles. We buy supplies. This is the last stop before the mountains and the border.

The road beyond Shatoi is scarred with craters and the blasted hills spill rocks down to the road. It is quiet and cold and we are silent. The Russians are using their new helicopters with night vision here. Crocodiles they call them. There is tension even when there is nothing out there.

Now the river runs lower on the left and the hills are steeper on the right. I figure out how far we have to go until the border and then safety. Seventeen kilometers. We get out of the car to relieve ourselves. There is a great booming in the distance. It is not our concern anymore. We are leaving. The night is clear and it is so cold the stars blink. The mountains rise up around us. The war is a long way away now. We get back into the car and drive the twisted road until we are stopped dead in our tracks by an eerie sight. We have not left the bombing behind, the bombing is now ahead of us. There is still no escape from this war.

High above us is a glowing oval of flickering light floating in the sky. It is too big to be a flare, too high to be a bomb blast. We stop the car and stare. I strain from the back seat to see it better. I want to get out of the car to take a picture. The guide says, "No." The light moves and changes. From the back of the car the blue tint on the window makes the light appear to change color from blue to yellow. I force my way out of the car to get a better look. Our driver has never seen anything like this before. Outside it takes me a while to understand what I am looking at. The mountains are on fire. They are sending missiles ahead of us to seal off the road.

We are standing 2000 feet below the peaks of the steep pine- covered mountains. The Russians are trying to destroy the last lifeline to the outside world with Scud missiles. Missiles that explode and burn on impact. The ring of fire is the result of the trees being incinerated as the fiery impact spreads southward creating a jagged oval ring.

We get back into the car and start driving. There is nothing we can do now. Our future once again is in someone else's hands. We are now 12 kilometers from the border. The winding road has been blown into a narrow precipitous path. The impact craters are 20-feet deep in some spots. The hills above have been hit sending tons of rock down onto the road. Somehow there is just enough space to get by. The road narrows to being just the ridge between two giant craters at one point. The air is full of smoke from burning pine trees. The river rages in an icy torrent below us. As we round a bend six kilometers from the border there are two more mountains on fire. The flames climb up the steep side of the mountain and seem to drip into the valley below.

As the walls of the canyon rise up, the road is no longer a road but a thin ribbon of flat dirt cut through the side of avalanches. We see a truck coming in the opposite direction. Good news again. The road is open to the border. The smoke is blinding. We are getting closer. But to what? The war is here now. Twisted machinery pushed off to the side of the road floats by in our weak headlights. Not content with killing children, women and even the dead, the Russians are now attacking the mountains, as only fools would.

Suddenly the road disappears completely as the car slithers down into the icy river. There is no longer a road so we drive through the river. There is no concern about land mines now. Only the need to get into Georgia before the next missiles strike. The canyon is now a chasm and the tall cliffs above us provide some sense of protection. Or do they? If a missile did land in this narrow slot there would be no place to hide.

Finally, in the icy night we see a crudely made road that climbs out of the river. On either side the towering black cliffs block the stars. We have finally reached the camouflage bunker that serves as the Chechen border and the door to the outside world.

We have escaped Chechnya.

Note: One week later Russian paratroopers land to seal off the road to Georgia.

—RYP

Colombia
★★★★★

Coca Loco Land

News Item:

FARC SETS UP FM RADIO STATION IN SWEDEN

Reports recently indicate the Revolutionary Armed Forces of Colombia (FARC) will go into the technological arena time and time again to further their cause. FARC has set up a radio station in Stockholm to help with their continuing propaganda campaign and legitimize their cause. The station's name Radio Cafe Stereo transmits on FM 88.4 from 0815-1045 daily.

Amazing.

Sweden, a country that hasn't fought a war since the last time it hosted a beach volleyball tournament, is now playing host to the Western Hemisphere's longest running insurgency, a nearly four-decade-old war that has cost some 35,000 lives in the last ten years alone. And for the listening pleasure of Colombian officials tuning in from capitals across Europe come these soothing words when Radio Cafe Stereo signs on in the morning: "We invite our listeners to actively participate in the seminars, rallies, marches and seizures of Colombian Embassies in Europe."

Easy listening 88.4.

Like the Tamil Tigers in Sri Lanka and Osama bin Laden in some outback cave in Afghanistan, FARC is using the Free World to get its message across, which apparently is: "We can e-mail press releases or rocket-propelled grenades."

Welcome to Radio Flee Colombia.

Each day, at least 10 people are killed in Bogotá—61 murders for every 100,000 people in any given year. During most years, more than 3500 people are murdered in the capital. In Cali, there are a whopping 90 murders for each 100,000 people; in Medellín, the murder rate is a staggering 228 murders for each 100,000. Consider the murder rate in Dallas, Texas—217 people murdered during the entire year of 1997.

Colombia's overall murder rate of 81 per 100,000 is nine times higher than the U.S. average, making it among the most violent countries in the world for murders. Others say it is only 53 per 100,000. Okay. Violent death is so ingrained in Colombian life that the health department has listed violence as the leading cause of death for individuals over ten years old. To date, there isn't a known vaccine for a bullet to the head. Bogotá spends $12 million a year to process violent deaths, at $3,250 per case. Relatives must fill in 25 different forms to bury their dead. Over 25 percent of mental illness in Colombia is directly related to violence.

The victims fit a neat pattern: male (90 percent, one or more bullet holes) and young (61.2 percent are under 34). Firearms account for some 37 percent of the deaths. For those who like to play the odds in this beautiful land, your insurance company will tell you that there are 4 kidnappings and 73 murders every day. A car is stolen every 24 minutes, and 142 houses are broken into every day. At least Russian roulette gives you better odds.

Ninety percent of the murders go unsolved. As one diplomat recently said in Bogotá: "If someone is determined to get you, chances are they're going to get you." And get away with it.

The statistics do little to reveal the entire story of what is happening in Colombia. Colombia is turning into a lawless nation that functions on the edge, barely keeping the lid on anarchy. Colombia's wealthy citizens, not to mention its intellectuals, have fled to escape kidnapping, extortion and murder threats. The drug lords, criminals, revolutionaries and terrorists not only wage war against the government and infrastructure but among themselves.

In all, the price of the guerrilla war in Colombia since 1990 has cost in excess of US$20 billion, or 4 percent of the GDP yearly. Extortion, kidnapping, oil pipeline attacks and murders inflicted by a 15,000-plus rebel-strong force (there were a mere 215 insurgents in 1964) have cost the state oil company, Ecopetrol, more than US$550 million—through lost royalties, pipeline attacks, repair and security costs, and ransoms. Private-sector oil companies consider the loss of US$430 million—due to death, destruction and mayhem—as the cost of doing business here.

In Colombia, crisis management teams outnumber pipeline teams. Negotiations consultants are hired, not to strike deals on leveraged buyouts and

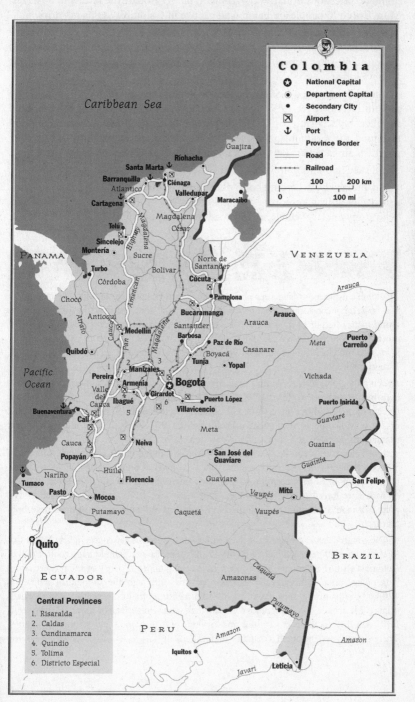

Colombia

- ⊛ National Capital
- ⊙ Department Capital
- • Secondary City
- ⊠ Airport
- ⊥ Port
- —— Province Border
- ·········· Road
- ┼┼┼┼ Railroad

0   100   200 km
0   100 mi

Caribbean Sea

Guajira

Ríohacha

Santa Marta
Barranquilla   Ciénaga
Atlántico   Valledupar
Cartagena   Maracaibo

Magdalena
César

Tolú
Sincelejo
Montería   Sucre
Bolívar

PANAMA

Turbo
Córdoba   Norte de
Santander

Chocó   Cúcuta
Antioquía   Pamplona

Quibdó   Bucaramanga   Arauca
Santander   Arauca   VENEZUELA
Medellín
Barbosa
Paz de Río
Boyacá   Casanare   Meta   Puerto
Carreño

Pacific
Ocean   1   2   3   Tunja   Yopal
Pereira   Manizales   Vichada
Valle   Armenia   Bogotá
del   4   Girardot   6
Cauca   Ibagué   5   Puerto López
Buenaventura   Villavicencio   Puerto Inírida

Cali   Meta   Guaviare

Cauca   Neiva   Guainía
Popayán   San José del   Guainía   San Felipe
Guaviare

Tumaco   Nariño   Huila
Pasto   Florencia   Guaviare   Vaupés   Mitú
Mocoa
Putamayo   Caquetá   Vaupés

Quito
ECUADOR   BRAZIL

Amazonas

Caquetá

PERU   Putumayo

Iquitos   Amazon   Amazon
Javari   Leticia

Central Provinces
1. Risaralda
2. Caldas
3. Cundinamarca
4. Quindío
5. Tolima
6. Distrito Especial

Pan American Highway
Atrato
Cauca
Magdalena
Magdalena

drilling concessions from the government, but to procure the release of hostages. More than 800 people are being held captive in Colombia as this ink dries.

Of all the folks killed here since 1990, more than half of them were innocent bystanders. One pipeline near the Venezuelan border was blown up 229 times during a 260-week period. That's almost as regular as the fireworks every night at DisneyWorld.

Colombia has slated US$4.2 billion for military spending in 1999, a nearly 60 percent increase over 1998. But the Andres Pastrana government has extended an olive branch (more like the tree's trunk) to Colombia's insurgents and promised the Colombian people he would make peace with the rebels. The guerrillas are indeed talking peace, but are blowing away people at the same time.

And they're doing both very effectively.

And humanely, according to FARC leader Manuel Marulanda, who recently issued Colombian motorists a neat little safety tip: drive at least 500 meters behind any military vehicle, on any road. You won't find that in any AAA manual.

Colombia is the most dangerous place in the Western Hemisphere and, like Vietnam in the early '60s, is not considered by our government to be a war zone, which is why some people are saying it may be our next Vietnam. We like it quiet over in our hemisphere. But facts tell otherwise: A 35-year-old war, 35,000 dead, 800,000 displaced, U.S. troops on the ground or in swamps and Uncle Sam pumping in $1.5 billion in known military aid in a three-year period. Nice vacation spot.

Even on a global scale, Colombia is a dangerous place. Worldwide terrorism took a record-high toll around the world in 1998, with 741 people killed and 5,952 injured. About 40 percent of the worldwide attacks—or 111 of them—were aimed at U.S. targets. The majority, or 77, were bombings of multinational oil pipelines in Colombia. Latin America's longest running insurgency has a special flavor—56 percent of the dead are civilians, with only 5 percent killed with a gun in their hands. To flee the fighting in the countryside, more than 100,000 refugees—or *desplazados*—flood into the capital of Bogotá each year. More than 1 million Colombians have been forced from their homes by the war. In 1998 alone, 380,000 civilians were forced to flee their homes. That same year, 1,231 people were killed in 194 politically-motivated murders. Since mid-1997, at least 9 human rights workers have been murdered.

The country's rebel groups are at the zenith of their power. They control nearly half of Colombia (about 40 percent). Some 15,000–17,000 guerrillas are fighting in or control 600 of Colombia's 1,061 townships. Their coffers have been pumped up lately by the proceeds from kidnapping, drug trafficking and extortion payoffs. Although the Colombian military is 120,000-troops strong, only about 20,000 soldiers are professionally trained, and morale is waning. Meanwhile, the *desplazados* complain their plight isn't served by the army's propensity for "cowardly" locating its garrisons and facilities next to schools and community centers. There's just something about a man in a uniform. . . .

Andres Pastrana and the Government

President Andres Pastrana—who defeated drug-link, allegation-plagued Ernesto Samper and rival Horacio Serpa in mid-1998 to assume the throne of South America's hell—inherited both an escalating 35-year-old guerrilla-cum-paramilitary war and an economy cracking at the seams for the first time in 50 years. Within days of being sworn into office, Pastrana jetted off to the jungle for a clandestine meeting with FARC leaders and has since ceded enough of Colombia to the rebels that they can apply for WTO status, draft a foreign policy and establish diplomatic relations with other countries—16,000 square miles, or 42,000 square kilometers (about the size of Switzerland), for essentially nothing in return. Except more death and abductions. In May 1999, Pastrana's defense minister, 17 generals and 300 of his most experienced and battle-hardened officers resigned to protest the protracted concession, reducing the army's capabilities to that of the Swiss Guards. Look for a permanent partitioning of Colombia at a theater near you. Or a good, old-fashioned civil war.

Colombian Military

http://www.ejercito.mil.co

Bolivarian Movement for a New Colombia, Revolutionary Armed Forces of Colombia or Fuerzas Armadas Revolucionarias de Colombia (FARC)

FARC had its origins after World War II as a Marxist group under the leadership of now 60-something Manuel Marulanda Vélez, aka Tirofijo (Sure Shot), and the Central Committee of the Communist Party of Colombia (Partido Comunista de Colombia—PCC). FARC officially began in 1966 and had only 500 fighters by the end of the '60s. Outside support in the 70's allowed FARC to expand and by the end of the '70s, they were numero uno in Colombia.

In 1984, FARC went legit as a political party (UP), but hard-liners split off to continue the armed struggle under Ricardo Franco Front (Frente Ricardo Franco). It didn't help that former revolutionaries turned politicos were being assassinated by government hit squads for their troubles. FARC is the largest and oldest rebel group operating in Colombia.

The group specializes in armed attacks against Colombian targets, bombings of U.S. businesses, kidnappings of Colombians and foreigners for ransom, and assassinations. Their funding comes from extortion (ransom payments) and income from the trafficking of drugs (predominantly cocaine). FARC has well-documented ties to drug traffickers and Cuba. The dope bucks provide much needed hard currency for Cuba, whose economy has been in tatters since the collapse of the Soviet Union.

FARC is the largest, best-trained, best-equipped (using high-tech gadgetry like cell phones, sophisticated radio equipment and laptop computers to coordinate attacks) and most effective insurgent organization in Latin America—the one Western terrorist group voted "most likely to succeed" by U.S. intelligence services. Many consider FARC to be the "military" arm of the Communist Party of Colombia (PCC). The leadership of FARC is composed largely of disaffected middle- and upper-class intellectuals, although it recruits from the peasant population in an effort to maintain a popular base. FARC also draws support from traditional left-wingers, workers, students and radical priests. The popularity of FARC has been undermined by the questionable practice of kidnapping peasants and murdering them as "collaborators" and "traitors" if they're not cooperative.

FARC's 47th Front is particularly known for its kidnapping-of-foreigners prowess. On March 23, 1999, the 47th Front snatched a German and a Swiss national—a month earlier, two Spaniards and an Algerian.

FARC is the principal force behind National Simón Bolívar Guerrilla Coordinator (SBGC), which includes all major Colombian insurgent groups. FARC was able to muster this coalition due to its closer ties with Colombian narcotics traffickers than the other insurgent groups. The relationship appears to be the strongest in those areas where coca cultivation and production and FARC operational strongholds overlap. In exchange for FARC protection of narcotics interests, the guerrillas have received money to purchase weapons and supplies. There is evidence that various FARC fronts have actually been involved in processing cocaine.

And the group has also publicly admitted to killing at least three Americans. FARC said that members of one of its guerrilla cells executed three U.S. citizens in March 1999 who had been working in Colombia as advocates for the U'wa indigenous tribe when they were abducted and later killed by FARC guerrillas.

On June 15, 1997, FARC, in a major publicity coup, released 70 Colombian soldiers, some of whom had been held for more than nine months. (Media attention, in fact, is one of the group's biggest goals. They've set up a radio station in Sweden, press offices in Mexico and Costa Rica and regularly e-mail to the media their accounts of battles with government troops. You can check out their web site listed below.) However, hopes for a possible path toward peace were dashed shortly afterward when FARC resumed full-scale offensive operations. In November 1998, FARC was "granted" a Switzerland-sized swath of land in Colombia's south by the government in an "olive branch" gesture. Government troops were to return to this so-called DMZ after 90 days, but didn't. They haven't. And they probably won't.

The FARC had a cash flow of $530 million from protection money, kidnapping, extortion and even cattle rustling in 1997; $348 million of that income is linked to drugs through protection of growers, shippers and labs. Forget Internet IPO's.

FARC has never been one united group and in the late 80's had 40 different groups fighting in various regions.

Voz de la Resistencia (6238 kHz),

Comision Internacional
Apartado Postal 27552
C.P. 06761, Mexico D.F., Mexico
http://www.contrast.org/mirrors/farc/
farc-ep@comision.internal.org
elbarcino@laneta.apc.org
http://burn.ucsd.edu/~farc-ep/

Autodefensas Unidas de Colombia
http://www.colombialibre.org/

Revolutionary Armed Forces of Colombia
http://members.tripod.com/~farc
Radio Cafe Stereo transmits on FM 88.4 from 0815-1045 daily from Stockholm, Sweden

Miller Time

Colombian commandos have enjoyed some recent successes in whacking FARC brass. FARC honcho Miguel Pascuas was blown away by cops on March 11, 1999, at his luxury penthouse in Cali. FARC Bogotá regional commander Vladimir Gonzalez—or "Miller Perdomo"—was turned into a Swiss cheese by security forces the next day in a firefight near the rural village of San Juan de Sumapaz, southeast of Bogotá. Miller called the shots in the 1998 abduction of four American bird watchers. Grab a cold one, boys.

National Liberation Army (NLA), or Ejercito de Liberacion Nacional (ELN)

A rural-based, anti-U.S., Maoist-Marxist-Leninist guerrilla group formed in July 1964 by Cuban-inspired Roman Catholic priests, the ELN raises funds by kidnapping foreign employees of large corporations and domestic cattle ranchers and holding them for lofty ransom payments. The ELN is a political-military organization that draws its support from among students, intellectuals, peasants and, surprisingly, the middle-class workers of Colombia. The ELN conducts extortion and bombing operations against U.S. and other foreign businesses in Colombia, particularly the deep-pocketed petroleum industry. The group has inflicted major damage on oil pipelines since 1986.

The ELN is number two in Colombia but they try harder. In 1964 Fabio Vásquez Castaño took a page out of Fidel's book and created the Ejército de Liberación Nacional, or ELN. Since Colombia is a hell of lot bigger than Cuba, they contented themselves with raising money by robbing banks, holding small towns to show who's boss and generally destabilizing the area in the Santander department.

Paramilitaries and the military almost wiped out the ELN in the early '70s. The government was convinced that they had wiped them out in 1973. A hard core of around 500 fighters rebuilt the ELN by shifting to bank robberies, audacious kidnappings, including the president's brother), and high-level assassinations including inspector-general of the army, General José Ramón Rincón Quioñes.

The ELN did not sign the 1984 cease-fire until their hero, Fidel Castro urged them to do so. The ELN is probably the most aggressive and creative of the three rebel groups in Colombia. Their favorite things to do on a Friday night is blow holes in the Cano Limon Covenas oil pipeline (over 700 times since 1982) .

Depending on what source you believe, the ELN number between 2,000 and 5,000 members, many of whom have been trained and armed by Nicaragua and Cuba. The ELN seeks ". . . the conquest of power for the popular classes . . ." along with nationalizations, expropriations, and agrarian reform. ELN leader Ike de Jesus Vergara was arrested in Bogotá in March 1997 and the number-four man, Diego Antonio Prieto, was gunned down by Bogotá police in June 1997. Imprisoned, as of mid-1999, were ELN leaders Francisco Galan and Felipe Torres. (Nicolas Rodriguez appears to be calling the shots these days.) But the losses haven't slowed the ELN down. Their kidnappings-for-ransom keep the coffers stuffed. Wealthy ranchers are the bull's-eyes. According to the cattle farmers organization, 250 of its members were abducted during the first seven months of 1998; 18 ended up dead.

Other operations include assassinations of military officers, airliner hijackings, offing of labor leaders and peasants, multiple armed robberies, various bombings, raids on isolated villages, weapons grabs on police posts and army patrols, and occupations of radio stations and newspaper offices. The ELN is currently perfecting attacks on petroleum pipelines and facilities, seeking to damage Colombia's economic infrastructure and investment climate. The Cano Limon Covenas pipeline, the largest in Colombia, was attacked no fewer than 40 times during the first half of 1997. The ELN has sabotaged the pipeline hundreds of times over the last decade, causing more than US$1 billion in damage. When operating normally, the pipeline ships 175,000 barrels of oil a day, about 45 percent of Colombian oil exports. The ELN regularly operates near the oil fields in Casanare and neighboring Arauca Departments looking for foreign hostages to grab.

Perhaps because it thought that FARC was getting too many headlines with its land concessions, the ELN decided to splash some ink of its own. On April 12, 1999, five well-dressed ELN rebels (one attired as a priest!) hijacked an Avianca Airlines domestic flight shortly after it took off from Bucaramanga and forced it to land at a jungle landing strip in southern Bolivar Department, where they, and a waiting force of ELN fighters, whisked the 41 hostages off into the forest. Then, to make the Society page, ELN insurgents kidnapped Diomedes Diaz, the son of a famous Colombian singer, on May 16, 1999. The rebels claimed they seized the plane and cradle-robbed the crooner's kid to show the world they weren't a "spent force." Indeed.

Spanish-born leader and former priest Manuel Perez died in 1998. The group's top commander is Nicolas Rodriguez, who has met with representatives of the pope. One can only wonder what they talked about. The top military strategist, Antonia Garcia, is busy financing the group through kidnappings.

Ejercito de Liberacion Nacional (ELN)

http://www.voces.org/
http://www.berlinet.de/eln/index.htm

Popular Liberation Army (EPL)

The EPL is like a spinoff from a hit sitcom. Not quite as big and nasty as the two main groups. The EPL kidnapped 40 people in October of 1999. Their earlier attempts at rising up the charts by kidnapping a folksinger didn't work. No word yet on whether the EPL is offering franchise opportunities. The EPL's income comes in at a measly $13 million derived primarily from extortion. They have about 500 members throughout Colombia.

The Jaime Bateman Cayon Group (MJBC)

These guys are a tiny offshoot of the now defunct 19 April Movement (M-19). These days, they've been limiting their attacks against the government to a series of ATM bombings in Bogotá.

The U.S. Military

Although U.S. State Department officials met covertly with FARC leaders in Costa Rica in December 1998, the U.S. government has unofficially declared war on the drug trade in Colombia and, therefore, FARC. Currently, there are officially 200 U.S. advisors in Colombia training troops. Although covert U.S. involvement in Colombia is low key presently, further disintegration of Colombia's infrastructure would undoubtedly lead to an increased presence. As it is, even with only some 200 U.S. army trainers currently inside Colombia, the rebels are really pissed at the gringos. The United States is providing a record US$240 million package to Colombia to help in the fight against drugs, including some pretty lethal hardware like weapons and aircraft. The United States sold 12 UH-60L Blackhawk helicopters to Colombia for $169 million, as well as 24 M60D door-mounted machine guns along with 920,000 rounds of 7.62-mm ammo. U.S. Southern Command Chief General Charles Wilhelm is supervising the creation of a U.S.-backed Colombian mobile army battalion specializing in antidrug operations. The rebels are whining that *they're* the real targets. They are.

Paramilitary Groups (AUL)

America's gift to the macho Latin landowners has been formalized and well-trained death squads. In an effort to combat Soviet influence, the United States helped strategize and train paramilitary organizations to nip revolutions in the bud.

Colombia's paramilitary organizations can trace their roots to the 1960s, when the nation adopted a new American counterinsurgency strategy.

The military hired and trained locals, then landowners and drug lords created their own armies, most for protection and intimidation. There are about 5,000 to 7,000 armed paramilitary men in Colombia.

There is an umbrella group led by Carlos Castaño Gil called Autodefensas Unidas de Colombia (AUC), which also runs the Autodefensas Campesinas de Cordoba y Uraba (ACCU).

These "self-defense groups" are not illegal under Colombian law and, despite UN urging to outlaw them, continue to find both government and military support. As one Colombian colonel phrased it: "The army sees the enemy of its enemy as its friend."
www.colombialibre.org

How to Survive an Anaconda Attack

According to the Peace Corps manual for volunteers who work in the Amazon jungle, here is how you survive an anaconda attack (edited for space).

1. Do not run. The snake is faster than you.

2. Lie flat on the ground, put your arms tight against your sides and your legs tight against each other.

3. Tuck your chin in.

4. The snake will begin to nudge and climb over your body.

5. Do not panic.

6. The snake will begin to swallow you feet first.

7. You must lie perfectly still. This will take a long time.

8. When the snake has reached your knees, reach down, take out your knife, slide it into the side of the snake's mouth between the edge of its mouth and your leg. Quickly rip upward, severing the snake's head.

9. Be sure you have your knife.

10. Be sure your knife is sharp.

United Self-Defense Forces of Colombia (AUC)

The most dangerous right-wing paramilitary group is the United Self-Defense Forces of Colombia (AUC), with an estimated 3,000–5,000 fighters. Carlos Castaño, the AUC leader erroneously reported to have been killed by FARC forces in 1998, oversaw 185 massacres and political killings in 1997 alone, leaving 2,100 people dead. When Senator Piedad Cordoba, a member of the opposition Liberal Party, head of the Senate's human rights commission and an outspoken critic of paramilitary gangs, was abducted from her doctor's office on May 21, 1999, it was Castaño who made the announcement. Castaño has vowed to fight FARC rebels controlling the southern demilitarized zone, even if the government won't. Carlos jams to *Evil Ways*.

The Orejuela Brothers and the Cali Cartel

How powerful is the drug business in Colombia? Gilberto and Miguel Rodriguez Orejuela, brothers who head the notorious Cali cartel and are considered the most infamous drug traffickers in Colombia's history, were each sentenced to a mere ten years in prison in January 1997 for smuggling hundreds of tons of cocaine into the United States. They could get off in five and have been busy running their operations unabated from the slammer. But under Pastrana's regime, and its new willingness to allow Colombian citizens to be extradited (Colombia's ban on extradition was lifted in November 1997), Uncle Sam could get his hands on these boys—if so, they won't be seeing daylight in their lifetimes. Meanwhile, Cali has sunk into depression since the crackdown on the Cali cartel. Once enjoying huge prosperity through laundered drug cash, Cali now suffers an unemployment rate of 19.5 percent.

Eastern Plains Cartel

This fledgling, little-known cartel, based in southeastern Guaviare Department, has the distinction of boasting Colombia's largest cocaine lab ever discovered by authorities. The 1.5-square-mile complex was capable of processing 1.5 tons of raw cocaine per day before it was raided in January 1997. That would be half the amount of cocaine shipped daily to the United States by Colombian drug traffickers. The lab had its own airstrip and employee housing quarters and was protected by FARC guerrillas.

A passport and a return/onward ticket are required for stays up to three months. Minors (under 18) traveling alone, with one parent, or with a third party must present written authorization from the absent parent(s) or legal guardian, specifically granting permission to travel alone, with one parent or with a third party. This authorization must be notarized, authenticated by a Colombian embassy or consulate, and translated into Spanish. Visas are not required for citizens of the United States, Canada or Great Britain for stays up to 90 days.

For up-to-the-minute information regarding entry and customs requirements for Colombia, contact the nearest consulate in Los Angeles, Miami, Chicago, New Orleans, New York, Houston or San Juan, or the embassy in Washington D.C.: **Colombian Embassy,** *2118 Leroy Place NW, Washington, DC 20008, Tel: (202) 387-8338.*

An onward ticket is not always requested at land crossings but you may be asked to prove that you have at least US$20 for each day of your stay in Colombia. Thirty-day extensions can be applied for at the DAS (security police) office in any city.

Entering Colombia by land usually presents no problems at the frontiers. But note that when leaving Colombia by land, you'll need to have an exit stamp from the DAS. You may not be able to get this stamp at the smaller frontier towns. Get the stamp in a city. Otherwise, you may be detained.

Cities within Colombia are served by Avianca, Aces, SAM, Intercontinental, Satena and Aires airlines. The bigger cities are reached on a daily basis, the smaller ones less frequently, sometimes once a week. By air, Avianca and American Airlines fly regularly to Bogotá from the United States, Cali and Barranquilla. There is an airport tax of US$18. Prices are higher in the high season (June–August, December). Purchase intra-Colombia tickets inside the country.

Buses are a great way to get around, but incidents of thefts are increasing. The air-conditioned buses are often quite frigid when the air-conditioning is working. When it isn't, they're hot, since the windows don't open. Bring your own food, as rest stops are infrequent. Additionally, expect the bus to be periodically stopped and boarded by police. Your identity will most likely be checked. Occasionally, a photocopy of your passport will be sufficient. Make one and have it notarized. Buses leave according to schedule, rather than when they are full. Colombia's VELOTAX minibuses are efficient. However, other buses experience frequent breakdowns.

Taxis are plentiful. Take only metered taxis. But if one cannot be found, negotiate and set a fixed price before you enter the taxi. Women should not take taxis alone at night (see "Dangerous Things").

The roads in Colombia are often dilapidated and unmarked. Avoid driving at night; Colombian drivers are careless and often reckless.

Everywhere

In an average Colombian day there are 2 bank robberies, 8 highway robberies, 87 murders and 204 assaults or muggings. At least you'll have armed guards if you're kidnapped. An April 1999 State Department warning recommended that all travel be deferred to Colombia. If you decide not to heed it, you will be the target of thieves, kidnappers and murderers. In 1997, there were 1,537 terrorist crimes committed. Civilians and soldiers are routinely stopped at roadblocks, dragged out of their cars and summarily executed in Antioquia Department. Tourists are drugged in bars and discos, then robbed and murdered. Expats, missionaries and other foreigners are favorite targets of terrorist groups, who kidnap them for outrageous ransom amounts that climb into the millions of dollars.

Should you be victimized or seek revenge due to a misfortune, expect little comfort or sympathy from the police, military, and judicial or diplomatic folks; they're busy covering their own asses from the threat of terrorism, drug cartels and crime lords. Since 1990, some 5,000 police officers have been killed. Only about 12 percent of the crimes committed in Colombia ever reach the judicial system.

Santa Marta

The north end of town and the Rodadero Beach areas are extremely dangerous. Do not travel alone into these areas. Daylight armed robberies of tourists are commonplace. Thieves will often relieve their victims of their clothes as well as all other valuables.

Bolivar Department and Barrancabermeja

Bolivar Department in Colombia's far north has become a killing field. Massacres by right-wing paramilitary death squads caused 6,000 villagers to flee their villages near the Serrania de San Lucas in June 1998 alone. The rural department has essentially, since then, been cleansed of its population, most of which has ended up in the dangerous, lawless oil city called Barrancabermeja. But these *desplazados* find little peace there. A May 1998 massacre there left 30 dead. Sniper fire in the streets of Barrancabermeja is common. Barrancabermeja is Colombia's Sarajevo.

The Darien

Pressed against the Panama border, Uraba is the murder capital of Colombia—more than 700 people were killed in Uraba by leftist guerrillas in 1996. The country's richest banana-growing region, it's also home to myriad drug runners, leftist guerrillas and paramilitary outfits. Uraba's annual murder rate of 254 per 100,000 people is the highest in Colombia. How bad is Uraba? Local officials are pleading for UN intervention and for a peacekeeping force to be installed. The area around the Darien Peninsula is a major transit point for contraband goods and a center for drug processing. The FARC group provides protection for the drug labs. Two Austrian and two Swiss tourists were kidnapped while they went to visit a nature preserve in March of '97. Their kidnappers demanded US$15 million and FARC wasn't going to use that cash to save the rain forest. Two of the victims were killed in the government rescue attempt.

Cartagena

Professional pickpockets abound, especially at the beaches. They especially like to strike in crowded areas. Cameras are a favorite trophy for thieves here. Scams in Cartagena are numerous. Other crooks pose as tour guides. Some of them can be rather touchy if you turn down their expensive excursion offers. If you're offered a job on a ship bound for the United States or other parts of South America, don't believe it because this is most assuredly a con. To its credit, though, Cartagena is probably the safest place in Colombia.

Medellín

Despite being a major drug traffickers' center and the new murder capital of Colombia, the city is a remarkably friendly place. Medellín had 4,472 murders in 1997, more than 12 a day. However, it's not the drug-lords you should be afraid of here. Rather, it's petty thieves and street thugs. Medellín has been experiencing a rash of bombings, most attacks being carried out by the FARC. On one day alone in June 1997, FARC bombed the union offices of a lingerie maker, two private homes in Caicedo neighborhood, five city buses and, for the *pièce de résistance*, guerrillas booby-trapped a FARC flag, which exploded when a man tried to remove it at Antioquia University.

Valle Department

Everywhere off the main roads in Valle Department is extremely unsafe due to guerrilla activities. Beware particularly of Cauca Department E off the Pan-American Highway. Tourists should avoid this area entirely. Areas of Cra 6 are also extremely dangerous, including Parque Bolivar and the market. There has also been guerrilla activity in the Purace National Park area, particularly near the Popayan-La Plata Road. In Inza, women should not be on the streets unaccompanied.

Other Guerrilla Areas

The Departments of Boyaca, Norte de Santander, Casanare, Caqueta, Huila, Putumayo, Cesar, Guajira, Arauka, Meta, as well as the Turbo/Uraba region.

The Upper Magdalena

You'll constantly encounter riffraff here, touting everything from drugs, gold and emeralds to pre-Columbian art. The items are always fake, except for the drugs.

Bogotá

There were 3,531 homicides in Bogotá last year. That's the good news. It's down from 4,352—its high in 1993. It still has a murder rate of 61.2 per 100,000 residents. Narco-traffickers and guerrillas have threatened and carried out terrorist attacks against Colombian officials, foreign embassies and other targets. Expect to travel in fear of violent crime, particularly in the south of Bogotá. Tourist areas are infested with thieves, pickpockets and opportunists. The richer, northern suburbs of Bogotá have experienced a rash of car bombings. If you survive the 7.5-mile ride into Bogotá from the airport, be forewarned that crime is prevalent in the vicinity of hotels and airports. Large hotels, travel agencies, corporate headquarters and other institutions that display U.S. corporate IDs are targeted by terrorists for bombing attacks.

Colombia East of the Andes

This area can be hazardous to your health, with the exception of the city of Leticia in the Amazonas Department and adjacent tourist areas in Amazonas.

North Coast/Barranquilla/Isla San Andres

Cali is the home of two of the major drug cartels. Expect plenty of fighting between the two rival groups. The island of San Andres is a major drug shipment area. Cartagena is considered relatively safe, due to the increased presence of police protecting the lucrative tourist trade. Expect tourist crime.

Barranquilla is the site of guerilla attacks on businesses and government centers. The busy port is a major center for drug traffickers. Guerrillas like to regularly attack the naval base near the airport at night. Outside the city limits is the domain of bad people, particularly at night.

Cali and Valle de Cauca Department

During the first five months of 1997, 721 murders and 18 kidnappings were committed in Cali and Valle de Cauca Department. It's hard to believe, but these figures represent a 27 percent downward trend in murder and kidnapping in the area—that's if the figures can be believed (1997 was an election year). Rarely does the crime rate go down while unemployment is rising, as it is in Cali. Wanna get a job here? Good luck; the unemployment rate is 17 percent. In 70 percent of the crimes committed in Cali, either the perpetrator or the victim is under 17 years old. In 1995, 1,243 minors were arrested for crimes ranging from robbery to murder.

Cali-Buenaventura Highway

The highway between these two cities has become prime pickings for guerrillas and common thugs. Kidnappings have increased markedly on the highway, most performed by FARC rebels and bandits. The road is also the venue for a surge in truck jackings by "land pirates."

Kidnapping—or "Miracle Fishing"

Remember the last time you asked your boss how much you were really worth? Well, you may find out on your next trip to Colombia. There were a record 2,338 "official" kidnappings in Colombia in 1998, 30 percent more than in 1997. In 1997, there were a reported 1,822 cases of kidnapping, a 13 percent increase over the 1996 figure 1,612—itself a 35 percent increase over 1995. Among those abducted in 1997 were 33 foreigners. About half of the abductions were carried out by leftist rebel groups. The police and/or army rescued 239 of the 1,997 victims. Half were freed after ransom payments. And at least 138 died while in captivity. The body snatchings earned their abductors a cool US$74 million in 1997.

Between 1994 and 1999, citizens from 44 countries were abducted. Venezuelans topped the list with 98 victims. But—surprise, surprise—guess who got the silver? Americans—46 of 'em in the same period. Twenty-six Italians were kidnapped, 23 from Germany, 21 each from Spain and Equador, 12 each from France and the U.K.; nine Canadians were snatched, followed by 8 from Lebanon (you figure that one out) and five from Mexico.

A nonprofit group that aids victims and monitors kidnapping rates offers only slightly different stats: 2,216 people were abducted in 1998, up from 1,693 in 1997, 1,528 in 1996 and 1,068 in 1995. More than 530 ranchers were kidnapped in 1998 and 34 of them killed. Ransoms earned victims' abductors about US$70 million in 1998.

These are just the reported cases. In reality, kidnapping has become a US$250–$350 million industry in Colombia. An average of at least six people are kidnapped a day here. The problem is so bad that newspapers publish maps revealing the most likely spots insurgents are to grab victims during holiday periods. The locals call it "miracle fishing"—kidnappers set up roadblocks and determine motorists wealthy enough to be snatched. Between October 1998 and March 1999, officials tallied 19 major rebel roadblocks that led to 129 kidnappings.

Fewer than 1 in 30 kidnappers are ever caught and sentenced. Fewer than half the kidnappings that actually take place are ever reported. Luckily, Colombians make up the bulk of the victims. Most never report the abductions, fearing it would just advertise their culpability.

Bird-watching

On March 23, 1998, four Americans were abducted at a roadblock in the forests east of Bogotá by armed FARC guerrillas. The tourists were armed with DEET, bird-watching guides and ignorance. They were later released after the guerrillas discerned the Americans were indeed bird-watchers, and not U.S. operatives. For any real U.S. undercover agent, being a birder would be a tough cover. Oh, the ransom for bird watching? $5 million. That's a lot of binoculars.

Murder

Colombia has the highest murder rate in the world with Johannesburg and Washington, D.C., not far behind. For every 100,000 people, 81 are offed. That's about nine times the rate in the United States. Although guerrilla groups do have some hand in the slayings, a full 75 percent of the country's murders are committed by common criminals. In 1997, 24,647 people were murdered in Colombia (a 7 percent drop over 1996), an average of 67 per day. Medellín, considered the murder capital of Colombia, also saw a drop in homicides in 1997, posting 4,472 murders—16 percent fewer than 1996. Oddly enough, law enforcement officials credit their weapons-for-toy-vouchers program for getting guns off the streets, though the decrease may simply be explained by the fewer people that are actually left to buy toys.

Massacres

In addition to kidnapping and murder, Colombia keeps statistics on massacres like sportswriters report baseball box scores. In the first quarter of 1997, 164 people were killed in massacres in Colombia, compared to 72 people in the first quarter of 1996, a 12 percent increase. During a two-week period in November–December 1997, a half-dozen massacres by right-wing death squads left 57 people dead. Colombia's rate of violent crime is unequaled anywhere else in the world. Normally playing down the significance of such grisly statistics, one government official disarmingly admitted in April 1997: "In Colombia, the notion of the value of human life has largely been lost."

Flying

In Colombia, many radar and ground tracking stations are damaged by rebels and drug smugglers to protect illegal drug shipments. More than 1,000 people have died in Colombian air accidents since 1986. Hijacking domestic airliners is becoming a bigger hit with the rebels these days. On April 12, 1999, the ELN hijacked an Avianca Fokker 50 airliner as it flew from Bucaramanga to Bogotá, forcing it down in an area near the northern San Lucas Mountains. At least 41 hostages were carted off into the jungle, including an American.

Being Mayor

More than 50 Colombian town mayors were murdered during the first six months of 1997 alone, making Colombian politics little more than campaign trails of blood.

Being the Mayor's Bodyguard

The Office of Administrative Security employs 2,000 men and women as bodyguards for presidents, cabinet ministers and other government officials. More than 113 of them have been killed in the line of duty over the last ten years. Deaths have declined, though, since Pablo Escobar was whacked by the cops in December 1993. Escobar was notorious for his legions of assassins who went after public figures and their *guardaespaldas,* or "those who protect your back."

COLOMBIA

Sicarios

Sicarios are Medellín's teenage assassins. Police claim that as many as 2,000 of these prepubescent killers—typically hired by drug dealers, the Medellín cartel, businessmen and even police to off their rivals—are on the streets of Medellín. Independent sources say that between 5,000 and 7,000 young people in the city have committed murder for pay at least once.

Oil Pipelines

There are 40 foreign oil-producing companies in Colombia. Occidental Petroleum (Oxy) is the country's largest. The Cano Limon oil field (along the border of Venezuela and Colombia) yields Colombia's largest oil deposits. The 470-mile pipeline cost over a billion dollars and is the focal point for guerrilla activity. Nasty men have blown up the pipeline over 400 times since it came on line in 1985. In 1988, an Oxy engineer was kidnapped and sprung for an impressive US$6 million dollars. To make things fair, the government of Colombia took responsibility for the repair of the pipeline every time the bad guys punched a hole in it. It takes about 36 hours to repair the bomb blasts. About 190,000 barrels of crude oil flow through the pipeline every day. The joke is that the rebels claim that the pipeline is robbing the Colombians of their natural resources. The real criminal seems to be the Colombian government, which skims 85 percent of every dollar generated by the oil. There is a $1.20 a barrel "war tax" to help fight the guerrillas and a tax of 12 percent of all profits taken out of the country. Occidental Petroleum has shut down its Cano Limon oil field because of continual attacks by rebels. They say it costs them $100,000 each day they're off-line. Some 11,000 Colombian soldiers are guarding oil installations. The Casanare field run by Oxy has reserves estimated to be $40 billion, with the potential daily output of half a million barrels a day.

Heroin

With the U.S. appetite for cocaine at a relative nasal trickle, the Colombian cartels have turned to heroin, making Colombia the world's third largest exporter of heroin. Of the hauls seized in the United States in 1993, only 15 percent came from Colombia. The figure more than doubled to 32 percent the following year, and doubled again to 62 percent in 1995. Colombian traffickers have tapped their Asian, Italian and Afghan contacts for the expertise in growing poppies and refining opium in the Andes. In 1997, sample purchases of street heroin by DEA agents sold in the northeast indicates that 90 percent of America's heroin may now be coming from Colombia. As many as 600,000 Americans now use heroin as their drug of choice. The Colombian government has spent over $1 billion on drug eradication programs, some $300 million of which has come from Uncle Sam, with another $1 billion pledged by the UN over the next ten years. That's not much compared to the $3 to $5 billion the drug trade pockets in Colombia.

Scopolamine

Scopolamine (or Burundanga, as it is called locally) is a drug Colombian thugs use to incapacitate tourists in order to rob them. It's spiked into drinks in bars, and into cigarettes in taxis. The drug renders victims unconscious and causes serious medical problems. Colombian doctors report that hospitals receive an estimated 2,000 Scopolamine victims every month in Bogotá. Keep an eye on your cocktail.

Picking Bananas

Banana growers have been targeted by both ELN and FARC guerrillas for their alleged support of right-wing death squads. Since 1989, more than 3,000 banana workers have been whacked in rebel attacks. A large number of banana workers in the country are members of the Hope, Peace & Liberty political party, a former radical leftist guerrilla group that gave up its armed struggle in 1990. Many of the slayings are in revenge for the movement giving up the fight.

Doing Good

Missionaries and human rights activists are some of the favorite people to be killed in Colombia. Nine human rights activists were murdered in 1999. An American missionary was shot twice in the head in broad daylight as he walked down a street in Bogotá.

Phony Cops

A common scam is to approach an obvious tourist as an alleged "policeman," saying that he is checking for counterfeit U.S. dollars and wants to "check" the foreigner's money. The person gives the criminal his/her money, receives a receipt, and the "policeman" disappears. Others request that the victim accompany him "downtown." You have just been kidnapped. In Bogotá, gangs of phony cops have been targeting houses for robbery whose occupants are out and tricking domestic staff and nannies to gain entrance.

Bombs

Bombs don't drop from the sky here. They usually drive up to you. Car bombs are deliberately detonated in crowded central locations. Buses are bombed, as well as oil pipelines, refineries, hotels and office buildings. Bombing is a deliberate attempt to capture publicity and strike fear into the populace. The victims are incidental.

Driving

Colombia's roads are in poor condition. Many routes aren't marked. Avoid driving at night. Many vehicles have dim headlights, if any at all. Other drivers are reckless. Cattle are unwitting, as they pause to pee in the middle of the road at midnight. Steer clear of any military vehicles, as they are often rebel targets.

Taxis

Women should never travel alone at night in taxis. Both sexes are subject to popular scams where the driver feigns a mechanical breakdown. The passenger is asked to get out of the car and help push the taxi to a "jump-start," which separates passengers from their luggage. The driver will then start the car and drive off. Use only well-marked taxis; do not share a ride or enter a cab with more than one person, even though many cabdrivers will tell you that your travel mate is for protection—remember, you only need to be wrong once. Lock the doors, and be prepared to have Scopolamine sprayed in your face by keeping alert and a window cracked (not enough to let people reach in).

Buses

Bus travel in the south of Colombia can be hazardous. Thieves haunt buses in this area waiting for passengers to fall asleep. Then, guess what they do? Buses between Bogotá and Ipiales and between San Augustin and Popayan are frequented by scam artists/thieves who offer doped chewing gum, cigarettes, food and sweets before taking everything you've got. Theft, druggings, extortion and kidnapping occur frequently on buses in both the city and rural areas.

Hotel Rooms

Hotel rooms of foreigners are infrequently raided by the police looking for drugs. Having a witness around may prevent them from planting drugs in the room. But, then again, it may not.

Drugs

Colombia supplies the planet with 80 percent of its cocaine. But get caught scoring a gram on a Cartagena beach, you may as well snort your return ticket home. Despite what we said about the few criminals that get to justice in Colombia, if you get arrested for any drug-related crime, expect threats of lifelong incarceration and spending a few thousand bucks bribing your way out of jail. The government will do little to help, as they hold the belief that gringos are the root of Colombia's drug ills (and they're right). Any foreigner who wants to cut out the middlemen and go into competition with the Colombian drug dealers should watch the movie *Scarface* a few times. Strangely enough, every year some yahoo ends up in a Colombian jail for doing exactly that.

Hassles with Police

Many police officers and soldiers will shake you down for doing everything from taking pictures to walking on the beach at night. The best bluff is to demand to see their supervisor and walk quickly in the direction that takes you farthest away from them. If the police really do arrest you, get on the horn to the consulate ASAP. They can't do much if you really screwed up, but they're all you've got.

Medical care is adequate in major cities, but varies in quality elsewhere. Health problems in Colombia include the presence of cholera, though cholera is found largely in areas outside the cities and usual tourist areas. Visitors who follow proper precautions regarding food and drink are not generally at risk. Doctors and hospitals often expect immediate cash payment for health services. U.S. medical insurance is not always valid outside the United States. In some cases, supplemental medical insurance with specific overseas coverage is considered useful. If you are the victim of a Scopolamine attack, remember to seek medical assistance immediately. Scopolamine is usually mixed with other narcotics and can cause brain damage.

Spanish is the official language. English is common in major cities and tourist centers. The Colombians like to party, so expect massive crowds and price hikes during local holidays. Electricity is 110V/60hz. Local time is the same as New York. The local currency is the peso, about 837 to the U.S. dollar at press time.

Temperatures are fairly high throughout the year. It gets cooler and wetter the higher you go. Seaside areas are muggy. Heavy rain falls between April and October.

Business hours are from 8 A.M.–noon and from 2–6 P.M. Monday–Friday. Bank hours in Bogotá are from 9 A.M.–3 P.M. Monday–Thursday, and from 9 A.M.–3:30 P.M. on Fridays, except the last Friday of the month, when they close at noon. In other major cities, they're open from 8–11:30 A.M. and from 2–4 P.M. Monday–Thursday. On Friday, they're open until 4:30 P.M., except the last Friday of the month, when they close at 11:30 A.M.

Embassy Location/Registration

Upon arrival, U.S. citizens are urged to obtain updated information on travel and security within Colombia and to register with the following:

Consular Section, U.S. Embassy
Calle 38 No. 8–61
Bogotá, Colombia
Tel: [57] (1) 320-1300

U.S. Consulate
Calle 77, Carrera 68
Centro Comercial Mayorista
Barranquilla, Colombia
Tel: [57] (58) 45-8480 or 45-9067

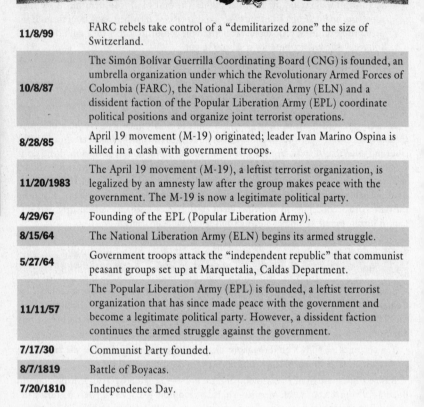

11/8/99	FARC rebels take control of a "demilitarized zone" the size of Switzerland.
10/8/87	The Simón Bolívar Guerrilla Coordinating Board (CNG) is founded, an umbrella organization under which the Revolutionary Armed Forces of Colombia (FARC), the National Liberation Army (ELN) and a dissident faction of the Popular Liberation Army (EPL) coordinate political positions and organize joint terrorist operations.
8/28/85	April 19 movement (M-19) originated; leader Ivan Marino Ospina is killed in a clash with government troops.
11/20/1983	The April 19 movement (M-19), a leftist terrorist organization, is legalized by an amnesty law after the group makes peace with the government. The M-19 is now a legitimate political party.
4/29/67	Founding of the EPL (Popular Liberation Army).
8/15/64	The National Liberation Army (ELN) begins its armed struggle.
5/27/64	Government troops attack the "independent republic" that communist peasant groups set up at Marquetalia, Caldas Department.
11/11/57	The Popular Liberation Army (EPL) is founded, a leftist terrorist organization that has since made peace with the government and become a legitimate political party. However, a dissident faction continues the armed struggle against the government.
7/17/30	Communist Party founded.
8/7/1819	Battle of Boyacas.
7/20/1810	Independence Day.

Congo
★ ★ ★ ★

Heart of Désiré

It's hardly surprising that Laurent Désiré Kabila and the late Mobutu Sese Seko (born Joseph Désiré Mobutu) share the same middle name. Leaders of Africa's dark heart since the 19th century raped this lush, mineral-rich region with impunity, turning what is potentially the richest African nation into a stinking cesspool of squalor and greed. The media predicted a new era of stability for the Congo, but history has more clout than optimism.

Like a child born prematurely, Zaire became the Democratic Republic of Congo on May 16, 1997, after a seven-month pregnancy. The "pregnancy" in this case was brutal, short-term insurgency led by veteran guerrilla Kabila, who swept his ragtag rebel army westward to Kinshasa and toppled longtime dictator Mobutu in a mere seven months. For Mobutu, the end was not a pretty picture. He suffered from a wicked case of prostate cancer (and some say AIDS). But the real cancer that killed Joe Mobutu was born of 32 years of greed, corruption, brutality, ethnic hatred and chaos. (CIA-installed Mobutu, a onetime key U.S. ally, plunged the former Zaire into despair and unimaginable poverty during his

CONGO

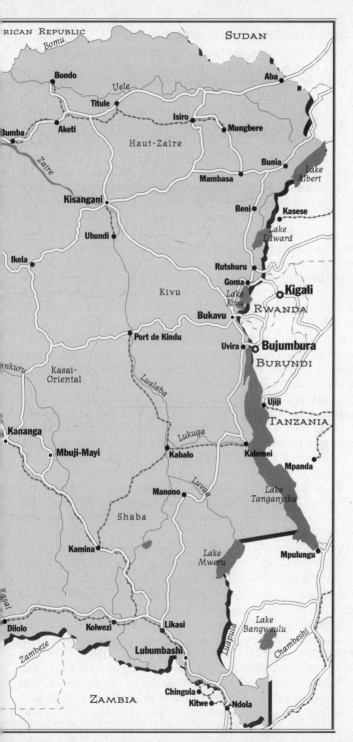

three-decade rule, amassing for his own coffer of a fortune in diamonds (US$4 billion) to make him one of the richest people in the world.

The Democratic Republic of Congo should be the envy of Africa. Twice the size of Texas, it is the African continent's third-largest country, after Sudan and Algeria. It boasts fertile soil, vast mineral wealth and the world's eighth-longest river. This natural force is powerful enough to provide electricity for the entire African continent. Instead, its 44 million people are among the poorest in the world, and among the world's most likely to hack each other to pieces.

There is no other country on the continent that more typifies the deep, tormented core of darkest Africa. The Portuguese first poked around the area in the 15th century, but it was the Belgians who began the plunder in earnest. Belgian King Leopold colonized Congo in the 19th century and duped his stronger European rivals into thinking his sortie into Africa was simply an honorable humanitarian mission. Instead, he made the Belgian Congo his personal treasure chest, amassing a fortune in diamonds and rubber plantations.

His employees were slaves, whose hands and feet he had cut off as punishment for not meeting quotas. One interesting twist is that Leopold made the Congo his own personal property. Likewise, Congo's natural resources and a healthy dose of Western aid made Mobutu one of the world's richest men. How honest is Kabila? A good litmus test will be the $615.5 million the government made off diamonds in 1998.

Joseph Conrad based his famous tale of depravity and corruption on this dying, diseased land when it was called the Belgian Congo. It is hot, violent and dark. Congo is everyone's favorite hellhole—corrupt, fetid, dangerous and deadly. Whether it's the bloodshot-red eyes of your first customs inspector or the apocalyptic way the earth reclaims the symbols of civilization, you will always remember your first trip to the dark heart of Africa: abandoned bulldozers, wooden houses, a sense of carnivorous danger. So into this history of greed, depravity and corruption comes Marxist, former terrorist and Tutsi-backed Laurent Kabila. When 1.2 million Hutu refugees streamed into northeastern Congo (then Zaire), they joined a substantial number of former Rwandan Hutu soldiers and government officials already there. From their makeshift camps in Congo they began staging raids against the then Tutsi Patriotic Front, which controlled Rwanda. In July 1996, the killing of Tutsis spread from Rwanda to Congo.

This was when Paul Kagame (see "Rwanda, Players") put together and trained 2,000 Tutsi fighters from Zaire and sent them back into their homeland to resist the Zairean attempt to oust all Tutsis from Zaire.

Instead of a bloodbath, the Zairean soldiers fled, leaving a curious power vacuum in Kivu province. Realizing that he could not just take over Zaire, the Rwandan Kagame dialed up Uganda leader Yoweri Museveni (who had supported Kagame's fight to oust the anti-Tutsi government in Rwanda in the early '90s). Museveni suggested that his old bushfighter pal, Kabila, would be an ideal next-door neighbor for Rwanda and Uganda. So Kagame faded away and, in two weeks, Kabila—a low-budget rebel who was visited (and dumped) by Che Guevara in the 1960s but who couldn't get arrested for jaywalking in Kinshasa—now was the leader of a revolution, thanks to Kagame, Museveni and, of course, the CIA.

The Name Game

Many people are confused by the names given to this festering region. In 1483, Portuguese Admiral Diago Cao arrived at the mouth of a large river. He asked the locals who said "Ndazi" (river) which the Portuguese misheard as Zaire. Since the Portuguese had named the river Zaire they automatically called anything upriver or in the basin Zaire. In November 1908, the Belgian parliament changed the name to the Belgian Congo as a warning to other colonial predators. Half a century later in 1960, independence brought the name Republic of Congo, when the politicians had enough time to come up with a constitution and create 21 autonomous provinces. In 1964, it was renamed the Democratic Republic of the Congo. The fact that there was another country peopled by the Bakonga tribe didn't matter. It was called Congo (Brazzaville) vs. Congo (Kinshasa). Mobutu not only changed his name but decided to create the Republic of Zaire to shift the focus off of the Bakonga tribe. After all, they just lived around the mouth of the river. Meanwhile, commie Kabila kept fighting for the "Democratic" Republic of the Congo even though he had no intention of holding democratic elections and was not a Bakonga by birth.

But Kabila did an about-face on his buddies. He sacked his Tutsi government ministers and did nothing about the Hutu rebels using Congo as a base for attacks on Uganda and Rwanda. So it came as little surprise when Rwandan and Ugandan forces showed up in Congo to help a new group of rebels—the Congolese Rally for Democracy (RCD), or Congolese Democratic Coalition (CDC)—take a whack at Kabila. Then it became a game of musical chairs. Shortly after the CDC insurrection was launched in the east in August 1998, no fewer than six African nations had taken sides and the war was on. A year later, it had dissolved into a bloodbath of attrition, with the rebels in control of the eastern 50 percent of the country and swinging their sights at Congo's diamond mines.

The objects of their own Désiré.

The wars in the DRC are like watching National Weather Service satellite shots in fast-forward. As one typhoon builds up from another country, then blows itself out over land, another ferments and festers in the heavy steam of the African tropics—young, immature, silly with rage and ready to strip all that was temporarily repaired.

Laurent Kabila's platform to the presidency in May 1997 was an agenda of bazookas, butchery and battles that hasn't quite ended. What exists is Africa's first continental war as allies, interlopers, mercenaries and refugees battle each other in ever-shifting, ever-spiraling death spasms. Production is at a standstill in the DRC. Food prices have skyrocketed. Monthly foreign exchange earnings have dipped to under $10 million from nearly $50 million before the latest rebellion. Kinshasa's dark at night and the phones don't work. The lines at fuel stations make the U.S. gas lines of the 1970s look like the ticket booth at a weekday Montreal Expos game. Half the country's children can't afford to go to school. And Congo's nasty little jungle schoolyard brawl has dragged in six other African countries, ironically, to stop war in their own countries. Keep your seat belts fastened; Désiré hasn't ridden this one out yet—and Africa just loves a good demolition derby.

Laurent-Désiré Kabila

Born in Kalemi, Kabila is not from any major ethnic tribe in the Congo. With his seven-month KO of Joey Mobutu, this guy's either the George Foreman or Idi Amin of modern Africa. Kabila, in his late 50s, has finally achieved his dream of taking over an area the size of Western Europe. His job now is to figure out how to govern more than 250 tribes and rebuild an economy that has been sliding over the abyss. If he does it the right way, Congo could become an affluent country with its copper (Shaba), diamond (Kasai) and gold mines. Kabila is a down-home, old-line Marxist who battled Mobutu for three decades. Camped out in the cool jungles around Lake Tanganyika, he never made much headway but did convince the Soviet Union, Cuba and China to send his rebels lunch money. Back then, his group had the snappier sounding name of the People's Revolutionary Party and the name he had for his country to be was the Democratic Republic of the Congo.

In his days as a jungle fighter (Kabila hosted Che Guevara in the 1960s before Che decided Désiré's boys made better detox patients than revolutionaries), Kabila got to know Yoweri Museveni, now leader of Uganda. It paid off big-time when Paul Kagame was looking for a front man to cover his back. When it became apparent in early 1997 that Kabila's march to Kinshasa would hit little flak, Kabila doffed his military fatigues in favor of business attire, ready to cut deals rather than throats. One mining firm gave Kabila's government US$50 million as down payment to dig for copper and cobalt as well as a private jet. In 1998, diamonds earned Kabila's government a cool $616.5 million. Meanwhile, Kabila has banned all political parties and essentially created a military dictatorship run by Tutsis-turned-Hutus. He's lost Museveni's support, as well as that of neighboring Rwanda, as Rwandan and Ugandan Hutu rebels continue to freely use Congo soil as a base for their attacks on those two countries.

After many of his original government started their own rebellions, Kabila has filled government positions with his relatives, built a support base of cronies from Katanaga and has developed all the hallmarks of a classic African dictator.

Alliance of Democratic Forces for the Liberation of Congo-Zaire (ADFL)

The new wind blowing is just as stench-filled as the old wind. The ADFL was formed October 18, 1996, in Lemera, South Kivu, but is an outgrowth of Kabila's old Marxist group, the Parti de la Revolution Populaire, founded in the '60s. The Rebel Alliance, as it's popularly called—whose official seal is Disney's Lion King—is an ever-expanding army of rubber-booted soldiers who trudged some 1,700 kilometers on foot through the jungles and mountains to reach Kinshasa in only seven months. These guys should've been sponsored by Timberland. To help fund their drive to the capital, the rebels taxed foreign journalists. Visiting a rebel-held area cost journos nearly US$600. At arrival in Goma, correspondents paid a US$70 fee, US$60 for press credentials, US$65 for a safe passage pass and another US$8 as an arrival fee. With eastern Congo lacking an international telephone system, reporters had to bring in their own satellite phones, which the then-rebels taxed US$350 a pop. When leaving, there was a US$20 departure tax and another US$11 in "airport fees." If you thought Kabila's rebellion wasn't given enough media coverage, now you know why.

Congolese Rally for Democracy (RCD), or Congolese Democratic Coalition (CDC)

"First we will take Kinshasa, then we will sort out Congo's political future," promised RCD military commander Jean-Pierre Ondekane after these rebels took up arms against the Kabila regime in August 1998. A year later, Congo's political future was still being sorted out, mostly because of Ondekane's inability to take even the first task at hand—capturing Kinshasa. At first, the RCD seemed it would take the capital in a matter of weeks. Kabila was caught with his pants down. Rwanda and Uganda were providing the RCD with logistical support, weapons and even the soldiers to go along with them. It was a good bitch-slap. Kabila fell to his knees, but they were padded with Angola, Namibia and Zimbabwe, turning Congo's civil war into a good ole'-fashioned African bush rumble. Although, RCD's got about half the country in its mitts, these guys may not be grabbing much more. The guerrillas have been pummeled by defections and splinter groups, and now operate basically as two different factions. The rebs' original leader, a guy whose name sounds like an Annette Funicello movie—Ernest Wamba-dia-Wamba—was replaced by Emile Llunga. Wamba formed his own RCD wing and made buddies with Uganda (sort of). Llunga, on the other hand, enjoys the support of Rwanda. Toss in the MLC (see below) and Congo becomes a boiling pot of headhunters' stew. Don't ask us to figure it all out. It's simply Africa solving African problems with African solutions.

Movement for the Liberation of Congo /Mouvement de Liberation Congolais (MLC)

Not seemingly bothered by the rift in the ranks of the RCD, Jean Pierre Bemba's MLC has pretty much had the north of Congo for themselves. Bemba's guerrillas are supported by Uganda. As Kabila is the portrait of rebel-turned-businessman, Bemba takes the opposite spin—businessman-turned-guerrilla leader. Bemba demands to be taken seriously, though he isn't trusted by elements of the RCD and the Rwandan government.

Union of Republican Nationalists for Liberation (URNL)

A squeak from the bleachers, no one—we mean no one—is quite sure who the hell these guys are. On March 4, these boys—with the hippest sounding acronym ("Urinal") since Myanmar's junta—captured the town of Bolobo on the Congo River, saying they would prevent food supplies from reaching Kinshasa. So obscure is the URNL, they took the town, about 300 kilometers northwest of Kinshasa, without a single shot being fired, which is unusual in most rest rooms.

Angola and Zimbabwe

The Angolans entered the current fray near the end of August 1998, supporting Kabila's rag-tag army with their own spit-and-polished infantrymen and aircraft, not so much to save Kabila's ass, but to keep Angolan UNITA guerrillas from finding sanctuary in the region of Congo that borders Angola. Zimbabwe, for its part, seemed to join Kabila's party just to keep their troops lubed. In June 1999, on the eve of another round of peace talks in Lusaka, Zimbabwe's President Robert Mugabe sent into Congo an additional 3,000 troops. Mugabe's not much interested in ethnic snot-slinging matches. Though the Zimbabwean president claims he's defending Congo's sovereignty, he's in it for the bucks. Kabila's offered Mugabe huge mineral concessions in exchange for the rental of Zimbabwean troops. Zimbabwe's own figures show that they spent $166 million between January and June on their war effort in the Congo.

Rwanda, Burundi and Uganda

It all really started when Rwanda thought Kabila would be a good neighbor and protect Tutsis being slaughtered by Hutu's inside eastern Zaire. To keep it all honest, by the end of August 1998, Burundi, Rwanda and Uganda jumped into the ring in favor of the RCD. It was a bit more than that, actually. Like Angola, both Rwanda and Uganda supported Kabila's 1997 drive to Kinshasa to oust Mobuto Sese Seko, under Kabila's assurances that he would bounce Rwandan and Ugandan Hutu rebels out of the former Zaire and the frontier zones with Rwanda and Uganda. Kabila had no such intentions. To the contrary, he started accepting forced resignation letters from Tutsi government officials, while the state radio broadcasted pep talks urging the slaughter of all Rwandan

Tutsis. Burundi has been a little less overt in its support for the rebels, if one calls Burundian army choppers commuting CDC rebels around the Congolese countryside covert. Afterall, Bujumbura, Burundi's capital, is so close to the Congo border that it could be taken by Congo soldiers without having to get their passports stamped and actually march in.

Mobutu Sese Seko Kuku Ngbenda wa za Banga (formerly Joseph Désiré Mobutu)

Joe Mobutu's an ex-player, but it would be unfair to readers not at least keep him in just for yuks in this dismal play. The late self-proclaimed and former "Redeemer," "Liberator," "Helmsman," "Messiah," "Guide" and the "cock who will jump on anything" (we are not making this up) isn't doing a lot of redeeming, liberating, steering or guiding anymore. Most of his estimated US$4–$8 billion in ill-gotten wealth is safely out of the country and tucked into his family's Swiss banks. The Swiss froze a US$2.75 million villa on Lake Geneva, but the former dictator had 24 other houses around the world to crash at.

How did he get so rich? Well, for example, when the German company OTRAG was looking for a place to test satellite rocket launchers, Mobutu gave them a chunk of his country as big as Belgium. The fee was $50 million, which Joe simply deposited in his personal account. He managed to siphon off aid money coming in and sales of raw resources going out. When that wasn't enough, he would simply write himself a check from the main mining concessionaire. In 1978, he made Gecamines write him a check for the entire year's export sales ($1.2 billion). That's a lot of villas. Most foreign aid loans or projects benefited him directly and nobody every wanted to repossess Zaire. He would siphon CIA money destined for UNITA (which was fighting the MPLA) in Angola to the south and any money sent to the government to fight communism (a.k.a. Kabila) went straight into his pockets.

At the end, his wealth didn't help, nor did he have any friends. He died in Morocco surrounded by about 40 hangers-on and his immediate family. He was 66. Considering that most Congolese don't live to see their 60th birthday, Mobutu Sese Seko did pretty well for the son of a maid from Gbadolite. His Israeli bodyguard, leopard-skin cap, harlequin outfits and ivory cane became fashion statements among dictator wannabes and fans of Eddie Murphy. Not a man with an eclectic taste in women, Mobutu's mistress was his wife's twin sister. For now, his numerous offspring will live well on the boulevards of Paris.

Maji-Maji Ingilima

These young folks (also called *mai mai*) make warfare in Africa fun. They would feel right at home in Compton. The *mai mai* are ganja-stoked, witchcraft-practicing teenage streetfighters who wear faucets, rosary beads and garden hoses as jewelry and worship water. They wear a cool grass headdress that makes them invisible in battle. Their name means "powerful water," a super-duper magic potion they whip up that protects them from bullets (although the headdress and magic potion do not come with a money-back guarantee). They are just local kids letting off a little steam and aren't quite up on the political situation. They have fought on both sides of the war and, of course, been killed in large numbers by both sides. The *mai mai* also make for great party hosts; they practice cannibalism and have attacked Hutu settlements. They are primarily from the Hunde, Nande and Nglima tribes near Goma. The main goal of the *mai mai* is to protect their villages around Bunia. Don't forget to lock up your gardening tools.

Banyamulenge

Ethnic Tutsis who live in the Mulenge mountains of South Kivu province started the ball rolling. Although they have lived in Congo for hundreds of years, their incentive to rebel against Mobutu's forces was only triggered after being ordered by Zairean soldiers in September of 1996 to move to Rwanda along with the Rwandan Tutsi refugees or face being hunted down and killed. Bad move. The ethnic Tutsis in Congo were denied citizenship in 1981 and things have been tense ever since. Muller Ruhimbika is one of the topkicks here but Kagame calls the shots. Their party name is Alliance Democratique des Peuples (ADP) and their leader is Douglas Bugera from Rotshuru. The Banyamulenge were the dominant force in Kabila's rebel army. Now Kabila doesn't have an army.

Interahamwe

The Hutu militiamen who led the genocide in Rwanda have lived in Congo refugee camps and prevented the more than one million refugees from returning home to Rwanda. These are the perpetrators of the 1994 genocide in Rwanda, which left some 800,000 Tutsis and "moderate" Hutus dead. These folks are the reason—at least the stated reason—for Rwanda's anger at Kabila. Hutu rebels use Congo territory, with Kabila's blessing, for staging attacks on the Rwandan government and, of course, ethnic Tutsis.

The Tutsis

The Nilotic Tutsis tend to be the educated and wealthier of the ethnic groups in eastern Congo. The Tutsis originally migrated south from the Rift valley as cattle herders 400 years ago and eventually settled near and intermarried with the agrarian Hutus. They created the two countries of Rwanda and Burundi (where they make up about 15 percent of the population) and are also found in eastern Congo and southwest Uganda. The Tutsi ruled the Hutus as serfs in Rwanda, whereas in Burundi a tribe called the Ganwa (unrelated to either the Hutus or Tutsis) ruled both. Later, the colonial rulers favored Tutsis in selected governmental posts, and even though missionaries would educate Hutus, there always remained both an imbalance and an integration. This odd symbiotic and volatile relationship is the reason why it is difficult to make clear ethnic or political distinctions in the killing and violence that will continue to affect the area.

Les Mongoles

Not a biker gang, but yet another militia group active in the Kivus and opposed to the RCD. Thuggery and stealing seems to be the sum total of their political agenda.

Front contre L'occupation Tutsie (FLOT)

The group has a political wing, the Union des Forces Vives Pour la Liberation et la Democratie en RDC-Zaire (UFLD), and is thought to be behind hate radio broadcasts in the Bukavu region in 1998.

In March 1999, the U.S. State Department warned travelers to stay away from Congo because of the continuing civil war. But if you still must go, a passport, a visa and a vaccination certificate showing valid yellow fever and cholera immunizations are required for entry into Congo. Before Mobutu's fall, visas were not issued to nationals of countries practicing "discriminatory" visa policies toward the Congolese. Although the government did not name the countries to which this edict was applied, U.S citizens did have difficulty obtaining tourist visas. *DP* talked with the new brass at the Congo embassy in Washington and was told "no problem" regarding the availability of tourist visas. Keep in mind that some travelers have been obliged to transit Brazzaville in neighboring Republic of the Congo to reach Kinshasa, which means a Congo (Brazzaville) visa may also be necessary. U.S. citizens should apply at the Congo embassy in Washington, D.C., well in advance of any planned trip. Visa fees range from US$45 for a transit visa to US$360 for a six-month multiple-entry visa. Most visitors will opt for the one-entry, one-month visa for US$75, or US$120 for multiple entries for the same period.

You will need a valid passport, proof of inoculation against yellow fever, a copy of your return ticket as well as application forms and two passport photos. If you show up in person, it takes 48 hours for a visa to be issued or 24 hours if you are a diplomat.

For more information, the traveler may contact the following:

Embassy of the Democratic Republic of Congo

1800 New Hampshire Avenue NW
Washington, DC 20009
Tel.: (202) 234-7690/91

Congo's Permanent Mission to the UN

2 Henry Avenue
North Caldwell, NJ 07006
Tel.: (201) 812-1636

Border Crossings

A special exit permit from Congo's immigration department and a visa from an embassy of the Congo are required to cross the Congo River from Kinshasa to Brazzaville, in the Congo. Unofficially, expect to see a special visa price be invented on the spot, and don't be surprised if your money disappears quickly into the same official's pocket.

There are three ferry crossing points for overland traffic between Congo and the Central African Republic. They are located at Bangui, Mobaye and Bangassou.

Of the 146,500 kilometers of local roads, only 2,800 kilometers are paved. Most intercity roads are difficult or impassable in the rainy season. When driving in cities, individuals often keep windows rolled up and doors locked. At roadblocks or checkpoints, documents are displayed through closed windows. A government "mining permit" may be required to travel to large areas of the country, regardless of the visitor's purpose in going there. This permit must be obtained before entering the "mining zone." Requests for *cadeaus*, or bribes, are the norm. If you bring a camera you will absolutely need a permit that says you are a journalist. The cost is whatever you get dunned after they arrest you for not having a permit.

The Entire Country

Although, on paper, there are several flights each week between Kinshasa and European cities, schedules are often disrupted by security problems in Kinshasa or when the soldiers in neighboring Brazzaville start shooting it up. There have been instances of bullets and shell fragments falling on Kinshasa from fighting in Brazzaville. Civil disturbances, including looting and the possibility of physical harm, can occur without warning in all urban areas of Congo. At press time, the eastern cities of Goma and Kisangani were in the hands of rebels fighting President Laurent Kabila's government. Congolese security personnel are suspicious of foreigners (French nationals are *tres outre*) and sometimes stop travelers on the street for proof of immigration status or can charge you with mythical infractions. Both Americans and Britons have been arrested as spies by Kabila. Border control personnel scrutinize passports, visas and vaccination certificates for any possible irregularity and sometimes seek bribes to perform their official functions. Travelers are urged to be cautious and polite if confronted with these situations.

Crime

In a country where there is little law, where underpaid police and soldiers are often criminals, you have to park your moral indignation when visiting. Morality, legality and right-or-wrong issues have to be sidelined in the interest of survival. Customs officials have an unwritten law of extracting about US$100 from all Western travelers who enter Congo. All border officials will hit you up for some type of *cadeau,* or gift. Once inside, you may wish you were being jacked up by a uniformed border guard rather than the street criminals who will continually hit on you. There is plenty of armed street crime, especially in Kinshasa, where violent crime is commonplace. Vehicle thefts, including hijackings at gunpoint, are on the rise.

Congo is quickly reverting to an agrarian, or barter, economy. Congo has also become a predatory environment where the use of deadly weapons has led to the deaths or serious injury of several expatriate citizens. As the economy continues to collapse, crimes such as armed robbery, vehicle theft and house break-ins increase accordingly, with the foreign community and travelers expected to become more frequent targets. If you look to the police for help, you may find yourself being taken for even more.

Levis

Not too many Congolese women wear the pants in their family these days. Nor anywhere else for that matter. Women caught wearing Western-style trousers are publicly stripped.

Taking Photos

Photography of public buildings and military installations is forbidden, as is photography of the banks of the Congo River. Offenders can expect to be arrested, held for a minimum of several hours and fined. You need a special permit if you are a photojournalist. In the tradition of West and Central Africa, most folks carrying professional-looking cameras are arrested on a regular basis. If you don't know how these infractions are resolved read the chapter on "Bribes."

Carrying Money

The inflation rate has gone from 14 percent to around 200 percent—a month. While U.S. dollars and traveler's checks can, in theory, be exchanged for local currency (the Congolese franc) at banks in Kinshasa, banks often do not have sufficient cash on hand to make transactions. Visitors may be given an unfavorable rate of exchange and the process can be very time consuming. Participating in the unofficial, "parallel" money exchanges that flourish in some areas is illegal and dicey since Kabila has cracked down on the black market. Some foreigners have been picked up for infractions of this type and their money has been confiscated. Credit cards are accepted at a few major hotels and restaurants. It is illegal to take Congolese francs out of the country. Don't fall for the "we're plainclothes police and we need to see your money" scam.

The Police

Cops make a maximum of about US$50 a month, if and when they get paid. There's no back pay if the accountants miss a payday. That's where you come in. If you are stopped by the police for whatever reason, you will be expected to become a foreign investor in Congo's economy. You don't have to give them anything, but to wriggle away takes time and bluster. Tourists are rarely beaten or actually charged with crimes (unless they get uppity) so smile, jabber and smile. If you are waylaid by a real criminal, don't bother reporting it. The police and government soldiers have been traditionally responsible for much of the crime in Congo, especially violent crime.

GETTING SICK

It is almost pointless listing the various health problems in Central Africa since most of them originate here. Getting sick in Congo is as inevitable as it is debilitating. This is the home of Ebola and a future incubator of some of the world's nastiest diseases. If you come down with anything, try to get on the next plane out to Joburg or Europe. Medical facilities are extremely limited and unsanitary. Any long-term visitor should purchase medical insurance that pays for Medevac costs to Europe or the United States (See the "Diseases" chapter).

NUTS AND BOLTS

Congo is big (905,365 square miles), diverse (more than 250 tribes) and dirt poor. The infrastructure has crumbled. More than 80 percent of the population is unemployed and most portable resources are smuggled out of the country. Most of the country's gold and over half of the diamonds are smuggled out to avoid lining the government's pockets. The rest of the gold, copper, oil, coffee, diamonds and other natural resources that are officially produced are quickly vacuumed out of the ground and shipped off to the U.K., Canada, Japan and the United States. One thing to keep in mind is that the region's former alignment with France has radically changed to a U.S./U.K. alignment under Kabila. The French are not unwelcome, but things could be a little tense if you light up a Gauloise.

The average monthly wage here is around $20, most phones don't work, and 50 percent of children cannot afford to go to school.

DP reader Chris Toliver, a photographer who covered the revolution, says the Hotel Membling or Hotel Intercontinental is your best bet, but expensive ($200 a night, $30 for dinner) There is the C.A.P. Protestant mission for $35 a night with meals included. They will also set you up with drivers, interpreters and cars. The inflation rate in Congo, at 2,870 percent (during *DP*'s March 1997 visit), was the highest in the world; the GNP is actually lower than it was 30 years ago and the word "industry" is an oxymoronic term used to describe Congo's anemic 10 percent of capacity output. The Congolese Franc is the official currency, but the U.S. dollar (bring fives and tens) is now the real currency for visitors. Congo is a country sitting on top of 70 percent of the world's cobalt, one that produces nine tons of gleaming gold every year.

The official language is French; the local tongue is called Lingala. Most Congolese are Christian. The population is about 44 million and shrinking.

Embassy Location

U.S. Embassy in Congo
310 Avenue des Aviateurs, Unit 31550
APO 09828
Tel.: [243] (12) 21532/21628

Resources

Forces of Freedom
P.O. Box 411884
Craighall 2024
South Africa
Tel.: +2783-212.22.76
Fax: +2711-404.27.23
E-mail: support@congo.co.za
http://www.congo.co.za/indexen.htm

7/7/99	Peace treaty hammered out but rebels refuse to sign.
8/98	Civil war again erupts in Congo, with three different factions and three foreign countries fighting to oust Kabila, who is backed by Zimbabwe, Namibia, Angola and for a short time Chad.
9/8/97	Death of Mobutu.
5/16/97	Mobutu gives up presidential powers and flees the country. Kabila renames Zaire as the Democratic Republic of Congo.
5/4/97	Mobutu-Kabila peace talks break down.
1/8/97	The Republic of Congo becomes the Democratic Republic of the Congo.
10/26/96	Tutsi soldiers slaughter Hutu refugees in Zaire. Hutus use refugee camps as bases for attacks on Tutsis in Burundi.
9/96	In eastern Zaire, Tutsis revolt after officials try to banish them. Kabila takes the helm of the rebellion and attacks refugee camps to snuff former Rwandan Hutu soldiers. Kabila begins sweep across eastern Zaire.
7/96	Mobutu leaves for cancer treatment in Switzerland.
10/27/71	Democratic Republic of the Congo is renamed the Republic of Zaire.
11/24/65	Revolution Day commemorates the establishment of the Second Congolese Republic by General Joseph Mobutu (now Mobutu Sese Seko) following his seizure of control of the government on this date.
5/25/63	The Organization of African Unity (OAU) was founded on this date. The day is celebrated as Africa Freedom Day. The OAU was organized to promote unity and cooperation among African states.
6/30/60	Independence Day. The Belgian Congo becomes the Republic of the Congo.
10/14/30	Birthday of former President Mobutu.

In a Dangerous Place: The Congo

Into Africa

"Hey, boet," the EO office manager yells through the phone, "get your bags packed, we're sending a flight up to Lubumbashi tomorrow." And the next day I'm on a silver Sabreliner flown by the owner, a bombastic American soldier-of-fortune from New Jersey, who must have tipped the scales at something over 350 pounds. I'll call him Slim. Slim and the chunky co-pilot, a South African doctor on a jolly sabbatical as EO's medical officer, are up front and three more of us scrunched in the back between boxes of food and medical supplies. Across from me is Slim's American mechanic, Bubba, who appears offended by life in general and stares resentfully at the ceiling. The other passenger is a tall, shy and unassuming chopper pilot whom I couldn't help glancing at with awe. Here was the stuff of legend, a name I'd heard since my first faltering steps covering the wars of southern Africa. The holder of more serious medals than you could shake a stick at, this former South African Air Force pilot should have had the chiseled jaw and narrowed eyes of a Texas lawman. He didn't, but I'll call him Wyatt Earp anyway. So there we are, Slim, Doc Holliday, Wyatt, Bubba and your DP reporter, heading for the gunfight at the OK Corral

Most of my African war zones have been reached after days of being shaken to pieces in captured Russian trucks or rattley old Land Rovers crawling along dirt tracks in low gear. Let me tell you that a twin-engine little number like the Sabreliner is better. We streaked over South Africa and Zambia at something like 30,000 feet and 500 mph, then began to descend.

There on the horizon was Lubumbashi and the long runway built in the quieter days of colonial rule. Slim radioed the tower for landing instructions. The message came back to make a low pass for identification. For all his size and irritating bombast, Slim had a handle on his Sabreliner. He rolled in, dropped the nose, and screamed down one side of the airstrip. Half-a-dozen trucks squatted along its length. Anti-aircraft guns tracked us. Or would have if the crews had been awake. They weren't taking any chances on getting surprised with another Kitona-style surprise attack, no sirree. We circled until someone woke the drivers to move their trucks. I could see straightaway that this was a seriously professional African army. Those rebels had better watch out.

We shut down next to a Russian four-engine Ilyushin cargo plane. First stop was the Hotel Karavia, where we checked in behind the hung-over Russian flight crew, then headed down the potholed road to a walled villa where the EO officers had taken up residence. Once through the steel gate ("Jesus Christ, will someone wake up the guard..."), there was a certain down-at-the-heels charm about the place. The lawns were burned to a frazzle, the stucco was peeling, and bougainvillea vines threatened to rip the roof off. A swimming pool with dead frogs floating on a few inches of green scum dominated the terrace. A large cage at the back of the garden held two rare pygmy chimpanzees the South Africans had saved from the locals' stewpot. One, a sweet natured grandmother, loved grooming anyone who came near her. Oscar, the feisty young male, had his own way of showing interest - like leaping up against the wire and doing his level best to pee or jerk off on you. For a second I desperately wished Mark Rugged were here in his brand new safari suit, talking to Barb back in New York. "As you can see behind me, Barb..."

Inside, worn furniture and coffee tables overflowed with much-thumbed girlie, biker, tattoo and Soldier of Fortune magazines, as well as deeply philosophical paperbacks from the pen of the well-known author Anonymous. I could see that the one dog-eared copy of World's Most Dangerous Places was in good company. Then there were the tools of the trade: stacks of ammunition boxes and brand-new Kalashnikovs lying across neatly arranged combat webbing and rucksacks, all ready for instant donning. The ops room, jammed with radios and wallpapered with maps, was the sanctum sanctorum of Ian, EO's intelligence officer, a tall and cynical chum who saved my life in Sierra Leone. (Thinking I was being left behind in Indian Country, I'd leapt for a departing helicopter and was dangling by my fingertips a hundred or more feet above a rapidly shrinking earth, when he grabbed a wrist and hauled me inside. I like quick thinking folks.) Seeing him and the others was sort of like a college reunion, and over beer and barbecue we swapped lies and war stories. "I'll ask John Numbe, our DRC liaison, to organize an interview with Kabila tomorrow," said Tim, the senior guy. (Lest you're wondering, no EO names here are real. That was part of the deal. Anyone outside that circle, however, is fair game.)

Back at the Karavia I dove from the path of stampeding ladies bidding for Slim's attention. Greeting them with avuncular familiarity, Slim patted a steatopygious bottom or two and promised to invite them to a scholarly seminar in due season. The chorus of, "Sleem, Sleem, moi, moi," was diverted by the Russian flight crew entering the bar. The dark wave turned and washed towards the Russkies, who also seemed to be on close speaking terms with them. How strange, I thought, stepping into the elevator, I'll bet those ladies don't speak a word of Russian.

After a sleepless night of swatting mosquitoes and listening to giggles and slurred Russian through the paper-thin walls, I stepped out of my room to see a scantily-clad lady tapping at a door. "Niki?" she said softly. "Niki?" I wandered bleary-eyed downstairs for breakfast on the patio. Bubba appeared, silently took a chair across from me and stared resentfully at the menu. Then he stared resentfully at his coffee. "Nice day," I ventured. "So what?" Bubba said resentfully. It turned out that Bubba was one of life's victims. Whether deserved or not, I cannot say, but the Born Again would undoubtedly find a parallel somewhere in the Good Book. Seems Bubba had come to Zaire a few years earlier as an aircraft mechanic for one of those really big American televangelists. You'd know his name if I mentioned it, even if you never watched television in your life. You probably saw it on the front page of the National Enquirer while you were waiting in the check out line at the supermarket. EVANGELIST FOUND NAKED BEHIND ALTAR -"I was only explaining to these ladies how we're all naked in the eyes of the Lord," said the Reverend Billy Rabbit. I can't remember now if this TV preacher had dropped his wad on women, drugs, 100-foot yachts, or whatever else the gullible sent checks for him to do after praying for them, but he was down to his last million or so. So he had mounted an expedition to Zaire. Not to look for lost souls and convert the heathen, as you're probably thinking. Don't be silly. He was looking for diamonds to convert his bank account. Sadly, things didn't work out and he headed back to the gold mine of preaching to the pitiful. And, like the good Christian he was, forgot to pay Bubba or even tell him he was leaving. Just sort of slipped his mind, probably, though I'm sure he repented and asked the Lord's forgiveness later. But Bubba had more grit than you'd give him credit for at first glance. Taking a liking to the country, he started a couple of businesses, settled down and was doing all right. Then Slim hired him. But Bubba wasn't very happy. I don't think he liked Slim too much. Of course, I don't think Slim liked Bubba too much, either. In fact, there was sort of a poetic circularity of loathing about their relationship. But Slim needed his silver steed kept in flying condition, and Bubba liked the bucks. So I guess they were stuck with each other. Tripping back upstairs for my cameras, I saw the same lady still tapping at the door. "Niki? Còest moi, Niki."

Over at the villa, my Sierra Leone savior is plugging the latest intelligence about the rebels into his laptop. Tim, a taciturn former Special Forces officer, is waiting impatiently for a call from Commandante Numbe about the promised interview with President Kabila. A couple of the guys are sprawled on couches, looking at pictures of girls their mothers would not approve of, while others are outside working on their tans. For those who have never been there, 95% of a working merc's contract is spent waiting. And I wait with them. And wait. Meanwhile, at the back of the garden Oscar is leaping back and forth in anticipation of someone getting close enough. Back at the hotel, Emanuelle is still tearfully tapping. "Còest moi, Niki.-

Using schoolboy French, I persuade EO's Congolese driver to take me in search of Numbe. We stop at an office, which hasn't been painted or washed since the Belgians left in 1965, and I'm handed a form that has spaces for my name, place and date of birth, marital status, father's name, mother's maiden name, their places and dates of birth ... . It turns out that I'm filling in a request for Congolese citizenship. Seems my French is worse than I thought. We head for the airport. At the gate, guards level RPGs and machine guns at us. The driver leans out of his window and shouts. The guards shout back. The driver shouts again. More guards come running. By now we're surrounded by lots of shouting guards, all of them pointing guns. I shrink, wondering what the French is for, Say you're sorry, turn around and let's get the fuck out of here. Suddenly everyone is laughing at the little misunderstanding and we're waved through. To our left a long line of locals are ducking through the perimeter fence and climbing the stairs to the cargo hold of the Ilyushin-76. When not shuttling between Lubumbashi and Tripoli to swap diamonds for guns, the entrepreneurial Russians do a little private charter service to Kinshasa and back. They are packed in by the hundreds, it's standing room only and one poor soul without the fare sails out the door and lands in a heap twenty feet below. The crew huddle under the wing, glancing grumpily at their watches. Pilot Niki is late. Immediately in front of the passenger lounge is a hive of activity around three 727s wearing faded liveries. Sweating soldiers and forklifts are unloading pallets heavy with ammunition crates. My driver points at a uniformed Congolese officer supervising the operation.. "Voila! Còest Commandante Numbe." Hooray, I think, hopping out with a winning smile. Numbe promises the interview to morrow, hisses at the driver to get me out of there, then turns back to calculating how much he's made on this little transaction. You'll probably be surprised if I tell you that he lied. But let's be fair. Would you spend valuable time telling your side of the story to a journalist when the main purpose of the war was to stuff your pockets? Get serious.

I'll spare you the subsequent excruciating details. Oh, I could include more snippets about all-night Russian drinking sessions, Slim's hijinks, Bubba's glowers, Rolex-encrusted Congolese officers who spent more time partying at the Karavia than preparing for war, and the philosophical Ethiopian flight crew whose 707 was grounded when an army truck crashed into a wing. My EO hosts, all professional warriors, suffered with me, but at least they were getting paid to wait. When it finally became clear that I might have to spend weeks here and still not have the story, I winged my way back to Pretoria.

By way of postscript, it turned out that I may have been luckier than I imagined. A respected Angolan journalist who arrived after me foolishly mentioned to Commandante Numbe that he was going to expose the sheer incompetence of the army. He has not been seen since. Two Hind gun ships were eventually provided by Kabila. They were so poorly maintained that one suffered mechanical failure and crashed. EO were finally given the green light to attack a strategic rebel stronghold, but the first two attempts saw their Congolese troops mutiny. On the third attempt, some 30 black and white South Africans had engaged the rebels (killing six Serbian mercenaries, it was later learned) when they were promptly attacked from the rear by the men they were leading. Fighting both rebels and "allies" simultaneously, they broke contact and scattered into the bush. Almost a week later, Wyatt found 13 of them from the air, but the second decrepit gun ship didn't have the power to lift them out. Kabila refused permission to send a recovery aircraft -- it was being used to ship his diamonds to waiting buyers, for goodness sake -- forcing EO to send in a rescue team on the ground. Learning the location of eleven more South Africans held hostage by their Congolese troops, EO launched an extremely dangerous operation that brought them back alive. By now it was clear that the army they had been hired to train and lead had no interest in being shot at. It was time to get out of Dodge. Numbe's threat to hold them was solved by locking him up and convincing Kabila that they needed a few days leave back in South Africa. Big Daddy, counting the millions he had already stashed in overseas accounts, couldn't be bothered by details, and gave them the nod. It was the last he saw of EO.

Which just goes to show that, like a war correspondent's, the life of even the best freelance warrior has its ups and downs. And can be damned inconvenient at times, too.

—-**Jim Hooper**

Dagestan
★★

Wolf Pact

The Chechens are big on wolves. They cruise silently through the foggy mountains of the Caucasus mountains without borders or any enemy except man. A fitting symbol for the Chechen rebels, who don't really see the ancient lines created by their former Russian masters. It's also fitting that the personal mark of Shamil Basayev is a wolf's head. Shamil is a Chechen named after a great Chechen rebel in the 1800s, but now he is spraying his mark on another tiny autonomous region in the Caucasus. The goal of Basayev and Khattab is to create a corridor that would unify Azerbaijan, Dagestan and Chechnya into an "imamate," or an area ruled by an Imam, or religious leader. Similar to the emirates found in the Gulf. Areas under this rule would include Kabarda, Balkariya, Ingushetiya, Karachayevo-Cherkessia and Azerbaijan (See "Russia").

If you look at a map of Russia, Dagestan looks like the nose of the Russian beast. Now it has a bloody nose. Shamil and between 500 and 2,000 (depending on if you use Chechen or Russian numbers) stormed into Dagestan and brought down the wrath of 15,000 Russian crack troops. Nothing new for Shamil, since he had been there, done that in the wars in Chechyna, Azerbaijan and Abkhazia.

He was the number-two man in the Chechen rebels, and when boss man Dudayev was nuked by a missile while making a sat phone call, he became the boss (not of the country, but of the rebels). With Chechnya pretty much independent, he has turned his eyes eastward to complete a great swath of Islamic peoples that would become part of a new Islamic country. Or so the Russians tell the story.

The northern Caucasus has only 8 percent of the population and 1.5 percent of the territory of the Russia Federation but this impoverished area provides about 99 percent of its headaches. The only reason they hang on to the mountainous region is the pipeline that runs through it.

The people who now live in Dagestan were doing fine, enduring the odd incursion by Arabs and Mongols, until the Russians came in 1722 under Peter the Great. The Cossacks needed land and the Russians gave it to them in the mid-16th century. No sooner had the embattled people of the northern Caucasus in 1785 when the Russians had to put down a six-year Islamic revolt led by Sheikh Mansur in Dagestan and Chechnya—sound familiar? You know, part of the those who do not learn from history are doomed to repeat it stuff you slept through in school.

The governor, General Ermolov (1816–27), immediately built a chain of fortresses and began punishing the rebels (déjà vu, anyone?), which led to another revolt, led by Imam Shamyl, which lasted for 25 years. The Caucasian War (1834–59) led to the Russians deporting everyone to Siberia to freeze to death and half a million others to flee to the Ottoman Empire.

When the old Russian empire collapsed (déjà vu anyone?) in 1917, there was a major uprising in the northern Caucasus, establishing a Muslim emirate. A constitution in 1936 established the Dagestan, Chechen-Ingush, North Ossetian, and Kabardino-Balkar Autonomous Republics and Karachai-Cherkessian and Adygei Autonomous Oblasts. But after World War II the Chechens and Dagestanis were accused of collaborating with the Germans in 1942, and another half a million people were sent in boxcars to Kazakhstan and Siberia (deja vu anyone?). The truth is that a few villages didn't like what the Russkies were doing and Shamil came calling and so began the second war in Chechnya. Balkars and Karachai were allowed to return in 1956, Chechens and Ingush in 1957. Things haven't been getting better. The area is a patchwork of minorities. The northern Caucasian republics have over 20 groups of different peoples (those with populations over 5,000) and in Dagestan there are 10 major ethnic groups and another 25 smaller groups and clans. Languages include Indo-European, Turkic and Caucasian. Then there are religious groups that include Christians, Jews and Muslims. The real friction began when Wahhabi Muslims (the same flavor of plain-Jane Islam you find in Saudi Arabia but not as PR-unfriendly as the Deoband Taliban style.) began to do charity work and invest in southern Dagestan. They focused on a few strategic villages and soon began to create mini militias. The Dagestani government banned Wahhabism in 1997 and arrested a number of leaders. Some escaped or fled to Chechnya. It was these same villages that were occupied by Basayev and his Saudi/Jordanian commander Khattab. The Dagestanis don't like or want religious extremism and the mini declaration of independence went over like an AA meeting in the Kremlin.

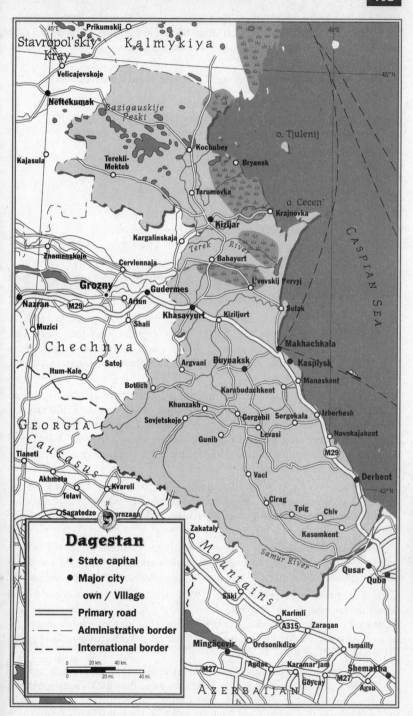

Dagestan

- **State capital**
- **Major city**
- own / Village
- ——— Primary road
- – – – Administrative border
- — — — International border

0   20 km.   40 km.
0   20 mi.   40 mi.

Although Dagestan stayed out of the Chechen revolt, Shamil and the Chechens offer "jihad to go" with a side of terrorism. Shamil has always said he would take the war to Moscow. I guess Dagestan was a little closer.

Link Page for Dagestani Sites
http://src-home.slav.hokudai.ac.jp/eng/Russia/n-caucasus-e2.html#dagestan

Dagestan
http://www.kavkaz.com/

Official Dagestani Government Page (click on English Button in top right)
http://serv.datacom.ru/dagestan/

State Council of Dagestan
http://caspian.hypermart.net/dagestan.html

Welcome to Dagestan
http://www.geocities.com/CollegePark/Union/6282/index.htm
http://www.dagestan.su/

Welcome to Dagestan (Cyrillic)
http://www.ppc.pims.org/csrc/Dagestan_Gathering_Storm.htm

Dagestan is larger than Chechnya, has around three dozen ethnic groups and would complete the eastern side of an Islamic corridor stretching from The Caspian to the Black Sea, or some say a wild and wooly contraband highway from East Turkmenistan to Albania, Karachi to Istanbul. Anyone want to invest in a chain of Motel Jihads?

Dagestan means "land of the mountains," but there aren't any tourist brochures to tell you this. It's a tiny (50,000 square kilometers or 31,000 square miles) backwater place that has a chunk of the oil-rich Caspian Sea to call its own. Dagestan is like Austria with gunships or Scotland with terrorists. You'll find about two million people who are determined not to intermingle. They're too busy fleeing, hiding or attacking.

There really is no economy unless goatherding becomes a fast-track career. Russians suck the oil and electricity out of Dagestan. The big ticket here is the oil pipeline that crosses to Russia from Azerbaijan and of course recycling artillery shells.

Magomedali Magomedov is currently the guy the Russians would like you to believe is in charge. When the leaders of the new insurgency declared a separate Islamic republic and a holy war, he called 911 and the Russian troops descended.

The first attack was on August 7, 1999, when 1,500 rebels pushed into mountainous villages, in Dagestan from Chechnya. The man in charge was technically the acting prime minister of Chechnya, but his boss has nothing to do with it. As President Maskhadov told *DP:* "Basayev is a private citizen and is free to do what he likes."

When the smoke cleared, Russia insisted they killed 1,000 rebels; the rebels say 44. The Russians say they lost 47; the rebels say more than 400. Pretty much par for the course down here. The rebels came back just as they promised a few weeks later and it looks like the war in Chechnya will keep them busy for a while.

Russian Wag the Dog

What if you held a war and nobody came? Dagestan is controlled on a local level by warlords, militia and, of course, Russians. Russia thought it was having the DTs when it needed to send 15,000 troops to put down the rebellion. The first press releases said the Russians were going to annihilate the rebels. When they found out Shamil was in charge, they scribbled that out and changed it to "push them back" to Chechnya.

When Russian internal security services were caught loading explosives into (that's *into* for the politically naive) an apartment building in Ryazank, they dismissed the population's worst fears by saying they were testing their readiness. The massive attack on Chechnya fueled by unproven accusations of Chechen terrorists planting bombs in apartments was greeted by Shamil Basayev as a political gift. He thanked Boris Yeltsin for reuniting Chechens in their hatred of Russians.

Islam

Any historian can tell you that empires fall when they extend themselves into alien territories. Dagestan is about as different as you can get from Moscow—Muslim, mountainous and with a history of kicking the crap out of invaders. Dagestan is an Islamic country, an area where religion can quickly overturn political affiliations. The last great rebel against the Russians was also named Shamil, but he was a Dagestani. He founded an imamate that lasted from 1834 to 1859. He lost in August 25, 1859, when the Tsar's troops took Gunib, the last base of the Imam. In 1877, another religious uprising took place in Dagestan, Chechnya and Adygheya and was brutally suppressed. The locals like the Russians around until they start cutting into the smuggling business.

Poverty

Over 80 percent of Dagestanis are unemployed.

Shamil Basayev

Although he is a Chechen and studied geography, Shamil has a problem with seeing the border between Dagestan and his native country. Shamil Basayev was born in Vedeno, Chechnya, in 1963. He is named for Imam Shamyl who fought the Russian army for 40 years before finally surrendering in 1859. Shamil is bearded, soft spoken and well liked by the press. He can be identified by a scar on his forehead from a motorcycle accident and now a missing right foot.

He graduated from a secondary school in 1982 and worked as a laborer at the Aksaiskiy state farm in the Volgograd region for about four years. He was a student at the Moscow Institute for land-tenure engineers in 1987, but flunked and left in 1988. Some say he passed. It is said that he was involved with one of the Chechen mafyia groups in Moscow until he first showed up on the military radar when he took part in the White House defense in the August 1991 uprising in Moscow. Shamil joined the troops of the Confederation of Caucasian Peoples in 1991 and ran against Dzhokhar Dudayev in the presidential elections in Chechnya in October 1991. Later he become the head of Dudayevs bodyguard. Its hard to figure out why he likes politics since one month later, on November 9, 1991, he took part in the hijack of a TU-154 passenger plane from the Mineralnye Vody airport to Turkey. Shamil was protesting the state of emergency in his country. The hijackers surrendered to the Turkish authorities and managed to return to Chechnya after negotiating the release of their hostages and the plane. This act made him a company commander of President Dudayev's troops. He is a colonel—a rank received from the Confederation of the Caucasian Peoples.

Basayev became the prototypical mujahedin. In late 1991 and early 1992, he fought in Nagorno-Karabakh for the Azeris and received training in Pakistan or Afghanistan at the muj bases. He also recruits from these Pakistani-run bases for his forces in Chechnya.

In August 1992 Basayev raised a battalion of Chechen volunteers to fight in Abkhazia. He became deputy defense minister of Abkhazia and headed the Gagry front.

In February 1994 Basayev and his men returned to Chechnya as an independent armed group—the Abkhaz Battalion. Basayev was appointed commander-in-chief of the armed units of the Confederation of Caucasian Peoples. There he fought the Russians again but ultimately lost. In summer 1994, things fell apart in Chechnya and Shamil and his 500-man Abkhaz Battalion of hardened vets fought with Dudayev. They fought against Ruslan Labazanov and Russian troops around and in Grozny. Basayev ran the defense of Grozny in the first 3 months of the 20-month-old war. He led 1,500 men in an audacious three-pronged attack on the garrison town of Grozny, reaching the center within half an hour.

Dudayev appointed Basayev commander of the southern front, and later commander of all the armed forces of Chechnya.

On June 14–20, 1995, Basayev was on his way to take the war to Moscow in buses but took a brief rest stop to take an entire hospital hostage and successfully negotiated his way home for 75 men and himself. They grabbed 2,000 hostages and gathered them in the hospital at Budennovsk, the Russian Stavropol territory, trying to force the Russians to suspend combat operations in Chechnya. This event technically made Basayev a wanted man by the Russian Prosecutor's Office.

Not surprisingly his political idols include Che Guevara and Garibaldi. Surprisingly, it also includes Charles de Gaulle and Franklin Roosevelt. He is married to three wives with a son and a daughter. One of his wives is from Abkhazia. He is said to have lost 11 members of his family during the Chechen war. *DP*'s favorite Shamil quote: "It does not matter to us when we die, what matters is how we die. We must die with dignity." Yee hah.

Shamil also has a direct connection between the past and the present. Basayev's great-great-great-grandfather died in wartime service as a deputy to the famous hero, Imam Shamyl. A great-grandfather died fighting the Bolsheviks, and another relative died when Stalin deported 800,000 Chechens to Kazakhstan and Siberia in cattle cars in 1944. The Basayev family's two-story stone house, built in the year 1010, was destroyed by Russian bombs. In one raid, Baseyev had lost his village, his home, his mother, two children, a brother, a sister and six other relatives. Should he be pissed?

http://www.muslimmag.org/webversion/caucasus/basayev_interview.htm

Ibn-ul-Khattab

Khattab is a descendant of Dagestanis who fled to Jordan to escape Russian genocide. Some say he is a Bedouin rich kid who wants to play Gucci muj. He technically became a general in the Chechen Army at the tender age of 29. Born in 1970 to an affluent family in the Arabian Gulf, Khattab speaks Arabic, Russian, English and Pashto and has been fighting since 1987 in Afghanistan, Tajikistan, Chechnya and Dagestan. He was trained in Jalalabad, Afghanistan, by Hassan As-Sarehi, the commander of the famous Lion's Den operation in Jaji, Afghanistan, in 1987. He fought in Afghanistan until 1983 and in Tajikistan for two years. He wears a driving glove on his right hand to hide two fingers missing after a homemade grenade explosion. He returned to Afghanistan in early 1995 but went to Chechnya in the spring of 1995 with eight volunteers. He fought for four years and helped to train recruits. He also fought at Khartashoi in 1995; Shatoi in 1996; Yashmardy in 1996; Grozny and Dagestan in 1997; and again in Dagestan and Chechnya. Khattab has a thing for videotaping his battles in Tajikistan, Afghanistan and Chechyna, and some of the results can be seen on the London-based Azzam Web site.

DP's favorite quote: "We know the Russians and we know their tactics. We know their weak points; and that is why it is easier for us to fight them than to fight other armies."

Azzam Publications
http://www.azzam.com

Wahhabism

Not a new dance or the latest Madonna exercise routine, but a wellspring of support for jihads around the world (see "Terrorism") and the belief of many of the "Arab" mujahedin. Khattab and Osama bin Laden could be called Wahhabists due to their rejection of Western influence and adherence to the tenets of Islam but they are not. Saudis, Pakistanis and Kuwaitis are among the top contributors to Wahhabist causes (which also include charitable and relief work). They make a once-only benefit payment of US$1,000–1,500, and then they pay out US$100–150 every month. For each new recruit brought in, the person who brought him receives US$50–100. The Wahhabi sect has support in villages of Karamakhi and Chabanmakhi, about 30 miles south of the capital. Their goal is to create a unified Muslim state of Chechnya and Dagestan.

Wahhabism

Abu l-Wahhab (1703–1792) was the founder of the Islamic school of the muWahhiduns, now known as Wahhabism. Wahhab studied in Medina with teachers of the Hanbali school and spent a number of years traveling, or on hejira. He lived four years in Basra, five years in Baghdad, one year in Kurdish areas, two years in Hamadhan, and one year in Esfahan, around the mid-1730s. In Esfahan, he studied philosophy and Sufism before contuing to Qom. After Qom, Abdu l-Wahhab returned to Uyayna and started to preach his message. He also wrote the Book of Unity. *This made him unpopular, and he found refuge in the town of Dar'iya, where chieftain Muhammad Ibn Sa'ud gave him protection. Abdu l-Wahhab became the religious leader, leaving the secular power in the hands of Ibn Sa'ud, the family that runs Saudi Arabia. Abdu l-Wahhab died a natural death at the age of 89.*

The Wahhabi Movement really began in the mid-18th century and called for a renewal of the Muslim spirit, with cleansing of the moral, and removal of all innovations to Islam. This simpler, older form of Islam has much support in the Gulf States and Saudi Arabia and Kuwait.

The term "wahhabism" is not used by the MuWahhidun, but was given to them by their opponents. It is now used by both European scholars and most Arabs. The term "muWahhidun" in Arabic means unitarians. The muWahhiduns are known for their conservative regulations, which have an impact on all aspects of life. The muWahhiduns started in 1912 to establish agricultural colonies, where people from different tribes lived together. The inhabitants of these colonies were known as brothers, or ikhwän. Each colony could house from 1,000 to 10,000 inhabitants. The colonies were established near water sources and were defended by arms. Mud huts were built in place of traditional tents.

The Prohibitions of Wahhabism

No object for worship other than Allah

Holy men or women must not be used to win favors from God

No other name than the names of Allah may enter a prayer

The Prohibitions of Wahhabism
No smoking of tobacco
No shaving of beard
Rosaries are forbidden
Mosques must be built without minarets and all forms of ornaments

Source: Encyclopedia of the Orient

There are approximately 1,500 young Dagestanis studying Arabic and Islam in Saudi Arabia, Iran, Turkey and Pakistan. Each year about 14,000 *hajis* go from Dagestan to Saudi Arabia.

Dagestan is part of Russia (See "Russia").

Dagestan is technically an autonomous republic in Russia with just over two million residents and an area of 50,300 square miles. It's also one of the few places in Russia that is experiencing a population increase. The capital is Makhachkala, with a population of 369,700 people. The coastal part of the territory is 26 meters below sea level, and the mountain region rises 4,466 meters above sea level. The climate is variable in the mountain area and temperate in the coastal part. As is expected, it is very hot in the summer and very cold in the winter.

Lezgistan

Just when you thought they had run out of "stans," along comes a few hundred more from Dagestan. The Lezgi are just one of 35 or so ethnic groups that want its own homeland in the Azeri/Dagestan region. In fact, Dagestan could put India to shame for the amount of different ethnic groups crammed into its tiny area.

Today, there is a mishmash of ethnic groups, all pushing for their own agenda. The Avar Popular Front, named after Imam Shamyl; the Dargwa movement Tsadesh (Unity); the Kumik Tenglik (Equality); the Lak Kazi Kumukh; the Lezgian Sadval (Unity); the Nogai Birlik (Unity); and the Kizlyar community of the Ter Cossacks army.

Many of these groups are supported by ethnic emigrants like the Avar, Dargwa, Ter Cossacks and the Lezgi diaspora. For such a small place, there are everything from Jews to Azeris to Russians to Chechens to direct descendants of Arabs living in Dagestan. Chechens only make up 3 percent of the population and Russians 9 percent. There are 30 different ethnolinguistic groups amongst the 2.1 million residents (1.2 percent of the population of Russia). Today the largest group is the Avars, found in central and western Dagestan.

Most Dagestanis are Sunni Muslims. Azeris, Russians, Armenians and Georgians are Christian. There are also mountain Jews.

Kinfolk

When the rebels come storming into the towns on the border it's only because there are about 60,000 Chechens in the Khassavyurtovskii and Novolakskii districts. But there are about 300,000 Russians living in the cities, predominantly in the Kizlyarskii and Tarumovskii districts. If you wonder why the entire population doesn't just rise up and throw off the Russian yoke, you need to know that there are a few other ethnic and family ties in the region.

There are about half a million Avars who are related to the Andiyan (Andi, Akhvakh, Bagulal, Botlikh, Godoberin, Karatin, Tindal, Chamalal) and the Didoyan (Bezhtin, Ghinukh, Gunzib, Khvarshin, Tsez-Didoi) peoples that live along the lower reaches of the Andi Koysu and Avar Koysu rivers. The Archin live along the upper reaches of the Kara-Koysu River.

There are about a quarter of a million Darghins, including the Kaitag and the Kubachi in central region. An equal bumber of Kumyks are found in the lowlands and foothills. About 200,000 Lezghins live in southern Dagestan.

After that, you are left with Laks (91.7 thousand) in the central mountains; Tabassarans (73.2 thousand) in the foothills and lowlands of the southeast; the Nogais (28.3 thousand) on the Nogai steppe in the north; the Rutuls (15 thousand) on the upper Samur; the Aguls (13.8 thousand) in the Chirakh-Chay River basin; the Tsakhurs (5.2 thousand) along the right tributaries of the Chirakh-Chay River; mountain Jews and Tats (18 thousand) in the cities. Where's Jesse and his rainbow coalition when you need him?

Avars

The muslim Avars are really the dominant political group here. Just take a look at who controls the rubles. Hadji Makhachev, now the director general of the Dagneft oil corporation and an Avar Dagestan, is rich in oil and gas. Makhachev has two criminal convictions and is former rebel leader. In the early 1990s, he became the leader of the Avar National Movement and chairman of the Imam Shamil Popular Front. He had his own army of several hundred well-trained fighters and took part in most of the republic's ethnic conflicts, defending the interests of the Avars.

The Avars are of Persian descent who were first overrun in the 8th century by the Arabs, who brought in Islam. Then the Mongols overtook them, and then Russia in 1803. They fought under Imam Shamyl until 1858. The Avar language was latinized, and then switched to the Cyrillic alphabet in 1938. At the same time Russian was made the only language of instruction in the schools. In the 1960s, teaching Avar was prohibited.

Lezgi

Most of southern Dagestanis are Lezgi (about 12 percent of the entire population). There is the same number of Lezgi right across the border in Azerbaijan. Lezgin on both sides act in unison, ignoring the border between them.

In 1992, Sadval organized mass campaigns by Lezgin on both sides of the Russia-Azerbaijani border, demanding the creation of a single republic of Lezginistan to be part of the Russian Federation. The Lezgi mafyia is a powerful force in Russia.

Chechens

The Chechen community in Dagestan live on territory that was part of the Chechen-Ingush ASSR until late 1944, and has aligned itself with President Aslan Maskhadov to create a free and independent Chechen state that would incorporate their districts.

When Chechens returned in 1956 to their villages, from which Stalin deported them in November 1944, they felt they were treated like second-class citizens in Dagestan. In

April 1998, then acting Chechen premier Shamil Basayev created the Congress of Peoples of Chechnya and Dagestan, whose declared aim is to unite the two republics in an independent northern Caucasus state. Military actions began in two villages in Dagestan's Botlikh Rayon on August 7, 1999, when a few hundred Chechen rebels and Arab volunteers, led by Shamil Basayev and field commander Khattab, took control, but eventually left.

Naqshbandi/Islam

The Naqshbandi order is a moderate form of Islam that includes among its adherents the president of Chechnya, the sultan of Brunei, Malaysian royals and his uncle, the grand mufti of Lebanon. A sect of Sufism founded in the 14th century in Uzbekistan, it stresses the spirit rather than the letter of Islam. Their theology can be so all-encompassing, folding in elements of other religions and philosophies, that orthodox Muslims often regard them as heretical. Sufi orders are banned in Saudi Arabia.

There are only about a dozen sejhs in Bosnia, but some ten thousand dervishes throughout Bosnia, and tens of millions of Naqshbandi followers from Asia through North America, including the Chechen Muslims, the KDP of Kurdistan and the singer Cat Stevens. These dervishes do not whirl. They practice Zikir, a guided meditation that "purifies" the spirit.

Kidnapping

Although most of the attention is on the 160 or so kidnap victims held in Chechnya, many of them were originally kidnapped in Dagestan. Russian naval captain Andrei Ostranits was kidnapped in Makhachkala, Dagestan. He is being held for $30,000 ransom in Chechnya. A representative of the International Red Cross Committee, Ribero Geraldo Cruz from New Zealand, was kidnapped in Nalchik, Kabardino-Balkariya, forcing the Red Cross to suspend its work in the northern Caucasus.

DANGEROUS DAYS

10/1/99	Russians invade Chechnya . . . again.
9/9/99	A series of explosions in Moscow apartments is blamed on Chechens.
8/10/99	Dagestan declares independence.
7/99	Basayev and Khattab begin operations in Dagestan.
8/6/96	Chechen fighters reverse the war, driving Russian troops out of Grozny.
1/17/96	Russian troops attack Chechen fighters and their hostages die in the village of Pervomaiskaya on the Chechnya/Dagestan border.
1/9–24/96	Chechen commandos, led by Salman Raduyev, take 2,000 people hostage at a hospital in Kizliar in the republic of Dagestan.
8/96	Russians sign truce deferring independence of Chechnya for five years.
12/94	Boris Yeltsin starts 20-month war; 80,000 die.
5/13/91	Dagestan declares sovereignty.
10/91	Dudayev declares independent republic of Chechnya.
1956	Khruschev allows diaspora return to Dagestan.

DAGESTAN

1944	Stalin orders deportation of Chechens and Ingush for collaborating with Nazis.
1834–1856	Imam Shamil unites tribes to create Muslim state.
1722	Peter the Great annexes Caspian Sea regions of Dagestan. Starts a 150-year war to conquer the northern Caucasus region.

In a Dangerous Place: Dagestan

Front Row Seats

One can never lead a normal life as a war photographer. As soon as the words "hostilities have broken out in . . ." are heard on CNN, it is expected that there will be a flow of videotapes and photographs that cover and explain the conflict. Most journalists are dispatched in a hurry and get in-country before the borders are closed. Others must make their way in by whatever means necessary. *DP* is part of the latter.

The large networks and news-gathering organizations pay extraordinary amounts of money not only to send in news teams but also to charter airplanes, couriers and even military planes to get their dispatches out of the country. Satellite telephones and transmitters make it easy to send reports now, but the units are expensive and heavy to pack.

When Russia sent its troops into Grozny, there were plenty of journalists and reporters. As the situation became embarrassing, the Russians began to simply round up and send journalists out of the country. Previously, Dudayev had expelled all Russian reporters because of their inflammatory articles. When the Russian and Western press began to highlight the Russian incompetence and division, the Russians rounded up the Western press. Unlike major conflicts where the press are carefully clothed, fed, housed and "spun" by briefings, press releases and carefully prepared interviews, Chechnya was the opposite. Russian troops couldn't care less if they shot at the glint of a camera lens or a sniper's telescopic sight. Mortars, bombs and shells dropped by the Russians cared even less.

We wanted to see for ourselves, so we sent in a correspondent to try to understand the situation firsthand. The story of just what it takes to get into a war zone like Chechnya will give you some idea of the new face of reporting war.

We made our preliminary arrangements before leaving Istanbul with the Caucasus Peoples Federation, a group that was supporting Dudayev's fight in Chechnya, or Chechenstan as it is locally known. The plan was to allow us to go in with a group of "volunteers," or mercenaries, via Baku in Azerbaijan through Dagestan and then on to Grozny. Although they could provide some forms of transportation to the border, from Hasalyurt we would have to walk for about three days through the mountains in the middle of winter to reach Grozny. Although we were being sent in under the protection of the Chechen forces, there was no guarantee who would be in charge once we arrived.

We set off the day before Christmas with minimal survival gear: our cameras, a stove, some tins of fish and warm clothing. We fly to Baku, in Azerbaijan, to meet the people who will take us into Grozny. The "friends" turn out to be members of the Lezgi Mafia, one of the toughest groups in Russia and the Transcaucasus region. The Lezgi number about 1.5 million and live in the north of Azerbaijan and in south and central Dagestan. Our goal is to fly 1,800 kilometers east to Baku and then travel 400 kilometers north along the Caspian Sea through Dagestan and then west 50 kilometers over the border into Grozny.

These entrepreneurial bandits have decided that since things are heating up (and as they don't know the difference between *DP* and NBC), they will need a $5,000 transportation fee. Now normally when you make a business transaction in any country, you have some basic understanding of the value of money, and the intentions and general cost of a service. When you are dealing with the mafia in Azerbaijan, however, there is no guarantee that you will not end up a frozen cadaver with a slit throat two miles out of Baku.

Seeing how we have a plan B, we have nothing to lose by negotiating this fee down to a paltry $1,000, which includes transportation, food and lodging, but no cable TV.

Plan B was the official Russian tour of Chechnya. Most Westerners are not aware of Moscow's new entrepreneurial spirit. Journalists who are accepted can arrange a $4,000 junket into Chechnya from Moscow via military transport. We opt for the lower-priced, more adventurous ground operator version via the locals.

We make our deal over tea and cigarettes, and, once accepted, we are as good as kinfolk with these tough characters. Although we are kissing cousins, we also agree to pay our fee once we are over the border in Hasalyurt. The man who is to take us there tells us we will have company. He is bringing in ten mercenaries and volunteers from Iran, Uzbekistan and Tadjikistan who will be joining us ten kilometers short of the Azerbaijan-Dagestan border. Oh, he mentions casually, a load of antitank missiles as well. We don't ask him how much money this one trip will clear but it is obvious that war is good for business in these parts.

One of his men drives us two hours north to Quba in a Lada, complete with reflective tinted windows. The mafia may have money, but they sure don't have taste. We stay at an old Russian farmhouse surrounded by apple orchards as far as the eye can see. Now abandoned, it was a way station and safe house for the Lezgi mafia. In the courtyard are two tractors with the antitank rockets. The men are packing oranges, apples, flour and other agrarian items to camouflage the clearly labeled crates.

We are awakened early the next morning and set off north toward Qusar, a town about 25 kilometers short of the Dagestan border. We are now traveling in three groups. The first group consists of two Lezgi, who would travel ahead of us to meet with the local officials, grease the border guards and ensure our safe passage into Dagestan. Behind us come the volunteers, now happy farmers bringing in foodstuffs. The border is officially closed, but the guards just stare dispassionately at us and never bother to even wave us down or check our passports. We thought the mirrored windows were bad taste; now we know their function. Inside Dagestan, we stay in the car until we reach an old Lenin Pioneer

Camp, a relic of the Russian regime, where primary and high school kids learned the ways of the revolution. It is the Soviet version of our Boy Scout camps.

That night we have a typical Azeri meal—smoked meat and smoked fish, washed down with homemade vodka strong enough to remove paint. Tonight will be cold, but the fire from the vodka will warm us up.

After our feast, we set off down a small side road that leads to the official checkpoint at the border. The cart track is used by the local farmers and is too bumpy to allow large trucks. There is little reason for a 24-hour border patrol, and, by "coincidence," there is no border patrol that night. As we travel along the gray Caspian Sea into Derbent, we learn some unsettling news. Moscow has replaced the local police and border guards with special security team members known as Omon. This is indeed a bad "omen." Security is tight because one of Dudayev's assistants has made a visit to Turkey and asked for the Turks to send assistance to Chechnya via Azerbaijan. The sudden heavy presence of the Russian military is to cut off any aid coming to the embattled capital of Grozny.

We are told this by a Lezgi mafia customs official. The fellow who holds this oxymoronic post advises us that in order for us to continue through Dagestan, we will need to become citizens of the Dagestan Autonomous Region.

That night, a man from the local police force brings two blank passports and we become Dagestanis for $300 each. It is a busy night as we fill out forms and complete the passports. Before dawn the next morning, it seems that our new status is to be rewarded. Our transport is a brand-new BMW bought (or stolen) in Germany. We leave our old passports behind as partial payment and to avoid being searched and arrested as spies. Dagestan is a war zone with a penalty of two years in jail for crossing the border illegally. The Russian soldiers are also empowered to detain and/or execute people whom they suspect as volunteers or spies.

I wonder who Sefail Musayev is, but I carry his passport thankfully. The fact that we cannot speak a word of Russian makes every border crossing a gut wrencher. The Russians are not in any mood for levity, but our Azeri driver/guide manages to chat and joke our way through a total of seven checkpoints. At each tense checkpoint my hair turns a little grayer, the lines on my face are etched deeper and I wonder what the hell I am doing here. When we reach the bustling city of Mohachkale (or Makhachkala), we finally can breathe. From here it is 170 kilometers to the border of Chechnya. From this point on, our driver knows nothing of the conditions ahead.

We drive on in our beautiful new BMW, feeling like royalty, although we are the last people the Russians want in this area. We come to Kizlar, and our driver stops to talk with a Chechen contact family, who works as a link between the Chechen Mafia and the Lezgi. We ask about the Reuters journalists who are based in Hasalyurt. We have made an earlier deal to use their transmitter and satellite phone. The news is not good. The day before, the Russians severely bombed the Hasalyurt-Grozny road, knocking out a number of bridges. The journalists who were staying in the local sports stadium and using it as a base for their forays into Grozny were rounded up and sent back to Moscow.

After coming this far we have no way to send out our information and no one to take us across the border; all that lies ahead of us is a bombed-out wasteland.

After much discussion with the Chechen family, we learn there is one chance. If we can make it to Babayurt, another border town, we can try to contact a group of Chechen volunteers who are to cross the border soon. They mention that we will be safer in Chechnya, since the Russians are increasing their crackdown on foreigners and volunteers in Dagestan daily.

Kizlar is about 40 kilometers north of Hasalyurt, and Babayurt is halfway in between. One of the refugees from Kizlar staying in the house offers to come with us to help us get into Chechnya and to ease our way past the checkpoints that await us. Our luck holds, because the Russians have concentrated their Omon special forces south of Hasalyurt and the checkpoints to the north are manned by local Dagestanis. We meet up with a group of 20–30 Chechen volunteers who are preparing to cross the border that night. We discuss the various ways into the country. Most agree that to try to walk over the mountains into Grozny is futile since the snow is now 4 to 5 meters deep. The 130-kilometer trip will take at least a full week, with an excellent chance of being attacked by jets or helicopters during the day.

We decide to tag along with the heavily armed volunteers. We begin our trip in a convoy of cars and cross the empty border post. Around midnight, the drivers of the cars drop us off and return. We will continue on foot. We walk for six or seven hours, covering 20 kilometers of frozen lowland impeded only by a slight snow cover. We let the main group of armed volunteers go on ahead of us. Our group was not armed, but if they meet up with the Russians, we are close enough to hear the sound of gunfire before we stumble into the same trap.

The cold is numbing, and we plod on through the night like zombies. The wind whips and slaps our faces, making icicles on my mustache. The moon is our only light. After a while, we come upon a dirt track that leads to the village ahead. The wind not only brings cold and pain; it now brings the sound of heavy gunfire, alternately fading and building. Our temperatures begin to rise, as we go through the fields leading down to the village. Rockets and automatic weapons crack and thump in the crystal-clear night. As we crunch our way down to the village, the light of the dull blue sky begins to rise like a curtain at the start of a movie. The sound of the Russian helicopters increases from a muted drumroll to a thunderous chorus.

My cold hands reach for my frozen cameras in anticipation. This is the play for which we have come, the drama to which we have fought so hard for admission. Now on with the show.

—**Sedat Aral**

East Timor
★★

Timor Bomb

Timor means "east" in Malay, but it has become the wild west of Indonesia. It was violently invaded by Indonesia in 1975 and then violently freed by plebiscite in September 1999. The wholesale destruction of everything the Indonesians built in East Timor has been calculated to put the region behind where it was in 1975. The future does not hold much hope for Timor. But then again, the island of Timor has always been a hot-spot of sorts.

It might have started when the Portuguese and the Dutch split the island, creating a formal boundary in 1859. Rebellions between 1984 and 1912 started the process of pacification. Before then it was just a little friendly headhunting with the winner returning the loser's cranium to its family. It used to be sandalwood and now it's only coffee that makes the rusty wheels of industry turn slowly. Timor's only other claim to fame is it's proximity to Australia, making it a major battleground in WWII, resulting in the deaths of between 40,000 and 60,000 Timorese. Timor is the largest and furthest east island of the lesser Sundas. With Australia only 500 kilometers to the south, its only hope is the oil deposits that may lie in its newfound territorial waters.

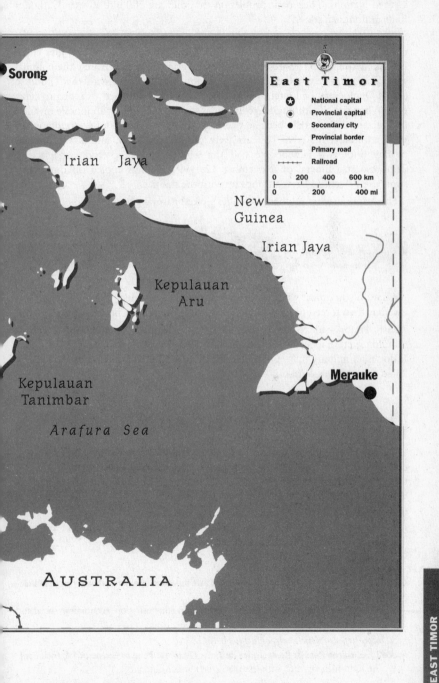

Sorong

Irian Jaya

East Timor

★ National capital
◉ Provincial capital
● Secondary city
—— Provincial border
═══ Primary road
＋＋＋ Railroad

0 200 400 600 km
0 200 400 mi

New
Guinea

Irian Jaya

Kepulauan
Aru

Kepulauan
Tanimbar

Arafura Sea

Merauke

AUSTRALIA

If you are a student of history, you know that East Timor is technically a nonautonomous 32,350 square kilometer territory of Portugal, according to the United Nations. Their basic problem is that they are 700,000 Roman Catholics in an Indonesian state.

There was a brief glimmer of independence on August 11, 1975, when five political parties sprang up from the Portuguese military's promise to give them independence. The Timorese Democratic Union (UDT) overthrew the colonial government, only to plunge the tiny region into civil war with the Timorese Social Democrats, or Fretelin, who used Portuguese-supplied weapons to seize Dili. When the left-leaning Fretelin began to win, big brother Indonesia invaded on December 7. Fretelin became guerrilla fighters and were slowly decimated by the Indonesian military. Tourists were allowed in 1989, and things looked peachy until two newspeople had the gall to videotape troops massacring Timorese at a funeral on November 12, 1991. Things cooled off until UN-supervised elections heated things up with the militias.

The future may be submerged—unexploited natural gas in the Timor Gap.

What do you expect when a Portuguese colony is invaded, then built-up by the invader, then forced to give it back to the, gasp, people? Chaos of course.

East Timor had to be destroyed so that Indonesia could make money rebuilding it. Expect chaos, then calm then corruption and a lot of richer Indonesian military men. Oh yeah, and over 100,000 East Timorese have been killed figuring this out.

The two main political parties are UDT and ASDT/FRETILIN, but there are a number of other political parties like the Apodeti and others. Three weeks after the revolution of April 25, the governor of East Timor created the Commission for the Autodetermination, which aspires to bring out to legality all the incipient political associations.

UDT (União Democrática Timorense, or Timor Democratic Union)

The first and most popular party, with support amongst old-line Portuguese and older Timorese

E-mail: udttimor@mo.unitel.net
http://www.unitel.net/udttimor/

ASDT/FRETILIN Frente Revolucionaria de Timor Leste Independente (Revolutionary Front of Independent East Timor)

Youngish lefties that support the usual reforms in administration, economical, social and political arenas.

http://www.geocities.com/SoHo/Study/4141/

Apodeti Associacao Popular Democratica de Timor (Timorese Popular Democratic Association)

The Indo-friendly party, with less-than-secret links to Indonesia.

The three minor parties are The KOTA (Klibur Oan Timur Aswain), or "sons of the mountain warriors," an old-school party that wants restoration of powers to the liurais (who can trace their ancestry back to the Topasse period) in order to constitute a democratic monarchy, with the king to be elected amongst the liurais. Other lefty parties include the Timorese Democratic Labor Movement and the Democratic Association for the Integration of East Timor

Ray Rala Jose "Xanana" Gusmao

Gusmao was born in the East Timorese town of Mana Luto on June 20, 1946. He studied at a Jesuit seminary and went to Dili High School. After compulsory service in the colonial forces, he moved to Australia after winning East Timor's poetry prize in 1974. He became involved with the FRETILIN independence group and returned to East Timor in November 1975, a week before the invasion by Indonesia.

He became the leader of FRETILIN's military wing in 1978 and was a romantic symbol of liberation among the people. He negotiated a three-month cease-fire in 1978 and was captured and sentenced to life in prison in 1992. It was reduced to 20 years in 1993. His wife, Emilia, and his two children live in Melbourne. He has returned to East Timor.

Jose Ramos-Horta

The Nobel Peace Prize winner is Timor's biggest spokesperson and works closely with UN special envoy to Timor, Jamsheed Marker.

Bishop Carlos Belo

Belo is considered the spiritual leader of the Roman Catholic Timorese. He was born in 1948 in the town of Bacau. He was exiled in Portugal and then Rome until his return to Timor in 1999. He was cowinner of the Nobel Peace Prize, with Jose Ramos-Horta, and continues to be a stable voice for reconciliation.

The Militias

There are a lucky 13 different milita groups in Timor. Their common goal is to maintain control of the region and people for Indonesian business and government mucky-mucks. They originally sprang up to battle the rebels, FALINTIL, on less than Queensbury rules. They exist to replace the direct involvement of ABRI or the civilian police and TNI, the Indonesian National Army. They are not directly linked to the central military and government in Jakarta but rather to the old-guard military and businessmen who have their fingers in the timber and coffee industries. and enemies of Habibe. Many of the militia members are press-ganged or intimidated into joining and come from areas outside East Timor. Their stated enemies also include journalists and UN workers. Their goal is to drive outsiders off the island so they can kill independence supporters. Accordingly, about 130 journalists helped them by hauling tail out of the Makota Hotel within days of the independence vote.

Aitarak (Thorn) led by Eurico Guterres

Eurico Guterres and the Aitarak (Thorn) like to think that Timor will become a "sea of fire." He says he heads the anti-independence militias, groups of young men in black shirts and red berets with direct ties to the Indonesian government who kill and maim citizens. In the tumultuous year before independence, over 1,000 civilians were murdered by the militia. In one case, 57 were shot and chopped as they cowered in a churchyard west of Dili.

Other Military Groups

Halilinta and Gardapaksi militias in western East Timor

Mahidi, led by Cancio Cavalho

Mati Hidup Demi Integrasi (live or die with integration) Mahidi

Besi Merah Putih (Red and White Iron)

Kelompok Naga Merah (Red Dragon Group) a paramilitary group aligned to the Indonesian Army

Pemuda Pancasila (Pancasila Youth—right wing military intelligence thugs)

Portugal

If you consider Angola and Mozambique as their shining examples of colonial development then it's amazing that any Timorese survived. When the Indonesians invaded, the illiteracy rate was 70 percent, there were 20 kilometers of paved roads and two hospitals. The Portuguese had essentially abandoned East Timor, and there was little hope for any future development.

Indonesia

The Indonesians, under Sukarno and Suharto, had a thing called Mapalindo, the idea that anything with rocks belonged to Indonesia. It made perfect sense to suck up the fly-speck half of Timor they didn't own and make it the 27th state. To be fair the Indos pumped in around $200 million to build 10 hospitals, 600 schools and 4,200 miles of roads.

There are plenty of bemos and buses. You can also rent cars or motorbikes. The airport is five kilometers west of Dili. Make sure you agree on a price before jumping in a taxi. Indonesia has an interesting ferry system. And depending on which government airline is bankrupt, there is frequent milk-run service to Denpassar, Kupang, Yogyarkarta and Surabaya.

Four centuries of misrule by Portugal and 24 years of Indonesian occupation have left. Eighty percent of Timor, 700,000 people, live below the subsistence level. Despite Indonesia pumping in half of $1,113 GDP, things are not getting better in East Timor. Per capita income is about $300 a person. Thirty-five percent of the people are illiterate—only 1,000 Timorese have college degrees, and that was back when things looked good.

Useful Links

Timornet

http://www.uc.pt/Timor/TimorNet.html

Resources on the Web (University of Portugal)
  http://www.ci.uc.pt/Timor/netret.htm
Government of Indonesia
  http://www.sdn.or.id/sdn/sdnp-new/htdocs/link/gov.html
UN in East Timor
  http://www.un.org/peace/etimor/etimor.htm
Amnesty International
  http://www.amnesty.org/ailib/aipub/1998/ASA/32102498.htm
East Timor Action Network
  http://www.etan.org/

02/99	New President B.J. Habibie weighs independence for East Timor. Talks at UN begin.
1996	East Timor Bishop Dom Ximenes Belo and activist José Ramos Horta awarded Nobel Peace Prize.
11/12/91	Massacre at Dili's Santa Cruz cemetery carried out by Indonesian troops
1/98	Australia recognizes Jakarta's rule of East Timor.
1984	First uprising against Indonesias
1983	U.N. Commission on Human Rights adopts resolution affirming East Timor's right to independence. Widespread hunger and continued battles between Indonesia troops and rebels.
1976	Indonesia declares East Timor its 27th province. As much as one-third of the 650,000 population may have been killed in fighting. UN maintains Portugal is administrating power.
8/11/75	Five political groups are created after promises of independance by Portugal
1975	Portugal withdraws from East Timor Indonesian troops invade the island.
1949	Dutch give up their colony, creating Indonesia.
1912	Uprising against Portugese.
1849	Dutch and Portugese officially split the island of Timor
1500s	Portugal begins settlement of east Timor
02/99	New president B.J. Habibie weighs independence for East Timor. Talks at UN begin.
1996	East Timor Bishop Dom Ximenes Belo and activist José Ramos Horta awarded Nobel Peace Prize.
11/12/91	Massacre at Dili's Santa Cruz cemetery carried out by Indonesian troops
1/98	Australia recognizes Jakarta's rule of East Timor.

EAST TIMOR

1984	First uprising against Indonesias
1983	UN Commission on Human Rights adopts resolution affirming East Timor's right to independence. Widespread hunger and continued battles between Indonesia troops and rebels.
1976	Indonesia declares East Timor its 27th province. As much as one-third of the 650,000 population may have been killed in fighting. UN maintains Portugal is administrating power.
8/11/75	Five political groups are created after promises of independance by Portugal
1975	Portugal withdraws from East Timor Indonesian troops invade the island.
1949	Dutch give up their colony, creating Indonesia.
1912	Uprising against Portugese.
1849	Dutch and Portugese officially split the island of Timor

In a Dangerous Place: East Timor

Maulindo's Feet

Like a stubborn mantra, Maulindo's feet still trudge through my head. Under star and moon, through sun and shadow, over roots and rocks, up, down and right into paddy, mountain and river, I stomped for a fortnight through the wilds of East Timor with only Maulindo heels in my vision. In my exhaustion, my thirst, and my fear, those guerrilla feet were my beacon, blueprinting a path of stealth and survival.

Palmcorder in hand, I went to East Timor to try to puncture the information blockade clamped on the island since the Indonesians invaded the freshly independent Portuguese colony in 1975 and set about obliterating a third of its 700,000 inhabitants. A few brave journalists have managed to contact the guerrillas resisting such genocide since the country was opened to foreigners in 1989, manna to a people who feel forgotten by the world. One of the last to try was Jill Jolliffe, an Australian who has been trying to make the world listen to the East Timorese since her first visit just before the invasion. After interviewing the guerrilla leadership in 1994, she was arrested while traveling to a second meeting, and expelled.

It was her journey I was setting out to complete. My assignment: to spend two weeks in the bush with the guerrillas of the National Council for Maubere Resistance (CNRM), recording their life, thoughts, stories and, if I could, combat. Getting in and out sounded like the hardest parts—and maybe for other journalists they had been. What I didn't realize in my naiveté was that I wasn't actually going to be doing quite what other journalists had done.

Day 1

As soon as you pass the military checkpoint that marks the division between West and East Timor, the change in atmosphere is almost palpable. Having spent three weeks crossing Java, Bali, Flores and West Timor to establish bogus tourist credentials, suddenly there are no longer the curious, smiling, friendly faces that throughout Indonesia are either the traveler's boon or bane, depending on how often you've had "Hello, mister" shouted at you that hour.

Instead, there are averted eyes, twitching shoulders and a general attempt to ignore my blatantly white presence. Getting into a crowded taxi in the capital, Dili, I feel like a leper as everyone shifts uncomfortably. It's only when I get out that I snatch my first glimpse of what I hope is the real East Timor—an old man inside flashes me a shining grin. It's night on an empty street and the taxi's driving off, so maybe it's just about safe to have this brief interaction with a foreigner.

This feels like a country saturated in the kind of fear that Stalin or Hitler would have relished—fear of anything in uniform (and the military are clearly the style-arbiters in Indonesia, with even parking attendants looking dressed for parade), fear of agents not in uniform, fear just of the inquisitive neighbor, and fear of the foreigner. All foreigners are covert journalists to the Indonesian authorities and no one wants to be seen having even eye contact with someone free to tell the outside world that Big Brother is alive and thriving in East Timor.

I say "free," but no one really has a sense of freedom here. Through checkpoints and hotel registers, foreigners are monitored every step of the way, and if you really want to get to the heart of things you have to disappear. Which is what I do tomorrow.

Day 2

I am smuggled out of Dili by the CNRM civilian network—the Clandestine Front—to a "safe" house not a ricochet away from an Indonesian army barracks. There I am greeted by the widest and wildest grins I've ever seen. For a moment I almost think they are mad, so persistent and broad is the show of teeth. And then they show me the broken hands, broken feet and unbroken spirit that are the Indonesian legacy each bears, and I realize that they're just genuinely happy that I'm here. Why? Because I've actually arrived? Because a foreigner gives a damn? Or is there also a sense of wonder at my naïveté in asking to do what I'm asking to do? Too cheerfully they tell me that in the 21 years since the invasion, no journalist has spent as long as two weeks with the guerrillas, none has marched with them into the interior, and certainly no one has ever filmed them in combat.

Now this is news to me. I am not a brave person and have never really worked out the difference between that quality and stupidity. When I'm going into a dangerous situation, I prefer to have the reassurance that at least someone else has trodden the same path before, so that at least in moments of shit-scaredness I can point them out to myself and assure myself, "Look, they're still mobile/ unmutilated/breathing."

But before I can properly wake up to the real risks of my situation, I am whisked out of the house under cover of midnight to cross Indonesian lines to the base of the local guerrillas. "Lines" is something of a euphemism, as in fact there are no such things here. It seems to be mainly a question of the resistance finding some small piece of bush where they can hunker down and quietly avoid the

Indonesian army, which means—and this too is news to me—that there isn't really a safe area in the whole country.

And so the fear comes—my first experience of nightwalking, Timor-style. There is one thing and one thing only that matters—the feet of the person in front. That is your universe entire, the focus of all your attention. Look up, look sideways, just blink too long and you may lose the precise trail being trod. And may stumble. And may make noise. And may be shot at.

You haven't actually been told, East Timor being a thrifty place information-wise even when you're on the inside, but you can assume the Indonesian army's pretty close when you have to walk with such care. Yet it's when the dim arm ahead of me points to a spot fifty meters away and the feet get extra-cautious that I realize they're much too close, and the fear hits. Surely even the deaf could sense our tremors, let alone an alert Indonesian guard on the listen for all our leaf-rustling, twig-cracking, stone-crunching. And if not these, then at least the hurricane of my breathing, which I suddenly realize sounds panicked.

Thinking my body may be panicking, my mind joins in. This is unexpected. I was sure I could take this, but suddenly my heart is bumping against my temples, my throat is threatening to gag as I try to still the hurricane and, worst of all, fear feeds off fear as the thought flurries through my brain that my nerves have taken me by surprise and jumped ship and maybe I can't take this. It's only the beginning after all. I'll be jibbering after two weeks. What happens if I can't cope. What happens if . . .

And then—nothing happens. Nothing happens, thank-god-please-Christ-I-promise-I'll-believe-in-you, and at three in the trembling morn, I crawl into an anonymous thicket to shake the hands of David Alex, the commander of this sector of resistance, and his merry band of nine, before subsiding onto a groundsheet in the lull of being safer and the dire certainty of soon being a lot unsafer.

Day 3

I put it down to first-night frights, though the feeling of anxiety never leaves, just lessens. I was led to believe that the armed forces of the National Liberation of East Timor, or FALINTIL as the CNRM's army calls itself, controlled some territory about which it moved freely. David Alex tells me there's territory that is safer, but none they can call theirs. I can tell it isn't here because everyone's whispering. If you can't even talk at normal volume in the middle of the countryside, things must be pretty insecure. I'm even asked not to film the treetops around us in case they are later recognized by the enemy.

Mr. Alex has the reputation of being the most combative leader in FALINTIL, constantly disrupting the Indonesian's composure with short, sharp attacks. At 49, he has spent twenty years in the bush and hasn't seen his wife or son for eighteen of those, though they live, depending on his movements, between only 20 to 100 miles away— the Timorese mile being the longest on earth. Any visit would invite reprisals on his family by the Indonesians. He is a small, wiry man with intense eyebrows and a quiet disposition, though whether that's a natural trait or the result of 20 years of whispering I don't know. What I do know is that I have an innate respect for anyone who's been shot five times and given up so much to live a life this tough for so long in defense of the basic rights of his people. Also, I want to absolutely admire, trust and believe in him because my life is now in his hands.

Fortunately, he has taken care to provide a young translator or communication would-be semaphoric. He was a student activist, imprisoned and tortured by the Indonesians ("They kept me like this for three days," he tells me as he strings a chicken upside-down) and is the virgin amongst these guerrillas, having no gun and only one combat experience. His nom de guerre (a necessity for all guerrillas in order to avoid Indonesian persecution of their families) is Tara Leu.

Like everyone else here, he has lost members of his family to the Indonesian terror and makes clear to me the relativity of the term "virgin" in Timor when he says that he and a friend knifed an Indonesian soldier to death in Dili. It surprises me, coming from his young and fresh face, but then the gentle cheerfulness of all these guerrillas belies the fear in which they are held by the Indonesian soldier. There is no military machismo here, none of the brutalization of men under arms, just expert adaptation to a life that has been forced upon them.

Days 4–6

Planning the next combat has become the focus of my whole visit. While he constructs a crude homemade bomb, David Alex emphasizes that they never attack simply to kill Indonesians, but to equip themselves with guns, bullets, even uniforms. Having no assistance from any outside sponsor, their arsenal is made up entirely of whatever weapons they can capture from the Indonesian Army (which does have sponsors, such as the United States and the United Kingdom), or bullets I'm told they buy at $2 apiece from some black marketeer in the same army.

They can't attack in this area for fear of Indonesian reprisals on the local population and are planning to ambush an army convoy about a 40-minute drive away. A 40-minute drive, but, with detours to avoid army patrols, a journey by foot that will last a week.

We crouch in the thicket for three days while the attack is organized through messages sent along the bush telegraph to other units in the sector. There are four military regions in Timor, and the one David Alex controls boasts 150 guerrillas, most of them split into small groups like this one. The feeling of hierarchy is slight, but David Alex is clearly much respected by all of his men. Tara Leu calls him Father, and indeed his future is in the commander's hands. The decision is still being made about whether he would be more useful in the bush or should be sent abroad first to either use his English as an activist or learn the medical, electrical and mechanical skills that the guerrillas lack. The easier second option seems to appeal to Tara Leu most, but above all he wants whatever is best for the cause and will happily do what David Alex asks of him.

Though I can't actually talk (or whisper) to them, everyone is wonderfully friendly and certain characters are making their mark. There is Haksolok (which means happy), a young soldier who seems to live up to his name and whom I originally think too handsome and well turned-out to take seriously enough, but am assured is a deadly shot and consummate guerrilla; Augostino, another quiet type who always seems to be trying to catch my eye just to give a smile; and Leki Luru, a bereted member of the Clandestine Front whom I'm told is absolutely trusted because he gave nothing away under the torture I can see the scars of. It is he who brings me the first worrying news that resistance agents in the Indonesian camp say the military know a foreigner checked into Dili for a night, then vanished from hotel registers. Automatic conclusion: journo on the loose. It's reassuring, though, to know the resistance have spies on the inside. I just wonder about the other way around . . . .

Day 7

We leave the base for the combat zone and I see that it isn't with just muted conversation, suppressed coughs and silent laughter that the guerrillas conceal themselves. What looked like a well-established camp in minutes becomes a seemingly never-inhabited piece of thicket as they unbind and spread clumps of bush, rescatter carefully-stored leaves and stones, bury any ashes or debris, and generally eradicate every mark of man. These must be the most environmentally-friendly campers in the world—which, of course, is one of the reasons why they're still alive after 21 years.

And so we start to march at night and Maulindo's feet become my necessary idol. A thousand thoughts (like 101 good excuses to stop the Indonesian army shooting you if captured) scurry through your head when you're doggedly marching for hours with only feet to watch, but you must never lose your concentration on those sure heels in front. Like silent Chinese whispers, each stumble sends out a warning that ripples, hopefully, all the way down the line to the clumsy gringo, who must concentrate or he will fall and gash his knees on the brittleness of volcanic rock, or find the dead branch breaking off his support, or feel the earth give way and flail embarrassingly down the sheer slope.

It's the concentration as much as the effort that wrings the sweat from you on a night march, trying to distinguish crevice from shadow, root from moonstreak. You squint desperately to make out those feet in the starlight, squint in panic when a cloud drowns even that. You become able to differentiate shades of night of which you were never aware—starlight obscured by cirrus or cumulus, by branches bare or leafed, the reflection offered by light path or dark soil. And by one's own so-glaringly-pale, nay, luminous, target of white skin.

And so Maulindo's feet have become my guiding stars, and at the same time the man himself has become for me the embodiment of the East Timorese guerrilla. At first he seemed nondescript and I took him for the cook, imagined him a farmer if the invasion hadn't happened. But each day he grows quietly in stature. I begin to see the subtle beauty in his face, the sharpness in his eyes, the tightness in his jaw. I am full of admiration for the way he emerges as an expert all-rounder—as path-finder, camp-constructor, natural healer and soldier. It turns out he was only seventeen when he took to the bush, after which his father was imprisoned and exiled for supporting him. Maulindo seems to have learned all the skills of the guerrilla and yet is modest and unshowy about them. He is still waters, deeply and quietly warm, yet deadly if backed into a corner, and epitomizes the natural expertise and defiance that the Indonesians have forced the resistance to master. Like David Alex, he has been in the bush for 20 years, and it is onto one of them that I shall latch in time of danger.

Day 8

After a week in the bush I actually see more than the thicket a few feet in front of me, or what I can glimpse by starlight. It's been deemed safe enough to march a bit by day, and the beauty of the scrubby hills makes it all seem easy for a while.

Until we have to climb the bloody things. I didn't expect it to be this punishing. Up, down, up, down, like human yo-yos. The scariest idea is having to run up one of these hills with Indonesian soldiers behind us. In that sheer exhaustion I fear I'd just surrender—shoot me, but let me lie down first. And drink some water.

Safety. Thirst. Those two words define my thoughts. When I'm still, thinking, waiting, it's safety I worry about, though less and less—I'm either used to the insecurity or more blasé because nothing's happened yet. But as soon as we start to move, the torment is thirst. We cross tauntingly parched riverbeds and water is scooped from old pools of rain I wouldn't wash my hands in. It's becoming a running joke as I piston away with my small purification pump, but everyone wants to use it, there being bad stomachs all around. Even this water is rare, though, and never cold enough or too iodine-soured by the pump to really quench anything. Cold, clean, frequent water has become my obsession. By night I seek it in my dreams, by day I would sell my mother and other relatives cheaply for just a glass. It has become as vital as Maulindo's feet.

Day 9

This morning we hear the cork pops of distant shots. David Alex makes radio contact with the other guerrillas we're joining—a complicated business in itself, nothing in guerrilla life being easy. First of all a tall antenna is joined together, then slotted onto an even taller branch (they never measure whether the branch will fit, just somehow whittle it expertly to the right diameter), and then someone hauls this twenty to thirty feet up a tree on top of a mountain to get the best transmission. The contact brings us seven extra men. Safety in numbers.

The use they make of the natural environment never ceases to amaze me in its speed and resourcefulness. Haksolok shot a stag today and within an hour Augostino had dismembered, smoked and stored the entire carcass. It will feed all of us for a week or more and is a welcome change to the rice with some vegetable, which has been the constant menu so far. At least now it'll be rice with something else.

Days 10–11

Today I feel doubly safe as we are now 34. We have been joined by Taur Matan Ruak, the FALINTIL chief of staff, and his men. He greets me with much warmth as it turns out I'm the first journalist he's met in his 20 years of conflict. He is an exuberant, talkative figure, his hair and beard long and corkscrewed to look like a truly '60s guerrilla, eyes darting and slightly manic when they're not covered by shades that make him look even more like one of the Grateful Dead. And, along with David Alex, he has a bounty of 40 million rupiah on his head.

He explains to me about lulik, which might be defined as the East Timorese version of lucky charms, but is taken far more seriously. Here Portuguese Catholicism has been adapted by traditional animism to create the kind of superstitious Christianity one might associate with Europe in the Middle Ages, but without the fear or bigotry. While all the guerrillas wear crosses or carry pictures of the Virgin, nothing is as important as their individual lulik. This can be anything—from a twig to a photograph to an old Portuguese flag—the essential thing is that the individual believes it will protect them.

As a born-again atheist I find this animistic side to their beliefs more sympathetic than the Catholic one, but am surprised when Tara Leu, university student, tells me with a straight face about a man who recently turned into a snake because he drank bad water. It must be true, he swears, because the local priest testified to it. They take my skeptical levity with good humor when I say that's why I'm purifying my water. And my further cynicism at stories of babies flying after birth and other miracles is well understood. They believe, I don't—no problem. But clearly in a situation as desperate as East Timor belief may be the only thing that keeps you going.

And here you need everything you can grab hold of to keep going. There can be few harder lives on the planet. "Sometimes it rains so hard we have to sleep standing up," I am told. Some of these men haven't slept in a bed or under a roof, let alone with a woman, for 20 years. The younger ones have grown up mainly on battery power or candle light. Every day they eat rice, rice, rice, and are tormented by illnesses they have no doctor to diagnose, let alone cure. All have left their surviving loved ones behind and, while supplied by trusted elements of the nearly universally supportive population, have to avoid the majority for fear of the odd informer.

The stress of this kind of life is betrayed most at night while the most vivid shooting stars I've ever seen ignore wishes overhead. Eve never heard so many people moan in their sleep. I don't know what they're dreaming and am reluctant to ask, but the ubiquity of the nightmares seems to say more about what Indonesia has done to the East Timorese subconscious than volumes of history.

Day 12

The most punishing march yet—eight hours by night to the place of combat, stomping through rivers, up vertiginous mountains, balancing along the dim rims of paddy fields. My exhaustion wipes out the Achillean protection of Maulindo's heels and I teeter into the muddy rice so often I just want to give up, until a scorpion decides to spur me on by implanting its barb into my groping hand. Finally, on top of some cruel mountain, Tara Leu points out lights that can't be more than 20 miles away. "That's where we came from," he says. What? A week ago? I can still see where we were a week ago?

Day 13

Unlucky for who? Today is FALINTIL day, the 21st anniversary of the taking up of arms by the Revolutionary Front for the Independence of East Timor (FRETILIN). Nothing quite demonstrates the solidarity of the East Timorese better than the fact that FRETILIN has now formed a united front (the CNRM) with the parties that fought it before the invasion—even the one that originally wanted union with Indonesia but has since discovered the lethal disadvantages of such a choice. And today FALINTIL are going to celebrate the anniversary with an ambush.

Before we take up positions around the main road, David Alex briefs his men. Trigger discipline is emphasized because of the shortage of bullets, and a tough fatalism comes to the fore. The word solidarity, which we use every single day, we need to show in the field, he warns. "But if some of us fall, too bad. Anyone who we feel has no chance of survival, we let them stay there, even if the enemy ends up killing them. This game is not new to us . . . ."

From 5 A.M. to 3 P.M. we huddle in yet another thicket overlooking a road down which an Indonesian army truck or two should pass at some point. It looks like a great setup—I have a hidden overview from which I can film the first resistance combat recorded by an outsider. There are 34 of them, a hefty number by FALINTIL standards, comfortably disproving absurd Indonesian claims that there are only fifty guerrillas in the whole country—in fact there are probably over ten times that, a number restricted mainly by the weapons available, and they manage to keep 17,000 Indonesian soldiers well-occupied. We're under the unique dual command of David Alex and Taur Matan Ruak. And through me they want to show the world that they're still alive and very much kicking. I relax a little in the heat . . . .

But it doesn't happen. Something else does.

Suddenly I'm being frantically ushered out of the thicket. Again I'm not getting any information. "What's happening?" I whisper. "Well, someone—maybe one of the local population trying to curry Indonesian favor—has informed and we've been surrounded."

Oh . . . FUCK!

As we leave the thicket, shouting breaks out, followed with frightening rapidity by gunfire. A lot of gunfire. Instinctively I retreat, ignoring the fundamental rule I've been taught—under fire, do what David Alex does, stick to him like glue. Tara Leu shouts me forward and then I do run after David Alex—into the middle of a field. A wide open field. Shots are coming from everywhere and I haven't a clue who's firing or what I should be doing to avoid them. Follow David Alex, follow David Alex . . .

And then I realize the fundamental problem in the fundamental rule—David Alex has an M16, I have a Sony 780. His shots are aimed to kill. Mine are not. He can distinguish between his men in Indonesian uniform and the Indonesians in Indonesian uniform. I cannot. He has some idea of where the danger is. I most certainly do not. Above all, he has to fight, and sticking right behind him suddenly seems suicidal. As something big explodes nearby, I dive by the only tree in the wide open field and watch David Alex march at full height up to a ridge and fire with purpose at an enemy I still can't see. I point the camera in his general direction as I use my eyes to try to figure out where the danger is. After David Alex has shot in three very different directions I realize it's pretty much everywhere.

Tara Leu shouts at me to come and film a dead Indonesian soldier as a guerrilla strips the corpse of gun and grenades. I don't feel great about it, but I'll feel the reasons later, because now I'm watching David Alex rally his men and sear himself forever into my memory as he strides up to another ridge, still not ducking, and fires at another enemy. It's a sight I'll never forget, this frail-looking 49-year old with bad feet, a bad stomach, the constant whisper, heading into the onslaught with absolute indomitability. And later, as we hurtle into the hills and he has given his rifle to someone else, a noise in the bushes makes him instantly, instinctively beeline towards the threat with only a machete as defense. The noise turns out to be friendly, but watching this man snap into decisive, fearless action, I do begin to learn a definition of real bravery. It is neither foolhardy, vengeful or careless—simply necessary.

Things have been moving too fast, and it'll probably be weeks before I catch up with the fear I should've felt. The perversity is that the more frightening the situation, the less frightened one feels. In such circumstances there isn't time to be aware of fear. The chattering mind dives for cover, survival takes over and panic disappears. It was far harder crossing the lines the first night.

The guerrillas are clearly on a survival high when we stop for a brief rest, but I can't share in their glee when they display the ID cards of the two Indonesians that Haksolok and Maulindo killed. My head is filled with how nasty a rifle shot can really sound, so much sharper, more destructive and meaner than TV or film can make you comprehend. The dead Indonesian I filmed doesn't feel like a vanquished invader, just some poor sod who unexpectedly had the last day of his life and got exactly what I'd been praying not to get.

Amidst the guerrillas'Castaño relief and the defiant abuses shouted down the hills at Suharto and his offspring (and no doubt the relishing of being able to turn up their volume for once), there must be some sense of disappointment. They were caught out and possibly only escaped bigger losses because they discovered the Indonesian advance guard early and avoided the probable reinforcements coming down the road.

The final reported tally is two Indonesians definitely dead, two M16s, their magazines and some mortar shells captured, one guerrilla dead, another missing and two lightly wounded. It doesn't seem a great deal after all the time and effort involved, but Taur Matan Ruak says it was worth it. It is something, after all, and in East Timor something means more than in most places.

One of the wounded guerrillas was shot in the stomach. I watch him clutching a bruised abdomen and am told that somehow the bullet didn't enter, because his lulik protected him. I can almost believe it, because these people seem indestructible. One of them is said to have been shot 30 times, another carried a bullet in his belly for weeks before coughing it up and Taur Matan Ruak himself says he was hit on the head by a mortar. They were all saved by their lulik, of course. I give up trying to distinguish fact from embellishment in the face of the scars so many bear and the glazed eye of one guerrilla who was shot in the head when he was eight.

The other wounded is Augostino who is no longer smiling and has neat bullet entry and exit holes in the flesh at the back of his neck, making him either the luckiest or unluckiest live guerrilla today, depending on your philosophy. What amazes me is the lack of attention he receives, both physical and social. It seems that he's expected to bounce back from his wound because there really isn't any choice and maybe too much sympathy will just delay that. I mention I have some iodine, but it isn't till six hours later that anyone takes me up on it.

More important to them is the fact that I've seen the combat and therefore many others will too, which makes getting me back safely their top priority. As we flee across the hills, my whiteness is covered (and temperature brought to boiling point) by balaclava, scarf and socks for gloves and any civilians encountered are shouted brusquely out of my path.

It comes to a head at night as the 32 of us try to file quietly past a small Indonesian army post in the woods. We fool them, but not a nearby dog which barks its treacherous throat off. A West Timorese militiaman appears and is told who we are—it can't exactly be disguised. The two or three Indonesians shout "FRETILIN!" One of the guerrillas fires a shot to scare them (and certainly me) and they disappear. I'm very confused, as surely these people and the militia are meant to oppose us in some way. Instead the militiaman just checks David Alex's false ID card while I hide my whiteness in doing up my broken laces. I learn afterwards that he'd have been taken prisoner if I'd been discovered, but I still don't understand the point of checking the ID cards of declared guerrillas. I never do get a satisfactory explanation, but I'm getting used to that.

Day 14

Taur Matan Ruak and his men leave us at daybreak with hearty handshakes from each one. I'm sad to see them go, both because of what we've briefly been through together and the fact that again we are only ten.

It's a certainty that after the attack the Indonesians are going to be out on the warpath, vengefully combing the sector for us. We learn later that they executed a civilian near the combat site for suspected collaboration, and on the edges of earshot I can hear helicopters. Suddenly the original base seems dreamily safe. We're marching non-stop to get back there, Indonesian patrols permitting.

Day 15

Which they don't. Today we spend five hours lying in silence in yet another thicket while a patrol just sits and relaxes by the luscious cool flowing water of a nearby river. I've developed a phlegmy cough and spend all morning trying to suppress it, yet as soon as David Alex says the Indonesians are near—hey, presto, instant cure.

Finally we sneak out and march through the night over wonderfully flat land. Now there is a moon—just a sliver, but it feels like an arc-light. It makes Maulindo's feet less important, yet, of course, if you can see better, then they can see you better. But again, nothing happens and we arrive unscathed back at the base. I collapse in relief.

Day 16

Naïve relief. Today the Clandestine Front bring us news that the guerrilla who was killed in the combat had a camera on him containing many lovely snaps of yours truly in the company of all these notorious friends of Indonesia. Snaps which can of course be distributed to every exit point in the country. Now I am worried.

I shave off my beard, hoping to find a way out where they won't look at my hairy passport. The videotapes have always been going out a different way, but now I have to leave anything remotely suspicious behind—camera, mic, notes, even sleeping-outside-and-not-in-a-nice-tourist-hotel kind of gear. I'm out of here (I hope) and I can't say it breaks my heart. It's been the toughest fortnight of my life.

Day 17

This afternoon, David Alex gives a speech to 30 or so villagers who have trekked into the bush, none of whose faces I can film for obvious reasons. I'm told they're all members of the Clandestine Front, which seems a huge percentage for such a small village, but I can fully believe it. They leave food for the guerrillas, and clearly Mr Alex is held in some kind of awe. He is, after all, a national hero here, in the style of a Che or Giap.

Leki Luru returns from the nearest village with the best news I've heard all my life—one of the resistance's inside agents managed to destroy the captured film of me before it was developed. Quite how they'd get away with that I don't know, but I desperately want to believe. Before I leave, they perform a lulik ceremony to ensure my bon voyage. Haksolok and others strangle three cocks in front of a makeshift altar of candles and bark while a shaman intones Latinic litanies. It's a startling synthesis with Catholic icons prominent as local whisky is passed round as communion and the entrails of the cocks are read. What this oracle reveals is that the East Timorese have had a hard life for 20 years and should keep on resisting. I suggest I could have told them that with my insides intact, and they're nice enough to laugh. Yet if it keeps them going . . .

At dusk I leave the camp. Despite wanting to escape so much, I do have tears in my eyes as I say goodbye to these ten amazing men. All along I have suspected, and now I truly know that they are the most remarkable people I have ever met. It has been a real privilege to know them, one I can only compare with knowing the besieged people of Sarajevo, but greater even than that—because this has been longer, so unreported and has no end in sight. I leave with a certain pride at having been through it, guilt at not staying longer, shame at wanting to leave, but above all sadness that I may never see them again—not the guerrillas, but these individuals, Haksolok, Leki Luru, Augostino, Amico, Laku Wani, Bere Du, Gali Ria, Tara Leu, David Alex, and Maulindo. The last thing I do is shake his feet.

As I cross into the nearest village, the sun is setting in the most Hollywood way— sharp oranges streaked by yellow finger-of-God beams and inky wisps of cloud. I almost laugh at its kitschiness, but try to persuade myself it's a good omen.

It is. In the early morning hours when the Indonesians are less alert, I am driven behind tinted windows out of the scared, brave land of East Timor and finally reach a place where I no longer have to hide or whisper.

But in my head the mantra treads on. I know that, despite the help it gets from the United States, United Kingdom, Australia, Netherlands, and others, Indonesia can never defeat the East Timorese—in the same way that the Americans couldn't beat the Vietnamese, or the Moroccans the Western Saharans, or the nationalist Bosnian Serbs the Bosnian people. The East Timorese have been too brutalized, bereaved and butchered to ever dream of giving up. They have survived their own Holocaust and desperately need the world to know they are still there and always will be. They are fighting not just for the basic right of self-determination, but for their very existence. And if the Indonesians haven't beaten them in 21 years, they never will. Like Maulindo's feet, the resistance will continue—tired but active, stealthy but sure, occasionally stumbling, always persisting. On and on they tread, through my head, through politics, through the shame of the world, hoping one day to rest in peace.

—Dom Rotheroe

Ethiopia/Eritrea
★★★★

Africa's Locked Horns

The Nobel Peace Prize winner for misery in this little Horn of Africa turf war goes to the weather. While heads of state from at least a dozen African nations have been sitting around the continent's Hyatts trying to resolve wars in Congo, Angola and Sierra Leone, the African solution to the African problem on the Horn is simple.

Rain.

No mediators. No peacekeeping force. No accords. No peace talks. No ceasefires. No Evian. No party favors and African Renaissance T-shirts. Period. The peacemaker in the Horn is Mother Nature. When the three-month rainy season arrives in July, the boys in uniform bunk down and listen to crumpled reggae tapes. Visit families. Have seaside picnics. Mow the lawn. The deluge of water is so predictable and overwhelming that no one even bothers trying to end this war with a Waterman pen.

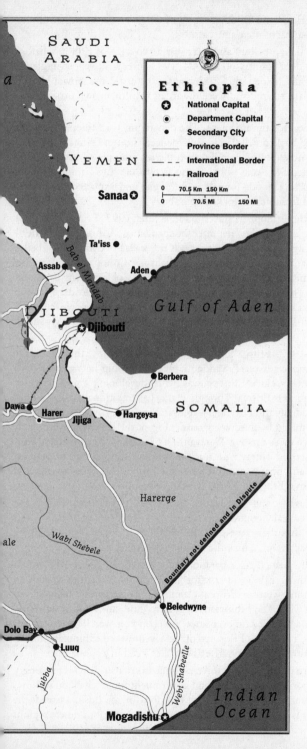

Ethiopia

But what turned Eritrea and Ethiopia—two of Africa's coziest neighbors for much of the 1990s—at each other's throats?

Eritrea is a former Italian colony and later was a province of Ethiopia before becoming an independent country on May 24, 1993, after a 30-year struggle for freedom. The Eritreans helped the Ethiopians overthrow the Soviet-backed Mengistu Haile Mariam regime and were rewarded with their own little coastal sliver of sovereignty.

It seemed a good deal for the Eritreans. The new regime in Ethiopia that sent Mengistu packing had backed Eritrean independence. Though Eritrea was tiny in comparison with its neighbor (3.5 million people to Ethiopia's 59 million), it had an ocean—the Red Sea—and ports. It was free to tap into Ethiopia's huge marketplace by importing goods for sale in Ethiopia, and exported goods and produce to the world from its landlocked neighbor.

The Eritreans and the Ethiopians stayed buddies after 1993. Eritrea even kept using the Ethiopian currency, the *birr*, after independence. Although the 1,000-kilometer border between the two countries was never clearly delineated—being based on old colonial maps drawn up by the Italians—Ethiopians looking for work crossed freely into Eritrea. And tens of thousands of Eritreans lived and worked in Ethiopia. There were some small squabbles over the border between Eritrean president Isaias Afwerki and Ethiopian leader Meles Zenawi, but they seemed to be the two-kids-in-a-sandbox variety. And the two sides always shook hands at the end.

But in November 1997, Eritrea introduced its own currency, the *nafka*, for what it called "economic reasons." Suddenly the relationship between the two countries became a little rockier. Ethiopia was swiftly developing Tigray province in the north, which adjoins Eritrea. Though Tigray has traditionally been a grain and cattle center, suddenly the Eritreans were watching the province emerge as a manufacturing hub, fueled by massive investment from the Zenawi government. It didn't help that Zenawi is a native Tigrayan. The Eritreans felt threatened, as if the Ethiopians had seeded Tigray with nuclear weapons silos instead of cement, bicycle, trucks parts and pharmaceutical factories. Eritrea had never sustained a truly working economy. Ethiopia was its working economy.

For their part, despite the cordialities between Zenawi and Isaias, the Ethiopians were never really comfortable with losing the ports of Massawa and Assab—never happy that their access to the outside world was controlled by a tiny, impoverished backwater. Thus, the building blocks of war.

The Eritreans finally pushed their paranoia over the edge in May 1998 when they grabbed land under Ethiopian control in the disputed Badme triangle in northern Ethiopia/southwestern Eritrea, claiming they were only taking what was theirs to start off with. The Ethiopians begged to differ and a full-scale World War I–type land battle has been on ever since. An economic war. The war started on May 6, 1999, when a group of Eritrean officers went to tell Ethiopian officials that they were on Eritrean territory. They were shot dead in a shoot-out.

The war in the Horn isn't like the drunken, zonked-out insurgencies in Congo, Angola and Sierra Leone—where rebels and government forces chalk up victories based on a body count of civilians and then best feet for the bush. Instead, the Eritrea/Ethiopia war is being fought in the desolate, mountainous desert regions along the border where, if you believe either side, thousands of soldiers die in a

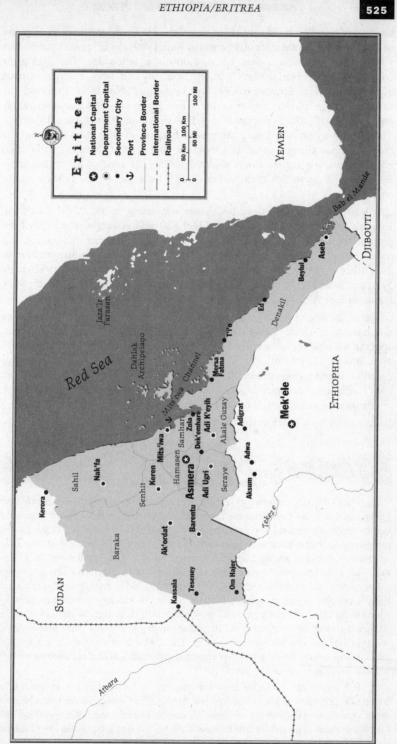

single, daylong assault. The war here makes the Maginot Line seem like a menu of champagnes. In one three-day period in June 1999, the Eritreans claimed that 4,000 Ethiopian soldiers were killed, 2,000 in a single day. The Ethiopians counted 8,000 Eritrean soldiers "out of action." By mid-1999, Ethiopia boasted it had put 24,450 Eritrean troops "out of action." Not to be outdone, the Eritrean foreign ministry announced that Eritrean forces had killed a seemingly preposterous 18,000 Ethiopian troops between June 10 and June 16, 1999. There's no way of ascertaining the precise figures—as both sides scoop up the corpses before giving journalists a look-see—but tens of thousands have been killed on the war's three fronts since May '98. The conflict has forced some 500,000 civilians to flee their homes while 3 or 4 million are facing drought conditions.

At least 70,000 troops from both sides are duking it out in the wasteland. Ethiopia recently purchased six MiG-23s at $20 million a copy, which have been pummeling Eritrea's coastal city of Assab. The artillery barrages are constant. In a number of places along the front, the opposing armies are but 50 meters from each other. Fighting moves from hill to hill. There aren't any jungles to hide in. Each side scrambles to cop as much craggy real estate as possible before the rainy season in East Africa makes fighting virtually impossible.

Like in the rest of Africa, the UN has kept the Eritrea/Ethiopia war at a safe distance. After Uncle Sam's debacle in Somalia in '93, there's been no real appetite for sending white folks (or black guys dressed up like white folks) with guns into the Dark Continent, for any reason. Though the Security Council has called for the implementation of an 11-point peace plan that would push Eritrea back to the soil it occupied before May 6, 1998, there doesn't seem to be much enthusiasm on either party's behalf to sign it.

The real plan for peace in the Horn of Africa, it appears, is in the clouds.

Laid-back Eritrea kicked back with seven years of peace before and after independence from Ethiopia in 1993, but then threw the first punch in May 1998 in what briefly became the world's largest conventional war, involving perhaps a half-million troops and all the goodies that go into creating mass carnage. Eritrea says it's reclaiming territory rightfully its own. Ethiopia says this fratricidal war was born from economic jealousy. The current war is like a binge alcoholic—a guy who spends a week murdering millions of brain cells, then sobers up a month before repeating the scene. More than 60,000 (perhaps 100,000 by press time) ethnic Eritreans living in Ethiopia—mostly pregnant women, the elderly, children and the sick—have been deported to Eritrea as a "security measure," huge numbers of them never having set foot in the country. But maybe it's better than the alternative—staying in Ethiopia. More than 5 million people in Ethiopia are at risk from a new famine. The UN has been trying to dig up a cool $50 million to nip it in the bud. But they don't have too many takers, as long as Ethiopia continues to spend $1 million a day on the war effort.

The only serious external backer in the war appears to be Libya, which has reportedly been training Eritrean pilots and funneling arms into Asmara. The Colonel just can't keep his paws out of a good game of African musical chairs. Meanwhile, Eritrea's capital of Asmara is still laid-back, going about its business of little business. Cafés line the seaside esplanades like a Mediterranean Riviera town. Journalists are shuttled to the front lines and get back in the evening in time for a couple of cold ones. The only thing different is you don't see a lot of guys around old enough to shoot a gun. Sounds like Nice in 1916.

Prime Minister Meles Zenawi, the Tigray People's Liberation Front (TPLF) and the Ethiopians

Zenawi was born in 1955 in Tigray and spent a few years at medical school in Addis Ababa before founding the TPLF in 1975. For 16 years, he battled Ethiopian dictator Mengistu Haile Mariam, and became chairman of the Ethiopian People's Revolutionary Democratic Front (EPRDF), a coalition of rebels battling the Ethiopian dictatorship, in 1989. On May 28, 1991, the EPRDF sent Mengistu packing for a distant villa. Zenawi became prime minister on August 23, 1995. He has been hailed as a renaissance man by Washington for leading Ethiopia down a road to peace and democracy during his reign, a model African leader representing stability in the Horn. But Zenawi also holds the dubious distinction as one of the Committee to Protect Journalists' (CPJ) Ten Enemies of the Press. Behind the George Washington exterior, some see an autocrat bent on suppressing the dissing of his regime. He busted 16 journos in 1997; most of them were held without being charged. And his expulsion of tens of thousands of ethnic Eritreans in 1999 smacks nothing short of ethnic cleansing. But Ethiopia has spun itself as the victim here rather effectively and the West has little stomach to get involved.

Ethiopian Government

www.nicom.com/~ethiopia/ind.htm
http://www.ethiopianembassy.org/

Eritrean Resistance Movement

http://home.swipnet.se/~w-26522/index167.htm

President Isaias Afwerki and the Eritreans

Before the outbreak of war, Afwerki and Zenawi were considered by Ethiopians and Eritreans alike to be brothers, although recently more in the Cain and Abel mold. They are in fact related. And like Zenawi, Isaias was considered to be the model new African renaissance leader, directing his fledgling nation, like neighboring Ethiopia, down a path to peace, stability and democracy. Isaias has had grand plans for Eritrea; he's been trying to mold the small state into Africa's version of Singapore or Hong Kong. His detractors sling mud over his attempts to make Eritrea self-sufficient through a 2 percent tax on the monthly salaries of Eritreans living abroad and by exporting coffee for the Ethiopians. They accuse him of banning all political parties and censoring journalists, and of building concentration camps in Barentu and Sawwa for political opponents. Others point out his close ties with Libyan leader Muammar Qaddafi. He also occupied the Yemeni Hanish Islands in the Red Sea for a couple of years before bowing to an international court decision that the isles did indeed belong to Yemen. He's made enemies with all his neighbors, including Sudan, Djibouti and Ethiopia—and, of course, Yemen across the Red Sea. The Eritrean People's Liberation Front (EPLF) in Eritrea still runs a tighter post revolution ship. Even 53-year-old President Isaias of Eritrea drives himself to work every day.

Eritrean Government

http://eritrea.org
http://www.netafrica.org/eritrea/index.html

Eritrean Government

www.geocities.com/eureka/park/5875/eritrea-ethiopia.html

Libyan Leader Colonel Muammar Qaddafi

Choosing the Ethiopian/Eritrean war after getting his own horns locked in Uganda over the Congo conflict, Libyan leader Colonel Muammar Qaddafi has been dying to put some ink on something now that he's allowed to take airplane rides since handing over the Lockerbie suspects—and although he looks cool dressed up like a cross between Tom Wolfe and Eddie Murphy on the red carpets of African airports, the only treaties he's signing these days are air charter contracts. Qaddafi in 1999 mediated—or meddled—in nearly every schoolyard fight between Pretoria and Khartoum, including bloodbaths in Congo, Sierra Leone and Eritrea—entirely without results. He sent peacekeepers into Uganda to end the war in Congo; they didn't. In July 1999, Qaddafi announced that both sides in the Ethiopia/Eritrea war agreed to an immediate halt to all military operations, ahead of signing a ceasefire. They didn't. Qaddafi was trying to get enough airplane trips in so he could use his frequent flyer miles to get to the annual OAU meeting in Algiers, the first one he's been to in 22 years. It's been so long since Muammar ordered room service that he stayed in a tent outside the conference venue. But you can't blame The Leader. In Libya, shuttle diplomacy for the last 12 years was a fender bender on the road to Zuwarah. No wonder the Colonel has been asking for a window seat these days.

Eritreans

All this ammo and hardware has to be paid for in cash. Military spending is burning up 20 percent of the total budget of the government of Eritrea. Eritreans living overseas are expected to contribute 2 percent of their income to the home country. This foreign aid is expected to raise $400 million.

Ethiopian Oromo Liberation Front (OLF)

The OLF has bases in Somalia's Gedo region and the main base is in Coriolei, 77 miles southwest of Mogadishu. Previously they were found in Kenya, in the Moyale area.

Al Ittihad Al-Islamiya

Ethnic Somali rebels supported by Hussein Aideed and the Somali National Front.

Somalia

Ertirea supports Hussien Aideed and the OLF through Balidogle.

Rahanwein Resistance Army

A Somali group, supported by Ethiopia, opposed to Hussein Aideed.

Kenya

Kenya is now providing troops to fight the OLF rebels. As payback Ethiopian troops attack the Somali forces of Aideed to take some pressure off Kenya. Naturally Aideed went to Muammar in Libya for help. Muammar is a big supporter of Taylor in Liberia and Sankoh in Sierra Leone. Where will it end?

Ethiopia

Passport and visa are required. A U.S. passport must be valid for three months beyond the intended stay. A visa for both tourist and business travel is valid for three months after issue for a stay of not more than 30 days. One passport photograph is required, along with a yellow fever vaccination certificate (if arriving from infected area within five days) and a copy of round-trip airline tickets. The consular fee is $70 per visa. Apply at:

Ethiopian Embassy

2134 Kalorama Road, NW
Washington, DC 20008

Tel.: (202) 234-2281/2
Fax: (202) 483-8407

The U.S. State Department issued a travel warning on April 21, 1999, advising U.S. citizens to defer all travel to Ethiopia due to the fighting with Eritrea.

Eritrea

Passport and visa are required. A U.S. passport must be valid for six months beyond intended stay. A visa for both tourist and business travel is valid for three months after issue for a stay of not more than 30 days. One passport photograph is required, plus a yellow fever vaccination certificate (if arriving from infected area within five days) and a copy of round-trip airline tickets. The consular fee is $25 per visa (single entry) and $30 (multiple entry). Multiple entry visas are not always granted, and to get one you'll need to include a letter why you need it. Business travelers need to compose a "business letter of responsibility" typed out on company letterhead explaining the purpose of the trip and a guarantee of financial support. Apply at:

Embassy of Eritrea

1708 New Hampshire Ave., NW
Washington, DC 20009
Tel.: (202) 319-1991
Fax: (202) 319-1304

Although Eritrea has re-established normalized relations with Sudan, overland travel between the two countries can be hazardous. In November 1998, Djibouti severed relations with Eritrea in response to the war with Ethiopia. The border areas are highly volatile. Don't even think about it. Djibouti also suspended all air service to Asmara by Djiboutian air carriers.

The U.S. State Department issued a travel warning on June 15, 1999, advising U.S. citizens against travel to Eritrea due to the fighting with Ethiopia. U.S. embassy personnel who were evacuated after the war broke out have been authorized to return to Asmara, but the U.S. government has not allowed the return of children of U.S. embassy employees.

Ethiopia possesses 28,500 kilometers of roads, with about 4300 kilometers of them paved. The Ethiopian segment of the Addis Ababa/Djibouti railroad line is 681 kilometers long. There are 10 airports with paved runways, 76 others unpaved. Sounds like it should be pretty easy to get around. It's not. The train is excruciatingly slow, as are the buses. In the boonies, you can hail the buses from alongside the major roads. In the cities, tickets need to be purchased a day ahead of time. Flying is the best bet. Ethiopian Airlines isn't entirely dismal and has a good internal network. It's also cheap.

Eritrea is even tougher to get around, but there's not as much to get around. Taxis will make the trip from Asmara to the front lines for a price. There are only some 5 kilometers of operating railway in Eritrea. And bombing Eritrea's airports at Asmara and Assab has become trendy with the Ethiopians.

Ethiopian/Eritrean Border

With Ethiopian tank commanders pretending to be Rommel driving Kugelwagons, all border areas with Eritrea should be avoided. Make a wide tack from security operations and do not try to intercede with police on behalf of Eritreans or anyone else. Armed attacks, targeting foreigners, have occurred in Ethiopia throughout the past year. Avoid travel to the Tigray region or that part of the Afar region bordering Eritrea. Think twice before visiting public places such as markets, restaurants, bars, nightclubs and hotel lobbies and stay away from these places as much as possible. It is best to stay at larger hotels that offer better security. Particularly nasty areas in the country are Harar and Dire Dawa, as well as the Somali region and the Bale Zone of the Oromiya region. In Addis Ababa, three coordinated grenade attacks against public places killed one Ethiopian and injured numerous people, including several foreigners. A few years back bombs at the government-owned Ghion and Wabe Shabelle Hotels killed five Ethiopians and wounded numerous Ethiopians and foreigners. In southern Ethiopia, along the Kenyan border, reports of banditry are not uncommon. Isolated incidents of violence have occurred in the vicinity of Lake Langano and Awassa. In eastern Ethiopia, two foreigners were killed and one wounded in daylight shooting incidents in Dire Dawa. A year later a grenade attack at a hotel in Harar wounded five foreign nationals. In several of these incidents, the attacks appear to have targeted foreigners. Since the mid-1990s, there have also been several clashes between various opposition elements and government forces around Harar and in the Somali Regional State, particularly near the border with Somalia. The Awash-Mile Road has been the site of shootings, apparently by bandits operating at night or the predawn hours. In western Ethiopia, military units have skirmished on rare occasion with forces alleged to be of the Oromo Liberation Front (OLF) in the vicinity of Nekemte. The westernmost tip of the Gambella region is subject to political violence originating from Sudan and interethnic conflict.

In Eritrea, the border between Eritrea and Sudan is also tense, and there have been occasional reports of Sudanese aircraft making bombing runs in border areas. In addition, there is a risk of encountering banditry or Eritrean Islamic Salvation (EIS), formally called the Eritrean Islamic Jihad, terrorist activity near the Eritrean-Sudanese border in areas north and west of the road between Keren and Barentu, and along the coastline north of Massawa. EIS insurgents have laid new land mines and EIS attacks have occurred in these areas. Bandits unrelated to the EIS prey the coastline south of Massawa.

Ethiopia

Land Mines

While travel on paved and unpaved roads is generally considered safe, land mines and other antipersonnel devices can be encountered on isolated dirt roads that were targeted during Ethiopia's civil war.

Being a Journalist

Journalists are routinely arrested in Ethiopia for criticizing the government. Prime Minister Zenawi makes no bones about his feelings for reporters, who have awarded him a slot on the Committee to Protect Journalists' (CPJ) Ten Enemies of the Press list. Zenawi arrested 16 journalists in 1997. Most busted reporters are never charged.

Flying a Plane

On August 29, 1999, Ethiopians shot down a civilian N35OJF Lear Jet for flying 25 miles in from the Eritrean border. The English pilot and Swedish copilot died in the crash. The plane was owned by Execujet Aviation Group and was being flown to South Africa from a fueling stop in Luxor, Egypt. The pilots had cleared their flight plan with Ethiopian, Eritrean and Djibouti airspace personnel before taking off.

Photo Albums

Bridges, dams, military installations and certain buildings and public places may not be photographed, but such sites are rarely clearly marked. Travel guides, police, and Ethiopian officials can advise if a particular site may be photographed. Photographing prohibited sites may result in the confiscation of film and camera.

Eritrea

Land Mines

Land mines and unexploded ordnance litter the countryside in many areas and continue to cause injuries and deaths. Although a demining effort is underway, it is wise to consider all areas that are not well traveled as potentially dangerous due to live mines. Areas north and west of Keren are known to be heavily mined.

Ethiopia

Ethiopia isn't Kansas. Yellow fever vaccinations are compulsory, and the country has more than its fair share of AIDS, malaria, parasites, contaminated drinking water and bilharzia—not to mention land mines.

Medical facilities in Ethiopia are extremely limited. Although physicians are generally well trained, even the best hospitals in Addis Ababa suffer from inadequate facilities, antiquated equipment and shortages of supplies (particularly medicine). Emergency assistance is limited. Serious medical problems requiring hospitalization and/or medical evacuation to the United States can cost thousands of dollars or more. Travelers must bring their own supplies of prescription drugs and preventative medicines. Doctors and hospitals often expect immediate cash payment for health services. The Medicare/Medicaid program does not provide for payment of medical services outside the United States. Please check with your own insurance company to confirm whether your policy applies overseas, including provision for medical evacuation. Please ascertain whether payment will be made to the overseas hospital or doctor, or whether you will be reimbursed later for expenses that you incur. Some insurance policies also include coverage for psychiatric treatment and for disposition of remains in the event of death. Travelers to Ethiopia are strongly urged to consider supplemental medical/travelers' insurance because these policies are inexpensive when compared to the costs of a medical evacuation.

Eritrea

Medical facilities in Eritrea are extremely limited. Serious medical problems requiring hospitalization and/or medical evacuation to the United States can cost thousands of dollars or more. Travelers must bring their own supplies of prescription drugs and preventative medicines. Doctors and hospitals often expect immediate cash payment for health services. The Medicare/Medicaid program does not provide for payment of medical services outside the United States. Check with your own insurance company to confirm whether your policy applies overseas, including provision for medical evacuation. Ascertain whether payment will be made to the overseas hospital or doctor, or whether you will be reimbursed later for expenses you incur. Some insurance policies also include coverage for psychiatric treatment and for disposition of remains in the event of death.

Ethiopia

Ethiopia is nearly twice the size of Texas but landlocked since Eritrean independence on May 24, 1993. The population is 58.5 million and Ethiopians can expect to live to a whopping 40 years old. Fifty percent of the population is Muslim, while about 40 percent are Ethiopian Orthodox. Animist and other religions comprise the balance. The official language is Amharic, while English is the major foreign language taught in schools and is used extensively. The Oromo make up 40 percent of Ethiopia's population; Amhara and Tigrean people comprise another 32 percent.

Per capita annual income is even lower than in Eritrea, at $530. Ethiopia is one of the poorest countries in the world. How poor is it? Ethiopia ranks 172 out of 174 countries for life expectancy, health care, education and income. Only Sierra Leone and Niger are ranked lower. Its currency, the birr, is pegged to the U.S. dollar (US$1 = 5.000 birr). Ethiopia's major exports include coffee, leather goods and gold, which formerly left the country via Eritrea's ports of Assab and Massawa, but those links have been cut off since the current conflict began. Ethiopia has a total of ten airports with paved runways and 4,300 kilometers of paved roadways.

Eritrea

Eritrea is just a little larger than the state of Pennsylvania and borders the Red Sea between Djibouti and Sudan. Another southerly neighbor is its good buddy Ethiopia. The Red Sea is one of the world's busiest shipping lanes. The climate is hot and dry and there are frequent droughts. The infrastructure, what little of it was there to begin with, has been decimated by civil war, and the conflict with Ethiopia doesn't help. Eritrea also suffers from deforestation, soil erosion and overgrazing. The population is 3.85 million, made up of ethnic Tigrinya (50 percent), Tigre and Kunama (40 percent), Afar (4 percent) and Saho people (3 percent), and is a blend of Muslims, Coptic Christians, Roman Catholics and Protestants. The major languages are Afar, Amharic, Arabic, Tigre and Kunama.

The average annual income for Eritreans is a miserable $600, making Eritrea one of the poorest countries in Africa, if not the world. Before the war, Ethiopia accounted for nearly 70 percent of total exports. In 1997, Eritrea introduced its own currency, the nafka; about 7.5 nafka equal one U.S. dollar.

Embassy Locations

The U.S. Embassy in Ethiopia (Addis Ababa)

Entoto Ave.
P.O. Box 1014
Addis Ababa
Tel.: (251-1) 550-666, ext. 316/336
Fax: (251-1) 551-094

The U.S. Embassy in Eritrea (Asmara)

Franklin Roosevelt Street
P.O. Box 211
Asmara
Tel.: (291-1) 12-00-04
Fax: (291-1) 12-75-84

Web Resources

Eritrea groups opposed to the Eritrean government

Eritrean Liberation Front—Revolutionary Council—Part of the Eritrean National Alliance

http://home.erols.com/meskerem/eritrea.htm

Eritrean Islamic Jihad Movement
http://www.webstorage.com/~azzam/html/jihad_in_ogadin.html
Eritrea Online
http://www.primenet.com/~ephrem/body.html
Tigrian Alliance for National Democracy
http://members.aol.com/alpha6986/tand/tigrian.html
Voice of the Oromo Liberation
http://www.visafric.com/Dimtsi_hafash.htm
United Front of Ethiopians
http://www.ethiopia.org

7/1/99	Libyan leader Muammar Qaddafi erroneously announces that Eritrea and Ethiopia have agreed to a peace deal.
5/6/98	Eritrea invades disputed territory in the Badme triangle.
11/97	Eritrea introduces its own currency, the nafka, replacing the Ethiopian currency, the birr.
12/94	New constitution is promulgated in Ethiopia.
5/24/93	Eritrea gains independence from Ethiopia.
4/27/93	Eritrean independence is proclaimed after landslide vote in independence referendum.
5/29/91	Isaias announces the formation of a provisional government in Eritrea.
5/28/91	Ethiopian People's Revolutionary Democratic Front topples the government of dictator Mengistu Haile Mariam, setting up the prospects for Eritrean independence.

India
★★★

Kashmir Sweat

It is a miracle that India even exists. Being a powerhouse nation of just under a billion people with so many ethnicities and religions, it should have ripped itself into a bunch of dinky fiefdoms long ago, each with hundreds of years of history, separate religions, dialects and customs. Like a terminally ill patient, India deals with the ugliest boils and rashes first. Its big problems are in the extreme south with the Tamil Tigers, and in the north with Sikh, Muslim and tribal separatists. Every time a bomb goes off (and they go off a lot), the suspects include Indians, Pakistani agents, Kashmiri separatists, Sikh terrorists, Maoist tribal rebels, Tamil Eelam guerrillas, Muslim militants, drug traffickers and even gangsters. Mother Teresa was the only one exempt from suspicion. And she's dead.

India bristles at its colonial-made borders, complete with equally belligerent neighbors like China, Pakistan and Myanmar. Although the core of India has the gray industrious bustling of a Third World country, its borders are very much warring outposts complete with bunkers, artillery duels, terrorists raids and MiG-21s.

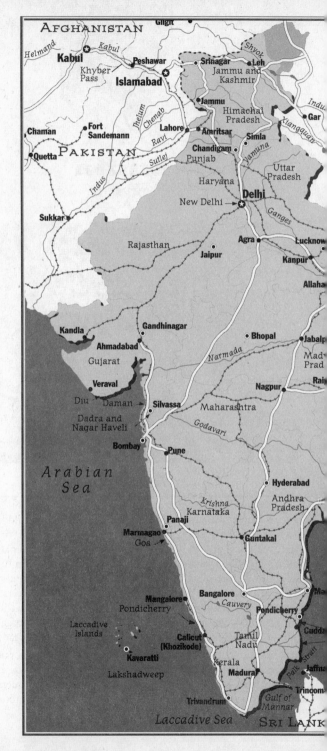

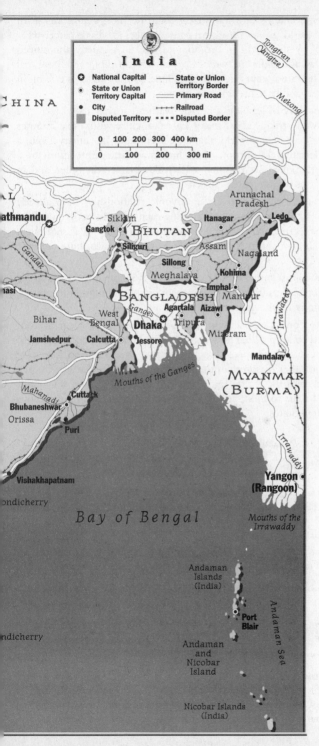

India

Legend:
- ⊗ National Capital
- ⊙ State or Union Territory Capital
- • City
- ▮ Disputed Territory
- —— State or Union Territory Border
- Primary Road
- +–+–+ Railroad
- ▪▪▪▪ Disputed Border

| 0 | 100 | 200 | 300 | 400 km |
| 0 | 100 | 200 | 300 mi |

CHINA

Tongtran Qangtze

Mekong

Arunachal Pradesh

athmandu

Sikkim
Gangtok
BHUTAN
Siliguri

Itanagar
Ledo

Assam

Nagaland

Sillong
Meghalaya
Kohima

Gandak

Imphal
Manipur

asi

BANGLADESH

Ganges
Agartala
Aizawl

Bihar
West Bengal
Dhaka
Tripura

Jamshedpur
Calcutta
Jessore

Mizeram

Mandalay

Mouths of the Ganges

MYANMAR
(BURMA)

Mahanadi
Cuttack

Bhubaneshwar
Orissa
Puri

Irrawaddy

Vishakhapatnam

ondicherry

Yangon
(Rangoon)

Bay of Bengal

Mouths of the Irrawaddy

Andaman Islands
(India)

Andaman Sea

Port Blair

ndicherry

Andaman
and
Nicobar
Island

Nicobar Islands
(India)

One of the ugliest scenarios on the horizon could be India's nuke race with Pakistan. While the world ignores the global consequences of what is perceived as a Hatfield-and-McCoy stick fight in the boonies, the CIA quietly announced recently that Pakistan and India are two of the planet's top choices for potential serious instability. It is a war kept out of the headlines as the two sides face off in high altitude bunkers and have firefights on glaciers.

India has the capability of lobbing a nuclear warhead within 1,000 feet of a target 150 miles away, striking most major Pakistani cities within five minutes after launch. In this part of the world, that's close enough. In January 1996, a mosque in the Pakistani-held portion of Kashmir was turned into mush by a conventional rocket; it killed 20 worshipers. Each side blamed the other, and an artillery and small arms squash match ensued.

India and Pakistan, in their relatively embryonic relationship, have already fought three wars. Pakistan has gone home crying each time. In between official wars both countries recruit, train and field separatist extremists—Pakistan funds the nasties in the Indian-controlled region of Kashmir, while India fans the flames of hatred in Pakistan's Sind area.

In the tortured northeast, tribal groups based deep in jungle hideouts fight for freedom and to keep settlers from drowning them out. Bombings, kidnappings, riots and assassinations are the general tone.

Not one to miss out on a gang banging, China is also part of India's multifront diplomatic fray. Just to keep China honest, India fought a brief border war with the Sinos back in 1962. Since then, though, the two countries' relations have improved—if for no other reason than their mutual respect for the size of each others' populations, and the realization that a conventional ground war might take a few hundred years to fight, and still leave each country with populations the size of the United States.

India is a relatively safe country with some nasty exceptions. Breathing, driving and hiking can quickly end your life here. Long famous for being one of the dirtiest, most overcrowded countries in the world, travelers now visit the far-flung and scenic regions of Kashmir or the northeast to escape the troubles.

Those who see the traditional sites should be forewarned by the roadside spectacle of mangled buses, lorries and people. India has the most dangerous road system in the world.

The Indian Army

The Indian military has about 1.3 million personnel, making it the fourth largest in the world. About half of them are posted in Kashmir. It is the largest force India has ever fielded against a secessionist rebellion. The Indian government subscribes to the domino theory: If Kashmir is allowed to break away from India, other parts of the country with separatist groups would follow and India would exist no longer. To battle its numerous insurgencies, the government will be establishing a counter-insurgency force of 60,000 troops, the largest of its kind in the world. The move comes after India reassessed its security threats, determining (finally) that its most dangerous enemies are not Pakistan and China—but domestic rebels. Currently, internal problems are handled by India's paramilitary forces totaling around 600,000.

Indian Army
http://armedforces.nic.in/

Indian Army in Kashmir
http://www.armyinkashmir.org/

Recruitment Page
http://www.subcontinent.com/indianarmy/index.html

Prime Minister of India
South Block
New Delhi, India 100 001
Fax: (91) 11-301-0700

Kashmir

In the disputed northern state of Jammu and Kashmir, more than 25,000 people have died just in the last nine years. Indian military estimates there are around 2,500 Pakistani-supported mujahedin in the region.

Pakistan's Inter Services Intelligence (ISI)

India's biggest thorn in their side. This is Pakistan's slightly more militarized and crudely transparent version of the CIA. They are no less obvious in their activities than our corn-fed, tow-headed operatives in short sleeved checkered shirts from J.C. Penney.

The Directorate for ISI was founded in 1948 by British army officer, Major General R. Cawthome, then deputy chief of staff in the Pakistan army. After the British left, the president of Pakistan (Field Marshal Ayub Khan) expanded the role of the ISI in maintaining military rule in Pakistan. This included monitoring opposition politicians. It is a testament to the ISI efficiency that when Prime Minister Shariz made noises about shutting down the ISI training camps, he suddenly found himself without a job and the military in charge. Staffed by hundreds of civilian and military officers, and thousands of other workers, the agency's headquarters is located in Islamabad. The ISI has about 10,000 officers and staff members. The ISI began using militants in Kashmir under President Zia Ul Haq in 1988. They are not just busy in Kashmir but in helping the Taliban in Afghanistan, in Koyalapattinam, a village in Tamil Nadu, supporting the Liberation Tigers, operating training camps near the border of Bangladesh training groups to fight in the northeastern states (United Liberation Front of Seven Sisters [ULFOSS]), National Security Council of Nagaland (NSCN), People's Liberation Army (PLA), United Liberation Front of Assam (ULFA), and North East Students Organization (NESO). The ISI is said to have intensified its activities in the southern Indian states of Hyderabad, Bangalore, Cochin, Kojhikode, Bhatkal, and Gulbarga. They are also supporting groups in Andhra Pradesh like the Ittehadul Musalmeen and the Hijbul mujahedin. They are also accused of training and supplying Uighur fighters in Xianjang province in Western China. They currently train and support at least six different groups in Kashmir totaling 5,000 to 10,000 fighters.

http://www.fas.org/irp/world/pakistan/isi/index.html

The Jammu and Kashmir Liberation Front (JKLF)

The leader of the local JKLF is Halil Hyder, and its headquarters is in Anantnag, 44 miles from Srinagar. It has been fighting since 1990. Founded in 1977 and led by President Yasin Malik, the JKLF wants to make Muslim Kashmir independent from Hindu India. The ball got rolling in 1988 when one of the leaders, Amanullah Khan, got together with the Srinagar-based Islamic Students League. They typically plant bombs and engage in antigovernment activities.

Amanullah Khan

Jammu Kashmir Liberation Front
Lower Plate
Muzafferabad
Azad Kashmir, Pakistan
Fax: (92) 058-2504
E-mail: jklf@isb.comsats.net.pk

Harkat-ul-Mujahedin (HUM)/ Harkat-ul-Ansar (HUA)

The Harkat-ul-Ansar (HUA) of Pakistan started in central Punjab in Pakistan in the early 1980s under the name the Harkat-ul-Mujahedin (HUM) with headquarters at Raiwind in Punjab.

HUA chief Parvez Ahmad Gazi was popped by Border Security Force troopers in May, as was new HUA head Peer Baba. And Sanaullah's predecessor, HUA Supreme Commander Arif Hussain Sheikh, was whacked in a cross fire between police and separatists on March 17, 1997. HUA is the union of Harakat ul-Jihad and Harakat ul-Mujahedin. The leader is Maulana Saadatullah Khan (until of course he gets popped). HUA is the main recruiter and trainer (with help from the Pakistani Secret Service) of young Kashmiri's and out of work mujahedin from Pakistan. If you are looking for mujahedin time to add to your resume, they will train you for five weeks in the dark arts of light weapons, land mines, booby traps and covert operations and then send you marching over the mountains to raise havoc in Indian-occupied Kashmir. The group is also known for sending eager fighters into Bosnia (all gone home now), Tajikistan (Tajik resistance), Myanmar (training Muslim rebels in the Arakan mountains) and other Muslim holy wars. They have become sort of a Burger King jihad around the world. They also provide much needed medical, food and other relief besides military. And you should know that HUM has banned any U.S. citizens from visiting Kashmir.

Hizbul Mujahedin (Fighters for the Party of God)

The new players and leaders of Kashmir's struggle for independence are now the largest military force against the Indian government.

Syeed Salahuddin, whose real name is Syeed Mohammed Yusuf Shah, is the commander of the Hizbul Mujahedin. It receives financial backing and support from Pakistan. Pakistan's prime minister Benazir Bhutto wants the Muslim majority states of Jammu and Kashmir out of Hindu-dominated India and aligned with Pakistan. The rebels claim they are fighting for *azad* Kashmir, or free Kashmir. Currently, there are about 15,000 active rebel fighters with several subfactions among them. The rebels operate in small hit-and-run groups in cities like Srinagar, or from remote bases in Kashmir. Pakistan has fought two out of three of its last wars over Kashmir, and the situation is expected to remain tense for years to come. The geopolitical volleyball started when Britain sliced up India and Pakistan in 1947, based on geographic divisions rather than religious ones. At the time, India promised to hold a plebiscite among all Kashmiris to determine whether the territory should be part of India or Pakistan. It backed down, and the conflict has been going on ever since.

All-Party Hurriyat (Freedom) Conference

This is an alliance formed by the numerous guerrillas who use secession from India as a common rallying point. Omar Farooq is the leader of the All-Party Hurriyat Conference, the umbrella group formed of 32 rebel organizations. Farooq is also the hereditary Mir Waiz of Kashmir, the religious leader of the region's Muslims. The losers seem to be the Hindus of the region. At last count, there were about 400,000 Hindu refugees from the Kashmir Valley in refugee camps around the state's winter capital of Jammu.

All-Party Hurriyat Conference (APHC)

Mirwaiz Manzil
Rajauri Kadal
Srinagar, Jammu and Kashmir

Jamiat ul-Mujahedin (JUM)

The JUM is a pro-Pakistan Muslim separatist group known for its bombings in Jammu and Kashmir states in northeastern India. Its leader, "Supreme Commander" Ghulam Rasool Shah, was arrested in June 1997. The JUM takes its directions from Pakistan's Inter Service Intelligence (ISI), claim Indian officials. New Delhi accuses Pakistan of fighting a proxy war against India by arming and training separatist groups such as the JUM, charges the U.S. State Department generally concurs with.

Bit Players: Al Umar/ Al Barq/ Muslim Janbaz Forc/ Lashkar-e Toib /al Faran

These groups are mostly Afghans sent in to raise havoc by the ISI with the help of Hezbi Islami and other fundamentalist groups inside Afghanistan and Pakistan. Al Faran was a nom de guerre of Afghans who took Western trekkers hostage and then killed them after a shoot-out.

The Northeast

Naxalites

The various radical communist groups all are descended from the armed peasants who operated in the 1960s under the banner of "Naxalites." They take their name from the Naxalbari, or "chicken neck," the strategic 20-kilometer stretch of land running between Nepal and Bangladesh.

http://www.hrw.org/reports/1999/india/India994-06.htm

Asamese: United Liberation Front of Assam (ULFA)

Assam supplies half of India's oil and 15 percent of the world's tea, but its people have nothing to show for it. The ULFA, drawn from the ranks of those who call themselves Asamese, was supposed to cede its fight for a socialist state in Assam when it signed a peace deal with the government in January 1992. The hard-liners said "screw that" and began a campaign of kidnapping and extortion against the rich tea growers. The Indian Tea Association quickly put together a 7,000-man private army to protect itself from ULFA thugs. Their bases are in Bhutan.

There have been reports of large-scale extortion and attacks on police stations throughout Assam by both ULFA and the National Democratic Front of Bodoland (NDFB), formerly called the Bodo Security Force. Security forces have stepped up their operations against the militants and rounded up large numbers of both suspects and weapons. Assam state officials, however, are hoping that the government in New Delhi will send in a paramilitary force to end the rebels' kidnappings. For now, Assam is an especially dangerous place if you grow tea. Crumpets, anyone?

http://www.uptontea.com/ta.htm

The Bodos/ National Democratic Front of Bodoland and the Bodoland Liberation Tiger Force

The Bodos comprise some 800,000 people out of Assam's 25 million inhabitants. Bodo tribals living in northwest Assam between the north bank of the Brahmaputra River and the foothills of the Himalayas for 30 years have been duking it out with the Bengali Hindus and the Indian government for a homeland that would split the state in two. The Bodos are pissed at the swarms of Bengali immigrants that have settled on their traditional tribal lands over the past 20 years, as well as the wholesale raping of the environment by illegal loggers. They like to chop up Bengali villagers and blow things up (trains, bridges, etc.). The struggle became truly violent, however, only after 1985. The Bodos claim some 1,200 of their people were slaughtered by Indian security forces before the 1993 autonomy agreement. The pact was never carried out by the government and the Bodos renounced it in 1996. However, the Bodos are divided by factionalism. The National Democratic Front of Bodoland (NDFB) and the Bodoland Liberation Tiger Force (BLTF) have been hacking up each other with as much fervor as they do immigrants and government security forces. Some 5,500 people have been killed in the insurgency since 1987. Their bases are in Bhutan.

http://www.assamtribune.com/

The Nagas/ the National Socialist Council of Nagaland

The radical Naga movement is considered the godfather of India's rebel factions and includes groups such as the National Socialist Council of Nagaland (NSCN), known for its massacres of civilians, namely ethnic Kukis. Naga militants are fighting for a separate homeland composed of Nagaland (in the northeast) and areas in adjacent states where Nagas have settled. Nagas in both Nagaland and adjacent Manipur charge that ethnic Kukis have settled on ancestral Naga land. The bloodbath in the northeast continues unabated. Other groups include United National Liberation Front of Manipur and the National Democratic Front of Tripura.

http://www.assam.org/assam/

East/Center

Maoist Peoples War Group and the Maoist Communist Center

The Scheduled Tribes, also known as *adivasis* (the original inhabitants), are about 500 tribes who were here before the Aryans arrived in 1500 B.C. The Maoist Peoples War Group (PWG) and the Maoist Communist Center (MCC) are just some of the hard-line Maoist groups that raise hell in and around Bihar. They want the Indian government to take land from the rich and distribute it to the poor. Obviously they didn't pay attention in history class. Guerrillas of the PWG concentrate their attacks in Andhra Pradesh and Bihar targeting cops and government officials, using homemade, remote-controlled land mines. The group also operates throughout the Dandakaranya region straddling four states: Orissa, Maharashtra, Madhya Pradesh and Andhra Pradesh.

Ranvir Sena

Ranvir Sena is a death squad bankrolled by landowners. There has been a two-decade war between land owners and communist groups who seek land reform. Ranvir Sena, a militia group formed by upper-caste landlords, often clashes with the Peoples War Group (PWG), the military arm of the Communist Party of India, over issues relating to the redistribution of land to the poor. Ranvir Sena has not been known to target foreigners and only kills peasants in remote villages. Their main targets are supporters of the Communist Party of India/Marxist-Leninist (CPI/ML), usually shot while they sleep. They also attack members of the Maoist Communist Center (MCC) a faction of the predominately lower-caste Peoples War Group. To date over 25,000 people have been killed since 1990.

Punjab

The Sikhs

The Sikhs want their own turf, and India doesn't want them to have it. They are led by Sohan Singh, a 78-year-old doctor who was captured by the Indian government in November of 1993. Typically proud and bellicose, a small segment of Sikhs wants to establish an independent homeland called Khalistan, or Land of the Pure. The Sikhs target security forces and other government symbols in their bomb attacks. The problem is that the bombs, although they may lean left or right, don't have political affiliations— and kill a lot of innocent people. Sikhs comprise only 2 percent of India's population, but they are a majority in Punjab state. The center of the Sikh terrorist movement is in the capital of Punjab, Chandigarh. Pakistan is sympathetic to the Sikh movement. Although the Indian government claims that the movement has been shrinking since its leader was captured, there are still a lot of angry bad boys in turbans with the last name of Singh (all Sikhs carry the name Singh, meaning "lion").

Khalistan Affairs Center
851 National Press Bldg.
Washington, DC 20045
Tel.: (202) 637-9210
Fax: (202) 6379211
E-mail: kac@cyberspace.org
Web site: khanda.unl.edu:80/~sikhism/kac

Police Chief Kunwar Pal Singh Gill

What was India's answer to putting down the Sikh rebellion? They hired a poet. But you won't find Gill giving readings at a gay encounter session in the East Village any time soon. Gill's the kinda guy who loves the smell of napalm in the morning. The Indian government gave him carte blanche for whacking rebel Sikhs in the '80s, and he cashed in. He turned a force of nervous flatfoots into a death machine. He handed out promotions and cash prizes for corpses without asking for evidence of guilt. Gill has retired, but the lawlessness he created in Punjab hasn't. Gill is still active, though, accusing Amnesty International of being a pro-separatist front.

A passport and visa (which must be obtained in advance) are required for entry into India for tourism or business. Visas range from 15 days to six months and can be had in single-entry or multi-entry versions. The only visa extendable is the six-month version. Evidence of yellow fever immunization is needed if the traveler is arriving from an infected area. Convicted drug offenders in India can expect a minimum jail sentence of ten years and heavy fines. Indian customs authorities strictly enforce the laws and regulations governing the declaration, importation or possession of gold and gold objects. Travelers have sometimes been detained for possession of undeclared gold objects. For further entry information, the traveler can contact the following:

Embassy of India

2536 Massachusetts Avenue, NW
Washington, DC 20008
Tel.: (202) 939-7000, 939-9849 or (202) 939-9806
Or contact the Indian consulates in Chicago, New York and San Francisco.

Bombay International Airport is a 45- to 60-minute car ride from Bombay and about 23 miles northwest of the city. There is a departure tax of US$10 for international flights, US$3 for Southwest Asian flights.

Between India and Nepal, border crossings are open at Biranj-Raxaul, Kakarbhitta-Siliguri and Sunauli-Gorakhpur. Sunauli is the best entry point if coming from Kathmandu to Delhi or elsewhere in northwestern India. Overland travel between Dhaka and Calcutta is possible. The only border checkpoint open with Pakistan is Lahore-Amritsar. This crossing can also be made by train.

The major airports in India are at Bombay (Mumbai) and Delhi. Other international flights arrive at Madras and Calcutta. A taxi from the airport to the center of New Delhi runs about Rs150. In Bombay it will cost you Rs170 and takes about an hour; in Calcutta, about Rs120. You can prepay in New Delhi and Bombay, but drivers will haggle a fixed price with tourists.

Indian Airlines has an extensive network inside India. In addition to the four international airports, 115 other airports serve domestic routes. The international carrier, Air India, also runs some domestic flights. These folks are facing some competition these days from upstarts Jet Airways and Sahara Indian Airlines.

The size of the railway network was estimated at approximately 63,900 kilometers (37,850 miles) in 1990. India's railway network is the largest in Asia and the second largest in the world. The rail system is the lifeblood of the Indian people. There are a number of different classes of trains—and the reservation system can be confusing for all classes. Foreign visitors can take advantage of the tourist quota allotment. Train passengers have been subjected to robberies and schedule disruptions due to protest actions. There are six classes of bus service—from ordinary to deluxe sleeper. The private buses tend to be faster and more comfortable than the state buses. Travel by road after dark is not recommended.

Restricted Areas

Permission from the Indian government (from Indian diplomatic missions abroad, or in some cases, from the Ministry of Home Affairs) is required to visit the states of Mizoram, Manipur, Nagaland, Meghalaya, Assam, Tripura, Arunachal Pradesh, Sikkim, parts of Kulu district and Spiti district of Himachal Pradesh, border areas of Jammu and Kashmir, areas of Uttar Pradesh, the area west of National Highway 15 running from Ganganagar to Sanchar in Rajasthan, the Andaman and Nicobar Islands and the Union Territory of the Laccadive Islands. All are considered dangerous areas except the Andamans and Islands where the government tries to preserve the indigenous people's way of life from the Nikon-equipped eco-yuppies. Oh, before the Andamans were pacified sailors, they ate anyone who washed ashore.

Kashmir

In 1989, the Muslims became violent in opposing Indian rule. There are 6 million people in Kashmir; 4 million of them are Muslim. Since 1989, about 25,000 people, mostly Muslims, have been killed. Half the toll has been civilians. Most of the casualties have been in the Kashmir Valley area around Srinagar. Kashmir is currently divided, with some parts under the control of Pakistan rebels and others under the auspices of the Indian army.

The Kashmir Valley drew 500,000 to 700,000 tourists a year in the 1980s. No more. Now, each week about 50 people lose their lives in Kashmir due to violence. It is even more frightening to know that the executed Norwegian tourist, Hans Ostro, contacted three Indian government tourist offices to inquire about the danger and was told that there were no risks. Terrorist activities and violent civil disturbances continue in the Kashmir Valley in the states of Jammu and Kashmir. There have been incidents in which terrorists have threatened and kidnapped foreigners. Undoubtedly, though, Pakistan is the biggest influence on India's foreign relations. India and Pakistan have duked it out on the battlefield three times since World War II—in 1947, 1965 and 1971. Today, it is very much a hot insurgency fought in a cold place.

Relations between the two became less strained only after Rajiv Gandhi replaced his mother as India's prime minister. In December 1985, Rajiv Gandhi and Pakistan president Mohammed Zia ul-Haq each pledged not to throw the first punch, particularly jabs aimed at the nations' nuke sites. The hot spot is the overlapping area that is known as the line of control. Both India and Pakistan claim an area of the Karakoram mountain range that includes a well armed 50-mile front along the 21,000-foot-high Siachen glacier region. The two countries have established military outposts in the region and armed clashes have occurred. The UN has one of its oldest and smallest field missions here (UNMOGIP). Forty-four South Koreans sit here to monitor how many times the combatants break the 1949 cease-fire agreement. Their job in life is "to observe and report, investigate complaints of cease-fire violations and submit its finding to each party and to the Secretary-General." And then what? The disputed area includes the following peaks: Rimo Peak, Apsarasas I, II and III, Tegam Kangri I, II, and III, Suingri Kangri, Ghaint I and II, Indira Col and Sia Kangri. The line of control was created in July 1972.

Increased violence in Kashmir, the one Indian state where Muslims comprise a majority, has brought about a greater likelihood that the two countries will again go to war. India claims that Pakistan is fueling the flames by encouraging and supporting Kashmir secession from India. Of course, rather than Kashmir becoming an independent entity, Pakistan would like to be the sponge that absorbs it. The Indian governor of Kashmir charged Pakistan in January 1994 with hiring more than 10,000 Afghan mercenaries to help Kashmiri rebels in their efforts against the government. Although media attention has been focused on the kidnapping and execution of only a group of Western hostages, there have been over 2,000 kidnappings since 1991. Half of the victims survive.

UNMOGIP
http://www.un.org/Depts/DPKO/Missions/unmogip.htm
Jammu Kashmir
http://www.jammu-kashmir.com/

Assam and India's Northeast

India's northeast is treated like a rich mother-in-law by New Delhi—hit up for its riches but never invited to dinner. Connected to the rest of India only by a thread, but exploited like a pipeline, India's northeast has been racked by a half-century of separatist insurrection, tribal wars, massacres, terrorism and guerrilla warfare. Little wonder—some 200 aboriginal groups comprise the northeast's population. Every day, someone is killed due to strife in one of the seven northeast states, at least five of which are suffering from violent insurgencies, mostly tribal-based. AIDS and drug smuggling are rampant. The states have been stripped of their oil and tea and have received little in return, spawning separatist groups like the All Tripura Tiger Force, ULFA, the Bodo Liberation Tigers and the National Democratic Front of Bodoland. However, India's "chicken neck"—as the 20-kilometer wide strip of Indian land separating Nepal and Bangladesh is called—doesn't necessarily divide the good guys and the bad guys. The Bodos have been in a slugfest with the Assamese—to protect their language and culture—and even with each other. Meanwhile, Manipur, with a 2,000-year history as a colorful kingdom with a constitution dating from 1180, is better known these days as just another deadly stop along the heroin funnel from Burma. More than 60 people were killed during a single two-week period in July 1997. Most of the killing here is related to the Naga's fight for independence (more than 1,500 people have died in Nagaland alone), the battle for control of Burma's drug smuggling routes and good ol' Hatfield and McCoy shoot-outs. Separatist guerrillas have started enforcing their own antidrug policy: narcotics users are shot in the head after three warnings. In Assam, tea plantation owners are raising a private army of 7,000–8,000 retired soldiers to guard the plantations. The 200 tea estates will also continue to pay protection money to the insurgents.

Punjab and Uttar Pradesh

Separatist violence continues in the Punjab and nearby regions outside Punjab state. Gangs have kidnapped and held for ransom foreign company executives. Militants and robber gangs operate in the area in and around Jim Corbett National Park and Dudhwa

National Park, as well as on roads leading to Hardwar, Rishikesh, Dehra Dun and Mussoorie. The most active and violent have been Sikh militants, who stepped up their attacks in 1997 on thickly populated targets, including transportation depots and marketplaces. The Sikhs are fighting for an independent homeland in Punjab, Khalistan (Land of the Pure). On July 8, 1997, 33 people were killed and 66 injured after a bomb exploded aboard a passenger train in southwestern Punjab state. Since 1984, when Prime Minister Indira Gandhi was blown away by her Sikh bodyguards, more than 25,000 people have been killed in the conflict in Punjab.

The cops, in their effort to put down the rebellion, have been as ruthless as the secessionists. More than 70 police officers have been charged with murdering alleged separatists.

Shiite Muslims have been raising havoc in Uttar Pradesh state, particularly since the June 1997 arrest of Shiite leader Maulana Kalbe Jawwad.

Delhi

In Delhi, several bombings have resulted in casualties and property damage. The targets are areas of public access, such as public transportation facilities, bazaars and shopping areas, and restaurants. In the states of Jammu and Kashmir, and Punjab in northern India, the terrorist threat is considerably higher. Bombings, kidnappings and assassinations are common occurrences in these regions. The State Department is advising American citizens not to travel to Kashmir and to avoid nonessential travel to Punjab.

Foreign residents throughout India usually employ *chawkidars* (residential guards) outside their homes. Police assistance throughout northern India can be requested by dialing 100 from any public phone; 100 connects to the nearest police control room, which can usually dispatch a patrol vehicle.

Bombay (Mumbai)

There has been an increase in the number of organized criminal gangs operating in Bombay, and police confirm that the problem exists throughout Maharashtra state. Drug gangs have proliferated in the larger cities, and police report these gangs have moved into some of the most affluent areas of Bombay. In 1994, there were three drive-by shootings in the Malabar Hill area of Bombay. Home burglary still remains the most prevalent crime in Bombay, often committed by servants or other persons with easy access to the residence involved.

Calcutta

Insurgent activities, including killings and kidnappings by the United Liberation Front of Assam (ULFA) continue in the northeast. Despite army intervention, violent dissidence continues in parts of Assam. Local ULFA militants have carried out coordinated kidnappings throughout the state. A Russian mining engineer was killed and a number of Indian hostages taken, including several high-ranking officials. Political clashes occur sporadically in different parts of west Bengal and Bihar. Americans who are members of the Ananda Marg have been victims of mob violence in some areas of West Bengal and Bihar states (especially Calcutta and the Purulia district) and are not welcome by state government authorities, who, upon locating such individuals, usually detain and deport them.

The crime situation in West Bengal and Orissa relates to petty thefts, etc. However, in Bihar, there have been killings and other violence stemming from caste and tribal differences. Travel by road after dark is not recommended, and train passengers have been subjected to robberies and schedule disruptions due to protest actions.

The South

Sri Lanka is a thorn in India's side because of the ethnic conflict between Sri Lanka's Sinhalese majority and the island's Tamil minority.

In May 1991, Prime Minister Rajiv Gandhi was killed in Tamil Nadu by a suicide bomber. Members of the Sri Lankan Tamil terrorist group, Liberation Tigers of Tamil Eelam (LTTE), commit acts of terrorism and violence throughout southern India.

Insurgents and Separatists

There are more than 100 rebel factions, with 10 being militarily significant, and about 60 intergroup clashes occur each year. Thousands of Kashmiri youths have received rudimentary training in Afghanistan and Azad Kashmir that takes two weeks to three months. Although there are plenty of weapons supplied by Pakistan, there is little organized fighting. Typically a mine will be laid across a road and a military convoy will be under attack by small-arms fire from a group of 5 to 10 insurgents. The insurgents then run away and do not press their advantage. The ratio of deaths for insurgents to military is about five to one. There are also about 1,000 volunteers, primarily from Afghanistan (500), Saudi Arabia (80), and Sudan (200) fighting in Kashmir.

Being Kidnapped

About 500 people are kidnapped in Kashmir each year, including Westerners. Over 2,000 people have been kidnapped in Kashmir since 1990. Less than half of them survived the ordeal.

The Hostages in Kashmir Campaign
Independent House
112 Borough Road
Middlesbrough, England TS1 2ES
Tel.: [44] (1642) 339090
Fax: [44] (1642) 339191
E-mail: jbowman@itl.net
Web site: www.hostagesinkashmir

Prithvi Rockets

The name "Prithvi" means "earth." The latest models of these nuke-capable projectiles, first tested in January 1996, have a range of 150 miles and can strike most major Pakistani cities within only a few minutes after launch. The short-range version can carry a 1000-kilogram payload. Although the Indians have some fine tuning to do on their accuracy, these little puppies are quite capable of mass death and destruction. It simply remains a matter of on whom and what they fall.

The Roads

According to the National Transportation Research Centre in Trivendrum, Indian roads are the most dangerous in the world. With one percent of the total vehicles in the world, India accounts for 6 percent of total road accidents and has the highest accident rate in the world at 34.6 per 100,000 people. Out of the half a million people that will be killed on the roads worldwide, over 60,000 of those deaths and 300,000 of road injuries will occur in India. More people are killed on India's roads than on the rails.

Bus and Train Stations

Bus depots and train stations—particularly in the north, including Delhi, and the northeast—have become favorite targets of separatists, who employ remote-detonated bombs in their ongoing campaigns of murder and terror. Almost daily attacks typically kill and injure dozens of people. Between 300 and 500 people die in train crashes each year. Much of the train system in India is manually controlled. The first train began in 1853; in 1997 there were still 85 steam trains operating. Eleven million people ride the 39,000 miles of rails each day. The death rate per mile of track equals that of Europe.

Political Rallies

Various separatist groups love to blow up politicians using suicide bombers. These bombs usually contain way too much explosive material and nasty things like ball bearings. Needless to say, they bury what's left of the politician in a sandwich bag and a lot of people die. Political rallies in India are much safer on TV.

Police Crackdowns

The army likes to talk to folks early in the morning. Between 3 and 4 a.m. they will seal an area off, roust folks from their beds and take them to an open area. They are divided into young, middle-aged and old. Women are allowed to return to their homes. Then the men are paraded in front of "cats," hooded informers who point out Kashmir insurgents. (The term "cats" comes from Concealed Apprehension Technique.) Anyone who looks like a bad guy is taken away for further interrogation. Some of the men never return home.

While the male population plays *What's My Line,* soldiers go through the houses, searching for weapons. In many cases, the unprotected women have been raped and the homes looted.

The Indian Army is known for their violent and poorly planned hostage rescue attempts, village shoot-outs and brutal interrogations of prisoners. Although we don't expect many *DP* readers to become prisoners, it is not uncommon to stumble in on a village shoot-out as we did in Kashmir. As for being rescued by the military if you are a hostage, you have a 50/50 chance of surviving . . . if you duck.

AIDS

There are 3.8 million Indians with HIV and 200,000 with AIDS. India is predicted to have the highest incidence of AIDS in the world by the year 2000.

Press Releases

On July 8, 1996, Muslim guerrilla Ikwhan Jammu kidnapped 19 journalists for 10 hours. It was a year after the kidnapping of German Dirk Hasert. The journalists were on their way to a press conference held by the Muslim mujahedin in Achabal (40 miles from Srinagar), another guerrilla group. Ikwhan held the journalists because their editors refused to stop publication of their newspapers after they refused to publish one of the group's press releases.

Malaria

Calcutta, West Bengal and northeastern India are once again suffering from serious outbreaks of malaria. Calcutta is reported to be the worst hit of the country's major metropolitan cities. Reports suggest that this is a continuation of a longer trend of higher incidences of malaria in general and of malignant and chloroquine-resistant strains in particular.

Yanni

Five Indian farmers threatened to set themselves ablaze in protest to a March 1997 concert in front of the Taj Mahal by Greek-born New Age musician Yanni. The farmers claimed that some 250 acres of crops were destroyed to make way for a stage for the concert. Crops aside, the sodbusters may have mistaken "easy listening" for "easy glistening" in the publicity announcements.

Delhi Belly is a bitch here. The chances of seeing India without frequent side trips to the john are slim. More serious intestinal problems include typhoid, cholera, hepatitis A and parasites. Don't be shy about consulting an Indian doctor. They know their stuff and they are reasonable. Adequate medical care is available in the major population centers but limited in rural areas of the country. The key is to take preventive measures against malaria, hepatitis, meningitis and Japanese encephalitis, which also includes taking precautions to avoiding getting bit by mosquitoes. Dengue and Japanese encephalitis are mosquito-borne viral diseases that pose a danger in rural areas during the rainy season. Travelers arriving from countries where outbreaks of yellow fever have occurred will be required to furnish a certificate for yellow fever vaccination. Cholera and gastroenteritis occur during the summer monsoon months, mostly in the poorer areas of India. The best protection includes eating only at better-quality restaurants or hotels, drinking only boiled or bottled mineral water and avoiding ice. Take along medication for intestinal problems and read up on the free information provided by the Centers for Disease Control.

India has three main regions: the mountainous Himalayas in the north; the Indo-Gangetic Plain, a flat, hot plain south of the Himalayas; and the Peninsular Shield in the south, where India's neighbors Sri Lanka and the Maldives are located. The coldest months are January and February, with sweltering heat between March and May. The southwestern monsoon season is from June to September. The post monsoon, or northeast monsoon, in the southern peninsula occurs from October to December.

India is hot, dirty and humid throughout most of the year. The north is cool in the highlands and alpine above that. If you are looking to latch onto some bacteria, southern India is the place to do it. Bombay may be the dirtiest city on earth and there will be plenty of people to pass on germs to you. The hottest months are April to July, the wettest months from June to August.

There are more than 900 million people crammed into India's 3.3 million square kilometers (1.3 million square miles). About 40 percent of India's people live below the poverty line, defined as the resources needed to provide 2,100 to 2,400 calories per person per day. About 70 percent of the population lives in the countryside. The official language is Hindi, but English is the second language and is widely spoken. All official documents are in English. In keeping with India's diverse makeup, 18 languages are recognized for official use in regional areas, of which the most widely spoken are Telugu, Bengali, Marathi, Tamil, Urdu and Gujarati, each with its own script. Hindus do not eat beef. Muslims avoid pork. Sikhs do not smoke. Strict Hindus are also vegetarian and do not drink.

Banking hours: 10:30 A.M.–2:30 P.M., Monday to Friday; 10:30 A.M.–12:30 P.M., Saturday. Business hours: 9 A.M.–noon, 1–5 P.M., Monday to Friday. Stores are open 9:30 A.M.–6 P.M., Monday to Saturday. The workweek is Monday through Friday.

The rupee (about 31 to the U.S. dollar) is the currency and should be changed only through banks and authorized money changers. Electricity is 230–240v/50hz.

Embassy Locations

U.S. Embassy

Shanti Path, Chanakyapuri 110 021
New Delhi
Tel.: [91] (11) 600651

U.S. Consulates General

In Bombay:

U.S. Consulate General
Lincoln House
78 Bhulabhai Desai Road
Bombay 400026
Tel.: [91] (22) 363-3611

In Calcutta:

U.S. Consulate General
5/1 Ho Chi Minh Sarani
Calcutta 700071
Tel.: [91] (33) 242-3611, 242-2336,
242-2337

In Madras:

U.S. Consulate General
220 Mount Road, Madras 600006
Tel.: [91] (44) 827-3040, 827-7542

Other Useful Numbers

Ministry of Communications

Sanchar Bhawan, New Delhi 110 003
Tel.: 383600

Ministry of External Affairs

South Block, New Delhi 110 011
Tel.: 301-1813

Ministry of Tourism and Civil Aviation

Parivahan Bhavan, Sansad Marg, New
Delhi 100 001
Tel.: 351700

Web Resources

The Times of India

http://www.timesofindia.com/

Oneworld Online

http://www.oneworld.org/news/asia/
india.html

SAPRA (Security and Political Risk Analysis India)

http://www.subcontinent.com/sapra/
sapra_3.html

The Hindu

http://www.webpage.com/index.h tml

IndiaExpress

http://www.indiaexpress.com/news/

The Hindustan Times

http://www.hindustantimes.com/

Deccan Chronicle

http://www.deccan.com/

India Abroad

http://www.indiaabroad.com/

News India

http://www.newsindia-times.com/

The Afternoon Dispatch and Courier

http://www.afternoondc.com/
index1.htm

Deccan Herald

http://www.deccanherald.com/

The Ministry of External Affairs of the Indian Government

http://www.meadev.gov.in/

The Consortium Of Indian Military Websites

http://www.bharat- rakshak.com/

Press Information Bureau of the Government of India

http://www.nic.in/India-Image/PIB/

U.S. State Department Consular Information Sheets

http://travel.state.gov/india.html

The Ethnologue

http://www.sil.org/ethnolo gue/coun-
tries/Inda.html

12/23/99	Kashmiri separatists hijack an Air India plane in Kathmandu and fly to Kandahar. Taliban refuses to help hijackers.
11/12/96	Midair crash of a Saudi 747 and a Kazakh cargo plane kills 349 people in the world's worst midair disaster.
8/13/95	Norwegian Hans Christian Ostro is found beheaded near Anantnag, 37 miles from Srinagar.
7/4/95	Al-Faran guerrillas kidnap two Britons and two Americans near Pahalgam, 55 miles from Srinagar.
10/94	Rebel leader Shabir Shah released from prison.
6/94	Two Brits are kidnapped and released unharmed 17 days later.
3/93	Three hostages are swapped for seven guerrillas.
12/6/92	Hindu extremists destroy the 16th-century Muslim mosque at Ayodhya in India's Uttar Pradesh state. The subsequent rioting and Muslim-Hindu clashes that engulfed India, Pakistan, Bangladesh and other nations results in over 1,000 deaths. Hindus claim the mosque was built on the birth site of the Hindu god Rama, a claim disputed by Muslims.
8/92	Two army engineers are kidnapped and killed after the government refuses to release 17 jailed rebels.
2/92	India plants mines along border with Pakistan to stop traffic of insurgents between countries.
11/91	The manager of the state-run radio station is kidnapped and exchanged for a guerrilla.
9/91	A former Kashmiri minister and her husband are kidnapped and freed in a raid one month later. The brother-in-law of an Indian minister, a policeman, an insurance worker, and a bank employee are kidnapped the same month. They are exchanged for rebels but not until a hostage's severed thumb is sent as proof.
7/91	Four government officers are kidnapped and executed three months later.
6/91	Eight Israeli tourists are kidnapped. Six escape and one dies in the attempt. An oil executive is kidnapped and released 53 days later.
5/21/91	Former Prime Minister Rajiv Gandhi is assassinated during a campaign rally in Tamil Nadu state.
3/91	Two Swedish engineers as well as a daughter and a wife are kidnapped. The wife and child are released but the men are not released until 97 days later.
2/91	A pregnant 29 year old is kidnapped and swapped for five rebels.
3/90	Kashmiri political leader Mir Ghulum Mustafa is kidnapped and killed.

12/90	Indian army fires on demonstrators, killing 38 in Srinagar. Separatists begin a military campaign for independence.
12/89	Guerrillas kidnap daughter of Indian home minister and swap her for five insurgents.
1/6/89	Two of Prime Minister Indira Gandhi's Sikh bodyguards are hanged for her assassination on October 31, 1984.
1/3/89	Muslim Kashmiri militants begin their campaign for independence from India.
7/6/87	Seventy-two Hindus are killed in an attack by Sikh militants on a bus in the Punjab.
4/29/86	Sikh militants seize the Golden Temple of Amritsar in Punjab and declare the independent state of Khalistan. They are expelled by government of India forces the next day.
6/23/85	A bomb explodes on an Air India flight over the North Atlantic following its departure from Canada, killing all 329 passengers on board. A second bomb explodes at Narita Airport in Japan, killing two people. Sikh extremists claim responsibility for both bombings.
12/3/84	A chemical leak at Union Carbide's Bhopal plant results in 2,000 deaths and nearly 150,000 injuries.
10/31/84	Indian prime minister Indira Gandhi is assassinated by her Sikh bodyguards. Anti-Sikh rioting following the assassination results in thousands of Sikh deaths throughout India.
8/9/84	The head of the Indian security forces that stormed the Sikh golden temple of Amritsar is assassinated by Sikh terrorists.
6/6/84	Indian troops stormed the golden temple of Amritsar, killing 300 Sikhs.
2/11/84	Maqbool Butt, founder of the Jammu-Kashmir Liberation Front, is hanged in a New Delhi jail for the 1965 murder of an Indian intelligence agent in Kashmir. Militant Muslims have marked the anniversary of his death with sometimes violent demonstrations in Jammu and Kashmir.
1/26/50	India's constitution is promulgated and India becomes a republic within the Commonwealth. (Republic Day is also called Constitution Day.)
1/30/48	Mahatma Gandhi is assassinated.
8/15/47	Independence Day.
4/13/1699	Sikh religion was founded by Guru Gobind Singh.
7/13	Martyr's day in Kashmir. It commemorates the deaths of Kashmiri nationalists during the British raj.

Tehran

Iran

Party Like It's 1399

The country where the United States is still referred to as the "Global Arrogance" or the "Great Satan." Better than being the "Little Satan," I guess (that privilege is reserved for the Brits). Yes, 20 years after the Islamic Revolution, the official vocab list hasn't changed a whole lot. In some respects, though, it's hard to blame them if they're a tad xenophobic. There's more than one example of spooky Yanks and crafty Brits plotting to remove Iranian governments they didn't find suitable to their tastes. In 1953 the Iranian Prime Minister, Mosaddeq, was removed in a coup when he tried to nationalize the Anglo-Iranian Oil Company. He was ousted after Britain's MI6 and the CIA financed military officers to overthrow him. In Iran, by the way, if you're a bit too clever, you're called a Winston, after the last great British imperial leader, Winston Churchill. Churchill is widely regarded as a brilliant example of the archetypal cunning imperialist. Very devious and just as dangerous. In fact the Brits may be the Little Satan, but in Iran they are regarded as far more dangerous and devious critters (this will probably upset the boys at Langley) than the Yanks,

IRAN

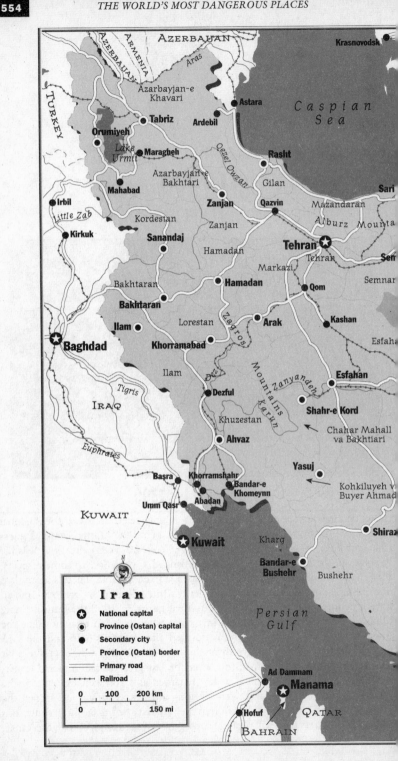

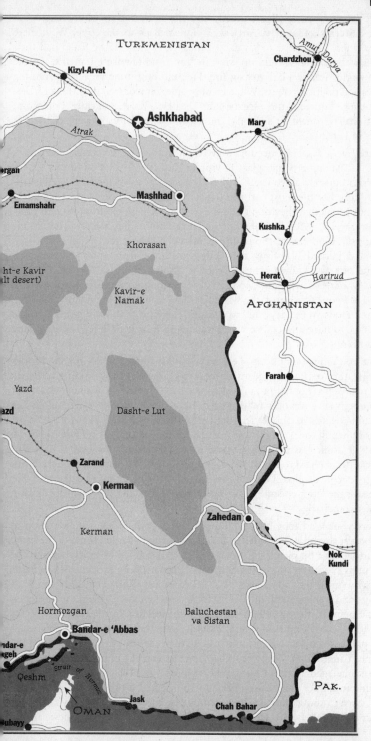

who are seen as having all the muscle and the cash, but are rank amateurs at Middle Eastern skulduggery. Anyway, I digress. Back to the coup. Well, there ain't really anything more to say except that the Big and Little Satan had their own ideas about who should do what in Iran. And it wasn't Iranians. To the outside world, Iran is a country on fire. Fire and brimstone preached from the mosques and political pulpits. When most people think of Iran they think of U.S. flags being burned, the Hezbollah, Islamic Jihad, suicide bombings, international terrorism (it's a long and nasty list) and lots of very dead U.S. Marines in Lebanon.

Despite Iran's desperate need to wipe us off the face of the earth (after Israel, that is), it still is a pretty nice place to visit, as long as you don't mind the "Death to America" posters as you talk with a local about his relatives in Pacoima or Beverly Hills. For the most part the Iranians are actually a pretty decent bunch. That's not to say that they don't like the odd anti-U.S demo from time to time. On February 11, 1999, Iranians celebrated the 20th anniversary of the Islamic Revolution. Hundreds of thousands of people gathered in Tehran's Freedom Square and burned U.S flags as an effigy of Uncle Sam while chanting that melodius and well-known song, "Death to America." This, after all, is still a country where you will find Morals Police cruising around the place. Morals Police! I ask you? Of course, the wisecracks are saying they should be patrolling the White House these days. Bill would sure think twice about slipping into the Oval Office to have intercourse with some intern if he knew a few lashings were coming his way.

In case you're planning a trip, here are a few identification tips for the Morals Kids. First, they're probably bearded, but what gives them away is their tendency to beat people up (not hard to miss then, are they?), especially women who don't dress properly (like wear the full-length chador) or who do subversive things like hold hands or kiss in public. As you can probably guess they're not the most popular bunch in town. In fact, people are getting a bit pissed off with them. In April 1999, some less than happy person even chucked a grenade at a Morals Police car. Kinda hard to blame them, really. The official rhetoric, though, belies a country deeply divided. Old-style mullahs may still be trying to make sure that no one sees the latest episode of *Baywatch,* but lipstick and stockings are making a discreet comeback.

Not everyone is a happy bunny, though. The overwhelming mandate given to the reformist (by Iranian standards) President Khatami has left some of the more hard-line clerics a bit pissed off, to say the least. For much of 1998, beneath the veil of unity, a vicious power struggle took place between moderates and hard-liners who miss the good old days of Ayatollah Khomeini, *fatwas,* death sentences and war against Iraq. That's not to say there hasn't been the odd open squabble between the ayatollahs. Grand Ayatollah Hussein Ali Montazeri, once tipped to succeed Khomeini, found himself under house arrest for opening his gob in public. Well, less for opening his gob than actually criticizing (tut tut) the Supreme Thunderbolt Thrower (Khameini, to you) in public. Another cleric who has managed to "confuse public opinion" is Mohammed-Ali Nejad al-Hosseini, an ally of the above. That got him jailed by the Special Court for Clergy. Nice to know they have one, a court that is. So, who's this new kid on the block in Iran? Well, he's a cleric (no surprise), he wears a suit (that's new) and he wants to reform Iran (that's even newer). President Khatami, though, has a bit of an uphill slog in front of him. Never mind that he won the 1997 elections with a massive 70 percent of the vote (from a turnout of 90 percent). If it was that easy the girls would be in miniskirts by now. Basically he wants better relations with the West, without Burger King and Coca-Cola running the country. But there are a whole load of kids with long beards in robes who would still like to see Israel nuked. In addition, Khatami wants a bit more consensus in how Iran is run, rather than a series of *fatwas*. Not a too popular line with the old guard, I'm afraid.

Towards the end of 1998 things got a bit vicious. Iran had its own version of murder mystery whodunnits, all for real. A number of prominent writers and liberals fell victim to a string of gruesome murders. It started with the stabbing to death, in November, of Dariush and Parvaneh Frouhar, a husband and wife team who were a bit too critical of the Supreme Thunderbolt Thrower. There quickly followed the disappearance of three other prominent writers (who, coincidently, just happened to be critics of the hard-liners), before they reappeared a while later—dead. You didn't really have to be Agatha Christie to figure this one out. And . . . lo and behold a couple of months later, it was admitted that the killings had been the work of secret police death squads, with links to the intelligence services (Iranian intelligence services, that is). No big surprise when you consider that Iran's intelligence services are not under the control of the moderate President Khatami, but dear old Ayatollah Khameini. The conservatives huffed and puffed, but didn't blow anyone's house down. Instead they went for the all-time Iranian favorite of blaming "outside forces" for the killings. Not really very original. Most people, for some obscure reason, were under the impression that it had been distinctly inside forces that were responsible. The Iranian intelligence chief was given a wide-ranging choice of being fired or resigning. An investigation was launched. Alas, it never got very far. The man who was accused of responsibility for the killings, Saeed Emami, the deputy minister of intelligence, committed suicide in prison. Oh dear, suddenly all the leads had kinda just, er, vanished. "What a pity," many of the hard-liners were muttering, sotto voce.

Murders aside, Iran's hard-liners have had to try a few other, more discreet tacks to undermine president Khatami. What better than the tourist industry to keep the image of fire and brimstone going? Tourist industry? What tourist industry? Well, actually, yes, there's now a bustling little tourist industry going in Iran. Which is probably why the odd busload of tourists have been stoned (i.e., had stones thrown at them), a German businessman was shot dead and three Italians kidnapped, amongst other little incidents. Someone spooky doesn't like westerners. Or reformers who cozy up to Westerners.

But as the reformers in question happen to hold rather a lot of the political cards, including the presidency and an overwhelming democratic(ish) mandate, the Koran Thumpers have gone for the subtle (and sometimes not so subtle) attack by proxy. Take the case of Golamhussein Karbaschi (who's he?). He is, or was, the popular mayor of Tehran . . . and a reformist. Need one say more? Well, okay, then. Someone fixed him up on corruption charges and he was sentenced to 20 years in the slammer, 20 lashes (someone's obviously into S&M here) and banishment from public office for life. It says a lot about Iran's power struggle that he wasn't actually sent straight to the slammer. Karbaschi did a bit of traditional haggling with the judges on appeal and got the sentence down to 2 years in the clink (no lashes . . . someone will be disappointed), a fine and a 10-year ban from public office.

Then, of course, there have been the not so subtle attempts to undermine moderates. Like spraying the HQ of a moderate party with machine gun fire. A hell of a way to make your point. But then there really are some people you can't expect moderation from. In this case it was operatives from the intelligence ministry—er, sorry, I'll take that back. It was a group who no one had really ever heard of before calling themselves the Fedayeen-e-Iran. They're pretty active kids actually. It's a complete coincidence (of course) that quite a few of them also happen to work for the hard-line intelligence services, answerable only to the Great Thunder Bolt Thrower.

Then, as we at *DP* tend to say rather a lot, things got out of hand. In July 1999 a small and peaceful student demonstration in Tehran was broken up by religious vigilantes and police. Using their usual kid gloves tactics one student was killed and several injured. The raid sparked the largest wave of unrest Iran has seen since the 1979 revolution. Things just kinda boiled over, I guess. Tens of thousands of Iranians, pissed off with hard-line mullahs, took to the streets in protest, eventually engaging in running battles with the police. It looked like the whole place was about to go a bit wobbly. And it did. For a while everything teetered on the brink. The students carried banners of Khatami, and cussed Khameini something chronic. The police and Islamic vigilantes got heavy. Extra orders were put in for tear gas, but no one bothered with rubber bullets. Altogether about seven people were killed and hundreds were injured. A bit of a clampdown ensued. About 1,400 people were arrested. Reinforcements were whistled up to quell the rioters. They arrived in the form of the Islamic Basij militia who roared around the streets chanting the hardly original lines of "death to America" and clubbed anyone in sight. Just so that no one else got any ideas about demonstrating against the government, four people were secretly (well, it can't be that secret if *DP* knows) sentenced to death for leading the riots. In reformist circles people got a bit wound up as to whether the riots would give the hard-liners the excuse to crackdown and reassert their foundering control. But the slippery new Prezzy wasn't having that. A pro-government demo was organized, and with a bit of management the 100,000 demonstrators chanted all the right slogans, which were pro-Islam, pro-government (death to America, of course) and pro-students. Do what? Pro-students? The rioting rabble?

As said, it was a bit slippery of the Prez; but by having a demo pro the students as well as everybody else it marginalized the hard-liners. Since then, things have cooled a bit, leaving everyone free to continue with their daily behind-the-scenes power struggle.

So where does all this leave Iran and the outside world? Well, the Little Satan (the Brits) and the Iranians have sorta kissed and made up. Both countries now have ambassadors from the other. Salman Rushdie has been quietly swept under the carpet by both sides, who are probably both hoping that the guy will have a convenient heart attack and save everyone lots of bother. You know, like the general embarrassment there would be if some fruitcake actually did slice him up in the name of Islam. Awfully inconvenient these hand-wringing liberal writers can be sometimes. That really just leaves Uncle Sam, still unable to get over the humiliation of having his embassy stormed all those years ago. At the same time, though, the United States wants desperately to reestablish relations with Iran before the bloody Europeans get all the lucrative oil contracts. Probably just to piss the United States off, France signed a large oil agreement with Iran in April 1999. The United States was not happy. They weren't getting the cash. And there's a whole US$300 million of it. No wonder the U.S isn't chuffed. So big Bill made a few of the right noises, saying something like he understood Iran or some such rubbish, intended to placate the mullahs and give a bit of support to nice President Khatami. The "little peace offering" met with "the little stick" from Iran, when Iranian officials made the usual derogatory comments about the United States, the slight difference being the tone was a little lower than the habitual all-out "death to America" stuff. You never know, there may be a U.S embassy in the Islamic Republic yet! *DP* thinks the Iranians should give a little here. After all, they did beat the Great Satan in the 1998 World Cup.

Leaving aside the international scene for a minute, Iran also has a minor problem of "terrorism." It just wouldn't be a fun place if there weren't any subversives rocking around the shopping centers, would it? For "terrorism" in Iran, you can read the Mujahadeen-e-Khalk Organization (MKO), or the People's Mujahadeen. They're based in Pyrotechnic City (Baghdad) in neighboring Iraq. They're a kinda lefty Islamist sorta group who got squeezed out of things by the mullahs at the beginning of the Iran-Iraq war. And they're bad losers. They keep the place lively with the odd bomb attack and assassination. In August 1998, the MKO whacked the former head of the prisons. In fact *DP* gives the MKO a pretty high mark for their apparent ability to carry out assassinations with a degree of competence. In April 1999 the MKO topped one of Iran's top generals. Lieutenant General Ali Sayyad Shirazi, the Iranian deputy chief of staff, was shot outside his home by men dressed as street cleaners. The Tehran God Botherers were not impressed. They threatened to launch missile attacks on Iraq (which *DP* guesses would make them technical allies of the U.S.?). The Iraqis wriggled and squirmed and then sent a letter to the United Nations saying there were no MKO bases in Iraq. After all, we all know that Iraq's one of the most peace loving nations on earth. Bit silly, really, when a few days later the MKO issue a statement (dateline: Baghdad) saying that the bombs that went off were nowhere near its HQ. Iran declined to comment on the bomb attacks, but you won't get a free membership in Mensa if you figure out the who the culprits might have been.

You Got the Wrong One Baby, Uh-huh

In January 1995, the Ayatollah Ali Khameini issued a religious decree apparently banning the consumption of both Coca-Cola and Pepsi, American soft drinks that had recently been reintroduced into Iran. Khameini was asked by a local paper, "Assuming drinking Coca-Cola and Pepsi politically strengthens world arrogance and financially helps Zionist circles, what would the Islamic decree on the issue be?" Khamenei replied, "Anything that strengthens world arrogance and Zionist circles in itself is forbidden." Only time will tell which real thing Iranians consume, Islamic dogma or the right one, baby. You probably won't be surprised to learn that satellite dishes are also banned.

I know it's hard to believe, but Iran actually has one of the most democratic societies in the Middle East. Perhaps that's just a sad reflection of the perilous state of democracy (or lack of it) in the region. But it's a bit more complicated than that. Iran, for example, has six main newspapers. Unlike the normal waste of space and trees that pass for newspapers in the region, there is actually a debate going on in them—if you ever manage to learn Farsi and read them. The debate, at the end of the day, is what role Islam should play in civil society? Answers in less than a thousand words, please. You won't find this kind of debate in Saudi Arabia. Quite who will win the debate and how remains to be seen. In the meantime, the political game of snakes and ladders between hard-liners and reformers, continues in Tehran. Watch this space for the *Return of the Jihad*.

Iran has two demands of the Great Satan: (1) gimme back our frozen assets, and (2) mind your own business. Hey what's their beef? Uncle Sam only spent $20 million trying to overthrow their Uncle Ayatollah. That's less than we spend on daily cruise missile–grams to their neighbor Saddam. Americans are still obsessed with blindfolded U.S. embassy staffers being paraded around Tehran's streets decorated with blazing Uncle Sam piñatas. It's nearly 20 years later and now we're the ones with blindfolds. Iran has elected a moderate (well in Iran, he's a moderate) cleric by the name of Mohammad Khatami, who actually wears a suit instead of bed sheets. The voter turnout was the highest in Iran since the mullahs came to power in 1979. Americans can travel freely in this country if they don't mind being shadowed like North Korean agents at a used plutonium sale. For now, Iran is open, the gals are loading up on the Revlon (under the chadors of course) and *Baywatch* via satellite dish is slowly eroding the old Iran we've come to hate. Oh, don't forget that hard-liner Ayatollah Ali Khameini still tosses the lightning bolts in this nation of very heavily clothed people.

Ayatollah Mohammed Ali Khameini

"Ayatollah" means "sign of god," and this ayatollah is Iran's spiritual leader and big cheese. A hard-liner and a fundamentalist to the max, he still holds most of the power after the May 1997 election of Khatami to president.

Government of Iran

http://www.gov.ir/

The Revolutionary Guards

This group of 120,000 well trained, politically indoctrinated soldiers were originally a bearded rabble of zealots run by ad hoc neighborhood groups, or Komitehs. They earned their reputation for fearlessness in the Iran-Iraq war. And it is a reputation well justified. These, after all, were the kids who would deliberately walk into minefields only concerned that their corpses would be in one piece for the funeral. The man in charge is Yahya Rahim Safavi, who was appointed by hard-liner Ayatollah Ali Khameini. So if you ever wonder who is large and in charge, it is not the nice moderate president.

Islamic Basij Militia

Subordinate to the Revolutionary Guards, the Basij militia is drawn from the poorer ranks of society. That's why they can be relied upon to beat the rich kids who don't play by the official rules, like dressing properly and watching devilish foreign television (*Baywatch*) on satellite channels.

President Mohammad Khatami

Moderate Khatami overwhelmingly defeated rival Ali Akbar Nateq-Nuri—by a margin of 20 million votes over Nuri's 9.7 million votes—in the presidential elections of May 1997. Khatami is being hailed as "Ayatollah Gorbachev," but it remains to be seen what kind of reforming he can do. But this guy's no Jack Kennedy. Khatami was born in 1943 to a fundamentalist cleric and highly vocal critic of Shah Mohammed Reza Pahlavi. Khatami followed in his dad's footsteps, being assigned to Hamburg, Germany, in 1978 to head an Islamic center dedicated to political change in Iran. He returned to Tehran after the shah fled Iran and Khomeini returned from exile in Paris. He was Iran's minister of culture and Islamic guidance in the 1980s, where he gained his reputation as a "cautious liberal." During his tenure at that post, Khatami allowed Western newspapers and magazines into Iran. He also lifted a ban on women singing in public, although the audiences were required to be all-female. Hey, it's a start. If Khatami moves at all with reforms, it will be gradually. He was ousted from ministerial power in the early 1990s during a backlash to lipstick and nail polish being worn by women. Sorta shows you what he's up against.

Khatami

The President
Pastor Ave.
Tehran, Iran
Tel. 98 (21) 61 61
http://www.gov.ir/khatami/khbio-e.htm
E-mail Khatami@president.ir

Islamic Iran Participation Front

The goodies. The party was set up to stand behind President Khatami. The founders include a vice president, seven deputy ministers as well as a group of hacks, a poet and a film producer. Set up in 1998, it represents what the reformers would like to present as the "New Face" of Iran—Islamic, democratic and ready to debate rather than bomb their way to Paradise.

Ali Akbar Nateq-Nuri

Ali Akbar Nateq-Nuri may have lost to Khatami, but he's not going to go away. Many in Iran believe Ali Akbar Nateq-Nuri lost the May 1997 polls solely because it was thought he, as president, would have decreed that women in public wear the long, hooded traditional chador, a one-piece garment about as popular in Iran as *Satanic Verses*. The real fabric of Iran may have been evidenced by the high turnout at the polls. Nateq-Nuri still leads the ultraconservative parliament and remains Khatami's nemesis.

Former President Ali Akbar Hashemi Rafsanjani

You may remember him as the patient towel-headed guy who politely endured Mike Wallace's dumb questions on *60 Minutes* as he tried to show that Iran wants to be buddies; but Mike wanted to spank him for something that happened 20 years ago.

What Mike didn't know was that Rafsanjani was the good guy. During his term, he attended the economy and repaired the damage left by the war with Iraq. He worked to get Iran reacquainted with the international community by expanding world ties and by arranging the release of hostages held by terrorist groups with ties to Iran. Rafsanjani had tougher problems than being grilled by Mike. He has narrowly escaped seven assassination attempts. Rafsanjani is credited with persuading Khomeini to finally agree to a cease-fire in the war with Iraq in August 1988.

http://www.cyberiran.com/government/constitution.html

Ali Mohammed Besharati

He's the influential interior minister. A former Revolutionary Guard, Besharati was one of the students who seized the U.S. embassy in 1979. His latest action was to unsuccessfully ban Iran's embarrassingly popular satellite dishes—which he views as instruments of Western filth—when he learned that *Star Trek* and *Baywatch* were getting better ratings than *Muslim Mullahs! Live From Mahabad!* and *Good Morning, Tehran*—with Ali Mohammed Besharati.

http://www.unhcr.ch/refworld/un/chr/chr95/country/55.htm

Mujahedin Khalq Organization (MKO)

The MKO is a 20,000-strong Iranian resistance force based in Iraq. But unlike other liberation groups, some 35 percent of the group's soldiers are women, as are nearly three-quarters of its officers. Training at Al-Ashraf Camp inside Iraq, just out of reach from Iran's howitzers, the fully armed MKO doesn't collect paychecks and bestows near-deity status to its female leader, Maryam Rajavi, whom the rebel group hopes to install as Iran's next president.

Have these folks got a chance against the mullahs? MKO troops have taken a vow of celibacy until Iran's government is toppled, so at least we know they're motivated. The MKO is one of the few armored liberation groups. The MKO can field 160 T-54/55 tanks (which they probably got from the Moscow military museum) and dozens of rocket launchers, APCs, towed howitzers and even attack helicopters. Even so, these guys and gals are more talk than action. The organization was 50,000 strong after the Islamic revolution, with nearly half a million supporters. About 5,000 activists have been executed in the government's crackdown, and more than 25,000 imprisoned. They lost a lot of kudos fighting against Iran during the Iran-Iraq war. After the cease-fire in the Iran-Iraq war, the mujahedin invaded Iran but were crushed by the Iranian armed forces.

National Council of Resistance of Iran (NCR)

Based in the United States, the NCR is the spoutpiece of the MKO. It's all a bit silly really, because the MKO is supported by that well-known U.S ally in the region, Saddam Hussein. Remember him? So here we can almost sum up U.S. foreign policy in the region: The NCR does lots of lobbying in Congress. The NCR is the political wing of an organization (the MKO) that the State Department has blacklisted as a terrorist organization. The said "terrorist" organization operates from Baghdad. But its politicos raise cash to overthrow the mullahs. Yeah, something's definitely wrong here.

http://menic.utexas.edu/menic/countries/iran.html

Khomeini Money

In 1989 the Iranian government used its official government currency presses to print the first of about $10 billion in counterfeit U.S. currency. The U.S. bills of 100-dollar denominations were originally used to finance terrorists in the Bekaa valley. There were little if any clues to the bills' origin (some say the zeroes have flattened tops).

The U.S. government estimates that there is around $400 billion in U.S. currency outside of the country. The paper used is the same paper used by the U.S. mint, and, in many cases, the bills cannot be detected even by optical scanners. The bills continue to appear, and have been spotted most recently in North Korea. In dangerous places where U.S. currency is the standard, DP has taken to carrying only 20s and not accepting any $100 bills printed in the '80s. The new $100 bill should solve this problem for now.

Not only is it legal to travel to Iran, but the country is planning to open its first U.S. tourist office in New York City. The staffers at Iran's U.N. mission in New York got a little giddy and loosened their guard with *DP* after the elections. "Iran is very safe!" he proclaimed. "We love Americans! Many Iranians want to be just like Americans. Tell me when you're coming. I will tell you how to leave the airport (without being followed)!" U.S. passports are valid for travel to Iran. However, U.S.-Iranian dual nationals have often had their U.S. passports confiscated upon arrival and have been denied permission to depart the country documented as U.S. citizens. To prevent the confiscation of U.S. passports, the Department of State suggests that Americans leave their U.S. passports at a U.S. embassy or consulate overseas for safekeeping before entering Iran. To facilitate their travel in the event of the confiscation of a U.S. passport, dual nationals may obtain in their Iranian passports the necessary visas for countries that they will transit on their return to the United States, and where they may apply for a new U.S. passport. Dual nationals must enter and leave the United States on U.S. passports. The U.S. government does not have diplomatic or consular relations with the Islamic Republic of Iran. The Swiss government, acting through its embassy in Tehran, serves as the protecting power for U.S. interests in Iran and provides only very limited consular services. Neither U.S. passports nor visas to the United States are issued in Tehran.

Iran Touring and Tourism

Deputy Minister for Tourism and Pilgrimage Affairs
Ministry of Culture and Islamic Guidance
Hajj and Pilgrimage Building, Third floor
Azadi Avenue
P.O. Box 13445-993
Tehran, Islamic Republic of Iran
Tel.: (98-21) 6423042, 6432098, 6432107
Fax: (98-21) 6433842, 6432088
Telex: 21-2089
E-mail: toursmec@www.dci.co.ir
http://www.itto.org/

Information on Iran

http://tehran.stanford.edu
Visa and passport are required. The Iranian government maintains an interests section through the Pakistan Embassy in Washington, D.C.: *Embassy of Pakistan, 2209 Wisconsin Avenue NW, Washington, DC 20007, Tel.: (202) 965-4990*

Mehrabad International Airport is seven miles west of Tehran, about a 30-minute drive. Airport facilities include a 24-hour bank, a 24-hour post office, a 24-hour restaurant, a snack bar, a 24-hour duty-free shop, gift shops, 24-hour tourist information and first aid/vaccination facilities. Airline buses are available to the city for a fare of RL10 (travel time: 30 minutes). Taxis also are available to the city center for approximately RL1,200–1,500. There is a departure tax of RL1,500. Transiting passengers remaining in the airport are exempt from the departure tax.

IRAN

Once inside Iran, transportation by private car (with driver) or with a guide (who will be assigned to keep tabs on you) is recommended.

Nowhere/Everywhere

Forget about crime. A pickpocket would have two strikes and then he could audition for *Flipper* sequels. The problem in Iran is everyone wants to know what you're doing here. U.S. citizens traveling in Iran have been detained without charge, arrested and harassed by Iranian authorities. Persons in Iran who violate Iranian laws, including Islamic laws, may face penalties that can be severe.

The eastern and southern portions of Iran are major weapons and drug smuggling routes from Pakistan and Afghanistan. Drug and arms smuggling convoys may include columns with tanks, armored personnel carriers and heavily armed soldiers. Right now, Iran is a brave new world for U.S. travelers. Most of the country can be considered safe (that's the good news), but it's still very much a police state (the bad news).

Party! Party! Party!

No you moron, not the Spuds Mackenzie, Prince, Jeff Foxworthy, hair band up all night, sleep all day, kind. Political parties. There's a lot of parties going on, but you won't find them in Iran. For now you can find them on the Web.

Iranian Democratic Movements
http://www.d-n-i.org

Communist Party of Iran
http://www.pi.se/webpage/
communist.party.of.iran/index.html

Constitutionalist Movement of Iran, The
http://www.irancmi.org/index2.htm

Organization of Iranian People's Fedaian
http://193.80.248.16/
iran.kar.fadai.aksariyat/
http://www.fadaii-minority.org/

Iraqi National Congress
http://www.inc.org.uk/

Organization of Iranian People's Mujahedin
*http://www.iran-e-azad.org/
farsi/index.html*

Tudeh Party of Iran
http://www.demon.co.uk/mardom/
tudeh.htm

Workers-Communist Party of Iran
http://www.wpiran.org/index.html

Uncle Sam

The Iranians (or at least those who haven't immigrated to America) have been foaming at the mouth about "Raygun," "Boosh" and now "Cleentun" for so long that they forgot we are fairly decent folks. You won't find outright hostility, but you may be hard-pressed to keep up if you get into a "Did not! Did too!" argument.

Charity

Iran is a major sponsor of SIIA and resistance groups like Hezbollahor the Hazari in Afghanistan. Iran has decided to bypass Syria as a transshipment point for weapons. They also send significant amount of weapons and arms to Massoud in the North of

Afghanistan. Next time you bump into those swarthy Iranians in the double breasted suits on those secret flights say hi for DP.

Drugs

If you think Iran means lots of dope and stoned evenings then put this book down now. Iran has executed nearly 2,000 drug smugglers since 1989. Possession of 5 grams of heroin or 3 kilograms of opium will be quite sufficient for you to be strung up.

Iran is on the front line of the war against drugs. And it really is a war. In 1998, 140 tons of drugs were seized by Iranian security forces. Between 1996 and 1998, 2,500 policemen and soldiers were killed by drug smugglers. Iran's border with Afghanistan means that there is a continual flow of very heavily armed Afghans moving backwards and forwards across the border with large amounts of heroin. And they don't like being asked for their passports. Over ten days alone in July 1999 25 smugglers were killed and one ton of drugs seized. The main drug route comes through the province of Khorasan, bordering Afghanistan and Pakistan.

Imported Goods

On May 6, 1995, President Clinton signed an executive order prohibiting exporting goods or services to Iran, re-exporting certain goods to Iran, new investments in Iran or in property owned or controlled by the government of Iran and brokering or other transactions involving goods or services of Iranian origin or owned or controlled by the government of Iran. These restrictions have been added to those already contained in the Iranian Transactions Regulations that prohibited unauthorized importation of Iranian-origin goods or services into the United States.

For information regarding the issuance of licenses, contact the Licensing Division, The Treasury Department's Office of Foreign Assets Control at: *Tel.: (202) 622-2480).* FAC issues licenses only for goods that were located outside of Iran prior to imposition of these sanctions on October 29, 1987. Goods in Iran after that do not qualify for authorization from Customs criteria for authorization. Iranian-origin goods, including those that were in Iran after October 29, 1987, may enter the United States if they qualify for entry under the following provisions administered solely by Customs: (1) gifts valued at US$100 or less, (2) goods for personal use contained in the accompanied baggage of persons traveling from Iran valued at US$400 or less, or (3) goods qualifying for duty-free treatment as "household goods" or "personal effects" (as defined by U.S. law and subject to quantity limitations). Inquiries about these provisions should be directed to Customs in the U.S. port where the goods would arrive.

A yellow fever vaccination is required for travelers over the age of one year coming from infected areas. Arthropod-borne diseases and Hepatitis B are endemic. Malaria is a risk in some provinces from March through November. Food- and water-borne diseases, including cholera, are common, as is trachoma. (Snakes and rabid animals can also pose a threat.) Basic medical care and medicines are available in the principal cities of Iran, but may not be available in outlying areas. There are 3 doctors and 14 hospital beds for every 10,000 people. The international travelers' hot line at the Centers for Disease Control: *(404) 332-4559,* has additional useful health information.

Iran is hurting because of the long drop in world oil prices. The rial fluctuates on the free market as much as 15 percent a day. About 3,000 rials are equal to US$1. Inflation is between 60–100 percent a year, and a thriving black market takes advantage of outrageous official rates. Government employees make the equivalent of US$60 a month, and many Iranians are forced to take two jobs to get by. Iran is home to more refugees than any other country in the world. There are an estimated 2.2 million Afghans, 1.2 million Iraqis and 1.2 million others who have fled the strife in Pakistan, Azerbaijan and Tajikistan. The country is held together by a wide net of informers. But give Iran credit—like most exporters of terror, it's a peaceful country.

About three times the size of Arizona, Iran is a constitutional Islamic republic, governed by executive and legislative branches that derive national leadership primarily through the Muslim clergy. Shi'a Islam is the official religion of Iran, and Islamic law is the basis of the authority of the state. Islamic ideals and beliefs provide the conservative foundation of the country's customs, laws and practices. Shiites comprise about 95 percent of the country. Sunnis make up about 4 percent. The literacy rate is at about 75 percent. Iran is a developing country.

The workweek in Iran is Sunday through Thursday. Electricity is 220V/50Hz. Languages are Farsi, Turkish, Kurdish, Arabic and scattered English. Only about half of Iran's population speaks Farsi.

Temperatures for Tehran can be very hot in the summer and just above freezing in the winter. The northern part of the country can experience very bitter winters. Iran has a mostly desert climate with unusual extremes in temperature. Temperatures exceeding 130°F occasionally occur in the summer, while in the winter the high elevation of most of the country often results in temperatures of 0°F and lower.

There is no U.S. embassy or consulate in Iran. The United States does have an interests section at the Swiss embassy in Tehran:

Swiss Embassy, U.S. Interests Section
Bucharest Avenue
Argentine Square
17th street, No. 5
Tehran
Tel.: [Tel.:98] (21) 625-223-224 and 626-906

2/20/99	6,800 people run for office in elections. 760 are not allowed to run by th Conservative Council of Gaurdians. Reformers win big.
5/24/97	Khatami, a moderate, is elected president.
7/3/89	The Ayatollah Khomeini dies.
2/14/89	Khomeini announces a death decree on *Satanic Verses* author Salman Rushdie, an Indian national, resident in the United Kingdom.
7/3/88	The U.S.S. *Vincennes* mistakenly shoots down an Iranian Airbus airliner over the Persian Gulf.

IRAN

12/4/84	Four Islamic Jihad terrorists hijack a Kuwaiti airliner bound for Pakistan from Kuwait and order it flown to Tehran. Two U.S. aid personnel are killed during the hijacking, while two others, another U.S. aid official and an American businessman, are tortured during the ordeal. Iranian troops storm the aircraft on December 9, retaking it from the hijackers.
6/28/81	The prime minister and 74 others are killed in the bombing of the legislature.
1/20/81	U.S. embassy hostages are released. Fifty-two American hostages are freed after 444 days in captivity, following an agreement between the United States and Iran arranged by Algeria.
9/19/80	Iran-Iraq war begins.
7/27/80	Death of the shah of Iran.
4/25/80	The day operations to rescue American hostages fails in the desert of Iran, due to operational shortfalls and an aircraft accident.
11/4/79	The U.S. embassy is seized and 63 people are taken hostage.
4/1/79	Islamic Republic Day, commemorating riots by Islamic fundamentalists in Isfahan.
3/10/79	Death of Kurdish leader Mullah Mustafa Barzani. (Kurdish regions.)
2/11/79	Revolution Day. Celebration of the victory of the Islamic revolution.
2/4/79	Iranian revolution begins. Iran's Shiite clerics start their takeover of the government.
2/1/79	Khomeini returns from exile and calls for the start of the "Ten Days of Dawn," commemorating the ten days of unrest, ending with Khomeini taking power on February 11 (the "Day of Victory").
1/16/79	The shah departs Iran.
11/4/78	Student uprising against the shah.
9/9/78	The shah's troops open fire on protesters in Tehran, killing several hundred demonstrators.
11/4/64	Ayatollah Khomeini is exiled to Turkey.
6/5/63	The Ayatollah Khomeini is arrested by the shah's police. It is also the Day of Mourning and Revolution Day.
1/22/46	Kurdish Republic Day.
2/7/1902	Birth date of the Ayatollah Ruhollah Khomeini.
6/28	Revolutionary Guard's Day.
3/21	Persian New Year. Kurdish New Year celebrated.

IRAN

Iraq

The Garden of Needin'

We promised to bomb then into the Stone Age. But Fred and Barney live much better than the average Iraqi. We called their leader names, but he didn't cry. We dropped and continue to drop millions of dollars of high-tech hardware on him, but he keeps rebuilding. Much to the annoyance of the Uncle Sam and the gang, Iraq is still being run by the one guy we all know and love . . . yes, Saddam Hussein, the man on whom the United States regularly offloads several tons of ordnance whenever he gets uppity, He still rules the roost in Baghdad. And, apart from periodically blowing the place to pieces, the United States doesn't quite know what to do. U.S. and British planes have made approximately 110 sorties to bomb Iraq this year alone. The reason? Because Saddam just won't do what he's told, which is to say that he wants the sanctions lifted, the no-fly zones repealed and northern Iraq back under his loving tender care—all penalties imposed after the Gulf War.

It all started—this time round—back in 1998, when Saddam decided to show who was boss in Iraq. So, to wind the United States and its allies up a bit, he

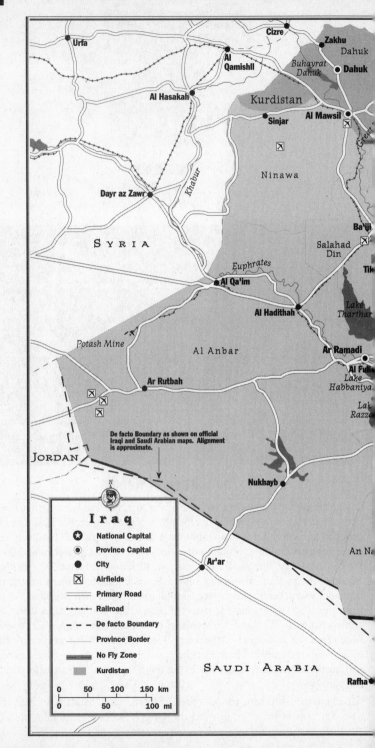

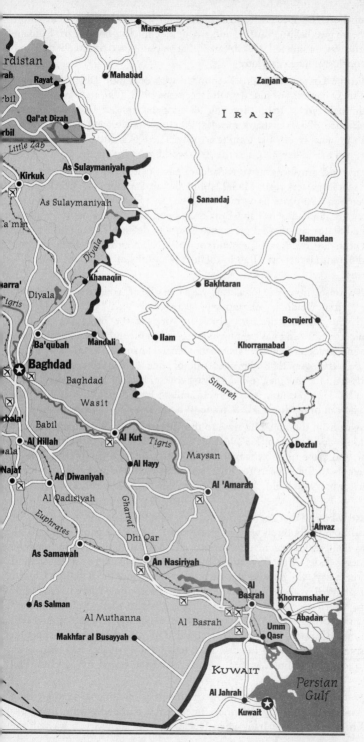

kicked out the UN inspection teams searching for weapons of mass destruction (all that nerve gas, ballistic missiles and a couple of nuclear bombs that Saddam has stashed away), a simple UN/CIA affair that was supposed to take 90 days and is still inconclusive nine years later.

What did the United States do? Responded with operation Desert Fox. Who thinks up these names? For four days in December 1998, U.S. and British planes blasted the hell out of Iraq. Targeting 97 sites throughout Iraq, the United States unleashed 325 Tomahawk missiles, 90 cruise missiles and quite a few B-52s. And with what result? Er, nothing actually. The UN is out, Saddam is in and the media had a field day. Oh, and the Arab world got very upset.

Then for good measure this year, Saddam has violated the no-fly zones 110 times by sending a few rusty MiG-23s into the air and targeted USAF planes flying over Iraq 190 times using radar lock on. In 11 weeks between February and March the United States and Britain dropped 274 bombs on 105 targets. The United States says that 25 percent of Iraq's air defense system in the no-fly zone has been destroyed. In all, a grand total of 1,100 bombs have been dropped on 359 different targets over Iraq in the first 8 months of 1999. But Saddam's not flapping.

Saddam's consolation prize for all this was a message of "solidarity and fraternal greetings" from Vladimir Zhirinovsky, aka "Mad Vlad," Russia's leading comedian who masquerades as a politician—or is it the other way around? Meanwhile, the bombing has continued pretty much off and on. In Baghdad the man responsible for air defense, Lieutenant General Shaheen Yassin, claimed that "it will be very soon that our skies will be free of hostile crows." What? Somebody send the guy on a spin doctoring course. Has all this fazed Saddam at all? Not a bit. He's put up a bounty of 25 million Iraqi dinars (US$14,000) for anyone who can bring down a U.S. plane. Who says the guy's short of cash?

Quite apart from thumbing his nose to the United States, Saddam's been busy on the domestic scene, too. He's had his three wives to look after, the kids to keep apart and those tiresome family squabbles to handle. Then there have been coup attempts to foil, officers to shoot, sanctions to bust, dissenters to execute and a nuclear bomb to build. All in all Saddam's had a busy year. It's tough at the top.

It can safely be said that Saddam has not only kept his place on Uncle Sam's list of the Bad Boys Club, but is way out ahead of the rest of the gang, although his pal Slobo in Belgrade has made a serious effort at catching up – and may be drawing level. Fidel, Muammar and Kim, though, are all lagging streets behind Saddam these days. So, how do you get to be a member of the Bad Boys Club? I hear you ask. Well, you can make an early start by sponsoring a little international terrorism, which is always helpful for the career minded. Saddam invited Palestinian terrorist Abu Nidal to stay in Baghdad. Nidal is the head of the Fatah Revolutionary Council. He was also responsible for the attempted assassination of the Israeli ambassador to London back in the '80s, which Israel used as an excuse to invade Lebanon. As said: a good qualifying round for Saddam. Full marks.

But if you really want to make your mark there's nothing better than invading another country. A country that the United States is friendly with, that is, as opposed to a country like Iran, when Uncle Sam will furnish you with all the weapons you need. Try Kuwait. Then, if you want to reach the dizzy heights of stardom, just take on the world—and stay in one piece. Well, I guess we all know that story.

What are the membership privileges of Uncle Sam's Bad Boys Club? Well, you don't get to go on holiday to the United States for a start. You get all your foreign assets frozen. You definitely do not get to do business in the United States, and you get a guarantee of as many cruise missiles as you can handle being chucked at your country. You also get to have lots of international politicians denouncing you as a monster (and at the same time hoping that no one remembers the time they were flogging you with weapons). But the really cool part is that you get to run a country that frustrates and embarrasses every attempt by the world's only superpower to suppress you.

In 1998 the U.S. Congress passed the Iraq Liberation Act, which granted US$97 million to Iraqi opposition groups. Opposition? What opposition? The latest cunning ploy by the United States to get rid of Saddam has been to launch as many cruise missiles, bombs and Tomahawks at him as possible, keep the fingers crossed, and hope that it will provoke a rebellion. Better rethink boys.

The downside is that the Western press gets to make fun of you. Some people just have no respect! In March 1997, Saddam Hussein sued a French magazine for defamation for referring to the Iraqi dictator as an "executioner," a "murderer," a "monster" and "a perfect cretin." Apparently, what really upset Saddam was the bit about being called a "perfect cretin." It's unlikely he'll get Kuwait back in damages. Kuwait, for its part, has sued Saddam for equally inflammatory remarks and for damages stemming from Iraq's attacks on Kuwaiti oil fields. Somebody call Johnny Cochran.

Iraq's plummet into the depths began in earnest in 1980. That year, Saddam launched the war against Iran, which lasted until August 1988. Iraq had long-standing border disputes with Iran and Kuwait, and a fierce animosity toward Israel. In addition to this, Saddam and President Hafez al Assad of Syria have a deep personal hatred of each other that goes back years. After the August 1988 cease-fire with Iran, Iraq supplied arms and money to the Christian forces of Michel Aoun in Lebanon to relaunch the war there against the Syrian army. It invaded and annexed Kuwait in August 1990, with the intention of seizing funds from Kuwait's banks and investment companies for the reconstruction of Iraq.

During the Iran-Iraq war, many countries supplied Iraq with arms in contravention of international conventions (as well as their own laws) that precluded arms supply to countries at war. Here are some of them: the United States, the former Soviet Union, France, Germany, the United Kingdom, Italy, China, Chile, Brazil and East European countries. Iraq has used chemical weapons against Iranian forces and subsequently against the Kurds in northern Iraq.

For now, Iraq is one of the world's great travel bargains. You'd have a hard time finding things to buy, however, no matter what budget you're on. But if you want to top your tank off, you're in luck. The collapse of the Iraqi dinar from its official rate at about $3.20 to its real rate of about a thousand times less means that when you buy a full tank of gas using dinars, you pay less than an Uncle Sam's penny. Gasoline costs .0009 cents a gallon, or 0.07 dinars a liter. But if you make other transactions at the official rate, beware. Don't reach out and touch someone; telephone calls from Baghdad to the United States can cost $158 a minute.

The embargo on Iraq imposed after Iraq's invasion of Kuwait, and a scarcity of U.S. dollars, is pulling the value of Iraq's currency to the value of used Charmin. In a country where educated people make about 2,000–3,000 dinars a month ($2–3!), there is little to buy and even less to buy it with. Just imagine a country where a crisp U.S. 100-dollar bill will bring you nearly 5,000 25-dinar notes. It's positively retro! The currency is worth so little that people pay for goods, where they can find them, in wads of 100 25-dinar bills wrapped with rubber bands. Shopkeepers don't even bother counting the notes. All in all, invading Kuwait seems to have been a bit of a costly mistake. Iraq has lost some US$150 billion in revenues since 1991.

After the Gulf War, Allied forces had destroyed, neutralized or captured 41 of the 42 Iraqi army divisions in the war zone of Kuwait and southern Iraq. The coalition estimated the number of Iraqi prisoners of war at 175,000 and the number of Iraqi casualties at 85,000–100,000, out of an estimated 500,000 soldiers positioned in the combat area. Iraq lost 3,700 of its 5,500 main battle tanks, 1,857 of its 7,500 armored vehicles and 2,140 of its 3,500 artillery pieces. Ninety-seven of Iraq's 689 combat aircraft and six of its 489 helicopters were destroyed. One-hundred-sixty combat aircraft were flown to Iran, where they were impounded as war reparations. Nine airfields were destroyed, as well as 16 chemical weapons plants, 10 biological weapons plants and 3 nuclear weapons facilities. Yet Baghdad continues holding onto thousands of pieces of civilian and military equipment that it had stolen from Kuwait during its occupation of the country.

Iraq currently possesses approximately 9,000 pieces of military equipment, including trucks, jeeps, armored personnel carriers and missiles, as well as perhaps 6,000 civilian items. These items were supposed to have been returned under the 1991 UN Security Council Resolution. And those are just the harmless things in Saddam's inventory. He otherwise has 6 fully operational ballistic missiles, 25 more hidden and stashed away, and one nuclear bomb minus its fissile core. The reader will also sleep better knowing that Saddam has still got VX nerve toxins, a mobile biological weapons production facility and freeze-dried anthrax. Any of which would kill most of New York in a matter of minutes.

Dr. Germ—Roses are red, violets are blue and my chemicals are all for you.

Iraq's biological and chemical weapons program is masterminded by 43-year-old Dr. Rihab Taha, aka Dr. Germ. To the substantial embarrassment of the British government she took her Ph.D. in plant toxins (don't you just love the smell of roses!) at the University of East Anglia between 1981–1984. But don't worry, Iraq is really up on animal rights, so none of the bio and chem weapons were ever tested on animals. They were tested on Iranian prisoners of war instead.

Iraq has rebuilt much of its infrastructure, including the phone system, electrical plants, government buildings and bridges—not to mention its all-important chemical weapons facilities. The Iraqi people have shown themselves to be a very resilient bunch, not that they really have a lot of choice. For those Baghdad residents who are not fortunate enough to live near a government ministry they get a whole half an hour's electricity a day. Saddam's is not the first dictatorship they have endured, and it won't be the last. Economic embargoes tend to have greater ramifications on innocent citizens than on the dictators who led them into it. Despots rarely go hungry. They're occasionally assassinated, but usually with full stomachs. Saddam still sports that tire around his waist, while his people are being starved to death.

In fact, *DP* learned that Saddam is perhaps a little concerned about his increasing weight. Among the "essential items" that have been imported to Iraq this year is a liposuction machine worth US$16,000. And just to make sure Saddam can keep up the flashy smile, a teeth whitening laser (worth US$126,000) has also been imported into Iraq. Of course, it's all absolutely essential.

Among the other vital necessities that have been imported have been silicon breast implants at US$ 750 a shot and viagra pills. Did you know that despite three marriages, Saddam's son Uday has yet to conceive? The Iraqi authorities maintain that an astonishing 1.5 million babies have died in Iraq as a direct result of the U.S.-led sanctions. Doubtless this is why other "vital necessities" include acne cream, crystal glasses, crates of whisky and champagne, not to mention cigars. By the way, 20 capsules of common antibiotics such as amoxycillin cost US$1.60 and 20 doses of penicillin cost just 50 cents.

Saddam seems to be somewhat confident of a long reign, despite the United States' claim that its embargo will ensure his demise. How do we know he is so confident? Well, since the Gulf War, he has spent US$2.2 billion building or rebuilding more than 74 palaces in Iraq. In April 1997, Saddam threw himself a lavish 60th birthday bash, complete with a Tigris River procession of 60 Turkish yachts, to remind everyone he was still alive. Saddam's birthday bash this year was a more modest affair. He merely held it at one of his summer resorts while the loud speakers in Baghdad all played "Happy birthday, Mr. President." Now 62, Saddam is in good health. He has a team of 12 Russian doctors on call 24 hours a day. This leaves him in tip-top form for fun on the river.

Saddam's vewy vewy pwoud of his yacht, the *Al Mansur*. And so he should be: it is 394 feet long and can accommodate over 200 of his buddies. If you're ever invited you should know that every room is also bugged. More recently Saddam has been building a special holiday resort on the shores of Lake Tharthar, north of Baghdad, for fun and frolics for the faithful. Saddam's own little palace in his hometown of Tikrit is a modest complex that consists of 13 different palaces with the interiors lined with gold and marble.

But it's not all fun and games ruling Iraq. Oh no. Quite the opposite. There's some serious work to be done. There's full-time sanction busting to be organized, relatives to kill, countries to threaten and TV appearances to maintain. Most of Saddam's cash comes from border trade with his neighbors. He's been exporting cheap oil to Jordan and Turkey ever since the Gulf War ended, and more recently to Syria. The U.S. turns a very big blind eye to this because it says that Jordan and Turkey are U.S. friendly and need the cash. The United States neglects to say that without this money Saddam would be utterly unable to pay his security forces. Syria is also not mentioned. All Saddam's cash goes on important things like paying the different branches of his secret police and the elite Republican guard—in other words, the people who keep him in power by torturing and murdering anyone who expresses anything less than undying love for Saddam.

No one really knows how many people have been executed in Iraq this year. But one of the more prominent people to bite the bullet was Shiite cleric Ayatollah Mohamed Mohamed Sadeq al Sadr, who was killed with his two sons in the city of Najaf. Sadr is just the latest in a long line of influential Shiite clerics who have fallen foul of Saddam and Co. Sadr, the third cleric in less than a year to get zapped for opening his gob, joins his cousin, who was whacked in 1980 by Saddam's cousin, Ali Hassan al Majid.

Coups 'R' Us

Want a risky job? Then join the Iraqi army. You'll have a hard time getting any insurance, though. And if you're a General, your best bet is to take early retirement. More military officers are executed in Iraq than in any other country in the world. In January 1999, Lieutenant General Sachit al Janabi, the deputy army chief in southern Iraq, was one of eight conspirators executed for allegedly plotting to assassinate Saddam.

When he's not signing execution warrants it's those tiresome family feuds that Saddam has to deal with. In 1995 his delightful son, Uday, shot his uncle Watban al Tikrit in the leg at a drinking party. Watban had been silly enough to argue with Uday about a car that Watban had and Uday wanted. This prompted two of Saddam's sons-in-law, Hussein Kamal al Majid and Saddam Kamal al Majid to leg it to Jordan, out of terror of the ever erratic Uday. Saddam was not chuffed with Uday for any of this. What did he do? Had petrol poured on all Uday's sports cars and then burned them. Back to the errant sons-in-law languishing in Amman. After a few months in Jordan, Saddam offered them a pardon if they would return. With growing calls from the Iraqi opposition that they be tried for crimes against humanity, the pair decided to take their chances in Baghdad. A silly choice, as it turned out.

On arrival in Baghdad their two wives were granted divorces within 24 hours. Almost the same evening their homes were surrounded and sealed off by security forces. Uday and his father-in-law, Ali Hassan al Majid, rocked up and the two prodigal sons-in-law found themselves under heavy machine gun, mortar and rocket fire. Eventually killed, their bodies were thrown onto the garbage dump after al Majid and Uday had emptied their pistols into the heads of the errant duo. I mean, what is this? The Iraqi version of the Jerry Springer show?

The UN reports that most of Iraq's population is experiencing mass deprivation, chronic hunger and endemic malnutrition, along with the collapse of personal incomes and a rapidly increasing number of destitute, jobless and homeless people. Sounds like a great place for a bargain vacation. For now the Iraqis can sell oil for food. The UN oil-for-food program began in 1996. It was resisted for months because of Iraqi concerns about loss of sovereignty (i.e., Saddam not being able to spend the cash on toys for the boys, like nuclear weapons). The UN allows Iraq to sell $10.4 billion worth of oil a year on condition that Iraq uses the revenues to buy food and medicine for its people. Yeah, some chance.

Meanwhile, Saddam is willing to pony up $14,000 for anyone that can shoot down a hostile jet in Iraqi space.

Publicly Saddam may be squawking, but his accountants are having some new deposit slips printed up. In fact, Saddam is reckoned to be one of the world's richest men. He is personally estimated to be worth around US$4 billion upwards and would rank number 47 in *Forbes* magazine's list of billionaires if it wasn't for the fact that he had stolen it all. Or is it just that he gets a really cool salary as president of Iraq?

Meanwhile, the Iraqi dinar continues to plunge. About 1,800 dinars fetch a buck these days. And the dinar won't catch up any time soon. U.S. Secretary of State Madeleine Albright declared in March 1997 that economic sanctions against Iraq would remain as long as Saddam stays in power. The sanctions have decimated the Iraqi people.

Considering that Baghdad is was once the breadbasket of the ancient world and part of the Fertile Crescent, the boys in Baghdad have done a good job of screwing it up—despite having enough oil to make Saudi Arabia look like a dry sump in Lubbock. Instead of basking in its riches, Iraq is poor, the consequence of Saddam's maniacal insistence on becoming the superpower of the Middle East. The Gulf War was a laughable attempt by Saddam to shun international diplomacy and snatch oil-rich Kuwait. Either Saddam didn't pay attention during history class or he just likes expensive fireworks, because he qualified his country for the Third World Club in a mere three months

President Saddam Hussein al-Tikriti

Saddam, the president, supreme commander, head of the National Command Council and self-styled Hero of al-Qadisiay, Knight of the Arab Nation, descendent of the Prophet, son of Imam Ali Ibn Abi Talib, is still the man. He had an early start at being a bastard. He was born out of wedlock on April 28, 1937, in the village of al-Ouja, an hour drive north of Baghdad. The man who sired him died before he was born. He got the name Saddam or "the stubborn one" because his mother tried to unsuccessfully abort him by strenuous labor. He was raised by an uncle, Khairallah Talfah, an Iraqi army officer who was jailed for a botched coup attempt against King Faisal II. He moved with his uncle to Baghdad in 1955 after he killed his first victim (shot in the back) at the ripe old age of 14. He was considered bright, cruel and violent. In his youth, he entertained himself and his friends by torturing and killing dogs and cats by sticking a red-hot steel rod up their anuses and in their eyes.

He joined the Ba'ath Party (Party of Arab Renewal) in 1957 and participated in an assassination attempt on Iraq's General Kassem on October 17, 1959. Saddam bungled it, was injured and fled to Syria for six months. He then went to study law in Egypt in 1962 and returned to Iraq after Kassem was deposed and executed in public.

Saddam married his cousin Sajida Talfah (the oldest daughter of Khairallah Talfah, the man who raised Saddam) in an arranged marriage in 1963. She bore two sons: Uday was born in 1964 and his second son, Qusay, was born in 1966. To show how close fruit falls from the tree in Iraq, he made his wife's brother, Adnan, defense minister and his wife's father the governor of Baghdad. You should also know he had Adnan killed. All in all, Saddam has had 40 of his relatives whacked.

The tables turned when Marshall Arif took power and arrested and jailed Ba'ath Party members, including Saddam. Saddam escaped and finally returned when Arif was deposed in 1968. This time Saddam became the ruling Ba'ath Party's deputy secretary general and chief inquisitor under President al-Bakr. Saddam kept busy executing hundreds of citizens, cozying up to the Russians and handing out jobs to fellow Tikritis. On May 16, 1979, al-Bakr died from heart failure. His heart stopped because he had been poisoned. The "stubborn one" had come from being a bastard to becoming the head bastard by the age of 43.

Saddam was famous for launching the 20th century's longest official war. The war with Iran killed one million people and lasted eight years. His big claim to fame was the invasion and rape of Kuwait. Under direct orders from Saddam, Iraqi soldiers are said to have removed more than 10,000 luxury vehicles (sold at public auction in Bagdad for $125 million), 3,216 bars of gold, 63 tons of gold coins and anything else of cultural or economic value, and had it shipped back to Iraq.

Saddam's banker was half brother and former head of the Mukhabarat, Barzan al-Tikriti who used to live in Geneva. (Why is it that so many of Saddam's family always end up being referred to in the past tense?) He was officially Iraq's rep at the UN, but he spent most of his time stashing away Saddam's bucks and buying weapons, including nukes. But in a fit of paranoia, Saddam had him recalled to Baghdad, accused him of cozying up to the CIA and put him under house arrest. Barzan, you will not be surprised to know, had a few problems with Uday. Thinking it might be a good idea to skip base, Barzan hopped on a plane for the United Arab Emirates and asked for political asylum.

Saddam has modestly bestowed a number of titles upon himself. He is president and chairman of the Revolutionary Command Council (RCC), regional secretary of the ruling Ba'ath Party, head of the 100,000-strong Popular Militia and commander in chief of Iraq's armed forces. In his youth, Saddam's dream was to become an officer in the Iraqi army. Alas, it was not to be. Saddam was rejected by the Iraqi military's officer training academy for his poor school grades. Never fear, when he became Prezzy in 1979 he made himself C in C of the armed forces, skipping all those tiresome ranks in between. One of the reasons Iraq screwed up so badly in its war with Iran was that C in C Saddam hadn't a clue about directing a war. No surprise, as he was never a soldier. He obviously never had a chance to study *Soldier of Fortune*, but still insisted on directing the war personally.

When he needs help running the country, he hires homeboys from Tikrit, north of Baghdad. The Tikritis are known as a minor league mafia who have graduated to running Iraq. But Saddam's absolute rule rests on more than just his popularity. He once shot dead a general who rashly disagreed with him in a cabinet meeting. Officially Saddam is chairman of the RCC, ex-officio, president of the republic. The president appoints ministers and judges, and laws are enacted by presidential decree. The country is currently divided into four zones of control. Saddam's cousin, Ali Hassan al Majid, governs Basra and much of the south. Majid has a good record for population control, which is such a concern of the World Health Organization (WHO) these days. It is unlikely, though, that Majid will be asked to write WHO pamphlets on how to keep the national population low. Majid's preferred methods are chemical weapons and firing squads. In northern Iraq, Majid managed to lower the Kurdish population by about 200,000 (out of 4 million) in less than a year at the end of the Iran-Iraq war.

Saddam's son Qusay and two generals control the other three sectors. But even they can't touch Majid for rapid population control.

Saddam is swiftly using up his nine lives. He survived a failed military coup in May 1991, and he offed 18 senior army officers just to make sure he could get a good night's sleep. In 1984, one of his stand-ins was assassinated by the Shiite Dawas (see "Marsh Arabs [the Ma'dan] and the Shiite Dawn Party"). His current body double is Faoas al-Emari, a man who has a hard time getting an insurance policy. It isn't known how many times the United States tried to take him out during the Gulf War. In June 1991, he fired 1,500 senior army officers and 180 senior police officers as a reward for following his orders during the Gulf War. Assassination attempts are the biggest concern for Saddam. After one attempt, more than 200 current and former officers and civilians were arrested, including the commander of the Republican Guard's tank battalion, Brig Sufiyan al-Ghurairi, and former parliamentarian Jasser al-Tikriti. All the plotters hailed from Saddam's hometown of Tikrit, as well as from Mosul and Ramadi. The attempt appears to have been the first in which members of the Tikrit clan played an important role in trying to remove their favorite son.

Saddam has developed a not-too-paranoid fear of being poisoned by shaking someone's hand. So if you happen to run into him, no soul shakes and definitely no tongue. If you're really lucky you get to kiss Saddam's armpits. His favorite song? The subtle and melodic, "Saddam, Oh Saddam, You Great and Powerful One." In October 1995, he held a plebiscite to see if Iraqis wanted him, and—surprise!—he received 99.9 percent of the vote. It is assumed that the 45 people who voted against him in Baghdad were either blind or shot as they were exiting the polls.

Saddam is one hell of a guy. In fact, he's like Qaddafi with cojones, or an Assad with more bluster and a guy who regularly takes on the entire Western world, his own people, his relatives and just about anybody who isn't him. Whatever you believe, one thing for sure is Saddam Hussein still calls the shots in Iraq.

For those of you who want to check out the official Iraqi Web site, try the following:

www.iraqi-mission.org

or for more on Saddamania try

http://www.inc.org.uk/Saddambackground.html
http://www.inc.org.uk/iraqiarm.htm
http://www.iraqfoundation.org/

The Bad Boys Club: Current and Recent Past

What do all these guys have in common? They like uniforms; they're on a first-name basis with editorial cartoonists; and they're all current or former targets of CIA plots.

Dues-Paying Members	
Fidel Castro	Cuba
Muammar Qaddafi	Libya
Saddam Hussein	Iraq
Kim Jong Il	North Korea
Emeritus	
Manuel Noriega	Panama
Ayatollah Khomeini	Iran
Daniel Ortega	Nicaragua

Uday Hussein al Majid al-Tikriti

The ultimate bastard son and spoilt brat, on whom all future aspiring bastards should model themselves. Tall, good looking—if you like the type—and sporting something of a slight limp these days, Uday is the real life Iraqi version of American psycho. Uday takes great pleasure in raping, murdering, gambling, partying and generally doing just about anything he wants to do including killing his father's butler, which landed him in jail for a short period. He was born June 18, 1964, and has a younger brother, Qusay, who runs all sections of the Mukhabarat (Iraqi secret police). Uday had a good headstart at being a psycho. At the tender age of four, his equivalent of Sunday school consisted of being taken to the torture chambers by Dad to watch the afternoon entertainment. Uday's weekend evenings are spent watching some of his vast video collection of people being tortured.

Uday is the editor of *Babel*, a newspaper known for its thoughtful editorials and sharp critiques. On April 1, 1999, Uday ran a headline in *Babel* saying that Russia had threatened the United States with a nuclear strike if sanctions were not lifted against Iraq. Turn to page two: It's . . . an April fool's joke. Ha ha. "Iraqis, you have only yourselves," Uday reminded his readers.

Like most of his family Uday likes to have a body double for insurance purposes. One of his doubles was Latif Yahia. Unfortunately, his resemblance to Uday was only passing. Not to worry. The ever-resourceful Uday had a plastic surgeon alter Latif's face to the required standards. When Latif decided to do a bunk, Uday got himself another double, Jutyar al Salihi. But he didn't like the pension scheme either and fled to Jordan in 1999.

Accordingly, there were few tears shed when, on December 12, 1996, he got a taste of his own medicine. Uday was speeding to Baghdad's al-Masur Club when six men sprayed his supposedly bulletproof Porsche with machine gun fire. Uday was hit eight times by bullets through the windshield. Uday had a hard time finding anyone who would treat him until Fidel Castro's personal doctor arrived. The upshot was that he lost part of his calf muscle and one lung. The group responsible was called Al Nahdah (The Awakening). They were tipped off about Uday's movements by a man called Ra'ad al Hazaa, whose uncle had his tongue cut out by Saddam and was then executed.

Uday has been married three times. His third wife is Hiba, the daughter of Ali Hassan al Majid. Uday has rightly been incensed by scurrilous and unfounded reports—by the ever irresponsible press—that the latest attempt to put him six feet under has also left him impotent, with a delicate part of his anatomy shot off. Uday, by the way, has no children. His brother, Qusay, has three children. Check out one of Uday's newspapers at:

http://www.index.com.jo/iraqtoday/index.html

Qusay Hussein al Tikriti

Uday's little brother. At the age of 33 he is now the second most important man in Iraq, after Dad of course. Qusay is responsible for the military, intelligence and security services in Iraq. These include organizations such as the Special Security Organization (SSO)—one of the most secretive organizations in Iraq—which is responsible for hiding Dad's nuclear weapons. Qusay and Uday are rivals, with a poisonous dislike of each other. Unlike Uday, Qusay is less a playboy than just plain old ruthless. Your average family man, Qusay also helps Dad with the annual prison purges and signs the execution warrants when Dad's a bit busy. Younger Qusay might be, but he has outdone older brother in everything. He is number two in the country and has three children. Uday has none and has been the laughing stock ever since he had his intestines reorganized.

Chemical Ali

Saddam's cousin and current governor of the south of Iraq, Ali Hassan al Majid, makes Saddam, Uday and Qusay look like bungling amateurs when it comes to mass murder. In fact, there are probably quite a few dictators around who could use Majid's population disposal services. Al Majid is called Chemical Ali because he decided the best way to solve the Kurdish rebellion was to gas them. He orchestrated the gassing of Kurdish villages carried out by low-flying helicopters with express orders to kill every living thing in the area, including plants and wildlife. This was all part of Operation "Anvil" at the end of the Gulf War (the first one that is), which saw the widespread use of chemical weapons against the Kurds in northern Iraq. Anfal had eight different phases and successfully solved the Kurdish question in Iraq. It also killed 200,000 Kurds.

In March 1988, in the town of Halabja, 5,000 Kurds died writhing in agony and 10,000 were seriously affected when Iraqi jets dropped chemical bombs on the town.

Surgical Bill

We're too lazy to do the math at *DP,* but here is WAG at what was dropped on Iraq. In the 109,000 sorties flown by a total of 2,800 fixed-wing aircraft, half were bombing runs. Over 20,000 sorties were flown against 300 strategic targets in Iraq and Kuwait; 5,000 were flown chasing down SCUDs, and 50,000 were against Iraqi forces in southern Iraq and Kuwait. Over 200 Tomahawk cruise missiles were fired from ships and submarines for the first time in combat.

The ordnance dropped totals about a quarter of a million bombs, 22,000 were "smart," 10,000 of these were laser-guided and 10,000 were guided anti-tank bombs. The remaining 2,000 were radiation-guided bombs directed at communication and radar installations. More than 3,000 bombs (including sea-launched cruise missiles) were dropped on metropolitan Baghdad.

Do You Want Fries with That?
(One Smart War Special to Go)

This is a partial list of what we delivered to Saddam during the past few years:

2,095 HARM missiles

217 Walleye missiles

5,276 guided antitank missiles

44,922 cluster bombs and rockets

136,755 conventional bombs

4,077 guided bombs (see below)

170,000 selections of the following

> Mk 82 (500 lbs)
>
> Mk 83 (1,000 lbs)
>
> Mk 84 (2,000 lbs),
>
> M117 (750 lbs)
>
> BLU-82 Daisy cutters (a 15,000-pound bomb containing GSX gelled slurry explosives), HE, fuel air explosives (FAE) or ethylene oxide fuel and about 80,000 cluster bombs

IRAQ

Do You Want Fries with That?
(One Smart War Special to Go)

Guided bombs included:

AGM-130, an electro-optically or infrared-guided 2,000-pound powered bomb

GBU-10 Paveway II, a 2,000-pound laser-guided bomb

GBU-101 Paveway II, a 2,000-pound laser-guided bomb with I-2000 hard target munition

GBU-12 Paveway II, a 500-pound laser-guided bomb, anti-tanks

GBU-24 Paveway III, a 2,000-pound laser-guided, low-level weapon (with BLU-109 bomb and mid-course auto pilot) used against chemical and industrial facilities, bridges, nuclear storage areas, and aircraft shelters,

GBU-27 Paveway III, a 2,000-pound laser-guided bomb with I-2000 hard target munition

Despite the sexy Sega press conferences most of the ordnance was delivered Vietnam style by the venerable B-52 flying at 40,000 feet and releasing 40–60 bombs of 500 or 750 pounds each. (A direct violation of Article 51 of Geneva Protocol I which prohibits area bombing)

GBU-28, a 5,000-pound "bunker busting" laser-guided bomb.

The North: The Kurds

Only a few days after the Gulf War ended, major insurrections broke out in both the south of Iraq and particularly in the northern Kurdish provinces, where Kurd rebels seized large areas of territory by the first week of March 1991. Iraq's "elite" Republican Guards used repugnant brutality in suppressing the Kurdish rebellion. Kurd refugees fleeing the wrath of the Republican Guard numbered 2 million or more along Iraq's borders with both Turkey and Iran. The U.S. and Great Britain dispatched troops to northern Iraq in an effort to entice the Kurds to return home and force the Iraqi army to leave the northern region.

When the Iraqi army pulled out of the north they left a political vacuum which was filled by the two main rival Kurdish groups, the Kurdistan Democratic Party (KDP) and Patriotic Union of Kurdistan (PUK), which continue to administer different parts of the region.

The U.S.-protected area is called Kurdistan. Of the 19.2 million people in Iraq, 21.6 percent are Kurds (73.5 percent are Arabs). There is a legitimate argument for the state of Kurdistan since the Kurds were left out of any postcolonial country carving. The Iraqi army has been doing bad things to the Kurds away from the scrutiny of the world. They have used a variety of methods to exterminate the Kurds, including bombing, starvation and chemical weapons. One major problem the Kurds have had is that no Iraqi government wants to let them control the oil fields in the Kirkuk area, which the Kurds claim as theirs. (See "Kurdistan.")

http://www.kdp.pp.se
http://www.puk.org

The CIA

Sometimes you wonder when the boys in Langley screw things up that maybe they rehearse and script it so our enemies think they screwed up. But there is no hiding that perhaps 300 Iraqis died in 1996 in a failed CIA attempt to overthrow Saddam Hussein. The blundering almost cost the United States northern Iraq and was one of the agency's biggest failures in its 50-year history. The attempt to oust Saddam was spawned by the CIA's belief that Saddam was ripe for a downfall after the defection of his son-in-law Lt. Gen. Hussein Kamil al Majid in 1995.

In early 1996, President Bill Clinton approved $6 million (not a whole lot when you come to think of it) for a covert ops group set up by the CIA called the Iraqi National Accord. Drafted from the ranks of former Iraqi officers, its mission was to destabilize Baghdad through bombing attacks. Saddam responded by having his tanks roll through Arbil in Iraqi Kurdistan after a Kurdish leader invited him into the region to solve the inter Kurdish fighting—by crushing the other side.

Saddam took advantage of this to waste every CIA operative who was unfortunate enough to be in town. Three thousand Iraqis and Kurds on the CIA payroll had to be evacuated out of Iraq through Turkey and Guam to the United States, where, we presume, more than a handful had their faces and fingertips changed. The CIA has spent some $100 million since 1991 in an effort to bag Saddam Hussein.

The South Marsh Arabs (the Ma'dan) and the Shiite Dawa Party

This area between the Tigris and the Euphrates has been home to the Ma'dan for over 5,000 years. The people live on islands and travel using ancient dugout canoes. Many of their villages are actually man-made floating islands. There is also a group of about 10,000 insurgents who fight against the government of Iraq. Although the people allude to it as the Garden of Eden, it is a hot, humid place infested with mosquitoes, fleas and ticks. Winters are cold, with gales coming from the mountains of Kurdistan to the north or Iran to the east. Saddam has been bulldozing villages and using tanks, poison and air raids to show his displeasure. In Iraq, there are about 50,000 Shiites living in the areas once considered to be the Garden of Eden. Some are Sabeans who predate Islam. Saddam's government is Sunni, even though 55 percent of Iraqis are Shiites. The Shiites in the south are supported by Shiite Iran. The Dawa is a group founded by Ayatollah Baqir al-Sadr who played host to Ayatollah Khomeini when he was on the run. Because of a deal struck by Saddam with the then Shah of Iran in 1978, Khomeini was physically tossed out of the holy city of Najaf, Iraq, and split for Paris. Chemical Ali personally strangled Ayatollah Baqir al-Sadr and had his two sisters hanged. The Dawa party was—surprise, surprise—banned and is now covertly headquartered in Basra.

For now, Saddam is busy building dams, draining the marshes and pouring poison into the rivers (he loves to play with chemicals, doesn't he?) in an effort to simply eliminate every living thing in the marshes. When he gets bored of poisoning the people, crops and animals, he has his army pound on them with artillery, strafe them with gunships and drop large bombs on them. If things are a little slow, he has his soldiers burn hundreds of acres of weeds just to give them something to do.

http://www.arab.net
http://www.inc.org.uk/marshes.html

Uncle Sam, the Allies and Armageddon

It is hard to say whether we wanted to flatten Iraq or just drop off a lot of old ordnance. They didn't let many journos in on the Mother of All Battles. Even Saddam parked the journos until he could find enough dead babies to photograph. We fought a war, managed to shoot more of our own people than the enemy did, and then handed everything back to the same people and went home. It's no wonder that Saddam announced he had won the war because in fact, he did. He stripped Kuwait faster than Uday can get a transvestite naked and then left the smoking bits for us to fix. He even got so bored he did the spank-the-kid, kick-the-dog routine by SCUDing Israel just so he'd have a live version of Space Invaders to watch from his bunker. Despite the fact that we dropped 227,000 bombs (of which only 8,000 were "smart"), we only killed 3,000 civilians. It seems you could kill that number of people just by dropping rocks or pennies out of B-52s. We didn't take out "the Stubborn One" and we didn't even mess up those nice pictures of him all over Baghdad. However, we did bomb a civilian shelter and, yes, Iraq has a bad habit of camouflaging their military installations to look like suburbs. But all in all, we didn't do a very good job.

We left about 400,000 soldiers, 2,200 tanks, 2,500 APCs, and 1,650 artillery pieces. We dropped over 120 million pounds of explosives in just under a month, and we didn't even make one of those big craters that people like to visit after the war. And God forbid we mention how much those cruise missiles cost and how many people each one didn't kill.

There are about 300 combat aircraft left that are hampered by the two no-fly zones monitored by the West. Why didn't we leave Saddam with a slingshot and two rocks? Well, seems that George Bush was more worried about Iran, so he whittled Saddam's toys down to Third World size.

http://www.inc.org.uk/palaces.html

UNSCOM

How you can you have a "latest six month report" from a 90-day project? Well, if you are the UN, no worries mate. On April 3 the UN passed Security Council Resolution 687 (1991), which essentially ordered Saddam to drop his drawers for a full short arm inspection. Well, a few years and one Scott Ritter later, the UN is on Security Council Resolution 1205 (1998), which unanimously condemns Iraq's actions and demands that Iraq rescind immediately and unconditionally its decisions of October 31 and August 5. Not a whole lot has transpired.

http://www.un.org/Depts/unscom/

Supreme Council of the Islamic Resistance in Iraq (SCIRI)

There were about 10,000 rebels in southern Iraq under an umbrella called the Supreme Council for the Islamic Revolution in Iraq. They are about the only real opposition to Saddam (discounting the Kurds in the north), with genuine people on the ground fighting the regime. Some have regrouped in the north. Many were killed in 1991 by Saddam Hussein during the aborted uprising. They have joined with the Iraqi National Congress (INC) and are based in Sulaymanya (Kurdistan)

SCIRI

Dr. Hamid al Bayati
27a Old Gloucester Rd.
London, WC1N 3XX
Tel.: [44] (171) 371 6815
Fax: [44] (171) 371 2886
E-mail: 101642.1150@compuserve.com

Iraqi National Congress (INC)

The CIA bankrolled the INC in the SAS hotel in Vienna, Austria, in 1992. The tab was $15 million and the idea was to combine all the anti-Saddam groups under one organization. Ahmed Chalabi, former Jordanian-based Shiite Iraqi and ex-banker, was picked to run the INC. Now wanted in Jordan on fraud charges, he sensibly lives in London (See "Kurdistan.") The INC is a bit of a defunct organization to be honest. It's an umbrella organization with no one under the umbrella. The Kurds, for example, are not part of the INC.

Iraqi National Congress
17 Cavendish Square
London W1M 9AA
Tel.: 0171 665 1812
Fax: 0171 665 1201
E-mail: pressoffice@inc.org.uk
http://www.inc.org.uk/
http://www.afsc.org/iraq/chalabi.htm

Iraqi National Accord

The Saudis and the CIA bankrolled this group as an alternative to the INC. Led by Ayad Alawi, an Iraqi doctor from Baghdad, it is headquartered in London, UK. The CIA kicked in $10 million to get things going, but used the INC to raise hell in Kurdistan. (See "Kurdistan.")

http://www.iraq-free.demon.co.uk

Iran

Saddam hates Shiite Iran and wasted hundreds of thousands of Iraqis in a bizarre WWI-style retro war of trenches and artillery duels. He kicked things off on September 22, 1980, when 400,000 Iraqis troops invaded Iran across an 800-mile front. Eight years later, the war ended with no winner. For their part the Iranians detest Saddam. No big surprise there, I suppose.

Travel Warning

The Department of State warns all U.S. citizens against traveling to Iraq. Conditions within the country remain unsettled and dangerous. The United States does not maintain diplomatic relations with Iraq and cannot provide normal consular protective services to U.S. citizens.

The Iraqi embassy considers Iraq safe for travel, and they are probably about 80 percent right. It's the 20 percent you have to worry about. Border crossings between Jordan and Iraq are closed; all others are open. Crossings from Turkey are backed up but are orderly and efficient.

You must be a reporter or use a foreign passport. Passports and visas are required. On February 8, 1991, U.S. passports ceased to be valid for travel to, in or through Iraq and may not be used for that purpose unless a special validation has been obtained. Without the requisite validation, use of a U.S. passport for travel to, in or through Iraq may constitute a violation of 18 U.S.C. 1544, and may be punishable by a fine and/or imprisonment. An exemption to the above restriction is granted to Americans residing in Iraq as of February 8, 1991, who continue to reside there, and to American professional reporters or journalists on assignment there.

In addition, the Department of the Treasury prohibits all travel-related transactions by U.S. persons intending to visit Iraq, unless specifically licensed by the Office of Foreign Assets Control. The only exceptions to this licensing requirement are for journalistic activity or for U.S. government or United Nations business. The categories of individuals eligible for consideration for a special passport validation are set forth in 22 C.F.R. 51.74. Passport validation requests for Iraq should be forwarded in writing to either of the following addresses:

Iraqi Embassy

> *1801 P Street, NW*
> *Washington, DC 20036*
> *Tel.: (202) 483-7500*

Deputy Assistant Secretary for Passport Services

> *U.S. Department of State*
> *1111 19th Street, NW, Suite 260*
> *Washington, DC 20522-1705*
> *Attn: Office of Passport Policy and Advisory Services*
> *Tel.: (202) 955-0231 or 955-0232*
> *Fax: (202) 955-0230.*

The request must be accompanied by supporting documentation according to the category under which validation is sought. Currently, the four categories of persons specified in 22 C.F.R. 51.74 as being eligible for consideration for passport validation are as follows:

[1] Professional reporters: Includes full-time members of the reporting or writing staff of a newspaper, magazine or broadcasting network whose purpose for travel is to gather information about Iraq for dissemination to the general public.

[2] American Red Cross: Applicant establishes that he or she is a representative of the American Red Cross or International Red Cross traveling pursuant to an officially sponsored Red Cross mission.

[3] Humanitarian considerations: Applicant must establish that his or her trip is justified by compelling humanitarian considerations or for family unification. At this time, "compelling humanitarian considerations" include situations where the applicant can document that an immediate family member is critically ill in Iraq. Documentation concerning family illness must include the name and address of the relative, and be from that relative's physician attesting to the nature and gravity of the illness. "Family unification" situations may include cases in which spouses or minor children are residing in Iraq, with and dependent on, an Iraqi national spouse or parent for their support.

[4] National interest: The applicant's request is otherwise found to be in the national interest.

In all requests for passport validation for travel to Iraq, the name, date and place of birth for all concerned persons must be given, as well as the U.S. passport numbers. Documentation as outlined above should accompany all requests. Additional information may be obtained by writing to the above addresses or by calling the Office of Passport Policy and Advisory Services at *(202) 326-0231 or 955-0232.*

U.S. Treasury Restrictions

In August 1990, President Bush issued Executive Orders 12722 and 12724, imposing economic sanctions against Iraq, including a complete trade embargo. The U.S. Treasury Department's Office of Foreign Assets Control administers the regulations related to these sanctions, which include restrictions on all financial transactions related to travel to Iraq. These regulations prohibit all travel-related transactions, except as specifically licensed. The only exceptions to this licensing requirement are for persons engaged in journalism or in official U.S. government or UN business. Questions concerning these restrictions should be directed to:

Chief of Licensing Section, Office of Foreign Assets Control

> *U.S. Department of the Treasury*
> *Washington, DC 20220*
> *Tel.: (202) 622-2480*
> *Fax: (202) 622-1657*

In the past year, most foreigners detained at the Kuwait-Iraq border, regardless of nationality, have been sentenced to jail terms of seven to ten years for illegally entering Iraq.

During 1992 and 1993, Iraq detained nine Westerners—three Swedes, three Britons, a U.S. national, a German and a Frenchman—on charges of illegally entering Iraq. They were released by late 1993 after much diplomatic energy. In March 1995, two Americans were held and sentenced to eight years in prison. Tom Jerrold and an ABC news crew were also detained, but were released after the UN intervened. Brent Sadler, who interviewed the two Americans in the Iraq jail, was asked for his written permission to be in the jail, even when accompanied by a Polish diplomat negotiating the release on behalf of the U.S. State Department!

There have been attacks against foreigners, and antagonism is still high in the Western world. Many Egyptians and other Arab expatriates were killed by disgruntled, unemployed Iraqi ex-soldiers. Don't forget that expats were held hostage by Hussein from mid- to late-1990 during the Mexican standoff between Iraqi and Allied forces over the Iraqi annexation of Kuwait. All travelers and foreigners in Iraq run the risk of being detained, harassed and questioned, particularly in the south near the Kuwaiti border. The Iraqi embassy referred us to Mr. Ganji at Babylon Travel, *(312) 478-9000,* for readers who want more details about travel to Iraq.

AIDS Test

Iraqi government officials have seemingly watched so many soap operas and pay-per-view dirty movies while out of the country that they think all Westerners are sex-crazed adulterers, fornicators and deviants.

Therefore, all visitors over age 12 and under 65 who plan to stay in Iraq for longer than five days (official visitors have 15 days) must call on the Central Public Health Laboratory in Al Tayhariyat al Fennia Square between 8 A.M. and 2 P.M. to either present HIV and syphilis (VDRL) certificates or arrange for a local test at a cost of ID100. HIV and VDRL certificates valid for Iraq may be obtained in the U.K. by arranging a blood test with a general practitioner. The sample should then be tested by a Public Health Laboratory Service listed on the blank certificate and attested by the Foreign Office and the Iraqi embassy in London. Failing to comply with these requirements carries a fine of ID500 or six months imprisonment. A yellow fever vaccination certificate is required for all visitors arriving from an infected area.

Iraq has 38,402 kilometers of paved roads. Expressway No. 1—a 1200-kilometer, six-lane freeway—connects Baghdad to Kuwait in the south and runs to Jordan and Syria in the west. A 630-kilometer freeway (Expressway No. 2) runs north from Baghdad to the Turkish border, where it links up with the modern freeway connecting southeast Turkey to Ankara and Istanbul. Another Baghdad-Basra route is planned via Kut and Amarah and will be known as Expressway No. 3.

There are 2,032 kilometers of rail network, including the 461-kilometer Baghdad-Kirkuk-Arbil line, the 528-kilometer Baghdad-Mosul-Yurubiyah standard line and the 582-kilometer Baghdad-Maaqal-Umm Qasr standard line. The 516-kilometer line between Baghdad and al-Qaim and Qusaybah on the Syrian border was opened last year. The 252-kilometer northern line between Kirkuk, Baiji and Haditha, which connects the Baiji oil refinery with the al-Qaim fertilizer plant, was opened in 1988.

Iraq's main port of Basra is inoperative because of the closure of the Shatt al-Arab waterway during the war with Iran. Several Iraqi naval vessels were sunk in the waterway during the Gulf War.

Iraq has an international airport at Bamerni, 17 kilometers south of Baghdad. Another international airport was planned for Mosul, with a 4,000-meter runway capable of handling 30 landings and takeoffs a day. Domestic regional airports at Arbil (3,000-meter runway), Amara and Najaf (for small 50-seater aircraft) were also planned. Iraqi Airways has a fleet of four Boeing 747s, two Boeing 737s, six Boeing 727s and two Boeing 707s.

You can rent a car from the airport. You will need both national and international driving licenses. You can also take the bus service for the 17-kilometer trip from the city center to the airport. In Baghdad, the double-decker buses are cheap and can take you just about anywhere you want to go; don't forget to buy your tickets at the kiosks first. There are also private mini-buses and shared taxis. A train service operates three times a day from Baghdad to Basra; don't plan on comfort or air-conditioning unless you're lucky. You can choose from three class services with sleeping accommodations, restaurant cars and air conditioning. You can take the train between most of Iraq's major centers (Baghdad-Mosul, Baghdad-Arbil and Baghdad-Basra).There is also regular bus service from Baghdad to other major cities and regular flights between Baghdad, Basra and Mosul. Domestic airports are at Mosul, Kirkuk and Basra, as well as Baghdad.

Taxis must be negotiated in advance. During the war, *DP* paid $1,200 to get out of Baghdad to Turkey (but we didn't have to tip). Taxis have meters, but it is legal to charge twice the amount shown on the meter. After 10 P.M. there is a surcharge.

Baghdad

The city where any pyrotechnic would be right at home. While most people have to wait for November 4 to see fireworks, Baghdad residents get a regular eyeful, all for free on a regular basis. The United States and Britain continue to bomb Baghdad whenever Saddam misbehaves. This is now largely ignored by the media which has grown bored of it. Occasionally someone tries to kill Saddam or one of his sons, making life tricky for passersby. And just for fun Iranian intelligence has left bombs behind for the Mujahadeen-e-Khalk, an Iranian opposition group based in Baghdad. You too can design you own video game, start with this keen free map:

http://www.reliefweb.int/mapc/mid_east/cnt/irqbag.html

The Kuwaiti Border

The Iraqis are sore losers. U.S. citizens and other foreigners working near the Kuwait-Iraq border have been detained by Iraqi authorities for lengthy periods under harsh conditions. Travelers to that area, whether in Kuwait or not, are in immediate jeopardy of detention by Iraqi security personnel. Journalists and oil workers have been detained. And there are untold numbers of land mines waiting to be unearthed. Feeling nervous? Don't be. "We are able to defend our borders with courage and fight to the last soldier and we have a reserve force at the ready that can be on the battlefield in 24 hours," said Kuwait's chief of staff Lieutenant General Ali Al Mounen. It just depends if the discos are closed or not.

Prison

The one place you don't want to end up in. They're very crowded in Iraq and you don't get to see your lawyer (ever). The food is rubbish and the beds are lumpy. The good part is that you won't be staying for very long in an Iraqi prison. Or is that the bad part? When things get too crowded Saddam has his annual version of spring cleaning, which is to say there are mass executions. In late 1997 and 1998 hundreds, possibly thousands, of prisoners were executed throughout Iraq under the direction Saddam's younger son, Qusay.

IRAQ

Art Patrons

Any visitor to Iraq (no, you can't fly over and drop bombs to be considered a tourist) marvels at the statues and monuments to the great leader. It's fairly common for middle east dictators to plaster their likenesses on everything from car stickers to the sides of apartment buildings. If you ever wonder why those statues of those military men in Basra are pointing across the Shatt al-Arab waterway, that's the direction of their enemy, Iran. But Saddam and Iraq are over the top. He claims not only at least 50 palaces but is working on the world's largest mosque, a double-decker bridge, the tallest tower in the Middle East in Bagdad and a monument to the "Mother of all battles." He is already famous for his "Celebration," a 24-ton crossed-swords monument built from the melted down guns of Iranians.

Soccer Games

Monday night's a great night for football! In July 1996, in a soccer game in Libya involving a team sponsored by Libyan leader Muammar Qaddafi's eldest son, murder and mayhem broke out after the referee made a call against Saadi Qaddafi's team. Junior's players began beating up the ruffled ref and players on the opposing team. When fans started to heckle Saadi and his team, Saadi's bodyguards responded by spraying the stands with bullets. Spectators shot back. When the cordite finally settled, the body count stacked up to as high as 50.

Not to be outdone, Saddam's eldest son and head of the Iraqi Football Federation, Uday—the Middle East's master of motivating halftime speeches—had members of the Iraqi national team tortured after Kazakhstan beat Iraq 3–1 on June 29, 1997. Uday ordered several members of the team to a secret prison at the offices of the Iraqi Olympic Committee, where the players were caned on the soles of their feet and beaten on their backs. Then they were forced to jump into a sewage tank to help the wounds go sceptic. As another punishment, they were forced to kick a concrete football around the prison yard. Needless to say there are no longer large queues of young men trying to join the Iraqi football team. Wanna feel how Iraqis (or in this case Assyrians) feel about soccer? Check out:

http://www.aina.org/aol/bulls/stars.htm

The diseases you should be vaccinated against are typhoid, cholera and hepatitis. Tap water should be sterilized before drinking, and visitors should avoid consuming ice. Milk is unpasteurized and should be boiled. Comprehensive medical insurance covering repatriation is essential, unless you want to get even sicker in an Iraqi hospital. Health and sanitary conditions weren't too good before the war, and they are worse now in all the major cities. Water, refuse and sanitation services are nonexistent, especially in the south, where outbreaks of typhoid, hepatitis, meningitis and gastroenteritis had reached epidemic proportions by late 1993. An outbreak of cholera was contained. Hospitals and other medical facilities were also damaged during the war and vital electricity supplies disrupted. Many expatriate doctors and hospital staff left the country. Stocks of pharmaceuticals have been depleted, and there are severe shortages of even nonprescription drugs. Essential drugs are almost nonexistent. If you need or think you may need medication or drugs, bring plenty with you. You can always donate or sell what you don't need on your way out.

Iraq has a population of 21.5 million. Although 53.5 percent of the population are Shia Muslims, the minority Sunni Muslims (41.5 percent) are politically dominant.

The Iraqi currency, for what little it's worth, is the Iraqi dinar (ID). One ID = 1000 files. Banks are generally open from 8 A.M.–12 noon. Government offices are generally open 8:30 A.M.–2:30 P.M. Businesses are open 8 A.M.–2 P.M. Shops, when they have anything to sell, don't follow the clock, opening at dawn, closing for lunch when the sun is high, and reopening when the day cools off around 4 p.m. Small shops tend to open very early, close during the middle of the day, and then reopen from around 4 P.M. till 7 P.M. or later. Food markets open around 9 A.M. and close at midday, or when supplies are exhausted. The Islamic year contains 354 or 355 days, meaning that Muslim feasts advance by 10 to 12 days against the Gregorian calendar each year. Dates of feasts vary according to the sighting of the new moon, so they cannot be forecast precisely.

There is a neutral zone between Iraq and Saudi Arabia, administered jointly by the two countries, with Iraq's portion covering 3,522 square kilometers. The country's most fertile area is the centuries-old floodplain of the Tigris and Euphrates Rivers, from Turkey and Syria to the Gulf. The northeast of Iraq is mountainous, while the large western desert area is sparsely populated and undeveloped. The northern mountainous region experiences severe winters, but the southern plains have warm winters with little rain and very hot, dry summers. The temperatures in Baghdad are between 40°F and 60°F in January, and between 75°F and 90°F in July and August. The average annual rainfall is 28 millimeters.

Alcohol is available only in international hotels. During the Ramadan, fasting month, both smoking and drinking in public are forbidden.

Money Hassles

The Iraqi dinar is virtually worthless (3.2 to the U.S. dollar officially; 1,000 to the dollar semiofficially and 3,000 dinars to the buck on the black market). The shortage of foreign currency has created a thriving black market, although the penalties for its use are severe, with heavy fines and possible imprisonment. The difference in exchange rates is vast between the black market and the official rates. You must declare your funds on entry, but few people do. It is legal to bring only ID25 into Iraq and take out ID5. Any amount of hard currency may be imported, but this must be declared on entry, and receipts must be obtained for any expenditure in Iraq. The balance and receipts must be shown upon leaving the country. Credit cards are not generally accepted, and traveler's checks are virtually useless. Iraqis traveling abroad may take out ID100.

Embassy Location

There is no U.S. embassy or consulate in Iraq. The U.S. government is not in a position to accord normal consular protective services to U.S. citizens who are in Iraq. U.S. government interests are represented by the government of Poland, which, as a protecting power, is able to provide only limited emergency services to U.S. citizens. The U.S. interests section of the embassy of Poland is located opposite the Foreign Ministry Club (Masbah Quarter):

U.S. Interests Section, Embassy of Poland

P.O. Box 2447 Alwiyah
Baghdad, Iraq
Tel.: (964-1) 719-6138, 719-6139, 719-3791, 718-1840

11/3/99	Saddam says he is ready to kick U.S. troops from the gulf.
12/17/98	Operation Desert Fox: Baghdad is bombed for four days after UN weapons inspectors were expelled from Iraq.
11/22/98	UN weapons inspectors leave Iraq.
8/31/96	Iraqi forces enter Arbil at invitation of KDP.
5/96	Iraq is permitted to sell $2 billion worth of oil over six months to buy food and medicine.
10/15/99	Presidential elections achieved 99.96 percent yes vote and 99.47 percent turnout for Saddam Hussein, leaving only about 3,300 unaccounted voters among 8.4 million.
4/16/91	U.S. President George Bush announces that U.S. troops will enter northern Iraq to create a safe haven for displaced Kurds around Zakhu.
3/2/91	Iraq signs a cease-fire agreement with allied forces, ending the Persian Gulf War.
02/27/1991	Allied forces in Kuwait and Iraq suspend military operations against Iraq.
2/24/91	Allied forces launch the ground assault against Iraqi forces occupying Kuwait.
1/30/91	Iraqi and multinational force elements have their first combat engagement in Khafji in the Persian Gulf War.
1/17/91	The start of hostilities between the multinational forces and Iraqi forces. The beginning of Operation Desert Storm.
8/2/90	Iraqi forces invade Kuwait and seize control of the country.
8/15/86	Turkish troops raid Kurdish rebel camps in Iraq.
11/26/84	Relations with the United States restored.
6/7/81	Israeli warplanes attack an Iraqi nuclear power plant near Baghdad.
9/19/80	Iran-Iraq war begins.
3/10/79	Death of Kurdish leader Mullah Mustafa Barzani (Kurdish regions).
6/1/76	During this month, Syria enters the civil war in Lebanon on the side of the Christian Phalange and against the Palestinians and their Muslim allies. In response, Abu Nidal renames his terrorist group then based in Iraq the Black June Organization and begins attacking Syrian targets.
7/17/68	Ba'ath Party seizes power.
2/8/63	Revolution Day.
2/3/63	The Ba'ath Party takes power in a popular revolt.
7/14/58	Republic Day. Celebrates the coup by General Abdul Karim Qasim during which King Faisal II and Prime Minister Nuri as-Said are killed.
4/8/47	Iraqi Ba'ath Party founded.
1/22/46	Kurdish Republic Day.
4/28/37	Saddam Hussein's birthday.
03/21	Kurdish New Year celebrated.

Israel
★★

Eye to Eye

Burdened by American cash and a sense that the Arab world is not as unifed or wealthy as they thought, it appears that Israel and its neighbors are beginning to see eye to eye. New émigrés who lack a knifelike hatred for Arabs and who have a need to just get on with things are slowly eroding the hawkish base that has made Israel both a pariah nation and a model for new countries.

On November 4, 1995, Israeli prime minister Yitzhak Rabin was gunned down at point-blank range by an unrepentant 25-year-old Jewish extremist, Yigal Amir. The Jewish-Palestinian struggle came full circle, as Israel discovered the biggest threat to the peace accord may not be HAMAS, the Palestinian terrorist group bent on Israel's destruction, but may come from right-wing Jewish extremists within its own precarious borders.

The leader of Shin Bet (the General Security Service, or GSS—Israel's secret service apparatus), known only as "K" under Israeli law, resigned after taking responsibility for a dearth of GSS precautions in preventing the assassination of Rabin. But it's interesting to note that "K" was long aware of the kinetic dangers posed by the enemy within; his college master's-degree thesis had been on the need of Israel's security forces to be prepared not only for the Palestinian threat, but also that from Israel's own hard-core religious right.

Reach Out and Kill Someone

Israel paid a Gaza businessman one million dollars and a false passport to deliver a booby-trapped cellphone to 30-year-old Yehiya Ayash in the Gaza Strip. The phone was a loaner while Ayash's phone was being repaired. Yehiya Ayash was from the West Bank and is credited with the string of suicide attacks and bombings. He did not know that the phone had high explosives in the earpiece set up to be detonated by audio signal. The security people made a call to Ayash and then triggered the explosion. It is not known whether the call made to Ayash was collect or not. The businessman is suspected to be in hiding in the States, where his son lives.

Despite the Israelis' need and demand for a homeland, their Arab brethren refuse to see things eye to eye; it's more like eye for an eye. Despite the peace agreement reached with the PLO, the trading of eyes and teeth between Israel and its numerous enemies continues at unprecedented levels. The increase in terrorist threats against Israel, particularly in the wake of the historic Israeli-Palestinian pact, has turned out to be more than merely the holy smoke of bored car bombers.

America's checkbook diplomacy convinced Israel and the Palestine Liberation Organization (PLO) to recognize each other's right to exist on September 9, 1994, with the historic signing of a Declaration of Principles by Rabin and PLO chairman Yasir Arafat. It would be fair to say that the increase in attacks, deaths and political violence is escalating due to the intense opposition to the agreement by extremist Palestinian groups such as HAMAS and right-wing Jewish groups.

While most of the world has lauded the pact as the most significant peace agreement in decades, enemies of Israel and Israeli settlers in the Occupied Territories, believing they'd been bought out by the United States—which essentially they were—have nothing but revenge in mind for Arafat. These "enemies" include some heavy hitters. Both Abu Nidal of the Fatah Revolutionary Council and Ahmed Jibril, leader of the Popular Front for the Liberation of Palestine General Command (PFLP-GC), have threatened to assassinate Arafat for treason. George Habash, head of the Damascus-based Popular Front for the Liberation of Palestine (PFLP), said the agreement would, ironically, increase *intifada,* the uprising on the West Bank and the Gaza Strip. He was right. Right-wing Jewish settlers and HAMAS alike have launched terrorist attacks in an attempt to discredit and dissolve the agreement.

Earlier that year, on May 4, 1994, Rabin and Arafat signed a long-awaited pact allowing Palestinians limited self-rule in the Gaza Strip and Jericho. Under the agreement, Israeli forces were withdrawn from designated areas, turning enforcement over to a Palestinian police force. A week later, the first contingent of nearly 150 Palestinian police officers entered the Gaza Strip from Egypt. (The agreement calls for an eventual force of 9,000 officers to police what is to become Palestine.) The new cops were greeted with flowers by inhabitants in the Strip. Not so by HAMAS and other radical factions.

While I was doing a radio interview, one listener phoned in and was surprised to hear me include Israel in *DP*'s list of war zones. Then, on April 10, 1996, Israel

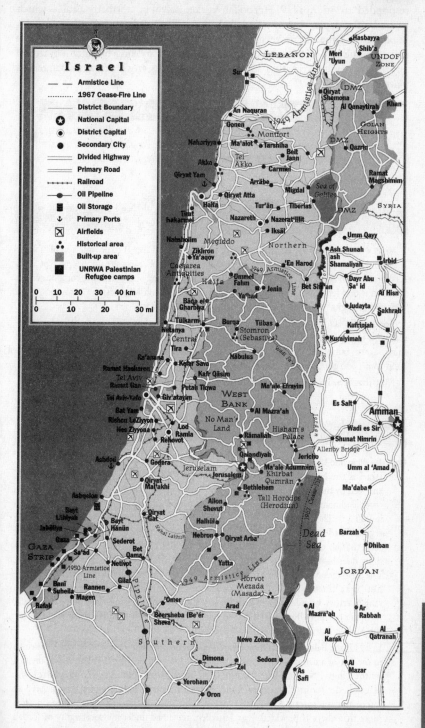

Israel

- – –   Armistice Line
- ·······   1967 Cease-Fire Line
- —   District Boundary
- ★   National Capital
- ◉   District Capital
- ●   Secondary City
- ═══   Divided Highway
- ───   Primary Road
- ┝━┥   Railroad
- ●━━●   Oil Pipeline
- ▮   Oil Storage
- ↓   Primary Ports
- ☒   Airfields
- ⁞⁞⁞   Historical area
-    Built-up area
- ▮   UNRWA Palestinian Refugee camps

0 10 20 30 40 km

0 10 20 30 ml

responded to an April 9 Hezbollah rocket salvo in northern Israel—which injured 40 people—by invading Lebanon. Hezbollah continued to launch hundreds of Katyusha rockets into northern Israel despite the invasion. Attacks still continue into 2000 even though prospects are looking brighter—but until Israel finds true peace within and with its neighbors, it will remain a dangerous place.

Terrorism Strikes Back

In March 1998, hackers attacked the Prime Minister Netanyahu's Netvision Web site, redirecting it to the Penthouse site. Netanyahu's wife's site led visitors to Playgirl magazine. The Israeli government has not decided which Palestinian Web sites to rocket yet.

Israel was carved out of Palestine by the British after World War II to provide a home for the Jews. The Arabs who had inhabited the region for hundreds of years were not happy. Not at all. Like most colonial border carvings, both sides are still arguing about it. What complicates the situation is that Jerusalem is a holy site for Christians, Jews and Muslims. It's a stew pot, filled with just the right spices and garnishes for one helluva long war.

The Israelis' landgrabs in Egypt, Jordan, Syria and Lebanon have not made them very popular with their neighbors. Peace agreements with their once bellicose neighbors have cooled things down, but HAMAS, Hezbollah and their hometown supporters of Iran, Syria and Lebanon aren't just going to forgive and forget.

Now that Syria is looking to talk instead of bankrolling terrorists, things may calm down.

God, the Bible and History Books

Israel is the homeland for the chosen people, the Israelites. Children of Abraham, enslaved by the Egyptians, led out of Egypt to Israel by Moses around 1290 B.C., the ten commandments, Mount Sinai, King David, a period of peace until the death of Solomon in 900 B.C. Then a whole lot of smiting as Assyrians, Greeks and Romans conquered the region. The Jewish revolt in the middle of the second century B.C. created an independent state that lasted for almost a century under the Maccabees. Jesus shows up about this time, does his thing and gets crucified. Then the Muslims capture the area in A.D. 638. The Crusades followed, and then the Ottoman empire. The British captured Palestine from the Ottomans in 1917 and promised the great grandfather of the present Jordanian king that they would create an independent state. What they were really doing was trying to figure out how Britain, France and Russia (the Sykes-Picot agreement) would divide the Middle East.

In 1917, the Balfour Declaration created by Britain promised Jews who helped the British in the war of a national homeland in Palestine. After World War II Palestine was divided by the United Nations. The partition gave Jews part of Palestine; the West Bank was placed under Jordan; Gaza came under Egyptian control; and Jerusalem was declared an international territory. A year later in 1948 the State of Israel was established on areas more than the UN provided. East Jerusalem remained under the sovereignty of Jordan until 1967, when Israel used the Six Day War to occupy the rest of Palestine. History provides no clear indication of whether Israel is owned or intended to be controlled by one single race, religion or political movement. Jews come from one of two major groups: the Sephardic, who control local politics, and the more numerous Ashkenazi, who control national political power.

Zionism, Judaism, Race, Religion and Politics

There are about 15 million Jews on this planet. About a third of them live in Israel. Like in any country, it would be unfair to assume that they all agree on anything, ranging from ultraorthodox Haredim to cell-phone-chattering, bikini'd babes in Tel Aviv.

Zionism was created in 1897 when Jewish leaders formally called for the restoration of the Jewish national home in Palestine, where Jews could find sanctuary and self-determination, and work for the renascence of their civilization and culture. It was formalized by Theodor Herzl, who helped it become a strong nationalist movement in reaction to the persecution of Jews in Europe and around the world. The Torah says that Judea and Samaria were promised to the Israelites; some take it further to include all the land from the Euphrates (in Iraq) to the banks of the Nile River in Egypt.

Zionism finds its modern support in the wealthy Jews in the United States and Britain and its roots in ancient pogroms in Russia and Eastern Europe.

The Hebrew language, the Torah, laws in the Talmud, the Jewish calendar and Jewish holidays and festivals such as Shavuot all originated in Israel. This would be fine if the reality of the 17 percent Arabs (15 percent by religion) weren't part of the population mix of Israel. Over the last few years, about 60,000 to 77,000 people immigrate to Israel each year. Any group that can get 1.5 percent of votes can get one of the 120 seats in the Knesset. Currently, parliament is divided between the Ashkenazi-favored Labour Party (which wants peace) and the Likud Party, a Sephardic-supported group which maintains a hawkish view of Israel's future. That, of course, is far too simple a breakdown, as over a dozen parties shift and mutate in Israel's ever-changing political scene.

http://www.us-israel.org/jsource/zion.html
http://menic.utexas.edu/menic/countries/israel.htm

Coke vs. Pepsi in Iran and Now Burger King Jihad in Israel

Just a few minutes north and east of Jerusalem, Burger King opened the 47th Burger King in Maale Adumin, a Jewish settlement in the disputed West Bank. The problem is that it was not on Jewish land. The Jews then decided to boycott all Burger Kings in the country. Burger King ordered the restaurant to stop operating. The Israeli franchise owners disobeyed. The Jewish Anti-Defamation League said that Burger King was now an enemy of Israel. The Jewish settler mayor of Malle Adumin lashed out, "They are Burger King. They are very strong. I expect them to behave like a king, not like a chicken." Burger Kings in Israel are operated by a southern Californian, Meshulam Rilis, the owner of the legendary Hollywood mansion, Pickfair, and former husband of Pia Zadora. Burger King representatives say they thought the restaurant was in Israel.

Russia

The early founders of Israel came from Russia (like David Ben-Gurion, born in 1886 in Plonsk) and over 700,000 Russians have flooded into Israel since the demise of the Soviet Union. Currently Russians make up 15 percent of Israel's population.

The Israeli Military

Without the Israeli army, Israel would cease to exist. A tiny nation with a reputation for striking first, Israel has been on the offensive rather than the defensive for most of its short life.

The Israelis spend about 20 percent of their budget on defense. Uncle Sam kicks in another $1.8 billion a year. The bill for the United States to keep Israel alive is $5 billion, making it our biggest aid receiver. Troops are stationed in the occupied zones, throughout the country and along the border with Lebanon, where a security zone is controlled by the South Lebanese Army (SLA), a militia funded by Israel. The military is a big part of any Israeli's life in Israel. Military service is four years for officers, three years for men and two years for unmarried women. Annual compulsory reserve duty continues up to the age of 54 for men, 24 for single women. Because of the Palestinian *intifada,* or uprising, annual compulsory reserve duty was increased to 62 days from 42 days in 1988. Jewish and Druze citizens are conscripted, but Christian, Circassian and Muslim citizens are exempt. However, they're permitted to volunteer.

Of Israel's 5.8 million people, more than one-sixth are Arabs. Troops are also stationed along the border with Lebanon, where a security zone is controlled by the South Lebanese Army. The security zone is designed to prevent guerrilla attacks on the country. In addition, troops are stationed on the Golan Heights. The navy patrols the eastern Mediterranean and the Red Sea. Israel has a strategic cooperation agreement with the United States, signed in 1982.

The fear of an Arab chemical or missile attack has prompted the Israeli government to research and develop increasingly sophisticated weapons. It was the largest foreign participant in the United States' Strategic Defense Initiative (SDI). The United States paid 80 percent of the cost of the Arrow antimissile system, which Israel can use for its own defense. In addition, the navy is developing an interceptor system capable of destroying missiles, ships and aircraft within a 12-kilometer range. An intelligence-gathering satellite is being developed. Its aim is to reduce dependence on U.S. intelligence sources. Although it has never been confirmed, Israel is believed to have the capacity to manufacture nuclear weapons.

Israel Defense Forces
http://www.idf.il/

Government of Israel

Politics in Israel are never easy. Whipsawing between hard-liners and moderates, the country moves slowly toward building stable relationships with its angry neighbors. The current regime has set its sights firmly on peace.

Prime Minister
3 Kaplan Street
Jerusalem, Israel
E-mail: rohm@pmo.gov.il
http://www.israel.gov.il/eng/mainpage.htm
http://www.israel.gov.il/eng/eemail2a.htm#16

Yasir Arafat and the Palestinian National Authority

The official government of the Palestinians, it is a direct outgrowth of the actions of the PLO (see below) and the only hope for the Palestinians living in occupied areas and camps. Will it work? So far, so good, with the opening of the airport, the hope for tourism in the Gaza strip (a big gambling attraction for Israelis) and continuing removal of restrictions on Palestinians.

http://www.pna.net/

Palestine Liberation Organization (PLO)

The PLO began in 1964 as a Palestinian nationalist umbrella organization dedicated to the establishment of an independent Palestinian state. After the 1967 Arab-Israeli war, control of the PLO went to the most dominant of the various *fedayeen* militia groups, Yasir Arafat's al-Fatah. In 1969, Arafat became chairman of the PLO's executive committee, a position he still holds. In the early 1980s, the PLO became fragmented into several contending groups but remains the preeminent Palestinian organization. The United States considers the Palestine Liberation Organization to be an umbrella organization that includes several constituent groups and individuals holding differing views on terrorism. At the same time, U.S. policy accepts that elements of the PLO have advocated, carried out, or accepted responsibility for acts of terrorism. PLO chairman Arafat publicly renounced terrorism in December 1988 on behalf of the PLO. The United States considers that all PLO groups, including al-Fatah, Force 17, the Hawari Group, the Palestine Liberation Front (PLF) and the PFLP, are bound by Arafat's renunciation of terrorism. The U.S.-PLO dialogue was suspended after the PLO failed to condemn the May 30, 1990, PLF attack on Israeli beaches. PLF head Abu Abbas left the PLO executive committee in September 1991; his seat was filled by another PLF member.

In the early 1970s, several groups affiliated with the PLO carried out numerous international terrorist attacks. By the mid-1970s, under international pressure, the PLO claimed it would restrict attacks to Israel and the Occupied Territories. Several terrorist attacks were later performed by groups affiliated with the PLO/al-Fatah—including the Hawari Group, the PLF and Force 17—against targets inside and outside of Israel.

Formerly the No. 1 bad boy of terrorism, Yasir Arafat and his fashion-conscious wife have gone mainstream. It remains to be seen whether he can be as powerful in peace as he was in war. Arafat's administrative skills are primitive at best, his health is failing and his handling of economic issues in the autonomous zones of Jericho and the Gaza Strip have come under fire—the protests fueled by Arafat's own assertions that the peace accords would bring greater prosperity to Palestinians. Skeptical investors are staying away from the Gaza Strip, at least until the former terrorist charts an economic course for the newly liberated Palestine.

http://www.pna.net/plo/

Hezbollah

The most dangerous thorn in Israel's side is Hezbollah, the Iranian-backed Shia group that continually battles Israel on its northern border. Under the religious guidance of Sheikh Fadlallah, the most senior cleric in Lebanon, Hezbollah members are typically Shiites recruited from the various Palestinian refugee camps. The Israelis conduct numerous retaliatory attacks against these camps in revenge for Hezbollah's shelling and rocketing of Israel.

Shortly after the revolution in Iran, the country began recruiting the most fanatical Shiites to set up its first major military base outside Iran, at Zabadani in Syria. The Iranians sent in about 5,000 Pasadaran to Lebanon to help the fight against Israel. A thousand of these troops fought the Israelis in the Shouf Mountains. After the fighting ended, 500 Iranians stayed behind in the Bekaa (or Biqáa) Valley under the protection of Syrian forces. The Baalbak area became something of a Silicon Valley for terrorism, where a number of special-interest groups lived and trained, from Abu Nidal's headhunters to the Libyans. The Bekaa Valley became the world headquarters for terrorism in 1982. Supplied from Damascus and supported by Iran, these Iranians quickly consolidated their dominance of Hezbollah. Soon, Hezbollah would become a federation of 13 Islamic terrorist movements (11 Shiite and two Sunni). Decisions are made by a religious council. Although Sheikh Sayyid Muhammad Hussein Fadlallah says he is not the movement's leader, it's known that his authority is absolute, even if not secured with a title. He was born in 1943 or 1944 in Najaf, Iraq, to a family originally from Lebanon. He rose to prominence after the Iranian revolution. He is an author of two books on Islam: *Islam and the Concept of Power* and *Dialogue in the Koran*. His religious preachings and his political beliefs are one and the same: Jihad is absolute and all encompassing and the war must be fought by whatever means necessary.

Hezbollah's Sayyid Abbas al-Mussawi has vowed that the terrorist group will continue its struggle until the city of Quds (Jerusalem) is liberated. Israel invaded Lebanon in April 1996 in an attempt to oust Hezbollah, which continued to pound northern Israel with rockets. The recent spat with Lebanon displaced 10 percent of the population of Lebanon, destroyed 200 homes and caused $600,000 in damage. Israel fired 11,000 shells and launched 1,000 aircraft sorties. Despite the cultural and scenic attractions of the Holy Land, you could end your vacation as a puff of holy smoke. You stand a better chance of being caught in a terrorist attack in Tel Aviv than in most cities of the world.

For more information, see "The Players" section in the Southern Lebanon chapter.

E-mail: hizbollahmedia@hizbollah.org
Note they don't answer e-mails unless you are media and have very specific questions. As for visiting, they advise that you just show up.

http://www.hizbollah.org/

Harakat al-Muqaama al-Islamiya (HAMAS)

HAMAS was formed in August 1988 in the West Bank by Sheik Ahmad Yassine as competition to al-Fatah (Arafat's group) for political leadership of the 1.8 million Palestinians in the occupied zones. Yassine was a refugee in 1948 and is well connected to the Ikwhan, or the Muslim Brotherhood, in Egypt. He controlled all the Muslim organizations in Gaza as a holy man. When the *intifada* began, he created HAMAS to lend support and provide an alternative to the PLO. In May 1989 he was charged with manslaughter and sentenced to 15 years in prison. The nearly blind, paraplegic, 61-year-old Sheik Ahmed Yassine was released in October 1997 to kick start the peace process. Yassine was one of 11 children, and remains poor despite the fact he handled millions of dollars in funds. He lived in a three-room flat in the Sabra area of Gaza City. He was jailed in 1989 and was released either because the Israelis did not want him to die in prison or as a token gesture for a botched Mossad hit on another HAMAS leader. The lack of terrorist acts since his release means that the aging and ailing Yassin and Arafat have struck a deal to chill out and see if the Israelis live up to their word (and to cash those U.S. peace checks).

Currently, the group is supported by about 30 percent of the Palestinians in the Gaza Strip and is more powerful than Fatah, the PLO's military wing. The *intifada* (which began in the summer of 1988) hardened HAMAS into the most ardent and powerful group defending the Palestinians' perceived right to not only self-determination, but to the destruction of Israel. Part of their success strategy is a decentralized structure based on the Muslim Brotherhood, a popular Islamic fundamentalist group. HAMAS has been having its lunch handed to it by Shin Bet (the Israeli Secret Police). In August of '95, Shin Bet held a news conference to gloat over the capture of Abdel Nasser Issa, 27, and his apprentice, considered to be the head bomb maker for HAMAS. Both men credited Yehiya Ayash—aka "The Engineer"—as the man who taught them their bomb-making skills in the Gaza Strip. Issa is accused of recruiting and transporting suicide bombers. The arrest also confirmed that the group's spiritual mentor, Sheik Izzadine Khalil, is now in Damascus. Khalil was deported from Israel in 1992.

But in a turn of events for HAMAS, Ayash was assassinated by Shin Bet in January 1996 in a daring cellular phone explosion in Gaza City. Most Israelis rejoiced, while others pondered how many Palestinians Ayash had taught his trade to and how many of those would employ their new skills to avenge their mentor's death.

For now, there are plenty of angry 14- to 20-year-olds to toss rocks, pull triggers and vaporize themselves for HAMAS. The only university these kids have a chance of attending is the ultra-radical Islamic University of Gaza.

HAMAS is short for *Harakat al-Muqaama al-Islamiya* (Islamic Resistance Movement), but also means zeal or enthusiasm in Arabic. HAMAS members are not the well-trained military terrorists of al-Fatah but a youthful cadre of young Palestinians mostly enlisted from the poorest parts of the Occupied Territories. Most believe that they will find salvation and martyrdom by destroying Israel. Every member is sworn to destroy Israel and to create a new Islamic state based on the Koran. Initially, their campaign of rock throwing turned to stabbing Israeli citizens, including teenage schoolchildren. After HAMAS killed five Israeli Defense Force members, 415 HAMAS members were exiled to southern Lebanon by the Israelis, provoking an international outcry. In the seven years of *intifada*, Israelis have killed more than 2,000 Palestinians. HAMAS has slain more than 575 collaborators and more than 160 Israelis. The attacks have escalated in their frequency and nature, including the recent bombing of a Tel Aviv bus. HAMAS is expected to continue to terrorize Israelis into the foreseeable future, and Yasir Arafat and his Palestinian police will be expected to control HAMAS, thereby pitting Muslim against Muslim to maintain peace with the Jews, creating another schism in the Middle East. The Jordanian chapter, which was shut down in late 1999, was the most hawkish of the bunch and was credited with the July 1995 bombing in Ramat Gan.

HAMAS is gaining hard-core supporters from former PLO sympathizers. It has an office in Tehran, where they get financial support and receive military training from Hezbollah.

http://www.hamas.org/

Izz ad-Din al Qassam Brigade

The military wing of HAMAS is the smallest section of the group, numbering only a few hundred young men. But the group's political followers number in the tens of thousands. HAMAS, like Hezbollah, has created schools, clinics, mosques and financial support systems for the poor, widows and orphans. The group even sponsors a soccer team.

Volunteers to the Qassam Brigade are trained in Sudanese camps and in southern Lebanon by Hezbollah. The Iranians provide more than US$30 million a year (compared to ten times that provided to fund Hezbollah), including use of a radio station in southern Lebanon that broadcasts messages of revolution into Israel. The HAMAS base of power is in the West Bank and Gaza Strip. They have managed to create an alliance of the 10 Palestinian groups including the PLFP and the DFLP. The leadership of HAMAS is young and highly educated. HAMAS runs information offices out of Amman, Jordan (Ibrahim Ghosha and Mohammed Nazzal); Tehran; Lebanon (Mustapha Kanua), and Khartoum, Sudan (Mohammed Siam). Their U.S. rep (Moussa Abu Marzouk) operates out of Damascus, Syria.

There is some danger of the military wing splitting off from the more moderate political HAMAS.

Unofficial HAMAS page

http://www.hamas.org/

Official HAMAS site (Palestinian Information Center—Beirut, Lebanon)

http://www.palestine-info.org
http://www.palestine-info.net/hamas/

Just Another Day

There were 463 terrorists attacks in 1997 compared to 268 in 1996. Most attacks were in Hebron and West Bank.

2 bombings

4 suicide bombings

18 knife attacks

21 shootings

29 Israelis killed

50 roadside bombings

100 attacks prevented

340 Molotov cocktail attacks

400 stone throwing

414 Israelis injured

Source: Shin Bet

Bit Players

Abu Nidal

Nidal (real name: Sabry al-Banna) was born in Jaffato to a wealthy family (like all good terrorists). His dad had 13 wives and he was one of 24 kids. No wonder he had to raise a little hell to get attention. He worked in Saudi Arabia, where he joined the Baathist Party. He got involved with Arafat's al-Fatah group when it was formed in Kuwait in 1959. He was sent to open a PLO office in Khartoum in 1969 and was tossed out for recruiting Palestinian students to the cause. He then tried the same thing in Baghdad for the PLO and did better. The Iraqis thought that Arafat was a wussy and that big bad Nidal should be the PLO chief so they supported his efforts to run the Iraqi PLO, which included a radio station, newspaper and student scholarships. He became a tool of the Iraqis and a thorn in Arafat's side as he invented Hollywood-like cover names (Black September, Black June, Al Aqab, etc.). He split from Arafat (who was happy to have a little bit of Palestine instead of demanding total expulsion of the Jews) in 1973 and actually tried to assassinate Arafat with death squads. His attempt to kill the Israeli ambassador in London triggered the Israeli invasion of Lebanon in the early '80s, which triggered a long civil war. Nidal is semiretired now, but is an example of how much damage nations can do with a classic bad boy terrorist toy. He was last seen in Baghdad.

Popular Front for the Liberation of Palestine (PFLP)

This group of about 800 Palestinians follows a Marxist-Leninist doctrine and disagrees with Arafat's deal with the Israelis (Oslo, 1993). The group is led by 56-year old Bassam Abu-Sharif, who was famous for blowing up the Pan Am, Swissair and TWA airliners in Jordan. The PFLP lost a lot of steam when Wadi-Haddad was taken out in 1978. Qaddafi and Assad provide most of the folding green for this hard-line group, which is based in Syria and Lebanon. Abu Sharif has rejected terrorism and has even written a book with a former Israeli intelligence officer called "Best of Enemies.'

Popular Front for the Liberation of Palestine-General Command (PFLP-GC)

PFLP-GC's leader Ahmad Jabril (b. 1938) regarded, and still does, Habash's PFLP as a bunch of wimps, so he and his men split in 1968 to focus on killing and maiming, while Habash employed just a little less violence to achieve his ends. Because Jabril was a captain in the Syrian army when Assad was minister of defense at the time Israel took the Golan Heights, it's understandable why the PFLP-GC is tighter with Syria than latex on an aerobics instructor. The PFLP-GC is headquartered in Damascus. Iran chips in when they run short of funds.

The group's sensationalist suicide attacks, employing everything from hang gliders to hot-air balloons, has given its "airline" the fewest number of members of any frequent flyer program found in Palestine. Although not as large as the vanilla-flavored PFLP, the PFLP-GC is still a major threat to Israelis.

Palestine Liberation Front (PLF)

This is a breakaway faction of the PFLP-GC (which is a breakaway faction of the PFLP, which is a breakaway faction of the PLO). If this sounds like a scene from Monty Python's *Life of Brian*, you're not far off. The PLF is led by Abu Abbas, or Muhammad Abbas, (b. 1938) who usually hangs out in Libya with his buddy Qaddafi or in the Bekaa Valley. Abbas' group is tiny, possibly nonexistent. Their most famous job was the attack on the *Achille Lauro* and the less than admirable killing of wheelchair-bound Leon Klinghoffer. They are estimated to have 50 members. Now based in Iraq.

The Palestine Islamic Jihad (PIJ)

A small group founded in the '70s that seeks the creation of an Islamic Palestinian State. Based in Syria, backed by Iran, they carry out suicide attacks against Israelis in the West Bank, Gaza Strip and Israel. They have threatened to attack U.S. interests in Jordan. Based in Israel, Jordan, Syria and Lebanon.

Democratic Front for the Liberation of Palestine (DFLP)

The Hawatmeh faction does not go along with the Arafat-brokered peace and continues its opportunistic attacks and raids.

Right Wing Groups: Kach/Kahane Chai

Kach was founded by the late Rabbi Meir Kahane and Kahane Chai (Kahane Lives) was founded by his son Binyamin Kahane. These groups are considered terrorist groups by the Israeli government. There are random incidents of far right-wing Israelis and external Jewish groups such as the Kahane Chai and Kach, as well as individuals, striking against Palestinians and moderate Jews. These groups present little danger to Americans.

Ben Gurion International Airport is 20 kilometers from the center of Tel Aviv. Taxis are common and a bus service runs every 15 minutes. A passport, an onward or return ticket and proof of sufficient funds are required. A three-month visa may be issued for no charge upon arrival and may be renewed. Anyone who has been refused entry or experienced difficulties with his/her visa status during a previous visit can obtain information from the Israeli embassy or nearest consulate regarding the advisability of attempting to return to Israel. Arab-Americans who have overstayed their tourist visas during previous visits to Israel or in the Occupied Territories can expect, at a minimum, delays at ports of entry (including Ben Gurion Airport) and the possibility of being denied entry. To avoid these problems, such persons may apply for permission to enter at the nearest Israeli embassy or consulate before traveling. For further entry information, travelers may contact the following:

Embassy of Israel

3514 International Drive, NW
Washington, DC 20008
Tel.: (202) 364-5500

Or contact the nearest Israeli consulate general in Los Angeles, San Francisco, Miami, Atlanta, Chicago, New Orleans, Boston, New York, Philadelphia or Houston.

The major airport is Ben Gurion International Airport with a smaller civilian airport in Tel Aviv. There are also airports in Jerusalem, Haifa, Eilat, Herzlya, Mahanayim and Sodom. National airline El Al operates international flights to Europe, North America and some African countries.

Israel has a modern road system, although it abounds with crazy drivers. Road accidents have been on the increase in the last decade, due mainly to deteriorating road conditions. There are approximately three fatalities for every 100 million kilometers traveled. Emergency rule has been lifted in Batman, Bingol and Bitlis provinces.

Hassles with Police

Israel has strict security measures that can piss off visitors. Prolonged questioning and detailed searches take place at the time of entry and/or departure at all points of entry to Israel or the Occupied Territories. American citizens with Arab surnames can expect extra-close scrutiny at Ben Gurion Airport and the Allenby Bridge from Jordan. Cameras or video equipment are always suspect and items commonly carried by travelers—even toothpaste, shaving cream and cosmetics—may be confiscated or destroyed for security reasons, especially at the Allenby Bridge. During searches and questioning, access may be denied to U.S. consular officers, lawyers or family members. Should questions arise at the Allenby Bridge, U.S. citizens can telephone the U.S. consulate general in Jerusalem for assistance at *[972] (02) 253-288*. If questions arise at Ben Gurion Airport, U.S. citizens can phone the U.S. embassy in Tel Aviv at *[972] (03) 517-4338*.

Broadcasting and the Press

Journalists are required to submit all relevant items to the censor's office for approval before transmitting them abroad or issuing them in the local media. The occupied territories are officially open to media coverage, but local commanders may close specific areas for a limited period "for operational reasons." Various measures were also enforced on newspapers in Israel and on foreign media correspondents, most of whom are Israeli citizens. The army has sometimes imposed news blackouts. The media has regularly complained about security forces personnel impersonating journalists in order to obtain information about the Palestinian *intifada*, and putting journalists' lives at risk.

Israel Television and Israel Radio are owned by the government and run by the Israel Broadcasting Authority (IBA). Its central committee members oversee programming. Israel TV broadcasts on one national channel in Hebrew and Arabic, funded by viewer license fees and, more recently, by commercial sponsorship.

Jerusalem Post
http://www.jpost.com

The Occupied Territories

The West Bank has since been reopened but travel restrictions may be reimposed with little or no advance notification, and curfews placed on cities or towns in the Occupied

Territories may be extended or, if lifted, reimposed. Palestinian demonstrations in the West Bank and the Gaza Strip have led to violent confrontations between the demonstrators and Israeli authorities, resulting in the wounding or death of some participants. Demonstrations and similar incidents can occur without warning. Stone throwing and other forms of protest can escalate. Violent incidents such as stabbings have occurred. Vehicles are regularly damaged.

Northern Israel

See "Southern Lebanon."

East Jerusalem

Although the Department of State had warned all U.S. citizens against traveling to East Jerusalem, the West Bank and Gaza, the consular section of the U.S. consulate general at *27 Nablus Road, East Jerusalem*, remains open. Traveling by public or private transportation in parts of East Jerusalem less frequented by tourists, however, remains dangerous. If visitors must travel to other areas of East Jerusalem, including the Old City, or to the West Bank, they may consult with the U.S. consulate general in Jerusalem, and in the case of travel to the Gaza Strip, with the U.S. embassy in Tel Aviv, for current information on the advisability of such travel.

Buses

One and a half million Israelis use the bus every day, almost 25 percent of the population. There have been nine suicide attacks on buses since April 1994, resulting in 67 people killed. Injuries run at two to three times the death rate. One American tourist was among the dead. Violent incidents have also involved bus stops. The U.S. embassy is advising its employees and American citizens in Israel to avoid use of public transportation, especially buses and bus stops. This restriction does not apply to tour buses. Although Israelis must take the bus, only thrill seekers and cheapskates need expose themselves to what is Israel's most dangerous form of transportation.

Driving

There are about 1.5 motor vehicles involved in road accidents per 1 million kilometers traveled. There are 3.2 fatalities for every 100 million kilometers traveled.

Rocket Attacks

Rocket attacks from Hezbollah positions in Lebanese territory can occur without warning close to the northern border of Israel.

Land Mines

In the Golan Heights, land mines in many areas have not been clearly marked or fenced. Walk only on established roads or trails.

Being Arrested in the West Bank and Gaza Strip

U.S. citizens arrested or detained in the West Bank or Gaza Strip on suspicion of security offenses often are not permitted to communicate with consular officials, lawyers or family members in a timely manner during the interrogation period of their case. Youths who are over the age of 14 have been detained and tried as adults. The U.S. embassy is not normally notified of the arrests of Americans in the West Bank by Israeli authorities, and access to detainees is frequently delayed.

Medical care and facilities throughout Israel are generally excellent. Israel has one of the highest doctor-patient ratios in the world, about one doctor for every 339 patients. Travelers can find information in English about emergency medical facilities and after-hours pharmacies in the *Jerusalem Post* newspaper. Water is normally safe to drink, but bottled water is a better choice for the cautious. Tap water outside the main towns is not safe for drinking.

Israel is a small country, about 20,700 square kilometers (7,992 square miles), that forcibly occupies the Golan Heights (annexed from Syria in 1981; 1,150 square kilometers, 444 square miles), the West Bank (annexed from Jordan; 5,878 square kilometers, 2,270 square miles) and the Gaza Strip (363 square kilometers, 140 square miles). The territories currently occupied and administered by Israel are the West Bank, Gaza Strip, Golan Heights and East Jerusalem. The Israeli Ministry of Defense administers the Occupied Territories of the West Bank and Gaza Strip.

The population includes 635,000 Muslims, 105,000 Christians (almost all Arabs) and 78,000 Druze. Although Israel claims Jerusalem as its capital, the claim—especially to East Jerusalem, annexed in 1967—is disputed by most countries. The currency is the new shekel (IS), with 100 agorot to the shekel. The weather is arid, warm and mild most of the year with hot days and cool evenings. Because of its higher elevation, Jerusalem is quite cool, and even cold in the winter. In Tel Aviv and along the coast, the weather is more humid with warmer nights.

The Jewish Sabbath, from Friday dusk until Saturday dusk, is rigorously observed. Stores close on Friday by 2 P.M. and do not open again until Sunday morning. Most cinemas and restaurants are closed on Friday night. In most cities during the Sabbath there is no public transport (except for taxis), postal service or banking service. It is considered a violation of the Sabbath (Saturdays) to smoke in public places, such as restaurants and hotels. The same is true on the six main Jewish religious holidays.

Jewish dietary laws *(Kashrut)* prohibit the mixing of milk products and meat at the same meal. Kashrut is strictly enforced in hotels. Because of this, some restaurants serve only fish and dairy dishes while others serve only meat dishes. Pork is banned under religious laws, but some restaurants serve it, listing it euphemistically as white steak.

Banks are open from 8:30 A.M. to 12:30 P.M., and from 2 P.M. to 6:30 P.M. on Sunday, Tuesday and Thursday, and from 8:30 A.M. to 12:30 P.M. on Monday, Wednesday and Friday. Businesses are open from 8:30 a.m. to 7:30 p.m. Sunday to Thursday; some are open 8:30 A.M. to 2:30 P.M. on Fridays. Government offices are open from 7:30 A.M. to 4 P.M. Sunday through Thursday.

Embassy and Consulate Locations

U.S. Embassy

71 Hayarkon Street
Tel Aviv, Israel

U.S. mailing address

PSC 98, Box 100
APO AE 09830
Tel.: [972] (3) 517-4338

U.S. Consulate General

27 Nablus Road
Jerusalem

U.S. mailing address

PSC 98, Box 100
APO AE 09830
Tel.: [972] (2) 253-288 (via Israel)
Tel.: [972] (2) 253-201 (after hours)

Useful Addresses

Ministry of Communications

P.O. Box 29515
Tel Aviv
Tel.: [972] (3) 5198247
Fax: [972] (2) 5198109
http://www.mfa.gov.il/

Ministry of Tourism

24 King George Street
P.O. Box 1018
Jerusalem 91000
Tel.: [972] (2) 754811
Fax: [972] (2) 253407 or (2) 250890

2/1/00	Israel vows retaliation against Hezbollah for death of SLA 2nd in command
1/29/00	Peacetalks between Israeland Palestinians follow unsuccessful talks between Israel and Syria
10/5/99	Safe passage for Palestinians and foreign visitors begins between Israel and Gaza, Judea and Samaria.
7/30/97	Fifteen people are killed in two suicide bomb blasts in Jerusalem.
4/10/96	Israel invades HAMAS positions and cities within Lebanon after a Hezbollah rocket attack on northern Israel injures 40 people.
11/4/95	Prime Minister Yitzhak Rabin assassinated by right-wing extremist.
10/11/94	The Palestine Liberation Organization (PLO) Central Council approves Chairman Yasir Arafat's peace deal with Israel by a vote of 63 to 8, with 11 members abstaining or absent.
9/13/94	Israel and the Palestine Liberation Organization sign a peace agreement in Washington, D.C., outlining a plan for Palestinian self-rule in the Israeli Occupied Territories.
9/9/93	The PLO and Israel sign a mutual recognition agreement.
12/17/92	More than 400 suspected members of HAMAS are forcibly expelled from Israel into Lebanon, following the kidnap-murder of an Israeli border policeman. The expellees are refused entry into Lebanon and forced to camp in the Israeli-controlled security zone in south Lebanon.
12/16/91	The United Nations General Assembly repeals the 1975 resolution which said Zionism is a form of racism.

5/15/91	Palestinian Struggle Day.
1/15/91	Abu Iyad, the second-ranking PLO leader, and two other high-ranking PLO officials are assassinated by a guard suspected of working for the Abu Nidal Organization (ANO).
10/8/90	Eighteen Arabs die during clashes with police at the Temple Mount religious site.
5/20/90	A lone Israeli gunman kills eight Arab laborers in Rishon le Ziyyon, south of Tel Aviv. Nine workers are injured. The gunman is identified as a discharged Israeli soldier.
7/28/89	Israeli commandos seize Shaykh Obeid from a village in southern Lebanon and detain him in Israel on allegations of involvement in terrorist activity on behalf of Hezbollah.
12/9/87	Date used to mark the beginning of the *intifada*, or uprising on the West Bank and the Gaza Strip.
10/1/85	The Israeli Air Force bombs the headquarters of the Palestine Liberation Organization (PLO) in Tunis.
5/17/83	Israel signs an accord with Lebanon for the withdrawal of Israeli troops from most of southern Lebanon.
6/6/82	Israel invades Lebanon.
6/4/82	Israeli planes bomb Beirut.
3/26/79	Egyptian-Israeli peace treaty.
9/17/78	Camp David accords signed.
3/16/78	Israeli forces invade Lebanon.
7/4/76	An Israeli raid on Entebbe airport in Uganda frees 103 hostages from a hijacked Israeli airliner.
10/6/73	The Yom Kippur War begins.
9/6/72	Palestinian Black September terrorists massacre Israeli athletes at the Munich Olympics.
5/30/72	Members of the Japanese Red Army (JRA) kill 26 people in a massacre at Lod Airport.
2/21/70	Suspected members of the PFLP-GC place a bomb on a Swissair passenger jet en route from Zurich to Tel Aviv, resulting in the death of all 47 passengers.
7/22/68	Members of the Popular Front for the Liberation of Palestine (PFLP) hijack an El Al flight en route to Tel Aviv and forced it to land in Algiers. The attack marks the first aircraft hijacking by a Palestinian group. The hijackers are said to have believed Israeli General Ariel Sharon was on the flight. The passengers and crew are detained by Algeria for six weeks.
6/5/67	The Six Day War ends.
5/31/67	Israeli troops capture East Jerusalem in the Six Day War.
1/1/64	Fatah Day. The Palestine Liberation Organization (PLO) is founded at a meeting in Jerusalem.

4/14/49	Holocaust Memorial Day.
3/21/49	Palestinian Solidarity Day. Arab solidarity day with the Palestinian people against Israel.
5/14/48	Israel is proclaimed a state, as the British mandate in Palestine expires. Arab armies launch attacks on Israel immediately following the proclamation. The Arabs call this event "Nakba" (the Catastrophe) and protest on this day.
5/14/48	The first Arab-Israeli war begins shortly after the State of Israel was proclaimed.
5/7/48	Israeli Independence Day, as observed by Arabs in the Occupied Territories.
11/2/17	Anniversary of the Balfour Declaration, which promised a Jewish homeland in Palestine. Demonstrations in the Occupied Territories and the Gaza Strip area have occurred on this date.

KOSOVO
★★

Pieces in Our Time

There's no doubt about it. Slobodan Milosevic is definitely angling for Saddam's chairmanship of the international Bad Boys' Club and the not-so-glamorous award of "dictator-to-get-his-country-trashed-the-fastest." The United States almost ran out of cruise missiles trying to persuade Slobo that he would be better off without Kosovo as part of the former Yugoslavia. Overall, between March 24 and June 10, a total of 37,465 air missions were flown, averaging 486 missions a day, which supposedly destroyed 30 percent of Serb heavy weaponry in Kosovo—400 Serb artillery pieces, 270 armored personnel carriers, 150 tanks, 100 planes and 5,000–10,000 Serb soldiers. Total cost? When all the bills came, NATO spent about $4 billion dollars according to *Jane's Defence Weekly*—$70 million in the first night of bombing alone.

That was the estimate until someone had a chance to check the damage on the ground. The actual grand total of all those weeks of bombardment? Well, er, actually 13 Serb tanks out of 300. Not very impressive when you come to think of it. The cunning Serbos took a leaf out of the Russian manual of "how to hide your tank from NATO" a bit too successfully. *DP* was on the ground when NATO forces entered Kosovo, and can assure you that after months of bombing, the Serbs appeared to be in remarkably good shape. Dummy tanks were scattered around the place just for NATO bombers to have a bit of harmless target practice. It made great TV pics for all the bored journos sitting on the border, but that was about all. The slippery Serbs even sent a few guys to sit outside NATO airbases and drink coffee all day, when they weren't busy on the phone to their mates to say that another dozen F-16s had just taken off and would be arriving in about 20 minutes. Then of course, there was the odd NATO balls up for Slobo and the gang to crow over. Bombing the Chinese embassy was really not a very clever move. Old maps, someone in the Pentagon muttered. Perhaps they should have taken a dekko at the local tourist maps of Belgrade, which clearly marked the embassy.

Next on the list, NATO managed to bomb a convoy of refugees. Thirty seconds later Slobo was on the TV denouncing the "deliberate and horrendous massacre." If that's not the kettle calling the pot black *DP* doesn't know what is. What Slobo didn't mention was that refugee columns were often used by the Serb military as cover to move their own equipment. Perhaps he just kinda forgot to mention it.

So, was the bombing campaign another monumental waste of time and bombs? Not quite. But it does rather depend on your point of view.

In 72 days the former Yugoslavia was reduced from a slightly impoverished Eastern European country to a heap of rubble. Slobo might have thought he was being smart when he expelled almost the entire Albanian population from Kosovo, but it was Uncle Sam who had the smart bombs. Before Slobo could finish his nightly bottle of plum brandy, Belgrade had become the European version of Baghdad at night. Just about every bridge in Serbia was destroyed, as was every factory that produced anything larger than peashooters. In short, Serbia has now joined the ranks of the Third World. So much so that the average wage in Serbia has now dropped below those in Albania—a sure sign that Serbia really is in deep sh*t. And before Serbia managed to qualify for a new and exclusive class of Fourth World countries Slobo got on the TV and announced victory. Just who Slobo thought he was kidding when he went on air to assure Serbs that Kosovo would remain an integral part of what is no longer Yugoslavia remains something of a mystery. But whoever was listening, it certainly wasn't Kosovo's Albanian population (or anyone outside Serbia for that matter).

For Kosovo's Albanian population, the real misery began when NATO started its air campaign. Slobodan Milosevic and the Belgrade Boys put operation "horse shoe" into action. And Kosovo became Europe's latest charnel house. An estimated 10,000 Kosovar Albanians were massacred as Serbian paramilitaries ran amok, looting, killing and raping their way across Kosovo. Kosovo was systematically emptied of its inhabitants. For the first time since the Nazis, Europe once again saw men, women and children packed like cattle onto trains and shipped anywhere but home. The systematic killing of Albanian Kosovars started the night NATO began bombing. Many decided not to wait for the paramilitaries to knock on their doors, and fled to neighboring Macedonia or Albania. An estimated 1,300,000 Kosovar Albanians fled in terror, taking whatever they could with them.

Not that they kept much for very long. After years of practice in Bosnia the Belgrade Boys can strip a country faster than Saddam Hussein can sign an execution warrant. Zeljko Raznatovic, aka "Arkan," and the gang weren't gonna pass up an opportunity like this in a hurry. With his pal Frenki Simatovic, Arkan got down to the nuts and bolts of gathering the gang together. The word went out that "Ethnic Cleansing Ltd." needed extra personnel. CVs to be sent promptly to either Arkan or Frenki. The standards were stringent: prior experience not absolutely necessary, but helpful. A criminal record? That's a plus point. A good eye for valuables? Useful. A pyschopathic hatred of Kosovar Albanians? You're hired. Monthly salary about US$5,000, one Kalashnikov and as many bullets as you want included.

Rich Kosovars were forced to pay up to DM 20,000 if they wanted to leave their country alive. For Serbia's paramilitaries it was payday with a vengeance. For their masters it was just another business transaction—quite a big one. Fleets of trucks carried the goodies back to Serbia and a few very rich people became even richer.

So, where did it all go wrong? Sometime back in the '80s, according to the analysts—the 1380s, that is. In 1389, the Serbs were defeated by the Ottoman Turks at the battle of Polje in what is now Kosovo, which left a chunk of southeastern Europe under the hands of the Turks. Six centuries later, the Serbs are still sore; and a lot sorer after NATO finished dropping a few hundred thousand bombs.

More recently it all started (again) in 1989. In fact most of the modern-day woes of the Balkans can pretty much be traced to one man, step forward . . . Slobodan Milosevic. Well, perhaps that's a bit unfair. After all, the Bosnian war was triggered by Croatia's declaration of independence and its quick recognition by Germany. That in turn put the Serbs on the defensive . . . but if you want detailed analysis of the Balkans, you'd better take five years off and go back to school.

But what is fair to say is that as Yugoslavia collapsed, Slobo gravitated from a commie apparatchik to a Serbian nationalist, playing the nationalist card to climb his way to the top of the slippery political pole. And that is where the beginnings of the recent Kosovo conflict were sown. Commemorating the battle of Polje, Slobo told the gathered faithful that no one would ever be nasty to them again and promised Serbs a "greater Serbia." Just to emphasize his point, Slobo stripped Kosovo of its autonomy and abolished education in Albanian. A wave of unrest was triggered. The local Serbs got all the plum jobs and the majority Kosovar population were generally ignored, unless they were nationalists, in which case they were shoved in prison to cool their heels for a while.

If you think that Slobo has not been wildly successful in his career as a Serbian nationalist, you'd be right. Since Slobo gravitated from prime minister to prezzy, he lost the war against Croatia, leaving 600,000 Serbs from Krajina living in refugee tents in Serbia. He didn't really come out of Bosnia too well either. And now out of a perhaps 200,000 Serbs who used to live in Kosovo, there are somewhere in the region of 20,000 left. The rest have legged it to Serbia fearing (quite rightly) revenge attacks by Kosovar Albanians. In fact at the end of the day the Serbs have more refugees than any other ethnic group from the former Yugoslavia.

But let's not get ahead of ourselves here. Back to Kosovo. In 1998 the Kosovo Liberation Army emerged. Not that anyone really knew much about them for some time. They excelled at chopping up Serb farmers, were reasonably capable at taking the odd potshot at the occasional policeman and, well, that's about it really. The Serbs (or Yugoslav authorities, as you're supposed to call them) responded in a typical commie and authoritarian manner: they started torching the place. (Even before NATO's campaign began there were about 200,000 Kosovar Albanian refugees knocking around the place.) Paramilitary police, known as MUP, trooped round to the houses of known KLA guerrillas and shot them. If they were in a bad mood they killed the families as well. Charming. But the KLA weren't a whole load better. Highly factionalized and based on clans, the KLA lacked anything resembling a coherent military structure. Quite apart from being paranoid and secretive, Kosovar exiles in Switzerland raised cash and claimed to speak for the KLA. In fact, quite a lot of people claimed to speak for the KLA. On the ground in Kosovo, hacks who thought they had good contacts with KLA-exiled leadership quite quickly found that the kids inside Kosovo couldn't give a damn what some guy in Switzerland said.

The moderate Kosovar Albanian leader Ibrahim Rugova, famous for his monosyllabic press conferences, began to get edged out as the violence gained momentum. While he preached peace and got praise from Uncle Sam, everyone else was doing their best to start a war. As the violence began to spiral European governments began to reluctantly sit up and take notice. In October 1998, NATO huffed and puffed and threatened air strikes against Serbs on the ground. A few Serb military forces withdrew and the KLA promptly moved into the vacated areas. The fighting continued. The threat of airstrikes had done . . . er, nothing, except give the KLA a slight edge. So the Serbos got pissed. They took out their irritation on the village of Racak in January 1999. About 45 villagers were massacred in reprisal for KLA activity in the area.

Things got heavy. Western leaders made big noises. The Serbs said that the people killed were KLA. The CIA stepped in and helpfully leaked a phone conversation between two of Slobo's senior sidekicks. The Yugoslav deputy prime minister, Nikola Sainovic, and the senior Serb police commander in Kosovo, General Sreten Lukic, had had an indiscreet blab on their mobile phones, with the former asking the latter how many people he had managed to kill and what the best way to cover it all up was. Whoops.

The United States got seriously involved. The various sides were all persuaded to sit down and negotiate a solution to the war. The United States produced the paperwork and told everybody to sign it. Amongst other things, after three years there was to be a referendum on independence for Kosovo. The Serbs refused to sign. Things got military. NATO started the bombing campaign; but unlike the operation against Iraq in 1991, they didn't bother asking the United Nations this time.

The rest, as they say, is history. Slick Willy said there would be no ground troops. The Serbs chuckled and set about kicking the Kosovar Albanian population out of Kosovo, hoping the alliance would never hold. About 1.3 million Kosovars fled in the largest mass migration since World War II. Western politicians had a great time preaching morality and vowing that the Serbs would pay, but ground troops were out of the question. Hey, I mean, someone might actually get killed! You don't say? Kosovars were under the impression that quite a lot of people were being killed.

So NATO went to war, but were so scared of losing a soldier that the bombers were not allowed to fly below 15,000 feet, which is why refugee convoys ended up getting hit, because the politicians wouldn't allow the pilots to fly low and identify their targets. Do the math: one NATO pilot is worth 80 Kosovar Albanian refugees. Pretty fucking stupid way to run a war. The amazing thing was that it worked, with the only people dying being Kosovars and Serbs (who didn't really matter). About the only U.S. casualties were two Apache pilots who crashed their helicopters in Albania. Oh yes, does anyone remember the Apaches? Those wonder weapons that were going to win the war overnight? Yeah, right. Why weren't they deployed? It's simple. They would have been blown out of the skies. One F-117A Stealth fighter was downed in the first days of the war and three U.S. soldiers wandered over to the wrong side of the Macedonian border to make their debut appearance on Serb television.

Slobo decided he had had enough after 79 days. Kosovars poured back into Kosovo and started cleansing the place of the Serbs who hadn't fled. The Russkies pulled a fast one on NATO and sent their troops in first. NATO looked very silly indeed for a while. Luckily for NATO, like their counterparts in Chechnya, the Russkie troops were soon out of fuel and food, and generally could only sulk at the airport. And that, in a nutshell, was the Kosovo conflict.

The Serb troops all departed and NATO forces, known as K-for, entered with a couple of thousand journos who made the usual mess of getting in the way. And a couple of hacks were gunned down by unidentified gunmen on the first day NATO forces entered Kosovo, their bodies left unceremoniously on the roadside. One hundred mass graves were found scattered around the province, with an estimated 10,000 Kosovars buried in them. Under the terms of the withdrawal agreement there are theoretically supposed to be a few hundred Serb border guards and customs officers. They're in no hurry to go back, though. Well now, that's a surprise!

That's not to say the Serbs don't talk up. A Serb general threatened to send back what passes for the Yugoslav army if NATO did not allow Serb policemen back to their posts. "We will have to use force to reclaim our territory," General Radovan Lazarevic told the Nedeljni Telegraf weekly. Yeah right. You kinda wonder what planet they're living on sometimes.

Building Peace in Kosovo
http://www.state.gov/www/regions/eur/kosovo_hp.html

So, where has all this left Kosovo? In a bit of a mess to say the least. Kosovo may be free, but it's far from a happy place. The Serbs thoughtfully left a number of mines behind, and there is enough unexploded NATO ordnance lying around the place to keep deminers happy for years to come. The few remaining Serbs are now being harassed and killed by Albanians. Whatever K-for commanders might say, there is a high level of violence in Kosovo as old scores are settled. Kosovo is supposed to be policed by the United Nations, known for their large salaries, expensive land cruisers, nice pistols on the hips and comprehensive uselessness. In October

1999, a Bulgarian UN officer was shot dead (after he was beaten first, of course) when he was mistaken for a Serb by a mob of youths. Pristina's unidentified gunmen had struck again. The KLA, led by Hashim Thaci are supposed to have been disarmed and are now acting as an unofficial police force. They're known as the Kosovo Protection Corps, (Kosovo Extortion Racket more likely). The place is held together by K-for, without which all Serbs would be trekking towards Serbia and anarchy would rule the day. The UN is supposed to be responsible for feeding Kosovo, but luckily for Kosovars there is a thriving black market, without which they would all starve.

Slobodan Milosevic

Born in 1941 in the town of Pozarevac to the southeast of Belgrade, the young Slododan didn't have the happiest of childhoods. Both his parents committed suicide. At school he was remembered for being bossy and organized. At university he was in charge of the ideological section of the communist party—a bundle of laughs that must have been. He married Mirjana Markovic and they have had two nice children. By 1984, Slobo had crawled his way up the political ladder to be the head of the Belgrade Communist Party. During his eight years in power, there have been four wars in the former Yugoslavia and over 300,000 deaths. Is it just that the guy is misunderstood? Slobo is the archetypal politician, which is to say that he will use anything to get and stay in power. Reading the sign of the times in the 1980s, he used Serb nationalism to get his place at the top. The problem was that there was a fair amount of Croatian nationalism as well. Germany helped with the destruction of Yugoslavia and the rise of Serb nationalism by recognizing Croatia. That got the initial bloodbath going. On and off it has continued ever since. When the Kosovo crisis escalated into NATO's bombardment, Bill Clinton signed a secret executive order giving the go-ahead to depose Slobo. That probably explains why, like Saddam, he is still there. Slobo holds the distinguished position of being the first serving head of state to be indicted for war crimes. What *DP* wants to know, Bill, you old smoothie, is why Saddam (far worse than Slobo) has not also been indicted? C'mon now. Answers on the back of a stamp, please. Just to piss Slobo off, hackers were hired to hack into his bank accounts in Greece, Cyprus, Russia, Hong Kong and the Cayman Isles. Even the Swiss played ball and froze the bank accounts of more than 300 people linked to Slobo and the Belgrade Boys. But Slobo's having the last laugh. He's still there. For those of you *DP*er's that might want to drop in on Slobo on a visit to Belgrade, we can inform you that he likes to hang round the Beli Dvor (White Court), which was the palace of Yugoslavia's last king. The daughter, Mariana, runs Belgrade's TV and radio station. Their son, Marko (now 25), prefers the nightlife and is a disco owner and car enthusiast.

Socialist Party of Serbia

http://www.sps.org.yu/engleski/index.html
Spokesperson: Ivica Daãiç
E-mail: ivica@sps.org.yu

The Slobadan Milosevic Fan Club

http://home.wxs.nl/~gertvonk/milosevic.html
Serb-friendly site: http://www.kosovo.net/

The Kosovo Liberation Army (KLA) / Ushtria Clirimtare e Kosoves (UCK)

Okay, time for a bit of multiple choice. Depending on whom you talk to the KLA were: (a) "a paranoid rabble" (journalists); (b) "terrorists" (the Serbs); (c) "a semi-useful rabble" (NATO); or (d) "freedom fighters" (Kosovars) or "CIA stooges" (Europeans). Rumors abounded. MPRI had a contract to train the rabble via their previously trained

Croation generals, the SAS were seen training, Canadians were doing a little artillery spotting, the CIA was packing off volunteers to join the KLA. How do we know? They were being handed copies of *DP* by their CIA handlers and being told to read the chapter on Albania. But as in most wars they were probably a little bit of everything and a whole bunch of nothing. Returning volunteers told *DP* that they should be called the KIA (for "killed in action").

Whatever they were, they were certainly controversial until NATO started the bombing campaign, when they were awarded the status of "temporary goodies." After all, they were fighting Slobo, too. Actually, a lot of them were just kids who had either been turfed out of their homes or returned from abroad to fight for their country (once the bombing campaign started). Who controlled them is another matter. Initially the KLA started with 500 men in 1992 and then really got going in 1998, when suddenly there were 17,000 of them. For the most part, they were clan based with a dash of Marxism in there somewhere, and they really weren't very effective. But a vast Kosovar diaspora in Switzerland and Germany meant that there was plenty of cash heading to Kosovo to buy all sorts of useful things like guns. Some KLA kids were also doing a bit of drug running just to keep the old bank account in the black. So who actually led the KLA? Bloody good question. As the bombing campaign got going the answer was pretty much no one. Whoever it was, they were not renowned for tolerance: when Ibrahim Rugova, the more moderate Kosovar leader, reportedly made a deal with Milosevic, he was sentenced to death by the KLA high command. What a bunch of charmers. In the second week of the bombing campaign, Hashim Thaci—the supposed KLA leader—formed the Provisional Government of Kosovo. They didn't bother consulting public opinion, which would admittedly have been tricky; but they were never much good at the democratic stuff, anyway. A former Croat army brigadier general, Agim Ceku, was appointed as the KLA head of staff to try and knock everything into shape. At its peak there were about 10,000 KLA troops running around in Albania and along the border. Another 2,000 were actually inside Kosovo doing the fighting. The man who eventually emerged as top dog was the 29-year-old Hashim Thaci, who has since made all the running in Serb-free Kosovo. By the time the KLA actually managed to get going, the war was over. In all, they had managed to liberate about 21 square kilometers of Kosvo, which I guess shows you how relevant they were. Anyway, the war's over now. So their temporary goody status has been revoked. Thaci's KLA now go under the name of the Party for Democratic Progress for Kosovo. It may say something about the true roots of the KLA that it can be magically transformed into an emergency rescue corps. Flatfoots with total arsenal of 200 pistols. The clever dicks are saying that "Democratic Progress" would be a lot quicker without them. A poll, conducted in October, found that the PDPK would get a whole 20 percent of Kosovars' vote. People have been a tad unhappy at being bossed around by brats with guns who drive around in flashy cars.

Kosovo Crisis Center
http://www.alb-net.com/kcc/kospress/index.htm

Ibrahim Rugova and the League for Democratic Kosovo
Rugova was the man that everybody wanted to do business with. Maybe it was the natty scarf, maybe it was the intellectual flair. It didn't quite work out. The former prime minister of Kosovo, Rugova was an adherent of nonviolence. He looked good, sounded good (when he opened his mouth) and the West liked him. It all started going pear-shaped, though. As the fighting got going in 1998, there was a growing wave of sympathy for the KLA, who preferred to fight rather than talk. If Western governments noticed this, they ignored it. When the bombing campaign reached its peak Rugova was written off as having been too cozy with the Serbs, or at least not doing anything for the Kosovar refugees. Now, though, he's the Comeback Kid. Kosovars pissed off with the useless and

unorganized attempts of the KLA to run the place (or not run it as the case is) have once again decided that Rugova is their kind of politician.

The United Nations, NATO and the Crusaders

The people everybody loves to hate. It took them from June until October to even start thinking about issuing license plates to cars. Was NATO good or bad for Kosovo? Before NATO started bombing, there were about 2,000 dead over a year or so and 200,000 refugees. After NATO started bombing 1.3 million became refugees and over 10,000 were killed. It was the first war since the crusades that was fought for peace. Hmm. Well, to be fair, most Kosovars thought that it was worthwhile, and *DP* guesses their opinion counts more than most. All in all, it took the world's most powerful military alliance 79 days to kick Slobo out of Kosovo. The NATO bombardment of Kosovo and Serbia saw a total of 37,465 sorties flown, paid for by you, dear reader.

NGOs in Kosovo
http://call.army.mil/call/fmso/NGOs/ngo.html

UN
http://www.un.org/peace/kosovo/pages/kosovo1.htm

NATO
http://www.nato.int/

Health Information Network for Advanced Planning (HINAP)
(For updates from various NGO in Kosovo and Albania)

http://www.who.int/hinap/albania/sources/misc/150699.htm

Arkan and Frenki (Ethnic Cleansing Ltd.)

Definitely the side without the goodies. Arkan (aka Zeljko Raznatovic, his real name) made his reputation in Croatia in 1991 when he organized a private army, the Serb Volunteer Guard (SDG / SSJ) "Tigers" in 1992.

Wanted for the Vukovar massacre (one of the worst episodes in the Croatian war) by the international tribunal based in The Hague, Arkan has of late taken to appearing on CNN and emphasizing that he's really just your average family man (he probably is in the Balkans). But his relations with CNN has not always been so good. In 1997, he threatened to sue the company when CNN ran a story "Wanted" in which poor old Arkan was accused of being all sorts of nasty things—like a murderer, for instance. The poor guy must have been heartbroken. You won't be surprised to hear that CNN wasn't really that worried about being taken to court. In 1991, Arkan served six months in a Croation slammer for possession of arms. So I guess he technically has a criminal record. Not that it affects his career prospects too much. Actually, in his youth Arkan was known as a bit of a wild kid. (No surprise that, I guess.) He obviously saw the civil war coming, so to get a bit of practice he spent much of his time robbing banks in Europe. It has stood him in good stead ever since. When NATO started bombing Kosovo, Arkan vowed to fight to the bitter end and turn the conflict into Europe's "Vietnam." But NATO wasn't too worried either; Arkan was far too busy sending the boys around to pick up whatever Kosovars had left behind—that is, when they weren't busy digging mass graves. Other things in his busy schedule include sitting in the Belgrade parliament (when he's not busy organizing ethnic cleansing). In all this, Arkan was helped by his pal Frenki Simatovic. Frenki used to be a senior policeman. But, you know, the pay sucks and the hours are antisocial. Instead, Frenki decided to set up his own little gang. Known for their trademark dark green cowboy hats (the harmless bit) and their penchant for ethnic cleansing (the nasty bit), they had a great time in Kosovo until NATO spoiled everything. The Hague indicted Arkan in 1997 for unspecified war crimes. He is also accused of committing atrocities during the 1991 Serb rebellion in Croatia and later in Bosnia. He is married to a glamorous folksinger, Ceca. In May 1998, Arkan was reelected chairman of the Party of Serbian Unity (SSJ) for four years by the unanimous vote of the SSJ Assembly. He can still muster about 3,000 men.

Ethnic Cleansing

http://www.state.gov/www/regions/eur/rpt_9905_ethnic_ksvo_4.html

Kosovars

As is usually the case in sports and warfare, there is always one guaranteed loser. In this instance, the Kosovars have a semiautonomous disaster zone. Mined, destroyed and impoverished, they now have to figure out how to get on with things. What industry there was has been destroyed by Serbs, putting people back on the fast track for non-jobs in farming, small repairs and NGO domestics. The UN hires about 1,800 locals. Out of 153,000 union workers, only 31,000 actually have a job that pays money. National income dropped from 2.2 billion in 1994 to less than 800 million today, according to the Yugoslav government. Essentially expediting the unemployment, economic decline and brain drain started by Milosevic in 1990.

There are three ways. Via Belgrade, Macedonia or Albania. If you go via Belgrade you will need a valid passport and permission from the authorities. It is the most difficult way. Much easier is to go via Skopje in Macedonia or Kukes in Albania. A valid passport is required on all counts. A visa, from the latter two places is not. For journalists K-o accreditation can be got in Pristina.

Kosova Information Center

Qendra për Informim e Kosovës
c/o Shoqata e Shkrimtarëve të Kosovës
RR. Beogradi P.N.
38000 Prishtinë
Tel.: +381 38 24234
Fax: +381 38 27660
E-mail: kic_pr@zana-pr.ztn.apc.org

United Kingdom

http://www.albanian.com

Kosovo Information Centre

136 Buckingham Palace Road
London, SW1W 9SA
Great Britain
Tel.: +171 730 1050
Fax: +171 730 8973
E-mail: kic-uk@kosova.demon.co.uk

You won't find much in the way of a public transport system in Kosovo these days. The best way to get around is to hire a car. This can be done either in Macedonia, Albania or inside Kosovo itself. Stay tuned to the news.

http://www.kosova.com/
http://www.alb-net.com/misc-pages/links.htm
http://src-home.slav.hokudai.ac.jp/eng/cee/kosovo-e.html
http://www.stratfor.com/crisis/kosovo/default2.htm

Watch for the remaining Serb enclaves. Unless you're Russian, you will not be popular. There is still a high level of violence in Kosovo, and everyone has an AK tucked under the bed. It's also not really a very clever idea to wander too close to the border with Serbia, either. The Serbs still tend to slip across from time to time. K-for does not have the manpower to patrol the whole area as much as they should, and the UN . . . well, forget it. In October, two journalists working for European Broadcasting simply disappeared. A week later it was discovered that they had inadvertently wandered across the border (or been snatched) and arrested by the Serbs. They spent a week in prison and only got out when a negotiator working for a British security company arranged their release. They hadn't had a fun time. There are still mined areas, especially close to the border with Albania and Macedonia.

Being a Serb

The boot's on the other foot now. And Kosovars are not in a forgiving mood, whatever the public utterances of their political leadership may be. Of the 200,000 or so prewar Serb population there are now about 20,000 left, which says it all, I guess. Antipersonnel mines, dangerous anywhere, there are plenty of them. K-for has set about marking as many of the mine fields as possible. That doesn't mean that they are all accounted for.

Crime

Ever since the Serbs left Kosovo, crime has rocketed. The Albanian mafia has decamped from Albania to Kosovo. Empty Serb flats were soon commandeered. Kalashnikov-wielding figures have halted cars and lorries near borders to ask for "taxes," only to melt away when NATO troops roar up into view.

Serbia Info

http://www.serbia-info.com/

Land Mines

The media has decided that Kosovo is the most heavily mined place on earth. NATO calculates there are hundreds of thousands of mines, booby traps and unexploded munitions strewn across the province. Most of the mines are courtesy of the Serbs along the borders with Albania and Macedonia. Bridges, roads and the infrastructure are also mined.

There is medical care in Kosovo. Your best bet is to get to an NGO for medical care and eventual shipment to Europe or back home.

Kosovo is in a bit of a limbo. Technically it is part of the former Yugoslavia; but you've got to be a blithering idiot to think that Kosovars will ever accept rule from Belgrade again any time in the next thousand years or so. (There are quite a lot of blithering idiots around.) So the place is run by the UN and K-for, at the moment. Theoretically there will be a referendum on independence in three years time. The local currency is the German deutsche mark or the American dollar. We kid you not. Either of those two currencies will be all you need for a stay in Kosovo. German DM are preferred. Anything and everything is available on the black market. There are plenty of guns floating around, though that's one of the negatives. There is electricity in all the main towns, but not in many of the villages—which is no surprise as many of them were burned to the ground. Bottled water is recommended.

Almost all of Kosovo's postwar 1.8 million population are Muslim. The Christians—in the form of the Serbs—have mostly fled. The best place to stay in Pristina is the Grand Hotel. Lots of people stay with the locals. Expect to pay about US$30 a night if you do so. The language is Albanian, but in places like Prizren many people also speak Turkish.

Albanian Embassy

Embassy of the Republic of Albania
2100 S Street, NW
Washington DC 20008
Tel.: (202) 223-4942
Fax: (202) 628-7342
Kosovar links: http://www.albanian.com/main/related.html

6/12/99	Russian troops enter Pristina three hours before arrival of NATO troops.
6/10/99	Serb troops begin withdrawal and bombing campaign is suspended.
6/9/99	NATO and Serb commanders agree on withdrawal schedule and terms.
6/7/99	NATO and Serb commanders fail to agree on terms of pull out. Talks suspended.
6/3/99	Belgrade accepts peace plan proposed by Russian and EU envoys.
5/29/99	Two Australian aid workers are convicted in Belgrade of spying and are jailed.
5/22/99	NATO bombs KLA barracks a day after it was visited by the international press.
5/10/99	Belgrade says it is withdrawing troops from Kosovo. Western powers dismiss the statement.
5/7/99	NATO bombs Chinese embassy. Three Chinese journalists are killed.
4/1/99	Three bruised U.S. soldiers appear on Serb television.
3/24/99	NATO launches cruise missile and bombing attacks over Kosovo.
3/23/99	Serb parliament rejects NATO demands to send peacekeepers into Kosovo.

3/20/99	All 1,380 OSCE monitors withdraw from Kosovo. Yugoslav army reinforcements arrive.
3/18/99	Kosovar Albanians sign international peace deal in Paris. Serbs boycott the event.
3/15/99	Peace talks resume in Paris.
3/11/99	U.S House of Representatives backs deployment of U.S. troops in Kosovo as part of peacekeeping operation.
2/6/99	Talks held at Ramboiullet, France. Milosevic refuses NATO deployment. KLA refuse to disarm.
1/18/99	UN war crimes prosecutor Louise Arbour refused entry to Kosovo to investigate.
1/16/99	Forty-five ethnic Albanians massacred at Racak by Serb forces.
10/27/98	Serb security forces withdraw en masse; NATO reverses decision to use air strikes.
10/24/98	UN Security Council authorizes deployment of OSCE monitors in Kosovo to verify end of fighting.
10/13/98	Richard Holbrooke outlines deal to avoid air strikes. NATO gives Milosevic four days to end offensive.
10/1/98	Series of killings of ethnic Albanians at hands of Serb forces reported.
9/24/98	NATO issues ultimatum to Milosevic to stop violence in Kosovo or face airstrikes.
8/16/ 98	Serb forces announce capture of last rebel stronghold, the mountain town of Junik.
3 /22/98	Kosovars vote for president and parliament. Serb authorities dismiss polls as illegal.
1991	Albania's parliament recognizes the independence of Kosovo.
1989	Kosovo is stripped of its autonomy inside the Yugoslav Federation.
1974	Yugoslav constitution grants Kosovo autonomy.
1389	Serbs defeated at battle of Polje by Ottoman Turks.

In a Dangerous Place: Kosovo

A Potentially Nasty Moment

Could there be any place more trashed than Kosovo after three months of NATO bombing and Serbian paramilitary handiwork? Plenty of places, you can be sure. But it was with good reason that Kosovars were coming out of their houses with dazed-looking expressions. Their towns and villages had, over a three-month period which had seen most of them cower inside, been reduced to varying degrees of rubble.

I had entered Kosovo just days earlier from Albania with the German NATO contingent. Careful and methodical planners the German army might be, but the press contingent certainly managed to spoil their entry into Kosovo. With a couple of hundred press jeeps and cars blocking the road to the border the Germans had had little option but to let the press cross the border first.

The one hitch was that the Serb military was still very much in evidence, too. Neither were they in much of a mood to accommodate the international press corps.

Driving through the countryside, we round a bend to find dozens of Serb troops sitting on the verge, beside the road. Three months of bombardment didn't seem to have done them much harm. Stopping at one point along the road, we watch as Serb military trucks emerge from local houses—in alarming numbers. Every empty village seems to have housed troops; and short of flattening most of Kosovo, there seems to have been little NATO could have done against the Serbs on the ground.

Rounding a bend, we come face-to-face with a Serb checkpoint. It's manned by a half dozen special police, known by the acronym of MUP, more generally known as "Ethnic Cleansing Ltd." They have decided that this is as far as we will be traveling. They ask for our passports before eventually saying that they have no objection to us going on to Prizren, the nearest town, but that our Albanian driver has no visa and must stay behind.

We drive back a few hundred meters and debate what should be done, in the midst of which a German armored column storms past. Follow the tanks, we tell the driver. We swerve in between a tank and an armored car and follow the column. The Serbs, though, are having none of it. Almost immediately, the paramilitaries are out in front, waving down press cars—this time with the AKs pointing at the cars. "JUST FOLLOW THE FUCKING TANK!" we shout at the driver. There's no way they'll open up with about 300 German troops following behind us—or so we hope. But the driver allows himself to be waved over to the side of the road, and we watch helplessly as the armored column goes past. Reportedly, the Serb military are refusing the Germans access to Prizren, which accounts for the reinforcements heading towards the town.

We beat a tactical retreat from the checkpoint and wait to see what will happen. The whole area begins to get more and more crowded as Serb forces gather for what will be their withdrawal from Kosovo. Buses carrying troops are going backwards and forwards past us as we film. Mostly they ignore us; either giving the three-fingered Serb victory sign or raising the middle finger. Two buses, though, decide to stop, and a couple of soldiers get out and start shouting at us to stop filming. We're stuck on a deserted piece of road, alone, with pissed-off Serb soldiers. Not a good situation.

It will not be until some hours later in Prizren that we will learn that two German journalists have been killed by unknown assailants on the Prizren–Pristina road. And if the assailants are unknown, the strong suspicion is that they are Serb, in one form or another.

The soldiers move on, though, which is something of a relief all around. It doesn't, though, solve the small problem of the roadblock ahead. This is eventually solved by the German NATO contingent. We are told to form a convoy. At the front is a jeep with a German officer; at the back is a tank. Once again, we drive to the checkpoint. For what seems like an eternity we wait, until suddenly the tank behind us pulls out and drives to the checkpoint.

"Well," said the smiling German officer later, "I asked them nicely if they would allow you through, they said 'no.' So I radioed for the panzer and asked them if they wanted to carry on the argument. They said 'no.'"

For the first time in months the people of Prizren have taken to the streets en masse. People put on their best clothes and come out to welcome the NATO troops in a heady atmosphere of excitement. Flowers are thrown on the German soldiers and young girls crowd around the embarrassed troopers with gusto.

It's a beautiful city and has been more or less untouched by the bombing. But the Serbian troops still have to pull out according to the agreed schedule. At the morning press briefing the German NATO officer tells us we should avoid going along the road back to Albania. "There are about 300 Serbian troops there. They are due to leave today, but they have been drinking alcohol all morning . . . I very much advise you to avoid that road."

As it is, we watch the Serbs leave from the town instead. I am with Jeff of the *Philadelphia Enquirer* and a veteran of Bosnia. We have been interviewing local people on the outskirts of town when we notice a large Serb convoy go past. We catch up with the convoy in the town. Escorting the Serbs on their way out are two German armored cars and troop carriers. We get out and start filming. All the Serb troops are still armed, and they don't look in a particularly good mood. I am still filming as the sound of automatic fire resonates from a nearby quarter. The German tanks start up and head in the direction of the shooting. I suddenly realize that we are alone with a convoy of about 700 Serb troops, some of whom are now taking up firing positions. Our car is about 100 meters down the convoy, which is a long way to walk past pissed-off Serb soldiers unslinging their weapons. As casually as possible I walk back to the car, looking neither left nor right. "Okay," says Jeff, once I get back to the car, "let's get out of here." He tells the driver to reverse slowly back down the road. Looking back at the line of trucks I notice a Serb soldier wandering down the street. He is half naked and holding an assault rifle. Half-naked soldiers. Definitely not a good sign. "All in all a potentially nasty moment," is Jeff's verdict once we are clear.

If Prizren had come through the war relatively unscathed, Djakova was another story. A mere half an hour away, large sections of the city had been razed by the Serbs in the first days of the war. We travel there the following day and are amongst the first journalists to arrive. The local Albanians are walking around the town with the dazed expressions of people who are just beginning to wake, as if from the grip of a terrible nightmare from which there had been no possibility of escape.

We walk through what had once been the center of the town, the main shopping area. There is nothing left. Almost every shop has been torched—and not by bombs dropped from the air. There is also a pungent odor of decaying flesh coming from beneath the rubble. "I very much doubt," says Jeff, "that what we are smelling is dead animals." We stop to talk to two girls. They are sisters and one speaks English. It is the first time they have left their house in nearly three months and we are the first foreigners they have seen. "We didn't quite believe that the Serbs could have gone," explained the older sister. Suddenly the younger girl starts crying. She tries to stop but can't. She just sobs, as if she can't believe the war is over and she is still alive.

In the following day, we travel around the villages. Almost every village has its corpses, usually charred and blackened by flame. Areas of freshly moved earth are the usual indicators of mass graves, and there seem to be plenty of them. The retreating Serbian army has left graffiti on the walls of local homes: "Fuck you NATO," it reads in red paint.

—**Roddy Scott**

Kurdistan
★★★★

Blood Kurd'ling

Kurdistan is one of those Alice in Wonderland type countries that do not officially exist. The Kurds are the largest ethnic group in the world without a country of their own. Take a step through the looking glass, though, and you'll find the Kurds geographically split between modern-day Iraq, Turkey, Iran and Syria. Welcome to Kurdistan. Historically, the Kurds have been cut something of a raw deal. When the Ottoman Empire collapsed after World War I the Kurds were promised an independent Kurdistan by the British under provisions made by the 1920 Treaty of Sevres. In 1923, though, the Brits changed their minds and cut a deal with Kemal Ataturk, the calculation being that it would be better to have an anti-communist Turkey than an independent Kurdistan. The 1923 Treaty of Lausanne left the Kurds viciously shortchanged, but then you'd expect that from perfidious Albion. Since then modern Kurdish history has been one of rebellion and repression.

As many as 12–15 million Kurds live in southeastern Turkey (a third of Turkey's politicians are of Kurdish origin), 5–7 million live in Iran, 1.5 million

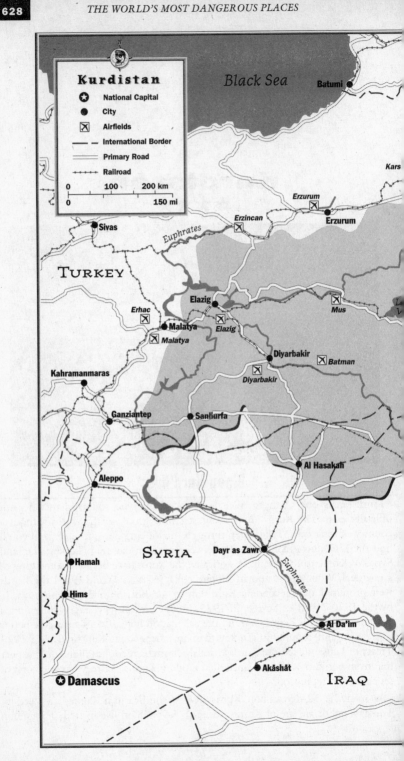

Kurdistan

☆ National Capital
● City
☒ Airfields
— — International Border
—— Primary Road
+++ Railroad

0   100   200 km
0   150 mi

Black Sea

Batumi

Kars

Sivas

Euphrates

TURKEY

Erzurum

Erzincan

Erzurum

Elazig

Mus

Erhac

Malatya

Elazig

Malatya

Diyarbakir

Batman

Kahramanmaras

Diyarbakir

Ganziantep

Sanliurfa

Al Hasakah

Aleppo

SYRIA

Dayr as Zawr

Euphrates

Hamah

Hims

Al Da'im

Akâshât

☆ Damascus

IRAQ

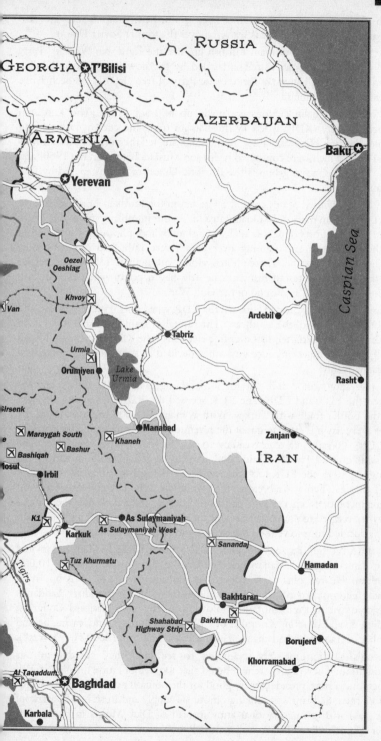

live in Syria and about 4 million live in northern Iraq. There are also approximately 1.5 million Kurds scattered over the former Soviet Union.

Currently, there are four main Kurdish groups: the Kurdistan Workers' Party (PKK) represents Turkish Kurds and is led by the now imprisoned Abdullah Ocalan. In Iran, the Kurdistan Democratic Party of Iran (KDPI) has been active politically but not militarily.

The other two main factions are made up of Iraqi Kurds. The Kurdistan Democratic Party (KDP) is led by the Barzani tribe, the current leader being Massoud Barzani. His grandfather, Ahmed Barzani, led the initial Kurdish revolts in the 1930s, which were continued by his son Mustafa Barzani in the 1960s and 1970s. The other main group is the Patriotic Union of Kurdistan, led by Jalal Talabani.

In 1991 the United States created a safe haven for Kurds in northern Iraq to protect them from nasty old Saddam Hussein. In our humble opinion, this was in part due to the efforts of people such as Çoskun, whose photos of Kurds fleeing into the mountains and fighting over bread were published internationally, including *Time* magazine. These photos, along with graphic TV footage, helped force the United States to instigate the safe haven policy when the Kurdish rebellion was crushed at the end of the Gulf War.

The area is currently divided between the KDP, who control the northwest, and the PUK, who control the southeast. The capital of Iraqi Kurdistan is Arbil. In 1992 Iraqi Kurds held their first ever free elections. The KDP beat the PUK with a small majority, but being nice guys, they decided to split the seats in the new parliament evenly.

The nice guy stuff didn't last for long, though. In 1994 warfare erupted between the PUK and KDP. The PUK accused the KDP of hogging the cash from the border trade with Turkey. With as many as 1,000 trucks crossing the border every day it is estimated that the revenue derived from taxing the trucks is about US$100 million a year. Needless to say, the KDP control the border. The KDP said "don't." The PUK said "do," leveled the antiaircraft guns and started blasting. In 1995 the PUK took the self-declared Kurdish capital of Arbil after fierce fighting. There was a breather for a while when the United States brokered an agreement between the two parties in Dublin, Ireland. When the United States then refused to put up the cash for the elections (a whole $2 million), both factions decided to resolve their differences with artillery instead.

This time, though, Barzani dumped Uncle Sam for Uncle Saddam and invited the latter into Iraqi Kurdistan to kick the PUK out. On August 31, 1996, 10,000 Republican Guards plus tanks rocked up outside the gates of Arbil. With Saddam's elite soldiers issued with real bullets the PUK left in a hurry. Saddam's folks got down to the busy task of blowing up the Iraqi National Congress, rounding up and shooting a number of CIA-trained flunkies, and leaving behind a number of Iraqis who had changed into Kurdish uniforms (See "The Players").

Clinton's election meisters scrambled to see how they could spin this confrontation. They vaguely remembered that footage of cruise missiles, stealth bombers and a stern president were good for the opinion polls. What they forgot was back then, Saddam was choking off our oil supply and Bush had Swartzkopf in the field with a multinational army instead of Dick Morris in bed with a hooker. Darn, it all worked so well for the Republicans.

About 69 percent of Americans supported Clinton's decision; 0 percent of Americans know how many people the cost of one cruise missile will feed. (DP figured that 44 cruise missiles at $1.5 million each equals $113.20 per Kurd in Iraq). Saddam was totally unfazed. His new Kurdish allies went on to capture the rest of Kurdistan over the next few days. The PUK retreated to their headquarters in Zahle, way up on the Iranian border, for some counseling and weapons.

It didn't take long for the PUK to hatch a plan. A month later they stormed down from the border (with a bit of help from Iran), recapturing most of their traditional areas. This time Saddam didn't come running to Barzani's aid. He simply informed the PUK that if they took the town of Degala then he would come back into the conflict again. A tad miffed, the PUK called a halt to the offensive, sat back in Sulymanya and waited for their next opportunity. Things really went haywire in October 1997. Earlier in the year the KDP had allied themselves with the Turks in their war against the PKK operating from the border area. With most of the KDP peshmerga tied up along the border the PUK rubbed their hands with glee and started planning the next offensive. October saw the beginning of the PUK blitzkrieg, and boy, was the KDP in trouble. It was double double, toil and trouble, when the PKK kids then moved down from the border and joined in the offensive for a lark. The KDP dialed 911 (or 312 as the case was) and the Turkish military came storming in with everything they had. A month of fighting saw the PUK reluctantly call a halt to the offensive. With the preferred option of exterminating the KDP no longer an option, the PUK decided to negotiate. After months of wrangling, both Kurdish leaders went to Washington in September 1998, where they signed a temporary—sorry, a permanent—peace agreement. Totally fixed and unfair elections were due to be held in June 1999, but as *DP* goes to press have yet to be held. Watch this space for round four of the Kurdish wars.

In Turkey the Kurdish struggle is led by the Kurdistan Workers' Party (PKK) whose leader, Abdullah Ocalan—aka "Apo"—has moved from a comfy house in Damascus to an even more comfy one in Rome. Who says a revolutionary can't have his creature comforts? Well, to be fair, he has since moved into the rather less salubrious confines of a Turkish prison, after his capture in Nairobi, Kenya by Turkish intelligence operatives. He has always sensibly left the fighting to the kids who are actually in southeastern Turkey, or "northwestern Kurdistan," as he wistfully calls it. After 15 years of all-out war with the PKK someone in the Turkish government decided to add up the cost: US$179 billion, 4,000 trashed villages, 3 million internal refugees and over 37,000 dead.

Despite the war, which started in 1984, between the Turkish military and the PKK in the southeastern provinces of Turkey, the Kurds as a people do not necessarily support the PKK's demand for a united Kurdistan. The chances of an independent Kurdish state being carved from hunks of Turkey, Iran, Iraq and Syria are about as likely as Saddam Hussein being nominated for the Nobel Peace Prize. Many, if not the majority, sympathize with the PKK's anti-Turkish motivation. The August 1999 announcement of a cease-fire by the PKK has meant that there is currently considerably less fighting. How long the situation will last is another matter. But over the years the Turkish military have torched about 4,000 villages in their bid to destroy the PKK. In turn the PKK have gunned down civilians who weren't quick enough to shout "long live Apo."

The PKK controls much of the countryside at night and sets up roadblocks to "tax" the local drivers and kidnap any foreigner dumb enough to be traveling after dark. During the day the Turkish Special Teams (Özel Timler) take back control and go PKK hunting. About 20 or so foreigners foolish enough to hang around the southeast have also been kidnapped by the PKK. If you're kidnapped you can expect to be doing a lot of hiking through the mountains as the PKK will want to take you far from the reaches of the Turkish military. You can also expect to be shelled and bombed. If it's not your ideal holiday, you can take consolation in the fact that you are guaranteed to come back a few pounds lighter. Far more effective than dieting. All the foreigners kidnapped have subsequently been released unharmed.

Not content with waging a war in Turkey, the PKK have also carried out bombings in Europe. A wave of attacks against Turkish embassies and businesses in 1993 sent the alarm bells ringing amongst European governments. With some 2 million Turks—a quarter of them Kurds—in Germany the government quickly banned 36 Kurdish organizations rather than see the battleground spread to Germany. The German government got so panicky that they actually sent a high-ranking member from the German secret service to have a chat with Ocalan in Damascus in 1995 (more like a grovel to beg Apo to reign in some of the wilder PKK elements). More recently, the German prosecutor has declared that the PKK is not, after all, a terrorist organization.

Kurdistan is a mess. Iraqi Kurds have been fighting successive Baghdad governments as well as other Iraqi Kurds, Turkish Kurds and the Turkish military. Vast mountainous regions mean that there are lots of places for the guerrillas of one side to hide and then whack the others. The Turkish Kurds, though, still use the Iraqi border as a springboard for attacks against Turkey. The Turkish military have virtually occupied a slab of the border zone since May 1997, under a media blackout, to fight their rebels in private. Some Iraqi Kurds have helped them. Others have helped the Turkish Kurds. In September 1998 the two main Iraqi Kurdish factions signed a peace deal in Washington. A mishmash of tribal and political allegiances with intelligence operatives from half a dozen countries running around makes it one of the most interesting and dangerous places in the world. But for the first time in Kurdish history Iraqi Kurds at least control their own destiny.

The United States/CIA/Iraqi National Congress and His Munificent Excellency the Very Honorable Saddam Hussein (and Sons)

Well, yes, here we come to one of one of the most entertaining foul-ups—depending on where you stand—in the recent annals of intelligence. In their heady desire to oust Saddam for someone with a prettier face, the CIA decided dole out the cash to the Arab opposition. Thus the INC was born: a motley crew of more parties than people. Led by

Ahmed Chalabi, a former banker wanted on fraud charges in Jordan, they set about the task of collecting Uncle Sam's cash and hatching a plan to depose Saddam. With a lack of secrecy that Austin Powers would have been proud of the INC installed itself in the Ankowa district of Arbil and set about plotting the downfall of Saddam. All well and good, you might be thinking to yourself. Not quite. Their willingness to welcome defectors from Baghdad—can you see where this is going?—made for more than the odd security slipup. As you might just have guessed, Saddam's kids promptly installed themselves at all the right levels, keeping their buddies in Baghdad informed of all goings-on. Not a great start. And, as they say, things could only get worse. And boy, did they get worse.

In 1996 the Dublin peace accord, which had been signed by the PUK and KDP began to fall to pieces. (The inside story on this is that the Turks told the United States that no way was there going to be any elections in Kurdistan. It might just encourage Turkish Kurds to get ideas of their own. The United States said okay and withdrew support for the elections.) Clashes started between the two factions. This time, though, Massoud Barzani tried another tact. He invited Saddam to help him kick the PUK and anyone else he didn't like out of Arbil. Did the CIA know this was coming? Well, actually they did. *DP*'s intelligence network in the region says that it was no big secret that Barzani was negotiating with Baghdad. Some in the CIA saw all this as just the opportunity to get rid of Saddam. The scenario amongst CIA officers on the ground went like this: Saddam comes to Arbil. The Kurds—in the form of the PUK—fight like hell. The United States comes to their aid with massive airstrikes taking out Saddam's tanks. The Kurds move on to Baghdad and the Iraqi military rebel. A re-enactment of 1991, except this time the United States supports the rebellion and . . . bye bye Saddam. That is, of course, what they told the PUK. So the PUK guys—or so they told *DP*—came up with an ultra-cunning plan to defend Arbil, only to find that where the CIA said one thing the State Department and the Pentagon had other ideas. Whoops! So Saddam rocked into Arbil . . . . no United States support for the PUK, who leg it from town and, well, you know the rest. Bill sends in the missiles and gets the ratings. The PUK get shafted. CIA operatives flee for Turkey. Saddam chuckles.

Iraqi National Congress

9 Pall Mall deposit
124 -128 Barlby Rd, London. UK W10 6 BL
Tel.: [44] (181) 960 4007
Fax: [44] (181) 960 4001, PR [44] (181) 233 9034
In Sulymanya, Iraq
Tel.: [873] (68) 234 6239
Fax: [873] (68) 234 6240
http://www.inc.org.uk

Jalal Talabani and the Patriotic Union of Kurdistan (PUK)

Uncle Jalal (as Talabani is known) and the boys really got going in 1975. The latest Kurdish rebellion had just been crushed by—guess who?—yes, dear old Saddam. It should be said that the United States and the Shah of Iran had just withdrawn all military support for the Kurds. Saddam had just given the Shatt-al-Arab waterway to Iran. In return for such generosity the Shah of Iran decided that he no longer needed to support the Kurdish rebellion. Oooopps! In turn some of the boys decided to blame Mullah Mustafa Barzani, the then Kurdish leader, for being a "lackey of imperialism" in overly depending on Iranian support. This being the '70s, quite a lot of them had commie tendencies. So, they wrote a letter to Jalal, who was then Mullah Mustafa's rep in Egypt, asking him to take the reins in the new party, which split from the KDP to become the PUK. As said, the kids cast around for an ideology and decided to plump for Marx with a bit of Lenin thrown in . . . come on, it was the '70s after all!

The PUK flag is green and its headquarters are at Zahle, deep in the mountains on the Iranian border. It gets some military support from Iran. The main areas of PUK support are the southeastern parts of northern Iraq. The PUK militia comprises about 25,000 men. They control their area from Sulymanya, which is a thriving hub of spies and revolutionaries. Turkish intelligence (known as MIT) and the PKK both have offices in Sulymanya. The Kurdistan Democratic Party of Iran (KDPI) and Iranian intelligence also both have offices there. In addition the CIA, MI6 and Saddam's mukhabarat all have a number of operatives running around town. Ya better be careful who ya talk to.

Jalal is something of a talker, which means that if—like *DP*—you're interviewing him it is often hard to get a word in edgeways. Fluent in English, Jalal will warble on ad lib with great charm. There's nothing he likes better than swanning around the international circuit. An invitation to Washington will see him making tracks to the airport almost before the invite has hit the doormat. He lives outside Sulymanya and also has a house in Damascus.

That said, Jalal is also knocking on a bit these days, which has left the rest of the gang wondering who will take over once he ups it. Seeing as you're a *DP* reader, we'll give you the inside scoop on the PUK leadership contenders. First, there's Kossrat Rassul, the current PUK prime minister. Kossrat's from Arbil. In the old days he used to covertly direct PUK assassination squads against Saddam's buddies in Arbil. Unfortunately, someone welched on him and he had to make some rather fast tracks to the mountains from where he continued the good fight. A member of the KDP described Kossrat as "an absolutely ruthless killer" as well as "utterly charming." *DP* will vouch for the "utterly charming" bit. Following fast on Kossrat's heels on the KDP hate list is Jabbar Farman, who was also called an "absolute killer." Jabbar—you will not be surprised to know—is the PUK's military commander. He also has an impeccable anti-Saddam record. In the '70s, he was locked up for a few years in the charming Abu Gharib prison, where most people tend to come out in very small pieces—or one big box. Jabbar survived and subsequently became the terror of Iraqi soldiers, leading PUK fighters on raids against Saddam and Co. As you can imagine, there's a fair amount of infighting and clawing behind the scenes in the PUK politburo. Yes, they still call it a politburo.

Patriotic Union of Kurdistan

Tel.: [44] (181) 642-4518
Att: Latif Rashid
USA Tel.: (703) 345-3056/
UK Tel.: [44] (181) 993-2196
France Tel.: [33] (1) 3916 0473
Turkey Tel.: [90312] 4402199
Germany Tel.: [49] (30) 344 8738
http://www.puk.org

Massud Barzani and the Kurdistan Democratic Party (KDP)

Massoud is the fourth son of Mullah Mustafa Barzani. Now leading the KDP he is the opposite of Jalal. A quiet, softly spoken man, he is clannish and tribal. His closest advisers all hail from the Barzani family. Who supports him? I hear you ask. Different countries at different times is the answer. In 1996 it was the Iraqis who were dolling out the cash and weapons and about 10,000 Republican Guard just for good measure. In 1997 it was the Turks who supported him when he took on the PKK along the Iraqi-Turkish border. As DP was going to press he was still getting support from Turkey. Barzani also gets all the cash from the technically illegal border trade with Turkey. He doesn't give any of it directly to the PUK—which rather miffs Jalal and the kids, and has been a contributing factor to the fighting between the two groups.

The KDP flag is yellow and the traditional area of support is the northwestern part of the Kurdish enclave. The KDP headquarters is Salahudin, a half-hour drive north of the self-declared Kurdish capital of Arbil. Barzani himself lives in one of Saddam's old palaces called Sereroche, just outside Salahudin. Barzani is still fighting the PKK along the Turkish-Iraqi border region with the Turkish army supporting him. The KDP say that for as long as the PKK have the bulk of their military forces inside Iraqi Kurdistan—as opposed to Turkish Kurdistan—they will continue to fight the PKK. Could be a long war, say the pundits. That said, the PKK has announced a cease-fire with the KDP. Could peace really be breaking out in Kurdistan? Nah, surely not!

Kurdistan Democratic Party
2025 I Street NW, Suite 1108
Washington, DC 20006
Tel.: (202) 331-9505
Fax: 331-9506
http://www.kdp.pp.se/
http://home1.swipnet.se/~w-11534/

Necherwan Barzani

Massoud Barzani's nephew and likely successor, Nachevan, is the eminence grise of the KDP. He is rarely seen and does not often give interviews. When Saddam's psychopathic brat, Uday, was so untragically gunned down in Baghdad Nachevan roared off to his bedside. Uday, you will not be surprised to know, is Nachevan's business partner in sanctions busting, i.e., selling oil to Turkey. Otherwise Nachevan would probably have finished off the assassins' job. What else would you do to someone who has lobbed chemical weapons at your village? Otherwise, though, he rocks round Baghdad in a Ferrari and is the key decision maker in the KDP after Massoud. And according to the slightly jaundiced view of a PUK politburo member, Nachevan "is a bit too much of a ladies' man."

The Turkish Military and Police Forces

With more than 350,000 Turkish troops and security personnel in southeastern Turkey, you'd have thought that they might be able to keep a lid on it all. To a certain extent they have, but only just. Not too cool on the old human rights bit, though. Always a fourth force in Turkish politics, the military has staged three coups in modern Turkish history. There are two things the military hate: Kurds and Islamists. In 1997 it forced Necmettin Erbakan and his Islamist-led government to resign without actually leaving their barracks. Turkish intelligence (known as MIT) also operates out of Sulymanya, where it has an office dedicated to monitoring the PKK, which has an office a little further down the road. *DP* wonders what happens if they ever get stuck in a traffic jam together. A couple of icy smiles, perhaps?

The Kurds

Definitely not God's chosen people. Split between Turkey, Iran, Iraq and Syria with a smattering in Armenia, the Kurds have been persecuted by all the aforementioned countries—except Armenia. Ayatollah Khomeini sent the firing squads into Iranian Kurdistan, Saddam sent his delightful cousin, Chemical Ali (Ali Hassan al Majid), and doses of nerve gas, to Iraqi Kurdistan and the Turkish military have trashed Turkish Kurdistan, embarking in the largest forced depopulation since the 1930s. The Kurds missed out savagely in the post World War I peace deal and were sold down the river by the British, who had promised them an independent state. Typical of the double-dealing Brits though, they turned around and did a deal with Kemal Ataturk instead. Bye-bye Kurdistan. It was a blow that the Kurds have never recovered from. To make matters worse, the Kurds have never—like the Palestinians—been united. Possibly this is because that they face four different enemies.

Today, the vast mountainous territory that all Kurds call Kurdistan is poor, underdeveloped and riven by sporadic warfare. Tourists have been repeatedly kidnapped by the PKK in southeastern Turkey. Aid workers have been murdered in northern Iraq. And extra-judicial murder and torture are generally the lot that most Kurds can expect for opening their mouths.

Kemal Ataturk

The Father of All Turks never really saw eye to eye with the Kurds. Actually he banned their language, said that Kurds were "Mountain Turks" and imprisoned anyone who disagreed with this view. While he was an enlightened revolutionary for the Turks, he ignored the Kurds. Well, actually, he kind of totally trashed them big time. As a Turkish nationalist and war hero he sought to assimilate the Kurds into Turkish society whether they liked it or not. And they didn't. Turkish was made the only language permitted to be taught in schools and the process of forced assimilation began. For the 10–15 million Turkish Kurds a life of cultural and political denial had just begun.

Abdullah Ocalan (aka Apo)

Apo, please come home . . . to be hanged. It's not quite known what kind of miss-you cards the Turkish government sent Apo while he was in Syria, but they didn't work.

Abdullah Ocalan was finally captured by Turkish intelligence operatives in February 1999. It's all a bit shady but *DP* has the scoop. In late 1998 the Turks were getting just a bit unhappy with Apo running the show out of a nice little villa in the suburbs of Damascus, so they decided to bomb Syria. Which is to say that they told the Syrians, "lose the man with the potbelly and the funny mustache or Damascus is history." Rather than lose Damascus the Syrians lost Apo, who took a plane to southern Cyprus, slunk off to Russia before landing in Italy on a false passport. The Italians didn't quite know what to do. The Germans did, though, and issued an arrest warrant for Apo—before they realized that maybe they really didn't want 200,000 German Kurds going ape as their leader was hauled through the courts. The extradition order was quietly rubbed off the menu and the German public prosecutor took a long holiday.

So for a few weeks Apo had a nice comfy villa on the outskirts of Rome. The Turks were not happy. All those plans and it looked like the bastard was going to end up with better accommodation than they had planned for him. That is, until Apo disappeared from all our radar screens. Here one minute, gone the next. Abdullah Ocalan had left Italy, said the Italian government, wiping its collective brow with relief. So Apo set off on another odyssey to find asylum somewhere other than Turkey. He rocked up in Moscow, only to find the Ruskies uninterested. A few Greeks then hid him in Greece before carting him off to their ambassador's residence in Nairobi. Nairobi . . . hmm . . . not the best of choices perhaps when you consider that in the aftermath of Mr. bin Laden's little bomb, the place is crawling with CIA and FBI agents.

Needless to say, they were soon listening in to Apo's desperate cell phone calls to anyone who might be able help him. Someone in Washington got on the blower to someone in Athens and gave them a mega bollicking for harboring the "terrorist Ocalan." Turkish intelligence agents, tipped off by Washington, flooded into Kenya. The Greeks told Apo that they were all going for a short ride. Apo's car, though, took a small diversion into the hands of . . . Turkish intelligence. Drugged and rushed to the airport, the next thing poor old Apo knew, he was in a plane heading for Istanbul.

After a quick trial, whichwas naturally extremely fair and considered all sides of the argument, Apo was sentenced to death. His last-minute plea that he could solve the Kurdish problem in Turkey if his life was spared fell, quite rightly, on deaf ears. As we all know—and as the Turkish government never tires of telling us—there is no Kurdish problem in Turkey. There is only a minor problem of some mindless terrorists, who happen to be Kurds. Sorry, as the Turkish government has just—again, quite correctly—

reminded *DP*, these people are Turkish citizens who live in the east and sometimes call themselves Kurdish. There is *not* a Kurdish problem in Turkey. Get it?

Then, in August 1999, from his prison cell, Apo announced a unilateral cease-fire and the withdrawal of all PKK forces from Turkey. Er, come again? Well, yes, all PKK forces are supposed to be leaving Turkey. Quite what the kids on the ground make of all this remains to be seen. But when *DP* visited the PKK kids in southeastern Turkey, they didn't appear to have any plans to start trekking out. Could it be that Apo just can't bear the thought of being a middle-aged prisoner with bad food and no more journos queuing up to visit him?

The Turkish government meanwhile, has said, "No negotiations with terrorists." So much then, for . . . er . . . peace. That said, there have been various noises made about not hanging Ocalan and letting him off with life imprisonment. How nice.

Abdullah Ocalan (latest—and probably final—address):
Imrali Prison
Imrali, Turkey

The Kurdistan Workers' Party (PKK)

The Parta Kakerin Kurdestan (or PKK) got going in 1978, in Siverek. They started off a Marxist-Leninist organization fighting for independence or autonomy in what they rather wistfully call "northwestern Kurdistan," for which you can read "southeastern Turkey." Their top dog, Abdullah Ocalan, used to run the show out of a comfy house in Damascus. That was, until the Turks got really quite pissed with the Syrians and threatened to unload a whole few tons of bombs on them unless they changed their tune. The Syrians denied Ocalan was in Damascus and the next thing anyone knew, "Apo," as his followers call him, had rocked up in Italy. The Italians were a bit fazed, to say the least, to have Turkey's most wanted man on their doorstep. A few weeks later Apo was on the move, and nobody knew where. Reports surfaced of him in Russia, Armenia, Greece and then, as we all know Nairobi (see above).

"Apo" used to be seen on MED-TV (until it, like him, got closed down) which served as a platform for fans to listen his reasoned calls for dialogue with the Turkish government; or, depending on his mood, long-winded rants. An old-style Marxist, he has never really managed glasnost convincingly, though he has tuned down his demands for an independent state carved out of Turkey, Iraq, Iran and Syria. Autonomy, he says, is the goal of the PKK. Get stuffed, says the Turkish military.

It wasn't just the PKK, but quite a lot of Kurds who got just a bit upset by Apo's enforced departure from the scene. Europe was rocked by demonstrations, with young Kurds pouring petrol over themselves, and there was a wave of panic that it might all get out of hand.

In Turkey the PKK began a series of bomb attacks in the west of the country. Turkish tourism plummeted. Department stores were firebombed, suicide bombers blew themselves up in the middle of Istanbul and everyone began to get a little bit nervous. The PKK promised to start a whole new war in west Turkey with plastic explosive on the dining-out menu for most restaurants.

In the meantime, the kids with the guns are mainly being trained in northern Iraq. The PKK has several training camps in the Qandil Mountains near the border with Iran. Most of the PKK guerrillas are recruited in southeastern Turkey, but quite a few are now being recruited in northern Iraq. Next door to Qandil there is Hajji Omran—a vast mountainous area where Iran, Iraq and Turkey meet—which also serves as a major base for the PKK. Abdullah Ocalan's little brother, Osman, tends to hang out in Qandil but also has a house in Sulymanya. More recently Osman has been hanging out in Iran. You might like to know that Osman used to spend a fair amount of time on the old sat phone to big brother. How do we know? Because Turkish intelligence operatives spend their whole time in Sulymanya, listening to big brother and little brother chatting away. How do we know that? Ah, well, that is a secret.

Since poor old "Apo" started living in the new accommodation provided so kindly by the Turkish government the PKK has established a—hold your breath now—Presidential Council. This comprises Cemil Bayik, code-named Cuma, Murat Karrayillan, code-named Cemal, Osman Ocalan, code-named Ferhat, Duran Kalakan, code-named "Abbas" and . . . that's about all I can be bothered to list for the moment.

In southeastern Turkey the military have had a fair amount of success curbing the activities of the PKK, mainly because they've burned all the villages. Over 4,000 villages have been torched by the military in the southeast. When *DP* had a chat to some of the PKK guys in northern Iraq they said that there is only less fighting because the soldiers no longer come up into the mountains, so they don't shoot them. They insisted, though, that their forces are still alive and well and in control of the mountainous regions in south eastern Turkey. Hmmm. *DP* has its doubts.

In fact, the PKK is definitely on a military back foot. At its peak, between 1991–93, PKK guerrillas controlled large sections of southeastern Turkey. There were nightly gun battles in Cizre, Silopi, Nusayabin and numerous other towns dotted round the south east. Turkish soldiers were being sent back to the west of the country in boxes at an alarming rate. In Ankara alone as many as ten coffins a day would arrive containing bodies of recruits killed by the PKK.

Nowadays the fighting is more or less concentrated deep in the mountains. The chances of the PKK swooping down from the mountains in broad daylight—as they did in 1995—and snatching a gaggle of tourists foolishly traveling through the region are remote indeed. That said, the PKK have managed to hold some of the valleys in provinces such as Tunceli, Bingol and Van, despite the best efforts of the Turkish military. In Tunceli the PKK controls Kutu Deresi (Box Valley), a deep 30-kilometer-long gorge that the Turkish military have never managed to take. As *DP* goes to press the PKK have announced a cease-fire and a withdrawal of their forces from Turkey in a bid to open negotiations with the Turkish government. The Turkish military didn't care and have continued operations.

It still isn't a good time to go mountain hiking in southeastern Turkey.

Kurdistan Information Center

10 Glasshouse yard
London EC1
[44] (171) 250 1315
Fax: [44] (171) 250 1317
http:// www.kurdistan.org

American Kurdish Information Network

2623 Connecticut Ave., NW
Washington. DC 20008-1522
Tel: (202) 483-6444
Fax: (202) 483-6476
E-mail: akin@kurdish.org
Web site: http://burn.ucsd.edu/~akin

Medya-TV

The TV station that has replaced Med-TV, the station that used to drive the Turkish government wild. Med-TV was the voice of the Kurdish rebel movement: the PKK. To the acute embarrassment of the British government it was broadcast from London. The station was named after the Medes (the ancient name for the Kurds). But the guys overstepped the mark when Osman Ocalan got on the blower—after his big brother was snatched by the Turks—and in typical Ocalan family style ranted and raved that everything was a "target." The Brits quickly closed it down on the grounds of "incitement to violence." As you may have guessed from the name, Medya-TV is a similar operation, but only broadcasts eight hours a day and has two nice men from Britain's Independent Television Commission checking all the programs for content.

For millions of Kurds, though, the TV station still defines them and gives them a sense of cultural identity. Tune in any time and you'll be able to find out just how splendidly the PKK's latest offensive is going, combined with tirades of anti-Turkish polemic.

Medya Broadcasting Ltd.
The Linen Hall
162-168 Regent Street
London W1R 5AT
Tel.: [44] (171) 494-2523
Fax: [44] (171) 494-2528
E-mail: med@med-tv.be
Web Site: http://www.ibibe/med/www/intro.htm
MED-TV is broadcast on Intelsat and Eutelsat (ESC II F2 transponder 25, 10 degrees east; downlink frequency 10971.667 MHz [P-V] polarization vertical) between 1400 and 2300 GMT.

To enter Turkey you need a valid passport good for at least six months. A visa is required for U.S. nationals. Visas for three months are available for US$20 and will be given on entry. Getting to Turkey's Kurdish areas means either a long bus journey or a short plane ride to Diyarbakir in the southeast. From there you will be able to travel around depending on the whim of the local police or military commanders.

Entry to northern Iraq (Iraqi Kurdistan) is next to impossible without some kind of covert contact in the region. Even *DP* staffers have a hard time. Roddy Scott was tossed out in 1997 and 1998. Turkey has closed the border to aid workers and journalists—though they may be reopening it in 1999. Yeah, some chance! Hacks planning a tour of southeastern Turkey should—to avoid tedious hours of questioning by the police—direct inquiries to:

General Directorate of Press and Information
Office of the Prime Minister
56 Konur Sokak
Ankara, Turkey
Tel.: (312) 417-6311
Alternatively, you can go for the full-blown undercover tour. This involves a very good taxi driver who knows the game and the checkpoints as well as just about everything else. If you get spotted, though, expect even more hours of tedious questioning as well as losing all your film.

Can be a tad hazardous. While local services in Turkey provide an efficient transport bus/minbus system you could well be turned back by the military—if they spot you. Travel at night is for morons and locals only. The PKK stop cars and sometimes burn lorries. Local militias stop traffic pretending to be PKK and rob travelers. That said, during a spate of foreign tourist kidnappings in 1995 all the victims were traveling during the day.

In northern Iraq the war between the KDP and PKK has left the border region security at an all-time low. Large areas are now under the control of the PKK at night. If its not wave your white flag time, try an armored vehicle with about 20 bodyguards. You might get through.

Rezerv Yor Seet Noww!

The following is a sampling of the regulations on a passenger ticket for the Turkish domestic carrier Bodrum Airlines. Their use of English is impeccable, wouldn't you say?

1. **You cannot give back your ticket, but if you annonce us before 24 hours your depart that you cannot fly you can use your ticket with in one year. After passing one year, you can not fly with your ticket.**

2. **You have to get in touch with contuar befe 30 mitutes of the departure, atherwine you don't get on the board and you don't have any rights for justice.**

3. **If someone gets ticket by doing tricky, Bodrum Airlines has rezerved the rights that there is no must to give a permation that passenger gets on the board.**

4. **Bodrum Airlines is not able to carry out flight schadule if an unusual thinks take place like bed weather, NOTAM, float, fire, eath queke, war, gone of elefricity, natural disaster, etc.**

5. **Do not allawe to drink alcaol and smoke cigarets on board.**

Northern Iraq (Southern Kurdistan)

In May 1997, 30,000 Turkish troops stormed across the border to whack PKK bases in the mountains. As the press was definitely not invited to attend the event, it's all been a bit tricky finding out the scoop. A few months later, though, the Turkish military waxed lyrical about how the PKK had all been eliminated. Odd then that, over two years later, they're still there fighting the PKK, as they have charged over the border again at press time. Since then *DP* has been one of the few, if not only, publications to get into northern Iraq and, er, thrown out again.

Southeastern Turkey (Northwestern Kurdistan)

In October 1997 the PUK launched a major offensive against the KDP. The KDP had been helping the Turkish military against the PKK on the border. All hell broke loose when the PKK kids put on the warpaint and decided to join in the offensive. Poor old KDP. With the KDP about to go down and out for the count they had to whistle up help. It came in the form of the Turkish military who hammered the PUK with F-16s and Leopard MBTs. With a very sore head the PUK sulkily went back to Sulymanya crying foul. Come on guys, it was two to one to start with!

In 1998 the Turkish military captured Sakik, aka Fingerless Zeki), in northern Iraq. (Well, actually he surrendered to the KDP and the Turks nabbed him as he trundled off from Dohuk to Erbil.) Sakik, formerly the PKK's Tunceli commander, became regional commander in northern Iraq and the list of his charge sheet makes more extensive reading than *DP*. Since then, there has been all-out war between the Turkish military and KDP on one side and the PKK on the other in the region. All under a rather unsporting media blackout.

Murder

Since the start of the PKK war there have been about 3,000 unsolved murders in southeastern Turkey. As most of these people were Kurdish activists, suspicion has rather unsurprisingly fallen on the Turkish military. The government tries to blame the PKK. Relatives of victims who try and bring charges against military personnel stand an excellent chance of becoming victims themselves.

Guarding Villages

To root out remaining pockets of rebel resistance in eastern Turkey, the government relocated some 3,000 subsistence farmers who were thought to be PKK sympathizers. Those with the brains to keep their political sympathies to themselves—about 70,000 folks considered loyal to the government—were rewarded with a gun and $200 a month in cash and instructed to defend their villages, hardly night watchman's pay in eastern Turkey. Not a cool thing to be doing if you want to collect your pension. The biggest PKK massacres have, unsuprisingly, been perpetrated against village guards. An average of ten village guards are killed every month. This job sucks.

Medical care in the area known as Kurdistan is rudimentary and far below Western standards. The only care of any value is given by NGOs operating in the area. Diyarbakir in eastern Turkey provides the best medical services in the region. For serious illnesses or injuries, this is where you'll want to start. Then get your ass to Istanbul.

Kurdistan is the homeland for the world's 25 million or so Kurds. The largest ethnic group in the world without an official country of their own, the Kurds just won't give up fighting for what many consider a lost cause.

A mountain people, their language is similar to Persian; but centuries of isolation have created a number of dialects. The two main ones are Kurmanji and Sorani. The former is spoken in Turkey and the latter in Iraq and Iran. Another dialect is Zaza, mainly spoken in Turkey. Most Kurds are Sunni Muslims. They are descended from the Medes.

Business hours in eastern Turkey are the same as in the rest of the country, from 8.30 a.m.–noon and 1.30 P.M.–5/5.30 P.M. Monday through Friday. Turkish post offices are recognizable by the black PTT letters on yellow background. Postal service is efficient and modern, as are telecommunications.

There are no such luxuries in northern Iraq. There are, though, numerous satellite telephones, which cost about $2 a minute.

Local time in northern Iraq is GMT + 3 hours April–September and GMT + 2 hours October–March. Electricity is available in most towns and is 220V/50Hz. Bottled water is recommended. The currency in Turkey is the Turkish lira (460,000 TL = 1 US dollar). In northern Iraq the currency is the dinar (20 ID = 1 US dollar). Hotels can be found in Salahudin, Arbil, Dohuk, Zakho and Sulymanya. The best hotel in Arbil is the Arbil Tower Hotel *(Tel.: 23797),* which costs about US$15 a night, has a well-stocked bar and decent food. The manager is Mr. Said. If you're in Dohuk, the only place is the Lowkama Hotel, at around the same price. In northern Iraq it's cash only. Hundred dollar bills are the advisable currency to carry. In southeastern Turkey, credit cards can be used in most sizeable towns.

Web Resources

Komala
> http://www.pi.se/webpage/comm unist.party.of.iran/Komola/Komola.html

Kurdish Parliament in Exile
> http://www.ariga.com/peacebiz/peacelnk/kurd.htm

National Liberation Front for Kurdistan (ERNK)
> http://www.megabaud.fi/~ernk/

Kurdistan Democratic Party
> http://www.kdp.pp.se/

Kurdistan Workers' Party,
> http://www.uni-passau.de/~lindeman/ kurd.htm

Patriotic Union of Kurdistan
> http://www.puk.org

Peoples' Liberation Party—Front (DHKC)
> http://www.ozgurluk.org/dhkc

3/8/99	From his prison cell Ocalan offers a cease-fire and withdrawal of PKK forces from Turkey.
2/20/99	Turkish intelligence operatives capture Abdullah Ocalan in Nairobi, Kenya.
9/12/98	KDP and PUK sign peace agreement in Washington.
3/17/98	Turkish troops capture Semdin Sakik, PKK regional commander in northern Iraq.
5/14/97	Turkey sends some 50,000 troops into northern Iraq to destroy PKK bases. An estimated 3,000 people are killed.
8/31/96	Forty-thousand Republican Guards take Arbil.
3/30/95	Medya-TV begins broadcasting.
4/16/91	U.S. president George Bush announces that U.S. troops would enter northern Iraq to create a safe haven for displaced Kurds around Zakhu.
3/2/91	Iraq signs a cease-fire agreement with allied forces ending the Persian Gulf War.
2/27/91	Allied forces in Kuwait and Iraq suspend military operations against Iraq.
1/17/91	The start of hostilities between the multinational forces and Iraqi forces. The beginning of Operation Desert Storm.
8/2/90	Iraqi forces invade Kuwait and seize control of the country.
8/15/86	Turkish troops raid Kurdish rebel camps in Iraq.
9/19/80	Iran-Iraq war begins.

3/10/79	Death of Kurdish leader Mullah Mustafa Barzani (Kurdish regions).
6/1/76	Workers' Party of Kurdistan formed.
1/22/46	Kurdish Republic Day.
4/28/37	Saddam Hussein's birthday.
3/21	Kurdish New Year celebrated.

Monrovia

Liberia
★★★

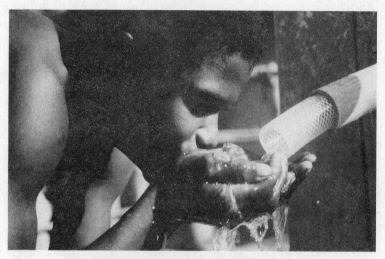

Chuck Taylor and His All-Stars

It's good to be king. In Liberia things have quieted down and Charles Taylor is now faced with trying to figure out how to run Liberia.

The war hogs in their Banana Republic jackets remember the old days fondly. Where else would one go to see a cast of outrageously wild characters dressed in odd-but-uniform military gear and going by names that would make a sailor blush? Back then Libyan-backed, self-proclaimed criminal Charles Taylor surrounded himself with the finest military men (all so competent that they were promoted directly from volunteer to general) Liberia could muster. General No-Mother-No-Father, General Housebreaker, General Fuck-Me-Quick and the gregarious General Butt Naked were just some of the colorful and oft-defeated warriors. General Butt Naked was particularly visible since he fought battles in his prime-evil buff—his only uniform was a pair of scuffed tennis shoes and his only armor the protective stench of stale liquor no bullet would dare penetrate. Ah, the good days. But them days is over. These days you'll find Butt Naked preaching the word of God on Broad Street in Monrovia as a born again

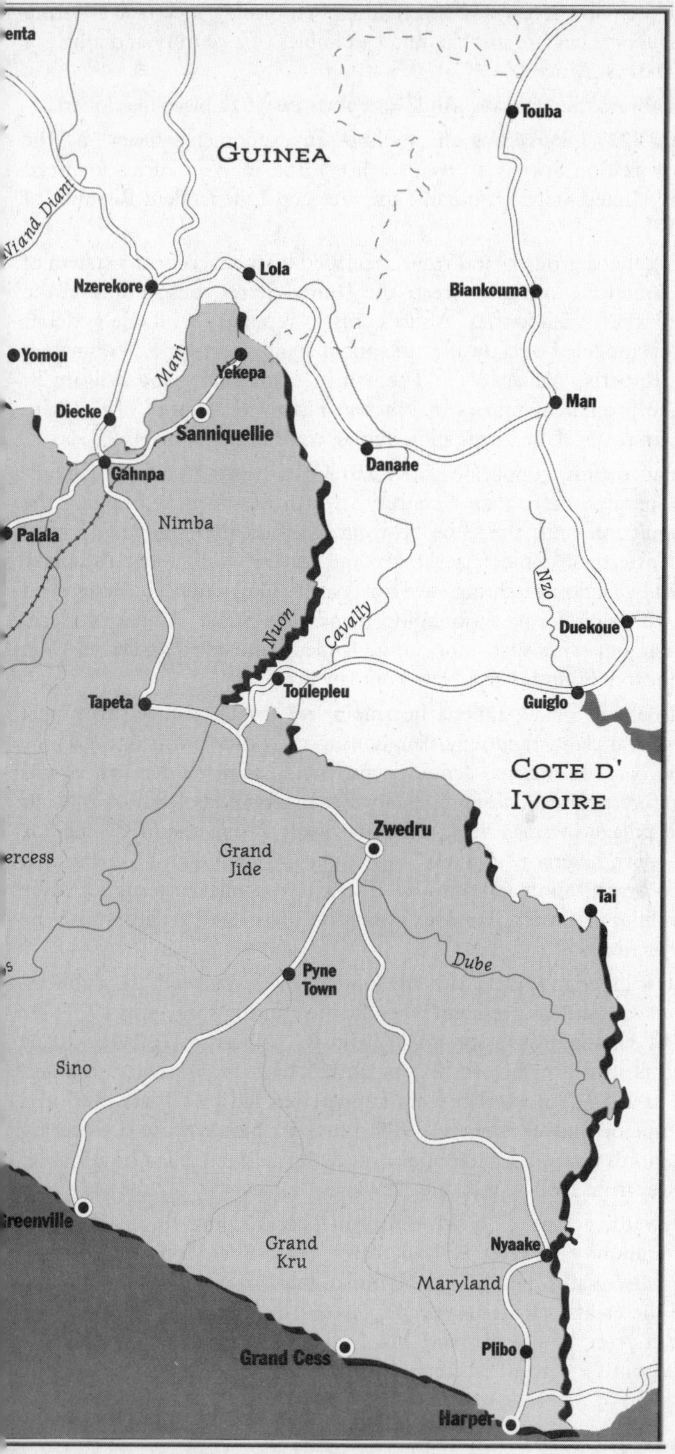
enta
Touba
Guinea
Niand Diani
Lola
Nzerekore
Biankouma
Yomou
Mani
Yekepa
Man
Diecke
Sanniquellie
Danane
Gahnpa
Nimba
Palala
Nzo
Nuon
Cavally
Duekoue
Toulepleu
Tapeta
Guiglo
Cote d' Ivoire
Zwedru
ercess
Grand Jide
Tai
Dube
Pyne Town
Sino
Greenville
Grand Kru
Nyaake
Maryland
Plibo
Grand Cess
Harper

preacher. Back then his choir was young children brandishing sticks and swearing like diseased sailors. They are just the finest examples of a century and a half of civilization in darkest Africa.

Well, there's always the next war. And war comes easy to a place like Liberia.

Founded in 1822, Liberia was an attempt—an experiment, really—by the American Colonization Society to create a homeland in West Africa for freed slaves from the United States. It became the Free and Independent Republic of Liberia in 1847.

It's interesting that a group of individuals so jaded by the racial strata system of 19th-century America chose to re-create the United States constitution on the other side of the Atlantic. As Africa's first "republic," Liberia's debut government was modeled directly after the one it sought to escape. With names like Joseph J. Roberts, William V. S. Tubman, Charles Taylor and William R. Tolbert Jr., the prominent figures in Liberian history read more like a Palm Beach polo team roster than a struggling, ragtag community of displaced slaves.

The attempt at creating a duplicate America in Africa, however, never came full-circle, namely because more than a century's worth of efforts at bringing the aboriginal population onto the same "playing field" as the emigrants proved unsuccessful. Instead of democracy, liberty and all that stuff, Liberia's course became marred by factional fighting, civil war, partitioning and bloody coups led not by men with sinister, nasty-sounding names like Stalin, Arafat, Noriega, Hitler or Amin, but with such innocuous, landed-gentryish handles as Doe, Taylor and Johnson. Sounds like a New York law firm.

Instead of freedom for all, Liberia became a free-for-all, reduced to primal clashes among rival clans, randomly slaughtering each other with old machine guns from the back of ancient, dented jeeps. Bands of marauders cut swaths across the rain forest plateau, donning Halloween masks and bolt-action rifles, as they rape and pillage in small villages before finally razing them. Calling the situation in modern Liberia a "civil war" is giving it too much status—crediting it with too much organization and purpose. The reality is villagers slaughtered by tribal-based militias that mark, like dogs pissing on a tree, their territory with the skulls of their victims.

One of the few Liberian leaders with any longevity was William V. S. Tubman, who was in his sixth term as president when he died during surgery in 1971. He was replaced by his longtime associate, William R. Tolbert Jr. Tolbert actually lasted nine years in office, before he was ousted by a mere master sergeant, Samuel Doe, in 1980. Yet another coup attempt was led by Charles Taylor, a senior official in Doe's government, in 1989. Leaving a bloody wake in capturing most of the nation's economic and population centers, Taylor failed by a whisker to wrestle power from Doe by mid-July 1990.

Shortly afterward, a six-nation West African peacekeeping force called the Economic Community of West African States Cease-Fire Monitoring Group (ECOMOG) essentially partitioned Liberia into two zones. The first encompassed the capital of Monrovia and was led by President Amos Sawyer. The other half, run by Taylor and his National Patriotic Front (NPFL), amounted to about 95 percent of Liberian territory.

Reconciliation and peace agreements were signed and ignored like journalists' bar tabs. A March 1991 conference failed to get anything accomplished except for the reelection of Sawyer as interim president. Despite a peace agreement in 1991, fighting continued to flare. Another peace agreement and cease-fire in July 1993, which established an interim government and set up general democratic elections, crumbled a short time later in November.

Gambia, Nigeria, Mali, Ivory Coast, Switzerland and Benin are among the venues that have hosted Liberian peace talks since Taylor launched the civil war the day before Christmas in 1989. Some ended with agreements hailed at the time as historic. All proved to be failures.

The 12th agreement, signed in Benin with UN guarantees, seemed the most likely to succeed. It ended up in tatters. Only 3,000 of Liberia's estimated 60,000 fighters—many of them teenagers addicted to drugs along with killing and raping civilians—were disarmed.

At least a third of Liberia's prewar population of 2.5 million fled the country after fighting broke out on December 24, 1989, when Taylor invaded Liberia from the Ivory Coast. In 1993, the UN estimated 150,000 had died, but stopped counting after that. (As of mid-1997, most estimates put the death toll at nearly 200,000.) It became nearly impossible for relief workers to operate in rebel-controlled areas. A peace accord signed in August 1995 called for countrywide ECOMOG deployment and disarmament of factional fighters, but 10 months later neither of these processes had gotten off the ground.

In April 1996, Monrovia was again launched into lawlessness. Fighting resumed in earnest between the rival factions. In only three days, Monrovia toppled into anarchy. Thousands fled the capital city in panic. As many as 20,000 Liberians descended upon the residential annex of the U.S. embassy. U.S. military commandos evacuated about 2,000 frightened American citizens and other foreigners by chopper to the Sierra Leone capital of Freetown, starting in the middle of the night on April 8, as Monrovia's airport was destroyed in the fighting. Evacuations continued for at least two months.

Yet a disarmament program, part of an ambitious transition program (and the war's 14th peace agreement) developed by the Economic Community of West African States (ECOWAS)—designed to dissolve Liberia's armed factions—became tremendously successful only nine months after Monrovia's anarchy. By February 1997, more than 10,000 fighters had been demobilized and 5,000 weapons recovered.

Up until July 24, 1997, Liberia was run by a six-member interim Council of State led by charismatic chairwoman Ruth Perry, who replaced Taylor stooge Wilton Sankawulo in this, Liberia's 14th, peace accord since 1989.

Before the Perry-led Council of State, the country was terrorized by up to 60,000 young (sometimes under 15), brutal, drunken and armed thugs who dressed up in masks, wigs and ballroom gowns and wielded rusty guns and vicious tempers to steal food and rape and butcher people. Bandits and terrorists continue to wax and dismember each other in the countryside, although the overall level of violence has dropped considerably.

In July 1997, Charles Taylor was elected with an impressive margin (even though earlier he swore he wouldn't run for office and he would go into business instead). Things are eerily calm in Monrovia outside of the odd gunfight and his countrymen and many enemies are waiting to see what Chuck and his All-Stars will do now that they have center court.

Fly the Friendly Flag

Ever notice that small type that follows those cool cruise ads? It usually says Liberian Registry. Yes, you read right, Liberia, the country without a postal system, phone network or even a government, sells a lot of flags and registrations. Over 1,600 ships totalling 59.8 million gross tons fly the Liberian flag. In fact, the $50 million in fees paid to the Liberian government comprises 90 percent of the revenue to the government in tough times. It is called a flag of convenience, and shipping lines escape many of the taxes and restrictions imposed by more sedate countries. Liberia maintains that it spends 10 percent of its earnings training ship inspectors and says they are second to none in safety. The government of Liberia is run by a six-member council that includes tribal chiefs, warlords and politicians. Charles Taylor, a former civil servant and now lead member in the council who started the civil war in 1989, now says that none of the funds is used for the military, but instead go towards schools, travel and payroll.

The checks are cashed by an American company called International Trust Company, which manages the registration business for the government of Liberia. The International Maritime Organization is permanently based in London, England.

The second most popular country to register ships? Why, the conflict-, crime- and drug-free country of Panama, of course. To register your ship contact: Bureau of Maritime Affairs, P. O. Box 10-9042, 197 Ashmun Street, 1000 Monrovia 10, Liberia

Liberia was once the most Americanized country in Africa. And, in a way, maybe it still is: violent, treacherous and floating calmly (for the moment) in a violent backwater eddy of outside agitation, tribal hatred and old-fashioned greed. This is a country created by former slaves who brought American surnames and American-style politics to Africa. And, it appears, racism, guns and crime. Liberia now barely functions as a country. The prolonged civil war has reduced the country to a subsistence economy. More than 150,000 were killed in the civil war between 1989 and 1997. The most recent peace agreement (the country's 14th since 1989), signed in August 1996, has been relatively effective in disarming the various factions. Chuck Taylor took the July 1997 elections and quickly put his brother and sister-in-law into his cabinet and left some seats open for his former warlord enemies. Things are calm now and it remains to be seen whether ethnic tensions and the mess with Sierra Leone will force Chuck Taylor to put his All-Stars back on the field again.

Dahkpannah Charles Ghanky Taylor and the National Patriotic Front of Liberia (NPFL)

Chuckie, the supreme Zo (chief of chiefs), has pulled off the big one. This member of the Gola tribe is now the prez. Not bad for a son of a servant and a Baptist teacher from Arthington. The only blemish seems to be that Chuck is still wanted in Boston for a 1985 jail break and that his boys played a big part in stacking up the 20,000 stiffs that didn't survive the last war. Charles Taylor (born 1948) started the miserable war in Liberia back on Christmas Eve, 1989. Rumor has it he had been brushing up on Revolution 101 in Libya. The last time anyone knew his whereabouts was back in 1984, when he was Director of the Liberian General Services Agency in charge of buying stuff for the Liberian government. He was accused of embezzling $900,000 from the Liberian coffers, and then he fled to the United States, where he was captured for extradition back to Liberia. He bragged about how he sawed through the bars of the laundry room after bribing his jailors with $30,000. That economics degree came in handy. He went to live in the Ivory Coast, where he assembled an army (actually about 150 people) with the help of the Ivorian president, whose brother-in-law, William Tolbert, was executed by Samuel Doe. He gathered together another 4,000 soldiers from the Gio and Mano tribes from eastern Liberia and began his "rebellion" in 1989. What he actually did was knock Liberia's delicate infrastructure into the toilet for the next 50 years at least. So how does a guy with pals like General Fuck-Me-Quick, Baby Killer and Butt Naked do in politics? Well, he got a personal phone call from Prezzie Bill, Jimmy Carter came over to make sure the elections were nice and tidy, and even Jesse "don't stand too close to me" Jackson is one of his buds. Former attorney general Ramsey Clark was the lawyer who defended him during his 16 months as a guest of the U.S. prison system. Oh, did I tell you that he is violently anti-communist and a devout Baptist?

So now that he is ensconced in the Presidential Mansion (he actually lives in a swank setup in Congoland) Chuck has taken to wearing suits instead of military fatigues, appropriate for a man with an economics degree from Bentley College in Waltham, Massachusetts. He is a Baptist who has a fondness for the music of Mahalia Jackson, Dirty Harry movies and good living.

How long will the good times last? It's hard to say in a country where life is worth less than a Coke. His enemy is the Krahn tribe (about 2 percent of the population), led by warlord Roosevelt Johnson. Taylor unsuccessfully tried to take Monrovia in 1990 and 1992. When politics did what bullets couldn't, Taylor was made part of a ruling committee, but he overstepped his authority when he tried to arrest Johnson. All hell broke loose, and the United States had to send in the marines to evacuate the embassy and the foreigners stuck in the crossfire. Taylor's choice of media is the KISS-FM radio station in Monrovia. As one of Chuck's new tourism ideas, he has ordered all expat Liberians to return home to get new passports. Uh-huh. We'll be right there, Chuck. Why so hard up for money? According to Chuck, the Liberian government is bankrupt and can't even fight off insurgents from Guinea who have attacked the northern part of the country.

Charles Ghanky Taylor
Executive Mansion
P.O. Box 10-9001
Capitol Hill
1000 Monrovia 10, Liberia
E-mail: EMansion@liberia.net
http://www.liberian-connection.com/lc-govn.htm

Diamonds Are Forever

When Charles Taylor married his girlfriend on January 28, 1997, he promised her he would not run for president, but would instead open a business. He lied.

Alhaji Kromah, Roosevelt Johnson and the United Liberation Movement of Liberia for Democracy (ULIMO)

Warlord Kromah leads one wing of the ethnically divided United Liberation Movement (ULIMO), and was a member of the six-member collective presidency called the Interim Council of State. His boys are at relative peace with the other two main factions—the Liberian Peace Council and the NPFL—and control the western portion of the country.

The ULIMO-J faction, led by Chief of Staff Roosevelt Johnson, likes to war with the ULIMO Mandingoes when things get slow. Johnson usually wins. But Johnson can't see the forest for the trees and is now content to trade lead with ECOMOG and the forces of Charles Taylor over a diamond mining concession dispute. He certainly wasn't happy with his former cabinet post of minister of rural development. To show his countrymen and the world how seriously he took his job, he kept his hacker bush boys fed by hijacking food aid convoys moving through his territory on their way to the thousands of displaced Liberians and refugees from Sierra Leone's smoldering civil war in the north. He was seemingly out of the peace process and the inner circle of Liberian political power until Taylor tried to have him arrested in April 1996. The fighting lasted two weeks between the rival factions, and Johnson negotiated directly with the U.S. government for a cease-fire.

Samuel Doe and the United Liberation Movement of Liberia for Democracy (ULIMO) and Armed Forces of Liberia (AFL)

The now dead Doe, a Krahn, was a 28-year-old master sergeant who put an end to the line of wealthy coffee-colored descendants of freed black slaves from America when he overthrew and executed Tolbert and 13 ministers. That he televised their executions didn't bode well for Liberia's future. When a coup was attempted, Doe's soldiers drove around Monrovia, publicly displaying the offenders' severed testicles. Hey, its like show and tell around here.

Sam Doe was applying his newfound financial genius. He managed to plunge the country deeper into debt by printing new money to pay the bills, while bumming millions of dollars in foreign aid. He did manage to cut all government workers' salaries by $10.

He was offered safe passage out of Liberia by the U.S. government (we provide free chauffeur service to all our favorite dictators), but he turned it down. Probably because Doe lived in luxury on the fifth floor of the Executive Mansion, with his two pet lions (which he fed with his many victims) and protected by his Israeli-trained bodyguards. Until one day in September of 1990, when he went to visit the ECOWAS headquarters. (See "Prince Johnson.") His memory lives on with the Krahn tribe and the highfalutin-sounding ULIMO group, which controls small pockets near the Sierra Leone border (from its base in Freetown) and Tubmanburg.

Prince Yormie Johnson and the Independent Patriotic Front (IPF)

Johnson originally was allied to Taylor when he first attacked Doe in 1989. He then broke away with 1,000 of his better-trained troops from the Gio tribe, leaving Taylor with the larger but less effective Mano tribal troops. In 1990, when Taylor controlled the countryside, Johnson controlled most of Monrovia, killing and torturing at random. About 200 of Johnson's men captured Doe when he went to the ECOWAS headquarters. They later cut off his ears and tortured him to death while videotaping the festivities. His dismembered body was paraded around Monrovia. Johnson and Taylor both claimed the presidency and set off another round of bloodshed. The fighting lasted seven weeks between the rival factions and as it raged Johnson was flown by U.S. Marines to Accra, Ghana to attend peace talks. None of the other warlords showed up and Johnson complained bitterly when both the Americans and ECOMOG refused to take him back to Monrovia.

Armed Forces of Liberia (AFL)

The AFL was formerly the national army under the Doe regime, and largely comprised of ethnic Krahns—Doe was a Krahn. By 1992, as a result of the civil war, the AFL maintained only limited authority and most of its equipment had been destroyed or rendered useless. The army these days is essentially just another faction.

During the April and May 1996 clashes in the capital, Krahn fighters loyal to Johnson were based in an AFL barracks downtown. Although its high command said the AFL was not involved in the conflict, many of its soldiers were thought to be fighting alongside fellow Krahns loyal to Johnson and Boley against the forces of Charles Taylor and Alhaji Kromah. Two men claim to be the AFL's chief of staff. Abraham Kromah was "appointed" to the position by the virulently anti-Krahn NPFL while Brigadier General Phillip Karmah inherited it when his predecessor was killed early on in the spring clashes in the capital.

"General" Butt Naked and the All-Star Generals

Taylor's ad hoc generals weren't the only colorful characters. Top of the Pops was the 25-year-old Krahn fighter, Joshua Milton Blahyi, who led the Butt Naked Brigade. Their claim to fame was going into battle in their birthday suits as a sign of defiance and invincibility. Young boys cheered the amply endowed "general" when he "swung" through the capital on his motorbike and fought wearing only Chuck Taylors. The exalted moniker was actually bestowed on him by journalists and was not of his own making. Originally he was a thug and robber who was recruited as a fighter for Roosevelt Johnson in 1994. He says he began his evil ways at age 11 in a satanic ritual requiring him to perform human sacrifices. He went into battle naked to ensure his safety on the battlefield. He has admitted to butchering a number of small children, many killed while they played. He says his transformation from killer to saver occurred in June 1996, when he was standing nude on the New Bridge waiting to kill some people and God appeared to him. "He said I was a slave to Satan, not the hero I considered myself to be." Butt Naked attended theology school in Nigeria, now is a born-again preacher in Monrovia and can be heard singing out against sin and evil.

http://www.aracnet.com/~atheism/tocapox5.htm

Juju

Just about everyone here is more than a little superstitious. Taylor is a numerology freak (seven is his lucky number). Religion and mysticism blend perfectly as people assume that bullets will bounce off, witches cast spells and that devils walk the forests snatching small children (partly true). Human sacrifice and cannibalism are very real here, but not expected to emerge as the next fast food franchise concept. It is believed by some that eating an opponent's still-beating heart gives them strength. Numerous body parts were used as everything from sign posts to footballs during the last war. Hey, I'm not trying to gross you out, it's a dangerous place alright.

http://www.liberian-connection.com/article1.htm#taylor

Please Laugh Generously

Taking a page out of Jeff Foxworthy, there seems to be a severe shortage of humor in Liberia as evidenced by the edited version of "You know you are Liberian if . . .

The fattest girl in school is always the best at knock foot.

You know how to open a can with a knife.

You know how to open a bottle with your teeth.

They call condensed milk white man snot (that's nasty!).

They sing hymns very loud and off key.

They call tooth picks "African dessert."

You ask them where they are going, they say, "Somewhere."

They brush their teeth with fire coal.

Source: The Liberian Connection

LIBERIA

Kids

During the last nightmare, between 6,000 and 15,000 children were recruited by Liberia's various factions. Encouraged to be brutal and kill without remorse, these are the same kids who hang around asking for money. Just under 4,700 were demobilized between 1994 and 1996. The youngest fighter on record according to UNICEF was six years old. Sure kid, how much candy you want?

Political Parties

Founded in 1878, the True Whig Party ran the country until the 1980 coup, after which it was banned. It was revived in 1991. Since then it's pretty much every man or woman for themselves. One only has to look at the credentials of the current leader to see how far democracy has come. As for the true political aspirations of warlords gone straight, hey, you figure it out. Ask them yourself:

http://www.liberian-connection.com/lc-govn.htm

Rubber, Timber and Iron

There is little left in Liberia, except for rubber plantations, the rain forest and the iron rusting the ground. The Firestone Company owns the largest rubber plantation in the world, about one million acres that it originally leased for six cents an acre back in 1926. The world's largest rubber estate, about 30 miles east of the capital, is now better known as a former battlefield.

http://www.isop.ucla.edu/mgpp/sample06.htm

The roads leading from Monrovia are passable for limited pre-approved travel, but they can be dangerous. Liberia is accessible by road from Danane, Ivory Coast. Travelers who plan a trip to Liberia are required to have a passport and a visa prior to arrival. Additionally, in order to be granted a visa, you must present to a Liberian embassy a letter stating the purpose of your visit and another from a doctor confirming you have no communicable diseases. Evidence of yellow fever vaccination is required. An exit permit must be obtained from Liberian immigration authorities upon arrival. There is no charge for a visa. *West Africa Safaris, P.O. Box 365, Oakdale, CA 95361, Tel.: +1-209-847-7710; (888) 454-7710, Fax: +1-209-847-8150 (Liberia Office, Raymond Bldg., Number 5, Broad and Gurley Streets, Monrovia, Liberia Phone: +231-225-070)* has a camp on Sinoe River in Sapo National Park and can give you solid advice on visiting Liberia: *http://www.wtgonline.com/data/lbr/lbr000.asp.*

Further information on entry requirements for Liberia can be obtained from the following:

Embassy of the Republic of Liberia
5201 16th Street, NW
Washington, DC 20011
Tel: (202) 723-0437 to 723-0440
Fax: (202) 723-0436
E-mail: Liberia-Embassy@msn.com
http://www.liberiaemb.org

Liberian Embassy in London
Tel.: +44-0171-221-1036
The closest British Embassy is in Abdijan. Canadians should contact their embassy in Accra.

U.S. Embasssy
11 United Nations Drive
Monrovia
Tel.: 226 370
Fax: 226 148

The embassy is open 10 A.M. too 4 P.M. Monday to Friday. The temporary address is the following:

5303 Colorado Avenue, NW
Washington, DC 20011

When traveling by road in Liberia, extreme caution is urged even when roads are open. Motorists are frequently hassled at checkpoints manned by stoned, hungry, unpaid and impoverished soldiers. Cigarette rolling papers—indeed, any kind of paper to make joints with—will increase your popularity immensely, as will booze, cigarettes, etc. But it's not a good idea to travel by road without someone who has done so before, and who knows how to deal with the fighters. As far as payoffs go, there is no rule of thumb—as little as you can get away with. Flashy watches, jewelry, sunglasses, etc., should be kept well out of sight and will be asked for as presents. Try to show your papers without actually handing them to the guard.

Roads leading out from Monrovia are passable but dangerous, more so at night. Travelers to the interior of Liberia may be in danger of being detained, harassed, delayed, injured or killed to use the usual jargon. The embassy tells us that the only area traditionally considered "safe" is inside the capital of Monrovia, since the Liberian Council of State does not control many areas outside of town. Tourism info can be accessed at *http://www.wtgonline.com/data/lbr/lbr000.asp*.

You can send money via Western Union to the Liberian Bank for Development & Investment located at the corner of Ashmun and Randall Streets in downtown Monrovia. It is housed in the former Citibank building. *Tel: (231) 227140/41.*

If you think they won't steal your watch or car remember that during the last flareup, the UN had 489 vehicles stolen (worth $8.3 million). Only 11 have been returned.

Monrovia

Monrovia's crime rate is high, regardless of the level of tensions. Foreigners are targets of street criminals, police and anyone who wants to advance their financial status. Residential break-ins are common. Just about all officials will ask for some type of gift. Just act stupid and hand them a Mr. *DP* sticker.

Things are still volatile here so it is important to check in with your embassy if you want a chopper ride out if things go to hell again.

Anywhere Outside of Monrovia

Once you are outside of Monrovia you are about as far away from help as you can get. Numerous roadblocks will ensure that any item of value will not be yours when you return. Keep in mind that you are in a country full of very tweaked, desperate and trigger-happy fighters.

Web Resources

http://www.liberian-connection.com/
http://www.hirondelle.org
http://www.liberia.net
http://www.africanews.org/west/liberia/

Embassy Locations and Useful Telephone Numbers

U.S Embassy

111 United Nations Drive
P.O. Box 10-0098
Monrovia
Tel.: (231) 226370/226154

Maddison Weon

Ulimo-J deputy chairman. Good contact
for Ulimo-J leader Roosevelt Johnson
Tel.: (231) 226763/8 or 225804

Liberian National Police Force

Tel.: 225825 or 222113

Emergency

Tel.: 115 (Don't hold your breath)

GETTING SICK

All visitors more than one year old must have a yellow fever vaccination certificate. Malaria and Hepatitis B are widespread, and arthropod-borne diseases such as river blindness and sleeping sickness can also be a hazard. There are 15 hospital beds and one doctor for every 10,000 people.

NUTS AND BOLTS

Liberia is a big, hot, nasty place situated on the west coast (Ivory Coast) of Africa, bounded by Guinea and Sierra Leone on the north and Cote d'Ivoire on the east. Monrovia, with a population of about half a million, is the capital. Liberia's total population is estimated at 2,839,000, with about half the inhabitants living in urban areas. The currency is the Liberian dollar. Officially there is parity between the United States and Liberian dollars, but ubiquitous money changers will give around 50 Liberian dollars to the greenback. (Take a bag instead of a wallet—the notes only come in five-dollar denominations.)

Liberia has a tropical climate, with temperatures ranging from 65°F to 120°F. The rainy period extends from May through November and is characterized by frequent, prolonged and often torrential rainfall. Humidity is high, usually between 70 and 80 percent.

There are 16 indigenous tribes in Liberia, including Kpelle, Bassa, Gio, Kru, Grebo, Mano, Krahn, Gola, Gbandi, Loma, Kissi, Vai and Bella, which make up 95 percent of the population; Americo-Liberians (descendants of black Americans who moved here) account for 5 percent. Are these people American Africans in PC speak, or are they African American Africans? Liberia is officially a Christian state, although indigenous beliefs are held by 70 percent of the population. Muslims comprise 20 percent and Christians only 10 percent of the population. English is the official language. There are close to 20 local languages derived from the Niger-Congo language. About 20 percent of the population uses English. Illiteracy stands at about 60 percent.

Lodging, water, electricity, fuel, transportation, and telephone and postal services continue to be uneven in Monrovia. Such services are nonexistent or severely limited in rural areas. All electrical power is supplied by generators. Mail delivery is erratic. Parcel delivery service and courier mail service is available to and in Monrovia.

U.S. citizens who register at the U.S. embassy in Monrovia may obtain updated information on travel and security in Liberia. Don't be surprised if you meet them at the departure lounge at the airport.

Embassy Locations

U.S. Embassy (in the capital of Monrovia)

111 United Nations Drive, Mamba Point
Tel.: [231] (2) 222-991 through 222-994
Fax: [231] (2) 223-710

Liberian Consulate (in Canada)

1080 Beaver Hall Hill, Suite 1720
Montreal, Quebec, Canada H2Z 158
Tel.: (514) 871-4741
Fax: (514) 397-0816

The U.S. embassy's mailing address:

P.O. Box 10-0098
or APO AE 09813
or P.O. Box 98
Mamba Point, Monrovia

1/10/00	Two ex-members of Taylor's NPFL rob Charles Taylor's home, just one of a rash of robberies by AK toting masked men. Just two of 60,000 demobbed, unemployed fighters.
7/19/97	Charles Taylor wins 75% of the popular vote.
4/6–5/26/96	Monrovia and Liberia are again plunged into civil war. Corpses litter the capital's streets and 2,000 Americans and other foreigners are airlifted from the American Embassy.
12/14/89	Charles Taylor launches his rebellion from neighboring Ivory Coast.
1/06/86	New constitution is inaugurated.
4/12/80	President William Tolbert is overthrown in a coup led by Staff Sergeant Samuel K. Doe, who subsequently suspends the constitution and imposes martial law.
5/25/63	OAU—Africa Freedom Day.
7/26/1847	Independence Day.
2/11	Armed Forces Day.

Mexico
★★

Run for the Border

"So close, yet so far," is the headline on one travel agent's brochure. Honesty in advertising, finally.

A one-hour plane ride plane or a 30-second drive in a Winnebago, and you're there—in Mexico. Its currency is about as useful as a moist towelette. Drug dealers ring its borders like souvenir stands. Separatist insurgents in the south threaten to topple Ernesto Zedillo's government with toy guns and ski masks. Church groups raise money for real guns. Hired assassins from the U.S. cruise through the San Marcos border checkpoint without a visa, do their deed, catch a floor show in Tijuana, get a dozen free windshield washes and are back home in West Covina in time to catch Thalia in a *Mari Mar* rerun.

Tourists are attacked by Volkswagen Bugs in Mexico City. The president's son is the victim of a carjacking attempt—by a policeman. A policeman actually catches a pair of carjackers—attempting to carjack *his* car. A pizza vendor is robbed 23 times in a single year. The country's most violent rebels, the EPR, hold press conferences from their headquarters, only a short bus ride away from a

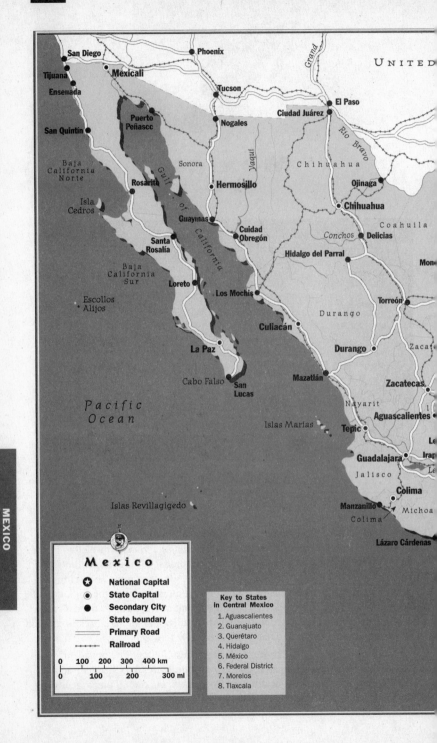

UNITED

San Diego
Tijuana
Ensenada
San Quintín
Phoenix
Mexicali
Tucson
Nogales
El Paso
Ciudad Juárez
Puerto Peñasco

Baja California Norte
Sonora
Yaqui
Chihuahua
Rio Bravo
Ojinaga
Rosarito
Isla Cedros
Hermosillo
Chihuahua
Coahuila

Guaymas
Cuidad Obregón
Conchos
Delicias
Santa Rosalía
Hidalgo del Parral
Mon

Baja California Sur
Loreto
Los Mochis
Torreón

Escollos Alijos
Durango

Culiacán
Durango
Zaca

La Paz
Mazatlán
Zacatecas

Cabo Falso
San Lucas
Nayarit
Aguascalientes

Pacific Ocean
Islas Marías
Tepic

Guadalajara
Le
Irap
Lé

Jalisco

Islas Revillagigedo
Colima
Manzanillo
Michoa

Colima
Lázaro Cárdenas

Mexico

⊛ National Capital
⊙ State Capital
● Secondary City
State boundary
Primary Road
Railroad

0 100 200 300 400 km
0   100   200   300 mi

Key to States in Central Mexico

1. Aguascalientes
2. Guanajuato
3. Querétaro
4. Hidalgo
5. México
6. Federal District
7. Morelos
8. Tlaxcala

MEXICO

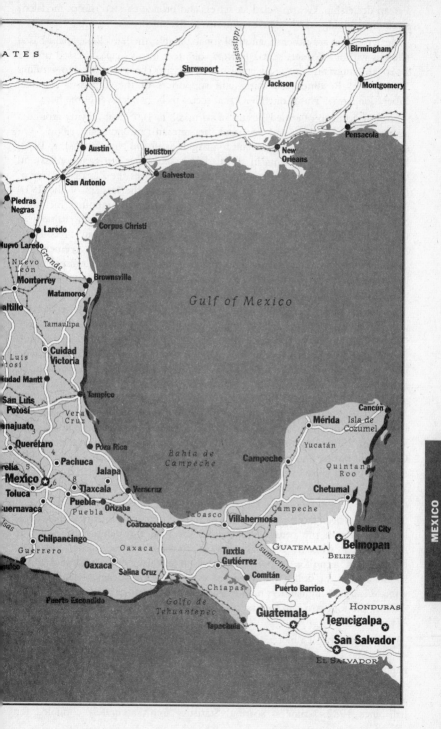

Ferrari dealership, G-string-clad jet-setters and bronze-chested (if not medaled) swan divers doing sans-bunjee-cord jumps in Acapulco.

Mexico's woes are either so laughable or so pitiable, the Barcelona, Spain-based Clowns without Borders sent a fearless volunteer into Chiapas dressed up like Bozo to entertain villages victimized by clashes between Mexico's ruling Institutional Revolutionary Party and supporters of the Zapatista National Liberation Army. This is one NGO that seems to be perfectly at home here.

Imagine a bunch of armed Texans in ski masks in 100° heat rallying around a statue of Sam Houston and declaring the state an "autonomous region." On second thought, it isn't that difficult to imagine at all. On New Year's Day 1994, hundreds of armed peasants in ski masks—brandishing bolt-action rifles and sticks—declared their autonomy. They called themselves the Zapatista Army of National Liberation, after Emiliano Zapata, one of the leaders of the 1910 Mexican Revolution. They stormed a number of Chiapas communities, including San Cristobal, Ocosingo, Altamira and Las Margaritas. The uprising came with the January 1, 1994, implementation of the North American Free Trade Agreement. The Zapatistas said, and continue to say, that the agreement will essentially strip the *indigenes* of claims to their ancestral land. The tour buses that previously descended upon San Cristobal and the surrounding indigenous Indian villages in droves slammed on their brakes and stayed away.

Adventure nuts, daredevil tourists and bleeding heart Eurokids have been visiting the town of La Realidad in Chiapas since 1994, including high-profile visits in 1996 to Subcommander Marcos by filmmaker Oliver Stone and former French president Francois Mitterand's globe-trotting PC wife. Zapatourists who want to follow in the footsteps of MTV and graying left-wingers can now make the pilgrimage down the muddy path to the Zapatista camps deep in the jungle near Toluca. But they're not much welcomed anymore, with some 60,000 Mexican army theater ushers doing the collecting of tickets and pointing a flashlight to an empty seat. Subcommander Marcos made a rare appearance addressing 2,000 supporters on May 9, 1999, in southern Chiapas state near the Guatemala border—so near he could have been the Dalai Lama in exile. Still donning his trademark ski mask and pipe—the mask of Zorro—Marcos delivered a speech denouncing Mexico's political system. But few tourists could make the matinee.

Mexico has been faced with a triple-whammy. Not only have the Chiapas rebels been a thorn in the country's side, and the EPR threatening the discos at Acapulco, but, while the central bank wasn't looking, the peso crashed. Investors began makin' a run for the border in droves in January 1995. The peso dropped so low against the dollar that Mexicans stopped robbing other Mexicans. With armed insurgent highlanders brandishing black flags emblazoned with a red star stalking the southern rain forests, it's a wonder so many still venture to this part of the world.

It's thought that if a mere 5 percent of Mexico's 96 million people took to the streets, Mexico's criminal-laden government would collapse. But why isn't it happening? Namely, because folks are too busy trying to survive. As one Mexican activist commented: "Mexico is a culture of survival." About half of the working-age population in Mexico is unemployed. Families have seen their savings cut in half since 1982. Crime is soaring. Statistics aren't accurately compiled for

Mexico's crime rate, but it is widely believed that crime between 1994 and 1999 has jumped an astronomical 80 percent in Mexico City alone. There has been a 100-percent increase in violent car thefts in the capital. Vigilante groups, private security "firms" and government-sanctioned thugs, called "Los Chombos," are doing what the cops won't: offing the bad guys—and also the good guys.

The Federal District's 741 security firms employ 37,000 people, 10,000 more than the number of cops on the district's streets. Drug dealers and runners and other shadowy types have gone missing in the hundreds. They are called the "narco-disappeared." Union leaders and their followers are also increasingly failing to show up at home at night for dinner. Let's call them the "labor-disappeared." Now the cops are being replaced by soldiers. Some complain it gives the military too much authority. Others respond, "Hey, they've got bigger guns."

For the traveler, Mexico is filled with extremes. Whether you want the coke-dusted lifestyle of the rich and famous on the Mexican Riviera, or like to shop for .45 caliber ammo behind the saloon in Sonora, Mexico has a little danger for everyone.

Of the top 10 countries visited by U.S. citizens, only Mexico has a State Department advisory for travelers. What can you say about a country that's rapidly becoming one of Mercedes-Benz's biggest markets and yet a full quarter of the population lives in extreme poverty? Mexico is where the Third World runs smack into the First World—like putting Mogadishu next to Santa Barbara, with a 1,820-mile border between them. Tell any red-blooded American he's gotta stay here for more than a week, and he'll be scrambling over the chain-link fence and dashing for Escondido. Even in the far south, where Mexico blends seamlessly into Guatemala, there is turmoil, where you can seamlessly blend into a shallow grave.

Rafael Sebastin Guillen Vicente (a.k.a. Subcommander Marcos) and the EZLN
(Starring in *Che for a Day,* **or** *The Adventures of Subcomedian Marcos*)

Although the image of the intellectual revolutionary is an appealing one in Latin America, there are few Latinos who are willing to lead a heroic group. Che Guevara did, and now it seems like the son of a furniture store owner in Tampico is going for it. Rafael Guillen, er, sorry, Marcos, is a former college professor (with a degree in sociology) from a well-off family in the state of Tamaulipas.

Alas, his revolution will never match Uncle Fidel's nor Chairman Mao's nor even that of his real idol, Sandino. Vicente was born on June 19, 1957, and educated at the National Autonomous University of Mexico. He left in 1980 with a degree in sociology, earned a graduate degree, and became an associate professor at Xochimilco south of Mexico City.

In 1984 he left for Managua, where he taught and learned about revolution. He returned to Mexico in the late '80s to start up the Zapatista National Liberation Army. Its acronym—EZLN—sounds like the call letters of a soft pop radio station.

MEXICO

The pipe-smoking, balaclava-wearing "Marcos" appeared on January 1, 1994, when the rebels suddenly said they were mad as hell and not going to take it anymore. What attracted the world's press was the '60s aura of a group of peasants led by a charming, wisecracking mystery man who never appeared without his trademark disguise, shotgun bandoleer, pistol and pipe. He communicated with the press via video press release, satellite phone, fax machine and word processor. Adventurous types, including filmmaker Oliver Stone, beat a path to his "secret" jungle hideaway for a high-profile rebel audience, or what filmmaker Ms. Wild calls a "post-glasnost revolutionary Woodstock." He was long on rhetoric and short on results. His methodology was to "capture" a town with his ragtag army (some armed with sticks carved to look like rifles), then hightail back into the bush before the troops arrived. Most of the victims were innocent villagers killed by bombs or wild cross fire when the rebels didn't move fast enough. Some Mexican authorities claim the EZLN are led and supported by 20 Cubans, 40 U.S. citizens, 60 Europeans and 300 Guatemalans (who can provide escape routes into neighboring Guatemala after attacks) leading 2,500 Zapatista combatants. These figures are undoubtedly inflated to justify the 50,000 to 70,000 Mexican troops now ringing EZLN hideouts in Chiapas.

Marcos is now making the transition to political respectability, though the government, ironically, isn't thrilled with Marcos bucking for a Nobel Peace Prize. In an April 1999 nonbinding poll, voters overwhelmingly granted Mexico's 10 million native Indians special constitutional rights via EZLN negotiations with the government. It was certainly the most emulous—and successful—effort by the EZLN since their 1994 insurrection began. To save face, the army has apparently been staging Zapatista "desertions"—the public surrendering of handfuls of guerrillas along with their weapons.

A Bedtime Story

Subcommandante Marcos had a bit of a problem getting the English language version of his book published in the States–a fiery autobiography laced with Marxist rhetoric? Not really a children's story. The Story of Colors, about Mayan gods, was published by Cincos Puntos Press in El Paso. It seems the NEA refused to pay the $7,500 advance. The author photo shows Marcos with his trademark balaclava and bandolier. Nightmares, anyone?

EZLN Web Sites

Ejercito Zapatista de Liberacion Nacional
http://www.ezln.org

Zapatista Front of National Liberation
http://www.peak.org/~joshua/fzln/
http://www.peak.org/~justin/ezln/ezln.html

Popular Revolutionary Army (EPR, PRA, PROCUP-PDLP)

When you're number two you try harder. Or kill faster. Unlike the laid-back, amiable, college-educated and Internet-savvy ranks of the Zapatistas, the EPR are some mean dudes. Marxist/Leninist/Maoist-mean, like the Shining Path and the PKK.

The EPR first showed up on June 28, 1996, when 80 masked men with automatic rifles announced their presence at a political rally in Guerrero state. They say they are made up of 14 organizations. Their 45-point wish list includes canceling foreign debt and nationalizing any U.S.-held interests. They did not discuss back end points and credit type size on movie deals. The government wrote them off as one-shots, the press scrambled (unsuccessfully) for witticisms and some people thought they were army stooges sent in to provide an excuse to send in government troops. Meanwhile, the tourists on the beach in Acapulco and shopping for silver in Oaxaca thought they might be in 1950s Cuba, but Club Med in Huatulco is a lot further than 90 miles to safety.

In September of '96, the EPR officially started a second uprising in Mexico by launching coordinated attacks in 5 of Mexico's 31 states. When it was over, scores were dead; an EPR ambush whacked 20 police officers. For now the EPR attacks government, military and police installations, and although their attacks take place in heavily touristed areas, they do not focus on attacking foreign travelers; they just want to scare off the turistas. Enterprising journalists, beware; the EPR did kill two security guards at a newspaper that refused to run their press release.

Popular Revolutionary Army Web Site

Ejercito Popular Revolucionario (EPR) and Partido Democratico Popular Revolucionario (PDPR)

http://www.pengo.it/PDPR-EDR/
http://www.xs4all.nl/~insurg

Info on Activities

http://www.eden.com/~tomzap/epr4.html

Che Wannabes

Since April 1998, two new armed insurgencies in Mexico have announced themselves to the world. Currently there are at least 14 rebel groups active in Mexico. Locals call them *encapuchados*, or the hooded ones. The first, on April 28, was the Oaxaca state–based National Indigenous Revolutionary Liberation Army (EIRLN), whose agenda is to attack "whatever group might attack it," not dissimilar to what a pack of South African baboons might issue to the press—if baboons could actually send press releases. After apparently hiring a new PR firm, EIRLN cleared things up a little for the befuddled media with a new mandate: to fight the government for "peace, justice and democracy in the name of those with no name, no face, with nothing." That criteria would appear to narrow down its potential constituency to "no one." Still more work to be done on the acronym, which sounds like the name of a power forward on the Minnesota Timberwolves.

Yet another EPR offshoot announced itself in mid-1998: the Revolutionary Army of the Insurgent People (ERPI). Again, a PR problem, as insurgent people often fight for themselves. The name implies there's already been a split in its ranks. Based in Guerrero state, ERPI argues that the EPR's terrorist attacks are counterproductive, or at least less productive than dialogue. Ironically, the ERPI was first heard from not in an attack on government forces but, instead, when government troops staged their own massacre on June 7, 1998, in the village of El Charco, 70 miles west of Acapulco, killing at least 20 people.

Anybody got a press kit on the Armed Revolutionary Southern Command, Popular Revolutionary Insurgent Army or the Clandestine Armed Forces of National Liberation?

Zapatista or Blast-ta-Piece-a-s? The *DP* Guide to Revolutionaries

Before you run off to La Realidad to hang with the latest poster boys of the revolution you should know the difference between the EZLN (who don't kidnap, torture and kill people) and the EPR (who do).

Zapatista or Blast-ta-Piece-a-s?
The *DP* Guide to Revolutionaries

The EPR are hard-core terrorists and criminals. Although they wear cute green camouflage and wear brown face masks for the press, the EPR usually operates in 12-man cells in urban areas in plainclothes. If in uniform, the EPR have red and green arm patches and assault rifles. They are very heavily armed, politically indoctrinated and will go out of their way to protect their identity if stumbled upon.

They have bombed U.S and Japanese corporate offices, robbed dozens of banks and kidnapped prominent businessmen in Mexico. Tourists are not specifically targeted but the EPR uses plenty of ammo in their attacks. A tourist was hit by the cross fire at the Huatulco Club Med.

Their training bases are deep in the Sierra Madre mountains. They practice hit-and-run raids and shoot to kill. They are closer to terrorists, have little grassroots support and are in the DP dictionary under "bad guys." If you really want to know if you are in trouble, the EPR wear cloth bags over their head with goofy homemade slits for the eyes.

The Zapatistas are a homegrown Indian group led by poorly trained but laid-back commanders. Most cells are village-based, with no real distinction between the military arm and the political arm. There was only one actual clash, in January 1994. They wear a yellow and red star patch and favor balaclavas. Chances are some will be carrying sticks and their guns will be rusty. The Zapatistas welcome foreigners as insurance policy against military excesses and the government does turn back people at checkpoints in the area. In August 1996, over 2,000 people visited five Chiapas villages in a weeklong convention (called the Intercontinental Encounter for Humanity Against Neo-Liberalism) to hear Marcos crack a few jokes and tell a few stories. By the way, trivia fans, Oliver Stone is a DP reader and Marcos turned down his chance to star in his own feature-length movie. Stay tuned for Revolutionary Land, *coming to Orlando soon.*

President Ernesto Zedillo

Accused of being weak and indecisive and smarting from his recent trashing of the peso, Zedillo ordered the Boris Yeltsin manual, "How to Stamp Out Insurrections." He initially bombed the hell out of Chiapas and ended up with truckloads of dead peasants. He then adopted a conciliatory stance, and, after the peso was lower than a cucaracha's belly button, he sent the troops in again. This time, the stock market went up and the white ruling class applauded, while the working class protested. The bottom line is that Zedillo has the tanks, men and helicopters; Marcos doesn't.

Presidente de la Republica
Palacio Nacional
Mexico City, Mexico
Fax: (525) 271-1774
http://www.presidencia.gob.mx/pages/f_ofna_presid.html

Juan García Abrego (El Muñeco) and the Gulf Cartel

As the reputed supplier of a third of the cocaine that reaches the United States, Abrego ("The Doll") was the first international drug trafficker to get his name pasted to post office walls as an elite member of the FBI's Ten Most Wanted list. He joked to his captors after he was busted by the FBI in January 1996 that "I never thought you'd get me." And he probably had a good reason to think they wouldn't. You see, "the Doll" was cozy with former Mexican President Carlos Salinas de Gortari's brother Raúl. In fact, Raúl used to party regularly with the boys of the cartel, one of Mexico's big four, and stashed some US$84 million into frozen Swiss bank accounts. The stinger was Raúl Salinas de Gortari's alleged trip to Colombia to pick up US$10 million from the Cali drug cartel, which he then tried to use to fund Luis Donaldo Colosio's bid for the presidency. When Colosio turned down the contribution, he was wasted by the Gulf cartel in March 1994. Raúl is now in prison for plotting the September 1994 murder of one of Mexico's top politicians. One thing for sure, while Carlos Salinas de Gortari was in office, the Gulf cartel rose to the top rank among Mexico's drug syndicates. Now this conglomerate of traffickers is on the downslide; 70 of its members have already been convicted in three U.S. states.

http://fuentes.csh.udg.mx/CUCSH/Sincronia/reding.html

Amado Carrillo Fuentes ("Lord of the Heavens") and the Juárez Cartel

With the capture of Abrego and other gold-chained fat dudes of the Gulf cartel, the Juárez cartel emerged as Mexico's strongest dope alliance. Cartel kingpin Amado Carrillo Fuentes, who died after a botched face lift in July 1997, was the most powerful drug lord in Mexico and was chummy with the Cali cartel. He was accused of facilitating huge jet loads of dope into Mexico from Colombia, thus his moniker. From Ciudad Juárez, the coke moves to American cities like Los Angeles, Dallas, Houston and New York. Until his death, Carillo managed to elude one of the most extensive dragnets by drug agents on both sides of the border. After his death, more than 50 people died in a gang war on the streets of Ciudad Juárez.

Marion Villanueva

This ex-governor of Cancún (Quintana Roo) claims he is so honest, that he fled Mexico in March 1999 because of a "government conspiracy" to bust him on charges of siphoning money from political donations and links with South American drug cartels, most notably the Juárez Cartel. Villanueva claims he was being harassed by antidrug agents and "decided to lose them." The DEA thinks he's hidden US$10 million in secret bank accounts in California, Switzerland, the Cayman Islands and the Bahamas. Reportedly, he's been in hiding in the next best places to scuba dive other than Cancún—Panama, Cuba and Belize.

http://www.fas.org/irp/congress/1997_hr/s970312c.htm

Miguel Caro Quintero and the Sonora Cartel

Quintero's northwest Mexico–based gang mostly runs ganja into Nogales, Arizona, and other western states but also dabbles in the white stuff. Quintero assumed the helm of the cartel after his brother Rafael was busted for the murder of DEA agent Enrique "Kiki" Camarena. The softspoken Quintero is under indictment in Denver and Tucson and is considered armed and dangerous by our DEA. If you see him call 1-877-WANTED2.

Rancho El Papago, Mexico
Caborca, SO., Mexico
http://www.usdoj.gov/dea/fugitive/denver/caro-quintero.htm

The Arellano Felix Brothers and the Tijuana Cartel

Ruthless and territorial, Benjamin Arellano Felix is supposedly running the most violent dope syndicate in Mexico (his brother is wasting away in a Mexican jail cell). The cartel is behind the massive quantities of methamphetamine that have been flooding into San Diego, Los Angeles and points east. Arellano Felix's enforcers are thought to have been the trigger men in the 1993 assassination in Guadalajara of Catholic cardinal Juan Jesus Posadas-Ocampo. This Tijuana-based cartel has already penetrated the Mexican military—which has taken over Mexico's antinarcotics efforts—perhaps all the way up to the president's bodyguards. Graduates of Mexico's most prestigious military academy are known to serve as security advisers to the Arellano clan, and the gang has employed former army officers as assassins to whack any potential witnesses against it. In Tijuana and Mexico City, at least seven federal prosecutors and a state attorney have been murdered in slayings connected to the cartel. There were 315 murders in Tijuana in 1997, most of them drug related.

The DEA and the FBI

The DEA and the FBI have considered each other deadbeat Princeton flatfoots for years. The DEA guys think they're cool because they're above politics and can meddle in the sovereignty of every banana and bongo junta with MFN status on the globe, not to mention MFN wannabes, centuries-old monarchies, Mother Russia and Uncle Sam. The fibbies are making a run at catching the splinters of the disintegrating CIA's turf, having never been content with hanging out in step vans and tapping phones in cheap motels. The two have kissed and made up for the purpose of nailing Mexican narco-monarchs and *contrabandistas* who, for decades, have been ponying guns, liquor, flake, smack and blue jeans across the Rio Grande. Together, they scored a coup with the García Abrego bust. Maybe a bigger one than they think. García Abrego may know enough mud in the Mexican government to cause the country's greatest crisis since the 1910 revolution.

http://www.emergency.com/clmbdeal.htm

Kidnapping Gangs

There are approximately 600 official kidnappings in Mexico each year, around 1,860 over the last three years, and those are just the ones that are reported. With most families of kidnap victims believing it a waste of time to report the crimes to police (and the cops themselves being involved in a number of the abductions), it was only a matter of time before Mexico's bad guys would take the cue from their Colombian buddies and organize. The Arizmendi kidnapping gang—under the protection of two senior officers of Mexico City's anti-kidnapping unit as well as officials from Mexico and Morelos states (the kidnap capital of Mexico)—has snatched at least 15 victims, earning payoffs of more than US$6 million. A Tijuana kidnapping gang snatched an American in September 1998, who was rescued by police 10 days later.

Kidnapping Insurance

http://www.hiscox.com
kidnap.internet@hiscox.com

All U.S. citizens visiting Mexico for tourism or study for up to 180 days need a tourist card to enter and leave the country. The tourist card is free and may be obtained from Mexican consulates, Mexican tourism offices, Mexican border crossing points and from most airlines serving Mexico. If you fly to Mexico, you must obtain your tourist card before boarding your flight; it cannot be obtained upon arrival at an airport in Mexico. The tourist card is issued upon presentation of proof of citizenship such as a U.S. passport or a U.S. birth certificate, plus a photo I.D. such as a driver's license. Tourist cards are issued for up to 90 days with a single entry or, if you present proof of sufficient funds, for 180 days with multiple entries. Upon entering Mexico, retain and safeguard the pink copy of your tourist card so that you may surrender it to Mexican immigration when you depart. You must leave Mexico before your tourist card expires, or you are subject to a fine. A tourist card for less than 180 days may be revalidated in Mexico by the Mexican immigration service.

If you wish to stay longer than 180 days, or if you wish to do business or perform religious work in Mexico, contact the Mexican embassy or the nearest Mexican consulate to obtain a visa or permit. Persons performing religious work on a tourist card are subject to deportation. U.S. citizens visiting Mexico for no more than 72 hours and remaining within 20 kilometers of the border do not need a permit to enter. Those transiting Mexico to another country need a transit visa that costs a nominal fee and is valid for up to 30 days.

Embassy of Mexico

1911 Pennsylvania Ave., NW
Washington, DC 20006
Tel.: (202) 728-1600
http://www.embassyofmexico.org

Mexico has extensive road, rail and air systems. Travelers in the remote areas should be very careful at night or when stopped outside of town. Robbery is common in these areas. Roads may seem well paved but huge potholes, animals, people and large objects can be found around blind corners.

During heavy seasonal rains (January–March), road conditions become difficult and travelers can become stranded. For current Mexican road conditions between Ensenada and El Rosario, travelers can contact the nearest Mexican consulate or tourism office or the U.S. consulate general in Tijuana.

Between 4 and 6 million U.S. citizens visit Mexico each year, while more than 300,000 Americans reside there. Although Mexico is "just across the border," it cannot be compared to Canada in terms of safety, health and crime threats. Remember that you are entering a country struggling to leave its Third World status. All tourists (both Mexican and American) are best targets for criminal acts simply because they routinely carry cash and expensive goods. Expect to be viewed as an easy mark for robbery whenever you travel to major cities and tourist areas in Mexico. There are an average of 35 homicides yearly in Baja (not including Tijuana), 40 percent of which are connected to the drug trade. Most of the murders are in Tijuana and most of these executions occur in daylight.

Chiapas

Travel throughout Chiapas, Mexico's southernmost state, may be delayed due to security checks. Chances of meeting a rebel roadblock are reduced after the recent military crackdown. Sometimes you may run into a roadblock put up by locals. Roadblocks in the Chiapas region can be as simple as a piece of string held up across the road. Many times rebels or locals will ask for articles of clothing. Journalists are also restricted in their movements. Interviews with Subcommander Marcos, although fairly easy to obtain, frequently involve long waits (up to a week or more) and a late-night rendezvous in a remote location.

The town of San Cristobal in the state of Chiapas is relatively quiet. The situation could become unstable in areas of Chiapas state outside of San Cristobal. Locals claim that law and order has ceased to exist in Chiapas, despite the presence of government troops. The army rarely intercedes in local disputes, even when they turn deadly.

The Mexican government is highly suspicious of foreigners traveling in the Chiapas region. In May 1997, 12 foreigners—including Spanish, Dutch, German, French and Italian nationals—were deported for participating in a protest march by Chol indians demanding the release of political prisoners.

http://flag.blackened.net/revolt/zapatista.html

Highways 15, 40 and 1

Beware of Highway 15 in the state of Sinaloa and of Highway 40 between the city of Durango and the Pacific coast areas. These are particularly dangerous and are where a number of criminal assaults have occurred. Avoid express Highway 1 (limited access) in Sinaloa altogether—even in daytime—because it is remote and subject to bandits.

Never sleep in vehicles along the road. If your vehicle breaks down, stay with it and wait for the police or the "Green Angels." Do not, under any circumstances, pick up hitchhikers; not only do they pose a threat to your physical safety, but they also put you in danger of being arrested for unwittingly transporting narcotics or narcotics traffickers in your vehicle. There are checkpoints and temporary roadblocks where vehicles are examined.

http://www.eden.com/~tomzap/driving.html
http://www.mexconnect.com/mex_/fqdriving.html
http://www.mexonline.com/drivemex.htm

Tijuana

What you have thought or read about Mexican border towns is true. Tequila-happy gringos looking to break every rule in the book, señoritas with hearts of gold, hardened and impoverished immigrants all controlled by a police force that makes the Keystone Kops look like the Delta Force. Don't blame the cops for all the raucous bloodletting and bad times. In the last four years, more than 20 Tijuana cops have been gunned down, so forgive them if they are a little trigger-happy or looking for a handout. Cops in Tijuana must not only supply their own uniforms, but they drive beat-up cop cars that Americans dumped years ago. They even have to buy their own bullets, and they do all this on a salary of about US$179 a month.

http://tijuana.com/

Jalisco State

Jalisco possesses the highest crime rate in Mexico. In 1996, there were 15,899 car thefts, 5,935 muggings and 5,926 store robberies. Today, there is an average of six truck hijackings per day. In one four month period, 18 banks were robbed and there were nine armored truck hijackings. Two-thirds of the crimes were committed by first-time offenders. Helluva retirement place.

http://www.jalisco.gob.mx/

Guerrero

And you thought Acapulco was famous for G-strings and cliff diving. You're relatively safe on a banana boat ride, but travel within Guerrero's interior is an invitation to a house of horrors. The state is home to two insurgent groups, as well as bandits, smugglers and drug traffickers. A lesson in "eco-trekkers meet narco-traffickers 101." Political violence erupts regularly between backers of the Organization of Peasants of the Southern Sierra (OCSS) and the ruling Institutional Revolutionary Party (PRI). More than 37 grassroots OCSS and PRI supporters have been gunned down over the last $3^{1}/_{2}$ years. In Guerrero state, 50 of every 100,000 people suffer a violent death. Stick to the beaches.

http://www.mpsnet.com.mx/mexico/guerrero.html

Mexico City

If you wanna get jacked around, Mexico City—with its population of 17 million—is a good place to start. An average of 443 criminal suspects are nabbed each day in Mexico City. More than 700 crimes are reported each day in the capital. Twenty-three percent of Mexico city residents said they have been victims of crime, usually robbery. About 75 percent of the victims said they did not bother to report the crime.

Mexico City police admit an average of 182 violent crimes each day. Murder has become one of the 10 leading causes of death in Mexico. More than 15,000 people are murdered each year. Forty percent of the victims are between the ages of 15 and 29. There are 12.62 murders committed per 100,000 people in Mexico City. Fifty percent of the killers get away with it. According to one late-1998 study, Mexico City is the tenth most deadly metropolis in North America and Europe. Little wonder—there are a million muggings and 70,000 car thefts in the capital each year. Crime against foreigners has risen dramatically since 1995. Most of the activity has been street crime. Pickpocketing, armed robbery and purse snatching are common. Using ATMs is a kiss of death. Thugs and other nasties hang in the shadows. Use only highly visible ATMs inside commercial establishments and only in daylight. Thieves have been known to beat up victims for their PIN codes and then abduct them overnight so as to use the machine the next day. The good news? Now ritzy hotels are offering crime insurance to guests. A fee of between $2 and $2.50 added to the hotel bill covers loss of goods and money.

http://www.mexicocity.com.mx/mexcity.html
http://www.juridicas.unam.mx/mtexto/

Street Kids

There are more than 13,000 homeless kids living on the streets of Mexico City, a number that has doubled over the last three years. More than 75 percent of the street kids are boys, and nearly two-thirds of all the street kids have criminal records. Handing out candy may not be such a good idea.

http://www.jbu.edu/business/sk.html

Protests

There are an average of 7.7 protests a day in Mexico City. Between January and May 1997 there were a total of 1,164 marches and demonstrations in the capital involving some 520,000 people. The leftist Democratic Revolutionary Party (PRD) led the tally with 295 marches, mandating a carbo-load diet for its supporters. On April 20, 1999, students at the National Autonomous University of Mexico (UNAM) in Mexico City went on strike to protest a decision to impose tuition fees. The protesters took control of most of the 40 schools and facilities of the university, which, with about 267,000 students, is the largest in Latin America. On the same day, 150,000 students from Mexico's National Polytechnic Institute staged their own little pep rally over unpaid wages to the school's 12,500 workers. Go, team, go.

Los Chombos

Cesar Chavez wannabes beware. Company-hired thugs known as "Los Chombos" stave off fledgling labor actions through intimidation and the occasional explosive disintegration of an unlucky union leader's kneecap. For about 30 bucks, a gang member will forward a threat to a labor leader. For US$500, the gang will punch a bullet hole into the guy, but in a bodily location where he'll live to brag about it six months later at union meetings after the cast is removed. For a negotiated fee, they'll make the dude "disappear." Mexico City is the most dangerous place to organize labor activities. But, personally, I wouldn't organize a gathering of lettuce pickers for anything more than a Corona and a wedge of lime anywhere in Mexico.

Express Kidnapping

Wanna make a quick peso? Kidnappers pull in around $165 million in ransoms every year in Mexico. Simply abduct some guy and demand a little cerveza dinero for his release. "Express" kidnapping has become all the rage in Burritoville in the last year. Kidnappers simply snatch their mark and demand a small ransom sum. That makes the money easy to raise for the victim's family and doesn't burden the abductors with hiding and feeding their victims for a couple of months while the victim's family bargains with the IMF for a huge ransom loan. Express kidnapping—when you absolutely, positively need to get your loved one back home in time for dinner.

MEXICO

The Kidnap Classifieds

In the first five months of 1998, there were 12 kidnappings of high-ranking business execs in Mexico City. How are they targeted? Kidnapping gangs scan the business sections of local newspapers to choose victims.

Fast Food Kidnapping

Like the Eskimos have dozens of names for snow, kidnapping in Mexico has become so ubiquitous—it's starting to approach Colombia's figures—the locals are redefining their newest national pasttime. "Fast food" abductions involve snatching some poor soul for their ATM card and PIN number. They hold their victim for a few hours (or a day or two) while his or her bank account is flushed. A U.S. embassy employee was the victim of a "fast food" attack in 1998. Each year there are some 2,000 kidnapping-for-ransom crimes committed in Mexico. The "Express" and "Fast Food" varieties don't fall under this stat.

Car Thefts

Mexico is the easiest place in the world to own a car with a Kelly *Blue Book* value of exactly US$0. In the first two months of 1999, 6,128 insured vehicles were stolen in Mexico. The final tally for 1999 is expected to exceed 43,000. The chances of getting your car back? About 1 in 6. And these are just the insured vehicles. Fully 66 percent of all vehicles in Mexico are uninsured—and their thefts not officially tallied. But even scarier than the number of rip-offs is the violence that usually comes along with them. Violence is involved in about 55 percent of all car thefts. The day of the week your car is most likely to get popped? Friday. A good day to keep the garage door locked—and get your pizza delivered. If the delivery boy doesn't get his car stolen on the way.

Playing Goalie

In February 1999, the father of Mexican National Soccer Team goalie Jorge Campos was abducted because, well, his son was goalie on the Mexican National Soccer Team. He was released a week later after a US$150,000 payoff. Though the perps in this case were caught, there doesn't seem much deterrent in Mexico for bad guys to go after high-profile figures. Only 6 in every 100 crimes reported to the police are solved. Only half of those found guilty spend any time behind bars. The message is clear: the Mexican National Soccer Team had better have a better outing at the next World Cup in Seoul than they fared in France.

Credit Cards

In a six month period, there were 13,852 cases of credit card fraud in Mexico. Foreigners are targeted in restaurants and hotels by seedy employees who steal your credit card number and drain the account like Tiger Woods putting a two-foot birdie. By the time you notice, you're back at home and the MasterCard statement arrives, showing a three-grand payment on a satellite dish (you've already got one!), a two-grand charge on frozen burritos and industrial kitchen equipment, $200 spent on tinted car windows and a lowered suspension and, of course, a $300 debit on a new pair of Tony Lamas.

Driving

Poor roads, infrequent repairs and lack of repair stations make motoring in Mexico a true adventure. It is not uncommon to be driving for 50 miles along a newly paved highway only to find a four-foot-wide chasm marked by a single branch. You have more to fear from cows than rattlesnakes, since livestock like to sleep on the warm asphalt at night. Many routes have heavy truck and bus traffic, some have poor or nonexistent shoulders, and many have animals on the loose. Also, some of the newer roads have very few restaurants, motels, gas stations or auto repair shops. If you have an accident, you will be assumed to be guilty, and, since you are a "wealthy foreigner," all efforts will be made to detain you until you until you are a little less wealthy.

An oncoming vehicle flashing its headlights is a warning for you to slow down or pull over because you are both approaching a narrow bridge or place in the road. The custom is that the first vehicle to flash has the right of way and the other must yield.

Drugs

Sentences for possession of drugs in Mexico can be as long as 25 years plus fines. Just as in the United States, purchase of controlled medication requires a doctor's prescription. The Mexican list of controlled medications differs from the U.S. list, and Mexican public health laws concerning controlled medication are unclear. Possession of excessive amounts of psychotropic drugs such as Valium can result in arrest if the authorities suspect abuse.

Drugs are a major part of Mexican life. Some areas are considered to be run by narcotics dealers. Drug dealers can be spotted by their love for Chevy Suburbans and Jeep Cherokees, Ray-Bans and AK-47s hidden behind the seats.

Because Mexican authorities need to show Uncle Sam they are cracking down on drugs, the government rigorously prosecutes drug cases where the defendant can't cough up enough money to get out of it. Under Mexican law, possession of and trafficking in illegal drugs are federal offenses. For drug trafficking, bail does not exist. Mexican law does not differentiate between types of narcotics: Heroin, marijuana and amphetamines, for example, are treated the same. Offenders found guilty of possessing more than a token amount of any narcotic substance are subject to a minimum sentence of seven years, and it is not uncommon for persons charged with drug offenses to be detained for up to a year before a verdict is reached.

Emergencies

It's best if you avoid them, because it may take awhile to be assisted. (If you think 911 is a sports car, welcome to Mexico.) In Mexico, "rapid response" is simply your reaction to the gravity of your predicament. During one six month period, there were 72,548 emergency calls received in Mexico City. In more than 4 percent of those requiring emergency police, fire or ambulance assistance, no one bothered to show up. In many other instances, it took more than an hour for a response. The situation is so bad, the city has contracted with a private "08" service to help handle the flood of calls. The catch? You have to be a paid subscriber. Sort of like cable for hypochondriacs.

Firearms

Last year 123 U.S. citizens were arrested for bringing guns into Mexico, some just for having bullets in the car and no gun. Do not bring firearms or ammunition of any kind into Mexico, unless you have first obtained a consular firearms certificate from a Mexican consulate. To hunt in Mexico, you must obtain a hunting permit, also available from the consulate. Travelers carrying guns or ammunition into Mexico without a Mexican certificate have been arrested, detained and sentenced to stiff fines and lengthy prison terms. The sentence for clandestine importation of firearms is from six months to six years. If the weapon is greater than .38 caliber, it is considered to be a military type, and the sentence is from 5 to 30 years. In some areas of Mexico, it is not wise to carry anything that might be construed as a weapon. Some cities, such as Nuevo Laredo, have ordinances prohibiting the possession of knives and similar weapons. Tourists have even been arrested for possessing souvenir knives. Most arrests for knife possession occur in connection with some other infraction, such as drunk and disorderly behavior. Strangely enough, Mexicans are allowed to bring into the United States three weapons and a whopping 1000 rounds of ammo.

Ah Chi Wow Wa! What a Shot!

On November 11, 1998, a 68-year-old Swiss tourist, Ernest Schmidt, thought he'd get a little Real TV footage. It seems there was a robbery on the the Chihuahua-Pacific Railway, which runs through the scenic Copper Canyon. Los banditos forgot to bring their film agent and promptly shot Ernest three times in the chest and the head. Cut! That's a wrap.

Mexican Jails

The Mexican judicial system is based on Roman and Napoleonic law and presumes a person accused of a crime to be guilty until proven innocent. There is no trial by jury nor writ of habeas corpus in the Anglo-American sense. Trial under the Mexican system is a prolonged process based largely on documents examined on a fixed date in court by prosecution and defense counsel. Sentencing usually takes six to ten months. Bail can be granted after sentencing if the sentence is less than five years. Pretrial bail exists, but is never granted when the possible sentence upon conviction is greater than five years.

Mexico has the highest number of arrests of Americans abroad—over 2,000 per year—and the highest prison population of U.S. citizens outside of the United States—about 425 at any one time. If you get busted in Mexico, contact a consular officer at the U.S. embassy or the nearest U.S. consulate for assistance. U.S. consular officers cannot serve as attorneys or give legal assistance. They can, however, provide lists of local attorneys and advise you of your rights under Mexican law.

http://www.state.gov/www/global/human_rights/1998_hrp_report/mexico.html

Phony Cops

Be aware of persons representing themselves as Mexican police or other local officials. Some foreigners have been the victims of harassment, mistreatment and extortion by criminals masquerading as officials. You must have the officer's name, badge number and patrol car number to pursue a complaint. Make a note of this information if you are ever involved with police or other officials. Do not be surprised if you encounter several types of police in Mexico. The Preventive Police, the Transit Police and the Federal Highway Police all wear uniforms. The Judicial Police, who work for the public prosecutor, are not uniformed.

Real Cops

Mexico's cops are routinely involved in extortion, kidnapping, robbery and counterfeiting gangs. For a $125 payoff to their commanding officers, a cop in Mexico City can get assigned to a busy intersection in the capital, netting him a cache of extortion money at the end of a day's work. The cops charge six bucks to overlook a parking violation, $12.50 for running a stop sign and $30 to back off from calling a tow truck. Mexico can boast the world's most corrupt police forces; so corrupt are they, in fact, that the Zedillo government has replaced a huge chunk of Mexico City's forces with soldiers. Real cops popped a Norwegian tourist in October 1998 and kidnapped and raped three girls in Tiahuac district in July 1998, and 19 cops were busted after whacking three youths in October 1997. The pretext most bad cops use when detaining foreigners is an immigration document check. Here's a *DP* tip-off: Ordinary cops aren't empowered to check immigration documents.

Goody Two-Shoes

Over 100 foreigners have been expelled from the Chiapas region since 1998 as undesirable. Mexican law prohibits foreigners from becoming involved in, or stating opinions about, Mexican politics. No, Marcos didn't do the film deal with Oliver Stone.

VW Beetle Taxis

Tourists don't even think about hailing Volkswagen Bug taxis on the street anymore. The incidents of violent crimes against foreigners in these vehicles is escalating. In 1997 alone there were 653 registered reports of crimes against foreign tourists, 160 of them assaults by taxi drivers. Tourists are not only robbed, but beaten silly. Drivers often work as cohorts of other thieves, who stop the cars at knife- or gunpoint. Use taxis only from authorized taxi stands (CTO or *sitio* stands). In Mexico City, beat feet from the taxis parked outside the Bellas Artes Theater, as well as those parked in front of discos, nightclubs and other venues tourists frequent. The safer Mexico City radio taxis can be reached at *271-9146, 271-9058, 272-6125, 516-6020* and *566-0077* or Servi Tazis 5 *516-6020* and Radio-Taxis at *5 566-0077*. *DP*'s advice? Tip generously.

Good medical care can be found in all major cities, and many U.S. prescription drugs are available over the counter. Most major hotels have a doctor on call who can treat everything from venereal diseases to broken bones. Health facilities in Mexico City are excellent, and are generally quite good in the major tourist and expat cities, including Cancún, Acapulco, Puerto Vallarta, Mazatlan, Merida, Manzanillo and Guadalajara. Care in more remote areas is limited.

In some places, particularly at resorts, medical costs can be as high as or higher than in the United States. If your health insurance policy does not cover you in Mexico, it is strongly recommended that you purchase a policy that does. There are short-term health policies designed specifically to cover travel.

Immunizations are recommended against diphtheria, tetanus, polio, typhoid, and hepatitis A. For visitors coming directly from the United States, no vaccinations are required to enter Mexico. If you are traveling from an area known to be infected with yellow fever, a vaccination certificate is required. Malaria is found in some rural areas of Mexico, particularly those near the southwest coast. Travelers to malarial areas should consult their physician or the U.S. Public Health Service and take the recommended dosage of chloroquine. Although chloroquine is not considered necessary for travelers to the major resort areas on the Pacific and Gulf coasts, travelers to those areas should use insect repellent and take other personal protection measures to reduce contact with mosquitoes, particularly from dusk to dawn when malaria transmission is most likely.

Montezuma's revenge is as sure as hangovers from cheap tequila. Drink only bottled water or water that has been boiled for 20 minutes. Avoid ice cubes. A good rule of thumb is, if you can't peel it or cook it, don't eat it. If symptoms of diarrhea present themselves and persist, seek medical attention, because diarrhea is potentially dangerous. Air pollution in Mexico City is severe. It is most dangerous during thermal inversions, which occur most frequently from December to May. Air pollution plus Mexico City's high altitude are a particular health risk for the elderly and persons with high blood pressure, anemia, or respiratory or cardiac problems.

Mexico has a population of 95,800,000, with Mexico City being the largest population center with some 17 million people. Mexico's climate varies from arid desert in the north to tropical in the south. About 97 percent of Mexicans are Roman Catholic; the remaining 3 percent are Protestant. The official language is Spanish. English is understood in highly touristed areas, but not in the countryside.

Telephone and fax service is good in the major cities and direct-dial calls to the U.S. can be made from the tourist centers and major cities. In the boonies, if you can find a phone, an international operator may be required to make an international call. Almost every town in Mexico has a post office. Most are open from 9 A.M.–5 P.M. Mexican businesses are also open during the same hours, most taking a one-hour break for lunch (some close for 2 hours). The electrical current is 110V/60C. Mexico's currency is the peso (7.5 pesos = US$1).

In an emergency, call *[91] (5) 250-0123*, the 24-hour hot line of the Mexican Ministry of Tourism. The hotline is for immediate assistance, but it can give you general, nonemergency guidance as well. In Mexico City, dial *06* for police assistance.

If you have problems filling out a police report or in filing a report, you can call the Silver Angels. This group helps tourists who are victims of crime file a police report.

If you have an emergency while driving, call the Ministry of Tourism's hotline to obtain help from the Green Angels, a fleet of radio-dispatched trucks with bilingual crews that operate daily. Services include protection, medical first aid, mechanical aid for your car and basic supplies. You will not be charged for services, only for parts, gas and oil. The Green Angels patrol daily, from dawn until sunset. If you are unable to call them, pull well off the road and lift the hood of your car; chances are good that they will find you.

Embassy and Consulate Locations

American Embassy

> Paseo de la Reforma 305
> Mexico 06500, D.F.
> Tel.: [52] (5) 211-0042
> Fax: [52] (5) 511-9980
> http://www.usembassy-mexico.gov/

American Consulate

> Circunvalacion No. 120 Centro
> Mazatlan, Sinaloa
> Tel.: [52] (678) 5-22-05
> Fax: [52] (678) 2-1775

American Consulate

> Paseo Montejo 453
> Merida, Yucatan
> Tel.: [52] (99) 25-5011
> After Hours (emergencies)
> Tel.: [52] (99) 25-5409
> Fax: [52] (99) 25-6219

American Consulate General

> Avenue Lopez Mateos 924-N
> Ciudad Juarez, Chihuahua
> Tel.: [52] (16) 134-048
> After Hours (emergencies)
> Tel.: (915) 525-6066
> Fax: [52] (161) 34048 ext. 210 or
> [52] (161) 34050 ext. 210

American Consulate General

> Avenida Constitucion 411 Poniente
> Monterrey, Nuevo Leon
> Tel.: [52] (83) 45-2120
> Fax: [52] (83) 42-0177

American Consulate General

> Progreso 175
> Guadalajara, Jalisco
> Tel.: [52] (36) 25-2998,
> [52] (36) 25-2700
> Fax: [52] (36) 26-6549

American Consulate

> Avenida Allende 3330, Col. Jardin
> Nuevo Laredo, Tamaulipas
> Tel.: [52] (871) 4-0696 or
> [52] (871) 4-9616
> After Hours (emergencies)
> Tel.: (512) 727-9661
> Fax: [52] (871) 4-0696 ext. 128

American Consulate

> Calle Monterrey 141, Poniente
> Hermosillo, Sonora
> Tel.: [52] (621) 723-75
> After Hours (emergencies)
> Tel.: [52] (621) 725-85
> Fax: [52] (62) 172375 ext. 49

American Consulate General

> Tapachula 96
> Tijuana, Baja California
> Tel.: [52] (66) 81-7400 or
> (706) 681-7400
> After Hours (emergencies)
> Tel.: (619) 585-2000
> Fax: [52] (66) 81-8016

American Consulate

> Avenue Primera No. 2002
> Matamoros, Tamaulipas
> Tel.: [52] (891) 2-52-50 or
> [52] (891) 2-52-51
> Fax: [52] (89) 138048

1/26/00	Mexico pledges $450 million to fight drug trafficking. Two-thirds of cocaine entering the U.S. comes from Mexico.
6/7/97	The ruling Institutional Revolutionary Party suffers its biggest electoral setback in its 69 years in power in Mexico.
3/23/94	Leading presidential candidate Luis Donaldo Colosio is assassinated.
1/1/94	Chiapas uprising begins.
5/5/1867	Archduke Maximilian of Austria, who was established as emperor of Mexico in 1864 by Napoléon III of France, is deposed by Benito Juárez and executed in 1867.
12/6/1822	Establishment of the Republic.
9/16/1810	Independence from Spain is declared by Father Miguel Hidalgo. The war for independence continues until 1822, when the Mexican Republic is established.

MEXICO

Yangon

Myanmar

Politically Incorrect

Watching tourism surge and hard currency flow into its former Third World neighbors such as Thailand, Malaysia, Vietnam and Indonesia, the generals of SLORC (the State Law and Order Restoration Council) figured that their own ancient temples, smiling people and steaming jungles were ripe for the picking—so they bulldozed villages, press-ganged the citizenry into slave labor and started razing the rain forest. Oh, isn't that how you attract tourists?

The generals' bizarre version of tourism, human rights and overall heavy-handedness has made Burma (whoops, Myanmar) the most politically incorrect destination on earth. While its buddies along the Pacific Rim sponsor tourism and award lucrative contracts to companies to build up the infrastructure and create tourist attractions, Myanmar saves a few bucks by having its general population do it—at gunpoint.

A few tourists showed up for the heavily promoted Visit Myanmar Year 1996 (which actually ran until the end of 1997 so the numbers would look good), but had to duck out of the way of occasional student demonstrations, mobs of SLORC Youth skinheads and truckloads of pissed-off Buddhist monks firebombing Muslim mosques. Yes, there's been a flood of foreign investment here over the last couple of years, mostly by ASEAN countries tucked behind the bombastic banner of "constructive engagement." And, yes, new hotels are springing into the Rangoon (Yangon) skyline like mushrooms after a May shower. But the high-tech and electonics industries are a little more hesitant. You see, unauthorized possession of a fax machine, modem and even a walkie-talkie is punishable by several years imprisonment. Sort of limits the market.

Then there are the drug lords. Notorious Khun Sa, who once supplied the U.S. with more than half of its heroin, "surrendered" to SLORC in January 1996. His brutal punishment? A cushy villa in Yangon, ten personal aides, four cars, a military escort, a personal Taiwanese doctor, a hotel and real estate empire, twice-weekly golf outings with the generals and the concession to run Yangon's bus system. He supplements his income with a line of ladies' shoes that fetch 20 grand a pair. That's what we call doing time.

To keep the "Prince of Death" (as Khun Sa translates into) in retirement funds, the generals look the other way while he runs a chain of methamphetamine factories ringing the Thai and Laos borders that rivals the number of Iowa's Pizza Huts. *Yaa baa,* as the Thais call it, has become all the rage in Thailand, where everyone from school kids to truck drivers gobble the stuff down like breath mints. It has killed hundreds. To get more of the youngsters hooked, Mr. K's freedom-fighters-turned-jungle-chemists coat the little devils with chocolate. Yummy.

There's also the ugly boil on SLORC's smiling face; the insurgent Karen National Union (KNU) has been slugging it out in a jungle rumble with various Yangon regimes since 1948 for a defined homeland, making its efforts the longest running rebellion in Southeast Asia. SLORC, trying to rake the leaves in its back yard as it enters ASEAN, has pushed more than 100,000 Karen refugees into camps in Thailand over the last few years. An early 1997 dry season offensive—which all but wiped out the KNU—sent some 20,000 people streaming across the border alone, many recounting horrific tales of rape and torture at the hands of the libido-savaged Burmese regulars along with their doped-out DKBA stooges—former freedom fighters who sold out to SLORC for a crate of AKs and some syringes.

Between SLORC, the KNU and Aung San Suu Kyi—the Nobel Prize–winning activist who was officially released after six years of house arrest but may as well still be under it—Myanmar makes for a bad soap opera. But let's go back a bit.

In keeping with the trend among developing and newly independent states to throw off the stigma of their colonial past, Burma became Myanmar in 1989 in a Joe Mobutu-like attempt to instantly decolonize the country. (Burma has always been called "Myanma"—that's right, no "r"—in the Burmese language.) Somerset Maugham turned in his grave when Rangoon became Yangon and the Irrawaddy became Ayeyarwady.

SLORCies and their fans will point out that Myanmar has been a nation of bellicose rulers and brutal suppression since 2500 B.C., when the Yunnan enslaved the Pyus along the upper Ayeyarwady River. Throughout its various occupations by the Mons, the Arakanese, the British and the Japanese, there have

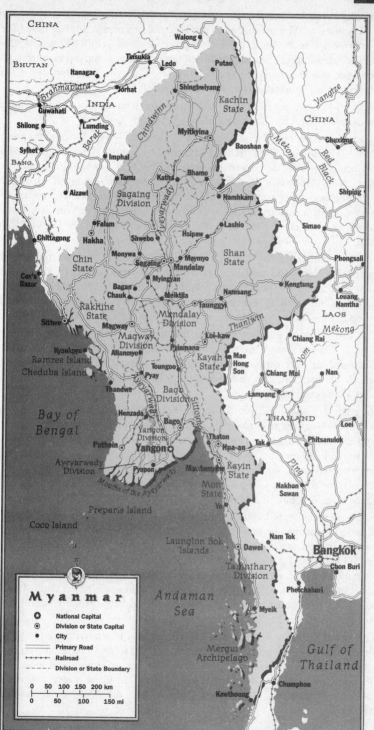

CHINA

BHUTAN

Walong

Tinsukia

Ledo

Putao

Itanagar

Jorhat

Shingbwiyang

Brahmaputra

INDIA

Kachin
State

CHINA

Guwahati

Yangtze

Myitkyina

Shilong

Lumding

Borak

Baoshan

Chuxiong

Sylhet

Imphal

Chindwinn

Bhamo

Metong

Shiping

BANG.

Tamu

Katha

Red

Aizawl

Namhkam

Black

Sagaing
Division

Lashio

Simao

Chittagong

Falam

Hsipaw

Phongsali

Hakha

Shwebo

Ayeyarwady

Cox's
Bazar

Chin
State

Monywa

Maymyo

Shan
State

Louang
Namtha

Sagaing

Mandalay

Bagan

Myingyan

Namsang

Kengtung

LAOS

Chauk

Meiktila

Mekong

Sittwe

Rakhine
State

Taunggyi

Thanlwin

Mandalay
Division

Loi-kaw

Chiang Rai

Magway

Kyaukpyu

Magway
Division

Pyinmana

Ramree Island

Allanmyo

Kayah
State

Mae
Hong
Son

Chiang Mai

Nan

Cheduba Island

Toungoo

Thandwe

Pyay

Lampang

THAILAND

Loei

Ayeyarwady

Bago
Division

Henzada

*Bay of
Bengal*

Bago

Sittoung

Loei

Yangon
Division

Thaton

Tak

Phitsanulok

Pathein

Yangon

Hpa-an

Ping

Ayeyarwady
Division

Pyapon

Mawlamyine

Kayin
State

Nakhon
Sawan

Mouths of the Ayeyarwady

Mon
State

Ye

Preparis Island

Coco Island

Launglon Bok
Islands

Dawei

Nam Tok

Bangkok

*Andaman
Sea*

Taninthary
Division

Chon Buri

Phetchaburi

Myeik

*Gulf of
Thailand*

*Mergui
Archipelago*

Chumphon

Kawthoung

N

Myanmar

⊛ National Capital

⊙ Division or State Capital

• City

——— Primary Road

+++++ Railroad

- - - - Division or State Boundary

0   50 100 150 200 km

0   50   100   150 mi

been tales of ruthless excess and exotic splendor. Unlike the nepotistic concept of royal hierarchy in Western countries, it was considered normal for Burmese rulers to exterminate heirs, rivals or the offspring of rivals. Until the mid-1800s, Burmese rulers burned, beat and drowned not only any potential claimants to the throne but also their children and servants. Hey, so what's the big deal about enslaving a few thousand peasants to build a road?

Today, the despotism continues. It's called something right out of a *Get Smart* episode: SLORC. A foreboding name in a forbidding land.

Myanmar was cocooned from the world by General Ne Win, who seized power in 1962. His 26-year reign plunged Myanmar backward. He ruled until 1988, when pro-democracy demonstrators won and Ne Win stepped down. But the military refused to honor the results of an election it itself organized. More than 3,000 Burmese protestors were killed when SLORC wrested control of the government in a military crackdown. The 80-something Ne Win lives in the shadows and is a close friend of current intelligence chief Major General Khin Nyunt.

The 21-member military junta of General Than Shwe continues to violently suppress dissidents and uprisings, and has firmly consolidated its vise on the nation by coming to "peace terms" with 15 of the 16 active rebel factions in Myanmar. Only the KNU continues to snipe at Burmese troops in remote jungle hamlets in the southeast of the country, but to date can claim no town as its base.

The current boy's club government has started to lure a steady stream of politically incorrect, eager investors, but the bulk of the 42 million Myanmars are condemned to exist on an average per capita income of US$200. Even the normally idealistic causes of insurgent groups have been replaced by the need for profits from opium production.

In getting ready for Visit Myanmar Year 1996, and true to form, the government—to prepare for the jumbo jet–loads of camcording Honshu islanders—chain-ganged not only criminals and dissidents but regular folks to help rebuild monuments, palaces, temples and attractions. In Mandalay, the junta ordered each family to contribute at least three days of free labor. Mandalayans could pay US$6 a month to be exempted from this drudgery. The average wage is about $6 a week in Mandalay.

There are an estimated 26,000 insurgents in and around Myanmar fighting for various causes at any one time, though most of them have at least temporarily laid down their arms through various peace (and drug profit sharing) agreements with SLORC. But figuring out who's fighting who is like getting an urchin out of a gill net. The military regularly abducts villagers in rural areas to serve as porters in its war against the insurgents, and to build roads to get there. Porters also come in handy after razing and pillaging refugee camps inside Thailand; their wives make suitable disposable lovers.

The forbidden zones and the Golden Triangle may lure adventurers, but there is little to see or do in these mostly rural and deforested areas. As the government creates an uneasy but profitable peace with rebel groups, more and more areas will open up to tour bus–bottomed "adventurers." In many places, you will be expected to have an MTT guide, who's very disinterested in anything adventurous.

Rangoon (whoops, Yangon) has the feel of 1938 Berlin. To hell with a cop on every corner, this place has got a loaded troop carrier on every corner. If it isn't NLD college kids out for a Sunday stroll en masse, truckloads of pissed Buddhist monks (or "external stooges" dressed up like monks, according to SLORC) are hurling Molotov cocktails at Muslim mosques. There are so many plainclothes spooks on the street, SLORC might consider eschewing a uniform budget altogether. Myanmar lucked out and hopped onto the ASEAN hayride in July 1997 along with Laos and Cambodia. The only one that really deserved it was Laos. Meanwhile, Unocal is forging ahead with its $1 billion natural gas pipeline, Aung San Suu Kyi remains as accessible as Carlos the Jackal, and the last remaining insurgency, the KNU's struggle, is getting smoked in the south. Myanmar is the very definition of "hard line."

Aside from politics, there's also news to upset eco-types: Myanmar grows about 75 percent of the tropical teak left in the world. The government, the Karens and the Shans, along with about 20 Thai logging companies, are rapidly sawing everything down before the political winds shift direction. According to some estimates, in 10 to 15 years, there won't be enough teak left to put together a decent deck chair.

Everyone

In Myanmar, you can't tell the bit players without a program. Even *DP* dares not dive too deeply into the various military, political, narco, ethnic, regional and ideological groups that want a piece of Myanmar for themselves. There are estimated to be at least 35 insurgency groups fighting or operating inside Myanmar (19 of them under the leadership of Karen leader Bo Mya), although most of them have made a precarious peace with Yangon. Depending on who's counting, they range in size from a handful of overeducated hotheads living in refugee camps, bad-ass shoot-to-kill drug smugglers, archaic political parties, regional warlords, and well-meaning but poorly equipped tribes to large, well-equipped armies of over 25,000 soldiers, complete with armored divisions. There are four major ethnic divisions, with 67 recognized tribal groups, with the majority Burmese living along the fertile center. Keep in mind as you travel around the country that most border and northern areas have some sort of grudge match going on at any one time. The Karen Nationals have been fighting for independence since 1948. The various groups fighting the SLORC are united under the name Democratic Alliance of Burma, but virtually all factions have made peace with Yangon over the last two years.

http://freeburma.org/

SLORC and the Generals

With a 400,000-man army, the 21-member junta comprised of the ruling families and selected investors holds all of the marbles here, at least in the majority of the country. These guys are mostly seen in public and the media petting goats, kissing babies, inspecting chickens, being deified by famous monks and passing out numbers to queues of foreign businessmen.

http://www.odci.gov/cia/publications/chiefs/f192.html

The Golden Land

http://www.myanmar.com/e-index.htm

Permanent Mission of the Union of Myanmar to the United Nations and other International Organizations, Geneva
http://www3.itu.int/MISSIONS/Myanmar/

People's Desire

- Oppose those relying on external elements, acting as stooges, holding negative views.

- Oppose those trying to jeopardize the stability of the State and the progress of the nation.

- Oppose foreign nations interfering in the internal affairs of the State.

- Crush all internal and external destructive elements as the common enemy.

—*Daily announcement appearing in the* New Light of Myanmar.
http://www.myanmar.com/nlm/

These folks have zero tolerance for dissent—in any form over any issue. Aung San Suu Kyi remains in isolation, most of her key supporters are in jail after dissident round-ups in May 1996 and May 1997. And the KNU has been all but crushed.

Monks

Ethnic groups and freedom fighters aside, even Buddhist monks aren't immune from a little storm trooping to keep them in line. After an alleged incident in March 1997 involving the rape of a young Buddhist girl by a Muslim businessman, monks in Mandalay decided to have a little tea party at the area's Muslim mosques. SLORC troops killed one of the rampaging monks and then slam-dunked Mandalay with a dusk-to-dawn curfew. The violence spread south to Yangon before it was quickly squashed.

Drugs

Recent announcements of peace between insurgents and the government are assumed to be "live and let live" agreements, which allow the Wa and Shan people to concentrate on the more lucrative business of opium rather than vying for political power. Consequently, for the first time since World War II, it appears the Yangon government has control over its entire 1,600-kilometer border with Thailand. Myanmar is the second largest producer of opium in the world.

http://www.usdoj.gov/dea/pubs/briefing/toc.htm

Wood

Although some parcels of Myanmar are controlled by insurgent groups, there exist tacit agreements between SLORC generals and Thai logging companies permitting rebel factions to smuggle hardwood and gems out of the country into Thailand. In turn, the logging roads created by this lucrative trade provide the government an expedient route to send in troops during the dry season to put pressure on the insurgents.

Karen National Liberation Army (KNLA)

The largest insurgent group is the Karen National Liberation Army of the Karen National Union (KNU), headed by 70-year-old Saw Bo Mya and based in Manerplaw before the brutal SLORC crusher offensives of the mid-1990s, which dispersed the remaining rebels to the jungle. Converted to Christianity by missionaries at the turn of the century and allied with the British during World War II, they have been fighting for their own independence since Burma was granted its independence without provision for a Karen homeland. The Karen battle for sovereignty has been ongoing since 1948, one of the longest struggles for freedom in Asia. They are funded through their control of the smuggling routes between Myanmar and Thailand. About 100,000 government troops, supported by ethnic Wa militia and the Buddhist DKBA (Democratic Karen Buddhist Army), are squeezing the life out of the Karen rebels. By reaching at least temporary peace agreements with most of the other factions battling Yangon, SLORC can now direct its full attention to the KNU.

The Karens are divided by religion, with Buddhist and Christian factions. The Buddhist faction (DKBA) has aligned itself with the Myanmar government and has been brutalizing and razing KNU refugee camps inside the Thai border. Meanwhile, aging and soon-to-retire Bo Mya continues to direct strikes against Burmese troops from a mobile base camp inside Myanmar. The rebels' strength, however, has been decimated to fewer than 2,500 fighters.

http://www.Karen.org

The Thais, Refugees and Natural Gas

For more than 20 years Thailand has provided safe haven for Myanmar's Karen refugees, which number more than 100,000. The Thais have built and maintained the numerous border camps and even footed the bill without appealing to the international community for help. Noble by any standards, save for those of Thai companies looking to make a killing off Myanmar's abundant natural resources. With more of Thailand's investment abroad ending up in the generals' coffers, Thailand appears to have shifted its policy on refugees. For the first time, there were reports in early 1997 of the Thai army forcibly repatriating Karen refugees. With a US$1 billion gas pipeline aimed at Thailand's front yard at stake, a little cooperation between Bangkok and Yangon isn't surprising. The Petroleum Authority of Thailand (PTT), with a 25 percent stake, is expected to be the big winner with the Yadana field pipeline. As some companies are pulling out of Myanmar, PTT is plunging in headfirst. It has acquired a big stake in a second gas pipeline project, which would connect the Yetagun field with Bangkok. The company's gas purchase is estimated to generate US$200 million for Yangon and the developing consortium. This is on top of the US$400 million a year that PTT will be paying the generals for Yadana gas. But if Thailand's refugee policy has indeed changed, it marks an about-face of Bangkok's longtime course to permit ethnic guerrilla groups to find refuge along its border with Myanmar, which will, in turn, provide the Thais a buffer between themselves and their longtime bitter enemy—but now ASEAN neighbor—the Burmese. Regardless, for PTT and other Thai concerns in Myanmar, life's a gas.

The Kachin Independent Organization

This is a seriously dwindled group of rebels—formerly 5,000 strong—also known as the Kachin Independence Army (KIA). The Kachins are animists and Christians of Tibeto-Burman descent who originally migrated from China. Found in northern Myanmar, they are funded in part through the mining of rich jade deposits in the area. The jade is then sold to China. At one time this group was the primary organizer of opium transportation to the Thai border. Although the KIA has been mostly KIAed (killed in action) since several recent SLORC blitzes against its strongholds in Kachin state, Putao remains off-limits to visitors, suggesting the mopping up isn't entirely completed.

The National League for Democracy (NLD)

The National League for Democracy is the opposition party that won the May 1990 general elections by a landslide, capturing 82 percent of the vote—and whose rarely seen dissidents have mostly all hidden in the jungle since then, when the Myanmar military suppressed a nationwide uprising for democracy. They've come out of the closet recently with the 1995 release from house arrest of NLD leader Aung San Suu Kyi, but may have to step back into it after walking out on SLORC's late-1995 constitutional convention and the subsequent government suppression of Ms. Suu Kyi's activities and movements.

Aung San Suu Kyi

The charismatic and brave figurehead of the NLD. She stood in front of SLORC's rifles during the student riots of '88, was busted by the evil generals and received a Nobel Prize for her efforts. Placed under house arrest in 1989, she wasn't heard from until her release in the summer of 1995. She's chosen not to leave Myanmar, but instead to engage in "constructive dialogue" with SLORC and to consult with her NLD colleagues to find a way of bruising the SLORC bullies without winding back in the slammer. SLORC sees her as more of a nuisance (albeit a major one) than a threat, as Euro and ASEAN conglomo-cash is beginning to flow into Myanmar, ensuring the generals a lasting reign. But the foreign investment well may dry up suddenly if they lock Suu Kyi inside again. After her release from house arrest as many as 10,000 people jammed the street in front of her lakeside compound to hear her weekly addresses. But roads leading to her home have been blocked now for months and she's no longer allowed to speak in public. She and some supporters have been rousted by Khin Nyunt's Ray-Ban cops a number of times, leading to an estimated 1,000 arrests. Some 260 NLD members were busted shortly before a party congress in May 1996, and another 50 or more ahead of a party meeting in May 1997 to mark the seventh anniversary of the May 27, 1990, elections that would have swept the NDL to power if recognized by the jealous generals. With Myanmar joining ASEAN it seems the road's going to be even tougher for the Iron Lady.

You can try getting to Suu Kyi's house. During our last trip, we were stopped by soldiers a couple of hundred yards away. University Avenue in Yangon is barricaded off near her house. Her address is 5456 Tekkhtho Yeiktha Avenue in Yangon. Her home phone number is *530365.*

http://theodore-sturgeon.mit.edu:8001/peacejam/aung/aung.html
http://www.communique.no/dvb/

SLORC Bullies Hurl Tomatoes in Bid to Get Drafted into the Majors

Former Los Angeles Dodgers manager Tommy Lasorda has found pitchers everywhere from the desert of Mexico to the base of Mount Fuji. He may want to start sending some scouts to Yangon for a new generation of hurlers. SLORC figures if they start gunning down NLDers like they did in 1988 with real bullets, the world will back out of oil and pipeline deals and half-finished hotels. So, through sheer political genius, they've resorted to hiring thugs to lob tomatoes at Suu Kyi and her supporters. The generals figure a few tomatoes and a few messed-up hairdos won't make the pages of the New York Times. *So they've enlisted the services of the Union Solidarity and Development Association (USDA)–ostensibly a government-sponsored social welfare association, but in reality a gang of shock troops and a Cleveland Indians farm team–to practice their pitching skills at NLD demonstrations. In one instance, in February 1996, as Suu Kyi was speaking at a memorial ceremony for former Burmese prime minister U Nu, a Toyota pickup filled with crates of tomatoes rolled up; the tomatoes were intended to be lobbed at the participants by USDA fledgling Florida Marlins. They refused to fire the tomatoes at the crowd, thinking that crates of jackfruit (a much larger fruit) were to be supplied instead.*

The Khun Sa Gang (formerly the Shan United Army, or Mong Tai)

The Mong Tai army was the private plaything of ruthless druglord turned hotel mogul Chang Chi Fu, also known by the thespian title Khun Sa (the Prince of Death; see below). It broke up into factions in June 1995, charging their leader with spending too much time tinkering with his dope business and not enough fighting for freedom. (Khun Sa theatrically claimed the defections occurred because he is half Chinese.) And government troops seized the drug warlord's mountain stronghold at Ho Mong in January 1996. The cagey guerrilla commander cut a deal with SLORC in which he turned over his territory and what was left of his army to the government in exchange for amnesty. Problem is, it seems he didn't tell his guerrillas. One Mong Tai army officer who made it into Thailand shortly before SLORC took the base said, "We were told our commanders were negotiating with SLORC for a cease-fire—but it turned out they were allowing the Burmese troops to take over our bases." Oh, well. Khun Sa has maintained all along that he was never an opium trader but a freedom fighter, and that he taxed drug runners moving through his territory to help fund the Shan liberation cause. An unknown number of the former soldiers remain loyal to Khun Sa and have been tasked with building and operating at least a dozen methamphetamine factories in the jungle along Myanmar's borders with Thailand and Laos.

Khun Sa

Khun Sa (a.k.a. the Prince of Death or Mr. K), wanted by the U.S. government for heroin trafficking, was the world's largest single supplier of heroin until he "surrendered" to SLORC in January 1996. The U.S. government credits Khun Sa with providing a full two-thirds of the world's heroin supply when he was in business. Rather than rotting and languishing in some Third World piss-stained jail cell, Mr. K, as he's referred to by his close associates, instead lives opulently with the generals in Yangon. He has a number of hotel interests and runs the capital's bus system. It's golf twice a week with the generals and a military escort when he leaves home. His choice of restaurants doesn't need to be marred by how busy they might be. Soldiers simply clear the place out. Mr. K and his ten aides—who followed him from his Ho Mong headquarters—can then dine in peace before taking Khun's four cars back to the compound for some afternoon pitch-and-putt in the back yard. Then, after a little nap, it's time to get that annoying diabetes checked out by his very own live-in Taiwanese doctor. Nonetheless, his best buddies say that Mr. K is both bored and stressed by Yangon and yearns for the mountains of Shan State and his former glory as a ruthless drug warlord. Not that he's left them entirely; his Khun Sa gang runs a network of methamphetamine factories where his poppies used to grow. Much of the dope ends up in Thai high schools and the glove boxes of long-distance truckers.

http://www.usdoj.gov/dea/pubs/briefing/2_8.htm

Can I Get a Dictionary?

A partial listing of Myanmar's insurgent groups, illegal political parties and rebels.

All Burma Students Democratic Front (ABSDF)

Burmese Communist Party (BCP)

Chin National Front (CNF))

Democratic Alliance of Burma (DAB)

Karenni Liberation Army (KLA)

Karenni Peoples United Liberation Front (KPULF)

Kayah New Land Revolution Council (KNLRC)

Kuomintang (KMT)

Ma Ha Faction of the Wa Army

Mon Liberation Front (MLF)

National Democratic Front (NDF)

National Coalition Government of the Union of Burma (NCGUB)

Pa-O Shan State Independence Party (PSSIP)

Can I Get a Dictionary?

Palaung State Liberation Organization (PSLO)

Tai National Army (TNA)

Shan United Revolutionary Army (SURA)

Shan United Army (SUA)

United Pa-O Organization (UPO)

http://www.amnesty.org/ailib/aipub/1997/ASA/31602097.htm

Visas are required of all travelers to Myanmar ages seven years and over, for a stay of up to 30 days (formerly, you couldn't stay in the country for more than two weeks). From Bangkok, visas now only take about two to three days to be processed and cost 800 Thai baht (US$32). Tourists can travel independently in Myanmar, but aren't permitted to stray from the "approved" tourist sites. Tourist visas are not extendable except in rare circumstances (i.e., you want to become a monk). Once inside Myanmar, a business visitor may possibly apply for an extended visa with the invitation and recommendation of a state enterprise. For a tourist visa, you'll need three passport-sized photographs.

Check with:

Myanmar Embassy
132 Sathon Neua Road
Bangkok, Thailand
Tel.: 66-2-233-2237

Myanmar Embassy
2300 S St., NW
Washington, DC 20008
Tel.: 202-332-9044

Sneaking into Myanmar can be easily done by hiking over land or along logging roads into the country from Thailand. Troubles you encounter won't be with the government but with the various ethnic and rebel groups, who will have no qualms about shooting you and leaving you to rot. You can try contacting the various groups through expat sympathizers; however, don't try this from inside the country. Another alternative is having a couple of 13-year-old schoolkids-turned-commandos sneak you across the border near Mae Hong Son in Thailand for a nominal fee.

Entry by air into Myanmar is via Yangon International Airport, the country's only international gateway besides Mandalay (which is serviced from Chiang Mai, Thailand). Daily flights take less than an hour between Bangkok and Yangon. Myanmar Airways (MAI) has recently purchased new aircraft (Boeing 737-400s) for use on its routes to Singapore, Bangkok and Jakarta and has upgraded its safety agenda far enough to get off of the FAA's ☆#% list. Thai International offers slightly better service than Myanmar Airways between the two capitals, but only three times a week. There are also direct flights available from Singapore, Calcutta, Kathmandu, Dacca, Moscow and Beijing on a variety of Third World airlines.

MAI flies twice a week to Singapore and Jakarta. Jakarta has become the seventh foreign city that MAI flies to, in addition to Bangkok, Hong Kong, Singapore, Kuala Lumpur, Dhaka and Kunming. The MAI international fleet consists of three Boeing 737-400s. Flights to and from Bangkok have been increased from twice daily to three times daily. MAI flies to Singapore once a day.

Yangon International Airport is situated about 19 kilometers northwest of Yangon, and there may or may not be a BAC bus to transport passengers into the major hotels. If you are traveling on a package tour, transfers are definitely provided. Expect to pay about US$6 if using local taxis (and don't forget to bargain a little).

A departure tax (US$6) is included in tour package prices. Or pay it yourself at the airport if traveling independently.

Getting there by sea was formerly an option by cruise boat. You can't get into the country by sea today, but check for the current regulations, as they change constantly. In February 1997, a group of foreign tourists visited the Mergui archipelago off Myanmar's southern coast aboard the 51-foot ketch rig trimaran *Gaea*. Operated by Southeast Asia Liveaboards, the boat made the run, with official permission from SLORC, from Thailand's coastal city of Ranong. There's every reason to believe the company will continue making regular cruises to the Merguis in the future. For the time being, voyagers aboard the *Gaea* can expect some degree of intrigue, like being stopped by Myanmar navy coastal patrols, which haven't yet gotten word the cruises (which are restricted to the inner islands only due to an ongoing fishing rights dispute in the outer islands between the Burmese and the Thais) are kosher with the generals in Yangon. For more information, contact Thailand-based **Southeast Asia Liveaboards** at 66-76-*340406; Fax: 66-76-340586; or e-mail seadiver@loxinfo.co.th.*

Yangon is the country's major port, and it lies at the mouth of the Ayeyarwady River. Visitors are welcome to travel upriver on private cargo ships or conveyances owned by the government-run Inland Water Transport Corporation to either Mandalay or Nyaung-U (for Bagan). The journey is hot, picturesque and overly time-consuming, but still popular now that you can get a 30-day visa.

Cruise ships in the Far East area often schedule calls at Yangon, but thus far, no company has been successful in arranging regular visits.

The overland route between Thailand and Myanmar, where visitors could travel from Mae Sai, Thailand, to Kengtung, Myanmar—an eight-hour trip by road each way—was closed at press time. Travelers using this route had been limited to a three-day/two-night trip (East-Quest and others offer tours). At press time, groups could no longer enter Myanmar by land from Tachilek, Three Pagodas Pass and Kawthaung in Thailand. The opening of a China overland route, from Kunming in Yunnan province, which was under consideration for independent travelers, has been shelved for the time being. Tour groups have made the crossing in the past. Things change all the time regarding land crossings. Check regarding all land crossings beforehand. There have been numerous instances of fighting along the border with Thailand, particularly opposite Tak, Kanchanaburi, Ratchaburi and Chumphon provinces in Thailand.

Transit, at least the mechanized means, in Myanmar has gotten better in the last few years. Now one can comfortably get around via minibus, train, modern aircraft and new, comfortable bus coaches. In Bagan, it is possible to find a guide with a Jeep or Land Rover.

Taxis have red license plates and can usually be found outside major hotels, but agree on the fare before setting off. Private cars with drivers go for about $50 a day, and motorcycles and bikes can be rented for $25 and pennies a day, respectively.

City buses are overly crowded and not recommended for Westerners, who tend to take up too much room and cause a terrible commotion if they don't understand something. MTT and perhaps a dozen other private companies operate buses from Yangon up-country. Buses to Mandalay take about 13 hours. Regular bus services today connect Yangon and Mandalay, Mandalay and Bagan, Bagan and Taunggyi, and Taunggyi and Mandalay.

The rail network in Myanmar is growing quickly (some say with the help of slave labor). The Yangon-Mandalay line is the trunk route in the country, with a number of branches. Special counters to help tourists have been opened at the stations in Yangon, Thazi and Mandalay. At present, there are about 2,739 miles of railway spreading across the country. About 1,000 additional miles are being constructed in states and divisions that were formerly under the control of rebel insurgents and dope traffickers.

The train station for overland destinations is between Sule Pagoda Road and Upper Pansodan Street across from Aung San Stadium in Yangon. Here, there are regular long-distance train connections with Mandalay, Prome, Thazi and Pegu. Regular express trains running daily between Yangon and Mandalay take about 12–14 hours. Visitors to Bangan and Inle Lake have to get off at the Thazi station and take a bus from there. To Bagan the bus trip takes about four hours, and from Thazi to Shwe Nyaung (Inle Lake) about five hours.

In addition to Myanmar Airways, two other air carriers serve Myanmar's domestic routes: Air Mandalay and Yangon Airways. As both are relative upstarts, it's difficult to appraise their safety levels. Myanmar Airways has rocketed their safety standards over the last few years and it's safe to assume that Air Mandalay and Yangon Airways subscribe to the same levels as the national carrier. The last crash of a Myanmar carrier was a Myanmar Airways F-27 that crash-landed at Myeik airport in July 1996. Domestic flights offered by the three carriers connect Yangon with the following cities: Bagan, Heho, Kawthoung, Mandalay, Myitkyina, Myeik and Tachilek.

Myanmar possesses hundreds of navigable rivers and streams and a huge deltaic region in the south below Yangon. Inland Water Transport operates a large network of waterways tansportation plans. Most tourists to Myanmar take a cruise down the Ayeyarwady River, a daylong trip from Mandalay to Bagan/Nyaung Oo. The journey takes 12 hours. In the Ayeyarwady Delta, travelers can take a boat to Pathein (Bassein). The trip from Yangon takes one day (16–20 hours). Other delta destinations are also possible, such as Labooda and Hpayapon. Boats depart from Lan Thit Street Jetty in Yangon.

Up the Lazy River

Myanmar not only has about 50 steam engines still in service, they still operate hundreds of ancient riverboats that go back as far as the 1880s. These paddlewheelers (now converted to diesel) chug up the 8,000 kilometers of navigable rivers in Myanmar, carrying passengers and freight. Many are used as ferryboats. There are now newer luxury versions, but the hardcore can still read their Rudyard Kipling poems on the deck of a slow-moving 19th-century paddleboat.

You might need permits to travel outside the standard tourist rut (Yangon, Mandalay, Bagan, Inle Lake, Taunggyi). Permits are letters generated from MTT and approved by the military. MTT or Yangon-based travel agencies will arrange for these. You will need to have a guide or driver and a pretty clear idea of where you want to go. You will not know which areas are specifically out of bounds until you apply to go to them. You can try to travel without a permit (many do), but be prepared to be turned back at any one of the military checkpoints throughout the county. Soldiers at checkpoints in partially controlled zones, like the Chin, Mon, Kayin or Shan states, will rarely bend the rules. You can, however, enter from Thailand illegally and take your chances with the insurgent checkpoints. You can fly into some areas much easier than by road. In many cases, the roads are controlled by insurgent armies. The need for permits and the areas that are considered dangerous or hot change regularly, so check with the local embassy or the MTT in Yangon.

You can fly in from Chiang Mai to Mandalay and Bagan. Pwin Ol Lwin, or Maymyo as it was formerly known, is an old British hill station that still has 153 horse-drawn carriages left over from colonial times. The Burma Road in the Shan hills is the major trade route with Yunnan in China.

The Golden Triangle area in Myanmar can be reached by train from Mandalay. You can also make the arduous 160-kilometer trip from Kengtung to Tachileik. Additionally, travelers have been able to get from Kengtung to Mai Sai in Thailand's Chiang Rai province. But the border is shut, and you'd probably get popped anyway.

Lashio is a mecca for adventurers, for this is where the Burma Road begins its long, winding path into China. Mogok is 115 kilometers from Mandalay and is the site of jade and ruby mines controlled by rebels on odd days, and the government on even days. You can see (and purchase) the fruits of their labors by posing as a buyer at the annual gem auction each February in Yangon.

Good maps are not available. Bartholomew, Nelles and Hildebrand are the best brands for maps of the country. The local MTT office in Athenian and Mandalay can provide street maps.

DP likes to group Myanmar in a group of countries that includes Turkey, Egypt, Cambodia, Russia, the Philippines, Israel and Colombia—countries that aggressively seek tourists even though they are, uh, well, kind of having a few problems in the hinterlands. Like Cambodia, if you stay on your leash and visit all the nice monuments, you will be fine. But if you head into the boonies, you are guaranteed to meet a lot of pissed-off folks. Those won't be rolled up election posters they're pointing at you.

Shan State (the Far North and Southeast)

So, where do you stay away from (or run to, depending on your taste in travel)? Well, start with any hilly, northern area bordering Thailand, China and Laos. This is where drugs are grown, sold and refined. (See "Drugs" for more than you ever wanted to know about the opium trade.) Shan state is home to the Shan, Kachin, Karen, Wa and other ethnic groups, all of whom have armies and control movement inside and across the borders. The mountainous areas are ideal for growing opium poppies. This region is headed by a narco government run by warlords with large armies.

Mon State (Southern Area)

The Mon and the Karen insurgents hide out in this strip of land that parallels the Thai border. Although there was a cease-fire in 1995 between the government and the Mon National Liberation Front, the Mon still duke it out with the Karen over control of the smuggling checkpoints into Thailand. Banditry along the highways by armed groups is prevalent in daylight.

Chin State

The ethnic Chin want their own remote mountainous country, and guess what they want to call it? Yep, Chinland. These folks need a little better feel for Marketing 101. The Chin are Tibeto-Burmese who are primarily animists. Of course, where there are happy animists, there are Christian missionaries handing out faded Ninja Turtle shirts and Adidas shorts. The government has also sent in Buddhist missionaries to tug their souls in another direction.

There are many people with Indian or Bengali ties, so the government is also actively persecuting the Muslims, forcing many to flee to neighboring India or Bangladesh.

Rakhine State

Rakhine state is stirred up by the activities of the Arakan Rohingya Islamic Front and the Rohingya Solidarity Organization, extra-agitated folks from among the quarter of a million Muslim refugees who live across the border (not by choice) in scenic, affluent Bangladesh.

Travel Restrictions

Traveling in Myanmar these days, although far less restrictive than in the past, is still like a bumper car ride. Just when you get out of first gear, you smack into a nasty little ethnic insurrection, a warlord state or a general's poppy field and have to double back to find some way around it. And just to add a little more confusion to the situation, package groups are permitted in some places where independent travelers are prohibited.

SLORC has a name for the indies: Foreign Independent Travelers (FIT). For everything naughty you can say about the government, you will indeed give them fits. They come up with some pretty cute acronyms, and this one is an accurate one.

Forget what you've read elsewhere; this is where you can and cannot go inside Myanmar—and how you can and cannot get there.

Kachin State

1. Both package tours and FIT are permitted to travel to Myitkyina either by plane or train.

2. Both package tours and FIT are allowed to Hopin, Mohnyin, Mogaung and Indawgyi by train. Prior permission is required to travel to these regions by car. Do not attempt to head out to these places by car unless you have written permission from the MTT or Ministry of Hotels and Tourism.

3. Package tours and FIT are allowed to travel to Jinghkrang, Myitsone, Waingmaw and Washaung in Myitkyina.

4. Package tours and FIT are no longer permitted (at press time) to go to Putao due to a pesky little secessionist war. Package tours could formerly get in by plane, with FIT having to sign up on a tour to get there. Putao should open up again after the body count. The problem here is with the Kachin Independent Army (KIA), a dwindling band of about 5,000 or so fighters. You'd want your own country, too, if you had mountain loads of jade in your backyard. Today, though, the KIA lives up to Myanmar's uncanny propensity for choosing for itself appropriate acronyms—it's mostly Killed in Action. But these folks remain infestive, nonetheless. Check with the MTT to see if the restriction has been lifted.

5. If Putao opens up, package tours visiting Manse, Mu Daung, Noi Nan, Machambaw, Hun Nan, Mulashidi, Ho Pa and Ko Pa can only do so through an authorized MTT tour supervised and guided by either a staff officer or an assistant manager of the Ministry of Hotels and Tourism. A detailed itinerary to the Putao area has to be submitted to MHT in advance.

6. Package tours and FIT are allowed to Bamaw by plane or by boat.

Northern Shan State

Package tours and FIT are permitted to Lashio through the inland route by planes, trains and automobiles.

Southern Shan State

1. Package tours and FIT are permitted to travel to Taunggyi, Inlay, Pindaya, Kalaw and Yatsauk through the inland route by planes, trains and automobiles.

2. Package tours and FIT are permitted to travel to Kyaing Tong and Tachilek by plane only.

Kayah State

Foreigners, either on a package tour or traveling independently, cannot travel to any area within Kayah State.

Rakhine State

1. Package tours and FIT are allowed through the inland route to Sittway, Mrauk U, Ngapali, Thandwe, Gwa and Taungkoke by plane, train or automobile. Travel is not permitted to Ahm and Kyauktaw.

2. Package tours and FIT are permitted by car to Kantharyar via Ngathaing Kyaung-Gwa Road, and to Ngapal via Pyay-Taungkoke Road.

Kayin State

Package tours and FIT are permitted to Tharmin Nya, Pa-an and Hlaingbwe either by train or car.

MYANMAR

Mon State

Package tours and FIT are no longer allowed to Kyaik Htiyo, Kyaik Hto, Thaton, Kyaik Maraw, Mawlamyaing, Balukyun, Thanbyuzayat and Kyaik Kami by either train or by car. The Christian Karens of KNU down there have been been getting their butts hammered by both SLORC troops and fighters of the government-backed Democratic Karen Buddhist Army (DKBA), a splinter group of the Karen National Union (KNU) that has been beating up on its Karen brothers with SLORC arms for the last couple of years. Recent fighting in early 1997 sent more than 90,000 refugees streaming across the border into Thailand's Tak Province. There are perhaps 11,000 KNU rebels slugging it out with about 17,000 SLORC troops in the region.

Tanintharyi Division

1.   Package tours and FIT are allowed to Myeik, Dawei, Maungmagan, Kawthaung and Lanpi Kyun by either plane or boat.

2.   Foreigners are not permitted to travel to Zadetgyi Kyun, either independently or as part of a tour package.

Yangon Division, Mandalay Division, Bago Division, Magway Division and Ayeyarwady Division

Package tours and FIT are permitted without any restrictions to travel by boat or car within these divisions.

Sagaing Division

1.   Package tours and FIT are allowed by car to Alaungdaw Kathapa, Po Win Taung, Monywa, Twin Taung, Butalin, Kyauk Ka, Yinmar Pin and Yeshantwin.

2.   Package tours and FIT are allowed to Khamti by either plane or boat. Travel to any area outside Khamti is prohibited.

3.   Package tours and FIT are allowed to Homalin by boat. Travel to any area outside Homalin is not permitted.

4.   Package tours and FIT are allowed to Kale by plane. However, travel outside a four-mile radius of the town is prohibited.

Chin State

Foreign tourists, both tour groups and FIT, are prohibited from traveling anywhere in Chin State due to another annoying separatist blood feud, this time between SLORC and the Chin people of northwestern Myanmar. The Chin are of Tibeto-Burmese stock, and are primarily animists with ties to Bangladesh and India.

The Ayeyarwady River

Package tours and FIT are permitted to cruise along the Ayeyarwady River on the following routes: Mandalay/Bamaw/Mandalay; Mandalay/Bagan/Nyaung U/Mandalay; Yangon/Mandalay/Yangon; the delta regions and Mawlamyaing/Pa-an/Mawlamyaing.

Other Restrictions

Mogoke

Authorized travel and tour companies arranging package tours to Mogoke are required to make booking arrangements through the Union of Myanmar Economic Holdings Ltd. However, MTT—a division of the Ministry of Hotels and Tourism—can make its own arrangements for package tours to Mogoke. Tours here can only be arranged by car, and travel to Hpakant is prohibited.

Border Crossings

At the time of this writing, independent travelers were not allowed to enter or leave Myanmar through any land border. The border at Tachilek is intermittently open to foreigners traveling to and from Thailand, but visitors are not permitted outside Tachilek and must return the way they came into the country. Package tourists have more options.

Northern Shan State

1. Visitors coming from China with a valid border pass are allowed to enter Myanmar through Muse, Namkhan, Kyu Koke and Kun-Lone checkpoints provided they are part of a package tour organized by authorized travel and tour companies. It is then possible to proceed by car up to Lashio.

2. Visitors entering Myanmar through the Lwe-je checkpoint with a valid border pass are permitted to continue on to Bamaw Township if they are members of a package tour organized by an authorized travel and tour company.

Southern Shan State

1. Visitors entering from Thailand with a valid border pass can enter Myanmar at Tachilek, but are restricted in their movements once there. Travel by road or plane to other parts of the country is prohibited.

2. Visitors entering through Wun Pone with a valid border pass are allowed only as far as Tachilek.

3. Visitors entering through Mai Lar are not permitted to visit Kyaing Tong. The government said it will give consideration to this restriction in the future.

Legal Border Pass Destinations

Foreign travelers on tour packages with valid visas and border passes entering Myanmar through a border checkpoint listed below are permitted to the areas mentioned here:

Muse, Namkhan, Kyu Koke and Kun Lone checkpoints

1. Package tours arranged by authorized travel and tour companies are allowed to enter through Muse, Namkhan, Kyu Koke and Kun Lone checkpoints and proceed on to Mandalay and Yangon via Lashio by plane, train or automobile.

Lwe-je

1. Package tours arranged by authorized travel and tour companies are allowed to enter through Lwe-je and proceed on to Mandalay and Yangon via Bamaw either by plane or boat.

The Name Game

Despite all the PC babble about Myanmar being the bad guys' name for Burma, don't believe it. Myanmar is the name of the country and Burmese (or Myanmars) the name of the people. Burmese is the language found around the capital city of Yangon and is spoken by ethnic Burmese. The region has been called Myanmar as far back as the 13th century, by Marco Polo, no less. It makes more sense to call the country a name other than just one of the many ethnic groups. Imagine if America were called India, after what was its largest ethnic group. All the generals were doing was a little colonial housecleaning when they renamed the country and many of its cities.

Myanmar experiences the typically Southeast Asian tropical monsoon climate, with hot, humid lowlands and cool highlands. The wet monsoon season is from June through September, the cool dry season from November to April.

The official language of Myanmar is Burmese; a number of ethnic languages are also spoken. Burmese is a completely indecipherable script for most casual visitors. English signs have been removed so bring a phrase book if you want to do anything more than eat or sleep. It is helpful to know that Burmese have one given name between one to three syllables, usually preceded with a form of address. In Burmese, use Oo (uncle) for adult males, Ko (elder brother) for males of the same age, Bo for leader, Ma (sister) for young girls, Daw (aunt) for older women, and Saya (master) for teachers or employers. Other ethnic groups use variations on this theme.

Buddhists comprise 85 percent of the population, while animists, Muslims, Christians and other indigenous religion followers comprise the rest. Sixty-eight percent of Myanmar's population is Burmese; however, there are five major ethnic groups (Shan, 11 percent; Karen, 7 percent; Kachin, 6 percent; Arakanese, 4 percent; and Chin, 2 percent). The Shan are found in the northeast. The Karen straddle northern Thailand and eastern Burma and pay little attention to the border between the two countries. The Mon populate the same fertile area as the Karen and are ethnically related to both the Khmers and the Burmese. The Burmese live primarily in the central plains along the Ayeyarwaddy River and were the builders of the great monuments at Bagan.

The literacy rate stands at 81 percent. The monetary unit is the kyat. The free market exchange rate at press time was nearly 300 kyat to the U.S. dollar, but should should settle down again to about 167 kyats to the dollar. The free market rate is now legal, replacing the ridiculously artificial rate of 6 kyats to the buck.

Big Brother

The military rulers of Myanmar keep a very close watch on their own people and particularly hnakaung shays, or long noses. That probably means you. Do not converse freely with strangers. It can be safely assumed that anyone who loiters near you or reappears often in your travels is a paid intelligence operative.

Telephone calls can be made from hotels and the Central Telegraph office in Yangon. International calls go through operators (watch what you say and who you call). There is no guarantee of a phone line being available or even usable. Telexes can be sent from major hotels as well as the telegraph office.

It costs six kyats to post an airmail letter, but don't count on it getting there anytime soon. Buy the stamps and mail your postcards or letters from Bangkok. MTT, *77-79 Sule Pagoda Road*, is the main source for travel info in Yangon. There are also offices in Mandalay, Bagan and Taunggyi.

Voltage is 220/50 cycles when it works.

Note: February and March are bad times to visit due to the influx of gem buyers into Yangon for the annual auction.

Embassies/Consulates

American Embassy
581 Merchant Street
Box B
Yangon
Tel.: [95] (1) 282055/6 or 282059

Australian Embassy
88 Strand Rd.
Yangon
Tel.: [95] (1) 280711

United Kingdom Embassy
80 Strand Rd.
Yangon
Tel.: [95] (1) 281700, 281702

Permanent Mission of Myanmar to the U.N.
10 East 77th Street
New York, NY 10021
Tel.: (212) 535-1311/0/1716
Fax: (212) 737-2421

Embassy of the Union of Myanmar (USA)
2300 S Street, NW
Washington, DC 20008
Tel.: (202) 332-9044-5

Money Hassles

The currency of Myanmar is the **kyat** (pronounced "chat"), which is divided into 100 pyas. Notes are used in denominations of 1, 5, 10, 15, 20, 45, 50, 90, 100, 200, 500 and 1,000; make sure markings are in both Burmese and Arabic numerals. SLORC seems to have a sense of humor, after all; without warning, it has had a tendency of arbitrarily banning certain denominations, as it has done with the K100 note. Coins are available in denominations of 1 kyat and 1, 5, 10, 25 and 50 pyas. Coins are difficult to decipher because they are marked only in Burmese numerals.

Insider Tip: No 50s, No 100s

You may find yourself in a situation where the change offered consists of either K50 or K100 notes marked "Union of Burma Bank." Do not accept them. They are no longer legal tender. Myanmar people possessing large amounts of these notes became impoverished after the government banned the circulation of them. The worthless notes have been known to be passed on to naïve foreign tourists.

Unlimited amounts of foreign currency, whether in cash or traveler's checks, may be brought into the country. But remember that what is declared upon entry must be accounted for upon departure. There are plenty of taxi drivers and tourist guides eager to offer a "better than official rate" for your dollars, so proceed at your own risk (see "Derring-do and Burma's Bogus Buck System" below). Keep the currency conversion form with you at all times, and present it to the customs officials upon exit. Loss of this document can be very troublesome. It's likely you won't be asked for the document when you leave, as it's easy to bribe your way out of the mandatory changing of US$300 into Foreign Exchange Certificates (FECs) in the first place—and the Customs officers know it. Unless your entire tour has been prepaid in U.S. dollars outside the country, your hotel may demand payment in foreign currency or by credit card. Keep the receipt as an extra precaution.

Unspent kyats cannot be reconverted to U.S. dollars at the time of your departure. If you are unfortunate enough to possess enough kyat near your departure time that makes reconversion necessary, hope that you have a friend in Yangon. You'll have to do it on the black market. But a word of caution: there are far fewer folks around who change kyat into dollars than who change dollars into kyat. Ask only those you trust where to find someone to make this transaction for you. If the friend is a good one you can expect to pay the black marketeer 1 kyat for each 160 kyats or FEC$1 you want to reconvert into U.S. dollars.

Foreign Exchange Certificates (FECs)

Myanmar, quite simply, is the most tourist-unfriendly country in the world to exchange money. FECs come in the same denominations as U.S. dollars and when used as such, they possess an equal value. They can be used for payment anywhere U.S. dollars are accepted, such as hotels and upscale restaurants. They cannot legally be converted into U.S. dollars, however. So if you play by the rules, you'll have to spend at least US$300 during your stay in Myanmar— even if you're a businessman only in town for an afternoon meeting.

If you don't want to play by the rules, there are a couple of ways around this. Simply ask the exchange clerk if there is any possible way you can avoid having to change the $300 into FECs. More than likely he or she will respond that, for a gift, of course there is a way. In all likelihood, for a "gift" of US$10, the clerk will require you only to exchange US$100. This is really only marginally worth it if you're going to be in-country for only a few days (marginally because it saves you the headache of finding a black marketeer who will exchange dollars for your FECs; see below). If you're going to stay in Myanmar for the duration of your visa, this isn't a deal, as you'll spend the 300 bucks anyway.

Although the government says any amount of currency you exchange over US$300 can be redeemed in U.S. dollars, don't count on it. Most, if not all, banks that cash traveler's checks will only do it with FECs, even if you show evidence that you've already exchanged US$300 into FECs. You are again forced to deal with the prospect of leaving the country with useless currency. Cashing a traveler's check is a two-step process if you want dollars. First it must be cashed into FECs at a bank, then into dollars on the black market or an FEC exchange center, with each middleman taking his own chunk out of it. Expect to lose US$4 or more for each US$100 you want exchanged into U.S. dollars.

Derring-Do and Burma's Bogus Buck System

In the tradition of the country's propensity for generating uncannily appropriate acronyms for its various factions and functions—i.e., SLORC, KIA (Kachin Independence Army, or "Killed in Action") and FITs (Foreign Independent Travelers, who give the government plenty)—has been born FECs, or Foreign Exchange Certificates. (I'll leave the pronunciation of the acronym to the reader's imagination.)

For a negotiated "gift" of US$10 to the FEC exchange clerk at Yangon airport, you in all probability will be permitted to only exchange US$100 instead of the required US$300. At this point you and the bureaucrat exchanger will share a perceived covert camaraderie, as if you've both just stuck one to SLORC, a similar feeling shared by a couple of college kids who've just scrawled a "Free Suu Kyi!" slogan at the base of Shwedagon Pagoda and then ducked into a toilet. To further inflate your newly found sense of subversive self-importance is the fact that your new friend is wearing a SLORC uniform. How exciting!

Then the final reinforcement: the clerk leans and whispers to you that you can stick it further up SLORC's backside by exchanging your FECs on the black market at a rate of 150 kyats to the U.S. dollar. A deft smile crosses her lips, as if she's just given you the key to smuggling a trunkload of Jews out of 1939 Hamburg. My, the good fight feels good, despite the clerk handing you an official government receipt saying you exchanged only US$100, even signing it—the same receipt you are theoretically required to show Customs when you depart the country—proving that you exchanged US$300.

With the formula for revolution memorized, you accept the offer of your taxi driver (also, it turns out, a freedom-lover and coconspirator! And a real, live demonstrator, to boot!) to exchange your FECs into kyats on the black market at a rate of 150 kyats to the dollar. He seems overly in a hurry to perform this service for you, as if your FECs were stamped with an expiration date, like milk, and he senses a sour effluvium was emanating from your wallet. You take him up on the offer as he pulls down a dark alley and instructs you to wait in the car—there could be guys in Ray-Bans and Hawaiian shirts hanging around.

It isn't until you check into your hotel, after the driver has squealed his tires, that you discover from the receptionist that the black market rate is actually 167 kyats to the dollar, that the hotel will be quite happy to do that for you, or that you can visit a clearly marked FEC exchange office downtown on Thein Byu Road that will be equally delighted to perform the same service. And you'll find out that the black market rate is no longer the black market rate. It's the official rate.

So much for the revolution.

Internet Sites

http://www.freeburma.org
http://danenet.wicip.org/fbc
Two places to find information on Aung San Suu Kyi and contact other people interested in a democratic Burma (calling the country Myanmar is *tres outre* for these folks). There is also an electronic service called BurmaNet that will distribute information on the goings

on inside Myanmar. You might want to let all your boycott tuna, save the whales and Body Shop pals join in what is the '90s most "in" protest. To be politically correct, you're not supposed to visit Myanmar so that your dollars don't fall into the evil hands of the generals. *DP* takes no sides but you might actually want to visit Myanmar and form your own opinion.

http://theodore-sturgeon.mit.edu:8001/peacejam/aung/news/newsindex.html

In a Dangerous Place: Myanmar

The Barking Dogs

Another dog-hot day came to a close at the dusty Wanka (Huaykalok) Karen refugee camp near Mae Sot and the Moei River—the silty ribbon of lazy backwater that meanders between northern Thailand and the free-fire zone of eastern Burma. It was the kind of day that moved at the pace of a snapshot— nothing unusual for the thousands of ethnic Karens who call Wanka a temporary home, stowaways from the protracted fighting between the KNU and SLORC.

That night, though, life at Wanka would be turned upside down.

Camp Leader Mary On had heard the "barking dogs" before, a reference to the DKBA, or "SLORC stooges," who were always making threats at the Democratic Korean Buddhist Army (DKBA). But the 6,800 Karen refugees here at Wanka hadn't expected so much so suddenly.

It started with chirping on the walkie-talkies, as they, and the rest of the camp, were preparing for sleep. On and a couple of aides listened to the voices. The language was Burmese, not Karen—an ominous sound along this part of the Moei River.

"The words were 'act swiftly and methodically,'" On says. Before On had time to make sense of what she was hearing, flames began spitting skyward from the roof of the camp's primitive clinic.

Then the raiders came for Mary. She dashed for the brush. There were the shouts and cries of women and children in the disconnected orange darkness, and the staccato reports of AK-47s being discharged. The soldiers reached On's spartan hut and set it aflame—and then swiftly and methodically razed hundreds of homes in the camp during the next 75 minutes of terror.

At 11 P.M., Wanka was engulfed in flames, but the job was only half-finished when the marauders heard sirens in the distance. Mistaking the sounds for an approaching company of Thai soldiers, the 137 Burmese and DKBA soldiers slipped from the Karen camp—along with 50 porters, charged with hauling anything that could be found in Wanka of value—across the Moei River into the blackness of the Burmese jungle.

At least 20,000 ethnic Karen had spilled into Thailand during this final bloody overture in early 1997 by SLORC in its race to "reconcile" the country in time to join the Association of Southeast Asian Nations by July. Of course, this ascent into legitimacy would necessitate silencing the KNU, the longest single running insurgency in Asia and the only faction of the 16 separate groups fighting the Yangon regime that had not made peace with SLORC. In all, some 100,000 Karen refugees were forced into camps inside Thailand by March 1997.

The KNU has been fighting various Rangoon/Yangon governments since 1948 in its bid for independence. The current regime, considered the most brutal since Burma forged its own independence from Britain the same year, has made crushing the remaining pockets of KNU guerrillas—scattered along the Thai border near the provinces of Tak, Ratchburi, Kanchanaburi and Chumpon—its main priority in 1997.

SLORC deployed more than 100,000 troops in 1997 to mop up the remaining 3,000 or so KNU fighters still active in the jungle, guerrilla forces still fiercely loyal to KNU president General Bo Mya and the four platforms of Karen patriarch Saw Ba Oo Gyi: "Surrender is out of the question; we will retain our arms; the Karen state must be realized; we will decide our political destiny."

Shortly after the raid on Wanka near Mae Sot, both refugees and fighting spilled over into Thailand at Umphang, about 200 kilometers south of Mae Sot. Burmese regulars with their butterfly nets set on automatic were chasing Karens through the forest—in this case, Thai forest—and the Thais began firing back. Flashpoints dotted the Thai-Burma map: Umphang, Songklaburi, Kanchanaburi, Ratchaburi—even as far south as Chumpon. Refugees began streaming across the border in Kanchanaburi; some were being turned back. Generals both from SLORC and the Thai army met at Tachilek to smooth feathers and get their photos taken in starched uniforms.

Mae Sot enjoys many of the benefits of Thai prosperity; modern, clean banks, service stations and hotels flank well-paved roads. Souvenir markets spill into the street at the unfinished Friendship Bridge on the Moei River. A smattering of Western tourists apply sunscreen and point camcorders toward forbidden Myanmar on the far side of the brown river. Unshaven Burmese men dressed in *longyis* lurk in the shadows of the gem stalls hawking hidden cartons of Marlboro; their mastery of English vocabulary is limited to the word "Marlboro." When this one-word sales pitch is combined with a smoking gesture of two fingers to the lips, it appears as if a Marlboro is what the salesman seeks rather than what he is offering. Naively believing the former, I hand one such black market vendor a cigarette from my own pack of Marlboros. Bemused, he lights it anyway.

The Wanka refugee camp is pitched in a giant, rolling field of parched grasses and brush. It is a brown, dusty and desolate moonscape that seems to have been selected by a freshman at refugee camp design school—or an A student. Every available twig and crusted banana leaf has been utilized to shelter this rickety, unsturdy city of 6,831. The little vegetation here has been scorched to the color of old tobacco. Smoke lofts lazily in the midday heat from lean-tos and small hootches.

A procession of rail-thin, *longyi*-clad men and women stoically accompany a tiny coffin down a rutted path past their sun-skewered thatched homes to the camp's Christian cemetery. They pass a spirited volleyball match between Wanka's more fit being contested beneath "the Dome," a canopy of corrugated, oxidized aluminum sheets perched atop makeshift bamboo scaffolding to shade the players from the searing sun. It is Wanka's version of a national stadium.

But what is most noticeable is the destruction of what little is here to begin with. Squares of scorched earth stick out in the landscape like a bad effort at Game Boy. What were trees are now charred stumps. Three of the bare, blackened trunks rise together like the crosses Christ and the two thieves were executed on.

Mary On is walking on a narrow dirt path sluicing through a gauntlet of charred frames and ash-covered foundations that had been homes before the SLORC raid. A small child sifts through the soot at the base of one gutted dwelling, panning the ash like a gold prospector in search of anything that might be of value. At first, it is not apparent that Mary On is a woman at all. She is diminutive and brushes her short wavy hair from a wide left part, like a schoolboy whose mother fusses with his trusses for him. She is also smoking a pipe and wearing golf trousers with a white belt.

On is the camp leader at Wanka; she is also the vice chairman of the Karen Refugee Committee and has been the KNU's matriarch since firing her first machine gun at Yangon troops in the early 1960s. On was born in 1934 in Yangon, the daughter of strict Baptists. Her father was active in the Karen rebel movement early on. By the time she was serving on the front lines with KNU guerrillas in the Pegu Mountains, there was little doubt where her loyalties were, and equally as little doubt she was prepared to die for them: the KNU's Four Principles. Throughout the 1970s On smuggled guns to the Karen guerrillas operating in the Delta and, in the 1980s, fought Yangon troops from the KNU base at Wanka. When that was finally overrun in 1984, she was asked to oversee the refugees at Huaykalok.

And On runs a tight ship. The lives of the camp's inhabitants are regimented; the children are remarkably disciplined and well-behaved. Wanka is meticulously clean, despite having been almost entirely razed by the SLORC and DKBA raiders. There was a school here with an American teacher. He left after the attack. The camp has yet to rebuild its clinic, as well as the makeshift churches that were destroyed in the fires. Despite the destruction, perhaps because of it, there is serenity here, a lack of urgency and despair. The rutted, dusty road that snakes through Wanka is flanked by the flimsy shacks still left standing; many serve as stores, selling sundries, food and "household" items. The camp's water is drawn from artesian wells. NGOs such as the American Refugee Committee help feed the population and aid the sick.

"The most important thing is to be clean," On says, her English flawless. "Most of the men are off fighting the SLORC, so I have to implore the camp's women about cleanliness. Cleanliness is the way to survive under these conditions." The words of a headmistress, but also the words of someone who is as comfortable with an M-16 as with a kitchen spoon. On is part Mother Teresa, part Joan of Arc. More part Joan of Arc.

"The KNU will fight to the end, to the single last person," she says. "The SLORC and the barking dogs know this. Stooges, all of them—like a Mickey Mouse under the table of the SLORC. The SLORC acts with their name. There are seven million Karen people in Irrawaddy Division. We will not be defeated. All we want is peace. And if we get peace, we would go back tonight. We wouldn't wait until tomorrow."

The KNU held four rounds of negotiations with SLORC between December 1995 and November 1996, and was seeking a fifth round of peace talks when Yangon launched a massive dry season offensive against the Karens in January 1997. Although the Yangon-backed DKBA, a KNU spin-off that sold out to SLORC, is blamed for most of the attacks on Karen refugees living inside Thai territory, thereby sparing SLORC from accusations of direct military involvement on foreign soil, On knows better.

"These aren't DKBA who crossed into Thai territory and burned our camp," she says. "This is what the SLORC wants you to believe. The men that night were mostly SLORC regulars. There were 107 SLORC soldiers, 30 DKBA barking dogs and 50 porters to carry all of our belongings and food away. What they couldn't carry away they burned. Their leaders were SLORC commanders. They ordered everyone from their homes. Their commands to the villagers were in Burmese, not in Karen.

"The soldiers demanded that we return to Burma. The villagers asked them: 'Are you going to put us in forced labor? Are you going to throw us in prison?' (The commander) said he couldn't guarantee it. 'Then of course we will not go,' the villagers said. It is better to stay in Thailand as a refugee than go back to Burma as a slave."

There had been some forewarning of the raid. A few days earlier, On had received a letter from the "barking dogs," signed by Chit Thu, demanding that the refugees return to Burma or face violent consequences. But On had received such threats before, and thought this latest note to be merely another SLORC wolf cry.

"We were totally unprepared for the attack," she says. After setting fire to the clinic, the soldiers set off for On's home about 200 meters away. On was hiding. "I never sleep in the same place. I am always moving."

The soldiers set fire to On's home first, then began randomly torching the camp's 1,360 flimsy homes. When they had finished, 690 had burned to the ground. Porters with bamboo baskets were ordered to strip the houses and small stores clean before they were set afire. Women screamed and tried to salvage their belongings. Soldiers shouted that they would be killed and fired into the air. The raiders next burned two Baptist churches, a Pentecostal church and ransacked the camp's Catholic church, according to On. They spared the camp's Buddhist monastery.

Finally, at 11 P.M., came the sirens. The SLORC and DKBA attackers, along with their porters, fled Wanka across the Moei River. The sirens were not those of the Thai army, but of a Mae Sot fire fighting detachment. "We didn't get any help at all," On says.

On is not quick to bite the hand that feeds them, however. Since 1984, Thailand, with little help from the rest of the world, has welcomed and provided food and shelter for hundreds of thousands of refugees and ethnic insurgents battling the Yangon regime. "We owe the Thai people a lot. The Thais have given us peace for 13 years," On admits.

Thailand's generosity is born of two reasons: out of mercy for those displaced by war, and the strategic advantage anti-Yangon groups ringing Thailand's border give Bangkok in the form of a buffer between two traditionally hostile nations.

But it is Thai strategy that worries On. News that at least 900 Karens, fleeing into Kanchanaburi province to escape the early 1997 fighting, were forced back into Myanmar is foreboding to Thailand's displaced Karens. Thailand, in recent years, has raced to do business with SLORC's generals, to capitalize on Myanmar's opening economy. And it doesn't inspire Thailand's humanitarian concerns that Karen guerrillas are the only remaining obstacle to Myanmar's $1 billion natural gas pipeline—being built by French oil company Total and U.S. fuel giant Unocal through Myanmar's Tenasserim region—which will ensure Thailand of much of its energy needs.

Meanwhile, On and the Karens at Wanka patiently wait for the day they can walk the few meters back into Myanmar as free people. On's assertions that ultimately, somehow, the United Nations and the United States will mediate the Karen crisis to a favorable resolution sound hollow, however, but indeed reflect a different reality: the Karens are simply outgunned, and that vested interest in their struggle is waning. This suggests, of course, that vested interest is the only interest outsiders have ever had in the KNU, and that as the last of Myanmar's 16 ethnic insurgencies to still do battle with SLORC, it will become the 16th footnote in the legacy of SLORC's internationally sanctioned dictatorship.

"If you've come to see the Karen, you will see the Karen in a museum," On says. "This is the policy of the SLORC."

For the KNU, the barking dogs are also biting. For the first time since World War II, Myanmar's entire 1,600-kilometer border with Thailand is thought to be under government control. But despite losing its bases of operation, General Bo Mya's fighters continue to pick and peck at Myanmar troops in the jungle. It's the mischievous gleam in On's eyes that reminds a visitor that the Karens are to Myanmar what Vietnam was to the United States, what Afghanistan was to Russia—and have been for 50 years. On is part of the reason Yangon might postpone its hunt for a curator.

—**Wink Dulles**

Lagos

Nigeria
★★★

Formula 419

Four-one-nine. That's Nigeria's code for criminal fraud. Travelers know that a trip to corrupt, impoverished Nigeria can make even the hardened adventurer swear off travel to Africa entirely. For nearly three-quarters of its 40-year history, Africa's most populated country has been bullied and bilked by military despots who promise elections and then spend more time shopping at Harrods than running the country.

Finally, in May 1999, Nigeria got its first democratically elected president since 1979. Of course, he's a general—but at least he was elected. We're taking bets on how long the Olusegun Obasanjo government will last. He's taken over an economy in its most dismal shape since independence from Great Britain in 1960, feuding ethnic groups and depressed oil prices, the country's only significant foreign exchange earner. It's unlikely that Obasanjo will stuff his personal coffers with oil money, not with ethnic Ijaw activists attacking pipelines and other Nigerians lighting Marlboros while filling Coke bottles from sabotaged petrol pipes.

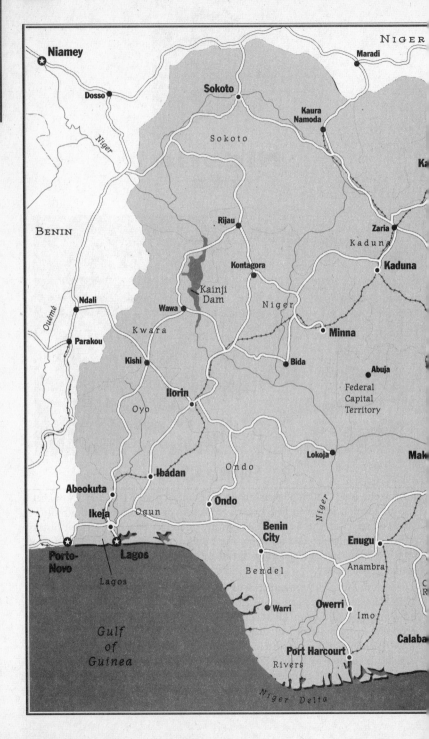

In the meantime, what do the enterprising Nigerians do to bolster their economy? In keeping with its tainted image as one of the most corrupt nations in Africa, there are a number of quasi-sanctioned, clever scams that sucker in dozens of unsuspecting foreigners every year (see below).

Nigeria's biggest export is oil (with Uncle Sam slurping up about half). Yet that darn oil money keeps getting lost. Former president (and, of course, army general) Babangida managed to misplace US$12.2 billion dollars worth. A black hole if there ever was one. By mid-1999, at least US$770 million of stolen state cash had been recovered from Abacha's relatives and cronies.

Shell Oil Co. has sucked about US$30 billion worth of Nigerian oil since its discovery in 1958, yet the Ogoni tribe still lives in poverty in the swamps. When they tested the trickle-down theory, their leaders (including Ken Saro-Wiwa) were hanged in November 1995, and the Ogonis chased into the swamps. Another black hole.

As one would expect, even though the Christian south is where the oil riches are coffered, the government has always been from the Muslim north.

Grow Hair, Pick Up Chicks and Make Big Money in Nigerian Oil Deals!

Nigerians have finally figured out how to bring corruption and misery straight to you without you having to leave the comfort of your office. Nigerian business scams are confidence schemes, designed to exploit the trust you develop in your Nigerian partner and to bilk you of goods, services or money. The scams are flexible, and operators adapt them to take the greatest advantage of the target— you.

Every week, the U.S. embassy in Lagos tries to console victims of these scams by which businesspeople have lost sums ranging from a few thousand to upwards of one million dollars. Patsies who have traveled all the way to Nigeria to clinch these "lucrative" deals have been threatened, assaulted or even killed. Local police couldn't care less, and Nigerian officials find the whole thing funny. The U.S. embassy can't do much more than lend you a toothbrush and a quarter to call your mother for airfare. Some Nigerian immigration officials have begun to warn folks upon arrival at Lagos airport, but the lemmings keep arriving to pick up their pot of gold.

Scams range from attempts to engage American businesspeople in fictitious money-transfer schemes to fraudulent solicitations to supply goods in fulfillment of nonexistent Nigerian government contracts. Most scam operators are sophisticated and may take victims to staged meetings, often held in borrowed offices at Nigerian government ministries. They do their research and can often provide plausible, but nonexistent, orders written on seemingly genuine ministerial stationery, replete with official stamps and seals. Nigerian business scams are not always easy to recognize, and any unsolicited business proposal should be carefully scrutinized.

It is not possible to describe how each of several hundred different scams works in Nigeria, but they all center on greed (yours), gullibility (yours) and money (yours).

This scam stuff is so much fun that we won't even dwell on the conflict (Muslim north versus Christian south) that ripped the country apart during the Biafran War, the billions of oil dollars that go straight into the pockets of the select few, or the overall poverty and population growth that plague this large country. For now, we just keep seeing how many suckers will travel here looking to make their fortune.

For information on how to verify the legitimacy of unsolicited proposals from Nigerian businesses/government agencies, contact the Nigeria Desk Officer, Office of Africa, US Department of Commerce, Washington, DC 20230.

As OPEC's fourth-largest oil producer, Nigeria is oil-rich and human-rights poor, the scam capital of the world, a boot camp for fatigue-clad banana dictators, and the Bermuda Triangle of currency. For all but 9 of its 40 years of independence, Nigeria has been ruled by the military. But in May 1999, army general and former Nigerian strongman Olusegun Obasanjo became Nigeria's first elected president since 1979, replacing the boys chomping on stogies behind Ray-Bans working for General Sani Abacha and later General Abdulsalami Abubakar after Abacha died in mid-1998. Abacha and Abubakar (to a lesser extent) and a previous succession of military rulers siphoned off the country's multibillion dollar annual oil earnings, returning hardly a trickle to Nigeria's oil-producing regions. Years of pilfering (for example, in one hand-in-the-cookie-jar case, Nigeria Airways said in February 1996 that the US$100 million paid by the government in 1992 to create an international airline had vanished without a trace) have left 108 million Nigerians largely without power, communications, education, health care and, ironically, fuel. In the final weeks of Abdulsalami's rule, a torrent of unbudgeted spending slashed Nigerian foreign reserves from $7 billion to $4.6 billion. The budget deficit for the first quarter of 1999 surpassed the military government's projections for the entire year. Officials said the first quarter deficit at 38 billion naira (US$410 million) compared with the yearly projection of 34 billion naira. Ouch.

Obasanjo has his work cut out for him. More than 250 ethnic groups in Nigeria's population of 108 million have been manhandled by eight different military rulers since 1960. And the situation looks only bleaker. Fully two-thirds of the 55,000 people in Nigerian jails have never had a trial. In the Niger Delta, the Pengassan oil workers' union are threatening to pull out unless their grievances are addressed. And the local Ogonis, whose land Nigeria's oil is pumped from, have demanded a greater share of the wealth. In short, after 15 years of military rule, Nigerians are going to demand greater freedom and wealth—and if it doesn't come quickly (it won't), Obasanjo probably won't be around too long, and Nigeria will continue to be what it's always been: a capricious non-nation of back-stabbing clans and ethnic groups thrown under the same flag by colonialism.

When You Gotta Go, You Gotta Go

A group of chanting, dancing and shouting youths were seen parading down the streets of Kano with an unusual object on the end of a long stick. It was the head of Gideon Akaluka, an automotive spare parts dealer who had been accused of using the Koran for toilet paper. He was originally arrested and detained for the charges, but a group of Islamic youths broke into the jail, beheaded him and presented his head to their traditional leader, the emir of Kano. The emir sent a messenger to tell the crowd that they had acted in a barbaric manner and that he was shocked. The crowd reacted by caning the courier with 100 strokes. There was never any proof of the victim's guilt brought forward. Don't expect many job applicants at Kano Express Couriers.

Ladies and Gentlemen, the President—Olusegun Obasanjo

Yeah, you heard that right, folks. Nigeria's finally got a president. An elected one, at that. And the whole darn election was monitored and pronounced legitimate, unsullied and free of ballot-box stuffing by guys like former U.S. president Jimmy Carter and ex-South African president Nelson Mandela. If a fellow like Carter, who is currently enjoying the strong credentials of having been weak in office, can say there was no vote rigging, then, believe me, there was no vote rigging. Obasanjo became the first elected president in Nigeria in 15 years on May 29, 1999, succeeding military ruler General Abdulsalami Abubakar who, himself, seized power after the sudden death of Nigerian tyrant Sani Abacha in June 1998. Obasanjo is a sixty-something pig farmer who also lists on his CV military dictator, innumerable offspring from innumerable marriages, accomplishments in snooker, squash and table tennis as well as an explosive temper. Obasanjo was Nigeria's military ruler who relinquished power to the country's last elected civilians in 1979. He was trained as a soldier in Britain and India and led a Nigerian army commando unit in the 1967–1970 Biafran civil war that almost single-handedly defeated the rebels in that conflict. Later, he was sentenced to 15 years in jail for plotting a coup against Abacha. Now Obasanjo inherits Nigeria's worst economic crisis since independence from Britain in October 1960.

Olusegun Obasanjo
President
State House
Abuja, Federal Capital Territory, Nigeria
Fax: [234] (9) 523-2138
http://www.lagos-online.com/head_of_state.htm

The First Ladies

In the U.S., there was Lady Bird and then Pat; there was Betty and her Palm Springs dope rehab clinic. Rosalynn's husband "felt lust in his heart." Nancy said no to drugs. Though Barbara looked Bushed–like she could have been George's mother–she didn't have any competition. Only Hillary Rodham wasn't quite sure if she was America's only First Lady. Meanwhile, Olusegun Obasanjo makes Bill Clinton look like a Franciscan friar. When Stella Abebe married Obasanjo in 1977, she wasn't entirely sure how many other women were married to Obasanjo as well. Even if there is the opportunity to grab Hillary-like headlines alongside her husband these days, Mrs. Obasanjo will undoubtedly face stiff competition. Obasanjo's obsession with women, his harem and a string of concubines are legendary. As one local reporter observed: "Gen. Obasanjo repeatedly has a giant appetite for women. Inevitably, Stella's entry into Obasanjo's life meant that she walked straight into a crowded field of Obasanjo's women." But Stella is the gal most often seen at Obasanjo's side in public. Nevertheless, if Obasanjo ever decides to host a bilateral summit, the visiting first lady should best prepare herself for a photo op that'll look like a group shot of Miss Africa preliminary contestants. Let's all hope that it's not Tipper Gore.

http://www.lagos-online.com/1999_constitution_of_the_federal.htm

General Sani Abacha's Ghost

Yeah, he's dead, but his legacy lives on. As Nigeria's seventh military dictator, Sani Abacha took destitution, murder, repression, corruption and greed to a new stratosphere. This guy made Idi Amin look like a bona fide Berkeley philanthropist. The fat man was unscrupulous, power mad and paranoid. He rarely left Nigeria (who the hell would have him over for a state dinner anyhow?) and was involved in the last three coup attempts before finally taking the government's reigns on November 17, 1993. His first act was to abolish all democratic institutions, including the senate, the national assembly and the state councils. As well, he banned all political parties. He swept in military rule and purged the government of all civilians and the army of officers loyal to former president Major General Ibrahim Babangida, who himself seized power through a coup in August 1985. Without any political or ideological agenda at all, Abacha busied himself stuffing his pockets with embezzled cash—and lining those of the brown-nosing northern primroses—and executing dissidents. On March 22, 1999, US$75 million in missing state funds was located and recovered from former state ministers, cronies and relatives of Abacha. Those seizures brought the total amount recovered to date from Abacha's heists to just over US$760 million. This guy may have been no Suharto (US$15 billion pilfered), Mobuto Sese Seko (US$5 billion), Ethiopia's Haile Selassie (US$2 billion) or the Philippines' Marcos (US$10 billion), but Abacha could definitely get invited to the same blackjack table as Baby Doc Duvalier—who ripped off Haiti for US$500 million.

Buck Naked

In August 1998, hundreds of pissed pensioners, who hadn't received a pension payment since 1993, went on a rampage in Kogi State and beat a local official senseless, leaving him in the streets naked. In all probability, the official hadn't been paid his salary since 1993 and probably reported to work the next day naked.

Truth Commission

Nigeria's taking a cue from South Africa; President Olusegun Obasanjo has established a Truth Commission to investigate assassination and other human rights abuses in Nigeria since 1994. Like a *Dallas* rerun, don't expect a lot of people to tell the truth, or even stick around to lie for that matter. More than 40 two-star generals have so far been bounced by Obasanjo. Two hundred other high-ranking officers are also expected to be sacked. One man Obasanjo is certain to subpoena is Lieutenant Colonel Frank Omenka, the former director of military intelligence under Sani Abacha's regime. "Colonel Terror," as Omenka is popularly known, didn't even dare show up at small claims court in June 1999 over a property dispute. Think he'll pull a P. W. Botha? Obasanjo has vowed to purge the military of all but "apolitical officers," which in Nigeria is an oxymoron.

Shell Oil Company

Oil accounts for 90 percent of Nigeria's foreign exchange and most of it is getting pumped out by Royal Dutch Shell. Shell's been catching a lot of flak from bleeding heart groups—from human rights lobbies to environmentalists. Some of it's deserved, some isn't. Shell has also been dissed for offering too few jobs to local folks, but also lauded for having pressured the government to develop the area. Nigeria sits atop a confirmed 20 billion barrels of oil. Shell (Nigeria Shell) accounts for half of the government's income. So what's the big deal about the unexplained loss of a few billion dollars here or there? On the other hand, the oil giant is involved in a US$3.6 billion liquefied natural gas project that's gotten a clean slate from the green crowd and can only be for the welfare of all Nigerians. Militant activities, including ethnic strife between Ijaw and Itsekiri tribesmen, have been on the increase in the oil-producing Niger River Delta, forcing Shell to reduce its output.

http://www.shell.com

The Ogonis

The Ogoni people are a small minority in Nigeria—perhaps numbering 500,000—but Abacha systematically raped their oil-rich land, and, of course, the Ogonis have nothing to show for it. So when Ken Saro-Wiwa decided to champion the group's rights, he and eight of his buddies were promptly executed by the government. Nigeria was suspended from the Commonwealth (which is like getting a bimonthly bye in the weekly bridge club), and Britain—in protest—recalled its ambassador, who was back in his Lagos digs by the middle of January 1996, only a couple of months after Saro-Wiwa was hanged and Abacha had his wrists slapped by the West. Now, it's back to the business of pumping for petrobucks. Hey, life goes on.

http://www.gem.co.za/ELA/ogoni.fact.html

The Yorubas and the Odudua Peoples' Congress (OPC)

Although President Olusegun Obasanjo is an ethnic Yoruba, he's not one of their buddies. Mostly because Obasanjo is in bed with the army and maintains strong ties with the Hausa-speaking north of the country, which has dominated Nigeria's military leadership for decades. The Yorubas are looking to carve a separate Yoruba state out of southwestern Nigeria. OPC youths often clash with the cops in Lagos and get carved up themselves.

http://landow.stg.brown.edu/post/nigeria/yorubarel.html

Militant Ijaws (Federated Niger-Delta Izon Communities)

The Niger Delta's largest ethnic community is the Ijaw people. In October 1998, Ijaw militants seized 20 fuel pipeline flow stations and closed the taps, shutting off a third of Nigeria's 2 million barrels-a-day exports. They control large swaths of the swamp south of Warri, patrolling their soggy surf & turf in speedboats and left unmolested by government troops for the most part. Like rock hounds, the Ijaws chisel away at the pipelines, hacking holes and disrupting the flow of billions of dollars worth of oil. They say they're not pissed at the oil companies, but at the government, instead. Dan Ekpebide, the movement's leader summed up the Ijaw's objectives: "If you give a man a fish, he will eat for a day. If you teach him to fish, he will eat for life." (He meant to say: "If you fill a man's fuel tank up, he will drive for a day. If you teach him to drive, he'll get better gas mileage.") We're not sure what that means in the context of commandeering oil pipeline pump stations, but it's a good sound bite. On April 19, 1999, at least two ethnic Ijaw activists (followers of the Egbesu cult of the Ijaw god of war) were killed by security forces at Ikebiri as they attacked an oil pipeline operated by Italy's Agip oil company with guns, machetes, spears, rocks—whatever they could get their hands on. In early June 1999, at least 50 people were killed in an Ijaw speedboat attack against ethnic Itsekiris near Chevron's tank farm at Arunton. But rather than sticks and stones, the Ijaws were packing automatic weapons. These guys are taking cues from Sri Lanka's Sea Tigers and are becoming the Navy SEALS of Nigerian clan clashes.

http://www.nigerianext.com/Ijawupdate.html

National Democratic Coalition (NADECO)

NADECO is a coalition of pro-democracy and human rights groups that has been accused of a rash of bombings in 1997. All the bombings have fit the same profile: the targeting of an army transport vehicle using a remote-controlled device. Fifteen suspected members of NADECO, including Nobel Prize–winning writer Wole Soyinka, were charged in March 1997 with conspiring to wage war on the nation and the detonation of bombs. Of the 15 busted, 11 were already in jail and the remaining 4 out of the country, including Soyinka. To date, the government hasn't identified any of the attackers in the dozen or so blasts since December 1996.

http://www.bellona.no/e/press/nigeria.htm

A passport and visa are required. Visas, at no charge, are valid for one entry within 12 months of issue. You'll need one photo, a yellow fever vaccination, proof of onward/return transportation and, for a tourist visa, a letter of invitation. Business visas require a letter from counterparts in Nigeria and a letter of introduction from a U.S. company. For further information, contact the following:

Embassy of the Republic of Nigeria

2201 M Street, NW
Washington, DC 20037
Tel.: (202) 822-1500 or 1522
http://www.lagos-online.com/nigerian_missions_abroad.htm
http://www.lagos-online.com/visa_requirements.htm

Consulate General (in New York)

Tel.: (212) 715-7200

If you think you are going to save money by flying Nigeria Airlines from Europe, think again. Remember, NA flights are banned from entering the U.S., and one of its new Airbus A310s was nabbed by the Belgians for nonpayment of debt. Another NA plane had to make an emergency landing in Algiers and has been sitting there for months waiting for spare parts. Many flights are canceled because politicians borrow the planes to go shopping in Europe or just feel like visiting their money in Saudi Arabia.

Nigeria is primarily dependent on road transportation. During the oil boom in the mid-1970s, a number of long-distance roads were built—but arteries have become dilapidated in recent years due to the civil war and shrinking government revenues. And the accident rate in Nigeria is nearly the worst in the world. There is a nominal railway system, but even this has fallen into disrepair.

Lagos

The capital is a free-for-all, plagued by acute crime. Violent crime committed in broad daylight is the norm, and foreigners are particularly targeted and sometimes murdered for no reason. Shakedowns, muggings, carjackings, robberies, assaults, armed break-ins and even murders are frequently committed by uniformed police and soldiers in the capital. The Nigerian government has not heeded urgent U.S. embassy requests for the perpetrators to be disciplined. Unlike other coconut coalitions in the Third World, Nigeria possesses a capital city that is every bit as dangerous as the countryside.

http://lagos.citynews.com/

The Rest of the Country

Factional fighting continues in Nigeria. Areas of noted danger include the border region in the northeast near Lake Chad—where outbursts of communal violence are common—usually involving clashes between Muslim fundamentalists and Christian proselytizers, southern Nigeria along the Niger River and regions in and outside Lagos in the southwest. Armed break-ins, muggings and carjackings are especially prevalent in the north.

There has been an increase in the number of unauthorized automobile checkpoints. These checkpoints are operated by bands of police, soldiers or bandits posing as or operating with police or soldiers, whose personnel should be considered armed and dangerous. Many incidents, including murder, illustrate the increasing risks of road travel in Nigeria. Reports of threats against firms and foreign workers in the petroleum sector recur from time to time. Chadian troop incursions have reportedly occurred at the border area in the far northeast, near Lake Chad.

http://www.nigeria.com/News_Room/Newspapers/newspapers.html

Bakassi Peninsula

Nigeria and Cameroon have been duking it out in the disputed Bakassi Peninsula, where the two nations have long been at odds. Since February 1994, the armed forces of the two nations have frequently clashed in the peninsula, a series of impoverished islands in the oil-rich Gulf of Guinea, which each claims to be its territory. Elf-Sarepca, the Cameroonian unit of France's Elf-Aquitaine, and several other oil firms are exploring for crude oil there and just south of the islands.

http://www.icj-cij.org/icjwww/idecisions/isummaries/icnsummary960315.htm

Disorganized Crime

Nigeria has one of the highest crime rates in the world. There are 94 murders and 1,256 thefts for every 100,000 people. Murder often accompanies even the simplest burglary.

Organized Crime

In April 1996, German police uncovered a Nigerian organized crime ring that was operating throughout Europe, and which was allegedly involved in counterfeiting, drug running, and credit card fraud. Over the past few years, German police investigations of these crimes have inevitably led them to Nigeria. Since 1990, the Nigerians have worked the following fraudulent trick: Offers were made to private individuals and medium-sized companies via letters or fax that they should help with the transfer of millions of dollars from Nigeria to Germany. In return, between 30 and 40 percent of the amounts were promised. In reality, however, the gangsters were interested in collecting high amounts for alleged charges in Nigeria from those whom they were cheating. By investigating these scams, the Germans were able to uncover that the Nigerians suspected of the crimes obviously were part of well-organized, internationally active groups.

Nigeria's organized crime enterprises are active in at least 60 countries. And the United States provides Nigerian scam artists a barrelful of suckers. The U.S. Secret Service estimates that Nigerian advance fee fraud letter scams cost Americans US$250 million a year. But back to basics. The South African government says Nigerian criminal operations have penetrated the entire southern African region, with enterprises in heroin and cocaine trafficking, alien smuggling, document fraud, car theft and gang activities.

Fuel Shortages

Nigeria possesses four major oil refineries and produces 2 million barrels of oil a day but can't even gas up its own cars. Nigeria's gas crisis of 1997 brought traffic to a standstill. Thousands of commuters in Lagos had nowhere to go and no way of getting there. Queues of cars outside empty fuel pumps made the U.S. gas lines of the 1970s look like the turnstiles at a Chicago Cubs game.

Pipelines (Fill 'er Up)

Vandals, youths and "rebels" routinely tap Nigeria's fuel pipelines for the much needed gasoline they can't find anywhere else. On October 17, 1998, at one brick pumping station in Ataiworo, a valve some of the vandals were siphoning from got stuck open. Gasoline came gushing from the pipeline, drawing entire villages packed down with pop bottles and buckets to collect the bounty. Then some idiot decided to play Marlboro Man and lit a fag. In Nigeria's biggest human disaster, more than 700 people were killed in the ensuing fireball. A thousand more, barely alive, lay hideously charred in the local hospital. Their families snatched them from their beds as rumors spread the pilferers would be arrested.

Lawmaking

Voodoo or doo-doo design? An omen for the new Nigerian government? Or was it just a helluvalot of rain? And will it cause cancer? The inauguration of Nigeria's new House of Representatives turned into a brief ceremony on June 4, 1999, when suddenly the roof of the House Chamber caved in on the fledgling lawmakers, sending many scurrying for their lives. The cave-in of the ceiling showered legislators with waterlogged asbestos. Olusegun Obasanjo's Truth Commission may add a few minutes to its agenda after the lung cancer lawsuits start getting filed.

"New Breed" Churches

These instant churches promise to their followers wealth, jobs and other miracles. Thousands of Nigerians now take part in religious moneymaking rituals, which can occasionally get out of hand. In one instance in Imo state, outraged crowds burned down the houses of suspected "new breed" church members after the discovery of the head of a missing child, two tongues, skulls and other human remains on the grounds of the Overcomers Church. These churches have sprung up all over Nigeria. The only folks getting rich, though, are their owners/pastors, who trot the globe in private jets and show up for sermons in imported luxury cars.

Vigilantes

Vigilantes roaming Ebute Metta in Lagos state have struck fear into both the local populace and the gendarmes alike. In just a few days in June 1999, one group killed 11 suspected thieves by picking them up from their homes and setting them ablaze.

Uniforms

Many petty and violent crimes committed against foreigners are performed by bandits dressed in police or military uniforms. Bandits regularly murder foreigners without provocation. As well, foreigners are frequently robbed, assaulted and/or killed by legitimate police officers and soldiers, who are never reprimanded or punished by the government. Pickpockets and confidence artists, some posing as local immigration and other government officials, are especially common at Murtala Muhammad Airport. In addition to harassment and shakedowns of American citizens by officials at airports and throughout Nigeria, there have been reports of violent attacks by purported government officials on Americans and other foreigners.

Going to University

University life is never dull. It seems over 500 kids have been expelled from Nigeria's 39 universities for indulging in a little organized mayhem. Over 32 people have died in two years, 12 in the first few months of 1999, and their deaths have been attributed to secret societies, or cults, with colorful names like the Pirates, Black Ax, the Buccaneers and the Green Berets. It seems that after the government banned student unions with political agendas, the groups quickly grew from their origins in the '80s on the University of Jos in the north and have now infiltrated places like the Edo State University Ekpoma, whose students have set up "Operation Flush," which enables students to "identify cultists and

NIGERIA

make the school uncomfortable for them." The cultist groups were created to correct the ills of Nigerian society. I guess they would get an "F" so far.

Road Travel

Road travel is extremely dangerous throughout Nigeria, but particularly in the south and the northeastern border near Lake Chad. Unauthorized automobile checkpoints are set up regularly in rural areas and manned by armed bandits or police/military personnel with the sole purpose of hijacking, assaulting and/or robbing motorists. Foreigners are targets for carjackings, robberies and violence. Most of Nigeria's roads are pothole-ridden and nearly impassable.

Flying

The U.S. FAA has prohibited aircraft from Nigerian Airlines from landing in the United States due to the unsafe upkeep of the airline's fleet. Additionally, the quality of fuel used in the airliners doesn't meet international minimum requirements—it's low-grade, often dirty and spiked with other ingredients that don't help planes stay off the ground.

You don't want to get sick in Nigeria. In recent times, more than 2,000 of Nigeria's doctors have fled to the United States, with another 2,000 opting for Saudi Arabia, the Gulf States, Canada and Britain. Health services are generally limited to the cities, and are only affordable for wealthy Nigerians. Modern medicine is nonexistent in rural areas. Public health has crashed with the government's pilfering of anything of value sent into the country. Yellow fever, chloroquine-resistant malaria, trachoma and yaws are the biggest medical threats in Nigeria. Malaria is found in all parts of the country, including all urban areas, and the risk is present all year. There is a 17 percent risk of malaria exposure. Dracunculiasis, meningitis, lassa fever, leishmaniasis (both cutaneous and visceral), rabies, relapsing fever, African sleeping sickness and typhus (endemic flea-borne, epidemic louse-borne and scrub) are prevalent. Muslim northern Nigeria is the area worst affected by the meningitis scourge that has killed thousands of people in the Sahal belt of West Africa. Nigeria is also receptive to dengue fever, and schistosomiasis may be found throughout the country. There is one doctor for every 6,134 people in Nigeria.

Outbreaks of meningitis, cholera, measles and gastroenteritis swept across the arid areas of West Africa in March and April 1996, particularly in Nigeria. Around 70,000 people in 17 African countries have been afflicted by meningitis alone, and nearly 9,000 have died, more than half of them in Nigeria. The health problem was seen as so grave by Saudi Arabia that it banned all Nigerians from entering the Kingdom to perform the annual pilgrimage, or hajj, to the Islamic world's two holiest shrines. Meningitis is inflammation of the brain and spinal cord. If treated in time, its victims can be saved, although complications can bring deafness or loss of the fingers.

The Federal Republic of Nigeria is a tropical country (356,668 square miles, or 923,770 square kilometers) with two different climatic zones. The south is hot, rainy and humid for much of the year, while the north is equally hot but dry from October through April.

Nigeria is a federation of 30 states now under the control of an elected government, but past governments have been marred by corruption and instability. Muslims comprise 50 percent of the population, while Christians make up 40 percent. The Hausa-Fulani, Yoruba and Ibo ethnic groups total 65 percent of the population, and an estimated 250 other ethnic groups comprise the other 35 percent. The official language of Nigeria's 108 million people is English.

There are more than 20 English-language newspapers in the country, but they were heavily monitored and supervised by the military junta. Foreign journalists were routinely expelled for citing corruption in the government. We'll see what happens to press freedom under the Olusegun Obasanjo regime.

The literacy rate is 51 percent. Less than 20 percent of the population graduates from secondary school. The official currency is the naira, divided into 100 kobo.

5/29/99	Olusegun Obasanjo takes office as the first elected president in Nigeria in 15 years.
7/98	Moshood Abiola dies, setting off protests that leave 55 dead.
6/98	Sani Abacha dies suddenly of presumably natural causes.
3/96	Nigeria moves troops into Cameroon.
3/21/96	Abacha signs a law permitting the military junta to dismiss any local councilman without cause.
1/19/96	UFNL claims responsibility for a plane crash that killed the son of military dictator Abacha.
11/10/95	Writer and Ogoni rights champion Ken Saro-Wiwa and eight colleagues are executed by the Abacha government.
11/17/93	General Sani Abacha's coup makes him Nigeria's seventh military ruler.
6/23/93	General Ibrahim Babangida annuls elections; military remains in power.
6/18/93	It is leaked that Moshood Abiola won the presidential elections comfortably over Bashir Tofa.
5/92	Two hundred people are killed in ethnic clashes.
7/3/86	Former President Shehu Shagari and former Vice President Alex Ekwueme are released after spending 30 months in detention.
5/23/86	Fifteen students are killed in clash with police.
8/27/85	Major General Ibrahim Babangida takes over the government in a military coup.
1/15/66	A group of army majors (mainly Ibo) fail in Nigeria's first coup attempt.
10/1/60	Independence declared.

North Korea

Il or Illin?

At Pyongyang's Mansudae Hill, a line of street cleaners who look more like housewives (which, of course, they actually double as), armed with straw brooms, march stooped over like a bad ensemble at Pasadena's DooDah Parade. Like a 17th-century Zamboni machine, they clear what little dust has accumulated on the walkway in front of the Korean Revolution Museum before a giant bronze statue of the late North Korean leader Kim Il Sung. Kim's massive right arm is eternally locked forward in a handshake with the clouds, which was about all he was able to shake hands with during his neurotically xenophobic, despotic and frequently brutal 46 years of rule of a country that may as well be on Mars.

Shaking hands with nothing. The image lingers with you, even after reading the romantic, campy description in the city's official guidebook: "The statue of Kim portrays his sublime figure looking far ahead, with his left hand akimbo and his right raised to indicate the road for the people to advance."

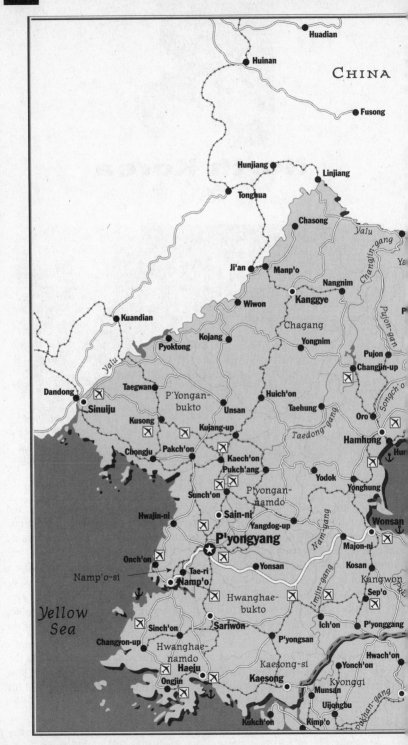

North Korea

- ⭐ National Capital
- ◉ Administrative Capital
- ● Secondary City
- Administrative Boundary
- Primary Road
- Secondary Road
- ┼┼┼┼ Railroad
- – – – Demarcation Line
- ▬▬▬ Demilitarized Zone
- ⚓ Primary Ports
- ☒ Airfields

0	25	50	75 km
0		25	50 mi

The road to the 38th parallel, no doubt.

The Great Leader departed for the Great Unknown on July 18, 1994, succumbing to illness that he tried vainly to thwart with a combination of meteorology and herbs. Millions of North Koreans have made pilgrimages to the statue and other shrines, openly weeping for a man who they were taught since birth created the dawn of each new day. Literally. It must have come as quite a shock when the sun rose the morning after Kim headed for that great *juche* in the sky.

Myth and legend shrouded Kim Il Sung. His legendary heroics against the Japanese during World War II, by all historical accounts, never occurred. His greatest victory was a stalemate in the Korean War, at the cost of a half million North Korean lives. He might also claim a victory of sorts in the arrest of more than 20 million people.

North Koreans are taught that Kim was the inventor of everything from centuries-old scientific and physics theories to such modern conveniences as the automobile and the toaster. Some believe he's walked on the moon. By law, every North Korean household must possess at least two portraits of the Great One. Not Gretzky, but of Kim. That's overachievement.

Certainly not overachieving is Kim's son, 59-year-old Kim Jong Il—the Great Leader's "hair" apparent and a Jenny Craig "before" model with a penchant for used Rodney Dangerfield leisure suits, permed Quaddafi-style tresses, lifts in his shoes and a bevy of kidnapped Japanese concubines he's got stashed in a collection of countryside villas. A virtual hermit, the younger Kim makes Howard Hughes look like Monica Lewinsky on a book-signing tour.

After more than four years of grieving for his dead dad, it was expected that Kim Jong Il would finally get some kind of a promotion—say, to president maybe? No way, José. Instead, on September 5, 1998, Kim Jong Il was named by the Supreme People's Assembly to "the Highest Post of the State." Whatever that is. Now the SPA isn't exactly a grass roots movement in the DPRK—a grass roots movement in North Korea is a group of starving villagers out in the forest foraging for food—but there may be a festering boil somewhere deep in the cavity of the Korean Workers' Party's bottom with this euphemism. Rather than appoint Kim as president, the state's previous highest position, the SPA simply abolished the post altogether.

And they may have had a good reason. Cognac-guzzling Kim Jong Il is both a reported lush and an alleged terrorist. He's been implicated as the mastermind behind a number of terrorist attacks, including a Korean Air jetliner explosion that took 115 lives in 1987. He is believed responsible for North Korea's nuclear program (the bomb part, anyway), as well as the foiled assassination attempt on the South Korean president in Myanmar that instead blew away 17 high-level South Korean officials in 1983.

It is also thought that North Korea's recent binge in amphetamine and opium trafficking to kickstart its moribund economy is being personally directed by The Chubby One.

In April 1997, a cache of 154 pounds of amphetamines with a street value of US$95 million was found on a North Korean freighter in port at Hiroshima, Japan. Dope is grown or manufactured in the DPRK (Democratic People's Republic of Korea) and then smuggled through diplomatic channels to Pyongyang's embassies abroad, where it is then sold to domestic dealers, or by North Korean diplomats themselves on the street level. It's believed that huge quantities of opium go through Russia via North Korean workers commuting to timber projects there. Late in 1998, the Narcotics Suppression boys at Bangkok, Thailand's Don Muang Airport seized 2.5 million tons of ephedrine—a principal ingredient in cheap, garage-lab amphetamines—enroute to Pyongyang from India. The pawns of Pyongyang insisted the chemical was intended for the development of bronchodilators. So we now know that not only are North Koreans starving, but they're all suffering from chronic asthma, as well.

But the mythmaking continues. Kim Jong Il was actually born in Siberia in 1941, but because most North Koreans have never heard of Siberia, Jong Il was reborn in a log cabin near North Korea's famed Mount Paektu beneath two rainbows and a bright, previously undiscovered star (Bambi had to have been close by). He is reputed to have written hundreds of books, all epic masterpieces, and six operas in the course of two years. He can stop rain (but apparently not flooding) and predict the discovery of natural resources (apparently plutonium).

However, the Dear Leader isn't a been-there, done-that type of fellow. He's reportedly been abroad only once, to neighboring China—and that was probably by mistake. No backpacks in this dude's closet. In all likelihood, he's met only a couple of Westerners in his entire life. Trying to get hip in time for his formal ascension to power, Jong practiced his English (and probably his Korean, too) to *Star Trek* reruns and the *Larry King Show*.

His face fills the television screens every night, at all times and on every channel. The man who claims "socialism is not administrative and commanding" may have a different relationship with communism than with alcohol. He is reported to spend nearly three-quarters of a million dollars a year on Hennessy cognac, specifically the Paradis line. That's commanding. Yet, he remains the subject of adulation. Normally bright, responsible scholars and educators from North Korea and abroad reduce themselves to writing driveling, soppy odes to this inglorious, silver-spooned papa's boy. Sample this, written by a doctor at Delhi University in India:

> *Dear leader Kim Jong Il*
> *Friend of masses, savior of*
> *humanity*
> *Increased efforts of yours inspired*
> *the masses*
> *You have awakened them*
> *To build modern DPRK*
> *Brick by brick*
> *Made them independent and masters*
> *of their own destiny*
> *Dear leader Kim Jong Il*
> *A rising star on the horizon*
> *Shown the path of salvation*
> *Of realism*
> *Removed flunkeyism in the face of*
> *Severe odds*
> *Dear leader Kim Jong Il*
> *A versatile personality*
> *I salute you*

Removed flunkeyism? Whoa.

The "My Automatic Rifle" Dance

In North Korea, propaganda has become an art form. Perhaps the most entertaining reading we've come across at *DP* is the "consumer" magazine that comes out of Pyongyang—*Korea Today*, of the DPRK. There are magnificent book reviews, all on Kim Jong Il's hundreds of books. No room for anything else. And no comments such as "The plot is frayed; the characters develop like a fungus. The author has talent, but should have restricted it to flyer writing for the PTA." Nope, nothing like that. You'd end up in the gulag for a few centuries.

The harshest criticism we spotted was surprisingly scathing, though: "Many of the world's people call Kim Jong Il the giant of our times. This means that he is unique and distinguished in all aspects—wisdom, leadership, ability, personality and achievements." (*Korea Today*, No. 3, 1992.) The writer was anonymous, fearing for his life if his byline were to be published. There's coverage of some great plays and performing arts shows. One particularly caught our attention, a tear-jerking rendition of the "My Automatic Rifle Dance," performed by two voluptuous (in North Korea, that means fed) actresses prancing about the stage with their AKs.

Korea Today publishes cutting-edge, bohemian poetry that mainstream periodicals wouldn't have the balls to print:

> *My song, echo all the way home from the trenches.*
> *When I smash the American robbers of happiness,*
> *And I return home with glittering medals on my chest,*
> *All my beloved family will be in my arms.*

Cool stuff. Want to subscribe? Write: The Foreign Language Magazines, Pyongyang, DPRK.

For more laughs, write The Korean People's Army Publishing House (Pyongyang, DPRK) for a copy of their enormously popular *Panmunjom*, a chronicle of North Korea's innumerable military accomplishments. There are some great combat shots, with captions like "U.S. imperialist troops of aggression training South Korean puppet soldiers to become cannon fodder in their aggressive war against the northern half of Korea." Another innocuous shot of a group of soldiers is depicted as, "A U.S. military advisor and the South Korean stooges are on the spot to organize the armed invasion of the northern half of Korea." Another photo shows a 1953 armistice meeting between North Korean and UN officials breaking up, and is appropriately captioned: "The U.S. imperialist troops of aggression hastily leave after their crimes have been exposed at a meeting held at the scene of the crime."

But the *DP* runner-up in the book goes to a 1976 shot of an American soldier using a chain saw to cut down a tree. The caption: "The U.S. imperialist troops of aggression committed a grave provocation, cutting down a tree."

And the winner? A fuzzy shot of a letter from Secretary of State John Foster Dulles to a South Korean colonel, dated June 20, 1950. The caption reads: "Secret messages exchanged between the south Korean puppets and the U.S. imperialists to invade the north, and Dulles' secret letter instigating the puppets to start a war." It took a magnifying glass, but we read the letter:

The dinner which you gave in our honor last night was something I shall always remember. The setting was really glorious, the company distinguished, the entertainment most interesting to us and last, but not least, the food was delicious. The antique vase (you gave us) will grace Mrs. Dulles' living room in New York and always keep fresh the memory of our visit with you.

For even more knee-slaps, check out the Korean Central News Agency's new web site. *DP*'s favorite headline is "U.S. Stands Alone on Land Mine." Although graphically as creative as a pancake, you're sure to howl at the copy, which continually adulates Kim Jong Il as having "perfectly controlled the complicated situation of the world." Of course, don't expect much on the mess the leader has perfectly controlled in his own back yard, namely four consecutive years of famine that one UN official said could turn into "one of the biggest humanitarian disasters of our lifetime."

Korean Central News Agency
http://www.kcna.co.jp

Despite the famine, which a U.S. congressional report says has killed up to 2 million people since 1995 (the DPRK admitted in May 1999 to a figure closer to 220,000 between 1995 and 1998), and having been dependent on international aid since the same year, the DPRK appears to have enough food to export. Okryukwan, the North's most famous restaurant and known for its *naengmyon*—cold buckwheat noodles—opened its first branch in Seoul in May 1999. With the ingredients imported from North Korea, Okryukwan has become Seoul's latest hip, up-market eatery.

Regrettably, for most North Koreans, "up-market" is an old lady selling yams by the side of the road in Ji'an, China. But the hundreds, maybe thousands, of North Korean spies planted in the South finally have a decent place to eat.

No one's quite sure. But the rest of the world's getting a clearer picture—during the first five months of 1999, there were 39 North Korean defectors. North Korea has been, along with Iraq, the US military's greatest concern since the end of the Cold War. At least 25 percent of the DPRK budget goes into the military, and although on paper, its army is close to twice the size of South Korea's and with twice the arsenal, South Korean President Kim Dae Jung doesn't see it going anywhere anytime soon. Namely because Jung-Il's war machine has run out of gas and spare parts. Thus, Kim's "Sunshine Policy" with the North—engagement with and aid to Pyongyang. Rather than bucking for a Nobel peace prize, Kim sees the pragmatism in keeping the North from imploding. South Korea's own shredded economy is ill-equipped to assimilate twentysomething million starving North Koreans who've never seen a baseball game.

The DPRK is perhaps the most closed society on the globe. It is also perhaps the most lobotomized. Obtaining information from abroad is illegal, as is picking up hitchhikers. Even bicycles were illegal until 1990. North Koreans can't even visit many areas in their own country. Talking to a foreigner is grounds for arrest. At press time, the few foreign expats living in Pyongyang were not permitted to leave the city.

The Chubby One has been stung by four years of famine—caused by floods and maladroit mismanagement of farmland—and a string of defections, including the high-profile bailing from the North of Hwang Jang Yop in February 1997 (and a number of lesser officials since). Hwang was number six (or 26 depending on who you talk to) in the pecking order and the architect of Pyongyang's *juche* ideology of self-reliance. How well that concept has worked is evidenced by Pyongyang's willingness to store Taiwan's nuclear waste for US$200 million worth of rice. Not to mention, of course, the US$1 billion admission ticket Pyongyang is trying to sell for a visit to the suspected underground nuclear facility at Kumchang-ri. That's self-reliance. As Mr. Hwang was recently quoted as saying: "At a time when workers and farmers are starving, how could we consider people sane who loudly say they have built utopia for them?"

Kim Il Sung

Yeah, he's dead. But long live the Kim. The effects of playing God for 46 years don't go away overnight. The North Koreans still show, and will continue to show for years, blinding adoration of their beloved pinko deity, except for, perhaps, the estimated 20,000 political prisoners held in the country. But, remember, in North Korea, you're a political prisoner if you don't turn on your television in the morning.

http://www.korea-np.co.jp/pk/001st_issue/97072012.htm

Kim Jong Il

The Dear Leader isn't seen around a lot. More likely he's at a Blockbuster somewhere in L.A., either stocking up on copies of *Rambo*, *Godzilla* and *Goodfellas* or abducting waitress/actresses. Jong's a movie freak; he owns perhaps 20,000 videotapes. It's also widely believed that Jong once kidnapped a South Korean actress and director and held them captive for nearly a decade while he played Dino de Laurentis. He shot a series of anti-Japanese films that make Crichton's *Rising Sun* look like the Meiji Constitution.

http://www.korea-np.co.jp/pk/dprk_leadership/category07.htm

The Military

North Korea has approximately 1.2 million troops, most of them massed along the border with South Korea. The balance are starving and roaming the streets of famine-struck cities and rural areas with their AKs hitting the "people" up at gunpoint for food and money. Fortunately, for the time being, Jong has their support, as the Dear Leader apparently has no plans to socialize the military, whose elite members enjoy such Western luxuries as Mercedes, Marlboros and mint-flavored Crest. But the military appears to be running out of gas for its 4,000 (whoa!) tanks and 600 combat aircraft. U.S. officials report that the North Korean air force has reduced its training missions near the DMZ by 75 percent.

Passport and visa are required. Visas must be arranged prior to arrival in Pyongyang, usually through a tour packager. The best places to procure North Korean visas are in Bangkok and Macau. You must pay for your entire trip before you depart, as you will be part of a government-organized tour. The North Korean Visa Office is a better bet than the North Korean embassy in Beijing. Perhaps even a better bet is through M.K. Ways in Bangkok *(57/11 Wireless Road, Bangkok 10330; Tel.: [66] (2) 254-4765, 255-3390, 254-7770, 255-2892)*. The company specializes in tour packages to Indochina, but has introduced packages to North Korea in an exclusive agreement with the government.

Tours of North Korea vary in length, but most are for 14 days. You'll need three passport photos and approximately US$15 for the visa. If asked if you are a journalist, it would help facilitate the process to say no. Inside the country, you may be able to extend your visa, but, again, you'll have to pay in advance for accommodations and guide services. Your guide should be able to make the necessary arrangements.

By air, you can get to Pyongyang via Beijing on Air China or Air Koryo. Pyongyang is also serviced by Aeroflot. Pyongyang Airport (Sunan) is 24 kilometers from the capital, about a 45-minute drive. By train, you can enter North Korea from Beijing via Tianjin, Tangshan, Dandong and Shinuiju. You'll be met at the Pyongyang station by your guide. The Pyongyang/Beijing train runs four times a week, and there's thrice-weekly service to Moscow via Khabarovsk. By boat, you may want to try the ship that runs from Nagasaki, Japan to Wonsan on North Korea's east coast. Other international ports include Chonjin, Haeju, Hungnam, Rajin, Songnim and Nampo (Pyongyang).

http://travel.state.gov/nkorea.html

GETTING AROUND

You won't have much choice in the matter. Most likely, you'll be with a government guide in a government vehicle and you'll go where the government wants you to go. U.S. citizens may spend money in North Korea only to purchase ordinary travel necessities such as hotel accommodations, meals and goods for immediate personal consumption in North Korea. There is no longer any per-diem restriction on these expenses, and the use of credit cards for these transactions is also authorized. Because the sanctions system prohibits business dealings with North Korea, unless licensed by the U.S. Treasury Department, purchases of goods or services unrelated to travel are prohibited. There exists only the skeleton of a public transit system in North Korea: very few buses, virtually no cars and no domestic flights (open to foreigners). Travel by train is your best bet if you're not traveling by car. Again, you'll have no say. But trains are usually used to visit some of the more popular tourist sites (a three-word oxymoron). There is no bus service between the cities. Pyongyang possesses a two-line metro and regular bus services.

http://www.dpr-korea.com/english.html
http://www.duke.edu/~myhan/b_NK.html

German Tours
Privatanschrift: Wielen,
Schaarberg 3, 24211 Wahlstorf
Tel.: 04342/889695
E-mail: DEGE@GEOGRAPHIE.UNI-KIEL.DE
Web site: http://www.uni-kiel.de:8080/Geographie/Dege/dege.htm

DANGEROUS PLACES

The Entire Country
The North Koreans think all Westerners who visit the country are spies. North Korea is host to few foreign tourists, and those who do get in will only see areas of the country targeted by the government for them to see. All visitors are accompanied by a government guide. You will be subjected to intense propaganda wherever you go. And you will never be permitted to stray off the beaten path unattended, although you might be occasionally permitted an unattended evening stroll around Pyongyang. Crime is not a problem in

North Korea. There is wide speculation that thieves and criminals get the death penalty. In this regard, no area of North Korea can be catgorized as unsafe. There is no U.S. embassy in North Korea.

http://www.path.ne.jp/~n-bikkal/n-korea.htm

The DMZ

And you thought Mexicans had it tough. The 38th parallel dividing North and South Korea is perhaps the most heavily fortified border in the world. On the southern side, some 37,500 U.S. troops lie in waiting for Kim Jong Il's horde to come crashing though the gates—in this case, the side of a mountain. For nearly 50 years, the North Korean army has been digging tunnels through the granite mountains on its side of the border into South Korean territory, ending them with only a few meters of rock and soil between the North's stockpiled invading force—artillery equipment, tanks, helicopters, warplanes and troops—and South Korean "sunshine." War is little more than a tap of an ice pick away.

http://www.fas.org/nuke/guide/dprk/index.html

Insulting the Great Leader, or the Dear Leader

Want to end up in the slammer fast? Here's how: Tell your guide that Kim Jong Il wears Kim Jong Suk's (his mother) army boots. Or, perhaps, mention you believe that the U.S. would kick North Korea's ass in soccer or in a ground war. Or mutter your suspicion that Kim Il Sung was gay. You get the point.

Giving Gifts

Never give North Koreans gifts of any nature, especially Western items, foreign currency or any currency. Although the individual might gracefully accept your generosity (most won't), you're setting that person up for trouble. Remember, you're a spy. Anyone you come into contact with will be assumed to be collaborating with your efforts to pass information and gather intelligence. Silly, but true.

Touching a North Korean Woman

Regardless of how she might come on to you (she won't, by the way), never touch a North Korean woman. Don't even shake hands. This will be construed as an immoral act and will undoubtedly get you both in trouble. In the DPRK, a prostitute is a misspelled place to get cancer.

Spies, Subs and South Korean Fishing Nets

Like beached orcas, North Korean spy subs need a new sonar setup. Hooking DPRK submarines is like a little Sunday afternoon bass fishing. In September 1996, a 320-ton North Korean sub found itself inadvertently rubbing the parasites off its belly on a beach along the South's east coast. The ensuing 53-day manhunt for the 26 spies who fled from it resulted in 24 of them being shot dead. In June 1998, a North Korean midget spy sub got itself tangled up in the nets of a South Korean fishing trawler. The nine crew members shot themselves dead rather than be captured. Dolphins don't have that option. The next month, the corpse of an armed DPRK commando was found near South Korea's Tonghae naval base, along with his tiny sub, which had room enough for four others—who can probably be found right now scarfing down a bowl of cold buckwheat noodles at Okryukwan.

Bow Shots

In April 1999, the Japanese discovered a pair of North Korean spy trawlers (with Japanese markings) snooping around in their waters, and decided to have a look-see. When the trawlers started high-tailing it back to North Korea, the Japanese got their first taste of a firefight since World War II. But there was a catch. It wasn't an actual firefight. You see, the Japanese are prevented in their post-WWII constitution from using force unless fired upon first. Because the DPRK spy boats didn't shoot at anyone, all the Japanese navy could do was fire bow shots—from an armada of warships and helicopters—for a few hours as the trawlers raced home unscathed. (If only that had been policy at Pearl.) No reason anymore for Japan's allies to go to the expense of staging war games with their buddies in the Pacific. The North Koreans'll do it for free. And speaking of bow shots, in late August 1998, the DPRK lobbed a Taepo-don ballistic missile over the Japanese peninsula, the rocket's cone landing in the Pacific, the first stage in waters near Alaska. Alaskans didn't complain because Exxon had nothing to do with it, and nothing leaked. But the Japanese and the Pentagon quickly cried foul, while Pyongyang insisted it had merely launched a satellite—which is probably true, as the Dear Leader previously had no access to the Playboy Channel.

Home Rocket Kits

Korea does have a business, a very good one at that. Build it at home rocket kits. Seems they will sell whatever bits you need to complete your own chemical, HE or nuclear missile program. (Instructions included, please read manufacturers warning label before operation.)

Pakistan's "Ghauri" and Iran's "Shahab-3" missile are GMC/Chevy-like copies of North Korean protoypes. Iran now can reach out at anyone from Sudan to India to most of Western Europe with its 1,250 mile range arsenal. Pakistan is supposed to have nukes that screw into the top of theirs. North Korea saves the best for home use. They can fire a missile that would hit anywhere in South East Asia, Russia or the caribou in Alaska. That's if they get the thing pointed just right.

Famine

How bad is it? According to South Korean intelligence officials, North Korea's population has dropped to 22 million from 25 million in 1995. By mid-1997, grain rations were down to 3.5 ounces a day per person, the result of two years of flooding and bureaucratic mismanagement of agricultural lands. In North Korea, 4.82 million tons of grain are needed as food for the country's twentysomething million people every year. In 1996, grain output dropped to 2.5 million tons in unhulled state. And most of that had been cut with grass and tree bark. In 1995–96, the famine affected at least 5.2 million people, left 500,000 homeless and ruined 359,936 hectares of arable land. In 1997, food rations dropped to a level four times lower than normally considered essential for a healthy population. By mid-1999, it was thought that more than 2 million North Koreans have starved to death, though the government has admitted to about 220,000 deaths. The country has only about half the grain it needs to feed its people and has been dependent on international aid since 1995. Perhaps *juche* needs a douche.

http://members.tripod.com/~nkorelief/

North Korea has a shortage of medical supplies, facilities and doctors. Western medicines and remedies are even more rare. On the plus side, the water is potable, and the hygiene and sanitation very good. Also, you won't find the food stalls that are seen throughout the rest of Asia. North Korea is squeaky clean.

NORTH KOREA

NUTS AND BOLTS

After the Japanese surrender of 1945, Korea was divided into two directorates: The USSR occupied the north, while the United States controlled the south below the 38th parallel. In 1948, the division between the two zones was made permanent. Trade was cut off between the two zones at the advent of the Cold War in the late 1940s.

The Democratic Peoples Republic of Korea (DPRK) is very much a communist nation. Before the demise of the Soviet Union, the DPRK imported nearly three-quarters of a million tons of oil from the USSR per year. These supplies have been essentially cut off. North Korea is nearly US$6 billion in debt.

The country is covered almost entirely by north-south mountain ranges and is about the size of Pennsylvania.

The language in North Korea is Korean, with indigenous elements in the vocabulary. Religions in North Korea include Buddhism and Confucianism. However, religious activities within the country basically don't exist. There is no public worshipping of deities in the DPRK. The currency is the won. The won=100 jon. Per-capita income is US$1,000.

The time in North Korea is GMT plus nine hours. Electricity is 220 V/60 Hz. Overseas phone calls can be made from the major hotels, and IDD is available in certain establishments. Mail can be received at some hotels and the Korea International Tourist Bureau. But it will be read by the government. Fax services are readily available.

The climate in North Korea is cold and dry in the winter with warm summers. More than 60 percent of the annual rainfall occurs from June through September.

The capital of North Korea is Pyongyang.

Koreascope
  http://www.koreascope.org/english/index.htm
Durham University Korean Page
  http://www.dur.ac.uk/~dmu0rcp/aksepage.htm
Harvard Korean Page
  http://www.fas.harvard.edu/~hoffmann/

DANGEROUS DAYS

8/31/98	Pyongyang launches a ballistic missile over the Japanese peninsula.
7/12/98	Dead DPRK commando found near South Korea's Tonghae naval base.
2/12/97	Leading party ideologue Hwang Jang Yop defects to the South Korean embassy in Beijing.
11/12/94	An American army helicopter is shot down in North Korean airspace. One pilot dies in the crash and the other is repatriated more than two weeks later.
7/18/94	The death of the Great Leader, Kim Il Sung.
7/27/53	The armistice ending the Korean War was signed.

9/15/50	UN Commander General Douglas MacArthur makes an amphibious landing at Inchon, behind North Korean lines, and routes the North Korean army.
6/27/50	U.S. President Harry Truman orders U.S. combat units into action to enforce the UN condemnation of North Korea's invasion of South Korea.
6/27/50	The United Nations condemns North Korea's attack of South Korea and decrees a withdrawal of the invading forces.
6/25/50	North Korea mounts a surprise invasion of South Korea.
5/1/48	The establishment of the Democratic People's Republic of Korea.

Islamabad

Pakistan
★★★

Dodge City with Skiing

It just goes to show, doesn't it? You can't turn your back for five minutes before the Karachi Kids are up to all sorts of things in *DP*'s absence. The boyz in Pakistan have had a very busy time of late: there've been nuclear bombs to test, a minor war to conduct with India over Kashmir, attempted assassinations to carry out (or dodge), and the usual political squabbles with games of musical chairs to play between the military and the politicians; then of course they've had to spare a bit of time to trash the imperialist hyenas (the Brits) at cricket. No, the big news in Pakistan this year, or at least just as *DP* was going to press, is that when the music stopped the military were all sitting in the right seats. The politicos were all left standing. Or to be more accurate the Prime Minister was left sitting under house arrest, wondering if it really had been such a good idea to fire his military chief of staff. Probably not, on balance. That said, given that the last military dictator in Pakistan died in an awfully convenient plane crash, perhaps General Musharraf had better watch his steps (or his flights). For the moment, though, Pakistan is back under tender, loving military rule; and no one appears to care

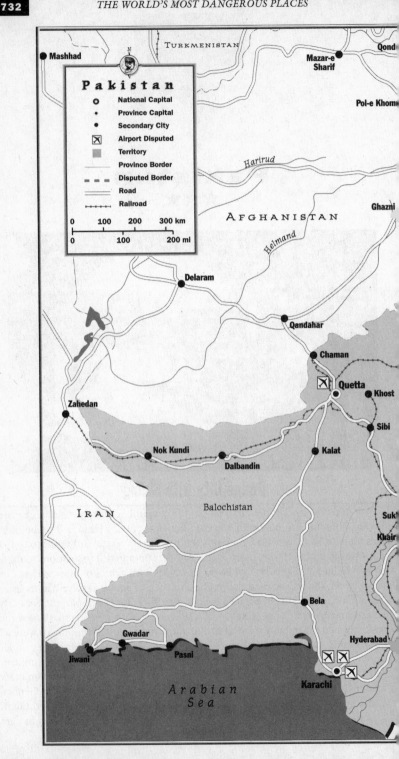

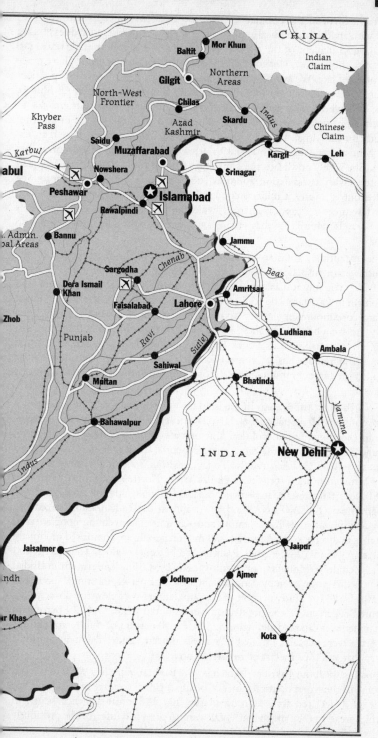

very much. Most of the population were too busy switching back to MTV to bother with anything as radical as a protest. I mean, what difference does it make when about 5 percent of the population actually bother paying their taxes? No big surprise there, when you consider the mess the politicos appear to have made of the place of late. We at *DP* aren't too hot on politics, but Pakistans's politicos really are in a league of their own. Take Benazir Bhutto. Her father, Ali Bhutto, was the chap who got his neck stretched by the last military ruler, General Zia ul-Huq when he took over in 1977. He was hanged after there were more votes counted (for him) than there were people voting! His daughter, herself an ex-Prime Minister, has been sentenced to a few years in the clink on corruption charges. She wisely now leads the opposition from abroad. Nawaz Sharif has had to contend with assassination attempts (he got away), corruption charges (he wriggled out . . . just), a military coup (which he didn't handle very well), and now a few more corruption charges while the generals spin a coin for heads (guilty) or tails (a retrial . . . that's to say another toss of the coin until it comes up heads).

In the meantime, Pakistan rather unsportingly had its membership of the Commonwealth suspended. Some people have no sense of humor. The good news, which you might have guessed by now, is that it doesn't really matter who is in control in Pakistan. The country still attracts planeloads of trekkers, hippies, and hard-core mountain climbers to discover some of the world's most rugged scenery, smoke a bit of hash and explore many of the wild and dangerous areas. British adventurers, such as writer Rudyard Kipling and explorer Sir Richard Burton, maintained a healthy respect for the "wily Pathans," who have always controlled the remote mountainous regions of northwest and the arid southwest of Pakistan.

The North-West tribal areas of Pakistan have never really felt the presence of any government, let alone tourists. Here Pashto-speaking tribes and warlike clans maintain their own social, political and military structures, free from politics, taxes and MTV. Many of the more entrepreneurial tribes still view travelers and visitors as walking CARE packages. Today, Pakistan is a crude welding together of four semiautonomous provinces Punjab, Sind, North-West Frontier Province (NWFP) and Baluchistan. It also encompasses federally administered tribal and northern areas (FATA/FANA) and lays claim to the Indian-administered but mostly Muslim states of Azad Jammu and Kashmir. The teeming population of Pakistan is as diverse as it is large. Its 130 million people are comprised of Punjabi (56 percent), Sindi (23 percent), Pashtun (13 percent), Baluchi (5 percent) and others, including Mohajirs, or Urdu-speaking Muslim emigres from India. Pakistan is dirt-poor, even by African standards. The per-capita annual income in 1992 was US$410. Thirty percent of the population lives below the poverty line, and only 35 percent of the population can read and write. Only 20 percent of Pakistani females can read and write, and barely 40 percent of children of primary school age were actually enrolled in schools. Poverty aside, Pakistan remains a country that still tops the list of any adventurer.

The bad news about Pakistan, (which is why Pakistan rates in *DP*), is that it has had some of the worst political violence of any regional country that is not in the middle of a declared war. Starting in the mid 1980s the violence began in Karachi, spread to the Punjab and as *DP* went to press had infected the previously immune diplomatic center of Islamabad. Doesn't sound good. Cheap weapons and heroin, freely available from neighboring Afghanistan have fostered a massive gun culture that almost equals the United States'; drug addiction (there are estimated to be as many as 4 million drug addicts in Pakistan) and rampant corruption are also the norm in Pakistan. That, of course, is the here and the now.

If you wanna know the "why" for all this, well, it goes back to the last guy who liked military parades and shoving the politicos on trial: General Zia ul-Huq. To get to the point, he rammed through a whole load of religious laws in the '80s that suited the Sunni majority, but not the 10–15 percent Shia population. (The first step on the proverbial banana skin.) Then he set up the madrassehs, or religious schools, for the not-so-rich-kids. They might have been called religious schools, but when Saudi Arabian "Wahabi" sects began to sponsor the schools they ended up churning out the Sunni Islamic version of *Terminator II*. Not much to look at maybe, but sure as hell packs a punch. (You don't, by the way, get any prizes for guessing where the Taliban emerged from.)

To get the picture here, you've got to see all this happening within the context of the Afghan (predominately Sunni) "jihad" against the Soviets and the (mainly Shias) Iranian revolution and the ensuing Iran-Iraq war. It's kinda complicated and—I'm afraid —gets even more complicated. Suffice to say both Sunni and Shia political parties began to get religious with something of a martial flavor to their daily "let's all tune in to God" meetings. The Sunnis and Shias, from tolerating (and even liking) each other began to exchange bursts of gun fire instead of "hellos." So a whole load of tit for tat killings started, which quickly spiralled into all out massacres of worshippers of the other faith. All rather unpleasant, really. Groups emerged, leaders were killed, more violent splinter groups emerged . . . it's all horrifically complicated and about as easy to untangle as a couple of mating cobras. But, at risk of ridicule, we at *DP* will have a go.

In the Sunni corner a whole string of groups emerged dedicated to trashing Shias: the Sipah-e-Sahaba Pakistan (SSP), previously known as the Society for the Soldiers of the Companions of the Prophet (at least they shortened the name), set themselves up in the Punjab. Needless to say, they were not wild about Shias. In 1990 their top dog, Nawaz Jhangvi, bit the dust in a hail of bullets. Not to be outdone a few of the less literate Shia kids set up the Sipah-e Mohammed Pakistan (SMP) and had a laugh a minute gunning down just about anyone who was Sunni that they didn't like. Some even less literate Sunnis boyz took one look at them, said "what a bunch of wimps" and set up their own little—more fanatical anti-Shia—group, the Lashkar-e-Jhangvi (LJ), named after the wasted chief of the SSP. If you're a *DP*er and ever happen to be in the Punjab you might like to know that these kids like to hang around Shia mosques. They can be identified by the large machine guns and their tendency to spray bullets in an indiscriminate manner. So, that's the local side of things dealt with.

Well, sort of . . . I guess I'd better mention that relations with India haven't been too cool recently. Pakistan still has claims over Kashmir, and in 1999 the two countries had a bit of a squabble over the region. It started with the infiltration of a few (thousand) guerrillas from Pakistan, continued with an artillery duel on the border, got a bit heavier as troops from both countries battled it out for a couple of months, but cooled down before either side used their nukes. I mean, after all, what politician wants to go down as the ass who got half his country destroyed in an afternoon? So, two questions. Did Pakistan gain anything from its nice little two month war with India? And why did they start it? The answer to the first question is pretty much, er, a resounding "no." To the second, well . . . they figured that a bit of a war (with both sides armed with nukes), might panic the international community enough to make them persuade India to redraw the borders over the disputed areas. But as nobody gave a damn what was happening on some godforsaken mountain top in the middle of nowhere, it didn't work. In 1998 Pakistan officially joined the nuclear club, exploding five nuclear bombs in the Baluchistan desert. Just to rub the point in, Pakistan's equivalent to Dr. Strangelove (nuclear scientist, Dr. Abdul Qadeer Khan), held a bit of a press conference to have a quick gloat over how his atomic bomb was better than India's, not to mention that the Pakistani Ghauri missile was much better than the Indian Agni missile (that's what he said, at least). Everyone else started putting in orders for underground nuclear shelters. He's the top man in Pakistan when it comes to building nuclear bombs. He's also top of a few other lists, too. Dr. Abdul Qadeer Khan (for it is he) is wanted in Holland for stealing classified information from the Almelo uranium enrichment plant. The Dutch government has kindly offered to put him up for free for a whole 4 years if he ever wants to drop by Amsterdam again. The international Atomic Energy Agency would also like a chat with Dr. Khan over minor allegations that he even (very naughty, this) offered to sell atomic secrets to the Thief of Baghdad (yes, our very own Saddam Hussein). If you, too, want to meet Pakistan's equivalent to Dr. Strangelove, then *DP* will give you a head start. He likes to hang out at the top secret Kahuta plant, where the uranium enrichment program is run, not far from Islamabad.

For those of you *DP*ers thinking of a trip to Pakistan, you should know that U.S. citizens aren't really flavor of the decade at the moment, at least among some sections of Pakistani society (the heavily armed, lunatic section, that is). In August 1999 a Pakistani religious scholar (mufti) declared that U.S. citizens were all fair game. Nizam-ud-din Shamzai's charming little declaration that "the spilling of American blood is permissible" came on the anniversary of the U.S. cruise missile attacks on Afghanistan and Sudan. If you're wondering what result the U.S. missile strikes actually had on the region, well . . . they reinforced Osama bin Laden's image of the Che Guevara of the Islamic world and gave the religious fruitcakes in Pakistan lots of excuses to make the kind of noises described above. Oh yes, they failed conspicuously to even come anywhere close to hurting bin Laden as well. Another monumental waste of cash and missiles; but, hey, at least it looks good in this age of sound bites and 30-second media attention span.

Pakistan was the first country created as an Islamic state. By law, the country's president must be a Muslim. The legal system follows both the Islamic code of justice, or Sharia, and old British laws. Even the banking system must abide by Koran dictates that say it is improper to charge or pay interest. Bank customers actually share the profits and losses with the institutions where they do business. However, fiscal common sense still supersedes religious zeal, when, every year, just prior to Ramadan, customers withdraw their entire bank accounts to avoid the Zakat tax, a 2.5 percent levy on certain bank accounts charged annually on the eve of Ramadan.

Pakistan (Islami Jamhuria-e-Pakistan, or the Islamic Republic of Pakistan) became independent on August 15, 1947, when Britain sliced up India in response to public pressure to create a separate Muslim state. East Pakistan seceded and became the separate country of Bangladesh in March 1971. Pakistan aligned itself with the United States and was a vital supply line for anti-Communist Afghan insurgents in Afghanistan. Population growth is among the world's highest, the literacy rate is low and deteriorating, and the unofficial unemployment rate is greater than 25 percent. Agriculture still accounts for about 70 percent of total exports.

Good for What Ails You

Travelers to Muslim countries are used to getting goofy on too sweet tea and whooping it up on watery yogurt. Ingesters of the fermented liquid form of the hop, grape and grain will be happy to learn that alcohol in Pakistan can be prescribed for medicinal purposes. Although alcohol is banned in Pakistan under Islamic law, you can order hard liquor and beer by the bottle through room service at the swank hotels in the large cities. You must fill out a form (for non-Muslims only), pay a small fee (about a dollar), and then sit in the quiet solitude of your room feeling like a junkie on methadone treatment. Malt beverages (beer without alcohol) are commonly available, and some remote areas feature homemade brews.

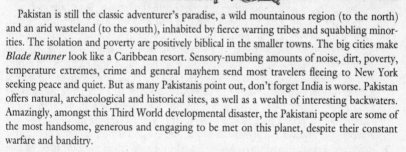

Pakistan is still the classic adventurer's paradise, a wild mountainous region (to the north) and an arid wasteland (to the south), inhabited by fierce warring tribes and squabbling minorities. The isolation and poverty are positively biblical in the smaller towns. The big cities make *Blade Runner* look like a Caribbean resort. Sensory-numbing amounts of noise, dirt, poverty, temperature extremes, crime and general mayhem send most travelers fleeing to New York seeking peace and quiet. But as many Pakistanis point out, don't forget India is worse. Pakistan offers natural, archaeological and historical sites, as well as a wealth of interesting backwaters. Amazingly, amongst this Third World developmental disaster, the Pakistani people are some of the most handsome, generous and engaging to be met on this planet, despite their constant warfare and banditry.

Pakistan has been pushed closer to the edge by the massive influx of weapons and refugees caused by wars in Afghanistan and conflict with India. There are a lot of guns in Pakistan with a lot of people who use them on a regular basis. Tourists are kidnapped for ransom but have not been harmed or executed (though a Swede was killed in 1991 in a messy government rescue attempt). Your health is definitely at risk; everything from cobras to dengue-carrying mosquitoes can end it all rather suddenly. Mountainous highways and insane drivers make Pakistan's roads a killing ground. Much of the country is not under the control of the government but ruled by tribes. Professional bandits prey on poor and rich alike. What better place for a stroll through the countryside?

The Army/Government

If you're wondering why it is that the military seem to think they are the only people capable of ruling the country, its simple . . . because they are just about the only people capable of ruling the place. The Pakistanis love a man in a uniform. Just ask Benazir Bhutto. Leave aside the scenery, the hippies and the fact that Pakistan is a nice place if you don't mind suicide squads on the road . . . the place is a shambles: there has been a near civil war in the country between the MQM and the government in Karachi. There is constant butchery between Sunnis and Shias, the vast majority of the population is under 25 and unemployed. And the military are about the only institution who actually have the capability and discipline to get anything done in the place . . . except defend their own country, that is. They have managed to lose just about every war they ever started (and even the ones they didn't start). But they still love to rattle their rusty colonial-era sabers at the huge Indian army to their east and watch their backs as Afghanistan descends into the apocalypse. Warring tribes in Baluchistan, Sind, the North-West Frontier, and the tribal areas keep the army's bullets from corroding in their clips, while criminals and ethnic terrorists in Karachi, Quetta and Hyderabad make soldiers sleep with one eye open. Having China as a neighbor to the north and Iran to the west does not make flower power high on the political agenda either. The government, bolstered by total armed forces of 587,000 is actively stirring up revolt in what they consider to be occupied (by India) Jammu and Kashmir. In fact, they nearly went a bit too far during the latest round of "we've got more artiller shells than you have" with the Indians. But in the end, well, everybody kinda got a bit bored and agreed to start it all up again sometime next year. Pakistan supplies much of the Middle East's cheap labor and is the world's prime low-cost supplier of military troops. About 30,000 military contract personnel from Pakistan were serving with the UN in Saudi Arabia, Libya, Oman, the United Arab Emirates and Kuwait in mid-1989, mainly in an advisory capacity. On a less peace oriented mission Pakistani military officers have also been turning up in Afghanistan doing a little more than advising the Taliban. There have been complaints that the government actually makes money by renting out its poorly paid troops to serve in UN peacekeeping missions. The UN compensates Pakistan at a higher rate of pay, and the government allegedly pockets the difference. Pakistan is and always has been run by the army. Even when the latest corrupt politician is turfed as in October of 1999, it doesn't really surprise the locals. You have to give Pakistan an A for effort when it comes to defending their Muslim state.

Considering how often the polis get turfed by the military, and considering that Ali Bhutto was strung up and his son was killed mysteriously in France, and General Zia Ul-Haq died in a mysterious plane crash—it's a wonder anybody wants to run this country. Also if you have any tips on how to solve Pakistan's exploding birth rate, poverty and belligerent neighbors send a postcard to the:

"Why I Want to Run Pakistan Sweepstakes"

Office of the Prime Minister
c/o Pakistani Military
Islamabad, Pakistan
Fax: (+92) 51 821 835
http://www.na.gov.pk

The Caretaker

To insiders, there is a troubling unknown variable regarding the coup in Pakistan in the man who led it: General Pervious Musharraf. *DP* reader D N Moorty. sends us this backgrounder on the good General and current caretaker of Pakistan's bright democratic future. While described as a straight maní and a soldier of soldiers many unconfirmed reports indicate that he personally gave the green light to the Kargil military incursions of last MayñJuly, in which Islamist radicals played a prominent role. The Pentagon has expressed satisfaction about nuclear command and control in Pakistan, that's probably because they are pointed at India not Honolulu. Nukes have always remained under the firm control of the army, even though there have been recent public discussions in Pakistani defense journals about the possibility of transferring nuclear command and control to the prime minister. The 12 October '99 coup was popular. There was widespread perception in the country that former prime minister Nawaz Sharif presided over a highly corrupt and inept government. Then again every government is considered to be highly corrupt and inept, you just can't protest the fact when the military is in charge. He had disturbed the relationship between his office, the president and the army by taking away the president's power to dismiss the prime minister. Although he used constitutional means to bring about his desired changes, his cajoling of opponents and his autocratic style had left him with a very small coterie of supporters. There were no signs of protests even in the streets of his home, Lahore, after his abrupt dismissal and arrest. Pakistanís stance on the Kashmir conflict will almost certainly harden. India has more to gain by accepting the present line of control (LoC) in Kashmir as the international border between the two countries than Pakistan. In Pakistan, such an outcome would be seen as a defeat ó not merely the kind of defeat it encountered in the aftermath of the recent skirmishes in Kargil, but a massive dent to national pride of the same proportion as the dismantlement of East Pakistan by India in 1971. This would be catastrophic for anyone in power. India's reaction to Nawaz Sharifís ousting has, in fact, been noticeably mute. India's National Security Advisory Council met to take stock of events and concluded that Musharrat was too busy for the time being to avenge the defeat in Kargil.

Nevertheless, General Malik did place the Indian Army on high alert. Again, the Bin Laden factor comes into play: not only may the Pakistan Army want to regain its lost prestige, but Osama bin Laden and his band of fundamentalists have declared a jihad against India. Given the stalemate, an early resolution of the Kashmir conflict does not seem feasible, so both India and Pakistan will continue weaponising their growing inventories of sophisticated missiles. However, since neither India nor Pakistan really wishes to seek a political solution for Kashmir, the army-led regime in Pakistan is not likely to be any more co-operative with India than the government of Nawaz Sharif. Even if there is a civilian government in Pakistan soon the resolution of this dispute is still improbable, as it requires major concessions by one or both sides, and neither side can produce them in the near future. Yet as long as it remains unresolved the dispute will continue to tick like a time bomb, except that since May 1998, when both India and Pakistan became overt nuclear powers, it is a nuclear one. Finally, like the USA, China has waited before taking any major steps related to its ties with Pakistan. General Musharraf's dealings with the radical Islamists of his own country and with the Taliban regime of Afghanistan will also serve as major litmus tests for China's next moves regarding Pakistan. China has been increasingly concerned regarding the reportedly growing contacts between the Taliban and separatist elements in its Xinjiang province. However, the heavy dependence of Pakistan on China for its military wherewithal may turn out to be one of the most potent variables in moderating the ties of the Pakistani military vis-à-vis the domestic Islamist hardliners and the Taliban.

The Inter Services Intelligence (ISI)

A very dubious bunch indeed. But then, most spooks are. Forget to whom they're supposed to be answerable. Most of the time they're not. Answerable, that is. Pick any crisis in the region and you can pretty much bet that there'll be a shady character or two from ISI running around there somewhere. To a very large extent indeed they have bankrolled the Taliban in Afghanistan with enough cash and weapons to keep the war there going well into the next millennium. In fact the Taliban was pretty much created in the 'deeni madressahs' (religious schools) in Pakistan. The aim, of course, is to secure influence in Afghanistan for Pakistan...its just that it doesn't really seem to be working. The Talibs might take the cash, but they sure as hell don't take the orders. Well, not the ones they don't like at any rate. Much the same is applied to Kashmir, where various separatist groups are trained and sponsored in Pakistan. Unsurprisingly, the Indians aren't too chuffed. So, how does it all work? What's the modus operandi, so to say? Its fairly straight forward. Pakistani volunteers travelling to Afghanistan are bussed across the border at Torkham and Chaman. ISI operatives have linked up with right wing Pakistani religious parties such as Jamiat-e-Ulema Islami and together they have managed to send an estimated 8,000 Pakistani volunteers to fight in Afghanistan under the Taliban. The more senior ISI operatives to be hanging around Afghanistan have been Colonel "Gul" in Khandahar and Colonel 'Imam' in Herat. the other groups that the ISI have to liase with are Lashkar-e-Tayyaba (operating in Kashmir), Tablighi-e-Jamiat (Afghanistan) and Harakat-e-Ansar, also called Harakat-ul-Mujahedin (which again operates in Afghanistan). The latter is dedicated to spreading the "jihad" abroad and has also been added to the State Department's lovely list of terrorist organisations. As said, ISI don't really bother asking any of Pakistan's (usually useless) politicians for permission for any of the above. In fact they get quite ratty if any politico tries to shove his oar in on any of their nice little operations running on the side. Just take a look at old Prime Minister Nawaz Sharif. He thought he could start closing down ISI training camps for the kids going to Pakistan and Afghanistan.

Needless to say he is now in the ranks of the unemployed, while the military put their boots up on his desk. The directorate of Inter Services Intelligence was founded in 1948 by British army officer, Major General R. Cawthome. Then it was Britain's means of snooping around and quietly sending arms to whoever they liked at the time. Things haven't really changed that much. ISI is mainly made up of military officers. Its a bit like the CIA on a more paramilitary scale with a bit less subtlety than the Langley Boys. (One shivers at the thought). Altogether there are as many as 10,000 members of ISI; its a lot, I know, but they have got all those dinky little wars, (Tajikistan—on and off—Afghanistan, Kashmir, etc.) to keep their fingers on and the weapons flowing in. Don't ever think its easy being a spook. but at least with the new military government in Pakistan there won't be any more interfering politicos on the scene for a while.

The Mujahedin

One of the problems of training people to fight in foreign wars under the banner of religion is that they sometimes come home. There are an estimated 10,000 mujahedin (mainly Pakistanis) in Pakistan, excluding those who are still fighting in Afghanistan and Kashmir. The Taleban, in neighboring Afghanistan, began in Pakistan; and their austere version of Islam has been supported ever since by Pakistan. There are also hundreds of mujahedin from Libya, Egypt, Yemen, Jordan, Palestine, Algeria and Tunisia based, recruited and trained in Peshawar, and the border regions between Pakistan and Afghanistan. This was all very well when the nasty old Sovs were running around in Afghanistan. In those days turban clad figures ready to do or die for Islam (as long as they killed commies) were positively encouraged by just about everybody. But the Soviets left Afghanistan over a decade ago. The Muj haven't quite got round to leaving, yet. Sorry, they have, but in all the wrong directions. Like, er, Nairobi . . . The inner circle of the mujahedin consists of 300 Egyptians. The regional branch of the Islamic Jihad is directed by Mohammed Shawky Islambuli, brother of the assassin of President Anar el-Sadat.

Some 30 Egyptian

Eight of these Egyptians constitute the central command of the Islamic Legion, a terrorist and political group active in Egypt, Eritrea, Kenya, Tanzania, Sudan, Algeria, Libya and Lebanon. Some of the mujahedin leaders have fled to Jalalabad from Peshawar. The Arab mujahedin have ties with fundamentalist Muslims in the United States. Ramzi Ahmed Yussef, a suspect in the bombing of the World Trade Center in New York was trained from 1987 to 1990 in Peshawar camps in the ranks of the Islamic Jihad groups under the orders of Dr. Ayman al-Zawahiri.

Haraket-ul-Mujahedin

They started off as Haraket-ul-Ansar in 1993, but got bored with the name. But they're a busy bunch. The aim of the party is to direct wannabe mujahedin to the right conflicts and make sure that they fight with the right people. Mainly they're now sending folk to Kashmir, Tadjikistan and Afghanistan. They've got (or had) training camps in eastern Afghanistan. But those camps kinda bit the dust a bit in August 1998 when the United States sent them a "miss you" card in the form of several cruise missiles. You don't have to be a genius to work out that one of the guests in their camp was the elusive Osama bin Laden, who the CIA is desperate to make a permanent resident in the United States.

The Mohajirs and the MQM

As of the beginning of 1995, the Mohajirs are the principal disturbers in the Karachi area. The Mohajirs are Urdu-speaking Muslim immigrants who came here from India after the partition between Pakistan and India in 1947. Their political/military group, the Mohajir National Movement (MQM), is directly battling police and strong arming locals. They were (and I guess, still are) led by Altaf Hussein, who skipped to London in the early 1990s; he has since been charged with just about everything under the sun except child molesting. There are six major political and religious groups in Karachi. In total, they have 1,000 armed guerrillas and snipers operating at any one time.

MQM-Haqiqi (The Real MQM)

Another reason why Karachi is not a cool place to hang out in (see below). The MQM Haqiqi split from the mainstream MQM in February 1991. Led by Afaq Ahmed, the group was getting a bit irritated with the authoritarian style of Altaf Hussein. So far, so bad. But things really got out of hand when military intelligence (a misnomer if ever there was one) decided to arm the splinter groups as a counterbalance to the mainstream MQM. The end result? A low level war between the rival factions when they weren't busy popping off soldiers and policemen. No, it wasn't the smartest move the military ever made.

The "Afghans"

There are 3 million "Afghan" refugees in Pakistan, most living in squalid mud-walled refugee camps outside of Peshawar and Quetta. Many others live in UNHR tents in small mountainous villages and deserts. They have been there so long that they consider their life better than what is happening inside Afghanistan. There is little chance for education or a greater economic future, but most are waiting for things to settle down in war-wasted Afghanistan.

The Mohajirs (The Unreal Ones?)

As of the beginning of 1995, the Mohajirs are the principal disturbers in the Karachi area. The Mohajirs are Urdu-speaking Muslim immigrants who came here from India after the partition between Pakistan and India in 1947. Their political/military group, the Mohajir National Movement (MQM) (founded in 1986) is directly battling police and strong-arming locals. There are six major political and religious groups in Karachi. In total, they have 1,000 armed guerrillas and snipers operating at any one time.

GETTING IN

A passport and visa are required. The visa must be obtained from a Pakistani embassy or consulate before arrival at the point of entry. Information on entry requirements can be obtained from the embassy of Pakistan or the Pakistani consulate general. There is a $20 fee for the visa and a $10 fee for rush delivery. Business visitors and tourists are required to carry a valid Pakistan visa in their passports that must be obtained prior to entry. Pakistani requirements to legally cross the country's borders are different for each nationality. U.S. citizens must have a visa issued by a Pakistani consulate as well as a valid U.S. passport. Make sure you apply for your visa in the country of your residence, since you will be told that only the embassy in your home city or country can issue visas.

Do not bring in alcohol: it will be confiscated. Crossing from Afghanistan officially is forbidden for foreigners, although many of the remote tribal areas do not observe any immigration formalities. Currently, the Afghanistan–Pakistan border is closed, but it is easy to sneak across—if you don't mind the mines, the bandits and are a fully qualified mountaineer. Only UN personnel, locals, aid agencies and journos (with the right Taliban visa) are allowed to cross the border officially. The Iranian border can be crossed using weekly train service (Zahedan-Quetta), or by a painfully slow 22-hour bus trip (Taftan-Quetta). Folks who like avoiding those messy passport stamps can expect to be arrested and discover the joys of the local prisons.

You can enter from China via the efficient, but weather-sensitive Karakoram Highway. The road is open from May 1–November 30 if Mother Nature obliges. The route continues to the famous trading town of Kashgar, but the bus ride will test the stamina and intestines of any traveler. Coming in from India is via train (Lahore-Wagh) or a four-hour bus ride (Lahore-Amritsar) but subject to closure due to Sikh attacks. Check with the government or the embassy for exact restrictions and closures. The only land border crossing with India is Amritsar.

Embassy of Pakistan
2315 Massachusetts Avenue, NW
Washington, DC 20008
Tel.: (202) 939-6200
http://www.pakistan-embassy.com/

Pakistani Consulate General
12 East 65th Street
New York, NY 10021
Tel.: (212) 879-5800

GETTING AROUND

Safe travel inside Pakistan is subject to weather, regional idiosyncrasies and plain luck. Bandits prey on buses and trains; the roads are makeshift, and if the robbers don't get you, the dilapidated buses might. Pakistan is a patchwork of tribal- and government-controlled areas, sprinkled liberally with bandits who couldn't care less who "rules" the area. Most travelers have a great time, despite the chaos.

Substantial areas within North-West Frontier Province are designated tribal areas, outside the normal jurisdiction of government law enforcement authorities. Travel within these areas is particularly hazardous. Tribal feuds or conflicts between smuggling factions may incidentally involve foreigners. Even in the settled areas, ethnic, political or sectarian violence may target foreigners. Car hijackings and the abduction of foreigners are occasionally reported from the tribal areas. If visitors must enter the tribal areas, a permit must be obtained from the Home Department, which may require that an armed escort accompany the visitor.

Driving

Today, Pakistan is busy spending the millions appropriated to it by the World Bank to upgrade its highways. Unfortunately, no one has been taught to drive. The white lines on those freshly made highways are an old colonial anachronism. Drivers weave, honk, squeeze, yell, wave, swerve and do everything except brake when faced with an oncoming car.

Considering the Pakistanis' creative use of their roadways, it is not surprising that, despite all the press about dacoits (local bandits) and civil unrest, the greatest potential for injury while traveling through Pakistan is the chance of being involved in a crash or being smacked like a cricket ball when crossing the street. To give pedestrians and other drivers a chance, Pakistanis decorate their vehicles with as many bright and shiny objects as possible. If you do happen to take a bus around the country, *DP* advises you to keep your eyes closed, unless you really are after a thrill a minute.

Of a total 35,258 miles of roads in Pakistan, 24,952 (a generous 70 percent) are paved. The torturous terrain requires major engineering feats to put in roads. Most of the country can only be traversed via pack-trails and footpaths. The main highway is the Grand Trunk Road between Karachi and Peshawar. The multilane highway linking Karachi with Hyderabad is also a major route, permitting crazed drivers to get more out of their sheet-metal buckets than Isaac Newton would ever advise. The Indus Highway, the other north-south artery, is being improved, and there will eventually be a highway connecting Peshawar with Karachi, via Islamabad and Lahore.

The most impressive highway is the 1,200 kilometers Karakoram Highway, built over a 20-year period to link the remote Chinese market town of Kashgar with Peshawar to the south. The road is a mind-blower for its mountainous scenery and is frequently closed due to landslides, snowstorms, floods and other topographical afflictions. Various adventure groups offer bicyling tours for the eco-adventurous. Obviously, the hundreds of ever smiling drivers would think nothing of adding one more shiny decoration to the side of their overloaded trucks.

On paper, Pakistan borrows the British rule of driving on the left. In reality, driving is a death-defying blend of the German habit of operating motor vehicles with the pedal to the floor, the Italian habit of talking with their hands, and the Asian custom of ignoring mirrors, or side and rear windows. The fact that most Pakistani roads are designed for Alexander's (the Great) camels keeps it interesting. If you want less control over your destiny, you might want to hire your own talkative driver and deathtrap car from the Pakistan Tourism folks. A 4WD jeep is preferable for more rugged trips in the north. Suzukis and Jeeps are popular. You will need a large security deposit and will be dinged about eight rupees per km and 200 rupees per day. Or, you can negotiate a fixed rate if you know your itinerary.

In the cities, yellow taxis are cheap and should be hired round-trip, since they tend to gravitate to hotels and are hard to find elsewhere. Wildly decorated buses are cheaper, but remember they expect you to jump on (and off) while they are moving. Don't forget the seats by the driver are for women and don't be shy about yelling before your stop.

http://travel.state.gov/pakistan.html

By Rail

As with many other former British colonies, Pakistan was built around its aging railway system. The country is linked by the north-south railway between the southern port of Karachi and the city of Peshawar in the North-West Frontier Province. The line runs through most major population centers.

Pakistan Railways offers 8,775 kilometers of track, 907 stations, 78 train stops, 714 locomotives, 2,926 passenger coaches and 32,440 freight wagons. Sixty percent of Pakistan's track and

30 percent of its rolling stock are supposed to be scrapped, but are in use every day. Express trains have been held up by dacoits on the link between Karachi port and Lahore. You'll have a choice between second, economy, first, and air-conditioned classes. Go for the air-con class, since rail travel is cheap, slow and nostalgic in this class. The other classes are just torture. Bedding, toilet paper, soap and towels are not supplied on first-class couchettes but can be rented from the reservations office. The train between the Afghan border and Peshawar is the most interesting, as two steam trains (one at each end of the train) labor up and back down the Khyber Pass every Friday. Currently, Westerners are not allowed on this train, since it goes through the locked-down Khyber area.

http://danger-ahead.railfan.net/reports/rep99/

By Air

For those of you who want to avoid the mind numbing terror of Pakistan's roads, you will be happy to know that there are indeed loads of internal flights all around the country. Air travel, particularly to the northern areas, is often disrupted due to weather conditions. Regional airlines in the north have to fly below some of the world's tallest mountaintops. Islamabad/Rawalpindi International Airport is five miles northwest of Islamabad and a 20-minute drive by taxi. State-run Pakistan International Airlines (PIA) maintains tardy but vital service to 41 international and 33 domestic destinations. There are 112 airfields, of which 104 are usable, 75 have a permanent surface. There are 31 runways over 8,000 feet. Domestic tickets are cheaper when bought inside Pakistan. Pakistanis pay about half what you will pay. Airfares are laughably cheap (about US$10–$80 for any internal leg). You must pay in rupees. International flights to Karachi or Islamabad should be bought in major European or Asian bucket shops. Pakistan International Airways has the dubious task of flying very used equipment around the world's most hostile flying environments. Soaring mountains, dust, high winds, turbulence, down- and updrafts and the extra maintenance required to keep planes airborne may be the reasons why the landing announcement is a Muslim prayer: "Ladies and Gentlemen, Inshallah (God willing), we will be shortly landing." The feeling of flying heavily loaded turboprops well below many of the world's highest mountains is, quite frankly, a thrill. The turboprops can be very bumpy, and don't be surprised to find passengers praying fervently on rough flights. Despite the white-knuckle flights, air travel is still the recommended means of transportation between major cities in Pakistan. Keep in mind that many flights are overbooked, but seats on these flights can be bought by sweet-talking (and, of course, bribing) an airport porter.

http://www.piac.com/index.htm
http://www.rpi.edu/dept/union/paksa/www/html/pakistan/trans.html
http://www.piads.com.pk/

Insider Tip

Pakistan is a land of frustrating red tape, but there are many ways to cut through it. For example, you can be told that a flight is overbooked, only to find out that a flight with one connection to the same destination is available. You can be stopped from entering a region by an emphatic border guard, only to walk 20 yards further along the border and walk right through. There is little that cannot be bought, solved, rented or fixed in Pakistan for a moderate fee. In fact, getting around problems is a major source of income for enterprising Pakistanis and "Afghans." There was little DP could not do or make happen in Pakistan with a little financial lubrication. So, when in doubt, whip it out (your rupees). A case in point.

A newly made friend asked me if I could get him a visa to America. I said, "It's not like Pakistan, you can't just pay people off."

"Surely you can pay the police 2000–3000 rupees (about US$100) to get me in? I could be your gardener."

"Sorry, no way."

"What kind of country is that?" he said in disgust.

Trekking

Since many of the major historical sites have been pounded to rubble by invading armies, and the vast deserts to the south do not inspire too many nature photographers, Pakistan realizes that most of the tourism is related to its spectacular northern mountain scenery. You will find this area of Pakistani tourism well run and efficient. In a country where you would have a hard time finding a decent motor-coach tour, you can climb a major mountain with great ease (or at least make the preparations). To facilitate understanding and access, tourism officials have divided the country into open, restricted, and closed zones for trekkers. Open zones go up to only 6,000 meters. Travel above that point is classified as mountaineering and requires a separate permit. The best source for information and permits is through the various trekking packagers well in advance of your trip (permits can take months).

Climbing

Although Everest is number one on the list of climbers, K2 (8,611 meters, 28,251 feet) really is the tougher climb. It is also one of the world's most dangerous climbs. Only 119 people have made it to the top of K2, compared to the 600 that have planted a flag on Mt. Everest. What makes K2 the most dangerous mountain in the world is its annual death toll. When *DP* was in northern Pakistan, there was a reward to find the bodies of two climbers who had disappeared in an avalanche.

Everest is on the border with Nepal and Tibet and costs a staggering $50,000 for six climbing permits. K2 is a bargain at $10,000 for six climbers. These are just the climbing fees, and with supplies, porters and excess baggage fees, climbing the big peaks is a sport for not only the brave, but also the rich.

http://www.findaguide.com/pages/pkclimbh.htm
http://www.infohub.com/TRAVEL/ADVENTURE/RECREATION/ASIA/pakistan.html

You will need an exit visa to leave the country. Although you may adhere to the paper chain faithfully, expect to get a quizzical look if the immigration official notes certain "irregularities" and requires additional funds to let you catch your plane out. If you are carrying anything that can be interpreted as being an antiquity, you are in trouble again. You'll need an export permit for rugs, and don't think for a moment that the nifty pen-gun you bought in Darra Adam Khel is not going to be spotted and confiscated. If you're bringing some smoking green back with you, expect it to be discovered by sniffer dogs at Karachi and Lahore airports. Please note that although hashish and heroin are as easy to buy in Peshawar as Snickers bars in Pacoima, there is much money to be made (5,000 rupees last we checked) turning frugal hippies in to police. The naïve stoners will then have to pay up to US$5,000 to the concerned but financially adept police to save their skin. Remember, you will need to keep your exchange receipts to change your grubby rupees into more stable currencies. Most people take care of exchanging their money in the bazaar (watch out for bogus US$100 bills printed in Syria, Iran and Lebanon before 1989). Remember to keep enough for your taxi, something to eat at the airport, 200 rupees for your departure tax. Everything else can be paid for in dollars. Some banks only cash traveler's checks and do not take foreign cash.

Karachi

Some consider Karachi to be the most dangerous city in the world. About five to ten people die every day as a result of political violence in Karachi. Karachi is a dirty, bustling port town, with a population of more than 5 million people. Robbery and kidnapping are often carried out with the distinct intention of creating terror and instability among the populace. Bombings have occurred at Pakistan government facilities and public utility sites. Vehicular hijacking and theft by armed individuals are common occurrences. Persons resisting have very often been shot and killed. Overly detailed and gory reports of murders, bombings, robberies and assassinations fill the papers every day.

The bustling port of Karachi is a war zone, thanks to the MNM. The name means Refugees National Movement and is led by Altaf Hussain (who conveniently lives in sedate London). The Urdu-speaking Mohajirs feel they are discriminated against (which they are) by the Sinhis. There is also a lot of banditry, drug feuds and Sunni/Shiite violence that is blamed on the MNM. There is even a splinter group called the MNM Haqiqi—or the real MNM.

Every day this dirty, sprawling metropolis of 13 million people tosses five or six bodies into the back of a police van for identification. In 1995 there were 2,100 people killed in Karachi, strikes crippled the economy, and people feared for their lives. Now only a couple of hundred die each year. The government's reaction was to declare open season on the MNM. In many cases suspects are rounded up (many with a price on their head) and simply shot later. There is a new law that allows cops to shoot to kill if they even think you are about to commit a terrorist act. If they don't hit you, they have to arrest you. Terrorists can get seven years just for being suspected of stirring up sectarian hatred.

There is also a ping-pong series of killings between minority Shiites and majority Sunnis that keep the morgue busy. If you get bored waiting around to be shot or kidnapped, you can spend a few hours crabbing or rent a camel on the beach.

http://www.usia.gov/abtusia/posts/PK2/wwwhamcn.html
http://www.karachipage.com
http://www.alephx.org/karachi/
http://www.brecorder.com

The North-West Frontier Province

An area created in 1901 by the British who could never figure how to "civilize" the many tribes and clans, the NWFP is still the land of *badal*, or revenge. It is the oldest continuously lawless area in the world. Home to the "wily Pathans," this rugged land of green valleys and snowcapped valleys has never been fully conquered by Alexander, Moghuls, Sikhs, Brits or even the Russians. The North-West Frontier Province has an affinity with Afghanistan in the west and is known for its well-armed populace. Its a place where the local farmers like to guard their crops with antiaircraft guns, with Stinger missiles inside the house for emergencies. Not a big surprise, really, when we tell you that the "crops" in question happen to be hash and opium. And snoopy outside visitors are often regarded with some suspicion. It's the kind of place where the locals might invite you to stay a while longer than you had planned. Especially so if the government gets any ideas about trying to eradicate the crops. Nothing better on the bargaining table than a couple of foreign tourists to concentrate everybody's minds. To be fair, though, opium production in the NWFP appears to be on the decline these days. Of the 800 (recorded) tons produced in 1980, by 1998 there were 24 (recorded) tons. Instead of producing, though, Pakistan has become more of a conduit for some of the annual 2,000 or so tons that are produced in Afghanistan. Peshawar, the largest city and capital of the province, could be accurately described as Dodge City without the benefit of a Wyatt Earp. Weapons are carried and sold openly on the streets. The city is the home of over 1 million Afghan refugees who live in three large mud cities. If you're in town and want to find a decent watering hole, the best (and only) place is the American Club; but you'll need someone to sign you in.

http://www.frontierpost.com.pk/

Khyber Pass

It would be an understatement to say that it is dangerous to travel overland through the tribal areas along the Khyber Pass from Peshawar to Kabul. The North-West Frontier areas are ruled by the Afridi tribes and are not under the control of the Pakistani government or police. Many, if not most, make money smuggling hashish, heroin and contraband into Pakistan. If you can get past the checkpoint at the smuggler's market (just walk through the gate in the north market square into the Afridi bodyguard complex) expect eight more Pakistani army checkpoints until you reach Afghanistan. Once you are in Afghanistan, you are on your own. There are many deadly tribal feuds over things as important as stolen goats or errant wives, so lightening some dumb foreigner of his vehicle or belongings does not even appear on their list of "things not to do." Car hijackings and the abduction of foreigners are occasionally reported from the tribal areas. If visitors must enter the tribal areas, a permit must be obtained from the Home Department, which may require that an armed escort accompany the visitor. (P.S. Khyber pass is Cockney rhyming slang for ass.)

http://www.dawn.com
http://www.afghan-network.net

Sind Province

Hundreds of years ago, travelers called Sind province the Unhappy Valley because of its burning deserts, freezing mountain peaks, dust, lack of water and general fear of the predatory tribes. Today it should perhaps be called the Very Unhappy Valley. Competing groups of Sunnis and Shias, Mohajirs and Sindhis all try their best to lower the population tally of the other groups. The result is frequent assassinations, firefights, bomb attacks, murders and overall mayhem. Several American businessmen have also been gunned down in Karachi. The government likes to blame these killings on whoever is convenient, (i.e., out of favor at the time). When the various kids with guns get a bit bored they take time off to do a bit of freelance banditry. Hey, c'mon, they've gotta earn a living somehow! Just keep your fingers crossed its not you they stumble across one fine evening.

Dacoits are well armed and will attack travelers even with your trusty police escort. They have been known to stop entire trains or vehicle caravans, often kidnapping and killing passengers. Anyone contemplating travel into the Sind interior should first contact the American Consulate *(8 Abdullah Haroon Road, Karachi, Tel.: 515081)* for advisability. Gunmen can be hired from travel groups or on the street (not advised) for about 4,000 rupees a day. You will have to pay for your bodyguard's room and board. Sind province still has a fairly healthy kidnappings-for-ransom business.

http://sindh.net/
http://www.sindh.gov.pk/index.shtml

Hyderabad

In Hyderabad, there have been recurring outbreaks of ethnic and sectarian violence which have been characterized by random bombings, shootings and mass demonstrations. Recent incidents have resulted in several deaths and the unofficial imposition of curfews. There have also been numerous incidents of kidnapping for ransom.

http://www.hyderabad.co.uk

Islamabad and Rawalpindi

Welcome to the Twin Cities: Dirty Rawalpindi and squeaky-clean Islamabad, the capital of Pakistan, are only 10 kilometers and two worlds apart. Islamabad is the showcase city for the embassy folks, and Rawalpindi is where all the real people live. The crime rate in Islamabad is lower than in many parts of Pakistan, but it is on the rise. In the recent past, Americans have been the victim of armed robberies and assaults, although these types of incidents are not frequent. Thefts from the massive walled residences are common. As usual, they are typically inside jobs. Most incidents experienced by the American community are committed by servants employed in the household. Rawalpindi has experienced some bombings in public areas, such as markets, cinemas and parks.

http://www.jang.com.pk/thenews/jul99-daily/09-07-99/metro/islam.htm

Lahore/Punjab Province

The Punjab Province has been the site of numerous bomb blasts occurring at cinemas, marketplaces and other public areas. A professional criminal element exists in the Punjab (operating mainly in the interior), with kidnapping for ransom, robbery and burglaries all being carried out by gangs of professional criminals. There are frequent armed clashes between Pakistani and Indian army groups along the border area and in east Punjab and particularly in the disputed territory of Kashmir. Lahore is placid but famous for rip-offs of tourists in cheap hotels, bogus traveler's checks and other tourist crime.

http://www.lcci.org.pk/

Kashmir

Once upon a time—a long, long time ago . . . in a galaxy far, far away—Kashmir was one of the most popular tourist destinations in the world. Not any more. Instead Kashmir now takes up a rather large slice of both Pakistan and India's defense budget, with both sides playing that well known game of "our-artillery-is-more-accurate-than-yours" along the 700-kilometer-long Line of Control. Things heated up a bit in 1999 when Indian soldiers went back up the Siachen glacier, as the snows melted, to find that the high ground had been taken by a large number of guerrillas who had infiltrated from Pakistan. And the aforementioned guerrillas didn't seem to want to leave or have their passports stamped. In nearly two months of fighting there were an estimated 3,500 casualties. The problem originated in 1947, when the princes who ran the "princely states" cut a quick deal with mainly Hindu India instead and screwed their predominately Muslim subjects. The Kashmir dispute, which caused the 1948 and 1965 wars with India (Pakistan was whipped both times), remains unresolved. The Simla Agreement after the 1971 Bangladesh war adjusted the boundary between the Indian state of Jammu and Kashmir and the Pakistani state of Azad and Kashmir. The Muslims in the Indian state of Jammu and Kashmir demand greater autonomy from Hindu India.

The separatist elements in the province, particularly the Jammu and Kashmir Liberation Front (JKLF), and the Shura-e-Jihad (a Kashmiri based organization that is made of seven separatist groups) openly receive training and military equipment from Pakistan.

So today, Kashmir has turned into a war zone with both sides owning and squabbling over large chunks of land. Much of the trouble goes back to the period of the Afghan conflict (the one with the Russians), when Pakistani parties allied and trained with Afghan mujahedin to kick ass out of the Russians. Some of the less academic groups thought that it would be cool to have a bit of jihad in Kashmir as well. So, while Pakistani groups like Jamiat-i-Islami trained alongside their mates in Afghanistan (in the case of the latter it was Hezb-i-Islami, led by Gulbuddin Hekmatyar), what no one really noticed at the time was that all these groups had close connections with Hezb-ul-Mujahedin, the armed wing of the Kashmiri Jamiat-i-Islami political faction. Oops!

Jammu and Kashmir Liberation Front (JKLF)

http://shell.comsats.net.pk/~jklf/index.html
http://www.geocities.com/CapitolHill/Lobby/8215/index.html

Information

http://www.jammu-kashmir.com

Baluchistan/Quetta

The province of Baluchistan that borders both Iran and Afghanistan is notorious for cross-border smuggling operations. It should really be in our "Forbidden Places," since few if any permits are given and you must have the permission of the local tribal chief to move in relative safety. Why anyone would want to travel to Quetta, southern Afghanistan, eastern Iran or the bleak Pakistani coast is a good question. We say relative safety, because kidnapping for money is as popular here as it is in the tribal regions up north. Any student of geography will quickly figure out that the fastest way from landlocked Afghanistan is through remote Baluchistan. The major drug smugglers (actually smuggling may be too ludicrous a term to apply here) run large truck and even camel caravans from Afghanistan to the coast.

This region also has a high occurrence of armed robberies, probably because just about everybody carries a gun. Terrorist bombings have occurred frequently in the region, primarily concentrated among those districts along the Afghanistan border. There is limited to no provincial police. Those hardy persons considering travel into the interior should first notify the province's home secretary, travel in a group and limit travel to daylight hours and see a psychiatrist. Although the Pakistani government tells *DP* that permission from the provincial authorities is required for travel into some interior locations, I couldn't help but wonder which government folks would be around to check.

http://www.pak.org/khazana/Provinces/Baluchistan/

Bogus Boogie

When the International Federation of the Phonographic Industry, the global cop for pirate CDs, comes to town, music store owners will want to run for the hills. Over 92 percent of all CD and tape sales in Pakistan were bootlegged copies.

Crime

Pakistan is a special place when it comes to crime. There are three levels of crime. The first is the friendly constant pressure to relieve the unwitting of their possessions. Just as the wind and rain can erode granite mountains, the traveler to Pakistan will find his money slowly slipping from him. Perhaps this is not a crime, since the victim is consensual, but it nevertheless is not an honest transfer of funds.

The second level is petty crime, the fingers rummaging through your baggage, the wallet that leaves your pocket or the camera that disappears from the chair next to you. Everyone will caution you on petty theft. Here, theft is an art, almost a learned skill. These crimes happen to the unwary and unprepared. Lock your zippers, do not leave anything of value in your hotel room, and do not tell people your schedule. The luggage of most airline and bus passengers looks like a Houdini act with locks, rope, sewn-up sacks, and even steel boxes used to keep out curious fingers. Mail must be sent in a sewn-up sack to prevent theft. Naturally, thieves love the many zippered, unlocked backpacks of foreign trekkers. The best solution is to put your luggage in a canvas or vinyl duffel bag, and keep all valuables on your person. Do not carry any money in pockets, and use money belts as well as decoy wallets when traveling. (Decoy wallets are cheap wallets with old credit cards, pictures and addresses of your worst enemy, and Iraqi dinars.)

The third level is where Pakistan outshines many other areas: The cold calculated art of kidnapping, extortion and robbery. There is little any traveler can do to prevent this crime in certain areas. People who have regular schedules and who travel to crowded markets, along well-known paths, or do not have good security are at risk. Check State Department reports and contact the local embassy for the latest horror stories. All large cities have security agencies that can provide advice, drivers and bodyguards for reasonable daily rates.

Dacoits

Possibly the most lucrative night job in Pakistan. Many *dacoits* are professional bandits aligned along tribal lines who hold normal day jobs and then head out into the country for a little extra cash at night. Unlike the greasy thugs of Russia or the gold-toothed banditos of Mexico, *dacoits* are usually bad guys for hire led by educated or civil service level young men. They cannot find employment, so they use their organizing and planning skills to support political parties, back up rebel units, raise operating funds and expand operations areas. Despite the genteel background of the leaders, the actions of their members are bloody and crude. *Dacoits* will stop buses and trains, rob, rape and murder, and generally create a bloody mess. They also use kidnapping as a way to generate funds and "flip the bird" to the local government. Expect to be a well-treated but powerless pawn, as the *dacoits* negotiate with the strapped local government (not your fat, rich, home government) for payment for your release. Your biggest problem may be a heavy-handed (but fiscally efficient) rescue attempt staged by the government on your behalf. Stay out of remote tribal areas or areas known for *dacoitry*.

Ethnic Clashes

Pakistan is the botched result of seven weeks of bad planning by Sir Cyril Radcliffe in 1947 in an effort to separate warring Muslims from the Hindus. The hastily created border caused instant riots and violence, sending 6 million people from each region fleeing across the new border. It is estimated that up to a million people were killed. Today, with 60 million Muslims in India and more than 10 million Hindus in Pakistan, there is little hope for peace. Demonstrations often get ugly in Karachi and Hyderabad, where Sindhis and immigrant groups in Karachi and Hyderabad duke it out. Between January 1990 and October 1992, Pakistan-trained militants killed 1,585 men and women, including 981 Muslims, 218 Hindus, 23 Sikhs and 363 security men. In three years, over 7,000 Kalashnikov rifles, 400 machine guns, 400 rocket launchers, 1,000 rockets, 7,000 grenades, 2,000 pistols and revolvers, and thousands of mines were seized. One of the keys to staying alive in heavily armed areas is to not bring a knife to a gunfight. If you visit Pakistan, you might want to bring your own army.

Cheap Guns

The border regions of Pakistan are (and traditionally have been) a Wild West region, with most tribal, ethnic and criminal groups being well armed with cheap weapons brought in from Afghanistan or manufactured on demand. There are few tribes that don't possess large arsenals and have fierce rivalries against one another. Most urban residents employ *chowkidaars*, or private guards, for protection. If you are not caught in the middle of a firefight, you may be worse off at a wedding or party. In the tribal areas, Pathans have a bad habit of celebrating weddings using their AK-47s as firecrackers and shoot bursts into the air, ignorant of Newtonian physics.

Reader Mike Squirrell sends in the following: Darra Adam Khel has been closed to foreigners for years but if you take local pickups from Peshawar (if you ask, the locals will hide you from the peering eyes of cops at checkpoints), make sure you tell the driver to take you all the way through town to avoid being stopped by the tribal police. At the first gun shop, ask the owner to invite the police to escort you, and a little baksheesh (about 100 rupees per cop) will get you a guided tour and a wave out of town. You can't actually buy the guns, but you can fire them. (Choose a Chinese- or Russia- made gun to fire since the Pak-made ones can explode in your face.)

The Pathans (Pahktuns)

Pakistan's Pathan community still wants to unite with the Pathans in Afghanistan to create Pahktunistan. No major shooting or activities yet but remember that the Taliban are mostly Pathan and have displaced a Tajik government.

There are good medical facilities in all major towns in Pakistan. You may need it after your first fly-blown kabobfest. Pakistan may not be the dirtiest place in the world, but it is enough to make some Siberian mining towns look positively pristine. Expect to get the runs, unless you have a PVC gastrointestinal tract. Some folks go gaga over the spicy food, and other folks end up crouched over a grubby pit toilet learning the hard way that fiery spices and peppers burn as bad going out as they do going down. Take the normal precautions you would take in any third-world country and carry medicine for diarrhea.

You need proof of a cholera vaccination if arriving from infected areas. You should get a typhoid shot and take malaria prophylaxis. Yellow fever vaccination and certificate are required if you have visited a country in the endemic zone recently.

Inoculations against yellow fever and cholera are required for visitors arriving in Pakistan within five days after leaving or transiting infected areas. In addition, immunizations against typhoid, polio and meningitis are recommended, as are prophylactic antimalarial drugs. Malaria is present throughout Pakistan at altitudes below 2,000 meters. Remember, even if you are heading straight for the mountains, you can still get bitten in the airport waiting lounge in Karachi. Hepatitis and tetanus are further health risks in Pakistan, as are amoebic dysentery and worms. Bilharzia (schistosomiasis) and elephantiasis (filariasis) are also endemic diseases, although not widespread. Follow the usual precautions for countries with poor sanitation. Military hospitals, frequently open to fee-paying local civilians and foreigners, often provide the best facilities.

Pakistan is a land of hard extremes. The climate is generally arid and very hot (very, very hot), except in the northern mountains, where the summers are hot and winters are very cold (very, very cold). The best time to visit Pakistan is between October and April. Karachi and Lahore are pleasant; Islamabad can get cool. The average annual temperatures in the southern city of Karachi are between 55° F and 93° F. Summer brings the monsoon season, but rainfall is negligible at other times of the year. After April, the temperatures climb from mid-July through September during the monsoon season, which can dump up to 16 centimeters of rain. North of Islamabad is mountainous, with a temperate climate. Summers are cool, winters cold, and the average annual rainfall is 120 centimeters.

The currency is the rupee; about 32 rupees to the U.S. dollar. You can only bring up to 100 rupees into Pakistan but who would? The rupee is best purchased at a bank, not at your hotel. Many money changers will try to foist off the faded dirty notes, but don't take them. They will be tough to exchange back. You will need to carry around the paperwork you get when you swap dollars for rupees. Most folks change their money at the market. Credit cards are worthless outside the major cities, but good old AMEX has offices in Islamabad, Rawalpindi, Lahore and Karachi. Don't expect much help from AMEX other than cashing a personal check up to $500 or replacing your card. The best exchange rates are on the black market. Merchants will give you a slightly better exchange rate if you pay in U.S. dollars. You will not get a receipt for the transaction, since the transaction is illegal.

Baksheesh is the Pakistani version of tipping. When people help you, it's normal and expected that you will drop a few rupees (about 10 percent) in their palm. Don't forget to haggle, haggle, haggle. Having a local guide do your haggling for you (shopping, bus, hotel, air fares, taxis, bribes, souvenirs) can easily save you his fee. You can bring in as much foreign currency as you want, but it must be declared upon arrival.

Electricity is 220V/50Hz. The electrical system can only be described as deadly, and shorts and blowouts are common. Be careful plugging in appliances around wet areas. Many water heaters are electric. Do not turn lights or appliances off with bare feet or in the shower.

If you hate crowds and crave danger, Pakistan provides excellent opportunities for winter sports, including mountaineering and hiking in the Himalayan hill stations. Folks who like to ski will be glad to know that there are absolutely no downhill ski facilities in this mountainous paradise. Pakistan features the longest continuous drops on the planet (heli-boarding anyone?) as well as breathtaking scenery. The AK-47s, pistols and 50-caliber machine guns are dirt-cheap in Peshawar but a bitch to bring home as hand luggage. Down below, where the Indus River makes the Punjab and Sind fertile, temperatures are more moderate, with an average of 60° F in January to an average of 95° F in the summer. Baluchistan consists of deserts and low bare hills. Here and in northern Sind, temperatures can climb over 120° F in the summer.

Normal office hours from Saturday to Wednesday are from 9 A.M. to 2 P.M., with at least one hour for lunch. Offices close earlier on Thursdays, usually at lunchtime. Friday is the weekly Muslim holiday. Banks are open from 9 A.M. to 1:30 P.M. from Saturday to Wednesday, and until 11 A.M. on Thursday. Urdu (the national language) and English are the official languages of Pakistan. Punjabi, Sindi, Pashtu, Baluchi, Seraiki and other languages and dialects are also spoken. Most children and older adults speak English.

Many people confuse Pakistani cuisine with Indian food. Kebabs, *tikkas* (spiced grilled meats) and curries are the staples; they're served with *naan* (flat bread). The most popular drinks are tea (black or green), *lassi* (a milk drink) and Western-style soft drinks, which are widely available.

Polo

One of Pakistan's most famous exports (besides drugs and terrorists) is polo. Afghans and Pakistanis love polo, a violent-spirited game that is as close to horse-mounted warfare as one can get. The British picked it up while stationed here and it quickly became the upper-class macho sport of Britain. You can still see polo games played by soldiers, cops and just regular folks in Chitral and Gilgit. Today, the best polo players in the world are from Argentina. The Argentinian gaucho put back a lot of the violence and death-defying elements of the game. Before polo, the Argentinians played puto, a tamer form of the Afghan game of buzkashi. Instead of a headless goat being manhandled around a huge field, the Argentinians would whack a duck with sticks. The most violent form of polo in Argentina is the Creole style. Ponies are ridden hard, bones are broken, and each seven-minute chukka, or period, is guaranteed to be full of action.

Useful Addresses

Associated Press of Pakistan (APP)

House 1, Street 56
F 6/3 POB 1258, Istanbul
Tel.: [51] (8) 26158
Fax: [51] (8) 13225

Canadian Embassy in Pakistan

Diplomatic Enclave, Sector G-5
P.O. Box 1042
Islamabad
Tel.: [92] (51) 211101

Pakistani Embassy in Canada

151 Slater Street, Suite 608
Ottawa, ONT. K1P 5H3
Tel.: (613) 238-7881
Fax: (613) 238-7296

Pakistan International Airlines Corp. (PIA)

Head Office Building, Quaid-i-Azam
International Airport
Karachi
Tel.: (21) 4572011
Fax: (21) 4572754

Pakistani Embassy in United States

2315 Massachusetts Avenue, N.W.
Washington, D.C. 20008
Tel.: (202) 939-6200
Fax: (202) 387-0484

Pakistan Tourism Development Corp. Ltd.

House No. 2, Street 61, F-7/4
Islamabad
Tel.: 811001

UK Embassy

Diplomatic Enclave, Ramna 5
P.O. Box 1122
Islamabad
Tel.: 822131
Fax: 823439

U.S. Embassy in Pakistan

Diplomatic Enclave, Ramna 5
P.O. Box 1048
Islamabad
Tel.: [92] (51) 826161
Fax: [92] (51) 214222

Embassy Location

The Consular Section

Located separately in the USAID build-
ing
18 Sixth Avenue, Ramna 5

The Consulate General

8 Abdullah Haroon Road
Karachi
Tel.: 568-5170

The U.S. Consulate General

Sharah-E-Abdul Hamid Bin Badees
50 Empress Road
New Simla Hills
Lahore
Tel.: 636-5530

The U.S. Consulate

11 Hospital Road
Peshawar Cantonment
Peshawar
Tel.: 279-801, 279-802, 279-803

The U.S. Embassy

Diplomatic Enclave, Ramna 5
Islamabad
Tel.: 826 161

U.S. Ambassador to Pakistan Thomas W. Simons, Jr.

P.O. Box 1048,
Unit 6220, APO AE 09812-2200
Tel.: 92-51-826161

10/12/99	General Pervious Musharrat overthrows Prime Minister Nawaz Sharif.
4/14/99	Pakistan responds to Indian missile test by test-firing its Ghauri II long-range missile.
4/11/99	India test-fires long range version of its nuclear capable Agni missile.
11/5/98	Fresh attempts on negotiations in New Dehli, amid tense military standoff on the Siachen glacier, the world's highest battlefield.
6/12/98	Pakistan and India invite each other for talks, but fail to agree on agenda.
5/28/1998	Pakistan says it has conducted five nuclear tests in response to India's tests weeks before.

4/6/98	Pakistan tests long-range (1,500 km) Ghauri missile.
8/14/97	Pakistan marks 50 years of independence.
2/6/92	Pakistan declares capability to build nuclear bomb, but vows not to build the bomb.
4/7/91	Shia Muslims mark the death of Hazrat Ali, fourth caliph of Islam.
8/5/88	Arif Hussain al-Hussaini, a leading Shiite religious and political leader in Pakistan, is shot to death in Peshawar.
7/17/88	An airplane carrying President Zia Ul-Haq and U.S. Ambassador Arnold Raphel crashes, killing everyone aboard.
9/5/86	Twenty-one persons, including two Americans, are killed in an abortive hijacking of Pan Am flight 73 by four Arab gunmen.
4/10/86	The daughter of former President Bhutto, Benazir Bhutto, returns from exile in Europe.
7/18/85	Shahnawaz Bhutto, son of executed President Zulfikar Bhutto and older brother of Pakistani People's Party Leader Benazir Bhutto, dies under mysterious circumstances in France.
7/14/85	Bombing of Pan-Am office.
11/22/79	The U.S. embassy in Islamabad is attacked and burned by Islamic militants, following rumors that the United States was involved in the violent takeover of the Grand Mosque in Mecca, Saudi Arabia.
4/4/1979	Former president of Pakistan Zulfikar, Ali Bhutto, is executed by the Pakistani government under President Zia. The terrorist group al-Zulfikar, founded by his two sons, is named after him.
7/5/77	Army Chief of Staff Mohammad Zia leads an army coup to seize power and becomes chief martial law administrator.
6/8/62	Martial law, which was imposed in 1958, is lifted and the national assembly convenes.
3/23/62	A new constitution is promulgated by President Ayub Khan.
10/7/58	President Iskander Mirza, supported by senior military officers, seizes power and imposes martial law.
9/6/57	Defense of Pakistan Day.
3/23/56	The national assembly adopts a new constitution that rejects Pakistan's status as a dominion and becomes an "Islamic Republic" within the commonwealth. Also known as Pakistan Day.
8/14/47	Independence Day. Pakistan becomes a self-governing dominion within the British Commonwealth.

PAKISTAN

Rhythm and Blues

Glancing at the wisps of cloud below the road, I thought about what Tariq had said the night before while we were waiting for our mutton kebabs on the Sangum Hotel's riverside terrace.

"Our saying is, Allah already has decided exactly how much food you will eat in this world, and exactly where you will eat it. So much food, in so many places," said Tariq, an Azad Kashmiri who is *Dawn* newspaper's man in Muzaffarabad. He took a small piece of imaginary goat between his fingers and popped it into his mouth to emphasize his point.

That morning, as we crossed the treacherous mountain road to the Neelam Valley, where the Indian and Pakistani armies pound each other daily across disputed Kashmir's Line of Control, Tariq's bit of fatalistic folk wisdom relieved my mind of any needless worry.

The road that crosses the 9,000-foot-high Nakka Pass is a testament to the audacity of the Pakistan Army's engineers. They were compelled to build it in 1994 when direct Indian fire across the LoC closed the otherwise less hazardous river road. The detour links two points that are no more than 15 kilometers apart on the map, but by Land Cruiser it is three hours and 40 klicks of switchbacks that cling to sheer cliffs, where overloaded buses and top-heavy trucks vie for position on a single, occasionally paved lane, without benefit of guardrail. The drop is typically 500 to 1,500 feet before you hit anything, not counting any Dogpatch-style cliff-hugging huts you might take out on the way down.

The corporal behind the wheel cranked the Pakistani pop tunes. The major who was our host for the day looked over his shoulder at us perched in the back of the stripped-down army land cruiser, and grinned through his moustache.

"We brought some Karachi journalists on this road two months ago," the major said. "They had loose movements every 15 minutes!"

He remarked with pride that it took only seven months to build this road, at a cost of 17 lives and several bulldozers. As we climbed higher and the river got smaller below us, I thought back to the first time I ever heard the Sex Pistols, in a small boat amid big waves off Surat Thani in 1977, when Anders the Swede began singing "Noooooooo future! Noooo future! No future for you!" I had been out of Asia for 20 years, but remembered that when it is pointless to be actually concerned, there is nothing to do but laugh. Besides, in Pakistan it was apparent there is a natural rhythm everyone was tuned into except us ferengi, a rhythm that allows donkey cart and speeding Toyota, careening bus and wobbling bicycle, child at play and herd of goats to share the road, in an incomprehensible traffic that flows effortlessly in many conflicting directions at once, at least until the mysterious logarithm craps out and everything comes to a complete halt or a bus plunges.

The Nakka Pass road trumped all previous Pak highways, but we negotiated the cliffs without incident, suffering our blow-out on a mellow stretch beyond the pass instead. We wound our way down through majestic pine forests, past white marble outcroppings to villages of tin-roofed chalets and cornfields on thumbnail-sized terraces, crossing and recrossing the same energetic mountain stream 8 or 10 times until we finally entered the Neelam Valley proper. Tall stone walls built along the last few switchbacks to shield traffic from the Indian firing positions across the river.

We knew the threat was real, having visited the Combined Military Hospital in Muzaffarabad, where we watched an orderly change the dressing on a screaming eight-year-old girl's bullet wound, and saw the eyes rolling in the head of an incoherently moaning young man whose ribs were shattered on both sides and guts churned up in the middle by a bullet that went in under one arm and came out under the other. After a heavy shelling campaign in June that followed the nuclear test blasts of May, the wards were full of depressed-looking men and women and frightened-looking children with their vital organs and limbs perforated by shrapnel—which, it turns out, will go through innocent flesh as well as wicked like hot steel goes through butter. The stench of urine from the nearby latrines triumphed over the otherwise impressive stink of disinfectant. It was sweltering, crowded and full of flies, and as we left we agreed that we did not want to have to go back there.

The peasants say their villages are targeted by the Indians because they support the mujahedin. The Indians say the Paks hide their artillery in the villages, which the peasants deny. The Indians also say the Paks hit civilians on their side because they don't support the mujahedin. For whatever reason, more than 200 people, mainly civilians, were killed by shelling on both sides in the summer after the nuke tests, and more than 600 were wounded.

The 50-year-old conflict that demands artillery duels is complex, and numerous websites will give you many versions of it. Search key word "Kashmir" and have a party. Essentially, the Hindu maharaja of mainly Muslim Kashmir ended up going with India after the British left in 1947. The Paks felt it should have gone to them. After three wars, they've ended up with a South Asian version of Northern Ireland, with a Korean DMZ quality to it—except that there is nothing demilitarized about the Line of Control, and the behavior of both sides pales the terrorism and police excesses of Northern Ireland.

In Pakistani-held Azad Kashmir, refugees will show you stumps where they say their legs or hands were hacked off by machete-wielding Indian soldiers in retaliation for supporting the mujahedin. The Indians say these must be landmine victims. You can chat with the refugee camp chief about the crying toddler his men smothered as they shepherded 1,400 villagers between Indian Army posts in a flight through the mountains. In Indian Jammu and Kashmir, you can meet the Hindu bride who saw her groom and all the other men in the bridal party shot dead before her eyes.

In nine years, the estimates of those tortured to death or summarily executed by Indian security forces, massacred or assassinated by mujahedin or ripped apart by shelling ranges from 25,000 to 80,000, depending on who you hear it from.

On the road to Neelam Valley, the major told us about his seven months as a cherry lieutenant getting his obligatory blooding on the Siachen glacier. The world's highest battlefield at 22,000 feet, it is considered by some observers to be emblematic of the murderous absurdity of this stalemated conflict. The Indians landed troops there in 1984 and the Paks, insistent that that was their godforsaken stretch of ice and rock, counterattacked. In the 14 years since, the two sides have fought a frigid form of trench warfare, sucking on oxygen tanks and poking their heads out of heated bunkers long enough to lob a few mortar rounds at each other several times a week. Rockfalls and frostbite claim more casualties on both sides than enemy fire. Rather than an absurdity, the major insisted that it was an honor to serve on the glacier that is one of the sources of the Sindh, Pakistan's great river, known to the west as the Indus, a cradle of early civilization. He was blase about the hardships.

"You become accustomed to the conditions," he said, noting that those who serve there get the best of everything the Pakistan Army has to offer. "You get to call your family once a week," he added.

Driving up the valley beside the rushing Neelam, the major informed us, "We are now under observation." He cheerfully pointed out star-shaped potholes and a shrapnel-riddled bus by the road. We pulled into Athmuqam and parked behind a building, out of sight of a mountaintop about two klicks away where the major said the Indian artillery spotters were.

He advised us to keep under the trees to avoid attracting their attention and tried, but failed, to keep the few remaining locals from glomming onto us. We were far too irresistible an oddity—two Americans stumbling among Athmuqam's roofless, scorched houses and splintered trees. Our entourage grew to 10 or so—nearly everyone else in this town of 5,000 had fled to stay with relatives elsewhere—and each vied for the honor of showing us his own destroyed hovel.

We had been surveying the damage for about 45 minutes and were walking down an open road—full mob in tow—when a loud explosion sounded in the trees nearby. It was a noise felt in the gut as much as it was heard—a real attention-grabber—and I remember thinking something to the effect of, "FUCK! THEY'RE SHOOTING AT US!" As our party dropped to a crouch and began scrambling over a stonewall, the major suggested that that was a ranging shot; we'd been spotted and the next one would be on our heads. He advised that we run like bastards for a bunker in the other direction.

Running along an irrigation ditch, jostling with a lot of pajama-clad men and feeling indescribably naked, I discovered how mortar fire can sharpen the concentration, as with each step I was able to pick out the next mudsplotch I'd throw my face into if need be. We ducked into the nicest bunker in town, a reinforced concrete cellar under the local schoolteacher's substantial but incendiary-gutted house. There, we found his small daughter hiding under a mattress like a puppy terrorized by thunder. We were safe for the moment, dripping with sweat and gasping from our 100-yard dash but suddenly feeling really good. As Winston Churchill put it, "There is nothing in life so exhilarating as to be shot at without effect." By which he meant, it's great when they miss. The major and I joked about the rudeness of these Indian mortarmen who interrupted his tour, and I explained that my wife would probably raise a big stink with the Indians if she knew what they were up to.

"No, no, we never tell our wives what happens here," tutted the major. When nothing more fell, he announced that the tour was over—further travel up the road would invite a barrage and he would be in big trouble if he managed to get two Americans and a *Dawn* correspondent killed. We made our way out through a ravine, again feeling like ants under a magnifying glass as we crossed a couple of clearings, and took the shell-pocked road out of town at about 50 miles an hour with a flat tire. It was a minor incident, not a big deal in a place where mayhem is commonplace, and we were irked that our visit had ended so abruptly. It had cost us a week of drinking tea and chitchat with bureaucrats in Rawalpindi and Islamabad to get there—better than 17 cups in five different offices by my count—and one half-heartedly lobbed Indian mortar round had cleared us out.

The Indian state of Jammu and Kashmir still held out its charms, and we flew there a few days later. In the 1948 war, the Indians ended up with the nice part of Kashmir, the part you always hear about—the fabled valley with its lakes that mirror the foothills of the Himalayas, houseboats, and the quaint winding streets of old Srinagar. The Paks got the part suitable mainly for goats, hydropower and white-water rafting, although they will look at you like you are demented when you propose the latter. The Indian-held Vale of Kashmir is paradise on Earth, as the Moghul Emperor Jehangir gushed in poem, but only as long as your definition of paradise includes no beer (the mujahedin stopped all sales of devil water with some strategic grog-shop smashings nine years ago); poor sanitation; being stuck in traffic a lot with a cow's ass six inches outside one window and black clouds of diesel exhaust being pumped in the other; and lots of machine gun nests.

Local reporters confirmed the government's claim that Srinagar is much more relaxed since the Indian crackdown began to show some results a couple of years ago, and despite the presence of large numbers of Kalashnikov-toting soldiers everywhere, it is apparent the throngs in the streets aren't too concerned. A movie theater and a four-star hotel recently reopened, and no foreigners have been abducted since the five disappeared in 1995. No one is offering any better information on where they may be, but the general impression is that incident turned into such a counterproductive nuisance for the Pakistanis and the militants themselves that abductions are out. Caution in trekking is advised, however, and Ladakh probably makes more sense than the Pir Panjal range. A German told us he enjoyed his trip into Ladakh immensely, although he said the CAUTION, VEHICLES MAY BE EXPOSED TO SHELLING sign near the Pakistani line in Kargil was somewhat alarming. Movement for foreigners is easier around Indian Jammu and Kashmir than Pakistani-held Azad Kashmir and no special approval is needed to get there, but expect to be turned back from forward LoC areas and anywhere they are busy killing mujahedin.

To even enter Azad Kashmir, a letter of approval from the Ministry of Information or the Ministry of Kashmir Affairs is needed. It is a long ride back to Islamabad if you don't have it, although the cops at the border post are nice and may offer you tea first for a chance to speak English and break the tedium.

Unlike the heavily armed presence in Srinagar, Aazad Kashmir has few signs of the conflict or soldiers until you get to the LoC, except for the ubiquitous graffiti in Urdu—ALLAH COMMANDS THAT WE BUILD THE ATOM, etc. But you will be openly followed by plain-pajama cops on motorscooters who will pretend that they are from the Ministry of Information. There was no sign that we were tailed in Indian Kashmir, where the cops apparently have other things to do.

Grenade attacks on bunkers in and around Srinagar have been down to about one a week recently and there has been only sporadic, low-intensity fighting in the countryside. The official line is that the guerrillas are moving into surrounding, less militarized regions, where Hindus have been massacred by unknown gunmen (militant groups deny it, saying the Indian forces do it to make them look bad: the Indians say that's nonsense). Except for the occasional grenade-tossing, the main militant activity within Kashmir proper in the summer after the nuclear tests appeared to be getting surrounded and killed to the last man by Indian troops. At least, that's what the Indian brass claimed, and local press and militant groups did not offer an alternate assessment. Soldiers raised no objection when we popped out of a door and into their rooftop bunker to photograph a busy traffic intersection over their shoulders, and 100 feet from another bunker, a pair of Kashmiris didn't hold back with an impromptu denunciation of what they consider an occupying force.

"Everyone fears to say anything here. We hold our tongue. They hold our tongue!" the fat man volunteered, not bothering to keep his voice down. "Freedom!" blurted his thinner, intense-eyed pal. "We want freedom. No India! No Pakistan! Freedom!"

But whatever the solution ultimately is to be, one Kashmiri journalist said wryly, "They won't ask us."

Many Kashmiris appear to be tiring of a conflict that has cost them much in money and blood. The Indians claim the militants today are all "Pakistani-inspired foreign mercenaries"—and they obligingly trot out Kashmiri militants who have surrendered for interviews. Many former militants who continue to oppose the Indians as "politicals" say they are periodically rounded up and roughed up, and their less prominent comrades still risk torture and execution even though they have renounced violence. Former militant Yaseen Malik of the JKLF, who was brave enough to risk a five-story drop while trying to evade arrest (he failed to make the 15-foot leap to another rooftop and nearly crippled himself crashing through the roof of a kitchen four stories down), said the move away from violence was necessary to show who the true aggressors are. But he insists that the tide of history will eventually smile on Kashmir.

"There was a time when people thought Germany would never be united, because there was a mighty USSR," Malik said. "But that USSR collapsed. You cannot rule the people against their will forever."

For the second year, the Indian Army was confident of its ability to squelch the militants that the holy Yatra was allowed to go ahead. So we headed to Chandanwari to witness the pilgrimage, a three-day trek through mujahedin-infested mountains to one of the holiest sites in Hindudom. At 9,500 feet, where a tributary of the Jhelum gushes out of last winter's dirty snowpack, we joined the queue of Hindu faithful waiting in the crisp mountain air to get patted down and walk through a homemade metal detector. It was the highest of our many Kashmir friskings and overall the most pleasant, given the surroundings.

Thousands of pilgrims were making their way up the trail—rich and poor together, nearly naked holy men smeared with ashes, old people in makeshift litter chairs, and young children on bony horses—all singing in praise of Lord Shiva.

Their destination at Amarnath is a place where a slow water drip from a crack in the cave's ceiling has created an ice stalagmite as tall as a man. Hindus call in Shiv Ling—the Penis of Shiva the Destroyer.

You'd probably have a hard time putting together a cross-section of Americans like that to hike three days through guerrilla-infested mountains for free money, let alone God, and look so happy about it. But more than 100,000 Hindus a year cross a 15,000-foot pass to reach that cave. By worshipping there, Hindus earn points toward escaping the endless cycle of reincarnation, so it is worth the trip. "It is our homage. It gives us a feeling of calm, peace and calm," said Bombay travel agent Harshad Joshi, who was making the trip on a malnourished pony. The Yatra had the atmosphere and color of a joyous medieval festival, except for all the automatic weapons and camouflage.

"We found three mines on the road ten days ago. If a vehicle had passed, boom! They'd have been blown off the road. Destroyed," said Pvt. Jaswind Singh, who was wearing a black scarf tied pirate-style over his head. He expressed enthusiasm for killing mujahedin and said he liked Kashmir because he got plenty of opportunities to do that. Pvt. Karamsingh Desai, manning a light machine gun in a rocky nest by the glacier, said, "Everywhere you look in these mountains there are our soldiers. The mujahedin can't get close to the yatris. They must be thinking about it, but it would be very difficult for them."

He added, "I am grateful to God that I can serve the Yatra."

Elsewhere, the mujahedin still are able to make their point from time to time. On the way to Wandhama, an hour north of Srinagar, our hired Ambassador was run off the road twice by fast-moving Indian army truck patrols with one man over the cab on the machine gun and another with a big stick who whacked the roof of the car when we didn't go into the ditch quickly enough. In this area, the locals glared suspiciously from the roadside and the Border Security Force foot patrols eyeballed our speeding car warily. When we arrived, we found a pastoral scene that looked like a study of light and dark in an 18th-century Dutch farmyard, except for the air of evil about the place. The hamlet seemed deserted, but soon the village idiot appeared, a vacant-eyed youth who gibbered as he wandered among the ancient trees and the blast-scarred ruins of the Hindu compound.

The retarded boy was made to understand that we wanted to talk to someone and scooted off. A few minutes later, a line of Muslim elders walked over from their part of the village and squatted to talk about the night when gunmen came down from the mountain to kill Wandhama's Hindus.

Haji Ghulam Mohidin Baba's weathered old face dissolved in anguish as he recalled the sight of his neighbors lying scorched and bullet-ridden on the ground.

"Mothilal! Mothilal!" he cried, his voice wavering as he called out the name of the dead Hindu elder. "He was so nice. He was so gentle . . . Their mothers were like our mothers. Their sisters were like our sisters. Their children were like our children.

"We have lived by each other for centuries. No one knows how long. I was there when Mothilal's children were married. He was there when my children were married.

"The killers came on the holy night of Shab-i-Qadar, when the Muslim men were all in the mosque praying, chanting Koranic verses that drowned out the sound of gunfire a kilometer away," Haji Baba said. "Around 1 A.M.," he said, "the womenfolk came from our houses and said, 'It's firing, firing!' We ran here and crouched behind that stone wall. This house and that temple were in flames. We shouted, 'Hindus! Hindus! Are you there?' . . . We couldn't go down there. There was heavy gunfire. We called to the Hindus but nobody answered, and the firing kept going on. We all ran to the next village. There was panic. We had great fear. There was confusion. Children were separated from their mothers."

"Now," he said, "the wreckage of the Hindu compound seems like a haunted place."

"Only God knows who did this. Only God knows why this happened," he said. "We can't get that scene out of our minds. We stay away from there. We don't go down that road anymore. We use the other road to leave the village. There is no peace of mind."

—**Jules Crittenden**

Manila

The Philippines
★★

A Marriage of Inconvenience

The Philippines have seemed to both accept and reject the cultures and influences that have swept through here. These laid-back Malays that can embrace rabid fundamentalism, sex tourism, fanatic Roman Catholicism, Spanish machismo, Russian communism, Asian traffic, American jeepneys, bad '80s lounge music and survive the odd natural catastrophe with a smile and a shrug. The first time visitor to the these 7,000 islands would find it hard to believe that this is also an island of pirates, kidnappers, assassins and rebels.

In the '50s, the Philippines had the strongest economy in Southeast Asia, if not all of Asia, surpassing even those of South Korea, Japan, Thailand and Malaysia. Today, however, nearly half of all Filipinos live on the poverty line. The Philippines is rapidly spiraling from being a mini-America to being a Third World country. Accordingly there are problems in the land of the crescent and the cross. The biggest headache (if you discount the Filipinos love for Las Vegas style lounge music) is the desire of the Moros to be separate from the North. But it's not a real war, more like a forced marriage of inconvenience.

The Muslim separatists of Mindanao have been around for a while. It would be an understatement to say that the King of Spain was a little shocked to find Muslims in the far east just a few years after they had finally expelled the Umayaids from Granada. The Spanish tried for 300 years to extinguish the flame of Allah; they couldn't. Neither could the Americans during their 50-year rule of the islands; nor could the Japanese during their occupation of the country during World War II. Although various Philippine governments have negotiated with the principal Muslim extremist group, the Moro National Liberation Front (MNLF)—with varying degrees of success—an even nastier, deadlier faction emerged, the Moro Islamic Liberation Front (MILF).

The government claims the MILF is only about 60,000 poorly trained guerrillas yet the minuscule MILF has most of the government's 115,000-soldier army on Mindanao to contain the separatists. The MILF itself claims 120,000 troops, but the number is closer to 40,000 combatants, only about a third of whom are on "active duty" at any given time. Even at that number, the MILF is far stronger than the communist New People's Army of the mid-1980s. And just to give the movement a little international flavor and foreign intrigue, as many as 1,000 MILF members were sent to fight in Afghanistan in the 1980s. The current Muslim uprising in the Philippines has been going on for a quarter of a century and has killed more than 120,000 people.

The relationship between the government and the rebels is like a bad marriage. The government could easily eradicate the MILF or the NPA but they choose not to. Partly because it distracts the people's attention on the lousy economy and also because they get so much damn military aid to fight the nonwar.

War, Hell, It's Just New Year's Eve!

New Year's Eve is a dangerous time in the jungles of Mindanao. The MILF has decided to crack down on the number of injuries caused by happy fire on New Year's. Ghazali Jaafar, deputy chairman of the Moro Islamic Liberation Front, said the movement's fighters have been warned they will be punished for firing their weapons to commemorate the new year.

"For every bullet fired, the penalty would be equivalent to planting at least 20 banana plants," Jaafar said. The government retaliated by ordering their soldiers not to fire their weapons during New Year celebrations or they will be dismissed.

First of all, Muslims comprise only about 5 percent of the Philippino population, there are 4 million Muslims in the Philippines—which is 83 percent Catholic and the only Christian state in Southeast Asia. Because of active settlement of Christians in Mindanao the Moros are greatly outnumbered by government supporters on Mindanao itself. They manage to keep most of the 115,000 Philippines army in Mindanao. Secondly, since the 1987 constitution was ratified, any successional or autonomy move must be approved by a plebiscite, and both Moro groups would lose handily on Mindanao. So it looks like jihadland for a while longer.

Mindanao is one of the more tense places that *DP* has visited. Checkpoint after checkpoint was manned by loosely identified gun carrying men. There is always

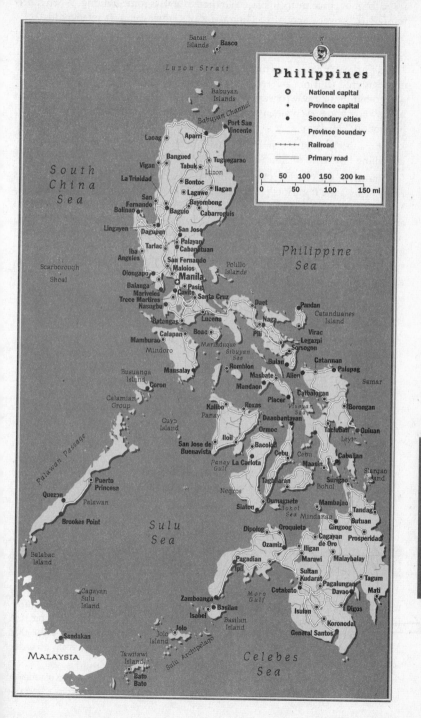

some form of peace treaty in place and there is always some fighting. When rebels tell *DP* to "be very, very careful" on the way to their camp, It's dangerous.

It seems that despite or because of the number of armed men, violent crime and kidnapping (or stealing people as it is called here) is the biggest fear.

The fear meter really gets turned up when you enter the Sulu seas. Foreigners are registered (but not offered any protection) as they leave airports and locals will go out of their way to warn you of the crime here. Our driver packed a 45 in his cowboy boots even when he entered a heavily armed bank "for his personal protection." Hee yaa.

The real no go parts of the Philippines are Basilan and Jolo where the rapidly dwindling boys club of Abu Sayeff is slowly being picked off.

Up north in the provinces you are bound to hear of the NPA or New People's Army. This is the remnants of the Huk rebellion who fought with the Americans against the Japanese. We thanked them by hunting them down and creating an army of 25,000 in 1987. They are down to about 5,000 now and depending on which way the economy goes they will shrink or grow as angered and impoverished youths take to the hills. The communist New People's Army is a spent force which sporadically makes the headlines these days with an assassination or kidnapping or two.

The Hours Suck but Think of the Accrued Holidays

Hiro Onada makes the Energizer Bunny look like a piker. Second Lieutenant Onada fought World War II for 30 years. The fact that nobody bothered to tell him that Japan surrendered in 1945 didn't stop him from hanging on until 1974. The 73-year-old Onada hid out on the island of Lubang in the Philippines, living off wild animals and plants. A Japanese journalist found Onada in 1952, but Onada thought he was a U.S. spy. In a way you can't blame him since he could see the activity at Subic Bay and the constant U.S. military activity made him believe that the war raged on. His orders were to stay in Lubang if the Americans captured it and to wage a guerrilla campaign. His only companion, Private Kinshinchi Kozuka, was shot by Philippine police after 19 years on the island.

He was finally convinced to give up his fight when Norio Suzuki, a Japanese adventurer, conveyed a direct order by his commander to surrender. He now teaches at an outdoor survival school in the Fukushima prefecture of Japan.

Don't be fooled by the modern veneer of the Philippines. It is a have and have not country where outsiders are spared much of the brutality and injustice. Muslim and communist separatists have been battling various Manila governments for nearly 30 years, resulting in more than 10,000 firefights between insurgents and government troops during that time. More than 120,000 people have been killed. As both rebel groups told me, the government needs the rebels to keep peoples' minds off how bad the economy is.

The government has kept a relative lid on the extremist problem—in the interests of promoting tourism—until the recent terrorist plot to kill the Pope and blow up numerous airliners simultaneously. Meanwhile, army rebels are busy plotting the next coup of the month. In all, the mayhem keeps the hotel rates down.

The Government

The Philippines seems to be run by either whoever used to be Minister of Defense or whoever the hell is in between Minister of Defense—a housewife, a movie actor (yeah like we should make fun of that). For now the land that taste forgot is run by a clone of Wayne Newton.

President of the Philippines
http://www.erap.com

News from the Government
http://www.opsphil.com/

Tourism
http://www.tourism.gov.ph

Hashim Salamat & the Moro Islamic Liberation Front (MILF)

An offshoot of the MNLF that sprang up in 1978 in the wake of the Tripoli-brokered autonomy agreement between Manila and the Moros, the MILF has no word for "compromise" in its Islamic dictionary. MILF troop strength is estimated at between 20,000 and 40,000 by independent analysts, but no one seems to know for sure. The MILF itself claims a force of 120,000 members, 80,000 of them armed in 13 major camps in 7 provinces—while the Philippine government says the group numbers no more than 8,000. The military guesstimates 60,000. *DP* estimates that the MILF is about 12,000 active fighters with plenty more on call. More than 1,000 Filipino Muslims in its ranks fought against the Soviets during the war in Afghanistan, although Philippine military intelligence says no more than 300 did. When *DP* paid a visit, we found the MILF to be highly disciplined and equally as radical. The MILF doesn't simply seek autonomy (as the more moderate MNLF has sought) but complete secession of Mindanao from the Philippines and the creation of a fundamentalist Islamic state—and will settle for no less. The Front's military commander, Al-haj Murad, a genial and modest man boasts of possessing six full divisions of soldiers; however, it seems to be a rotating army, with only two divisions on duty at any given time. This may explain the massive gap in estimates of the group's strength. MILF leader Hashim Salamat is a tough guy to get hold of—military commanders and many of the Front's other bellwethers have never set eyes on him—but does give regular religious sermons on radio broadcasts in Mindanao. *DP* had no problem setting a chin wag and a guided tour at his base camp. The first American in a long time to say hi to the MILF. Salamat received his religious training in Egypt and Pakistan in the 1960s (he was heavily influenced by Syed Abul Ala Mau'dudi of Pakistan's Jamaat i Islami Party and Syed Outh of Egypt's Muslim Brotherhood) and formed the Moro National Liberation Front in 1970. His training in the Middle East made him a lot of bearded buddies with bombs, so he had no problem arming his spin-off gangsters when he founded the MILF. These days, the MILF is busy funding itself through the kidnapping of Taiwanese diplomats and Chinese-Filipino businessmen and by attacking Philippine military detachments and burning schools. They also like to bring along high-tech video cameras on their raids so they can pop the footage off to TV stations in time for the 11 o'clock news.

Al Haj Murad
Vice Chairman for Military Affairs, Central Committee & Chief of Staff

Bangsamoro Islamic Armed Forces (BIAF)
Tel.: (064) 421 34 86
E-mail: Alhijrah@microweb.com.ph
Or for the latest in rebel dish, subscribe to the

MILF Maradika

The Editor
Post Office Box 535
9600 Cotabato City
Philippines

The Abu Sayyaf Group (ASG)

The Abu Sayyaf Group (ASG) is an Islamic fundamentalist faction with zero tolerance for the Christian government. It first appeared in August 1991. The ASG began as Tabligh (Spread the Word), an organization founded in 1972 by Iranian missionaries who came to the Philippines to spread the doctrines of Ayatollah Ruholla Khomeini. The ASG figured the poor Muslim communities of the Philippines were a good place to wage a secessionist jihad.

Tabligh's military arm became known as the Mujahedin Commando Freedom Fighters (MCFF), and later tagged as the Abu Sayyaf Group—named after charismatic leader Abdurajak Janjalani Abubakar, a mestizo Ilongoo-Tausug who was educated in Saudi Arabia and went by the handle of Abu Sayyaf (Father of the Sword). Abubakar was also trained in Libya and fluent in Arabic. He was killed in combat with government troops on December 18, 1998, and the group has been in disarray ever since. The ASG was partially financed by Iran, Pakistan and bin Laden. The group is based in the remote parts of Basilan island and can muster only about 120 armed combatants. The hard core of "Afghans" is down to less than a dozen. Is it still dangerous? When poking around the mosques in the Sulu region I was politely told, "We wouldn't just wander into your home would we?" Keep on the latest from the Sulu seas:

http://www.inquirer.net

The Moro National Liberation Front (MNLF)

A formidable and brutal Muslim insurgency group for a quarter-century is now a paper tiger. The MNLF signed a peace agreement with the Ramos government on September 2, 1996. Today, the MNLF is a mainstream political entity that has spawned the more militant MILF. Some 7,500 former guerrillas are now being trained and paid to fight alongside government troops to battle the even nastier MILF and the remnants of the Abu Sayyaf group. The former guerrillas get $170 and a monthly allowance of $30. The MNLF chairman, Nur Misuari is now in charge of a four province Autonomous Region in Muslim Mindanao. How long will the honeymoon last? Until the money stops flowing.

http://www.c-r.org/acc_min/index.htm

The New People's Army (NPA)

The communist NPA is an outgrowth of the Maoist Communist Party of the Philippines founded in 1968. In 1969 they created an armed group called the New People's Army, the most powerful insurgent group in the Philippines. At their peak in 1988 there were 26,000 guerrillas and supporters but government fighting, assassinations, amnesties and defections have whittled them down. Also the biggest bane of rebel groups, a good economy has cooled their ardor for war. Once figured to be an anachronism, a recent government study found that the NPA have increased the number of guerrillas to 6,700, up 10 percent from 1996. *DP* figures the hardcore members are only about 3,000. They are gaining members in Mindanao and losing them in the north. It's really all about economics here. Former President Fidel Ramos' principal objective was to pursue peace with the NPA, which has been largely accomplished. José María "Joma" Sison is now in exile in the Netherlands. Ramos scored a success when he was able to persuade another

NPA leader, Leopoldo Mabilangan, to leave the group. Mabilangan was later assassinated by NPA operatives.

New Peoples Army

NDF International Office
P.O. Box 19195
3501 DD Utrecht
The Netherlands
Tel.: +31 30 23.10.431
Fax: +31 30 23.22.989
E-mail address: ndfp@hkstar.com
Web site: http://www.geocities.com/~cpp-ndf/npa.htm

The Alex Boncayo Brigade (ABB) or Sparrows

The ABB is a lethal leftist death squad led by Sergio Romero (who's real name is Nilo de la Cruz) that has taken scores of lives in its 10-year history. These guys are supposed to be the assassin branch of the Communist Party of the Philippines but in reality don't get along with the more moderate NPA. Most recently, the group has been offing Chinese businessmen in sort of an ethnic cleansing of the ranks of the Philippines' industrialists. The leader Nilo who was charged with 200 murders, was nabbed and is awaiting trial and sentencing. They have reduced his sentence so that no judges or government officials wake up with horses heads in their beds. The government has drawn up a list of more than 160 ABB members targeted for arrest. Right now they are down to about 20 active members. As Nilo told me, "thank goodness for pro bono human rights lawyers."

Revolutionary People's Army/Alex Boncoyo Brigade (RPA-ABB)

A mix of a Maoist hit squad (see Sparrows) and a Marxist agrarian land reform group. The tongue twisting rebel group is active on the island of Negros. *DP* just happened to be the first one to ever film them. We didn't have the heart to tell the guy with the bright orange Nike basketball outfit about the benefits of cammo, but they are a serious bunch. Three of them were wasted after our visit. They are working to pressure the landowners and the military for land reform, and they promised me they won't hurt tourists.

Uncle Sam

You were just waiting for some post colonial angst weren't you? The Philippines was America's only colony, an odd result of the Spanish American War. Commodore Dewey sent a cable to President McKinley after sinking the Spanish fleet in Manila bay: "Have taken Manila, what shall I do with it?" That wasn't the bad part. After we fought with the Moros and fought with the Communist rebels against the Japanese, we glued the southern area of Mindanao into a big Philippines and gave them independence. In 1915 the Americans allowed Christian northerner to settle in the lands of the Muslim south. In April of 1940 the sultanate of Bangsa Moro was recognized and incorporated into the independent country of the Philippines. We got a few military bases and a whole lot of pissed off Moros who would be just as happy being left alone. If you hang around the south long enough without being kidnapped you'll get an earful in the mosques. The kicker? Some of the Moros want us to intervene militarily for their independence against the Philippine government.

Operaton Cold Shower

In March of 2000, thousands os U.S. and Philippine troops will carry out the first large scale military exercises in five years? The biggest danger? According to the top brass it's not Chinese Sams or terrorist bombs. It is attacks of passion by prostitutes at Angeles City, next to Clark Air Force base. Our secret weapon? "Sports" says U.S. Major General James Donald, his Philippine counterpart and DP buddy, Orlando Mercado (and Minister of Defense) says the American troops "will be provided with alternative activities, mostly sports activities, in the camps to keep their testosterone levels down," Maybe Operation Balikatan, or "Shoulder to Shoulder" should be called "Operaton Cold Shower".

Sniffing Out Terrorists

Most white-bread folks think it's easy to spot a terrorist. It's the guy with dark skin, a big nose, a scraggly beard with a towel wrapped around his head. Problem is that less than 0.01 percent of all guys who look like this are terrorists. And Timmy McVeigh fit this profile about as well as Roseanne fits into Pamela Anderson Lee's swimsuit. The Philippines think they have a better formula for sniffing out terrorists. The Immigration Bureau's Civil Security Unit (CSU) advises immigration officers to detect the following when assessing if an arrival might be a terrorist: foul foot odor and calloused skin. That's right. Passport stampers are advised to eyeball guys carrying only one bag, whose eyes are darting around the room. This qualifies the might-be nasty for a strip search, according to the CSU. Strip searchers should then be on the lookout for calloused elbows and hands, marks on the stomach and chest, and athlete's foot—all of which suggest the potential perpetrator has undergone rigid military training. In 1996, immigration inspectors turned away some 200 arrivals as suspected terrorists because of smelly feet. Probably half of them were gardeners from Brunei on vacation.

Wanna Buy Baby Gang (WBBG)

Yeah, you read it right. Philippine security forces are hunting a gang that snatches babies and children and sells them to childless Filipino and foreign couples. The group, called Wanna Buy Baby Gang, preys on babies and children aged eight months to two years. The going price per child is US$20,000 if the buyer is a foreigner and 20,000 pesos (US$785) if the client is a Filipino. The chief of the anti-kidnapping unit of the National Bureau of Investigation (NBI) said the existence of the gang was reported by parents who had been victimized. Women gang members carry out the abductions by applying to work as maids. After gaining the trust of their employers, they disappear with the babies. The gang has reportedly taken over 30 babies and small children in recent years. (We couldn't make this stuff up if we tried.)

http://www.erap.com/web/mostwanted/index.htm

Sex Workers

Rene Ofreneo of the University of the Philippines estimates that there are 400,000 to 500,000 prostitutes in the country—equal to the number of its factory workers.

http://worldsexguide.org/
http://www.ecpat.org/
http://www.fhi.org/en/aids/impact/mapmnl.html

Pirates

Pirates are a very real part of the southern Philippines. Zamboanga is a historic trading center, where luxury goods from Indonesia, Malaysia, Singapore and China are as plentiful as the raw materials from the sea and jungles that surround the city. The goods are brought in on *tora-toras*, flat-bottom boats, that are usually loaded to the gunnels with cheap TVs, beer, cigarettes and other prized items.

The "pirate" ships are an assortment of rusting freighters, aging ferries, modern speedboats, *basligs*—the large boats with outriggers to avoid capsizing in the heavy seas—and speedy canoelike *vintas* with their colorful sails.

The amount of trade in high-ticket items from duty-free ports, such as Labuan in Brunei, make legitimate traders easy targets for pirates who employ everything from *parangs* (machetes) to machine guns to kill their victims.

http://www.maritimesecurity.com/

A passport and onward/return ticket as required. For entry by Manila International Airport, a visa is not required for a transit/tourist stay up to 21 days. Visas are required for longer stays; the maximum is 59 days. You'll need to fill out an application and provide one photo, at no charge. Company letter needed for business visa. AIDS test required for permanent residency; a U.S. test is accepted. For more information contact the following:

Embassy of the Philippines

1600 Massachusetts Avenue, N.W.
Washington, D.C. 20036
Tel.: (202) 467-9300
http://www.dfa.gov.ph/d-cntnts/dfa-lnks.htm

Or nearest consulate general at:

Hawaii, Tel.: (808) 595-6316   *New York, Tel.: (212) 764-1330*

Illinois, Tel.: (312) 332-6458   *Texas, Tel.: (713) 621-8609*

California, Tel.: (213) 387-5321 and   *Washington, Tel.: (206) 441-1640*
(415) 433-6666

Arrival into the Philippines from abroad is primarily through Manila's Ninoy Aquino International Airport, a modern facility with 14 jetways. Located in nearby Pasay City, the airport is less than 30 minutes away by car to any major hotel and services an average of 170 international flights weekly. Manila is just over an hour by air from Hong Kong, 3 hours from Singapore, 5 from Tokyo, 17 hours from San Francisco and 22 hours from New York.

Several Southeast Asian regional carriers have direct flights into Zamboanga, Mindanao, and proposed international airports are due for Cebu City and Zamboanga.

PTICs are located at Ninoy Aquino International Airport *(Tel.: 828-4791/828-1511)*, Nayong Pilipino Complex, Airport Road *(Tel.: 828-2219)* and on the ground floor, Philippine Ministry of Tourism (Ermita) building near Rizal Park in Metro Manila *(Tel.: 501-703, 501-928)*. Field offices are situated in Pampanga, Baguio, Legazpi, La Union, Bacolod, Cebu, Iloilo, Tacloban, Cagayan de Oro City Davao, Marawi and Zamboanga. The Department of Tourism hotline is *Tel.: 501-660/728.*

In North America, the Philippine Tourist Office has the following locations:

Philippine Center

556 Fifth Avenue   *Suite 1212, 3460 Wilshire Boulevard*
New York, NY 10036   *Los Angeles, CA 90010*
Tel.: (212) 575-7915   *Tel.: (213) 487-4525*

Suite 1111, 30 North Michigan Avenue
Chicago, IL 60602
Tel.: (312) 782-1707

The Philippines might be the world's second most popular sex tourist destination after Thailand. Although the U.S. squids have packed up and shipped out, horny foreigners keep the hookers gainfully employed in places like Angeles, Sabang and Subic City. If this is your thing, get hold of *Asia File* and subscribe to their newsletter, which handles the particulars of these places pretty thoroughly:

Asia File

P.O. Box 278537
Sacramento, CA 95827-8537
Fax: (916) 361-2364
E-mail: asiafile@earthlink.net

Accommodations, food and travel in the Philippines offer some of the best bargains found in Asia. The National Railway serves the island of Luzon, from Lagaspi in the south to San Fernando, La Union, in the north. Car rentals are available in the major cities, with or without a driver. Jeepneys are cheap and plentiful in Manila and other large towns. Domestic flights connect Manila daily with about 50 other towns, cities and rural areas. Where scheduled flights do not serve, there are aircraft for charter. Local service is bare-bones basic, with nothing offered but plastic cups of water. Allow plenty of time before departure for security inspection. Around the archipelago there are inter-island sea vessels with first-class accommodations that sail between several different ports daily.

If you find yourself in a pinch, or need quick transport out of the Philippines, you can charter a boat from Sitangkai for the 40-km trip to Semporna in the Malaysian state of Sabah. This, of course, is completely illegal. However, there are a slew of boats that make the trip from the Philippines to the busy market in Semporna. Keep in mind that Sabah has its own customs and immigration requirements, so you'll need a separate stamp when you move back and forth from Sabah to peninsular Malaysia. These waters are also home to Sulu pirates, actually a combination of minor smugglers and armed thugs who prey on large commercial vessels. Pirates have also been known to rob banks and terrorize entire towns in coastal Sabah. Just inquire at any fishing village or dockside hangout in Sitangkai. Usually, you'll have to cross at night, and don't be surprised to pay two to three times the normal rate of P$150. Going the other way is also easy; there are boatmen who can hook you up with the many speedboats that are for rent in Semporna. Be careful dealing with the Ray-Banned entrepreneurs you meet along the docks. They might turn you in for the reward money and simply pocket the sizable fee you paid them to get you across.

Leaving from Ninoy Aquino International or Domestic Airport can be a drag due to the tight security inspections. The airport taxes are P$500 for international flights and P$25 for domestic flights.

Mindanao

More than 10,000 firefights between government soldiers and rebel separatists as well as countless bombings and other politically motivated slayings have left 50,000 people dead over the last 30 years in the Philippines, most of them on the island of Mindanao. Sultan Kudarat is particularly dangerous. Government soldiers are regularly attacked by MILF guerrillas in this area, and surrounding parcels of land change hands regularly. Dangerous as well is Zamboanga, where a wave of bombing attacks by ASG terrorists rattled the city for six days in March 1996.

Basilan

This island is the strong hold of Abu Sayeef but is in an area where law and order are strictly homemade. Inquire at the local mosques and civil centers to understand just exactly what the crisis of the moment is. Best advice is to let the locals steer you clear of the kidnapping and attacks on foreigners that occur here.

The Spratlys

OK, OK so the worst thing that happened to *DP* was that we got sunburnt. The Minister of Defense, Orlando Mercado (see Government), flew us out on a tourist junket to see the newest thing in ecotourism. Well it's not bad if you don't mind a lot of drunk soldiers, chopped-down palm trees, rusty anti-aircraft guns, abandoned military gear and old bunkers. As for danger, well the air force pilot said he wouldn't buzz the brand-new Chinese Motel 6's on Mischief Reef "because sometimes they throw their garbage at us." Lock and load the Glad bags gunny . . . we're going in.

To get China's version:
http://www.fmprc.gov.cn/
To get the Philippines version:
http://www.fmprc.gov.cn/
To keep up on the nail biting news:
http://headlines.yahoo.com/Full_Coverage/Asia/Spratly_Islands_Dispute

Crime

Crime is high throughout the Philippines, particularly in urban areas. Many stores employ armed guards. There are 30 murders and 3 rapes per 100,000 people. There are 72 thefts for every 100,000 people.

Kidnapping

The kidnapping rate in the Philippines has risen 48 percent over the last year. If you're a Chinese businessman living and/or working in the Philippines, consider wearing a mask or seeing a plastic surgeon, as you're the favorite target of kidnappers. Kidnappers like snatching Chinese for ransom, because their companies/embassies/families invariably will pay up. Kidnappers realize that if they take a Westerner, they'll have to feed the poor SOB for a couple of months, only then to get stormed by police commandos. In 1995, more than 160 people were abducted in the Philippines—many of them belonging to rich ethnic Chinese families—hauling in more than a US$3.6 million booty for the kidnappers. One syndicate demands 50 million pesos ($1.2 million) and gets it for their victims. That's positive cash flow. Through the first eight weeks of 1997, kidnap gangs had seized 42 victims—most of them ethnic Chinese—making the Philippines the kidnapping capital of Asia. The official kidnap rate in the Philippines is about 13.5 victims per month (most anti-crime groups say the figure is much higher, about 1,000 people are kidnapped every year in the Philippines). There are an estimated 40 different kidnapping syndicates in Manila alone. In 1997, kidnap gangs in the Philippines collected a total ransom of 7.1 million dollars from 249 victims, nearly triple the 2.5 million dollars they earned from 241 victims in 1996.

Kidnapping by the Numbers

Kidnapping has become such a way of life in the Philippines that gangs now accept checks to cover their ransom demands. At least three Filipino-Chinese businessmen were quickly freed by kidnappers after they issued checks ranging from US$11,500 to US$38,000. One anticrime watch official stated that he doubts "if they gave stop payment instructions because the kidnappers would certainly have gotten back to them."

YEAR	NO. OF KIDNAPPINGS	RANSOMS PAID
1992	123	51
1993	104	28
1994	205	41
1995	199	N/A
1996	241	N/A
1997	370*	N/A

Source: Pinkerton (Asia) Limited
* estimated from DP sources

Being a Journalist

Investigative journalists in the Philippines may want to consider forwarding their CVs to "Hard Copy," or just simply getting the hell out of the Philippines. On June 3, 1997, Danny Hernandez, news editor of the *People's Journal Tonight*—the country's most popular tabloid daily—was shot dead in a taxi cab. He is believed to have been assassinated for his anticrime reporting. Another anticrime journalist, Albert Berbon of radio station DZMM, was assassinated outside his home in December 1996. A leading anti-crime group then stated: "If a radio reporter of the caliber of Bert Berbon could be killed in Mafia fashion, then it would not be difficult to comprehend that an ordinary Filipino citizen could be killed any time by people who wish them harm."

Shots for smallpox and cholera are not required for entry, but cholera shots are suggested when the Philippines appears on a weekly summary of areas infected (according to the World Health Organization). Yellow fever vaccinations are required of all travelers arriving from infected areas. There is one doctor for every 6,413 people in the Philippines. Medical care in the Philippines outside of Manila can be below Western standards, with some shortages of basic medical supplies. Access to the quality facilities that exist in major cities sometimes requires cash-dollar payment upon admission. Most of the general hospitals are run privately. Malaria, once a big problem in the Philippines, has been eradicated in all but the most rural regions. Tuberculosis, respiratory and diarrheal diseases pose the biggest threats to travelers. The U.S. embassy and consulates maintain lists of health facilities and of English-speaking doctors. Drinking only boiled or bottled water will help to guard against cholera, which has been reported, as well as other diseases. More complete and updated information on health matters can be obtained from the Centers for Disease Control's international travelers' hotline, *Tel.: (404) 332-4559.*

The world's second-largest archipelago after Indonesia, the Republic of the Philippines comprises 300,000 square kilometers (777,001 square miles) on 7,107 islands in the South China Sea between Borneo to the southwest and Taiwan to the north; only 4,600 are named and a mere 1,000 are inhabited. The islands are in three main groups: the Luzon group, the Mindanao group and the Sulu and Visayan group. The country's 65.2 million inhabitants speak Tagalog and English. Roman Catholics comprise 83 percent of the population, Protestants 9 percent, Muslims 5 percent, and Buddhists 3 percent. There are more than 100 ethnic groups in the country.

The Philippines has one of the developing world's highest literacy rates. Nearly every child in the country finishes primary school and nearly three-quarters of the population completes secondary school. The education system is based on the U.S. model. Although relatively highly educated, about 50 percent of Filipinos live at or below the poverty line, namely because economic expansion falls short of the country's population growth rate. The official currency is the Philippine peso. Approximately 26 pesos equal US$1. Hard foreign currency and traveler's checks are easily exchanged at banks, hotels and authorized money changers throughout the country. Credit cards are also now widely accepted.

Local time in the Philippines is GMT plus eight hours, i.e., exactly 13 hours ahead of Eastern Standard Time. Manila is in the same time zone as Beijing, Taipei, Macau, Kuala Lumpur, Singapore and Hong Kong, but one hour ahead of Seoul and Tokyo. It is one hour ahead of Bangkok and Jakarta, and one and a half hours ahead of Yangon.

The local water is generally potable, except in remote rural areas. Hours of business in the Philippines are from 8 A.M. to 5 P.M. Monday through Friday, with most offices closed from noon to 1 P.M. or so. Banks open from 9 A.M. to 4 P.M. Monday through Friday. Shops in major tourist centers open at 9 or 10 A.M. until at least 7 P.M. daily.

Telephone, telex and fax services in the Philippines are surprisingly poor, and communication with the outside world is slower than you'll find in other parts of the Far East. Overseas calls take from 30 minutes to an hour to put through and are expensive, although IDD has arrived at the better hotels.

The local current is 220V/50 cycles—when there is power. One of the biggest infrastructural problems in the Philippines is electricity. The country experiences frequent and lengthy power outages on 258 out of the 297 working days each year.

Although the Philippines exports copper and is the world's largest supplier of refractory chrome, perhaps 90 percent of the country's natural resources have yet to be tapped, as the Philippines hasn't been largely surveyed.

Embassy Locations

United States Embassy

*1201 Roxas Boulevard-Ermita 1000
Manila, The Philippines
Tel.: (63-2) 523-1001
Fax: (63-2) 522-4361
http://www.usia.gov/posts/manilaemb/*

The Canadian Consulate

*Fourth floor, Philippine Air Lines Building
Ayala Avenue
Makati
Tel.: 876-536.*

THE PHILIPPINES

12/18/98	Leader of Abu Sayeff killed in fire fight.
9/96	Moro National Liberation Front agrees to a peace plan with the government.
2/25/86	Marcos flees into exile in the United States.
8/21/83	Opposition leader Benigno Aquino shot to death by military police as he arrives in Manila after returning from self-exile.
1/17/81	President Ferdinand Marcos ends eight years of martial law.
7/4/46	Philippines gains independence.
12/8/41	Japan invades the Philippines.

In a Dangerous Place: Negros

The Phantoms

I am to meet a company of NPA rebels on the run from the military, a group that has never been photographed before, and the odds are good that they may all be dead by the time I get there. They are on the run from the army, so they say they can only wait and talk to us for an hour, no longer. Then they must move on.

Making my covert contact with the rebels is easier than I thought. When I arrive at the airport on the island of Negros there is a man with a withered hand and a big, toothy smile holding a large sign that says ROBERT TELKON AND COMPANY.

Our four guides use aliases to greet us and then talk to each other using their real names. Oops. So much for security.

The trip will be delayed. There are troop movements by the Special Action force. The camp is on the move. It is better for us because the camp is only two hours away instead of seven.

There are three battalions of Philippine government troops on the island, about 3,000 troops in all. Two are here in Bacolod, one is in the south. The special forces group is in the south, and they are carrying out an operation today. There are rebels here because there is sugar cane. Sugar cane is a peasant crop. Like coffee or cotton, it is hard seasonal work, manual labor and low pay.

There are 25,000 haciendas, or sugar cane plantations. There are 50 families that are the major landowners. The biggest landowner, the Cojuanco, owns thousands of hectares. The cane cutters are indentured laborers, and the landlords call the shots. The cane cutters tell us they get 600 pesos per hectare—not each but for however many people and days it takes to finish. It takes them two days to weed a hectare, there were nine people working and they get the equivalent of 30 cents a day. Agricultural workers, by Philippine law, should get 100 pesos a day.

We are in the newest, swankiest hotel in town—twenty dollars a night. I don't even want to figure out how long it would take a sugar worker to afford a night here. It might sound strange to hole up in a businessman's hotel, but it is the place that we will stand out the least. Our guides leave us here to watch four overweight golfers load a mountain of golf bags on the back of a shiny Chevy dual-cab pickup truck as the guides roar away on their motorbikes.

Negros is split down the middle both by culture and by a ragged, denuded cordillera. The people align themselves with the people on the facing slope of the neighboring island. We are in Negros occidental where they speak Ilokano; the other side of the island speaks Cebuano.

The Victoria Sugar Mill is the largest sugar mill in Southeast Asia. It has been in operation for 78 years. It's more of small town than just a mill. Gray flakes of burnt sugar float down like snow. Everybody is gone because it's Sunday.

On the morning we are to meet our peripatetic rebels (at a secret location of course), our guide zooms up in a very noisy dirt bike. He doesn't hang around long but zooms up and down the street like a buzzing fly. For once everybody is on time. We head out into the cool dawn and begin our journey high up into the mountains.

The odds of an ambush by the military are high in the dawn hours, so it is probably the worst time, place and conditions to visit rebels on the run. The people in the hills know our escorts well. There is lots and handshaking and welcoming when we pass through villages.

The most striking things about the mountains are the coolness and that they have been completely devastated by clear-cutting. There is simply nothing left that would resemble the triple-canopy rainforest that covered this archipelago. In place of jungle are scrubby ferns and a hodge-podge of trees amongst scattered villages and plantations.

The road winds up and down and round and round. I pull out my GPS to figure out exactly where we are going. My contact says my GPS is making our rebel contacts nervous. I look over to see them sleeping, their heads bobbing in time to the sways in the road. Uh huh.

Needless to say the rebels are in the hills, but exactly where is unknown. Originally we were told that we would drive seven hours and then walk for three. Then it became drive five, walk two. When we arrive on Negros, there is a development. The rebels have been chased closer to us.

Soon a blue arc forms and the clouds are painted a dusty pink. A 300-meter waterfall appears. Steep volcanic canyons and black boulders sit like sculptures in reflective rice paddies. It takes about three hours and a few backtracks to avoid the military, but we soon arrive on the slope of a mountain with a few ramshackle nipa huts. Then, like your first sighting of big game on a safari, rebels appear. Attired in faded green camouflage, festooned with worn and polished weapons and wearing canvas sneakers with red shoe laces. We have a brief powwow to set up filming. This group is a company of the Revolutionary Proletariat Army–Alex Boncoyo Brigade or RPA–ABB, a breakaway faction of the NPA formed in 1996 who work with the urban members of the Alex Boncoyo hit squad. There are about three dozen men, mostly in their twenties and thirties. There are three *manara,* the local name for the black-skinned mestizo Filipinos.

The troops are lined up in threes and go through their drill for us. They get most of it right and it is easy to see that the military skills lie with the two or three leaders. They play rebel in the jungle, posing for us with their battered rifles stolen from the Philippine army. They also have some newer M-16s with grenade launchers, obviously stolen or captured from the special forces groups.

They kill a pig in our honor, and just as lunch is getting ready, we learn that a RP special forces group is now in the village we just passed and heading our way. We have to disperse fast as a blocking force is sent down the road to protect us. We quickly pack up our gear and begin humping up the mountain. The camp followers carry the cooking pot and the soldiers listen carefully to the radio comms.

They are listening to the radio communication of the Philippine army. They also smoke homemade cigarettes. We have a sit-down chat with the local commander, his military head and his spokesperson.

Essentially, they split with the NPA because they want a more functional solution to the plight of the poor. They also consider the landowners and warlords to be their enemy. I ask why they attack the military instead of the kids in the military. They say the military does the bidding of the landowners. We have a pretty low-key conversation on whether having an insurgency actually harms the people because of lack of investment. They welcome investors (although I heard the word capitalist used as a form of insult many times). Would they harm or kidnap foreigners? Not at all. Their fight is with the landowners (although the ABB takes considerable pride in having assassinated the station chief of the CIA in Manila). It's a good interview. The right questions. The right answers. How do they feel when they kill a brother Filipino in the military? They are forced to because their reaction is to defend themselves. Do they initiate attacks on the military? Yes but only as part of the greater revolutionary struggle and in conjunction with their comrades' political agenda. Uh huh.

They decide to ask me a few questions. They want to know what people think of them. I tell them that acronyms and socialist dogma are the quickest way to get people to turn off. There is no shortage of revolutionary groups here, so their revolution-lite formula is going to get lost in the mix. (Wastes great, less killing?)

They are obviously thrilled to see a camera crew from the States, so they don't quite know what to do. They set up their ever-present red flag with the unpronounceable Tagalog long form of their group behind every interview and they make a bad-boy motif in the background with all the best weapons and meanest looking fighters. The guy with orange dayglo basketball shorts and lime-green shirt probably needs a little jungle camouflage training.

When things quiet down, they invite us to a meal of greasy pig and rice. Then the rebels get to do their laundry.

Seven days later, three of our newly made friends die in a shootout with the military.

—**RYP**

Russia
★ ★ ★

Bled Red 'til Dead

Russia has gone from superpower to Third World in a mere six years. Or Red to dead without even gaining a toehold on optimism that drove the success of some of its former republics. Not the actual country but the government has descended from being all beneficent, all powerful and all knowing to being a cabal of old men stuffing their pockets with tattered rubles as fast as they can. The real money is being made by people who never see the inside of the Kremlin. Gangsters, businessmen, private citizens, killers and even rebels.

But if its people are any richer than they were under the hammer and sickle (they're not), they're certainly not living any longer. War, disease, drugs, unemployment, crime, poverty and all those other frills of freedom are taking their toll on the erstwhile resilient Russians with a vengeance.

Male life expectancy has fallen a staggering seven years, to 58, since the flag of freedom was hoisted over the Kremlin. Men in Russia today live 15–17 fewer years than their counterparts in the United States and Western Europe. Russian men were more likely to reach 60 a century ago than they are today. Russia is

Commonwealth of Independent States

1. Adygea
2. Karachay-Cherkessia
3. Kabardino-Balkaria
4. North Ossetia
5. Checheno-Ingushetia

0   **400 km**

0   **400 mi**

SVALBARD
(NORWAY)

Arkhangel'sk

Barents
Sea

Kara
Sea

Baltic
Sea

FINLAND

Murmansk

Kaliningrad

ESTONIA

LATVIA

Karelia

White Sea

Arkhangel'sk

Pechorskoye
More

LITHUANIA

Pskov

St. Petersburg

Leningrad
Oblast

Arkhangel'sk

Nenetsia
AOk

Novgorod

BELARUS

Vologda

Komi

Yamalia
AOk

Tver'

Smolensk

Yaroslavl'

Bryansk

Kaluga

Moscow

Ivanovo

Kostroma

Moscow

Vladimir

Permyakia
AOk

Khantia
Mansia
AOk

Kursk

Orel

Tula

Ryazan'

Nizhniy-
Novgorod

Kirov

UKRAINE

Lipetsk

Belgorod

Tambov

Mordovi

Chuvashia

Penza

Mari El

Udmurtia

Perm'

Voronezh

Ul'yanovsk

Tatarstan

Sverdlovsk
Oblast

Saratov

Samara

Bashkortostan

Tyumen'

Tomsk

Rostov

Volgograd

Orenburg

Chelyabinsk

Kurgan

Krasnodar
Kray

1

Kalmy

Stavropol'
Kray

Astrakhan'

Omsk

Novosibirsk

Kemero

2

3

4

5

GEORGIA

Dagestan

KAZAKHSTAN

Altay Kray

Kh

ARMENIA

Gorr
Alta

AZERBAIJAN

Aral Sea

CHIN

IRAN

Caspian Sea

TURKMENISTAN

UZBEKISTAN

Lake Balkhash

being ravaged by a disease. It is CIS-positive, malignant with the growing pains of liberty, which Russians are abusing like a chemically dependent pharmacist. Russian men are 20 times more likely to be murdered than Western European males. In 1996, Russian men committed suicide and boozed themselves to death twice as much as they did in 1990. The war in Chechnya took the lives of some 4,300 Russian soldiers. Tobacco causes nearly 300,000 deaths every year. Not surprising when you consider that 77 percent of Russian males smoke $3 billion worth of cigarettes a year. It kinda makes those nuclear reactor leaks, environmental hazards, heavy metal pollution and toxins, crime and civil war seem like mere entertainments in the vodka soaked existence of the typical Russian.

Suddenly communism doesn't look so bad anymore. Poverty was a lot easier when you could blame it on the U.S. imperialist aggressors. The only reason fewer people are feeling the pangs of indigence in Russia today is that there are fewer Russians around to feel anything. There have been a million more deaths than births each year in Russia since the days of the crowds at Lenin's tomb. If the population continues to fall by a million a year, in a half-century Russia won't be much more populous than the Los Angeles basin—but without the palm trees. A victory of sorts for Planned Parenthood, but a bad day for baby formula makers.

In December 1991, the Cold War ended when the Soviet Union collapsed. The high-flying Russian revolution had finally run out of gas and crashed. The jagged pieces totalled 12: Armenia, Azerbaijan, Belarus, Georgia, Kazakhstan, Kyrgyzstan, Moldova, Russia, Tajikistan, Turkmenistan, Ukraine and Uzbekistan. And most of these states are going through a secondary breakup, as ethnic and religious factions fight for sovereignty, usually with the help or antagonism of "Mother Russia," Iran or gangsters. After their brief taste of independence (and financial insolvency), many of these independent states are thinking about realigning themselves with Moscow.

Russia is the largest country that emerged from the former USSR. In 1992, Russia introduced an array of economic reforms that not only freed the prices on most goods and services, but set the course for a downward economic spiral that continues today.

Although President Boris Yeltsin survived a national referendum on his ability to lead the country in 1993, he dissolved the legislative bodies still left dangling from the Soviet era and signed a peace treaty. On October 3, 1993, tensions between the executive and legislative branches of the government escalated into armed conflict. With the help of the military, Boris got to keep his whopping $21,000 a year salary and free Moscow apartment.

A December 1994 attempt to take Grozny in the rebel Republic of Chechnya revealed in a rebel rout of the Russian forces precisely how weak the Russian war machine had become, and subsequent events showed even greater disorganization. Yeltsin may think he is in charge, but it became apparent that when push comes to shove, the army will decide. Renegade commanders refused to follow orders or never received them. Russian soldiers captured by the insurgent Chechens revealed that they were without food and maps—essentially that they had no direction nor any idea of what the hell they were doing. Russian corpses littered Grozny like dead worms after a heavy rain. Although the vastly superior forces eventually took the Chechen capital in 1995 only to retreat in August 1996, they've faced a repeat of Afghanistan since.

However, crime may be Russia's biggest export in the next decade. The brutal control of a central government has been reborn in the form of Russian Mafias. In Russia, there are an average of 84 murders a day; many are contract killings, according to the Ministry of the Interior. In 1996, at least 200 Russian business executives were whacked by the Chechen Mafia in Moscow alone. Compare the rate of 16 murders per 100,000 in Russia to the U.S. rate of 9 per 100,000, and you can see why even trigger-happy Americans look like Buddhist monks next to the Russians. Someone is murdered in Russia every 18 minutes. Sixty percent of the murders are for material gain, and 20 percent are thought to be murders of gangsters by rival gangs. In fact, there are more gangsters than there are police in Russia. Less than half of all perpetrators are ever brought to justice.

There is more afoot than just thuggery in Russia. Tired of polishing their ICBMs and rotating their nuclear weapons, some army units have decided to strip them down into more economically attractive components and, by doing so, generate a little cash. In 1993, there were 6,430 reports of stolen weapons, ranging from assault rifles to tanks. To date, there have been more than 700 reports of nuclear material being sold to various buyers outside and inside Russia. On the black market, a kilo of chromium-50 can go for $25,000, cesium-137 for $1 million and lithium-6 for $10 million. Prospective customers for these goodies are Iran, North Korea, Libya and other nations looking for a big bang for their money.

Russia's myriad woes defy being capsulized. Chechnya is giving Colombia and the Philippines a run for their ransoms as the kidnap capitals of the world. Five Russian TV journos snatched earlier in 1997 are still missing. A police crackdown has netted dozens of hostage-takers. The Russian military remains in shambles. More than 10 Russian soldiers die each day from non-combat causes—including suicide and malnourishment. The Chechens should have just waited for the Russkies to off themselves. (The Russian population decreases by 1.2 million people a year.) To boost dismal morale and put more potatoes on the officers' plates, Russia has started peddling antiaircraft missiles to Cyprus, despite threats of force from Turkey, which would assuredly kick Boris' behind in a full-auto pistol polo match. Now that Yeltsin has been invited into the Boys Club of the Eight, he gets his mug on CNN more, but still has to deal with Russia's nemesis supreme: Afghanistan. Afghanistan has been a burr between Moscow's buns for two decades—hastening the collapse of the USSR—and the Taliban doesn't bode well for Mother Vodka. Once again, Moscow is faced with possible military intervention (a Russian oxymoron), as Afghanistan has become a staging ground for Islamic insurgents seeking to topple the Russian-backed government in Tajikistan. Drinking games aside, Boris fears a domino effect if the Taliban gets a foothold in Tajikistan. Turkmenistan and Uzbekistan would surely be next. Russia's military can hardly afford another ass-kicking.

It's amazing enough that the Kremlin's button-pushers even possess this information at all. Kremlin intelligence (another Russian oxymoron) has been as ravaged as the army. The dreaded KGB has been replaced by the threaded FSB, who are so hard up for good spies and information other than Iditarod scores that they've set up a telephone hotline to bring Russian agents spying for foreign intelligence services back into the fold. That's right! Turncoat agents can now call a special number and turn themselves in! Callers are immune from prosecution and can continue to collect CIA, MI6 and Mossad paychecks, but are asked in return to provide those spook agencies with bogus information. Wow. In Russia, a mole is a birthmark with a bunch of hairs growing out of it.

Russia has reverted back to a 19th-century society of potato farmers. But potato farmers with nukes. The middle class, a key to a successful democracy, is dissolving like cheap dentures in an acid bath. The rank-and-file of the army haven't been paid in months. Russia will never be the West. Look for a military coup and a scenario that makes the Cold War look like a hockey game.

It Doesn't Get Much Worse . . .

The President has decreed that government officials will have to exchange their Mercedes and other luxury imported cars for domestic Volga sedans. The luxury cars will be sold by the government at open auctions. This comes at a time when millions of Russians haven't seen a paycheck for months. Some bureaucrats have put in a request for two Volgas to replace a single Mercedes because Volgas "break down so much," said one.

The Russian Mafia (*Organizatsiya* or Mafyia)

In 1996 there were 8,000 criminal gangs in Russia. In 1993 there were 5,700, over 300 of them operating internationally. The Ministry of Internal Affairs (MVD) has estimated that 40 percent of private business, 60 percent of state-owned enterprises, and more than half of the country's banks are controlled by organized crime. One wonders how the other half survives. Banks are considered to be insolvent since the crash of August 1988. The rest are suspected of being money-laundering fronts for the government and businesses. Most private enterprises pay protection of up to 30 percent of their profits to organized crime.

In a land of extremes, it's still surprising that there are 1,500 contract killings a year, 8,000 missing and 30,000 violent crimes in Moscow alone. Big shots, or *Shkafy*, own more new Beemers and Mercs than Orange County. The Mafyia is not only here to stay, but it keeps the country working. Who else is going to give you good deals on everything from cheap fuel to nuclear warheads. Imagine what things would cost if the government got their hands on it.

There are 150 major criminal societies controlling 35,000 enterprises. Most crime in Russia is controlled by eight "families," such as the Chechens, the most powerful group and descendants of a centuries-old tribe who still control the Caucasus Mountains. The Chechens specialize in bank fraud and extortion. Some $12 billion gets flushed out of Russia each year into accounts in Switzerland and Cyprus equal to the total of outside investment flowing into the country. The Russian Mafyia is reputed to have about $10 billion in Swiss bank accounts. Half of Russia's banks and 80 percent of the joint ventures involving foreign capital have connections with organized crime.

http://www.mafia.spb.ru
http://www.alternatives.com/crime/menu.html
http://personal.inet.fi/tiede/johan.backman
http://www.yorku.ca/nathanson/default.htm

Show Me the Rubles!

The average Russian makes $1,700 a year. An army lieutenant makes $1,000 a year and a senior civil servant makes a $2,000 a year salary. The Russian prime minister makes righteous bucks: $8,000 per year. Even Boris isn't in the 28-percent tax bracket. The Russian president makes a mere $21,000 a year, about the same as an experienced sandwich-maker at Subway.

The Economy

What economy? The gross domestic product of Russia has declined each year since 1989, apart from the death-kick increase of 0.8 percent in 1997. Inflation rages like a Malibu hill fire between 18 and 30 percent. Russia owes over $160 billion in debt. Most banks have been insolvent since August 1998. Do you want me to keep going on?

http://www.csis.org/ruseura/rus_econ.html

The Government

What government? The latest prime minister of the week harangued the Duma on combating terrorism: "We must not slobber or snivel."

http://www.gov.ru/

The Next President

Vladimir Valdimirovich Putin was born in Leningrad on October 7, 1952. He graduated from the Law Department of Leningrad State University (LGU) in 1975, embarking immediately on a career with the first chief directorate (foreign intelligence) of the KGB. To make it short, he is a man with the goods on everyone and somebody who is interested in rebuilding the Russian economy. Putin ran the FSB (the reborn KGB) during the Kosovo conflict in the initial stages of the Dagestan conflict. He may be a WWIII scenario planner's worst nightmare. A spook that answers to no one. A capitalist with an iron fist. His "you want a piece of me?" internal policy would give Stalin a woody. He doesn't even bother deporting thousands of people from the Caucasus. Instead he has a Swanson TV dinner approach to warfare. He just has his citizens chopped up, napalmed, frozen and starved in place and of course served up lovingly on TV as dead terrorists. The truth is much darker, and so Russian. But everyone loves a tough guy.

The Army

The army is slowly building back its power base in Russia and the CIS but is still as disheveled and unruly as a Moscow drunk. When Russian troops stormed Pristina airport in the Balkans, the politicians were red faced. Seems like the generals were doing a little internal foreign policy planning. When the Kremlin made some mumbles about easing off in Chechnya in the fall of 1999, the military made it clear that they could run the country just fine without the benefit of spineless politicians. That doesn't mean the Russian army will be all it can be. It's still made up of drunken lifers brutalizing ill-trained farmboys and working for corrupt mafyia-controlled generals. The only difference is they are drunk officers and scared, pink-cheeked boys with guns, and in Russia that guarantees a decent living. And the mafyia is a more regular employer than the government.

In some areas, army commanders rent out weapons and men are hired out as mercenaries to the highest bidder. It's not a very tight ship. More than 6,000 crimes involving corruption and embezzlement were committed in the Russian armed forces in 1996, double the figure of three years ago. More than 20 generals were being investigated as of mid-1997, many in housing schemes. An estimated 110,000 troops lack proper housing, and 428 soldiers committed suicide in 1996. In the spring of that year, Yeltsin announced that conscription would end in Russia by 2000, causing Moscow's Generation Xers to party in the streets. It was an empty campaign pledge. Russia cannot afford an all-volunteer army until 2005 at the earliest, Boris' defense minister has said. Bummer.

Induced by a chronic food shortage, many soldiers have resorted to begging. And thousands of soldiers died in 1996 from acts of torture and ill treatment by other soldiers. The Kremlin's army has shrunk to a measly 1.7 million soldiers. Russia's version of web-surfing is draft-dodging. A reason for the army's decline is quite simple, really: Russia took over 85 percent of the Soviet Union's armed forces and only 65 percent of its economic potential.

http://www.milparade.ru/

Perestrelka

No, not *perestroika*, a word used by Mikhail Gorbachev to symbolize reforms. *Perestrelka* means "shoot-out" in Russian and is a better description of what is going on in Russia today.

The military vacuum in Russia has allowed the rise of the *vory v zzakone*, or thieves-in-law. A class of thugs created before the revolution and toughened in Soviet gulags, these gangsters are enamored with pomp and circumstance and even possess private jets. The government estimates that there are 289 thieves-in-law operating in Russia and 28 other countries around the world. Below these very wealthy and powerful Mafia figures are the gangs. There are about 20 criminal brigades, or gangs, that control Moscow with L.A.-style monikers for their neighborhoods. There are estimated to be 5,800 gang members in Russia. The gangs aren't quick or smart enough to control the country, so it's left to the *vory v zzakone* to reap the profits of absolute control.

There are four levels of Mafia in Russia. The lowest stratum consists of shopkeepers who sell goods at inflated prices to afford protection money. The enforcers are burly, loud men with a fancy for imported cars (usually stolen). They'll also double as pimps, gunrunners and drug dealers. The businessmen are unfettered capitalists who steer most of the lucrative deals the Mafia's way.

Finally, at the top of the food chain, is the "state Mafia." They are the controllers of a large percentage of the money earned by the lesser Mafia. These politicians/gangsters allow the lower echelons to operate in peace and without fear of prosecution. They have driven away a lot of Western investment and businessmen who find themselves forced to retain a local "partner" in their enterprises.

http://www.acsp.uic.edu/oicj/pubs/cji/110413.htm

Big Business

It should come as no surprise that a handful of "czars" call the shots in the Kremlin. Their only competition is the high-ranking members of the Russian military. In the end, he who has the most rubles wins.

http://www.megastories.com/russia/oligarchs/glossary.htm
http://www.westga.edu/~bquest/1997/moscow.html

The Roof/krysha

You just don't do business in Russia without a roof. A protector that guarantees that you stay alive long enough to pay your monthly dues. These groups are usually affiliated with FSB (formerly known as the KGB) and local authorities. Naturally there is also an accommodation with the local mafyia, thugs and neighbors.

In a concession to modern economics, many of these groups will only dip their beak into your profits, giving you a chance to get into the black. If you try to get smart you'll of course end up in the red.

Russian Gangster Slang

Wanna talk the talk, drochit'?

ochko   ass

Russian Gangster Slang

it pizda	*shits*
chelovek ne obremenenni' intelectom	*fuckwit*
nehoroshiy chelovek	*trip-ass motherfucker*
pakhan	*boss*
hui	*penis*
cyka	*bitch*
perdol'ka	*baba*
zaebis	*that'll roll*
drochit'	*jack-off*
Merin	*Mercedes*
Kaban	*Mercedes S-class*

Source: http://www.razvod.com/rus/fenya/fenya.htm

A passport and Russian visa are required for all U.S. citizens traveling to or transiting through Russia by any means of transportation, including train, car or airplane. While under certain circumstances travelers who hold valid visas to some countries of the former Soviet Union may not need a visa to transit Russia, such exceptions are inconsistently applied. Travelers who arrive without an entry visa may be subject to large fines, days of processing requirements by Russian officials and/or immediate departure by route of entry (at the traveler's expense). Carrying a photocopy of passports and visas will facilitate replacement should either be stolen.

All Russian visas, except transit visas, are issued on the basis of support from a Russian individual or organization, known as the sponsor. It is important to know who your sponsor is and how they can be contacted, as Russian law requires that your sponsor apply on your behalf for replacement and extension of or changes to your visa. The U.S. embassy cannot act as your sponsor. Tourists should contact their tour company or hotel in advance for information on visa sponsorship.

For current information on visa requirements, U.S. citizens can contact the Russian consulates in New York, San Francisco or Seattle or the embassy:

Russian Embassy

> *2641 Tunlaw Road, NW*
> *Washington, DC 20007*
> *Tel.: (202) 939-8907, (202) 939-8913, (202) 939-8918*
> *Fax: (202) 483-7579*
> *http://www.russianembassy.org/consulate.html*

All foreigners must have an exit visa in order to depart Russia. For short stays, the exit visa is issued together with the entry visa; for longer stays, the exit visa must be obtained by the sponsor after the traveler's arrival. Russian law requires that all travelers who spend more than three days in Russia register their visas through their hotel or sponsor. Visitors who stay in Russia for a period of weeks may be prevented from leaving if they have not registered their visas. Errors in the dates or other information on the visa can occur, and it is helpful to have someone who reads Russian check the visa before you depart the United States.

Many areas along Russia's southern borders are not manned, and checkpoints are only on main roads. Russian soldiers can be bribed due to their low pay and acceptance of side income.

Internal travel, especially by air, can be erratic and may be disrupted by fuel shortages, overcrowding of flights and various other problems. Travelers may need to cross great distances, especially in Siberia and the Far East, to obtain services from Russian government organizations or from the U.S. embassy or its consulates. Russia stretches over 6,000 miles east to west and 2,500 miles north to south. Winter can last a long time.

Unlike the old days, you can go just about anywhere you want these days. You don't even need to use Intourist to get around. The cheapest way into Moscow from Cheremkhovo airport is via the regular bus. You can use rubles. Taxis usually require long waits and one *DP* reader suggests having your sponsor pick you up at the airport. You can also pick up a private car from one of the many people who will try to offer you one. Expect to pay $50 in real money (not rubles) or the equivalent amount in cigarettes. For about the same price, you can arrange a car in the arrivals section. You must use a credit card. In Moscow, most taxis demand U.S. dollars, or one to three packs of cigarettes, or R10 to R20.

About half the roads in Russia are paved. The worst time to traverse Russian roads is during the spring, when the rural roads become muddy rivers. About 20 percent of the roads are simple tracks. The railways are the major means of transport, with most routes spreading out from Moscow on 11 major trunk lines. There are 32 railway subsystems within the former Soviet Union. The main route is the passenger artery through Russia along the Trans-Siberian Railway, which travels east from Moscow across Siberia to the Pacific and China, Mongolia and Korea.

Traveling by sea is also an efficient way to get around Russia, particularly in the Baltic. Twenty-seven former Soviet passenger ships form the largest such fleet in the world.

Russian airlines service 3,600 population centers inside Russia. Airlines are viewed as buses with wings, so don't expect much. They are adding new Western aircraft to the various Russian airlines, so ask what kind of plane you'll be on. The severe winters can affect schedules and flights into places like Tajikistan, and airlines are subject to fuel shortages.

The telecommunications infrastructure remains underdeveloped. Only 30 percent of urban and 9 percent of rural families have telephones. More than 17 million customers have ordered telephones, but are still waiting (sometimes for years) to have them installed.

All items which may appear to have historical or cultural value—icons, art, rugs, antiques, etc.—may be taken out of Russia only with prior written approval of the Ministry of Culture and payment of a 100 percent duty. Goods that are purchased from street vendors can be problematic and expensive to export. Russian customs laws state that any item for export valued at more than 300,000 rubles (value is established by customs officials at the time of export—for example, just prior to a traveler's departing flight) is subject to a 600 percent export tax. Items purchased from government-licensed shops, where prices are openly marked in hard currency, are not subject to the tax. Request a receipt when making any purchase. Caviar may only be taken out of Russia with a receipt indicating it was bought in a store licensed to sell to foreigners. Failure to follow the customs regulations may result in temporary or permanent confiscation of the property in question.

Embassy and Consulate Locations and Phone Numbers

Moscow

Novinskiy Bulvar 19/23
Tel.: [7] (095) 252-2451.
After-hours duty officer: Tel.: [7] (095) 230-2001/2601.

U.S. Consulate General in St. Petersburg

Ulitsa Furshtadskaya 15
Tel.: [7] (812) 275-1701.
After-hours duty officer, Tel.: [7] (812) 274-8692.

U.S. Consulate General in Vladivostok

12 Mordovtseva
Tel.: [7] (4232) 268-458/554 or 266-820.

Consulate General in Yekaterinburg

Tel.: [7] (3432) 601-143
Fax: [7] (3432) 601-181
Provides emergency services for American citizens.

The situation remains unsettled in Russia's north Caucasus area, which is located in southern Russia along its border with Georgia. Travel to this area is considered dangerous. The regions of the Chechen Republic, the Ingush Republic and the North Ossetian Republic have experienced continued armed violence and have a state of emergency and curfew in effect.

The Caucasus

How much does Russia love Chechnya? After a survey by the Audit Chamber, the nonpartisan, independent state auditor for Russia went through the files, it was discovered that of $3 billion earmarked for reconstruction of the Chechnya economy after the war ended, there was documentation for only $2 billion. Less than $150 actually reached Chechnya. They probably used it for postage. To study the convoluted backgrounds and problems, here is a potpourri of sites:

I Fall to Pieces . . .	
Abkhazia	*http://www.abkhazia.org/*
Adygeia	*http://www.angelfire.com/co/adygheya/*
Chechnya	*http://src-home.slav.hokudai.ac.jp/eng/Russia/n-caucasus-e.html*
Dagestan	*http:www.dagestan.ru/*
Kabardino-Balkaria	*http://www.fotw.net/flags/ru-kb.html*
Karachai-Cherkessia	*http://www.ozemail.com.au/~karachay/ncauc.html*
Ingushetia	*http://www.unpo.org/member/ingush/ingush.html*
North Ossetia, Alaniya	*http://www.friends-partners.org/old-friends/ossetia/*

Georgia/Sarkartvelo

Georgia, or Sarkartvelo as it's known locally (or as it should be known "the country that can't shoot straight), is the southernmost region of Russia and the first republic to give Mother Russia the finger. Naturally, fighting began immediately in the south Ossetia region and the Mingrelia area has killed hundreds. In May of 1991, Zvaid Gamsakhurdia was elected president of Georgia with an overwhelming majority of the popular vote (86.5 percent). Not content with popular support, Zvaid began to conceive and implement very undemocratic statutes, such as "making fun of the president gets you six years in the slammer." He also put his money on the wrong ponies when he backed the coup plotters who failed to overthrow Yeltsin. He cracked down on the southern Muslim state of Ossetia, which instigated a revolt effective enough to force him to flee on January 6, 1992. The opposition, which consisted of his prime minister and foreign minister (who had backed Yeltsin), invited Eduard Shevardnadze, the former Soviet foreign minister and first secretary of the Georgian Communist Party, to be chairman of the state council. OK so he made a few mistakes.

The return of old hard-line communist hacks did not satisfy the Muslim Abkhazian separatists, under Chechen Shamil Basayev who, feeling their oats, had taken over the Abkhazian region along the Black Sea.

The Russians meddled and brokered a cease-fire, which was quickly broken on September 16, 1993. Despite a pistol-waving Shevardnadze, the rebels took over the strategic Black Sea port of Sukhumi. The bizarre twist is that Shevardnadze blames the Russians for setting him up by brokering a phony cease-fire and then letting the rebels take over the country. The fact that the "rebels" were using Russian-supplied weapons and equipment confirmed the perception that the Russians were backing the Abkhazians. In September 1999, Russia lifted the border restriction off the top of Abkhazia allowing weapons and goods to flow in. This was in retaliation to Georgia's refusal to seal their northern border with Chechnya. Dagestan, Ingushetia and North Ossetia have all welcomed Russian troops in providing a sealed border except for the snow mountain passes to on Georgia's 50-mile-long northern border with Chechnya. Next rumor, the Chechens will set up a government in exile in Tiblisi, which will of course prompt Russia to find some reason to kick poor Georgia back into the arms of Moscow.

http://www.parliament.ge/
http://www.sakartvelo.com/
http://sergi.virtualave.net/sakartvelo/

Moscow

In Moscow alone are 5,000 murders and 20,000 incidents of violent crime every year. The local population easily recognizes U.S. tourists and business travelers as foreigners because of their clothing, accessories and behavior. American visitors tend to experience a relatively high incidence of certain types of crime, such as physical assaults and pickpocketing of wallets, traveler's checks, passports and cameras on the street, in hotels, in restaurants and in high-density tourist areas.

http://www.state.gov/www/about_state/business/com_guides/1999/europe/
russia99_09.html

St. Petersburg

St. Petersburg has a crime rate 30 percent higher than Moscow's. The area around Gostiniy Dvor and the underground passage on Nevsky Prospekt, as well as train stations, the food markets, the flea markets and the so-called "art park" are frequent stages for street crime against foreigners. It is estimated that 20 percent of the foreign businesses are controlled by the Russian Mafia. Most groups who try to set up businesses in the city find they are hit up for a $10,000 fee to arrange the "necessary contacts." If you are edgy, bodyguards can be hired for about $600 a month (U.S. dollars only). Not bad, when you figure that the average monthly wage is about $20. Most crimes are committed in broad daylight, since the police will do little, if anything, to help or track down your assailants. If you are staying in one of the better hotels in St. Petersburg, have them send a car for you at the airport. If not, you can take a taxi into town for about $30. If you want a car for the entire day, figure on spending about double that.

http://www.times.spb.ru/
http://www.spb.ru/

Emergency Numbers

Fire	**Hard Currency Taxi**
Tel.: 01	*Tel.: 298-6804, 298-3648*
Police	**Western-Style Medical Care**
Tel.: 02	*Tel.: 310-9611*
Ambulance	**American Express**
Tel.: 03	*Tel.: 311-5215*
U.S. Consulate	**Delta Airlines**
Tel.: 274-8692	*Tel.: 311-5819/20/22*
Taxi	
Tel.: 312-0022	

The Chechens

A remote trans-Caucasian region just north of Georgia, the Republic of Chechnya is home to Russia's largest and most powerful crime families. In fact, they have a friendly neighborhood branch in what may be your own hometown (Boston, Philadelphia, Chicago, Los Angeles and New York).

The Chechens in Moscow are split into three main criminal factions. The most powerful is the "central," followed by the "Ostankinsky" and the "automobile." Finding these groups used to be easy, as they operated from plush Moscow hotels until the war. The centrals could be found in the Hotel Belgrade, the Golden Ring and the Russia Hotel. Here, they controlled drugs, prostitution, restaurants, Moscow markets and the retail trade. The Ostankinsky takes its name from the Ostankinsky Hotel. The group is also headquartered in the Voskhod and Baikal hotels. Their specialty is the transfer and shipment of all types of goods (including drugs) between Moscow and their home base of Chechnya. The "automobile" group brings in cars from Western Europe and looks after seven gas stations.

The transport and sale of drugs are a major source of income for the Chechens. They also employ the time-honored method of extortion to supplement their income. Everyone from street vendors to major international corporations have to cough up about 10 percent of their gross or face the music. The Chechens are linked to the three main Italian Mafia families as well as members of the former Soviet government, the KGB and former Soviet Communist Party members.

Chechen Government
http://www.amina.com/

Chechen "Rebels"
http://www.kavkaz.org/
http://andrsn.stanford.edu/Other/redmaf.html

Airlines

Airline passengers are more likely to be killed in Russia than anywhere else in the world. There are about 315 different airlines in Russia, rapidly dwindling to around 53 when the dust settles. The number of fatalities per million passengers has risen from 1 in 1990 to 5.5 in 1993. The breakup of Aeroflot into hundreds of regional carriers that cannot afford to properly maintain their planes has a lot to do with it. Pilots, who make an average of $21 a month, have even spoken out. Oh yeah, and 65 Russian airlines went bankrupt in 1997, and all those horror stories you've heard all are true.

Aeroflot

4, Frunzenskaya Naberezhnaya;
20/1, Ulitsa Petrovka;7, Korovy
Val; 19, Ulitsa Yeniseyskaya
Moscow, Russia
Tel.: 155-5045 926-6278
http://www.aeroflot.org

Shari'a and Jail

Shari'a in Chechnya dictates that convicted murderers have their throats slit, while non-Muslims committing the same offense can expect a cozy, lifelong stay in the slammer. However in a survey among Russian prisoners whose death sentences had been commuted to life terms in prison, 20 percent said they preferred death. Lifers are sent to brutal, hard-labor prison camps in Siberia. Many are confined to tiny cells for 23 hours a day. *DP* tourist trivia: You can now take tours of Moscow's funkier jails for $2 a ticket.

Water

Fully 70 percent of Russia's tap water is not safe for human consumption. See "Vodka."

Vodka

Talk about a hangover; in Russia, one of every six bottles of Russian-made vodka is hazardous for human consumption. Some 340,000 cases of counterfeit vodka that were brought to Moscow in June 1997 aboard 70 railroad cars were sent to a chemical plant for reprocessing into car windshield cleanser and brake fluid, perhaps because these concoctions are more palate-friendly.

http://www.epact.se/acats/vodka.html

Crime

In a place where hiring a hit man to kill someone costs only $200, you had better watch your step. Foreigners are targets of crime in Russia, especially in major cities. Pickpocketing and muggings occur both day and night. Street crimes are most frequent in train stations, airports and open markets; on the Moscow-St. Petersburg overnight train; and when hailing taxis or traveling by the Metro late at night. Groups of children who beg for money sometimes pickpocket and assault tourists. Foreigners' hotel rooms and residences have also been targeted. Some victims have been seriously assaulted during robberies. If you receive a replacement for your lost or stolen U.S. passport from the U.S. embassy or a consulate in Russia, your exit visa must also be replaced, with assistance from your sponsor, so that the passport number written on the visa matches your new passport. This normally requires a Russian police report.

Older people are also targets of crime in Russia. In addition, there has been a sharp rise in the number of taxi drivers killed while on duty. Policemen have been killed at their posts. And, to make matters worse, Russian jails are becoming overcrowded. Even more so if you decide to hire a guard. There are 9,800 private security firms registered in Russia, and of the 5,000 firms inspected by the Interior Ministry, 10 percent had criminal connections.

http://www.alternatives.com/crime/menu.html

Extortion

Apart from the street muggings, which are the most dangerous thing in Russia, extortion is number two. If you're lucky, you'll get mugged and hit up for a bribe. Russians say that 70 to 80 percent of businesses pay extortion demands to criminal groups. Only about 10 to 15 foreigners file extortion charges each year. No it is not tax deductible.

http://www.itaiep.doc.gov/bisnis/country/ruscrime.htm

Uncle Sam

Russia is like the eternally drunk, lying, slovenly brother-in-law we'd rather suck up to than get into a fistfight with. So we give them money when they need it, lecture them when they go overboard and try to steal as many of our secrets back as we can. For now Americans shouldn't feel that nervous when visiting Russia, but it never hurts to have a friend in-country. Two guesses where the billions in IMF, Uncle Sam money goes—to fight wars and in politicians' pockets.

U.S. Embassy—Moscow:

Novinsky Bulvar 19/23.
Tel.: 7 095 252-2451; Fax 7 095 956-4261
After-hours emergencies: 7 095 252-1898 or 255-5123.

U.S. Consulate-General—St. Petersburg

Thomas Lynch, Consul-General
Ulitsa Furshtadkskaya 15
Tel.: 7 812 275-1701; Fax 7 812 110-7022
After-hours emergencies:
Tel.: 7 812 274-8692 or 271-6455.

U.S. Consulate-General—Vladivostok

Jane Miller Floyd, Consul-General
32 Pushkin Street
Tel.: 7 4232 268-458 or 300-070
Fax: 7 4232 300-091 or 300-072

U.S. Consulate-General—Yekaterinburg

Daniel Russell, Consul-General
15A Ulitsa Gogolya, 4th Floor
Tel.: 7 3432 564-619 or 564-691
Fax: 7 3432 564-515.

Les Miserables/Russian Politics/Springtime for Boris

Just a couple of weeks of press clippings on the political scene in Russia: Gennady Tuganov, chief coordinator of the St. Petersburg branch of the Liberal Democratic Party (LDP), was killed in a contract killing. Yeltsin is threatened with impeachment votes on a regular basis for everything from illegally dissolving the Soviet Union to launching the war in Chechnya.

Aslan Maskhadov, the leader of Chechnya escaped an assassination plot on April 10, 1999 when a bomb went off along the route Maskhadov was set to travel on to a rally. The U.S. Embassy was the target of mass demonstrations and running protest actions. Police and gunmen exchanged shots in front of the embassy on March 28 after attackers tried to fire a grenade at the building.

Andrey Galushko, first deputy governor of Omsk Oblast survived an assassination attempt on March 22, 1999, when gunmen sprayed his car with automatic-weapons fire. Galushko was wounded in the attack and his driver was killed. The attack on the deputy governor was thanks to Galushko's efforts to crack down on the mafyia. Yuri Shutov, a deputy in the St. Petersburg Legislative Assembly, was arrested on suspicion of heading a criminal gang, the Tambov—the leading gang in St. Petersburg. Moscow police arrested

19 members of the radical right-wing Russian National Unity movement, under Alexander Barkashov. The members of the neo-Nazi-type group like to dress in black uniforms and were handing out pamphlets near subway stations when they were taken into custody. Communist State Duma Deputy Viktor Ilyukhin recently said that Jews were responsible for the "genocide" of the Russian people. His remarks followed an earlier statement by Deputy Albert Makashov demanding that Jews be rounded up and jailed. Tune in next week for *As The Russians Crumble* . . .

Some More Helpful Hints from the Locals	
Last year the locals told you how not to get robbed. The folks at the *L A Times* Moscow bureau have compiled a helpful guide to help you sort out all those confusing demands for bribes or vzyatki:	
Stopping a major criminal investigation	$100,000
Cancelling a contract killing	$50,000
Getting an arrest warrant withdrawn	$10,000
Avoiding the military draft	$5,000
Clearing an imported car through customs	$3,500
Getting permission to install a flashing police light on private car	$1,500
Access to an important official	$1,000
Getting a phone installed quicker	$600
Getting your driver's license without a test	$400
Passing a university exam	$150
Avoiding arrest for DUI	$100
Minor traffic stop	$12
Avoiding speeding ticket	$2

Source: http://www.latimes.com

GETTING SICK

Medical care in Russia is usually far below Western standards, with severe shortages of basic medical supplies. But it is free. Access to the few quality facilities that exist in major cities usually requires payment in dollars at Western rates upon admission. The U.S. embassy and consulates have a list of good facilities and of English-speaking doctors. Many expats travel outside of Russia for most of their medical needs. Travelers may wish to check their insurance coverage and consider supplemental coverage for medical evacuation.

Typhoid can be a concern for those who plan to travel extensively in Russia. Drinking only boiled or bottled water will help to guard against cholera, which has been reported, as well as other diseases. More complete and updated information on health matters can be obtained from the Centers for Disease Control's international travelers' hotline, *Tel.: (404) 332-4559.*

RUSSIA

The Russian Federation is the largest republic of the CIS; it's almost twice the size of the United States. Moscow, with nearly 9 million residents, is the largest city.

The Russian Federation officially came into existence in December 1991. Russia is a presidential republic, containing 22 autonomous republics that maintain an uneasy balance between the Russian president and the Congress of People's Deputies (parliament). In practice, the power base is much more complex. Russia's vast size (10.5 million square km) and population (148 million) could make the region ripe for exploitation by Western investors; the corrupt infrastructure, however, makes business profits unlikely for years to come.

Russian is the official language, although there are many local ethnic tongues. English is widely read but not yet fluently spoken. Translators, of varying abilities, will be found in all sizable organizations. The country boasts a nearly 100 percent literacy rate.

Business hours are from 9 A.M. to 1 P.M., with a break for the typical heavy Russian lunch between 1 and 2 P.M. Some stores close from 2 to 3 P.M. Banks are open from 9:30 A.M. to 12:30 P.M., with currency exchanges open longer. You can change money at Sheremetyevo II International Airport in Moscow 24 hours a day. Also, the American Express office in Moscow can cash your AMEX traveler's checks into dollars.

Russia is $160 billion in debt but still manages to keep finding major oil fields. The former USSR had about 6.4 percent of the world's oil reserves and was the world's largest producer and exporter of natural gas. However, poor management has led to annual decreases each year since the 1980s.

Gas comes from western Siberia; the largest areas are Urengoi and Yamburg. New fields on the Yamal peninsula are waiting for development. The former USSR was the world's third-largest coal producer (after China and the United States). Russia possesses the world's largest explored reserves of copper, lead, zinc, nickel, mercury and tungsten. It also has about 40 percent of the world's reserves of iron ore and manganese. Figures released in September 1990 show confirmed iron reserves of 33.1 billion tons. The world's largest gold deposits at the Sukhoi Log reserves are estimated at more than 1,000 tons, much of which is smuggled out of Russia through the Baltic States. Russia is also trying to retain more control over its diamond reserves. The government created the Federal Diamond Centre, granting parliament more control over the industry. The intent is to weaken control over Russia's diamonds by De Beers, which has operated a supply cartel and maintained Russia's output at 7,500,000 carats per year.

Russia will be a net food importer for some time to come. Even when there are record harvests, shortages of labor cause the crops to rot in the fields.

Arms sales continue to be an important part of Russia's exports, although there is worldwide concern that a lot of high-tech systems are getting into the wrong hands.

The official currency is the ruble; it's pointless to post its rate against the U.S. dollar, since it changes as frequently as most people change their underwear. We are not even going to hazard a guess how little the ruble will be by the time you read this. U.S. currency is still preferred in Russia. There are 100 kopeks to the ruble.

Electricity is 220V/50Hz.

Money Hassles

Traveler's checks and credit cards are not widely accepted in Russia; in many cities, credit cards are only accepted at establishments catering to Westerners. Old, or very worn, dollar bills are often not accepted, even at banks. Major hotels or the American Express offices in Moscow or St. Petersburg may be able to suggest locations for cashing traveler's checks or obtaining cash advances on credit cards. Western Union has agents in Moscow, St. Petersburg and some other large cities that can disburse money wired from the United States.

Resources

ITAR-TASS
> http://www.itar-tass.com/itar-tass.htm

Interfax
> http://www.interfax-news.com/

All about Russia
> http://www.russianinfo.com/

Russian Studies Database
> http://www.nupi.no/russland/russland.htm

Russia Today
> http://www.russiatoday.com/

Better Living through Chemistry

Russia's drug addicts number 1.5 million (or 1 percent of the entire population), and the figure keeps growing. Illegal hemp fields in Russia cover an area exceeding 40 million hectares. During a recent eight-month period, Russian law enforcement bodies made arrests in connection with 40,000 drug-related crimes, seizing 13.3 tons of various drugs. Police have busted 3,300 gangs engaged in drug trafficking and sale. From 30 to 35 percent of the drugs are imported. In Moscow and St. Petersburg, however, the figure reaches 80 to 90 percent.

The price of one gram of cocaine in Moscow is from 400 to 900 percent higher than in New York, for which reason the Russian drug market looks very attractive to the international Mafia. The drug trade in Russia is a $100 million-a-year business. The police force fighting drug dealers today numbers as few as 3,500. Police are especially concerned that a new synthetic drug—trinisilsyntholin—is being produced in Russia. It formerly had only been produced in the U.S. The substance is so strong that one gram of it is enough to make 10 liters of narcotics more powerful than heroin or cocaine. Imported drugs, such as heroin and cocaine, are now sold everywhere in Russia. In Moscow, for instance, the price of one gram of heroin ranges from $200 to $300.

1/14/99	Russian troops enter Grozny . . . again.
10/1/99	Russians invade Chechnya . . . again.
9/9/99	A series of explosions in Moscow apartments is blamed on Chechens.
8/10/99	Southern Dagestan declares independence, but the Russian military change their mind.
7/2/96	Yeltsin wins Soviet election.
12/31/91	President Bush recognizes the independence of all 12 former Soviet republics and proposes the establishment of full diplomatic relations with 6 of them, including Russia. Russian President Yeltsin responds formally and positively on December 31, 1991, the date officially considered to be when the United States established formal diplomatic relations with Russia.

12/25/91	Mikhail Gorbachev resigns as president of the Soviet Union and transfers control of the Soviet nuclear arsenal to Russian President Boris Yeltsin. A few hours later, the United States recognizes Russia as the successor state to the Soviet Union. These actions mark the end of the Soviet Union, 74 years after the Bolshevik revolution.
12/21/91	Russia joins with 10 other former republics of the Soviet Union (which ceased to exist on December 25, 1991) in establishing the Commonwealth of Independent States. The Commonwealth was expected to have military and economic coordinating functions and would be headquartered in Minsk, Belarus.
8/19/91	Coup attempt fails, which symbolizes the end of communism in Russia and the breakup of the Soviet Union. Violent demonstrations occur in Moscow in August 1992, resulting in several deaths.
5/2/45	Berlin falls to the Soviets.
2/1/43	Germany's 6th Army surrenders to Soviet forces in Stalingrad.
6/22/41	German invasion of USSR.
11/7/17	Revolution Day, considered the most sacred day by Russian communists.

Rwanda
★★★★

Tutsi Pop

One of Africa's oldest proverbs—"When elephants fight, the grass gets trampled"—couldn't be better suited for the slaughter of Central Africa. Nearly a third of sub-Saharan Africa's 42 countries are mired in international or civil wars. Rwanda's got its candle wick dipped into both. How can one of the tiniest, lushest countries in Africa become one of the largest killing fields in the world? Tribalism.

Rwanda, like neighboring Burundi, is a rather simple (for most African states) hybrid of two tribes: the Hutus and the Tutsis. A four-year uprising made minor headlines every time Tutsi guerrillas would infringe on the territory of Rwanda's famous silverback gorilla families. When full-scale war broke out after the death of Burundi's and Rwanda's leaders in a plane crash, the majority Hutu tribe blamed the minority Tutsis and began indiscriminately slaughtering them. But the surprise success of the ragtag Tutsi rebels transformed them from freedom fighters into outright butchers. The Hutu-controlled government has been replaced by Tutsi rebels, and the wholesale massacre started being directed at the Hutus.

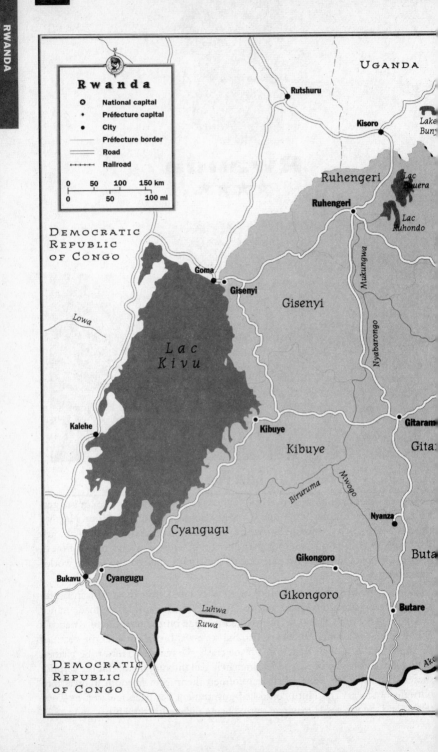

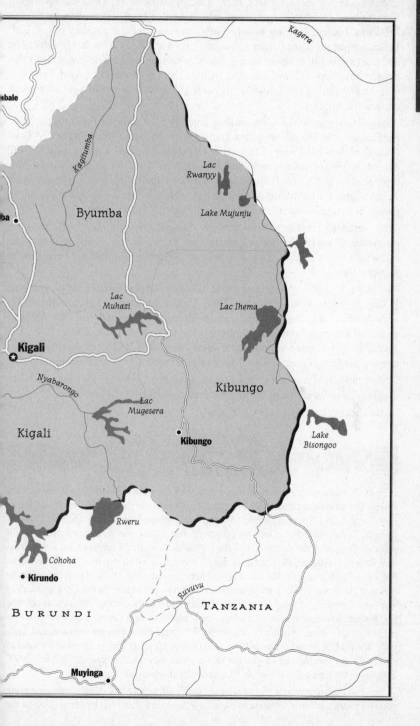

Now waves of refugees have been making tentative explorations homeward from eastern Congo (at least those who have not been slaughtered by Congo President Laurent Kabila's mostly Tutsi forces) under the auspices of the UN. Estimates put the Tutsi fatality toll at more than a million in the last few decades, and the number of refugees at more than twice that figure. The genocide in this decade has topped 1 million dead. Almost half of Rwanda's population of 8 million fled during the hostilities in April 1993; 10,000 per minute at its peak crossed the borders.

Rwandan leader Major-General Paul Kagame tried to bring the refugees back, particularly the Hutus, who fled the country en masse after Kagame's Tutsi Rwandan Patriotic Front (RPF) came to power in 1994. Kagame ordered the execution of any soldier who killed a civilian. That he was so serious was evidenced by the 1,116 Tutsi soldiers jailed by Kagame in 1996. Eighty of them were officers—most facing murder charges. Now, there are 130,000 people in prison in Rwanda awaiting trial in connection with the slaughter.

For refugees returning from eastern Congo, though, there has been no guarantee of safety. Former neighbors have turned hostile. Some returnees are ostracized, some accepted, some murdered. Returning Hutus have been shot as war criminals.

In 1998, Rwanda became embroiled in Congo's latest installment of civil war, aiding guerrillas seeking to oust DRC President Laurent Kabila, who Kigali accuses of hosting the defeated former Rwandan army and the *Interahamwe* militia which engineered the 1994 genocide in Rwanda. In late May 1999, the Rwandan government announced a cease-fire with Kabila's troops, that would remain in effect as long as Kigali felt its border with Congo was secure.

"Anything which waters down that guarantee plunges us back into the conflict," one Rwandan government minister warned of the cease-fire.

Like sucking on a Tutsi pop, perhaps?

In 1959, a faction intent on maintaining Tutsi privilege in Rwanda assassinated several Hutu leaders. Hutu rage slaughtered 100,000 Rwandan Watutsi, and the carnage was on—a 22-year genocide that, in 1994 alone, would wipe out half a million Watutsi and moderate Hutus in Rwanda. Today, Rwanda is a state paralyzed with fear. Illiteracy in Rwanda stands at over 50 per cent. Because of the slaughter, half the population is under 15 years old. Rwandan President Pasteur Bizimungu and Uganda leader Museveni have a firm grip on a Tutsi power bloc. But a new Hutu insurgency has arisen in northwest Rwanda. Some 6,000 Hutu extremists are hiding in the dense jungle, waiting for their comrades—participants in the 1994 genocide—who joined innocent refugees in their flight to Zaire (now Congo, or the DRC) and fought the new Rwanda government from their refugee camp bases in eastern Congo. Now they're returning to Rwanda—sneaking in from Congo over the Virunga chain of extinct volcanoes and, ironically, aboard UN aircraft. Many of these *interahamwe* guerrillas were recruited and trained in eastern Congo and blended in with the refugees that were forcibly repatriated in late 1996. They know the terrain and the locals. The government apparently doesn't.

You may want to postpone that endangered gorilla sightseeing tour. Hutu rebels are making good on their threats to off foreigners, particularly Americans. Hutu rebels operating out of the northeastern DRC targeted and whacked American monkey tourists in March 1999, prompting the U.S. State Department to warn against all travel to Rwanda. Hutu guerrillas are not an endangered species in Rwanda. About 130,000 Hutus are now imprisoned in Rwandan jails awaiting their day in court on genocide charges. About 1,000 have actually been brought before a judge.

Paul Kagame and the Rwandan Patriotic Front (RPF)

The man is a Rwandan Tutsi, born in Rwanda, and residing there today. Although Kagame is technically Rwanda's vice president, he is the most powerful man in the Tutsi homelands of Rwanda and Burundi and probably the most powerful man that either of those two precarious states have known since they both became independent in 1962. But most of his life he lived in Uganda, during that country's most wretched years—and there's the twist. The very wretchedness of that period helped bring the Watutsi and their son Kagame back to Rwanda.

The Uganda in which Kagame matured was a nether world, a place of attenuated pain, both psychological and physical. This, the Watutsi shared with their Ugandan hosts and helped them bear, first the nightmare of Amin, then two more nightmares. With little more outside help than refugee Watutsi could provide, the people of Uganda finally ended those nightmare years, and when they did, the Watutsi were not without influence.

First among these influentials was young Paul Kagame, Rwandan refugee, intelligence chief for all of Uganda . . . and a key organizer of the RPF. The Tutsi front was formed by the guerrilla years its leadership had spent with Yoweri Museveni's National Resistance Army, which drew its strength from popular support. This meant, above all, discipline. Rape was punishable by death, and a summary execution for just such an offense was meted out to a Tutsi fighter in the midst of 1994's 14-week war for Rwanda. The front demanded no privileges for the Watutsi, though there was little rhetorical nonsense, either: It was clear that majority rule would be balanced by minority rights. And there was clearly a danger that with meager resources, it could not control the climate of terror.

As a member of Uganda's military, Kagame was able to apply for a course in tactics given by the U.S. Army Command and General Staff College at Fort Leavenworth, Kansas. In fact (and reflecting in part Tutsi chutzpah), Kagame was in Kansas in October 1990, the very month he and a close comrade-in-arms, Fred Rwigyema, had planned to invade Rwanda. The invasion went ahead anyway, and it went well, until France put together a combined force of French troops, Zairois troops, Belgian troops and French-trained Hutu paras. In 1991, his movement launched its last frustrated invasion. Again, it went well, but with the prospect of intervention again hanging on the horizon, he stopped short in the north and agreed to talks. These were to drag on for two years in the Tanzanian town of Arusha at the foot of Mt. Kilimanjaro. At last, late in 1993, Rwanda's hard-line president agreed in priniciple to terms that called for a moderate Hutu to be installed as president and another as prime minister. The hard-line president signed a formal cease-fire, Rwanda's even harder-line military was enraged, and a large question began to loom as to whether Rwanda's government would or could fulfill the terms to which it had agreed. As he watched from his camps along the Biumba road, this was the chessboard upon which Kagame had to focus all his strategic faculties: French armor in Hutu hands, French heavy weapons, a Hutu military for which France and Belgium had successfully bought time for a huge buildup—Hutu airborne troops and 30,000 regulars, all trained by the French. Against this, he had no armor and no heavy weapons, just mortars and rocket-propelled grenades that Uganda had to pretend it didn't supply. As for training, it's basically the homegrown discipline of

Museveni's children's crusade, plus Kagame's course, which was in tactics, not strategy, as American reporters were wont to boast.

President Pasteur Bizimungu

Though he's the boss, Kagame (who also runs the military) is the dude calling the shots, and firing them, as Kagame has been doing in neigboring Congo to help rebels oust DRC President Laurent Kabila. Kagame announced a cease-fire in May 1999 as Libyan leader Mu'ammar Gaddafi commenced on his world tour—complete with chartered airliners and a bevy of buxom bodyguards—bucking for a Nobel Peace Prize by trying to end the fighting in the DRC. The author of the "Green Book" stands a better chance of being nominated than Bizimungu, whose grandest accomplishment as Rwandan leader was a ride aboard Air Force One with Bill Clinton to visit Ugandan President Yoweri Museveni in Kampala in March 1998. The flight was so short, the Boeing 747 couldn't get enough altitude for Bizimungu to use his Walkman.

Mwalimu Julius Nyerere

A great teacher of lessons, not all of which should be taught. Tanzania's soft-spoken leader, now deceased, is influential still: For Africans, he remains *mwalimu*, the teacher. In fact, without portfolio, he is more influential than most African heads of state. What he retired from, the presidency of backward, resource-poor Tanzania, was never the prime source of his influence. The decline is due almost entirely to the failure of his most ambitious ideas. He is known, will long be known, for a magnificent idea that has failed magnificently. Nyerere tried to craft, from the Swahili word for family, *ujamaa*, something between a voluntary Israeli kibbutz and a compulsory Chinese commune. It rarely worked. It cost millions. Whole villages were uprooted. Labor was forced. It never came close to paying its way. Today, the effort is largely abandoned. Regardless, he was a man of integrity, remains a powerful teacher of integrity, and many believe Africa needed more leaders like him.

Congo President Laurent Kabila

Kabila was born by Rwandan politics whether he admits it or not. The success of his rebellion against Mobutu Sese Seko was due to the support of U.S. connections and Paul Kagame. Now Kabila's holding most of the marbles in Kinshasa and has his own massacre to cover up. He'll have to think quick to account for some 250,000 Rwandan Hutu refugees missing in his reborn Congo. Kabila let a UN team into Congo to check the allegations out. But with a new civil war raging against Kabila, supported by Kagame, Rwanda, Uganda and Burundi, most of the body bags won't get tagged. Rwanda's army says it is fighting with the rebels to ensure security on its border with the former Zaire. It has accused Kabila of breaking bread with and handing out Kalashnakov souvenirs to Hutu hardliners responsible for the 1994 genocide of minority Tutsis and Hutu moderates.

Interahamwe Militia/Ex-FAR (Forces Armees Rwandaises)

Remnants of the Hutu militias and former Rwandan armed forces responsible for the 1994 genocide, many of them fighting alongside the Mayi-Mayi and Kabila's forces. They often link up with Congolese Hutu fighters.

Peuple en Armes Pour la Liberation du Rwanda (PALIR)/Armee Pour la Liberation du Rwanda (ALIR)

PALIR and its armed wing ALIR, is the *interahamwe* version of a political organization. PALIR has been weakened by the return of ex-*interahamwe* fighters to Rwanda, but the group has claimed responsibility for the kidnapping of foreign tourists.

Colonel Mu'ammar Gaddafi and the Libyans

Ol' Mu'ammar's been making up for lost time since handing over to an international court two suspects alleged to be involved in the 1988 bombing of a Pan Am jetliner over

Lockerbie, Scotland. He's been trotting around Africa with his armed detail of female mud-wrestlers trying to make peace in the DRC. Gaddafi is emerging as Africa's version of Jimmy Carter, doing it with the style (and wardrobe) of Don King. Though he looks more like a WWF fight promoter than an actual statesman, he seems to be relishing in his newly-attained mobility and his ability to bring the warring factions of the Great Lakes to the peace table. In May 1999, Gaddafi hosted a meeting in the Libyan city of Sirte between Ugandan President Yoweri Museveni and Congo President Laurent Kabila at which the two signed a declaration of intent aimed at securing a peaceful solution to the crisis. Then he sent 62 Libyan troops to Uganda's Windsor Lake Victoria Hotel in Entebbe for some prepeacekeeping cocktails, even though they weren't "sanctioned"—a word the Libyan leader has found confusing as of late. At least he gets to take plane rides these days. The colonel was getting damn tired of bouncing around Africa in a jeep while his buddies were jet-setting around the Dark Continent in wet-leased Boeings.

http://www.headlines.co.za/news/may99/congo14.htm

The UN International Criminal Tribunal for Rwanda (ICTR)

An understaffed, unqualified, mismanaged, overpaid and bumbling UN International Criminal Tribunal for Rwanda (ICTR) is overseeing the genocide trials of a handful of Rwanda's slaughterhouse curators. As of mid-1999 there were only 38 people detained under the ICTR's custody and a mere four trials completed. Only in a little league atmosphere like this could any credibility be given to the defense arguments that the killing of 800,000 Tutsis and moderate Hutus was not genocide but "mass killings in a state of war where everyone is killing his enemies," as was stated by defense lawyer De Temmerman in his defense of notorious Hutu *interahamwe* warlord Georges Rutaganda. The Hutus claim that the massacres were a spontaneous uprising which they tried to prevent. Laughable, but similar arguments have won the release of *interahamwe* officers and continuances for monsters like Jean-Paul Akayesu, who is suspected of ordering the wholesale slaughter of Tutsis and encouraging Hutus to murder their own grandchildren, nephews, nieces and in-laws.

A UN report concluded the ICTR is dysfunctional "in every administrative area." The tribunal has a cash fund of US$600,000 but no written rules for disbursing it. The financing head doesn't have a degree in financing, accounting or administration. The procurement head has never bought anything for the UN in his life. Some personnel don't get paid for months while others receive duplicate paychecks. The prosecutors have decided the court makes a good forum for arguing among themselves. Of the court's 44 lawyers, 21 are from Europe, 12 are from Africa and 11 from North America. How bad is it for the boys in sky blue? UN Office for Internal Oversight chief Karl Paschke admitted in an understatement: "Justice (in Rwanda) has been delayed."

Bedside Manner

In June 1999, ICTR judges condemned former Rwandan governor Clement Kayishema to life in prison after announcing a guilty verdict in his two-year genocide trial. Kayishema not only ordered the massacres of tens of thousands of Tutsis hiding in churches and schools in his area, but personally incited killers with a megaphone and sometimes fired the initial shot. During the trial, survivors scarred with machete and bullet wounds testified that Kayishema—formerly a medical surgeon trained in Europe—sliced babies in half with a sword. Kayishema is affectionately known by his "patients" as the "Butcher of Kibuye." Kayishema was found guilty of murdering Tutsis at Mugonero hospital, where he once worked, by luring thousands of Tutsis into the stadium at Kibuye with the promise of security. His prescription? "Shoot those Tutsi dogs!" he commanded his followers.

RWANDA

NGOs

There are some 4,600 Western-based NGOs working in the Third World. When 2 million Rwandans, mainly Hutus, fled the country in mid-1994, more than 200 aid organizations were on the scene instantly. These "refugee cities" soon became headquarters for extremist Hutu former government militias plotting their next civil war in Rwanda, the same folks responsible for the slaughter of some 800,000 Tutsis and moderate Hutus earlier in 1994. NGOs spent more than $1 billion between 1994 and 1996 supplying food, water and shelter to Rwandan refugees. The refugee camps in eastern Congo today have been feeding and clothing Hutu nasties who have apparently started feeling nourished enough to head back to Rwanda to stir up trouble. The UN estimates that 25 percent of its food is stolen.

http://www.reliefweb.int/IRIN/archive/rwanda.htm

Diplomatic ties have been restored between the United States and Rwanda. Passport and visa are required. Multiple-entry visa (extendable) for a stay of up to 1 month requires a US$30 fee (cash, check or money order), two application forms, two photos and immunization for yellow fever. Exact date of entry into Rwanda is required with application. Include prepaid envelope or $1.50 postage for return of passport by certified mail.

At the height of the hostilities, when *DP* asked about entry permission, a spokesperson replied, "We know nothing." Later, after things had calmed down, it seemed the embassy staff had developed a sense of bureaucratic humor. When we asked if there were any Americans in jail in Rwanda, we were told, "We have none; they have been behaving so far." You should know the first of the 12 conditions for entry and stay in Rwanda is that "proper attire and conduct are required of persons staying in Rwanda." The embassy maintains that it is safe to travel in Rwanda. The U.S. State Department, on the other hand, issued a travel warning in March 1999 suggesting quite the opposite.

Embassy Locations

Rwandan Embassy in United States

*1714 New Hampshire Avenue, NW
Washington DC 20009
Tel.: 202-232-2882
Fax: 202-232-4544
E-mail: rwandemb@rwandemb.org
http://www.rwandemb.org/*

Embassy of the Republic of Rwanda

*1714 New Hampshire Avenue, NW
Washington, DC 20009
Tel.: (202) 232-2882*

Canadian Embassy in Rwanda

*Rue Akagera, BP 1177
Kigali
Tel.: 73210
Fax: 72719*

Rwandan Embassy in Canada

*121 Sherwood Drive
Ottawa, Ontario, Canada K1Y 3V1
Tel.: (613) 722-5835/722-7921
Fax: (613) 729-3291*

U.S. Embassy in Rwanda

*Boulevard de la Revolution
BP 28, Kigali
Tel.: [250] (7) 5601/2/3
Fax: [250] (7) 2128*

Permanent Mission of Rwanda to the UN

*124 East 39th Street
New York, NY 10016
Tel.: (212) 696-0644/46*

Consulate General in Chicago

Tel.: (708) 205-1188

Consulate General in Denver

Tel.: (303) 321-2400

Rwanda has a total road length of 3,036 miles; a mere 286 of them are paved. There are neither railways nor ports. There are eight airfields in the country, three of them with a permanent surface.

Air Rwanda flies internally from Kigali to Gisenyi and Kamembe. Occasionally, you can fly between Gisenyi and Kamembe. Due to the amount of foreign aid into the country, Rwanda's road system isn't too bad. As in neighboring Burundi, the roadways are served by a fleet of relatively late-model Japanese minibuses. The buses leave most towns when they are full. Larger government buses also traverse Rwanda's roads, although they are fewer and farther between. They cost less than the minibuses, but take longer to get to their destinations.

The Entire Country

The entire country of Rwanda can be considered unsafe. Travelers are regularly the victims of theft, petty crime and murder. Sporadic violence is a problem in Kigali as well as in the interior. Fighting caused thousands of refugees to flee into neighboring Burundi as well as other countries in the region. In 1996, Paul Kagame ensured the safety of returning refugees and a trickle began returning to Rwanda, many to find their land and dwellings seized by squatters. The northwest has recently swelled with extremist Hutus, many returning from refugee camps in the DRC. This area has become a hotbed for insurgent activity and the border region has become a haven for rebels in the DRC. Kabila's air force has been bombing Rwandan border towns to flush the guerrillas out. Travelers should use extreme caution everywhere in Rwanda. Do not travel into the troubled areas of Kigali or anywhere in or near Gisenyi. Do not travel after dark.

Prisons

With 130,000 Hutus jailed in Rwandan prisons awaiting genocide trials, it comes as no surprise that their buddies still battling the Pasteur Bizimungu government from the hills would like to see these guys see the light of day again to help out the cause. Hutu rebels frequently raid Rwandan prisons and jails in attempt to free their comrades. In February 1998, some 5,500 Hutu insurgents attempted to storm the Nyakabanda prison, but, amazingly, were repulsed by security forces.

Being a Nun

To be a Catholic nun in Rwanda not only takes a helluvalot of faith, but also—shall we say—a big set of rosary beads. In March 1998, Hutu rebs snatched two Spanish and five Rwandan nuns near Gisenyi. Two months earlier, six Rwandan Catholic nuns and three from the DRC were murdered by Hutu rebels, also in Gisenyi. Nuns here may want to rethink their "habits."

Being a Priest

In April 1999, Bishop Augustin Misago was busted on genocide charges. He's the highest-ranking church official to be 'cuffed and printed on a genocide rap in Rwanda. Misago joins 19 other Rwandan priests who have been jailed on suspicion of aiding the 1994 killings. Rwandan President Pasteur Bizimungu and Tutsi survivors of the massacres in Gikongoro Prefecture said Misago refused shelter to Tutsis trying to escape death from Hutu mobs. Survivors of the genocide routinely claim that thousands of Tutsis were hacked to death by Hutus in Catholic churches and missionary-run schools, sometimes with the "blessing" of the prelates and priests.

Getting Acquitted

Vigilante attacks against folks acquitted of genocide charges are on the rise. Fortunately, not a lot of those charged end up free. At the end of 1997, 20 cleared genocide suspects were murdered in Butare after getting released from prison. In August 1998, vigilantes slaughtered 14 people 50 miles south of Kigali with machetes, hoes and knives who were alleged buddies or relatives of acquitted genocide suspect Emmanuel Gasana.

Brewing Beer

Apparently, Hutu rebels aren't quite satisfied with Rwanda's local beers—Primus and Mutzig. A January 1998 attack on a busload of workers on their way to Rwanda's only brewery killed 34 people and wounded 25 others. The innocents were "fire-brewed" in their bus after guerrillas threw gasoline on it and set it ablaze. Primus doesn't have an alcohol content to achieve the same results. Tastes great! Less filling! The debate in Rwanda rages on.

Growing Up

About 85,000 Rwandan children are the head of their households, namely because their moms and pops were slaughtered back in 1994. Children hosted in Rwanda's 47 orphanages dropped from 100,000 following the genocide to about 5,000 in 1999. Only some 6,800 have been reunited with their parents. Another 3,000 are street children. Adopting a Rwandan kid may become more stylish than a Cambodian tot.

The Lakes

There are very large man-eating crocodiles and an abundance of germs to be found in all lakes and large rivers in Rwanda.

Land Mines

Land mines are especially prevalent in Byumba, Cyangugu, Kigali and Kigali rural prefectures. Avoid unpaved roads and don't tip-toe through the tulips in uncultivated fields.

Medical facilities, doctors and supplies are dangerously scarce in Rwanda. There is one doctor for every 33,170 people under normal conditions and 15 hospital beds for every 10,000 people in the country. There are 34 hospitals and 188 health centers in this tiny country, so the traveler has some access to treatment. Cholera and yellow fever inoculations are required. Tetanus, polio, typhoid and gamma globulin vaccines are advised, as are antimalarial prophylaxes: DPT, measles and mumps vaccines are recommended for children. Tap water is not potable.

About the size of Vermont and located in east central Africa, Rwanda (the capital is Kigali) is a landlocked country just south of the Equator bordering Uganda to the north, Burundi to the south, Tanzania to the east, and Zaire to the west. There were estimated to be over 8 million people in Rwanda before the holocaust. They live packed at 789 people per square mile: 85 percent are Hutu, 14 percent Tutsi. Almost half of the Tutsis were murdered during the genocide.

Rwanda is home to rare mountain gorillas and the bizarre topography and plant life of its forests found in Parc National des Volcans. The gorillas of the park have been mainly unharmed in the nation's unrest due to its remoteness and that most Rwandan park guards have remained on duty. At last count, there were only 650 mountain gorillas left on the planet, of which 320 live in the 125-square-kilometer Parc National des Volcans in Rwanda's northern mountains.

The currency is the Rwanda franc (RFr). There are 100 centimes to the RFr. There are 222 RFr to the U.S. dollar. Local time is two hours later than GMT, seven hours later than U.S. EST. Electricity is 220V/50Hz. Hutus comprise 85 percent of the population; the Tutsi account for 14 percent. Sixty-five percent of the population is Roman Catholic. Protestants make up 9 percent, Muslim 1 percent and indigenous beliefs 25 percent.

Kinyarwanda and French are the official languages, and Kiswahili is used commercially. Illiteracy stands at 50 percent. Rwanda has a tropical climate that varies slightly with altitude. The major rainy seasons are February through May and November through December, with an average annual rainfall of 31 inches.

Web Resources

http://www.rwandemb.org/rwsites.html

12/98	Rwanda sends troops into the Democratic Republic of Congo to aid rebels fighting the government of Laurent Kabila.
6/97	Perhaps 250,000 Hutu Rwandan refugees are feared dead in a slaughter by Congo President Laurent Kabila's rebel troops in eastern Congo.
6/18/97	Two UN World Food Program employees are killed by gunmen.
4/28/97	Rebels murder 17 schoolgirls and a Belgian nun.
11/96	Rwanda war crimes trial resumes in Arusha, Tanzania.
8/12/94	Thousands of Rwandan refugees begin moving toward Zaire from southwest Rwanda.
7/19/94	Pasteur Bizimungu is sworn in as president at a ceremony at the parliament building in the capital of Kigali. Rebel commander Major General Paul Kagame is named vice president and defense minister.
7/18/94	The rebel Rwandan Patriotic Front (RPF) claims it has won Rwanda's civil war.
7/15/94	A tidal wave of Rwandan refugees pours into neighboring Zaire.

7/4/94	Rwandan rebels capture the capital of Kigali and the last major government-held southern town of Butare.
4/6/94	President Juvenal Habyarimana is killed in a plane crash, sparking nationwide fighting.
1/28	Democracy Day.
7/01	Anniversary of Independence.
7/05	National Peace and Unity Day.
10/26	Armed Forces Day.

Freetown

Sierra Leone
★ ★ ★ ★

Operation No Living Thing

Welcome to Sierra Leone. RUF rebels—in a drunken, coke-clouded, ganja-dazed nine-year insurgency against a couple of handfuls of governments and dime-store juntas—don't much concern themselves with the PC-sounding, ditty little battle euphemisms of the Western world for their terror-filled offensives. Nothing cute like Operation Desert Storm, or Operation Battle Sword. Nothing that sounds like WWF tag-team night in Indianapolis. Instead, RUF military campaigns go by codes like Operation Burn House (for a series of arson attacks), Operation Pay Yourself (a campaign of looting and pillaging) and the brutally self-explanatory Operation No Living Thing. The rebels always had a way with words and machetes. Even when rebel leader Fodah Sankoh tried to do a little whistlestop glad handing they sounded hollow and horrible. "You, who we have wronged, you have every human right to feel bitter and unforgiving, but we plead with you for forgiveness." Small comfort to the legions of armless or legless children who now must figure out how to survive in Africa's poorest country.

Libya trained the motley, human flesh-eating RUF as best it could, and mayhem has served as Sierra Leone's constitution ever since. There have been more deaths in Sierra Leone than Kosovo, more mutilations, more refugees, more rapes and more human rights violations. Sierra Leonians constitute the largest group of refugees in Africa. Yet aid groups in Sierra Leone bitch about their budgets being cut and diverted to Kosovo. As one analyst asked: "Would there have been this much international neglect of Sierra Leone if a bunch of white people were running around with their limbs hacked off?" Indeed.

The former British colony of Sierra Leone gets its sustenance from diamonds. It also yanks enough bauxite, gold and iron ore out of the ground to keep it mildly solvent. But diamonds are the lifeblood of this sweaty little backwater.

Sierra Leone hasn't had it easy. In 1787, Sierra Leone (Lion Mountain) became an experimental community for freed slaves after British do-gooders bought a swath of 52 square kilometers and called it Province of Freedom. Within three years, 90 percent of the former slaves and white settlers in the territory had died of tropical diseases. Of the 1,200 freed slaves who fought for King George during the American Revolution and were brought to Province of Freedom shortly afterward, 800 were dead in two years. Some 50,000 freed slaves were dumped into this sweaty hell-hole between 1807 and 1864.

Britain ceded independence to Sierra Leone in 1961, and the country formed a republic in 1971. In 1992, the people overwhelmingly voted to conduct democratic elections, which was a cue to the folks who were draining the diamond coffers that it was time for a coup. In April 1992, Captain Valentine Strasser seized control of the government and ruled whichever pieces of the pie he could govern.

The problem with the word "democratic" in Africa is that it is an antonym of the word "tribal." In Sierra Leone, where 52 percent of the population are animists, 39 percent are Muslim and 8 percent are Christian, it doesn't make for a recipe for democracy.

The rebels were at the doorstep of the capital Freetown until Strasser rented a group of mercenaries under the command of well-known American merc Bob MacKenzie. MacKenzie had fought in Vietnam, with the SAS in Rhodesia, and in El Salvador, and he had trained HVO (Croat-Bosnian Defense Force) troops for Colonel Zeljko "Nick" Glasnovic 1st Guards' Brigade at Capaljina in Bosnia. The British government (unofficially, of course) asked him to head a group of Ghurkas from Nepal to safeguard the diamond mines in Sierra Leone and push back the rebels. When MacKenzie was killed two months later (some say cannibalized by the rebels), the Ghurkas flew home. Pretoria, South Africa–based Executive Outcomes saw an opportunity and put together a small army of 200 South African mercenaries, complete with an air force and supply jets. They began training the Sierra Leone army and got to work liberating the diamond fields. The army was pumped up to about 14,000 men (and children).

Battles mainly consisted of brief encounters, with both sides discharging only a single clip before running like hell in the opposite direction. Both the army and the RUF rebels were whacked out of their brains on ganja and booze, which made for low casualties. Executive Outcomes carved disciplined killers out of the government

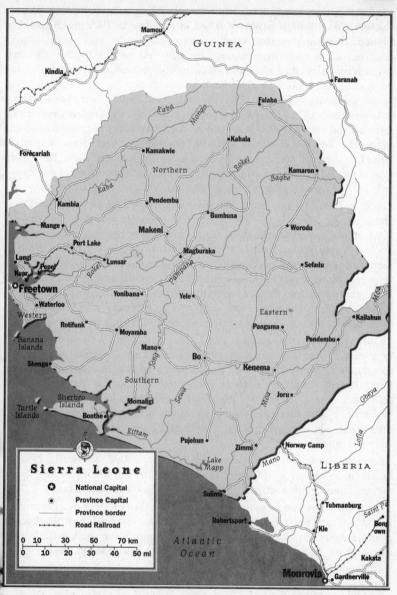

Sierra Leone

- ⊛ National Capital
- ⊙ Province Capital
- —— Province border
- ┼┼┼ Road Railroad

| 0 | 10 | 30 | | 50 | 70 km |
| 0 | 10 | 20 | 30 | 40 | 50 ml |

army ranks, and the face of the war changed. The body count started rising (thanks in part to EO's very own Russian Hind Mi-24 helicopter gunship air force flown by Belorussian mercenary pilots), and the rebels went into retreat. Sierra Leone soldiers stopped selling their weapons and uniforms to the RUF rogues, and the diamond fields were returned to the hands of Strasser and De Beers.

The diamond mines were the first targets for repossession, as Strasser hired the mercs on credit, with a promise of US$500,000 a month payment in diamonds. Hardly surprising, as Executive Outcomes is reportedly owned.

The rebels took great pleasure in not only killing folks but taking Western hostages. Seven foreigners were grabbed in two days by RUF rebels and then released. Then the insurgents snatched seven Italian nuns, who were summarily killed, but at least spared from becoming Sunday night meatloaf. Because the drug-crazed rebels enjoy their victims as meals, most foreigners split Sierra Leone and the government mobilized all available troops to prevent the insurgents from getting any closer to Freetown. To date, more than 24,000 Sierra Leonians have fled into Guinea and 50,000 have been killed in the six years of fighting since 1991. There are still some 120,000 Sierra Leone refugees awaiting repatriation in Liberia and another 240,000 in Guinea. But why bother coming back? Some hospitals in Sierra Leone report that up to 100 people a day die from starvation. The eastern areas of the country are especially volatile. Sierra Leone's population of 4 million is suffering from food shortages and a general disintegration of society.

In Sierra Leone anyone with a gun seems assured of a term in office, and their fifteen minutes in the sun—but rarely a few moments past that. On May 27, 1997, an obscure army major with the name of a Brooklyn rapper, Johnny Paul Koroma, deposed democratically elected President Ahmed Tejan Kabbah in Sierra Leone's third military coup in five years. Koroma accused Kabbah of being "nurtured on tribal and sectional conflict," and cited the government's failure to end a rebel uprising and low pay as reasons for seizing Kabbah's office. The U.S. ambassador to Sierra Leone, John Leigh, was probably closer to the mark when he remarked the coup's organizers were simply "out to line their own pockets."

Kabbah was Sierra Leone's first elected president in five years, and is credited with negotiating a November 1996 peace treaty designed to end the government's five-year civil war against rebels of the Revolutionary United Front. In fact, things seemed to be going pretty well for the respected Kabbah before his ouster, so well the Nigerians waited only long enough for U.S. Marines to evacuate foreigners out of the capital before pummeling it with shells from offshore in an effort to reinstate the Sierra Leone leader, who fled safely to Guinea during the coup.

Koroma schmoozed RUF leader Sankoh and the RUF, formed in 1991 by Sankoh in an alliance with Charles Taylor's National Patriotic Front for Liberia, suddenly found itself nominally in power in 1997 after Koroma's coup.

But Johnny Boy's coconut junta was ousted in February 1998 by a determined ECOMOG, and Kabbah was reinstalled as president. Sankoh's guerrillas became guerrillas again and were joined by the crux of Johnny's army back in the bush to regroup with the assistance of Liberia and Burkina Faso. Sankoh was arrested in Nigeria and charged with treason.

In October 1998, RUF was ready and began intensifying their attacks against ECOMOG's 15,000 soldiers and the Sierra Leone army after 24 members of Koroma's junta, including senior RUF officers, were executed and Sankoh was sentenced to death. In December, the rebels launched an all-out offensive on Freetown, occupying most of the capital for a brief period in January 1999 before being driven back into the jungle.

But it became obvious by the spring of 1999 that neither side could win an outright military victory without turning the country into a moonscape and Sankoh was released by Kabbah to pursue peace talks in the Togolese capital of Lome. Though, publicly, Kabbah vowed to carry out Sankoh's death sentence, he also admitted he would pardon the rebel leader if that's what it would take to attain peace in Sierra Leone.

After four months of diplomatic fisticuffs, including six weeks of direct talks between Kabbah and Sankoh and some less than gentle prodding by Liberia's president and RUF *compadre* Chuck Taylor, a peace deal was reached in Lome on July 6, 1999. Both Taylor and Togo President Gnassingbe Eyadema came out smelling like roses. And Sankoh, who a few months earlier was getting goosed on death row, was slotted for a cabinet post and given a full pardon.

The price of peace in Sierra Leone? Amnesty for the rebels and at least four ministerial posts for RUF in the Kabbah government.

The war in Sierra Leone is fought by children, many as young as eight. They're not the cuddly variety. Their Kalashnikov teddy bears reek of cordite. It is not a war of ideology, as no wars fought by eight-year-olds can be, but one of diamonds, wealth, poverty and 30 years of resentment among the destitute rural masses of the interior against the rich folks of Sierra Leone's capital, Freetown. It has its roots in more than a generation of government ineptness and greed, and the civil war in neighboring Liberia. Like Angola's UNITA guerrillas, rebels of the Revolutionary United Front (RUF)—a rebel group of black Muslims formed by former army photographer Foday Sankoh—have a perversion for hacking off the limbs of villagers, keeping them from farming their fields of casava, rice and vegetables. And to keep them from eating, of course. They then send the newly stumped bleeding and traumatized into towns held by the government, not so much as a warning, but as a further strain on government resources to care for the victims.

Between December 1998, when RUF renewed its war on Freetown, and February 1999 at least 5,000 people were killed. One government pathologist counted 7,335 corpses from the January 6, 1999, RUF offensive alone. Woman and young girls were raped systematically by the guerrillas. The population was routinely used as human shields. The mutilations since December have been countless. Entire compounds of families have been emptied, the villagers lined up while the rebels jokingly decide which ones to shoot and which ones to let go, or carve a drum stick off of one of the villagers. In one instance, to prevent a small child from bringing his newly severed hand to a hospital for possible reattachment, RUF insurgents sliced the amputated limb in half.

For its own part, the Nigerian-led ECOMOG "peacekeeping" force comprised of soldiers from Nigeria, Ghana and Guinea have hardly been angels. Summary executions of rebels and suspected rebel sympathizers have been the order of the day. Little effort has been made by the peacekeepers to prove the guilt of their victims. An early 1999 UN report accused ECOMOG of a "totally unacceptable" level of atrocities.

Well call it fox in the hen house politics. Former coup leader Johnny Paul Koroma will head a commission responsible for overseeing implementation of the accord that ended eight years of civil war and Kabbah confirmed the appointment of rebel Revolutionary United Front leader Foday Sankoh as head of a commission to oversee exploitation of mineral resources including gold and diamonds.

Who says war crime doesn't pay?

Sierra Leone is a slice of life. Literally if you're one of the 100,000 people who've had a limb sawed off since Foday Sankoh and his RUF tree-trimmers got into the personal landscaping business back in '91. The country has been a tin-pot dictatorship with a rotating list of guest stars and small-time military dictators (with the odd elected president once in a while). When peaceful, Sierra Leone lives off the largesse of outside mining companies. It is the world's second-largest producer of titanium oxide (an ingredient for paint pigment) and a major source of diamonds. When not peaceful (which is pretty much all of the time), it lives off the largess of death and debauchery. For now, it's a nasty place run by heavily armed, Ray-Banned army punks who zoom around the capital and countryside in pickup trucks. A peace treaty was signed between Sankoh and Sierra Leone President Kabbah in July 1999 in Lome, Togo, granting unconditional pardons to guys like Captain 2 Hands, Betty Cut Hands and Dr. Blood, and anyone else who has made it damn tough for Sierra Leonians to pick their noses and do crochet. Nevertheless, the UN put their John Hancock on the deal, ending for the time being a civil war that makes Kosovo look like a weekend paint-pellet fight in the Michigan woods. RUF/AFRC rebels, flocking into Freetown to party with relatives they haven't seen in two to eight years are hiding their weapons rather than surrendering them to ECOMOG. We'll see what happens after they get a little UN-sponsored R&R.

Voodoo Ju-Ju Boom-Boom

Pubescents, beware. In Sierra Leone, the Jombobla secret society is striking terror into the hearts of anyone tuffed at the groin. The group has launched a campaign of sexual violence in the south and east of the country. Jombobla (which translates from the Mende language as "remover of pubic hair") has terrified even its most staunch skeptics with its alleged supernatural powers. In a two-week period in 1997, the group raped at least 10 women in and around the town of Bo. Group members attack women wearing ju-ju charms and a fetish around the neck. After doing the dirty deed, they pluck the pubic hairs from their victims to make empowering fetishes or talismans. Ouch.

Ahmed Foday Sankoh and the Revolutionary United Front (RUF)

RUF specializes in atrocities. Mutilation of civilians is their favorite tactic. Most armies in the world are made up of Bravo Company, Charlie Company, 101st Airborne, etc. Not RUF. Their fighting units go by the tags of Burn House Unit, Cut Hands Commando, Blood Shed Squad and Kill Man No Blood Unit, whose specialty is beating people to death without a drop of blood being spilled. The Born Naked Squad strips their victims nude before killing them. Some noted commanders of the Cut Hands Commando include Captain 2 Hands, Commander Cut Hands (a 15-year-old boy), Dr. Blood, Betty Cut Hands (a woman), OC Cut Hands and Adama Cut Hands. RUF soldiers' eating of victims is not uncommon. The most favored entrées are the liver and heart. Another nasty trick the guerrillas employ on captives is the slashing of ankle tendons and neck muscles. Nice guys. Makes the Khmer Rouge look like a ladies' field hockey team.

Sankoh, RUF's leader, is a former army corporal and photographer. A member of the Jemme tribe, he joined the Royal West African Forces in 1956 and was trained as a wireless operator by the British. In 1961, Sankoh was put in jail for taking part in an attempted coup against Joseph Momoh. Pardoned in 1980, he traveled to the United States to meet with black Muslim groups. Returning to Sierra Leone, he put together a cadre of like-minded revolutionaries and knocked on Gadaffi's door for some bullets and bucks. While there, he was introduced to Charles Taylor, the chief instigator of Liberia's misery. Taylor used the border areas of Sierra Leone for his bases, and Sankoh received guns and support from Taylor during the late '80s and early '90s. In April 1992, a group of peach-fuzz army officers calling themselves the National Provisional Ruling Council (NPRC) overthrew the new government of Momoh, and 28-year-old Valentine Strasser took over, only to be bounced by another soldier who then set up democratic elections. All of this transpired without Sankoh even being invited to the inauguration or getting to threaten the boss. Strasser did bring in Executive Outcomes, who pushed Sankoh's tattered RUF rebels even further into the bush and obscurity. Sankoh was arrested during an early 1997 trip to Nigeria but emerged as Johnny's No. 1 man after the coup.

But it's been a roller-coaster ride for Sankoh. Under Koroma, he was Deputy AFRC Chairman and second-in-charge in Sierra Leone. But when the Nigerians found out, they hustled him from his five star suite at the Abuja Sheraton to house arrest in a neighborhood said to also be the upscale holding pen for Moshood Abiola the democratically elected but jailed president of Nigeria. Kabbah's regime sentenced Sankoh to death, only to release him in April 1999 to kickstart the peace process. With the July 1999 treaty in the books, Foday's enjoying another 15 minutes in the sun as a ranking member of Kabbah's cabinet. The guy commutes regularly between death row and a red carpet.

Sankoh's 3,000-man RUF, formed in 1991, is predominantly Muslim and consists mainly of ragtag adolescents and villagers forced into fighting. Libya has been a major supplier of arms and money to RUF. The group has an office near the Liberian border and a press office in Abidjan (run by Sankoh's brother, Alimany Sankoh) in Ivory Coast.

Government of Sierra Leone
http://www.sierra-leone.org/govt.html

Ahmad Tejan Kabbah

Sierra Leone's first civilian president in five years promised to make peace with the RUF rebels and nearly succeeded. On April 23, 1996, Tejan Kabbah and rebel leader Foday Sankoh met in the Ivory Coast and announced a truce in order to detail peace and disarmament accords. Later that year, a peace accord was signed, ending the five-year civil war. But the peace didn't last long. At the end of February 1997, the government claimed to have intercepted a radio message delivered by Sankoh calling for his troops to begin a major offensive against the government. Fighting between RUF and government troops began anew. Kabbah was overthrown in yet another coup in May 1997 and sweated it out in Guinea until February 1998, when ECOMOG got the throne back for him. Now he's forced to play patty-cake with Sankoh at cabinet meetings.

Sierra Leone Web Site
www.sierra-leone.org

Sierra Leone Civil Defense Forces
www.slcdf.org

The Nigerian Army and ECOMOG

The Nigerians weren't happy with Johnny Paul Koroma seizing the government and sending their buddy Kabbah scampering through the bush to Guinea. They began lobbing shells into Freetown as soon as all the foreigners had been evacuated by U.S. Marines. With a force of about 10,000—two-third's the make-up of ECOMOG—the

Nigerians scored one of the greatest accomplishments in their military annals by finally ousting Koroma and reinstalling Kabbah as president in February 1998. But Nigerians weren't doing an a-go-go in the streets—as were the residents of Guinea and Ghana, ECOMOG's other players—after the July 1999 peace treaty was signed. Instead, Nigerian President Olusegun Obasanjo came under major heat for announcing his troops would remain in Sierra Leone. Most Nigerians don't see the sense in pumping buckeroos into an expensive peacekeeping operation abroad while their own country is awash in poverty. And the Nigerian government has been tight-lipped about its intervention in Sierra Leone. Casualty figures aren't released, nor are any other details about the conflict. But you can bet your backside that Obasanjo is just making sure that Johnny and Foday don't start up another game of King of the Hill.

Johnny Paul Koroma and the Armed Forces Revolutionary Council (AFRC)

This totally unknown army major seized power in May 1997 and charted Sierra Leone toward more squalor after having just gotten out of jail for a previous coup attempt. Koroma invited RUF leader Foday Sankoh into his cabinet and declared the army would be running the government until 2001. That didn't sit well with the Nigerians who were contemplating invading SL in earnest. Peace talks in Abidjan were quashed in August 1997 after Koroma's announcement of "four more years" for the soldier-boys, and his government began to implode. ECOMOG kicked ass, and by February 1998, Johnny was just another ex-president, one of enough in Sierra Leone to fill out the cut in a celebrity charity golf tournament. Koroma joined Sankoh's boys back in the jungle, and while he didn't appear on *The Price Is Right* in Lome, he definitely was pulling some strings. Now he is back in the government and in charge of making sure the integration of the rebels with the government goes peacefully.

The United Nations

The United Nations isn't sure what it signed. It put pen to paper on the July 1999 peace accords, and then added a handwritten caveat to the agreement saying that the general amnesty clause in the accords wouldn't apply to rebels who partook in war crimes, genocide, crimes against humanity and "other gross violations." Which pretty much means that all of Foday's boys could be corralled into a box car and sent off to The Hague. The United Nations will be expanding its presence in Sierra Leone essentially bank rolling the Nigerian military to keep a lid on things.

http://www.un.org/Depts/DPKO/Missions/unosil_p.htm.

The Kamajors

These obscure, traditional hunters from the south and east of Sierra Leone have been thrown into the conflict, as well. But no one can quite figure out which side they're on. The hunters, originally hired by local chieftains to protect their villages from RUF attacks and considered a militia of the government army, have been throwing sticks and stones at both sides using crude, homemade rifles. But there's no doubt about it; these are nasty folks to deal with. They're making a reputation for themselves through summary execution of RUF rebels they capture and by kidnapping aide workers for ransom. They accuse government troops of pillaging and plundering civilian property and blaming it on the rebels. For now the Kamajors control large parts of the outlying jungles and are siding with Kabbah. Allegedly whipped into shape by EO/Sandlines they were instrumental in helping ECOMOG take out Koroma's junta in February 1998.

http://www.hrw.org/hrw/worldreport99/africa/sierraleone.html

Sierra Leone's borders are as lax and corrupt as you can imagine. Most visitors are Lebanese diamond traders who zip in and out with small amounts of stones. Someone who enters with a backpack and a ponytail might provoke a few minutes of respectful silence before being relieved of all his possessions. Visas can be had for a stay of 30–90 days and can be obtained at Sierra Leone embassies and consulates. The country maintains embassies in the United States, Great Britain, Germany, Belgium, Sweden, the Netherlands, Egypt, Austria, Switzerland, Spain and Italy—to mention the major sources of visas. In countries where Sierra Leone does not maintain an embassy, it may be possible to obtain a visa through the British High Commission. The Sierra Leone embassy in the United States:

Sierra Leone Embassy
1701 19th Street, NW
Washington, DC 20009
Tel.: 202-939-9261
http://www.embassy.org/embassies/sl.htm

If you are a U.S. citizen applying for a visa through the Washington embassy, you will most likely be required to provide a letter from both your employer, stating that you've indeed got a job to which you must return, and your bank, stating that you have enough funds to motivate you to return. Officials at the embassy may require you to first send a self-addressed stamped envelope for a list of visa requirements. A 90-day single-entry visa costs US$20. You'll need two passport-sized photos and quite possibly proof of your round-trip airline ticket. Allow two weeks for processing.

Although entry permits for Sierra Leone can be obtained in West African states, visas and entry permits cannot be had at the border.

The single 52-mile (84-km) railroad line was abandoned in 1971. Most roads are hellish; the airlines bring in the odd supplies and whisk the wealthy away for shopping sprees in Paris or London. Freetown is perpetually under siege; the countryside is slowly being upgraded from absolutely deadly to very dangerous. It will be a long time yet before travelers can wander through the rain forests in Sierra Leone looking for rare orchids.

Illegal Diamond Mining

Diamond mines are considered off-limits to all outsiders, and, if bumbling travelers happen to stumble upon them, they will be extremely lucky if they are merely detained and lectured on their stupidity. If you come across diamond smugglers, you'll likely end up in a shallow, hastily dug grave.

http://www.mbendi.co.za/indy/ming/mingsl.htm

Being a Journalist

Local journalists are routinely rounded up, arrested and beaten by government thugs. The French-based reporters' rights group, Reporters Sans Frontieres, occasionally sends in lawyers from Brussels to Freetown to bail out and defend busted reporters. They, too, are usually beaten up and busted.

http://www.cpj.org

Malaria in the severe falciparum (malignant) form occurs throughout the country and is chloroquine-resistant. Tungiasis is widespread. Many viral diseases, some causing severe hemorrhagic fevers, are transmitted by ticks, fleas, mosquitoes, sandflies, etc. Relapsing fever and tick-, louse- and flea-borne typhus occur. Sleeping sickness (human trypanosomiasis) is regularly reported. Foodborne and waterborne diseases are highly endemic. Bilharziasis is present and widespread throughout the country, as are alimentary helminthic infections, the dysenteries and diarrheal diseases, including cholera, giardiasis, typhoid fever, and hepatitis A and E. Hepatitis B is hyperendemic; poliomyelitis is endemic, and trachoma widespread. Frequently fatal are navirus hemorrhagic fevers which have attained notoriety. Rats pose a special hazard; lassa fever has a virus reservoir in the commonly found multimammate rat. Use all precautions to avoid rat-contaminated food and food containers. Ebola and Marburg hemorrhagic fevers are present but reported infrequently. Epidemics of meningococcal meningitis can occur. Echinococcosis (hydatrid disease) is widespread in animal breeding areas. One atlas of the world lists even childbirth as a communicable disease in Sierra Leone. So be careful—there is only one doctor for every 13,153 people in the country. Witch doctors provide the only "health care" available outside the capital.

Sierra Leone was founded in the late 18th century by the British as a settlement for Africans freed from slavery. The country's nasty brother to the south, Liberia, was established by the Americans for the same purpose. In retrospect, even the snowiest of doves has conceded this was a bad idea. So, for now, the British content themselves with relieving the country of its natural resources (mainly diamonds and bauxite) and meddling into the questionable affairs of a questionable government.

Sierra Leone is the classic West African hellhole. The country can proudly boast the lowest life expectancy of any country in the world (41.5 years). It also has the second-highest infant mortality rate on the globe, and leads the human race in overall destitution and despair in other key categories as well. Zany and paranoid, the government executed 26 people in December 1992 for plotting to topple the regime—while most were in jail at the time!

Sierra Leonians bathe in rain water, and they have plenty of opportunities for showers. It rains about 195 inches a year in Freetown and on the coast, making the country the steamiest and wettest in coastal West Africa. During the *harmattan* season from November to April, it can be hot and dry. Most of Sierra Leone is fetid lowlands with scenic mountains in the northeast.

The currency is the *leone*, which is worth nothing, perhaps due to the country's 81 percent inflation rate. Unemployment is endemic and Sierra Leonians make an average of US$145 a year, making it the sixth most impoverished nation on Earth. The official language is English. Electricity is 220V/50Hz.

http://www.sas.upenn.edu/African_Studies/Country_Specific/S_Leone.html
http://hypertextbook.com/eworld-links/salone.shtml

Embassy Location

The U.S. Embassy is located in the capital of Freetown

Corner Walpole and Siaka Stevens Street
Freetown
Tel.: 26481

10/25/99	Sankoh and Koroma are integrated into new government.
1/16/99	Foday Sankoh is released.
1/03/99	Major offensive by rebels forces evacuation of Freetown.
3/10/98	President Kabbah returns to Freetown.
7/30/97	Kabbah announces that the military will run the government until 2001.
5/27/97	Major Johnny Paul Koroma overthrows Kabbah as president.
5/10/97	Fighting between RUF rebels and government forces resumes in earnest.
11/30/1996	President Tejan Kabbah and RUF leader Foday Sankoh sign peace agreement to end the civil war.
1/16/96	Captain Valentine Strasser is deposed in a military coup.
9/92	Liberian-backed RUF rebels begin offensive against the NPRC.
6/20/92	Three British mercenaries are arrested and accused of plotting to overthrow the government.
5/29/92	President Joseph Momoh is deposed by Captain Valentine Strasser.
1991	ULIMO rebels from Liberia set up camp in Sierra Leone.

Sierra Leonabonics: Local Words of Wisdom

If you wonder why Sierra Leone politics are so convoluted, a good place to start might be looking at what passes for words of wisdom. Sierra Leonean proverbs would challenge the deepest clearest thinker but could provide some good hooks for the latest rap songs.

KRIO (English Pidgin) SAYING:	TRANSLATION:
Kakroch noh de go na makit, boht i de it pamai.	The cockroach doesn't go to market, but it eats palm oil.
We yu go na kohntri, if yu mit pipul dehn de dans wit wan fut, yusehf foh dans wit wan fut. Boht if yu dans wit tu fut, dehn go koht di ohda wan ohnda yu.	When you go to a country where the people dance on one foot, you should dance on one foot as well. If you dance on two feet, they'll cut one of them from under you.
Sehn kakroch foh go kohl fohl.	Send a cockroach to go call a chicken.

Sierra Leonabonics: Local Words of Wisdom

Trohki wan bohks, boht in han shoht (boht i noh geht han).	The turtle wants to box, but its arms are too short (but it has no arms).
Nohbohdi noh de was wata.	Nobody washes water.
If kakroch se i de dans, kohl kak, leh i kam nak sangba foh-ram.	If the cockroach says he will dance, call the cock, have him come and beat the drum for him.
Mblama! Mblama! luk motoka tinap!	Mblama! Mblama! There's the vehicle!
Sira-man dohn fohdohn wit in motoka.	The Lebanese has had a car accident.
We fohl wet, i wet.	When a chicken is white, it's white.
If yu tek tehm kil anch (maskita) yu go si in goht.	If you kill an ant (mosquito) carefully, you will see its guts.
If yu yams wet, kohba-ram.	If your yam is white, cover it.
Wan fingga noh go ebul opin baksai.	One finger can't open up an anus.
Yu wan kaka, boht yu noh wan it.	You want to shit, but you don't want to eat. (You want the reward, but you don't want to work to get it.)
Yu noh jehntri, yu se yu noh de it dohg.	You're not rich, you say you won't eat dog. (Beggars can't be choosers.)
Mohnki nohba [noh go] lehf in blak han.	A monkey will never be rid of its black hands. A bad person, especially a thief, will never give up his bad ways. (A leopard won't change his spots.)

Source: Sierra Leone website that carries krio proverbs and stories.

Somalia
★★★★★

Clan Bake

It's tough running a country whose only natural resources are camels, bananas, frankincense, spiny lobster tails, shark fins, kidnapped aid workers and pirated yachts—a country which generates its tax revenue from roadblocks, license plates, pirate-collected port duties and whatever spare change is left in the sand.

Up north in breakaway Somaliland things have been pretty calm, save for the fallout from the Ethiopia/Eritrea war. The eastern half of this tiny area is called Sanaag and is controlled by a clan that does not agree with Mohammed Ibrahim Egal's presidential ambitions. Self-elected Egal has put the lid on his half of Somalia—called Somaliland. The country of Somaliland (not to be confused with Somalia or Disneyland) prints its own money in Britain, has a funky homemade flag (it may humor our readers to know that the Somali flag is based on the blue UN flag) and is protected by a ragtag army of about 15,000 kids and unemployed qat junkies. The main airport is closed (so what?), and its ill-defined border with Ethiopia to the south is a free-fire zone ruled by reject extras from a Mad Max movie.

Heavily armed clans dodge land mines in the rocky wastelands in their technicals, rusty tanks and camels. Its main exports are goats, sheep and camels to Saudi Arabia and the Gulf States. Oh, I suppose we should mention that Somalia's 1700-mile coast has great beaches. Foreign yachtsmen from Europe are occasionally invited for a little beach blanket bingo as they putter on by off the coast.

Somalia (like most blown-to-hell countries) was actually a pretty cool place about 1,000 years ago. Known in ancient times as Punt (an appropriate political strategy these days), it was the home of the Queen of Sheba, spices, and traded with China and other Arab nations. Today Somalia is an arid, high-speed cross between Sergio Leone's *Once Upon a Time in the West,* Mad Max and a '60s drugs 'n' biker movie, or maybe more like *Star Wars'* wasted brown planet of Tatooine without the colorful bar scene. If you like looking on the sunny side, there is a web site titled "Visit the Somali Republic, the Jewel of the Indian Ocean. The Cross Roads of Africa . . . The Gum of the Sea Ways, The Real Paradise for the Hunter, The Country of Peace, Culture and Stability." The site lures tourists with phrases like "Mogadiscio, with its stable climate, is a paradise for the tourist." A quick peek at the airlines, however, lists a subsidiary of BOAC, an airline name that has been defunct for about 20 years. Oh well, maybe you should postpone your trip for the next century when they have the annual clan get-togethers on the streets of Mog.

The syrupy home-spun web hype forgets to mention that Somalia's clans have been drilling holes in each other ever since the first Somalis decided to marry someone other than their sister. How long will this clan-banging go on? Well, until they run out of bullets and somebody ties down every rock in this parched, godforsaken country. Recently, the clans have cloaked themselves with high-falutin political names so that it sounds more like a church gathering than a street fight. Names such as the Somali Salvation Democratic Front or the Somalia National Alliance may conjure up visions of crew-cutted, white-shirted, apple-cheeked kids riding around tree-lined neighborhoods with Korans, but that is far from accurate. These clans are more likely to be scrawny, bug-eyed (from chewing qat), flip-flopped kids who charge around the shattered 100-degree-plus streets in smashed-up Toyota pickup trucks featuring jury-rigged, welded .50-caliber or anti-tank guns stolen from Uncle Sam's cache. Since a good living in Somalia is $3 a day, we figure the kids are allowed to roar around drunk or stoned and shoot off a few armor-piecing rounds at each other. To be fair, some Somali sources describe the young drug-whacked kids as militiamen, "unpaid volunteers who fight, not on orders but out of desire to defend their communities." They conclude by saying, "A well-organized civilian militia, protected by the right to keep and bear arms, is still the most effective protection for the security of a free state." Uh, yeah, and I'll take that shiny new watch you're wearing in the name of freedom and security.

But before we dive into the players, you must know that there are really three equally lawless Somalias.

The dodgy Republic of Somaliland in the northwest with the capital of Hargeisa; Somali, the land that makes up the long southern coastal section and the home of the Digila and more agrarian Rahanweyne clans; and the northeast with Bosaso as its hub. The capital of the south is the hotly contested city of Mogadishu. To further complicate the divisions, Djibouti is actually half-Somali.

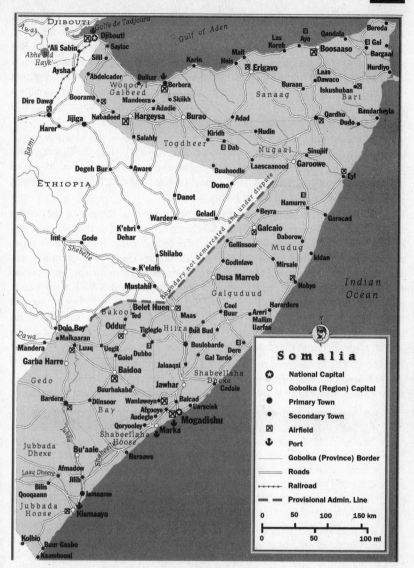

Beirut was easy to figure out compared to Somalia. The breakaway republics are not recognized by any international body, although perhaps they should be.

Only the southern part makes the news—that section of Siad Barre's defunct Somali Republic which was formerly Italian Somaliland. The south is simply lawless territory inhabited by nomadic Somalis and ruled by clans. The northern part, formerly British Somaliland, misses the headlines and is sometimes portrayed as considerably more peaceful. Unlike the south, the north has had something of a government—the government of Somaliland—since the fall of Barre's republic, and even, at times, a head-of-state.

Yet overall, it's been an orgy of blood feuds in Somalia. After the rebel United Somali Congress (USC) captured Mogadishu during the last week of 1990 and toppled Barre's despotic regime (although it at least was a regime), Somalia watched its last government—or anything resembling it—go down the drain. Siad fled and the USC installed Ali Mahdi Mohamed as temporary president. But the USC was marred by internal bickering and bloodshed within its ranks, and from them rose General Mohamed Farah Aideed. Aideed and Ali Mahdi signed a UN-bullied peace agreement in March 1992, but it broke down as perhaps a million Somalis fled the country's famine and clan warfare. Soldiers looted UN food supplies the world body was unable to protect.

Enter the United States and Operation Restore Hope. Eighteen hundred American marines landed in Mogadishu on December 9, 1992, the first of nearly 30,000 troops to arrive here with the mission of restoring some semblance of order. (Hussein Aideed, the general's son, was one of the U.S. Marines.) Aideed and Ali Mahdi grudgingly shook hands.

On January 11, 1993, a general cease-fire was agreed to. But it, like the dozens before it, hadn't a prayer. After Somalis became accustomed to the strange aliens called Americans, they decided to off a couple and even dragged one corpse through the streets of Mogadishu. CNN got it all on tape and the Pentagon, not wanting any more bad publicity and angry mothers, brought the boys home. U.S. efforts to bring Aideed down were like a Philadelphia SWAT team attack: they kept turning the wrong house into Swiss cheese. So Uncle Sammy washed his hands of the whole Somali affair in November 1993. With the Americans gone, Somalis were again permitted to resume killing, raping and maiming each other. Only this time they had more UN leftover toys to play with.

The only bright spot was the May '97 peace accord between Aideed (currently the self-proclaimed president of Somalia) and his chief rival, Ossan Hassan Ali Ato's Rahanweyne Resistance Army (RRA). Fighting still goes on between other clans.

Sylvester and Elvis

The Islamic Court in north Mogadishu, the closest thing resembling an administrative body since the overthrow of Mohamed Siad Barre in 1991, has warned that clean-shaven men had better grow beards—in the Islamic tradition—or suffer the consequences. The court's leader, Sheikh Ali Sheikh Mohamed, brought a clean-shaven youngster before a gathering of faithful and ordered the crowd to boo at the kid. "Those who shave like Elvis Presley, Sylvester Stallone and the U.S. Marines will not go unpunished," Ali Sheikh proclaimed.

The youngster was decidedly sans Elvis' sideburns, being barely old enough to sport a tuft of pubic hair, much less a cascade of ZZ Top whiskers. But prepubescent teenagers and secular governments aside, it's Gillette and Schick that have to be worried the most about the rise of Islamic fundamentalism.

The 26 factions of the National Salvation Council (NSC) are trying to get a central government together in the south but have been stymied by Hussein Farah Aideed—an ex-U.S. Marine with a disdain of idle rifles—whose trumped-up charges of "foreign intervention" have served as an excuse to keep the bullets whistling. As many as 60,000 Somalis have been killed since 1991—300,000 have died due to war-induced starvation. There has been no central government since 1991. Some semblance of order has returned to north Mogadishu, if only because folks there want to hang on to their limbs. The Islamic *shari'a* courts are the law here (you know, the folks who cut off hands for stealing)—the Jenny Craig of criminal justice. You, too, can lose weight fast. Meanwhile, Somalia has become the Ho Chi Minh Trail of the Ethiopian/Eritrean war. Hussein Aideed's forces are being beleaguered by the Ethiopian-backed Rahanwein Resistance Army as the Eritreans and Ethiopia duke out their own border war in Somalia's front yard. Aideed and the Somali National Front have enlisted the Eritreans' help, turning Somalia into a Rent-A-Battlefield for foreign armies. The Ethiopians have sent at least 5,000 soldiers into Somalia to ostensibly swap lead with the Ethiopian resistance group, the Oromo Liberation Front, who are trained by Aideed. The Eritreans have been sending arms to Aideed, who's been training the OLF at Coriolei, about 45 miles southwest of Mogadishu. The loser? The Somalis: a million people face serious food shortages and 400,000 are on the brink of starvation.

The Clans and Everybody Else

In this clan war, if your mama's from a different family tree than Aideed's, you are the enemy. There are more than 500 clans and 20 political groups in Somalia. The Lisan subclan clashes with Aideed as do the forces of Ali Atto and Ali Mahdi. The Yaalahow militia controls the Mecca and Medina districts of Mogadishu, depending on what day it is. Break out those phonebooks and history books if you want to figure this one out. If you can figure out the backgrounds and shifting alliances between the Habr Gedir, Marehan, Abgal, Majertein, Murusades drop us a line.

Hussein Mohammed Aideed

"Aideed" means "rejector of insults." In Hussein's case, it also means "AWOL." Ironically, Somalia's newest warlord, Hussein Mohammed Aideed, is a corporal in the United States Marine Reserve who served as a translator for the Marines in Somalia in 1992–93, and who has been conspicuously absent from his Pico Rivera, California, artillery unit since 1995. Hussein Aideed is the son of the slain General Mohammed Farah Aideed, and once worked as a $9-an-hour municipal clerk for the city of West Covina, California, and graduated from high school there. He joined the Marine Corps Reserves in 1987, last reporting for duty in July 1995. He moved back to Somalia shortly afterwards. Aideed was first brought to the United States as a teenager by his mother, Asli Dhubat, Gen. Aideed's first wife. Interviewed by the Associated Press in Somalia, Aideed said he valued his Marine experience: "I'm proud of my background and military discipline," he said. "Once a Marine, always a Marine." His CO isn't in complete agreement, however. Aideed's top foreign policy advisor also spent time in the United States; he was a Washington cab driver for three years—making him overly qualified in this "regime." When *DP's* Rob Krott hired about 100 U.S. Somalis for a Department of the Army project, about 10 percent were Washington area cab drivers. If you want to shoot the breeze on your next trip you can find Aideed in his headquarters in Southern Mogadishu.

Osman Hassan Ali Atto/Rahanweyne Resistance Army (RRA)

Originally the financier of Aideed Sr., Atto replaced Aideed in June 1995, when the United Somali Congress–Somali National Alliance (USC–SNA) called a Congress. Atto called for the UN to come back and rebuild Somalia. Pretty please.

Mohamed Farah Aideed and the Somalia National Alliance

"President" Mohamed Farah Aideed was killed in factional fighting in late July 1996. According to his enemies, he died "while killing people." Aideed liked the old school form of *kritarchy*, or traditional government, while his opponent Ali Mahdi wanted to be a Western puppet. Aideed led troops that killed 18 U.S. soldiers in 1993. That action resulted in the United States withdrawing its forces and blocking the UN effort to reconstruct the country. His Somalia National Alliance had been duking it out with Ali Mahdi's Somali Salvation Alliance. In reality, the chance of either side actually controlling all of Somalia is nonexistent. Aideed collected taxes from—or shot—anyone who crossed his "green line." His son has now taken on the mantle of being self-proclaimed president.

Aideed spent the end of the 1960s and early 1970s in prison for planning a coup against Barre. Barre for some reason freed Aideed and made him ambassador to India, Sri Lanka and Singapore to get him out of town. Aideed repaid him by forming the United Somali Congress (USC) which deposed Barre. Despite a lack of popular support, Ali Mahdi proclaimed himself President of the Republic of Somalia. In June 1991, Aideed was elected chairman of the United Somali Congress by a two-thirds vote, but Ali Mahdi refused to step down. By October 1991, Ali Mahdi had formed a government of eight ministers with the support of Italy. Naturally things went to hell very quickly and the fighting started. Ali Mahdi started it but Aideed had almost won when the UN stepped in. Mahdi was surrounded in Mogadishu allowing Aideed to go after Barre in the south. Siad Barre's army in southern Somalia had been looting food stores causing much of the famine. Mohamed Siad Barre, the ex-president of the Somali Republic, whose excesses finally undid him, was cozy with Egypt and a buddy of Boutros-Ghali's when Boutros-Ghali was with Egypt's Foreign Ministry. When Barre's man Aideed became Barre's enemy Aideed, Boutros-Ghali, understanding the exercise of power, targeted Aideed. He worked against him before the UN intervention, and it was during his tenure as secretary general, with his men ensconced in Mogadishu, that he allowed the U.S. functionaries to get so worked up over Aideed that they shifted the focus of the UN mission there. As Boutros-Ghali looked on, the United States went after Aideed.

The UN Security Council issued an arrest warrant for Aideed but he managed to elude both UN forces and U.S. troops. The United States never got Aideed. (Strangely enough while all this was going on *DP* saw Aideed attending a rubber chicken dinner in Nairobi on the front page of the local newspaper.) Despite the price on his head and the number of spooks who we assume can read a newspaper, nothing ever happened and the military continued its search-and-destroy mission at great cost in both money and, later on, lives. Between 6,000 and 10,000 Somalis were killed and 18 U.S. soldiers died.

Aideed was weakened by the defection of his sugar daddy, the wealthy Osman Ali Atto. Atto stepped on a land mine, and he lost most of his left foot. His dissatisfaction with Aideed split the Haber Gedirs.

Ali Mahdi Mohamed

Ali Mahdi Mohamed controls the relatively sedate northern area of Mogadishu. He is allied with Osman Ali Atto, who formerly bankrolled Aideed's fight for power. Atto and Aideed battled it out in the south, with casualties per day between 60–100 people killed and 10 times as many wounded. Ali Mahdi, the other "president" of Somalia, is backed by the Somali Salvation Alliance and supported by the Saad and Abgal clans. Ali Mahdi presents himself as a moderate and is in favor of alignment with the West. His brand of Islamic justice has led to amputations, stonings and floggings in the northern Mogadishu areas he controls. In the last year, the SSA has judged at least 500 cases and ordered five executions, 21 amputations and 421 floggings. In one case, a court of 12 religious leaders sentenced a man to stoning for rape. He was shackled to the ground and stoned to death with cinder blocks hurled by an enthusiastic crowd. Naturally, the media was invited to film the festivities.

http://www.reliefweb.int/IRIN/cea/countrystories/somalia/19990504a.htm

The Habr Gedir Clan

Mohamed Farah Aideed's Habr Gedir clan (actually a subclan of the Hawiye) comes from the Mudug region. The hot, dry and destitute condition of the Mudug region ensures that only the strong survive. Aideed's driving ambition was to forge a Somali state. When his U.S. pursuers boasted of getting so close to catching him that his bed was still warm, reporters invited into that "still warm" sanctum found a book on Thomas Jefferson on the bedside table. But this was not merely a man who, as head of the Habr Gedir clan, was unable to accommodate other clans. Within his own Habr Gedir, vicious infighting has erupted between extended families.

Somaliland

The little area that sits on the right shoulder of Ethiopia is for all intents and purposes a separate country from Somalia. It has no racing technicals, no ad hoc shootouts no looted aid vehicles. It has a population of 3 million people (half of them nomadic) who live in peace and tranquility with ten million goats. The government will tell that they also have $500 in revenue from exiles and $27 million in revenue from the sale of those goats. Oh yes on the balance sheet are also five million sheep and an equal amount of camels. They would like to be independent but they don't have enough money to print passports.

The Somaliland Page
http://www.users.interport.net/~mmaren/somlandarc.html"

Somaliland Cyberspace
http://www.anaserve.com/~mbali/

Ethiopia and Eritrea

The Ethiopians, allied with the Somali People's Democratic Party, have at least 5,000 troops inside Somalia battling Aideed's forces, the Eritreans, Al-Ittihad (an armed Islamic Group based in Somalia) and the insurgent Ethiopian group, the Oromo Liberation Front. For a little R&R from their mega-border war with Ethiopia, Eritrean soldiers spend their holidays from the front in Somalia helping Aideed, the Somali National Front and the OLF. This has become a regular terrorist all-star game. Or a "technical" demolition derby. Ethiopia and Eritrea have been trying to outflank each other since squabbles over their common 1,000-mile-long border erupted into the world's largest ground war in May 1998. The folks in Cape Town are no longer safe. Ethiopian advances have brought much of southern Somalia under their control.

http://www.un.org/Docs/sc/reports/1997/s1997135.htm

Al Hahad, or Al-Ittahad

The Saudis are backing a small group of Islamic fundamentalists based along the Juba River on the Ethiopia border. They have also been attacking Ethiopia which simply sends in troops to the lawless area of Somalia and kills as many as they can (see "Ethiopia").

The Crusaders

Not the guys that went to the holy land, the United Nations, the United States and the rest of the aid organizations that try to do something meaningful. It goes something like this. Aideed Sr. (who was elected by the Somali Congress with 66 percent of the vote) had just about whupped the other factions when the United Nations stepped in and decided that it was going to run Somalia. Naturally, Aideed declared war on the United Nations and the United States. Millions were spent on aid infrastructure in Somalia and most of it was destroyed or pillaged. As one Somali UN employee said to *DP* in Somalia, looting is "a more efficient form of aid distribution."

United States and United Nations troops killed between 8,000 and 10,000 Somalis while in-country.

Visas are not available at either the airport in Mogadishu nor at any of the border crossings. From the United States, unless you're an aid worker or have been specifically invited by whomever's in charge at the time, forget it. However, it may be possible to obtain a visa from Somalia's embassies maintained in Kenya, Egypt, Djibouti and Tanzania. In Nairobi, try the International House (Mama Ngina Street). For a three-month visa, you'll need three photographs and a letter of introduction, preferably from your embassy. You should be able to pick up your visa the next day. In Cairo, try the Somali mission on Dokki Street. Here, you'll definitely need a letter from your embassy stating the purpose of your journey, as well as proof of onward travel by air. There are no land-crossing visas issued. Here, you'll also need three photos. Processing takes a day. In Tanzania, Somali visas are issued at the Italian embassy:

Italian Embassy

> *Lugalo Road*
> *P.O. Box 2106*
> *Tel.: 46352/4*

Somalia has a consulate in Djibouti and this may be the easiest place to get a Somali visa:

Somalia Consulate

> *Boulevard del Republique*
> *BP 549*
> *Tel.: 353521*

U.K.: Embassy of the Somali Democratic Republic

> *60 Portland Place*
> *London, England, W1N 3DG*
> *Tel.: [171] 580-7148*

United States: Somali Permanent Mission to the United Nations

> *425 East 61st Street, Suite 703*
> *New York, NY 10021*
> *Tel.: (212) 688-9410*
> *Fax: (212) 759-0651*

The road network in Somalia is thoroughly dilapidated. About a tenth of the 27,000 miles are paved. Well actually 600 miles used to be paved. There are surfaced roads between Mogadishu, Kisimayo and Baidoa in the south, and between Hargeisa, Berbera and Burao in the north. There is the skeleton of a bus network in the south and no public transportation in the north. Fifty percent of the Somali people are nomads, and the camel is the principal form of transportation in the country. The IDA agreed to repair the road network in Somalia but has yet to get started on the work, for obvious reasons. It seems the Somalis like to steal every ADI vehicle they can get, chop the roof and slap a stolen .50-caliber machine gun on the back. The only way to get around, at present, is to hitch a ride with one of the few aid agencies remaining in the country. In the past, lifts have been available with United Nations High Commission for Refugees vehicles in Mogadishu and other areas. In Mogadishu, you can try hiring a cab or motorbike driver, but you'll probably be abducted or shot, or both. The twice-weekly Somali Airlines flights between Mogadishu and Berbera and the weekly flights to Hargeisa and Kisimayo from Mogadishu have been suspended.

If you do attempt to travel by road, make sure you bring along some friends. Technicals (ideally, with .50-caliber guns) come in very handy at the many roadblocks, which are just a way for the locals to make money. A show of force or a short burst above their heads will force them to ponder the relative value of dying for a few dollars. There are no fixed prices for renting a technical with *mooryaan*, or teenage gunmen, but there will be plenty of offers. It is estimated by the United Nations that there are 2 million assault rifles in Mogadishu alone.

There is supposed to be a $20 departure tax when the airport opens, but you should keep in mind that when the UN left, they needed heavy armor and hundreds of marines. The UN probably promised to mail in their $20 when Somalia gets a postal service to deliver it, a bank to cash it and a government to spend it.

Xeer

The traditional Somali constitution is called the Xeer. Pronounced like hair with a lougee. The main reason Somalia is a *DP* is because the factions just can't get it together long enough to form a cohesive government.

Kidnapping/Attacks

Aid workers run the risk of being kidnapped. The good news is that ransoms are relatively low—$100,000 per person for 10 aid workers kidnapped in April 1998. Somali gunmen also shot up a chartered UN plane a month earlier as it tried to land at Sakoweyne. A UN doctor was ambushed and murdered.

Piracy

A backpacker crewing his way to Egypt is just the latest victim for Somali pirates. He was shot dead wrestling with his attackers on a yacht. Yachts are the Somalis' favorite target but they will also go after rusting freighters being towed.

Why is piracy getting big? Well, duh, there's no one left on land to kidnap. So the clans set their sights at sea. Somali pirates nabbed two Finnish pleasure craft sailors in April 1999 off the coast of the country, and in June, four German yachtsmen were seized by high-seas kidnappers operating under the umbrella of the Somali Salvation Democratic Front faction. All the sailors were later released after intervention from clan elders. Pirates in Somalia fancy speedboats and will pretend they are officials on official business. Who would know the difference? If you're skippering anything more luxurious than an inner tube, make a wide tack from the Horn. Or you could end with more than a three-hour tour.

http://paladin-san-francisco.com/libpirac.htm

The South

The guerrilla force that overthrew Siad Barre in Mogadishu—the Somali National Movement—got its start in the north, and having seen to Barre's overthrow, it has long since gone back to the north. The problem in the north is that the victorious guerrillas turned the government over to an interim president—Abdirahman Tour—who at worst was bent on destroying his own government because he wanted to see a reunited Somali Republic (he has ties to the old Barre regime and to Egypt, which supported Barre) and at best was simply unable to contain clan warfare. In fact, clan warfare began in the north when the president sent armed men from his own clan, the Habre Younis, to seize Berbera, the north's chief port and the turf of the Issa Musa. Already ensconced in the capital at Hargeisa, it now appeared as if he were set. At least for a few months.

Along came an old man now commonly acknowledged to be brilliant, Ibrahim Dhega Weyne. Under his direction, the Issa regrouped and took Berbera back. With that, the two clans repaired to a mountain village, where for 17 days they argued fiercely.

The Green Line

Nope, this ain't a Los Angeles rapid transit line, but the front line in Somalia's civil war. It runs in Mogadishu on a southeast axis down Afgoye Road with Atto controlling the area around the former U.S. embassy and Somali National University and Aideed Jr. controlling the south and the port of Merca. Atto's area borders on the Medina district, where he is backed up by Mussa Sudi, an ally of Mahdi.

The North/Somaliland

In October 1994, fighting broke out between President Mohamed Ibrahim Egal, who is supported by the Habir Awal, Gadabursi and Saad Musi clans, and the Idegale militia, who are aligned with the Habir Younis. Normally, a peaceful area, the fighting quickly sent 150,000 refugees fleeing from the capital of Hargeisa. The Idegale make a little folding money by controlling the airport and charging a tax on all who use it. The government muscled in, and that's when the fighting started.

The Habir Younis (now remember, they support the Idegale Militia) appealed to Aideed and were sent a plane full of rifles and ammo. Egal (the guy who runs the country) called Ali Mahdi Mohamed (Aideed's enemy in the south) and received a nice letter in return but no guns. So Egal hit up his buddies, the North Koreans, and then got busy fighting. The fighting spread to the Garhadjis (a subclan of the Idegale and Egal in Burca, Sheikh and Burao). The government forces didn't do so well, so now the Garhadji militias have most of the government weapons in their possession. To make things more complicated, Egal does not have support from the majority of people but is pushing for an independent Somaliland. His opponents want to join up with Somalia. His predecessor, President Abdurahman Tur of the Habir Younis clan, was voted out and is now hanging out in Mogadishu under the protection of Aideed Jr.

Even though Egal has done a good job of whipping Somaliland (not Somalia) into fiscal and governmental shape, not one Western country will recognize its sovereignty. Go figure. Okay, now who's ready for a pop quiz on Somalia politics?

SomalilandNet

http://www.compmore.net/~hersi/index.html

The Northeast/Punt

Breaking up is not that hard to do in Somalia. Instead of outside forces trying to create a unified nation based on colonial principles, individual regions like Somaliland have simply ignored Mogadishu and gone on with their lives. "Puntland" has been established in the Northeast, and "Hiranland" and "Jubbaland" are being suggested (along the lines of Disneyland with their own separate worlds)? Although the UN poo-poos these microkingdoms, Somaliland has a government, stamps, money, a police force, safe streets, education and healthcare.

http://www.abyssiniacybergateway.net/somalia/

Bandits and Clans

All Somalis can trace their ancestry back to six clans. Back then, Sir Richard Burton (who got a spear through the cheek as a souvenir of his visit) called them "a fierce and turbulent race of republicans." Today there are 26 main factions broken into sub-clan groups, and in a big powwow its not unusual to see 500 or so leaders show up. Most of the factions are simply extended families engaged in blood feuds. They take no prisoners, and if you stumble onto anybody's turf, expect to be treated accordingly (i.e., shot or macheted). Where clans don't rule, bandits do. Bandits control large rural areas and snipe around in the cities, as well. Police forces are present in some cities, but are essentially impotent and refuse to stand up to the clans and bands of thugs. They have few resources and are as likely to be targeted for death as anyone else. Muslim *shari'a* law, which has replaced any form of institutional legal system in Somalia, is enforced in a noncohesive fashion by clan elders.

http://www.sil.org/ethnologue/countries/Soma.html

Khat (Qat)

Although technically not dangerous by itself, most of the gunmen cruising around the country have that tweaky, faraway look that sends chills down the spine of visitors. Khat is also one of the underpinnings of the economy here resulting in the occasional shootout over territory or delivery routes. Those who don't fight battles or raise camels grow khat, an amphetamine-like stimulant that, when chewed, provides a mild high. Khat is preferred fresh, and Federal Express would be green with envy to watch the bundles of khat being airfreighted out of Mogadishu to Yemen and the Gulf States. Khat can also be used as a form of currency.

http://www.sas.upenn.edu/African_Studies/Hornet/qat.html

Technicals

Every American teenage kid's fantasy is to drop a big 454 into an old Chevy Nova and terrorize the neighborhood. Here every Somali's fantasy is to drop an antiaircraft gun onto the back of a Toyota pickup truck and terrorize the country. Actually, a technical might be a great way to get through the morning commute. Technicals are essentially anything with wheels to which Somalis can bolt a belt-fed machine gun. Homemade technicals were invented in Lebanon in the '80s when warring groups wanted to hit and run (and make a lot of noise). Technicals became the ride of choice when the locals found out that the UN workers would hire them as security. Needless to say, it was harder to find a Toyota Land Cruiser with a roof after that. Thank goodness it only rains bullets here.

http://www.dodccrp.org/Proceedings/DOCS/wcd00000/WCD0004B.HTM

Journalists

No need for nasty letters to the editor here. The Somali warlords are a well-read bunch, and if they take issue with something you've written, they send a *mooryaan* to knock on your door and deliver their response. Four Somali journalists were executed by followers of Aideed for offending him in an article they wrote in a UN-sponsored paper. An Italian journalist was executed after being mistaken for an executive of an Italian banana exporter. Most journalists do not sign their name on local articles for fear of reprisals.

http://www.cpj.org/countrystatus/1998/Africa/Somalia.html
http://www.ixpres.com/netnomad/

Food

As of mid-1999, 1.2 million people were facing serious food shortages in Somalia, with 400,000 on the brink of starvation. With the Ethiopians and the Eritreans using Somalia to try and outflank each other (which they'll probably do down to Antarctica), uncontrolled crop pests, its own messy civil war and no rain for two years, Somalia is on the abyss. Of the total emergency food aid requirements for 1998/1999, only about a quarter—52,000 tons—was delivered. Somalians have been dining on a cuisine of dried leaves, roots and the shells of coffee beans—an entree that might cost 50 bucks at Spago's, but in Somalia is a better bet than Jenny Craig at losing weight real fast. Naturally there are frequent attacks on food convoys by bandits.

http://wwwnotes.reliefweb.int (Go to Somalia)

Bananas

Ali Mahdi's men have fired at banana boats trying to dock in the ports of Mog. You see Aideed is Ali Mahdi's mortal enemy and Aideed controls the banana trade. Now we don't know what happens if you are carrying a banana through customs, but we should warn *DP* readers that a customs inspector might ask, "Is that a banana in your pocket or are you just showing your support for Aideed?" Money raised from the sale of bananas by the Sombana and Somalfruit companies is used by Aideed's clan to buy weapons and fuel.

Killing People

With all these guns and hair-trigger tempers, it doesn't take more than a few minutes for a clan fight to break out and people to get killed. The only consolation we can offer you if you are convicted of killing someone is that the *shari'a*, or Islamic law, mandates that you must pay 100 camels. If you are a woman, the penalty is 50 camels. Meanwhile our government does a study looking into human rights with such meaningful topics as "The right to organize and bargain collectively." Obviously they have never been stopped at a Somali roadblock.

http://www.state.gov/www/global/human_rights/1998_hrp_report/somalia.html

Monopoly Money

Hussein Aideed's idea of prosperity for all is simple: just print more money—a shitload of it. He's obviously earned a degree from the Milton Bradley Institute of Micro(scopic) Economics. Somalians have been rioting over hikes in transport, food and other commodities as the presses at Aideed's mint churn out Somali shillings overtime— millions of dollars worth in 1999. Dozens have been killed and an untallied amount injured by armed guards firing on mobs trying to bust into businesses where the bogus bucks are being hoarded. "Go to jail" isn't on the Somali game board.

Foreign Trade Department
Mogadiscio
Somalia
Postal Address:
PO Box 928
Mogadiscio, Somalia
Tel.: +2521 21453
Telex: 3143 mincom sm

The World Bank actually did a study on Somalia. You can download or they can send it to you printed on a single Post-it.

http://www.worldbank.org/data/countrydata/aag/som_aag.pdf

Stuff You Never Wanted to Know Except under "I'll Try Somali Trivia for $500, Alex"

The Cushitic language wasn't written until 1973. Feuding is a principal pasttime of the Somalis. Principally, they feud over the control of *barkados*, water for hire stations. Frankincense from the Boswellia tree is among the country's most prized exports. There are two rainy seasons, the *gu* and the *dayr*. And you better cough up the *diya* or the *abbaan* will lay down the *shari'a*, baaby.

http://meltingpot.fortunecity.com/lebanon/254/marchal.htm

GETTING SICK

The state-run medical system has collapsed in Somalia, and only rudimentary care is available through NGOs (when they aren't being shot or kidnapped). Statistically there is supposed to be one doctor for every 4,640 people in Somalia. Good Luck. Diarrhea, communicable and parasitic diseases are rampant in the country. Chloroquine-resistant malaria is present in all parts of the country. Larium should be used for chemical prophylaxis. Cholera, dracunculiasis (Guinea worm), cutaneous and visceral leishmaniasis, rabies, relapsing fever and typhus (endemic flea-borne, epidemic louse-borne and scrub) are prevalent. Somalia is also receptive to dengue fever, as there have been intermittent epidemics in the past. Meningitis is a risk during the dry season in the savanna portion of the country, from December through March. Schistosomiasis may also be found in the country and contracted through contact with contaminated freshwater lakes, streams or ponds. A yellow fever vaccination certificate is required for all travelers coming from infected areas.

There's also a pesky little problem with Tumbu Fly, a local maggot that burrows into human skin, munching on flesh all the way. The larvae grows big enough to rip out flesh before it turns into a fly. You don't see a lot of horror movies in Somalia because real life beats David Cronenberg every time. The best place to be evacuated to is Riyadh, Saudi Arabia.

NUTS AND BOLTS

Somalia is flat hot place wrapped around Ethiopia like a bandage. The north has hills 3,000–7,000 feet (900–2,100 meters). The rest is a wasteland of dirt. Located in the Horn of Africa, British Somaliland and Italian Somaliland formed independent Somalia in 1960. The population is 9.3 million with a 12 percent mortality rate. Somalia covers 637,655 square kilometers (246,199 square miles). Best time to go? Well the term hot as hell would be the phrase of choice describing the climate most of the year. June–September is hot with cool evenings. October–May hot enough to give cockroach heatstroke. If you like your heat wet, head to Mog, where the humidity is a constant 80 percent, with the occasional breeze.

Somalia is not really set up to be the next big tourist attraction in Africa. Its long coastline has some of the nicest sand beaches on the continent, but the waters are infested with sharks and there is little shade. Believe it or not, there is a tourist office in Mogadishu. Let the phone ring a long time (if you can get through). Most journos stay at the Sahafi Hotel in Mogadishu.

Somalia National Agency for Tourism
Box 533
Mogadishu, Somalia
Tel.: 3850 or 3479

March to June and September to December are the rainy seasons. Nomadic grazing is the name of the game here, with temperatures hot and landscape arid. The country is 100 percent Sunni Muslim; the entire population is ethnic Somali. English is widely spoken, and Italian is popular in the south. Somali is a difficult language and uses the Roman alphabet. Somali has been a written language only since 1972 so understandably just 24 percent of the country is literate. Things like telephones (country code 252) electricity (220), gas or food are in short supply, so look for a hotel with a roof and a generator.

Money is the Somali shilling broken down into 100 centesimi. The money is a little funky since Aideed reprints new money with the old 1996 date. The new Somali shilling is worth less than Old Somali shillings. Hotels run about 45 shillings a day. Depending on which region you are in most of the city folk speak Arabic, Italian or English. For the latest in Africa currency exchange rates check out:

http://www.mbendi.co.za/cyexch.htm

Somalis like to be called by their nicknames. The slender Somali frame creates a lot of nicknames like *Ato* (thin) or *Dheere* (tall).

Somali has some very benign pockets where you can find pay satphones ($1 a minute outside the country, free inside), banks and other niceties.

Contacts

For more information contact:

Australia
(represented by its embassy in Kenya)

P.O. Box 39341
Riverside Drive (just off Chiromo Road)
Nairobi, Kenya
Tel.: [254] (2) 445-034
Fax: [254] (2) 444-617

Canada
(represented by its high commission in Kenya)

Comcraft House
Haile Selassie Avenue, Box 30481
Nairobi, Kenya
Tel.: [254] 221-4804
Fax: 254-226-987

British Embassy

Waddada Xasan Geedd Abtoow 7/8
P.O. Box 1036, Mogadishu, Somalia
Tel.: 20288.

United States (represented in Kenya)

U.S. Liaison Office for Somalia
U.S. Embassy
Moi and Haile Selassie Avenues
Nairobi, Kenya
Tel.: [254] (2) 334141, FAX: (2) 340838.
Mailing address: P.O. Box 30137, Nairobi,
or Unit 64100, APO AE 09831

Somalia News Update

Department of Cultural Anthropology
Uppsala University
Tradgardsgatan 18
S-753 09 Uppsala, Sweden
E-mail: Bernhard.Helander@antro.uu.se

Web Resources

There is absolutely nothing that is up-to-date on Somalia and even less that is accurate. The web is a good starting point for recent news reports. Most of these sites all link back to the same places.

NomadNet

http://www.ixpres.com/netnomad

Virtual Library (links)

http://www.columbia.edu/cu/libraries/
indiv/area/Africa/Somalia.html

SomaliNet

http://somalinet.com/

State Department info on Somalia/
Area Handbook

http://lcweb2.loc.gov/frd/cs/sotoc.html
http://www.odci.gov/cia/publications/
factbook/so.html

Arab Net

http://www.arab.net/somalia/
somalia_contents.html

Mbendi Country Profile

http://www.mbendi.co.za/cysocy.htm

Greater Horn Initiative

http://www.info.usaid.gov/regions/afr/
ghai/

SOMALIA

7/99	More Ethiopian troops enter Somalia to fight Aideed- and Eritrean-backed forces, bringing the number to more than 5,000.
6/24/99	Four German yachtsmen kidnapped at sea and then released.
3/19/99	A firefight breaks out between warlord Musa Sudi Yalahow's militia and Mogadishu Governor Hussein Ali Ahmed's militia in northern Mogadishu. At least 40 people are killed and 70 injured. Initial hostilities between the two groups began on March 13 over taxation rights.
3/21/96	Five UN aid workers are taken hostage at the Balidogie airport.
9/95	Aideed and 600 men seize Baidoa in the south.
6/95	Osman Hassan Ali Atto is elected as chairman of the Somali National Alliance.
3/95	UN forces withdraw from Somali.
6/5/93	Twenty-six Pakistani peacekeepers and 50 Somalis are killed in a battle with Aideed's men.
3/93	Aideed and the four tribes of northwest Somalia adopt the Somali constitution called Xeer (pronounced "hair"). Two more clans join on June 4.
12/9/92	In Mogadishu, 1,800 U.S. Marines arrive, prior to 28,000 other American troops, for the start of Operation Restore Hope.
3/3/92	Under UN pressure, Ali Mahdi and Aideed sign a cease-fire.
1/25–31/92	United Somali Congress rebels capture Mogadishu.
91–92	Massive famine. Seventy-five percent of the country's 6 million people are at risk of starvation.
6/91	Aideed is elected chairman of United Somali Congress.
10/31/80	President Siad Barre declares a state of emergency.
10/21/69	Bloodless coup brings Siad Barre to power.
7/60	British Somaliland and Italian Somaliland are united to become independent Somalia.

SOMALIA

Sri Lanka
★★

Body Count

Perhaps in no other insurgency in the world are the foes so anal about body counts as in Sri Lanka's bitter 16-year civil war. Each day brings not only bombings, suicide attacks and jungle battles to the headlines of Sri Lanka's newspapers, but also the number of folks who were whacked in the attacks.

Daily, the numbers rack up like computer ATP rankings—300 rebels dead, 500 injured; 25 government troops dead, 73 injured, and so on. Rather than fighting, the insurgent Liberation Tigers of Tamil Eelam (LTTE) spend most of their time—thanks to their London PR office—in a media battle with the Colombo government disputing the body count. Both sides in the conflict steadfastly refuse to let *DP* help with the math. Journalists aren't allowed to cover this little civil war. *DP* went in only to cool our heels watching fire-walking performances for tourists. However, no matter whose calculator is on the blink, one thing is for sure: some 55,000 Sri Lankans have been killed in this inglorious ethnic conflict since 1983. The LTTE says it has lost only about 10,000 soldiers in 16 years. As usual it is civilians that make up the bulk of the casualty list.

The bitter conflict in Sri Lanka hasn't only claimed the lives of combatants and innocent civilians. It can also chalk up a president, the Navy commander, the government's opposition leader and the husband of President Chandrika Kumaratunga, not to mention India's Prime Minister, Rajiv Gandhi.

Just when things seem to be going the government's way, the pesky Tigers blow a few Sri Lankan navy ships out of the water, lay siege to major army bases. and retake strategic towns along the Jaffna Road, the country's most important artery. Or, of course, they also revert to their time-tested tradition of car-bombing Colombo skyscrapers into tiny glass shards, shredding a couple of hundred innocents in the process. These guys make Northern Ireland's IRA look like a bunch of schoolkids with scraped knees pounding caps with a rock.

Perhaps even more ingrained into our memories than tattered duchesses staggering half-naked and bloodied out of Harrods—or body parts twitching on the street alongside a blown-up Kosovo bus—are scenes of downtown Colombo, ripe with screaming Sinhalese, fresh from amputations they hadn't paid for. The glass is falling like a hard rain, unheard by the hundreds whose eardrums have exploded like an aerosol can tossed into a fire.

Although the Sinhalese and Tamils have been at odds with each other for more than 2,000 years, much of the tension and fighting that has gripped the island has occurred only in recent years. The fighting began in earnest after a Tamil Tiger ambush of an army patrol in the Jaffna area in 1983. Sinhalese all over the island then went on a rampage for the next three days, murdering and looting Tamils and burning down their villages. Perhaps 2,000 Tamils were killed in the uprising.

The north and the east of the island have been war zones for the better part of 14 years. Although areas in the south are still relatively safe, nowhere on the island is actually Tiger-free. The former LTTE "capital" of Jaffna was taken by government troops on December 5, 1995. The entire Jaffna peninsula was wrested by the army in May 1996. But the rebellion continues. Even visiting the ruins at Anuradhapura and Polonnaruwa is risky. The Batticaloa region remains the Tamil Tigers' principal area for staging operations in the south.

President Kumaratunga, during her election campaign in 1994, promised to find a peaceful means of ending the war, and the government offered a proposal for "devolution" to the Tigers, granting Tamil provinces in the north and east nearly complete autonomy. The government move was lauded both internationally, by moderate Tamils, and by Sri Lanka's imposing and Tiger-backing neighbor, India. But a restless military persuaded Kumaratunga, whose ruling coalition party had a majority of only one vote, to launch an attack on Jaffna and the north on October 17, 1995. Government forces were spectacularly successful in capturing Jaffna in December, but took heavy losses. According to the government, 500 soldiers died while nearly 2,000 Tigers were killed. The guerrillas, of course, claimed the reverse figures in their continuing war of body counts.

By 1988, the entire country was in turmoil and the economy was crippled. In 1999, Government forces had increased tenfold (to 126,000 soldiers) since 1983 to battle the Liberation Tigers of Tamil Eelam (Tamil Tigers, or LTTE). More than 55,000 people have died since 1983. The Tigers have been pushed back into the jungle where leader Velupillai Prabhakaran vows to continue their fight.

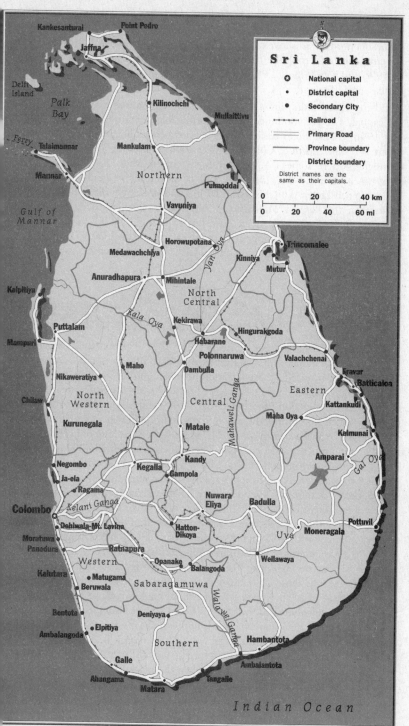

President Kumaratunga claimed in January 1996 that the war would be won in 12 months. She was wrong. Today, more than 6 percent of Sri Lanka's gross domestic product is shoveled into the 16-year-old civil war. In May 1996, government forces took the Jaffna peninsula. But it hardly declawed the Tigers. In 1996 and 1997, the LTTE rocked the capital with a series of massive bomb blasts, including the Central Bank and the World Trade Center.

And the Tigers didn't lick their wounds simply by trashing a few buildings in the capital. They've continued to be a formidable military force in the field. In July 1996, LTTE forces besieged the key northern military base of Mullaittivu about 170 miles north of Colombo. They took the base on July 22 after a five-day siege, where some 1,400 government troops were killed. Although the government claimed the base was still in government hands, Tamil Tiger spokeswoman Helen Whitehead told *DP* in London a rather different story: "We have taken the base at Mullaittivu," Whitehead said. The siege marked the bloodiest fighting of the conflict. And just to keep Colombo on its toes, two LTTE bombs aboard a commuter train in the capital killed nearly 70 innocents on July 24 that same year. In December of 1999 the president was barely missed being blown to bits.

Since independence from the UK in 1948, Sri Lanka has been under emergency rule for more than half of its young life. And sixteen years of civil war with the Tamil Tigers (since 1983), leaving more than 55,000 Sri Lankans dead, won't end overnight. As Sri Lanka's Foreign Minister Lakshman Kadirgamar recently said: "Guerrilla wars don't finish like that. The Second World War finished on a particular day. I don't think this one is going to finish in that way." But who says war is hell? The civil war with the LTTE has been the best thing to happen for the island's economy since independence. The war has provided 400,000 new jobs—from the army's recruitment of poor, young villagers in the south to the hiring of 150,000 round-the-clock security guards for the private business sector. Then, of course, there are the army's vendors. Not bad for a nation of 18 million people. Then you've got your refugees. Unlike most places, like Kosovo, where you can simply tip-toe though the forest and suddenly find yourself inside another country in a tent with a UN-issue sterno stove and a kilometer-long line at the potty, Sri Lanka's more than 540,000 refugees have had to fly off the island. These days, between 15,000 and 18,000 Sri Lankans say adios to their homeland each year, keeping those 747s fuller than a Muslim cleric's belly the day after Ramadan. Each year, they send some US$500 million back to their families at home, which contributes to the island's US$4 billion "black economy." Right now, the road to Jaffna may be closed, but as such, it's a road to riches. If the army finally takes the road, the Tigers will dissolve back into jungle. The US named the Tamil Tigers to their list 30 foreign terrorist organizations in October 1997. The major danger to travelers is when the Black Tigers get dressed up in C-4 and dynamite corsets and head into town to join a political rally. Don't ever offer to pull a thread on someone's clothing in Sri Lanka. In a nutshell? As

President Chandrika Kumaratunga admitted at a recent ceremony: her country has so far failed to build a nation.

Velupillai Prabhakaran and The Liberation Tigers of Tamil Eelam (LTTE)

The LTTE began in 1976, and today it is the largest Tamil separatist guerrilla group and perhaps the most ruthless and efficient terrorist cell on the planet. (Yup, terrorists, at least according to the U.S. government's list of 30 foreign terrorist organizations.) They began the military fight with the Sri Lankan government in 1983. The Tigers have maintained their hard-line position on separatism and conducted numerous military and terrorist acts to further their cause. They are most famous for their suicide attacks on prominent politicians. These attacks not only snuff their intended victims, but, because of the type of bomb employed (usually a very powerful explosive unleashing a volley of shrapnel or metal pellets), they usually take out a couple of dozen innocents as well. It is believed that LTTE members were responsible for the 1993 assassination of President Ranasinghe Premadasa.

Led by Velupillai Prabhakaran (http://www.eelamweb.com/pirabha.html), the LTTE maintains its own navy, called the Sea Tigers. Operating now in waters off the northeastern coastal city of Mullaittivu, each light boat carries five or six guerrillas who attack Indian navy ships or make landings to attack Sri Lankan army units. Sea Tigers also are suicide frogmen who blow up navy ships with self-detonated explosives.

Bombs are the favored method of Tamil suicide guerrillas. Suicide bombers are revered among the Tamils. Their pictures are defiantly and proudly displayed along the road and in the houses of their families. Their families are accorded a distinction equal to the mothers of saints. How do you spot a suicide bomber or Black Tiger? Despite the fact that an average Tamil lives until he is over 70, most suicide bombers are young, in their early 20s; they wear a pendant around their necks with a cyanide capsule dangling from the end. The cyanide will kill within 5 minutes when nibbled on as a snack.

Despite the LTTE loss of its "capital" Jaffna in December 1995, the Tigers remain a formidable force in deflecting the ongoing Victory Assured offensive by the government and causing huge government casualties. The army lost 1,400 men when the LTTE took Mullaittivu in 1996 and at least 600 when Kilinochchi was lost to the rebels in 1998. But the Tamils have also retaliated by slaughtering innocent villagers to slow the government offensive. Prabhakaran, widely believed responsible for the 1991 assassination of Indian Prime Minister Rajiv Gandhi and the 1993 snuffing of Sri Lankan President Ranasinghe Premadasa as well as a wave of other suicide bombings, is hiding out in the Vanni forests in the northwest plotting his next targets.

Tamil Tiger strength is estimated to be between 3,000 and 10,000, depending on who you talk to. They claim to have lost some 10,000 fighters in the 16 years of warfare. If you want to talk to some of the Tamil Tigers and get the scoop for yourself, you can—but you better have a good reason. They talked to *DP*, but only after "checking us out." The U.S. government believes that the LTTE is involved in smuggling drugs and Tamils have acted as couriers of narcotics to Europe. The LTTE gets its main support from Tamil Nadu in SE India and the Sri Lankan civil war is one of the few insurgencies that is fought on the ocean with gunboats.

Liberation Tigers of Tamil Eelam

211 Katherine Rd.
London E6 1BU

United Kingdom
Tel./Fax: 011-44-181-470-8593
http://www.eelamweb.com
Other groups to contact are World Tamil Association (WTA), World Tamil Movement (WTM), Federation of Associations of Canadian Tamils (FACT) and the Ellalan Source

http://intamm.com/organisations/orglist_us.htm
http://dspace.dial.pipex.com/liberation/

The Government

The current president and daughter of two former Sri Lankan prime ministers, Chandrika Kumaratunga, 53, didn't let the assassination of her husband by the LTTE get in the way of the peace process. In November 1994, she sent delegates to begin discussions on ending the then 11-year-old civil war. The protracted talks ended up with the government's proposed offer of autonomy for Tamil provinces in the north and east. Since that effort failed after the LTTE sinking of two naval vessels in April 1995 at the port of Trincomalee, she's been pounding the LTTE and everyone unlucky enough to be in the vicinity with everything she's got.

The 120,000-strong army (10 times the size it was in 1983) took the Jaffna peninsula from rebel forces in May 1996. The army sent in 30,000 troops for 50 days and after the smoke cleared 2,500 people had died. Jaffna had been the financial, military and medical base for the Tigers, who are now mounting an increasingly effective jungle insurgency. The army is now fighting to clear the 45 mile road to Jaffna. Thousands have been killed in this so-called "Victory Assured" offensive, which started in May 1997. A suicide bomber tried to kill her in Dec. 1999. She escaped with a serious eye injury.

The Defence Secretary, Ministry of Defence
15/5, Baladaksha Mawatha, Colombo 03, Sri Lanka
Fax: 00 94-1-541529
http://www.lankapage.com/wlib/gov.html

A passport, onward/return ticket and proof of sufficient funds (US$15 per day) are required. A tourist visa can be granted at the time of entry into Sri Lanka, and may be valid for a maximum period of 90 days. For business travel or travel on an official or diplomatic passport, visas are required and must be obtained in advance.

Business visas are valid for one month and require an application form, two photos, a company letter, a letter from a sponsoring agency in Sri Lanka, a copy of an onward/return ticket, and a US$5 fee. Include US$6 postage for return of your passport by registered mail.

Yellow fever and cholera immunizations are needed if arriving from an infected area.

For further information, contact the following:

Embassy of the Democratic Socialist Republic of Sri Lanka

2148 Wyoming Ave., NW
Washington, DC 20008
Tel.: (202) 483-4025
http://piano.symgrp.com/srilanka/
or nearest consulate:

California
Tel.: (805) 873-7224

New Jersey
Tel.: (201) 627-7855

Hawaii
Tel.: (808) 735-1622

New York
Tel.: (212) 986-7040

About a third of Sri Lanka's 47,070 miles of road are paved. There are 1,210 miles of heavily traveled railroad and 14 airfields; the only major airport is in Colombo. Trains are arguably more comfortable than buses, but are slower and don't service as many areas of the island as do buses. The train stations, although dilapidated, aren't nearly as crowded as those in India, where rail travel is the lifeblood of Indians. However, don't fall asleep on the trains. You'll more than likely get ripped off by a thief.

Tamil Eelam

The place they are fighting over. The island of Ceylon or Sri Lanka was originally divided between two distinct kingdoms. The Tamil Kingdom in the north and the Sinhala kingdom in the South. The British lumped them together and adminsitered them both from the capital of Colombo. When Ceylon was given its independence, the control of the entire island was handed to the Sinhalese government in1948. The same thing happened when the Americans bundled the Moros into the Philippine government after World War II and Kashmir along with India, etc., etc. So now you get the whole point. The Sinhalese called the place Sri Lanka and the Tamils call their homeland Tamil Eelam. There is also linkage with the Indian state of Tamil Nadu.

http://dspace.dial.pipex.com/liberation/index2.html
http://www.eelam.com/
http://mapsofindia.com/maps/tamilnadu/index.html
http://www.geocities.com/Athens/5180/tlinks.html

National Parks

Remote forested areas, such as Wilpattu and Galoya national parks, are considered especially unsafe. Rebels like the peace and quiet and may take exception to your need to explore and save their rain forest. They're doing just fine beneath their blanket of triple-canopy forest hidden in deep bunkers—excellent cover from air force helicopter and bomb attacks.

Jaffna

In retreating from their stronghold at Jaffna in November 1995, LTTE Tigers booby-trapped virtually the entire city with trip-wired antitank and antipersonnel mines. Anything that could be picked up—from books to cooking utensils to clothes on the floor—were booby-trapped by the fleeing rebels. The city's population plummeted from 120,000 to a mere 6,000 in just a few short weeks. Like Paris in August—with land mines.

Vavuniya to Kilinochchi

This is a 55-mile stretch of roadway under LTTE control that would link Colombo with the Jaffna peninsula if the government forces could just get their hands on it. For now, government troops on the Jaffna peninsula can be reinforced and resupplied only by air and sea. A fierce government offensive to seize control of the Vavuniya-Kilinochchi road began in May 1997 (involving some 20,000 Sri Lankan soldiers, supported by warplanes, chopper gunships, tanks and artillery) and dissolved in 1998 after the LTTE's capture of Kilinochchi.

North and East

Currently, fighting between the government forces and the LTTE continues in much of the north and east, with sporadic, but increasing, guerrilla attacks in Colombo and the south. Although the fighting is relatively confined to the north and east, security checkpoints have become the norm along major crossroads in and around Colombo, a result of the March 1991 LTTE bombing assassination of Deputy Defense Minister Ranjan Wijertaine, the June 1991 bombing of the Ministry of Defense's Joint Operations Command, the January 1996 bombing of the Central Bank of Sri Lanka in Colombo (just a few hundred yards from President Chandrika Kumaratunga's office) and the October 1997 bombing of Colombo's World Trade Center.

Colombo

The LTTE bombings here are just plain scary. On January 31, 1996, a blast took nearly 100 lives and wounded 1,400 others. On July 24, 1996, the Tigers blew up a train leaving Dehiwala, a southern suburb of Colombo. This detonation killed 57 people and injured 500 others. Another bomb blasted through the World Trade Center in 1997. However, other than the blood splattered by the LTTE, the level of criminal activity in Colombo is moderate in relation to other cities of the world. Violent crimes are on the rise, with a 20-percent increase in murders and rape reported in Colombo for 1998. The Sri Lankan police, though limited in resources, generally make every effort to provide assistance to foreign visitors. This is particularly so within the confines of Colombo. Police coverage tends to be less reliable outside of the city. Important police emergency telephone numbers for the greater Colombo area:

Police Emergency (24 hours daily)
Tel.: 433333
Cinnamon Gardens Police Station
Tel.: 693377
Colpetty Police Station
Tel.: 20131
Bambalapitiya Police Station
Tel.: 593208

Political Rallies

The Black Tigers, or suicide bombers, cast their votes and reduce the pool of voters by blowing themselves and anyone else in a 50-yard radius into small fleshy pieces. Using massive explosives packed around ball bearings, pellets and other homemade shrapnel, they can kill up to 60 people at a time. Prominent national leaders and senior military personnel have been targets and/or victims of terrorist violence, which, of course, makes anyone else in the neighborhood a target, as well.

http://www.agora.stm.it/politic/sri_lanka.htm

Religious Temples

The Sri Lanka government officially outlawed the LTTE after a devastating January 1998 truck bomb attack on the holiest Buddhist shrine on the island, the Temple of the Tooth, in Kandy. Sixteen people were killed and the temple so badly damaged, it made Angkor Wat in Cambodia look like Reverend Robert Schuller's Crystal Cathedral in Garden Grove, California. England's Prince Charles, who was to attend a ceremony at the Temple of the Tooth, had to high-tail it back to Colombo, not that he was really any safer there.

http://suif.stanford.edu/~saman/lanka/sri_lanka.html

Women

The 3,000-odd lasses who help make up the Tamil Tigresses don't seem to mind taking a bullet or two, either. Some 68 female LTTE guerrillas were whacked during the siege of Mullaittivu. And on July 4, 1996, a female suicide bomber adorned in designer explosive devices crashed into a Jaffna motorcade on her scooter trying to assassinate the minister of construction. He survived, but 23 people were killed and 60 others were injured by the blast. In May 1998, an elite Black "Tigress" hurled herself in front of a vehicle carrying a military general, killing the officer and his two bodyguards. The lady, of course, ended up as accessories in an organ transplant catalog and won't be seen on the cover of ELLE any time soon.

http://www.state.gov/www/global/human_rights/1998_hrp_report/srilanka.html

Homosexuals

According to Sri Lankan penal code, sex between men is punishable by 12 years in jail, while the existence of lesbianism is not acknowledged by the 1883 Penal Code.

Suicide

Although some 55,000 folks have died in the fighting between the LTTE and government troops since 1983, 70,000 others committed suicide during the same period. It appears there's a bigger market in Sri Lanka for Prozac than for Viagra.

http://www.tamilrights.org/news/1999n/hrwsl99.htm

Buses

The LTTE is apparently becoming more interested in civilian targets than military troops. A March 5, 1998 LTTE attack on a minibus left 30 dead and more than 300 injured. A bus depot was attacked in October 1997, leaving a security guard dead and 18 buses destroyed. A bomb exploded on a bus in Kandy, killing two and injuring 25 people, on April 11, 1999. There were four bombings in Colombo in March 1999 alone.

The Day after a Polio Vaccination

Sri Lanka enjoys exactly four days of peace a year. These are the days when UNICEF conducts its annual polio vaccination drive throughout the country. Both the LTTE and the government reward these days with a temporary cessation of fighting ("days of tranquility," they're called).

Operation "Victory Assured"

Victory Assured is the code name for the government effort, started in May 1997, to gain control over the entirety of the Jaffna road, linking the tip of the northern peninsula with Colombo and the south. But with the LTTE taking the key town of Kilinochchi in September 1998, victory, it seems, is hardly assured. In that attack, the army lost some 600 men; 400 others were injured. Sri Lanka's military said there were 1,200 deaths in the battle. The government claims to now control more than two-thirds of the highway. It may seem like a boast of sorts, but what it really means is that vital supplies, equipment and food for the forward units can only get about two-thirds of the way to where they actually need to go.

http://lcweb2.loc.gov/cgi-bin/query/r?frd/cstdy:@field(DOCID+lk0010)

Trucks

Truck bombs are so ubiquitous in the capital Colombo, any given lorry with some hardware store's decal on the cab could be packing a manifest of diesel and fertilizer and headed to a gleaming office skyscraper near you, turning your lunch break into a platter of white and dark meat served on shards of glass. A truck bomb obliterated Colombo's Central Bank in January 1996 and the Colombo World Trade Center in October 1997. A March 1998 decree made it illegal for heavy vehicles to enter Colombo Fort (downtown—the business district where the Presidential residence is located) without a special permit. If the driver is a Tamil, he needs a letter from his boss verifying he's never killed a Sri Lankan soldier nor blown up a Colombo bank teller on his coffee break. The Sri Lanka version of a "deathalyzer test."

http://www.mtholyoke.edu/acad/intrel/tamarms.htm

Dudes with Amulets Around Their Necks in Colombo

At any given time, at least 60 LTTE suicide bombers are dressed up like the Michelin Tire Man and combing the streets of Colombo searching for somebody important to blow up. Because security is so tight around President Kumaratunga and other high-ranking government officials, the bombers have started stalking anyone with a title or who's gotten his or her name in a newspaper—even leaders of the opposition. Assisted suicide has never been easier.

http://www.ipcs.org/states/sri-mal-index.htm

Sea Tiger Gunboats

The Sea Tigers (the marine version of the LTTE) operate small gunboats to conduct naval- and marine-style raids. Each boat usually carries five or six guerrillas. When *DP* used these boats in the Jaffna Lagoon to visit the Tigers, the boat in front of us was blown from the water by a naval shell. Usually, though, the high-speed boats manage to outrun the slower naval gunners. About 40 of these mini-warships are based on an island just off the coast of the rebel-held town of Mullaittivu.

Air Tiger Warplanes

The LTTE has added a miniature air force to complement its miniature navy. But we won't be seeing any computer-guided smart bombs any time soon. The Tigers have started employing microlight aircraft to attack government targets. There is speculation that the LTTE might begin using airborne suicide bombers to attack Temple Trees, President Chandrika Kumaratunga's official residence in Colombo. Don't expect headsets, peanuts or beverage service.

Crime

There's been an unprecedented crime wave in Colombo over the last two years with 18 criminal gangs counted so far. In 1998 1,066 rapes and 1,993 homicides were reported. This is a 20-percent increase in these crimes over previous years. With the LTTE wreaking havoc in the capital, it's been necessary to recruit more cops for security. These new flatfoots are taught too little, too fast and then sent out on the streets with machine guns and rocket launchers, concerned more with the guys taped up in dynamite sticks than guys with rocket launchers in their trousers.

The Inspector General of Police,
Police Headquarters,
Colombo 01, Sri Lanka

Political Rallies

Election violence is the order of the day in Sri Lanka, especially during provincial elections. Clashes between the United National Party (UNP) and the ruling People's Alliance (PA) resulted in two deaths during the week of March 29, 1999. On April 4, the UNP office in Kegalle was bombed, killing one and injuring three. According to the U.S. embassy, "Americans throughout Sri Lanka are advised to avoid political rallies and other mass gatherings, limit exposure to government and military installations, and use caution when traveling on public buses and trains and on domestic air carriers."

GETTING SICK

Medical facilities are limited—you'll find one doctor and 27 hospital beds for every 10,000 people. Doctors and hospitals often expect immediate cash payment for health services. Malaria is prevalent in many areas outside of Colombo. Visitors must take precautions against malaria, hepatitis and yellow fever prior to arriving in Sri Lanka. Rabies is common in many animals in Sri Lanka; take some comfort that the painful injections against rabies can be obtained locally. Tap water is laced with everything from amoebas to horses and should not be ingested unless boiled for a couple of decades, strained through an offset press and carpet-bombed with iodine.

Sri Lanka was once known as Serendib in ancient times and then as Ceylon under the Brits. The emerald isle is made up of a teardrop-shaped main island and groups of smaller islands 50 miles off the southern coast of India. Sri Lanka, with its lush jungles and dramatic interior, has been called one of the most beautiful islands in the world. Thirty-one percent of the island is mountainous jungle nestling ancient cities such as Polonnaruwa and Anuradhapura. The 833 miles of coastline are primarily pristine, coral-fringed beaches.

The major ethnic group is the Sinhalese (74 percent) followed by the Tamils (18 percent) and Moors (7 percent). Burghers, Malays and Veddhas comprise the last 1 percent. The Sinhalese are predominantly Buddhist and the Tamils are Hindu. Christians and Muslims make up only about 8 percent of the religious pie.

English is widely spoken in this former British colony. Sinhala is the official language, but Tamil is recognized as a national language. As one would expect in the Indian Ocean, the heat and humidity can wring you out like a wet sponge in a boxing match. Since the British were fond of colonizing tropical destinations with cooler hill stations, you can expect cool, moist weather up high. The average temperature along the coast is 80° F with little change all year. There are two cooling monsoon seasons, the southwest and the northeast monsoons, which dump about 100 inches of rain every year. The Sri Lankan currency is the rupee. Electricity is 230–240V/50Hz.

News from Sri Lanka

> http://www.is.lk/is/spot/
> http://www.lankapage.com/

Links

> http://www.mtholyoke.edu/acad/intrel/srilanka.htm

Embassy Location and Registration

Updated information on travel and security within Sri Lanka is available at the U.S. embassy:

U.S. Embassy

> P.O. Box 106
> 210 Galle Road
> Colombo
> Tel.: [94] (1) 448007
> Fax: [94] (1) 437345
> http://www.usia.gov/posts/sri_lanka/

U.S. citizens are encouraged to register at the U.S. embassy upon arrival in Sri Lanka.

Embassy Locations

Canadian Embassy in Sri Lanka

> 6 Gregory's Road
> Cinnamon Gardens
> Colombo 7
> Tel.: [94] (1) 695841
> Postal address:
> P.O. Box 1006
> Colombo, Sri Lanka

Sri Lankan Embassy in Canada

> High Commission of the Democratic
> Socialist Republic of Sri Lanka
> 333 Laurier ave. West Suite #1204,
> Ottawa
> Ontario, Canada, K1P 1C1.
> Tel: (613) 233-8449
> Fax: (613) 238-8448
> http://infoweb.magi.com/~lankacom/

12/19/99	President Kumaratunga is injured in a suicide attack by a female attacker.
11/2/99	Strategically important town of Oddusudan is captured by Tigers.
3/7/99	Military captures large area in Wanni District.
1/25/98	Suicide bombing destroys Buddhist shrine in Temple of the Tooth.
5/13/97	Government offensive "Sure Victory" begins to establish land link with Jaffna.
7/18/96	Over 1,200 Sri Lankan soldiers are killed in Mullaitivu by Tamil Tigers.
1/31/96	Colombo blast kills nearly 100 people, injures 1,400. LTTE is believed to be responsible.
12/5/95	Jaffna falls to government forces.
10/17/95	Government offensive of the north begins.
5/1/93	Assassination of President Ranasinghe Premadasa.
9/4/92	Dasain (Hindu) festival.
6/13/90	The Liberation Tigers of Tamil Eelam (LTTE) launch a renewed offensive against Sri Lankan government forces by storming at least 24 police stations in northern and eastern Sri Lanka. Several hundred police officers are taken hostage and a number of them are later killed.
8/18/87	Grenade attack on Sri Lankan parliament. One legislator is killed.
7/29/87	Indo–Sri Lankan peace accords signed.
7/20/86	Sinhalese rioting.
5/14/85	Tamil separatists kill more than 150 people in an attack on a Buddhist shrine at Anuradhapura.
7/23/83	The killing of 13 Sri Lankan soldiers in an ambush by Tamil militants touches off widespread anti-Tamil violence that leaves as many as 2,000 Tamils dead and 100,000 homeless.
5/22/72	Republic Day. Also known as National Heroes' Day.
11/24/54	LTTE founder's birthday. Prabhakaran birthday is marked by the LTTE as "Heroes' Week," which also commemorates LTTE members who have died in battle.
2/4/48	Independence Day.
5/24/563 B.C.	Birth of Buddha.
1/14	Tamil Thai Pongal Day.

Tiger Time (Comparative history Tamils vs. Sinhalese))
http://www.tamilnet.com/timeline/#early

SRI LANKA

Khartoum

Sudan
★ ★ ★

Black Tide Rising

Sudan is not the largest country in Africa. It is actually two countries. There is the north, a dry arid, Islamic land; and there is the south, a lush, animist and Christian land of black-skinned Nilotes. But the SPLA (Sudan's People's Liberation Army) is slowly making its way up north, flowing around and over the northern garrisons like a black wave. There is also another tide that has not begun to rise. It is estimated that Sudan has oil reserves equal to Saudi Arabia.

Sudan is cursed not only by poverty (a per capita income of only US$330), its size (it is the largest country in Africa) and a history of fundamentalist leaders who declare Holy War on the West, but it is also crippled by its dubious distinction of straddling the uneasy and unmarked border between the arid Islamic Arab north and the lush, animistic black south. These two cultures have never dwelled in harmony, and, in Sudan, they never will. The two tribes continue to battle, as the north persists in imposing its political will on the tribal south.

Sudan is 70 percent Muslim, 20 percent animist and 5 percent Christian—a bad mix on any continent. Ethnically, it's an even nastier brew: Sudan is 52 percent

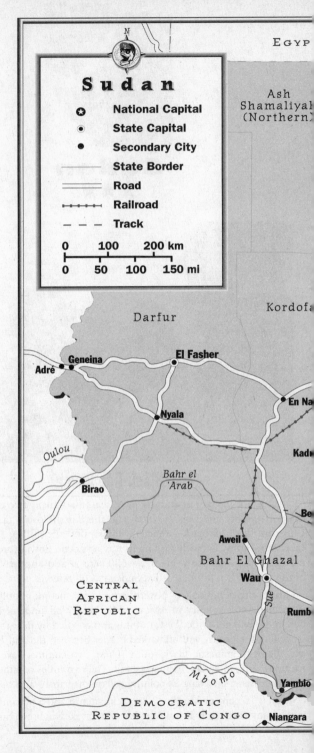

Lake
Nasser

Wadi Halfa

"Hala'ib Triangle"

Halaib

Administrative
Boundary

Dunqunab

Red
Sea

Ash
Sharqiyah
(Eastern)

Port Sudan

Suakin

Dongola

Karima

Haiya

Ed Damer   'Atbarah

Atbarah

ERITREA

Khartoum

Omdurman   Halfa' el
Gadida

Ak' ordat

Khartoum

Kassala   Teseney

Blue Nile

Wad Medani
Al Qadarif

Tekeze

Ed Dueim

Sennar

Obeid

Kosti   Al Awsat
(Central)

Atbara

El Jebelein   White Nile

Dinder

Gonder

Ed Damazin   Rosieres
Dam

T'ana
Hayk'

Kurmuk   ETHIOPIA

Debre
Mark'os

Asosa

Malakal   Sobat

Nek' emte

Upper Nile   Baro

Qanat Jungali Canal
(Construction
Halted)

Gore

Jima

Akobbo

Omo   Awasa

Jebel

Pibor Post

onglei   Kangen

Bor

Equatoria

Juba   Lake
Turkana

Administrative
Boundary

ei

Nimule

black, 39 percent Arab and 6 percent Beja. The hatred between the north and south has killed more than 500,000 people and driven 4.5 million others from their homes. One million have starved to death.

Even the rebel factions are known for their intolerance of each other. They wage warfare against each other, using starvation and terror as weapons of war. The SPLA rebel factions have been known to murder international aid workers and will not even guarantee safe passage for relief aircraft in case they may be providing food or medicine for enemy factions.

Since Iran has 21 years left on its leases of bases in Port Sudan and Suakin, there are thousands of Iranian soldiers stationed and training in Sudan. There is also an Iranian-funded radio station based in Port Sudan that broadcasts Islamic and Iranian propaganda to Egypt and other Arab countries. Sudan's strategic position and its holy alliance with Iran give it a powerful presence in the Red Sea and the Horn of Africa. Iran's recent meddling, and the resultant civil war in nearby Yemen, might provide a good reason to dust off the domino theory formerly applied to Southeast Asia.

Iran pays its new friend with oil and military supplies, while it receives strategic real estate and full cooperation from Sudan. Sudan also has new lethal exports to pay its militant friend: murder and mayhem.

Some side effects of this new export business include the terrorist attack on the World Trade Center in New York, the murders of more than 210 of the Algerian defense forces by Algerian fundamentalist groups and the continuing attacks on tourists and officials in Egypt. Although a Muslim country, Egypt is considered too soft on Israel and becoming too Westernized.

Since Sudan's independence in 1954, there has been a succession of military leaders and little relief from overwhelming poverty. In 1972, the Addis Ababa accord gave the south limited autonomy (an oxymoron) that ended the war against the Anyana guerrilla movement. But in the early 1980s, the SPLA came into being to fight the same battle. In 1984, Islamic law was introduced and the SPLA began fighting in earnest. The SPLA was supported by Cuba, Ethiopia, Libya and, strangely, by Israel. In 1985 Nimeiri's regime was overthrown in a coup and democratic elections were held. "Democracy" lasted until yet another coup in 1989 brought in the current ruler, General Omar Hassan Ahmad al-Bashir, in June of that year.

The Ethiopians have had their hands in the pie since November of 1987. Khartoum has also sought the assistance of Iran and Libya, including MiG-25s flown by Libyans. Even Iraq and the PLO (Palestine Liberation Organization) lent a hand by flying bombing missions over the south.

Ethiopia hasn't meddled in Sudan's affairs since the ouster of Mengistu, allowing the SPLA to go on a roll. They almost took the city of Juba in the spring of 1989, when a factional group led by Garang's second in command, Riek Machar, created SPLA/United. The two southern factions began to battle each other. In 1993, the two southern SPLA groups called a truce after killing thousands of each other's members. The CIA is busy working to get the two sides to kiss and make up.

The Islamic fundamentalist military government of al-Bashir finally launched its long-awaited offensive against the rebel SPLA in February 1994 in an effort to end the 25-year civil war. Tens of thousands of refugees have fled to the Ugandan border.

Today, southern Sudan south of Malakal is controlled by the SPLA, with the exception of the city of Juba and a half-dozen Sudanese army strongholds. But the government positions are isolated and have been cut off from Khartoum. Under the constant psychological pressure of imminent attack, they man their trenches and watch their food and medical supplies shrink by the day. By containing the Sudanese army units with relatively small numbers of men, SPLA leader John Garang can marshall his forces and supplies for the eventual assaults on the strategic garrisons of Juba and Wau. He is in no rush to do so; the longer he waits, the weaker his forces become.

Garang's chunk of real estate in the south is rich in gold, hardwood, cotton, tea, coffee and tobacco. The fertility of the soil is such that even during the height of the war, farmers sympathetic to the SPLA were able to feed the guerrillas with surpluses of rice, corn, sorghum, goats and cattle.

Meanwhile, in the northeast, the National Democratic Alliance is threatening the crucial road and rail links to Port Sudan. In Sudan's central-eastern region, the NDA is within striking distance of the hydroelectric dam at Damazine, the source of 80 percent of Khartoum's power. The NIF has not publicly admitted to losing any ground.

Sudan was formerly perhaps the largest recipient of Western aid, but most of that was cut off in 1991, after the government supported Saddam Hussein's efforts in the Gulf War. The Sudanese people now only receive emergency aid from outside relief agencies. Aid workers experience delays regarding travel permits and visas, and sometimes are arrested.

Only Islamic agencies are allowed to operate in government-occupied areas of the south, since the government claims many Western groups are fronts for Christian missionary work or intelligence-gathering. Dawa Islamia, the largest Islamic aid agency, with close links to the government, withholds food from Christian and animist Southerners unless they convert to Islam.

Sudan has been expelled from the World Bank, suspended from the IMF (and likely to become the first country to be thrown out of the International Monetary Fund entirely since the fund was created) and kicked out of both the Arab Monetary Fund and Arab Fund for Economic and Social Development. Sudanese experience 100 percent inflation per year.

Sudan is a big, bad, ugly place with a belligerent, extreme Islamic government hell-bent on choking the entire country under Islam's shroud. Khartoum is Terrorist Central. The country is one massive training camp for suicide bombers, hijackers, assassins, car bombers, grenade chuckers and synagogue saboteurs. Three guys who were involved in the plot to assassinate Egyptian President Mubarak are in Sudan getting their hair cut and nails done and watching the V Channel, despite an OAU call for the government to hand over the thugs. In all, there are an estimated 15,000 militants living or training in Sudan. This Allah's hornet nest hasn't gone unnoticed by the UN, though, who slapped diplomatic and travel sanctions on Khartoum in April 1997.

SUDAN

The Khartoum government has had its work cut out for it keeping the lid on the insurgent SPLA, whose numbers have swelled while chalking up battlefield wins in the south and east of Sudan in 1997 with CIA assistance. The mainly-Christian SPLA, through the efforts of the American covert intelligence community, has gotten an overhaul in recent months. Its warlord-style commanders have been diced from the ranks. Egypt, Eritrea, Uganda and Ethiopia have also boosted the SPLA's capacity to out-muscle Sudanese troops. The SPLA has teamed up with another rebel group, the National Democratic Alliance (NDA)—which includes the Beja Congress Armed Forces—and their joint offensives have overrun army garrisons in a drive west-ward from Ethiopia and Eritrea. These joint operations have posed the greatest threat to the Khartoum regime to date.

The NDA—based in Asmara, Eritrea—is moving to cut off Khartoum's access to the Red Sea. They've captured some towns in the east and pose a threat to hydroelectric projects in both Roseires and Kassala. A number of Sudanese opposition groups, with CIA support, are training their forces at camps in Eritrea. It is expected all of the camps will soon be united under the command of the NDA's leader, General Fathi Ahmed Ali. Eritrea makes no secret of its support for the rebels. Asmara cut ties with Khartoum in December 1994. To rub it in Sudan leader Omar al-Bashir's face, Eritrea gave the former Sudanese embassy to Sudanese rebels for use as a headquarters.

As he has done in other of the world's nastiest places, ex-prez Jimmy Carter has been bro-kering broken knuckles between Sudan's bullies. He doctored a brief cease-fire in 1995 and got four insurgent groups to bite his carrot in April 1997. The four southern groups—fresh with a surprisingly decent 501K package, including limited autonomy, rights to a secession referen-dum and permission to keep their guns—then formed an alliance, the Southern Sudan Defense Forces (SSDF), to help off the SPLA. We're not sure what kind of wrist-slapping Carter got by the CIA when he got home. As *DP* goes to press there is a pissing contest going on between islamist Turabi and President Bashir. Bashir is tired of fighting religious inspired wars with Eritrea, Uganda and in the south.

Dr. Hassan Abdullah al-Turabi

This is the man pulling the strings. Intelligent, well-educated and determined to be the first guy on his block to have his own fundamentalist state. He has described himself as being the symbol of a new movement that will change the history of humanity. His goal is to unify the billion or so Muslims under one guiding theocratic government. He was educated in London and earned his doctorate at Sorbonne in 1964. Five years later, he became leader of what was then a small and fanatical group of religious nuts. Turabi became the head of the Muslim Brotherhood, only to be banished from Sudan less than a month later, when General Nimeiri's Marxist coup made Turabi's style of religion out of style. Saudi Arabia took him in and the Brotherhood took hold among the 350,000 professional Sudanese working in oil-rich but skills-poor Saudia Arabia. They provided a source of funds, which Turabi used to send the brightest Sudanese to Western universities to get their Ph.D.s. The Brotherhood was busy turning out doctors, lawyers, writers and teachers, who would then take the message of Islam back to other Muslim countries. They created the Islamic African Relief Fund (now the Islamic Relief Association) to help with the millions of African refugees in sub-Saharan Africa. In the mid-1970s, they created Faisal Islamic Bank to handle the deposits of expat workers in the Gulf States. Islamic banks charge no interest, pay no interest and share profits with their depositors. The bank made loans to small businessmen, taxi drivers and shopkeepers.

After building a strong financial and political base from Saudi Arabia, Turabi returned to Sudan in 1977 as attorney general under Nimeiri's program of national reconciliation with former enemies. In 1983, Nimeiri declared *Shari'a*, or Islamic law, after a particularly vivid dream. Turabi was not the force behind the change. Although Turabi is extreme in his long-term plans, he is a moderate in affecting change.

The dramatic changeover did not affect the political climate as much as it influenced the financial health of Sudan. Nimeiri instituted the 354-day year, and taxes were abolished and replaced with voluntary tithing. Interest was abolished, and the resultant loss of revenue and fiscal chaos plunged Sudan into bankruptcy. Sudan was US$8 billion in the hole and sinking fast. When the government couldn't cut a check for US$250 million, they went into default with the IMF. By March 1985, Nimeiri blamed the country's slide into debt on the Islamic laws now ostensibly enforced by Turabi. Leaders of the Muslim Brotherhood were removed from political office, and Turabi was put in jail. Three months later, Nimeiri was ousted in a coup, and the first thing General Siwar el-Dahab did was dispatch a plane to fly Turabi back from prison to Khartoum. By then, Turabi was head of the National Islamic Front, originally an opposition party. But Turabi, once again, became attorney general. The Muslim Brotherhood was welcomed back into politics.

http://www.turabi.com
http://msanews.mynet.net/Scholars/Turabi/
http://www.dm.net.lb/rdl/1909/tourabi.htm

Lieutenant General Omar Hassan Ahmad al-Bashir

Al-Bashir was reelected as president in a fraud-tainted, "supervised" election March 23, 1996. He is the leader of the 15-member National Salvation Revolutionary Council, a junta comprised entirely of military officers. Reigning in a state of emergency and with a suspending constitution, al-Bashir has brought Sudan into the swelling ranks of despot-ruled countries in Africa. There have been only three periods of civilian rule since 1955. He continues to appoint National Islamic Front (NIF) loyalists, though more for their religious zeal than political skills. The NIF leader Dr. Hassan Abdullah al-Turabi was the minister of justice and attorney general under Major General Gaafar Mohamed Nimeiri and was the architect of both the 1983 and 1991 versions of *Shari'a* (or Islamic law). Before the new federal structure was introduced, *Shari'a* only applied to administrative and civil cases and not to criminal cases. The first victim of the new *Shari'a* was a Christian southern Sudanese petty thief, whose punishment was the "cross-amputation" of his right hand and left foot. Nimeiri was said to have fainted while attending his first amputation. Al-Bashir is not so squeamish about carrying out the wishes of al-Turabi's NIF. He is busy battling the 55,000 or so armed Southerners with his 68,000 soldiers. Iran's largesse in providing arms to al-Bashir is considerable, and there is circumstantial evidence that Iranian *mujahedin* in the guise of volunteers are serving with the Sudanese army. Iraq has also sent arms and technicians. China, with large oil concessions in the south, is also providing Khartoum with guns at bargain-basement prices. Drop al-Bashir a line at:

Lt. General Omar Hassan al-Bashir
People's Palace
P.O. Box 281
Khartoum, Sudan

Sudanese People's Liberation Army (SPLA)

Like the Shilluk and the Nuer, the Dinka are Nilotes, perhaps the tallest, blackest people in the world. For centuries, the Muslim north raided them for slaves, concubines, wives. For decades, they have been so ravaged by venereal disease that many clans are almost totally barren. When we drove overland from Malakal to the heart of the Sudd at Bor, warriors from a barren Nuer village raided a Shilluk village, carrying off several girls.

The minimum demands of the SPLA are for the abolition of Islamic Shari'a law, introduced by Bashir, and the creation of a new constitution. The breakaway faction of the SPLA is calling for the complete independence of southern Sudan. The SPLA is headed by Dr. John Garang de Mabior, a former Sudanese army colonel. He is a graduate of the Infantry Officers Advanced Course at Fort Benning, Georgia, and has a Ph.D. earned while stateside. Some see him as the next president of Sudan.

Garang's original job was to fight the rebels, but he ended up joining them instead. He worked his way to the top of the SPLA, mostly because he was on very close terms with Ethiopia's Lieutenant General Haile Mengistu Mariam. He feels that the simplistic principle of Muslim against Christian and black against Arab is too Western in concept. It is simply a matter of discrimination, which gets in the way of economic development and political power—a *raison d'être* echoed by German mercenary Rolf Steiner, who helped the Anya in the 1970s and was tortured, tried and imprisoned for his troubles. The current war is about life for the south not about death for the north. Iran is pushing Sudan relentlessly to create a fundamentalist Islamic state. The fact that the black Africans of the south predate the Muslims of the north is immaterial. The SPLA armed forces are estimated to number 55,000. Support, even clandestine training in the bush, has come from Israel and Ethiopia. Garang is chummy with Ugandan president Museveni, who has allowed SPLA movement on the Ugandan side of the border.

Sudan may have petroleum reserves nearing those of Saudi Arabia. Western concessionaires who previously flipped the SPLA the bird when it warned against collaboration with Khartoum, are now deeply worried about losing their investments, while those previously uninvolved are actively wooing Garang.

The SPLA currently controls five regions in the south where it maintains civil authority. They get weapons and support from Ethiopia and Eritrea. Sudanese rebels train in Eritrea. Following massive gains by the SPLA in 1997, southern Sudanese refugees in neighboring Kenya, Uganda, Congo and Central African Republic are returning to their homes en masse. Journalists or travelers need travel permits from the SPLA if they want to travel in the southern areas.

A peace accord was signed with the Lam Akol, SPLA-United Faction in April 1997, six other groups signed a peace agreement with the government. Akol's group is small group comprised of Shuluk tribesmen and their homeland is sitting on giant oil reserves.

The SPLA led by Garang is the last hold out.

The SPLA maintains offices in London, Washington, Asmara and Addis Ababa. You, too, can get the scoop but don't count on a well planned trip to front:

New Sudan Online
http://members.aol.com/NewSudan/Online.html
E-mail: NewSudan@aol.com

SPLA London
Tel.: 0171-209-5859

SPLA Asmara
Tel.: 29-11-181114
The press officer for the SPLA here is Yasir Kharman. The office occupies the former Sudanese embassy.

SPLA Addis Ababa
Tel.: 201394

Free South Sudan (not affiliated)
http://www.geocities.com/CapitolHill/Senate/4117/

Background
http://www.yasin.dircon.co.uk/sudan/whois/spla.htm

National Democratic Alliance (NDA)

The NDA is an awkward coalition between the SPLA and eight Muslim-based parties: the DUP, Umma, Legitimate Command, the Beja Congress, Alliance of Trade Unions, Alliance of Forces, the Federal Party and the Communist Party, all of which not only supported the imposition of Shari'a on the south, but also opposed southern autonomy or secession prior to the 1989 coup. For the Muslim members, many of whom were jailed or exiled by the NIF, the alliance gives them military muscle. Given that the Prophet Mohamed forbade Muslims fighting Muslims, the alliance provides the SPLA with a crucial shield against the involvement of most Muslim countries—Iran and Iraq being the exceptions—on the side of Khartoum in its declared jihad against the infidel southerners. The SPLA's stunning military success in 1997 also prompted mass defections of Muslim Popular Defense Force units to John Garang. Inasmuch as the SPLA (under the banner of the "New Sudan Brigade") provides over 95 percent of the NDA combatants, Garang heads the Joint Military Command of the NDA. His growing popularity and military might saw him named at a recent NDA conference in Asmara as the possible next president of all Sudan.

The National Democratic Alliance Headquarter

Asmara Eritrea
Tel.: +2911-127641
Fax.: +2911-127632

National Democratic Alliance Secretary General Office (UK)

Tel.: +44-1344-874123
Fax.: +44-1344-628077
E-Mail: aelmahdi@cygnet.co.uk

National Democratic Alliance Secretary General Office (Egypt)

Tel.: +202-5919408
Fax.: +202- 5932908, +202-2715979

NDA Web Page

http://www.umma.org/nda/index.htm

Good Links Page

http://www.safsudan.com/history.htm

Sudanese Alliance Forces

Based in Ethiopia and Eritrea and fighting against the National Islamic Front for a secular government.

Mr.Abdel Aziz Dafaalla Eritrea-asmara
USA: (703) 329-0560,
Canada: (905) 272-0819
Fax: 905 272 4760
E-mail: tali@chass.utoronto.ca.
Tel./fax: 002911127539
http://www.safsudan.com/saf.htm

The Iqhwan

The Muslim Brothers, the Iqhwan, in conversation simply *aqhi*, "brothers," the Arab world's oldest Islamic party, was founded in Egypt in 1928 and today is a force in Syria, Jordan and the Sudan. Trying to use his riveting personality to transform Egypt, Nasser banned them as reactionary. Under fire from the Nasserite left, Sadat brought it back to legal life as a counterweight. Today, Hosni Mubarak uses them as a foil to parry the Islamic radicals bearing down on his regime; he pressures them to renounce terror, and he makes sure the favors due Islam either go their way or the way they favor.

http://www.warwick.ac.uk/~suaaf/im.html

Uncle Osama's slightly used, low mileage slaves

Apparently bin Laden, according to the Sunday Telegraph, is snapping up deals on small children from the LRA and using them to pick marijuana on his farms in Nile valley just north of Khartoum. He also has large sunflower plantations worked by Sudanese slaves. Apparently bin Laden's boys pay one AK for every healthy young'un–Kony had complained that he had been cheated once, only getting 98 guns for 100 kids. The young Ugandan children are snatched by the LRA and then marched to Jabelin, Kony's HQ in the southern Sudan. Many of the girls are sent to Nsitu camp, 15 miles off Juba, where they are sold to Arab slavetraders. The children are sold and then flown out of Juba to their new owners. Kony's camp is supposedly just one of 17 terrorist training camps in Sudan. The LRA is an Acholi group that gets its leadership from Gulu. According to politician Betty Bigombe, who talked to Kony in 1994, Kony said, "Most of my commanders have AIDS, and if it was not because God gave me the power to cure AIDS they would all be dead by now."

The LRA began when 21-year-old Acholi woman Alice Lakwena said she was possessed with the spirit of an Italian priest who worked in the region a century ago. They had minor successes at first but then realized that they were not bulletproof, were wiped out and Lakwena fled to Kenya. Her cousin Joseph Kony (born 1959) created the LRA.

Slaves

Yes Virginia, slavery still exists in the Mahgreb and Sudan. Slave traders like to strike during dry weather in carefully planned raids. The women and children are snatched and then sold off as domestics or cheap labor. Since 1995 over 11,000 slaves have been freed in Sudan by the Swiss based group Christian Solidarity. They buy women and children for around $50 a head, and then take them back to the south. They have bought back over 5,000 slaves since 1995. The United Nations Children's Fund says the practice of buying back slaves actually encourages the practice.

E-mail: Cos-int@csi-int.ch

The Nonplayers

The tall and muscular Nuba people of Sudan used to number nearly 1.5 million. The latest and best estimates say only 200,000 remain. Is it because of disease and pestilence? Hardly. Rather, they've been banished to "peace camps" by the government to keep them fighting in support of the separatists in the south–and evidently from propagating, as well.

A passport and a visa are required to enter Sudan. Both a standard and business visa cost U.S. citizens US$50 and allow for a stay of up to three months. The approval process takes three to four weeks, sometimes longer, as applicants must be approved by Khartoum. Travel is not permitted in the southern area of the country under SPLA control. However, according to a Sudan embassy spokeswoman, travel is permitted overland to Eritrea in the east. The Sudanese government recommends that malarial suppressants be taken and that yellow fever, cholera and meningitis vaccinations be administered. Visas are not issued to those who have previously traveled to Israel. Business visas require a letter from a sponsoring company in Sudan with full details on length of stay, financial responsibility and references in Sudan. All borders are open, but questionable people who enter in the south may experience problems.

Journalists have been known to enter Sudan from the village of Periang, 500 miles northwest of the Kenyan border. From there, it is about 100 miles into the Nuba Mountains and SPLA-controlled territory.

Others enter from Uganda to interview pro-SPLA groups and leaders without a passport or visa. There is a minor catch: You need travel permits from an SPLA representative to enter the "New Sudan."

Accessing Sudan from the south is dependent on aid organizations willing to provide transportation from Lokichogio in Kenya, or Adjumani, Moyo, Koboko in Uganda, something they are unlikely to do without seeing a letter of laissez passer from the SPLA. Bring cigarettes and small gifts, and be prepared to meet starvation and disease head-on. There is little to help you tell the difference between freedom fighters and bandits. Both may happily shoot you for your boots or supplies. Accessing the south from Khartoum is impossible, especially using a letter from the SPLA. You will be arrested, tried under every Islamic law known and jailed forever in the deepest, darkest dungeon in Islamdom.

The trip to the center of Khartoum from the airport is about 4 kilometers. Negotiate and write down the agreed-upon taxi fare on a piece of paper before you get into the cab. There is a surcharge after 10 P.M. Remember, before you use our taxi tip, that 73 percent of the population is illiterate, according to the World Bank. Those travelers who enter illegally will be prosecuted under Sudanese laws. Contact the Sudanese embassy for more information:

Embassy of the Republic of the Sudan

2210 Massachusetts Avenue NW
Washington, DC 20008
Tel.: (202) 338-8565
Fax: (202) 667-2406
http://www.sudanembassyus.org/

Unforeseen circumstances, such as sandstorms (April and September) and electrical outages, may cause flight delays. The Khartoum Airport arrival and departure procedures are lengthy. Passengers should allow three hours for predeparture security and other processing procedures at the airport. There is little to no fuel in the south and vehicles must be hired from Uganda or other countries. Roads and much of the countryside is mined. Food is brought in through aid groups but there are times when no food is available. Outsiders may only travel in the south with the permission of the SRRA/SPLA. Visitors to the north will have visa's applications scrutinized by the government and may not be allowed permission to enter.

Government News Agency

http://www.sudanet.net/suna.htm

The South

Civil war persists in southern Sudan in the three provinces of Upper Nile, Bahr El Ghazal and Equatoria.

The West

Banditry and incursions by southern Sudanese rebels are common in western Sudan, particularly in Darfur province along the Chadian and Libyan borders, and in southern Kordofan province.

Khartoum

Western interests in Khartoum have been the target of terrorist acts several times in recent years.

Iraqi Military Sites

Iraqi missiles and fighter planes were positioned in Sudan to threaten the Saudi Arabian Port of Jeddah and Egypt's Aswan High Dam.

Terrorist Training Camps

Northern Sudan is considered very dangerous for Western travelers because of the large number of terrorist training bases here. There are Islamic fundamentalist and terrorist training camps outside Khartoum, along the coast and in other nameless places.

Black Gold, Canadian Tea

The SPLA want to capture or incapacitate the pipeline built by Canadian, Malaysian and Chinese concerns which now provides cash to the northern government. The Canadian wells formerly owned by Arakis (who wanted to hire mercenaries to protect them) pump out 150,000 barrels per day of crude oil.

http://www.talisman-energy.com/

Medicine Factories

The United States bombed the al-Shifa medicine factory in August 1998. After the owner decided to sue, the White House quietly unfroze $15 million of the Salah Idris' assets and sheepishly admits that maybe it made a mistake. Idris wants the United States to recover the $30 million it will cost to rebuild the pharmaceutical plant. The United States bombed the plant because they maintained it had links to bin Laden and manufactured the chemical used to make VX nerve gas. Idris has said the plant made medicines, including treatments for malaria and tuberculosis.

Politics

Their new constitution lifts a 10 year ban on party politics even welcoming former dictator Gaafar Numeiri after 14 years abroad. The United States still supports its allies of Ethiopia, Uganda, and Eritrea and Garang. The United States is also ramming Inter-Governmental Authority on Development (IGAD) designed to teach the southern Sudanese learn good governance (see IADP). They have also extended the Sudan Transitional Assistance for $6 million and will add more to the $100 million they provide in food supplies.

Dinner Parties

It is against the law in Sudan to have a gathering of more than four people at one time, making pick-up basketball games and AA meetings a real problem here.

Hassles with Local Police

Travelers to the north are required to register with police headquarters within three days of arrival. Travelers must obtain police permission before moving to another location in Sudan and register with police within 24 hours of arrival at the new location. These regulations are strictly enforced. Even with proper documentation, travelers in Sudan have been subjected to delays and detentions by Sudan's security forces, especially when traveling outside Khartoum. Authorities expect roadblocks to be heeded.

Medical facilities are as scarce as literate Sudanese outside Khartoum. Years ago the country had 158 hospitals with a total capacity of 17,205 beds. There were 220 health centers, 887 dispensaries, 1,619 dressing stations and 1,095 primary healthcare units. Although there were 2,122 physicians and 12,871 nurses working in the country, you can expect less than one doctor and nine hospital beds per 10,000 people. Don't expect squat in the rebel-held south. Some healthcare is provided free of charge through any NGOs, but keep in mind the north loves to bomb hospitals (they use that nice red X to line up on before they kick the 500 pounders out the back of the Antonovs. Travelers entering Egypt from Sudan will need to produce either a certificate of vaccination against yellow fever or a location certificate showing that they have not been in a yellow fever area. A valid cholera certificate is required of travelers arriving from infected areas.

Malaria, typhoid, rabies and polio are endemic. Bilharzia is also present, and visitors should stay out of slow-moving freshwater. Other prominent diseases include amoebic and bacterial dysentery, cerebral malaria, giardiasis (a hemorrhagic fever similar to Ebola) and guinea worm. The latter affliction is quite nasty. The eggs of the worm are ingested through river water. After hatching, the larvae cruise the blood system until finding a suitable home, where they mature and proceed to eat their way out of the body.

The arid north of Sudan is mainly desert with greener, agricultural areas on the banks of the Nile. Crops can only be grown during the rainy season (July to September). The south is mainly swamp and tropical jungle. The most important features are the White and the Blue Nile. The Blue Nile is prone to severe flooding. Mid-April to the end of June is the hot, dry season with temperatures above 110°F.

The official language is Arabic, but English is widely understood. The government is trying to eradicate the use of colonial-tainted English as part of its Islamification. Ta Bedawie and Nubian are also spoken, as are dialects of the Nilotic, Nilo-Hamitic and Sudanic languages. Evening meals are served around 10 P.M. The staple diet is *fool* (beans, or *dura*) eaten with vegetables. Disruptions of water and electricity are frequent. Telecommunications are slow and often impossible.

The strict Islamic code (*Shari'a*) has been in force since 1991.

Embassy Locations

The U.S. Embassy is located at *Shari'a Ali Abdul Latif* in the capital city of Khartoum. The mailing address is *P.O. Box 699, or APO AE 09829. Tel.: 74700 and 74611*. The work week is Sunday through Thursday. However, at press time, the embassy was closed due to the continuing turmoil. Visa information is at: *http://www.sudanembassyus.org/frvisa.html*

Other Web Resources

Government of Sudan
 http://www.columbia.edu/~tm146/sudan.html
Sudan.net
 http://www.sudan.net/

Sudan Home Page
   http://www.yasin.dircon.co.uk/sudan/
Arabnet
   http://www.arab.net/sudan/sudan_contents.html

1/29/00	President Omar Hassan Al-Bashir refuses to lift month-long state of emergency.
12/12/99	The President dissolves parliment and declares a three-month state of emergency. The move is designed to reduce the influence of Hassomal-Turabi.
7/20/98	Al-Shifa chemical plant is bombed by the United States. Later it is admitted that they might have made a mistake.
6/30/89	A group of officers led by general Omar al-Bashir overthrows the government of Sadiq Mahdi.
4/15/86	A U.S. embassy communicator is shot and wounded while riding home from the embassy in Khartoum. The shooting is believed to be in retaliation for U.S. air raids on Libya earlier in the day.
5/16/83	Founding of the SPLM/SPLA (The Sudanese People's Liberation Movement/Army).
1973	The current civil war begins as a small mutiny at a remote army garrison in southern Sudan.
3/1/73	U.S. Ambassador Cleo Noel and Deputy Chief of Mission George Moore are assassinated in Khartoum during the seizure of the Saudi embassy.
3/3/72	Anniversary of the Addis Ababa accords that ended the insurgency against the central government and granted southern Sudan wide regional autonomy on internal matters.
7/22/71	Anti-communist military elements loyal to Gaafar Nimeiri lead a successful countercoup and bring him to power several days after a coup by the Sudan Communist Party.
6/9/69	The south declare independence.
5/25/63	The Organization of African Unity is founded. The day is celebrated as Africa Freedom Day. The OAU is organized to promote unity and cooperation among African states.
1/1/56	Independence Day.

In a Dangerous Place: Southern Sudan

The All Metal Shell Casing Band

Its about three hours to the front lines and the protocol here dictates getting permission from the commander and then gathering up a crowd of well armed polite fellows who stare at you dispassionately as they bob and weave in the back of the pickup truck. They look like they are just along for the ride but they're here to make sure I don't get shot. This is the second time they've taken this area, and not everybody is thrilled with the SPLA's presence. My battered white Toyota has also been pressed into service as a low-budget FedEx since we spend a lot of time dropping off letters and picking up messages. There is no other truck or car on the road. Not good if they mine the roads.

Pickup surfing in the bed of our clanging truck, you get a few nice vistas of the blue-on-blue *jebels* (rock mountains) or granite outcroppings that add a dramatic perspective to the rolling green landscape.

Up close, everything is burnt from shell fire, grass clearing or air attacks. The scenery from the Juba road is low-budget-game drive style, without the game but with dozens of twisted blown up trucks along the sides. Lots of them. I start taking pictures at the tenth one and stop at about thirty. They are simply place markers here. They look liked carcasses picked by vultures. In fact they are picked cleaner than the human skeletons I am about to see.

We keep a sharp watch out for armed men. What's that up ahead? Troops! Animals? Finally. A colobus monkey and a herd of deer bolt accross the road, probably trying to find a way out of this shell-shocked hell.

My adventure watch from Dubai tells me its 39°C, or over 100°F for the more genteel. Hot enough to make your skin turn into a sponge from the sweat, and dry enough to parch you and make you weak after just ten minutes. Not as hot as the north, I am told, but well beyond comfortable. Not a place I would want to fight a protracted bush war.

The road is not bad. Typical red African dirt with the frequent "elephant holes" where the big trucks plow through and dig pits that strangle small pickups. We are lucky it is hot—that means it is dry.

The *jebels* are interesting, great towering chunks of solid-black granite. Almost the same black color and anamorphically exaggerated vertical perspective as the stork-like Dinkas that we pass walking the road. In some places there are the remnants of perfectly spaced experimental teak forests, the small scrawny type with big leaves, lots of thorny bushes and bright green spears of grass poking through charred black ground.

Just before we arrive at the front, we give a lift to a local demining team. My driver complains about his springs. I worry that they are just trying to skip checking the road ahead. They have been inspecting the road we are on for mines. I feel better since we were the first and only vehicle on this road this morning and the carcasses of twisted trucks are enough of a reminder to keep me alert.

I ask the group of five deminers where their equipment is. A man holds up a rusty-metal rod with a pointed end. Oh boy.

I ask him if he has more equipment. He says, "We have very many of these," and holds his stick up again. I decide to start looking for fresh dirt patches on the road.

Every check subjects us to a lengthy discussion on our purpose and permission. They actually have little swinging barriers on strings at each village. They act as if we might be a bus tour that somehow lost its way on an archeology trip. At one post I am rebuked by an angry armed, flip-flopped soldier for taking pictures, and then apologized to profusely for his outburst. I wonder what I was before that was so odious?

We are met at the front line by a man blowing an old shell casing with a hole. This seems to be what they do every time we roll by a troop emplacement. It's not the monotonal tooting that's interesting, it's the bloodshot, bugged-out eyes and fur helmet he is wearing that gets my attention. The yellowed-plastic welding goggles are a nice touch, too. He says this flute is what he plays to scare the enemy away. "When they attack I play this music and they all run away." He also has a very large-caliber antiaircraft gun lowered to ground level that might help out a bit. But who am I to argue?

The commander welcomes me into his cool thatch HQ. We are with the second brigade in sector 2. He has an old shortwave radio and a large paperback Bible on his very neat desk. He and his second-in-command are ex-seminarians. They remind me of polite school boys. Their official communiqués are written on schoolbook paper, each carefully written out in longhand and then laboriously and neatly stamped. I glance at his folder: a polite request for more ammunition, letters explaining politely why certain soldiers need to travel to different places. Such a polite war.

They are positioned south of Juba. He and his men have been here since March of last year. He is impatient to attack , but there are over 670,000 people in Juba and they are worried about local casualties when they attack. Right now they shell each other's front lines. Yesterday they had an exchange of artillery, and the day before they captured a supply truck. The SPLA had taken Juba before, and were pushed out when one of their key commanders defected to the north. Back then the people were eating lily pads and rats. Win or lose, the south really doesn't have a choice. If they don't fight this war the Arabs will simply starve or kill the southern people off. Asked if he has any message for the outside world, the commander asks formally, as if I could grant his wish, "Please ask the international community to put pressure on the Sudanese to stop using these Antonovs against our innocent civilians."

The Antonov (a bomber that drones overhead, either taking pictures, transporting material or dropping bombs) has been a dark nemesis since we arrived. There has been one circling today. On the menu today is water, so the commander passes out metal cups and asks us to drink up.

After our chat, a frontline tour is arranged. The perimeter is a jagged slit trench with round shooting positions. Their trenches encircle the camp and are manned by boys and men who look too thin to actually be real. They wear a collection of Eastern bloc uniforms that stop just below their knees and hang in tatters. Some wear berets, others wear East German forage hats and others go bareheaded. As the commander and I walk past each installation, they come to attention or man their weapons fiercely.

There is no electricity other than a single solar panel to power the radio, no structures other than mud bandas, no vehicles except blown-up ones used to support other structures, no food stores, just old Russian- and Chinese-made guns and raggedy soldiers either following us around or standing at an uneasy attention.

The soldiers sleep on grass mats in front of their foxhole; they eat food given to them by the locals; and they have even put their own crops in, but there has been no rain this year and they have received no seeds to plant for the rainy season. The commander asks why our president didn't visit us on his last tour. "We are a rich country and we will pay for the arms when we win. Why don't you send us 40 F-15s? We would be very happy. You please write that down and ask for us."

Our conversation is halted mid-sentence as the soldiers do that weird head cock, like a dog listening. The Antonov. I almost forgot. Naturally, I can't hear it, but they can. The blast from the antiaircraft shots smack me in the face. Even though my video camera is pointing right at the big gun about 20 yards away, I don't figure it out until I hear the ke-clang, ke-clang, ke-clang of the ejected shells.

The antiaircraft boys decided to let the bomber have it with their 37 mm carriage- mounted antiaircraft gun. The gun makes a hell of a noise, and you can faintly hear the shells exploding in the sky. The commander yells at them to stop firing since they look like a dog chasing its tail the way they are whirling around. It looked like they were riding a very loud carnival ride. They'll get him next time the Commander promises me. He apologizes for the interruption, and we continue our tour around the perimeter.

We pass the position of my flute-blowing, goggle-wearing friend. He is wearing a good ol' boy straw hat decorated with what used to be a skunk. He puts on his game face and his eyeballs almost pop through the yellowed-plastic goggles. Thankfully his ammo feeder looks more sanguine. "Looking very serious," is the term they use to describe him. The second wacky guy is a too-tall Dinka dressed like Boba Fet with his bandoliers of heavy bullets, Russian tanker's helmet and machine gun.

They decide to play a little music for me. He expands his musical repertoire with a homemade lyre made from an ammunition case. He plays me an atonal song with lyrics that basically say what you would expect them to say, something like, "We'll kick your scrawny Muslim asses all the way to Juba."

The other fighters keep time by banging on ammunition cases and some fighters do that lazy Zairoise shuffle that passes for dancing here. The whole line starts weaving and shuffling to the beat and there I am in the middle of *Sudanese Bandstand*.

Back at Yei, the town looks like your typical looted, abandoned, war-torn film-set. It's too quiet. All the safes have been dragged into the street and hammered open. The people who are still here use transmission cases, engine blocks and rear differential casings as seats. All the furniture and wiring is stripped, and there is an impressive collection of gutted cars and land rovers outside the official government buildings. Commerce consists of tiny stalls with plastic bags of salt, packets of coffee and homegrown peanuts. There are also toothbrushes, lollipops and soap. There is a meat market and a few tea shops that consist of two kettles on a tiny stove and a collection of mismatched dirty glasses.

The soldiers hang around under the big mango trees and sit motionless. They wear earrings, nail polish, faded tee-shirts and flip-flops, "Because we are guerrillas, we wear sandals but when we take the country, we can all have shoes." The fighters that come out of the field have a cheap green tarp rolled up and slung over their backs with string.

I am invited to stay at the commissioner's house. Not really his house—his real house was burned and looted, and the official government house is also bombed by the Sudanese. It's also too close to the hospital that gets bombed on a regular basis.

The commissioner comes from the same tribe as Idi Amin, the Kakua. A round bowling-ball head on a round massive body, the commish is so black he glistens. When he opens his mouth to laugh a bright pink hole and white teeth appear.

He wanders around in his flip-flops and brightly colored towel every morning listening to the BBC, a toothbrush protruding from his lips at a jaunty angle. Then he carefully packs emblems of his position into his battered briefcase and walks the few hundred yards to his office.

The commish talks about "those fucking organizations," referring to the UN and NGOs. "They only bring food only for the Sudanese people in Uganda. When we took Yei they went back to their villages, some of them have their homes destroyed, many of the houses have been burnt? How can they live?"

His point is that he can't figure out why the aide organizations don't bring food to the people instead of creating refugee camps outside Sudan.

To make his point, he invites us to visit his former home. All the major buildings have been stripped and destroyed by the Arabs. Now he has no money so he asks America to send him money so he can rebuild his home. His office has a blown safe, no glass and is cool and dark. He makes sure I close the door behind me and he unpacks the tools of his trade. The commish keeps busy. He goes to work each day with his tiny desktop flag, his official stamp and a dried out stamp pad. He methodically handwrites communications on three-hole-punch-lined schoolpaper. He then rings a bell and a messenger enters and snaps to attention with an odd little step-up, handclasp to side and a click of the heels—British and straight out of Monty Python. The stiff, chin-up messenger does not do a silly walk when he leaves, but I have to remember to teach him one. Yei even has a financial administrator who is waiting for some money to administrate. Over the last year they have done a good job of setting up a government, even though there aren't that many people to govern.

Agostini is also a government official, the executive director of administration, whose office is completely bare except for an "in" and an "out" basket, both of which are empty. I don't ask how a Sudanese got an Italian name, and I don't ask what he does all day with an empty desk. He wants to know, "Where do the African-Americans live?" Anywhere they want I guess. "Everywhere?" He is incredulous. "You know all the people are all the same, but during the time of John Kennedy I heard they didn't want blacks." The administrator wants us to bring "Lewis" blue jeans and a shirt and a black cowboy hat. "A big one. If you do this I will be very happy to you."

Lunch is a big deal here. Everyone packs up slowly, and though there are no clocks, everyone manages to be sitting back at the commish's house at the same time. My little goat friend is smashed into bite-sized bits, and his intestines have been tied in knots and turned into stew along with the rest of his vitals. After lunch, our executive administrator friend wants to know where our whiskey is. "All Americans have whiskey," he protests when he finds out we don't have any. He tells us that it is very good that I stayed for lunch because the women killed and cooked the goat just for us. We talk about his favorite foods. He doesn't eat goat, but he likes raw mutton and chicken. His favorite? Bush rat, a large rodent they catch once in a while that he swears tastes just like chicken. The next time someone asks me what chicken tastes like. I'll say bush rat.

The next morning I am awakened by the sound of roosters, pots banging and spitting, mingled with the scratchy BBC radio report. It seems that the journalists have discovered that food is being used as a weapon in the war in Sudan. The northern government gives their approval, but the soldiers stop the convoys before they get to the people.

Outside, the commish is sitting holding court, as always, wrapped in his brightly colored towel with his red gel toothpaste and his dayglo green flip-flops. Listening to the BBC report, he reacts by saying, "The fucking Arabs don't want us. They just want the little ones so they can convert them. They want all the grownup ones dead. That is why they bomb us, starve us, kill us or drive us away." After breakfast I go for a walk through the small collection of bandas between the commish's house and the hospital. A young woman walks up to me and says very shyly and flatly, "Excuse me, sir. Can I talk to you? The Antonov bomber came here and dropped bombs on my house and killed my husband and small child. What shall I do?"

—**RYP**

Dushanbe

Tajikistan
★★★★

Tragikistan

Tajikistan is one of those "stan" places (like Afghanistan, Pakistan, etc.) we skip over in geography lessons. Its kissing cousins are Afghanistan (another stan-fabrication of a colonial power), Kyrgyzstan, Pakistan and Uzbekistan. Now Tajikistan acts as a lifeline to the beleaguered Afghan government under Ahmad Shah Massoud and a whipping boy for Mother Russia.

To say there is a civil war would assume that there are two clearly defined sides in a conflict. The truth is that in Tajikistan there is no solid definition—only that if a warlord doesn't like what the Russian-backed stooge of the week says, he fights back. You can always tell if a peace agreement is about to be signed by the number of bombs that go off in Dushanbe.

This beautifully mountainous, handsome-peopled but sparsely populated country is hard, ugly, deadly and controlled by tribes and clans. If space dictates simplification it could be said that the western third is lowland plain with most of the infrastructure and civilization while the country ascends in height and descends in civilized amenities towards the east. The borders are not marked because only

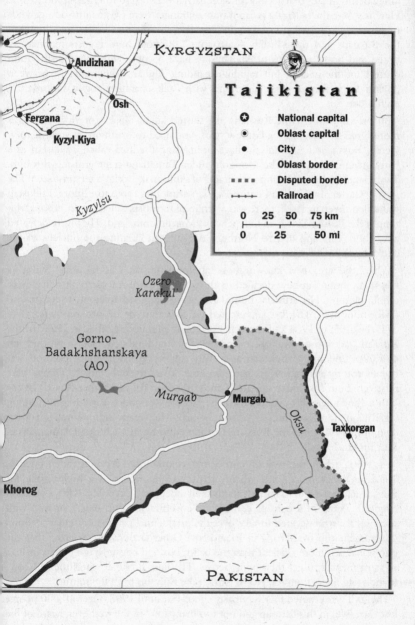

Afghan drug smugglers brave the narrow mountainous passes into its rough-and-tumble neighbors of Kyrgyzstan, Uzbekistan, Pakistan, China and Afghanistan.

The main geographical feature of Tajikistan is the Pamir, an almost impassable range of mountains that act as a physical barrier between southern Asia and Russia. Here is where the radiating Asian mountain ranges were twisted into a huge knot to create a vast wasteland of stark beauty. It is also the new buffer zone between the Russians and the Muslim "barbarians." Remote border posts manned by bored and brutal veterans of Afghanistan have become high speed distribution centers for the ancient but rapidly-expanding Afghan drug trade. In between buying drugs, they also fight skirmishes with Tajik separatists, rogue warlords and each other.

But if you thought the Russians just started killing Tajiks (or vice versa as is more often the case) in the last few years, you need to brush up on your history. China, Russia and Afghanistan have been using the area called Tajikistan as a battleground ever since the Mongols under Tamerlane came cruising through. Tamerlane's habit of making mountains of skulls make today's terrorist seem like Jimmy Carter. In 1717, an entire Russian army that came to explore Tajikistan was killed. Even in 1917, there was a group of terrorists called the *basmachis* who fought the Bolsheviks for an independent Muslim homeland. They were defeated after four years and fled to Northern Afghanistan creating the nucleus of the current Tajik rebellion.

When the area was known more appropriately as Central Asia, Stalin (a Georgian mountain boy) decided to chop his Southern real estate into five quasi ethnic clumps. His artificial boundaries were designed to lump together and divide minorities. The Russians created a Tajikistan to be an autonomous satellite of Uzbekistan in 1924 and then changed to a full union republic in 1929. In the Russian tradition of totally screwing up ethnic and indigenous history, they left 475,000 Tajiks in Uzbekistan and every important government position was usually run by a round-faced, hard drinking Soviet from the north. Things were relatively calm (or undocumented) under the iron fist of Mother Russia. In the '80s a fundamentalist group called the Islamic Resistance Party began pushing for Tajik nationalism and started to raise hell. They really didn't come into their own until 1990 when the Russians threatened to resettle Christian Armenians in Muslim Dushanbe.

In 1991, when the rest of post-Soviet central Asia declared independence, Tajikistan's lack of national wherewithal and importance as a buffer zone for Russia, delegated it to its current status as an independent republic. The population magically voted in a corrupt communist government. This didn't sit well with some locals, who decided to take over the presidential palace to install a coalition government run by Akbarshah Iskandarov. Other factions also realized that the gun was much more efficient than the ballot box and began to use bullets instead of stern memos to get their point across. The lines broke down as the Moscow-friendly old liners from the North battled the Kulyabis from the south.

The civil war erupted in a very nasty shoot-out until 1993. Over 40,000 people lost their lives in this flare-up and not too many folks in the west even heard of the massacre. The ethnic cleansing and precarious political structures opened the door to the Russian army who then stepped in to babysit their puppet ruler Imamali Rakhmanov (from the Kulyab district) and then proceeded to spank all the various warring factions. Seemingly blind to the history lesson dealt them in Afghanistan, Russia still views Tajikistan as a buffer zone and does not want nasty Islamic fundamentalists sneaking in to mess up their nice Moscow neighborhoods.

Tajikistan is a poor country where 90 percent of food and all fuel is donated by aid groups. The average wage is $5 a day and that's if you can find a job. Tajikistan is a low budget wasteland where a downsized Russian army can still afford to play the Great Game. Russia's army has also provided a high speed pipeline for heroin and hashish straight to Moscow via Spetnaz 'R' Us overnight military cargo service. The ruling clan is simply government de jour, but the Russians call the shots and pay a lot of bills here. For now the only tourist attractions are a ring of armed border forts manned by 25,000 Russian soldiers, weekly firefights with Afghan smugglers and Tajik rebels.

The Tajiks

It would be charitable to say that the Tajik Islamic Movement led by Sayid Abdullo Nuri represents the Tajiks in Tajikistan, but that would be overstating his importance. They want 40 percent control of the government, but they don't really represent all Tajiks.

His 2,000 or so rebels have been pounding away for 6 years (since the Soviet meltdown) at the Russian forts along the Afghanistan/Tajikistan border, and once in a while they lob a grenade in downtown Dushanbe, so the reporters don't have to travel so far to report the news. For now they are trying to make good on a peace treaty signed in May of 1997. An attractive option after President Rakhmanov survived an assassination attempt a month earlier. Nuri finally came to Dushanbe in September to kiss and make up. It seems his photo op was delayed by a wave of bombings. A peace agreement with Sayid Abdullo Nuri was signed after five years of exile. He will have about 560 fighters to make sure he stays alive in Dushanbe. They spent their nights wearing their headbands, large hunting knifes and AK dancing with the Russian whores in the courtyard of the Hotel Tajikistan.

The often Shia (some are Sunni) Muslim Tajiks are Persians originally from northern Afghanistan. They are Persians and consider themselves a superior race and have a millennium of cultural achievements to back it up. Their capital was Bukhara where some of Islam's brightest stars held court. Poets, philosophers, artists and calligraphers spread their skills throughout the Muslim world from here. There are about 5,000 Tajik fighters based in Northern Afghanistan. *DP*'s pal Ahmed Shah Massoud uses Tajikistan as a supply line, and is a hero to these folks, and will more than likely come to visit if the Taliban push him out of the Panshir valley. This could start the war going the other way. Tajiks are primarily Sunni Muslims with the Pamirs being Shia's. You can also find Tajiks in Uzbekistan (860,000), Kazakhstan (100,000) and the Xiajang region of China (30,000). For now, the Tajiks fight in four major groups that include The Democratic Front, The National Front and the following major groups.

Islamic Revival Party

About 2,000 fighters based in Kunduz, Afghanistan, Taloquan and Jalalabad, the IRP are supported and trained by Gulf state businessmen, Pakistani and Afghan fundamentalists,

Libya and Iran. Many trainers and support personnel are connected to Gulbuddin Hekmatyar's Jamaat-e-Islami and Pakistan's ISI. The IRP has a political office in Moscow.

Rebels 'r Us

Tajikistan is sort of the Wal-Mart for rebels. Iran, Osama and local warlords keep the market value up but they are cheaper to import than the Afghan trained ones. You can always pick up a few lean and mean fighters here for a little jihad. There is a group in Northern Tajikistan led by an Uzbek Islamist Juma Namangani, from the city of Namangan in the Fergana valley. He fled Uzbekistan to Tajikistan in the early 1990s to escape President Islam Karimov's clampdown on political and religious opposition, and became a field commander on the Islamic side in the Tajik civil war. If you look at a map of Tajikistan you'll notice how it hooks around the countries of Kyrgystan and Uzbekistan. This of course is not how the people, natural barriers or trade flow in the region. If you crack a history book you'll learn that the Tajiks (which are Persian in origin) created Khiva, Samarkhand and Bukara, the great cites of Islamic learning in what is the only tourist spot in Uzbekistan. Everyone from the Talibs to the Tajiks want it back. For now the Islamic rebels view Uzbekistan as being cut out of the same cloth as Russian and are waging war through direct and indirect means (through the Islamic Movement of Uzbekistan) while borders are bottled up tightly. There are also a number of Afghan Uzbeks (who fought under Dostum and Malik) who are looking for a little action.

The Russians

The Russians must have forgotten their history lessons and decided that Tajikistan is a lot easier to defend as a border than Afghanistan. (The first time the Russians came to Tajikistan in 1717, their entire army was massacred.) Maybe they didn't notice the mountains, nasty weather, hardened fighters and silly puppet government make for deadly politicians. The Russians spend about 3 billion rubles a year to keep 50 border posts open along a 900 km border with Afghanistan. The 25,000 troops include a number of Afghan veterans including OMON and Spetznaz commandos. The same folks who showed the Afghans how to get drugs into Europe without using camels. The Russians have about 200 T-72 battle tanks, 420 hard shell combat vehicles and artillery against a third as many rebels using cheap running shoes and beat up AKs. Considering the Russian draftees are offered $60 a month and three year contracts, it is not surprising that they are having a hard time finding grenade fodder to man the frozen border with Afghanistan. Local boys who volunteer can serve for only 6 months. If you have combat experience, you can be a contract soldier and serve 18 months for a lot more money. It is assumed that many Afghan vets (all the way to General level) actually choose Tajikistan because they can supplement their income with drug deals. There are about 150 contacts a year with rebels with a third ending up in firefights. The kill ratio is about 10 to 1 for the Russians with much of the activity occurring along the Pyandzh River at night. The towns of Pyandzh and the Kulyab region are the hottest.

When not selling weapons to Massoud the border guards like to shoot the rare Marco Polo sheep for food. (It'll cost you $20,000 for a hunting license if you want to bag one.)

The Pamiris (Ismailis)

The Pamiris barely survive in the high altitude valleys between the imposing peaks. Most have a hard time communicating with each other. The people are poor and in many cases destitute. Ninety percent of food is supplied by aid organizations and all fuel is brought in. Seems like just the place for a former playboy who was born in Switzerland and jet sets around the world to be a religious leader. The Pamiris are Ismailists who believe in a sect of Shia Islam, a religion that has no house of worship, icons, holy men or even holidays. Their leader is the Aga Khan, a direct descendant of Mohammed who keeps the Pamiris alive by the generosity of his Swiss based charity foundation. He is considered a living deity and his photograph is hung in every home. There are some 210,000 people with 45,000 arable acres, but little hope of any future improvement.

Aga Khan Foundation

1-3 Avenue de la Paix
P.O. Box 2369
1211 Geneva 2
Tel.: +41 22 909 7200
Fax: +41 22 909 7291
E-Mail: akfgva@atge.automail.com

Aga Khan Foundation, USA

1901 L Street, NW, Suite 700
Washington, DC 20036
Tel.: (202) 293-2537
Fax: (202) 785-1752;
E-mail: 71075.1561@compuserve.com
http://www.geneva.ch/AKF.htm

The Clans

Forget the Hatfields and McCoys, here you have the Pamiris from the Gorno-Badakhshan, the Leninabaders from the north, Kulyabis from the south, the Kurgan-Tyube, Garmis from east, Afghan drug smugglers, Tajik rebels from across the border and doped up Russian soldiers supplementing their paychecks. Some warlords are happy just to knock off a profitable business like the aluminum smelter such as Kadyr Abdullayev did in Tursunzode (west of Dushanbe). To make matters worse, the nearby Russian commander and his 200 soldiers, angered at Abdullayev's men stealing weapons from his garrison and tired of feuding warlords, disobeyed the President and shot their way into the town and wrested control away from Abdullayev and his rival.

Some, like Bakhram Sadirov (based in Kalainav, 52 miles east of Dushanbe), just snatch up 23 people (UN workers monitoring the cease fire, a government minister sent to negotiate a settlement and journalists covering the event) to help them in various negotiations; in this case to release his brother who was kidnapped by another warlord allied to the government. In short the political situation in Tajikistan is like having every NHL hockey team playing on the ice at the same time . . . using rocket launchers.

Although Tajikistan is officially part of Russia, you need specific permission on your visa to enter. These days travelers are allowed in, but it is still more of a journo spot. In the United States, visas for Tajikistan are issued by the Russian Embassy, Consular Division, *1825 Phelps Place NW, Washington, DC 20008, Tel.: (202) 939-8907,* or the Russian Consulates in New York, San Francisco or Seattle. For information about the country, you might also try the Tajik Mission to the UN, *East 67th Street, New York, NY 10021; Tel.: (212) 472-7645; Fax: (212) 628-0252.* Tajik visas granted by these offices are valid for a stay of five days. These visas are also valid in other Commonwealth of Independent States for five days, except in Uzbekistan, where they are valid for three days only for transiting to another country. Visas are required when you check in at a hotel. If travelers plan a longer stay, they may apply at the Ministry of Foreign Affairs for a longer visa. If you want to stay longer than 90 days you will need an AIDS test or supply a medical certificate. The Gorno-Badakhshan border requires a special advance permission. You can apply for a longer stay once in country. If you are bouncing back and forth between Uzbekistan, remember to get a double or multiple entrance Russian visa.

Also, you will need an exit visa to leave Tajikistan so whatever you said (or paid) to the nice immigration person may come back to haunt you on your way out. Worst case, there is the OVIR (immigration) office in Dushanbe that can try to iron things out. Road rats can try getting a visa at the Tajik embassy in Almaty in Kazakstan at *Ulista Emeleva 70, Tel.: [7] (3272) 611760, Fax: 610225.*

When airlines are going into Dushanbe you can take the six hour flight directly from London to Dushanbe via Tajikistan Airlines *(TIA, 154 Horn Lane, London, W3 6PG Tel.: (0181) 993-8885, Fax: 993-7504)* on Sunday and from Moscow about every second day. There is also a 1.5

hour flight to Delhi. You can also go once a week on the two hour Karachi-Dushanbe flight. If you find yourself in one of these places, sit back and enjoy the retro feeling of a creaky '60s-era Boeing 707 maintained by post Soviet-era mechanics. Aeroflot won't guarantee it, but they list a four hour flight from Moscow for about $300 one way. Because of frequent aid flights there are a variety of charter flights from Dushanbe with outbound space. Just head to the airport and beg or haggle. There is also a crime ridden but more reliable train from Moscow and a daily bus from Samarkand. Internal flights are often cancelled or delayed by lack of fuel, passengers or whatever.

Due to a lack of fuel, there are not many taxis. Taxis can be called in Dushanbe by dialing *24-66-29* or catching one at the Hotel Tajikistan. Negotiate and agree to a fare first. Take the bus into and around town. There are private buses that cruise Dushanbe. *DP* recommends hiring a private driver and car for about $30–$50 a day. A *DP* reader in Belgium tells us that he used a Kyrgz visa and used the "72 hour rule" which gives you 72 hours to get a visa for the FSR you are entering. Make sure you get clearance from the police in Osh to cross at Sary Tash.

Tajikistan is not a country designed for leisurely touring. Ninety three percent of the country is mountainous. Only 10 percent can be cultivated. Some tourist itineraries provide a three-day tour of which two and a half days are getting in and out of Dushanbe with a half day sprint from the hotel and back to see the Gissar fortress before it gets dark. Not much a draw for bus tours. The eastern mountains make most of the country an adventure, the civil war makes the driving interesting, and the general lack of infrastructure means you come in or you go out, but you don't cruise around. There are daily 22-hour train connections to Tashkent, Uzbekistan, but sit with your back to the engine to avoid most of the rocks thrown through the windows by guerrilla wannabes thinking that Russians are on board. There are three rail lines inside Tajikistan, but check to see if the track has been blown up and, of course, look out for thieves while on board.

You can try to hitch rides with the aid convoys and truck drivers going through the northern mountains into Kyrgyzstan and Uzbekistan. The alpine scenery along the Pamir Highway into or from Kyrgyzstan is worth the life-shortening ride, bad food and lack of accommodations. The embattled M41 highway along the border with Afghanistan is used only by Russian military vehicles. The high passes are snowed in from October to March. The M41 road between Osh, Kyrgyzstan and Khorog is kept open year round and is the most scenic, but once past Khorog, it becomes one of the most dangerous as it hugs the border between Afghanistan and Tajikistan.

There are supposed to be regular flights via Tajik Air to Khojand, Khorog and most major towns in Tajikistan, but once again weather, crashed planes and the availability of Stinger air to ground missiles dictate the flight schedules here. Reservations are not taken until 3–7 days before the flight. You have to buy your tickets at the airport since the locals get to pay a lot less at the airline offices. You can get the latest from **Tajik Intourist** *Tel.: 7 (3772) 21-68-92* or Russia's Intourist *630 Fifth Avenue, Suite 868, New York, NY 10111 Tel.: (212) 757-3884, Fax: (212) 459-0031* and good luck getting a straight answer.

You must be very specific about which cities you wish to visit and make sure they are clearly written in. There are a lot of checkpoints if you travel by road. Soldiers will shoot if you do not stop. When you do stop they will shake you down for a bribe. Smile and act stupid and they may give up on you. If you do not have the proper paperwork you will be sent back. You could also be detained and fined. For in-country security reports, contact the UN Military Observers

Team at Shevchenko Street in Dushanbe: *Tel.: [7] (3272) 21-01-47.* Travel anywhere within 15 miles of the Afghan border is very dangerous and controlled by Russian soldiers.

You can't take any antiques out of the country. That, of course, is the least of your worries. Antiques could be anything from the phone system to the political philosophy of the current rulers. You are also not allowed to take any local currency out. Again, this won't be too much of a problem since there is not much call for Tajik rubles in the cafes of Paris. The only place you might run into a customs person would be at the border with Kyrgyzstan. Needless to say, the border with Afghanistan is more concerned about folks trying to sneak in at night with rocket launchers and trucks full of opium. The only thing you should concern yourself with is how to get out of this godforsaken place with Afghan fighters to the south, mountains to the north and a whole lot of Central Asia to the north and west. Tajikistan is a long way from anywhere. The only thing your credit cards will be good for is scraping the ice off the dilapidated truck's windshield and your travelers checks will make good kindling on those nights in the mountain passes.

If you hire a driver to take you to Uzbekistan, remember that you may have to change cars at the border since the Uzbeks often do not let Tajik tagged cars in.

The M41 Highway

There is a road that heads east from Dushanbe and then winds south along the Afghan border that is off limits even to locals. You will be turned back at any one of the military checkpoints or even find yourself front and center at a Tajik attack on your Russian border stop. Many sections of the road are mined every evening by rebels. The rebels steal the mines the Russians lay down and then put them back in places where the Russians suspect least. Some people take the daily flight from Dushanbe to Khorog ($60) and then take a bus through the mountains into Osh, but don't count on regular departures or the weather being compliant.

Bus Stops

Bus stops are Tajik rebels' favorite place to shoot or roll grenades at Americans, Russians or people that look like Russians or Americans. If you have a death wish, wear your uniform (complete with U.S. or Soviet flag) and hang around Dushanbe for a while.

Dushanbe

The capital city of Dushanbe (Tajik for Monday, the day of the weekly market) is a dangerous place due to street crime and violence after dark. It's only three hours by tank from the Afghan border. Westerners are targeted not only in public, but in their hotel rooms. Even armed soldiers stay off the streets at night. UN vehicles have been hijacked in daylight. Bombings are frequent within the city. Call the U.S. embassy in Dushanbe for the latest: *[7] (3772) 21-03-56.*

Flying

When there is air service, the chances of crashing are good in Tajikistan. The Russians pay their pilots an additional sum to make the 45 minute flight between Dushanbe and Khorog—white knuckle flying at its finest. The high altitude prevents the aircraft from passing gracefully over some of the highest mountains in Russia. So the pilots simply fly in around, and by the peaks. You should know that you are flying over (or rather through) an active war zone (Yeah I know everyone's signed off on a peace treaty), and one unlucky flight was downed by Tajik rebels using a surface-to-air missile. You can call the London office of Tajikistan International Airlines (we're pretty sure they're not that busy) at *Tel.: (0181) 993-8885, Fax: 993-7504.*

http://www.angelfire.com/sd/tajikistanupdate/artorg.html

Opium

Three quarters of drugs coming from Afghanistan via Tajikistan go through Shurabad, Muminabad, and Pyanj districts. The border with Afghanistan and the presence of the Russian troops means that Russian Generals make Japanese efficiency experts look like slackers. Although the farmers don't have any axe to grind with foreigners, you may find yourself in an area controlled by smugglers. In 1998 there were 1,285 arrests of smugglers with opium being the drug of choice followed by weed and then heroin.

http://www.hri.org/docs/USSD-INCSR/1998/Europe/Tajikistan.html

Journalism

Over 40 journalists have been murdered in Tajikistan since 1992. CPJ counts only 29. Most of the killings are at the hands of the rebel groups who haven't quite learned how to send pithy and scathing "letters to the editor." There is no censorship of media in the 13 TV stations, 3 radio stations along with 202 newspapers and magazines, there just seems to be a very violent readership.

http://www.cpj.org/countrystatus/1998/Europe/Tajikistan.html

Do Gooders

Tajikistan would not survive if not for the direct provision of food, clothing, shelter and money of outside aid organizations. Is this good or is this bad? Hey go see for yourself. Right now the NGOs are about the only way an outsider can move around the country.

http://www.soros.org/tajik/ngotajik.html
http://www.cango.net.kg/

Open Society Institute—Tajikistan

Country Director: Zuhra Halimova
33 Rudaki St., Rooms 4, 5
Dushanbe, Tajikistan, 734001
Tel./Fax: (7-3772) 211-958 or 510-142
E-mail: zhalimov@osi.td.silk.org

Russians

Ethnic Russians, politicians and military men are popped off by wild eyed Tajiks rebels. So if you're an American with a potato nose, cauliflower ears and gold teeth, you might want to visit Brighton Beach or Istanbul instead.

The Alma

There have been over 500 eyewitness accounts of the *alma* or the *almasty* in Tajikistan. The *almasty* is Tajikistan's version of the yeti (or "that thing") and is said to be about 6 feet, 6 inches, weigh in at about 500 lbs. and walk on two legs. The man/animal has reddish-brown fur and can move along the ground at up to 40 mph. They root for berries amphibians and rodents. They are seen at night and run away when spotted. *Alma* youngsters look just like human babies except smaller.

Some scientists say they are Neanderthals driven into the wilderness by our ancestors, the Cro Magnons. Others say they are a result of active imaginations. But somewhere on the "Roof of the World" exists a large hairy creature. Is it dangerous? Not really. It is said that it will attack pack animals and scream a lot. There are ancient stories of similar creatures from Oregon to Chechnya to Mongolia to Borneo. So why not be the first one on your block to have a pet *alma*?

http://www.xproject-paranormal.com/CryptoZoo/hominids/index.html

Money Hassles

Tajikistan started printing its own version of the ruble in 1995. Remember that the lowly Tajik ruble is only worth 100 Russian rubles. You get about 400 rubles for a U.S. dollar. Needless to say, napkins and coasters might retain their value longer than this creative solution to insolvency. You can't take money out of the country. Credit cards are useless. Banks have no idea what a traveler's check is. Needless to say, the almighty dollar is good as gold here, but you will need Tajik rubles to buy airline tickets in country. Don't take or accept 100 dollar bills before 1993 because of the high amount of bogus Iranian printed C notes. Worst case is that money changers will discount your ragged greenbacks for up to 25 percent of their value. The locals pay a much lower price for just about everything, and if you get caught hiring a local to buy your tickets, you will get dunned for the difference or a bribe.

Tajikistan has malaria in the southern and lower regions. The water supply is not potable and bottled water should be your only source. Hepatitis A is a risk. Ticks are found in higher elevations in grassy and wooded areas. Rabies is a significant risk from local dogs, many of which are trained to attack strangers. Add meningitis, tuberculosis, schistosomiasis and typhoid (Dushanbe and south) to your disease list.

There has been a significant deterioration in the medical infrastructure in Tajikistan with many trained personnel having fled the country after the recent kidnappings. Tajikistan has a general scarcity of medical equipment and medicines. The potential exists for significant disease outbreaks, because of massive population displacement and a partial breakdown in immunization activities.

Electricity is 220V/50Hz of the two-pin European type. The language is officially Tajik, written in the Arabic script, Uzbek, and about a third of the people speak Russian. The moola is the Tajik ruble (100 kopeks to the ruble and about 400 rubles to the U.S. dollar). You can leave home without your American Express because Tajikistan is a cash-only economy. International banking services are not available and if there was a decent bank it would be knocked off within five minutes of opening. The phones are funky (the country code is 7 and Dushanbe is 3772) and the general infrastructure non-existent outside the major cities. The Tajik ruble is good for toilet paper, blowing your nose or souvenirs when you leave the country. The average income of Tajiks is around $2.50 a month so they don't see any rubles or dollars.

Since most of Tajikistan is above 3,000 meters, Tajikistan is frigid in the winter and hot and arid in the summer. The best times for masochists to visit would be between October and May to experience the blizzards or between June and October to be sandblasted in the heat by the dust storms. Well at least there's a breeze. March and May bring the most rain, the heat in June to August will fuse your Airwalks to the pavement with temperatures reaching well over 100°F. Only 7 percent of the land is arable and the rest is comprised of alpine hidey-holes for gun-toting mountain folk. For what it matters, American soap operas and trash TV are big during those long winter nights. Number one is *Santa Barbara*, a show with a plot about as convoluted and strange as the political situation in Tajikistan. The hotels usually don't serve food. You can stay in funky dachas or the upscale (for Tajikistan) tourist hotels along with the embassy staff and pilots. The only other major town is Khorog where you can risk your life to see the town's one tourist attraction: a bunch of faded, badly stuffed animals and a collection of Lenin photos.

Tajikistan is dangerous, mountainous, earthquake-prone and an ideal place to start *DP's* pick for the new Central Asian extreme sport: Helicopter gunship skiing, where contestants try to ski past machine-gunning Russian border guards and Hind-D gunships carrying five keys of opium gum on their back. Too whacko? Well how about Yeti hunting?

Embassy Locations

The U.S. embassy in Dushanbe is providing only emergency consular services. The Canadian embassy is in Moscow and Almaty, Kazakstan. *Tel.: [7] (3272) 50-11-51, FAX: 581-1493.*

U.S. Embassy (Dushanbe)
Oktyabrskaya Hotel (October Hotel)
105A Pospekt Rudaki
Dushanbe, 734001, Tajikistan
Tel.: [7] (3712) 21-03-56, no fax

Russian Embassy (US)
Consular Division
1825 Phelps Plaza NW
Washington, DC. 20008
Tel.: (202) 939-8918
There are Russian consulates in New York, San Francisco and Seattle.

Russian Embassy (Canada)
285 Charlotte Street
Ottawa, Ontario K1M 8L8
Tel.: (613) 235-4341
Fax: (613) 236-6342

Web/E-mail Users
http://www.soros.org/tajik/ tajkinte.html

The Embassy of the United States
irage@usis.td.silk.glas.apc.org

Tajikistan Update
www.angelfire.com/sd/tajikistanup- date/

Tajik Banks
http://www.soros.org/tajik/tajk- bnks.html

Soros Foundation
http://www.soros.org/

3/8/97	Rebels and government sign a pact to create a peace agreement.
4/97	President Emomali Rakhmanov survives a grenade attack in Khudjand by a 21-year-old Tajik.
2/8/97	Nine UN workers, Russian journalists and Tajikistan's security minister are kidnapped by warlord Bakhram Sadirov. They are later released with the help of Ahmad Shah Massoud.
9/10/92	Declaration of Independence.

9/7/92	President Rakhmon Nabiyev resigns after Islamic rebels forcefully take control of the government. The Islamic Party is overturned in a bloody coup late in October 1992. September 10 is recognized as the date of Tajikistan's declaration of independence. Islamic rebels have continued fighting since early September 1992.
12/25/91	President Bush formally recognizes Tajikistan and 11 other former Soviet republics. On that occasion, he also states that formal diplomatic relations will be established with six of the republics as soon as possible and that diplomatic relations will be established with the other six (Tajikistan being one of them) when they meet certain political conditions.
12/21/91	Tajikistan joins with 10 other former republics of the Soviet Union (which cease to exist on December 25, 1991) in establishing the Commonwealth of Independent States.
2/12/90	Twenty-five persons die as Interior Ministry troops fires on demonstrators massed outside the Tajikistan Communist Party headquarters in Dushanbe, the capital of Tajikistan. February 12 now is celebrated as "Memory Day," and an obelisk was unveiled on February 12, 1992, to commemorate the persons who died in February 1990.

In a Dangerous Place: Tajikistan

Cold Going Over

There is a joke in Tajikistan. Just one. And everyone you meet will tell it to you. It takes a long time and it's not that funny. But it's very Tajik. It goes something like this: An American, a Frenchman and a Russian are stranded on a desert island. They find a bottle with a genie in it. Each gets three wishes. The American and the Frenchman choose great wealth, a long life and to get the hell off the island. The Russian thinks for a while and asks the genie for 10 cartons of cigarettes, four cases of vodka and, oh, for my last wish, can you bring my friends back?

That's kinda how it goes in Tajikistan. They miss the Russians.

The people of Tajikistan have that hard squint and painful stoop that comes from working in the fields too long. Life now is subsistence. Even the dogs look tough and hard. Tajik dogs are big dogs with their ears cut off to prevent the wolves from ripping them off.

Along the way sheepherders, soldiers, policemen, and pink-cheeked stocky women all stare and wonder why I am here. There is very little that could be described as exotic, things are mostly hard tough and poor. I get a chance to take pictures and meet the people more than I really want because about every 20 to 30 minutes our car conks out and the driver must attach the bicycle pump to the gas line to move the gas up into the carburetor. It gives me a chance to stretch my legs and look around. There is not much here. People will sit on the side of the road all day just to sell four or five apples.

Dusty stores are packed with up to a dozen brands of cheap vodka and 4 to 5 brands of cigarettes, but not much else. Cigarettes are the equivalent of about 10 to 20 cents a pack.

Money is a funny thing here. Tajik rubles come in denominations of 200. Most of them are brand new and packed into nicely banded wads. You need 900 Tajik rubles to make one U.S. dollar (6,000 Russian rubles for a U.S. dollar). There just isn't a whole lot to buy with rubles. U.S. dollars are the preferred currency and the black market is the accepted form of transfer.

We pass through spectacular scenery as we cross back and forth over the river gorge that will take us up into the mountains. Landslides are a common occurrence and the road is broken up, bent and rebuilt on a regular basis. It is getting colder and colder but the sky is clear and I enjoy the ride. The only high drama occurs when we cross over one of the many bridges that shift us from side to side.

The bridges range from old, rusty, army Bailey–type bridges to the *Indiana Jones*– style swinging wood bridges complete with gaping holes, missing planks and crunching sounds. All that's missing is the horror soundtrack as the planks creak and crack. For fun I look straight down and have no problem seeing the thundering rapids interrupted occasionally by the odd solid plank.

As we continue to climb I keep asking where the summit is. "Don't worry you'll know," is the answer. The sun is beginning to disappear behind the mountains and we are still nowhere near the top. Finally as we reach the snow line we see people walking down. My guide Hamrakul says now we are getting near the summit. Our car has conked out again so I get out and look around. The wind is fierce and there are thick bullying clouds that scud and collide with the peaks. We are heading into a blizzard. I decide to walk up ahead to scout things out.

The people that are walking down are old hands at this game. They drive as far as they can and then resign themselves to spending the night in some type of crude shelter instead of sitting out the howling storm packed in their cars. As we turn a corner I see where we are heading. It doesn't look good. There are long lines of screaming, spinning cars being pushed up by crowds of men. The road is now pure ice with people breaking up clumps of dirt to add traction. The light is fading and the storm is in full force. It is damn cold but the exertion of walking up and down the hill pushing cars keeps me warm. The dull blue light finally fades into night and the wind increases, smacking my face with sharp ice crystals. We are miles from the summit.

Down here where you can still see, people are having fun. Nobody is yelling and everybody is helping out. It seems the hardest part is keeping the cars from slipping over the precipitous edge and rolling thousands of feet into the unseen white chasms below. Some cars zip right past, others have to be pushed like overloaded toboggans up the hill. It seems that along with our car's fuel problem, his clutch has given out and the chains I thought would save us are slicing into the exposed cords of our bald tires.

Since I have made the fatal mistake of being the only able-bodied male in the vehicle (the driver of course must drive), I get to push. Not just a little to get some momentum but physically push the car up the mountain. As our car slithers and screams on the slick ice, the chains fly off and hit me in the knees. I am dripping with sweat as we run into the back of a long convoy stuck ahead of us. I decide to walk up and help work on the front of the line, but after walking for over a mile I realize that we are nowhere near the summit and we won't be going anywhere tonight. As if to finalize our predicament, when I get back to tell our driver not to be in a hurry, our car refuses to start. Our battery is dead.

I had not planned on doing a little high-altitude camping in the dead of winter so I improvised. I simply emptied out all the clothing in my pack and stuffed them in my pants and jacket. I look like the Michelin Man, but it will suffice. I also had the foresight to pack gloves and a hat. I end up giving my gloves and hat to my fellow passengers as the temperature drops inside the small car. I end up wearing socks on my hands and pulling my watch cap down over my face. When it is still sub-zero, I do manage to fall asleep once or twice, but I wake up to find my extremities heading toward frostbite. It is the coldest night of my life. Having spent a lot of my life in northern Canada, I know that death by cold is not an unpleasant death because your brain slowly turns to Jell-O and you sit there frozen, happy and stupid until your heart stops beating.

I forced myself to get out of the car around 3 A.M. The blizzard had stopped and the stars were out. I marveled at the beauty of freezing to death in such a clear beautiful place. Occasionally we would hear the crunch-crunch of someone walking around outside. From inside the car, all that could be seen were the delicate patterns of ice crystals as they grew from the bottom of the windshield to the top. I was sure I saw a tableau of a wolf-headed monster chasing four maidens. By around 4 A.M., everything in the car was frozen solid. The children in the back along with Hamrakul and the women were passably warm because they filled up the entire back seat with blankets and each other. I had given them all the spare clothes I had and I just sat shivering in the front watching my watch tick off the minutes until the sun would restore my body temperature to 98.6.

By 5:30 I couldn't just sit and freeze to death so I told Hamrakul that I was going to walk over the pass and down to the next village some 20 kilometers distant. No one was coming for us and it really doesn't matter if you freeze in a car or fall down the edge of the precipice that runs along the side of the road. He had lost the feeling in his feet and hands and thought that was a fine idea. We left our clothes with the woman and her children and told her we would walk ahead to see if there was a tractor or shelter. So we bid our driver adieu and crunched up the mountainside until we saw the faint dull dawn begin. In the dim light, the white mountains glowed a deep blue. The sharp wind and piercing cold were replaced by an eerie quiet, disturbed only by the crunching of our boots on the fresh snow. Soon we were at the top and were surprised to find a brand new emerald green Cadillac Seville among the dozen or so abandoned trucks and cars. Their occupants were inside a destroyed weather station with a small curl of gray smoke coming from the chimney. The building was too full of people to even enter.

The drivers inside were waiting for the sun to come up since it was more dangerous to attempt the descent of the pass on the ice than the ascent. Even walking was lethal. As we crested the summit and began walking down, I slipped and fell flat on my ass. As I struggled to get up, I began to slide off the road.

Sheet-ice covered the road and there was a small edge of dirt before the cliff. Falling a few times, I learned to slowly put my foot down and measure my next step. As we gingerly walked down, the sun glanced off the tops of the massive crags. Later, when we hit our first patch of sun, it was like being recharged. For the first time, there was heat. As the light intensified, we could see the village below. About ten minutes straight down by parachute or hang glider, but miles as we walked back and forth along the steep switchbacks. Finally, we hitched a ride with a potato truck and basked in the strong mountain sun as the truck gingerly picked and slid its way down the mountain. In the village, we ordered soup, bread and tea at a chaikhana. The villagers had never met a Westerner and slaughtered a large sheep in my honor. They invited me to watch. I am not a fan of watching people or animals' last moments, but I politely sat there as the confused animal watched its lifeblood squirt out. Long after its blood had drained, it continued to breathe and then suddenly its brain starved of oxygen. The eyes glazed over and life was stopped. I wasn't really that hungry anyway.

—RYP

Ankara

Turkey
★★

Muddle East

The country where the Simpsons meet medievalism. In Turkey you can buy designer clothes, have a Burger King double Whopper, sunbathe on beautiful beaches, stroll around the backstreets of Istanbul, hit the night clubs, wax up the Mastercard and tune into CNN. That's the nice part—and there's a lot of it. Alternatively, you can get yourself kidnapped by Kurdish rebels, meet people who would make Ayatollah Khomeini look like a moderate or be in the wrong place at the wrong time when one of Turkey's numerous terrorist groups decides to liven up the place with a little car bomb. Yes, Britain is not the only country where shopping can be fun.

The modern Turkish state was founded by Mustafa Kemal Ataturk in 1923. Turkey has a strictly secular constitution, partially modeled on the French constitution. Turkey is a country where you'll see girls in mini-skirts, hear the latest pop music and be able to drink yourself under the counter without anyone raising an eyebrow. Well, not much anyway. Try and bring in a bit of hash, though, and you are in deep sh*t. Bear in mind that the only people allowed to bring dope or heroin into Turkey are authorized mafia members, who pay the

right people to turn both blind eyes and keep their heads firmly in the sand. You probably don't qualify as the former, so don't bother. Unless, that is, you want to spend a bit time in one of Turkey's prisons.

DP has been in the slammer in Turkey and can reliably inform you that a Turkish prison is not a cool place to hang out in. (Turkey's prisons are just one of many prisons *DP* has invariably been invited to stay in over the years.) But take consolation in the fact that if you are planning a career in terrorism, Turkish prisons are an excellent training ground. You will be joining a large number of Turks and Kurds who have been caught chucking bombs around the place and machine-gunning policemen. Strategically placed between the West and the East, Turkey is host to the U.S. Incirlik air base near Adana, which is periodically used to blast neighboring Saddam whenever he starts getting any ideas. The CIA

has numerous listening posts in Turkey, which are used to spy on Russia and Syria, and anyone else un–U.S. friendly, for that matter.

If you head to the east, though, you won't be finding much in the way of nightlife. Helicopter gunships and large numbers of troops are the most likely things and people you will see and meet. Why? Because there is something of a problem in the east. Well, actually there is war. The Kurdistan Workers' Party (PKK) has led a 15-year insurgency for Kurdish autonomy in the southeast. Most of the southeast is inhabited by ethnic Kurds.

If you want to see trashed villages—there are lots of them—young men in jeans with AK-47s manning checkpoints, who will probably ask you lots of questions, then head off to the east. If you're silly enough to travel at night, you might even get yourself kidnapped by the PKK.

So what's all this PKK palaver? Well, for a long time the Kurdish language was banned. Turkey even refused to admit that there were any Kurds in Turkey (Kurds number 12 million out of Turkey's 60 million population). Instead they were referred to as "Mountain Turks" and viewed as slightly retarded boys from the backwoods. Kurdish revolts in the 1920s and '30s were crushed with the usual mass executions and burned villages. Turkey feared that recognizing Kurdish rights would encourage Kurdish nationalism and possibly cause the breakup of the country. But by not recognizing Kurdish rights, they got the PKK instead, which represents the most pissed-off bunch of Kurds you can find.

The PKK is probably the most organized and effective of all the Kurdish groups. It has a large support network in Europe amongst the Kurdish community there, and raises much of its funds in Europe. The PKK is also the most radical of all the Kurdish groups. Adopting a Marxist-Leninist ideology and demanding an independent Kurdish state carved from Turkey, Iran, Iraq and Syria, the PKK began its war in 1984 (See Kurdistan). In the early years of its rebellion, the PKK was also the most violent of all the Kurdish groups.

The PKK has repeatedly killed teachers in the southeast, claiming they imposed Turkish culture on Kurds, as it is illegal to have any education in Kurdish. Kurds who sided with the state and were armed by the military really got it in the neck from the PKK. Sometimes they and their entire families were killed. Nasty stuff. Things began to get out of hand; and in 1987 emergency rule was introduced in 11 provinces in the southeast. The nasty stuff was equalled by the Turkish military, who torched thousands of Kurdish villages, sending thousands more boys and girls to the ranks of the PKK, who by 1991 were turning recruits back and telling them to wait.

Death squads were unleashed in the southeast, and thousands of Kurdish nationalists began to disappear, only to reappear on roadsides with bullet holes in their heads. Suspicion fell on the police. The number of Kurds entering police stations in perfect health, only to fall down the stairs, stub cigarettes out on themselves, try and plug into the electricity mains manually or jump out of windows rose dramatically.

As the PKK reached its zenith between 1991–1993 things really went haywire. The PKK were taking on the Turkish military in pitched battles, taking out big military camps and generally getting way out of control, even attempting to take sizeable towns such as Sirnak in 1992. Turkey's generals began to get very nervous indeed. A massive military crackdown, burning lots more villages and killing more people ensued. So, how many people have been whacked in this war so far? I hear you ask. Well, to date and by official Turkish government figures 37,000 people have been offed. And the real number is probably higher. In the nine-year period between 1987 and March 1996 the government figures that it knocked off about 10,663 terrorists while they only lost 3,400. Oh yeah, about 3,938 civilians got aced in the cross-fire and about 3,000 villages (give or take a few) have been razed to the ground by the Turkish army.

Is that a Grenade in Your Pocket or Are You just Happy to See Me?

Most of the PKK (and now the YAJK) suicide bombers are young women in their 20s. Often they prematurely detonate themselves when stopped at police checkpoints on their way to military barracks or police stations. Often the women carry grenades and explosives hidden under their jackets.

As for whether tourists should worry Abdullah Ocalan's brother, Osman Ocalan said that every Kurd will be a "living bomb" and "our people must make life an inferno for the Turkish state." And then, in Stern magazine, he said that there would be no harm to tourists who visit Turkey. Go figure.

In the mid-1990s the PKK went through a kind of glasnost, removing the hammer and sickle from its flag and tuning down its demands to Kurdish autonomy inside Turkey. The Turkish military were not impressed. So, the PKK said "ya boo sucks to you" and began to target the tourist industry for additional fun and games. At US$7 billion a year the tourist industry raises almost as much as the PKK war costs. Bear that in mind the next time you stop off in Turkey or look at posters of those sunny beaches. In 1993, there were seven attacks against tourist facilities by the PKK, injuring 27 tourists. The PKK also kidnapped 19 foreigners (one American) in southeastern Turkey. That same summer, a series of bomb attacks in Antalya wounded 26 persons; in Istanbul, a grenade was thrown under a tour bus, injuring eight persons, and a bomb was thrown at a group of tourists as they were sightseeing around the city walls, resulting in six injuries. A hand grenade was found buried on a beach southeast of Izmir, and there were reports of similar incidents in other areas along the west coast. In 1994, the attacks continued, PKK bomb attacks were conducted on some of Istanbul's most popular tourist attractions, including St. Sophia and the covered Bazaar, resulting in the deaths of two foreign tourists.

The PKK's head honcho is Abdullah Ocalan, aka Apo. Apo used to live in Syria; he now lives in jail, for now. He moved back to Turkey in February 1999, taking the plane directly from Nairobi, Kenya. He even got the flight for free. And he was helped to Turkey by some nice men from Turkish intelligence who had thoughtfully drugged him for the flight, just so he didn't get airsick or anything like that. Apo has since been given an island all to himself, just off the coast from Istanbul, and the Turkish government generously picks up the tab for his accommodation. He has obviously been treated well and has managed to lose much of his pot belly since his arrival in Turkey. Oh, I almost forget to mention, Apo has also been sentenced to death. The PKK didn't really appreciate Apo's rehousing arrangements by the Turkish government. In Europe, 15 Greek embassies in different countries were occupied by PKK supporters, after Greece was accused of helping the Turks capture Ocalan. (Actually it was the United States who played a key role.) In Bonn, Germany, Israeli security guards opened up when Kurds tried to storm the embassy killing three protesters. Across Europe, about 70 men, women and children poured petrol on themselves in protest against Apo's arrest. Then they got the zippos out. London and Moscow were just two cities where Kurds became part of a new outdoor central heating system. A wave of bomb attacks rocked western Turkey. Suicide bombers blew up themselves—and anyone else they could—in Taksim square in the center of Istanbul. Car bombs also went off near Ankara. The PKK threatened to unleash a whole new bombing campaign in the west of Turkey. As one PKK source told *DP*, "It's time to play ball in the Turkish half of the country." Perhaps it is fortunate that this was an activity that the PKK managed to carry out with staggering incompetence. The more effective car bombs were subcontracted by the PKK to TIKKO, a Turkish Maoist group with slightly better bomb-making technicians. Most of the suicide bombers killed only themselves, mainly injuring passersby. Sounds like they should be off to the Gaza Strip or west Belfast for a few lessons. It was enough, though, to reduce Turkey's 1999 tourist influx to a rather pathetic trickle in comparison to most years. Approximately 2.5 million people canceled their holidays to Turkey with a loss of US$2 billion. In poor old Apo's enforced absence from the scene, the PKK established a "Presidential Council" to run the day-to-day business of zapping Turkish soldiers. It comprises ten senior commanders, including Apo's little brother, Osman Ocalan (see "Kurdistan" chapter). But the PKK say that Apo is still their leader, until—I guess—he takes the big drop.

Then, in August 1999, from his prison cell, Apo announced a cease-fire and a withdrawal of all PKK forces from Turkey. Cynics see this as just another ploy by the fat man to avoid having his neck stretched. And before you ask—no . . . the Turkish government is not wildly impressed by the offer, nor in Apo's claim that he has a God-ordained mission to solve the Kurdish question in Turkey. The official line in Ankara is that there is no Kurdish question in Turkey, which is about as silly as you get really. Have a nice flight. . . . In 1998 a lone Kurd hijacked a plane flying from Adana to Ankara on the 75th anniversary of Turkey's founding. Armed with a hand grenade and pistol, he demanded to be flown to first Bulgaria and them Lausanne, Switzerland. The plane landed at Ankara. Turkish security officials pretended to be diplomats from the Turkish embassy in Sofia. The hijacker sounded off about Turkey's unitary cultural system and denial of Kurdish identity. The security guys strung him along in the cockpit and the special team climbed in the back door . . . and shot the hijacker dead.

More than 80 Turkish journalists, academics and writers have been imprisoned for speaking out on the Kurdish issue. One of the more prominent people to be carted off to the slammer in 1999 was Akin Birdal, head of Turkey's Human Rights Association (HRA). Birdal has had a rough time as head of the HRA. In 1998, two men walked into his office and shot him six times after the military leaked a report saying he was in the pay of the PKK. The supposed source of this much-vaunted report? Why, none other than that paragon of virtue and reliable info, step forward . . . Semdin Sakik, as "Fingerless Zeki," the forcibly retired former PKK commander of Tunceli province who was captured in northern Iraq in 1998. Birdal's most recent crime was to call for dialogue in solving the Kurdish question in the southeast. That got him nine and a half months for "incitement to racial hatred." After Apo got himself slung in the cop-shop, the Turkish Ministry of Foreign Affairs introduced a new set of literary guidelines to help the Turkish press in its coverage of the PKK and Apo saga. The PKK were to be referred to as a "criminal gang." Ocalan had to have the prefix "terrorist," villages that had been torched by the military had in fact been "evacuated," and

Kurds had to be called "Turkish citizens of eastern origin." Oh, and when Ocalan offered a cease-fire, it had to be described as "a cessation of terrorist activity." What the government neglected to say was that many, many "Turkish citizens of eastern origin" were hoping that the government would perhaps let them return to their "evacuated villages" and take advantage of the "terrorist Ocalan's offer of a cessation of terrorist activity." Generally speaking, though, the Turkish military have got the upper hand these days. Not surprising, given that there are about 350,000 security personnel in the southeast at the moment. Torching about 3–4,000 Kurdish villages has helped. The war has now been pushed deep into the mountains. But the PKK is still hanging in there, and in strongholds like Tunceli still manages to control strategic valleys like Kutu Deresi (Box Valley). On the Turkish terrorist scene, the Turkish Workers and Peasants Liberation Army—what a mouthful!—has been taking over the running from Dev Sol, who appear to be off on holiday these days.

As you can probably guess, TIKKO—as the former is known—is yet another of Turkey's leftist terrorist groups. And just to be different from the others, they're Maoist. They set off three car bombs around Ankara and Istanbul in March 1999. Further east, they've been busy gunning down civilians in Tunceli province. In September, a TIKKO suicide bomber in Tunceli managed to kill a grand total of one person: himself. TIKKO are not impressed with the PKK's declaration of a cease-fire. Somewhat sulkily, they've decided not to cooperate with the PKK anymore. Terrorism aside, Turkey, you should be aware, is prone to the occasional earthquake. In August 1999, an earthquake in the town of Izmit, near Istanbul, killed 15,486 people in a mere 45 seconds and injured another 24,376 by official statistics. The quake affected six provinces of western Turkey and is estimated to have caused US$10 billion damage to homes and property. Some of the wilder casualty figures given by the media reached 50,000 dead. But the truth is that nobody really knows how many people died and the government ain't telling if they know. Why did so many people die? Because certain Turkish construction companies didn't bother building the houses to the standards required under Turkish law, which incidentally are the same building standards as California. In order to make a fast buck and avoid too many overheads the construction companies decided not to bother using too much cement. Whoops! 15,486 people later they're wondering if it was really such a good idea. Interestingly, houses built by British firm, Balfour Beatty—to the correct standard—received only cracks in the structures, compared to most apartment blocks built by Turkish firms which . . . er . . . collapsed instantly. For the dazed survivors it took a while for any kind of help to come from the government, which also refused aid from Armenia. Eventually, well . . . 24 hours after the quake, the military rocked up to see what could be done. Instead of turning up with picks and shovels, though, they rolled up with M-16s. As one well-known Western hack rather unkindly put it, they're very good at burning and bombing thousands of Kurdish villages, kidnapping Apo, arranging a show trial, but they can't organize a soup kitchen! Oh you're so generous! In the midst of Turkey's earthquake, Osman Ocalan was interviewed on the pro-PKK Medya TV. The ever-thoughtful (mentally deficient?) Osman said that the quake proved Turkey's military could only destroy, rather than build. He offered to send PKK guerrillas to the earthquake zone to help find victims and rebuild the area as a gesture of goodwill between Turks and Kurds. I mean, what is this guy on?! It seems that like Big Brother, Osman is very good at talking a lot of BS. Either that or the man should be certified. Talk about the kettle calling the pot black! So, you know about terrorism, bombing and earthquakes in Turkey.

D'you wanna know what's really dangerous? *DP* can now tell you that both terrorists and earthquakes pale into the background when it comes to traveling around in Turkey. Yes, you are in more danger on Turkey's roads than anywhere else. It's a sad reflection on the competence of Turkey's terrorist groups that you are probably in more danger on the road than from them. Turkey has the worst road accident record in the whole of Europe. In 1997, approximately 5,000 people died on Turkey's 61,350 kilometers of roads. There are 15 times more deaths from road accidents in Turkey than in Great Britain, and twice as many as Spain, which has twice the amount of traffic. Public holidays are usually the worst time to go for a drive in Turkey. Between April 3 and April 11, 1998, 164 people were killed and 317 people were injured in traffic accidents as the Turkish populace left the big cities on the Sacrifice Holiday, the equivalent of a long bank holiday weekend. When the Turkish government introduces regulations that theoretically oblige every driver to have a body bag in his or her car, you know the situation is not cool! I say theoretically because Turkey has numerous laws, it's just that everybody ignores them (like the laws about building houses to earthquake standards). In an effort to get people to drive sensibly and soberly, the government has taken to putting signs along the road: DON'T BE A TRAFFIC MONSTER or STOP THE TRAFFIC MONSTER WITHIN YOU, they urge Turkey's drivers. It's a campaign the Turkish government says is working. In 1998, the death toll for the first two months on the roads was down by 9 percent. In January 1998, a mere 268 people were killed on the roads as opposed to 281 in January 1997. In February 1998, the toll was a piddling 269 compared to the previous year's 302. Still, *DP* can testify that driving in Turkey can be a truly terrifying experience (nothing compared to Pakistan, though). You want to increase the odds of your survival driving in Turkey? Well, don't drive between 6 P.M. and 4 A.M., which is when most accidents happen.

Knowing all this, you will probably not be surprised to hear that one of Turkey's biggest scandals revolved around a car accident. Near the town of Susurluk, on November 12, 1996, a Mercedes slammed into a lorry, killing three of the four occupants. The occupants consisted of one of the most wanted right-wing hit men in Turkey, a beauty queen, a police chief, and *DP*'s old buddy, Kurdish warlord Sedat Bucak. In the back of the car were pistols, silencers and ammo. It was the most glaring evidence of Turkish state collusion in death squads that has ever come to light. Bucak survived, but when he came around, discovered the joys of amnesia.

Although you will hear about terrorist activity in Turkey, it would be more accurate to say that—with over 37,000 people killed since 1984 in violent encounters with the PKK and the rest of the happy gang—the situation is better summed up as an ongoing civil war. The group with the most bucks and bullets is the PKK who, despite their leftist leanings, make some decent change babysitting drugs coming from the East and have a Smack 'R' Us franchise in Europe. They have a big enough allowance to afford a satellite lease and a TV station, so business must be good (also see the Kurdistan chapter). You may be wondering why the Turkish government doesn't bang on about the supposed PKK involvement in drugs. The reason is that more than a few Turkish politicians are involved in it themselves, not to mention the Kurdish tribal chieftains, who are paid handsomely to fight the PKK in the southeast of the country. But keep that quiet, okay?

The Military

The military has, continues to, and will run Turkey. Despite a revolving cast of democratically elected politicians, the army steps in when things get too silly for their tastes. There have been three military coups in modern Turkish history, in 1960, 1971 and 1980. That is not to say there are not democratic freedoms, it just means only the people who play ball get to have them. The military sees itself as the guardian of Ataturk's secular and nationalist legacy. There are two things the military really don't like very much, toga wearing Islamists and cocky Kurds. The Kurds are officially considered no different than any other minority in Turkey and logically they are entitled to all the benefits Turkish citizens have. But quite frankly that's a load of bollocks.

The government feels it has a lid on the PKK problem and has an annual spring outing to their headquarters in Zap just to piss them off. The government is so confident that it has now lifted the state of emergency in 5 of the 11 Kurdish dominated provinces. It's all a bit of a con, though. If you visit the provinces, now supposedly no longer under emergency rule—as *DP* has done—you will see the difference between them and those under emergency rule are . . . er, nothing actually.

The man the PKK keeps out of the ranks of the unemployed is General Huseyin Kivrikoglu, who is the Turkish Chief of Staff, responsible for zapping as many PKK kids as possible. The largest foray into Northern Iraq was in 1997 (in which *DP*'s Roddy Scott was in the wrong place at the right time and ended up being deported from Kurdistan). As many as 50,000 troops stormed after the PKK and left a supposed death toll of 3,009 guerrillas and 113 Turkish soldiers—a number the PKK vehemently deny. Since then the Turkish military has never really been out of northern Iraq, but rather rudely hasn't allowed any journos in either. Spoilsports. Special ops units under the control of the regional supergovernor conduct raids against the PKK and are known for their brutality and treatment of villagers and Kurdish journalists. (In plain language, they beat the shit out of you, like they did to *DP*'s Sedat Aral.) Their utilization of the latest American military hardware (i.e., Cobra helicopter gunships) against the PKK's guerrilla tactics and small arms (AK-47 rifles) gives the conflict a neo-Vietnam aura. The military was invited into Northern Iraq in October 1997 by the Kurdistan Democratic Party (KDP) to help clean up the PKK and the PUK. Complicated? Read the Kurdistan chapter for more info. Journos who want to poke around should contact:

Prime Minister's Office

General Directorate of Press and Information
56 Konur Sokak Ankara Turkey
Tel.: (312) 417-6311

Kurdistan Workers Party (PKK)

The biggest, best and baddest of the lot. The PKK is the best-organized and most active Kurdish group in Turkey. Founded in 1978, the PKK is a Marxist group led by the now captured Abdullah Ocalan, a former law student from Ankara University. Things got seriously military in 1984. Ocalan lived in Damascus and was supported by President Assad of Syria for 18 years. Syria was, and is, none too pleased about Turkey's ongoing efforts to build more dams, possibly stemming the flow of water into Syria. But when, in 1998, the Turks threatened to turn Damascus into the middle eastern version of the Waco compound the Syrians changed their tune, deciding that Ocalan might want to find alternative accommodation after all (see Kurdistan chapter). Unlike the Iraqi Kurds, the PKK is active in all parts of Kurdistan, being the best-known and most violent advocate of Kurdish independence. Towards that end, the PKK has not only declared war on Turkey, but they have aimed their sights on the tourist industry, claiming that income from tourism (US$7 billion a year) funds the Turkish government's war against the Kurds.

The 20 or so tourists that have been kidnapped in the southeast have all been released unharmed. Why? Because frightened tourists make for better interviews on CNN than dead ones. The PKK is most active in southeast Turkey, setting up roadblocks, placing land mines (the Turks apparently have lost the maps for all the minefields they have planted along the Syrian border) and blasting away at villages protected by "loyalists." The army has assigned about 60,000 locals to fight the PKK who are paid $200 a month—or get their homes burned down if they don't play ball. The army provides them with a gun and then hopes that not too many of them will be made an example of by the PKK. About one village guard is killed for every two soldiers. The military claims that their kill ratio is about 10:1 in favor of the loyalists and soldiers against the PKK. Yeah, I'm sure. The PKK has a lot of support amongst ex-pat Kurds. In Germany alone, there are more than 450,000 Kurds, about a quarter of the total Turkish population in Germany. The PKK, along with 35 other organizations, was banned by the German government in November 1993. The PKK has been accused of using this offshore group to extort money from Turkish businesses and professionals in Europe. There are estimated to be as many as 7,000 armed PKK guerrillas, with about 800 of them in mountainous Tunceli province, 3,000 elsewhere in southeastern Turkey and about 3,000 inside northern Iraq. Something like that, anyway. For those of you who were hoping to collect on the US$94,000 reward for information leading to the arrest of "Fingerless Zeki," whose real name is Semdin Sakik, tough! You've missed the boat. He was caught in northern Iraq in 1998. Zeki was the rebel commander in charge of the PKK troops in Tunceli province. (Literally "tunc eli" means "bronze fist" in Turkish. The region is called Dersim by the Kurds who live there and is the province where the PKK has almost 100 percent support from the local people.)

Back to Sakik, who, in the meantime, fell out with Apo in 1998 during a visit to Lebanon, fled to northern Iraq, surrendered to the KDP and was snatched by the Turks. He has since been sentenced to death. Before he got the hoof, *DP* met with Ocalan in the Beka'a valley in his efforts to stir up more spin on his anti-Turkish goals. The basic gist is that he wanted to spin the Turkish army's spring visits to his camps as minor setbacks and he often liked threatening everyone. The PKK has a number of unofficial offices in Europe, the United States and London. The people at the Kurdistan Information Center are helpful and informative—most of the time—if you give them a call.

American Kurdish Information Network   MED-TV

2623 Connecticut Avenue, NW #1
Washington, DC 20008 1522
Tel.: (202) 483-6444
Fax: (202) 483-6476
E-mail: akin@kurdish.org
http://www.kurdistan.org

The Linen Hall, 162-168 Regent
Street, London W1R 5AT
Tel.: (44) (0) 171-4942523
Fax: (44) (0)171-494-2528
E-mail: med@med-tv.be
http://www.med-tv.be

Kurdistan Information Center
> *10 Glasshouse Yard*
> *London EC1A4JN*
> *United Kingdom*
> *Tel.: 011-44-171-250-1315*
> *Attn: Mizgin Sen*

Kurdistan Workers Association
> *Tel.: 011-44-181-809-0743*

PKK (Kurdish Workers Party)
> *Mekte-Bi Amele-1 Kurdistan*
> *Barelias-Chotura*
> *West Bekaa, Lebanon*

Kurdistan Solidarity Committee
> *Tel.: 011-44-171-586-5892*
> *Attn: Estella Schmidt*

Patriotic Union of Kurdistan
> *Tel.: 011-44-181-642-4518*
> *Attn: Latif Rashid*

Kurdistan Solidarity Committee
> *Tel.: 011-44-171-586-5892*
> *Also check out www.ozgurluk.org. It's the unofficial PKK web site.*

Yak Girls/The Kurdistan Free Women's Union (YAJK)

Spice up your life! Well for a few microseconds anyway. YAJK is a new all-female suicide group started by Osman Ocalan the brother of Apo. The idea is that attractive young Kurdish girls can finagle there way onto military barracks and police stations and then pull the pin on their 24 hour Wonder Bomb. No word yet if concert promoters have discovered a way to launch this unusual combination of talent, energy and built-in pyrotechnics.

Warlords and Smugglers

Southeastern Turkey has become something of a repository for warlords and smugglers. In an effort to destroy the PKK, the military have recruited heavily from local Kurdish tribes such as the Jerkis around Van and Bucaks in the Siirt region. The head of the tribe is given about US$200 a month per man he enlists. Needless to say, it is not unheard of for the lists of armed villagers presented to the military to be a little inflated, which means that the money the top dog gets is a little more than he should be getting. Tsk tsk.

One of the most hardline anti-PKK warlords is Sedat Bucak, an MP for the True Path Party. Is it surprising that he argues that the war against the PKK must be fought to the bitter end? Er, not when you consider the loss of income that he will suffer in the unlikely event of peace breaking out. Of course, it could just be personal. Bucak has the distinction of being virtually the first person the PKK tried to assassinate—before they really got going—in 1978. If you're ever in Siirt, you can always try and look him up.

The other people you'll be hoping not to bump into are the local smugglers. The southeast is a major route for drugs coming from Afghanistan through Iran and westwards. The main route for smugglers is the Yuksekova (known as Heroin City) and Semdimli areas, way down by the border with Iran and Iraq. It's big business, and your presence probably won't be appreciated.

The Mafia: Godfathers and Bloodbrothers

Closely linked to both of the above, the Turkish mafia is the second biggest in the world, after the Italian mafia. They are instrumental in handling the drugs that flow from East to West and anything else they can get their paws on. They are also—in many cases—friendly with top Turkish politicians, that's when the politicos aren't actual mafia members.

Take for example the case of Alaatin Cakici. Once one of Interpol's most-wanted men, he is currently in prison in France. Prior to Turkey's April elections he was fighting a tough battle not to be extradited back to Turkey. After the elections he begged to be sent back to Turkey.

Make any sense? Only once you realize that the government had changed and the new kids on the block were also his best mates.

In September 1999, six mafia members serving a bit of time in Bayrampasa prison in Istanbul, shot their way through to another part of the prison and killed six members of a rival mafia.

The killings revolved around control of the annual prison turnover. Yes, prisons have what *DP* likes to call the Gross Prison Product (GPP). In the case of Bayrampasa, it is estimated at 500 trillion Turkish Lira a year! If you want to know the dollars, then divide by 470,000, which is the exchange rate.

For creature comforts, the pricelist for prison furniture—in case you're ever there—is the following: (all prices subject to 70 percent inflation and local corruption. Catalogues available upon request from the right guard) .

- One mobile telephone: 500 million
- One cup of hash: 30 million
- One gram of cocaine: 300 million
- One weapon: 10,000 DM (type unspecified—for clarification please to refer to warders)
- One fridge or TV: US$20,000

Dev Sol (Devrimci Sol, or Revolutionary Left

The Rocking Dev Sols are not a retro surf reverb rock group out of California, but a splinter faction of the Turkish People's Liberation Party/Front formed in 1978. They espouse a Marxist ideology and are intensely xenophobic, virulently anti-U.S. and anti-NATO. Dev Sol seeks to unify the proletariat to stage a national revolution. (Yawn.) The group finances its activities largely through armed robberies and extortion. Their symbol is a yellow star with hammer and sickle against a red background.

Dev Sol has conducted attacks against the U.S., Turkish and NATO targets but was weakened by massive arrests from 1981–83. In the early 1990s, the group killed several foreigners, including two Americans. Five members, including one of its leaders, were shot and killed in Istanbul on March 6, 1993. Dev Sol is down to several hundred hard-core radicals with several dozen armed militants. While other groups have concentrated their actions in Adana in recent years, only Dev Sol has attacked Americans. In February 1991, the group assassinated an American employee of a Department of Defense contractor outside his home in downtown Adana. The same year, the group bombed the American consulate and other U.S. affiliated organizations. Early in 1996, Dev Sol guerrillas murdered two prominent Turkish businessmen and a secretary in their offices in downtown Istanbul, to avenge the deaths of three prison inmates at Istanbul's Umraniye prison. Local state banks are a favorite target and have been bombed numerous times. Dev Sol is led by Karatas. But to be quite honest Dev Sol seem to be in semi-retirement these days, not having carried out a decent assassination for a while; and they're a bit of a bore anyway. You never know, maybe they've just heard about glasnost!

Hezbollah

This is where things get complicated. Turkish Hezbollah is not the same as the Hezbollah from Lebanon. Mainly operating in the east and southeast of Turkey, Hezbollah has been responsible for numerous attacks against Kurdish activists and businessmen. Imagine a terrorist group that preys on another terrorist group. Exactly how Hezbollah started and who started it is something of a mystery. However, given that the majority of the victims were PKK supporters and that very few arrests were ever made, there has been more than the odd aspersion cast on links between Hezbollah and the police. Well now, that's a surprise. Hezbollah's main base is Batman, in southeastern Turkey. Hezbollah comprises different factions. Those who kill people without the prior permission of the police tend to get into trouble. Like they actually go to prison!

Turkish Workers and Peasants Liberation Party (TIKKO)

A small group with a fetish for blowing up automatic teller machines (everyone's enemy) and banks in major cities. What fun. They have about 60 men operating in Tunceli province, in the southeast. They were allied to the PKK operating in the region, but think the PKK are a bunch of wimps for calling a cease-fire. They are also responsible for most of the car bombs that go off in Turkey. As they're a bit more competent at bomb making, the PKK have subcontracted them to do their dirty work in the cities. (The PKK kids don't know the difference between plasticine and plastic explosive.) In March 1999, TIKKO set off a number of car bombs around Ankara. Kawa Kawa is a legendary folk hero among the Kurds. The Kawa group was established in 1976 after breaking away from the Revolutionary Culture Association (DDKD), a pro-Soviet Kurdish group advocating uniting all the Kurdish people under the Marxist banner. Kawa's anti-Soviet stance was the reason for the break with the DDKD. Kawa also fell victim to dissension within its own ranks over the teachings of Mao Tse-tung.

Alevis

The Alevis are a Muslim minority who live in central Turkey but are unrelated to both the Shiites, who consider Ali to be the successor to Mohammed, or to the ruling Syrian Alawite faction. They adhere to a moderate branch of Islam started in the 13th century by philosopher Bektas Veli. Occasionally, there are violent demonstrations and riots in the Istanbul and Ankara areas. In March 1995, 16 people were killed in two days of riots.

A passport is required. A visa is not required for tourist or business visits of up to three months. For information on entry requirements to Turkey, travelers can contact the nearest Turkish Consulate in Chicago, Houston, Los Angeles or New York, or the embassy in Washington, D.C.: *Embassy of the Republic of Turkey, 1714 Massachusetts Ave., NW, Washington, DC 20036, Tel.: (202) 659-8200.* Or take a look at what appears to be the official Turkish government website: *www.turkey.com.* You won't find it particularly thrilling. When you get off the plane in Istanbul, you need to proceed to the line to the left of the longer lines. You'll know what we're talking about. If you want to head to the east then it's either a short plane ride or a long bus journey to Diyarbakir. There are numerous police, militia and army roadblocks with lots of operations taking place. Do not believe any tourism hype about a minor problem with rebels.

Embassy of the Republic of Turkey

2525 Massachusetts Avenue, NW
Washington, DC 20008
Tel.: (202) 612-6700
Fax: (202) 612-6744
E-mail:Turkish@erols.com or tcwash.cons@erols.com
http://www.turkey.org/

If you wish to travel to eastern Turkey, your request may be refused. There are numerous police, militia and army roadblocks with numerous police and special ops operations taking place.

DP has traveled extensively in southeastern Turkey, both alone and with an armed military escort consisting of armored personnel carriers and commandos using Land Rovers. Travel by road after dark is hazardous throughout southeastern Turkey and quite possibly you won't be allowed to travel at night, anyway.

In Tunceli province no traffic is allowed on the roads after 4 P.M. Depending on the situation, other provinces may or may not have similar restrictions, so plan your itinerary accordingly. Buses are common but are subject to lengthy searches at all checkpoints. As a foreigner you will probably be left alone (unless you are a journalist—in which case expect to be followed everywhere), although you may have to flash your passport from time to time at checkpoints. But it is not unheard of for foreigners to be subjected to lengthy questioning in the southeast. Much of the time this will be because soldiers or policemen are simply a bit bored or curious about you.

Not very many tourists go to the southeast. Well now, that's a surprise. Okay, now you might be asking yourself, "Cool, so how do I get to meet the PKK kids in the mountains?" Not easily, is the answer; and you'll need some damn good contacts who are possibly willing to risk their necks. The political wing of the PKK in Turkey is the Democratic Peoples Party, known as Hadep. A lot of the Hadep activists have close links to the PKK. More than a few Hadep people are also in prison. You too can join them in prison if you start messing around in the southeast. The Turkish government does not take kindly to foreigners poking their noses into the region.

But if you're the really determined type, then start in Europe—that's if you have no contacts in the region. The PKK has numerous front offices in Europe. But don't expect them to hand you anything on a plate. They will want to know who you are and why they should be giving you the time of day.

A word of warning, gentle reader. You should bear in mind that the Turkish security forces tend to monitor Hadep activists—and anyone else considered subversive—as closely as they can. Yes, you can be paranoid. So watch out for the guys with radios and something bulky stuck down their pants, and it isn't because they're pleased to see you. You won't be on a fun run if you're caught messing around with these people. A press card will help, but then you will have to be a genuine hack or hackette to get a Turkish government press card. (This is handy to flash if you're in trouble and a foreigner—sometimes. One journalist was stripped down to her underpants by pissed-off security police in Kiziltepe. Another hack was physically frogmarched back to the airplane at Diyarbakir airport on arrival and sent to Istanbul, even though he lived in Ankara.)

If you want to hang out with any of the Dev Sol boys and girls, the best place to start is London, which has a small but active Turkish community heavily influenced by the left. *DP* will give you a head start: go to Hackney.

Ataturk Airport, near Istanbul, is the main international entry and exit point for Turkey. Istanbul is an excellent link between the east and the west. You can also get plenty of cheap tickets and just about everyone speaks English. Turkish air carriers are modern and safe. Ankara's airport is the hub for domestic flights and about 20 miles from downtown.

Istanbul Ataturk Airport
Tel.: (212) 663-64-6

Izmir Airport
Tel.: (232) 274-24-05

0 Ankara Airport
Tel.: (312) 398-00-00

http://www.concierge.com/travel/c_planning/06_airports/mid/istanbul.html
http://eunuch.ddg.com/ISTANBUL/MISC/airlines.html

The Wild East

Eighty percent of the time you will be perfectly safe traveling in Turkey, but it's the 20 percent that will kill you—with only the Turkish traffic and driving standards to worry about. The PKK has announced a cease-fire and a "withdrawal" of all its forces from Turkey. How long this will last is another matter. It is reckoned that maybe only 700 PKK guerrillas (the commanders) will be leaving Turkey for a mega PKK congress in the Qandil mountains on the Iran-Iraq border. The rest of the kids will stay put. So hiking is still off the menu in southeastern Turkey. The Turkish military don't really care and have continued operations against the PKK all over the southeast.

Travel in Tunceli province might be particularly hazardous. TIKKO have continued fighting, occasionally zapping civilians for fun. Other provinces to steer clear of are Van, Hakkari and Sirnak. Over the past 15 years, several thousand Turkish civilians and security personnel have been killed in guerrilla attacks.

In the early '90s, the PKK began kidnapping foreigners in eastern Turkey to generate media attention for their separatist cause. Over the years, a number of foreigners, including Americans, have been held by the PKK and eventually released. On October 9, 1993, an American tourist was abducted by the PKK while traveling by bus on the main highway between Erzurum and Erzincan, in Tunceli province. Due to the tense security situation, the climbing of Mt. Ararat near the border with Iran continues to be extremely dangerous, even with the required Turkish government permits. If you're an American citizen give the embassy a call. But *DP* can tell you they will simply say "don't bother" if you're planning a trip to the southeast. So, now you don't need to give them a call, do you?

U.S embassy in Ankara is: [90] (312) 468-6110, or the American consulate in Adana, [90] (322) 454-3774
http://www.usis-ankara.org.tr/

The Touristed Southwest

Things are benign where foreign dollars flow. But visitors should stay aware of recent incident reports. Terrorist activity was mostly designed to frighten tourists off, rather than actually kill them. Most of the paranoia goes back to the summer of 1994 when the PKK conducted a series of hand grenade attacks against establishments frequented by tourists in Antalya and planted at least six hand grenades in beaches around Izmir and Kusdasi. The Antalya attacks injured Turkish nationals and tourists, as well as causing extensive property damage. In early 1999 there was a wave of bomb attacks after Ocalan was caught and brought back to Turkey. The situation has calmed since the PKK announced a cease-fire, but don't get your hopes up. TIKKO are still around and cease-fires have a habit of ending. The good news is that crime against Americans is rare in western Turkey other than the usual pickpocketing and petty theft. Generally speaking, you will be perfectly safe. I mean, hey, there should be another 8 million much fatter and slower tourists to give you cover.

TURKEY

Crime, Muggings and Bar Brawls

There is the usual petty crime against tourists, including pickpocketing, purse snatching and mugging. In Istanbul, incidents have been reported of tourists who have been drugged and robbed in nightclubs and bars, usually by other foreigners who speak English and French. Americans have been involved in fights at discos, and bar scams involving girls ordering drinks at inflated costs have been reported.

Pavions

There is a certain style of clipjoint in Istanbul and Ankara called a glitter bar, or pavion. Many are found around Taksim Square in Istanbul. The pretty ladies you meet will order enough drinks to melt your VISA card. Even if you drink yourself into a coma without the help of a local lass, your eyeballs will roll back in your head when you see the bill. Owners of pavions do not take kindly to debt restructuring or threats of recrimination. Many patrons have been robbed of watches or rings to meet payment. You will get little sympathy from the local cops.

Antiques

Unauthorized purchase or removal from Turkey of antiquities or other important cultural artifacts is strictly forbidden. Violation of this law may result in imprisonment. What is or not an antique can be the subject of heated debate as your plane is being loaded. At the time of departure, travelers who purchase such items may be asked to present a receipt from the seller as well as the official museum export certificate required by law.

Newspaper Publishing and Journalism

This can be a hazardous profession in Turkey, where papers are regularly closed down, editors fined and journos occasionally disappear. Although there is no prior censorship of newspapers in Turkey, it is illegal to publish anything that is deemed to advocate separatism or insults either Ataturk or the military. The punishment can range from fines or closure of the newspaper to imprisonment. Pro-Kurdish newspapers such as Ozgur Gundem have been closed and a number of hacks shoved in the clink for such offenses.

Drugs/Cold Turkey

In Turkey, the penalties for possession, use and dealing in illegal drugs are severe. You can expect a few years in the slammer. It's cold, cold Turkey if you get sentenced to a Turkish prison. Remember *Midnight Express*? That was a romanticized version of Turkish jails. Turkey is still a major drugs route for heroin coming from Afghanistan and hash from Lebanon. Stay well clear. The U.S. embassy security office can be reached at: *[90] (312) 426-5470, extension 354,* and the Air Force Office of Special Investigations at: *[90] (312) 287-9957.*

Medical facilities are good in the west, few in the east. In the southeastern city of Diyarbakir, there are recurring outbreaks of dysentery, typhoid fever, meningitis and other contagious diseases. Typically Turkey is a healthy place to travel.

NUTS AND BOLTS

The local currency is the Turkish lira, a limp currency that makes you an instant millionaire each time you exchange about 15 bucks. Turkey has high plateaus and Mediterranean coastal areas. The plateau areas in the east get very cold in the winter and very hot in the summer. The fall and spring are quite pleasant. Istanbul has moderate temperatures year-round, with summer temps in the 80s (F) and winter lows in the mid 40s (F). Istanbul gets about four inches of rain a month in the winter.

The bulk of tourists in Turkey are Russians, attracted by the proximity, beaches and cheap goods. Germans comprise the second-largest bloc, followed by tourists from England, Romania and Israel. Trivia for today: The world's first town was Catalhoywk in central Anatolia; it was founded in 6,500 B.C.

Embassy and Consulate Locations

U.S. Embassy in Ankara

110 Ataturk Boulevard
Tel.: [90] (312) 468-6110

U.S. Consulate in Istanbul

104–108 Mesrutiyet Caddesi
Tepebasl
Tel.: [90] (212) 251-3602

U.S. Consulate in Adana

At the corner of Vali Yolu and
AtaTurk Caddesi
Tel.: [90] (322) 453-9106

Adana local police emergency number

Tel.: (322) 435-3195

Americans who are victims of crimes may also call the consulate

Tel.: (322) 454-2145

DANGEROUS DAYS

2/15/00	PKK renounce warfare.
8/17/99	Earthquake shatters six provinces across Turkey, killing 17,000 people in 45 seconds and injuring another 24,000.
8/3/99	From his prison cell, Ocalan announces a cease-fire and withdrawal of all PKK forces from Turkey.
7/15/99	Ocalan is sentenced to death by Turkish court.
3/24/99	Bombs explode in Istanbul and Ankara in retaliation for Ocalan's capture.
3/20/99	Abdullah Ocalan is captured by Turkish military in Nairobi, Kenya.
11/10/1998	Abdullah Ocalan arrives in Italy.
10/9/98	Turkey threatens to go to war against Syria for harboring PKK leader Abdullah Ocalan.
4/23/98	PKK commander Semdin Sakik is captured by Turkish troops in northern Iraq.
5/10/97	Turkish troops invade northern Iraq under a media blackout.
3/4/95	Turkish troops invade northern Iraq.
5/19/95	PKK announce unilateral cease-fire.

10/6/93	PKK cease-fire ends after 35 unarmed and off duty soldiers are gunned down by rogue PKK commander near Bingol.
1/3/93	PKK announce unilateral cease-fire.
4/17/92	Turkish police kill 11 suspected Kurdish guerrillas in a series of raids in Istanbul. Kurds undertook several terrorist attacks in 1992 in Germany and Turkey citing this date.
8/30/91	August 30, 1991, is celebrated as Victory Day and made an official Turkish holiday.
5/27/91	May 27, 1991, is celebrated as Constitution Day and made an official Turkish holiday.
4/25/88	Hagop Hagopian, leader of the Armenian Secret Army for the Liberation of Armenia (ASALA)—aka the Orly group, 3rd October Organization—is shot dead in his home in Athens by two gunmen. No group claims responsibility for his murder.
9/6/86	Twenty-one Jewish worshippers are killed in Istanbul during an attack on a synagogue by an Abu Nidal terrorist team.
8/15/86	Turkish troops raid Kurdish rebel camps in Iraq.
8/15/84	The day that Kurdish Workers Party (PKK) elements first launch an attack against Turkish government installations.
10/8/84	Start of PKK war for independent Kurdish state.
1984	Start of PKK war for independent Kurdish state.
8/27/82	The Turkish military attaché in Canada is assassinated by Armenian extremists.
8/7/82	Nine people, including one American, are killed, and more than 70 are wounded in an attack on the Ankara airport by the Armenian Secret Army for the Liberation of Armenia.
1/28/82	The Turkish consul general to the United States is assassinated in Los Angeles by members of a group calling itself the Justice Commandos for the Armenian Genocide.
3/10/79	The death of Kurdish leader Mullah Mustafa Barzani (Kurdish regions only).
11/27/78	Considered to be the date on which the Kurdish Workers Party (PKK) was founded. PKK guerrillas may engage in terrorist attacks in connection with this date.
5/1/77	More than 30 leftists are killed during clashes with security forces in Istanbul.
10/24/75	The Turkish ambassador to France and his driver are shot and killed in Paris by members of the Armenian Secret Army for the Liberation of Armenia (ASALA).
1/22/46	Kurdish Republic Day.
11/10/38	Death of Kemal Ataturk.

10/29/23	Turkish National Day. The date commemorates the declaration of Turkey as a republic by Mustafa Kemal Ataturk and his inauguration as its first president.
3/16/21	Signing of the Soviet-Turkish border treaty that ended Armenian hopes of establishing an independent state.
4/24/15	Armenians observe this date as the anniversary of the alleged 1915 Turkish genocide of Armenians.
3/12/1880	Birthday of Kemal Ataturk, founder of the modern Turkish state.
6/16	June 16 is the anniversary date of the founding of the Turkish leftist terrorist group, 16 June. Until 1987, the group acted under the name Partisan Yolu. Since 1987, the group has claimed responsibility for numerous acts of terrorism, including the December 1989 firebombing in Istanbul of the Hiawatha, a U.S. Government–owned yacht.
3/21	Kurdish New Year, or Now Ruz, when traditionally the PKK launches its annual offensives.

In a Dangerous Place: Southeastern Turkey

Dead Kids Walking

The sun beats down unmercifully. Rivulets of sweat are coursing down my face and body. My clothes are wet with sweat and my rucksack feels like a lead weight strapped to my back. Ahead and on either side of me, vast mountain ranges reach far into the sky. I seem to be the only person trudging through the valley, and though I am constantly straining my ears, the only sound is that of my boots clumping over the rock-hard earth. Far in the distance I can see a few houses. I begin to change my course and climb the mountain slopes, hugging the mountainside and the trees dotted over it for cover.

Stopping underneath a tree, I sit on a rock and pull out my water bottle and gratefully take a swig. Reaching for the binoculars, I scour the slopes and valley for any sign of activity. I have been walking for two hours and have another hour to do before I will reach the rendezvous. I am searching for any sign of Turkish military activity. It would be hard to explain my presence here, walking through the middle of southeastern Turkey, the heartland of Turkey's Kurdish war. I have been mulling over excuses and explanations for the best part of several days, and there really aren't very many. Even more so when the people I am expecting to meet at the rendezvous point are the Kurdish guerrillas fighting the might of Turkey's army.

Five minutes later I set off again, negotiating the stone-littered paths and swerving through the trees. Through the misty haze of heat, I make out the outline of some houses. This time I don't change course. Ahead is the rendezvous. Trudging up the pathway, I hear the distant sound of rotor blades. I stop and watch the horizon. On the opposite side of the valley, just above the skyline, two helicopter gunships cruise shark-like through the air. I watch them, momentarily transfixed, until they dip back below the horizon and disappear from sight.

Arriving at the village, I am greeted by the stare of a curious child who quickly runs shouting to the nearest house slamming the wooden door. A woman peers out before ducking back into the house. Finally a man emerges. He is wearing the traditional baggy Kurdish trousers and a cummerbund around his waist. He beckons me forward into the house.

Inside I am offered first water and then a small glass of sweet tea. I sit grateful to have the rucksack off my back and be able to rest my feet. It is half past six in the evening. I will have to wait for some hours, possibly even a day or so, before the arrival of the PKK guerrillas. I ask the old man if he knows when "the friends"— as the PKK are referred to—might be arriving. "Usually they will come in an hour or so," he says, as dusk falls. So, perched on the wooden balcony, I sit and wait, watching the mountain slopes for any sign of human forms making their way down through the trees. But I see nothing and eventually give up. "Come on, you must be hungry," says the old man. "You should have something to eat." I say I would rather wait, and he leaves to herd the cattle into the wooden barricade for the night.

It is the sound of several pairs of feet trudging through the yard that alerts me to the presence of the guerrillas, and looking to my right I suddenly see figures emerging wraithlike from the darkening gloom. There are seven of them as they climb the steps of the balcony. I stand at the top and we shake hands one by one. Their faces are expressionless, their eyes dead. There is an aura of death around them. Kalashnikov assault rifles are slung casually over their shoulders with ammunition clips and hand grenades strapped to their waists. They are all wearing the traditional Kurdish dress. Some of them have badges pinned to their shirts. In green, yellow and red—the colors of Kurdish nationalism—the letters ARGK are emblazoned on the badges, National Liberation Army of Kurdistan, the military wing of the Kurdistan Workers Party or PKK.

Villagers crowd around to greet them. Once again, they go through the ritual of shaking hands and kissing the men on the cheek. We all go inside the house to eat. I notice they don't bother taking off their shoes, as is customary. Their sneakers are the "Mekap" make. A cloth is laid on the floor and food is brought. Children crowd shyly round the doorway to look at the guerrillas until the old man sharply tells them to leave, which they do to the sound of giggles and the patter of fleeing feet.

We chatter over food. I ask them about the amnesty that the Turkish government has offered PKK guerrillas since the capture of PKK leader Abdullah Ocalan. Have any of them thought of taking up the offer? One of the guerrillas grins and silently points several times at his neighbor, raising a finger to his lips. The whole group bursts into laughter, their eyes momentarily flickering superficially with life and humor.

We wash down the meal with diluted yogurt, called mastaw in Kurdish, and it is time to leave. Darkness is now complete. The assault rifles are picked up and once again slung over shoulders as we make our way out into the yard. A villager gives the guerrillas a bag full of food and cigarettes as we set off into the darkness.

The moon provides a soft yellowish light for us as we make our way through the trees and across the mountain slopes, quickly leaving the village lights far behind us. The only sound is the tread of our feet on the ground. Reflected by the moonlight our shadows flit across the ground, distorted by trees and rocks. The stars are brighter and clearer than I have ever seen. Every so often there is a streak across the sky as a shooting star expends its final energy.

We begin to climb the mountainside, my shoes slip on the loose stones sending a small avalanche cascading down. Halfway up we start traversing the slope. I try to look for the pathway we are supposed to be following, until I gradually realize that there is no path. There is just the mountainside at an angle of about 50 degrees. Across the other side of the valley I can see the occasional village light. A warm wind blows gently in my face. In the distance a flare rises slowly into the night sky. Falling back to earth it gives off an illuminating glow, a small temporary moon, lighting up the hilltops a few kilometers away. There's a degree of surrealism, as we walk so casually through the trees yet knowing that the now dimming flare represents the terrible threat of soldiers with night vision equipment and helicopters backing them up. A couple of hours walk sees us into another village. One of the guerrillas knocks softly on a door. A man opens the door and we all troop in. For the guerrillas it is time to catch up on the latest news of troop movements and drink some scaldingly hot tea. For me it is time to catch my breath, let the sweat cool on my body, drink several bowls of water and smoke some of my precious supply of cigarettes.

The villager asks who I am. "A journalist," say the guerrillas, "who has come to report on the situation."

"Welcome to Kurdistan," says the man. I just sit and nod, too tired to do much else. His wife and children sit at the back of the room talking with some of the guerrillas. We are offered food, but decline. With tea time over we set off once again. A horse is waiting for us at the door. One of the guerrillas takes my backpack, which is duly slung across the horse's back.

We head off again on what appears to be the standard nightly "village tour." We reach a river: the guerrillas slip quickly into the water, wading stealthily across. I follow suit, stealthily slipping into the water . . . slipping so far, in fact, that my legs are soon pointing at the sky and I land with a loud splash in the water. Hands quickly haul me to my feet again and I resume my attempt to imitate the guerrillas . . . failing pathetically as my feet slip once again on the stones in the riverbed.

It's a very wet hack who eventually reaches the other side of the river. I am given the horse to lead. About to ask why, I notice that the Kalashnikov's are now being unslung and there is a brief discussion in Kurdish. "Follow at least thirty meters behind us," says the commander. With a brief thrill of fear I watch as the guerrillas move off ahead of me into the darkness. This time they are moving slowly and are well spread out, sometimes kneeling on the ground to see if they can catch the outline of troops lying in ambush against the moonlight. I strain my eyes in an effort to keep the last guerrilla in sight. The moonlight fades, blocked by moving clouds. I lose sight of my escort. The only sound is that of the horse trying to munch at the grass on the ground.

Lost in the middle of the night, soaking wet, with a horse in the middle of a war zone. Not the ideal situation.

I strain my eyes even more and catch sight of movement. I blunder forward only to find that my eyes are playing tricks on me. It is a tree, and has definitely not been walking around. Every second now seems an hour as I cautiously move forward, wondering if it really had been such a good idea to link up with the PKK inside Turkey. No one else had ever done so. Fairly fucking obvious why, I think to myself acrimoniously. I wonder if I can perhaps somehow surrender. A cup of tea, a quick chat with the soldiers, a warm bed and off home. A delightful prospect. Probably a tad unrealistic, though. Better to just carry on, and if occasion demands perhaps a long whine for mercy might get me off the hook. Doubtful.

All in all it was probably no more than two minutes before I catch a glimpse of what actually is movement and an outline that, as I moved closer, quickly formed the shape of a guerrilla.

We're on the march again. Now the pace is fast and caution appears to have been thrown to the wind. We enter another village, quickly entering a house for more tea. The horse is left in the village as we leave and a guerrilla puts my backpack on his back. A hundred meters or so from the village the commander stops and we all sit down. "We're waiting for some friends," says the commander. A soft whistle cutting through the night is answered by a whistle from the commander. Three figures emerge from the darkness. I notice briefly that they have no weapons; but they join the group and we set off again.

We descend a gully. As usual there is no path, just a 70-degree slope of loose soil, which we slither down trying to brake the speed of our descent with our feet, sending several mini-avalanches of rock and loose earth cascading down the slope. I notice a large rock, about what I think is a couple of feet down. I jump down, but misjudge the distance. It's more like four feet and I land awkwardly, smashing my knee against the stone. We climb up the other side of the ravine, using branches from the bushes to haul ourselves up the slope. At the top there are thickset bushes. I can already hear guerrillas pushing their way inside, smashing down branches inside to make room for us to sleep, undetected from the exterior. I push my way inside and slump down on the ground, grateful for the warm summer night, and am soon asleep.

I wake to the distinctly unpleasant sound of several helicopter gunships buzzing overhead. But they are passing by, and the bushes are dense—concealing us well—even though movement inside is difficult. The guerrillas are already awake. I ask what's going on. There's a Turkish military operation going on says the commander, whose name I discover is Murat. I ask where. About 10 kilometers away, says Murat. Will troops be coming here? I ask. No, no, says Murat with a casual wave of the hand. To put me at ease another guerrilla cheerfully tells me how he has been in the valley for nearly three weeks. "The enemy launched a four-day operation here to find us," he says, "but we just moved ahead at night and then doubled back . . . you've got nothing to worry about." We spend the day listening to Kurdish folk music on a tape recorder and Turkish military radio reports coming through on the radio scanners. Above us is a constant roar of jet fighters and the drone of helicopters, supporting the operation just a few kilometers away. For lunch food given by the villagers is taken out of the bag. Tomatoes, cucumbers, cheese and bread appear to be the staple mountain diet.

I notice the three youngsters who had joined us the night before. "They're new friends," explained Murat, meaning new recruits. "We'll get them some weapons in a couple of days." I ask one why he has joined the PKK. "To fight for the rights of the Kurdish people," he says. I push a bit further and ask which village he is from and whether he is local. "My home was burned a year ago by the military . . . alongside our entire village," he says blankly, before adding, "I have been waiting all this time to join the PKK."

—Anonymous

Uganda
★★★★

Where Danger Still Hangs Out

The pearl of Africa, the mountains of the moon promises a sense of Africa renewed, pristine, undiscovered and perhaps pure. What Uganda offers, though, is a mist-covered glimpse into hell.

It is where Western tourists were ruthlessly hacked to death with machetes, a place where jails are stained with the brains of former inmates, where children are snatched and sold into slavery. A big, wide-shouldered place where even *DP* almost met their maker in a bomb attack. Uganda is a fertile and deadly place, always has been.

Back in January 1971, correspondents came out of State Department backgrounders in more than one capital, reporting, "This new guy Amin might be okay." ("Establishment military," authoritative sources had said; "we've dealt with him.") They were wrong.

Alas, when Yoweri Museveni's outlaw army began showing up on a distant bush horizon 15 years later, it wasn't so easy to get the scoop. He just wasn't the

State Department's type. All we could tell was that authoritative sources were uneasy. So we were uneasy, too.

We speculated about Museveni, the radical, about reports he'd been with FRELIMO in Mozambique, among Maoist Chinese on the Tanzanian island of Pemba. We heard reports that this renegade off in the shadows of the bush was even sending children into battle . . . and, hey, the reports checked out. He was. Now he runs the place.

We pictured a gang of bush-hardened cultural revolutionaries, armed with AKs and simple-minded slogans, about to drag Uganda right back into chaos, just as new and moderate leaders were at last in place to nurse that sorry realm back to life.

During his long march on Kampala through a shell-shattered free-fire zone in Buganda known as the Lowery Triangle (shattered largely by the government's North Korean shells), Museveni had slipped out to London. In fact, he was there during a period when any practical leader (and he is a practical man) could see his cause was lost. He had virtually no financial resources, no trained military resources. The triangle was hamburger, it was over, and guile with reporters was pointless.

We paid slight attention to him then, just as we failed fully to appreciate until too late that Uganda's "moderates" were crooks who killed more Ugandans than Amin. A little more attention to quiet voices and we might not have evoked such foolish dismay as we relayed third-hand reports about a bullet-riddled beast (so rudely subhuman in its ability to live after such punishment), slouching toward Kampala.

This beast, as we now know, was an army of some 20,000 adolescents and kids in their 20s—those the despairing Museveni had left behind. On their own, they had hung on, and at last, slowly, pushed on. Less dependent on authoritative sources, we might even have provided some modest inspiration in dispatches about a true children's crusade, about orphans left with no choice but combat, their families and their lands having been trashed first by Amin, then by the undisciplined, unpaid and rapaciously angry soldiers of Tanzania, and then again by Amin's old military, now led by corrupt "moderates."

We didn't deliver that story until Museveni's kids were on the cusp of victory in mid-1985. To this day, many are surprised to learn that Julius Nyerere's protégé, the school teacher Apollo Milton Obote, killed more Ugandans than Amin.

All this matters now because all of Central Africa is dangerous. Museveni had almost succeeded in removing most of Uganda from the world's most dangerous places. The State Department reports that snatch-and-grabs from cars stalled in Kampala traffic are common, but security in Kampala and Entebbe is by no stretch frightful. Uganda's frontier with Rwanda is notably less dangerous than the refugee-ridden frontiers that Tanzania, Burundi and Congo share with Rwanda. But throughout East and Central Africa, you hear that we ignore Uganda at the risk of getting taken by surprise yet again . . . and not just in Uganda.

Though President Yoweri Museveni is tossing his 15,000 troops and hardware at Congo leader Laurent Kabila in a jungle catfight, the man who didn't want to be king is actually making some parts of Uganda a decent place to make a living without the threat of getting whacked by crazed rebels or government troops on a binge for some beer money. Uganda's eight-percent annual growth rate is the largest in sub-Saharan Africa. However, most of the prosperity is being felt in the south, where Museveni is from, while the northern half of the country continues to be bogged down in butchery, debauchery, bribes and beggary. Northerners feel the government has neglected them and left them exposed to attack. The land is fertile. But the ongoing insurgencies of the Lord's Resistance Army and the Allied Democratic Forces are forcing farmers to flee into Uganda's larger towns and across the border into Congo. As fighting between the government and now well-trained and Sudanese-armed rebels spreads to central and western Uganda, there seems little hope for any peacemaking. Khartoum is pissed at Museveni for supporting Sudan's insurgency in the south, and Museveni isn't going to talk peace with a northern rebel backed by Sudan. It makes for a good, old-fashioned bush war. In March 1999, the U.S. State Department warned against all travel to Uganda in the wake of the killings of eight foreign tourists—including two Americans—in Bwindi National Park in southwestern Uganda by Hutu rebels. And Museveni's involvement in the Congo civil war means catching a rare glimpse of a silverback gorilla will become even rarer.

President Yoweri Kaguta Museveni

The president of Uganda is former guerrilla chief Yoweri Museveni. He was born in 1944, raises about 1,500 head of cattle and became a guerrilla fighter in 1971. With the help of Tanzanian troops, he ousted Idi Amin in 1979. He married Janet Kataha in 1973 and has four children.

When word of Museveni and his guerrillas began popping up in the mid-1980s, they were the most obscure of players. In Kampala, moderates of various stripes had been at work trying to pull Uganda from the pit into which Amin had shoved it.

Uganda is still struggling to recover. Large portions remain insecure. Its military (Uganda's National Resistance Army [NRA], now with a political wing, the National Resistance Movement) is poorly armed and underpaid (they make about US$30–160 per month). But Museveni, without seeking the role, has become the most powerful man in Central and East Africa today.

Though he gets dissed a lot in his own country for not doing enough against poverty, suppressing human rights and calling Uganda's no-party system a "democracy" (after 14 years in power, the president begins his second five-year "term" in 2002), Museveni's got a good PR spin on with his support of the Sudanese rebels (the SPLA), which makes him buddies with Washington. When U.S. Secretary of State Madeleine Albright swung through town back at the end of '97, she paid a visit to SPLA leader John Garang, boosting the legitimacy of Museveni's regime. Recently, Museveni has turned into a pop psychologist. He's been "studying" the families of young "terrorists" to see what makes them tick, and why they're so ticked off. "Government will approach their families and urge the parents to appeal to their children to give up and surrender before the army kills them," Museveni told a rally in June 1999. Museveni is Africa's Dear Abby.

Yoweri Kaguta Museveni
Princes' Road
P.O. Box 7069
Kampala
E-mail: museveni@starcom.co.ug
Tel.: 270331/9
http://www.uganda.co.ug/kags.htm

Timing

The U.S. embassy in Uganda was targeted for the biggest of the bomb attacks on U.S. installations. The one ton bomb never was delivered or exploded. The August 7 blasts killed 248 people in Nairobi, Kenya, and 11 in Dar es Salaam, Tanzania. Why there? Maybe because U.S. Special Forces are in Uganda training and supervising Ugandan troops in the annihilation of all Sudanese backed rabble-rousers. Arrests of suspected "terrorists" in Uganda often involves U.S. "security personnel." As a top cop in Uganda admitted near the end of 1998: "I'm not aware that Americans are involved (in the arrests), though I'm aware of their presence in the country." For now terrorist acts are remarkably underreported or described as "grenade attacks." Don't believe it.

http://travel.state.gov/uganda.html

Lord's Resistance Army (LRA)

The LRA, led by Major General Joseph Kony, a former altar boy, has been pouring freshly trained and armed guerrillas into Uganda from Sudan over the last couple of years. A far cry from their primitive beginnings in 1988 under his aunt Alice Lakwena who started the Holy Spirit Movement (a gal who said she could protect her fighters from bullets until they were wiped out). The LR is—get this—a Christian fundamentalist group. Their agenda is to create a theocratic state based on the Ten Commandments. There are daily occurrences of looting of convoys and hit-and-run firefights with the army, usually leaving scores of government soldiers and civilians dead.

Joseph Kony leads this savage group—armed and uniformed by Sudan—whose members believe their bodies will deflect bullets when smeared with tree oils. In June 1997, Kony ordered his men to avoid killing civilians and to await reinforcements from Sudan. In the first six months of 1997, the LRA was responsible for 400 deaths in the northern third of Uganda and the displacing of some 200,000 farmers. The LRA specializes in abducting children, whom they train and enroll in their ranks. Some 3,000 schoolchildren were abducted in 1995 and 1996 by rebels targeting them as recruits.

The strength of the LRA has been estimated by the government at 600 men, but Sudanese money has expanded the LRA into a real army. Kony says he has 6,500 men in three brigades that operate in groups of 30 or less. Despite their new military bearing it's hard to know if local Acholis have to still be careful not to be found within six miles of a road, riding a bicycle or motorcycle, and anyone keeping ducks or sheep will be killed. The LRA considers ducks and sheep to be unclean animals. The LRA has experienced a number of setbacks at the hands of Clabe Akandwanaho, the brother of Museveni.

Around 5,000 children have been kidnapped and escaped from the LRA, but another 5,000 are still being held in rebel bases in the Southern Sudan according to Amnesty International. The children are sold for weapons (one AK per child) to Arabs and some say to do gooder Christian groups that create a ready market for the children. If their statistics are correct the number of freed slaves equals the number of kidnapped children from Northern Uganda.

According to Tomy Masaba Bambi in London, Joseph Kony is no longer in his camp in Jablein 80 miles from Juba but under house arrest in an undisclosed location. Also senior

LRA leaders have had their passports taken away and were not allowed to leave the region. Kony was getting $7,000 a month from the Sudanese military until February 1999. There are two reasons suggested: one is that Turabi, under pressure from the United States, shut him down; the other is that Kony was also getting support from Kabila. The LRA has an office in London that keeps promising an intimate meeting with Kony. The LRA information office in Khartoum has been closed and its coordinator Yassin Ojwang moved to Aden. Their office in Nairobi lost its phone lines, and its secretary-general, Dominic S. Wanyama, and spokesperson, John Obita, were apparently sent to a refugee camp in Northern Kenya. For now the LRA can be contacted in London:

Alex Oloya
E-mail: aoloya@hotmail.com
London Mobile: 07931747202

Allied Democratic Forces (ADF)

These guys are Sudan-backed Muslim nasties formed from the radical Muslim sect Salaf Tabliq, the West Nile Bank Front (WNBF) and what's left of the National Army for the Liberation of Uganda (NALU; see below), and secessionist Rwenzururu movement. They operate out of the cool green mountains in Southwestern Uganda and they are trying to carve a niche for themselves along the Congo border. The ADF has been attempting to destabilize the Museveni regime since its beginning in the spring of 1996. They launched their first attack on Uganda from the Congo on November 16, 1996. The group first appeared in the southwestern part of the country (where it doesn't seem to enjoy a lot of support) and has been the meatiest insurgent cell to make an appearance on the Ugandan rebel landscape since 1994. The ADF is estimated to have between 600 and 1,000 members, recruiting mainly from among the Hutu Rwandan Army and from late President Mobutu Sese Seko's Forces Armees Zaireoises. They also like to snatch children and press gang villagers. Most of the clashes between the ADF and government forces have been occurring in and around the towns of Bundibugyo, Bumbombi, Kabarole and Kabunomi. And, true to form, most of the casualties have been civilians. Between 5,000 and 10,000 Ugandan villagers have fled across the border in the former Zaire to escape the fighting—only to find renewed fighting there between Ugandan troops and Congolese government troops loyal to Laurent Kabila. They are based in the southwestern area of Uganda in Ruwenzori mountains, Bundibugyo district but are also active in Kampala and other urban areas.

National Army for the Liberation of Uganda (NALU)

The NALU is a small rebel band with connections to former Uganda President Milton Obote. These gentlemen are pissed at the West's support of Museveni and in April 1999 announced they were going to "shoot and kill" foreigners. The NALU also claims credit for the killing of eight tourists (including two Americans) in the attack on the Buhoma camping site in Bwindi National Park on March 1, 1999, though the deeds appear to be the work of *Interahamwe* rebels instead. But these bad boyz aren't all sizzle and no steak. NALU guerrillas were behind the August 25, 1998 bombings of three buses in western Uganda that killed more than 30 people. They are based in Kisinga in the Kasese district.

http://www.reliefweb.int/IRIN/cea/countrystories/drc/19990630a.htm

Interahamwe

The Interahamwe militia was organized by the political party of the former Rwandan President Juvenal Habyarimana's political party, after the genocide in Rwanda, they fled to the eastern Congo. The Congolese refer to any ethnic Hutu combatant in Congo as Interahamwe, including Hutu who have lived in Congo for generations. The Interahamwe were responsible for the deaths of eight tourists in Bwindi. Their motivation was to destabilize Ugandas' fragile tourism industry because of Musevenis meddling in the war in the Congo. They are also opposed to the current Tutsi government controlled by Paul Kagame.

Neighbors

Museveni is Uncle Sam's golden boy. Never mind he has invented a single party democracy and likes to dabble in wars in Congo and Sudan. Museveni points to his 7 percent growth rate as if that balances the rebel groups and corruption of his regime. While his troops fight alongside Congolese rebels things at home are pretty nasty. He also supports the Christian SPLA against Khartoum which then supports the ADF and the LRA. Uganda's messing around in the Congo is why Angolan, Chadian, Zimbabwean and Namibian troops suddenly showed up.

http://www.intl-crisis-group.org/projects/cafrica/reports/ca04main2.htm

Homeys

Forty percent of Ugandans live in poverty, in some areas half of pregnant women have tested positive for AIDS in rural clinics, local banks are handing out unsecured loans to cronies, and government ministers resign. Outsiders figure corruption sucks $200 million a year down a black hole. The result is that Museveni is the longest reigning ruler of Uganda in history using a single-party "democratic" system.

http://www.africanews.com/monitor/

The Libyans

The Colonel hadn't taken an airplane outside Libya since his boys shot a Pan Am jetliner out of the sky over Lockerbie, Scotland, in 1988 before he surrendered the two suspects to an international court in The Netherlands in early 1999. Now Gadhafi's been busy jetting around Africa trying to keep the lid on the civil war in the Democratic Republic of Congo—starting with Uganda. Libyan peacekeeping forces arrived in Uganda in May 1999 with the intentions of deploying between Ugandan forces and forces loyal to DRC President Laurent Kabila. The problem was that no one asked them to.

http://www.geocities.com/Athens/8744/mylinks1.htm

A passport is required. Visas are not required of U.S. citizens. Visas can be had at border checkpoints, usually for a cost of US$20. Immunization certificates for yellow fever and cholera are required (typhoid and malaria suppressants recommended). For a business visa and other information, contact the following:

Embassy of the Republic of Uganda

Embassy of Uganda
5911 16th St., N.W.
Washington, DC, 20011
Tel.: (Tel.: 202) 726-7100-02
http://www.ugandaweb.com/ugaembassy/
email: ugaembassy@rocketmail.com

Permanent Mission to the UN

Tel.: (212) 949-0110.

From the United States, the best connections by air are made through Europe, Nairobi and Johannesburg. Sabena flies from Brussels to Entebbe, while British Airways flies to Kampala from Gatwick. Air France flies direct from Paris. Uganda Airways is the national carrier. By rail, there is twice-weekly service to Kampala from Nairobi and Mombasa. Ugandan Railway Corporation (URC) has in the past operated a ferry to Port Bell from Mwanza in Tanzania, but the service was suspended at press time. By road, border crossings are open at Malaba, Busia Mutuku, Kisoro, Arua and Lwakhakha. Drivers will need an international license and proof of insurance. There will be a fee for a temporary Uganda road license.

There is something to be said for the third-class train. There is a branch line to Gulu, and if it is running, it could be a reasonably safe way to get to Gulu and see the country. Driving to Gulu is discouraged; there have been numerous incidents. Hitchhiking is even less advisable, but you may end up hitching if you decide to drive. URC operates passenger service between Kampala and the towns of Jinja, Toroco, Mbale, Soroti, Lira, Pakwach and Gulu. There are also services to Kasese in western Uganda and a weekly service to Nairobi.

There are more than 2,000 kilometers of paved roads in Uganda and 6,000 kilometers of murram (dirt) feeder routes. Four-wheel-drive vehicles are preferable for both surfaces. The only fuel stations are along the major routes. Drivers should inquire with locals about the distances and times between towns and villages. International car-rental companies are based in Kampala and Entebbe. Taxis can be found at the airports and in the main towns. Fares are negotiable and should be determined before you set out. In Kampala, long-distance buses depart from the station near the stadium. Ferries run to the Ssese Islands from Port Bell and Bukakata when they're operating.

There is an eerie quiet in this once bustling country—akin to the sound of waiting for another boot to drop. Uganda can be seen as an inherently civilized country surrounded by nasty neighbors: Sudan to the north, Zaire to the west, Rwanda to the south. The white minority in Kenya to the east is betting on prosperity as a ravaged economy begs for outside investment. There are only about 85,000 or so visitors every year compared to Kenya's 800,000, but it is growing at about 10 percent each year.

Crime is common in Uganda, with violent crime being more common than not. Roadblocks around the country are just as likely to be manned by thugs. Taking pictures of the military is considered a crime. Border areas are not safe. The north is dangerous for any kind of travel. We can only vouch for two towns, Gulu and Moroto, and one outpost, the National Resistance Army Camp on the Kidepo River frontier with the Sudan. Moroto is a lovely place in this serene wilderness. There are even some decaying colonial structures surrounded by green, and a huge green mountain rises due east of the town. But as far as we know, this has always been the sort of African town where you sleep on the floor of the police post.

Gulu, on the road to the Sudanese frontier town of Nimule to the north, and the rail line to Pakwach on the Albert Nile to the west, offers considerably more, but outside of town, this country is just as dangerous. There are the proper, if faded, Acholi Inn (a reminder that this is the country of the Acholi, many of whom were killed en masse by Amin) and, a notch down, the Luxor Lodge (a reminder, perhaps, that the Khedive, through his agents in the Sudan, once claimed all Uganda as Egyptian territory). These days it's unlikely that either of these hotels would require reservations, but even if they do, it's not a police-post town: Both the Church of Uganda and the Red Cross Society are said to offer accommodations.

http://www.ugandaweb.com/

Kampala

There have been 20 bombs in the last two years that have killed 45 people.

http://www.utbsite.com/

Mbarara and Ankole Country

The maxim for most dangerous places is, don't go unless you have to. That's not what you hear about the town of Mbarara and Ankole country just north of Rwanda and Tanzania, where you still find, after years of the white man's devastating rinderpest, longhorn Ankole cattle. Not unlike Tutsi cattle, they are owned by a tall, dark aristocracy, descended like the Watutsi from northern invaders who seized a Bantu-speaking kingdom. Here, the serfs are the Hima people, the aristocrats, the Ankole.

This is the region through which Henry Morton Stanley (the explorer who presumed to discover Dr. Livingstone) passed in 1875 on his way to meet Mutesa, king of Buganda, and what you hear about it is don't let the danger keep you away.

For one, it's beautiful, often the spare, dry beauty of the savanna rather than the ever-lush beauty of Buganda just to the north. (Buganda's deep green light filtering through banana groves colors the Uganda of our imagination.) For another, there is both the human and animal population. Mbarara is not an unusual African town, but then you begin to realize how combat tore the place up, and how other towns, similarly battered, still languish in a decrepit state. It's bracing to experience the resilience of this much patched place. Gusty *jambos* in a town with cheap hotels sporting names like The Super Tip Top Lodge Bar & Restaurant; this is Africa? Wildlife is devastated, but just when you think it is utterly gone, there it is. And seeing it in such circumstances, the sudden appearance of a bull eland brings a melancholy rush.

http://www.utbsite.com/utbpg10.htm#ABOUT

Gulu and the North

Kampala, Entebbe, the Uganda of repute, is a place of enveloping warmth, lush-green, coffee-rich, a jacaranda breeze. The far north of Uganda is nothing like this. The country north of the Victoria Nile and Lake Kyoga is drier than the savanna in the far south—wide open land, often trackless, which even before the days of Idi Amin, travelers were warned to enter with no less than two four-wheel-drive vehicles. Today, you're warned to shun it altogether, unless you can rent a light plane to get in and out of secure redoubts like the army base on the Kidepo River frontier with the Sudan, a region whose land, people and animals are so close to the Pleistocene, and so palpably distant from the rest of the world, that you find yourself hypnotized.

This is Nilote country. Amin came from the Nilotic tribes that populate this harsh country; likewise, Obote. Meantime, Museveni's crusade came from the green south and west, the heartland of the old Bantu kingdoms.

The Acholi, the tribe that spawned Joseph Kony has suffered terribly. It is estimated that 300,000 Acholi have died in the last ten years.

The far north has always been a rough place, a place where men can still be seen with chest scars toting their kills (left breast for women, right for men), and cattle rustling has long been both a routine way of life and a routine way of death. Today, it's especially dangerous. Remnants of Amin's army are about, along with the Lord's Resistance, as well as outright *shiftas*. In this territory, the term *shifta*, meaning bandit, is likely to be used honestly, and not as a euphemism for guerrillas.

http://www.state.gov/www/issues/relief/gulu.html

Uganda a No-Go

Want to get out for a night on the town? U.S. government employees must have permission from the chief of mission to visit the following districts: Kotido, Moroto, Apac, Lira, Gulu, Kitgum, Kisoro, Rukungiri, Kasese, Moyo, Arua, Nebbe, Adjumani, Bundibugiyo, and Kabarole.

Travel Outside Kampala

Kampala is relatively safe, but outside the capital is a war zone. LRA guerrillas control the roads north of Kampala at night, and bandits those to the southwest. Teams of LRA rebels regularly ambush convoys to the north and have even tried to take the key northern city of Gulu. Ask local bus drivers in Kampala what is going on. Those burnt patches on the road used to be their coworkers and former passengers.

Buses, Bistros and Bars

On August 25, 1998, grenades or bombs exploded on three different buses in Uganda, killing some 30 people. Guerrillas and others often hide explosives in their luggage that aren't particularly pothole-friendly. They simply detonate accidentally. Other attacks are blamed on Allied Democratic Forces rebels. Grenades seem to be the preferred objects to get tossed around according to the press but often they get it wrong. In 1998, grenade attacks on bars and restaurants in Kampala killed at least 18 people and injured at least 30 others.

http://www.uganda.co.ug/hotels.htm

Safaris

In the best of times, driving into the country north of the Victoria Nile has entailed the sense of entering country so open and vacant that once you're off the track and in trouble, it could be weeks before you're found. Kampala safari operators maintain radio contact with safaris. Should things get hot, they'd likely get their clients out fast; there's a chance they could get you out aboard a light plane with an extra seat. A minor problem is that you might have to kiss your gear good-bye. Depending on distance and danger, count on paying anywhere from US$750 to $10,000. If there is anyone flying out of Entebbe or any other field, the best way to find out would be through Wilson Airport (not Embakazi, out of which the commercial airlines fly) north of Nairobi.

http://www.africa-insites.com/uganda/directory/airchart.htm

Gorilla Watching and Guerrilla Watching

In March 1999, two Americans and six other foreign tourists were murdered by Hutu rebels while on a gorilla watching tour in Bwindi National Park. Insurgent groups such as the National Army for the Liberation of Uganda (NALU) have made it quite clear that Westerners will be targeted in Uganda. Kidnapping for ransom is only a concept in Africa. If you're tagged, expect to be bagged.

Uganda Tourist Board

IPS Building
Parliament Avenue
P.O. Box 7211
Kampala

Tel:256-41-242196/7
Fax:256-41-242188
E-mail: utb@starcom.co.ug
http://www.utbsite.com/

Cattle Rustlers and the "Karimojong"

The Karimojong live in the northeastern part of the country, and at some point, got the idea in their heads that all cattle in the region belong to them. Their god-given right is backed by their Russian-made guns. On April 10, 1998, 11 people were whacked when two truckloads of AK-47-toting Karimojong raided a village in Mbale district. And cattle rustlers from Kenya are making life miserable for ranchers in the east. In one attack in May 1997, rustlers from Kenya killed 76 Ugandan villagers, including 50 children, as they made off with 300 head of cattle. More and more Ugandans in the northeast are asking themselves, "Where's the beef?"

http://www.uganda.co.ug/nilotic3.htm

Bicycles

The hospital in Lachor has started receiving children with their feet hacked off by rebels of the LRA. They have been losing their limbs as punishment for riding bicycles, which the rebels claim can be used to ferry information to the Ugandan army.

http://www.state.gov/www/global/human_rights/1998_hrp_report/uganda.html

You're on your own, friend. Any number of Western embassies in Kampala can, of course, advise where to get competent medical attention in Kampala, but Kampala isn't a dangerous place, nor for that matter are the actual towns of Gulu and Moroto, where there are also adequate (and, of course, inadequate) medical facilities. Yet, when a country has an average of one doctor for every 22,291 people, your chances of getting one are slim to none. AIDS is a big killer here, along with the usual Central African lineup of malaria, intestinal bugs, respiratory ailments and other tropical killers. Malaria is present throughout the country and chloroquine-resistant. Louse-borne typhus is especially prevalent where groups of people congregate together.

Uganda has a population of about 21 million people. The capital is Kampala, with a population of 800,000. The climate is tropical with hot lowland areas and cooler temperatures in the mountains.

The official language is English, but you'll also hear a lot of Swahili spoken. There are another 30 indigenous languages, the most common is Luganda. About two-thirds of the Ugandan people are Christians, while Islam makes up about 16 percent of the population.

The Ugandan currency is the Ugandan shilling (UGs1,000 = US$1). Credit cards are accepted at the major hotels, but not in the boonies. Banking hours are 8:30 A.M.–2 P.M. Don't expect cash machines to work. The phone lines are intermittent. Business hours are 8:30 A.M.–12:30 P.M. and 2–5 P.M. Telephone and fax services are available in the main towns. The IDD code for Uganda is +256. Uganda is on GMT+3. Electrical supply is generally 220V/50C. Ugandans drive on the left-hand side of the road.

News Sources

Africa News Online:

http://www.africanews.org/east/uganda/

The Monitor
http://www.africanews.com/monitor/

The New Vision
http://imul.com/vision/

3/1/99	Eight foreign tourists (including two Americans) are abducted and killed by Hutu extremists in Bwindi National Park while on a gorilla-watching tour.
4/4/99	Bomb at Speke's Hotel and Nile Grill kills 4, injures 12.
5/1996	Museveni wins elections with 72 percent of the vote.
1/29/86	Museveni is declared president after NRA seizes Kampala.
7/27/85	Milton Obote is ousted as president for the second time in a military coup.
5/27/81	Obote returns as president after nine years in exile.
4/10/79	Tanzanian and UNLF forces enter Kampala after driving out Idi Amin's forces.
10/78	Idi Amin's forces invade Tanzania.
6/76	Israel launches commando raid on Entebbe airport.
1/25/71	Idi Amin becomes president.

In a Dangerous Place: Uganda

One Night in Kampala

Kampala is a modern clean place. The people speak softly and are overly polite.

I visited the museum which, like most Third Word museums, is full of fluorescent-lit wooden display cases. They have a nice selection of primitive instruments and some rather bizarre minidioramas of primeval man.

I walk back along the golf course. The well-dressed people walk slow, but the cars pass by at breakneck speed. Outside the golf course is a new top of-the-line Mercedes, which wouldn't look so out of place if it weren't for the truck next to it with the "Society for the Reintegration of Demobilized Soldiers for the Reconstruction of Roads" sign on the door. The Asians have come back, and it seems they are doing quite well, thank you. The kids drive hopped-up European cars and wear the latest sunglasses. You might think this was Beverly Hills if it wasn't for the giant marabou storks perched on building tops.

The city is rebuilding and after ten years, you can barely find a bullet hole or destroyed building. The only sign that something might still be amiss is when you tell people you are going up north.

They will tell you that it is "sometimes not very safe there." Maybe if you talk to someone, they can tell you, "It is better to take the buses, because when it is dangerous, the buses will not go."

It is always interesting to see people's perspective on where they are. If you stay in Kampala, you will wonder what all the fuss is about. This is Africa's fastest growing nation economically and a polite colonial backwater.

After the museum walk, I have a gin and tonic outside on the veranda of the Speke Hotel. The Indian owners are renovating the place, but it still has the reeky ambiance of a good African hotel. The veranda is by far the best place to sit and view the park that surrounds the Sheraton on top of the hill and to watch the traffic go by. The sun goes down, and I head down for dinner. After an hour, I decide to get an early start since we have to catch a bus that leaves at 4 A.M. from the bus terminal.

I watch inane Indian videos on MTV and at 9:30 P.M., a bomb goes off outside the room. Rob rolls to the floor, and I jump up and grab my camera. Out on the street in the exact same table that I had sat in twice before today, at first victims say a bomb has been thrown from a passing car. The explosion has ripped apart three people and injured a few more. The people downstairs seem rather blasé, but they keep muttering "bomb." I go out to the sidewalk less than one minute after the bomb goes off, and I don't see the people because they are hidden by the columns. After rushing to the scene, I see pools of blood forming on the sidewalk when I arrive. There are three people slumped on the ground, but there is no moaning or screaming. The bomb was put right under my table. Rob jumps into action and tries to help the people. Luckily there is an American doctor having dinner, and he rushes out to help.

I help to lift the shattered people onto the back of pickup trucks while people stare bug-eyed at our efforts.

One waitress will probably lose her leg, one man is probably dead already and another has massive chunks of flesh out of legs and upper body. Two men are cut or wounded but will do fine. It is hard to tell if this is an attack on the hotel or on these specific people, or it could be an attack on tourists by any one of the three insurgent groups—except these folks are local.

The locals continue to stare and then, when one man runs, they all run away. Then they come back to stare. Meanwhile the blood spreads slowly on the ground. Finally some police in blue pickups show up and are just as confused as the onlookers. Rob and the American doctor try to provide first aid and lift them onto the beds of the truck. One man is put in a chair, and I can't help notice that he has a grasshopper sitting tenaciously on his head through the entire ordeal. Rob and I attempt to stabilize the wounded along with a group of foreigners who were having dinner.

My hands and camera are all slippery from the blood. I am torn between filming, helping and organizing. So I do all three at the same time. I do manage to make sure the police have been called, get towels, and help hustle the people to the hospital. Rob is trying to tell the gape-jawed onlookers and police to help, but they just stare and move away. Frustrated by their inaction, he shouts at them and then some go get cushions. If anything saves these people's lives, it will be because three westerners were here and Rob had brought a medical kit.

One westerner was sitting close by and is deaf from the blast. He has a large cut in his hand and is covered with a frosting of glass. So we bring him up to the room to stitch him up. He is a little dazed, so I tell him to go buy a lottery ticket. I am interviewed by the local press.

At 11:20 another bomb goes off. At first I think it is in the Sheraton up the hill. I jump in the back of the private security truck and we go to the scene. It is not the hotel, but a local restaurant, The Nile Grill. Once again, there are a few people staring into the darkness. The bomb was around back; there are three women laying there.

I gather the people and we slide blankets under them. Rob arrives on another truck and tries to stabilize them. One young woman is dead on the scene. The first woman I carry is conscious but very seriously wounded. As we lift her into the back of the pickup truck, her legs dangle over the side. They are shredded pieces of meat.

Rob goes to the hospital and I ride with the Saracen security guard. He is angry. The police do nothing, there is no ambulance and he is usually the one to inform the police of major problems. The police in Kampala make about $40 a month; my friend makes $100. But the police make it difficult for the private security companies to do their job. He is only 23, but he is dispirited because he is going nowhere. He was in the army or, as he says, "the war came to me in 1983." He has trained people, and they have gone on to better jobs. Saracen is a South African security company that guards about 800 establishments in Kampala.

As we race through the streets with his blue light flashing, we warn other hotels of the danger. We go to a nightclub where hundreds of people are milling around. They listen politely, but they don't seem to care. Back at the second explosion site, the military have shown up. The police are milling around. There are large eight-foot pools of congealed blood. I notice my hands and pants are covered in blood. They were three waitresses who apparently found a bag in the restaurant and took it to the back to see what was inside.

At 1:20, I think I hear another explosion, but I don't care. It is probably the start of the rains.

Rob tells me that when he got to he hospital with the second victims, he saw the original victims still lying there. He had to get a gurney to bring the people in. The first three people are still alive, but a doctor hands Rob a name tag of the young girl he brought in and he says, "Your friend is dead."

Her nametag said "Rebecca."

—**RYP**

Washington D.C.

The United States

★

How the West Was Stunned

Land of the free and home of the brave. And you'd better be damned brave here, because people are free to do pretty much anything they like. Behind white picket fences and two-car garages, husbands clobber their wives silly while their kids make crack deals over the phone with *Scarface* on the tube. A land where the license plates of one state reads: "Live Free or Die." Nice choice.

And dying we are.

In Littleton, Colorado, a couple of pimply-faced kids too squirrely to join their high school football team, and armed like a Navy SEAL team, whack 12 of their fellow students and a teacher before doing a sword-swallowing act with their assault rifles and chowing on a lead lunch.

And that was a copycat killing.

In Chicago, a World Church of the Creator white-supremacist fruitcake goes on a two-state ethnic duck-shoot that leaves two dead and nine wounded before

927

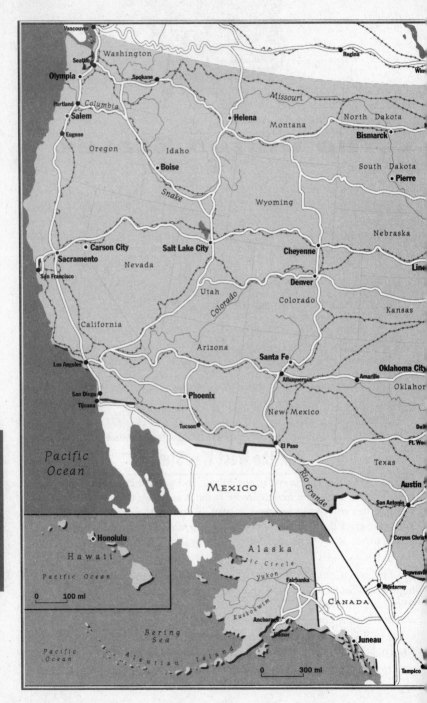

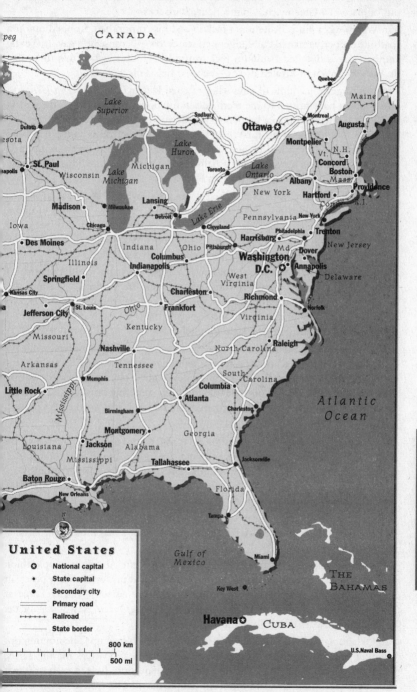

also dining on a .32-caliber Tootsie Roll. The victims' crime? They'd look a little out of place in a Greenwich, Connecticut, Starbucks.

In Wyoming, a kid is beaten in a pickup and his corpse then propped up on a roadside property stake like a bludgeoned scarecrow—because he's gay. In Texas, another guy is dragged behind a pickup until his limbs peel off his torso like drumsticks on a well-broiled turkey—because he's a black dude.

In Los Angeles, a couple of guys who watched DeNiro and Kilmer in *Heat* too much, pop a bank armed to the teeth and in full body armor, turning the streets of North Hollywood into a battlefield. Hollywood producers scramble on their Star Tacs to cut their deals for World's Scariest whatever deals as the bad boys walk around calmly, jacked up and spraying bullets. The cops are so outgunned they raid a gun shop for an arsenal usually reserved for beach landings. Was there a message? Hell Yeah! Great ratings on Fox.

This is a land where doctors kiss their wives good-bye and later lose their lives outside burning abortion clinics in Massachusetts, Virginia, Florida, Oregon, Ohio, Minnesota and California—the victims of preachers, former altar boys, and women who look more like manicurists than terrorists. Other docs doing the dishes in their suburban homes are assassinated with deer rifles.

In Idaho, Montana, Alabama, Louisiana, Georgia, Texas and Utah, the pride of white America, stash a decade's worth of Spam and freeze-dried food into the hills, practice with paint guns and plot the demise of everybody from the IRS to the FBI. In this land of equality and free speech, the JDL and Nation of Islam do their part to keep the hate at a scalding pitch.

In L.A., inner-city toddlers catch stray bullets from drive-by shooters, while, in New York, Islamic whackos use a rented van full of fertilizer makings to blow up the World Trade Center. In San Diego, a despondent plumber hotwires a tank, flattens some cars, and is shot to death after high-centering on a freeway divider. Rival rapsters in New York and L.A. gun down each other in a war of the coasts.

What would Ozzie and Harriet Nelson say?

In Miami, a renowned fashion designer out to fetch his morning paper—whose only crime is penning groin-high hemlines—is blown away by a young, bar-hopping trendie from West L.A. who looks disturbingly like another young, bar-hopping trendie from West L.A.—only that one is allegedly hacked up by a famous football and movie star.

Local police are now hiring ex-SEALs to teach them how to take down entire schools instead of trailers. Things are heating up. What's that miss? Your kitten's up the tree? Boom!

A recent Gallup poll discovered that 40 percent of the American people think that "the federal government has become so large and powerful that it poses an immediate threat to rights and freedoms of ordinary citizens." Delta Force at Waco. Black helicopters over urban cities. New World Order? Naw just your tax dollars hard at work doing something.

In Oklahoma City, the Alfred P. Murrah Building is blown up. The nondescript building has no significance other than being the headquarters for the DEA, Secret Service and the ATF. The aftermath is a nine story-hole, a crater 30 feet wide by 8 feet deep, and 168 innocent people killed. The methodology is very similar to that used in the World Trade Center bombing: a 1,000 to 1,200-

pound fertilizer- and diesel-based bomb packed into a rented Ryder truck and detonated by remote control or timer. Different folks, same strokes.

Farther south, some 300 miles away in Waco, Texas, the site of the Branch Davidian compound has become a popular local tourist attraction. The bomb blast in Oklahoma City occurred two years to the day after the attack by the ATF on the cult's compound. During the ATF raid, a brainwashed prophet, with an arms cache the size of the Serbs', had his followers blow their brains out as he torched his compound—and their children. Or so the government told us he did, until they found military advisors and inflammable tear gas canisters at the scene.

Mayhem, Tabloid Style

We used to chuckle at the tabloids, as we bought them with our groceries. Now we can't figure out if it's the news we're watching or promos for the latest B movies.

Hard times breed strange heroes. The hardscrabble days of early America bred the outlaws of the Wild West. Jesse James and Billy the Kid were popularized in East Coast dime novels. The Great Depression gave us Dillinger and Capone, Bonnie and Clyde. Today, in down-on-its-luck L.A., we are hatching a new breed of famous ne'er do wells. In Los Angeles, the land of "three strikes you're out" has become "do a crime, do the prime time." Are you watching a talk show or is it a Tyson bout? Is that a mass murderer or is he just working through some "issues"? What is wrong and what is right? Film at 11. Answers, never.

Must See TV	
Most closely followed news stories from 1986–1999	
Challenger explosion (July '86)	**80%**
San Francisco earthquake (Nov. '89)	**73%**
Rodney King verdict (May '92)	**70%**
Crash of TWA (July '96)	**69%**
Little Girl who fell in a well (Oct. '87)	**69%**
Columbine High School shootings (April '99)	**68%**
End of Gulf War (Mar. '91)	**67%**
Hurricane Andrew (Sept. '92)	**66%**
Southern California earthquake (Jan. '94)	**63%**
Iraqi invasion of Kuwait (Aug. '90)	**63%**

Source: Pew Research Center for the People and the Press

Here, random violence and thoughtless pain take on plot, character and movie deals, as two rich kids splatter their parents' brains against a wall with a 12-gauge for a couple of Rolexes. In Los Angeles, a former football hero and movie star is accused of nearly severing his ex-wife's head and brutally stabbing to death her acquaintance. Meanwhile, during his "getaway," traffic on plagued L.A. freeways comes to a halt; motorists emerge from their cars waving banners urging, "Go O.J.!" and "Save the Juice!" After the most publicized trial in history, the jury lets him go free.

Must See TV	
Most closely followed news stories of 1999	
Colombine shootings (April)	**68%**
Events after Colombine shootings (May)	**59%**
JFK Jr crash (July)	**54%**
Capture of 3 U.S. soldiers in Kosovo (April)	**47%**
NATO airstrikes against Serbia (early April)	**41%**
NATO airstrikes against Serbia (later April)	**41%**
Oklahoma and Kansas tornadoes (May)	**38%**
Kosovo (July)	**32%**
NATO strikes against Serbia (July)	**32%**
Impeachment trial of Clinton (February)	**31%**

Source: Pew Research Center for the People and the Press

Here, crime needs a subplot and linkage. A mother tosses her kids off a bridge and jumps in herself afterward. The news media immediately connects it to a woman in the South who rolled her two kids to their watery end—a woman who played the media like a fiddle in her search for her "kidnapped" children. A mother of a school shooting victim walks into a pawn shop to see a gun, loads it and shoots herself in the head.

Distraught people block crowded freeways, unfurl large banners and then blow their brains out on the freeway. Suicide by cop means clean shooting, an ambulance if they miss and wall-to-wall TV coverage. Everyone can be Hemingway now.

Crime also needs a surprise ending, a payback. Rodney King gets the crap beaten out of him, sues and gets millions. Reginald Denny gets the crap beaten out of him and hugs and kisses the mother of one of his attackers. The Unabomber's big demand is that he have his antitechnology manifesto published. We Americans like our crime. Just keep it fresh, surprising and very brutal.

Hey, America . . . What Time Is It?	
Every 2 seconds	**a criminal offense**
Every 3 seconds	**a property crime**
Every 4 seconds	**a larceny-theft**
Every 13 seconds	**a burglary**
Every 19 seconds	**a violent crime**
Every 23 seconds	**a vehicle is stolen**
Every 28 seconds	**an aggravated assault**
Every 60 seconds	**a robbery**
Every 5 minutes	**a rape**

Hey, America . . .
What Time Is It?

| Every 29 minutes | a murder |
| Every 30 minutes | news, sports and weather |

Sources: F.B.I. Uniform Crime Report, DP

You can find out about the goings on of the Army of God on the Abortion Rights Activist web site. Check out:

Abortion Rights Activist

http://www.cais.com/agm/main/aog.htm

We live in the land of the free, the home of the brave, where everyone has a right to do something, to speak his mind, to 15 minutes of fame, to a guest appearance on the *Ricki Lake Show.* What is wrong with this picture? It seems that Americans are punctuating their angry sentences with bullets. The beat goes on.

Some Samplings from *The Army of God* (U.S. version) Manual:

- If terminally ill, use your final months to torch clinics; by the time the authorities identify you, you will have gone to your reward.

- Use a high-powered rifle to fire bullets into the engine block of a doctor's car.

- Never make a bomb threat from anywhere but a pay phone.

- Hot-wire a bulldozer at a construction site, drive it to a clinic, jump off and let the bulldozer crash through the clinic wall.

- Drop butyric acid into dumpsters or boxes of trash when people are in the building.

- Put holes through clinic windows. The problem with .22-caliber weapons is the noise—the Fourth of July and New Year's Eve are great times for gunshots.

- Why get out of the way of an abortionist's car? The current lawsuit-crazy attitude can be used against baby-killers, and many awards have been received.

- Look up magazines such as *Soldier of Fortune* or *Survivalist.* Guaranteed that you'll be amazed, if not shocked, by the materials available.

As Not Advertised on TV

In the days of *Father Knows Best,* 91 percent of homicides were solved. Today, when it seems there are more TV cops than real ones, only about 65.5 percent become untangled. The majority of murders are committed by family members and acquaintances against each other. The chances that you will get killed by a stranger are only two out of ten, that is, if you take into account just the solved murders. When unsolved murders are tallied, the FBI estimates that 53 percent of all homicides are being committed by strangers, and that only 12 percent of homicides take place within families. Eighty percent of crimes are committed by same-race perpetrators. Robbery is committed by strangers 75 percent of the time, and aggravated assault is committed by a stranger 58 percent of the time. Eighty-seven percent of all violent crimes are committed against whites and Hispanics. Lone white offenders select white victims 96 percent of the time, and one black offenders select white victims 62 percent of the time. White rapists select white victims 97 percent of the time, and black rapists select white victims 48 percent of the time.

Although 51 percent of prison inmates are black, the balance is out of whack, since African-Americans make up about 12.3 percent of the U.S. population. The number of black males in prison between the ages of 25 and 29 is 7,210 per 100,000. A statistic that should shock and sadden. According to the Department of Justice, the homicide rate for whites is 5.2 per 100,000 and for blacks about 44.7 per 100,000. Urban killers tend to be male (90 percent) and young (15–29). Something is very wrong.

In 1960, 12 percent of the population reported owning one or more handguns. In 1976, 21 percent owned a handgun. Today there are well over 200 million handguns, with 4 million new guns being manufactured each year. Professor Gary Kleck of Florida State University estimates that 1500 citizens used guns to kill criminals in 1980. Police only kill about 500 criminals each year.

U.S. Incarceration Rate (per 100,000 people)	
States with Highest Incarceration Rate	
Texas	659
Louisiana	573
Oklahoma	536
Arizona	473
States with Lowest Incarceration Rate	
Vermont	135
West Virginia	134
Maine	112
Minnesota	103
North Dakota	90

In America one in every 175 people are in jail. Prison populations have doubled in the last 15 years. Maybe we should move to Chechnya, it's safer isn't it?

Within the next year or so the United States is expected to overtake Russia as the country with the highest per capita rate of prisoners, according to a March 1999 report by the private nonprofit group Sentencing Project. The United States, which already has the largest prison population in the world, houses some 1.8 million prison inmates, an incarceration rate five to eight times those of other industrialized nations. According to numbers released by the Justice Department that same month, the United States has 668 prison inmates for every 100,000 residents while Russia currently has 685 inmates for every 100,000 residents.

Cable Killa'

Should we blame the entertainment industry? Entertainment is no family affair. A cable industry–sponsored report says that 57 percent of shows feature violence. In 1995, the three major networks ran 2,574 stories on crime, four times the number they ran in 1991.

Top-10 Talk Show Subjects	
Parent-child relations	48%
Dating	36%
Marital relations	35%
Sexual activity	34%
Reconciliations	25%
Physical health	24%
Abuse	23%
Alienation	23%
Physical appearance	23%
Criminal acts	22%

Bang Bang Boogie, or Chock Full o' Nuts?

Americans know it's a jungle out there because they see it on TV; if it bleeds it leads, if it booms, we zoom.

Rocky Mountain Media Watch estimates that crime disaster and war coverage make up an average of 42 percent of all newscasts. On any given night the amount of violence is between 21 percent and 41 percent. UCLA researchers say that even though murders make up 2 percent of all felonies in Los Angeles, the news devotes 27 percent of its coverage to them. In the same study, it was disclosed that 50 percent of crimes committed by blacks in L.A. are violent and that 47 percent of crimes committed by whites are violent. There were about 30 percent more stories on black crimes involving violence than white crimes. Even though homicides have declined by 13 percent between 1990 and 1995 the number of crime stories on the three networks went up 336 percent—after being de-OJed. Oops, time to get Andy and Barney out of the newsroom.

We like crime, it gives Chuck Norris something to fight about every week. America is the land of the tough guy, people who don't take any crap, and will gun you down if you give them any lip. In New York, Bernard Goetz gets slammed in a $41 million lawsuit for gunning down thugs (while Eastwood makes millions in movies doing the same thing). Meanwhile, on the other coast, prosecutors won't file murder charges against a white man who guns down Latino taggers. Go west young man.

Being the boss man of the land of the free is no picnic. In America, four presidents have been assassinated. Two others have been shot. There have been nearly successful assassination attempts on three others. Three serious contenders for the presidency have been critically shot, two dead. They might even have to move the White House to Bogotá where we have more security and a nicer neighborhood.

The venerable building has been riddled with the bullets of drive-by shootings, bad snipers, even a crashed airplane. America is not a Pepsi commercial or the *Brady Bunch*. America is a dangerous place.

The president has called crime "the great crisis of the spirit that is gripping America today." He didn't say who was gripping at the time and whether it was a crime if you fired your gun but didn't aim. Viewers of films like the *Matrix* or

Basketball Diaries wonder if reality is weirder than fantasy or if the two just collide in school shootings, suicide by cops, and terrorist acts. The number of crimes recorded by police in the United States has risen by more than 60 percent since 1973. Violent crime, by the most conservative estimates, has risen by nearly 25 percent during that same period. The Statue of Liberty may well want to pull her arm down and take in the welcoming mat. In the United States, nearly 10 of every 100,000 people are the victims of a homicide. In 1900, only one person in every 100,000 could expect to become a murder victim.

The United States is a large modern country with devolving inner cities. There are more than 200 million guns in the possession of Americans. Most violent acts in the States are the result of robberies, domestic disputes and drug-related violence. Terrorist acts, ranging from the killing of abortionist doctors to the bombing of the World Trade Center, are highly publicized but not considered a real threat to travelers. The threat of robbery or violent crime in inner cities and some tourist areas is real and should be taken seriously. Travel in America is considered safe, and danger is confined to random violence and inner cities. Those seeking adventure can find it in a New Orleans bar at five in the morning or strolling through South Central L.A. after midnight.

Whackos

In most dangerous places, the players have a sense of purpose—through lineage or frustrated political or theological ambition. Here in America, we protect the right of an individual to make a fool of themselves. According to Southern Poverty and Law Center there are 474 hate groups in the United States, a 20 percent increase from the year before. There are also 163 web sites that disseminate racial hatred.

www.splcenter.org/

Aryan Nation, the KKK and Hate Groups

These are right-wing belligerent groups that specialize in pipe bombs and the intimidation of blacks, Jews and immigrants. Although not considered a threat to the social structure, they are a magnet for a strange new minority: Disenfranchised white poor . . . in an organization that insiders say that is primarily made up of FBI informants.

The KKK's existence is typically displayed in public rallies where a few klansmen can drive crowds into fits of apoplectic rage. Despite the Klan's request that they not be protected by police most cities go into high gear for these events. In 1999 in Ohio alone, there were about 24 Klan rallies that cost an estimated $800,000 in State and civic provided police security.

Just Another Day . . .

The date April 19 holds major symbolic value for right-wing extremists in the United States, being associated both with past historical events as well as terrorism. In the historical context, April 19, 1775, was the date of the Battle of Lexington. In the more current context, a number of militia groups associate April 19 with the Waco catastrophe, the Oklahoma City bombing, and the execution of Richard Wayne Snell, a white supremacist, who was executed on April 19, 1995, some 12 hours after the bombing of the Alfred P. Murrah Federal Building. Snell, convicted of two murders, including the shooting of a black Arkansas state trooper, had ties with two right-wing extremist organizations, the "Aryan Nations" and the "Covenant, Sword and Arm of the Lord" (CSA). Subsequent to the Oklahoma City bombing there were reports suggesting that convicted bomber Timothy McVeigh, planned and timed the April 19 bombing of the Alfred P. Murrah Federal Building to coincide with the Waco tragedy and the execution of Snell.

Another terrorist goon squad to hit the scene in 1996 was the Aryan Republican Army. On April 2, 1996, a pipe bomb tore through the offices of a Spokane, Washington, newspaper, followed by two men who ripped the paper off for $50,000, who then set off another explosion. They left a letter behind announcing the end of "Babylon," a popular buzz term white supremacists use to call the federal government. These guys get off using the names of federal agents when they rent getaway cars.

http://www.kkk.com/

Bring on the Port-o-Johns

In June 1996, The Ku Klux Klan adopted a half-mile stretch of Interstate 55 running through the south of St. Louis through Missouri's "Adopt-A-Highway" program. Backed by a court ruling protecting free speech, hooded and robed Klansmen took to the stretch of road with plastic garbage bags and rakes. Irate locals began using the section of highway as a dumpster.

Islam/Terrorists/Hair Gel

There are a million and a half Muslims in America. If one were to generalize you could say they were black men and women who seek to battle the poverty and lack of self-respect 400 years of American identity have left them with. The roots of Islam are in Chicago. Most people know of the rantings and expostulations of the self-promotional Louis Farrakhan (his news organ can be found at *http://www.finalcall.com/*) But few know of the Muslim American Society led by the son of Elijah Mohammed (the person that Farakhan is supposedly continuing the works of). Yes, there is divisiveness in the Muslim community in the United States, particularly between Muslim immigrants from the Middle East and South Asia, and the definitely more laid back style of homegrown Chicago Islam. Probably the most unfair and pervasive stereotype is that of skinny mujahedin turned cab drivers packing fertilizer into U-Hauls waiting for an activation call from bin Laden. Yes, they exist but they do live up to the reputation the media has given them.

Despite the seriousness given Islamic terrorists by American journalists, they tend to resemble the gang that couldn't shoot straight. According to one of *DP*'s buddies who was hired by the FBI to infiltrate Islamic groups stateside, you'd have a better chance finding bin Laden supporters at a Pillsbury Bakeoff. True, Islamic terrorists were behind the February 26, 1993, bombing of the New York World Trade Center (WTC), which killed six and wounded more than 1,000 others. The FBI and local authorities busted nine suspected Islamic terrorists associated with the bombing as well as other plots to bomb targets in New York, including the UN building and the Lincoln and Holland tunnels beneath the Hudson River. They also are alleged to have put plans together to assassinate both prominent American and Egyptian politicians. FBI agents and immigration authorities nabbed a blind Egyptian cleric named Sheikh Omar Abdel-Rahman (famous for allegedly issuing the *fatwa* that led to the assassination of Egyptian President Anwar Sadat in 1981) on felony charges in connection with the WTC bombing and the other proposed terrorist activities. Rahman and his nine followers were convicted in October 1995 of seditious conspiracy and will be guests of Uncle Sam (using your tax dollars, of course) for a long time.

However, on closer inspection, it seems that the sheik's bodyguard, Emad Salem, a former Egyptian army colonel, was an FBI informant who supplied 150 hours of audio- and videotapes of the entire plot. The videotapes even include shots of the men mixing their homemade fertilizer bombs. Many experts agree that it was a miracle that any of the crudely made bombs could go off at all. For those who have no interest in terrorism we should mention that Farrakhan sells some bitching hair gel and motivational tapes (*http://www.finalcall.com/sales/order-form.html,* Visa and Master Card accepted) and *DP* didn't appreciate the gestapo pat down and brush off on our last visit.

The Bin Laden Babies

Did The Stepford Wives *scare the hell out of you? How 'bout* The Omen? *Or* The Boys From Brazil? *Get ready for* The Bin Laden Babies, *an entire generation of freaked-out whackos from Afghanistan and Pakistan plotting embassy bombings and subway gas attacks on Boston, and they all go by the name of Osama. A bad movie? Maybe not. A survey conducted in the Dir region that borders the two countries revealed that Osama has now become the most popular name for a new boy. More than 500 infants in Pakistan's remote Khost region have been named after the infamous terrorist Osama bin Laden since 1998's embassy bombings in Africa. Businesses are even changing their names. There's now Osama Poultry Farms, a watchmaker named Osama Watches, the Osama Bakery, Osama Cloth House and Osama Public School. Bin Laden has become the Michael Jordan of the "Stans." Be like Ossie. No word, though, on when Nike will come out with its Air Osama running shoe.*

Muslim American Society
http://www.worldforum.com/ministry/abmnstry/mission.htm

American Moslem Foundation
http://www.oz.net/~msarram/

Nation of Islam
Maryam Mosque
7351 South Stoney Island Avenue
Chicago, IL 60649
Tel.: (312) 324-7619
http://www.noi.org/

North American Association of Muslim Professionals and Scholars
http://www.ecnet.net/users/mfmas/naamps/naamps.html

The Rugged Mountain Folk of Montana

This remote, rugged and mountainous state breeds individualism, for sure, but it also produces a disproportionate share of mental cases and whackos. Some of these folks have just been in the woods too long and eaten too many squirrels. Even the militia in Montana tell us that Montana has its unfair share of colorful folks. Montana is the home of the suspected Unabomber, Theodore Kaczynski, who was busted by the feds April 3, 1996, in his remote Montana cabin. The Unabomber killed three people and injured 23 during a 17-year mail bombing spree. Montana is also the home of extremist militiaman

John Trochmann (see "Militia of Montana" below), as well as Terry Nichols of Oklahoma City blast fame. And the state is the base for a bunch of zanies who go by the handle "Freemen" (they're not free any longer). These guys, devout white supremacist Christians who reject government authority, refuse to pay taxes and like to write bad checks. On March 25, 1996, a standoff began in Jordan, Montana, between 20 armed Freemen and more than 100 FBI agents after two of the Freemen's leaders were jailed over a $1.8 million fraudulent check scheme, the theft of television equipment and for threatening a federal judge. Even former Green Beret and borderline fascist James "Bo" Gritz couldn't negotiate this wolfpack's surrender. Even Trochman and his MOM get foamy at the mouth when *DP* calls to say hi. Toss in another chunk of meat.

Office Workers

There's an alarming trend of murder in the workplace. More than 1,000 Americans are murdered on the job every year. The U.S. Postal Service has had 34 employees gunned down since 1986. They still issue pepper for use against dogs. Hmmm, maybe it's time for Kevlar and .45s.

Your Tax Dollars

The FBI has the worst conviction rate of any federal law enforcement agency or so says a Syracuse University TRAC compiled by former *New York Times* reporter David Burnham. His point is that the FBI is responsible for everything from terrorism to civil rights to bank robberies and that federal prosecutors did not take action in one-third of the cases. Burnham says that the FBI has a 27 percent conviction rate compared to the DEA, INS and IRS. ON a ratio of dismissals to convictions the INS won with a ratio of 18 convictions for every dismissal, the DEA had a 7 to 1 ratio and the IRS limped in at 2 to 1.

The FBI describes that report as "meaningless" and says that their conviction rate is 69 percent of cases prosecuted.

Gangs

America's willingness to absorb large masses of refugees resulted in the importing of some of the nastiest and hardest groups of street gangs in any Western country. In New York, rival gangs of Puerto Ricans, Irish or blacks don't actually break out into spontaneous choreography when they want to settle a dispute. *West Side Story* has become *Apocalypse Now*. In L.A., fast cars and even faster weapons have elevated gangs into small armies. The weapons of choice are full-automatic weapons with semiautomatics reserved for rookies. Assault weapons, like the AK-47, Tec 9, MAC, UZI or shotguns are preferred. Most gangs are created along ethnic and neighborhood lines. Bloods and Crips are the new Hatfields and McCoys. The *gangsta* look has become big business now. Baggy pants, work shirts, short hair, and that unique gangsta *lean* have all been adopted by freckle-faced kids from Iowa. Gangsta music has towheaded kids reciting tales of inner-city woes, just as their parents were able to recite "Itsy Bitsy Teenie Weenie Yellow Polka Dot Bikini." The new proponents of this violent/hip culture seem to live life a little too close to their lyrics. Rappers Tupac Shakur and Notorious B.I.G. both probably wish they had been singing Barney's theme of "I love you, you love me." In Los Angeles, there are over 800 gangs with 30,000 members. There are at least 1,000 homicides every year and well over 1,000 drive-by shootings. According to figures presented to the White House, there are 500,000 gang members in 16,000 gangs in the United States. Eight hundred American cities are home to these gangs, compared to 100 in 1970. Fifty-seven percent of towns with over 25,000 residents have reported gang-related incidents.

But gangsterism in America is not black, white and Hispanic. Gang members come in all flavors. The most dangerous gangs in America are the new Asian gangs, groups of Cambodian, Vietnamese, Laotian and Filipino youths whose families came from the refugee camps, killing fields and dung heaps of Southeast Asia. Chinese-American gang members are being blamed for the February 25, 1996, murder of Cambodian actor Dr. Haing Ngor, a former refugee of the Khmer Rouge and the star of the 1984 movie *The Killing Fields*. After enduring four years of savage brutality under the Khmer Rouge during the guerrilla group's reign of terror between 1975 and 1979, the Academy Award–winning doctor was ironically slain in the land of the free, for a Buddhist amulet.

Crips
www.crips.com
Bloods
www.bloods.com

Thrill Rides

You have a one in three million chance of being injured on a thrill ride. Thirty-six people have been killed on rides since January 1987. In 1997 8,700 visitors were injured on roller coasters, ferris wheels and other whoop de do danger rides. Eighty percent of the injuries are caused by people who stick their feet out, stand up, or ignore warnings.

Your Next-door Neighbor

Four out of ten violent crimes in the United States are committed by relations or acquaintances of the victims.

Your Bed

You have a one in three chance of dying in bed.

Militias and the New World Order

Militias were once social centers for good ol' boys with a strong sense of gun love. Ignored by the mainstream press until the Oklahoma bombing, they were free to dress in army surplus gear and shoot off guns in the swamps of Florida or the mountains of Colorado. Now the more colorful members of the militia realize that being on TV doesn't do too much other than get you a fat FBI file.

Divisive, unruly and as media savvy as Reggie Jackson they quickly were demonized and ostracized. Given a few more long necks and a couple of pinches of Skoal, the more colorful and mercenary of the bunch could come up with coherent political agenda. But that is just the cartoon version the Feds would like you to believe. Militias are a very pervasive and deep rooted movement in areas where hard times, dull headed governments and jackboot agencies exist. As one militia leader told *DP*, "You are not going to see a real militia man on TV, but we're here . . . waiting."

The point is that militias don't exist to sell videotapes, parade around in designer cammo and fondle guns. The mainstay of the American militia movement is the same lifeblood that thumped King John, tossed the British under King George and will become vocal when our government forgets that. Are they the enemy? It depends which side you are on. If you live inside the Beltway or drive a Volvo you just might be.

**Team Delta Is Looking for a
Few Good Prisoners . . .**

Looking for a little weekend getaway for you and the wife?
Life looking too good after that Internet IPO. Looking for a
special gift for your boss? How about three days at Prisoner
of War Interrogation Resistance Program? For a measly
$695 each you can learn how to survive punishment, harass-
ment, bad food and no sleep. Their brochure says it all:
"Physical techniques (pain) are employed as required. . . .
The less a prisoner cooperates with the interrogators and
the guards, the more 'pain compliance' that prisoner can
expect." They promise "an extremely memorable experience."

> *Team Delta*
> *12th Street Gym*
> *204 S. 12th Street*
> *Philadelphia, PA*
> *http://www.teamdelta.net/boot_fit.htm*

The Southern Poverty Law Center has identified 440 self-proclaimed antigovernment militias. And they've infested every state in the union. The government calls them "Internet commandos," but is taking them quite seriously (see "The Babylonians"). Currently, there are 24
states where the higher-profile militias are in operation. California, Arizona, Nevada and Colorado make up the South/Western area while the Southeastern area includes Florida, Alabama,
Georgia, Tennessee, Arkansas, Missouri, North Carolina and Virginia. There is also a Northeastern area that is composed of New York, New Hampshire, Ohio, Pennsylvania, Indiana and
Wisconsin. There is no accurate count of exactly how many people belong to militias.

It is interesting to note that many of the militia groups are growing in popularity, thanks to
Janet Reno and the use of tanks and military forces against the Branch Davidians and the gen-
eral isolation of a Washington-based government. The most well-known militias in the good ol'
U.S.A. are the following:

> *http://www.splcenter.org/*
> *http://www.militia-watchdog.org/m1.htm*
> *http://members.tripod.com/ibfletch/index-militia.html*
> *http://pages.prodigy.com/geoffc/nwo.htm*

The New World Order

There is not enough space here to really lay out the New World Order, but in brief a small
group of bankers are working to control the world through politicians, business and
security groups like the United Nations. The word also pops up like when George Bush's
created the "New World Order" to crusade against Saddam Hussein prior to the 1991
Gulf War.

> *http://www.unn.ac.uk/societies/islamic/about/current/neworder.htm*

The Leaderless Resistance/Lone Wolves

The new tact is to encourage individuals to strike back without claiming affiliation or
creating groups that can be penetrated by federal agencies. The idea was proposed by a
U.S. military officer to combat communism in 1962. By removing the labels and public
gatherings the media has no hooks to hang on and no publicity. An unseen and unknown
revolution causes more fear in the enemy. Or is nobody home?

> *http://www.louisbeam.com/leaderless.htm*

Florida State Militia

A right-wing Christian group with about 500 members led by Robert Pummer. Favorite quote from handbook: "BUY AMMO NOW! YOU WILL NOT BE ABLE TO BUY IT LATER!

http://www.interlog.com/~vabiro/pubs/adl_mi~1.htm#Florida

Guardians of American Liberties (GOAL)

This Colorado-based group wants to be the mouthpiece for militias everywhere (probably in direct competition with the Unorganized Militia based in Indianapolis).

http://www.nizkor.org/hweb/orgs/american/adl/armed-and-dangerous/colorado.html

Lone Star Militia

Leader Robert Spence (who bills himself as an Imperial Wizard of the True Knights of the Ku Klux Klan) says he heads up 11,000 militia members. It is said that if it wasn't for FBI covert informants the KKK would have been extinct 20 years ago.

http://www.fas.org/irp/eprint/presley.htm

The Republic of Texas Militia

A hundred and fifty years ago these guys would have gotten some respect. In fact, Sam Houston would have been at the helm. But it's the late 1990s, so, instead, we get a guy named Richard McLaren, who refers to himself as the Ambassador of the Republic of Texas. The RTM emerged in 1995 with the agenda of seceding Texas from the union, claiming the state was annexed illegally in 1845. The "ambassador" took a couple of hostages in April 1997 to grab some PR, but now is without portfolio in some Texas dungeon.

Militia of Montana (MOM)

John Trochman heads a little family-run militia, video and book business in the wide-open lands of Montana. This white supremacy group is reported to be working closely with the Aryan Nations Church in Hayden Lake, Idaho. He is a particular fan of *DP* and despite the rather innocuous listing here likes to threaten us whenever we call.

P.O. Box 1486
Noxon, MT 59853
Tel.: (406) 847-2735
Web site: www.logoplex.com/resources/mom

Northern Michigan Militia

It's cold in Michigan, so cold that it can freeze the rational parts of most folks' brains. Considering the inclement weather and "band together or freeze" syndrome, it seems that joining a militia is the next favorite activity after ice fishing. Commander Norm Olsen manages to combine his skills as minister, gun store owner and former air force officer to lead his flock of 12,000 NMMS (Numbs?).

http://www.carnell.com/michiganmilitia.html

Police Against the New World Order

Although we couldn't find a Yellow Pages listing for the New World Order (we couldn't figure out if it was a Chinese restaurant or a church), apparently this group thinks "it's" out there. Probably the most famous and visible of the groups, PANWO, is captained by former Phoenix police officer Jack McLamb. McLamb was last seen nationally doing some expostulating with Bo Gritz at the ill-fated Waco compound.

http://www.police-against-nwo.com/

Unorganized Militia of the United States

Created by Linda Thompson, a lawyer from Indianapolis whose specialty seems to be suing the Federal government, This is the only nationally organized militia with far, far fewer members than the 3 million their PR claims.

The Babylonians
Bill Clinton/The Office of the President of the United States

What can you say about a man who can helm the world's most powerful armed forces without any military experience, bomb Afghanistan, boff employees and keep his job, bomb Iraq, lie under oath, cheat on his wife, bomb Serbia, fight impeachment, bomb Sudan, and make speeches about all the good moral stuff presidents are supposed to stand for. It's good to be king. Bill Clinton has sent more troops overseas than any other president since 1945.

The president is commander-in-chief because the Constitution allows him to make war. Since then, presidents have sent U.S. troops into action more than 200 times. In 1975 the War Powers Resolution was designed to bring an end to the undeclared war in Vietnam. The resolutions required that the president notify Congress before sending troops in harm's way. Those troops must be withdrawn within 60 days if Congress does not authorize their presence. Since 1980, U.S. troops have been sent to Panama, Grenada, Lebanon, Iraq, Iran, Haiti, Somalia and the Balkans. Only Bush got Congress's approval to send troops to the Gulf in 1991.

http://www.whitehouse.gov
http://www.whitehouse.gov/WH/Mail/html/Mail_President.html

Bob Hope Concert Tour Information (U.S. Troops Overseas)

Over 200,000 U.S. Troops are stationed overseas. Numbers change often

Germany	70,000
Japan	40,000
Yugoslavia	37,000 troops (reassigned)
Saudi Arabia	25,000
Bosnia	20,000 troops (1995)
Balkans	7,000
Bosnia	5,900
Panama	4,000 (2,000)
Cuba	1,000
Haiti	450
Macedonia	587
Ecuador	21

Peace Love and . . .

It may say something that half a million people went to Woodstock in 1969, but the biggest event of 1999 was not Woodstock's 20th anniversary (with 225,000 attendees) but a bunch of bikers in Sturgis (over 500,000 people). The latest incarnation of three days of peace love and profits featured $5 bottled water, riots, 40 arrests, one death (from heart failure) and 3,000 people seeking medical treatment. The highlight of the event was when candles handed out by a peace advocacy group were used to start fires to cars, trash and of course a wooden mural called the Peace wall.

http://www.woodstock.com

Executive Working Group on Domestic Terrorism

This secret task force meets at the Justice Department every couple of weeks and plots strategy against the burgeoning number of Boy Scouts turned bin Ladens. How much damage they're doing isn't certain, but since its inception in late 1995, the number of FBI investigations into militias around the country has increased 300 percent. The group is privately being called instrumental in stopping a Texas terrorist from blowing up Austin's IRS office in 1995.

http://www.fbi.gov/pressrm/congress/freehct2.htm

The Military

So what do you get for $242 billion a year? We are heading for a total armed forces of 1.4 million and downsizing in toys. Right now we have 95,000 troops in place in Korea and Japan and another 230,000 in the NATO countries. It looks like the new kinder, gentler military will shake out to be as follows. The Army gets a chintzy $71 billion to train, house and feed 797,000 troops. The Air Force gets $83 billion and runs ten active and five reserve tactical fighter wings, totaling 1,500 planes and 300 large transport planes, and finally the Navy burns up $87 billion a year to run 451 surface ships and 14 aircraft carrier battle groups.

http://www.defenselink.mil/

The Military/Industrial Complex

Today there are only six states in the world that are hostile to the United States: Cuba, Iraq, Iran, Libya, North Korea and Syria. So it seems that the United States, with its insatiable demand for deadly toys, has become the most dangerous player on the planet. Why? Because it seems that we like to practice on tiny islands or desert wastelands (you get better PR photos that way). Our pyrotechnic show-and-tell supports our $53.9 billion in sales between 1994 and 1998. The Avis to our Hertz is Russia with a pathetic 12.3 billion in sales in the same period. Who is our biggest customer? Taiwan sucked up $13.3 billion, followed by Saudi Arabia at 9.7 then Turkey, Egypt, South Korea, Greece and India. They get the previously owned, flown by an 18 year old only on weekend stuff. The good stuff, well, we keep that stuff. Uncle Sam pockets about $10 billion a year in sales of arms to other nations.

Consider the ultimate plaything: the modern aircraft carrier. Three billion a pop, four and a half acres of space, 6,000 people, can sail 22 years before refueling, can launch 25 different kinds of aircraft in 15 minutes. But we fight wars in Lebanon, Somalia, Kosovo, Kuwait, Colombia, Grenada, Panama, etc. Places where mules and slingshots could come in handy. Go figure.

War is high-tech, according to the boys in the Pentagon. Carefully planted stories about how our air launched missile inventory was down from 300 to a shocking 100, ship launched Raytheon built, Tomahawks down to 2,000 from 2,700, our B-52s are aging, angst, horror, fear and loathing. Coincidentally, the government needs a cool $6 billion to freshen up inventory, 10 percent for missiles. Boeing is busy building 230 more missiles to refill our warehouses.

The Navy blew off 400 Tomahawks against Iraq and Yugoslavia in December 1998. Was it a Y2K thing that would have made them obsolete anyways or just the best way to get some new toys? You would think everything we threw at the swarthy buggers was intelligent. Only 10 percent of the weapons fired during the Gulf war were smart bombs, but the videos we saw made us think otherwise.

Ever wondered why we sent B2s from Guam to bomb skinny teenagers with turbans? Ever wonder why we need stealth fighters but we show videotapes of their bombing runs? Ever scratch your head and wonder why we use a million and a half dollar cruise missile against Iraqi supply trucks? Ever wonder why we like to invade a little puke country with all those gizmos and then just leave? Now you know.

http://www.mnsinc.com/pogo/mici/
http://www.thirdworldtraveler.com/Economics/MilitIndusComplex_Privit.html
http://www.foreignpolicy-infocus.org/papers/micr/.

Dirty Harry on Steroids

Need to make an impression on unshaven, unfed ground troops? Here is just some of what Uncle Sam has in their sandbox. Ninety percent of the weaponry used in the Balkans were "smart" and expensive.

Nuclear Carrier	$3 billion	One carrier has a bigger air force than 75 percent of the world's nations
B2 Bomber	$2.3 billion	Carries 16 one-ton bombs
E-3 Sentry	$270 million	Surveillance, command and control plane
B1 Bomber	$200 million	Long-range bomber
F 117A Stealth	$45 million	fighter bomber
Tomahawk	$1–1.5 million	GPS and radar guided warhead
B52	$30 million	Aging war horse
F16 Fighter	$16 million	Compact multi-role fighter
F-15 Fighter	$43 million	State-of-the-art fighter
GBU-32 JDAM	$18,000	GPS-guided, delivers a 1–2,000 lb. payload
Paveway GBU-27	$55,000	Very accurate laser-guided 2,000 lb. bomb
AGM-130	$884,000	Rocket-powered, pilot steerable air-to-ground warhead with 30-mile range
AGM-154 JSOWO	$ 247,00	Satellite-guided missile that can cover a football-field-sized area with anti-personnel bomblets
AGM-88 HARM	$284,000	Air-launched radar-guided missile with a range of 17 miles
AGM-86C	$1,160,00	Air-launched cruise missile
GBU -15	$300,000	Glide weapon
AGM-130A	$280,000	Air-to-surface missile
AGM-65 Maverick	$17,000–100,000	Air-to-surface missile

The Mob

The Russians

The Russians started coming in the late 1970s and early 1980s—300,000 in all—when the Soviet government temporarily lifted immigration barriers allowing persecuted Soviet Jews to emigrate. Included in this batch was what the FBI terms as "second-echelon" criminals, who settled in Brighton Beach in Brooklyn. They basically beat up on each other, and the Feds stayed out of it. The second wave arrived after the collapse of the Soviet Union, when Russia upped the number of visas to the United States from 3,000 a year to nearly 33,000—a more than 10-fold increase. Savage and unrepentant, the Russian mob counts on fear to scare its enemies—and doesn't think twice about wasting cops. In 1994, the FBI—with the help of the Russian Ministry of Internal Affairs

(MVD)—got a tip on a top Moscow crime boss, Vyacheslav Ivankov, who was coming to New York to oversee the gang's U.S. operations. Ivankov was under surveillance once he got to the States and then made the mistake of extorting a couple of Russian emigrés who owned a Wall Street investment consulting firm. To show he was serious, Ivankov had one of the targets' father show up dead in a Moscow train station. Ivankov was later busted and ended up spitting at and kicking reporters after he was fingerprinted. The Feds have a lot more to learn about the Russian gangsters, who one MVD official categorized as "very tough, very smart, very educated and very violent."

http://members.tripod.com/~orgcrime/russexy.htm
http://www.razvod.com/links/clubs.htm
http://brightonbeachavenue.com/MainPage.html

The Triads and Tongs

The FBI knows quite a bit more about the Chinese *triads*, *tongs* and street gangs than they do about the Russians. The Chinese population in the United States has been spiraling for decades and has provided a far more penetrable profile for the Feds. They're well aware of the three tiers: the Hong Kong–based *triads*, the secretive criminal families that were on the scene well before the Sicilian mafia; the *tongs*, which are ostensibly Chinese-American business associations, but in reality crafty overseers of devious doings; and the Chinese-American street gangs brought in as enforcers. The *triads* and *tongs* do their biggest business bringing Chinese white heroin into the United States, but also dabble in the smuggling of Chinese illegal aliens. The *triads* get them to Mexico, or somewhere else knockin' on Uncle Sam's door, where the *tongs* take over and put the illegals to work at slave wages in sweat shops and whorehouses. For their freedom, they have to pay off the *tongs* from US$30,000–50,000.

http://www.fringeware.com/subcult/Chinese_Tong.html

Right-wing Groups

There is a movement afoot in America, distrust of big government and a need to push back. There are two dispossessed groups in America. The first is the large groups of racial minorities who live in the inner cities; the other is the much larger group of whites who for whatever reason cannot avail themselves of the American Dream. Most of these folks are content to listen to Rush Limbaugh and throw empty beer cans at their TV. Others gather together and create groups that commiserate and plot. Few ever do anything meaningful, but they do exist.

Luckily, none of the right-wing whacko groups are under the players sections. Although the names sound interesting, even a brief review of their political agenda or beliefs will convince you that many of these folks aren't firing on all cylinders. Most groups are poorly financed, loosely organized, like guns, think small, have few members, drink a lot of beer, live in the woods and usually have a pot-bellied leader who likes to go by a goofy name as exalted something or grand poobah.

The guys who do decide to get violent practice a pattern of violence similar to the "calendar terrorism" we saw executed by the leftist groups of the 1970s, when attacks coincided with specific historical events. Their MO is mostly bomb attacks. Explosives-related arrests accounted for 22 percent of criminal incidents involving extremists in a two-year period ending in December 1996. The bombmakers rely heavily on the *Anarchist's Cookbook* (*http://www.murzik.com/book*) for their lethal recipes. None have graduated to building nuclear devices (*http://www.pal.xgw.fi/hew*) or even put together a decent recipe book (*http://www.hartfordadvocate.com/articles/whitetrash.html*). For now the most vocal of the groups seems to grab the most media attention.

Ku Klux Klan

The Klan is probably the most well known hate group in the United States. Known for decorating the south with flaming crosses, they now are more of a parody of the old guard right wing in America. (It could also be those dorky bedsheets they have to wear.) The Klan in North America has some proponents like Louis Beam (leader of the Fifth Era Klan) of Texas and Dennis Mahon (who leans more towards Tom Metzger's WAR movement) of Oklahoma who demand revolutionary violence. There are Klan-lite groups like the one led by Arkansas-based Thomas Robb who portray the Klan as the white man's nonviolent NAACP. For now they are targets of the FBI and left wing groups who prosecute the group on behalf of its victims for any hate crime.

http://www.kukluxklan.org/women.htm

The New Abolitionists

Not quite Buckwheat ebonics, but a magazine advocates that white people reject their whiteness, or "abolish the white race as a social category." Their hero is John Brown, who is considered unwhite.

http://www.alliswell.com/newabolition/

White Aryan Resistance (WAR)

WAR is a group led by Tom Metzger, a television repairman who lives in rural Fallbrook, California. He lost everything he had in a landmark lawsuit which determined that he and the activities of his group were responsible for the beating and death of a man in the Pacific Northwest. He is still on the Web with his nasty cartoons for those who care.

http://www.resist.com/

Christian Identity Groups

It's hard to believe that you could get enough people for a cocktail party under the premise that the most egregious "theft of culture" in human history was perpetrated by Satan and the Jews to dispossess the Anglo-Saxon and kindred peoples of their birthright, but there are Christian identity groups that use this basic pretext at their core. These folks also believe that the world is heading into an apocalypse soon. These folks blame the Jews for making them live in trailer parks and shanties and say that it will be payback time when the millennium rolls around.

http://www.carm.org/c_christian_identity.htm

National Alliance

The National Alliance is a Neo-Nazi group begun after leader William Pierce wrote a book called the *Turner Diaries* (under the pen-name of Andrew McDonald). The radical right wing adopted the book about a Neo-Nazi underground group that kills Jews, blacks, and those whites guilty of "racemixing," as part of an effort to overthrow a Jewish-dominated government. The *Turner Diaries* is one of Timothy McVeigh's favorite books.

http://www.natall.com/index.html

Odinism

Odinism is a Christian-based religion that also includes ritual magic, anti-Semitism, and a desire to get back to the good old days when the Aryan race (Nordic/Germanic) was cool. Odinism has followers in Scandinavia, Germany, South Africa and America. Asatru is a belief much like Odinism, except for the racist part.

http://www.natall.com/index.htm

Wicca

Wicca is witchcraft but also a religion. It does not really concern itself with existence after death, nor does it really provide concrete rules to living happily, e.g., there are no Commandments. The only rule laid down by Wicca is to harm no one; violation of that rule results in retributory consequence. But what it is to harm someone, is not defined in the religion. That is left for everyone and everything to decide for themselves, because whatever it is that someone decides to do will be revisited upon them.

http://www.religioustolerance.org/wic_usbk.htm
http://www.spiritonline.com/wicca/

Church of the Creator

Church of the Creator was created by a charismatic and highly authoritarian leader, Ben Klausen, who ministers via mail order. The COC centers on the belief that all religions are false since Christianity was built on a Jewish fable. Reverend Ben (he called himself Pontifex Maximus) said that creativity is the thing, a blend of militant atheism, health-fadism and racism is where it's at. The problem is that Ben offed himself, yet his followers can still be found, primarily in Europe and the United States.

World Church of the Creator

Matt Hale runs this bigoted shoebox full of hate out of East Peoria, Illinois. Its most esteemed member was Benjamin Nathaniel Smith, who distinguished the order's preachings by going on a two-state "retreat" in July 1999 around the Chicago area—killing two and wounding nine others in some multi-ethnic target practice from his blue Ford Taurus before swallowing the molten puke of his own pistol. Smith took out some true riff-raff—a student and a college basketball coach. Way to go, Ben. Both of you.

www.creator.org

Posse Comitatus

Posse Comitatus, founded by William Potter Gale, fights the idea of income tax.

White Singles

Sorry, not a hate group per se (or would it be a love to hate group?), but a great place to meet Aryan friendly white chicks.

http://whitesingles.com/

Canadians

You too can make your own politically incorrect Web site, eh?

http://www.freedomsite.org/index1.html

Phineas Priesthood

The Phineas Priesthood is an ultra-right group known for its attacks on cops and gays. The PP has been characterized as "one of the most violent ideologies in the extremist movement today." It is a combination of religious faith, white-only membership and low-profile tactics, based on a Biblical tale of Phineas, who killed an Israelite who consorted with a woman who was not of the chosen people. Phineas' action saved the people of Israel from a plague that God unleashed on those who did not follow purity of race and religion codes. Connect the dots.

Skinheads

The Anti-Defamation League estimates that there are a minimum of 3,500 skinheads in the United States. *DP* does not know how many of them are actually prematurely bald men or Limp Bizkit fans.

http://www.skinheads.net/

The IRS

I know they are supposed to be a kinder and gentler organization but there are a number of groups who are formed solely to highlight the illegality and brutality of the IRS in paying the government's bills. This is a separate movement from race, religion or anti-big government.

http://www.irs.ustreas.gov/prod/cover.html

Informed Jury

Another cornerstone of some militias. The idea that the only democratic power we have left is the jury system wherein an informed citizen does not have to convict citizens of offenses they deem reasonable. This also ties into the IRS tax hot button but for now it doesn't hurt to learn more about the rights of individual citizens against big government.

http://www.fija.org/

Tree Huggers and Animal Lovers—Xtreme!

Activities by rights groups are centered around the abortion issue, but certainly aren't confined to it. Animal rights activists have been out doing dirty deeds, but their acts go largely unnoticed. The Animal Liberation Front (ALF), an underground animal rights group, claimed responsibility for a number of fires that caused damage in downtown Chicago department stores. Five of eight incendiary devices ignited, causing fires in Marshall Field's, Carson Pirie Scott and Saks Fifth Avenue stores. While death is not an objective in the actions of most rights groups—as it undermines their causes—each possesses its crazies, as terror and death serve as their tools.

The Animal Liberation Front (ALF)

The ALF (Alfie) originated in Britain in the early 1970s as an outgrowth of an animal rights group known as the Band of Mercy. Over the years, the group has engaged in a wide range of violent and non-violent activities ranging from low-level bombs and arson to protests and raids on farms to release animals. While the animal rights movement has been strongest in Britain, some of its activities have spilled over to the United States and onto continental Europe. Efforts by authorities to identify and neutralize ALF and other animal rights groups have had only partial success as the groups usually operate in small cells, are not tightly organized, and have no card-carrying members. As noted above, their tactics usually involve a wide range of protests, vandalism, product contamination, arson and low-level bombings. ALF slogans promoted in its literature are "learn to burn" and "devastate to liberate." Their targets include all industries engaged in the use of animals for experimentation, food, fur or sport as well as companies engaged in peripheral industries such as the transportation of animals or the use of animal extracts in their products. In the past, universities, research centers, research scientists and chemical companies have been prime targets. And these guys have caused some serious setbacks on some major medical research. On April 5, 1999, Alfie "commandos" ransacked laboratories at the University of Minnesota, taking dozens of research animals and causing an estimated US$1 million in damage. The raid and subsequent damage set back the facility's Alzheimer's research alone by two years.

http://www.animal-liberation.net/

Antiabortionists

It might seem like another small-time raid on an abortion clinic using a botched recipe from *The Anarchist's Cookbook*. On the morning of March 13, 1999, a bomb exploded outside an abortion clinic in Asheville, North Carolina. The blast didn't injure anyone and didn't cause much damage. But the clinic is one of several that received anthrax hoaxes during the previous month. More importantly, it is located 125 miles west of the area where the search for accused serial bomber Eric Rudolph is focused. Rudolph is suspected in the January 1998 Alabama abortion clinic bombing that killed a security guard and severely injured a nurse. There's a million bucks on his head. Could it be that Rudolph's still actively targeting clinics with a price tag on his ass and a massive FBI task force on his trail? It's possible—and if so, Rudolph would be to abortion clinics what Jesse James was to banks. The group of Americans that are most vulnerable to terrorist attacks are abortion providers. While millions get pumped into beefing up the security of overseas embassies, comparatively little goes into protecting abortion clinics. And the little that does is said to save more lives than the funds earmarked for overseas. Huh?

The Army of God

Not to be confused with Hezbollah (meaning "Army of God"), this group has taken responsibility for a series of bomb attacks in the late 1990s on gay discos and abortion clinics in Atlanta and elsewhere. The group has known sympathies with the Branch Davidian sect which got burnt to a crisp by federal authorities in April 1993. A gay disco bombed by the group was characterized in one press release as a "sodomite bar."

THE UNITED STATES

www.angelfire.com/al/abortionkillsbabies/aoginfo.html

Biotic Baking Brigade (BBB)

Probably the next in line for Osama bin Laden's spot on the top ten most wanted list is Agent Salmonberry who is determined to give corporate leaders their just desserts. He recently issued a *fatwa* proclaiming that all corporate traitors and environmental traitors and their lackeys in the non-profit sector would "be held accountable." *DP* did not catch if this statement was issued over lunch, but we want to thank Pinkerton's for giving us the heads up on this newest terrorist group. In March 1999 an oil company CEO was brutally hit with several pies. The terrorist group that took credit for the attack was the members of the Biotic Baking Brigade (BBB), a radical environmentalist group. Two men and two women took their position and then threw the pies at the CEO as he arrived at a San Francisco high school to give a talk on careers. The attack was in response to the oil company's ongoing activities in Nigeria. Three of the BBB group's members were sentenced to jail for a November 1998 pie attack on San Francisco Mayor Willie Brown. Other victims have included the February 1998 attack on Microsoft chairman Bill Gates in Belgium. Other recent BBB victims have included the executive director of the Sierra Club, a Nobel prize–winning economist and the director general of the World Trade Organization. It is not known if the pies are of Russian or North Korean origin.

http://www.nacic.gov/

Passport required. The United States has over 20 different types of visas indicating different reasons for travel. Visa type and length varies by country. Travelers from selected countries can stay for up to 90 days without a visa. New Zealand and Australian nationals need visas, not necessary for British citizens. Contact the nearest U.S. embassy or consulate to obtain visa information and requirements.

http://travel.state.gov/links.html

However you want. The United States possesses perhaps the most modern and comprehensive transportation systems in the world, both private and public. As public transportation in the United States is not nationalized, you can expect different levels of service in different areas. Whereas New York City possesses an intricate public transit infrastructure, public transit in Los Angeles is still in the development stage. However, intercity and interstate transportation links in the United States are considered excellent. Problem areas are principally inner-city areas at night. Avoid late-night trips in these areas due to the increased probability of crime.

http://www.bbb.org/library/travel/travel.html

Nevada

According to crime statistics, Nevada is the most dangerous state in the country, and has been since 1996. It is followed by Florida, Louisiana, Maryland, California, Arizona, New Mexico, Illinois, Tennessee and Alaska.

http://www.morganquitno.com/cr99dang.htm

Miami

Florida has the second highest crime rate of all 50 states and Miami is America's second most dangerous city. In 1995, 41.3 million tourists flowed through Florida, so it may not seem like a big deal when one or two of them are offed. A Dutch tourist couple on their way to a shopping center in west Dade was robbed and murdered on February 23, 1995. After a brief respite of two years, it seems that the tourist death toll is beginning to climb again. The Dutch tourists were lost in the seedy area of Liberty City in Dade County in the mid-morning. Many tourists are victims of bump-and-rob scams in which the perpetrator rear-ends the victims on the highway and then robs them as they pull over to exchange info. Miami is home to thieves who like to create confusion by spilling food, asking directions or bumping into you while their accomplice grabs your belongings. These folks tend to be from South America. In July 1997, fashion designer Gianni Versace was gunned down by a homosexual serial killer in Miami's trendy South Beach. Haitian seamen have been dropping like flies on freighters at Miami's docks. A July 1997 massacre aboard one freighter left six Haitian crewmen dead in an ongoing series of assaults on cargo ships by bad guys looking for drugs to steal. And speaking of drugs, the DEA's Miami office confiscated 16,465 pounds of cocaine during the first nine months of fiscal 1996. That was more than five times the amount seized in Houston and four times the amount nabbed in L.A. during the same period. In 1996, the U.S. Customs Service seized 70,000 pounds of cocaine, an increase of more than 50 percent over 1995. The Cali cartel makes Miami its North American home, and the DEA says South Florida is home to more cocaine traffickers than it was a decade ago. Sonny Crockett, where the hell are you?

http://www.miamicity.com/

Atlanta

This southern city has the dubious distinction of possessing one of the highest crime rates in North America. The FBI headed a counterterrorism network to neutralize any terrorist threats at the 1996 Olympic Summer Games in Atlanta. Then a pipe bomb allegedly planted by a "good ole boy" killed two innocent people and injured nearly 200 other attendees (the suspect was later deemed innocent). The Army of God was busy in Atlanta in 1997, bombing an abortion clinic and a gay disco. In January and February of 1996, there were 29 bomb threats in Atlanta. During the same two months of 1997, there were a whopping 112.

http://www.pactmetroatl.org/macc/macc.htm

Los Angeles

The men (and women) in blue that patrol the home of gangsta' rap are proud to announce that crime is actually down in L.A. Whether it is our videotaped beating of traffic offenders, turning thugs into music stars or putting on top-rated trials of former football heroes, L.A. must be doing something right. Total crime fell from 312,415 to 278,352 during a recent two-year period. Murders were down from 1,076 to 846. It would appear that no one has notified the 1,140 street gangs that rule the night in L.A.'s poor neighborhoods. There are an estimated 142,000 gang members in L.A.'s South Central—10,000 make their livings simply by selling crack—and the strip that connects downtown to the harbor like a digestive tract is still the most dangerous place in L.A. Apart from the 230 black and Latino gangs identified by the L.A.P.D., there are some 80 Asian gangs that specialize in burglary and carjackings. The L.A.P.D. has started issuing shotguns to its motorcycle officers to meet "the firepower carried by many criminals."

Nonetheless, there are nearly 2,000 willful homicides annually in the county, a place where folks can get away with murder. Only half of all homicide investigations result in arrests and charges. There's a conviction in only a third of the cases. In the early 1990s, murders involving gang members accounted for 38 percent of the cases. The figure is up to 45 percent today.

L.A. is also the bank robbery capital of the world. There were 1,126 of them in 1996, though down from 2,641 in 1992. Eighty percent of the heists are drug-related. Although the number has dropped, the ferocity in their execution hasn't. North Hollywood was turned into a war zone on February 28, 1997, when two gunmen in full III-A body armor, and packing AK-47s and an HK91A3 converted to full auto, took a Bank of America and then took on the LAPD. The crooks sprayed the cops with nearly 100 rounds in the Bank of America parking lot. Civilians and cops dropped like flies. Thoroughly outgunned, some of the officers sped off to a local gun shop to level the playing field. When it was all over the bad guys were dead, but not before they wounded 11 police officers and six civilians. Just to the south of L.A., in Orange County, so-called "takeover" robberies, where gunmen take customers and tellers hostage, jumped 140 percent between 1994 and 1996.

http://da.co.la.ca.us/

New Orleans

It's not the bad guys here that make "The Big Easy" so damned uneasy. It's the cops. The 1,285-member New Orleans Police Department can be considered the most corrupt and brutal major-city force in the United States, according to an FBI investigation into police abuses of civil liberties and overall corruption. Since 1993, more than 50 NOPD officers have been arrested on felony charges, including murder and rape. A few years ago, the week before Rodney King was clobbered by the cops in L.A., one *DP* writer was arrested and beaten by the police in New Orleans—he was hauled in on drug trafficking and prostitution charges after he had been seen giving an impoverished black guy (he's white) a few dollars for directing him to an ATM in the French Quarter. But the good-ole-boy attorney network in N.O. went to work for him. His attorney played golf with a prominent judge a few days later and got the charges dropped—and it only cost the writer five grand. During a subsequent attempt to sue the department and the city, he was informed that the highest damages he would receive would total no more than $3,000, that the city was bankrupt and that any damage award would be paid over 18 years.

Although the murder rate dropped 14 percent in New Orleans in 1995, the city still possesses the highest homicide rate of any major city in the country: 75 murders for every 100,000 residents. In the city's public housing developments, the murder rate is about 18 times higher than the nation's. In the French Quarter, it is best to stay south of North Rampart Street and keep to the center of the street. Do not stop if someone asks you for the time. The housing projects are rife with crime—Desire, Florida and B.W. Cooper are the worst. Do not visit the cemeteries after dark.

Anchorage, Alaska

Yes, Anchorage, though we hate to say it. This city of 260,000 has finally caught up to the 20th century. There are drive-bys, crack houses, handguns and Uzis—in the hands of teenagers. There were more than 25 homicides in Anchorage in 1995, tying a record. The Crips and the Bloods are here. Even the Mexican and Asian gangs have arrived, all wearing colors. And the legal climate in Alaska offers a warm welcome to young criminals and thugs, if the weather doesn't. Under Alaskan law, first- and second-time juvenile offenders are typically punished with a letter that is sent to their parents from authorities. "We still have laws from the *Leave It to Beaver* era," Alaska Governor Tony Knowles said, "for thugs from the *Terminator* age."

http://ucsbuxa.ucsb.edu/Police/1995/UCLA/UCLA.html

Still Murder Central

City	Total	Rate per 100,000
Washington	397	73
New Orleans	351	72
Richmond, Virginia	112	55
Atlanta	196	47
Baltimore	328	46
St. Louis	166	44
Detroit	428	43
Birmingham	113	42
Newark, New Jersey	92	35
Jackson, Mississippi	67	34
U.S.A. Average	19.224	7

Source: USA Today, FBI Uniform Crime Reports

Schools

School used to be a simple red building with a bell on top and belle inside. Today, some high schools use metal detectors and armed security guards to keep the peace. There have been 173 violent deaths in U.S. schools in a four year period. Recently in Los Angeles, a five-year study proved once and for all that schools are safer than the neighborhoods around them. According to the National School Safety Center, violence in the classroom has killed 251 Americans since the 1992–93 school year. California is the leader with 56 deaths, Colorado (15), Florida (14), Texas (13), Georgia (12), Washington (11), New York/Pennsylvania (10), and Illinois and Missouri (9). Is it guns, parents, video games, movies, hormones? Well, in one example Kip Kinkel, the 15 year old who shot 24 schoolmates (2 dead, 22 injured) in Springfield, Oregon, made a class presentation on how to build pipe bombs and read about his plans to kill everyone from his diary in Literature class.

http://www.vpc.org/press/9904col.htm

Fast Food Joints

Food service ranks fourth among the world's most dangerous occupations, behind cab drivers, liquor store employees and police officers. How frequently are fast food chain employees whacked? Of the 52 U.S. murders that occur each day, food service employees are the victims in two of them.

http://stats.bls.gov/oshcont1.htm

The South

The southern states lead the United States in per-capita murder rates. Seven of the ten states with the highest murder rates are in the South. The United States is the most murder-prone country in the developed world.

http://www.disastercenter.com/crime/

The Golden Gate Bridge

San Francisco's Golden Gate Bridge has the dubious distinction of being the most popular bridge for death. The Golden Gate Bridge District is finally getting around to considering a US$3 million steel wire fence to be erected across the bridge's span as a suicide barrier. More than 1,000 people have leapt to their deaths from the bridge since 1937, the year it opened.

http://www.goldengate.org/Misc/AnnualReport2.html

Murder

About 52 people are murdered each day in the United States. In 1996, 19,224 people were whacked (compared with 21,600 in 1995). The U.S. homicide rate is 17 times greater than Japan's, and 10 times the rate in Germany, France and Greece. Louisiana has the highest homicide rate in the country, with 18.5 murders per every 100,000 people. Anywhere in the South is dangerous; the southern states possess the highest rates in the country. But the place where you're most likely to be snuffed is in the nation's capital; a whopping 66.5 people are murdered in Washington, D.C., for every 100,000 people. Males between the ages 15 and 24 are most likely to commit murder. Men commit 91 percent of the murders in the United States.

For those of you currently contemplating committing a murder (automatically pegging it as Murder One!), you might want to consider your venue. Texas leads the nation—big time—in the number of executions since 1976 at 119, followed by Virginia and Florida at 39 each. Of the death penalty states—present and past—Idaho has capped the fewest guys: only one. Fifty-six murderers were put to death in 1995 in the United States, nearly twice as many as the year before. It was the largest number in four decades.

http://www.ihf-hr.org/reports/ar99/ar99usa.htm

Being Black

African-Americans make up about half of the murder victims in the United States. Young African-Americans are more likely to be killed than any other segment in the country.

Being an Immigrant in California

Immigrants are more likely to be wasted than people born in the United States. Between 1970 and 1972, immigrants were the victims in about 23 percent of the homicides in California, even though they represented only 17 percent of the population. Non-Latino white immigrants, most of whom emigrate from European countries, are more than twice as likely to be the victim of a homicide than U.S.-born whites.

http://headlines.yahoo.com/Full_Coverage/US/African_American_News/

AIDS

According to the U.S. Centers for Disease Control, in 1993, AIDS surpassed accidents as the leading cause of death for Americans between 24 and 44 years old. For every 100,000 people, about 35 die of AIDS, about 32 die in accidents. There are 275,000 adults living with HIV in the United States. There are 4,500 children under 13 with the virus.

http://sis.nlm.nih.gov/aidswww.htm

Diplomatic Immunity? Tops in Tickets

It can be assumed the foreign diplomatic in the United States gets away—in the name of "diplomatic immunity"—with a lot of stuff that would send the average Joe to jail for life, such as smuggling state secrets, jet fighter blueprints, Cuban cigars and Afghan heroin. But like everyone else in the greatest democracy on earth, diplomats have to pay parking tickets. These nations' diplomatic corps received the most tickets in New York City. Having the largest fleet, Russia led the way. But the *DP* Cheapskate Award goes to the boys from Pyongyang, with most tickets per vehicle. We don't imagine the parking change these guys figured they'd save went toward feeding its starving population. More likely toward Cuban cigars.

RANK	COUNTRY	No.
MOST TICKETS		
1	Russia	31,388
2	Indonesia	5,706
3	Bulgaria	5,527
4	Egypt	5,074
5	Nigeria	3,551
AVERAGE PER VEHICLE (PER MONTH)		
1	North Korea	38
2	Bulgaria	20
3	Kyrgyzstan	16
4	Russia	15
5	Kazakhstan	13

Source: Los Angeles Times

Big Rigs

While large trucks make up only 3 percent of all registered vehicles in the United States, they account for 21 percent of all deaths in crashes involving two or more vehicles. In 1995, accidents involving heavy trucks killed 4,903 people and injured 116,000. That makes for an average of 13 deaths every day in truck crashes. Twelve of the thirteen victims are occupants of passenger cars.

http://mchs.fhwa.dot.gov/

Handguns and Rifles

Americans own more than 6.7 million handguns (200 million of all types of guns), and aren't afraid to use them. About one-quarter of all American adults own a firearm. On a typical day, one million adults in the United States are packing heat and another two million have a gun in their car. Firearms send almost 40,000 Americans to their graves each year. The deaths and injuries from shootings aren't all borne of malice. In the last year, an Indiana woman fired a .410-gauge shotgun at her foot to remove a callus. A Kentucky man shot himself in the chest "to see what it felt like," he told paramedics. An Oklahoma man got hit with the ricochet after convincing a buddy the best way to kill a millipede crossing a sidewalk is with a .22-caliber rifle. Meanwhile, in Wyoming, a House committee approved a bill that would lower the minimum age for big-game hunters to 12.

http://www.nra.org/
http://www.handguncontrol.org/
http://pacdc.miis.edu/events/effects.html

It Was the Summer of '99			
Where	**Victims**	**Site**	**Date**
Johnson City, TN	2 killed	Law Firm	3/18/99
Salt Lake City, UT	2 killed, 4 wounded	Library	4/15/99
Littleton, CO	13 killed, 21 wounded	High School	4/20/99
Conyers, GA	6 wounded	High School	5/20/99
Las Vegas, NV	4 killed, 1 wounded	Grocery Store	6/3/99
Southfield, MI	2 killed, 4 wounded	Clinic	6/11/99
Atlanta, GA	7 killed, 1 wounded	Home	7/12/99
Atlanta, GA	9 killed, 13 wounded	Brokerage Firm	7/29/99
Pelham, AL	3 killed	Business	8/5/99
Los Angeles, CA	1 killed, 3 wounded	Community Center	9/10/99
Anaheim, CA	3 killed	Medical center	9/15/99
Honolulu, HA	7 killed	Copier Repair office	11/2/99
Seattle, WA	2 killed, injured	Shipyard	11/3/99

Source: *AP*, LA Times,

Being a Kid

Who says it's great being a kid? American youngsters are 12 times more likely to die by gunfire than their counterparts in other industrialized nations. And American children are five times more likely to be killed by any other means than their industrialized counterparts. In the United States, the homicide rate for children under 15 is 2.57 of every 100,000, compared to 0.51 per 100,000 in other industrialized countries. U.S. kids are also twice as likely to commit suicide. The U.S. rate is 0.55 for every 100,000 children. In the rest of the industrialized world, the rate is 0.27 per 100,000. Tricks are for kids.

http://www.child.net/violence.htm

Being a Cop (Andy of Mayberry meets Rambo)

Being a cop is tough. Here at *DP* we are pro police, even if they do pull us over for doing 140 m.p.h. on a street bike. But we gotta wonder when a New London, Connecticut, officer is not hired because he is considered too intelligent. Robert Jordan scored an IQ score of 125, 21 points higher than the national average score for cops. The city decided that smart cops would get bored and quit after going through expensive training.

More than 160 police officers were killed in the line of duty in 1995. California was the deadliest state, with 18 police fatalities. Florida and New Jersey had nine deaths each. Kids are mostly to blame. Between 1984 and 1993, 94 cop killers were under the age of 18. Each year, more than 66,000 police officers are assaulted and 24,000 are injured.

Cops are starting to look more like storm troopers than community civil servants. Between 1995 and 1997 the Department of Defense gave cops 1.2 million pieces of military gear. We're not talking camouflage BVDs here but sniper rifles, machine guns, assault rifles and armored personnel carriers. Using rapidly expanding paramilitary groups or SWAT (Special Weapons and Tactics) teams, cops can now facilitate the new phenomenon of suicide by cop with special sniper training, high powered weapons and other deadly skills.

Cops have taken to videotaping every pursuit or apprehension with $6,000 video systems installed in cruisers. Could this be a direct reaction to the amateur videotaping of Rodney G. King in Lake View Terrace in March 3, 1991? What's next? Live feeds straight to the Fox network, in car editing and sweetening? Stay tuned.

http://www.nleomf.com/News/LineofDuty/tributes.htm
http://www.morganquitno.com
http://www.bna.com/e-law/cases/heroes.html

Sidewalks

Ft. Lauderdale, Florida, is the most dangerous city in the country for pedestrians, based on fatalities relative to population and the number of people who walk to work in U.S. cities. Some 60 pedestrians die each year in this Florida city. The highest number of average annual pedestrian fatalities, however, belongs to New York City. About 310 pedestrians die on its mean streets every year. L.A. is a close second, with an average of 299 killed. Pedestrians account for 14 percent of all motor vehicle-related deaths in the United States each year. About 6,000 pedestrians are killed each year in the United States and another 110,000 injured. So much for getting healthy.

http://www.pedestrians.org/

Mortality

The big three are still heart disease, cancer and stroke, but then things get scattered around. Latinos and blacks are more likely to die of accidents, diabetes, AIDS and homicide than whites or Asians. Car accident deaths among young people are most highly concentrated in the southeast. Prostate cancer deaths are highest among black men along the south Atlantic coast, and for white men along the northern perimeter of the United States. The southeast has the highest rate of death from heart disease. Lung cancer deaths among white women are highest along the Pacific coast and the desert southwest. Most strokes occur along a belt from North Carolina to Mississippi. Call it different strokes for different folks.

http://www.cdc.org

Yourself

More people die in America as a result of suicide than murder. There are 31,000 homicides versus 19,000 suicides every year. Globally, suicide is the second leading killer of women aged 15 to 44 and the fourth leading killer of men, the number three cause of death for teenagers and the second highest cause for college students.

http://www.afsp.org/index.html

Appearing on *America's Most Wanted*

During its decade on the air, the television show *America's Most Wanted* has been directly responsible, as of the writing of this edition, for the capture of 433 robbers, killers and kidnappers, meaning, of course, ratings for the reruns won't motivate advertisers.

http://www.1800crimetv.com/

Excellent health care is available throughout the United States. Medical facilities and supplies, including medicines, are in abundance. The level of medical training of U.S. doctors is considered excellent. Foreign visitors without medical insurance will be expected to pay in cash or by credit card where accepted. No special precautions are required.

http://www.cdc.org

11/2/99	U.S. military bombs Iraq for the eighth continuous year.
3/24/99	U.S. military bombs Serbia.
8/20/98	U.S. military bombs Sudan and Afghanistan.
8/7/98	U.S. embassies in Nairobi and Dar es Salaam are bombed n Nairobi, where the U.S. embassy is located in a congested downtown area, 291 persons are killed in the attack, and about 5,000 are wounded. In Dar es Salaam, 10 persons are killed and 77 are wounded.
3/25/96	Standoff begins in Jordan, Montana, between 20 armed "Freemen" and more than 100 FBI agents after two of the Freemen's leaders are jailed over a $1.8 million fraudulent check scheme.
4/19/95	Alfred P. Murrah Federal Building in Oklahoma City is bombed, killing 167 and injuring more than 400.
3/4/94	Four are convicted in the bombing of the World Trade Center.
3/1/93	Law agents besiege Texas Davidian religious cult after six are killed in raid at Waco.
2/26/93	New York's World Trade Center is bombed by Islamic extremists.
6/5/68	Robert F. Kennedy assassinated.
4/5/68	Martin Luther King Jr. assassinated.
11/22/63	President John F. Kennedy assassinated.
9/6/1901	President William McKinley assassinated.
7/2/1881	President James A. Garfield assassinated.
4/14/1865	President Abraham Lincoln assassinated.

THE UNITED STATES

Coming Attractions

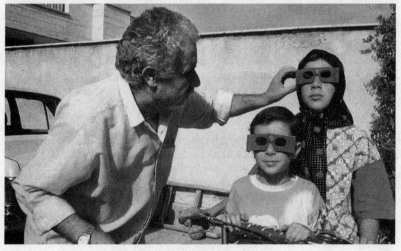

The Future's So Bright . . .

Over the last 10 years, there have been more than 100 wars with 20 million fatalities. So it would take a moronically optimistic person to assume that the next millennium will bring love, peace and happiness to this planet. This is the first year we sent down some star attractions to the minor leagues. Among them are Angola, Armenia, Georgia, Bosnia, Bolivia and other places we just got too damn tired waiting for something major to happen in. It would seem that most of the Coming Attractions are like '80s sitcoms—they just never go away, but then they never get big again either.

So with some trepidation and a roll of the dice, we open ourselves to possible ridicule as we present our low-budget trailer of things to come in the next *The World's Most Dangerous Places*.

Some starting points

http://cgs_grad.cgs.edu/~saxtong/ntlsm.html
http://paladin-san-francisco.com/index.htm

Akhazia

Akhaz Haze

It's okay if you don't know where Akhazia is. You can be forgiven if you don't know where Georgia is. But it will matter. Akhazia is in the western part of Georgia, which used to be the southernmost part of the Soviet Union—where Stalin vacationed, and where Jason sought the Golden Fleece. No, doesn't ring a bell. Okay, where Dannon did the yogurt commercials about the 100 year olds? Oddly enough Akhazia is the most southernly part of Russia because Russian peacekeepers have been patrolling the once tourist-crowded beaches since the nasty 14-month war ended in 1994. Ten thousand died but economics shrunk the population by three-fourths to 150,000. Now Akhazia is an independent country. Well, er, sort of—if you ignore Georgia's claim of sovereignty and of course Russia's AKed babysitters. Akhazia is also where Chechen Shamil Basayev learned how to kill Russians. So far now Akhazia sits landmined (30,000 at last count), embargoed (by Georgia), ruined and impoverished (by Russia) and fed by the Red Cross (33 percent of the population). The future looks hazy indeed. To understand more, see the demon spawn of the Soviet breakup: Chechnya, Dagestan, Trans Dniester and Nagorno Karabakh.

http://www.abkhazia.org

Central African Republic

CAR Cesspool

We'd like to warn you that it is getting more dangerous, but then it never has been safe in this pocket-sized cesspool. The only thing that keeps it from turning into Liberia or Zaire is the French paratroopers that baby-sit the potentate for a day. There are about 2,500 French citizens in the country.

In May 1996 the streets were slippery with blood as the French put down another week-long mutiny attempt. The French use CAR as a staging ground to defend Chad against Libya.

Ceuta and Melilla

It's a Dung Hole After All

DP can never be accused of painting the world with too broad a brushstroke. In these two minuscule Spanish exclaves on the north coast of Africa, it seems they have enough room for an insurgency group and plenty of room left over for drug smugglers, money launderers and the usual Casablanca-ish riffraff that haunts these places. A lot of Latin America nose candy comes here by ship to be then distributed throughout Europe.

The two areas were kept by Spain when they handed over Morocco in the 16th century. It has taken this long for a coalition called the August 21 group, led by Muslim activist Mohamed Abdou, to threaten Spain with further armed attacks. The August 21 group claimed responsibility for two car-bomb attacks in April 1995; no one was hurt. In a recent visit by the Spanish prime minister with the king of Morocco, they forgot to bring up the issue. It appears Spain shut Morocco up back in 1974, when they handed them their colony of Spanish

Sahara. The August 21 group sent a threatening fax and asserted that their cause was "as holy and noble . . . as other nationalist groups."

China

Breaking Up Is Hard to Do

China has its problems. In the next five years it is estimated that the current 100 million people who have migrated to the city to find work will swell to 200 million. Beijing has over 3 million who cannot find steady work. Forty million are unemployed. Inflation runs about 25 percent. One hundred million people are unemployed. Half of the 100,000 state owned businesses lose money and will be shut down or sold off. Eight hundred million peasants live a subsistence life and resent the new city based economic growth. There are serious doubts that China will be able to feed itself without importing massive amounts of food. After Xiaoping's death, things are relatively calm in China, but for how long?

If all of China's 1.2 billion people were to do anything at once, let alone jump off a wall, it would paralyze the country. This isn't good news for tourists and even worse news for the government because tourism to China has been surging in recent years. About 1.74 million foreign tourists visited Beijing alone in 1992, compared with less than 300,000 in 1978. In the first six months of 1993, 882,600 foreigners visited the capital city, up 13 percent over the corresponding period the preceding year. Throughout China, tourism brought in a whopping US$1.69 billion in the first five months of 1993, up 22.2 percent over the same period in 1992. That figure is a record.

China officially possesses no known terrorist groups (that is if you ignore Islamic groups in East Turkmenistan and liberation groups in Tibet since 1949), but a ride on one of their domestic airliners may make you wish they did—so the plane could be hijacked to a country with decent air traffic control. Unlike in other parts of the world, hijackers in China aren't trying to draw world attention to a cause (they wouldn't get it, anyway). They're not likely to make ransom demands. And it's not done for the love of God. They're simply trying to get the hell out. Taiwan is the favored destination. There are about 10 hijackings to Taipei a year and about a dozen that are foiled.

The good news is that 4,367 Chinese criminals were executed last year. About a couple more thousand were sentenced to death but for some reason they couldn't find time for the quick pop to the back of the head and a trip to the morgue to have their organs ripped out. Why good news? Well, it seems between 2,000–3,000 kidneys and corneas are available each year for transplant in China. Human Rights Watch has even accused China of keeping condemned prisoners alive until the organs are needed. Crimes are generally nonviolent; thefts form the bulk of them. Despite the executions, major crime incidents have risen by nearly 20 percent annually in the past four years.

If you don't want people in pieces you can also get them whole. China also has gangs that kidnap teenage women for sex trades and young boys for families that seem to plop out girls.

The Chinese Public Security Ministry has admitted the country does not have the resources to protect tourists from the rising rate of crime across the mainland. The Qiandao Lake incident may be a precursor of what's to come. There have been numerous recent incidents where tourists have been robbed, beaten and even murdered. However, in considering whether to report a crime in a country where residents can be executed for stealing a ball point pen or for hooliganism, the normal traveler is more likely to let that disposable camera go instead of making a federal case.

Dangerous Places

China loves a revolution except when other folks want to revolt. Like most dictatorships, freedom means enslaving and forcibly occupying other people's countries.

Tibet

China invaded Tibet in 1949, and, in the process, killed 1.2 million people, a tenth of the Tibetan population. Two hundred thousand Tibetans live in India. China has destroyed 6,241 monasteries. There are only 13 left. For now China just breeds and pushes the Tibetans out and the region is 60 percent Chinese.

East Turkmenistan

The Muslim Turks don't want to be Chinese, so groups based in neighboring countries keep the revolution at a simmer since after World War II.

East Turkistan Liberation Front

Turfan, Kamal
East Turkistan Information Center (Munich)
Tel.: 49 89 3170 6691 or 49 89 5440 4772
East Turkistan Center (Washington, DC)
Tel.: (703) 918-9560

Chinese Government

http://www.gov.cn/

International Taklamakan Uighur Human Rights Association

http://www.taklamakan.org/index.html

Eastern Turkistan Information Center

http://www.uygur.com/index.html

Eastern Turkistan National Freedom Center

http://www.uyghur.org/

Free East Turkistan

http://www.caccp.org/et/
http://www.geocities.com/CapitolHill/1730/index.html

Southern Mongolia or Inner Mongolia

Southern Mongolia Freedom Federation

http://members.aol.com/yikhmongol/smff.htm

Inner Mongolian People's Party

http://members.aol.com/imppsite/

Citizens Against Communist Chinese Propaganda

http://www.afn.org/~afn20372/pol/fm.html

Inner Mongolia People's Party

http://members.aol.com/imppsite/index.htm

Tibet

Tibetan Government in Exile

http://www.tibet.com/
E-mail: ayusef@aol.com

Getting In

Passports and visas are required. Most tourist visas are valid for only one entry. Travelers are required to obtain new visas for additional entries into China. Those who arrive without a visa will be fined a minimum of $400 at the port of entry and might not be allowed to enter China (or get out!). A transit visa is required for any stop (even if one does not exit the plane or train) in China. Specific information is available through the Embassy of the People's Republic of China or from one of the consulates general in Chicago, Houston, Los Angeles, New York or San Francisco.

Chinese Embassy in the United States
2300 Connecticut Avenue, NW
Washington, DC 20008
Tel.: (202) 328-2500.

U.S. Embassy in China
Xiu Shui Dong Jie 3
Beijing -100600
Tel.: [86] (1) 532-3831

The Comoros

Backwater Bungle

These fragrant islands in the Indian Ocean don't seem big enough for problems, but after 18 coups since independence, things never seem to cool down. In 1974, the four Comoran Islands were given the choice of independence or remaining under French administration. Grande Comore, Anjouan and Moheli chose independence, and formed the Comoran Islamic Federation. Mayotte voted by referendum to remain under Frence rule. In August 1997, residents of Anjouan Island (under seccessionist leader "president" Abdullah Ibrahim) decided to break away—back to French colonial rule. They may be on to something since sister isle Mayotte was doing much better economically under French control. France said thanks, but no thanks.

Machete sales soared, and when the main island sent in troops, they were forced to retreat with 105 captured, 40 dead and 30 wounded. Thinking this retro independence thing was a good idea, the smallest island of Moheli decided to declare its independence from the Comoroan Federation and elected an army officer to be "president." In early December 1998, 60 people died, thousands were displaced and property looted and destroyed after an assassination attempt against Founnd.

Congo Brazzaville

Two Out of Three?

OK, OK, choosing anyplace that starts with the name Congo is not the most clairvoyant choice for a war zone. Congo Brazzaville has the distinction of being a rather simple war to figure out. North vs. South, Bakongo (north) vs. Mbochi (south), Pascal Lissouba (a former geneticist and member of the Nibolek tribe) and his *Cocoyes* vs. Denis Sassou-Nguesso and his *ninjas*. Even Don King couldn't do a better job of rematches and foregone conclusions.

Congo-K (as it is called) got their independence from France in 1960. It took the commies four years to create the Marxist Leninist National Revolution Party (MNR) as the only party. Things fell apart in the CIA heavy late '70s and the president was assassinated and martial law was declared in 1977. Lissouba was elected in 1977. Marxist Denis Sassou-Nguesso turfed him. Now they are involved in a see-saw war with Angola backing both sides.

Scorecard		
Leader	Lissouba	Sassou-Nguesso
Party	Pan-African Union for Social Development (UPAD)	Congolese Labor Party (PCT)
Region South	North	South
Militia	Cocoyes	Ninjas
Tribe	Bakonga	Mbochi
1979	Winner	Loser
1992	Winner	Loser
1997	Loser	Winner
1999	Winner	Loser

The U.S. embassy is closed in-country but Congo-K have a mission at: *4891 Colorado Avenue NW, Washington, DC 20011, Tel.: (202) 726-5500, Fax: [1] (202) 726-1860.* The future looks bright, not because Congo is the fourth-largest oil producer in sub-Saharan Africa, but because Congo-K is becoming a popular dumping site for toxic waste for the Europeans.

Africa News
> *http://www.africanews.org/central/congo/*
> *http://www.odci.gov/cia/publications/factbook/cf.html*

Corsica

The Tourist War

Petru Pogglii, born in 1940, is the leader of the Corsican Nationalist Alliance. The CNA is an offshoot of the Corsican National Liberation Front/Front Liberation National Corsican (NLNC) founded in 1976. Their headquarters is in Carbuccia.

There are about 1,000 separatist rebels in a number of small gangs, most of whom are aligned with a liberation front. The gangs spend as much time fighting among each other as they do the French. Over the last 20 years, there have been 8,400 terrorist attacks and 100 deaths. A poll in 1996 showed that 86 percent of Corsicans are against independence. On July 2, a car bomb exploded in daylight in the middle of Ajaccio, killing one of the leaders of the Corsican FLNC and injuring another leader seriously. About 2 million tourists visit the island each year.

Cyprus

U(N) Can Never Go Home Again

The oldest UN mission in the world (UNFICYP) is living testament to the fact that you can keep the kids from squabbling, but you will never make them kiss and make up. It's the Greeks vs. the Turks. Both sides will tell you horror stories of what will happen once you cross the UN border. As usual, both sides are comprised of charming, hospitable people. The Turks created the unrecognized Turkish Republic of Northern Cyprus (TRNC) in 1983. They maintain 30,000 troops to occupy about 37 percent of the island. About 200,000 Greek Cypriots have never been compensated for the loss of their land. There are 198,000 Turks (double compared to 1960) and 650,000 Greek Cypriots. Meanwhile, gangsters from Eastern Europe fight amongst each other for control of nightclubs and entertainers.

Equatorial Guinea

Dictator of the Week

Coups could become a weekly event replacing soccer in this forgotten armpit of Africa. Back in 1969, Macias Nguema took over this oversized cocoa plantation and began systematically killing all his fellow politicians. By the time he was done, he had killed 50,000 of his own people, including every senior politician and civil servant, and 100,000 people, a third of the population, had fled.

When he was finally tried and executed in 1979, he had managed to spend the entire $105 million treasury. Since then, the remaining residents have been playing dictator for a week. One coup in 1986 only took 30 people to overthrow the government. Why not invite your church choir, and you too could be dictator for a day. The one good outcome is that there have been so few tourists that there technically is no tourist crime.

Greece

November 17: A Good Day to Die

The November 17 group is the most feared terrorist group in Greece and perhaps the most ruthless in Europe. The terrorist ring got its start with the December 1975 assassination of Athens CIA station chief Richard Welch while he was on his way home from a Christmas party, zapping him with what would become its signature grim reaper: a .45-caliber pistol.

Since then a .45 has been used in six more of its subsequent 20 executions, including 4 Americans, 13 Greeks and couple of Turkish diplomats. It doesn't sound like a particularly huge body count in these days of *Hezbollah*, GAI and Chechen whackos, but considering that not a single member of this shadowy group has been identified—much less arrested—it is. And the group has also conducted at least 35 other attacks on multinational companies and Greek tax offices, employing bombs that suggest their construction techniques were learned in the Middle East in the early 1970s.

Of all of Europe's homegrown radical assassins, only the November 17 group remains entirely an enigma. Italy's Red Brigades and the German arm of the Red Army Faction have been snuffed. Rebel Basque, Irish and Corsican separatists have been picked off like flies by INTERPOL. Action Direct in France was similarly destroyed. But November 17's 10–25 members continue to elude all attempts to expose and drain them.

The terrorists named themselves for the day in 1973 when a student uprising at Athens Polytechnic University was crushed by soldiers and tanks sent in by the ruling military junta. These guys don't work on a single agenda. When the

United States was supporting the military junta in Greece during the first decade of the terrorists' existence, the group blew away Americans. When Turkey occupied Cyprus in 1974, Turkish diplomats became the targets. For sure, November 17 is a Marxist outfit, professing hatred for both the United States and NATO, as well as the European Union. It's thought that its founding members belonged to a resistance group created by Socialist Premier Andreas Papandreou during the 1965–1975 military dictatorship. And there has been some indication that Papandreou knows who they are. But he's not talking.

The former East German police are believed to have been chummy with November 17, however attempts to retrieve information from their files have been futile. In the meantime, suspicions of connections with Middle East terror clans continue—as do .45 slugs to the head.

Indonesia

Archipeliblow

Indonesia is an archipelago of more than 13,000 islands, the largest of which are Kalimantan (Indonesian Borneo), Sumatra, Irian Jaya (West Irian), Sulawesi and Java. Nearly two-thirds of the population lives on Java, one of the most densely populated areas in the world. Sumatra contains 25 percent of Indonesia's land area and 20 percent of its population.

But it's on the far flung island of Timor where a lingering insurgency festers since the Indonesian invasion in 1975 (and annexation in 1976). The Timorese are not fond of their Indonesian rulers and continue to battle for their independence. More than 100,000 people are believed to have died in the Indonesian invasion of East Timor in 1975. About 200–450 rebels whack away at the soldiers while their leader and former poet; Jose "Xanana" Gusmao rots in Jakarta's Cipinang jail serving a 20 year sentence. Jose Ramos-Horta runs a slow steady PR campaign to keep East Timor in the limelight. The funny thing is the real ruler (according to the UN) is Portugal, not exactly known as a tread-lightly colonizer.

The Players

Free Papua Movement/Organasi Papua Merdaki (OPM)

Timor isn't the only place in the archipelago with guerrillas in the midst. Often, entirely forgotten are the ragtag rebels of the Free Papua Movement (OPM), who have been fighting the Indonesian government for the independence of Irian Jaya (High Victory) with sticks, stones and rusty flintlocks for the last 30 years. Irian Jaya was supposed to gain their independence in 1965, but Indonesia decided to not leave. These guys don't get into the news that much and are often called the "T-shirt" army because they're about as trained and equipped as a Connecticut cub scout den. For now, the Indonesian government gets a third of its oil exports from Irian Jaya.

But for a group of seven unlucky foreigners, the rebels may as well be the charge of the Light Brigade. In January 1996, two Dutch researchers, four British students and a German stumbled into a solitary OPM unit, probably out gathering nuts and berries; the guerrillas found the juicy, plump, white-skinned Westerners a godsend. Just think, real live hostages—frightened Anglo pussycats—just like the kind we pick up on our satellite dish! The world, and CNN, had discovered the OPM.

Now known by the outside world, they and their supporters have taken to the streets. On March 18, 1996, thousands rioted in the Irian Jaya provincial capital of Jayapura, torching vehicles, shops and other buildings. Three demonstrators were shot dead, one a policeman who joined the rioters and was blown away by a shopowner protecting his investment. Since 150,000 people have died in this conflict and many more will, don't expect a Visit Irian Jaya Year anytime soon.

http://www.converge.org.nz/wpapua/opm.html

Free Acheh Movement/Aceh Merdaka

Aceh is the northernmost tip of the Indonesian island of Sumatra. The rebels want independence or even a bigger share of the region's wealth, mostly natural gas wells, and they don't like the forced migrants from Java taking their jobs. In 1873, the Netherlands invaded the Kingdom of Acheh and in 1942 the Dutch gave up.

In 1949 the Dutch got even by tossing Aceh into the Dutch East Indies, and giving it to Indonesia. In 1976 the Acheh-Sumatra National Liberation Front, also known as Acheh Merdeka, or Free Acheh, was founded as an armed resistance group and a redeclaration of independence was issued. Leader of the group is Tengku Hasan M. di Tiro, or Prince Hasan Mohamad Tiro, who lives in exile. The fighting flared up in 1989 and over 200 people have died to date in the fighting between government troops and rebels. The National Commission on Human Rights has reported that at least 781 people were killed. Other estimates put the death toll at between 50,000 to 100,000 deaths since 1989.

http://www.interlog.com/~cafiet/background/acehback.html
http://www.unpo.org/member/acheh/acheh.html

Free Molucca Youth Movement/Republik Maluku Selatan (Republic of South Moluccas)

No, not a giveaway, but yet another independence movement caused by Jakarta perfidy and greed. The Moluccas was part of the Dutch East Indies during the colonial period. The Dutch were supposed to give the Mollucans their freedom in the transition of their territory to Indonesian rule in 1949, but they lied. The Moluccan people declared their independence, formed the Republik Maluku Selatan (Republic of South Moluccas) and was promptly invaded by Indonesian forces in July and September 1950. In December 1950, the Moluccan Army withdrew to Ceram. Their leader Chris Soumokil was captured and summarily executed in 1966. Jakarta decided to send thousands of Javan settlers to make the Moluccans a minority. In 1997 there were increased clashes due to the forced colonization of Moluccan lands by Javanese. Most of the fighting takes place on the island of Ambon against ethnic Chinese and Muslim Javanese settlers.

http://www.dlm.org/

Kenya

A Rift in the Valley

Tourism to Africa's most "civilized" country has declined due to attacks in game parks, lawlessness in the major cities and continuing tribal clashes in areas such as the Rift Valley. The bombings of the U.S. Embassy finished off whatever tourism was left. Somali bandits still cross the border and attacked UN relief workers in Wajir province. At least 35 security officers and 50 civilians have been killed in Wajir, Garissa and Mandera provinces. The Red Cross has suspended selected relief operations in the northern provinces due to bandit attacks and the theft of materials. The northwest corner and the borders with Somalia and Ethiopia have become a hot spot for cattle wars. It is estimated that over 10,000 Turkana tribespeople have been killed in cattle raids by better armed Pokots, Dinka and Somalis.

In Nairobi, armed robbers ambush expensive vehicles as they drive in exclusive neighborhoods: Mercedes Gelandwagons, Land Rover Defenders, Discoveries,

Range Rovers, Toyota Land Cruisers and Isuzu Troopers are their favorite targets. In Nairobi, 1,224 cars were stolen in the first six months of 1992. Twenty-five were stolen from the UN High Commission for Refugees alone. The M.O.: Carjackers cut off the intended victim, occasionally utilizing an accomplice to prevent a rear escape. Most carjackings take place after 7 P.M., but there have been incidents during daylight hours in populated places.

With more than half of the population of Kenya under the age of 15 and unemployment at over 60 percent, there is ample motivation for criminal behavior. Average per-capita income in Kenya is below US$450 a year. Add to the soup bloodthirsty cops and more than 330,000 refugees and thousands of automatic weapons from Somalia, and the continent becomes darker indeed. Displaced by the war in Somalia, rugged hardy bands of desperate Somali men go south in search of anything of value. Just hope you don't have what they want.

Kenyan police enjoy bragging that they've killed (not apprehended) 70 percent of the bandits operating in the game park regions. But that's little solace. There's no guarantee you won't run into elements of the other 30 percent.

Nairobi for tourists is about as close to a herd of frightening wildebeasts avoiding lionesses in Masai Mara. Jet-lagged and stumbling under luggage, they have no idea they have entered a criminal free-for-all. Savvy tourists take cabs even for short trips, keep arms inside cabs, hire private guards and get the hell out of Nairobi.

http://pacdc.miis.edu/events/eafrica.html

Laos

Bombies and Zombies

From 1964 until 1973, U.S. planes averaged one sortie every eight minutes over this unfortunate slice of Spam wedged between Vietnam and Cambodia. More than 285 million bombs were dropped over Indochina during the Vietnam War, a good number of them over Laos; a good number of those remain unexploded.

Many payloads were jettisoned by B-52s, which had to get back to their bases in Thailand in a hurry; other warplanes used Laos for target practice. But mainly, Laos was pounded into oblivion to prevent Pathet Lao guerrillas from advancing from their jungle bases in the northeast toward the capital of Vientiane, as well as to wreak havoc on North Vietnamese forces shuttling up and down the Ho Chi Minh Trail, which cuts a narrow swath through the mountains of Laos.

The Laotians call the unexploded ordnance "bombies," a cute term for the cluster bombs that today take scores of Laotian lives every month. And because farmers cannot take advantage of valuable agricultural land due to the "buried treasure," thousands more Laotians face malnourishment and starvation seemingly with zombielike indifference. In heavily carpet-bombed Xieng Khouang province northeast of Vientiane, hundreds of families subsist on virtually no food at all for three to four months of every year due to the "bombies" in the fields. These "bombies" are actually small bomblets (or cluster bombs)—but very lethal—that spill from large casings as they're dropped from aircraft. The bomblets, about the size of a tennis ball, number about 650 to the case. Covered in bright yellow plastic, they make a particular curiosity to children, who comprise 44 percent of all bomb accidents in Laos. Half these accidents result in death. You don't want to see what the other half look like. Thirty-one percent of all bomb accidents occur while children are playing, giving a new meaning to Romper Room.

There aren't many soccer fields in Laos.
http://www.pacom.mil/forum/laos.htm

Morocco

Sand Wars

Polisario is still doing its thing. To get a good spot for your beach chair contact Mohamed Abedaziz, leader of the Polisario Front: *E-mail: 100427.3223@compuserve.com;* or the Western Sahara campaign office in Leeds, U.K.: *Tel.: 44 113 245 4786.*
http://www.arso.org/index.htm

Nepal

Trek or Treat

What the hell are Maoists doing in the yuppie trekking capital of Nepal? Well about 90 percent of the country works as a farmer (well actually peasants, but that doesn't sound so PC). It all started on February 13, 1996, at about 3:45 P.M. when a small group of people, took over the office of the Small Farmer's Development Program of the state-owned Agricultural Development Bank in Chyangli VDC (Village Development Committee) in Gorkha district in central Nepal. A soft drink bottling factory and five other targets were attacked.

What does the Dr. Baburam Bhattrai and his United People's Front-Nepal, or UPF (a.k.a. Maoist Samyukta Jana Morcha, or SJM), want? Well they are pissed at feudal comprador and bureaucratic capitalism, and their state power. In English that means people who wear Nikes instead of make them. Does that mean you have to include Nepal along with Kashmir, Afghanistan, Peru and Colombia as places that are deadly to ecotourists. Probably not yet. Most attacks are against factories, police stations and villages, but not tourists. But then again they haven't been around long enough to learn how effective kidnapped tourists are in devastating the bourgeois economy. So far about 900 people have died in the fighting.

Communist Party of Nepal
http://www.blythe.org/mlm/misc/nepal/nepal.htm
Interview with leader
http://www.blythe.org/mlm/misc/nepal/interview.htm

Northern Ireland

Ununited Kingdom

A kingdom run by a queen, ununited by religion and of course what kings and queens did in the past. It's not surprising the English and the Irish don't quite know how to disentangle themselves. The IRA and Sinn Fien waffle back and forth between peace and bombing. For now it's peace talks, then it's bombing. It would be very hard to foresee any peaceful solution to clear away centuries of anger and hate. Send your solutions to:

Whoever is in charge
10 Downing Street
London, U.K.

Peru

Ok, so we watched them kill all the Tupac Amaru on live TV so things are back to normal, right? Wrong. Despite 30,000 dead since 1980 and a vicious campaign of executions and bombings things are not back to normal yet. No longer deserving of a full chapter in *DP* (although there are some pretty wacky players in Peru) Peru's deeply jungled Huallaga valley still is a dangerous place. The Tupac Amaru may be withering on the vine but the Shining Path is very much alive, albeit not in the numbers they once were and definitely not with the machismo that led to the capture of the Japanese embassy.

The Shining Path (Sendero Luminosa) was formed in 1980 and is a rural-based Maoist uprising. The basic idea is that you convince pissed-off peasants to rise up against rich, evil bourgeois and then you get to be a rich evil bourgeois. The difference is, you can drive a Volvo instead of a Mercedes. And, of course, meet more liberal arts chicks with hairy armpits.

The Shining Path used to have 10,000 members until firebrand Abimael Guzman was captured in 1992. Now the Path is down to less than a thousand members. They can be found in the central Andes mountains, the Ayacucha highlands and in the Huallaga valley in the Northwest Amazon jungle.

Filomeno Cerron Cardoso, aka "Comrade Artemio," is the latest leader of the Shining Path. He is in his thirties and known for being a go getter. He is comfortable in the jungles and a hard ass collector of taxes from the coca growers and timber traders. He has less political motivation and may be learning a few things from his counterparts in Colombia.

Oscar Ramirez Durand, age 46, a.k.a. "Comrade Feliciano," was nabbed by the army in the summer of '99 in central Peru. He had created his own group called Sendero Rojo, or Red Path. Commandos made a special point of mentioning that he was also captured with three female bodyguards. He was with about 200 supporters at the time. Man, the life of a South American rebel!

Peru People's Movement (MPP):
Study Circle Red Sun
Postboks 571
2620 Albertslund
Denmark
E-mail: srs@politik.dk
http://www.blythe.org/mlm/misc/peru/peru.htm

Senegal

Lovelorn

Sengal's southern Casamance Province has been home to the Movement of Democratic Forces of Casamance (MFDC) since 1982. They are fighting for autonomy from the central government citing neglect. They continue to indulge in shoot-outs, looting, and throat slitting incidents. Four French tourists never returned from one deadly region in April 1995, and locals are occasionally found slaughtered like sheep. Although the government will tell you everything is hunky dory, 50 rebels attacked a military camp in August.

http://www.reliefweb.int/IRIN/archive/senegal.htm

The Spratlys

Makin' Mischief

Tourists as the new secret weapon. Samsonite and Nikons on the front line. World War III fought by bus tours. Not so preposterous as you think. When Minister of Defense, Orlando Mercado, was confronted by *DP* for his new concept of sending eco-tourists to the military outposts of Pag Asa, he tossed us on a navy flight to see for ourselves. Our verdict? Those 40 mils need a good cleaning and oiling, and unless you like to drink cheap gin and jungle juice with bored Filipino armed forces, forget it. When *DP* was in the Spratlys this year, we couldn't help but notice how much the new Chinese fortifications on Mischief Reef looked like cheap motels. Maybe we were talking to the wrong landlord.

These flyspeck islands are custom-made for an international dispute. This group of islands just north of Borneo is floating on oil close to nowhere. China, Brunei, the Philippines, Vietnam and anybody else in the neighborhood who has a half-assed reason to lay claim to these isles is talking tough and showing off military hardware like gangs in a schoolyard. China has occupied the aptly named Mischief Reef. The Philippines sent its entire fighter air force (nine planes) to sit nearby and look tough. The other countries have gone running to the world court to mediate.

http://www.actionworks.org/guides/frlinks/spartly.htm

Taiwan

The Seed of World War III

Now it may be just coincidence that China is mentioned whenever World War III is mentioned. Chinese Premier Li Peng is not happy with Taiwanese president Lee Teng-hui, who's considering taking the lethal gamble of declaring Taiwan's independence from Mother China. The scarlet latter considers Taiwan a renegade province and will not tolerate such tomfoolery. China has been doing military "exercises" in the Taiwan Strait, lobbing missiles to within a few hundred meters of the Taiwanese coast, just to let the islanders considering independence know the next volley will fall on their heads. The U.S. Navy, in March 1996, sent two carrier groups close to the Strait in a show of force as the Chinese continued to splatter rockets into the waters off Taiwanese beaches. Sunbathers beware. If China decides to take the island by force, they've got a billion or so people who can help them out in the operation. Will Uncle Sam let it happen? Depends who you talk to. We keep selling Taiwan every used tank, missile and ship we can. Maybe we need China to reduce their inventory.

http://www.gio.gov.tw/

Venezuela

Ai Caramba!

Venezuela is in a bad spot. Not only do they have narco-nutty Colombia as a neighbor but they are wedged in on the left by loosey-goosey Guyana. Instead of just minding their oil-rich business, they also have been demanding that Guyana hand over more than half of themselves in a 35-year-old border dispute, and

President Pastrana, asked why, said to stop meddling in Colombia's affairs. The current president is a close confidante of Castro and doesn't like all those U.S. "crop dusters" flying over his country. Best of all, he has decided to set up an open dialog with FARC and ELN, Colombia's two biggest headaches.

http://www.embavenez-us.org/

In a Dangerous Place: Montenegro

Oh, The Life of a War Correspondent

I stood shivering in the dark wind over the bow, watching the forbidding beauty of the distant coastline emerge in the early dawn. Montenegro—Black Mountain. A great massif of ragged, saw-toothed blades stabbing out of the Adriatic. Despite vowing never again to set foot in the Balkans, I was back. Oh, I'd kept abreast of things through friends returning from the borders of Kosovo for a spot of R and R. And my colleague, Roddy Scott, who'd answered the clarion call of the dedicated war correspondent, had regularly rung from the squalor of Kukes in northern Albania. Sitting safely at home, I'd listened sympathetically, if not a little yearningly, to frustrated accounts of high adventure and low comedy in his efforts to make common good with the Kosovo Liberation Army before the war ended. But the bombing campaign was finished now, the Serbs were skeddadeling and Roddy had at last crossed the border to record the evils done. The war—at least that war—was over.

But war in the Balkans is like a pernicious bacterium; stamp it out here, and it sprouts afresh over there, its malevolent toxin intact and bubbling. If thumbing a few centuries of history fails to convince, one need look only at the four wars instigated by Serbian President Slobodan Milosevic since 1991. Given that the Federal Republic of Yugoslavia (FRY) had lost one state to each conflict— Slovenia, Croatia, Bosnia, and now Kosovo, and been whittled down to Serbia and Montenegro in just eight years, one had to wonder if Slobo suffered a long-term learning disability. ("Did you cut many throats in the war, Daddy?" "You bet, sweetheart, and I could have done a lot more if it hadn't been for those bad NATO people." "I'm sorry, Daddy.") But the miasma of Balkan intrigue, ethnic enmity and a genetic predisposition to self-destruction beggars logic. So, despite Slobo's most recent thrashing, Western eyes now focus uneasily on Montenegro. Will Serbia's last reluctant corepublic be the next flashpoint? Many of Milosevic's thugs had retreated into Montenegro, where 90 percent of the population called itself Serb. Even Frankie's Boys and Arkan's Tigers, the most brutal of the Serbian paramilitaries, were known to have established strongholds in the northern mountains. Supported by kith and kin and safe from attack in aerie hideouts, they'd chosen their moments to dash drunkenly across the border to rape, murder and loot, to the approval of their atavistic cousins back home. Strategically and more soberly, Montenegro was Serbia's last remaining access to the Adriatic. The recipe, with all the attendant ingredients, was there for the Fifth Balkan War of the 1990s. But I'd long since had my fill of the place. Gimme a merry band of mercs in the heart of Africa and I'm away. But schlepping around the Balkans on my own again? Uh-uh, not this boy.

The telephone rings. "Hey, Hoop, it's Robert." Robert is RYP, my boss at *Dangerous Places.*

"Hiya, Robert," I say warily. "How're things in California?"

But RYP has spent more time recently in far-off grumpy places than in California and isn't inclined towards small talk. "I need a piece on Montenegro—" he starts in his usual oblique way.

"Forget it."

But RYP isn't listening. "—to run with Roddy's stuff in the next edition of *DP.* Now that boy has some good stories, right from the thick of it in Albania and Kosovo. Not to mention Turkey and Kurdestan."

"Good for Roddy." After nine wars I've become mature and cautious. Yellow, actually.

"How are you on *DP* T-shirts?"

I sigh. He knows my weak point. *DP* T-shirts are cool. No wonder he made a zillion bucks once upon a time marketing Marvel comic books. "I gave away my last one in the Congo," I say pathetically.

"No sweat. As soon as I get your stuff I'll have Bev FedEx a bunch to you."

"Okay, Robert," I surrender.

In the old days you could fly right to Montenegro's capital of Podgorica. But the Coalition put an end to that by bombing the bejeezus out of the runways. Flying to Dubrovnik in Croatia and grabbing a taxi to the border was out too: the FRY army had blockaded the crossing with tanks and were refusing entry to foreigners. Especially foreigners with press cards. Same along the border with Albania. The softest entry, I heard, was the port of Bar, which was controlled by the Montenegrin Ministry of Interior Police (MUP), few of whom supported Belgrade. In fact, Montenegrin President Djukanovic had ordered all FRY troops to return to barracks and stack their weapons; until further notice, the loyal MUP would oversee Montenegro's security. Those FRY troops who were Serbs from Serbia were damned cranky at that and not all had taken it to heart; those who were Montenegrins first and Serbs second didn't think it such a bad idea. After all, Djukanovic was Western-friendly and had pretty much kept the country out of the war. Sure, there'd been some bombing, but only in an essential military sort of way. A few runways holed and a handful of missile and radar sites blown to smithereens, but none of the tiny country's infrastructure or industries had been touched.

A few days later I wing my way to the Italian port of Bari and wander down to the docks for a ticket on the ten-hour Bari-Bar ferry crossing. In America you have lines, in England we have queues. In Bari they've never heard of either one. Hopping up and down behind a heaving mob, I can see the agent's wife flicking through paperwork, supremely disinterested in the crush of beseeching customers. The agent's lumpen daughter stares vacuously, then frowns at the impertinence of a ringing telephone, before painting another fingernail. A dozen more people push ahead of me. I yelp as a Gypsy woman stomps the toe of my sneaker and scuttles in front. If ever there was a case for diplomacy, Balkan-style, this is it. Snarling, I dive into the scrum of shouting, gesticulating and highly aromatic Albanian truck drivers. An hour later, exhausted and panting, I grasp a bar of the ticket window in one hand and wave an expired UN press card and enormous wad of lira in the other. "Per favore, signora!" I wail, hanging on for dear life. She gives me a motherly smile. "Boat full. You come back tomorrow."

Thirty-six hours and a sleepless night later, I stand bleary-eyed at the ferry's bow as a predawn sky silhouettes the coastal spine of Montenegro. And feel the first of the butterflies stir my innards. Two hours later, we sail past the breakwater and the petroleum storage tanks that NATO had generously left off its target lists. We inch into the harbor, followed at a distance by two sleek fast boats: smugglers' boats that have spent the night ranging up, down and across the Adriatic for cigarettes, whiskey, perfumes and condoms. But the boats that really capture my attention are tied opposite our berthing pier: FRY navy corvettes saddled with sea-skimming Styx missiles expressly designed to give Western naval planners the vapors. They'd make a lovely snapshot for *Jane's Defence Weekly*, but I'm not encouraged by FRY troops lounging menacingly along the quayside. Having been interrogated, thumped and threatened by Serbs in the past, I cannot recommend it, and leave the camera bag tightly zipped.

Instead of charging the customs building en masse, à la the ticket office in Italy, my fellow passengers fall meekly into line under the gaze of a camouflage-uniformed giant smacking his palm with a nightstick. "Dobar dan," I wheeze ingratiatingly when I reach the customs officer inside. Good day. He looks at my passport. "Why you here?" Reportage, of course. "America, England no good," he snarls, loud enough to be heard throughout the hall. "NATO all shit!" Impressed by his command of the idiom, I about break my neck nodding in agreement. (Maybe you forgot about my yellow streak.) Satisfied I'm not importing guns, printing presses, Serb-Muslim interracial pornography or other proscribed contraband, he motions me to repack my bags. I turn to escape. "Stop!" He hands back my passport with a private wink. "Welcome to Montenegro," he whispers.

Outside, a taxi driver latches on to me. "Where go?" "Podgorica.: "Okay, okay, 600 dinara, nema problema!" Too hot to haggle, I follow him to a Lada that has seen better days. He opens the passenger door with a flourish and I settle inside. Broken springs under the threadbare upholstery immediately threaten to do my delicate parts an injury. He slides a length of wire coat hanger through the open window and around the central post, giving it a few twists, before dashing round the hood for a Le Mans start. First switching on a transistor radio hanging from the stump of a rear view mirror, he turns the ignition with a knife blade and we're off in a cloud of smoke and bolts. This, my friend, is where the dangerous part comes in. One minute rock walls are flashing by, the next I'm looking over a sheer precipice that drops forever. In some countries guard rails preclude sudden wingless flight. Not in macho Montenegro, where they're considered girlish or only for the timid. And Sterling Moss here is anything but timid. He drifts through a hairpin turn, bald tires squealing and scattering gravel on a two-foot shoulder that separates us from oblivion. Ahead, a column of four trucks climbs ponderously in first gear. Beyond them the road disappears into another hairpin. Sterling floors it. The engine bellows in protest through the broken exhaust. The door, which remains alarmingly ajar despite the coat hanger, bangs and rattles like a Jamaican out-of-tune steel band, and the shock-absorberless Lada hurtles towards destiny. My frantic scrabble for the seat belt draws a smirk of disdain. One truck. Two trucks. Three trucks. My feet threaten to rip through the firewall in search of the brake. Four trucks. The road disappears to the left. Ahead is freefall. The nose of an oncoming truck appears round the bend, horn blaring. I close my eyes. Why couldn't I have photographed those missile boats and been safe and sound in jail right now? We swerve back to the right, fishtailing on the edge of thin air as gravel ricochets off the underside, and then we're through. I glance weakly at Sterling, who, conducting with one hand, is singing along to a wailing Balkan love song issuing from the jiggling transistor radio. Unable to speak, I point at the tenth or twentieth roadside shrine draped in plastic flowers. Sterling interrupts his aria. "Many accidents this road," he shouts instructively, shaking his head at the sort of drivers one has to put up with these days.

If you're going to stay in Podgorica, the government-owned Hotel Crna Gora, at $150 a night, is as good—or bad—as any of the others in town. Done in traditional socialist style best described as stultifying, it boasts a restaurant where the portions are as large as they are inedible, and telephone service that's hopeless. The latter may be due to the fact that everything's routed through Belgrade, where NATO bombers took a keen interest in the telephone exchanges. (Hint: Carry your own GSM; it may take just as many tries to get through, but at least you can do it in your own time, rather than going through the glacial process of using the hotel operator.) In the lobby a Casablanca collection of spooks and smugglers lurk inconspicuously behind potted plants wreathed in cigarette smoke, while outside on the terrace one can observe the hustle and bustle of Montenegro's capital: black market money changers; cops in natty blue American uniforms; their bosses in natty blue and white American Buicks; more smugglers striking deals over endless cups of Turkish coffee; a gypsy-child mother suckling a baby as she moves expressionlessly from one table to another with palm outstretched; and the most astonishing parade of beautiful women you're ever likely to see this side of a modeling agency. (Every male correspondent I know who has done time here agrees that the region boasts more drop-dead gorgeous women per capita than anywhere else on earth. However, lest this give you ideas, remember it's the Balkans, where sharp knives and humorless male relatives offer the prospect of speaking several octaves higher forever more.)

Rental car ready, it's showtime for your intrepid *DP* reporter. I part the fronds of a potted palm. So where's the action? I ask the concierge But he's too busy striking a deal for a late model Japanese car that recently disappeared in Germany to do more than wave his hand vaguely and mutter, "Try the airport." The airport! Why didn't I think of that? It's one of the few places around still controlled by the FRY army. Thirty minutes later, I turn off the main road. From atop a bridge a scorch mark or two, courtesy of the coalition air force, livens the place. A red and white pole blocks the entrance. Three bewhiskered soldiers slowly lower bottles, pick up Kalashnikovs and sway to their feet. My pleasant "Gosh, hi, dobar dan, how are you guys today?" is met with blank stares. "Journalist," I explain helpfully. Three pairs of bloodshot eyes sink to the level of the window and I'm rocked by a disconcerting lack of oral hygiene. "America, England no good," a stubbled face growls. Practicing the recommended diplomacy for dealing with drunks carrying guns, I'm nodding like one of those stupid toy dogs that sit in the back windows of some folks' cars. "NATO all shit, fuck NATO," hisses another. Flecks of spittle spot my spectacles. I'm still nodding like a moron. "And fuck you, too," adds the third, giving lie to claims that an interpreter is essential in the Balkans. Welp, so much for the airport, I decide, wishing I'd paid more attention to the movies where the hero does something tricky with the steering wheel, whips around in the opposite direction and lays rubber till he's out of sight. Back on the main road, I make a note to ask RYP about an evasive driving course when I get home. Fat chance.

Okay, time to unlimber those investigative skills and get cracking on a scoop. This is for *DP*, after all. My reputation's on the line. Back at the hotel, the concierge is waxing his new car. I invite him for a coffee. "So what did NATO bomb?" I ask. "Oh, lots of stuff." "Like what?" "The airport." "Forget the airport." "Hmmmm," he thinks. "Did they hit any hospitals, schools, cows?" I ask provocatively, looking for an angle. "No," he says after a ponder, "they were pretty careful, but what do you think of my new car?" "Nice, but I need some dirt." "Wait!" he says excitedly, "they bombed something big near Ulcinj!" I spread my map, the excitement of the hunt throbbing in my veins. Ulcinj is down the coast near the Albanian border, a four-hour drive. "What was it?" "Something near a civilian beach," he shrugs. "Yeah?" My eyes gleam. I can see the slug already. NATO BOMBS CIVVIE SUNBATHERS. "At night," he adds. Oh.

Desperate, the next day I'm lunching at a seaside restaurant in Ulcinj. The waiter brings another ice-cold Heineken. "Any NATO bombing around here?" "Oh, yes, big bombas there"—he points farther down the coast—"other side Ada River near most-famous-in-Montenegro beach." Aha! I'm getting warm. "What did they hit?" "Yes, something for seeing airplanes." An early-warning radar dish, I cleverly deduce. "Yes, my brother there in army." I cringe. "Is he, like, okay?" "Oh yes. Montenegro army peoples here not want fight America, England, so they don't go to work when bombas start." He gives me directions to the most-famous-in-Montenegro beach. I cross the bridge over the Ada. The road curves sharply right, and my blood freezes at the sight of a manned checkpoint. I've missed a turn and driven straight into a hard-core FRY unit guarding the border with Albania. An Audi bearing German license plates pulls up behind, blocking my escape. Fumbling nervously with the gear shift, I stall. The Audi driver honks impatiently, then pulls out and passes, stopping at the checkpoint. The Audi's suspension heaves a sigh of relief as a German couple of quite majestic proportions climb out. Cheerful banter and money change hands. Beaming, the couple proceed to strip to the buff.

The Audi sinks as they climb in and disappear round a leafy bend. I'm still staring in astonishment as the guard saunters forward. "Hier ist ein nudischeprivatstrand," he says in pidgin German. A nudist beach! Those dirty-minded Serbs were manning a radar site on a nudist beach? Naked human shields! Perverts! I steel myself. This is what investigative journalism is all about. RYP would be proud of me. I step out in sandals and panama, a handful of cameras dangling strategically. "Keine photo-apparaten," the guard frowns. No cameras. I set them inside, holding nothing more than the 25 deutsche mark entrance fee. There's a snigger and a comment passed in Serbian. The snigger becomes a chuckle, one points, and they both guffaw loudly. I look down and see nothing remotely funny. By now they're in convulsions and pounding each other on the back. I recognize it for what it is, Serbian psychological warfare at its worst. Well, if I can't take photos, I rationalize, what's the point? and climb huffily into my clothes. Their laughter follows my retreat over the bridge. Oh, the life of a war correspondent.

—Jim Hooper

MR. DP'S
LITTLE BLACK BOOK

Save the World

Patching the Apocalypse

Civilization is a machine that does not offer an instruction manual. Worse, there isn't even a repair manual. It's not worth going into the various woes of the world, but the UN defined 1.3 billion poor people (poor is a relative word) who probably could use a little help. You could also focus on the 42 so called Highly Indebted Poor Countries (HIPCs), where people die sooner, work harder, eat less, get ill and just plain have the dirty end of the stick. The good news is that these are countries where a two-week visit can make an extraordinary difference. Your cherished vacation budget spent at Disney World doesn't really make a dent in the scheme of things. Two weeks in a small village in Africa will change those people's lives (and yours) forever.

So why isn't everyone parking their Winnebagos in Chiapas or pitching their North Face in the Sahel? These days, the hides of Americans are thicker than that of the endangered rhino. Reality TV have spawned like flies from maggots, and the affluent can watch the pain and suffering of total strangers intermingled with cheerful commercials selling online trading Web sites and new SUVs. The 4 o'clock, 6 o'clock, 7 o'clock, 8 o'clock, 9 o'clock and 10 o'clock news cut together the world's woes and wars into 15 minutes, complete with snazzy graphics, logos and maps. Designed to stop channel surfers and to fire freaks, television zooms in with nice clean images of blood, explosions, screaming and "you are there" action. The trouble is, you aren't there, and even if you are, television makes it seem more distant and less painful. Anything too disturbing can be cast away with a simple click of the remote control. Hey, it's not my problem. Or is it?

You can't save the world; you can't convince Serbs to stop wacking Albanians and vice versa; you can't convince the pope that birth control might actually be a good idea in some countries; and you probably won't get far telling our government to stop messing in other countries' affairs.

You might even be of the opinion that those knock-kneed little tykes are going to bite the bullet anyways so why waste your time? Corrupt governments, civil war and plain old poverty isn't new in these places.

If you actually go there, you might find things are very different than what you see on those infomercials and news stories. Most people get by—they don't have much but they get by. They might have to walk a mile to get water, make shoes out of truck tires or even share one tattered textbook in an open-air school, but they get by. This is the secret. Anything you can do for these people makes their life a little better. A box of books, teaching farming skills, organizing governments, an old computer to make a newspaper, even pitching in to build a schoolhouse is a real contribution.

People helping people can make a difference. One on one, face to face or even by mail. Whether it be teaching kids a song or working for ten years for their indigenous rights, every time you do something for someone, you change his or her life. Dangerous places need people who can help push back the danger. You don't need to be a bomb disposal expert or a facial reconstruction doctor to make a difference; by simply picking up a shovel you can do wonders.

So back to how you connect. Don't assume that being a "charity tourist" is the solution (as one Mexican anthropologist in Tijuana said to me in disgust). Visiting poor countries on the weekends with bags of faded T-shirts and Kraft Macaroni dinners is not the best way to approach poverty. You need to understand the unique needs of the region you are interested in. The United Nations Development Program *(http://www.undp.org)* specializes in analyzing problems of the developing world. Interaction publishes a bi-weekly newsletter, *Monday Developments,* which lists dozens of job opportunities at international organizations in each issue *(http://www.interaction.org/md/index.html)*. They also have a 450-page directory of groups you can contact.

Your first step should be to contact NGO Web sites and country Web sites that provide background. You will find that they come in two flavors: long-term relief and emergency relief groups. Then look into how you can help.

Interaction

A coalition of over 150 nonprofit groups working worldwide. With excellent resources for addresses and backgrounders

http://www.interaction.org/

University of Wales, Department of International Politics

A link site to nongovernmental agencies and relief organizations.

http://www.aber.ac.uk/~inpwww/res/relorg.htm

Doctors of the World (Links Page)

http://www.doctorsoftheworld.org/links2.html

Directory of Humanitarian Organizations

http://www.reliefweb.int/library/contacts/dirhomepage.html

Alertnet

The Reuters Foundation's news and communications service for the emergency relief community.

http://www.alertnet.org/

Disaster Relief

News page and links

http://www.disasterrelief.org

Links to Emergency Response groups

http://www.interaction.org/md/index.html

ReliefWeb

News and links the Humanitarian Relief Community.

http://wwwnotes.reliefweb.int/

Working Overseas

Once you get into the idea of helping people around the world, your tiny vacation may not be enough. How about making it your life's passion? Be forewarned, working overseas is a lot more romantic than it is financially rewarding. Yes, there are professional folks at the UN and big money groups that just want to make that tax-free "nut" of around a million dollars and buy that condo in Key West. But most people that work have to sacrifice to make it work. Most people just don't want to chuck it for a life of misery and poverty. Jobs overseas require training and lengthy job searches. There are some shortcuts: the military, the diplomatic corps, multinational corporations, even foreign correspondents all will guarantee you frequent-flier miles and broken marriages. There are also short deals like the Peace Corps or contract work or even Club Med. In any case, the world will be your workplace, and you will develop an understanding and enjoyment of the world few people will ever appreciate.

International Volunteer Program

Volunteer opportunities in Europe and America.

Société Française de Bienfaisance Mutuelle
210 Post Street, Suite 502
San Francisco, CA 94108
Tel.:[415] 477-3667
Fax: [415] 477-3669
E-mail: crystal6@ix.netcom.com
http://www.ivpsf.com/

Expat Network

A 5,000-member organization of mostly UK expats, they also provide a directory of 500 recruitment companies for overseas work. It costs about $100 to join.

http://www.expatnetwork.co.uk/

Vacation Work Publications

9 Park End Street
Oxford, England OX1 1HJ
Tel.: [44] (865) 241978
Fax: [44] (865) 790885

A British source for publications on summer jobs, volunteer positions and other new ways of travel. If you cover the postage, they will send you their latest catalog about books and specific publications on subjects that cover teaching or living and working in various countries around the world. A small sampling of publications can show you how to teach English in Japan, work on a kibbutz in Israel, choose an adventure holiday, get au pair and nanny jobs, find summer employment in France and much more.

Institute for Global Communications (IGC)

A central clearinghouse for "people who are changing the world." A little left of left, the site provides good information on a broad range of global subjects. Sites include ConflictNet, WomensNet, EcoNet and LaborNet. Not a direct job source, but a good way to keep up on global events and meet others.

P.O. Box 29904
San Francisco, CA 94129-0904
Tel.: (415) 561-6100,
Fax: (415) 561-6101
E-mail: support@igc.org
http://www.igc.org/igc/

The Federation of American Women's Clubs Overseas Inc.

A support network of over 16,000 members in 33 countries around the world.

http://www.fawco.org/

Overseas Jobs Express

Premier House, Shoreham Airport
Sussex BN43 5FF
Tel.: [44] (1273) 440220,
Fax: [44] (1273) 440229
E-mail: OJE-books@overseasjobs.com
http://www.overseasjobs.com

Club Med

Okay, you're not going to save the world, but you at least can get some training wheels at one of the 115 resorts they run. The idea is that you can get to some of the most godforsaken places and then contact the locals after your six-month gig is up.

You make about $450 a month, but you can stash most of it away. By then you should have made enough contacts to get a meaningful job. They interview in March and October.

Club Med's G.O. hotline:
407-337-6660.

Transitions Abroad

Box 3000
Denville, NJ 07834
Tel.: (413) 256-3414
Fax: (413) 256-0373
http://www.transabroad.com/

This bimonthly magazine is targeted for people who want to live and work in a foreign country. It includes a directory of international volunteer positions and lists job opportunities including teaching and technical positions. $38 for 12 issues.

Job Search Overseas

P.O. Box 35, Falmouth
Cornwall, TR11 3UB
Tel.: (0872) 870070
Fax: (0872) 870071

A monthly paper that collects international job ads from other sources for the working traveler.

Overseas Employment Newsletter

A newsletter published by Overseas Employment Services every two weeks in which they "describe in detail at least 300 currently available jobs for a broad range of skills, careers and positions in many developing nations and industrialized countries around the world." The same group also publishes a variety of useful books on the same topic.

http://www.overseasjobs.com/
Also:

http://www.advocacy-net.com/
overseasmks.htm
http://www.escapeartist.com/jobs/
overseas1.htm
http://joyjobs.com/
http://ser.org/jobs.html

STUDENT TRAVEL AND WORK EXCHANGE CONTACTS

Campus Travel

http://www.campustravel.co.uk

College Travel International

http://www.prairienet.org/rec/travel/
homepage.html

Council Travel

http://www.ciee.org/cts/ctshome.htm

ISTC

http://www.istc.org/

International Center for Educational Travel
http://www2.ios.com:80/~ncet/

STA Travel
http://www.sta-travel.com/

Student and Budget Travel Guide
*http://asa.ugl.lib.umich.edu/chdocs/
travel/travel-guide.html*
http://www.usia.gov/homepage.html

Global Citizens Network
Global Citizens Network sends small
teams of volunteers to rural
communities around the world to
immerse themselves in the daily life of
the local culture for several weeks. The
teams work on community projects
initiated by the local people, such as
planting trees, digging irrigation
trenches, setting up a schoolroom or
teaching commercial skills.

http://www.globalcitizens.org/

American Field Service Intercultural Programs
*220 East 42nd Street, Third Floor
New York, NY 10017
Tel.: (212) 949-4242, (800) 876-2377
Fax: (212) 949-9379
http://www.afs.org/*
Since 1947 AFS has been a global leader
in promoting intercultural
understanding through high school
student exchanges. AFS offers U.S.
students more than 100 programs in 46
countries around the world. Students
live and study abroad for a year or a
semester of high school, or they can
take time out between high school and
college to do valuable community
service work in another country. AFS
also offers opportunities for families and
high schools in the United States to
host selected students from 50
countries who come to live and study in
America for a semester or a year.

Volunteers Exchange International
*http://userhttp://www.sfsu.edu/
~jopam/*

Volunteers for Peace
*http://www.vermontel.com/~vfp/
home.htm*

World Learning Inc.
*Kipling Road, P.O. Box 676
Brattleboro, VT 05302-0676
Tel.: (802) 257-7751, (802) 258-3248
http://www.worldlearning.org/*
This organization offers a school for
international training in teaching
languages, intercultural management
and world issues as well as college
semester abroad programs in 30
countries. Citizen exchange and
language programs include summer
abroad programs for students and
seniors, corporate language projects and
youth adventure camps. Au pair
arrangements and exchange programs
are also offered. Projects in
international development and training
strive to improve economic and social
conditions around the world through
development management, human
resource development and development
training.

Youth Exchange Service (YES)
*4675 MacArthur Court, Suite 830
Newport Beach, CA 92660
Tel.: (800) 848-2121, (714) 955-2030
http://www.yesint.com*
An international teenage exchange-
student program dedicated to world
peace. If you are interested in hosting
an international teenage "ambassador,"
contact this group.

United Nation's Volunteer Programme
http://suna.unv.ch/

The Council on International Educational Exchange (CIEE)
*International Volunteer Projects
205 East 42nd Street
New York, NY 10017
Tel.: (888) COUNCIL
E-mail: info@ciee.org
http://www.ciee.org/*
Offering more than 600 projects in 30
countries, CIEE gives volunteers the
option to work in archaeology, nature
conservation, construction and
renovation, or social service. The
directory costs $15, a charge that CIEE
will deduct from the $295 project
registration fee. Write for a directory or
more information.

Operation Crossroads Africa

475 Riverside Drive, Suite #831
New York, NY 10115-0050
Tel.: (212) 870-2106
Fax: (212) 870-2055
E-mail: crw@loop.com (for brochure
and an application); oca@igc.apc.org
(for summer program: Africa/Brazil)
http://www.igc.apc.org/oca/

Operation Crossroads Africa has volunteer opportunities in several African countries as well as in Brazil. Since 1957, 10,000 Crossroads participants representing 500 universities, colleges, organizations, etc., have come together to work for a better world. Being a Crossroads volunteer is an intense living, working, and learning experience at the grassroots level.

VOCA-California

1008 S Street, Suite B
Sacramento, CA 95814
Tel.: (916) 556-1620
Fax: (916) 556-1630
E-mail: voca-california@voca.org
http://www.voca.org

Friendship Force

57 Forsyth Street, NW, Suite 900
Atlanta, GA 30303
Tel.: (404) 522-9490
Fax: (404) 688-6148
E-mail: 254-9295@mcimail.com
http://www.friendship-force.org/

The Friendship Force is a private, nonprofit organization whose purpose is to create an environment where personal friendships can be established across the international barriers that separate people.

Peacework

gopher://gopher.bev.net/00/
community/peacework
E-mail: 75352.261@compuserv.com
http://www.afsc.org/peacewrk.htm

Sponsors short-term international volunteer projects in developing communities around the world.

Partnership for Service Learning

E-mail: pslny@aol.com.
http://www.studyabroad.com/ps

Offers programs that combine structured academic studies with volunteer community service for summer, January term, semester or year.

Volunteers Exchange International

E-mail:Leids@Icyeus.igc.apc.org
http://www.ciee.org/

The U.S. committee of an international network of volunteers: the Federation of the International Christian Youth Exchange (ICYE).

Overseas Development Network

333 Valencia Street, Suite 330
San Francisco, CA 94103
Tel.: (415) 431-4204
Fax: (415) 431-5953
http://www.peacenet.org/odn/

The ODN is primarily for students who want to work overseas in an intern (read no pay) position. This is also called "alternative tourism" in the San Francisco area. The benefit is that you get to get in there and do something about hunger, poverty and social injustice. The 12-year-old organization has placed over 200 interns overseas and in the Appalachian area of the States (yes, Third World standards do still exist in America). If you want to do your good deeds even closer to home, ODN membership ($15 student, $25 for a regular member) will introduce you to other like-minded students. There are also positions with ODN requiring about 12–20 hours a week. You can gain experience organizing, promoting, writing and marketing and get a good "foot in the door" position if you want to get serious in global affairs. All positions are unpaid and require a minimum commitment of three months and eight hours a week. You can take part in a local ODN chapter, work to build sustainable locally initiated development programs within your local community or just contribute to the ODN's ongoing programs.

Peace Corps

1990 K Street, NW
Room 9320
Washington, DC 20526
Tel.: (800) 424-8580
http://www.peacecorps.gov/

When most people in the '60s and '70s thought about how they could change the world, the Peace Corps came to mind. It may surprise you to know that the Vietnam-era hearts-and-minds division of the U.S. government is still hard at work making the world a better place without killing or maiming.

The Peace Corps is pure American do-goodism from its Woodstock-style logo (the Peace Corps was formed in 1961) to its Puritan slogan "The Toughest Job You'll Ever Love" and goes straight to the soul of every Midwestern farm boy. The Corps appeals to the American love of doing good things in bad places. In the 30 years of the Peace Corps' existence, 140,000 Americans have heeded the call and the world has truly benefited by an outpouring of American know-how. Last year there were about 6,500 volunteers spread out over 90 countries. What do you get? Well, the answer is better stated as what do you give. Successful applicants go through two to three months of language, technical and cultural training for each "tour." You will get a small allowance for housing, food and clothing, airfare to and from your posting and 24 days of vacation a year.

While in-country, you will work with a local counterpart and may be completely on your own in a small rural village or major city. The payoff is that you can actually make things happen, understand a different culture and say that you did something about the world. Does the reality meet the fantasy? Apparently it does. The average length of time spent in the Peace Corps is six years with nine months of training. That works out to three two-year tours with the minimum training. All ex–Peace Corps volunteers we talked to said it was among the most rewarding years of their lives.

Getting in is not that easy, but once in, you join a club that can benefit you greatly in your career. Being an ex–Peace Corps member says that you are about giving and hard work and a little more worldly than most.

You must be a U.S. citizen and at least 18 years old and healthy. Most successful applicants have a bachelor's degree. You must also have a minimum 2.5 grade point average for educational assignments or experience in the field you want to enter. Although there is no limit on age, the Peace Corps is typically a young person's game and considered to be an excellent way to get a leg up in government and private sector employment. The government will give you $5,400 when you get out, find you a job in the government on a noncompetitive basis and even help you apply for the over 50 special scholarships available for ex–Peace Corps members.

The emphasis is on training and education in the agricultural, construction and educational areas. There are not too many fine-arts requirements, although they do have a category for art teacher. Couples with dependents are a no no, and couples are strongly discouraged. It helps if you know a foreign language, have overseas experience and have a teaching/tutoring background.

The Peace Corps does not mess around in countries that are overtly hostile or dangerous to Americans, like Peru, Colombia, Angola, Algeria and Iran. Also, you will not be posted to Monaco or Paris. You can be posted to Fiji, Thailand, Central Africa or most countries in the CIS. If you are curious, the Peace Corps recruiters hold two-hour evening seminars at their regional offices. Don't be put off by the slightly '80s banner of "Globalize Your Resume." You can meet with returning volunteers and ask all the questions you want.

CARE

Worldwide Headquarters
151 Ellis Street
Atlanta, GA 30303
Tel.: (404) 681-2552
Fax: (404) 577-4515
http://www.care.org/
CARE was founded when 22 American organizations joined to help European survivors of World War II. It is the world's largest private, nonprofit, nonsectarian relief and development organization. In 1994, CARE provided $367 million in goods and services to more than 30 million people in developing countries. There are programs for disaster relief, food distribution, primary health care, agriculture and natural resource management, population, girls' education, family planning and small-business support. Ongoing self-help projects are in place in 61 of the least developed countries of Africa, Asia and Latin America, and programs are in progress for the emerging economies of Eastern Europe and the former Soviet Union. CARE responds to disasters overseas and has sent emergency aid to victims of famine and war in Rwanda, Haiti and the former Yugoslavia.

Save the Children

50 Wilton Road
Westport, CT 06880
Tel.: (203) 221-4245
(800) 243-5075
Fax: (203) 222-9176
http://www.savethechildren.org/
SCF is a nonprofit, nonsectarian organization, founded in 1932, to make positive and lasting differences in the lives of disadvantaged children both in the United States and abroad. SCF has more than 60 years of experience in 59 countries and throughout the United States providing emergency relief and community development assistance. The group targets four key sectors: (1) health/population/nutrition, (2) education, (3) economic opportunities and (4) commodity-assisted development/emergency response.

UNICEF

338 East 38th Street
New York, NY 10016
Tel.: (212) 686-5522
(800) FOR-KIDS
http://www.unicef.org/
UNICEF is the leading advocate for children throughout the world, providing vaccines, clean water, medicine, nutrition, emergency relief and basic education for children in more than 140 nations. Children in Rwanda and the former Yugoslavia have been recent recipients of emergency relief. UNICEF is an integral but semiautonomous agency of the United Nations with its own executive board. Financial support for its work comes entirely from voluntary contributions. UNICEF's budget is not part of the dues paid by the member governments of the United Nations. An extensive network of volunteers work for UNICEF throughout the world, and local volunteers are always needed.

U.S. Committee For Refugees

1717 Massachusetts Avenue,
NW, Suite 701
Washington, DC 20036
http://www.refugees.org/
USCR in Review compiles statistics and reports from more than 100 field workers. The U.S. Committee documents and defends the rights of refugees worldwide, regardless of their nationality, race or religion.

The Soros Foundation

George Soros has created a chain of national foundations, an autonomous nonprofit organization to promote the development of open society. His largesse focuses primarily in the countries of Central and Eastern Europe and the former Soviet Union.

http://soros.org/

The Carter Center

One Copenhill
Atlanta, GA 30307
Tel.: (404) 331-3900
Fax: (404) 331-0283
http://www.cartercenter.org

Jimmy Carter has been busy since he left office. His peace negotiations in North Korea, Haiti and Bosnia have been effective in achieving short-term results as well as angering many hardliners with his friendly approach to our enemies. Carter shows that a mildmannered, ever-smiling good ol' boy from the South can play the perfect good cop to the U.S. military's bad cop. Jimmy Carter seems to be working overtime for the Nobel Peace Prize. Not because he needs more stuff to hang on his wall (he was awarded America's highest civilian award in August 1999), but because he really believes that all people have good in them and he has a responsibility to make the world a better place.

Jimmy and Rosalynn's "keep busy and do good" organization is the Carter Center. One of his big events is building homes in poor countries (along with hundreds of volunteers like you). He works out of a 100,000-square-foot complex, complete with chapel, library, conference facilities and museum, to fight disease, hunger, poverty, conflict and oppression in 30 countries. The center is always happy to receive donations and resumes of motivated individuals who want to volunteer their time.

Philanthropic Advisory Service (PAS) of the Council of Better Business Bureau

Tel.: (703) 276-0100
http://www.bbb.org/about/pas.html

PAS promotes ethical standards of business practices and protect consumers through voluntary selfregulation and monitoring activities. They publish a bimonthly list of philanthropic organizations that meet the Council of Better Business Bureau's Standards for Charitable Solicitations. The standards include Public Accountability, Use of Funds, Solicitations and Informational Materials, Fund-Raising Practices and Governance. Ask for a copy of *Give But Give Wisely* ($1.00). Many of the groups have E-mail addresses, databases and on-line services.

National Charities Information Bureau (NCIB)

Tel.: (212) 929-6300
http://www.give.org/

NCIB regularly publishes listings and reports on charities, monitoring which groups meet their standards. Ask for a copy of their *Wise Giving Guide*. Individual contributions of $25 or more and corporations and foundations contributing $100 or more will be sent the *Wise Giving Guide* for one year. NCIB also publishes detailed evaluations about organizations. As many as three reports at a time are available without charge.

Human Rights Groups

Human Rights Watch

350 Fifth Avenue,
34th Floor
New York, NY 10118-3299
Tel: (212) 290-4700
Fax: (212) 736-1300
E-mail: hrwnyc@hrw.org

Human Rights Watch is dedicated to protecting the human rights of people around the world. Their goal is to prevent discrimination, to uphold political freedom, to protect people from inhumane conduct in wartime, and to bring offenders to justice. There are a number of ways you can be involved and contribute to their activities.

http://www.hrw.org/

Amnesty International USA

322 Eighth Avenue
New York, NY 10001
Tel.: (212) 807-8400
http://www.amnesty.org/

Amnesty International began in London in 1961 and so far claims they have come to the rescue of 43,000 prisoners. Today, the staff of 200 monitors news and information and communications from around the world to seek out cases of mistreatment. Their goal is to pressure governments to end torture, executions, political killings and disappearances, to ensure speedy trials for all political prisoners and to effect the release of prisoners of conscience provided they have neither used nor advocated violence.

Their method is simple and easy to effect. They coordinate the writing and mailing of letters to the captors of prisoners of conscience. Their methods have been proven successful and the international group was awarded the Nobel Peace Prize in 1977 for their efforts to promote observance of the UN Universal Declaration of Human Rights.

The membership is over 500,000 people in over 150 countries. Together, they can create an avalanche of mail and global protest over the mistreatment of prisoners. *Tel.: (202) 544-0200.*

Cultural Survival Inc.

215 First Street
Cambridge, MA 02142
Tel.: (617) 495-2562
Fax: (617) 621-3814
http://www.cs.org

There are about 40 ethnic groups at risk around the world. But there is more talk about saving the rain forest than the people who live in it. Nomadic forest dwellers have no money, own no land and in many cases do not integrate into societies who are pushing them out of their homeland. Having seen the havoc wreaked on our own native Indians and Inuit, it is difficult to come up with viable alternatives to their eventual extinction.

This is an organization of anthropologists and researchers whose goal is to help indigenous peoples (like tropical forest dwellers) develop at their own pace and with their own cultures intact. Cultural Survival's weapon is the almighty dollar, and they put it in the hands of the groups they help. Working with indigenous peoples and ethnic minorities, they import sustainably harvested, nontimber forest products. What are those, you ask? Well, handicrafts, cashew and Brazil nuts, babassu oil, rubber, bananas, even beeswax. The end result is that indigenous peoples gain lands, develop cash crops and don't have to live in shantytowns or timber camps to support themselves.

Founded in 1972, the group has a variety of methods of achieving its goals: education programs, importing and selling products, providing expertise to larger aid groups and providing technical assistance to local groups seeking economic viability.

The organization has projects in Brazil, Guinea-Bissau, Guatemala, Ecuador, the Philippines and Zambia. Membership ($45) gets you a subscription to the *CSE Matters* and the quarterly journal *Cultural Survival Manual*. Ask for a free catalog of products. By purchasing the products for sale, you directly support the peoples who gather and manufacture them, something very rare in this world of markups and middlemen.

If you would like to work as an intern, they are looking for people to help crank out the newsletter, raise funds, handle the office work and expand the network of indigenous groups and supporters. To receive an application, contact Pia Maybury-Lewis, Director of Interns, Cultural Survival, *46 Brattle Street, Cambridge, MA 02138, Tel.: (617) 441-5400*, or fax your resume and a letter that explains your personal interests to *(617) 441-5417.*

Human Rights Watch

1522 K Street, NW
Suite 910
Washington, DC 20005
Tel.: (202) 371-6592
http://www.hrw.org/about/about.html
This organization promotes and
monitors human rights worldwide.
Human Rights Watch serves as an
umbrella organization to Africa Watch,
Asia Watch, Americas Watch, Middle
East Watch, Helsinki Watch and the
Fund for Free Expression.

UNHCR

P.O. Box 2500
1211 Geneva 2, Depot, Switzerland
Tel.: [41] 22-739-8502
http://www.unhcr.ch/
The United Nations High Commission
for Refugees works to prevent refugees
from being forcibly returned to
countries where they could face death
or imprisonment. It also assists with
food, shelter and medical care. *Refugees
Magazine* focuses on a different refugee
movement each month. The UN
defines a refugee as anyone who flees his
home country in fear of loss of life or
liberty.

Peace Brigades International

5 Caledonian Road
London, England N1 9DX
Tel.: [44] (171) 713-0392
Fax: [44] (171) 837-2290
http://www.igc.apc.org/pbi/index.htm
The Peace Brigades try to prevent
human rights violations by escorting
individuals at threat, carrying a camera,
holding all night vigils and other
nonviolent actions.

An interesting way to make a nonviolent
stand. Volunteers acts as human shields
or witnesses in areas where locals' lives
are at risk. Partly funded by British-
based Christian Aid.

Peace Brigades International—
International Office (PBI)

5 Caledonian Rd, London N1,
England
Tel: +44-171-7130392
Fax: +44-171-8372290
E-mail: pbiio@gn.apc.org
http://www.igc.apc.org/pbi/

Servicio Paz y Justicia en America Latina (SERPAJ)

Casilla 09-01-8667,
Guayaquil, Ecuador
Tel: +593-4-201451
Fax: +593-4-203600

War Resisters' International (WRI)

5 Caledonian Rd,
London N1 9DX, England
Tel: +44-171-2784040
Fax: +44-171-2780444
E-mail: warresisters@gn.apc.org

Reporters Sans Frontieres

International Secretariat
5, rue Geoffroy-Marie
Paris, France
Tel.: [33] 144-838-484
http://www.rsf.fr/
RSF was founded in 1985 and has
offices in Belgium, Canada, France,
Germany, Italy, Spain and Switzerland
with members in 71 countries. Their
job is to defend imprisoned journalists
and press around the world. Their
annual report offers tips for journalists
on 152 countries, including the ones
where journalists have been harassed,
threatened and murdered. The annual
report is available for US$20.

They will send protest letters and
provide lawyers (if possible) and other
forms of assistance to reporters in jail. If
you want to convert to journalism after
you are jailed, these folks can't help you.

The Journal of Humanitarian Assistance

Faculty of Social and Political Sciences,
University of Cambridge,
Free School
Lane, Cambridge, CB2 3RQ, UK
http://www-jha.sps.cam.ac.uk/

A Few Tips on Writing Letters to Governments

I encourage members to write letters, but telegrams are more effective in gaining the attention of the reader. State the purpose of your letter in the first sentence and make sure you end it with your request. If you are writing about a specific person, clearly state his name. The letters should be short. Be polite and state your concern as simply and honestly as possible. Always assume that the person you are writing to is a reasonable person. Tell the reader what you do for a living and what country you are from. Do not bring up politics, religion or opinions. Use the proper title of the addressee, write in English, write it by hand and sign the letter "Yours respectfully."

Peace Groups

These are comprised of mostly university or private funded think-tanks on developing peaceful solutions to conflict.

The Albert Einstein Institution
http://hdc-http://www.harvard.edu/cfia/pnscs/aei.htm"

The Center for Defense Information
http://www.cdi.org/

The Commission on Global Governance
http://www.cgg.ch/"

The Conflict Resolution Consortium
http://www.colorado.edu/conflict

Consortium on Peace Research, Education and Development
http://www.igc.apc.org/copred

The Cyprus Peace Center
http://www.isr.umd.edu/~pzaphiri/peace_center/index.html

Fellowship of Reconciliation
http://www.netaxs.com/~nvweb/for/

The Foundation for Prevention & Early Resolution of Conflict
http://www.conflictresolution.org/

Harvard University: The Program on Nonviolent Sanctions and Cultural Survival
http://hdc-http://www.harvard.edu/cfia/pnscs/homepage.htm

Initiative on Conflict Resolution and Ethnicity
http://www.incore.ulst.ac.uk/

Institute for Conflict Resolution Studies (ICRS)
http://www.vvaf.org/icrs

WarChild
http://www.warchild.org

UNICEF
gopher://hqfaus01.unicef.org:70/00.cefdata/.emerctyprof95/

Human Rights Watch
http://www.hrw.org/research/afghanistan.html

World Disasters Report (IFRC)
http://www.ifrc.org/pubs/wdr/95/

Institute for Global Communications: PeaceNet, EcoNet, etc.
http://www.igc.apc.org/

International Peace Research Association
http://www.antioch.edu/~peace//ipra/IPRA.html

International Peace Research Institute, Oslo
gopher://csf.Colorado.EDU:70/11/peace/orgs/prio

National Conference on Peace & Conflict Resolution
http://web.gmu.edu/departments/NCPCR/

Peace Brigades International
http://www.igc.apc.org/pbi/index.htm

Relief Web, a project of the UNDHA
http://www.reliefweb.intl

Stockholm International Peace Research Institute
http://www.sipri.se/new_location.html

Tampere Peace Research Institute, University of Tampere [Finland]
http://www.uta.fi/laitokset/tapri

U.S. Institute of Peace
http://www.usip.org

University of California: Institute on Global Conflict & Cooperation
http://www-igcc.ucsd.edu/IGCC2/igccmenu.htm

The Disaster Response Unit of Interaction (The American Council for Voluntary International Action)
http://www.interaction.org/ia/sitrep/afgan.html

United Nations High Commissioner for Refugees (UNHCR)
http://www.unhcr.ch

U.S. State Department Human Rights Report
http://www.usis.usemb.se/human/

Medical Aid Groups

There are angels in Rwanda, Somalia, Angola, Afghanistan and Iraq. They are not there to convert souls or play harps. They are not soldiers or politicians but white-coated volunteers who sew back limbs, pull out shrapnel from babies' heads and minister to the sick and dying. They are the men and women who try to ease the suffering caused by violent actions. Natural disasters also tax the resources and stamina of aid workers to the limit. If you don't mind stacking bodies like firewood or can live with the ever-present stench of too many sick people in one place, you will do just fine.

The world needs people who are capable of cleaning up the mess caused by governments. If there is a disaster, chances are you will see these folks in there long before the journalists and the politicians. These are nondenominational groups that are found in the world's most dangerous places. If you have medical skills and want to save more lives in a day than a tentful of TV evangelists in a lifetime, this is the place to be. Conditions are beyond primitive, usually makeshift refugee camps on the edges of emerging conflicts. Many groups will walk or helicopter in to war-torn regions to assist in treating victims. Many aid workers have been targeted for death because of their policy of helping both sides. There is constant danger from rocket attacks, land mines, communicable diseases and riots. These people are not ashamed to stagger out of a tent after being up 48 hours straight, have a good cry and then get back to work saving more lives. It hurts, but it feels good. Contact the following organizations for more information:

International Committee of the Red Cross

19 avenue de la Paix
CH 1202 Genève
Tel.: 41 (22) 734 60 01
Fax: 41 (22) 733 20 57 (Public
Information Centre)
The International Committee of the Red Cross (ICRC) is an impartial, neutral and independent organization whose exclusively humanitarian mission is to protect the lives and dignity of victims of war and internal violence and to provide them with assistance. It directs and coordinates the Iinternational relief activities conducted by the Movement in situations of conflict. It also endeavors to prevent suffering by promoting and strengthening humanitarian law and universal humanitarian principles. Established in 1863, the ICRC is at the origin of the International Red Cross and Red Crescent Movement.

http://www.icrc.org

Addresses of delegations

http://www.ICRC.org/eng/
delegations/

American Red Cross

National Headquarters
17th and D Street, NW
Washington, DC 20006
Tel.: (202) 737-8300
For 115 years, whenever there has been a disaster or war, these folks have been on the scene knee-deep in bandages, blood and cots, helping the injured and consoling those who have just lost everything. They always have a need for volunteers, particularly people with medical and technical skills. If you can't volunteer your time or skills, blood donors are desperately needed.

Doctors of the World

375 West Broadway, Fourth Floor
New York, NY 10012
Tel.: (212) 226-9890
Fax: (212) 226-7026
http://www.doctorsoftheworld.org/
home.html
Doctors of the World is a non-sectarian, international organization working in the United States and abroad that provides humanitarian assistance to those in the greatest need.

AmeriCares

161 Cherry Street
New Canaan, CT 06840
Tel.: (203) 966-5195, (800) 486-4357
AmeriCares is a private, nonprofit disaster relief and humanitarian aid organization that provides immediate response to emergency medical needs and supports long-term health care programs for people around the world, irrespective of race, color, creed or political persuasion. Since 1982 AmeriCare has delivered more than $1.4 billion worth of medical and disaster aid around the world. AmeriCare works with corporate America to secure large donations of supplies and materials. Cash contributions are used primarily for logistical costs. For every $1 donated, AmeriCare is able to deliver $22 worth of relief supplies.

Refugee Relief International

2995 Woodside Road
Suite 400-244
Woodside, CA 94062
One of *DP*'s favorite group of guys. Founded in 1982 to provide medical supplies and other aid for refugees and war victims. There are no salaried staff and volunteers pay their own expenses. All administrative offices are donated. RRI has assisted people in Afghanistan, Myanmar, the Balkans, Thailand and Cambodia. This small group of ex-special forces guys will guarantee that every dollar you spend gets sent up to the front-lines where civilians need medical attention the most. So cheap, they don't even have a Web site. That means your money is going where people need it most.

Physicians for Peace

229 West Bute Street, Suite 820
Norfolk, VA 23510
Tel.: (757) 625-7569
Fax: (757) 625-7680
PFP is an apolitical, nonprofit organization that helps to foster international peace and cooperation by improving health care.

Doctors Without Borders (Medecins Sans Frontieres)

11 East 26 Street, Suite 1904l
New York, NY 10010
Tel.: (212) 679-6800 (France: [72] 73-04-14)
Fax: (212) 679-7016
http://www.msf.org/
Doctors Without Borders, founded a quarter of a century ago, is the largest international emergency medical organization in the world. Every year, around 3,000 volunteers leave for three to six months of service in more than 70 countries around the world. Many of the countries are in a state of war. Sixty percent of the volunteers are medically trained and come from 45 countries around the world. Most are 25–35 years old. The organization assists victims of natural disasters and health crises like Ebola, and ministers to refugees and war victims. To deploy people as quickly as possible (within 24 hours when possible), special emergency kits were created with strict operational and medical procedures. Today, these kits and manuals are used by other international organizations around the world.

International Medical Corps

12233 West Olympic Boulevard, Suite 280
Los Angeles, CA 90064-1052
Tel.: (310) 826-7800
Fax: (310) 442-6622
E-mail: IMC@IGC.APC.ORG
IMC is a private, non-sectarian, nonpolitical, nonprofit organization established by U.S. physicians and nurses to provide emergency medical relief and health care training to devastated regions worldwide.

Save Yourself

Stay Alive! (At Least Until You Get Home)

There is much ink and photons on survival being wasted on adventure and travel these days. Most are knee-jerk stories about what victimized people should have done, written by people in the comfort of their media offices. Yemen, Chechnya, Uganda, Guatemala, Colombia and other countries have been the site of tourist and expat disasters. After talking to a number of people involved in these highly publicized kidnappings, murders, rapes and attacks, I can tell you that no amount of training would have predicted, prevented or averted what happened. Most of these people are smart, fearful, cautious and took a lot of precautions. What does come out of these incidents is that knowing what to do in a worst-case scenario does make the difference between being able to talk about it on Oprah versus being a statistic.

Armies have long known that training can replace thinking with ingrained reaction. The brain has a bad habit of pushing your "Holy shit, what are we going to do now!" button every time it hears a loud noise. This button immediately sets into motion helpful self-defense devices like shaky knees, dry mouth, buggy eyes, stammering, slack jaw and mental confusion.

There is the other side of the coin, described as "blissful ignorance," where backpackers think antiaircraft fire and wildly erratic katushyas and are just charming native celebrations. Both conditions can lead to a condition called "sudden reality check." This is caused by a rapid education in the truths and evils of not being prepared for danger.

Can you really train for the myriad of horrors that are out there? No. But you can dramatically shave the odds. I sat down to communicate what I have learned and I wrote a whole book on survival called *Come Back Alive* (Doubleday). When I turned it in, it was 64 chapters and over 700 single-spaced-pages long. The publisher of course cut it in half, which means that you don't know the half of it.

The point is that there are a lot of very simple things that can save your life. There are also a lot of courses and experts who can convey that information to you.

Ba Boom . . . Thunk

There are six universal types of soft body-armor you can choose from in the field.

They are heavy, hot and sweaty and provide little protection from mines, shrapnel or multiple guns shots . . . but they can save your life.

CLASS	STOPS	NOTES	COST
Level I	.22 LR and .38 special	*Offers minimal protection from the smallest types of pistols. Will not stop military rifle ammunition.*	$250
Level IIA	low-velocity .357; 9mm	*Will stop low-powered ammunition from standard handguns. Will not stop military rifle ammunition.*	$300
Level II	high-velocity .357; 9mm	*Will stop high-powered ammunition from standard handguns. Will not stop military rifle ammunition.*	$350
Level IIIA	.44 magnum; submachine gun 9mm	*Will stop high-velocity 9mm ammunition. Will not stop military rifle ammunition.*	$500–$700
Level III	High powered-rifle	*Will stop 7.62mm, 5.56mm (.223), .30 cal military rifle ammunition and shotgun slugs.*	$175
Level IV	Armor-piercing rifle	*Will stop armor-piercing ammunition from high-velocity military rifles. This type jacket is very heavy.*	$300
Trauma Plates (Steel or Ceramic Groin Plate)	Upgrades front and rear protection significantly as well as increasing weight	*Vests provide different amounts of coverage in the groin and arm area. A trauma plate is a solid piece of ceramic or layered Kevlar that stops high-velocity rounds aimed at the heart or groin.*	$20–$150

Source: Real World Rescue
Inter American Security Products http://www.interameri.com

What does that have to do with survival training? First of all, most people have never been in a life-threatening situation. We've seen movies, been challenged by bullies or read other people's accounts, but it is always different. Often people will use the word "dreamlike" to describe the event—a natural outcome of heightened senses and information overload playing things out in slow motion, but more like the look a rat has when a snake towers over it. Training can at least help you to recognize situations, react intelligently and minimize the trauma.

Journalist Safety Training

Many of these courses and all this information is available to non-journalists. There is a blurred line between tourists, stringers and journalists these days with small DV cameras and a trend in khaki adventure wear. The courses are expensive, but obviously worth whatever your hide is.

Groups such as Frontline, CPJ and Reporters Respond have no interest in providing travel planning tips to civvies, but if you are trying to break into the impecunious business of war reportage, they can offer some advice.

Centurion Risk Assessment Services Ltd.

Reed Cottage, Fleet Road, Elvetham, Hartley Wintney, Hants RG27 8AT U.K.
Tel.: (44) 7000 221221
http:www.centurion-riskservices.co.uk
Survival training for journalists, body armor and helmet rental.

AKE Ltd

Mortimer House
Holmer Road, Hereford. JR4 9TA UK
Tel.: 44 0 1432 267111
Fax: 44 0 1432 350227
E-mail: andy@ake.co.uk
http://www.ake.co.uk/
Monthly courses on surviving hostile regions in the UK.

Real World Rescue

1280 Robinson Avenue, Suite C
San Diego, CA 92103
Tel.: (619) 297 7114
http://realworldrescue.com
Provides safety/survival training for journalists and travelers.

Hacks, Save Your Skin

AKE is one of two British companies running Hostile Environment Courses (HETs) for journos. Based in Hereford on the Welsh border, the course is run by Andrew Kain and Paul Brown, both of whom spent over a decade in the British army's elite Special Air Service.

The course is structured as if the participants had never been near a war zone. It consists of five days of intensive lectures and a final day of field work (theoretically evacuating and treating severely wounded people from a war zone). Divided into two sections, the course concentrates on weaponry, the damage it can do and the accuracy of different types of weaponry and the (different) men behind the guns. Thereafter the course consists of a series of intensive lectures on emergency medical procedures and recognizing various diseases.

Andrew Kain takes participants through the different tactics employed by different armies, from guerrilla forces to former Eastern Bloc and NATO forces, with useful tips about recognizing military tactics and what to do in some of the more predictable situations. Paul Brown, a former SAS medic, lectures on everything from hypothermia and snake bites to open fractures and gunshot wounds. Almost half of the medical course is practical, with the participants learning how to splint broken arms and legs, treat burns and (all-important in a war zone) gunshot wounds.

Hacks, Save Your Skin

Lectures on antipersonnel mines, the different types and how they are placed and recognized combined with what to do if you tread on one from a medical perspective, make the course a must for hacks venturing into war zones. While the course organizers readily acknowledge that five days is the bare minimum needed for the course, it covers almost every life-threatening risk you are likely to encounter. It might not be nice being threatened by a thug with a pistol, but it's nice to hear from the experts that if the thug in question is more than 20 meters away his chances of hitting you are about zilch, and even less if you're running.

Adventure/Recreation Schools

School for Field Studies

http://www.bu.edu/cees/ugrad.html

A nonprofit group that runs 40 month-long and semester-length programs that allow students to gain field research experience. Targeted to high school and college students, the college credit courses are run all around the world. There is a wide choice of topics, from coral reef studies (the Caribbean), marine mammals (Baja, Mexico), tropical rain forests (Australia) and wildlife management (Kenya). Scholarships and interest-free loans are available.

SOLO (Stonehearth Open Learning Opportunity)

http://www.stonehearth.com

A school for professionals, SOLO is designed to teach wilderness guides what to do in an emergency. They offer a four-week, $1,200 Emergency Wilderness Training Certification course that will get you on the preferred list of just about any expedition. Shorter two-day seminars are taught around the country for $100. The areas of specialization are wilderness emergencies (such as frostbite, hypothermia, bites and altitude sickness), climbing rescue, and emergency medicine (wounds, broken limbs, shock and allergy). Participants are expected to have a basic grounding in climbing and outdoor skills.

National Outdoor Leadership School

http://www.nols.edu

This school gets past the superficial imagery of some survival schools and right down to business. People who want to make money in the outdoor adventure business come here to learn not only survival aspects, but the nuts and bolts of adventure travel outfitting. You can also take the 34-day, $2,100 NOLS instructor's class once you have passed a basic wilderness class. The emphasis here is on safety, since your future charges will be less than amused if they end up living off the land because you forgot to pack their favorite pudding. Choose from sea kayaking, winter camping, telemark skiing, backpacking or mountaineering. Some courses qualify for college credit.

Entry-level classes are in reality great adventure vacations depending on your area of interest. Mountaineering classes are taught in Alaska, British Columbia and even Kenya. Expect to spend two weeks to three months on location learning the specialized skills you will need to lead other groups. If you want to cram in a class on your vacation, then opt for their selection of two-week courses on horsepacking, winter skiing, rock climbing or canoeing. If you flunk, well you had a good time on a well-organized adventure tour.

Adventure Experience Organizations

British Schools Exploring Society

http://www.rgs.org

BSES sets up an expedition for young people (16^1/$_2$ to 20 years old) every year. The six-week expeditions are usually to the arctic regions (Canada to Russia) and are during the summer holidays. They have been sneaking in expeditions to tropical climes and offer four- to six-month expeditions to Botswanna, Greenland, Alaska and Svalbard.

Over 3,000 people have taken part since 1932, and interviews take place in London in November. Participants pay a fee to cover costs; membership to BSES is by election after the successful completion of a BSES expedition.

Outward Bound

http://www.outwardbound.org/

Do you want to develop that calm, steely-eyed approach, that strong warmth that exudes from those '40s male movie stars with an unshakable faith in your abilities and courage? All right, how about just being able to sleep without your Mickey Mouse nightlight on? Outward Bound starts with the mind, and the body follows. The program has been used with the handicapped, the criminal and the infirm, and it creates magical transformations in all. What is the secret? Well, like the tiny train that said, "I think I can, I think I can," OB teaches you to motivate yourself, trust your companions and step past your self-imposed limits. What emerges is self-confidence and a greater understanding of your fellow man.

Earth Skills

http://www.anamorph.com/earthskills.html

There is a school where you can learn tracking, survival, plant uses and general bush lore. The Earth Skills school was founded in 1987 by Jim Lowery to introduce people to the great outdoors in a very practical way. Most of the classes are over a three-day weekend and run between $50 to $160. The wilderness skill course is a three-day class that will teach you how to trap, identify edible plants, weave baskets, build shelters, start a fire with an Indian bow, make primitive weapons, purify water and generally learn how to survive more than 50 miles from a 7-Eleven.

The idea for the school was developed in 1941. Today, there are 31 Outward Bound schools around the world, with seven in North America: Colorado, Maine, New York, North Carolina, Oregon, Minnesota and Toronto.

Outward Bound has expanded to include executive training courses, but the results are not as glorious as anticipated. In one recent session, instructors in England divided executives into two groups and told them to rescue two injured people on the side of a mountain. One group then proceeded to steal the other's stretcher, brought their "victim" to safety, then stood and cheered while the other victim lay stranded on the mountain. Oh, well. Maybe learning to survive the urban jungle makes men tougher than we thought.

Survival Training

Boulder Outdoor Survival School (BOSS)

http://www.boss-inc.com/

If you want to live like a native (no, they do not offer casino management courses), check out the BOSS progam. The big one is the 27-day course in Utah, where you will go through four phases. For openers, you will spend five days traveling without food or water. The second phase is 12 days, with the group learning and practicing your survival skills. The third phase has you spending three to four days on a solo survival quest with minimal tools (no credit cards or Walkmans), living off the land until you finally make the grade by spending five days in the wild traveling a substantial distance. Graduation ceremonies are somewhat informal and muddy. For this, you pay about $1,300. Naturally, food, accommodations and transportation are not included. One added benefit is that most participants lose about 5 to 8 percent of their body weight after taking the month long course.

For those who don't have a month to spend on a forced weight-loss system, or can't miss reruns of *McGyver,* there are one- to three-week courses that range from basic earth skills and aboriginal knowledge for $550, to winter survival courses that include making snowshoes, mushing dog sleds and cold weather first aid for $565. The one that appeals to me is the seven-day desert and marine (as in water) survival course held in the Kino bay area of Sonora, Mexico. This course teaches you how to find your food underwater and on land, finding water, what there is to eat in arid lands and general desert survival knowledge. BOSS is consistently held above the others as the toughest and most rewarding survival school.

Scotti School of Defensive Driving

http://www.ssdd.com

For two decades this school has been teaching evasive and survival driving to personnel in 600 corporations in 28 companies.

Executive Security International

http://www.esi-lifeforce.com

Training school (est. 1980) for bodyguarding, self-defense, marine security and driving skills.

ETI Wilderness Survival Training Program

www.montrose.net/eti/surv.htm

Courses in Arctic, desert and plain old survival.

Travel Insurance

Go ahead, pick up the phone, tell the toothy rotarian with the bad comb-over that you are going to Chechnya and are worried about losing your camera. Can he write a travel insurance policy? Sure, a few years ago the disclaimer on your insurance pretty much guaranteed that the only thing insurance companies would pay for would be the cost of the postage to cancel your insurance after they explain all the things they didn't cover. Things like terrorism, acts of God, and even things like theft or loss without a police report. Good luck trying to find a cop, let alone a piece of paper and pencil in the places *DP* travels to. In most cases it's the cops that arrange to have our stuff stolen.

But things have changed. And of course so have the premiums. You can get kidnap insurance, AIDS insurance, cancellation insurance and I guess you could probably buy insurance in case something happens to your insurance company while you are away.

Tips for buyers: Use a broker and be up front with the type of coverage you need. Read the fine print and check quality of medical treatment (including any caps on coverage) and demand replacement value of your expensive items.

Access America
 http://www.accessamerica.com/

Travel Guard
 http://www.travel-guard.com/

CSA
 http://www.travelsecure.com/

Kidnap, Rescue, Extraction
 http://www.black-fox.com/

Travel Insurance
 http://www.chubbodyssey.com

Long-Term Travel Insurance
 http://www.worldwidemedical.com/

Extreme Sports Coverage
 http://www.worldcover.co.uk/

Medical Coverage
 http://www.intsos.com/

Emergency/Rescue

If you become seriously ill or injured abroad, a U.S. consular officer can provide assistance in finding medical services and informing your next-of-kin, family or friends. A consular officer can also assist in the transfer of funds from the United States, but payment of hospital and other expenses is your responsibility.

It is wise to learn what medical services your health insurance will cover overseas before you leave on your trip. If you do have applicable insurance, don't forget to carry both your insurance policy identity card as proof of such insurance, and a claim form. Many health insurance companies will pay customary and reasonable hospital costs abroad, but most require a rider for a Medivac flight back to the States. This is usually done via private plane or by removing airline seats. You will be accompanied by a nurse or medical assistant who will also fly back to the country of origin. Medivacs can burn money as fast the Lear Jet you charter, so plan on spending a minimum of five grand and up to $30,000. If you are really banged up, you may need more medical technicians, special equipment and a higher level of care during your flight. The Social Security Medicare program does not provide for payment of hospital or medical services outside the United States.

If you're getting toward the back end of your adventuring career, the American Association of Retired Persons (AARP) offers foreign medical care coverage at no extra charge with its Medicare supplement plans. This coverage is restricted to treatments considered eligible under Medicare. In general, it covers 80 percent of the customary and reasonable charges, subject to a $50 deductible for the covered care during the first 60 days. There is a ceiling of $25,000 per trip. This is a reimbursement plan, so you must pay the bills first and obtain receipts for submission to the plan. Keep in mind that many insurance policies may not cover you if you were injured in a war zone.

To facilitate identification in case of an accident, complete the information page on the inside of your passport, providing the name, address and telephone number of someone to be contacted in an emergency. The name given should not be the same as your traveling companions, in case the entire party is involved in the same accident. Travelers going abroad with any preexisting medical problems should carry a letter from their attending physician. The letter should describe their condition and cover information on any prescription medications, including the generic name of any prescribed drugs that they need to take.

Any medications being carried overseas should be left in their original containers and be clearly labeled. Travelers should check with the foreign embassy of the country they are visiting to make sure any required medications are not considered to be illegal narcotics.

International SOS Assistance
15 Rue Lombard,
1205 Geneva, Switzerland
Tel.: [22] 347-6161
Fax: [22] 347-6172
http://www.intsos.com/

Access America, Inc.
P.O. Box 90310
Richmond, VA 23230
Tel.: (800) 284-8300

Air Ambulance Inc.
Hayward, CA
Tel.: (800) 982-5806, (510) 786-1592

Aero Ambulance International
Ft. Lauderdale, FL
Tel.: (800) 443-8042, (305) 776-6800

Air Ambulance Network
Miami, FL
Tel.: (300) 327-1966, (305) 387-1708

Air-Evac International
8665 Gibbs Drive, Suite 202
San Diego, CA 92123
Tel.: (800) 854-2569

Air Medic—Air Ambulance of America
Washington, PA
Tel.: (800) 321-4444, (412) 228-8000

American Aero-Med
1575 West Commercial Blvd.,
Hanger 36B
Fort Lauderdale, FL 33309
Tel.: (800)-443-8042

Euro-Flite
3000 Wesleyan, Ste 200
Houston, TX 77027
Tel.: (713)-961-5200
Fax: (713) 961-4088

Euro-Flite
Vantaa, Finland
Tel.: (358) 870-2544

Air Ambulance America
Austin, TX
Tel.: (512)479-8000

Care Flight—Air Critical Care Intl.
Clearwater, FL
Tel.: (800) 282-6878, (813) 530-7972

National Air Ambulance
Ft. Lauderdale, FL
Tel.: (800) 327-3710, (305) 525-5538

International Medivac Transport
Phoenix, AZ
Tel.: (800) 468-1911, (602) 678-4444

International SOS Assistance
Philadelphia, PA
Tel.: (800) 523-8930, (215) 244-1500

Mercy Medical Airlift
Manassas, VA
Tel.: (800) 296-1217, (703) 361-1191

AIRescue
7435 Valjean Avenue
Van Nuys, CA 91406
Tel.: (800) 922-4911, (818) 994-0911
Fax: (818) 994-0180
(This number can be called collect by patients and customers from anywhere in the world.)

What to Pack

Use It or Lose It

You really cannot give solid advice on what to pack. If you say travel light, people feel cheated. If you provide a five page list of gizmos, you get yelled at for being a gadget hawker. I have traveled with nothing (after all my luggage was stolen) and lots (on assignment, complete with tripod, tape recorders, video cameras and camera), and having nothing is the way to go. Most travelers travel with less and less as they gain experience or as they get mugged and pickpocketed. You choose: lose it now or later. The only exception would be specialized expeditions, where you are expected to come back with footage or samples of your discoveries. Even if you consider porters for your gear, maintain your credo of traveling light. The web sites listed are some of my resources but not endorsements (Yes I get just as mad at high prices, low quality and fashion extras invading the adventure business). Anybody want to hire me to create decent equipment?

Luggage

What separates you from the locals is your baggage (not to mention that ridiculous hat you're wearing). I prefer a frameless black military bergen, a camera bag that snaps around my waist, and a mountaineer fanny pack. I tell people to avoid outside pockets, but I must have twenty of them, filled with dirty laundry and cold-weather gear. Sometimes I squash everything into a UN flour sack when checking on nasty airlines. Having multiple bags that attach to me keeps my hands free, confuses the hell out of customs inspectors and gives a theif something to think about when it's all **caribinered** together. Locks and twist-ties from garbage bags are good to slow down thieves. Put everything inside large heavy-duty Ziploc freezer bags, and then put those inside large garbage bags. Bring some spares of both types of bags. Some people like to use thick rubber "rafting" sacks, but in my experience they are useless, being neither waterproof nor durable. Inside my pack, I like to put a small Pelican case with the delicates and expensives. I also carry a second fanny pack for toiletries and personal stuff. I use clear Tupperware containers to store first aid, medicines, and other assorted small objects. Don't scrimp on your pack, but remember it will come back foul smelling, ripped and covered in dirt.

http://www.eagleindustries.com/
http://www.eaglecreek.com/
http://www.letravelstore.com/cargo.htm
http://www.timberland.com/
http://www.tamrac.com/

Tent

Do you really need a tent? Consider a hammock, a bug net or even a simple plastic tarp. You can substitute a groundsheet with rope for warmer climes or a jungle hammock for swamps. Or you can get extra friendly and crash with the locals. After your first night on the ground in the jungle, you will realize why the apes sleep in the trees.

http://www.gorp.com/gorp/publishers/menasha/gea_tent.htm
http://www.junglehammock.com/

Sleeping Bag

Get a light cotton-lined sleeping bag that has anything but down stuffing. A flannel sheet will do just fine in the summer. Down does not insulate when wet, so look into thin synthetics. I have never used a sleeping bag in DPs, since most people will provide a sheet or blanket.

http://www.outdoorreview.com/gear_reviews/Sleeping_Bags_name.html
http://www.hitthetrail.com/sleepbag.htm
http://www.backpacking.net/gearbags.html

Toiletry Kit

Combination comb/brush, toothbrush, toothpaste, floss, deodorant, toilet paper, tampons, condoms, small Swiss Army knife with scissors and nail file, shaver, shampoo, liquid soap. Tiny, tiny tiny and stick it all in a Tupperware container.

http://www.www.tupperware.com/

Compass/GPS

Even if you don't know how to use a compass, you should have one. If you take along the manual, you'll easily learn how to use your compass to tell time, measure maps, navigate by the stars, signal airplanes, and, God forbid, even plot your course if you get lost. The best compasses are made by Silva. I love the Garmin GPSs with the built-in maps. Military checkpoints and rebels don't. Some countries consider GPSs to be military equipment, so ask before you go. Or just tell them it's a radio.

http://www.inmet.com/~pwt/gps_gen.htm
http://igscb.jpl.nasa.gov/
http://www.laafb.af.mil/SMC/CZ/homepage/
http://www.gps4fun.com/l
http://joe.mehaffey.com/
http://www.silva.se/files/compass.html

Flashlight

You should carry three flashlights: (1) a tiny single-cell key; (2) AA-battery Maglight or other waterproof flashlight (get two or three because they make great gifts); and (3) a Petzl or REI waterproof head-mounted flashlight. Get lots of AA batteries.

http://www.petzl.com/
http://www.meiresearch.com/worklights/maglite/index.shtm
http://www.leeco.com/page021.htm.

Mosquito Netting

REI sells a nifty mosquito tent that will cover your head and arms. Mosquitoes like to start feeding as soon as you drift off to sleep, so this light tentlike mesh will keep your head and arms safe. It can also be used to catch fish, strain chunks out of water and strain gasoline. Bring bug repellent with the highest DEET content. Wash it though, because it may cause some nasty rashes if not washed off. In hotel rooms, mosquito coils can make life bearable. They do not scare off large rats.

Clothing

There is much debate on fabrics and clothing styles. In the arid tropics, cotton is about the only fabric worth wearing and will wash on rocks. In tropical countries, be careful of the germ buildup that synthetics create. Try loose-fitting light cotton shirts rather than T-shirts. After one week, everything you own will be stinky, damp and wrinkled, so it's best to rotate three shirts, three T-shirts, two pants, one shorts, three socks, three underwear, a hat, poncho, one pair of sneakers, hiking boots and flip-flops. And that's it.

http://www.actiongear.com/
http://www.cabelas.com/

Pants

The plain khaki army fatigues made in Korea are your best bet. Others swear by convertible short/pant combos. Be careful of shorts. Many Muslim countries don't think the sight of your naked legs is all that sexy. You'll get cut, dirty and burned as well. Cabellas, safari catalogs, Travelsmith and army surplus stores are an excellent source of outdoor clothing.

http://www.royalrobbins.com/
http://www.imsplus.com/ims_catalog_index.html
http://www.compfxnet.com/opshop/mil.html

Light cotton T-shirts

Preferably with the name of where you are from or a *DP* shirt (use as gifts later). Plan on buying your T-shirts where you travel to and pick up a few semi-formal shirts. In some countries they will make you an entire wardrobe in a day . . . and for pennies. Some people prefer synthetics for wicking and ease of washing.

http://www.patagonia.com

Wool socks

I avoid synthetic socks (and cotton socks). I like wool, or at least a good wool blend. You want your socks to maintain their shape and breathe, and good wool does that. Take three pairs—one to wear, one to wash and another to wear because you forgot to wash the first pair. Do not get the high-tech synthetic socks, just the funky rag type.

http://www.sock-monkey.com/sockmonkey.html
http://www.mightymedia.com/sockmonkey/
http://www.mtbr.com/reviews/Socks/smartwool_MTBsocks.html
http://www.thorlo.com/

Underwear

Loose cotton boxers; get groovy-looking ones so that they can double as swim trunks. Speedos are for the French and strip clubs.

http://www.topdrawers.com/

Shirt

Long-sleeved cotton, not too butch so you can wear it to dinner. Safari-style is fine because people expect you to look adventurous.

Poncho

One heavy vinyl, another cheap plastic to protect pack and camera gear and to sleep on.

http://www.totalsurvival.com/camping.htm

Hat

Wide-brimmed canvas hat. Tilleys are the best, but who wants to look like a geriatric on safari? Another choice is to pick up a cheap straw hat when you get there—natty and disposable.

http://www.tilley.com/
http://www.thingzoz.com/hats/bushhats.htm

Hiking boots

Lightweight mesh and canvas or leather, no foam padding if possible. Go for leather or canvas with replaceable soles so they can be repaired on the road. If you are doing some rugged work in remote regions, think about repair. Leather and separate Vibram soles can be patched; some of the new designs can't. I go custom with Viberg, the people that made my logging boots (still in perfect condition after 20 years).

http://www.viberg.com/
http://www.raichle.ch/
http://www.hi-tec.com

Sneakers

I use Chuck Taylor's Converse in beige (over 500 million pairs have been sold since 1917). Get 'em one size larger 'cause your feet will swell up. These are the world's greatest (and cheapest) jungle boots. Others swear by simple boots and shoes like the classic Timberlands or Rockports.

http://www.converse.com/athletic_originals/core_color_high.html
http://www.rockport.com/
http://www.timberland.com/

Food

It's not worth bringing a cooking kit. Even in the most devastated of places, someone prepares food. I do recommend bringing beef jerky, gum, energy bars, bags of nuts and other high-protein/high-fat munchies. Also, hot sauce is indispensable in eating that Third World slop.

http://www.ofd.com/mh/
http://www.webart.co.uk/clients/expedition.foods/index.htm
http://theepicenter.com/foodh2o.html

First Aid Kit

A prescription from your doctor or a letter describing the drugs you are carrying can help. Pack wads of antidiarrheals, electrolyte powder, antibiotics, insect-sting kit, antacids, antihistamines (for itching and colds), antibiotic ointment, iodine, water purifier, foot powder, antifungal ointment and a syringe or two. Also look into items like Vagisil, which can be used to dry feet out, Superglue to seal cuts, and other home remedies. Ask your doctor to prescribe any drugs you might need to complete your kit. Single-sided razor blades, a lighter, condoms, rubber gloves, IV drip (needle and bag) and small first aid kits are good to have.

http://gearreview.com/firstaidrev99.asp
http://www.adventuremedicalkits.com.
http://www.destinationoutdoors.com
http://www.orgear.com.
http://www.sawyerproducts.com
http://www.siriusmed.com/

Camera/Video/Binoculars

Bring the smallest, simplest camera that uses standard negative film. Bring two if it matters. Hi-8 tapes are now common worldwide (don't forget the PAL, SECAM and NTSC problem), but DV is the way to go. Some of the pocket-sized cameras from Sony and Canon are broadcast quality and can also double as digital tape recorders and still camera. You won't find tape or batteries unless you check the duty free shop at the airport. Don't bring binoculars. You can always bum somebody else's, unless you are going to Africa or want to avoid gunships—then they are a must. Leica and Zeiss roof prisms are the only ones to consider.

http://www.canon.com
http://www.leica.com
http://www.sel.sony.com
http://www.nikonusa.com/
http://www.fujifilm.com

Survival Kit

Survival kits are like an African fetish. We hope that just having these items around means we will never have to use them. Remember to keep this kit separate from your main pack, ideally in a belt mounted bag. Your entire pack should consist of first-aid kit, two space blankets, Bic lighters, Swiss Army knife (get the one with the saw), a whistle, Power Bars (get one of each flavor), string, extra money, your photocopied ID, fishing line with hooks (not too helpful in the desert), candle butts, Stop Trot or any other electrolyte replacement product and headache pills. Also bring a sewing kit, and buy a surgical needle shaped like a fishhook. You will need this to sew up your skin (sterilized with a lighter first) if you suffer a severe gash. Baby wipes are handy for many uses. Hydrogen peroxide is a nasty but useful disinfectant. Reader Trond M. Vågen from Norway also suggests tampons (for wounds), a small magnet (for a makeshift compass with needles or razorblades), magnesium fire-starting kit, and to cap it off, a small survival guide so you figure out how you got so lost.

http://www.sharplink.com/jkits/
http://www.gutz.com/
http://www.equipped.com/survlkit.htm
http://www.baproducts.com/survkit.htm

Water Bottle/Purifiers

Bring a metal water bottle that can be used to boil water in a pinch. The kind they sell as fuel bottles are fine and you should carry a small MSR stove for the purpose of disinfecting questionable water supplies. Purifiers and filters are helpful depending on whether you will be near sterile water supplies. The new Camelbak style "hydration systems" are fine until they freeze, puncture and leak all over your clothes or get contaminated. They are fine for external use and make a great addition to water but beware of their limitations.

http://www.msrcorp.com/
http://www.camelbak.com/
http://www.general-ecology.com/

Essentials

Your passport, airline tickets, money, credit cards, traveler's checks, drivers license, malaria pills, sunscreen, lip salve, spare contacts, glasses, sunglasses. Make two copies of all documents, including credit cards. Leave one at home, take one with you in a place other than the originals.

Letters of Recommendation

If you get in a jam or need special dispensations, it doesn't hurt to have plenty of glowing letters about you on fancy stationery. Lots of official stamps help too. Money is better.

Equipment Resources

http://www.gorp.com
http://www.out-there.com/htl_bpk.htm#Manufacturers
http://www.gorefabrics.com
http://www.rei.com/
http://www.emsonline.com/
http://www.fogdog.com/
http://w4.lns.cornell.edu/~seb/philmont-coop-b4.html
http://www.magellans.com/

Gifts

Most of the Third World views you as a rich capitalist pig. Because you think you are a *poor* capitalist pig doesn't let you off the hook when it comes to giving gifts. Keep it simple and memorable and have plenty to go around. Mirrors, beads and shiny paper were big in Columbus' time, but you are expected to do better than that today. Here are a few suggestions to make you the hit of the village:

Pens

Call an advertising specialty company to get cheap pens printed with your name and message on them. They will still be as cheap as drugstore Bics and a lot cooler as gifts.

http://dir.yahoo.com/Business_and_Economy/Companies/Marketing/Advertising/Promotional_Items/

Stickers/Cards

Buy a bag of them from party stores; if you can't resist a little self-promotion, have your own stickers printed up on foil and give 'em out to the eager hordes. You can also have your photo printed on stickers or use your computer, color printer and adhesive paper to make your own. Worst case you could just have a bunch of cards made up with your photo, name and E-mail address to hand out.

http://www.kinkos.com/

Cigarettes

I know it is not cool to smoke, but passing around smokes is a successful way to initiate male-bonding in the rest of the world. In the Muslim world, where men don't drink, they smoke enough to make up for it. Even if you don't smoke, carry a couple of packs of cigarettes as gifts and icebreakers. I know for a fact that peoples' intentions to shoot me have been altered by the speed with which I have offered up the smokes.

http://www.megalink.net/~dale/quitcigs.htm

Weird Stuff No Adventurer Should Be Without

Everyone tells you to pack light (including me), so here are all the little items that can make your day or night in the bush:

Psion Palm Computer

I used to carry a *Laptop* but this baby fits in your pocket, runs on AA batteries for a month and has everything, spreadsheets, language software, calculator, word processing, drawing and much more. You off-load your files onto a static memory chip so even if you get busted, your precious words of wisdom are safe.

http://www.psion.com/

Adventurer Watch

A number of companies make waterproof watches with all sorts of gee whiz features including alarms, compasses and dual dials for different time zones. My favorite is the *Casio* series with built-in compass, altimeter and more.

http://www.casio.com/

Books

Buy them by thickness. My faves are *Information Please Almanac*, the *Book of Lists*, Penguin compendiums of classic stories and fat chunky adventure novels like *Three Musketeers* or *Les Misérables*. The Bible or the Koran will do in a pinch, and I have been known to write a book out of boredom. Trade 'em or give them away as gifts along the way. We hope the first thing you pack is a guidebook. Also think about phrase books, survival manuals, and even poetry if you know all is lost. Address books are useful too.

http://www.amazon.com/

Maps

Good maps are very difficult to get in Third World countries. Especially in war zones. Spraying them with a spray fixative available at any art store will help to waterproof them. Consider the new GPS hand receivers that lets you download digital maps.

http://www.maps.com/
http://www.maptown.com/
http://www.lib.utexas.edu/Libs/PCL/Map_collection/Map_collection.html
http://www.reliefweb.int/mapc/index.html
http://www.un.org/Depts/Cartographic/english/htmain.htm
http://plasma.nationalgeographic.com/mapmachine/

Business or Calling Cards

If you are the sociable type, have a bunch of cheap cards with plasticized ink made up (be sure moisture doesn't make the ink run). Look in the phone book for a translator if you would like them in two languages. Leave enough room for your new friends to write their name and address on them. Make sure you also bring plenty of extra passport photos.

www.kinkocs.com

Shortwave Radio

Now that Sony makes those teensy-weensy shortwave receivers, you need never spend a 10-hour bus ride without entertainment.

http://www.grundig.com/produkte/audio/welt.html
http://tekgallery.site.yahoo.net/tekgallery/shorrad.html

Notebook and Pens

For the nontechnical, a notebook is an indispensable part of the travel experience. You will have plenty of time to wax poetic and capture your thoughts.

Caribiners

Use them to snap your pack to a bus rail or bike frame, hold items on your belt, hang things from trees, rescue people and use as a belt when you lose weight.

http://www.omegapac.com/

Yellow and Black Danger Zone Tape

I use the heavy striped tape to mark my luggage, tape rips, pack boxes and even fix my runners. I just point at the yellow tape on my waist bag, hold up the number of fingers for how many pieces of luggage and presto, instant recognition.

http://dir.yahoo.com/business_and_economy/companies/industrial_supplies/safety-products/

Syringes

Just visit a Third World hospital.

http://www.jandw.com/Syringes.htm

Razor Blades

Boils, slivers, infected cuts—all may require a little field surgery.

Hydrogen Peroxide

Cleans out cuts, hurts like hell, stops major infections.

Credit Card Survival Kits

> *Tool Logic*
> *2290 Eastman Avenue,*
> *Suite 110,*
> *Ventura California 93003*
> *Tel.: (805) 339-9725*
> *Fax: (805) 339-9712*
> *http://www.toollogic.com/*
> Credit card–sized knife, compass, screwdriver, etc. Ideal for gifts or back up survival.

Ziploc Freezer Bags

> Organizes, holds anything, waterproofs everything from passports to cameras. Use it for everything but food. The plastic transmits an icky plastic taste to food when kept in hot climates.

Trash Bags

> Heavy-duty garbage bags make great waterproofers. They also double as ponchos, groundcovers, umbrellas, water catchers, spare windows, sails and even garbage bags.

Tupperware

> It organizes and waterproofs, and you can eat out of it and give it away as gifts. Get the clear stuff and size it to the pockets or corners in your luggage.
>
> *http://www.tupperware.com*

Bubblegum

> Get the kind that Amerol makes in the tape form. It's sold in a plastic snuff tin. Get the dayglo pink stuff; it drives the natives crazy to watch you blow those bubbles.
>
> *http://www.topps.com/baz1.htm*
> *http://www.bubblegum.com/*

Empty Film Cannisters

> The clear kind that Fuji film comes in. Take the top off, squeeze them and they act like suction cups. Squeeze them with the tops and they are like tiny popguns. You can amuse the little ones for hours.
>
> *http://www.fuji.com*

Polaroid Camera

> I could create peace in the world and brotherly love if I just had enough Polaroid film to take pictures of every headhunter, mercenary, tribal warrior, soldier and politician. They love it, and smiles break out all around. Think about it: How many times does somebody take your picture where you work and actually give you a copy?
>
> *http://www.polaroid.com*

If any of our rabid readers have more gizmos or tips send them to: *ryp☆comeback-alive.com.*

Resources

http://www.rei.com/
http://www.emsonline.com/
http://www.fogdog.com/
http://www.gorp.com/gorp/gear/gearlink.htm

Those Hard to Find Items

Camouflage Passports

> *http://www.scopebooks.com/*

Bulletproof Rain Coat

> *http://www.counterspyshop.com/*

Hostage Tracking Sensors

> *http://www.spooktech.com*

Pith Helmet
> *http://www.actiongear.com*

Nightvision
> *http://www.73.com/a/0111.shtml*

Female Bodyguards
> *http://www.execops.com/execops.htm*

Tracked Military Vehicles
> *http://members.aol.com/militintl/classifieds.html*

Language Tapes
> *http://www.berlitz.com/*

Disguises
> *http://www.spybase.com/facial.html*

Expedition Vehicles
> *Mantec Services*
> *Unit 1*
> *The Green*
> *Hartshill*
> *nr Nuneaton*
> *Warwicks, CV10 0FW*
> *Tel./Fax: [44] (1203) 395368*

Manufacturers and suppliers of four wheel drive equipment. Also provide training, advice for expeditions and vehicle purchase advice.

Buddies
> *Adventure Team*
> *http://www.adventureteam.com/*

Good chat source for gear, advice and adventurous teammates or travel partners.

International Long-Distance Access Codes

Dial these numbers from within the countries to reach your preferred carrier.

COUNTRY	AT&T	MCI	SPRINT
Albania	00-800-0010	No MCI Access	No Sprint Access
American Samoa	6332-USA	633-2-MCI	633-1000
Angola	199	No MCI Access	No Sprint Access
Anguilla	800-872-2881	No MCI Access	800-877-8000
Antigua	800-872-2881	#2	800-366-4663
Argentina	001-800-200-1111	001-800-333-1111	001-800-777-1111
Armenia	8-14111	No MCI Access	8-10-155
Aruba	NO AT&T ACCESS	800-8888	800-8870
Australia	800-881-001	800-551-111	800-551-110
Austria	022-903-011	022-903-012	022-903-014
Bahamas	800-872-0881	800-888-8000	800-389-2111
Bahrain	800-001	800-002	800-777
Barbados	800-872-2881	800-888-8000	800-534-0042

COUNTRY	AT&T	MCI	SPRINT
Belarus	8-800101	No MCI Access	No Sprint Access
Belgium	0-800-10010	0800-10012	0-800-10014
Belize	555	815	812
Benin	102	No MCI Access	No Sprint Access
Bermuda	800-872-0881	800-888-8000	800-623-0877
Bolivia	0-800-1112	0-800-2222	0-800-3333
Bosnia	00-800-0010	No MCI Access	No Sprint Access
Brazil	000-8010	000-8012	000-8016
Brunei	800-1111	No MCI Access	No Sprint Access
Bulgaria	00-1800-0100	00-800-0001	00-800-1010
Cambodia	800-881-001	No MCI Access	No Sprint Access
Canada	800-225-5288	800-888-8000	800-877-8000
Cape Verde	112	No MCI Access	No Sprint Access
Cayman Islands	800-872-2881	800-888-8000	800-366-4663
Chile	800-800-0311	800-207-300	00-0317
China	108-11	108-12	108-13
Colombia	980-11-0010	980-16-0001	980-13-0010
Cook Islands	09-111	No MCI Access	No Sprint Access
Costa Rica	0800-011-4114	0800-012-2222	0800-0013-0123
Croatia	99-385-0111	99-385-0112	99-385-0113
Cyprus	080-900-10	080-900-00	080-900-01
Czech Republic	00-42-000-101	00-42-000-112	0042-087-187
Denmark	800-1-0010	800-1-0022	800-1-0877
Dominican Republic	800-872-2881	800-888-8000	800-751-7877
Ecuador	999-119	999-170	999-171
Egypt (Cairo)	510-0200	355-5770	356-4777
Egypt (All Others)	02-510-0200	02-355-5770	02-356-4777
El Salvador	800-1785	800-1767	800-1776
Estonia	8-00-8001001	No MCI Access	No Sprint Access
Fiji	004-890-1001	004-890-1002	004-890-100-3
Finland	9800-100-10	9800-102-80	9800-1-0284
France	19-0011	19-0019	19-0087
French Antilles	19-00-11	No MCI Access	No Sprint Access
French Guiana	19-00-11	No MCI Access	No Sprint Access
Gabon	00-001	No MCI Access	No Sprint Access
Gambia	00-1-11	00-1-99	00-155
Germany	0130-0100	0130-0012	0130-0013

COUNTRY	AT&T	MCI	SPRINT
Ghana	01-91	No MCI Access	01-99-00
Gibralter	8800	No MCI Access	No Sprint Access
Greece	00-800-1311	00-800-1211	00-800-1411
Grenada	800-872-2881	800-888-8000	800-877-8787
Guam	018-872	950-1022	950-1366
Guatemala	190	189	195
Guyana	165	No MCI Access	No Sprint Access
Haiti	183	001-800-444-1234	170-171
Honduras	123	122	121
Hong Kong	800-1111	800-1121	800-1877
Hungary	00-800-01-111	00-800-01-411	00-800-01-877
Iceland	800-9001	800-9002	800-9003
India	000-117	000-127	000-137
Indonesia	001-801-10	001-801-11	001-801-15
Ireland	800-55-0000	800-55-1001	800-55-2001
Israel	177-100-2727	177-150-2727	177-102-2727
Italy	172-1011	172-1022	172-1877
Ivory Coast	00-111-11	No MCI Access	No Sprint Access
Jamaica	0-800-872-2881	0-800-888-8000	0-800-877-8000
Japan (KDD)	0039-111	0039-121	0039-131
Japan (IDC)	0066-55-111	0066-55-121	0066-55-877
Jordan	18-800-000	18-800-001	18-800-777
Kazakhstan	8-800-121-4321	No MCI Access	No Sprint Access
Kenya	0800-10	0800-11	0800-12
Korea (DACOM)	009-11	0039-12	0039-13
Korea (KT)	550-HOME	009-14	009-16
Kuwait	800-288	800-MCI	800-777
Latvia (Riga)	7007007	No MCI Access	No Sprint Access
Latvia (Others)	8-27007007		
Lebanon (Beirut)	426-801	600-MCI	No Sprint Access
Lebanon (Others)	01-426-801	01-600-MCI	No Sprint Access
Liberia	797-797	No MCI Access	No Sprint Access
Liechtenstein	155-0011	155-0222	155-9777
Lithuania	8-196	No MCI Access	8-197
Luxembourg	0-800-0111	0-800-0112	0-800-0115
Macao	0800-111	0800-131	0800-121
Macedonia	99-800-4288	No MCI Access	No Sprint Access

COUNTRY	AT&T	MCI	SPRINT
Malaysia	800-0011	800-0012	800-0016
Malta	0800-890-110	0800-89-0120	No Sprint Access
Mexico	95-800-462-4240	95-800-674-7000	95-800-877-8000
Micronesia	288	No MCI Access	555
Monaco	19-0011	19-0019	19-0087
Montserrat	800-872-2881	No MCI Access	No Sprint Access
Morocco	002-11-0011	00-211-0012	No Sprint Access
Netherlands	06-022-9111	06-022-9122	06-022-9119
Netherlands Antilles	001-800-872-2881	001-800-950-1022	001-800-745-1111
New Zealand	000-911	000-912	0-800-760-877
Nicaragua	174	166 (Managua)	171
Nicaragua (other)		02-166	
Norway	800-190-11	800-199-12	800-198-77
Palau	02-288	No MCI Access	02-222
Panama	109	108	115
Paraguay	008-10-800	008-11-800	008-12-800
Peru	171	170	176
Philippines	105-11	105-14	105-16 (PLDT)
Philippines			105-01 (ETPI)
Poland	0-0-800-111-1111	00-800-111-2122	00-800-111-3115
Portugal	05017-1-288	05017-1-234	05017-1-877
Puerto Rico	800-225-5288	800-888-8000	800-877-8000
Qatar	0800-011-77	0800-012-77	0-800-017-77
Romania	01-800-4288	01-800-1800	01-800-0877
Russia (Moscow)	755-5042	8-10-800-497-7222	155-6133
Russia (Others)	8-095-755-5042	8-10-800-497-7222	8095-155-6133
St. Kitts/Nevis	800-872-2881	No MCI Access	No Sprint Access
St. Vincent	800-872-2881	No MCI Access	No Sprint Access
Saint Lucia	800-872-2881	800-888-8000	800-277-7468
Saipan	235-2872	950-1022	235-0333
San Marino	172-1011	172-1022	172-1877
Saudi Arabia	800-10	800-11	1800-15
Sierra Leone	1100	No MCI Access	No Sprint Access
Singapore	800-0111-111	800-0112-112	800-0177-177
Slovak Republic	00-42-000-101	00-42-000-112	00-42-087-187
South Africa	0-800-99-0123	0-800-99-0011	0-800-99-0001
Spain	900-99-0011	900-99-0014	900-99-0013

COUNTRY	AT&T	MCI	SPRINT
Sri Lanka	430-430	440-100	No Sprint Access
Suriname	156	No MCI Access	No Sprint Access
Sweden	020-795-611	020-795-922	020-799-011
Switzerland	0-800-55-0011	155-0222	15-9777
Syria	0801	0800	0888
Taiwan	0800-10-2880	0080-13-4567	0080-14-0877
Thailand	001-999-11-111	001-999-12-001	001-999-13-877
Trinidad & Tobago	No AT&T Access	800-888-8000	23
Turkey	00-800-1-2277	00-800-1-177	00-800-1-4477
Turks and Caicos	800-872-2881	No MCI Access	No Sprint Access
Ukraine	8-100-11	8-100-13	8-100-15
United Arab Emirates	800-121	800-111	800-131
United Kingdom	0800-89-0011	0800-89-0222	0800-89-0877
United States	800-225-5288	800-888-8000	800-877-8000
Uruguay	000-410	000-412	000-417
Uzbekistan	8-661-7440010	No MCI Access	No Sprint Access
Venezuela	1-201-0288	800-1114-0	800-1111-0
Vietnam	1-201-0288	1-201-9999	1-201-1111
Virgin Islands (U.S.)	800-225-5288	800-888-8000	800-877-8000
Virgin Islands (U.K.)	800-872-2881	800-888-8000	800-877-8000
Zambia	00-899	No MCI Access	No Sprint Access
Zimbabwe	1-201-0288	No MCI Access	No Sprint Access

International Long-Distance Access Codes

INDEX

T

U

V

W

Y

Z

World's Most Dangerous Places: Photo Credits

Robert Young Pelton, Jim Hooper, Alex Smailes

AFP/CORBIS: Atta Kenare, Pius Utmoi Ekpei, Ivestia, Rob Elliot, Swen Nackstrand, Joel Robine, Yuir Kochetkov

CORBIS: Barnabas Bosshart, Howard Davies, Jeremy Horner, Liba Taylor, Peter Turnley

GALLO IMAGES/CORBIS: Paul Velasco

IMAGES SANS FRONTIERES: Sedat Aral

REUTERS NEWMEDIA, INC./CORBIS: Andy Clark, Jason Reed, Arturo Bermudez

JIM SUGAR PHOTOGRAPHY/CORBIS